HANDBOOK OF
ADOLESCENT PSYCHOLOGY

THIRD EDITION

HANDBOOK OF ADOLESCENT PSYCHOLOGY

THIRD EDITION

Volume 2: Contextual Influences on Adolescent Development

Edited By

RICHARD M. LERNER

LAURENCE STEINBERG

WILEY

John Wiley & Sons, Inc.

This book is printed on acid-free paper.

Library of Congress Cataloging-in-Publication Data:

Handbook of adolescent psychology / edited by Richard M. Lerner, Laurence Steinberg.—3rd ed.
    p. cm.
   Includes index.
   ISBN 978-0-470-14921-8 (cloth : v. 1 : alk. paper)
   ISBN 978-0-470-14922-5 (cloth : v. 2 : alk. paper)
   ISBN 978-0-470-14920-1 (set)
    1. Adolescent psychology. I. Lerner, Richard M. II. Steinberg, Laurence D., 1952-
BF724.H33 2009
155.5—dc22

                                            2008038561

Printed in the United States of America
10 9 8 7 6 5 4 3 2 1

Contributors

Aida B. Balsano
Milton S. Eisenhower Foundation
Washington, D.C.

Erika Bagley
Department of Psychology
University of North Carolina
Chapel Hill, North Carolina

Deborah L. Bobek
New England Aquarium
Boston, Massachusetts

Jeanne Brooks-Gunn
Teachers College
Columbia University
New York, New York

B. Bradford Brown
Department of Educational Psychology
University of Wisconsin–Madison
Madison, Wisconsin

W. Andrew Collins
Institute of Child Development
University of Minnesota
Minneapolis, Minnesota

Jennifer A. Connolly
Department of Psychology
York University
Toronto, Ontario

Véronique Dupéré
Eliot-Pearson Department of Child
    Development
Tufts University
Medford, Massachusetts

Patricia L. East
Department of Pediatrics
University of California San Diego
La Jolla, California

Richard F. Elmore
Harvard Graduate School of Education
Harvard University
Cambridge, Massachusetts

Ulla G. Foehr
Research Consultant
Belmont, California

Andrew Fuligni
Department of Psychology
University of California Los Angeles
Los Angeles, California

Mary Agnes Hamilton
College of Human Ecology
Cornell University
Ithaca, New York

Stephen F. Hamilton
Department of Human Development
Cornell University
Ithaca, New York

Cecily R. Hardaway
Department of Psychology
University of North Carolina
Chapel Hill, North Carolina

Lisa Henriksen
Stanford University
Stanford, California

Diane L. Hughes
Department of Applied Psychology
New York University
New York, New York

Rachel Kaplan
Department of Psychology
University of North Carolina
Chapel Hill, North Carolina

James Larson
Harvard University
Cambridge, Massachusetts

Reed Larson
Department of Human and
    Community Development
University of Illinois
Urbana, Illinois

James Lauckhardt
Department of Psychology
Fordham University
New York, New York

Brett Laursen
Department of Psychology
Florida Atlantic University
Ft. Lauderdale, Florida

Tama Leventhal
Eliot-Pearson Department of Child
    Development
Tufts University
Medford, Massachusetts

Sarah Ryan Lowe
Department of Psychology
University of Massachusetts, Boston
Boston, Massachusetts

Joseph Mahoney
Department of Education
University of California–Irvine
Irvine, California

Caroline McIsaac
Department of Psychology
York University
Toronto, Ontario

Vonnie C. McLoyd
Department of Psychology
University of North Carolina
Chapel Hill, North Carolina

Emily E. Messersmith
University of North Carolina
Chapel Hill, North Carolina

Kelly M. Purtell
Department of Psychology
University of North Carolina at Chapel Hill
Chapel Hill, North Carolina

Jean E. Rhodes
Department of Psychology
University of Massachusetts, Boston
Boston, Massachusetts

Aimee Rickman
Department of Human and Community
    Development
University of Illinois
Urbana, Illinois

Don F. Roberts
Department of Communication
Stanford University
Stanford, California

Alice Schlegel
Department of Anthropology
University of Arizona
Tucson, Arizona

John E. Schulenberg
Department of Psychology
University of Michigan
Ann Arbor, Michigan

Elizabeth Scott
Columbia Law School
Columbia University
New York, New York

Lonnie R. Sherrod
Society for Research in Child Development
    and Fordham University
Bronx, New York

Sandra Simpkins
The School of Social and Family Dynamics
Arizona State University
Tempe, Arizona

Ciara Smalls
Department of Psychology
University of North Carolina
Chapel Hill, North Carolina

Jeremy Staff
Department of Sociology
Pennsylvania State University
University Park, Pennsylvania

Christina Theokas
The Education Trust
Washington, D.C.

Deborah Vandell
Department of Education
University of Wisconsin–Madison
Madison, Wisconsin

Jennifer L. Woolard
Department of Psychology
Georgetown University
Washington, D.C.

Nicole Zarrett
Psychology Department
University of South Carolina
Columbia, South Carolina

Contents

Preface

In 2004, in our preface to the second edition of the *Handbook of Adolescent Psychology*, we noted that 24 years separated the first and second editions of this work. At the time of the publication of the first edition, the field was one where relatively little empirical work was being conducted and where, as well, the major theoretical frame was psychoanalytic. There was present as well a little cognitive developmental theory, a touch of behaviorism, and just the beginnings (in the prescient chapter by Elder, 1980) of a dynamic, developmental systems model.

By 2004, 852 pages and 25 chapters (plus an afterword) were needed to summarize the vast empirical literature that had developed in the previous quarter-century. The chapters of the second edition revealed that the role of grand theories of adolescence, whether psychoanalytic or not, had waned, and that the sorts of mutually influential, person ←→ context relational models of development that Elder had discussed (represented as individual ←→ context relations) had become the predominant theoretical lens in the study of adolescent development, as they had within the field of human development more broadly (Damon & Lerner, 2006, 2008). In the second edition, the contexts in which adolescent development takes place received considerably more attention than had been the case previously. Moreover, the second edition reflected a growing interest in how theoretically-predicated, empirically-based knowledge about adolescence could be used to capitalize on the strengths of young people and promote their positive development.

We suggested in 2004 that the quality and quantity of the ongoing work in the scientific study of adolescence indicated that the field was remarkably active; that the increasing

numbers of high-quality researchers drawn to the study of adolescent development portended an even greater growth in knowledge than had taken place between the publication of the first and second editions of the *Handbook;* and that it was likely that the field's future would be marked by the rapid evolution of the theoretical and empirical emphases represented in the second edition of the *Handbook*. Our expectations have been confirmed, but the expansion of the field took place with a breadth and depth of scholarship that we could not have fully anticipated.

The publication of the third edition of the *Handbook of Adolescent Psychology* in 2009 represents only a 5-year period between the present and prior edition, about 25% of the time between the first and the second editions. However, within this relatively short period, the knowledge base with the field has exploded. The number of chapters we have included in this edition in order to fairly represent the range of high-quality scholarship defining the cutting edge of the contemporary study of adolescent development has increased by more than 50% and now fills two volumes.

Framing this scientific work are both theoretical models that stress processes of systemic, individual ←→ context relations (see our opening chapter on the history of scientific research on adolescence in volume 1) and scientific methods that include both sophisticated quantitative techniques to study change (Little, Card, Preacher, & McConnell) and rich qualitative, ethnographic procedures that give voice to the developing adolescent and insight into the nature of his or her social, cultural, and historical context (Burton, Garrett-Peters, & Eaton). The contemporary study of individual development reflects this dynamic between person and context—whether the focus of analysis is brain development (Paus), puberty (Susman & Dorn), thinking (Kuhn), social cognition (Smetana & Villalobos), moral cognition and prosocial behavior (Eisenberg, Morris, McDaniel, & Spinrad), identity and self (Côté), gender and gender role development (Galambos, Berenbaum, & McHale), autonomy and attachment (McElhaney, Allen, Stephenson, & Hare), academic motivation (Eccles & Roeser), spirituality and religious development (King & Roeser), or sex (Diamond & Savin-Williams).

The study of interpersonal relationships in adolescence—involving those with parents (Laursen & Collins), siblings (East), peers (Brown & Larson), romantic partners (Connolly & McIsaac), or mentors (Rhodes & Lowe)—illustrate that the process of adolescent development involves dynamic, mutually influential exchanges between the developing youth and significant others. Indeed, even when the focus of developmental analysis is on the features of the institutional or cultural contexts of adolescence, the relations between the characteristics of the young person and the features of the settings in which he or she develops constitute the basic process of change during this period of life. These relational processes unfold in schools (Elmore), after-school settings (Mahoney, Vandell, Simpkins, & Zarrett), workplaces (Staff, Messersmith, & Schulenberg), and neighborhoods (Leventhal, Dupéré, & Brooks-Gunn), and are influenced by poverty (McLoyd, Kaplan, Purtell, Bagley, Hardaway, & Smalls), the structure of the transition to adulthood within the United States and internationally (Hamilton & Hamilton), ethnicity and immigration (Fuligni, Hughes, & Way), mass media (Roberts, Henricksen, & Foehr), the legal system (Woolard & Scott), globalization (Larson, Wilson, & Rickman), and culture (Schlegel).

Theory and research about individual development, interpersonal relationships, and contextual influences on these processes underscore that the adolescent years are marked by both opportunity and vulnerability. This potential for intraindividual variation in the course and outcomes of individual ←→ context relations is brought into high relief in the burgeoning scholarship applying developmental science to help youth confront the normative and nonnormative challenges of the period and, as well, to promote their positive, healthy development. Scholarship about adolescent risk and resilience (Compas & Reeslund), positive youth development (Lerner, Phelps, Forman, & Bowers), and citizenship (Sherrod & Lauckhardt) rely on these bidirectional models to frame research. Similar use of these dynamic conceptions of development occurs in studies of internalizing problems (Graber & Sontag), externalizing problems (Farrington), substance use (Chassin, Hussong, & Beltran), developmental disabilities (Hauser-Cram, Krauss, & Kersh), and physical health (Ozer & Irwin), as well as in efforts to promote positive development through community-based programs and social policies (Balsano, Theokas, & Bobek). Together, then, the two volumes of the third edition of the *Handbook of Adolescent Psychology* depict a field that is enriching our understanding of the basic, relational process shaping trajectories of development across the adolescent period; providing important leadership in the study of human development over the entire life span; and offering innovative and scientifically grounded means to promote healthy development among young people in the United States and abroad.

There are numerous people to thank for their contribution to this edition of the *Handbook*. First and foremost, we owe our greatest debt of gratitude to the colleagues who wrote the chapters for the *Handbook*. Their careful scholarship and commitment to the field have allowed us to produce a volume that will benefit scientists, practitioners, and policy makers alike.

We are deeply grateful also to Lauren White, Editor at the Institute for Applied Research in Youth Development. Her expertise and tenacity in overseeing the day-to-day management of this work through all phases of manuscript development and production were invaluable to us. The overall quality of the *Handbook* is a direct result of her impressive ability to track and coordinate the myriad editorial tasks associated with a project of this scope, her astute editorial skills and wisdom, and her unfailing good humor and patience (with the editors as well as the contributors).

We also appreciate greatly the important contributions to this book made by Jennifer Davison, managing editor at the Institute. Her knowledge of the manuscript development and production process, and her talents for enhancing the efficiency and quality of the editing, were enormous assets that enabled this work to be completed in a timely and high-quality manner.

We are indebted to our editor at John Wiley & Sons, Patricia Rossi. Her enthusiasm for our vision for the *Handbook*, unflagging support, and collegial and collaborative approach to the development of this project were vital bases for the successful completion of the *Handbook*.

Several organizations that supported our scholarship during the time we worked on the *Handbook* also deserve our thanks. Tufts University and Temple University have provided the support and resources necessary to undertake and complete this project. In addition, Richard M. Lerner thanks the National 4-H Council, the Philip Morris USA Youth Smoking Prevention Department, and the John Templeton Foundation. Laurence Steinberg is especially indebted to Temple University for supporting a sabbatical leave during which most of his work on this book was completed.

Finally, we want to once again dedicate this *Handbook* to our greatest sources of inspiration, both for our work on the *Handbook* and for our scholarship in the field of adolescence: our children—Justin, Blair, Jarrett, and Ben. Now all in their young adulthood, they have taught us our greatest lessons about the nature and potentials of adolescent development.

R.M.L.

L.S

July, 2008

REFERENCES

Damon, W., & Lerner, R. M. (2006). *Handbook of child psychology* (6th ed., vols. 1–4). Mahwah, NJ: Lawrence Erlbaum.

Damon, W., & Lerner, R. M. (2008). Child and adolescent development: *An advanced course*. Hoboken, NJ: John Wiley & Sons.

Elder, G. H., Jr. (1980). Adolescence in historical perspective. In J. Adelson (Ed.), *Handbook of adolescent psychology* (pp. 3–46). New York: John Wiley & Sons.

PART I

Interpersonal Influences

CHAPTER 1

Parent–Child Relationships During Adolescence

BRETT LAURSEN AND W. ANDREW COLLINS

No aspect of adolescent development has received more attention from the public and from researchers than parent–child relationships. Much of the research indicates that despite altered patterns of interaction, relationships with parents remain important social and emotional resources well beyond the childhood years (for recent reviews, see Collins & Steinberg, 2006; Smetana, Campione-Barr, & Metzger, 2006). Yet it is a challenge to reconcile this conclusion with the widespread perception that parent–child relationships decline in quality and influence over the course of the adolescent years. The aim of this chapter is to specify the characteristics and processes of parent–child relationships that sustain the centrality of the family amid the extensive changes of adolescence. We will argue that it is the content and the quality of these relationships, rather than the actions of either parent or adolescent alone, that determine the nature and extent of family influences on adolescent development. We will also argue that divergence between academic prescriptions and public perceptions about parent–adolescent relationships can be traced to the relative emphasis that each places on potential individual differences.

The chapter reflects three premises that have emerged from the sizable literature on parent–child relationships during adolescence. First, relationships with parents undergo transformations across the adolescent years that set the stage for less hierarchical interactions during adulthood. Second, family relationships have far-reaching implications for concurrent and long-term relationships with friends, romantic partners, teachers, and other adults, as well as for individual mental health, psychosocial adjustment, school performance, and eventual occupational choice and success. Third, contextual and cultural variations significantly shape family relationships and experiences that, in turn, affect the course and outcomes of development both during and beyond adolescence.

The chapter is divided into four main sections. The first section outlines theoretical views of parent–adolescent relationships and their developmental significance. The second section focuses on the behavior of parents and children and on interpersonal processes between them, with particular attention given to the distinctive characteristics of parent–child relationships and how these relationships change during adolescence. The third section considers whether and how parent–child relationships and their transformations are significant for adolescent development. The fourth section focuses on variability in parent–child relationships during adolescence as a function of structural, economic, and demographic distinctions among families.

THEORIES OF PARENT–ADOLESCENT RELATIONSHIPS AND THEIR INFLUENCE

For heuristic purposes, we have divided theories of parent–adolescent relationships into two groups: those that describe changes in relationships across the adolescent years and those that describe the influence of parenting and parent–child relationships. The first set of theories is dedicated to explaining the significant transformations that take place in parent–adolescent relationships. The second set of theories is dedicated to explaining the contributions that parents and parent–child relationships make to individual adolescent adjustment.

Theories Addressing Relationship Transformations

Conceptual models of transformation in parent–adolescent relationships vary in whether their primary focus is on the adolescent or on the relationship (Laursen & Collins, 2004). The prevalent perspective for most of the last century was that adolescents' physical, cognitive, and social maturation undermined patterns of interaction in close relationships that were established during childhood. The implications of individual change varied from one theoretical perspective to another, the common focus being the relative turbulence and instability of relationships during adolescence relative to those during childhood. More recent models emphasize stable features of parent–child relationships. Enduring bonds forged between parents and children are assumed to be the foundation for continuity in the functional properties of the relationship that transcend age-related changes in the characteristics of participants and alterations in the content and form of their interactions.

Models of Individual Change

Theories of individual change focus on disruptions caused by adolescent maturation and their potential to destabilize parent–child relationships. These models hold that changes in adolescents provoke changes in families. Maturationist models assume that a period of diminished closeness and heightened conflict accompanies adolescent maturation and that these perturbations continue until parent–adolescent relationships and roles are renegotiated. Most models hold that a rapprochement follows this period of normative relationship

turbulence (Collins, 1995). Conflict should become less frequent and better managed, closeness should increase, and social interactions should grow more sophisticated and constructive as a result of transformations in relationships.

Psychoanalytic theorists (A. Freud, 1958; S. Freud, 1921/1949) assumed that hormonal changes at puberty give rise to unwelcome Oedipal urges that foster impulse control problems and anxiety, as well as rebelliousness and distance from the family. More recent psychoanalytic formulations place greater emphasis on adolescent autonomy striving and ego identity development than on impulse control (Blos, 1979; Erikson, 1968). These later models converge on the dual contentions that awareness of parental fallibility (deidealization) and psychic emancipation drive a wedge between parents and children that is exacerbated by the inner turmoil brought on by adolescent hormonal fluctuations. This account implies that heightened conflict and diminished closeness inevitably follow maturational changes, as adolescents grapple with psychic disturbances. Child withdrawal and disengagement should continue into young adulthood, although a measure of closeness may be reestablished after parents are no longer perceived as a threat to the ego, sometime after identity achievement is complete and intimate relationships with peers are established.

Evolutionary views also emphasize the role of puberty in transforming relationships, but propose that change processes stem from physical and cognitive advances that are designed to encourage adolescents to separate from the family in order to seek mates elsewhere (Steinberg, 1989). In this view, adolescent maturation threatens parental dominance, resulting in heightened conflict with and diminished closeness to parents. This prompts youth to turn away from their family to be comforted by peers who are experiencing similar relationship disruptions. Some envision a reciprocal process, whereby independence hastens pubertal maturation and vice versa

(Belsky, Steinberg, & Draper, 1991). Although evolutionary views stipulate no mechanism for reestablishing parent–child closeness during young adulthood, it may be that parental investment in offspring and the warmth experienced in earlier periods provide a foundation of positive affect and regard that enables both parties to transcend the difficulties of adolescence (Gray & Steinberg, 1999). Improved relations should follow the child's transition to parenthood to the extent that grandparents are interested in providing resources and assistance to help ensure the survival and reproductive success of the next generation (Crosnoe & Elder, 2002; Smith & Drew, 2002).

Other maturational models give cognitive development a central role in parent–adolescent relationship changes. In these accounts, advances in abstract and complex reasoning foster a more nuanced appreciation of interpersonal distinctions and an increasingly egalitarian view of relationships that were previously oriented around the unilateral authority of adults (e.g., Selman, 1980; Youniss & Smollar, 1985). As a result, adolescents increasingly aspire to reciprocity and equal power in their interactions with parents. The same cognitive advances underlie the emerging tendency to consider certain issues as matters of personal volition, even though they previously were under parental jurisdiction (Smetana, 1988). Parents' reluctance to transform the hierarchical relationships established in childhood into more egalitarian ones creates conflict and curtails closeness. Eventually, familial roles are renegotiated to acknowledge the child's enhanced status and maturity. Conflict should dissipate as relationship roles and expectations are realigned, but the long-term implications for relationship closeness and harmony depend on whether parents and children are successful in revising their relationship in a mutually satisfactory manner.

A fourth group of theorists view physical and cognitive maturation as sources of constraints and demands on adolescents but give equal emphasis to changes in social expectations

and the need to adapt to a variety of new situations during age-graded transitions. Four kinds of moderated maturationist models typify this approach. The first set of models implicates changes in parents as the source of alterations in parent–adolescent relationships (Steinberg, 2001). Parents' developmental issues related to careers, personal goals, and future orientation can exacerbate the difficulty of the adjustments required in parent–adolescent relationships. Parents are also confronted with diminished or extinguished physical and reproductive capabilities and fading allure at a time when adolescent sexuality and attractiveness are blossoming, both of which may aggravate conflict and disengagement (Steinberg & Steinberg, 1994). A strong orientation toward work and investments in other nonfamilial domains could mean that parents view adolescents' movement toward autonomy as positive, ameliorating some of the obstacles to relationship transformation (Silverberg & Steinberg, 1990). Reestablishing positive relationship ties may be difficult for those who experience the most disruption, particularly if parents are unable or unwilling to address factors in their own lives that exacerbated transitional turmoil.

Two related theories emphasize the role of parents' beliefs and expectations in moderating age-related changes in relationships with adolescent children. Generalized or category-based beliefs models (Eccles, 1992; Holmbeck, 1996) posit a straightforward link between parents' stereotypes and expectations about adolescence in general and parents' relations with their own adolescent children. Beliefs become a self-fulfilling prophesy: Those who expect adolescence to be a period of turmoil are more likely to behave in a manner that provokes relationship deterioration compared with those who expect adolescence to be relatively benign. The expectancy violation–realignment model (Collins, 1995) begins with the assumption that interactions between parents and children are mediated by cognitive and emotional processes associated with expectancies about the behavior of the other person. In periods of rapid developmental change, such as the transition to adolescence, parents' expectancies often are violated. In younger age groups, change may occur more gradually, so that discrepancies are both less common and less salient than in periods of rapid multiple changes, such as adolescence. Expectancy violations are assumed to be a source of conflict that eventually stimulates parents to realign their expectations. It follows that changes in the tenor of parent–child relationships over the course of adolescence will vary as a function of the accuracy of parental expectations; those with unrealistic expectations should experience frequent violations and more relationship disruption than those with accurate expectations. Expectancies should also shape relationship recovery. Parents who foresee improved relations, particularly those who anticipate altered expressions of relationship closeness, are more likely to successfully repair relationships than those who expect irreparable damage and those who expect a return to the perceived tranquility of childhood.

The second set of moderated maturationist models implicates changes in parent–older sibling relationships in alterations in parent–younger sibling relationships. Models differ in terms of their postulated consequences for younger siblings. According to the spillover model, changes in relations between firstborn children and parents dictate the timing of changes in relations between later born children and parents (Larson & Almeida, 1999). Relationships with later born children deteriorate and are renegotiated concurrent with (or shortly after) relationships with firstborn children. Thus, child maturation is more strongly related to parent–child relationship change in firstborn than in later born adolescents. Several mechanisms besides child maturation may be responsible for changes in relationships between later born children and parents, including sibling modeling and imitation, and a parental desire to avoid differential treatment. Parent–adolescent relationship decline and recovery may depend on the extent to which firstborn and later born children share the burden of conflict and role renegotiation. Relationships between parents and "me too" children should be more resilient because firstborns are apt to bear the brunt of negativity with parents and because younger children may continue to look to parents to satisfy more of their emotional needs (Whiteman, McHale, & Crouter, 2003).

A related theory also postulates birth order differences in changes in parent–adolescent relationships. The learning-from-experience model argues that parents hone their skills with firstborn children and are thus better able to cope constructively with developmental changes in later born children (Whiteman et al., 2003). According to this view, it is the magnitude of parent–child transitions that differs between firstborns and later borns, not the timing of change. Declines in warmth and increases in conflict should be greater for parents and firstborn children than for parents and later born children because parents have learned how to navigate transitions during adolescence. Improved parenting skills should not only minimize relationship disruption but should also help relationships with later born children recover more quickly and perhaps more satisfactorily than relationships with firstborn children.

The third moderated maturationist model implicates parent and child gender in changes in parent–child relationships. The gender intensification model argues that with the onset of puberty, parents increasingly assume responsibility for the socialization of same-sex offspring (Hill & Lynch, 1983). The original model suggested that parent–child closeness increases in same-sex dyads and decreases in other-sex dyads. Another possibility, however, is that same-sex parent–child relationships become closer than other-sex relationships because, although absolute levels of closeness decline in both, the latter deteriorates more than the former. The model also has implications for parent–child conflict: With the advent of puberty, same-sex parent–child relationships should experience greater turmoil than other-sex relationships, as conflict and role negotiation are focused on the parent who has most of the socialization responsibilities. Notwithstanding these different interpretations, there is general agreement that by the end of the adolescent years, children should have better relations with their same-sex parent than with their other-sex parent.

The fourth moderated maturationist model implicates schools and other extrafamilial peer settings in alterations in parent–adolescent relationships (Simmons & Blyth, 1987). According to this view, maturity-related expectations vary across peer contexts, accelerating or delaying demands for realigning relationships with parents. Settings that encourage contact between early adolescents and late adolescents may elicit parent–child relationship disturbance earlier than settings that limit contacts to same-age adolescents because the former may prompt young adolescents to seek greater rights and privileges than the latter. Thus, exposure to older peers may hasten the onset of parent–child relationship change and lengthen the period of estrangement and heightened conflict with parents. Reestablishing positive parent–child relationships after early, off-time transformations may be difficult in cases where closeness was discontinued prematurely and followed by a prolonged period of discord and dissatisfaction.

Models of Relationship Continuity

Some models of parent–adolescent relationships focus on forces that promote stability within the dyad, rather than on the impact of individual change on the dyad. The most prominent example, attachment theory, emphasizes the strong emotional ties between parents and adolescents. As a mutually regulated system, parents and children work jointly to maintain the relationship in a manner consistent with cognitive representations derived from their history of interactions with significant others (Bowlby, 1969). Thus, the quality of parent–child relationships is presumed to be stable over time. Manifestations of attachment

undergo gradual developmental transformations, but these changes are consistent with the underlying quality of the relationship, which tends to be durable (Ainsworth, 1989).

Attachment in adolescence is distinctive from attachment in earlier relationships, both behaviorally and cognitively. Strong emotional ties to parents may be indicated in subtle and private ways, including friendly teasing and small acts of concern, as well as in more obvious connections such as shared activities (particularly with fathers) and self-disclosure (particularly to mothers). Cognitive advances in adolescence make possible an integrated, overarching view regarding experiences that involve caregiving, caretaking, and confidence in the availability of significant others (Allen & Land, 1999). Consequently, whereas younger children view attachment in terms that are more specific to the parent–child relationship, adolescents are increasingly attuned to the similarities and differences between relationships with parents, other significant adults, friends, and romantic partners.

The functions of attachment relationships for adolescents, however, are parallel to those for young children. In both cases, parents serve as a secure base for exploring the environment. Whereas security facilitates the toddler's exploration of the immediate environment, security affords the adolescent a sense of confidence in family support for explorations outside of the family, including the formation of new relationships. Security also allows adolescents an opportunity to explore intellectual and emotional autonomy from the family, which includes the realization that parents are fallible and an appreciation of the advantages of amicably resolving disagreements (Allen et al., 2003). Put simply, the form of secure base behavior changes with age but the function remains essentially the same.

A key implication of attachment formulations is that relationship reorganization occurs gradually. Adolescents and parents with a history of sensitive, responsive interactions and strong emotional bonds should maintain these positive features throughout adolescence, although supportive interactions may be reformulated as the child matures. Adolescents and parents with a history of difficult, unresponsive interactions are also likely to experience continuity in the quality of their interactions. Dismissive youth may seek to distance themselves from parents as soon as possible, whereas preoccupied youth may be unwilling or unable to embrace demands for greater autonomy made by parents. These families may experience an increase in conflict and a decline in warmth, but this does not necessarily signal worsening relationships, but may instead represent a new manifestation of insecurity. Attachment theory does not rule out the possibility that increasing adolescent autonomy may give rise to modest age-related changes in the frequency with which affection and disagreement are expressed, but these changes are thought to reflect shifts in forms of expression, not in the fundamental quality of relationships between parents and children (Allen & Land, 1999; Allen & Manning, 2007; Carlivati & Collins, 2007). Greater significance is attached to the tenor of interactions between parents and children and the degree to which participants treat each other with mutual regard. These and other indices of relationship quality are directly tied to attachment security. Stability in attachment security implies stability in relationship quality both over time and across individuals.

Similar predictions characterize developmental applications of interdependence and social relations models (Laursen & Bukowski, 1997; Reis, Collins, & Berscheid, 2000). Interdependence is a hallmark of all close relationships and is manifested in frequent, strong, and diverse interconnections maintained over an extended time (Kelley et al., 1983). In an interdependent relationship, partners engage in mutually influential exchanges and share the belief that their connections are reciprocal and enduring. These enduring interconnections are internalized by participants and organized into mental schemas that shape expectations concerning future interactions.

Cognitive advances during adolescence give rise to a realization that the rules of reciprocity and social exchange govern interactions with friends but not parents (Youniss & Smollar, 1985). Greater autonomy provides an impetus for adolescents to seek changes in relationships with parents so that interactions incorporate many of the same principles of social exchange. Although the affiliation remains involuntary or obligatory, there is great variability in the degree to which parents and children remain interconnected during late adolescence and early adulthood. To the extent that affiliations become increasingly voluntary, exchanges may be revised to better reflect their costs and benefits to participants. The magnitude of change depends on the potential for children to lead independent lives: Children (of all ages) who are utterly dependent on their parents are less likely to insist upon equitable exchanges than children who are (potentially) self-sufficient.

Patterns of communication and interdependence established during childhood are assumed to carry forward into adolescence. As the child becomes more autonomous, the degree to which parent–child relationships change depends on the degree to which participants consider their exchanges to be fair, which is closely linked to perceptions of relationship quality (Laursen & Collins, 2004). Increased conflict may occur in poor quality relationships, along with a decline in closeness, as adolescents express a growing dissatisfaction with unequal treatment and unfavorable outcomes (Smetana, 1999). Participants in these relationships are usually ill equipped to navigate these challenges because they lack a history of collaborative interactions and a constructive process for resolving disputes. High-quality relationships, however, may change little during adolescence, or may even improve, as participants build on beneficent interactions to adjust exchanges in a mutually satisfactory manner. In sum, patterns of social exchange in close relationships are resistant to change because they are sustained by a web of interdependencies. When adolescents push to revise interactions with parents, change comes slowly and in a manner that typically extends trajectories of relationship quality from antecedent periods.

Interplay between continuity and discontinuity is a feature of parent–child relationships across the life span. Most models of parent–adolescent relationships acknowledge this interplay; few emphasize one without the other. Our depiction of models in terms of their relative emphasis on relationship change and stability obscures many theoretical subtleties, but it underscores an important conceptual distinction. Theories that focus on individual development inevitably emphasize universal changes in adolescents and their concomitant effects on relationships with parents. Theories that focus on relationship development inevitably focus on distinctive trajectories of parent–child relationships and their continuity with prior relationship functioning. These different orientations have important implications for models that describe the role parent–child relationships play in adolescent outcomes.

Conceptual Models of the Influence of Parents and Parent–Child Relationships on Adolescent Development

In this section we summarize conceptual models that address associations between parents, parent–child relationships, and adolescent development. Most models share the assumption that parents (and relationships with parents) shape adolescent outcomes, but there is little agreement on the particulars. We begin with a description of the various modes of influence, followed by an overview of proposed influence mechanisms. We then discuss hypotheses concerning the direction and magnitude of influence attributable to parents and parent–child relationships, closing with a summary of theories describing developmental variations in patterns of influence.

Modes of Influence

Approaches that describe modes of influence attempt to trace the paths through which parents shape child outcomes. Theories tend to be written in terms of concepts and processes, using the vocabulary of ordinary language. This differs from tests of hypotheses, which model links among variables using analytic terms. Consequently, the conceptual underpinnings of analytic models of modes of influence tend to be implicit rather than explicit. An explication of these analytic assumptions follows.

Perhaps the most obvious distinction in the analytic approach is that between correlated paths and causal paths. Some may be surprised that this issue remains a point of contention, given the extensive literature on parent–child relationships, but the issue continues to generate vigorous and legitimate debate. The argument that parent socialization contributes little to child outcomes hinges largely on the assertion that (1) most research on the topic is correlational; (2) causal designs yield sparse effects; and (3) genetically informed designs attribute minimal variance in child outcomes to shared environments (Harris, 1998). Scholars making the case that parents play an important role in child outcomes respond that (1) nonexperimental longitudinal designs reveal meaningful changes in child outcomes as a function of antecedent parent influence; (2) natural experiments and interventions reveal pronounced effects for parenting; and (3) traditional studies of heredity overlook gene–environment interactions and correlations, thereby underestimating parent socialization effects (Collins, Maccoby, Steinberg, Hetherington, & Bornstein, 2000). Both sides agree that little new can be learned from cross-sectional, correlational studies of parent behaviors and child outcomes.

In the most frequently proposed and tested models, parenting or parent–adolescent relationships are treated as predictor variables. Strictly speaking, parents are posited to be causal influences in these models, particularly (as is usually the case) when paths are not reversed to consider parent behaviors as outcome variables. Influence paths may be direct or mediated. Direct paths imply that changes in parent behaviors or in parent–adolescent relationships are responsible for changes in adolescent outcomes, whereas indirect paths suggest that parent variables act on proximal variables (e.g., home environment) that, in turn, have consequences for youth development. Mediated models have also been proposed in which parent variables serve as mediators, typically between contextual variables (e.g., neighborhood distress) and adolescent outcomes.

Linear and nonlinear relations between parent variables and adolescent development have been proposed for both direct and mediated models. In linear models, incremental changes in parenting or in parent–adolescent relationships are associated with commensurate changes in adolescent outcomes. In nonlinear models, the effects of the parent variable are not constant across its range. Often, the relation posited is one in which parenting or parent–adolescent relationships have linear (or even exponential) effects below a certain threshold, but above that threshold, effects of the parent variable are weak, nonexistent, or reversed (Hoff, Laursen, & Bridges, in press). Consider parent–adolescent conflict, which is thought to be beneficial at moderate levels, but detrimental at high levels (Adams & Laursen, 2007). Analytic models are not always as they appear: Studies that focus on one part of the range of a parenting variable (e.g., harsh parenting) and ignore differences outside that range implicitly model nonlinear or threshold effects, despite the appearance of testing a simple linear model.

Direct and mediated parental effects may be ascribed to heredity and to socialization. The once common practice of assessing effects with an additive model that apportions unique variance to genes (plus error), shared environments (parent influence), and nonshared environments (nonparental influence) has given way to more nuanced strategies. As a consequence, contemporary approaches recognize the need for multiple methodologies to pull apart variables that typically go together (Rutter, Pickles, Murray, & Eaves, 2001). Although few dispute the conclusion that genes shape child outcomes, the claim that nonshared environmental effects outweigh shared environmental effects (Plomin & Daniels, 1987) has been challenged for several reasons (Turkheimer & Waldron, 2000). Sampling and methodological biases tend to favor genetic and nonshared influences at the expense of shared influences. The assessment of individual level variation overlooks population level variation, failing to recognize that beneficial parenting behaviors common across individuals may be invariant, but are influential nevertheless. Further, sibling differences are not necessarily due to nonfamilial influences; differential perceptions and differential treatment arise within shared environments. Thus, genetically informed models remind us that heritability accounts for much of the variance that might otherwise be ascribed to the direct effects of parental socialization, but they are somewhat limited in their ability to disentangle shared from nonshared environmental effects.

Further pressure on either/or views of influence comes from models of bidirectional influence. Several such models have been proposed (see Kuczynski, 2003, for review). These models share the common assumption that children and parents are unique socialization agents who construct meaning out of their social experiences and who initiate purposeful behavior intended to influence the partner (Kuczynski & Parkin, 2006). Transactional models emphasize continual change in children and parents in response to recurring, reciprocal interchanges (Sameroff, 1975). One partner responds to the other's behavior, and the response influences the form of his or her subsequent behavior. Transactional models are not linear in the sense that stable behaviors in one partner cause stable outcomes in the other; they depict a dialectic of constantly changing dynamics that fosters qualitative change in the relationship and its participants. In contrast, circular causality models typically imply linear, microanalytic influences that contain a recursive loop in which cause and effect cannot be isolated. In one example, difficult child temperament and inept parenting combine to foster a vicious cycle of escalating coercion (Patterson, 1982). Finally, fit and coevolution models suggest that causality is located not in the interactions between parents and children, but in the system they construct and the degree to which their attributes and needs mesh (Thomas, Chess, & Birch, 1977). Linear effects may be hypothesized as a function of goodness-of-fit, or qualitative distinctions may be made according to the salient features of parents and children.

In another type of model, parent variables serve as moderators. These models typically start from the premise that there are qualitative differences between groups. As a consequence, associations between predictor variables and outcome variables differ for those who experience different types of parents or relationships. Parenting styles provide an example. Authoritative parents differ from authoritarian parents on a constellation of attributes that combine to create distinct child-rearing environments (Baumrind, 1991; Darling & Steinberg, 1993). Within each, similar parent behaviors may elicit different outcomes. For instance, adolescents with authoritative parents may be less likely to dissemble in response to parental requests for information than adolescents with authoritarian parents (Darling, Cumsille, Caldwell, & Dowdy, 2006). Parent moderators may enhance risk for some youth and buffer against adversity for others. Some argue that authoritarian parents may buffer against detrimental peer influences for youth in troubled neighborhoods, but the same parents may alienate youth in benign settings, inadvertently promoting fraternization with other alienated youth (Furstenberg, Cook, Eccles, Elder, & Sameroff, 1999).

All of the foregoing models invoke parenting or parent–child relationships as a substantive

influence or a meaningful outcome at some point in a causal sequence. Direct effects models imply that parents cause subsequent adolescent outcomes. Mediated effects models imply that parents cause change in an intermediary agent, which, in turn, causes change in adolescent outcomes. Bidirectional models imply that parent behaviors are both the cause and the consequence of child behaviors. In contrast, correlated change models argue that parent influences are limited to genetic contributions and to external causal factors that are either correlated with or responsible for the parent behaviors that are linked to child outcomes.

Agents of Influence

Models that assume participant driven effects, typically from parents to offspring, are still the primary framework for research on parent–adolescent relationships (Collins, 2002). They stem from an implicitly individualistic approach that focuses on associations between differences among the properties of individuals and differences among their behaviors and outcomes. Models that describe relationship driven effects are not uncommon, however, and research designs increasingly adopt this perspective (Laursen & Collins, 2004). Relationship-focused models reflect a systemic approach that focuses on associations between differences among the properties of relationships or systems of relationships and differences among the behaviors and outcomes of individuals (Reis, Collins, & Berscheid, 2000).

Early conceptions of family influence focused exclusively on parents: The parent cast a social mold for the child, which was responsible for his or her development (Collins, 2002). Few today would advocate this position conceptually, but research designs tell another story. Despite the growing acceptance of child-centered, relationship, and bidirectional frameworks, most research designs still entail the straightforward prediction of adolescent outcomes from parent behavior. Prominent in this regard are studies of parenting styles and parenting practices, and other topics that that have recently come to dominate the research landscape, such as parent psychological control. Most learning theory models of coercive training, inept parenting, and deviant modeling also fall into this category; the contributions made by temperamental difficulties in offspring have been added to recent formulations, but the research is overwhelmingly parent-driven, particularly as it applies to the second decade of life.

Child-driven or evocative models have greater currency in the study of young children than in the study of adolescents. In these models, offspring with certain characteristics or behaviors elicit particular responses from parents, which, in turn, shape child outcomes. The development of antisocial behavior in temperamentally difficult children is one example. Parents tend to respond to disruptive, aggressive children by withdrawing affection and reducing monitoring, which increases the risk of alienation and affiliation with deviant peers (Lytton, 2000). Child-driven models applied to adolescence typically focus on the influence of personality and emotional regulation. One recent model suggests that adolescent openness and disclosure elicits parent behaviors that are usually operationalized as monitoring (Kerr, Stattin, & Pakalniskiene, 2006). In this view, parent reactions to adolescent engagement and withdrawal shape subsequent adolescent outcomes and behaviors. This may strike some as circular causality, but the process is clearly categorized as child driven.

Considerable interest surrounds bidirectional models that address concurrent and over-time influences between children and parents. These models include child-driven effects and parent-driven effects, but it is one thing to hypothesize a model in which both participants in a relationship are agents of influence, and it is another thing to apply this model to actual data. Statistical obstacles have long plagued efforts to identify bidirectional effects as scholars have struggled to test reciprocal and joint influences (Laursen, 2005). Most conventional analytic procedures cannot easily incorporate data from both participants; those that do typically provide biased or misspecified results. Recent advances in dyadic data analyses can overcome these limitations, which will help to bridge the gap between theory and research (Card, Little, & Selig, 2008; Kenny, Kashy, & Cook, 2006). It is important to note that although dyadic analytic techniques were initially developed to describe the influence of one partner on another over the course of a specific interchange, they have been successfully applied to global perceptions of concurrent parent–adolescent relationships, including attachment security (Cook & Kenny, 2005) and perceived social support (Branje, van Lieshout, & van Aken, 2005). Modifications for longitudinal data have been proposed that will permit the analyses of nonindependent data across multiple time points (Kashy & Donnellan, 2008; Laursen, Popp, Burk, Kerr, & Stattin, 2008).

Relationship models start from the premise that parent–child relationships are more than the sum of the child's behavior and the parent's behavior. As a consequence, relationships are hypothesized to be important influence agents. Relationship influence mechanisms range from global indices of relationship quality (such as attachment security and support), to composites that describe positive and negative attributes of the relationship, to specific features of the relationship (such as communication and cohesion). Direct links are hypothesized between relationship quality and child outcomes, on the assumption that positive relationships are beneficial to development and negative relationships are detrimental. Relationship experiences are also filtered through relationship perceptions, which serve as a lens through which the child interprets the environment. This suggests an indirect effects model in which perceived relationship quality partially or wholly mediates associations between parent behavior and child outcomes.

Developmental Patterns of Influence

Conventional wisdom holds that parental influence wanes across the teen years relative to peer influences. Plato quotes Socrates's lament about the youth of his time: "They have bad manners, contempt for authority; they show disrespect for their elders and love chatter in place of exercise." More recently, Bronfenbrenner (1970) observed that adolescent concern with and conformity to peer norms increases with age as the school structure becomes more impersonal. That is, as schools get larger and contact with teachers becomes more superficial, youth band together to form their own culture; social pressures within the peer group increase, gradually eclipsing that exerted by adults. Similar claims of declining parental influence accompany theories of parent deidealization (Blos, 1979). According to this view, identity development and individuation require youth to separate from their parents. As adolescents recognize that parents are not infallible, they increasingly question and resist parent influence attempts. This creates an influence vacuum, which tends to be filled by peers.

But other scholars have noted that influence is not necessarily a zero-sum proposition. According to this view, parent influence is not necessarily tied to peer influence (Brittain, 1963). If absolute levels of influence are unrelated across relationships, change in influence accorded to one relationship does not necessarily prompt change in influence accorded to another. It follows that when peers become more influential, parents do not necessarily become less influential. In other words, the influence of parents may not decline in absolute terms over the course of the adolescent years, although it may decline relative to that of peers. A more nuanced version of this model holds that developmental changes in influence are domain specific (Kandel & Lesser, 1972). Different developmental patterns of influence may arise for different outcomes. For instance, peer influence may increase over matters such as attire but not over matters such as future career aspirations.

The models described thus far portray a steady growth in peer influence across the

adolescent years. Curvilinear models of peer influence have also been advocated (Devereux, 1970). According to this view, adolescents are especially vulnerable to peer pressure during the process of identity formation because, in the absence of a clear sense of self, they look to age-mates for guidance. Susceptibility to peer pressure purportedly declines in late adolescence with a rise in autonomous thought. In keeping with the notion of domain specificity, different curvilinear trajectories may apply to different outcomes (Berndt, 1979). For instance, normative increases in delinquent activity between early and mid-adolescence should accompany increases in peer pressure to experiment with deviant behavior; these pressures subside by late adolescence and so does the prestige of youth engaged in delinquent acts. Similar developmental trends would not be anticipated in peer pressure concerning internalizing problems or prosocial behavior.

Berndt (1999) offers an important caveat to the coda. It is typically assumed that parents and peers are opposing sources of influence. Adolescents are thought to be buffeted between the competing interests of family and friends. An alternative scenario holds that parents and peers are generally complementary sources of influence, providing a consistent message concerning adolescent behavior. Parents are hypothesized to have considerable direct and indirect leverage over the child's selection of friends (Parke & Buriel, 2006), so we should expect parents to encourage youth to befriend those who share their values. Another possibility holds that parent and peer influences are distinct during the early adolescent years, as adolescents struggle to establish and maintain unique identities, but that parent and peer relationships (and their influence) become gradually more integrated over time (Collins & Laursen, 2000). After youth establish an independent sense of self, sometime during mid-adolescence, peer group cohesion should decline and adolescents should spend more time in mixed-sex cliques and with romantic partners. By late adolescence, family and friend relationships are reintegrated as youth prepare for the challenges of young adulthood. This suggests that parents and peers become increasingly complementary forces across the adolescent years.

Magnitude of Influence

Until recently, the notion that parenting played a significant role in adolescent outcomes was taken for granted. Even today, after two decades of evidence suggesting that heredity accounts for a substantial proportion of the variance previously ascribed to parenting, it is still unusual to see models that hypothesize effect sizes. The focus remains squarely on statistical significance, with little or no discussion about whether large or small effects are expected. There are many good reasons to consider the magnitude of effects. First, if there is no conceptual distinction between strong trends and weak trends, there is no incentive to consider the magnitude of a particular trend. Second, models that fail to distinguish weak effects from strong effects suggest a simple main-effects model in which parents exert uniform influence over all aspects of adolescent development. Weak or null effects are counterfactual to this proposition, which leaves the door open to the assertion that parents don't matter. Third, those models that do not anticipate the relative strength of parent effects tell us only whether parents make contributions to outcomes but are of little use in explaining when and why these contributions are important.

Conceptual models hold practical and statistical implications for research. Moderated effects and nonlinear effects, which are central to many contemporary models, are difficult to detect without large samples (Fritz & MacKinnon, 2007). Furthermore, they typically yield small effects. Scholars who adopt these models must be prepared to argue that statistical procedures tend to underestimate their magnitude or else describe how small effects have important implications for development. Bidirectional models tend to be tested within a path or structural equation–modeling

framework, which can make the estimation of effect sizes less than straightforward. Effects for any one particular influence path are bound to be small after variance is partitioned across variables and relationship participants (Saris & Satorra, 1993). One consideration often overlooked is that models often dictate the selection of constructs. Event-based constructs may be less prone to bias from relationship cognitions but, as a consequence, they are less reliable and poorer predictors of outcomes (Burk, Dennissen, van Doorn, Branje, & Laursen, in press). Constructs that are highly stable also tend to yield small effects because they have insufficient variability to predict change in outcome variables. Finally, systemic models are apt to yield greater effects than individualistic models because the former encompass a wider range of variables than the latter. By the same token, interpreting systemic effects can be more difficult than interpreting individualistic effects because influence mechanisms may be less obvious.

A final point is that theories of relationship transformation have implications for models of parent influence on adolescent outcomes. Conceptualizations that emphasize change in parent–child relationships in response to the maturation of the child do not speak directly to patterns of adolescent adjustment because an accounting of normative changes experienced by all youth cannot anticipate individual differences in outcomes. Approaches that emphasize enduring characteristics of relationships should help to explain patterns of adolescent adjustment because they are predicated on the notion that some parents and some relationships are better equipped than others to help children successfully navigate the challenges of adolescence.

Maturational models assume that all families experience a period of heightened conflict and diminished closeness associated with adolescent physical and cognitive development. Differences in adjustment outcomes may be traced to the extent to which maturation is normative, both in its course and its timing. The notion that adolescence is a period of normative disturbance (Blos, 1979; A. Freud, 1958; Hall, 1904) stands in contrast with more recent assertions that youth whose physical development is internally asynchronous (e.g., pubertal maturation in the absence of emotional maturation) and youth who are off-time relative to peers are at risk for adjustment difficulties (Simmons & Blyth, 1987). The general premise that variation in parenting and parent–child relationships is a product of adolescent development, rather than a cause of maladaptive development, contrasts with theories of relationship continuity. These latter models do not assume that adolescence is inevitably a time of troubled parent–child relationships. Rather, they are predicated on the view that parenting and parent–child relationships at the outset of adolescence anticipate changes in individual adjustment over the course of adolescence: Youth in secure, supportive relationships should experience few difficulties coping with maturational changes. Youth in poor quality relationships may lack resources to cope with maturation and thus may experience an upsurge in interpersonal difficulties that heighten the risk of adjustment problems. These difficulties do not spring up overnight. Escalating conflict and emotional alienation are thought to be symptomatic of relationship distress that is evident in the years leading up to adolescence.

INTERPERSONAL PROCESSES AND RELATIONSHIP PERCEPTIONS

These theoretical views underscore a fundamental but often neglected point: Despite a long-standing orientation to the impact of parental actions, the significance of relationships with parents derives from joint action patterns. The meaning of most parental actions depends on the history of interactions between parent and adolescent and the immediate context of the action of each toward the other (Maccoby, 1992). This suggests that a focus on behavior alone provides a less-than-complete picture of the relationship; we must also consider how participants perceive their own behavior and that of their partner. There are systematic differences between parents and children in perceptions of their relationship. There are also individual differences in views of relationships. Put simply, interactions differ across relationships and these interactions are interpreted differently by parents and children, and by individuals with specific attributes. In this section we will describe these behavioral and perceptual differences and discuss some of their ramifications.

Most of the developmental research on parent–child relationships has focused on identifying aspects of the relationship that are subject to change and to charting the course of these normative alterations. As is the case in relationships generally, parent–adolescent dyads vary in the content or kinds of interactions; the patterning, or distribution of positive and negative exchanges; the quality, or the degree of responsiveness that each shows to the other; and the cognitive and emotional responses of each individual toward the partner and his or her behavior. In this section, we will describe continuity and change in parent–child relationships during adolescence and review the available evidence concerning age-related trends in parent and adolescent behaviors and perceptions as well as individual differences that affect them.

Parents and Adolescents as Relationship Participants and as Relationship Reporters

Thirty years ago, Olson (1977) made an important distinction between insider and outsider views of the family. The point is worth repeating (and the chapter is worth rereading), because it contains many subtle distinctions that tend to be lost or overlooked. There is widespread acknowledgment that family members experience family relationships differently. But what, exactly, does this mean? For starters, it means that mothers, fathers, and adolescent children have different expectations about their relationships. Fathers expect the family to be a respite from work; mothers anticipate family obligations to be a major source of stress and gratification; adolescents, whose emotional energies tend to be focused on peers, tend to hold utilitarian views of the family (Larson & Richards, 1994). These expectations are a product of schema, cognitive structures that interpret experiences on the basis of past interactions and that construct scripts that guide future interactions (Baldwin, 1992). Differences in relationship schema arise because the nature and the content of interactions differ across family members: Mothers have more mundane socializing interactions with children than fathers, and a much higher percentage of mother–child interactions fall into this category than father–child interactions. In contrast, fathers devote a higher proportion of their time with adolescents to recreational activities. These distinctions are amplified in households with more than one child. Participants interpret these interactions in terms of their relationship schema; fathers, looking to relax, seek to minimize socialization hassles with children, whereas mothers, who often experience negative affective spillover from work, may invest considerable emotion in otherwise mundane interactions with children.

Differences in schemas and experiences have important implications for reports about family relationships and interactions. Olson (1977) notes that reports differ not only between members of a family, but also between family members and observers. The relationship schema held by observers are not the same as those held by parents or children because observers have no common relationship history on which to base expectations and no emotional stake in the interaction. Does this mean that observer reports are more accurate? Not necessarily because, although observers may be less biased, they are also less informed. Observers may have difficulty distinguishing playful insults from hostility, and they may miss inside jokes or veiled

animosity (Gonzales, Caucé, & Mason, 1996). This is not to say that observer reports are unhelpful. There are many important uses for observer reports, particularly when one needs an objective take on microanalytic events. But self-reports are important for precisely the reason they are often shunned by researchers— namely, because they are biased by participant perceptions, expectations, and cognitions. The challenge for developmental scientists is how best to collect and utilize reports from both participants in a relationship, which are, by definition, not independent. To understand the true course of parent–adolescent relationships, we must distinguish stability and change as they are experienced by each participant. This requires longitudinal data for each reporter. To understand the role that parent–child relationships play in adolescent outcomes we must distinguish each participant's perceptions of the relationship from their perceptions of their own behavior and that of their partner. This requires analytic techniques designed for interdependent data (Kenny, Kashy, & Cook, 2006). There are very few circumstances in which the optimal research strategy involves (1) focusing exclusively on the views of a single relationship participant or (2) combining parent and child reports into a single score.

Parenting Styles and Practices

Interactional variations from one parent–adolescent dyad to another have been subsumed, in part, by the construct of parenting styles (Baumrind, 1991; Darling & Steinberg, 1993). Parenting styles characterize parents and their relations with specific children. *Authoritative parenting* denotes a complex amalgam of actions and attitudes that give priority to the child's needs and abilities while at the same time implying age-appropriate maturity demands. By contrast, *authoritarian parenting* is typified by interactions implying relative neglect of the child's needs in favor of the parent's agenda, strong demands for child compliance, and forceful methods for gaining compliance and punishing infractions.

Permissive parenting implies low demands from parents related to child-centered indulgence and self-direction on the part of the child. A fourth dimension, *uninvolved parenting*, refers to parent-centered inattentiveness and neglect of the child (Maccoby & Martin, 1983). These concepts almost certainly gain their explanatory power from diverse interactions whose influence is often mistakenly attributed to parents alone (Collins & Madsen, 2003). Indeed, parenting styles are defined in terms of the attitudes that parents have toward children and child rearing, the tenor of interactions between parents and children, and expressions of warmth and discipline. For example, Maccoby and Martin (1983) identified the defining features of authoritativeness as interactions that are high in reciprocity and bidirectional communication, whereas authoritarian and indulgent styles imply relationships in which reciprocity and communication are disrupted by the dominance by the parent (in the authoritarian style) or the child (in the indulgent style). As initially conceived, interactions between parents and children were both a marker and a product of different styles of parenting.

The distinction between the parent's attitudes about children and the parent's actions toward children becomes clearer in Darling and Steinberg's (1993) formulation, in which *parental styles* are global attitudes and emotional stances, and *parental practices* are specific strategies for gaining children's compliance, maintaining control, and enforcing expectations. Although relevant to relationships, styles and practices should not be considered indices of relationship quality; rather, these variables refer to the parent's views about the relationship and behavior within the relationship, respectively. Practices are postulated to be an outgrowth of styles, so styles have more influence over the overall quality of the relationship than practices. Neither is fixed; practices change as attitudes about parenting are modified and, presumably, parents modify styles on the basis of experiences with

particular practices in specific relationships. As their names imply, parental styles and parental practices describe parents, who are assumed to be the primary vehicle of influence in the relationship. Styles and practices are related to characteristics of parents, such as education and personality, but they are not traits; parents can and do adopt different styles and practices with different children (Baumrind, 1991).

Scholars have devoted considerable effort to the challenge of parsing authoritative parenting. Two areas of controversy merit mention. The first concerns distinguishing psychological control from other aspects of authoritative parenting (Barber, 1996; Gray & Steinberg, 1999). Despite recent studies suggesting that psychological control is distinct from autonomy granting (Silk, Morris, Kanaya, & Steinberg, 2003) and monitoring (Smetana & Daddis, 2002), the construct remains poorly understood, in part because some studies operationalize psychological control as an index of parenting style whereas others treat it as a parenting practice (Steinberg, 2005). The second area of controversy concerns the distinction between parental monitoring and adolescent disclosure (Kerr & Stattin, 2000; Stattin & Kerr, 2000). Although monitoring is typically defined as parents' attempts to elicit information about youths' activities and whereabouts, measures tend to conflate parental knowledge with parental efforts to stay informed (Stattin, Kerr, & Tilton-Weaver, in press). Stattin and Kerr argue that most parental knowledge comes from the voluntary disclosure of information by adolescents rather than the active solicitation of information by parents. Disclosure, they argue, is a product of family climate or parenting style, not parenting practices. These controversies underscore the need for scholars to separately consider information from parents and children because there are obvious confounds between the child's reports of their own behavior and their views of their parents' styles and practices.

In North American samples, authoritative parenting and indulgent parenting are more prevalent than authoritarian parenting and neglectful parenting. Most studies that describe parents of adolescents focus on mothers; some report the average of maternal and paternal scores; few examine mothers and fathers separately. There is some evidence to suggest that mothers and fathers in the same household tend to adopt similar or pure parenting styles (Steinberg, 2001). A recent study (Simmons & Conger, 2007) revealed consistency between parents but divergence between reporters: Both child reports and observer reports agreed that pure parenting prevailed in most households. Children indicated that indulgent parenting was the most common style, whereas observers indicated that authoritative parenting was prevalent. Cross-sectional findings imply that practices associated with authoritarian parenting decline across the adolescent years, practices associated with indulgent parenting increase across the adolescent years, and practices associated with authoritative parenting hold steady (Steinberg & Silk, 2002).

Positive Interactions and Perceived Support

In order to maintain relationships in the midst of rapid and extensive change, they must be adapted to the characteristics of individuals. The most obvious pressure on relationships comes from the physical, social, and cognitive changes in adolescents. At the same time, adolescents have a number of new experiences that differ from their experiences with family members. As a consequence, the importance of parents in adolescents' lives depends less on the physical power of parents and the extent to which they share experiences with their children and more on the emotional and instrumental support the family provides and the psychological bond between parents and children. Even so, there is considerable continuity between positive features of relationships during adolescence and those earlier in life, despite alterations in interaction, affect, and cognition.

Early studies pitting parents against peers found that the latter steadily gained influence at the expense of the former across the transition into adolescence and beyond (Bowerman & Kinch, 1959). Subsequent work underscored the limitations of this hydraulic perspective, revealing that relative parent and peer influences vary across domains. For issues relating to the future (e.g., school and career), parent influence remains greater than peer influence across the course of adolescence, but for issues concerning contemporary lifestyle (e.g., attire and leisure activities), peer influence increases during adolescence and eventually outweighs that of parents (Collins & Steinberg, 2006). Taken together, the literature suggests that relationships with parents remain the most influential of all adolescent relationships and shape most of the important decisions confronting children, even as parents' relative authority over mundane details of adolescents' lives wanes. Yet the issue is far from settled because important questions remain about the mechanisms of influence, the relative strength of parents and peers over specific forms of behavior, and the degree to which relative influences vary as a product of individual differences in family and friend relationships and in characteristics of youth.

Closeness is an umbrella term that describes the extent to which two individuals are connected behaviorally and emotionally. Commonly invoked indicators include interdependence, intimacy, support, trust, and communication. Although parents and adolescents who consider themselves close also report positive thoughts and feelings (Laursen & Williams, 1997), a minority appear to have highly interdependent and mutually influential relationships comprised predominantly of negative interactions in which one person neither feels positive about nor close to the other person (Collins & Repinski, 2001). The generally positive views attributed to parents and adolescents rest on findings that both report frequent, supportive interactions and a very low incidence of problems such as physical withdrawal and communication difficulties. This depiction of positive, well-functioning parent–adolescent relationships applies to families in cultures around the world (Collins, 1995; Collins & Repinski, 2001).

Continuities in relationships coexist, however, with significant changes in the amount, content, and perceived meaning of interactions; in expressions of positive affect between parents and adolescents; and in their perceptions of each other and their relationship (Collins, 1995). Closeness during adolescence is manifest in forms that differ from closeness in earlier parent–child relationships. For example, intimacy, as expressed by cuddling and extensive joint interactions, decreases as children mature, whereas conversations in which information is conveyed and feelings are expressed increase (Hartup & Laursen, 1991). These adaptations are appropriate responses to the maturity level and changing needs of the adolescent.

Developmental changes in closeness are well documented. Subjective rankings of closeness and perceived support and objective indices of interdependence decrease across the adolescent years (Laursen & Williams, 1997; Mooney, Laursen, & Adams, 2006), as does the amount of time parents and adolescents spend together (Larson, Richards, Moneta, Holmbeck, & Duckett, 1996). Both the form and the content of time spent together change. As children get older, they spend more time watching TV with their parents and less time sharing meals and going out together (Dubas & Gerris, 2002). Relative to preadolescents, adolescents perceive less companionship and intimacy with parents (Buhrmester & Furman, 1987) and report lower feelings of acceptance by parents and less satisfaction with family life (Hill, 1988). Although perceptions of relationships remain generally warm and supportive, both adolescents and parents report less frequent expressions of positive emotions when compared with reports during preadolescence. Decreases in expressed warmth appear to be steepest from preadolescence to mid-adolescence, tapering off or even rebounding by late adolescence. In relationships with

mothers and fathers, warmth expressed by daughters declines more than that expressed by sons, in part because the former start from a higher level than the latter (McGue, Elkins, Walden, & Iacono, 2005). Birth order appears to moderate these trends. First-born children report the warmest relationships with mothers and fathers across the course of adolescence, but firstborns also report the steepest drops in warmth from early adolescence to mid-adolescence (Shanahan, McHale, Crouter, & Osgood, 2007). Maternal experiences with older siblings predict subsequent maternal perceptions of relations with younger siblings; parents who have unsatisfactory relationships with older siblings tend to have similarly unsatisfactory relationships with younger siblings (Whiteman & Buchanan, 2002).

It is important to note, however, that descriptive data on age-related declines in closeness may overstate the significance of changes in parent–adolescent relationships. Many of the changes reflect a declining dependence on parents, but not necessarily erosion in the positive features or the importance of these relationships. This point may be obscured because research typically focuses on accumulated estimates of change at the group level without considering change at the level of the family. Longitudinal data from the Pittsburgh Youth Study revealed moderate to high levels of stability in parent and child reports of relationship qualities (Loeber et al., 2000). Across childhood and adolescence, the relative ordering of families on various dimensions of closeness remained fairly constant from one year to the next, even though the mean level of each variable fell. Other findings show that despite decreases across the adolescent years, parents remain second only to friends or romantic partners in perceived support during late adolescence (Furman & Buhrmester, 1989). Almost 20% of late adolescents nominated a parent as their closest relationship partner, and 25% rated these relationships as their most interdependent (Laursen & Williams, 1997). Taken together, the available findings portray a complex dynamic of relationship continuity and change that belies the conventional view of an abrupt descent toward distance and alienation.

Parent and adolescent views of the family are notable for their divergence, particularly during early adolescence. In general, children tend to see the family in terms quite different from parents. Maternal and paternal reports of their own relationships with an adolescent child agree more than the child's reports and that of either parent (Cook & Goldstein, 1993). Where mothers and fathers see unique relationships, adolescents see monolithic ones. Parents, especially mothers, tend to appraise the family more positively than adolescents do (Laursen & Collins, 2004). Mothers routinely report more warmth and affection among family members than adolescents do (Noller & Callan, 1988), which may be an attempt to ward off the decline in maternal life satisfaction that accompanies increasing adolescent autonomy (Silverberg & Steinberg, 1990). Another explanation of perceptual discrepancies is rooted in the different orientations of parents and children. Based on a round-robin, Social Relations Model design (Cook & Kenny, 2005), recent findings indicate that adolescents' perceptions of family support were primarily driven by their general views of the family, whereas parents' give greater weight to evaluations of specific relationships (Branje, van Aken, & van Lieshout, 2002). Discrepant expectations and mismatched perceptions of cohesion, expressiveness, and support are highest at the outset of adolescence; parent and child views gradually converge over time (Collins, Laursen, Mortensen, Luebker, & Ferreira, 1997; Seiffge-Krenke, 1999).

Closeness varies from one adolescent to another and from one adolescent–parent pair to another. Adolescents spend more time with their mothers and are more likely to share feelings with them. Adolescents are more likely to disclose information about personal matters to mothers than to fathers (Smetana, Metzger, Gettman, & Campione-Barr, 2006).

Fathers are often somewhat distant figures, who tend be consulted primarily for information and material support. Sons and daughters have similarly warm relationships with mothers, but fathers are typically closer to sons than daughters (Smetana, Campione-Barr, & Metzger, 2006). These trends accelerate across childhood and adolescence. One longitudinal study showed that parent involvement during childhood predicted closeness during adolescence, with stronger links between early father involvement and closeness to father at age 16 for girls than for boys (Flouri & Buchanan, 2002). Adolescent pubertal maturation, above and beyond age, has also been implicated in increased family distance, but the effects are small and inconsistent (Susman & Rogol, 2004); the timing of puberty appears to be a more potent predictor of changes in closeness than physical maturation per se.

Families adapt to individual and relationship changes in varying ways. Most families capitalize on greater adolescent maturity by fostering patterns of sustained interaction that promote a psychological closeness that depends less on frequency of interactions than was the case in childhood. They do so by adjusting interaction patterns to meet demands for adolescent autonomy (Collins, 1995). Families with a history of interpersonal problems, however, may lack the adaptive patterns needed for new forms of closeness during periods of relative distance and thus may be unable to surmount the barriers to effective relationships during adolescence (Grotevant & Cooper, 1986; Hauser, Powers, & Noam, 1991). Longitudinal evidence is consistent with the notion that some families experience greater diminutions in warmth and closeness than others. Youth who report the highest levels of support from mothers at the outset of adolescence experience little or no decline in perceived support across ages 11 to 13, whereas those who perceive the lowest initial levels of perceived support report steep drops in subsequent support (Adams, 2005). Similar findings emerge from measures of attachment, where the general trend indicating a decline in parent–child attachment across the adolescent years appears to be moderated by characteristics of the relationship (Buist, Deković, Meeus, & van Aken, 2002). Mother–adolescent attachment security remains steady and even increases slightly during mid-adolescence for nondistressed youth, but it declines dramatically for distressed youth (Allen, McElhaney, Kuperminc, & Jodl, 2004). With age, insecurely attached youth increasingly turn to peers to fulfill attachment needs (Markiewicz, Lawford, Doyle, & Haggart, 2006).

Negative Interactions and Perceived Conflict

Conflict, which is ubiquitous in close relationships, is especially prominent in families. Surveys of adolescents indicate that disagreements are most common with mothers, followed by siblings, friends, and romantic partners, then fathers; angry disputes arise more frequently with family members than with close peers (Laursen, 1995). When college students were asked to recount three memories that defined the person they came to be, almost all of the memories involving parents concerned conflict during the adolescent years (McLean & Thorne, 2003). Thus, significant meaning is attached to some parent–child disagreements.

There is considerable continuity in parent–child discord. Negativity begets more negativity. From one year to the next across the course of adolescence, children's negative feelings for parents predicted a subsequent increase in parent's negative feelings for children, and vice versa (Kim, Conger, Lorenz, & Elder, 2001). Family contentiousness during the adolescent years is best forecast by family disharmony during the preadolescent years (Stattin & Klackenberg, 1992), and parent–child conflict during the adolescent years predicts negative interactions between parents and children during young adulthood (Belsky, Jaffee, Hsieh, & Silva, 2001).

Negativity takes many different forms, but it is most commonly gauged in terms of interpersonal conflict. Disagreements are composed of discrete components with a sequential structure (Laursen & Collins, 1994). Like plays or novels, conflicts follow scripts consisting of a protagonist and an antagonist (the participants), a theme (the topic), a complication (the initiation), rising action and crisis (the resolution), and a denouement (the outcome and aftermath). Conflicts that adolescents identify as important differ from other conflicts primarily in terms of the intense negative feelings generated during and lingering after the interaction (Laursen & Koplas, 1995).

A few words about assessment are in order. Disagreement is common, but serious conflict is not. This poses a problem for measurement. Some scholars address this problem by asking parents and children to describe global perceptions of conflict in their relationship. Unfortunately, global rating scales of event frequency are heavily influenced by individual atributes, such as personality, and by overall perceptions of relationship quality (Schwarz, 1991). Other scholars ask participants to report on events using a recall period that spans an extended period of time, such as the past 2 weeks or month. This, too, introduces perceptual confounds. When compared to ratings of conflict immediately after the interaction, adolescent reports of the same interaction 6 weeks later shifted to be more consistent with their attachment-related representations (Feeney & Cassidy, 2003). When compared to peak ratings of emotion made at the close of the day, individuals who described themselves as neurotic recalled more negative emotions one month later, whereas individuals who described themselves as extraverted recalled more positive emotions one month later (Barrett, 1997). Still other scholars ask participants to report on recent events, such as those during the current or previous day. This minimizes perceptual confounds, but raises the risk that some youth will describe unrepresentative days; large samples ameliorate this liability to some extent, although it is still the case that the highly contentious are most accurately described. A running average of reports from several consecutive days may afford the least biased measure of conflict. By definition, the stability and reliability of reports of conflict from a single day will be lower than those that encompass longer time periods, which, in turn, will be lower than those from global rating scales; these differences have less to do with the assessment of conflict than with the fact that the variables confounded with conflict (e.g., personality, relationship representations) are highly stable (Burk et al., in press). One final concern: Participants infer meaning from the time frame given for the recollection of conflict; long periods imply rare, affectively laden events, whereas short periods suggest that the investigator is interested in frequent, mundane experiences (Winkielman, Knäuper, & Schwarz, 1998). These issues, combined with the absence of a common measurement metric, mean that considerable variability should be expected in accounts of parent–adolescent conflict.

Most disagreements between parents and adolescents concern mundane topics, famously tagged by John Hill (1988) as "garbage and galoshes" disputes. Findings from a small meta-analysis indicate that parent-adolescent disagreements are usually resolved through submission or disengagement; compromise is relatively rare (Laursen, 1993). Adolescents report that conflicts with parents have few negative repercussions for the relationship, despite the fact that coercive tactics prevail. The prototypical conflict between parents and adolescents involves a mundane topic, with a power-assertive resolution and a winner/loser outcome that elicits neutral or angry affect (Adams & Laursen, 2001). This form of disagreement is to be expected in obligatory affiliations where power is shared unequally and where interactions tend to take place on a closed field (Homans, 1961). During the adolescent years, children remain dependent on parents and have little choice but to engage them in matters of mutual concern. The continuity of the relationship does not depend

on getting along, so participants are free to adopt coercive strategies in conflicts without fear that the relationship will dissolve as a consequence.

Conflict with parents was once thought to increase in early adolescence and decline beginning in middle adolescence, but meta-analytic methods demonstrated that this presumed inverted U-shaped curve was an artifact of the failure to distinguish the frequency of conflict from its affective quality. Evidence from multiple studies actually reveals linear declines in the frequency of conflict with parents from early adolescence to mid-adolescence and again from mid-adolescence to late adolescence. Significantly, however, the anger associated with these conflicts increases from early adolescence to mid-adolescence, with little change thereafter (Laursen, Coy, & Collins, 1998). Thus, conflict rates fall as negative affect rises, leaving families with the perception of worsening discord. A recent challenge to this explanation argues that curvilinear trends in parent–child conflict take place at the level of the family, not the dyad (Shanahan, McHale, Osgood, & Crouter, 2007). According to this view, conflict between parents and all children in the household follows an inverted U–shaped function, beginning when the eldest child is an early adolescent. This spillover hypothesis opens a new avenue of research on a topic that many thought had been settled.

No reliable age differences have emerged in either the topics or the outcomes of parent–adolescent conflict, but there is some indication that conflict resolutions are somewhat altered across the adolescent years. The frequency with which adolescents submit to parents declines, accompanied by an increase in disengagement and, during late adolescence, compromise (Smetana, Daddis, & Chuang, 2003; Smetana & Gaines, 1999). Perhaps more important are changes in views concerning the legitimacy of parental authority and decision making (Smetana, 2000). Across the adolescent years, but particularly during early adolescence, parents and children renegotiate domains of authority. Adolescents view an increasing number of issues to be personal matters outside of parental authority, whereas parents continue to see the same topics as prudential or social-conventional matters that fall within their jurisdiction. Steinberg (2001) suggests that one reason adults see adolescence as a particularly contentious age period is that in the process of claiming authority over domains previously regulated by parents, youth may appear overly eager to reject the ways of their elders.

In contrast to the relatively detailed information available about parent–child conflict during adolescence, we know remarkably little about changes in parent–child conflict from childhood to adolescence and from adolescence to adulthood. Evidence is limited to a single cross-sectional survey indicating that children perceive conflicts with mothers and fathers to be more prevalent during adolescence than during childhood or young adulthood (Furman & Buhrmester, 1989). In the absence of an empirical literature, Laursen and Collins (2004) offered two speculative propositions regarding long-term developmental trends in parent–child conflict: (1) The level of negative affect in parent–child conflict probably is higher during adolescence than during any other age period, except perhaps toddlerhood; and (2) the prevalence of coercion and winner/loser outcomes in parent–child conflict gradually declines across successive age periods from toddlerhood to adulthood. To this we would add that parents and children view these developmental trends somewhat differently. Parents may regard the changes as signs of rejection and deteriorating relationships, whereas adolescents may regard them as evidence of an (overdue) acknowledgment of enhanced maturity. Those who perceive loss (i.e., parents) in response to change experience greater stress than those who perceive gain (i.e., adolescent children).

Viewing relationships through the prism of personal gain and loss helps to explain why parents and adolescents describe their interactions in different terms (Noller, 1994). Adolescents appear to have more accurate (or more honest) appraisals of unpleasant aspects of the relationship than do parents. Reports of family conflict from independent observers frequently match those of adolescent children, but neither observer nor adolescent reports accord with parent reports of the same events (Gonzales et al., 1996). Although fathers are stereotyped as the family member most likely to be out of touch, accumulating evidence implies that it is mothers who most often underestimate the incidence of parent–adolescent conflict and overestimate its severity. Not coincidentally, mothers also report the most negative repercussions from conflicts with adolescent children (Silverberg & Steinberg, 1990). Several explanations have been offered for mothers' relatively extreme responses. Chief among them is that conflict represents a personal failure for mothers because it is an indictment of their ability to serve as family conciliators and peacemakers (Vuchinich, 1987). Moreover, conflict is the primary vehicle through which adolescents renegotiate their role in the family, which inevitably diminishes maternal (but not necessarily paternal) authority (Steinberg, 1981). The fact that parent and child reports of conflict appear to converge during late adolescence suggests that disagreements, though often unpleasant, play an important role in aligning expectations and facilitating communication among family members (Collins, 1995).

Parents appear to become either more skilled or less invested in changes in relationships with later born children as compared with firstborn children. It is also possible that later born children learn how to better navigate relationships with parents by watching their older counterparts. In any event, second-born children report less conflict during early and mid-adolescence than firstborn children did during these age periods (Whiteman, McHale, & Crouter, 2003). Compared to second-born children, mothers and fathers discipline firstborn children relatively more often during early adolescence, particularly if they display high levels of emotionality (Tucker, McHale, & Crouter, 2003). This type of differential treatment is not necessarily detrimental. Adolescent perceptions of differential treatment are associated with parent reports of greater relationship hostility only when the child perceives the treatment to be unfair (Kowal, Krull, & Kramer, 2004).

The extent to which gender moderates the relation between parent–child conflict behavior and developmental changes in adolescents varies according to whether the focus is the frequency of conflict, the affective response to it, or the resolution. Rates of conflict and levels of negative affect are higher in mother–daughter relationships than in other parent–child relationships (Laursen & Collins, 1994). In the meta-analysis by Laursen and colleagues (1998), conflict rates declined more in mother–child relationships than in father–child relationships, but gender did not moderate changes in affective intensity. Conflict resolutions vary as a function of both parent and adolescent gender: Compromise is more common with mothers than with fathers, and disengagement is more typical of conflict with sons than of conflict with daughters (Smetana et al., 2003; Smetana, Yau, & Hanson, 1991; Vuchinich, 1987). In contrast, studies of negative affect and conflict resolution yield no reliable evidence that gender moderates patterns of developmental change. Too little attention has been given to understanding the role gender plays in differences between dyadic and triadic parent–child conflict. Adolescents clearly interact differently with one parent than they do with two parents (Vuchinich, Emery, & Cassidy, 1988), and some evidence suggests that conflict discussions are more constructive when they involve one parent than when they involve both (Gjerde, 1986). Fathers and sons are particularly likely to alter conflict behaviors in the presence of another parent (Smetana, Abernethy, & Harris, 2000).

Variations in conflict attributed to puberty depend on whether the indicator is pubertal status or pubertal timing. Pubertal status refers to absolute level of sexual maturity. Meta-analytic comparisons yield a small positive linear association between pubertal status and conflict affect, indicating that greater physical maturity is associated with greater negative affect (Laursen et al., 1998). No similar association emerged for pubertal status and the frequency of parent–child conflict. Observational studies of problem-solving interactions among fathers, mothers, and children suggest that family dynamics shift as a function of pubertal maturation (Hill, 1988; Steinberg, 1981). Fathers interrupt adolescents during discussions more in the middle phases of pubertal maturation than in earlier or later phases, successfully signaling their dominant role in family decision making. Adolescents and mothers mutually interrupted each other most often during mid-adolescence, as the former challenges the authority of the latter. In later pubertal phases, mothers interrupt less and appear to be less influential over the outcomes of group decisions than sons; mothers and daughters interrupt each other less and exert similar levels of influence over family decisions.

Pubertal timing is an indicator of adolescents' level of maturity relative to peers. Generally, early maturing sons and daughters experience more frequent and more intense parent–child conflict than do adolescents who mature on time (Laursen & Collins, 1994). Indeed, pubertal timing accounts for much of the variance in parent–adolescent conflict that might otherwise be attributed to pubertal status. Several explanations for the association between pubertal timing and parent–child conflict have been offered, most of which suggest that parents do not agree with adolescents that physical precocity is a sufficient basis for autonomy granting (Laursen & Collins, 2004). Evolutionary accounts take a more distal view, arguing that heightened parent–adolescent conflict accompanies early puberty and the onset of sexual activity, which helps to ensure reproductive success under conditions of environmental risk (Belsky, Steinberg, & Draper,

1991). Findings that heightened conflict precedes rather than follows the early onset of puberty (Belsky et al., 2007; Graber, Brooks-Gunn, & Warren, 1995; Moffitt, Caspi, Belsky, & Silva, 1992) underscore the notion that individual differences in parent-adolescent conflict are rooted in long-standing differences in family relationships.

Although families vary considerably, the extreme forms of conflict implied by the popular impression of storm and stress are neither typical nor inevitable. Bandura (1964) forcefully argued that difficult relations during the teenage years are generally circumscribed to those families that also had difficult relations during childhood. Subsequent reviews of the literature consistently conclude that turmoil characterizes a small minority of households with adolescent children—probably somewhere between 5% and 15% of North American families. As we will discuss later, individual adjustment is closely bound to interpersonal conflict (Smetana et al., 2006). Relationship difficulties usually have more to do with distressed family systems or individual mental health problems than with the challenges posed by adolescent development (Offer & Offer, 1975; Rutter et al., 1976). This serves as a fitting backdrop to findings from cluster analyses indicating that bickering is fairly common in some families, but only a small fraction have frequent and angry quarrels (Branje, van Doorn, van der Valk, & Meeus, in press; Smetana, 1996).

Conflict management processes also vary across dyads such that the significance of a disagreement depends on the perceived quality of the relationship. Feelings of positive connectedness promote the consideration of alternatives in a nonthreatening context; in less supportive relationships, disagreement may be interpreted as a hostile attack that requires an antagonistic response (Hauser et al., 1991). It is not surprising, therefore, that securely attached adolescents report fewer conflicts overall and are more likely to resolve conflict with parents through the use of compromise and

are less likely to rely on disengagement than dismissing adolescents (Ducharme, Doyle, & Markiewicz, 2002). One of the most important tasks confronting parents and children during adolescence is to renegotiate their roles and relationship; the overall tenor of the affiliation has an important bearing on the attitudes that each brings to the discussion.

To conclude, many families experience a modest upswing in conflict at the outset of adolescence, but disagreements typically are not a threat to relationships. Indeed, conflict during this period actually may strengthen relationships by providing a vehicle for communication about interpersonal issues that require attention. More than any other form of social interaction, disagreements offer parents and adolescents an opportunity to reconsider and revise expectations and renegotiate roles and responsibilities to be consistent with the autonomy typically accorded to youth in their culture. Most families successfully meet this challenge because they are able to draw on healthy patterns of interaction and communication established during earlier age periods. But for a small minority of families, the onset of adolescence holds the potential for a worsening of relationships. Families with histories of ineffective relationships are at risk for dysfunctional discord as they encounter pressures to realign relationships in response to the developmental demands of adolescence.

THE ROLE OF PARENT–CHILD RELATIONSHIPS IN ADOLESCENT ADJUSTMENT

Links between parent–adolescent relationships and the development of individual adolescents have been the focus of most of the research on families as contexts of adolescent development. Because the evidence on this point has been reviewed recently and extensively (Collins & Steinberg, 2006; Steinberg & Silk, 2002), this section is selective. It focuses primarily on how the recurring action patterns and emotional qualities of parent–adolescent interactions are related to key aspects of psychosocial competence in adolescence. The section is divided into two parts. The first is an overview of findings directly linking parent–child interactions to adolescent development. The second outlines illustrative evidence that parent–child relationships also play an important indirect role in adolescent socialization by moderating and mediating the impact of influences in and beyond the family.

Adolescent Outcomes Associated with Parent–Adolescent Relationships

Parental style, the dimension that is most closely related to the emotional tenor or quality of the parent–child relationship, is regarded as having motivational effects on the child's receptiveness to specific practices (Darling & Steinberg, 1993). It follows that the quality of parent–child exchanges and shared decision making, over and above the specific content of parental teaching, should contribute to the development of autonomous, responsible adolescent behavior by facilitating role-taking skills, ego development, and identity exploration (Grotevant & Cooper, 1986; Hauser et al., 1991). The evidence is consistent with this hypothesis: Mature levels of these competencies are associated with parent–adolescent relationships in which both individuation and connectedness are encouraged (Allen, Hauser, Bell, & O'Connor, 1994; Lamborn, Mounts, Steinberg, & Dornbusch, 1991).

Parental styles have been linked to a wide range of adjustment outcomes. In general, children of authoritative parents are most apt to excel in school and display the highest levels prosocial behavior, whereas children of neglectful or uninvolved parents tend to evince the most antisocial and health-risk behaviors and the least psychosocial maturity (Steinberg, 2001). Authoritative parent–child relationships are marked by parents' expectations of mature behavior in combination with interpersonal warmth, accepting attitudes, bidirectional communication, and an emphasis on training social responsibility and concern for the impact of one's action on others. Neglectful

parenting, in contrast, consists of relatively few expectations, low involvement with the child, and a rejecting, unresponsive, parent-centered attitude. Recent evidence suggests that the advantages of authoritative parenting and the disadvantages of neglectful parenting, found in community samples across cultures, may even extend to families of youth who commit serious criminal offenses (Steinberg, Blatt-Eisengart, & Cauffman, 2006).

Practices that are typical of authoritative families are linked to indices of positive adjustment. In studies of moral development and social responsibility, prosocial behavior is correlated with clearly communicated parental expectations for appropriate behavior, and with warmth and moderate power accompanied by reasoning and explanation (Eisenberg, Fabes, & Spinrad, 2006). Adolescents' perceptions of parental acceptance and involvement are correlated positively with self-confidence, identity exploration, and empathic behavior (Jackson, Dunham, & Kidwell, 1990; Kamptner, 1988). Observational studies of parent–adolescent interaction have shown that adolescents from families marked by high encouragement for expressing and developing one's own point of view manifested higher levels of identity exploration (Grotevant & Cooper, 1985). These conclusions are bolstered by longitudinal studies showing that high levels of bidirectional communication and mutual respect in parent–child relationships correlate positively with subsequent adolescent psychosocial maturity. Allen and colleagues (1994) report that parents' (especially fathers') behaviors that made it more difficult for family members to discuss their preferences were highly correlated with subsequent decreases in adolescents' ego development and self-esteem. In a similar study, Walker and Taylor (1991) found that advances in adolescents' moral-reasoning levels were best predicted by earlier parent–child interactions characterized by supportive, but cognitively challenging, discussions of moral issues. Although joint decision making is generally associated with the most favorable adolescent outcomes, longitudinal findings suggest that additional benefits may accrue to those who are gradually accorded autonomy over personal issues (Smetana, Campione-Barr, & Daddis, 2004).

A large body of evidence links certain parenting practices to maladaptive adolescent outcomes. Correlational findings imply that antisocial behavior and substance use are most strongly predicted by an absence of behavioral control; self-esteem and internalizing problems have the strongest links to warmth and autonomy granting; and school grades are uniquely associated with warmth, autonomy granting, and behavioral control (Barber, Stoltz, & Olsen, 2005; Gray & Steinberg, 1999). Studies of this type have been justly criticized for their reliance on concurrent data, but recent longitudinal evidence indicates that parenting practices predict subsequent changes in adolescent outcomes. Among youth affiliating with deviant peers at age 11, externalizing behaviors increased across the next 4 years for those whose parents reported low levels of behavioral control, but there was no change in externalizing problems for those whose parents reported high levels of behavioral control (Galambos, Barker, & Almeida, 2003). Parental warmth also forecasts decreases in adolescent externalizing behaviors; psychological control anticipates increases in adolescent internalizing (Doyle & Markiewicz, 2005). Some studies have raised the prospect that the influence of different parenting practices varies as a function of the child's characteristics. For instance, harsh parenting best predicts externalizing problems for undercontrolled youth but internalizing problems for overcontrolled youth (van Leeuwen, Mervielde, Braet, & Bosmans, 2004). Findings of this sort strongly imply that greater attention must be given to the match between parenting practices and child characteristics, because some child characteristics may amplify the risks associated with deleterious parenting.

Negative and positive features of parent–child relationship are only modestly intercorrelated, and each is known to make a unique contribution to adolescent outcomes. With regard to negative features, many studies have indicated that high levels of conflict are associated with psychosocial problems during adolescence and beyond. Reciprocated hostility between parents and early adolescents predicts subsequent conduct problems and depressive symptoms during mid-adolescence and high levels of expressed negative affect toward romantic partners at age 18 (Ge, Best, Conger, & Simons, 1996; Kim, Conger, Lorenz, & Elder, 2001). High levels of parent–child conflict during adolescence have also been linked to emotional maladjustment and poor-quality relationships with romantic and marital partners at age 25 (Overbeek, Stattin, Vermulst, Ha, & Engels, 2007).

Conflict is not uniformly deleterious, however. Its impact appears to vary as a function of the perceived quality of the relationship. Evidence suggests that conflict is inversely related to well-being if the relationship is perceived to be poor, but moderate amounts of conflict may be beneficial for those whose relationships are good (Adams & Laursen, 2007). Regardless of the quality of the relationship, the worst outcomes are generally reserved for those with the most conflicts. But when adolescents reporting no conflicts with mothers and fathers are compared to those reporting an average number of conflicts, the latter had higher school grades if they were in better but not poorer quality relationships and reported more withdrawal if they were in poorer but not better quality relationships. The negative tenor of conflicts in relationships perceived to be unsupportive undoubtedly plays a central role in these deleterious outcomes. Findings that poorly managed parent–child conflict is associated with adolescent depression, delinquency, and self-esteem (Caughlin & Malis, 2004; Tucker, McHale, & Crouter, 2003; van Doorn, Branje, & Meeus, in press) suggest that dysfunctional families not only have frequent disagreements but that these disagreements are typically angry and are resolved in a coercive, unconstructive manner.

Perceptions matter. New studies indicate that adolescent views of relationship quality predict the trajectory of subsequent individual adjustment. Studies of attachment security indicate that adolescent representations of parent–child relationships predict changes in internalizing and externalizing symptoms (Allen, Porter, McFarland, McElhaney, & Marsh, 2007). Adolescent attachment security also predicts increases in social skills and constructive interactions with romantic partners (Allen, Marsh, McFarland, McElhaney, & Land, 2002; Roisman, Madsen, Hennighausen, Sroufe, & Collins, 2001). Difficulties increase over time for adolescents who initially perceive low support from parents, whereas adjustment problems remain flat or even decline for those who initially perceive high support from parents (Brendgen, Wanner, Morin, & Vitaro, 2005; Deković, Buist, & Reitz, 2004). This is not just a matter of the troubled getting worse and the well-adjusted getting better; the same findings emerge for youth with comparable levels of behavior problems at the outset of adolescence (Mooney, Laursen, & Adams, 2007).

Adolescent reports are most likely to be indicative of positive adjustment when they converge with parent reports. Regardless of who sees the relationship in better terms, large discrepancies signal poor adolescent functioning. Specifically, divergent reports of relationship quality and parenting practices are associated with concurrent academic and behavioral problems (Feinberg, Howe, Reiss, & Hetherington, 2000; Mounts, 2007) and prospective declines in adolescent self-esteem (Ohannessian, Lerner, Lerner, & von Eye, 2000). Perceptions also matter in terms of whether adolescents see themselves as receiving the same treatment as a sibling. After accounting for absolute levels of each, differential warmth and control uniquely predict adolescent outcomes (Tamrouti-Makkink, Dubas, Gerris, & van Aken, 2004). Not surprisingly, effects are stronger for the sibling who perceives himself or herself to be the recipient of poorer treatment (Feinberg & Hetherington, 2001; Sheehan & Noller, 2002).

The increasing use of longitudinal designs bodes well for conclusions concerning parent influences. However, the largely correlational nature of findings from longitudinal data leaves open the question of process: What is the origin of associations between variations in family relationships and adolescent adjustment? Several possibilities have been proposed (Collins et al., 2000). One is that parents' child-rearing behaviors provide models of different patterns of social responsibility and concern for others. A second possibility is that different parenting styles engender differentially effective skills for autonomous, responsible behavior. In this respect, parent–child relationships provide continuities between childhood and the new demands of adolescence that facilitate the integration of past and future roles. Third, sensitive, responsive parental treatment of children and adolescents promotes positive emotional bonds that make the values and behaviors of parents more salient and attractive to adolescents. These three possibilities are not mutually exclusive. Indeed, multiple plausible mechanisms imply a more complex causal process than does a view that emphasizes the simple transmission of parents' values to the next generation (Kuczynski, 2003; Grusec, Goodnow, & Kuczynski, 2000). Adolescent adjustment clearly is facilitated by certain parental behaviors, but the operative processes almost certainly include dynamic properties of relationships between parent and child that foster the adolescents' desire or willingness to be influenced.

The debate on parental monitoring and child disclosure is instructive in this regard. Parental monitoring has long been assumed to be beneficial for adolescent development. Many scholars have reported that monitoring predicts concurrent and prospective adolescent outcomes. Although monitoring is conceptualized as an active process whereby parents solicit information about children and keep track of their activities and whereabouts, the conflation of measures of parental control and knowledge with measures of child disclosure calls into question the mechanisms of parent influence, raising the prospect that a family climate that encourages disclosure may be more important than parent monitoring efforts. Initial reports by Stattin and Kerr (2000; Kerr & Stattin, 2000) and a recent longitudinal replication (Kerr, Stattin, and Burk, in press) indicating that parental knowledge from child disclosure predicted concurrent adolescent adjustment more strongly than did knowledge gained by tracking and surveillance launched a flurry of empirical work. The finding that parental monitoring is of secondary importance in the prediction of adolescent outcomes has not been consistently replicated (Fletcher, Steinberg, & Williams-Wheeler, 2004; Waizenhofer, Buchanan, & Jackson-Newsom, 2004), which has stimulated an ongoing search for potential moderating variables.

One important distinction to emerge is that between voluntary disclosure and active attempts to keep secrets from parents (Frijns, Finkenaur, Vermulst, & Engels, 2005). Adolescents from authoritative homes and those who report high levels of trust and acceptance in relationships with parents are more apt to disclose information and refrain from lying and keeping secrets than adolescents who report low levels of trust and acceptance (Darling, Cumsille, Caldwell, & Dowdy, 2006; Smetana, Metzger, Gettman, & Campione-Barr, 2006). These findings raise the possibility that some parents find monitoring more effective and rewarding than others. We know that parents tend to decrease their monitoring of deviant youth, even though this results in a subsequent escalation of antisocial behavior (Dishion, Nelson, & Bullock, 2004; Jang & Smith, 1997; Laird, Pettit, Bates, & Dodge, 2003). Perhaps the parents of deviant children (for whom trust and acceptance are in short supply) respond to secretive and nonresponsive youth by reducing efforts to solicit information, which widens the gulf between them and diminishes the parent's potential for positive influence (Kerr, Stattin, & Pakalnaskiene, in press). Thus, family climate dictates the degree to which parental knowledge

is effective in shaping adolescent outcomes by creating conditions that foster or inhibit honest disclosure and effective supervision.

Parent–Child Relationships as Moderators and Mediators of Influence

Contemporary approaches to research on parenting have moved beyond the exclusive reliance on the global analyses of parental influence that dominated the field in the last century (Collins et al., 2000). Among the insights emerging from these more complex models of parenting is the recognition that, in addition to their direct impact on adolescent development, relationships with parents also may be significant as intervening mechanisms. In this section, we consider instances in which parent–adolescent relationships serve as *moderators* of relations between other sources of influence and adolescent outcomes and as *mediators* that help to account for or explain why a predictor is related to the outcome of interest.

The complex interplay between genetic and environmental influences on adolescent development is illustrated by recent findings indicating that parenting moderates the heritability of adolescent adjustment difficulties. The first example concerns the role of parental monitoring on adolescent cigarette smoking (Dick, Viken, Purcell, Kaprio, Pulkkinen, & Rose, 2007). A genetically informed twin design revealed that parental monitoring had a very modest direct influence on smoking (accounting for less than 2% of the variance), but the effects for monitoring as a moderator of genetic influence were dramatic: Genetic factors accounted for more than 60% of the variance at the low end of the parental monitoring continuum and less than 15% of the variance at the high end. A related study indicated that parental warmth similarly moderates genetic influence on adolescent antisocial behavior but not depression (Feinberg, Button, Neiderhiser, Reiss, & Hetherington, 2007). At low levels of warmth, genetics accounts for 90% of the variance in antisocial behavior, but at high levels of warmth, the contribution of genetics approaches zero. These findings render discussions about the relative importance of genes and parenting practices obsolete; child outcomes clearly depend on both.

As one set of relationships in a larger network of close relationships, parent influences moderate and are moderated by peer relationships and relationships with other family members. Most adolescents are embedded in networks of relationships that are similar in their perceived quality. Longitudinal evidence indicates that the majority of adolescents describe all of their parent and friend relationships as either high quality or low quality; fewer than one in four adolescents report diverging support from peers and parents (Laursen, Furman, & Mooney, 2006). Good relationships with friends can ameliorate some of the detrimental impact associated with poor relationships with parents (Gauze, Bukowski, Aquan-Assee, & Sippola, 1996), but there are limits to this buffering. Adolescents reporting a positive relationship with a parent or a friend (but not both) had somewhat better outcomes than adolescents with no positive relationships, but adolescents with uniformly positive relationships almost always had the best school grades, the highest self-worth, and the fewest behavior problems (Laursen & Mooney, 2008).

Parenting quality moderates extrafamilial stressors. Mid-adolescents experiencing high levels of school hassles demonstrated more competent functioning and less evidence of psychopathology if they rated their familial relationships as high quality rather than lower quality (Garber & Little, 1999). Moreover, the link between after-school self-care and involvement in problem behaviors was found to be buffered by parental acceptance and firm control, which are the dual hallmarks of relationships in authoritative families (Galambos & Maggs, 1991). The potential complexity of moderation is evident in research showing that the perceived quality of relationships with parents facilitated adolescents' modeling of parents' substance use. Adolescents who had a relatively good relationships with parents tended to follow their parents' example more than if the relationship was relatively poor (Andrews, Hops, & Duncan, 1997), implying that positive relationships with antisocial parents may be a source of risk.

These instances broaden simplistic cause-and-effect models of the impact of parent–adolescent relationships. Rather than focusing only on the assumption that parenting styles and practices *cause* the outcomes to which correlational findings have linked them, compelling evidence shows that parent–adolescent relationships contribute to adolescent development by modifying the impact of other sources of influence and by transmitting them to adolescents through moment-to-moment exchanges between parents and children. The next section includes examples that illustrate the process whereby parenting mediates associations from familial and extrafamilial stressors to adolescent adjustment outcomes. We know that children are active participants in the socialization process and that parents react to their children's behavior. Thus, parenting practices may buffer against or exacerbate child tendencies, as in findings where inept parenting mediates links between oppositional behavior in early adolescence and the subsequent trajectory of adolescent delinquent peer affiliation (Simons, Chao, Conger, & Elder, 2001). It is fitting, therefore, that scholars devote more effort to understanding and elaborating the various bidirectional models of parent–child relationship influence.

THE INTERPLAY OF CONTEXT AND RELATIONSHIP PROCESSES AND OUTCOMES

Although the significance of parent–adolescent relationships and influences is surprisingly consistent across social, economic, and cultural contexts (Barber, Stolz, & Olsen, 2005; Steinberg, 2001), forces outside of the parent–adolescent dyad nevertheless help to shape the nature and impact of interactions and their impact on adolescent behavior and adjustment.

Links between adolescent adjustment and differing contexts are well documented (e.g., Fuligni, Hughes, & Way, this volume). Recently, researchers have begun to examine the processes that account for these associations. In general, their findings have shown that, although differing contexts each exert certain direct influences both on parenting and on adolescent behavior and adjustment, it is often the case that parent–adolescent interactions serve as conduits by which contexts impinge on adolescent development or as buffers of the potential impact of contexts.

This section briefly outlines illustrative instances of parent–adolescent interactions as moderators and mediators of contextual influences. The first concerns changes in the family system associated with marital difficulties. The second focuses on links between adolescent–parent relationships and parents' work experiences and socioeconomic circumstances. The third considers the opportunities and constraints in parent–adolescent relationships associated with ethnic and cultural variations.

Characteristics of Family Systems

Adolescent development occurs within family systems, and apparently direct effects of features of, and especially changes in, the systems are well documented. Most prominently, differences between parent–adolescent relationships in generally harmonious families versus those marked by high levels of conflict and disruption in one or more of the relationships in the systems are frequently associated with sharply contrasting behavior and adjustment of adolescents (Hetherington & Clingempeel, 1992).

Impact of Parental Conflict

Children and adolescents who witness frequent, angry, unresolved conflicts between mothers and fathers become distressed and manifest depressive symptoms and behavior problems (Cummings & Davies, 1994). In addition, marital conflict is associated with increased conflict between parents and adolescents (Almeida, Wethington, & Chandler, 1999). This heightened conflict is associated with more negative adolescent behavior and poorer adjustment, even in cases where the parent–adolescent relationship is generally positive (Erel & Burman, 1995).

The accumulated evidence implies that marital conflict and other stressors may undermine parents' ability to maintain an authoritative parenting style. In many families links between marital conflict and adolescent internalizing and externalizing problems are mediated by high parent–adolescent conflict and associated harsh discipline (Buehler & Gerard, 2002; Low & Stocker, 2005). Moreover, according to longitudinal evidence, the nonconstructive resolution strategies that typify conflictful marital relationships are effectively transmitted to parent–adolescent relationships (van Doorn, Branje, & Meeus, 2007). Relations between children and fathers are particularly vulnerable to high levels of marital troubles (Krishnakumar & Buehler, 2000), suggesting that mediated effects may occur more frequently in father–adolescent relationships than in mother–adolescent relationships.

Divorce and Remarriage

High levels of marital conflict commonly eventuate in divorce, which can exacerbate the stress and emotional disruption that stem from the multiple physical, cognitive, and social changes of adolescence. Moreover, the transitions necessitated by divorce may entail other stressors, such as economic need and changes in domicile, neighborhoods, and schools, as well as continuing emotional distress for parents and reorganization of family roles and relationships (Hetherington, 1999). These multiple stressors contribute to temporary disorganization and disruption of parent–adolescent relationships. Mother–adolescent relationships in divorced families manifest higher levels of both conflict and harmony than do relationships in never-divorced families. Divorced mothers monitor their children's activities less closely and demand greater responsibility for family tasks than do married mothers. Divorced mothers also use more peremptory and coercive techniques to discipline and otherwise influence adolescents' behavior. For their part, adolescents in recently divorced families tend to feel anger and moral indignation toward their parents. Some adolescents react by pulling away from the family and behaving with aloofness toward both parents, a withdrawal that may help them adjust to the divorce. These changes in parent–adolescent relationships and influences, rather than direct effects of the divorce or remarriage, likely account for the links between transitions in family systems and negative behavior and adjustment in the adolescent (for review, see Hetherington & Stanley-Hagan, 2002).

Whether perturbed parent–adolescent relationships imply higher levels of parent–adolescent conflict in divorced than in never-divorced families is unclear. Some researchers found more conflict in divorced families in the 2-year period of adjustment, with a gradual return to levels similar to those of never-divorced families (Hetherington & Kelly, 2002). Others report that initial increased levels are sustained beyond the first 2 years (Baer, 1999), and still others found fewer arguments in single-parent families than in married households (Smetana, Yau, Restrepo, & Braeges, 1991). Two studies suggests that overall rates of parent–adolescent conflict in intact two-parent households and divorced single-parent households are similar, but that mother–adolescent conflict differs across households because mothers in single-parent households are engaged in disputes that otherwise fall to fathers in two-parent households (Laursen, 1995, 2005).

Custodial parenting arrangements vary. Disruptions in relationships with noncustodial fathers appear to be more extensive and long-lasting than in mother–adolescent relationships, showing links to adjustment and relationships of offspring a decade later during young adulthood (Burns & Dunlop, 1998; Hetherington, 1999). Regardless, adolescents who have regular, supportive contact with their noncustodial parent have different experiences than those for whom the noncustodial parent is rarely, if ever, in contact. Moreover, having support from an extended family member, such as a grandparent, is linked to single parents' success in maintaining authoritative parenting practices; extended family support is notably less important for sustained authoritative parenting in intact households (Taylor, Casten, & Flickinger, 1993). These differences in the significance of postdivorce arrangements vary to some extent with the recency of divorce and the number of ancillary changes that accompany divorce (Steinberg & Silk, 2002).

Are the implications of apparent disruptions in relationships unique to recently divorced parents and adolescents? Some evidence suggests that parental conflict and lack of harmony in the family have negative effects much like those observed in studies of the impact of divorce (Fauber, Forehand, Thomas, & Wierson, 1990). Moreover, the nature and extent of disruptions vary among divorced families, with more pronounced links for boys than for girls, especially when the mother is the custodial parent (Needle, Su, & Doherty, 1990). Adolescents who have experienced divorce tend to be somewhat less well adjusted than those who have not. A meta-analysis of parental divorce and child adjustment revealed modest differences between divorced and intact families in terms of secondary school student outcomes in the domains of academic achievement, conduct, psychological adjustment, self-concept, and parent–adolescent relationships (Amato, 2001).

The impact of remarriage on parent–adolescent relationships likewise varies considerably from family to family and adolescent to adolescent (Amato, 2000). Adjustment to remarriage appears to be more difficult initially for daughters than for sons (Hetherington & Stanley-Hagan, 2002). Whereas warmth and intimacy characterize mothers and daughters in divorced, single-parent families relative to intact, two-parent families, closeness in the former group declines somewhat when the parent remarries. In contrast, sons sometimes benefit from the introduction of a stepfather into the family. Their relations with mothers often improve, and stepfathers also report more positive relationships with boys than with girls. Findings from one study imply that some African American adolescents benefit more from remarriage than European American adolescents (McLanahan & Sandefur, 1994). In the final analysis, adolescents' relationships with parents and stepparents depend on several factors. Continuing tensions and conflict between an adolescent's biological mother and father generally make it more difficult for the adolescent to adjust.

In general, noncustodial parents who put the welfare and adjustment of their children before their own personal difficulties foster positive parent–adolescent relationships and high levels of authoritative parenting during family transitions. Recent findings show that adolescents who perceive little conflict between their parents and close relationships between themselves and their parents have fewer adjustment problems than do those whose parents are in conflict with one another (Brody & Forehand, 1990). One reason for this is that adolescents often feel caught between warring parents and have attendant fears of breaching their relationship with one parent or another (Buchanan, Maccoby, & Dornbusch, 1991).

Economic Status

In cases where parents either are unemployed or income is insufficient for the family, adolescents face well-documented developmental challenges. Among the multiple risks associated with economic strain are difficulties in familial relationships, including those between parents and adolescents. As with the effect of family system stressors, the operative factor appears to be deterioration of the parents' ability to maintain nurturant, authoritative parenting (Grant, Compas, Stuhlmacher, Thurm, McMahon, & Halpert, 2003).

Strong evidence indicates that the impact of family economic strain on adolescents is mediated by a rise in negativity and a deterioration of nurturant and involved parenting, which in turn is associated an increase in adolescent academic and behavior problems (Gutman & Eccles, 1999). Familial conflicts serve a similar mediating role in the link between family economic hardship and adolescent aggression and anxiety–depression (Wadsworth & Compas, 2002). Both chronic poverty (McLoyd, 1998) and sudden economic loss (Conger et al., 1992, 1993) are associated with greater parent–adolescent conflict, more negative behaviors, harsh, punitive parenting, and adverse adolescent outcomes in domains ranging from prosocial behavior to academic achievement.

Recent findings specify one process by which parent–adolescent relationships may exacerbate or buffer the impact of economic strain on adolescent behavior and adjustment. Early adolescents who experience chronic stress from family turmoil, poverty, and crowded, substandard living conditions generally manifest higher allostatic load (a physiological marker of cumulative wear and tear on the body) than adolescents with lower cumulative risk. This effect is most pronounced for adolescents whose mothers are low in responsiveness, implying that having a responsive mother is a resource for adolescents in stressful circumstances, whereas low maternal responsiveness is an additional risk factor (Evans, Kim, Ting, Tesher, & Shannis, 2007).

It should be noted that stressors and developmental challenges emanate not only from economic loss and disadvantage. As a group, children and adolescents from affluent families manifest problems such as depression, anxiety, and substance abuse to a greater extent than those from less affluent families (Luthar & Latendresse, 2005). This link between affluence and developmental risk is mediated by achievement pressures and isolation from parents. In many affluent families, material wealth appears to be accompanied by reduced contact between parents and their offspring, possibly resulting in poorer quality parent–adolescent relationships (Luthar & Becker, 2002).

Parental Work Roles

Parent–adolescent relationships often reflect the nature of parents' work roles and the stresses associated with them. Kohn (1979) argued that parents whose work requires conformity rather than individual initiative tend to value obedience over autonomy in their children's behavior. In addition, parents' work schedules—whether they are required to travel extensively, and even the distance between workplace and home—often influence what adolescents are expected or allowed to do (Gottfried, Gottfried, & Bathurst, 2002).

Until recently, researchers focused almost exclusively on maternal employment. Today, few studies show differences in closeness or other qualities of relationships for working and nonworking mothers (Galambos & Maggs, 1991; Keith, Nelson, Schlabach, & Thompson, 1990). Indeed, both sons and daughters of working mothers appear to have less stereotyped views of masculine and feminine gender roles than children with nonworking mothers (Hoffman & Youngblade, 1999).

In response, researchers have broadened their inquiries to address the impact that parents' work-related stressors have on their family lives. Findings show that work-related stressors may exacerbate marital and parent–adolescent conflicts. In one study, mothers and fathers were more likely to experience tense interactions with their adolescents when they also had experienced work overloads or home demands (Almeida et al., 1999). Tension spillover was more likely for mothers with adolescents than for mothers with younger children. Other findings have revealed that the link between parents' work pressures and adolescent well-being are mediated by parents' sense of role overload (Crouter et al., 1999). Having documented these problems, we still lack research that describes the processes by which parents and adolescents adjust to the competing demands of parents' work and family roles.

Ethnic and Cultural Variations

Little is known about variations in closeness among adolescents and parents who differ in socioeconomic status or ethnic background. One issue in comparing diverse groups is the best method for equating the degree of closeness associated with different norms and cultural forms of relating. The suggestion that closeness be operationalized as interdependence may provide a partial solution to this quandary by allowing for members of cultural groups to specify and report on the frequency, duration, diversity, and salience of activities that denote closeness in their respective contexts (Reis et al., 2000). Variations among families also reflect differences in ethnic and cultural heritages. Different cultures foster sometimes contrasting views of parent–adolescent relationships (Feldman & Rosenthal, 1991). For Korean adolescents, strict parental control signifies parental warmth and low neglect, whereas middle-class adolescents in North America typically regard the same behavior from parents as repressive (Rohner & Pettengill, 1985). Adolescents from European backgrounds report similar or greater closeness, compared to their peers from families with Mexican or Chinese backgrounds, yet those from the latter two groups experience a stronger emphasis on family obligation and assistance than do adolescents from European backgrounds (Hardway & Fuligni, 2006). Cultural comparisons generally show sizable overlaps in descriptions of relationships across differing cultural groups and equal or even greater diversity within than between these groups (Harkness & Super, 2002).

Cultural gaps in the nature and significance of parent–adolescent interactions are especially apparent in immigrant families. Parent–adolescent relationships vary across immigrant families and between immigrant families and those of the host culture, reflecting parents' varied cultural and normative patterns. For example, Asian American families in California reported more formal communication with their parents than did either Hispanic American or European American adolescents (Cooper, 1994). Asian American youth also expressed higher levels of familistic values, emphasizing the importance of respect for and duty toward parents and family. Some cultures foster relatively more attention to duty and filial piety than others (Hofstede, 1980), and these differences may affect the degree to which adolescents evaluate their relationships with parents and siblings in terms of the quality of interaction. Research findings suggest that patterns of parent–adolescent conflict differ between immigrant and nonimmigrant families in the United States (Fuligni, 1998), but not between different nonimmigrant subgroups (Smetana & Gaines, 1999). Similarly, Greek Australian adolescents reported more tolerance and acceptance of conflict than did Greek adolescents reared in Greece, but Greek Australian parents viewed conflict with their children much as the parents living in Greece did (Rosenthal, Demetriou, & Efklides, 1989).

Despite cultural and ethnic differences in the perceived qualities of relationships, several studies have documented consistent correlations between the characteristics of parental behavior toward adolescents and adolescents' behavior and development. In one multiethnic sample, adolescents' perceptions that their parents were authoritative, rather than authoritarian or neglectful, were correlated with personal maturity, school achievement, and low levels of behavioral and psychological problems (for an overview, see Steinberg, 2001). This correlation held for African Americans, Hispanic Americans, Asian Americans, and European Americans alike. Similarly, perceptions of parental rejection have been found to be correlated with poor individual outcomes in a number of different cultures (Rohner & Pettingill, 1985; Rohner & Rohner, 1981). In other words, although typical patterns of parental control may vary across cultures, family environments that emphasize mutuality,

respect for the child's opinions, and training for maturity seem to be most effective in helping adolescents develop attitudes and behaviors appropriate to their society. A recent study of the impact of racial identity and parent–adolescent relationships on adolescent functioning illustrates the complexity of these links. A sample of African American high school seniors revealed that correlations between racial identity and maternal support, on one hand, and depressive symptoms and anxiety, on the other, were mediated by perceived stress (Caldwell, Zimmerman, Bernat, Sellers, & Notaro, 2002).

It is clear that direct and indirect influences of relationships with parents extend to families in all cultures. However, the enterprise of amassing information on variations in the nature of these links is still in its infancy. Knowledge of indirect links is especially meager. The next phase of research incorporating ethnic and cultural diversity must attend to the more complex models of parenting that encompass multiple possible pathways of influence.

CONCLUSION

Contemporary research with parents and adolescents challenges traditional theoretical and methodological approaches to adolescent development. Conceptually, the growing body of findings on adolescents' close relationships implies that adolescent development can be understood more fully in the context of relationships with significant others and that relationships with parents remain central to these contexts. Methodologically, the findings imply the need for broadening the construct of adolescent outcomes to incorporate interpersonal competencies and developmental changes in them and also to adopt more complex models of the processes through which parent–adolescent relationships have an impact. The key task is to understand not only the developing individual, but also the interplay between individual growth and change in the nature and developmental significance of relationships with others.

REFERENCES

Adams, R. (2005). *Parent-child relationships across early adolescence: Changes and adjustment.* Unpublished doctoral dissertation, Department of Psychology, Florida Atlantic University, Boca Raton, FL.

Adams, R., & Laursen, B. (2001). The organization and dynamics of adolescent conflict with parents and friends. *Journal of Marriage and Family, 63,* 97–110.

Adams, R., & Laursen, B. (2007). The correlates of conflict: Disagreement is not necessarily detrimental. *Journal of Family Psychology, 21,* 445–458.

Ainsworth, M. D. S. (1989). Attachments beyond infancy. *American Psychologist, 44,* 709–716.

Allen, J. P., Hauser, S. T., Bell, K. L., & O'Connor, T. G. (1994). Longitudinal assessment of autonomy and relatedness in adolescent–family interactions as predictors of adolescent ego development and self-esteem. *Child Development, 65,* 179–194.

Allen, J. P., & Land, D. (1999). Attachment in adolescence. In J. Cassidy & P. R. Shaver (Eds.), *Handbook of attachment: Theory, research, and clinical applications* (pp. 319–335). New York: Guilford Press.

Allen, J. P., & Manning, N. (2007). From safety to affect regulation: Attachment from the vantage point of adolescence. In M. Scharf & O. Mayseless (Eds.), *Attachment in adolescence: Reflections and new angles. New Directions for Child and Adolescent Development* (No. 117, pp. 23–39). San Francisco: Jossey-Bass.

Allen, J. P., Porter, M., McFarland, C., McElhaney, K. B., & Marsh, P. (2007). The relation of attachment security to adolescents' paternal and peer relationships, depression, and externalizing behavior. *Child Development, 78,* 1222–1239.

Allen, J. P., Marsh, P., McFarland, C., McElhaney, K. B., & Land, D. J. (2002). Attachment and autonomy as predictors of the development of social skills and delinquency during midadolescence. *Journal of Consulting and Clinical Psychology, 70,* 56–66.

Allen, J. P., McElhaney, K. B., Kuperminc, G. P., & Jodl, K. M. (2004). Stability and change in attachment security across adolescence. *Child Development, 75,* 1792–1805.

Allen, J. P., McElhaney, K. B., Land, D. J., Kuperminc, G. P., Moore, C. W., O'Beirne-Kelly, H., et al. (2003). A secure base in adolescence: Markers of attachment security in the mother–adolescent relationship. *Child Development, 74,* 292–307.

Almeida, D. M., Wethington, E., & Chandler, A. L. (1999). Daily transmission of tensions between marital dyads and parent–child dyads. *Journal of Marriage and the Family, 61,* 49–61.

Amato, P. R. (2000). The consequences of divorce for adults and children. *Journal of Marriage and the Family, 62,* 1269–1287.

Amato, P. R. (2001). Children of divorce in the 1990s: An update of the Amato and Keith (1991) meta-analysis. *Journal of Family Psychology, 15,* 355–370.

Andrews, J. A., Hops, H., & Duncan, S. C. (1997). Adolescent modeling of parent substance use: The moderating effect of the relationship with the parent. *Journal of Family Psychology, 11,* 259–270.

Baer, J. (1999). The effects of family structure and SES on family processes in early adolescence. *Journal of Adolescence, 22,* 341–354.

Baldwin, M. W. (1992). Relational schemas and the processing of social information. *Psychological Bulletin, 112,* 461–484.

Bandura, A. (1964). The stormy decade: Fact or fiction? *Psychology in the Schools, 1,* 224–231.

Barber, B. K. (1996). Parental psychological control: Revisiting a neglected construct. *Child Development, 67,* 3296–3319.

Barber, B. L., & Eccles, J. S. (1992). Long-term influence of divorce and single parenting on adolescent family- and work-related values, behaviors, and aspirations. *Psychological Bulletin, 111,* 108–126.

Barber, B. K., Stolz, H. E., & Olsen, J. A. (2005). Parent support, psychological control, and behavioral control: Assessing relevance across time, culture, and method. *Monographs of the Society for Research in Child Development, 70,* 4 (serial no. 282).

Barrett, L. S. (1997). The relationships among momentary emotional experiences, personality descriptions, and retrospective ratings of emotion. *Personality and Social Psychology Bulletin, 23,* 1173–1187.

Baumrind, D. (1991). Effective parenting during the early adolescent transition. In P. A. Cowan & M. Hetherington (Eds.), *Family transitions* (pp. 111–163). Hillsdale, NJ: Lawrence Erlbaum.

Belsky, J., Jaffee, S., Hsieh, K., & Silva, P. A. (2001). Child rearing antecedents of intergenerational relations in young adulthood: A prospective study. *Developmental Psychology, 37,* 801–813.

Belsky, J., Steinberg, L., & Draper, P. (1991). Childhood experience, interpersonal development, and reproductive strategy: An evolutionary theory of socialization. *Child Development, 62,* 647–670.

Belsky, J., Steinberg, L. D., Houts, R. M., Friedman, S. L., De Hart, G., Cauffman, E., et al. (2007). Family rearing antecedents of pubertal timing. *Child Development, 78,* 1302–1321.

Berndt, T. (1979). Developmental changes in conformity to peers and parents. *Developmental Psychology, 15,* 608–616.

Berndt, T. (1999). Friends' influence on children's adjustment to school. In W. A. Collins & B. Laursen (Eds.), *The Minnesota Symposia on Child Psychology:* vol. 30. *Relationships as developmental contexts* (pp. 85–107). Mahwah, NJ: Lawrence Erlbaum.

Blos, P. (1979). *The adolescent passage.* New York: International Universities Press.

Bolger, K. E., Patterson, C. J., Thompson, W. W., & Kupersmidt, J. B. (1995). Psychosocial adjustment among children experiencing persistent and intermittent family economic hardship. *Child Development, 66,* 1107–1129.

Bowerman, C. E., & Kinch, J. W. (1959). Changes in family and peer orientation of children between the 4th and 10th grades. *Social Forces, 37,* 206–211.

Bowlby, J. (1969). *Attachment and loss,* vol. 1: *Attachment.* New York: Basic Books.

Branje, S. J. T., van Aken, M. A. G., & van Lieshout, C. F. M. (2002). Relational support in families with adolescents. *Journal of Family Psychology, 16,* 351–362.

Branje, S. J. T., van Doorn, M., van der Valk, I., & Meeus, W. (in press). Parent–adolescent conflicts, conflict resolution, and adolescent adjustment. *Journal of Applied Developmental Psychology.*

Branje, S. J. T., van Lieshout, C. F. M., & van Aken, M. A. G. (2005). Relations between agreeableness and perceived support in family relationships: Why nice people are not always supportive. *International Journal of Behavioral Development, 29,* 120–128.

Brendgen, M., Wanner, B., Morin, A. J. S., & Vitaro, F. (2005). Relations with parents and with peers, temperament, and trajectories of depressed mood during early adolescence. *Journal of Abnormal Child Psychology, 33,* 579–594.

Brittain, C. (1963). Adolescent choices and parent–peer cross pressures. *American Sociological Review, 28,* 385–391.

Brody, G., & Forehand, R. (1990). Interparental conflict, relationship with the noncustodial father, and adolescent post-divorce adjustment. *Journal of Applied Developmental Psychology, 11,* 139–147.

Bronfenbrenner, U. (1970). Reaction to social pressure from adults versus peers among Soviet day school and boarding school pupils in the perspective on an American sample. *Journal of Personality and Social Psychology, 15,* 179–189.

Buchanan, C. M., Maccoby, E. E., & Dornbusch, S. M. (1991). Caught between parents: Adolescents' experience in divorced homes. *Child Development, 62,* 1008–1030.

Buehler, C., & Gerard, J. M. (2002). Marital conflict, ineffective parenting, and children's and adolescents' maladjustment. *Journal of Marriage and Family, 64,* 78–92.

Buhrmester, D., & Furman, W. (1987). The development of companionship and intimacy. *Child Development, 58,* 1101–1113.

Buist, K. L., Deković, M., Meeus, W., & van Aken, M. A. G. (2002). Developmental patterns in adolescent attachment to mother, father, and sibling. *Journal of Youth and Adolescence, 31,* 167–176.

Burk, W. J., Denissen, J., van Doorn, M., Branje, S. J. T., & Laursen, B. (in press). The vicissitudes of conflict measurement: Stability and reliability in the frequency of disagreements. *European Psychologist.*

Burns, A., & Dunlop, R. (1998). Parental divorce, parent–child relations, and early adult relationships: A longitudinal Australian study. *Personal Relationships, 5,* 393–407.

Caldwell, C. H., Zimmerman, M. A., Bernat, D. H., Sellers, R. M., & Notaro, P. C. (2002). Racial identity, maternal support, and psychological distress among African American adolescents. *Child Development, 73,* 1322–1336.

Card, N. A., Little, T. D., & Selig, J. P. (Eds.) (2008). *Modeling dyadic and interdependent data in developmental research.* Mahwah, NJ: Lawrence Erlbaum.

Carlivati, J., & Collins, W. A. (2007). Adolescent attachment representations and development in a risk sample. In M. Scharf & O. Mayseless (Eds.), *Attachment in adolescence Reflections and new angles. New Directions for Child and Adolescent Development* (No. *117,* pp. 91–106). San Francisco: Jossey-Bass.

Caughlin, J. P., & Malis, R. S. (2004). Demand/withdraw communication between parents and adolescents: Connections with self-esteem and substance use. *Journal of Social and Personal Relationships, 21,* 125–148.

Collins, W. A. (1995). Relationships and development: Family adaptation to individual change. In S. Shulman (Ed.), *Close relationships and socioemotional development* (pp. 128–154). New York: Ablex.

Collins, W. A. (2002). Historical perspectives on contemporary research in social development. In P. Smith & C. Hart (Eds.), *Blackwell Handbook of Social Development* (pp. 3–23). Oxford: Blackwell.

Collins, W. A., & Laursen, B. (2000). Adolescent relationships: The art of fugue. In C. Hendrick & S. S. Hendrick (Eds.), *Close relationships: A sourcebook* (pp. 59–69). Thousand Oaks, CA: Sage.

Collins, W. A., Laursen, B., Mortensen, N., Luebker, C., & Ferreira, M. (1997). Conflict processes and transitions in parent and peer relationships: Implications for autonomy and regulation. *Journal of Adolescence, 12,* 178–198.

Collins, W. A., Maccoby, E., Steinberg, L., Hetherington, E. M., & Bornstein, M. (2000). Contemporary research on parenting: The case for nature and nurture. *American Psychologist, 55,* 218–232.

Collins, W. A., & Madsen, S. D. (2003). Developmental changes in parenting interactions. In L. Kuczynski (Eds.), *Handbook of dynamics in parent–child relations* (pp. 49–66). Beverly Hills, CA: Sage.

Collins, W. A., & Repinski, D. J. (2001). Parents and adolescents as transformers of relationships: Dyadic adaptations to developmental change. In J. R. M. Gerris (Ed.), *Dynamics of parenting: International perspectives on nature and sources of parenting* (pp. 429–443). Leuven, Netherlands: Garant.

Collins, W. A., & Steinberg, L. (2006). Adolescent development in interpersonal context. In W. Damon & R. Lerner (Series Eds.) and N. Eisenberg (Vol. Ed.), *The handbook of child psychology,* vol 3: *Social, emotional and personality development* (6th ed.; pp. 1003–1067). Hoboken, NJ: John Wiley & Sons.

Conger, R. D., Conger, K. J., Elder, G. H., Jr., Lorenz, F. O., Simons, R. L., & Whitbeck, L. (1992). Family process model of economic hardship and adjustment of early adolescent boys. *Child Development, 63,* 526–541.

Conger, R. D., Conger, K. J., Elder, G. H., Jr., Lorenz, F. O., Simons, R. L., & Whitbeck, L. (1993). Family economic stress and adjustment of early adolescent girls. *Developmental Psychology, 29,* 206–219.

Cook, W. L., & Goldstein, M. J. (1993). Multiple perspectives on family relationships: A latent variables model. *Child Development, 64,* 1377–1388.

Cook, W. L., & Kenny, D. A. (2005). The Actor–Partner Interdependence Model: A model of bidirectional effects in developmental studies. *International Journal of Behavioral Development, 29,* 101–109.

Cooper, C. R. (1994). Cultural perspectives on continuity and change in adolescents' relationships. In R. Montemayor, G. R. Adams, & T. P. Gullotta (Eds.), *Personal relationships during adolescence* (pp. 78–100). Thousand Oaks, CA: Sage.

Crosnoe, R. A., & Elder, E. H., Jr. (2002). Life course trainsitions, the generational stake, and grandparent–grandchild relationships. *Journal of Marriage and the Family, 64,* 1089–1096.

Crouter, A. C., Bumpus, M. F., Maguire, M. C., & McHale, S. M. (1999). Linking parents' work pressure and adolescents' well-being: Insights into dynamics in dual-earner families. *Developmental Psychology, 35,* 1453–1461.

Cummings, E. M., & Davies, P. (1994). *Children and marital conflict: The impact of family dispute and resolution.* New York: Guilford Press.

Darling, N., Cumsille, P., Caldwell, L., & Dowdy, B. (2006). Predictors of adolescents' disclosure to parents and perceived parental knowledge: Between- and within-person differences. *Journal of Youth and Adolescence, 35,* 667–678.

Darling, N., & Steinberg, L. (1993). Parenting style as context: An integrative model. *Psychological Bulletin, 113,* 487–496.

Deković, M., Buist, K. L., & Reitz, E. (2004). Stability and changes in problem behavior during adolescence: Latent growth analysis. *Journal of Youth and Adolescence, 33,* 1–12.

Devereux, E. (1970). The role of peer group experience in moral development. In J. Hill (Ed.), *The Minnesota Symposia on Child Psychology,* vol. 4 (pp. 94–140). Minneapolis: University of Minnesota Press.

Dick, D. M., Viken, R., Purcell, S., Kaprio, J., Pulkkinen, L., & Rose, R. J. (2007). Parental monitoring moderates the importance of genetic and environmental influences on adolescent smoking. *Journal of Abnormal Psychology, 116,* 213–218.

Dishion, T. J., Nelson, S. E., & Bullock, B. M. (2004). Premature adolescent autonomy: Parent disengagement and deviant peer process in the amplification of problem behavior. *Journal of Adolescence, 27,* 515–530.

Doyle, A. B., & Markiewicz, D. (2005). Parenting, marital conflict and adjustment from early- to mid-adolescence: Mediated by adolescent attachment style? *Journal of Youth and Adolescence, 34,* 97–110.

Dubas, J., & Gerris, J. R. M. (2002). Longitudinal changes in the time parents spend in activities with their adolescent children as a function of child age, pubertal status, and gender. *Journal of Family Psychology, 16,* 415–427.

Ducharme, J., Doyle, A. B., & Markiewicz, D. (2002). Attachment security with mother and father: Associations with adolescents' reports of interpersonal behavior with parents and peers. *Journal of Social and Personal Relationships, 19,* 203–231.

Eccles, J. S. (1992). School and family effects on the ontogeny of children's interests, self-perceptions, and activity choices. In J. E. Jacobs (Ed.), *Nebraska Symposium on Motivation,* vol. 40: *Developmental perspectives on motivation* (pp. 145–208). Lincoln: University of Nebraska Press.

Eisenberg, N., Fabes, R. A., & Spinrad, T. L. (2006). Prosocial development. In W. Damon & R. Lerner (Series Ed.) and N. Eisenberg (Vol. Ed.), *The handbook of child psychology,* vol. 3: *Social, emotional and personality development* (6th ed. pp. 646–718). Hoboken, NJ: John Wiley & Sons.

Erel, O., & Burman, B. (1995). Interrelatedness of marital relations and parent–child relations: A meta-analytic review. *Psychological Bulletin, 118,* 108–132.

Erikson, E. H. (1968). *Identity: Youth and crisis.* New York: W. W. Norton.

Evans, G. W., Kim, P., Ting, A. H., Tesher, H. B., & Shannis, D. (2007). Cumulative risk, maternal responsiveness, and allostatic load among young adolescents. *Developmental Psychology, 43,* 341–351.

Fauber, R., Forehand, R., Thomas, A. M., & Wierson, M. (1990). A mediational model of the impact of marital conflict on adolescent adjustment in intact and divorced families: The role of disrupted parenting. *Child Development, 61,* 1112–1123.

Feeney, B. C., & Cassidy, J. (2003). Reconstructive memory related to adolescent–parent conflict interactions: The influence of attachment-related representations on immediate perceptions and changes in perceptions over time. *Journal of Personality and Social Psychology, 85,* 945–955.

Feinberg, M., & Hetherington, E. M. (2001). Differential parenting as a within-family variable. *Journal of Family Psychology, 15,* 22–37.

Feinberg, M. E., Button, T. M. M., Neiderhiser, J. M., Reiss, D., & Hetherington, E. M. (2007). Parenting and adolescent antisocial behavior and depression: Evidence of genotype X parenting environment interaction. *Archives of General Psychiatry, 64,* 457–465.

Feinberg, M. E., Howe, G. W., Reiss, D., & Hetherington, E. M. (2000). Relationship between perceptual differences of parenting and adolescent anti-social behavior and depressive symptoms. *Journal of Family Psychology, 14,* 531–555.

Feldman, S. S., & Rosenthal, D. A. (1991). Age expectations of behavioral autonomy in Hong Kong, Australian and American youth: The influence of family variables and adolescents' values. *International Journal of Psychology, 26,* 1–23.

Fletcher, A. C., Steinberg, L., & Williams-Wheeler, M. (2004). Parental influences on adolescent problem behavior: Revisiting Stattin and Kerr. *Child Development, 75,* 781–796.

Flouri, E., & Buchanan, A. (2002). What predicts good relationships with parents in adolescence and partners in adult life: Findings from the 1958 British birth cohort. *Journal of Family Psychology, 16,* 186–198.

Freud, A. (1958). Adolescence. In R. Eissler, A. Freud, H. Hartman, & M. Kris (Eds.), *Psychoanalytic study of the child,* vol. 13 (pp. 255–278). New York: International Universities Press.

Freud, S. (1949). *Group psychology and the analysis of the ego.* New York: Bantam. (Original work published 1921.)

Frijins, T., Finkenauer, C., Vermulst, A. A., & Engels, R. C. M. E. (2005). Keeping secrets from parents: Longitudinal associations of secrecy in adolescence. *Journal of Youth and Adolescence, 34,* 137–148.

Fritz, M. S., & MacKinnon, D. P. (2007). Required sample size to detect the mediated effect. *Psychological Science, 18,* 233–239.

Fuligni, A. J. (1998). The adjustment of children from immigrant families. *Current Directions in Psychological Science, 7,* 99–103.

Furman, W., & Buhrmester, D. (1989). Age and sex differences in perceptions of networks of personal relationships. *Child Development, 63,* 103–115.

Furstenberg, F., Cook, T., Eccles, J., Elder, G. H., & Sameroff, A. J. (1999). *Managing to make it: Urban families and adolescent success.* Chicago: University of Chicago Press.

Galambos, N. L., Barker, E. T., & Almeida, D. M. (2003). Parents do matter: Trajectories of change in externalizing and internalizing problems in early adolescence. *Child Development, 74,* 578–594.

Galambos, N. L., & Maggs, J. L. (1991). Out-of-school care of young adolescents and self-reported behavior. *Developmental Psychology, 27,* 644–655.

Garber, J., & Little, S. (1999). Predictors of competence among offspring of depressed mothers. *Journal of Adolescent Research, 14,* 44–71.

Gauze, C., Bukowski, W. M., Aquan-Assee, J., & Sippola, L. K. (1996). Interactions between family environment and friendship and associations with self-perceived well-being during early adolescence. *Child Development, 67,* 2201–2216.

Ge, X., Best, K. M., Conger, R. D., & Simons, R. L. (1996). Parenting behaviors and the occurrence and co-occurrence of adolescent depressive symptoms and conduct problems. *Developmental Psychology, 32,* 717–731.

Gjerde, P. F. (1986). The interpersonal structure of family interaction settings: Parent-adolescent relations in dyads and triads. *Developmental Psychology, 22,* 297–304.

Gonzales, N. A., Caucé, A. M., & Mason, C. A. (1996). Interobserver agreement in the assessment of parental behavior and parent-adolescent conflict: African American mothers, daughters, and independent observers. *Child Development, 67,* 1483–1498.

Gottfried, A. E., Gottfried, A. W., & Bathurst, K. (2002). Maternal and dual-earner employment status and parenting. In M. Bornstein (Ed.), *Handbook of parenting,* vol. 2: Biology and ecology of parenting (pp. 207–230). Mahwah, NJ: Lawrence Erlbaum.

Graber, J. A., Brooks-Gunn, J., & Warren, M. P. (1995). The antecedents of menarcheal age: Heredity, family environment, and stressful life events. *Child Development, 66,* 346–359.

Graham-Bermann, S. A., Cutler, S. E., Litzenberger, B. W., & Schwartz, W. E. (1994). Perceived conflict and violence in childhood sibling relationships and later emotional adjustment. *Journal of Family Psychology, 8,* 85–97.

Grant, K. E., Compas, B. E., Stuhlmacher, A., Thurm, A., McMahon S., & Halpert J. (2003). Stressors and child and adolescent psychopathology: Moving from markers to mechanisms of risk. *Psychological Bulletin, 129,* 447–466.

Gray, M., & Steinberg, L. (1999). Unpacking authoritative parenting: Reassessing a multidimensional construct. *Journal of Marriage and the Family, 61,* 574–587.

Grotevant, H. D., & Cooper, C. R. (1985). Patterns of interaction in family relationships and the development of identity formation in adolescence. *Child Development, 51,* 415–428.

Grotevant, H. D., & Cooper, C. R. (1986). Individuation in family relationships: A perspective on individual differences in the development of identity and role-taking in adolescence. *Human Development, 29,* 82–100.

Grusec, J. E., Goodnow, J., & Kuczynski, L. (2000). New directions in analyses of parenting contributions to children's acquisition of values. *Child Development, 71,* 205–211.

Gutman, L. M., & Eccles, J. S. (1999). Financial strain, parenting behaviors, and adolescent achievement: Testing model equivalence between African American and European American single- and two-parent families. *Child Development, 70,* 1464–1476.

Hall, G. S. (1904). *Adolescence: Its psychology and its relations to physiology, anthropology, sociology, sex, crime, religion, and education,* vols. 1 and 2. New York: Appleton.

Hardway, C., & Fuligni, A. (2006). Dimensions of family connectedness among adolescents with Mexican, Chinese, and European backgrounds. *Developmental Psychology, 42,* 1246–1258.

Harkness, S., & Super, C. (2002). Culture and parenting. In M. Bornstein (Ed.), *Handbook of parenting,* vol. 2: Biology and ecology of parenting (pp. 253–280). Mahwah, NJ: Lawrence Erlbaum.

Harris, J. R. (1998). *The nurture assumption.* New York: Free Press.

Hartup, W. W., & Laursen, B. (1991). Relationships as developmental contexts. In R. Cohen & A. W. Siegel (Eds.), *Context and development* (pp. 253–279). Hillsdale, NJ: Lawrence Erlbaum.

Hauser, S. T., Powers, S., & Noam, G. (1991). *Adolescents and their families: Paths of ego development.* New York: Free Press.

Hetherington, E. M. (1999). Social capital and the development of youth from nondivorced, divorced, and remarried families. In W. A. Collins & B. Laursen (Eds.), *The Minnesota Symposia on Child Psychology,* vol. 30: *Relationships as developmental contexts* (pp. 177–209). Mahwah, NJ: Lawrence Erlbaum.

Hetherington, E. M., & Clingempeel, W. G. (1992). Coping with marital transitions: A family systems perspective. *Monographs of the Society for Research in Child Development, 57* (2–3, serial no. 227).

Hetherington, E. M., & Kelly, J. (2002). *For better or worse: Divorce reconsidered.* New York: W. W. Norton.

Hetherington, E. M., & Stanley-Hagan, M. (2002). Parenting in divorced and remarried families. In M. Bornstein (Ed.), *Handbook of parenting,* vol. 3: Being and becoming a parent (pp. 287–315). Mahwah, NJ: Lawrence Erlbaum.

Hill, J. P. (1988). Adapting to menarche: Familial control and conflict. In M. R. Gunnar & W. A. Collins (Eds.), *Minnesota Symposia on Child Psychology,* vol. 21: *Development during the transition to adolescence* (pp. 43–77). Hillsdale, NJ: Lawrence Erlbaum.

Hill, J. P., & Lynch, M. E. (1983). The intensification of gender-related role expectations during early adolescence. In J. Brooks-Gunn & A. C. Petersen (Eds.), *Girls at puberty: Biological and psychological perspectives* (pp. 201–228). New York: Plenum Press.

Hodgkinson, H. (1985). *All one system: Demographics of education, kindergarten through graduate school*. Washington, DC: Institute of Educational Leadership.

Hoff, E., Laursen, B., & Bridges, K. (in press). Measurement and model building in studying the influence of socioeconomic status on child development. In L. C. Mayes & M. Lewis (Eds.), *A developmental environmental measurement handbook*. New York: Cambridge University Press.

Hoffman, L. W., & Youngblade, L. (1999). *Mothers at work: Effects on children's well-being*. New York: Cambridge University Press.

Hofstede, G. (1980). *Culture's consequences: International differences in work-related values*. Beverly Hills, CA: Sage.

Holmbeck, G. N. (1996). A model of family relational transformations during the transition to adolescence: Parent-adolescent conflict and adaptation. In J. A. Graber, J. Brooks-Gunn, & A. C. Petersen (Eds.), *Transitions through adolescence: Interpersonal domains and contexts* (pp. 167–200). Mahwah, NJ: Lawrence Erlbaum.

Homans, G. C. (1961). *Social behavior: Its elementary forms*. New York: Harcourt.

Jackson, E. P., Dunham, R. M., & Kidwell, J. S. (1990). The effects of gender and of family cohesion and adaptability on identity status. *Journal of Adolescent Research, 5,* 161–174.

Jang, S. J., & Smith, C. A. (1997). A test of reciprocal causal relationships among parental supervision, affective ties, and delinquency. *Journal of Research in Crime and Delinquency, 34,* 307–336.

Kamptner, N. L. (1988). Identity development in late adolescence: Causal modeling of social and familial influences. *Journal of Youth and Adolescence, 17,* 493–514.

Kandel, D. B., & Lesser, G. S. (1972). *Youth in two worlds*. San Francisco: Jossey-Bass.

Kashy, D. A., & Donnellan, M. B. (2008). Comparing MLM and SEM approaches to analyzing developmental dyadic data: Growth curve models of hostility in families. In N. A. Card, T. D. Little, & J. P. Selig (Eds.), *Modeling dyadic and interdependent data in developmental research*. Mahwah, NJ: Lawrence Erlbaum.

Keith, J. G., Nelson, C. S., Schlabach, J. H., & Thompson, C. J. (1990). The relationship between parental employment and three measures of early adolescent responsibility: Family-related, personal, and social. *Journal of Early Adolescence, 10,* 399–415.

Kelley, H. H., Berscheid, E., Christensen, A., Harvey, J. H., Huston, T. L., Levinger, G., et al. (1983). *Close relationships*. New York: Freeman.

Kenny, D. A., Kashy, D. A., & Cook, W. L. (2006). *Dyadic data analysis*. New York: Guilford Press.

Kerr, M., & Stattin, H. (2000). What parents know, how they know it, and several forms of adolescent adjustment: Further support for a reinterpretation of monitoring. *Developmental Psychology, 36,* 366–380.

Kerr, M., Stattin., H., & Burk, W. J. (in press). A reinterpretation of parental monitoring in longitudinal perspective. *Journal of Research on Adolescence.*

Kerr, M., Stattin, H., & Pakalniskiene, V. (2006). What do parents do when faced with adolescent problem behavior? In J. Coleman, M. Kerr, & H. Stattin (Eds.), *Parenting of adolescents*. Hoboken, NJ: John Wiley & Sons.

Kim, K. J., Conger, R. D., Lorenz, F. O., & Elder, G. H., Jr. (2001). Parent–adolescent reciprocity in negative affect and its relation to early adult social development. *Developmental Psychology, 37,* 775–790.

Kohn, M. L. (1979). The effects of social class on parental values and practices. In D. Reiss & H. A. Hoffman (Eds.), *The American family: Dying or developing* (pp. 45–68). New York: Plenum Press.

Kowal, A. K., Krull, J. L., & Kramer, L. (2004). How the differential treatment of siblings is linked with parent–child relationship quality. *Journal of Family Psychology, 18,* 658–665.

Krishnakumar, A., & Buehler, C. (2000). Interparental conflict and parenting behaviors: A meta-analytic review. *Family Relations, 49,* 25–44.

Kuczynski, L. (Ed.). (2003). *Handbook of dynamics in parent-child relations*. Thousands Oaks, CA: Sage.

Kuczynski, L., & Parkin, M. (2006). Agency and bidirectionality in socialization: Interactions, transactions, and relational dialectics. In J. E. Grusec & P. Hastings (Eds.), *Handbook of socialization* (pp. 259–283). New York: Guilford Press.

Laird, R. D., Pettit, G. S., Bates, J. E., & Dodge, K. A. (2003). Parents' monitoring-relevant knowledge and adolescents' delinquent behavior: Evidence of correlated developmental changes in reciprocal influences. *Child Development, 74,* 752–768.

Lamborn, S. D., Mounts, N. S., Steinberg, L., & Dornbusch, S. M. (1991). Patterns of competence and adjustment among adolescents from authoritative, authoritarian, indulgent, and neglectful families. *Child Development, 62,* 1049–1065.

Larson, R. W., & Almeida, D. M. (1999). Emotional transmission in the daily lives of families: A new paradigm for studying family process. *Journal of Marriage and the Family, 61,* 5–20.

Larson, R. W., & Richards, M. H. (1994). *Divergent realities: The emotional lives of mothers, fathers, and adolescents*. New York: Basic Books.

Larson, R. W., Richards, M. H., Moneta, G., Holmbeck, G., & Duckett, E. (1996). Changes in adolescents' daily interactions with their families from ages 10 to 18: Disengagement and transformation. *Developmental Psychology, 32,* 744–754.

Laursen, B. (1993). Conflict management among close peers. In B. Laursen (Ed.), *Close friendships in adolescence. New Directions for Child Development* (no. *60*; pp. 39–54). San Francisco: Jossey-Bass.

Laursen, B. (1995). Conflict and social interaction in adolescent relationships. *Journal of Research on Adolescence, 5,* 55–70.

Laursen, B. (2005). Conflict between mothers and adolescents in single-mother, blended, and two-biological-parent families. *Parenting: Science and Practice, 5,* 347–370.

Laursen, B., & Bukowski, W. M. (1997). A developmental guide to the organisation of close relationships. *International Journal of Behavioral Development, 21,* 747–770.

Laursen, B., & Collins, W. A. (1994). Interpersonal conflict during adolescence. *Psychological Bulletin, 115,* 197–209.

Laursen, B., & Collins, W. A. (2004). Parent–child communication during adolescence. In A. Vangelisti (Ed.), *Handbook of family communication* (pp. 333–348). Mahwah, NJ: Lawrence Erlbaum.

Laursen, B., Coy, K. C., & Collins, W. A. (1998). Reconsidering changes in parent–child conflict across adolescence: A meta-analysis. *Child Development, 69,* 817–832.

Laursen, B., Furman, W., & Mooney, K. S. (2006). Predicting interpersonal competence and self-worth from adolescent relationships and relationship networks: Variable-centered and person-centered perspectives. *Merrill-Palmer Quarterly, 52,* 572–600.

Laursen, B., & Koplas, A. L. (1995). What's important about important conflicts? Adolescents' perceptions of daily disagreements. *Merrill-Palmer Quarterly, 41,* 536–553.

Laursen, B., & Mooney, K. S. (2008). Adolescent adjustment as a function of the number of perceived high quality relationships with parents and friends. *American Journal of Orthopsychiatry, 78,* 47–53.

Laursen, B., Popp, D., Burk, W. J., Kerr, M., & Stattin, H. (2008). Incorporating interdependence into developmental research: Examples from the study of homophily and homogeneity. In

N. A. Card, T. D. Little, & J. P. Selig (Eds.), *Modeling dyadic and interdependent data in developmental research*. Mahwah, NJ: Lawrence Erlbaum.

Laursen, B., & Williams, V. (1997). Perceptions of interdependence and closeness in family and peer relationships among adolescents with and without romantic partners. In S. Shulman & W. A. Collins (Eds.), *Romantic relationships in adolescence: Developmental perspectives. New Directions for Child Development* (no. 78; pp. 3–20). San Francisco: Jossey-Bass.

Loeber, R., Drinkwater, M., Yin, Y., Anderson, S. J., Schmidt, L. C., & Crawford, A. (2000). Stability of family interaction from ages 6 to 18. *Journal of Abnormal Child Psychology, 28,* 353–369.

Low, S. M., & Stocker, C. (2005). Family functioning and children's adjustment: Associations among parents' depressed mood, marital hostility, parent–child hostility, and children's adjustment. *Journal of Family Psychology, 19,* 394–403.

Luthar, S. S., & Becker, B. E. (2002). Privileged but pressured? A study of affluent youth. *Child Development, 73,* 1593–1610.

Luthar, S. S., & Latendresse, S. J. (2005). Children the affluent: Challenges to well-being. *Current Directions in Psychological Science, 14,* 49–53.

Lytton, H. (2000). Toward a model of family–environmental and child–biological influences on development. *Developmental Review, 20,* 150–179.

Maccoby, E. E. (1992). The role of parents in the socialization of children: An historical overview. *Developmental Psychology, 28,* 1006–1017.

Maccoby, E. E., & Martin, J. A. (1983). Socialization in the context of the family: Parent–child interaction. In P. H. Mussen (Series Ed.) and E. M. Hetherington (Vol. Ed.), *Handbook of child psychology,* vol. 4: *Socialization, personality, and moral development* (pp. 1–101). New York: John Wiley & Sons.

Markiewicz, D., Lawford, H., Doyle, A. B., & Haggart, N. (2006). Developmental differences in adolescents' and young adults' use of mothers, fathers, best friends, and romantic partners to fulfill attachment needs. *Journal of Youth and Adolescence, 35,* 127–140.

McGue, M., Elkins, I., Walden, B., & Iacono, W. G. (2005). Perceptions of the parent–adolescent relationship: A longitudinal investigation. *Developmental Psychology, 41,* 971–984.

McLanahan, S. S., & Sandefur, G. (1994). *Growing up with a single parent: What hurts, what helps*. Cambridge, MA: Harvard University Press.

McLean, K. C., & Thorne, A. (2003). Late adolescents' self-defining memories about relationships. *Developmental Psychology, 39,* 635–645.

McLoyd, V. C. (1998). Socioeconomic disadvantage and child development. *American Psychologist, 53,* 185–204.

Moffitt, T. E., Caspi, A., Belsky, J., & Silva, P. A. (1992). Childhood experience and onset of menarche: A test of a sociobiological model. *Child Development, 63,* 47–58.

Mooney, K. S., Laursen, B., & Adams, R. E. (2007). Social support and positive development: Looking on the bright side of adolescent close relationships. In R. K. Silbereisen & R. M. Lerner (Eds.), *Approaches to positive youth development* (pp. 189–203). Thousand Oaks, CA: Sage.

Mooney, K. S., Laursen, B., & Adams, R. E. (2006). Social support and positive development: Looking on the bright side of adolescent close relationships. In R. K. Silbereisen & R. M. Lerner (Eds.), *Approaches to positive youth development* (pp. 189–203). Los Angeles: Sage.

Mounts, N. S. (2007). Adolescents' and their mothers' perceptions of parental management of peer relationships. *Journal of Research on Adolescence, 17,* 169–178.

Needle, R. H., Su, S., & Doherty, W. J. (1990). Divorce, remarriage, and adolescent substance use: A prospective longitudinal study. *Journal of Marriage and the Family, 52,* 157–169.

Noller, P. (1994). Relationships with parents in adolescence: Process and outcome. In R. Montemayor, G. Adams, & T. Gullotta (Eds.), *Personal relationships during adolescence* (pp. 37–78). Thousand Oaks, CA: Sage.

Noller, P., & Callan, V. J. (1988). Understanding parent-adolescent interactions: Perceptions of family members and outsiders. *Developmental Psychology, 24,* 707–714.

Offer, D., & Offer, J. B. (1975). *From teenage to young manhood: A psychological study*. New York: Basic Books.

Ohannessian, C. M., Lerner, R. M., Lerner, J. V., & von Eye, A. (2000). Adolescent–parent discrepancies in perceptions of family functioning and early adolescent self-competence. *International Journal of Behavior Development, 24,* 362–372.

Olson, D. H. (1977). Insiders' and outsiders' views of relationships: Research studies. In G. Levinger & H. Raush (Eds.), *Close relationships: Perspectives on the meaning of intimacy*. Amherst: MA University of Massachusetts.

Overbeek, G., Stattin, H., Vermulst, A., Ha, T., & Engels, R. (2007). Parent–child relationships, partner relationships, and emotional adjustment: A birth-to-maturity prospective analysis. *Developmental Psychology, 43,* 429–437.

Parke, R. D., & Buriel, R. (2006). Socialization in the family: Ethnic and ecological perspectives. In W. Damon & R. M. Lerner (Series Eds.), N. Eisenberg (Vol. Ed.), *Handbook of child psychology,* vol. 3: *Social, emotional, and personality development* (pp. 429–504). Hoboken, NJ: John Wiley & Sons.

Patterson, G. R. (1982). *Coercive family process*. Eugene, OR: Castelia.

Plomin, R., & Daniels, D. (1987). Why are children in the same family so different from each other? *Behavioral and Brain Sciences, 10,* 1–16.

Reis, H. T., Collins, W. A., & Berscheid, E. (2000). The relationship context of human behavior and development. *Psychological Bulletin, 126,* 844–872.

Rohner, R. P., & Pettengill, S. M. (1985). Perceived parental acceptance–rejection and parental control among Korean adolescents. *Child Development, 56,* 524–528.

Rohner, R. P., & Rohner, E. C. (1981). Parental acceptance–rejection and parental control: Cross-cultural codes. *Ethnology, 20,* 245–260.

Roisman, G. I., Madsen, S. D., Henninghausen, K. H., Sroufe, L. A., & Collins, W. A. (2001). The coherence of dyadic behavior across parent–child and romantic relationships as mediated by the internalized representation of experience. *Attachment and Human Development, 3,* 156–172.

Rosenthal, D. A., Demetriou, A., & Efklides, A. (1989). A cross-national study of the influence of culture on conflict between parents and adolescents. *International Journal of Behavioral Development, 12* 207–219.

Rutter, M., Graham, P., Chadwick, O. F. D., & Yule, W. (1976). Adolescent turmoil: Fact or fiction? *Journal of Child Psychology and Psychiatry, 17,* 35–56.

Rutter, M., Pickles, A., Murray, R., & Eaves, L. (2001). Testing hypotheses on specific environmental causal effects on behavior. *Psychological Bulletin, 127,* 291–324.

Sameroff, A. (1975). Transactional models of early social relations. *Human Development, 18,* 65–79.

Saris, W. E., & Satorra, A. (1993). Power evaluations in structural equation models. In K. A. Bollen & J. S. Long (Eds.), *Testing structural equation models* (pp. 181–204). Thousand Oaks, CA: Sage.

Schwarz, N. (1991). Self-reports: How the questions shape the answers. *American Psychologist, 54,* 93–105.

Seiffge-Krenke, I. (1999). Families with daughters, families with sons: Different challenges for family relationships and marital satisfaction? *Journal of Youth and Adolescence, 28,* 325–342.

Selman, R. (1980). *The development of interpersonal understanding*. New York: Academic Press.

Shanahan, L., McHale, S. M., Crouter, A. C., & Osgood, D. W. (2007). Warmth with mothers and fathers from middle childhood to late adolescence: Within- and between-families comparisons. *Developmental Psychology, 43,* 551–563.

Sheehan, G., & Noller, P. (2002). Adolescent's perceptions of differential parenting: Links with attachment style and adolescent adjustment. *Personal Relationships, 9,* 173–190.

Silk, J. S., Morris, A. S., Kanaya, T., & Steinberg, L. (2003). Psychological control and autonomy granting: Opposite ends of a continuum or distinct constructs? *Journal of Research on Adolescence, 13,* 113–128.

Silverberg, S. B., & Steinberg, L. (1990). Psychological well-being of parents with early adolescent children. *Developmental Psychology, 26,* 658–666.

Simmons, L. G., & Conger, R. D. (2007). Linking mother-father differences in parenting to a typology of family parenting styles and adolescent outcomes. *Journal of Family Issues, 28,* 212–241.

Simmons, R. G., & Blyth, D. A. (1987). *Moving into adolescence: The impact of pubertal change and school context.* New York: de Gruyter.

Simons, R. L., Chao, W., Conger, R. D., & Elder, G. H. (2001). Quality of parenting as mediator of the effect of childhood defiance on adolescent friendship choices and delinquency: A growth curve analysis. *Journal of Marriage and Family, 63,* 63–79.

Smetana, J. G. (1988). Adolescents' and parents' conceptions of parental authority. *Child Development, 59,* 321–335.

Smetana, J. G. (1996). Adolescent–parent conflict: Implications for adaptive and maladaptive development. In D. Cicchetti & S. L. Toth (Eds.), *Rochester Symposium on Developmental Psychology,* vol. 7. *Adolescence: Opportunities and challenges* (pp. 1–46). Rochester, NY: University of Rochester.

Smetana, J. G. (2000). Middle-class African American adolescents' and parents' conceptions of parental authority and parenting practices: A longitudinal investigation. *Child Development, 71,* 1672–1686.

Smetana, J. G., Abernethy, A., & Harris, A. (2000). Adolescent–parent interactions in middle class African American families: Longitudinal change and contextual variations. *Journal of Family Psychology, 14,* 458–474.

Smetana, J. G., Campione-Barr, N. & Daddis, C. (2004). Longitudinal development of family decision making: Defining healthy behavioral autonomy for middle-class African American adolescents. *Child Development, 75,* 1418–1434.

Smetana, J. G., Campione-Barr, N., & Metzger, A. (2006). Adolescent development in interpersonal and societal contexts. *Annual Review of Psychology, 57,* 255–284.

Smetana, J. G., & Daddis, C. (2002). Domain-specific antecedents of parental psychological control and monitoring: The role of parenting beliefs and practices. *Child Development, 73,* 563–580.

Smetana, J. G., Daddis, C., & Chuang, S. S. (2003). "Clean your room!" A longitudinal investigation of adolescent–parent conflict and conflict resolution in middle-class African American families. *Journal of Adolescent Research, 18,* 631–650.

Smetana, J. G., & Gaines, C. (1999). Adolescent–parent conflict in middle-class African American families. *Child Development, 70,* 1447–1463.

Smetana, J. G., Metzger, A., Gettman, D.C., & Campione-Barr, N. (2006). Disclosure and secrecy in adolescent–parent relationships. *Child Development, 77,* 201–217.

Smetana, J. G., Yau, J., & Hanson, S. (1991). Conflict resolution in families with adolescents. *Journal of Research on Adolescence, 1,* 189–206.

Smetana, J. G., Yau, J., Restrepo, A., & Braeges, J. L. (1991). Adolescent–parent conflict in married and divorced families. *Developmental Psychology, 27,* 1000–1010.

Smith, P. K., & Drew, L. M. (2002). Grandparenthood. In M. Bornstein (Ed.), *Handbook of parenting,* vol. 3 (pp. 141–171). Mahwah, NJ: Lawrence Erlbaum.

Stattin, H., & Kerr, M. (2000). Parental monitoring: A reinterpretation. *Child Development, 71,* 1072–1085.

Stattin, H., Kerr, M., & Tilton-Weaver, L. (in press). Parental monitoring: A critical examination of the research. In P. Dittus,

V. Guilamo-Ramos, & J. Jaccard (Eds.), *Parental monitoring of adolescents.* New York: Columbia University Press.

Stattin, H., & Klackenberg, G. (1992). Discordant family relations in intact families: Developmental tendencies over 18 years. *Journal of Marriage and the Family, 54,* 940–956.

Steinberg, L. (1981). Transformations in family relations at puberty. *Developmental Psychology, 17,* 833–840.

Steinberg, L. (1989). Pubertal maturation and parent-adolescent distance: An evolutionary perspective. In G. R. Adams, R. Montemayor, & T. Gullotta (Eds.), *Advances in adolescent development* (pp. 71–97). Beverly Hills, CA: Sage.

Steinberg, L. (2001). We know some things: Adolescent-parent relationships in retrospect and prospect. *Journal of Research on Adolescence, 11,* 1–19.

Steinberg, L. (2005). Psychological control: Style or substance? In J. Smetana (Ed.), *Changing boundaries of parental authority during adolescence. New Directions for Child and Adolescent Development* (no. 108, pp. 71–78). San Francisco: Jossey-Bass.

Steinberg, L., Blatt-Eisengart, I., & Cauffman, E. (2006). Patterns of competence and adjustment among adolescents from authoritative, authoritarian, indulgent, and neglectful homes: A replication in a sample of serious juvenile offenders *Journal of Research on Adolescence, 16,* 47–58.

Steinberg, L., Lamborn, S., Dornbusch, S., & Darling, N. (1992). Impact of parenting practices on adolescent achievement: Authoritative parenting, school involvement, and encouragement to succeed. *Child Development, 63,* 1266–1281.

Steinberg, L., & Silk, J. S. (2002). Parenting adolescents. In M. H. Bornstein (Ed.), *Handbook of parenting,* vol. 1: Children and parenting (pp. 103–134). Mahwah. NJ: Lawrence Erlbaum.

Steinberg, L., & Steinberg, W. (1994). *Crossing paths: How your child's adolescence triggers your own crisis.* New York: Simon & Schuster.

Susman, E. J., & Rogol, A. (2004). Puberty and psychological development. In R. M. Lerner & L. Steinberg (Eds.), *Handbook of adolescent psychology* (pp. 15–44). Hoboken, NJ: John Wiley & Sons.

Tamrouti-Makkink, I. D., Dubas, J. S., Gerris, J. R. M., & van Aken, M. A. G. (2004). The relation between the absolute level of parenting and differential parental treatment with adolescent siblings' adjustment. *Journal of Child Psychology and Psychiatry, 45,* 1397–1406.

Taylor, R. D., Casten, R., & Flickinger, S. M. (1993). Influence of kinship social support on the parenting experiences and psychosocial adjustment of African-American adolescents. *Developmental Psychology, 29,* 382–388.

Thomas, A., Chess, S., & Birch, H. G. (1977). *Temperament and development.* New York: Brunner/Mazel.

Tucker, C. J., McHale, S. M., & Crouter, A. C. (2003). Dimensions of mothers' and father's differential treatment of siblings: Links with adolescents' sex-typed personal qualities. *Family Relations, 52,* 82–89.

Turkheimer, E., & Waldron, M. (2000). Nonshared environment: A theoretical, methodological, and quantitative review. *Psychological Bulletin, 126,* 78–108.

van Doorn, M. D., Branje, S. J. T., & Meeus, W. H. J. (in press). Conflict resolution in parent–adolescent relationships and adolescent delinquency. *Journal of Early Adolescence.*

van Doorn M. D., Branje, S. J. T., & Meeus, W. H. J. (2007). Longitudinal transmission of conflict resolution styles from marital relationships to adolescent–parent relationships. *Journal of Family Psychology.*

van Leeuwen, K. G., Mervielde, I., Braet, C., & Bosmans, G. (2004). Child personality and parental behavior as moderators of problem behavior: Variable- and person-centered approaches. *Developmental Psychology, 40,* 1028–1046.

Vuchinich, S. (1987). Starting and stopping spontaneous family conflicts. *Journal of Marriage and the Family, 49,* 591–601.

Vuchinich, S., Emery, R., & Cassidy, J. (1988). Family members as third parties in dyadic family conflict: Strategies, alliances, and outcomes. *Child Development, 59,* 1293–1302.

Wadsworth, M. E., & Compas, B. E. (2002). Coping with family conflict and economic strain: The adolescent perspective. *Journal of Research on Adolescence, 12,* 243–274.

Waizenhofer, R. N., Buchanan, C. M., & Jackson-Newsom, J. (2004). Mothers' and fathers' knowledge of adolescents' daily activities: Its sources and its links with adolescent adjustment. *Journal of Family Psychology, 18,* 348–360.

Walker, L., & Taylor, J. (1991). Family interactions and the development of moral reasoning. *Child Development, 62,* 264–283.

Whiteman, S. D., & Buchanan, C. M. (2002). Mothers' and children's expectations for adolescence: The impact of perceptions of an older sibling's experience. *Journal of Family Psychology, 16,* 157–171.

Whiteman, S. D., McHale, S. M., & Crouter, A. C. (2003). What parents learn from experience: The first child as a first draft? *Journal of Marriage and Family, 65,* 608–621.

Winkielman, P., Knäuper, B., & Schwarz, N. (1998). Looking back at anger: Reference periods change the interpretation of emotion frequency questions. *Journal of Personality and Social Psychology, 75,* 719–728.

Youniss, J., & Smollar, J. (1985). *Adolescent relations with mothers, fathers, and friends.* Chicago: University of Chicago Press.

CHAPTER 2

Adolescents' Relationships with Siblings

PATRICIA L. EAST

Sibling relationships are among the most enduring of interpersonal ties and serve as important contexts for individual development. Because siblings share a personal history and often the same parents, as well as the same family and neighborhood and community, they can be affected by the same influences. Moreover, the relationships that children and adolescents share with siblings typically have a profound influence on their development and their experiences within the family. For example, siblings have been known to affect one another's attitudes, behaviors, school success, and even one another's friendships. In fact, sibling relationships often serve as a basis for other, future close adult relational bonds (Conger, Cui, Bryant, & Elder, 2000). Thus, sibling relationships can serve as a window into one's past, as well as a lens through which to better understand one's future. All in all, sibling relationships are fascinating, dynamic, and unique relationships that can help unravel the basic processes of human development.

Most children have at least one sibling, though the number of siblings in a family varies as a function of their age and birth cohort (Rowland, 2007). Several demographic trends in the United States may lend greater relevance of the sibling relationship to individuals'

lives today than in the past. First, family size has diminished to where today the average child in the United States has only one sibling, thus creating the potential for greater intimacy and mutual reliance between siblings (Rowland, 2007). Second, the increasing longevity of the life span has served to elongate sibling bonds, with siblings serving as strong providers of support often up to late adulthood (Geotting, 1986). The recent increases in geographic mobility and in divorce and subsequent remarriage may also cause people to cling to the constancy and permanency a brother or sister can provide. Finally, with more parents absent from the home (due to employment or divorce), children may be more likely to serve as care providers to one another and to band together as a mutual support system (Chappell & Penning, 2005).

However, there is a contradictory nature to this closeness that makes sibling relations so unique. Because siblings are typically nested within the same family, they share common familial resources. Whether implicitly or explicitly acknowledged, siblings often compete for these resources, which include parents' time and attention, as well as the family's financial assets and material possessions (Behrman, 1997; Behrman, Pollack & Taubman, 1995).

Preparation of this chapter was supported by Grants R01-HD043221, from the National Institute of Child Health and Human Development, and APR-006013, from the Office of Population Affairs, Department of Health and Human Services. The author thanks UC–San Diego student Ashley Slonim for locating, typing, and managing the reference list for this chapter.

These forces, in conjunction with the intense closeness siblings experience, can promote strong rivalries that often persist throughout the life course (Cicirelli, 1995).

This chapter reviews sibling relationships, particularly as they occur during adolescence. There has been far less research conducted on sibling relations during adolescence than during childhood or infancy. Recently, however, the work on teenage sibling ties has increased, with many studies showing the importance of sibling relationships during adolescence (Dunn, 2005). In addition, several longitudinal studies have provided compelling evidence of the changes that occur in sibling relationships across adolescence, as well as the strong influence siblings have on youths' health and well-being (Kramer & Bank, 2005).

In this chapter, I first present theories pertinent to sibling relationships. I then focus on the developmental course of sibling relationships, noting the form and functions sibling ties serve during adolescence. Third, I consider the various influences that shape adolescents' relations with siblings, including family factors and qualities of parents' parenting. Fourth, I discuss how sibling relationships influence adolescents' developmental course and adjustment, particularly adolescents' friend and peer relationships and engagement in risky behaviors, such as drug and alcohol use. I next consider the large literature on the nonshared environmental influences on siblings, or the factors that explain why siblings within the same family are so different (Dunn & Plomin, 1990). This research includes studies of parents' differential treatment of siblings and the process of sibling deidentification. Finally, recent studies of siblings from diverse family, cultural, and socioeconomic backgrounds are reviewed, as well as studies that describe the nuances that pertain to step- and half-siblings.

THEORIES PERTAINING TO SIBLING RELATIONSHIPS

Before embarking on a review of the field of sibling research, it is essential to first discuss the various theories that have been applied to the study of sibling relationships. Below I discuss family systems theory, attachment theory, social learning theory, social comparison theory, social provision theory, and the confluence model. Although the confluence model is not considered a theory per se, it was a highly popular and hotly contested model in the social sciences for decades and significantly shaped the face of sibling research. Also, it should be noted that my selection of the theories reviewed is not all encompassing; rather, my emphasis is on perspectives that remain important in the field of sibling research today.

Family Systems Theory

Family systems theory maintains that family members are part of an interdependent, dynamic family system whereby the behavior of each individual or family subsystem has the capacity to affect other individuals or subsystems within the family (Kreppner & Lerner, 1989; Minuchin, 1988). Family subsystems refer to alliances within the family, such as the marital dyad, sibling relationships, and parent–child relationships. Family systems theory contends that change in either the individual or the family unit has an impact on the other. Thus, family relationships are in constant flux, affected by the development of individual family members, the family unit as a whole, and the ever-changing larger social ecology in which the family is embedded. A systems perspective brings attention to the dynamic interdependence of various subsystems within the family, with the presence of a parent altering siblings' interactions, for example (Buhrmester, 1992). Similarly, the presence of an older sibling can alter parents' expectations of a younger child (Whiteman, McHale, & Crouter, 2003). As applied to the study of sibling relationships, a family systems perspective posits that individual family members, family subsystem dyads, as well as the dynamics of the family unit as a whole have the potential to affect the quality and intensity of adolescents' sibling relations and vice versa (Brody, 1998).

Attachment Theory

Attachment theory describes a system of human behaviors that serve to bring an individual into closer proximity to an attachment figure, often the principal caregiver, in times of stress or duress (Bowlby, 1969). The caregiver's responsiveness and sensitivity to a child's affective signals function to provide safety and security which, when experienced over time, helps children develop a sense of trust and the ability to regulate emotional distress. Attachment theory has been applied to sibling relationships in at least three contexts. First, the quality of mother–infant attachment bonds has been compared across siblings, with most studies finding that attachment security is consistent across siblings (Rosen & Burke, 1999; Van Ijzendoorn, Moran, Belsky et al., 2000; Ward, Vaughn, & Robb, 1988), although this link may weaken in adolescence (Kiang & Furman, 2007). Second, a strong attachment bond between mother and child is known to contribute to warm and close sibling relationships (Brody, 1998; Brody, Stoneman, & MacKinnon, 1986). Third, it has been noted that children may develop a strong attachment to a sibling in cases wherein parents do not (or cannot) provide sufficient warmth or security. Such instances were noted by Bank and Kahn (1982) in their description of intense sibling loyalties, and in situations where a sibling provides a child's primary care, such as after a maternal death or when a mother is chronically ill (Sears & Sheppard, 2004; Stein, Riedel & Rotheram-Borus, 1999). In a process known as *parentification,* a child caregiver is responsible for fulfilling siblings' basic needs, and the sibling relationship is forced to renegotiate its traditional roles and functions (Lamorey, 1999).

Social Learning Theory

Social learning theory proposes that observational learning, or modeling, is one of the primary methods by which behavior is acquired (Bandura, 1989). Sibling modeling is believed to be the basis for why siblings engage in similar behaviors, with siblings (especially older siblings) serving as powerful socialization agents. It is known that children readily model a sibling's behavior (Stocker & Youngblade, 1999). Indeed, Patterson's (1984, 1986) research documents that children's aggressiveness is learned or modeled after witnessing a sibling's aggression. Similarly, behaviors observed during parent–child interactions often generalize to children's interactions with their siblings; for example, children and adolescents use conflict resolution patterns with siblings that they have observed or experienced with parents (Cummings, Goeke-Morey & Papp, 2004). Positive interactions between parents and children are also known to generalize to empathetic and prosocial sibling interactions (Stocker, Ahmed & Stall, 1997), and sibling similarity in attitudes, interests, and behaviors have been found to result from siblings' observations of each other (Whiteman, McHale, & Crouter, 2007a, 2007b).

Social Comparison Theory

Social comparison theory is vital to the study of sibling relationships. Social comparison theory contends that there exists a basic human drive to evaluate oneself relative to others (Festinger, 1954). Indeed, without these comparisons, we could not assess our particular strengths, weaknesses, or talents. Siblings are a critical "other" to be compared, as each child in a family is similar but also different in relevant ways. One implication of social comparison processes is that the particular people to whom we compare ourselves can greatly influence how we see ourselves. Social comparison processes are not only central to the quality of sibling relationships, but also to parents' expectations of their various children (Whiteman & Buchanan, 2002). There is, in fact, a large and growing literature on sibling comparison processes and impact on parents' parenting and expectations, and on youth's adjustment (Boyle, Jenkins, Georgiades, et al., 2004; Brody & Stoneman, 1994; Reiss, Plomin, Hetherington et al., 1994). For example, children's individual adjustment has been found to be more strongly related to how they compare to their siblings than how children behave in an absolute sense (Feinberg, Neiderhiser, Simmens, et al., 2000).

Social Provision Theory

In Sullivan's (1953) social provision theory, he proposed that different social relationships serve different social needs. Weiss (1974) later modified Sullivan's theory and characterized the socioemotional functions, or social provisions, provided by different types of relationships. Both Sullivan and Weiss maintained, though, that individuals have basic needs for "tender" attachments, playful involvement, and emotional intimacy, and that only particular relationships can meet specific needs. Furman and Buhrmester (1985a, 1985b) applied this theory to children's and adolescents' sibling relationships in attempts to discern the various functions that siblings serve. They found, on average, that most siblings provide important sources of companionship, affection, intimacy, nurturance, instrumental help, and support. Through their work, Furman and Buhrmester noted that siblings also fulfill a wide variety of roles, such as friend, playmate, companion, confidante, competitor, agitator, caregiver, teacher, protector, and role model (Buhrmester, 1992; Buhrmester & Furman, 1990; Furman and Buhrmester, 1985a, 1985b, 1992). Goetting (1986) took a similar functional approach in studying sibling relationships and noted that siblings provide one another large amounts of caretaking, companionship, and emotional support throughout the life course.

It is important to note that social provision theory laid the groundwork for the "compensation hypothesis" of sibling relationships, or the notion that siblings can compensate for the provisions of a functionally analogous but absent relationship, such as same-age friends or peers (East & Rook, 1992). Currently, there is a growing literature on the protective effects of supportive sibling ties in the context of absent or unfulfilling relationships with parents,

friends, and peers (Jenkins, 1992; Milevsky & Levitt, 2005; Stocker, 1994). Other studies also have shown that affectionate sibling ties can buffer children from stress and depression in the presence of parents' marital conflict and when experiencing stressful life events (Gass, Jenkins, & Dunn, 2007; Milevsky, 2005). These and other studies highlight the functional significance of sibling ties in adolescents' lives and confirm the crucial benefits that can be gained by close and supportive sibling bonds (Lamb & Sutton-Smith, 1982).

The Confluence Model

One of the most widely recognized developmental models applied specifically to siblings is the confluence model (Zajonc & Markus, 1975), which attempted to explain sibling differences in intelligence and achievement in terms of family size and birth order. In trying to account for the generally inverse relationship between intellectual ability and number of siblings, the model held that a family's intellectual environment was the average intelligence of everyone in the family, with children contributing less than parents to the summed average. Later born children, thus, were thought to be exposed to a relatively less intelligent environment, because the family environment included the lower mental ages of succeeding siblings. Children from large families in which siblings were close in age were believed to be most disadvantaged due to the average lower mental ages of their many young siblings. Although the theory adequately explained population-level IQ scores, it was less successful in predicting individuals' achievement and IQ, and generally grew out of favor (Rodgers, 2001). However, an important element of the confluence model is still being tested today, that of various children within a family succeeding to varying extents as a function of their birth order (Conley, 2004), birth spacing (Rosenzweig, 1986), and family constellation, including the gender of one's siblings (Conley, 2000; Conley, Pfeiffer, & Velez, 2007). This line of research on parents' differential investment in their various children constitutes an important component of siblings' nonshared environment and is reviewed later in this chapter.

The preceding theories have been useful in describing and explaining adolescent sibling relationships and are widely used today to better understand sibling influences on youth development. In the following section, I review the research on the nature and function of sibling relationships from childhood up to young adulthood.

THE DEVELOPMENTAL COURSE OF SIBLING RELATIONSHIPS

During childhood, sibling interaction is a major component of children's social experiences (Dunn & Kendrick, 1982). As noted by sibling researcher Dunn (2007), two characteristics of the sibling relationship that are immediately apparent during childhood are the emotional intensity and intimacy between siblings. The intimacy of siblings' experiences with one another, spending more time together than in any other relationship during childhood, breeds extreme familiarity (Bank & Kahn, 1982). Indeed, it is this intimacy and emotional vulnerability that lends itself to a special closeness and openness that few relationships can match.

However, during childhood, sibling ties are often characterized by a love–hate relationship, with children rating their siblings as supportive and loving, but also as aggressive and antagonistic. Relative to other social relationships, children engage in relatively high rates of physical aggression (hitting, fighting) with their siblings (Furman & Buhrmester, 1985a). In asking 4th and 5th graders to describe their sibling relationships, children characterized them as affectionate, but also rivalrous and hostile (Stocker & McHale, 1992). Using two independent samples of college students, Stocker found that college students also described their sibling relationships as warm and close, but also as conflictual and competitive (Stocker, Lanthier, & Furman, 1997). Thus, there appears to be some longevity to the emotionally ambivalent nature of sibling ties.

As children move into adolescence, significant developmental changes occur in their sibling relationships. Sibling ties typically become less conflictual and more egalitarian, as siblings spend less time with one another and the intensity of the relationship lessens (Buhrmester & Furman, 1990; Kim, McHale, Osgood, & Crouter, 2006). In fact, following a steady increase in sibling conflict up to about age 12, there is a rather abrupt decline in the frequency of conflict starting from grade 7 (Furman & Buhrmester, 1985b). Scharf and colleagues (2005), using an Israeli sample, also found decreases in sibling conflict from middle adolescence to young adulthood.

However, recent research indicates that the change in conflict might be different for different children within a family. In a four-year longitudinal study, Kim and colleagues found that sibling conflict declined after early adolescence at the same time (but at different ages) for firstborns and second-borns (Kim et al., 2006). Among firstborns, reports of sibling conflict began to decline at approximately 14 years of age. Among second-borns, sibling conflict started to decrease at about age 11 years. Given that the average age difference between the siblings in the sample was about three years, the authors concluded that the difference in age at the decline was secondary to an overall decrease in sibling conflict when the older child entered middle adolescence. It is likely that this decline in conflict is due to both an increase in emotional self-control and to youth spending more time with friends and romantic partners and in their own extracurricular activities. These results point to the importance of considering children's ever-widening social worlds when studying their sibling relationships. These findings also underscore the importance of examining the mutuality of sibling conflict, or the interdependence of individual behaviors when studied within a dyad (Hinde, 1979).

Although sibling conflict generally appears to decrease during adolescence, rivalry and competition show signs of increasing.

Specifically, sibling relationships become more polarized from middle childhood to early adolescence, when the relative developmental differences between siblings begin to diminish (Brody & Stoneman, 1994). Thus, different-age siblings become more alike as they get older, as the disparity in relative competencies and abilities between siblings decreases. This situation produces more opportunity for social comparisons (from both self and parents) and sibling rivalry. In fact, parents' social comparisons were found to be linked with increases in negative sibling relationship qualities and decreases in positive sibling relationship qualities across time (Brody, Stoneman, & McCoy, 1994a). (This issue of sibling rivalry and parents' differential treatment is discussed more below in the section "Why Siblings Within the Same Family Are So Different").

Across adolescence, sibling intimacy, or the warmth and closeness of the relationship, also appears to decline. During middle childhood, siblings typically report very high levels of intimacy (or during grades 2 to 4). But by early adolescence, intimacy declines to more moderate levels (at 7th grade), after which it remains fairly stable up to college (or at ages 17 to 19) (Buhrmester, 1992). Despite this decline, adolescents still report more intimacy (personal disclosure, emotional support) with siblings than they do with parents (Furman & Buhrmester, 1992; Hartup, 1983). Thus, siblings appear to remain relatively intimate during adolescence, even in the face of less contact.

However, other research studying roughly the same age periods as those described above indicates that siblings' intimate exchanges follow a curvilinear trend, with intimacy moderate during late childhood, relatively low during early adolescence, and at its highest point during middle adolescence (Cole & Kearns, 2001). Analysis of the gender makeup of the sibling dyad, though, may explain this trend, with an interaction between a change in sibling intimacy and whether the sibling pair is of the same or opposite sex. Specifically, mixed-sex sibling pairs report relatively low intimacy during middle childhood (or from roughly ages 7 to 11 years), but report an increase in intimacy during middle adolescence, or from ages 12 to 19 (Kim et al., 2006). Same-sex sibling dyads, though, show no significant change in intimacy across development. A similar developmental trend was observed among 13- and 15-year-old youth, with intimacy increasing across time for opposite-sex sibling pairs, but remaining stable for same-sex pairs (Updegraff, McHale, & Crouter, 2002). These age-by-gender interactions likely reflect youth's greater interest in heterosexual relationships during adolescence, which may foster more companionship with and advice-seeking from opposite-sex siblings. This trend suggests a unique developmental significance of sister–brother relationships during adolescence, or that of possibly preparing one for a romantic or eventual spousal relationship.

As children enter adolescence, gender also appears to become more significant for sibling ties, with brother–brother pairs becoming less close than sister–sister pairs (Dunn, Slomkowski, & Beardsall, 1994). Older adolescent brothers also report less warmth and closeness with their younger sisters than adolescent girls report with their younger sisters. Consistent with this trend, in a study examining Latino and African American youth, sister pairs reported higher increases in warmth and closeness from early adolescence to middle adolescence than did sister–brother pairs (East & Khoo, 2005). However, boys and girls may operationalize closeness within the sibling relationship differently. Sisters, for example, cite talking and caring for each other as markers of closeness, whereas brothers cited doing activities together as a confirmation of their closeness, a pattern also seen with respect to gender differences in friendships outside the family (Edwards, Hadfield, Lucey, & Mauthner, 2006). Nevertheless, by middle adolescence, older sisters appear to be more likely than older brothers to be in close, confiding relationships with their younger siblings.

There is also evidence that sibling companionship, or the amount of time siblings spend with each another in leisure activities, declines during adolescence (Buhrmester & Furman, 1987). For example, using a home-based time-sampling methodology, siblings were found to spend a vast majority of time together during the preschool and early elementary school years, but by adolescence, they spent a relatively small fraction of their time in direct interaction with one another (Larson & Verma, 1999). In another study of 4th-, 6th-, and 8th-grade students, a generally downward trend was apparent in the amount of time siblings spent in shared recreational activities (Cole & Kearns, 2001). Studying a later age period, Israeli adolescents also reported spending less time with siblings in general and in joint leisure activities from ages 16 to 24 years (Scharf, Schulman, & Avigad-Spitz, 2005).

Continuing into young adulthood, there appear to be further declines in both contact and proximity between siblings, starting roughly at ages 18–23 years (White, 2001). The decline in contact is strongly linked with a decline in proximity, as young adult older siblings are likely to leave home for college, a job, or to be with a spouse or partner. Nevertheless, most siblings still see or speak with one another at least weekly (Stewart, Verbrugge, & Beilfuss, 1998), suggesting an attempt to remain emotionally connected even though they may not live with one another.

Siblings' role structure also changes during adolescence, as the power differential between older and younger siblings narrows. During early and middle childhood, the older sibling is more dominant in the relationship, perceived as having more power and status (Furman & Buhrmester, 1992). But beginning at about age 11 or 12 years, older and younger siblings began to strike a balance in power, with both older and younger siblings able to adopt an authoritative role in the relationship.

Paralleling these developmental changes in power are critical changes in the amount of nurturance given and received from siblings from middle childhood to early adolescence. During middle childhood, there are large asymmetries between the amount of nurturance older siblings provide to younger siblings and the amount of nurturance younger siblings provide to older ones (Buhrmester, 1992). From approximately ages 5 to 12 years, older siblings typically are involved in helping younger siblings through caregiving and with school-related tasks. But when older siblings reached early adolescence (or roughly age 11 or 12 years), the amount of nurturance they provide to younger siblings decreases. Moreover, the amount of help and nurturance younger siblings give to older siblings increases during this time period. This results in a more egalitarian relationship, with both older and younger siblings providing and receiving relatively more equivalent levels of support from one another as the older child moves into adolescence. In a large sample of European adolescents, the amount of support given from older siblings to younger ones, and from younger siblings to older ones, showed a strikingly similar pattern (Branje, van Lieshout, van Aken, & Haselager, 2004).

The more egalitarian role structure of the sibling dyad during adolescence likely represents a critical milestone in the sibling relationship. In this case, the younger sibling might feel emancipated from the oppressive authority of the older sibling, and the older sibling might feel liberated from his or her caregiver role toward the younger sibling (Buhrmester & Furman, 1990; Furman & Buhrmester, 1985b). In all, though, this developmental trend seems to reflect a basic shift in the power and role structure between siblings as they enter adolescence.

Similarly, other research shows that both older and younger adolescent-age siblings are equally likely to go to one another for advice and support about family problems and emotional concerns (Tucker, McHale, & Crouter, 2001). However, younger siblings are more likely than older siblings to turn to their siblings for help with problems concerning school, peers and pressure to engage in risky behaviors, such as drug or alcohol use. This echoes an earlier trend that showed that younger siblings tend to place greater value on the support they receive from older siblings than vice versa and that youth felt closer with an older rather than a younger sibling during middle adolescence (Buhrmester & Furman, 1990). Both of these trends suggest that older siblings may develop into mentors for younger siblings during adolescence. Starting in early adulthood, though, birth order begins to have no influence on the amount of support given or received from one's siblings (Cicirelli, 1995). This trend toward equality in the sibling relationships continues until the middle and late adulthood years, by which point older and younger siblings give and receive equivalent levels of support (Connidis, 2005).

Cicirelli (1995) conducted an interesting retrospective study in which he asked middle-aged sibling pairs to rate the positive and negative qualities of their sibling relationship from childhood to middle adulthood. Results revealed that individuals' ratings of the positive qualities of their sibling relationship (such as enjoyment, trust, confiding, and understanding) declined sharply in adolescence and then increased in adulthood. This teenage dip was sharpest among sister pairs, whereas pairs of brothers evinced a flatter—albeit still downward—trajectory. Those who were younger siblings also rated their relationship less positively throughout their life course than those who were older siblings. Individuals' ratings of the negative qualities of their sibling relationships (such as arguing, competition, and antagonism) peaked in adolescence and then declined in adulthood. When asked to explain the changes, most respondents attributed them to the mood swings of adolescence and to becoming more engaged with others outside the family during this time. The subsequent improvement in the relationship that had taken place by young adulthood was attributed to increasing maturity and to an increased acceptance of each other. Almost all participants

acknowledged, though, that their sibling relationship changed dramatically throughout their lifetime.

One phase of the life course that is perhaps the most understudied in relation to individuals' sibling relationships is the transition to adulthood (Cicirelli, 1995; Stewart et al., 1998). This developmental transition is often accompanied by significant life-course events, such as leaving home to attend college, getting married, and starting full-time employment, all of which can significantly impact sibling ties. Indeed, contact between siblings is likely affected, as are the pattern of behaviors and the nature and dynamic of the relationship. However, findings on the nature of change in sibling relationships during this developmental period are mixed. Riggio (2006) reported decreases in sibling warmth and emotional closeness from adolescence into young adulthood. White (2001), using a large national data set, also found that sibling contact, proximity, and giving and receiving support declined starting at age 16 and continued to drop into middle adulthood. In contrast, Stewart and colleagues found increases in sibling warmth during this period (Stewart et al., 1998), and, Stocker and colleagues (1997) found that most college students still perceived their sibling ties as close and supportive. The Stocker et al. study reported no relation between the geographical distance between siblings and the characteristics of their relationship during young adulthood, whereas White (2001) found strong links between these variables, with greater proximity associated with more sibling support. Certainly, more research should be directed toward better understanding how sibling bonds change as youth transition to adulthood.

In all, the nature of sibling ties changes significantly as adolescents grow and develop. In general, sibling relations become more egalitarian and less conflicted and intense across the adolescent years, although there is some indication that siblings may become more outwardly competitive with one another. Emotional dependency, affection, and intimacy with siblings also generally wane across adolescence. These trends reveal a separation and individuation from siblings similar to that from parents and family described in the theoretical work of Blos (1979) and reflected in the empirical findings of Collins and colleagues (Collins, Gleason, & Sesma, 1997). Time spent with siblings and time engaged in joint leisure activities also generally decline during adolescence. These developmental trends are invariably linked to youth's increasing autonomy, as well as to changes occurring in other spheres of youth's lives, such as their increased engagement with friends, peers, and romantic partners, and in their own recreational pursuits. Finally, while age spacing and birth order generally decrease in importance across adolescence, gender and gender constellation appear to become more significant influences on sibling ties, with sister pairs and sister–brother pairs increasing in closeness during adolescence, but brother pairs not showing a similar pattern. In general, although the structure and nature of sibling ties change in important ways during the teenage years, youth's overall emotional attachments with siblings remain strong, close, and supportive (Cicirelli, 1995).

Certainly, though, not all sibling relationships are the same. Sibling ties are strongly influenced by family and parenting processes, as well as by each individual's temperament or behavioral disposition. Influences that shape the quality of youth's sibling relationships are reviewed next.

INFLUENCES ON THE SIBLING RELATIONSHIP

Numerous studies have shown that siblings develop different kinds of relationships depending on the family context in which they are embedded and the parenting they receive (Furman, 1995). Because siblings are nested within the same family, it is imperative to understand the sibling relationship in the context of the family system. Indeed, the origins of children's sibling relations are integrally tied to the family processes that precede the formation of the sibling bond, such as parents' marital relationship, parents' parenting, and the parent–child relationship (Brody, 1996, 1998; Hetherington, 1994).

The study of sibling relationships within the larger family context derives from both attachment theory and social learning theory. As discussed above, attachment theory contends that there is a coherence in individuals' close relationships, with children's early interactions with caregivers providing an internal working model that affects their expectations for and interactions with siblings and others (Sroufe & Fleeson, 1988). Similarly, from a social learning perspective, children are known to model the interactions they witness from others within the family (Cummings & Davies, 1994; Patterson, 1984).

Much of the earlier research on sibling relationships also examined how children's temperament, or behavioral style, is linked to the quality of sibling ties (Dunn & Kendrick, 1982; Minnett, Vandell, & Santrock, 1983). A number of studies have also looked at several of the above-mentioned influences simultaneously. When considered jointly, children's temperament, mothers' parenting, and child age account for more of the variance in the quality of the sibling relationship than that explained by birth order or gender constellation (Brody et al., 1994a, 1994b, 1996; Stocker, Dunn, & Plomin, 1989). This suggests that all of these factors (individual child characteristics, sibling constellation factors, family relationships, and family process variables) need to be considered simultaneously to fully account for variations in sibling relationship quality. Such multivariate studies are useful for understanding the full influence of these factors and the relative power of each in shaping youth's sibling bonds.

Associations Between Temperament and Youth's Sibling Ties

Most of the research on the links between individuals' temperament and the nature of their sibling ties generally indicate that sibling relations are more conflictual and less positive when siblings are temperamentally difficult (Brody, 1996; McHale, Kim, & Whiteman, 2006), and, conversely, that individuals with easy temperaments enjoy more favorable sibling relations (Brody et al., 1994a, 1994b; Stocker et al., 1989). However, interesting longitudinal associations have been found that forecast adolescent sibling relations from their childhood temperamental dispositions. For example, youth who are characterized as temperamentally easy at 7–9 years are likely to report more positive and less conflicted sibling relationships in early adolescence (ages 12–14) (Brody et al., 1994a). Child temperament was actually found to be more consistently associated with sibling relationship quality in early adolescence than in middle childhood, such that the association between temperament and sibling quality became more robust across age.

Other research has considered the temperament of each individual in the sibling dyad and concluded that a difficult temperament has different consequences for the relationship when manifested by older versus younger siblings. For example, an older sibling's difficult temperament was predictive of *less positive* sibling relations, whereas a younger sibling's difficult temperament forecast *more negative* sibling ties (Brody et al., 1994b). It may be that difficult younger children are more likely to initiate conflict, and difficult older children are more likely to withdraw from sibling interaction.

Other research has examined whether the behavioral disposition of one sibling has more influence than the other in shaping the nature of the relationship (Furman & Lanthier, 1996). In a study of college students and their siblings, it was found that individuals' extraversion, agreeableness, conscientiousness, emotional stability, and intellectualism were all significantly associated with sibling warmth, conflict, and rivalry (Lanthier, 2007). However, the older siblings' personality traits were more strongly associated with sibling warmth and rivalry than were these characteristics of the younger sibling. Thus, while the personality characteristics of both siblings play a large role in how they get along, the behavioral styles of older siblings may have more influence than those of younger siblings in determining the nature of the sibling bond.

The Contributions of Parents' Parenting and the Quality of the Parent–Child Relationship to Sibling Ties

As stated above, positive parent–child relationships are expected to contribute to the development of positive sibling relationships, according to attachment theory (Sroufe & Fleeson, 1986) and social learning theory (Bank, Patterson & Reid, 1996; Patterson, Dishion & Bank, 1984). An impressive consensus of research supports this link, with warm and affectionate parent–child relations consistently associated with positive and prosocial sibling bonds (Brody et al., 1987, 1992a, 1994b; Conger et al., 2000; Howe et al., 2001; Stocker et al. 1989), and with negative, intrusive, and overcontrolling parent–child relationships associated with unsupportive and aggressive sibling ties (Bank et al., 1996; Brody, 1996, 1998). Although conducted largely with preschool children, several studies have also documented that mothers' sensitive and nurturing interactions with a younger child influence how older siblings interact with their younger sibling (Bryant, 1989; Howe & Ross, 1990; Volling, 2005).

Longitudinal associations between parent-child relations and sibling relationships have also been documented. Specifically, as the parent–child relationship improves across age, so, too, do sibling relations (Brody et al., 1996). More time in shared dyadic activities with mothers and fathers predicts more positive sibling relations at a later time point, even after considering the effects of the older and younger siblings' temperament. Similarly, among elementary school-age children, those who had warmer father–child and mother–child relationships had the most affectionate and least hostile sibling ties during early adolescence (Stocker & McHale, 1992).

Parents' parenting style is also highly significant for the quality of sibling relations. Specifically, parents' attentive monitoring and equitable treatment of their adolescent children have been linked to less sibling conflict and more positive sibling interactions (Boll, Ferring, & Filipp, 2003; Brody, 1996, 1998; Conger et al., 2000). Parents' involved and nurturing parenting has also been associated with an absence of sibling conflict, both concurrently and one year later (Brody, Stoneman, McCoy, & Forehand, 1992). However, lax maternal monitoring during early adolescence has been found to be related to an older sister having more status and power within the sibling dyad during middle adolescence (East & Khoo, 2005). The suggests a scenario wherein an older sister might adopt a parental-supervisory role with younger siblings when the mother is unable (or unwilling) to monitor her children's whereabouts and activities.

Another aspect of parents' parenting that has been examined in studies of sibling relations is parents' mediation of their children's disputes (McHale, Updegraff, Tucker, & Crouter, 2000; Perlman & Ross, 1997; Smith & Ross, 2007). Research with 5- and 10-year-old children shows that when mothers provide guidance and reason, and when they directly discuss youth's emotions, interests, and the conflict negotiation process, siblings are better able to reason and to resolve their disputes (Smith & Ross, 2007). However, during adolescence, when parents directly intervene (by punishing siblings or solving the problem), conflict between siblings escalates (McHale et al., 2000). It may be that younger children's sibling relations profit from parental intervention, but that older adolescent siblings benefit most from parental nonintervention. Indeed, parents typically use different conflict management strategies with different-aged children (Kramer, Perozynski, & Chung, 1999). More developmental studies are needed to clarify the most effective conflict resolution strategies to be used with siblings at different ages.

Influences of Parents' Marital Relations on Youth's Sibling Ties

Most of the research directed at uncovering the influences of parent's marital relations on sibling ties has focused on how marital conflict is related to sibling conflict and negativity (Cummings & Davies, 1994; Stocker & Youngblade, 1999). However, a few studies have focused on the link between positive parental marital relations and affectionate sibling ties (Brody et al., 1992a, 1996; Conger et al., 2000; Stocker et al., 1997), and at least two studies have found that siblings form especially close and supportive ties in the face of excessive marital conflict (Dunn et al., 1994; Jenkins, 1992).

The association between marital conflict and poor sibling relations has been well documented. Dunn and colleagues (1999), using a community sample of families with 7-year-olds living in England, found that mother-partner hostility and lack of affection were related to greater negativity from older to younger sibling four years later. Stocker and colleagues also found that when mothers described their marriages as low in affection, 4th- and 5th-grade children reported more hostile and rivalrous relations with their siblings (Stocker et al., 1997).

In attempting to uncover the processes underlying these associations, a few studies have examined how parents' hostility directed toward their children might mediate the relation between marital conflict and sibling conflict. Indeed, parents who report high marital conflict are more likely to also engage in punitive parenting, and siblings' physical aggression toward one another is related to both (Erel, Margolin, & John, 1998). Results from another study show that parents who fight often with their spouse are more likely to also behave angrily toward their children, and it is the parental hostility directed toward their children that is linked to increases in sibling conflict

(Stocker & Youngblade, 1999). In addition, blaming a sibling for parents' marital conflict was found to be associated with high rivalry between siblings (Stocker & Youngblade, 1999). Thus, poor sibling relations appear to be closely intertwined with both high marital conflict and harsh parenting.

At odds with these trends, however, are reports that in the face of excessive or long-term marital conflict, siblings grow closer and provide large amounts of comfort and support to one another (Dunn et al., 1994; Jenkins, 1992). In these situations, children are likely trying to find solace and cope effectively by securing support from siblings. In fact, in responding to parents' angry exchanges, older siblings have been shown to increase their nurturing and helpful behavior toward their younger siblings, suggesting a protective, shielding role of older siblings in the face of marital conflict (Cummings & Smith, 1989). These results, which appear to contradict those previously cited, suggest that different levels of family conflict may affect children's sibling relationships differently. It may be important to look at the level, duration, and potential abusive patterns of marital conflict, as well as the levels of stress and anxiety experienced by children.

Collectively, the studies reviewed in this section add to theoretical models that emphasize the role of individual, family, and parenting processes in shaping youth's sibling ties. The available evidence supports the interdependent nature of family relationships, with marital relations affecting the parent–child relationship, which in turn affects the quality of sibling relations. However, it has also been shown that hostile and antagonistic sibling relations can exacerbate marital conflict, and a temperamentally difficult child can precipitate poor parent–child relations (Brody, 1998; McHale et al., 2006; Stocker et al., 1989). These family factors are invariably inexplicably linked in complex ways across development (Lerner, 2004; Lerner & Steinberg, 2004). Moreover, family dynamics constantly change as the family unit and family members

age and develop. For example, recent research indicates that having an older adolescent child shapes parents' expectations for their younger children when that child enters adolescence (Whiteman & Buchanan, 2002; Whiteman et al., 2003). Similarly, parent–child conflict has been shown to increase for all children in the family when the oldest child transitions into adolescence (Shanahan, McHale, Osgood, & Crouter, 2007). Certainly, it is important to study adolescents' sibling relationships within a larger and ever-changing family system (Lerner, 2004).

SIBLING INFLUENCES ON ADOLESCENT DEVELOPMENT AND ADJUSTMENT

Much research within the sibling relationship field has focused on how siblings positively and negatively influence each other and, in so doing, affect their adjustment. This area of study has generally taken one of two approaches in describing sibling relationship contributions to adolescent outcomes. The first approach draws from a social modeling perspective, which emphasizes the ability of children to actively shape and reinforce their siblings' attitudes and behaviors (Patterson et al., 1984). In this case, similarity in siblings' adjustment is attributed, in part, to modeling each other's behaviors. Here, the balance of power is important for a socialization influence, with the individual who holds more power or authority more likely to serve as a model or socialization agent (Whiteman et al., 2007a, 2007b).

The second approach to explaining sibling influence derives from a family systems perspective, whereby positive and healthy functioning within the family contributes to the well-being of individual family members (Minuchin, 1988). Here, sibling relationships contribute to developmental outcomes because siblings share the same family context, experience the same parenting, and are exposed to similar family functioning and dynamics.

From a family systems perspective, siblings would share the same vulnerability to internalizing and externalizing problems because of problematic functioning at the family-systemic level (Davies & Ciccetti, 2004). The research on sibling influences for adolescents' positive and maladaptive functioning is reviewed below.

Sibling Influences on Adolescents' Positive Functioning

Sibling Support Linked With an Absence of Adjustment Problems

Guided by the coping and social support literature (Cohen & Smye, 1985; Sandler, Miller, Short, & Wolchik, 1989), several studies have shown that sibling support is associated with adolescents' positive mental health. Specifically, adolescents who have close and supportive sibling ties report less loneliness (Ponzetti & James, 1997), less depression and anxiety (Branje et al., 2004; Kim et al., 2007; Milevsky, 2005), more positive feelings of self-worth (Stocker, 1994), and greater life satisfaction (Oliva & Arranz, 2005). However, such simple main effects assessed from correlational data are vulnerable to important threats to internal validity, or to plausible alternative explanations, mainly, that positive functioning on the part of individuals brings about supportive relations with others, including brothers and sisters (Dooley, 1985).

A more robust test of the benefits of sibling support is the presence of a protective effect, wherein support buffers an individual from harm in the presence of stress or stressful life events (Cohen & Wills, 1985). When this effect is evident, sibling support interacts with risk factors to buffer or offset their impact and thus moderate the effects of risk (Rutter, 1987). At least two studies have documented this more complex link, showing that high sibling support moderates the relationship between exposure to stressful life events and youth's functioning. In the first study, children who experienced many cumulative stressful life events (family deaths, accidents, illnesses,

separations, etc.) and had high sibling affection reported lower internalizing problems than children who had relatively unaffectionate sibling ties (Gass et al., 2007). In the second study, high sister support was found to buffer the relationship between ecological risk (poverty, family stress, poor-quality neighborhood) and adolescents' adjustment in school (Milevsky & Levitt, 2005).

Another support effect discussed in the sibling literature is "compensatory support," which refers to the more or less planned investment in a particular relationship knowing that one has failed in other kinds of relationships. In this way, compensation implies active seeking of social provisions in an effort to substitute or make up for a particular relationship deficiency (East & Rook, 1992). This type of compensation would be evident if those who perceive low support in one type of relationship seek support in another, functionally analogous relationship, or a relational bond that serves similar social functions as described in Weiss's theory of social provisions (Weiss, 1974).

This type of compensatory pattern has been shown in several studies, such that adolescents who have poor relationships with parents, friends, or peers develop especially close ties with siblings (East & Rook, 1992; Milevsky, 2005; Milevsky & Levitt, 2005; Seginer, 1998; Sherman, Lansford, & Volling, 2006; Stocker, 1994). Four of these studies also found that high support from a sibling partially compensated for low support in another social relationship with respect to measures of well-being (East & Rook, 1992; Milevsky, 2005; Milevsky & Levitt, 2005; Stocker, 1994). For example, among college students who reported low support from mothers, fathers, or friends, those who reported high support from a sibling were less depressed and less lonely than those who received low support from a sibling (Milevsky, 2005).

Thus, close sibling relations are an important source of support for adolescents, and such support is associated with positive psychological benefits. More importantly, there is evidence that sibling support can mitigate the negative effects associated with life stress and with the lack of support in other social ties.

Sibling Relations and Social Competence

There is accumulating evidence that children who grow up with at least one sibling have greater social skills and interpersonal understanding than children who have no siblings (Downey & Condron, 2004; Howe, Aquan-Asse, Bukowski et al., 2001; Tucker, Updegraff, McHale, & Crouter, 1999). Indeed, children learn critical conflict negotiation strategies with siblings, and are able to practice turn taking, compromise, and sharing within their day-to-day sibling interactions (Dunn & Slomkowski, 1992). Having a sibling can also help foster the development of many prosocial behaviors, such as helping, teaching, and nurturing (Brody et al., 1986; Smith, 1993). Although most of this research has focused on young children, some studies have examined the association between adolescents' sibling relationship qualities and the nature of their peer and friendship ties. Generally, these studies indicate that youth who have warm and intimate sibling relationships also have close friendships and are socially competent with peers (Brody & Murry, 2001; Updegraff et al., 2002).

Recent research has attempted to identify the processes underlying this link. It has been suggested, for example, that youth learn specific social skills within their sibling relationships, such as how to share intimate feelings and information with others, how to be emotionally empathetic, and how to understand another's feelings (Howe et al., 2001). Children who have warm and close sibling ties show a greater capacity for empathy and self-disclosure (Howe et al., 2001) and are more sensitive to others' feelings than youth who have less positive sibling relations (Tucker et al., 1999). In addition, in a European sample of adolescents, satisfaction with one's sibling relationship was linked with intimacy with a best friend and strong attachment and

trust with one's peers (Oliva & Arranz, 2005). Because all of these studies were correlational, drawing causal inferences is not possible. But the results as a whole are consistent with the notion that youth learn critical socioemotional skills related to emotional intimacy and empathy in the context of their sibling relationships, and that these skills are then used to foster positive, close relations with others.

Other research also has examined whether children learn prosocial and regulatory skills within the context of positive sibling relationships. Studying a sample of aggressive children, Stormshak and colleagues found that the warmth and support children received from siblings were correlated with children's emotional control and prosocial behavior displayed at school (including the inclination to help others and be friendly) (Stormshak, Bellanti, Bierman, et al., 1996). Similar results were found in a longitudinal study of African American sibling pairs, in which results from structural equation modeling indicated that older siblings' competence contributed to younger siblings' self-regulation, which in turn was related to younger siblings' social competence one year later (Brody, Kim, Murry, & Brown, 2003). These findings suggest that younger siblings learn emotional and behavioral control from a competent older sibling, in the form of self-regulatory behaviors, that then help with their friendships. Using the same sample and a similar analytic strategy, these researchers also reported that younger siblings' social and academic competence was linked to the earlier absence of sibling conflict (Brody & Murry, 2001). In this case, the absence of conflict may best allow siblings to interact fully and positively so that the prosocial behavior can be best observed. Frequent and intimate discussions with siblings also have been linked with adolescents' perceived self-competence at school and with peers (Tucker & Winzeler, 2007). It may be that such discussions with siblings provide adolescents a context for learning communication skills, norms for behavior, and how to be emotionally intimate.

Collectively, this literature suggests that essential social skills and prosocial behaviors are learned and practiced with siblings, and that these skills then help youth develop positive relations with friends and peers outside the family (Brody, 2004). Such skills include sharing, cooperating, self-regulation (anger management, conflict negotiation), and increased social understanding, perspective taking, and effective communication.

The Benefits of Successful Resolution of Sibling Conflict

During early childhood, sibling conflict is known to foster social and cognitive development by providing opportunities for children to learn how to discuss and defend their self-interests and negotiate resolutions to disagreements (Dunn & Slomkowski, 1992). However, until recently, not much was known about how sibling conflict might contribute to development in adolescence. It has been suggested that sibling conflict plays a role in adolescents' identity formation, with sibling disputes helping to clarify a sense of self-identity or defining who one is (Raffaelli, 1992). Sibling conflict during adolescence also likely serves to reinforce behavioral rules and norms, as well as teach about the limits of acceptable behavior and personal boundaries, such as defining how much provocation will be tolerated by another (Raffaeli, 1992). Adolescents also can learn important interpersonal skills from successful resolution of sibling conflicts, such as compromise, assertiveness, and peaceful negotiation. In addition, youth can learn the crucial skill of resuming interactions after a dispute has occurred, which likely has ramifications for future close personal relationships over the life course (Katz, Kramer, & Gottman, 1992).

The sibling relationship itself is also likely to benefit from successful resolution of disputes. For example, after a conflict with a brother or sister, individuals report a greater sense of trust, acceptance, and openness with their sibling (Bedford, Volling, & Avioli, 2000). Others report that the conflict with their sibling

was liberating, realizing that it was acceptable to disagree and to continue their relationship despite their disagreements. A study of school-age children found that children's sense of self and their social understanding improved as a result of a sibling conflict (McGuire, Manke, Eftekhari, & Dunn, 2000). Sibling conflict also has been shown to provide children opportunities for persuasive negotiation and to provoke adolescents to state and defend their differing perspectives (Ross, Ross, Stein, & Trabasso, 2006). In addition, the conflictual nature of children's sibling interactions can provide opportunities to learn affect regulation and behavioral control (Stormshak et al., 1996). In all, sibling conflict appears to provide unique opportunities for the development of many social skills that are beneficial to adolescents' other social bonds.

A word of caution is in order lest the preceding findings be interpreted as sibling conflict is optimal for development. Certainly, while some level of conflict between siblings is normative (Dunn & Kendrick, 1982; Dunn & Slomkowski, 1992), prolonged conflict, severe physical aggression, and continued hostile and caustic interactions between siblings is not normative and has a deleterious impact on children's and adolescents' psychological health and well-being (Stocker, Burwell, & Briggs, 2002). It is in only cases in which disputes can be successfully negotiated and resolved that the learning benefits of sibling conflict can be realized.

Sibling Influences on Early Adult Romantic Relationships

A number of researchers have proposed that the social skills learned in sibling relationships can be important for adolescents' romantic relationships (Conger et al., 2001; Rauer & Volling, 2007; Reese-Weber & Kahn, 2005). Because both sibling and romantic relationships share the same intensity, intimacy, and egalitarian structure, the sibling relationship may serve as an essential model for adolescents when they start to initiate romantic relationships. For example, the social skills discussed immediately above would likely relate to success or failure in one's early adult romantic relationships.

Guided by an observational learning hypothesis, Conger and colleagues (2000) tested a *sibling socialization continuity hypothesis*, or whether sibling interaction patterns observed during middle adolescence are predictive of later interactions with a romantic partner during early adulthood. Their results indicated that there was no relation between sibling affective behaviors during middle adolescence and behaviors with a romantic partner during early adulthood. However, in studying whether sibling conflict resolution patterns were indicative of concurrent conflict resolution patterns with a romantic partner, Reese-Weber and Kahn (2005) found that both positive (e.g., compromise) and negative (e.g., verbal attack, blaming) conflict resolution behaviors employed with siblings were also used with a current romantic partner. These results, which are consistent with social learning theory (Bandura, 1989), suggest that adolescents observe how conflict is handled in their interactions with siblings and reproduce these strategies in their relationships with others. In this case, because links were found for both positive as well as negative resolution strategies, youth who successfully resolve their sibling conflicts appear more able to also competently resolve conflict with romantic partners, whereas those who are unable to resolve sibling conflict appear to have more difficulty in resolving disagreements in their romantic relationships.

In an interesting study of whether sibling jealousy plays a role in young adults' romantic relationships, it was found that experiencing distress in one's romantic relationships was indeed related to retrospective reports of sibling jealousy in childhood (Rauer & Volling, 2007). Here, a preoccupied (insecure) attachment style with parents may spill over to one's later relationships, with a negative internal working model of relationships contributing

to conflict, ambivalence, and jealousy in one's later adult romantic ties. These findings underscore the notion that young adult interpersonal relationships often have familial origins or specifically, that there is consistency from earlier sibling relationships to later adult social bonds.

Sibling Influences on Adolescent Problem Behaviors

Delinquency and Antisocial Behavior

The literature on adolescent delinquent behavior has consistently emphasized the involvement of siblings in the development of antisocial behavior. Patterson (1984, 1986) cogently described how early aggressive exchanges between siblings, accompanied by ineffective parenting, reinforces the use of hostile interpersonal tactics that result in escalating cycles of attacks and counterattacks with siblings. Left unchecked, such exchanges serve as a training ground for developing a predominately aggressive, coercive interaction style (Patterson et al., 1984). Children with such aggressive interpersonal tendencies are most typically rejected by their more socially skilled peers, which leaves them vulnerable to developing associations with deviant peers, or those who are similarly aggressive and unskilled (Snyder & Stoolmiller, 2002). Indeed, many studies have shown that adolescents whose sibling relationships are characterized by elevated levels of aggression and conflict display high levels of antisocial behavior with peers (Bank, Burraston, & Snyder, 2004; Conger, Conger, & Scaramella, 1997; Criss & Shaw, 2005).

While earlier research on childhood aggression has focused on young children's hostile interactions with siblings and peers, more recent research has examined how continued exposure to a deviant model in the form of an older sibling is a significant risk factor in the development of antisocial behavior during adolescence (Shortt, Capaldi, Dishion, et al., 2003; Slomkowski, Rende, Conger, et al., 2001; Williams, Conger, & Blozis, 2007). This area primarily has utilized a social modeling perspective and focused on how propensity for delinquency is promoted through direct interaction with and modeling of a deviant sibling. For example, Slomkowski and colleagues (2001) found that the frequency of hostile interactions with an older delinquent sibling was directly related to the development of delinquency in an adolescent younger sibling, among both boys and girls (e.g., delinquency was operationalized as serious legal offenses, such as damaging property, breaking and entering, and physical assault). Similarly, extensive involvement with a coercive sibling at 6 years of age has been shown to predict highly antisocial behavior 10 years later (Compton, Snyder, Schrepferman, et al., 2003). In addition, adolescents who strongly identify with a deviant older brother are more negatively affected by exposure to their antisocial sibling than those who do not have as intense an identification (Ardelt & Day, 2002). Thus, intensive interactions with a coercive sibling can have powerful long-term effects on one's tendency to engage in delinquent behavior.

There is also evidence that a warm and close relationship with a delinquent older sibling is associated with a younger sibling's antisocial behavior. Criss and Shaw (2005) found this effect for both brother–brother and sister–sister dyads, and Slomkowski and colleagues (2001) found this effect for brothers only. In the latter study, warmth and closeness with a delinquent older brother was predictive of younger brother's delinquency 4 years later. It may be that receptivity to antisocial behavior and the modeling of deviant acts is more likely when siblings are close. It is also possible that brothers engage in deviant acts together, and thus a warm and close relationship reflects a "partners in crime" scenario (Slomkowski et al., 2001).

Further research in this area has examined how involvement with and exposure to an older sibling's deviant peers may exacerbate a younger sibling's early initiation into and progression toward antisocial behavior (Snyder, Bank, & Burraston, 2005). For example, sharing the same friendship network with a delinquent older sibling strongly predicts younger siblings' engagement in delinquent behavior, even after controlling for older siblings' delinquency (Rowe & Gulley, 1992). There appears to be a synergistic effect of being exposed to both a deviant older sibling and his (or her) older peer group, which can escalate the younger sibling's involvement in deviant activities.

Along these lines, Snyder and colleagues (2005) conducted a unique study that examined sibling influence on youth's involvement in delinquent activities across development. They found that sibling conflict during early childhood predicted older brothers' association with deviant peers during middle adolescence, which in turn was linked to younger brothers' coparticipation in deviant activities with the older brother at age 16. These findings point to a sequential progression of deviance training by both the older brother and his delinquent peers, with both sets of risks synergistically increasing a younger sibling's likelihood for delinquency.

As a whole, this research strongly points to the socialization role of siblings in the development of antisocial behavior. Specifically, sibling conflict during childhood provides the context for observing, developing, and practicing aggressive and antisocial behaviors, which generalize to interactions with others outside the family. Such behavior leads to association with deviant peers, which further reinforces coercive interaction styles. As delinquent acts escalate in seriousness, as is often the case during adolescence, the younger siblings of delinquent older siblings appear to be vulnerable not only to influences of the older sibling, but also to influences of the older siblings' deviant friends.

Sibling Influences on Drug and Alcohol

Use   Similar to studies of adolescent delinquent and antisocial behavior, there is a large literature that shows a high concordance between siblings' substance use (Ary, Tildesley, Hops,

& Andrews, 1993; Conger & Ruteer, 1996; Duncan, Duncan, & Hops, 1996). Unlike the literature on sibling effects on youth's antisocial behavior, though, slightly different processes have been used to explain sibling similarity in alcohol and drug use. For example, there is some evidence that siblings are equally susceptible to alcohol use during adolescence as a result of witnessing their parents' alcohol use or abuse (Ary et al., 1993; Duncan et al., 1996; McGue, Sharma, & Benson, 1996). Studies of twins and adopted siblings also have established sibling similarity in smoking and drinking during adolescence while controlling for genetic relatedness (McGue et al., 1996; Rende, Slomkowski, Lloyd-Richardson, & Niaura, 2005; Slomkowski, Rende, Novak, et al., 2005).

Siblings' similarity in substance use also has been conceptualized within a problem behavior framework, which postulates that proneness to problem behaviors is a function of ineffective social controls against such behaviors, particularly weak parental controls (Jessor & Jessor, 1977). According to this approach, siblings would be equally likely to use or not use substances because they perceive ineffective sanctions against such behavior. This has been substantiated by findings showing that sibling similarity in substance use is related to parents' permissive alcohol use norms (Brody, Flor, Hollett-Wright, & McCoy, 1998) and parents' actual alcohol use (Duncan et al., 1996) and abuse (Conger & Ruteer, 1996). In this case, high parental use and accepting attitudes about alcohol are related to the drinking behavior of both siblings.

There is also some suggestion that adolescent substance use can result from conflicted sibling relations, with substances used as a means to cope with or find solace from the high arousal generated by interacting with a hostile sibling. At least two studies have found that sibling conflict is associated with a younger sibling's use of substances as a coping mechanism (Hall, Henggeler, Ferreira, & East, 1992; Windle, 2000). The study by Windle (2000) also found evidence implicating possible

role-modeling effects, or younger siblings imitating older siblings drinking when under stressful circumstances.

Several studies also have explored siblings as socialization agents who have direct influences on adolescents' substance and alcohol use. These studies have generally focused on older sibling use accelerating that of younger siblings. For example, it is known that adolescent sibling pairs follow a similar developmental trajectory of substance use across time (Duncan et al., 1996). But increases in an older sibling's substance use have been shown to significantly escalate a younger sibling's rate of use 3 years later (Duncan et al., 1996). In this case, older siblings may be encouraging and reinforcing a younger sibling's use by providing the substances or by using substances together. Similar results were reported by Khoo and Muthen (2000), who studied the heavy drinking patterns of over 1,600 adolescent sibling pairs from ages 18 to 32 from the National Longitudinal Survey of Youth. Results indicated that heavy drinking tended to peak around 21 years of age for both siblings, but younger siblings initiated heavy drinking earlier than older siblings, and younger siblings' rate of heavy drinking during early adulthood tended to increase faster than that of older siblings. Thus, the trajectory of an older sibling's adolescent alcohol use (age of onset, rate, linear incline) may accelerate the trajectory of younger siblings' alcohol use.

Further investigations of sibling socialization effects on adolescent substance use have shown that sibling contact and mutual friendships increase siblings' similarity of adolescent smoking and drinking (Rende et al., 2005). The predictive value of mutual contact is consistent with the notion that siblings who choose to spend time together likely share a proclivity for deviant activities, such as smoking and drinking. Shared friendships also likely underlie sibling similarity in drug use due to social connectedness, or to deviant friends exerting like pressure for both siblings to use substances (Slomkowski et al., 2005).

Sibling Influences on Sexual Activity and Pregnancy During Adolescence

Numerous studies have documented that adolescentswho have sexually active older siblings are likely to have sex early (Haurin & Mott, 1990; Rodgers, Rowe, & Harris, 1992; Widmer, 1997). As in studies of delinquency and drug use, research on adolescent sexuality has pointed to two primary processes that explain sibling similarity in sexual behavior: sibling socialization and permissive family norms, or the lack of parental control that discourages norm-breaking and deviance (Crockett, Bingham, Chopak & Vicary, 1996; Haurin & Mott, 1990). When examining sibling similarity in adolescent sexual behavior, though, research to date has focused almost exclusively on sibling socialization effects as explanatory variables. Very little research has examined a link between siblings' similarity in sexual behavior attributable to exposure to common family norms. However, a few studies have examined an older sibling's sexual behavior and family or parenting processes simultaneously as predictors of youth's sexual onset. Results of these studies generally indicate that both an older sibling's age at first sex and parent's are significant predictors of adolescent sexual activity (Crockett et al., 1996; Whitbeck, Yoder, Hoyt & Conger, 1999; Widmer, 1997).

Research testing a sibling socialization hypothesis has examined effects related to sibling relationship factors, such as the closeness of the relationship (East & Shi, 1997), the dominance of the older sibling (East & Khoo, 2005), sibling pressure to be sexually active (East, Khoo & Reyes, 2006), the amount of time siblings spend together (Whiteman et al., 2007b), and whether siblings share a friendship network (East, Felice, & Morgan, 1993). In all of these studies, a sibling socialization hypothesis was supported, such that younger siblings are likely to engage in early sexual activity if they are close with, spend a lot of time with, and share similar friends with an older sibling who is sexually active. In the latter case, of siblings sharing the same friendship network, older siblings might be actively accelerating the sexual experiences of their younger siblings by exposing them to an older peer group, one that is likely to be sexually experienced or function as potential sexual partners for the younger adolescent (East & Shi, 1997). This type of facilitative process has been examined in several studies (Rodgers & Rowe, 1988; Rodgers et al., 1992; Rowe, Rodgers, Meseck-Bushey & St. John, 1989). An additional study that used a socialization framework also found that older siblings influence their younger siblings' sexual behavior primarily through altering their attitudes about when it is best to start having sexual relations (Widmer, 1997).

Investigating whether older siblings' socialization role might be harnessed for discussions about safe sexual practices, one study found that discussions about safe sex with an older, early adult sibling was associated with more positive attitudes toward safe sexual practices among adolescent younger siblings (Kowal & Blinn-Pike, 2004). In this study, girls who had older sisters were more likely to talk about these issues than either girls who had only older brothers or boys who had older sisters. Sibling discussions about sex were also more likely to occur when adolescents reported a positive relationship with their older sibling.

There is also strong evidence that adolescent girls who have a teenage childbearing older sister are at very elevated risk of adolescent childbearing themselves (Cox, Emans, & Bithoney, 1993; East, 1996a; East & Felice, 1992). The younger sisters of childbearing adolescents have also been shown to start having sex earlier (East, 1996b; East et al., 1993) and are five times more likely to become pregnant by age 18 than other girls their same race and socioeconomic status (East & Jacobson, 2001; East, Reyes, & Horn, 2007). Moreover, as the number of sisters who are teenage parents increases, so does younger siblings' (both younger brothers' and younger sisters') risk of involvement in teenage pregnancy (East & Kiernan, 2001).

This cycle of repeated early pregnancy and childbearing across siblings is likely due to two primary sets of factors: the risks that derive from siblings' shared background and the effects that stem from the older sister's pregnancy and birth on the teen's family and siblings. In addition, both of these factors may operate concurrently, thereby intensifying their effects. Regarding the former effect, of shared within-family risk factors, because siblings receive similar parenting, are exposed to the same neighborhood and community norms, and share a common biological predisposition for early puberty (which is linked to teenage pregnancy; Newcomer & Udry, 1984), they are equally likely to become or not become pregnant as adolescents.

Regarding the latter effect, or the impact of an older sister's pregnancy and birth on families and siblings, there is evidence that family stress levels increase and mothers' diligent parenting declines as a result of an older sister's early childbearing (East, 1999; East & Jacobson, 2003). Specifically, mothers are less strict, less communicative, and less watchful of their adolescent children after an older daughter has a child (East, 1999). In addition, within teenage childbearing families, mothers' harsh and punitive treatment toward their children increases in line with increases in family stress and the time mothers spend looking after their older daughter's child (East & Jacobson, 2003). Mothers' punitive treatment of their children within such families has also been associated with adolescents' substance use and sexual behavior. One could easily imagine a scenario wherein a teenager's childbearing creates a host of stressful circumstances that cause family strain and compromised parenting, which in turn contributes to the problem behavior of the other children within the household. This type of family-level process may precipitate repeated early pregnancies across children within the family and could explain the disproportionately high teenage birth rates among the sisters of childbearing teens (East, 1998; East & Jacobson, 2001, 2003).

Taken together, this research clearly demonstrates that older siblings have the potential to set standards of conduct and norms concerning sexual and childbearing behavior. Older siblings' sexual activity can exert a strong influence on when younger siblings start to engage in sexual relations, and an older sister's teenage pregnancy and birth can have profound effects on younger siblings, both by presenting a role model of early parenting and by increasing family stress and diminishing the quality of parents' parenting.

WHY SIBLINGS WITHIN THE SAME FAMILY ARE SO DIFFERENT

Developmental psychologists have long known that parents treat different children within a family differently (Baumrind, 1980). Much research across multiple fields shows that parents expend different levels of investment, in the form of time, attention, money, and emotional investment, on their individual children (Draper & Harpending, 1987; Foster, 2002; Kalil & DeLeire, 2004; Yeung, Linver, & Brooks-Gunn, 2002). Such differential investments are thought to account for disparities in siblings' achievement, adjustment, and life outcomes (Anderson, Hetherington, Reiss, & Howe, 1994; Blake, 1987; Conley et al., 2007).

Differential parental treatment of siblings constitutes an important component of siblings' nonshared environment within the family (Daniels & Plomin, 1985; Plomin & Daniels, 1987). Indeed, it is important to understand how siblings' experiences within the family differ if we are to clarify the environmental influences that make siblings within the same family so different (Dunn & Plomin, 1990; Hetherington, Reiss, & Plomin, 1994). In addition to being critical to the study of larger family dynamics, the study of differential parenting is useful for understanding the patterns of parental investment *across* children, and how such patterns matter for siblings' unique adjustment and developmental course (Bradley & Corwyn, 2004).

Almost all studies conducted to date have indicated that parents do in fact show different levels of warmth and negativity to their various children (Atzaba-Poria & Pike, 2008; Feinberg & Hetherington, 2001; Shanahan, McHale, Crouter & Osgood, 2007; Shanahan, McHale, Osgood & Crouter, 2007). Longitudinal studies indicate that differential parenting starts in infancy and continues all the way through early adulthood (Shanahan, McHale, Crouter et al., 2007; Shanahan, McHale, Osgood et al., 2007; Volling & Elins, 1998; Volling, McElwain & Miller, 2002). Recent studies have examined how parents' differential treatment of their various children shifts throughout development, such that one child receives more or less of the available resources at different points in development. For example, firstborns have been shown to experience warmer relationships with their mothers compared to second-borns throughout middle childhood and adolescence (Shanahan, McHale, Crouter, et al., 2007). Using this same sample, it was further found that firstborns experience elevated levels of conflict with parents between middle childhood and middle adolescence, whereas second-borns experience high conflict with parents in the later part of childhood (Shanahan, McHale, Osgood, et al., 2007). Had a within-family comparison approach not been used, these patterns pertaining to sibling-specific experiences would not have emerged.

It is important to recognize, though, that parents' differential treatment not only *contributes* to differences in sibling outcomes, but also likely *results from* siblings' unique physical and behavioral traits and aptitudes. Consistent evidence from the family economics field shows that families distribute available resources based on the unique qualities and potential of each individual child (Behrman, 1997; Foster, 2002; Mayer, 1997). In addition, several studies by developmental psychologists show that individual differences in sibling adjustment and intelligence play a key role in eliciting different responses from parents and others

outside the family (Feinberg & Hetherington, 2000; Plomin & Daniels, 1987; Scarr & McCartney, 1983). In all, this area of sibling research has provided a welcome departure from the study of single parent–child relationships *between* families and allowed for comparisons of different parent–child dyads *within* families and the importance these family subsystems have for individuals' development (Boyle, Jenkins, Georgiades, et al., 2004; East & Jacobson, 2000; Feinberg & Hetherington, 2001).

The study of differential treatment as it pertains to sibling relationships has had three primary foci. First, it has examined the implications of parents' differential treatment for youth's sibling relationships. Second, it has sought to determine the impact of differential parenting on siblings' adjustment. Third, there has been interest in the area of sibling deidentification, or the process of actively differentiating oneself from one's sibling so as to increase one's uniqueness and individuality. Each of these areas is reviewed here.

Parents' Differential Treatment and Sibling Relationships

Rooted in the writings of neo-Freudian Arthur Adler (1927) and the later experimental work on social comparison theory (Suls & Miller, 1977), several studies have documented that parental favoritism and preference gives rise to sibling rivalry and jealousy (Rauer & Volling, 2007; Volling et al., 2002). Indeed, much evidence has accumulated showing that if parents show more affection, attention, or warmth in their relationship with one sibling than the other, the siblings are likely to get along less well than the siblings in families in which parents and siblings do not describe such differential treatment (Brody & Stoneman, 1994; Feinberg & Hetherington, 2001; McHale, Updegraff, Jackson-Newsom, et al., 2000).

Brody and colleagues (1992a), for example, found that the degree of fathers' differential negative behavior predicted low rates of positive relational behaviors among both older and younger siblings (such as smiling, laughing, praising). Similarly, high levels of negative relational behavior by siblings (threats, insults, and sarcasm) were most characteristic of sibling dyads in families where differential paternal treatment was high. Differential paternal behavior accounted for more unique variance in sibling relationship quality than did mothers' differential behavior. The authors proposed that the greater impact of differential paternal behavior on negative sibling interactions may arise from the relative scarcity of fathers' attention compared to that of mothers.

Adolescent interpretations of their parents' differential treatment are also crucial for its impact on the sibling relationship. When children attribute such differential treatment as parents' lesser concern or love, the sibling relationship is likely to be less positive (Kowal & Kramer, 1997). Similarly, when adolescents perceive their parents' differential treatment as unfair and unjust, they are more likely to feel jealous and rivlarous of their sibling (McHale et al., 2000). Sibling jealousy is highest when youth perceive their disfavored status as unfair. However, when adolescents perceive their parents' differential treatment as equitable and fair, there are no apparent consequences for the sibling relationship (Kowal, Kramer, Krull, & Crick, 2002).

Parents' Differential Treatment and Adolescents' Adjustment

Consistent evidence across numerous studies has shown that parents' differential negative treatment is related to adjustment difficulties of the slighted child (Brody, Stoneman, & McCoy, 1992b; McGuire, Dunn, & Plomin, 1995; Richmond, Stocker, & Rienks, 2005; Volling & Elins, 1998). Low self-esteem (McHale et al., 2000), low self-worth (Shebloski, Conger, & Widaman, 2005), anxiety (Sheehan & Noller, 2002), externalizing behaviors, and problem behaviors (McGuire et al., 1995; Stocker, 1993, 1995; Tamrouti-Makkink, Dubas, Gerris, &

van Aken, 2004) have all been associated with differential negative parenting, that is, when parents are more harsh, critical, or punitive toward one child than another.

Because of the likely possibility that a child's poor functioning could precipitate differentially negative treatment, longitudinal studies are necessary to tease apart this association. At least four studies have used longitudinal analyses and concluded that changing patterns of parents' differential treatment are linked to across-time fluctuations in adolescents' adjustment (McGuire et al., 1995; McHale et al., 2000; Richmond et al., 2005; Shebloski et al., 2005). For example, as siblings became less favored by parents over time, their externalizing problems increase (Richmond et al., 2005). Declines in adolescents' self-worth were also found to be related to across-time changes in perceptions of parents' partiality (Shebloski et al., 2005). This effect was found for later born siblings only, though, with younger and less emotionally mature youth possibly more reactive to changes in parents' favoritism than older age youth (Shebloski et al., 2005).

Recently, investigators have attempted to study *the degree* of differences in mothers' and, separately, fathers' differential parenting and the implications for youth's adjustment (Boyle et al., 2004; Feinberg & Hetherington, 2001). Using data from three national longitudinal studies, Boyle and colleagues (2004) tested the hypothesis that highly incongruent levels of mothers' positive behaviors (praising) and negative behaviors (spanking) would be related to increased levels of children's emotional–behavioral problems after controlling for average levels of mothers' positive and negative behaviors. Their results were consistent with expectations, such that high levels of incongruency in maternal behaviors were associated with children's poor adjustment over and above the direct effect of mothers' parenting. This effect was stronger for negative maternal behaviors, such as spanking and disciplining, than positive maternal behaviors.

Similarly, other results indicate that the magnitude of differences in parents' differential parenting (in warmth/support and conflict/negativity) has a unique impact on youth's adjustment over and above the effect of the level of parenting directed toward each child separately (Feinberg & Hetherington, 2001). Like the Boyle et al. study cited above, Feinberg and Hetherington (2001) found that differential treatment was more strongly linked to poor youth adjustment when overall parenting was low in warmth and high in negativity. The relation between parents' differential treatment and adolescent adjustment was weak among youth whose parents treated them well, even when their siblings received warmer and more positive treatment. Thus, when one is exposed to both high levels of parental negativity, as well as *differentially higher* levels of negativity than one's siblings, one is more likely to exhibit poorer adjustment than when experiencing comparably high parental negativity without experiencing differentially more negative treatment.

Finally, some research has shown that siblings' perceptions of their parents' differential treatment is more consistently related to their well-being than is the actual level of differential parenting (Kowal et al., 2002). This suggests that the negative effects of parents' inequitable treatment are mediated through children's subjective appraisal of the situation, thus differential treatment that is perceived as fair (e.g., when a sibling who is having problems in school receives more parental assistance with homework than one who is doing well, or when a sibling who is older is granted more freedom) has a less deleterious impact on youth's adjustment than differential treatment that is seen as unjustified (Kowal et al., 2002)

Sibling Differentiation

There are numerous theories that posit that siblings develop specific roles and personality characteristics to purposively distinguish themselves from each another. These include role differentiation theory (Bossard & Boll, 1956), sibling deidentification theory (Schacter, 1982; Schacter, Shore, Feldman-Rotman, et al., 1976), and, in the genetics literature, contrast effects theory (Carey, 1986). Indeed, active sibling differentiation is thought to have originated in part as a survival function, whereby each child's individuality is maximized so as to increase the likelihood of child survival under different environmental conditions (Draper & Harpending, 1987; Lerner, 1984; Scarr & Grajek, 1982). More recently, however, sibling differentiation has been discussed as a defense mechanism to reduce social comparisons, and therefore the potential of sibling rivalry and competition (Feinberg, McHale, Crouter, & Cumsille, 2003). That is, sibling deidentification may serve a protective function against social comparisons, and may be motivated by siblings wishing to establish their own unique role and identity within the family (Brody & Stoneman, 1994; Whiteman et al., 2007a).

Although it is a fascinating concept, finding evidence that active sibling differentiation has occurred is difficult in part because the process is not always a conscious one. A few studies have tested this notion by proposing that sibling pairs most similar in age and gender would be most likely to differentiate (Schacter, 1982; Whiteman et al., 2007a). Schacter (1982), in fact, was able to demonstrate that consecutive-born sibling pairs were more different from each other than "jump pairs" (firstborns and third-borns), and that same-sex sibling dyads were more different from each other than opposite-sex dyads. However, Whiteman and colleagues (2007a) were unable to corroborate these findings.

In trying to understand the process of sibling deidentification, researchers have asked adolescents if they try to be like or different from their sibling in areas of athletics, academics, and conduct. Findings indicate that less than one-third of older siblings purposively try to distinguish themselves from their younger sibling, but that 40% of younger siblings report purposely differentiating themselves from their older sibling (Whiteman & Christiansen, 2008; Whiteman et al., 2007a). In supporting the notion that active differentiation is motivated to reduce sibling rivalry (or the potential for rivalry), those who deidentified with their sibling reported lower sibling hostility than youth who tried to be the same as their older sibling (Whiteman et al., 2007a). This effect was particularly strong for same-sex sibling pairs, such that girl–girl and boy–boy sibling pairs who differentiated from each other reported especially low levels of sibling negativity (Whiteman & Christiansen, 2008). Feinberg and colleagues (2003) also found that siblings who became more different over time in their relationships with their parents became closer to one another across a 2-year period.

Other research has shown that sibling deidentification tends to become more pronounced as individuals reach adolescence. Specifically, older adolescent-age siblings become more different from their younger siblings over time, in terms of sex-typed qualities (McHale, Updegraff, Helms-Erikson, et al., 2001). The authors speculated that sibling deidentification may be more likely to occur during adolescence, when youth are striving to establish their own unique identity.

In general, the research reviewed in this section highlights how nonshared environmental forces—such as parents' differential treatment and youth's active sibling differentiation—operate to reduce sibling similarity and accentuate sibling differences. These within-family processes are thought to be triggered by siblings' own unique individual traits, and have ramifications for the sibling relationship and adolescents' adjustment. Given that heterogeneity surely exists across siblings, with all siblings varying in their endowments, motivations, and physical traits (Scarr & Grajek, 1982), how families, parents, and the siblings themselves react to these differences is crucial for understanding the developmental course of sibling relationships. The work within this area also serves to highlight how sibling experiences are embedded within a larger family system of relationships and are best understood within that larger context (McHale et al., 2006).

SIBLINGS FROM DIVERSE FAMILY, CULTURAL, AND SOCIOECONOMIC BACKGROUNDS

The large scope of this chapter has precluded specific attention to the different dynamics of sibling relationships among adolescents from diverse family, cultural, and socioeconomic backgrounds. This is largely a function of the literature on siblings, which is comprised predominantly of studies on full biological siblings from White, middle-class families living in the United States. The knowledge of sibling relationships in other cultures and different socioeconomic backgrounds is sorely lacking. Some notable exceptions along these lines include the study of sibling interactions and caregiving within a cross-cultural perspective (Maynard, 2004; Rabain-Jamin, Maynard, & Greenfield, 2003; Zukow, 1989, Zukow-Goldring, 2002) and on sibling influences in low-income families (Criss & Shaw, 2005). This chapter also did not review the literature pertaining to the broad range of sibling relationships, such as the nuances that differentiate step-siblings, half-siblings, and adopted siblings. Recently, work within this area has highlighted the significance of the family context for shaping the nature of these sibling ties and for creating similarities or differences in siblings' adjustment (Deater-Deckard, Dunn, & Lussier, 2002; Kim, Hetherington, & Reiss, 1999; O'Connor, Dunn, Jenkins, et al., 2001).

Only recently have researchers begun to focus on Mexican American siblings (McHale, Updegraff, Shanahan, et al., 2005; Updegraff, McHale, Whiteman, et al., 2005) and siblings within African American families (Brody, Kim, Murry & Brown, 2003, 2004; Brody & Murry, 2001; McHale, Whiteman, Kim, & Crouter, 2007). The former work on Latino siblings suggests that the strong family ties characteristic to Latino families extend to adolescents' sibling bonds. Specifically,

Mexican American siblings describe themselves as more loyal and supportive of one another than non-Latino youth, and Latino adolescents place a greater value on sibling assistance, support, and future obligation than non-Latino youth (Fuligni, Tseng & Lam, 1999). Latino adolescents' familistic values (or sense of family obligations) also have been associated with more harmonious and involved sibling ties (Updegraff et al., 2005). Other research has pointed to a greater disparity of restrictions placed on daughters versus sons within Mexican American families than within other families, with such gender-specific differential restrictions related to differences in boys' and girls' adjustment (McHale, Updegraff, Shanahan, et al., 2005).

Other work has focused on sibling socialization processes within rural African American families. This research has shown that older siblings' competence is linked to younger siblings' competence by way of involved and supportive parenting (Brody et al., 2003; Brody & Murry, 2001). Another study sought to simply describe the sibling relationships of adolescents in two-parent, middle-class African American families. Results indicated the presence of positive, negative, and distant relationship types, with each type correlated in important ways to youth's ethnic identity, mothers' parenting, and the family's experiences of discrimination (McHale et al., 2005). In all, these studies highlight how sociocultural experiences are integral to the study of sibling ties, and they broaden the field in ways that have meaningful implications for today's adolescents and families. Given the changing demography of the American population, and given cultural differences in expectations governing family relationships, more research on sibling relationships in non-White populations is sorely needed.

CONCLUSIONS

Sibling relationships play a critical and formative role in human development. Indeed, sibling ties serve as a model for other social relationships,

with essential social skills learned and practiced with siblings. However, the functional significance of the sibling bond changes across development. From childhood to adolescence, sibling relations become less intense, less close and more egalitarian. Although the nature of sibling ties changes in important ways throughout the life course, youth's overall emotional attachments with siblings remain strong, connected, and supportive. Indeed, support from a sibling can have far-reaching importance to one's well-being, with close and supportive sibling ties able to mitigate the negative effects associated with life stressors and deficiencies in other social bonds. However, adolescents' sibling relationships also make significant contributions to many health-risk behaviors, such that the propensity for delinquency, substance use, and adolescent sexual activity and pregnancy is promoted through direct interaction with and modeling of a high-risk sibling.

Collectively, the research reviewed in this chapter adds to theoretical models and extant research that emphasize the role of the individual, the family, and parenting processes in shaping youth's sibling ties. Indeed, the study of sibling relationships allows for a clearer understanding of family processes and of the environmental influences that make individuals unique. For example, within-family comparisons of parents' treatment and expectations of their various children reveal how parents differentially invest in siblings, and how these differences channel siblings along quite disparate pathways. Yet, we know that parents' differential treatment of siblings can shift across development. In addition, family dynamics are constantly changing, as the family unit and family members age and develop. Certainly, it is important to study the sibling relationship within this type of developmental systems framework. This broader perspective allows for a more comprehensive understanding of the nature and function of adolescents' sibling ties, as well as the mechanisms through which siblings directly and indirectly influence one another's lives and development.

REFERENCES

Adler, A. (1927). *The practice and theory of individual psychology.* New York: Harcourt Brace.

Anderson, E. R., Hetherington, E. M., Reiss, D., & Howe, G. (1994). Parents' nonshared treatment of siblings and the development of social competence during adolescence. *Journal of Family Psychology, 8,* 303–320.

Ardelt, M., & Day, L. (2002). Parent, sibling, and peers: Close social relationships and adolescent deviance. *Journal of Early Adolescence, 22,* 310–349.

Ary, D. V., Tildesley, E., Hops, H., & Andrews, J. (1993). The influences of parent, sibling, and peer modeling and attitudes on adolescent use of alcohol. *International Journal of the Addictions, 28,* 853–880.

Atzaba-Poria, N., & Pike, A. (2008). Correlates of parental differential treatment: Parental and contextual factors during middle childhood. *Child Development, 79,* 217–232.

Bandura, A. (1989). Social cognitive theory. *Annals of Child Development, 6,* 1–60.

Bank, L., Burraston, B., & Snyder, J. (2004). Sibling conflict and ineffective parenting as predictors of adolescent boys' antisocial behavior and peer difficulties: Additive and interactional effect. *Journal of Research on Adolescence, 14,* 99–125.

Bank, L., Patterson, G. R., & Reid, J. B. (1996). Negative sibling interaction patterns as predictors of later adjustment problems in adolescent and young adult males. In G. H. Brody (Ed.), *Sibling relationships: Their causes and consequences* (pp. 197–229). Norwood, NJ: Ablex.

Bank, S. P., & Kahn, M. D. (Eds.). (1982). *The sibling bond.* New York: Basic Books.

Baumrind, D. (1980). New directions in socialization research. *American Psychologist, 35,* 639–652.

Bedford, V. H., Volling, B. L., & Avioli, P. S. (2000). Positive consequences of sibling conflict in childhood and adulthood. *International Journal of Aging and Human Development, 5,* 53–69.

Behrman, J. R. (1997). Intrahousehold distribution and the family. In M. R. Rosenzweig & O. Stark (Eds.), *Handbook of population and family economics* (pp. 125–187). New York: Elsevier Science.

Behrman, J., Pollack, R. A., & Taubman, P. (1995). Parental preferences and provision for progeny. In J. Behrman, R. A. Pollack, & P. Taubman (Eds.), *Parent to child: Intrahousehold allocations and intergenerational relations in the United States* (p. 23–42). Chicago: University of Chicago Press.

Blake, J. (1987). Differential parental investment: Its effects on child quality and status attainment. In J. B. Lancaster, J. Altmann, A. S. Rossi, & L. R. Sherrod (Eds), *Parenting across the life span: Biosocial dimensions* (pp. 351–375). New York: Aldine de Gruyter.

Blos, P. (1979). *The adolescent passage.* New York: International Universities Press.

Boll, T., Ferring, D., & Filipp, S. H. (2003). Perceived parental differential treatment in middle adulthood: Curvilinear relations with individuals' experienced relationship quality to sibling and parents. *Journal of Family Psychology, 17,* 472–487.

Bossard, J. H., & Boll, E. S. (1956). *The large family system.* Philadelphia: University of Pennsylvania Press.

Bowlby, J. (1969). *Attachment and loss,* vol. 1: *Attachment.* New York: Basic Books.

Boyle, M. H., Jenkins, J. M., Georgiades, K., Cairney, J., Duku, E., & Racine, Y. (2004). Differential-maternal parenting behavior: Estimating within- and between-family effects on children. *Child Development, 75,* 1457–1476.

Bradley, R. H., & Corwyn, R. F. (2004) "Family process" investments that matter for child well-being. In A. Kalil & T. DeLeire (Eds.), *Family investments in children's potential: Resources and parenting behaviors that promote success* (pp. 1–32). Mahwah, NJ: Lawrence Erlbaum.

Branje, S. J. T., van Lieshout, C. F. M., van Aken, M. A. G., & Haselager, G. J. T. (2004). Perceived support in sibling relationships and adolescent adjustment. *Journal of Child Psychology and Psychiatry, 45,* 1385–1396.

Brody, G. H. (Ed.). (1996). *Sibling relationships: Their causes and consequences.* Norwood, NJ: Ablex.

Brody, G. H. (1998). Sibling relationship quality: Its causes and consequences. *Annual Review of Psychology, 49,* 1–24.

Brody, G. H. (2004). Siblings' direct and indirect contributions to child development. *Current Directions in Psychological Science, 13,* 124–126.

Brody, G. H., Flor, D. L., Hollett-Wright, N., & McCoy, J. K. (1998). Children's development of alcohol use norms: Contributions of parent and sibling norms, children's temperaments, and parent–child discussions. *Journal of Family Psychology, 12,* 209–219.

Brody, G. H., Kim, S., Murry, V. M., & Brown, A. C. (2003). Longitudinal direct and indirect pathways linking older sibling competence to the development of younger sibling competence. *Developmental Psychology, 39,* 618–628.

Brody, G. H., Kim, S., Murry, V. M., & Brown, A. C. (2004). Protective longitudinal paths linking child competence to behavioral problems among African American siblings. *Child Development, 75,* 455–467.

Brody, G. H., & Murry, V. M. (2001). Sibling socialization of competence in rural, single-parent African American families. *Journal of Marriage and the Family, 63,* 996–1008.

Brody, G., & Stoneman, Z. (1994). Sibling relationships and their association with parental differential treatment. In E. M. Hetherington, D. Reiss, & R. Plomin (Eds.), *Separate social worlds of siblings: The impact of nonshared environment on development* (pp. 129–142). Hillsdale, NJ: Lawrence Erlbaum.

Brody, G. H., Stoneman, Z., & Burke, M. (1987). Family system and individual child correlates of sibling behavior. *American Journal of Orthopsychiatry, 57,* 561–569.

Brody, G. H., Stoneman, Z., & Gauger, K. (1996). Parent-child relationships, family problem solving behavior, and sibling relationship quality: The moderating role of sibling temperaments. *Child Development, 67,* 1289–1300.

Brody, G. H., Stoneman, Z., & MacKinnon, C.E. (1986). Contributions of maternal childrearing practices and play contexts to sibling interactions. *Journal of Applied Developmental Psychology, 7,* 225–236.

Brody, G. H., Stoneman, Z., & McCoy, J. K. (1992a). Associations of maternal and paternal direct and differential behavior with sibling relationships: Contemporaneous and longitudinal analyses. *Child Development, 63,* 82–92.

Brody, G. H., Stoneman, Z., & McCoy, J. K. (1992b). Parental differential treatment of siblings and sibling differences in negative emotionality. *Journal of Marriage and the Family, 54,* 643–651.

Brody, G. H., Stoneman, Z., & McCoy, J. K. (1994a). Contributions of family relationships and child temperaments to longitudinal variations in sibling relationship quality and sibling relationship styles. *Journal of Family Psychology, 8,* 274–286.

Brody, G. H., Stoneman, Z., & McCoy, J. K. (1994b). Forecasting sibling relationships in early adolescence from child temperaments and family processes in middle childhood. *Child Development, 65,* 771–784.

Brody, G. H., Stoneman, Z., McCoy, J. K., & Forehand, R. (1992). Contemporaneous and longitudinal associations of sibling conflict with family relationship assessments and family discussions about sibling problems. *Child Development, 63,* 391–400.

Bryant, B. K. (1989). The child's perspective of sibling caretaking and its relevance to understanding social-emotional functioning and development. In P. Zukow (Ed.), *Sibling interactions across cultures: Theoretical and methodological issues* (pp. 245–270). New York: Springer-Verlag.

Buhrmester, D. (1992). The developmental courses of sibling and peer relationships. In F. Boer, & J. Dunn (Eds.), *Children's sibling relationships: Developmental and clinic issues* (pp. 19–40). Hillsdale, NJ: Lawrence Erlbaum.

Buhrmester, D., & Furman, W. (1987). The development of companionship and intimacy. *Child Development, 58,* 1101–1113.

Buhrmester, D., & Furman, W. (1990). Perceptions of sibling relationships during middle childhood and adolescence. *Child Development, 61,* 1387–1398.

Bullock, B. M., Bank, L., & Burraston, B. (2002). Adult sibling expressed emotion and fellow sibling deviance: A new piece of the family process puzzle. *Journal of Family Psychology, 16,* 307–317.

Carey, G. (1986). Sibling imitation and contrast effects. *Behavior Genetics, 16,* 319–341.

Chappell, N. L., & Penning, M. J. (2005). Family caregivers: Increasing demands in the context of 21st-century globalization? In M. L. Johnson (Ed.), *The Cambridge handbook of age and ageing* (pp. 455–462). Cambridge: Cambridge University Press.

Cicirelli, V. (1995). *Sibling relationships across the life span.* New York: Plenum Press.

Cohen, S., & Smye, S. L. (Eds.). (1985). *Social support and health.* New York: Academic Press.

Cohen, S., & Wills, T. A. (1985). Stress, social support, and the buffering hypothesis. *Psychological Bulletin, 98,* 310–357.

Cole, A., & Kearns, K. A. (2001). Perceptions of sibling qualities and activities of early adolescents. *Journal of Early Adolescence, 21,* 204–227.

Collins, W. A., Gleason, T., & Sesma, A., Jr. (1997). Internalization, autonomy, and relationships: Development during adolescence. In J. E. Grusec & L. Kuczynski (Eds.), *Parenting and children's internalization of values: A handbook of contemporary theory* (pp. 78–99). New York: John Wiley & Sons.

Compton, K., Snyder, J., Schrepferman, L., Bank, L., & Shortt, J. W. (2003). The contribution of parents and siblings to antisocial and depressive behavior in adolescents: A double jeopardy coercion model. *Development and Psychopathology, 15,* 163–182.

Conger, K. J., & Conger, R. D. (1994). Differential parenting and change in sibling differences in delinquency. *Journal of Family Psychology, 8,* 287–302.

Conger, K. J., Conger, R. D., & Scaramella, L. V. (1997). Parents, siblings, psychological control and adolescent adjustment. *Journal of Adolescent Research, 12,* 113–138.

Conger, R. D., Cui, M., Bryant, C. M., & Elder, G. H. (2000). Competence in early adult romantic relationships: A developmental perspective on family influences. *Journal of Personality and Social Psychology, 79,* 224–237.

Conger, R. D., & Reuter, M. A. (1996). Siblings, parents, and peers: A longitudinal study of social influences in adolescent risk for alcohol use and abuse. In G. H. Brody (Ed.), *Sibling relationships: Their causes and consequences* (pp. 1–32). Norwood, NJ: Ablex.

Conley, D. (2000). Sibship sex composition: Effects on educational attainment. *Social Science Research, 29,* 441–457.

Conley, D. (2004). *The pecking order: Which siblings succeed and why.* New York: Pantheon.

Conley, D., Pfeiffer, K. M., & Velez, M. (2007). Explaining sibling differences in achievement and behavioral outcomes: The importance of within- and between-family differences. *Social Science Research, 3,* 1087–1104.

Connidis, I. A. (2005). Sibling ties across time: The middle and later years. In M. L. Johnson (Ed.), *The Cambridge handbook of age and ageing* (pp. 429–436). Cambridge: Cambridge University Press.

Cox, J., Emans, S. J., & Bithoney, W. (1993). Sisters of teen mothers: Increased risk for adolescent parenthood. *Adolescent and Pediatric Gynecology, 6,* 138–142.

Criss, M. M., & Shaw, D. S. (2005). Sibling relationships as contexts for delinquency training in low-income families. *Journal of Family Psychology, 19,* 592–600.

Crockett, L. J., Bingham, C. R., Chopak, J. S., & Vicary, J. R. (1996). Timing of first sexual intercourse: The role of social control, social learning, and problem behavior. *Journal of Youth and Adolescence, 25,* 89–111.

Cummings, E. M., & Davies, P. (1994). *Children and marital conflict: The impact of family dispute and resolution.* New York: Guilford Press.

Cummings, E. M., Goeke-Morey, M. C., & Papp, L. M. (2004). Everyday marital conflict and child aggression. *Journal of Abnormal Child Psychology, 32,* 191–202.

Cummings, E. M., & Smith, D. (1989). The impact of anger between adults on siblings' emotions and social behavior. *Journal of Child Psychology and Psychiatry, 34,* 1425–1433.

Daniels, D., & Plomin, R. (1985). Differential experience of siblings in the same family. *Developmental Psychology, 21,* 747–760.

Davies, P. T., & Cicchetti, D. (2004). Toward an integration of family systems and developmental psychopathology approaches. *Developmental Psychopathology, 16,* 477–481.

Deater-Deckard, K., Dunn, J., & Lussier, G. (2002). Sibling relationships and social–emotional adjustment in different family contexts. *Social Development, 11,* 571–590.

Dooley, D. (1985). Causal inference in the study of social support. In S. Cohen & S. L. Syme (Eds.), *Social support and health* (pp. 109–125). New York: Academic Press.

Downey, D. B., & Condron, D. J. (2004). Playing well with others in kindergarten: The benefit of siblings at home. *Journal of Marriage and Family, 66,* 333–350.

Draper, P., & Harpending, H. (1987). Parent investment and the child's environment. In J. B. Lancaster, J. Altmann, A. S. Rossi, & L. R. Sherrod (Eds.), *Parenting across the life span: Biosocial dimensions* (pp. 207–235). New York: Aldine de Gruyter.

Duncan, T. E., Duncan, S. C., & Hops, H. (1996). The role of parents and older siblings in predicting adolescent substance use: Modeling development via structural equation latent growth methodology. *Journal of Family Psychology, 10,* 158–172.

Dunn, J. (2005). Commentary: Siblings in their families. *Journal of Family Psychology, 19,* 654–657.

Dunn, J. (2007). Siblings and socialization. In J. E. Grusec & P. D. Hastings (Eds.), *Handbook of socialization: Theory and research* (pp. 309–327). New York: Guilford Press.

Dunn, J., & Kendrick C. (1982). *Siblings: Love, envy, and understanding.* Cambridge, MA: Harvard University Press.

Dunn, J., & Plomin, R. (1990). *Separate lives: Why siblings are so different.* New York: Basic Books.

Dunn, J., & Slomkowski, C. (1992). Conflict and the development of social understanding. In C. Shantz & W. Hartup (Eds.), *Conflict in child and adolescent development* (pp. 70–92). Cambridge: Cambridge University Press.

Dunn, J., Slomkowski, C., & Beardsall, L. (1994). Sibling relationships from the preschool period through middle childhood and early adolescence. *Developmental Psychology, 30*(3), 315–324.

East, P. L. (1996a). Do adolescent pregnancy and childbearing affect younger siblings? *Family Planning Perspectives, 28,* 148–153.

East, P. L. (1996b). The younger sisters of childbearing adolescents: Their attitudes, expectations, and behaviors. *Child Development, 67,* 267–284.

East, P. L. (1998). The impact of adolescent childbearing on families and younger siblings: Effects that increase younger siblings' risk for early pregnancy. *Applied Developmental Science, 2,* 62–74.

East, P. L. (1999). The first teenage pregnancy in the family: Does it affect mothers' parenting, attitudes, or mother–adolescent communication? *Journal of Marriage and the Family, 61,* 306–319.

East, P. L., & Felice, M. E. (1992). Pregnancy risk among the younger sisters of pregnant and childbearing adolescents. *Journal of Developmental and Behavioral Pediatrics, 13,* 128–136.

East, P. L., Felice, M. E., & Morgan, M.C. (1993). Sisters' and girlfriends' sexual and childbearing behavior: Effects on early adolescent girls' sexual outcomes. *Journal of Marriage and the Family, 55,* 953–963.

East, P. L., & Jacobson, L. J. (2000). Adolescent childbearing, poverty, and siblings: Taking new direction from the new literature. *Family Relations, 49,* 287–292.

East, P. L., & Jacobson, L. J. (2001). The younger siblings of teenage mothers: A follow-up of their pregnancy risk. *Developmental Psychology, 37,* 254–264.

East, P. L., & Jacobson, L. J. (2003). Mothers' differential treatment of their adolescent childbearing and nonchildbearing children: Contrasts between and within families. *Journal of Family Psychology, 17,* 384–396.

East, P. L., & Khoo, S. T. (2005). Longitudinal pathways linking family factors and sibling relationship quality to adolescent substance use and sexual risk behaviors. *Journal of Family Psychology, 19,* 571–580.

East, P. L., Khoo, S. T., & Reyes, B. T. (2006). Risk and protective factors predictive of adolescent pregnancy: A longitudinal, prospective study. *Applied Developmental Science, 10,* 188–199.

East, P. L., & Kiernan, E. A. (2001). Risks among youths who have multiple sisters who were adolescent parents. *Family Planning Perspectives, 32,* 75–80.

East, P. L., Reyes, B. T., & Horn, E. J. (2007). Association between adolescent pregnancy and a family history of teenage births. *Perspectives on Sexual and Reproductive Health, 39,* 108–115.

East, P. L., & Rook, K. S. (1992). Compensatory patterns of support among children's peer relationships: A test using school friends, nonschool friends, and siblings. *Developmental Psychology, 28,* 163–172.

East, P. L., & Shi, C. R. (1997). Pregnant and parenting adolescents and their younger sisters: The influence of relationship qualities for younger sister outcomes. *Journal of Developmental and Behavioral Pediatrics, 18,* 84–90.

Edwards, R., Hadfield, L., Lucey, H., & Mauthner, M. (2006). *Sibling identity and relationships: Sisters and brothers.* New York: Routledge.

Erel, O., Margolin, G., & John, R. S. (1998). Observed sibling interaction: Links with the marital relationship and the mother-child relationship. *Developmental Psychology, 34,* 288–298.

Feinberg, M. E., & Hetherington, E. M. (2000). Sibling differentiation in adolescence: Implications for behavioral genetic theory. *Child Development, 71,* 1512–1524.

Feinberg, M. E., & Hetherington, E. M. (2001). Differential parenting as a within-family variable. *Journal of Family Psychology, 15,* 22–37.

Feinberg, M. E., McHale, S. M., Crouter, A. C., & Cumsille, P. (2003). Sibling differentiation: Sibling and parent relationship trajectories in adolescence. *Child Development, 74,* 1261–1274.

Feinberg, M. E., Neiderhiser, J. M., Simmens, S., Reiss, D., & Hetherington, E. M. (2000). Sibling comparison of differential parental treatment in adolescence: Gender, self-esteem, and emotionality as mediators of the parenting-adjustment association. *Child Development, 71,* 1611–1628.

Festinger, L. (1954). A theory of social comparison processes. *Human Relations, 7,* 117–140.

Foster, E. M. (2002). How economists think about family resources and child development. *Child Development, 73,* 1904–1914.

Fuligni, A., Tseng, V., & Lam, M. (1999). Attitudes toward family obligations among American adolescents with Asian, Latin American, and European backgrounds. *Child Development, 70,* 1030–1044.

Furman, W. (1995). Parenting siblings. In M. H. Bornstein (Ed.), *Handbook of parenting,* vol. 1: *Children and parenting* (pp. 143–162). Hillsdale, NJ: Lawrence Erlbaum.

Furman, W., & Burmester, D. (1985a). Children's perceptions of the personal relationships in their social networks. *Developmental Psychology, 21,* 1016–1024.

Furman, W., & Burmester, D. (1985b). Children's perceptions of the qualities of sibling relationships. *Child Development, 56,* 448–461.

Furman, W., & Buhrmester, D. (1992). Age and sex differences in perceptions of networks of personal relationships. *Child Development, 63,* 103–115.

Furman, W., & Lanthier, R. P. (1996). Personality and sibling relationships. In G. H. Brody (Ed.), *Sibling relationships: Their causes and consequences* (pp. 127–146). Norwood, NJ: Ablex.

Gass, K., Jenkins, J., & Dunn, J. (2007). Are sibling relationships protective? A longitudinal study. *Journal of Child Psychology and Psychiatry, 48,* 167–175.

Goetting, A. (1986). The developmental tasks of siblingship over the life cycle. *Journal of Marriage and the Family, 48,* 703–714.

Hall, J. A., Henggeler, S. W., Ferreira, D. K., & East, P. L. (1992). Sibling relations and substance use in high-risk female adolescents. *Family Dynamics of Addiction Quarterly, 2,* 44–51.

Hartup, W. W. (1983). The peer system. In E. M. Hetherington (Ed.), *Handbook of child psychology,* vol. 4: *Socialization, personality, and social development* (pp. 103–196). New York: John Wiley & Sons.

Haurin, R. J., & Mott, F. L. (1990). Adolescent sexual activity in the family context: The impact of older siblings. *Demography, 27,* 537–557.

Hetherington, E. M. (1994). Siblings, family relationships, and child development: Introduction. *Journal of Family Psychology, 8,* 251–253.

Hetherington, E. M., Reiss, D., & Plomin, R. (Eds.). (1994). *Separate social worlds of siblings: The impact of nonshared environment on development.* Hillsdale, NJ: Lawrence Erlbaum.

Hinde, R. (1979). *Toward understanding relationships.* New York: Academic Press.

Howe, N., Aquan-Assee, J., Bukowski, W. M., Lehoux, P. M., & Rinaldi, C. M. (2001). Siblings as confidants: Emotional understanding, relationship warmth, and sibling self-disclosure. *Social Development, 10,* 439–454.

Howe, N., & Ross, H. S. (1990). Socialization, perspective-taking, and the sibling relationship. *Developmental Psychology, 26,* 160–165.

Jenkins, J. M. (1992). Sibling relationships in disharmonious homes: Potential difficulties and protective effects. In F. Boer & J. Dunn (Eds.), *Children's sibling relationships: Developmental and clinical issues* (pp. 125–138). Hillsdale, NJ: Lawrence Erlbaum.

Jessor, S. L., & Jessor, R. (1977). *Problem behavior and psychosocial development: A longitudinal study of youth.* New York: Academic Press.

Kalil, A., & DeLeire, T. (Eds.). (2004). *Family investments in children's potential: Resources and parenting behaviors that promote success.* Mahwah, NJ: Lawrence Erlbaum.

Katz, L. F., Kramer, L., & Gottman, M. (1992). Conflict and emotions in marital, sibling, and peer relationships. In C. U. Shantz & W. Hartup (Eds.), *Conflict in child and adolescent development* (pp. 122–149). Cambridge: Cambridge University Press.

Khoo, S. T., & Muthen, B. (2000). Longitudinal data on families: Growth modeling alternatives. In J. S. Rose, L. Chassin, C. C. Presson, & S. J. Sherman (Eds.), *Multivariate applications in substance use research: New methods for new questions* (pp. 43–78). Mahwah, NJ: Lawrence Erlbaum.

Kiang, L., & Furman, W. (2007). Representations of attachment to parents in adolescent sibling pairs: Concordant or discordant? *New Directions for Child and Adolescent Development, 117,* 73–89.

Kim, J., McHale, S. M., Crouter, A. C., & Osgood, D. W. (2007). Longitudinal linkages between sibling relationships and adjustment from middle childhood through adolescence. *Developmental Psychology, 43,* 960–973.

Kim, J., McHale, S. M., Osgood, D. W., & Crouter, A. C. (2006). Longitudinal course and family correlates of sibling relationships from childhood through adolescence. *Child Development, 77,* 1746–1761.

Kim, J. E., Hetherington, E. M., & Reiss, D. (1999). Associations among family relationships, antisocial peers, and adolescents' externalizing behaviors: Gender and family type differences. *Child Development, 70,* 1209–1230.

Kowal, A. K., & Blinn-Pike, L. (2004). Sibling influences on adolescent attitudes toward safe sex. *Family Relations, 53,* 377–384.

Kowal, A., & Kramer, L. (1997). Children's understanding of parental differential treatment. *Child Development, 68,* 113–126.

Kowal, A., Kramer, L., Krull, J. L., & Crick, N. R. (2002). Children's perceptions of the fairness of parental preferential treatment and their socioemotional well-being. *Journal of Family Psychology, 16,* 297–306.

Kramer, L. & Bank, L. (2005). Sibling relationship contributions to individual and family well-being: Introduction to the special issue. *Journal of Family Psychology, 19,* 483–485.

Kramer, L., Perozynski, L. A., & Chung, T. Y. (1999). Parental responses to sibling conflict: The effects of development and parent gender. *Child Development, 70,* 1401–1414.

Kreppner, K., & Lerner, R. M. (1989). *Family systems and life-span development.* Hillsdale, NJ: Lawrence Erlbaum.

Lamb, M. E., & Sutton-Smith, B. (Eds.). (1982). *Sibling relationships: Their nature and significance across the lifespan.* Hillsdale, NJ: Lawrence Erlbaum.

Lamorey, S. (1999). Parentification of siblings of children with disability or chronic disease. In N. D. Chase (Ed.), *Burdened children: Theory, research and treatment of parentification* (pp. 75–91). Thousand Oaks, CA: Sage.

Lanthier, R. P. (2007). Personality traits and sibling relationships in emerging adults. *Psychological Reports, 100,* 672–674.

Larson, R. W., & Verma, S. (1999). How children and adolescents spend time across the world: Work, play and developmental opportunities. *Psychological Bulletin, 125,* 701–736.

Lerner, R. M. (1984). *On the nature of human plasticity.* Cambridge: Cambridge University Press.

Lerner, R. M. (2004). Diversity in individual-context relations as the basis for positive development across the life span: A developmental systems perspective for theory, research, and application. *Research in Human Development, 1,* 327–346.

Lerner, R. M., & Steinberg, L. (2004). The scientific study of adolescent development: Past, present, and future. In R. M. Lerner & L. Steinberg (Eds.), *Handbook of adolescent psychology* (2nd ed.) (pp. 1–12). Hoboken, NJ: John Wiley & Sons.

Mayer, S. E. (1997). *What money can't buy: Family income and children's life chances.* Cambridge, MA: Harvard University Press.

Maynard, A. E. (2004). Sibling interactions. In U. P. Gielen & J. Roopnarine (Eds.), *Childhood and adolescence: Cross-cultural perspectives and applications. Advances in applied developmental psychology* (pp. 229–252). Westport, CT: Praeger.

McGue, M., Sharma, A., & Benson, P. (1996). Parent and sibling influences on adolescent alcohol use and misuse: Evidence from a U.S. adoption cohort. *Journal of the Study of Alcohol, 57,* 8–18.

McGuire, S., Dunn, J., & Plomin, R. (1995). Maternal differential treatment of siblings and children's behavioral problems: A longitudinal study. *Development and Psychopathology, 7,* 515–528.

McGuire, S., Manke, B., Eftekhari, A., & Dunn, J. (2000). Children's perceptions of sibling conflict during middle childhood: Issues and sibling (dis)similarity. *Social Development, 9,* 173–190.

McHale, S. M., Kim, J., & Whiteman, S. D. (2006). Sibling relationships in childhood and adolescence. In P. Noller, & J. A. Feeney (Eds.), *Close relationships: Function, forms and processes* (pp. 127–149). Hove, UK: Psychology Press.

McHale, S. M., Updegraff, K. A., Helms-Erikson, H., & Crouter, A. C. (2001). Sibling influences on gender development in middle childhood and early adolescence: A longitudinal study. *Developmental Psychology, 37,* 115–125.

McHale, S. M., Updegraff, K. A., Jackson-Newsom, J., Tucker, C. J., & Crouter, A. C. (2000). When does parents' differential treatment have negative implications for siblings? *Social Development, 9,* 149–172.

McHale, S. M., Updegraff, K. A., Shanahan, L., Crouter, A. C., & Killoren, S. E. (2005). Siblings' differential treatment in Mexican American families. *Journal of Marriage and Family, 67,* 1259–1274.

McHale, S. M., Updegraff, K. A., Tucker, C. J., & Crouter, A. C. (2000). Step in or stay out? Parents' roles in adolescent siblings' relationships. *Journal of Marriage and the Family, 62,* 746–760.

McHale, S. M., Whiteman, S. D., Kim, J., & Crouter, A. C. (2007). Characteristics and correlates of sibling relationships in two-parent African American families. *Journal of Family Psychology, 21,* 227–235.

Milevsky, A. (2005). Compensatory patterns of sibling support in emerging adulthood: Variations in loneliness, self-esteem, depression and life satisfaction. *Journal of Social and Personal Relationships, 22,* 743–755.

Milevsky, A., & Levitt, M. J. (2005). Sibling support in early adolescence: Buffering and compensation across relationships. *European Journal of Developmental Psychology, 2,* 229–320.

Minnett, A. M., Vandell, D. L., & Santrock, J. W. (1983). The effects of sibling status on sibling interaction: Influence of birth order, age spacing, sex of child, and sex of sibling. *Child Development, 54,* 1064–1072.

Minuchin, P. (1988). Relationships within the family: A systems perspective on development. In R. A. Hinde & J. Stevenson-Hinde (Eds.), *Relationships within families: Mutual influences* (pp. 7–26). Oxford: Clarendon Press.

Newcomer, S. F., & Udry, J. R. (1984). Mothers' influence on the sexual behavior of their teenage children. *Journal of Marriage and the Family, 46,* 477–485.

O'Connor, T. G., Dunn, J., Jenkins, J. M., Pickering, K., & Rasbash, J. (2001). Family settings and children's adjustment: Differential adjustment within and across families. *British Journal of Psychiatry, 179,* 110–115.

Oliva, A., & Arranz, E. (2005). Sibling relationships during adolescence. *European Journal of Developmental Psychology, 2*(3), 253–270.

Patterson, G. R. (1984). *Siblings: Fellow travelers in coercive family processes. Advances in the study of aggression* (pp. 173–215). New York: Academic Press.

Patterson, G. R. (1986). The contribution of siblings to training for fighting: A microsocial analysis. In D. Olweus, J. Block, & M. Radke-Yarrow (Eds.), *Development of antisocial and prosocial behaviors* (pp. 235–260). Orlando, FL: Academic Press.

Patterson, G. R., Dishion, T., & Bank, L. (1984). Family interaction: A process model of deviancy training. *Aggressive Behavior, 10,* 253–267.

Perlman, M., & Ross, H. (1997). The benefits of parent intervention in children's disputes: An examination of concurrent changes in children's fighting styles. *Child Development, 68,* 690–700.

Plomin, R., & Daniels, D. (1987). Why are children in the same family so different from one another? *Behavioural and Brain Sciences, 10,* 1–60.

Ponzetti, J. J., Jr., & James, C. M. (1997). Loneliness and sibling relationships. *Journal of Social Behavior and Personality, 12,* 103–112.

Rabain-Jamin, J., Maynard, A., & Greenfield, P. (2003). Implications of sibling caregiving for sibling relations and teaching interactions in two cultures. *Ethos, 31,* 204–231.

Raffaelli, M. (1992). Sibling conflict in early adolescence. *Journal of Marriage and the Family, 54,* 652–663.

Rauer, A. J., & Volling, B. L. (2007). Differential parenting and sibling jealousy: Developmental correlates of young adults' romantic relationships. *Personal Relationships, 14,* 495–511.

Reese-Weber, M., & Kahn, J. H. (2005). Familial predictors of sibling and romantic-partner conflict resolution: Comparing late adolescents from intact and divorced families. *Journal of Adolescence, 28,* 479–493.

Reiss, D., Plomin, R., Hetherington, E. M., Howe, G. W., Rovine, M., Tryon, A., et al. (1994). The separate worlds of teenage siblings: An introduction to the study of nonshared environmental and adolescent development. In E. M. Hetherington, D. Reiss, & R. Plomin (Eds.), *Separate social worlds of siblings: The impact of nonshared environment on development* (pp. 63–109). Hillsdale, NJ: Lawrence Erlbaum.

Rende, R., Slomkowski, C., Lloyd-Richardson, E., & Niaura, R. (2005). Sibling effects on substance use in adolescence: Social and genetic relatedness. *Journal of Family Psychology, 19,* 611–618.

Richmond, M. K., Stocker, C. M., & Rienks, S. L. (2005). Longitudinal associations between sibling relationship quality, parental differential treatment, and children's adjustment. *Journal of Family Psychology, 19,* 550–559.

Riggio, H. R. (2006). Structural features of sibling dyads and attitudes toward sibling relationships in young adulthood. *Journal of Family Issues, 27,* 1233–1254.

Rodgers, J. L. (2001). The confluence model: An academic "Tragedy of the commons." In R. Sternberg & E. Grigorenko (Eds.), *Family environment and intellectual functioning: A life-span perspective* (pp. 71–95). Mahwah, NJ: Lawrence Erlbaum.

Rodgers, J. L., & Rowe, D. C. (1988). Influence of siblings on adolescent sexual behavior. *Developmental Psychology, 24,* 722–728.

Rodgers, J. L., Rowe, D. C., & Harris, D. F. (1992). Sibling differences in adolescent sexual behavior: Inferring process models from family composition patterns. *Journal of Marriage and the Family, 54,* 142–152.

Rosen, K., S., & Burke, P. B. (1999). Multiple attachment relationships within families: Mothers and fathers with two young children. *Developmental Psychology, 35,* 436–444.

Rosenzweig, M. R. (1986). Birth spacing and sibling inequality: Asymmetric information within the household. *International Economics Review, 27,* 55–76.

Ross, H., Ross, M., Stein, N., & Trabasso, T. (2006). How siblings resolve their conflicts: The importance of first offers, planning, and limited opposition. *Child Development, 77,* 1730–1745.

Rowe, D. C., & Gulley, B. L. (1992). Sibling effects on substance use and delinquency. *Criminology, 30,* 217–233.

Rowe, D. C., Rodgers, J. L., Meseck-Bushey, S., & St. John, C. (1989). Sexual behavior and nonsexual deviance: A sibling study of their relationship. *Developmental Psychology, 25,* 61–69.

Rowland, D. T. (2007). Historical trends in childlessness. *Journal of Family Issues, 28,* 1311–1337.

Rutter, M. (1987). Psychosocial resilience and protective mechanisms. *American Journal of Orthopsychiatry, 57,* 316–331.

Sandler, I., Miller, P., Short, J., & Wolchik, S. A. (1989). Social support as a protective factor for children in stress. In D. Belle (Ed.), *Children's social networks and social supports* (pp. 277–307). New York: John Wiley & Sons.

Scarr, S., & Grajek, S. (1982). Similarities and differences among siblings. In M. E. Lamb & B. Sutton-Smith (Eds.), *Sibling relationships: Their nature and significance across the lifespan* (pp. 357–381). Hillsdale, NJ: Lawrence Erlbaum.

Scarr, S., & McCartney, K. (1983). How people make their own environments: A theory of genotype–environment effects. *Child Development, 54,* 424–435.

Schachter, F. F. (1982). Sibling deidentification and split-parent identification: A family tetrad. In M. E. Lamb & B. Sutton-Smith (Eds.), *Sibling relationships: Their nature and significance across the lifespan* (pp 123–151). Hillsdale, NJ: Lawrence Erlbaum.

Schachter, F. F., Shore, E., Feldman-Rotman, S., Marquis, R. E., & Campbell, S. (1976). Sibling deidentification. *Developmental Psychology, 12,* 418–427.

Scharf, M., Shulman, S., & Avigad-Spitz, L. (2005). Sibling relationships in emerging adulthood and in adolescence. *Journal of Adolescent Research, 20,* 64–90.

Sears, H. A., & Sheppard, H. M. (2004, January). "I just wanted to be the kid": Adolescent girls' experiences of having a parent with cancer. *Canadian Oncology Journal,* 18–25.

Seginer, R. (1998). Adolescents' perceptions of relationships with older siblings in the context of other close relationships. *Journal of Research on Adolescence, 8,* 287–308.

Shanahan, L., McHale, S. M., Crouter, A. C & Osgood, D. W. (2007). Warmth with mothers and fathers from middle childhood to late adolescence: Within- and between-families comparisons. *Developmental Psychology, 43,* 551–563.

Shanahan, L., McHale, S. M., Osgood, D. W., & Crouter, A. C. (2007). Conflict frequency with mothers and fathers from middle childhood to late adolescence: Within- and between-families comparisons. *Developmental Psychology, 43,* 539–550.

Shebloski, B., Conger, K. J., & Widaman, K. F. (2005). Reciprocal links between differential parenting, perceived partiality, and self-worth: A three-wave longitudinal study. *Journal of Family Psychology, 19,* 633–642.

Sheehan, G., & Noller, P. (2002). Adolescent's perceptions of differential parenting: Links with attachment style and adolescent adjustment. *Personal Relationships, 9,* 173–190.

Sherman, A. M., Lansford, J. E., & Volling, B. L. (2006). Sibling relationships and best friendships in young adulthood: Warmth, conflict and well-being. *Personal Relationships, 13,* 151–165.

Shortt, J. W., Capaldi, D. M., Dishion, T. J., Bank, L., & Owen, L. D. (2003). The role of adolescent friends, romantic partners, and siblings in the emergence of the adult antisocial lifestyle. *Journal of Family Psychology, 17,* 521–533.

Slomkowski, C., Rende, R., Conger, K. J., Simons, R. L., & Conger, R. D. (2001). Sisters, brothers, and delinquency: Evaluating social influence during early and middle adolescence. *Child Development, 72,* 271–283.

Slomkowski, C., Rende, R., Novak, S., Lloyd-Richardson, E., & Niaura, R. (2005). Sibling effects on smoking in adolescence: Evidence for social influence from a genetically informative design. *Addiction, 100,* 430–438.

Smith, J., & Ross, H. (2007). Training parents to mediate sibling disputes affects children's negotiation and conflict understanding. *Child Development, 78,* 790–805.

Smith, T. E. (1993). Growth in achievement and teaching younger siblings. *Social Psychology Quarterly, 56,* 77–85.

Snyder, J., Bank, L., & Burraston, B. (2005). The consequences of antisocial behavior in older male siblings for younger brothers and sisters. *Journal of Family Psychology, 19,* 643–653.

Snyder, J., & Stoolmiller, M. (2002). Reinforcement and coercion mechanisms in the development of antisocial behavior: The family. In J. B. Reid, J. R. Patterson, & J. Snyder (Eds.), *Antisocial behavior in children and adolescents: A developmental analysis and model for intervention* (pp. 65–100). Washington, DC: American Psychological Association.

Sroufe, L. A., & Fleeson, J. (1988). The coherence of family relationships. In R. A. Hinde & J. Stevenson-Hinde (Eds.), *Relationships within families: Mutual influences* (pp. 27–47). Oxford: Clarendon Press.

Stein, J. A., Riedel, M., & Rotheram-Borus, M. J. (1999). Parentification and its impact on adolescent children of parents with AIDS. *Family Process, 38,* 193–208.

Stewart, R. B., Verbrugge, K. M., & Beilfuss, M. C. (1998). Sibling relationships in early adulthood: A typology. *Personal Relationships, 5,* 59–74.

Stocker, C. M. (1993). Siblings' adjustment in middle childhood: Links with mother–child relationships. *Journal of Applied Developmental Psychology, 14,* 485–499.

Stocker, C. M. (1994). Children's perceptions of relationships with siblings, friends, and mothers: Compensatory processes and links with adjustment. *Journal of Child Psychology and Psychiatry, 35,* 1447–1459.

Stocker, C. M. (1995). Differences in mothers' and fathers' relationships with siblings: Links with children's behavior problems. *Development and Psychopathology, 7,* 499–513.

Stocker, C. M., Ahmed, K., & Stall, M. (1997). Marital satisfaction and maternal emotional expressiveness: Links with children's sibling relationships. *Social Development, 6,* 373–385.

Stocker, C. M., Burwell, R. A., & Briggs, M. L. (2002). Sibling conflict in middle childhood predicts children's adjustment in early adolescence. *Journal of Family Psychology, 16,* 50–57.

Stocker, C., Dunn, J., & Plomin, R. (1989). Sibling relationships: Links with child temperament, maternal behavior, and family structure. *Child Development, 60,* 715–727.

Stocker, C. M., Lanthier, R. P., & Furman, W. (1997). Sibling relationships in early adulthood. *Journal of Family Psychology, 11,* 210–221.

Stocker, C. M., & McHale, S. M. (1992). The nature and family correlates of preadolescents' perceptions of their sibling relationships. *Journal of Social and Personal Relationships, 9,* 179–195.

Stocker, C. M., & Youngblade, L. (1999). Marital conflict and parental hostility: Links with children's sibling and peer relationships. *Journal of Family Psychology, 13,* 598–609.

Stormshak, E. A., Bellanti, C., Bierman, K. L., & Conduct Problems Prevention Research Group. (1996). The quality of sibling relationships and the development of social competence and behavioral control in aggressive children. *Developmental Psychology, 32,* 79–89.

Sullivan, H. S. (1953). *The interpersonal theory of psychiatry.* New York: W. W. Norton.

Suls, J. M., & Miller, R. L. (Eds.) (1977). *Social comparison processes.* Washington: Hemisphere.

Tamrouti-Makkink, I. D., Dubas, J. S., Gerris, J. R. M., & van Aken, M. A. G. (2004). The relation between the absolute level of parenting and differential parental treatment with adolescent siblings' adjustment. *Journal of Child Psychology and Psychiatry, 45,* 1397–1406.

Tucker, C. J., McHale, S. M., & Crouter, A. C. (2001). Conditions of sibling support in adolescence. *Journal of Family Psychology, 15,* 254–271.

Tucker, C. J., Updegraff, K. A., McHale, S. M., & Crouter, A. C. (1999). Older siblings as socializers of younger siblings' empathy. *Journal of Early Adolescence, 19,* 176–198.

Tucker, C. J., & Winzeler, A. (2007). Adolescent siblings' daily discussions: Connections to perceived academic, athletic, and peer competency. *Journal of Research on Adolescence, 17,* 145–152.

Updegraff, K. A., McHale, S. M., & Crouter, A. C. (2002). Adolescents' sibling relationship and friendship experiences: Developmental patterns and relationship linkages. *Social Development, 11,* 182–204.

Updegraff, K. A., McHale, S. M., Whiteman, S. D., Thayer, S. M., & Delgado, M. Y. (2005). Adolescent sibling relationships in Mexican American families: Exploring the role of familism. *Journal of Family Psychology, 19,* 512–522.

Van Ijzendoorn, M. H., Moran, G., Belsky, J., Pederson, D., Bakermans-Dranenburg, M. J., & Kneppers, K. (2000). The similarity of siblings' attachment to their mothers. *Child Development, 71,* 1086–1098.

Volling, B. L. (2005). The transition to siblinghood: A developmental ecological systems perspective and directions for future research. *Journal of Family Psychology, 19,* 542–549.

Volling, B. L., & Elins, J. L. (1998). Family relationships and children's emotional adjustment as correlates of maternal and paternal differential treatment: A replication with toddler and preschool siblings. *Child Development, 69,* 1640–1656.

Volling, B. L., McElwain, N. L., & Miller, A. L. (2002). Emotion regulation in context: The jealousy complex between young siblings and its relations with child and family characteristics. *Child Development, 73,* 581–600.

Ward, M. J., Vaughn, B. E., & Robb, M. D. (1988). Socio-emotional adaptation and infant–mother attachment in siblings: Role of the mother in cross-sibling consistency. *Child Development, 59,* 643–651.

Weiss, R. S. (1974). The provisions of social relationships. In Z. Rubin (Ed.), *Doing unto others* (pp. 17–26). Englewood Cliffs, NJ: Prentice Hall.

Whitbeck, L. B., Yoder, K., Hoyt, D., & Conger, R. D. (1999). Early adolescent sexual activity: A developmental study. *Journal of Marriage and the Family, 61,* 934–946.

White, L. (2001). Sibling relationships over the life course: A panel analysis. *Journal of Marriage and Family, 63,* 555–568.

Whiteman, S. D., & Buchanan, C. M. (2002). Mothers' and children's expectations for adolescence: The impact of perceptions of an older sibling's experience. *Journal of Family Psychology, 16,* 157–171.

Whiteman, S. D., & Christiansen, A. (2008). Processes of sibling influence in adolescence: Individual and family correlates. *Family Relations, 57,* 24–34.

Whiteman, S. D., McHale, S. M., & Crouter, A. C. (2003). What parents learn from experience: The first child as a first draft? *Journal of Marriage and Family, 65,* 608–621.

Whiteman, S. D., McHale, S. M., & Crouter, A. C. (2007a). Competing processes of sibling influence: Observational learning and sibling deidentification. *Social Development, 16,* 642–661.

Whiteman, S. D., McHale, S. M., & Crouter, A. C. (2007b). Explaining sibling similarities: Perceptions of sibling influences. *Journal of Youth and Adolescence, 36,* 963–972.

Widmer, E. D. (1997). Influence of older siblings on initiation of sexual intercourse. *Journal of Marriage and the Family, 59,* 928–938.

Williams, S. T., Conger, K. J., & Blozis, S. A. (2007). The development of interpersonal aggression during adolescence: The importance of parents, siblings, and family economics. *Child Development, 78,* 1526–1542.

Windle, M. (2000). Parental, sibling and peer influences on adolescent substance use and alcohol problems. *Applied Developmental Science, 4,* 98–110.

Yeung, W. J., Linver, M. R., & Brooks-Gunn, J. (2002). How money matters for young children's development: Parental investment and family processes. *Child Development, 73,* 1861–1879.

Zajonc, R. B., & Markus, G. B. (1975). Birth order and intellectual development. *Psychological Review, 82,* 74–88.

Zukow, P. G. (Ed.). (1989). *Sibling interactions across cultures: Theoretical and methodological issues.* New York: Springer-Verlag.

Zukow-Goldring, P. (2002). Sibling caregiving. In M. H. Bornstein (Ed.), *Handbook of parenting* (2nd ed.), vol. *3* (pp. 253–286). Mahwah, NJ: Lawrence Erlbaum.

CHAPTER 3

Peer Relationships in Adolescence

B. BRADFORD BROWN AND JAMES LARSON

For decades, scholars have pointed to peer relationships as one of the most important features of adolescence. Peers have been alternately blamed for some of the more problematic aspects of adolescent functioning and praised for contributing to adolescent health and well-being. Recently, researchers have pushed the study of peer relations in exciting new directions, using more sophisticated methodologies to explore understudied aspects of adolescent peer relationships and mechanisms of influence. In this chapter, we review the issues that investigators have pursued over the past 5 years, since the last edition of this *Handbook,* that pertain to adolescent peer relations. We consider how findings from these studies improve our understanding of the role that peers play in the lives of adolescents and how these studies chart a direction for future research in the area.

SCOPE AND OBJECTIVES

This chapter is not intended to be a comprehensive review of scholarly work on adolescent peer relations, which now spans well over half a century, nor is it our intention to summarize all of the recent work related to peer interactions. We pursue the more limited task of calling attention to research that moves the field past well established features of adolescent peer relations and interactions toward a more integrative understanding of how peers affect adolescent development. We pay particular attention to conceptual and methodological innovations that underlie recent scholarship.

Because most researchers rely on chronological age or school grade levels to define their samples, we focus on studies that concentrate on young people between the ages of 11 and 22, or roughly from the beginning of secondary school (most typically, grade 6 in North America) to the end of college. Operationalizing adolescence in this way is controversial. Increasing numbers of young people are entering puberty prior to the transition to secondary school (see chapter 5, vol. 1 of this *Handbook*), lending credibility to the argument that adolescence, at least as it is defined by biology, may be drifting down the age span to the elementary school years. However, we maintain that there are still major social structural changes that are age-graded or tied to school transitions in technologically advanced societies (in which most research on peer relations occurs). Because these changes have a substantial effect on peer relations, it is sensible to confine our analyses to the age and grade levels that we have stipulated.

The field of peer relationships encompasses a wide variety of affiliations. We give scant attention in this chapter to three important components of the field: romantic relationships, sexually based interests and activities, and groups of young people engaged in formal activities organized and supervised by adults. Each of these components is a central concern of other chapters in this *Handbook* (see chapter 14, vol. 1; chapter 4, vol. 2; chapter 7, vol. 2 of this *Handbook*). Given recent efforts to integrate research across various facets of peer relations, however, we caution readers that this partitioning may inadvertently diminish emphasis on scholarly efforts to provide a more integrative portrait of adolescent peer relations.

Finally, some of the intriguing research on ethnic identity and ethnic discrimination treats those who share an ethnic background as a peer group, or uses ethnic peers as a basis for examining how ethnic background affects adolescents (see chapter 15, this volume). There is little doubt that aspects of adolescents' interactions with peers and the adolescent peer system contribute to ethnic identity development, or that peer relationships contribute to norms about discrimination or activities that reveal racial and ethnic prejudices, but most of the studies that we examined did not approach peers from this perspective. For example, Killen et al. (2007) asked a sample of U.S. youth from minority and nonminority backgrounds to indicate how wrong it would be to exclude a peer from a school- or community-based social activity because of the peer's ethnicity, and then to justify their decision. Responses pointed to age differences in attitudes about racially motivated exclusion, but did not speak directly to the peer dynamics that might underlie age differences. As a result, we do not include this or similar studies in our review.

To fully appreciate current work in the field one must understand the foundation on which it is built. Before examining recent research, we quickly review ten assertions derived from older studies about peer relations in adolescence. The assertions constitute conventional wisdom about peer relations from which recent studies have been derived. Then, following Hartup's (2006) advice for organizing the literature, we proceed with an analysis of recent research as it pertains to four major facets of peer relations and interaction. The first encompasses characteristics of individuals that have some direct bearing on social relationships. Studies of popularity or social status, aggression, friendship expectations, and peer crowd identification exemplify this category. We then turn attention to characteristics of relationships, including the degree of similarity or complementarity among friends, the quality of friendships, the nature of antagonistic relations, and features of peer groups. A third area of research concerns interpersonal processes that adolescents encounter in their relationships with peers. Peer influence is the dominant concern in this area, but there is also research on other social processes within friendships, antagonistic relationships (e.g., bullying behavior), and small groups. Finally, we consider contextual influences on peer interactions. In addition to the family and school, investigators have considered the role that ethnic or cultural background, and electronic media (especially, the Internet) play in adolescent peer relations. A few investigators have also engaged in cross-national comparisons of peer relations. We end with recommendations for future research on peer-related issues.

CONVENTIONAL WISDOM ABOUT PEER RELATIONS

As evidence accumulated over the second half of the twentieth century, researchers came to several conclusions about the nature of peer relations in adolescence. The basis for these conclusions has been covered in greater detail in previous reviews of the literature (Berndt & Murphy, 2002; Brown, 1990; Bukowski & Adams, 2005; Hartup, 1999; Savin-Williams & Berndt, 1990). We offer a brief summary here to set the stage for closer examination of recent scholarship:

1. *Peer relations become more salient in adolescence.* The transition from childhood to adolescence engenders changes in the individual, social context, and social norms that serve to elevate the importance of peers. Young people become likely to spend more time with age mates, often with reduced oversight by adults, and they put greater stock in the expectations and opinions of peers. In some arenas, peers compete with adults as a significant source of

influence on adolescent attitudes, activities, and emotional well-being.

2. *With the transition to adolescence, peer relations grow more complex.* Concomitant with the growing importance of peers is an increase in the complexity of the peer system. New types of relationships emerge in adolescence—most notably, romantic relationships—and new levels of the peer system become apparent, such as reputation-based crowds or a broader youth culture. In selecting friends, romantic partners, or friendship groups, young people grow more sensitive to the ramifications of a specific relationship for their status or reputation within the broader peer system. In other words, young people must negotiate peer relationships and issues on a broader set of levels than they did in childhood. This prompts researchers to differentiate more carefully between dyadic and group relations and to distinguish among different types of relationships at each level. The dynamics within friendships cannot be expected to be equivalent to the dynamics within other dyadic connections: romantic relationships, sexual liaisons, mutual antipathies, or bully–victim relationships. Likewise, the features of interaction based friendship groups are likely to differ from those of reputation based crowd affiliations. Although different types of relationship or levels of peer association are distinctive, they remain interdependent. For example, openness to and success in romantic relationships are contingent on experiences within the friendship group (Connolly, Furman, & Konarski, 2000), and friendship norms vary among crowds (Finders, 1997).

3. *Friendships and friendship groups are characterized by similarity, which is a product of both partner selection and influence.* A fundamental feature of friendships is that partners share many characteristics in common. Through systematic research, investigators have discovered that this is because similar background, tastes, values, and interests propel individuals to select each other as friends, and as these characteristics are affirmed within the relationship, the partners are likely to grow even more similar to each other (Cohen, 1977; Kandel, 1978). Moreover, if, over time, friends begin to diverge in attitudes and activities, the strength of their bond will diminish, often to the point that the relationship ends. The fact that similarity between friends is driven by the interaction of these three forces—selection, socialization, and deselection—makes it difficult to estimate the degree of influence that friends have on each other. Moreover, there are questions about whether adolescents remain equally susceptible to influence by a friend over the entire course of their relationship.

4. *Status or prestige is an important element of adolescent peer relations.* By definition, *peer relations* refers to associations among equals, but in reality the equality is confined to individuals who share the same life stage (fellow adolescents). Hierarchies emerge within aspects of the peer system, such that certain crowds have more status than others (Brown, Von Bank, & Steinberg, 2008; Horn, 2006), and cliques feature leaders and followers (Dunphy, 1969), if not an even more differentiated "pecking order" or dominance hierarchy (Adler & Adler, 1998; Savin-Williams, 1980). Even within friendships or romantic ties, which are dyadic relations supposedly founded on the principles of equality and reciprocity, one partner often appears to have more power than the other (Giordano, Longmore, & Manning, 2006; Updegraff et al., 2004). Within any group of young people, certain individuals are rated as more likable than others, or more popular than others (Cillessen & Rose, 2005). As adolescents consider or negotiate relationships with specific peers or peer groups, they must be sensitive

to status differentiations. The importance of status can vary among groups of young people (Peshkin, 1991), but the impact of the status dimension on peer interaction should not be neglected by researchers.

5. *Young people with good social skills are better adjusted than those with poor social skills.* Although intuitively obvious, it has been important for researchers to document that deficiencies in social skills place young people at risk for poor adaptation in terms of academic, social, and emotional outcomes. Much of this work has concentrated on childhood, when rudimentary social skills are learned and practiced. The changing peer landscape in adolescence, in which new types of relationships and levels of peer interaction emerge, calls for a broader set of social skills, underscoring the importance of continuing to study the development of social skills through this stage of life. However, measures of social self-concept and social skills often fail to assess the full range of skills that adolescents must develop to negotiate the social system effectively.

6. *Social acceptance is also a good indicator of adjustment.* Within a peer system young people can be grouped or ranked in terms of sociometric status as well as power or prestige. Across the last third of the twentieth century a vast literature developed tracking the characteristics of groups of children and adolescents identified by asking young people to nominate the peers (usually, school classmates) whom they like the most and like the least (or whom they most and least want to play with or have as friends or partners in a group activity). Applying a standard set of decision rules to these sociometric data, investigators differentiated groups of young people who were popular (widely nominated as well liked and rarely nominated as disliked), rejected (widely disliked and rarely liked), neglected (rarely nominated as liked or disliked), and controversial (receiving considerable nominations as liked and disliked). The groups differed substantially and consistently on various emotional and behavioral outcomes (Cillessen & Mayeux, 2004b). Subsequent longitudinal studies indicated that sociometric status predicted (at modest levels) these outcomes, but to a certain extent was also predicted by them.

Although useful as a fundamental indicator of peer acceptance, sociometric categories have several limitations. First, each category is not necessarily cohesive. Most notably, investigators found substantial differences in adjustment and behavior patterns of rejected youth depending on whether or not they were aggressive toward peers. Also, the sociometric categorization was always a relative judgment, dependent on the features of the criterion group. If an adolescent was assigned to a classroom containing a large number of affable and well adjusted peers, her chances of being categorized as popular were less than if she had been placed in a classroom with many shy or highly aggressive students. Most significant was that the category system failed to reveal *why* peers regarded some children as likable and others as disagreeable. Thus, the very convenient categorization system did not get at the heart of adolescents' relationships with peers.

7. *Self-perceptions of peer relations or the peer system are unreliable.* Early studies of peer relations and peer influences often relied upon respondents to report not only their own attitudes and behavior but also the attitudes and activities of significant peers. For example, estimates of peer influence were derived by correlating adolescents' reports of their own behavior and the behavior of their closest friend, friendship group, or generalized set of peers. Later investigations comparing these estimates to direct reports from (or observations of) the targeted peers revealed two

patterns. First, adolescents tended to overestimate the degree of congruence between themselves and their peers (Kandel & Andrews, 1987), so that inferences from many studies exaggerated the degree of peer influence. Second, adolescents also overestimated peer involvement in antisocial, unhealthy, or maladaptive behavior such as drug use, sexual activity, or inattentiveness to schoolwork (Prinstein & Wang, 2005). The implications of these findings are controversial, as scholars debate whether adolescents are likely to be influenced more by the actual attitudes or behaviors of peers or adolescents' *perceptions* of these peer characteristics. In any case, researchers have grown more cautious about relying upon adolescents to report on their peers' behaviors, preferring instead to gather information about peers directly from the appropriate associates of a target respondent.

8. *Peer affiliations and peer reputations are only moderately stable.* Unlike adolescents' relationships with significant others in the family, school (e.g., teachers), or community (e.g., health care professionals, activity supervisors such as coaches or music teachers), close peer associates are relatively ephemeral. Most early adolescents are likely to name a different peer as their best friend at the beginning and end of a school year. It is rare for a friendship group or clique to remain entirely intact over a 6-month period, and rarer still for early adolescents to retain the same romantic partner for this period of time. Studies suggest that sociometric status (being popular, accepted, neglected, or rejected) is not very stable, although more so for the rejected category than others (Jiang & Cillessen, 2005). Understandably, youth who retain the same sociometric classification over long time periods reflect the strengths or limitations of that status to a greater extent than sociometrically transient peers (Cillessen, Bukowski, & Haselager, 2000). The limited data that exist suggest that peer crowd affiliations often change as well (Kinney, 1993).

Two facets of adolescents' peer relationships point to stability, however. First, as individuals move through adolescence their friendships grow more stable and romantic relationships tend to last longer. Second, amidst routine changes in specific relationship partners and peer affiliations, adolescents do display stability in the *types* of individuals and groups with whom they affiliate. For example, individuals who are part of a predominantly aggressive clique at the beginning of the school year usually appear in an aggressive group at year's end as well, even if their group's specific membership has changed substantially (Cairns, Leung, & Buchanan, 1995).

9. *Peer influence is a reciprocal process.* A primary focus of studies of adolescent peer relations is the extent to which young people are influenced by peers. In most cases, researchers organize their studies to evaluate the degree of influence that some aspect of the peer system has on an adolescent, failing to take into account that adolescents influence others as well as being influenced by them. The reciprocal, transactional nature of peer influence is very difficult to capture in research studies, especially if the research is grounded in traditional socialization theories that are based on unilateral patterns of influence. We expect parents, teachers, coaches, or other adults to influence children to a much greater extent than they are influenced by them, allowing us to overlook reciprocal patterns of influence in these relationships more easily. Although investigators acknowledge the need to examine peer influence from a bilateral perspective, they still struggle to develop methodologies to accomplish this.

10. *Studies of peer influence must consider characteristics of the influence agent, the target of the influence, and the individuals' relationship.* An important step toward charting the reciprocal nature of peer influence is integrating three factors in a study's research design (Brown, Bakken, Ameringer, &

Mahon, 2008; Hartup, 2005). One is the characteristics of the individual identified (at least for research purposes) as the target of influence. Variability in adolescents' competence and self-confidence in a particular domain, along with their susceptibility or openness to peer influence, should affect the degree to which they are affected by others. Likewise, characteristics of the person or group identified as the agent of influence—expertise or credibility in a given domain and facility in exerting influence, for instance—should contribute significantly to the process. Finally, investigators must consider features of the relationship between influencer and influenced: the nature and strength of the bond, the amount of time they have been associated with each other, and so on. Placing all of these factors into a theoretical and measurement model is challenging, but as Hartup (2005, p. 388) notes, ignoring them is foolhardy: "Main effects conclusions in the peer contagion literature are, by and large, either oversimplified or dead wrong" (p. 388).

As new research builds on these fundamental assertions, investigators sometimes find it necessary to qualify them. Understandably, the assertions may not apply to all populations at all phases of adolescence in all historical circumstances. Nevertheless, they form a strong foundation on which to proceed with a better elaborated understanding of particular features of adolescents' interactions with age-mates. With this caveat, we turn attention to studies that build upon assertions 4–6 above in exploring individual characteristics that shape the type of peer relationships and experiences that adolescents encounter.

PEER-RELATED CHARACTERISTICS OF INDIVIDUALS

The Nature of Popularity

One of the mostly widely studied peer characteristics is popularity. In previous decades, investigators produced scores of reports based on sociometric data that allowed them to assign young people (mostly children) to standard sociometric categories—popular, rejected, neglected, average, or controversial—based on the frequency with which they were nominated as liked or disliked by peers (usually, school classroom mates). Members of various categories were compared on a host of personal characteristics or indicators of well-being, usually demonstrating a distinct advantage for popular youth, especially in comparison to rejected peers. These studies have faded, mostly because the paradigm has been pushed to its limits in providing new insights (Rubin, Bukowski, & Parker, 2006), but also because of two problems in applying the paradigm to adolescent samples. First, the structure of middle schools in North American and several other nations was not well suited to standard sociometric techniques. With students migrating among classrooms with shifting sets of peers throughout the day, there was not the small, stable social unit on which social relationships (and sociometric status) could be based. Equally troublesome was that adolescents had already co-opted the paradigm's primary construct, popularity, but imbued it with a different meaning than the one that sociometric researchers had in mind. Rather than being well liked, nominated frequently as someone that people wanted to play with or have as a friend, a popular adolescent was someone with high status or prestige—and, probably, power—in the teenage social system.

Two Forms of Popularity

In essence, researchers discovered that adolescence features two forms of popularity, one related to status and the other to being well liked. This discovery soon prompted investigators to explore the nature and distinctiveness of both forms, in terms of their stability, intercorrelation, relation to other personal characteristics, and influence on social and psychological adjustment. Although there is not complete consensus on labels for the two forms of popularity, they are most commonly referred to as *sociometric popularity*, referring to the degree to which individuals are well liked or sought out as activity partners or friends, and *perceived popularity,* indicating the amount of status or prestige assigned to a person (Cillessen & Rose, 2005). We will describe the literature with these terms.

Investigators have found that sociometric and perceived popularity are significantly correlated, sometimes to a high degree (de Bruyn & Cillessen, 2006a, 2006b) but more often moderately (Rose, Swenson, & Waller, 2004). An interesting longitudinal study of middle-class U.S. youth indicated that the correlation between perceived and sociometric popularity declined substantially between grades 4 and 9, especially for girls, to the point that among 9th-grade girls the two were no longer significantly associated (Cillessen & Mayeux, 2004a).

One explanation for the growing distinctiveness of the two forms of popularity is that as the peer system grows more complex across adolescence, groups emerge that are organized by status or prestige. It is common for young people to label one of the higher status groups the "populars," but this group is not necessarily well liked (Eckert, 1989). Likewise, members of groups with extremely low status (i.e., low perceived popularity) are not sought out for friendship (Kinney, 1993), so that it may well be the middle-status groups (with moderate perceived popularity) whose members are best liked, on average. Another possibility is that as status (perceived popularity) becomes a defining characteristic of crowds, likability (sociometric popularity) serves to further differentiate clusters of high-status youth. In interviews with a sample of Dutch early adolescents, de Bruyn and Cillessen (2006b) discovered two distinct subgroups of high-status youth. The "prosocial populars" were described as friendly, helpful, social, and academically engaged, whereas the "populists" were regarded as arrogant, cocky, aggressive, and antisocial. Applying cluster analysis to a similar sample of Dutch females of the same age, de Bruyn and Cillessen (2006a) found five groups varying in perceived popularity and school engagement. Both high status and

low status groups were further differentiated, in part, by their average level of sociometric popularity. The "popular studious" group was well liked by peers, whereas the "popular disengaged" group was not.

Stability of Popularity Ratings

To further understand the disaggregation of popularity ratings over time, it is helpful to consider the stability of these ratings. Few investigators have examined sociometric ratings over periods longer than a year. One important exception is a study by Cillessen and Mayeux (2004a), who tracked popularity scores of a sample of middle class U.S. youth from grades 5 through 9. Year-to-year stability correlations were quite high (0.50–0.90), but 4-year stability coefficients were more modest (0.40–0.50). Perceived popularity ratings were more stable among boys than girls, whereas sociometric popularity scores were more stable among girls than boys. Among girls, perceived popularity had higher stability coefficients than sociometric popularity; the pattern was not as clear among boys. Both ratings had lower stabilities across school transition years (from elementary to middle school, and from middle to high school) than nontransition years.

School transitions precipitate transformations in the peer social system (Kinney, 1993) and this process may serve to differentiate sociometric and perceived popularity. In some school contexts, for example, ethnic background becomes a stronger basis for friend selection and group formation as young people move into middle school. In a sample of 6th graders attending multiethnic schools in California, Bellmore, Nishina, Witkow, Graham, and Juvonen (2007) noted a within-ethnic group bias in sociometric popularity ratings of Latino, Asian American, and European American students: Each of these groups tended to nominate coethnic peers as well liked. African American students showed more of a global bias, naming coethnic peers as well-liked and disliked, but ignoring nonethnic peers in their nominations. As variables such as ethnicity become more salient to adolescents, they affect the identification or formation of in-groups and out-groups. In turn, this affects popularity ratings. It is wise for investigators to keep these social processes in mind as they trace individuals' popularity among peers across adolescence.

Correlates of Popularity

One variable that consistently differentiates sociometric and perceived popularity is aggression. As a general rule, aggression enhances one's status, but detracts from likeability (Cillessen & Borch, 2006; Sandstrom & Cillessen, 2006). Researchers have been intrigued particularly by the positive relation between aggression and perceived popularity because it defies the consistent findings in childhood samples that aggression detracts from a child's "popularity" (what becomes labeled as sociometric popularity in studies of older youth) among classmates. The association between aggression and perceived popularity builds over time. Rose, Swenson, and Waller (2004) found that aggression was negatively associated with young people's status among classmates in 3rd grade and not significantly related to status in grade 5, but then grew more positively related to status from grades 7 to 9. The pattern was stronger for measures of relational than physical aggression (also referred to as "overt aggression"). Becker and Luthar (2007) found that the connection between aggression and perceived popularity was as strong among urban, economically disadvantaged, ethnic-minority early adolescents as among their counterparts in an affluent, predominantly European American suburban school.

Longitudinal studies have begun to flesh out the association between aggression and popularity. Rose, Swenson, and Waller (2004) found that relational aggression significantly predicted girl's perceived popularity 6 months later in a sample of predominantly European American early adolescents, whereas physical aggression was negatively correlated with later perceived popularity over the same short period. Interestingly, initial rates of perceived popularity predicted later relational aggression scores in this sample, but not physical aggression. However, in a similar sample of 5th graders, Sandstrom and Cillessen (2006) found that perceived popularity did predict rates of overt aggression 3 years later, but only among boys. Across grades 5–9, Cillessen and Mayeux (2004a) reported that physical aggression was increasingly accepted by young people, but had diminishing effects on perceived popularity. However, whereas relational aggression became more denounced across this grade span, it was increasingly associated with perceived popularity, but especially among girls. Following adolescents from grade 5 through the end of high school, Cillessen and Borch (2006) concluded that girls must accept a trade-off: Relational aggression increasingly secures their status among peers, but at the expense of being well liked. Boys in this study were more successful at negotiating high status while remaining well liked, possibly because they were not punished as much by peers for their aggressive behavior.

The findings in these sociometric studies reflect interpersonal dynamics noted by ethnographers who have carefully examined interaction processes in girls' friendship groups (Adler & Adler, 1998; Simmons, 2003; Wiseman, 2002). Group leaders are observed to employ aggressive tactics (especially relational aggression), or direct their subordinates to do so, in order to preserve their position or maintain the integrity of the clique. Similar studies of boys' friendship group interactions during adolescence are lacking. Such studies of relationship processes are important to pursue to understand the connection between popularity and aggression more completely. Schwartz, Gorman, Nakamoto, and McKay (2006), for example, found that, across grades 9 and 10 in a sample of lower-class youth, as perceived popularity increased, so did inattentiveness to school, but only among youth who are high in aggression. Rose, Swenson, and Waller (2004) reported that the association between relational aggression and poor friendship quality was stronger among those who were high in perceived (as well as sociometric) popularity. Associations between aggression and popularity are not entirely straightforward and deserve closer scrutiny.

Investigators have attended to characteristics beyond aggression as correlates of popularity, finding that sociometric popularity is generally associated with positive adjustment and prosocial behavior, whereas correlates of perceived popularity are not as clear (Becker & Luthar, 2007; Cillessen & Rose, 2005). In an ethnically and economically diverse sample of high school youth in the United States, Mayeux, Sandstorm, and Cillessen (2008) found that, controlling for sociometric popularity, perceived popularity in grade 10 predicted rates of alcohol use and sexual activity 2 years later. The inverse was not true (except that cigarette use in grade 10 predicted later perceived popularity for boys), nor was sociometric popularity in grade 10 a significant predictor of problem behavior in grade 12.

Variable-centered analyses can mask the tendency for personal characteristics to correlate with popularity in different ways among subgroups of youth. De Bruyn and Cillessen (2006a) applied cluster analysis to self-, peer, and teacher ratings of popularity and academic behaviors to identify groups of Dutch girls, age 13–14. The five clusters that emerged ranged from high-status and studious girls, who displayed high sociometric popularity and prosocial behavior, to low-status, disengaged youth, who had poor academic records, were regarded as unlikable, and were often subjected to bullying.

Methodological Considerations

A major concern in sociometric studies of adolescents is obtaining an adequate sample to achieve reliable ratings. Unlike younger children, whose peer relationships are usually confined to a self-contained classroom, adolescents are likely to draw associates and establish their reputation among a larger network of peers. Asking adolescents to rate or even draw

nominations from this broader network of peers is a foreboding task. So is the challenge of obtaining high participation rates from an entire school grade. Internal review board policies in several countries, requiring documented parental consent for all participants, even those who are nominees but not respondents, further complicate data gathering, often resulting in biased samples with restricted participation among immigrant, minority, and economically disadvantaged youth.

In an effort to respond to these issues, Prinstein (2007) compared three ways of obtaining sociometric ratings: gathering data from as many students in the targeted grade level as possible (the standard, "full rating" procedure), relying on ratings from a random subgroup of students (a small, randomly chosen subset of the full sample), and using a panel of social experts (nominated by teachers as especially attuned to peer social dynamics). As a group, the experts enjoyed higher ratings (from the full sample) of sociometric popularity than either other rating group. Their judgments of perceived popularity were highly correlated with those of the full sample (around 0.90); correlations between the two groups on sociometric popularity were also substantial (around 0.60). Correlations between the random sample and full sample were also significant, but at slightly lower levels than the experts and full sample. Prinstein concluded that impaneling experts may be a viable alternative to drawing sociometric data from the much larger sample usually expected in sociometric studies.

The different patterns that emerge in person centered (cluster) analyses than variable centered approaches underscore the value of applying a variety of methods to examining popularity, as well as other characteristics associated with adolescent peer relations. The sociometric task used to rate adolescents' popularity varies among studies. Some investigators rely on nominations, whereas others have respondents rate each peer. The number of nominations permitted is sometimes limited and other times unrestricted. Questions used to elicit nominations for sociometric popularity vary, although, curiously, researchers tend to approach perceived popularity more directly by asking respondents who is "popular" (or how popular or unpopular a given student is) without elaborating on the meaning of popularity. The need for more standardized measures and strategies is debatable. Although standardization facilitates direct and valid comparison of findings across studies, it constrains the discovery of social dynamics that often emerge when slightly different methods are employed to address similar questions.

Summary

The burgeoning research on popularity in adolescence underscores the need to attend to features of the adolescent social system in seeking to understand how personal characteristics affect adolescent peer relations. The distinction between perceived and sociometric popularity is fundamental and dramatic, yet evolving over the course of adolescence. It may well depend on the composition of the peer system as well, although Becker and Luthar's (2007) research suggests that there are strong similarities in the meanings of these terms across different social ecologies.

Some may question whether popularity is best regarded as a personal characteristic that affects social relationships or a quality of relationships. Although most investigators regard it as the former, evaluations of an individual's popularity often reflect how an adolescent is perceived to be integrated into the social system. There are also hints that one's popularity changes as the social system changes (at school transition points). In future research, both perspectives on popularity should be considered.

Aggression and Victimization

Studies of peer-related aggression are not focused exclusively on connections to young people's sociometric status. In previous investigations, especially those dealing with younger populations, scholars have demonstrated that children high in aggression have comparatively more difficulty making and keeping friends, especially if they are inclined to attribute aggressive intent to ambiguous behavior of peers (Rubin et al., 2006). Often, these studies have focused on physical aggression, or what is now more commonly referred to as overt aggression. Current interest has concentrated on the prevalence and effects of different types of aggression, especially the distinction between overt and relational aggression. Using vignettes to measure hostile attributional bias in a sample of 4th- through 6th-grade girls, Crain, Finch, and Foster (2005) were surprised to discover that hostile attributional bias was not significantly related to adolescents' level of relational aggression (as rated by peers). It is possible that the vignettes failed to measure the cognitive processes captured by previous studies of the subject, but it is also possible that the bias applies less to those who are inclined to relational, as opposed to overt aggression.

French, Jansen, and Pidada (2002) speculated that the higher rates of relational aggression found among girls, compared to boys, in North America might be mitigated in more collectivist cultures. They compared references to aggression among 5th and 8th graders in the United States and Indonesia who were asked to name two peers they disliked and then explain why they disliked them. There were no significant cultural differences in references to verbal aggression, but physical aggression was mentioned more often by Indonesian youth. As in previous studies, girls noted relational aggression issues more often than boys.

Most recent studies of adolescents have focused on youth as victims rather than perpetrators of aggression, often exploring samples other than predominantly middle-class European Americans, who have dominated previous research. Storch and Masia-Warner (2004) found that rates of relational and overt aggression among students in an all-female, urban parochial high school (still predominantly White and middle class) were comparable to those previously reported in coeducational samples. Girls who encountered only relational aggression or both types of aggression were relatively high in social anxiety and loneliness. These associations were reduced (although still significant) among girls who received higher levels of social support from peers. In a primarily African American sample of adolescents, Goldstein, Young, and Boyd (2007) found that girls witnessed and experienced more relational aggression than boys. The more relational aggression these adolescents perceived, the more unsafe they felt at school and, among boys, the more likely they were to bring a weapon to school. Thus, at least in this context, relational victimization appeared to have similar consequences to the more physical forms of intimidation documented in previous research. In a sample of Italian mid-adolescents, Gini (2008) found, not surprisingly, that the more adolescents encountered overt or relational victimization, the less satisfied these youth were with their friendships. However, the association was mitigated among adolescents expressing a relatively low need for an affective relationship, but only with regard to relational—not overt—aggression.

These studies suggest that relational aggression may be as salient, if not more so, than overt aggression in adolescents' peer interactions, perhaps because over the course of adolescence, relational aggression becomes more common (and more widely accepted) than physical aggression. Not all investigators are convinced that type of aggression is the key factor in understanding the impact of victimization, however. Nylund, Bellmore, Nishina, and Graham (2007) assessed students' experiences with various types of victimization across 3 years in a lower socioeconoic status (SES), urban, multiethnic sample of U.S. early adolescents. Using latent class analysis, they discovered that amount of victimization differentiated respondents more clearly than type of victimization. Unfortunately, their measure of victimization included only one or two items per type, suggesting that the salience of degree of victimization (rather than type of aggression) may have been a measurement artifact.

The transformation across adolescence in the most common forms of aggression raises the issue of whether young people with particular personal characteristics remain equally vulnerable across this age period. Little attention has been given to this issue. Because aggression (especially overt aggression) is more common in early adolescence, most research has concentrated on this period. This may be sensible from an intervention point of view, but to fully appreciate how individual characteristics influence or are influenced by experiences with peers, investigators must devote more attention to older age groups. Likewise, as will become apparent later in this chapter, it would be useful to differentiate more clearly—both conceptually and methodologically—between identifying oneself as a bully or victim and being the perpetrator or recipient of aggressive behavior.

Friendship Motives and Expectations

Issues of popularity and aggression deal with peer relations more generally. Some research concentrates on personal characteristics related to particular types of peer associations. Much of this work is focused on friendship.

In previous decades, several North American scholars have traced developmental changes in the characteristics that young people consider most critical in their friendships (e.g., Bigelow & LaGaipa, 1980). From early to middle adolescence they have noted a transformation as young people ease up on efforts to retain intense, intimate, and exclusive friendships focused on mutual trust in favor of more relaxed alliances that recognize the needs of partners both within and beyond the relationship. Entry into longer term romantic relationships reduces the need for highly intimate friendship, and actually enhances the value of friends who remain loyal and committed through all sorts of interpersonal experiences.

Recently, some scholars have questioned whether the same transformations are anticipated among youth in more collectivist cultures, who not only emphasize interdependence in relationships more than their counterparts in individualistic cultures but may also delay romantic and sexual alliances until late adolescence. Gummerman and Keller (2008) compared friendships expectations in samples of Icelandic, Russian, German, and Chinese youth who ranged in age from 7 to 15. Differences across samples in how data were collected obfuscate interpretation of findings, but some cultural distinctions do conform to the authors' expectations. For example, older Icelandic youth put less emphasis on trust and sharing feelings, and more on simple conversation, than Russian and Chinese adolescents did. Such findings remind scholars that friendships, or peer relationships more generally, occur within a sociocultural context and can be heavily influenced by norms and expectations within the broader context—an idea to which we will return at the end of the chapter.

Even so, there are specific characteristics that can facilitate or inhibit adolescents' capacities to form effective friendships. Marsh, Allen, Ho, Porter, and McFarland (2006) demonstrated that, over time, early adolescents with high levels of ego development are more successful in forming close attachments to friends, establishing intimate friendships, and achieving a high level of (sociometric) popularity among peers. However, Parker, Low, Walker, and Gamm (2005) traced inclinations toward and reputations for jealousy in friendships among White, lower to middle-class rural early adolescents in the United States. Feelings of jealousy exacerbated a sense of loneliness, even among those who lacked friends and were not well liked. Girls reported more jealous feelings over friends than did boys and also had a stronger reputation for jealousy in general peer relations. Nevertheless, jealousy had equivalent effects across gender on peer victimization, loneliness, and social rejection. Jealousy regarding friends diminished with age, as one would expect from observations of age changes in friendship expectations in

individualistic societies (Bigelow & LaGaipa, 1980).

Peer Crowd Identities and Orientations

Complementing the work on individual characteristics that shape or affect friendships is a handful of studies concerned with adolescents' crowd affiliations. Recall that crowds are reputation-based clusters of youth, whose function in part is to help solidify young people's social and personal identity (Brown, Mory, & Kinney, 1994). Accordingly, it is reasonable to ask how adolescents select a crowd with which to identify, or are driven to this choice by personal characteristics.

Two studies have examined this process prospectively, tracing the personal traits or behaviors in preadolescence or early adolescence that predict crowd membership later in adolescence. Prinstein and La Greca (2002) examined how measures of depression, loneliness, anxiety, and self-esteem, gathered when a multiethnic sample of U.S. children were in grades 4–6 (Time 1), foreshadowed the peer crowd with which they identified 6 years later, in the middle of high school (Time 2). Mean scores for members of the four crowd comparison groups—jocks/populars, brains, burnouts, and average or no crowd affiliation—were significantly different on two of the Time 1 measures, and on all four measures when readministered at Time 2. The crowds also differed on cross-time trajectories for all four measures. The advantaged position that brain crowd members enjoyed on all four measures at Time 1 dissipated, to the point that they had marginally higher anxiety levels at Time 2 than other groups. By comparison, jocks/populars improved across time from relatively moderate to much healthier levels on all four outcomes. It is not possible to determine from these data whether these trajectories in adjustment measures presaged entry into particular peer groups or were affected by crowd identification that occurred earlier than Time 2, but the data suggest that there is some predictability prior to adolescence in young people's ultimate crowd identification.

In a related study, Stone et al. (2008) traced how self characteristics in grade 6 among a sample of working-class European American youth predicted crowd identities 4 years later, at about the same age as they were measured in the study by Prinstein and La Greca (2002). The crowd identities from which respondents chose were fashioned from a popular movie at the time of data collection and featured groups similar to those commonly observed using more systematic and ecologically grounded methods for identifying major crowds in a given social milieu (see, e.g., Brown, Herman, et al., 2008; or Prinstein & La Greca, 2002). Stone and colleagues used discriminant function analysis to determine how closely each crowd compared on members' Time 1 personal traits. The two functions emerging in each gender-specific analysis underscore the importance of academic orientation, athletic competence, and physical appearance in early adolescence as setting young people on trajectories toward certain crowd identities in mid-adolescence.

Two recent and simpler cross-sectional studies elaborate on the notion that crowd identifications are linked to personal characteristics. Both of these studies involve samples outside of North America. Heaven, Ciarrochi, Vialle, and Cechavicuite (2005) presented freshmen (age 12) in Catholic high schools in Australia with a list of five crowd types garnered from previous studies in the United States (including Prinstein & La Greca, 2002) and asked them which group was most like the "kind of students you hang around with." Comparing responses to participants' self-reports of parenting styles and depressive attributional style (DAS), they found that "rebels" were markedly higher than other groups on DAS, but low on exposure to authoritative parenting. The studious group had the most adaptive DAS. Delsing et al. (2007) used a more sophisticated strategy to identify crowds uniquely relevant to their sample of Dutch youth in grades 7–12. Factor

analyses were used to reduce the list of crowds to four major dimensions, which were then compared on measures of internalizing and externalizing problems. High scores on the achievement oriented and conventional dimensions were associated with low scores on externalizing measures, whereas high scores on the "alternative" and the urban crowd dimensions were positively associated with both internalizing and externalizing variables. In both studies, members of less conventional crowds displayed higher rates of problem behavior.

In a study of students from several multiethnic high schools in the United States, Brown, Herman, et al. (2008) pursued a different question: whether ethnic minority group members who identified with an ethnically defined crowd (as opposed to a group based on abilities, interests, or peer social status) were drawn to the crowd by factors associated with ethnic discrimination and isolation or variables associated with a positive ethnic identity. The study also compared the same youth, classified into ethnically oriented or nonethnic crowds as determined by peer ratings. In both analyses, the most consistent correlate of ethnic crowd affiliation was the ethnic homogeneity of their friendship network. There were additional correlates, some supporting the argument that ethnically based crowds exacerbate prejudice and discrimination, and others suggesting that they may facilitate positive ethnic identity.

The connection in Brown, Herman, et al.'s (2008) study between crowd identity and friendship networks, however, hints at a missing link in the research on peer-related personal characteristics. With rare exceptions, scholars have confined their study to one segment of the peer system: relationships in general, dyadic associates (mostly friendship), or crowd affiliation. Complementing these valuable efforts should be more studies that cut across segments. How are crowd affiliations conditioned by friendship networks? Why is the association between perceived popularity and aggression strong in one crowd or friendship group and not another?

Conclusions

The extensive literature concerning peer-relevant personal characteristics has yielded important insights about peer processes in adolescence, but its conceptual foundations are tenuous. Some scholars base their research on a broad array of theories, and others on no theory at all. This contributes to the segmented and disjunctive sense that one gets from reading this literature, and it compromises the task of comparing findings across studies or linking results across research questions. It would be helpful to have a core set of theories that can spawn a more systematic approach to issues in this area of research.

FEATURES OF PEER RELATIONSHIPS

Although it is certainly important to examine individual predispositions, abilities, and attitudes that allow adolescents to connect to peers, at some point the study of adolescent peer relations must turn to the actual relationships forged with age-mates. To a modest but increasing extent, researchers have moved beyond their prior concentration on peer-related characteristics of individuals to consider the characteristics of peer relationships. One classic concern that still receives some attention is similarity in friendship—the degree to which friends are more similar to each other than random pairings of individuals, or the traits on which similarity between friends is strongest. Because evidence of such similarity is overwhelming (our third point of conventional wisdom), most investigators have progressed to other topics. Chief among these is the quality of friendship. Yet friendship is not the only major type of affiliation that adolescents forge with peers. A small cadre of researchers has shifted focus from friends to enemies, examining the frequency and features of mutual antipathies. A common example of such dyads is the bully and her or his victim, but it also includes sets of antagonists who are on more equal footing. Finally, there is a small set of studies oriented toward

the features of peer groups. We comment on research in each of these four areas.

Similarity Between Friends

In the past, researchers devoted considerable attention to the degree and derivation of similarity between pairs of individuals who were close friends. Key questions included whether friends' similarity arose from selection (the process of choosing someone as a friend who is already similar to oneself), socialization (growing similar to one another through interaction), or both processes, and whether degree of similarity was an important factor in the quality or duration of the relationship or in partners' individual adjustment. Some fairly simple assessments of friend similarity still appear in the literature. For example, using the Add Health data set, Kao and Joyner (2004) discovered that most adolescents named a peer from their own racial or ethnic group as a best friend, and the higher a peer was on respondents' list of five closest same-sex peers, the more likely they were to report engaging in activities with the peer. Generally, however, analyses have grown more sophisticated.

Daddis (2008) used difference scores to compare beliefs about personal jurisdiction (i.e., beliefs about whether adolescents or parents should have authority over various decision; see chapter 7, vol. 1 of this *Handbook*) among dyads of friends (individuals who chose each other as close friends) or nonfriends (neither named the other as a friend). His expectation that friends would have more comparable beliefs was supported only occasionally, and the moderating effects of age, duration of the friendship, and degree of interaction were inconsistent and sometimes contrary to the author's hypotheses. Nevertheless, the methodological approach used in the study was promising. In a sample of urban, economically disadvantaged, ethnic minority early adolescents, Card and Hodges (2006) found that friend dyads (reciprocal nominations on a sociometric measure) shared more common targets of aggression than nonfriend dyads, and the more that dyad members had a reputation among peers as aggressive, the more targets of aggression they had in common. Their analyses point to the significance of coalitions in bullying behavior among youth with this demographic profile.

One of the most intriguing recent studies focusing on friendship similarity—and complementarity—is Guroglu, van Lieshout, Haselager, and Scholte's (2007) longitudinal analysis of bullying and psychological adjustment in a large sample of Dutch youth. The authors identified friend dyads (reciprocated nominations), then used dyad mean and discrepancy scores on self-reports of bullying and victimization, along with peer reports of various social behaviors, as the basis for a cluster analysis to identify different types of dyads. Three major clusters emerged: socially withdrawn dyads (high mean scores on victimization and low peer ratings of prosocial behavior, but also high discrepancy scores on most variables), prosocial dyads (high ratings for prosocial behavior and low scores on other variables, with generally low discrepancy scores), and antisocial dyads (high mean as well as discrepancy scores on antisocial behavior and bullying). The authors then used cluster analysis again, within cluster types, to further differentiate each type of friendship. As expected, they found that socially withdrawn youth often paired with a more socially accepted peer, and antisocial youth often befriended a peer with an antisocial but less bullying-oriented background. In other words, many friend dyads featured basic similarity, but also complementarity on certain characteristics. Subsets of dyads within the three major clusters were distinctive on several psychosocial outcomes; they also differed from classmates who did not have reciprocated friendships in distinctive ways.

These findings affirmed the authors' hypotheses, based on previous studies, that bullies often pair up with aggressively oriented peers who act more as assistants or audience, rather than coparticipants in their bullying exploits.

Likewise, socially withdrawn and victimized youth pursue friendships with a peer who is socially skilled enough to avoid victimization, and thereby shield the victimized adolescent to some extent from the ravages of peers. True similarity in friendship is most common among a subset of adolescents who are prosocial in orientation. Using similarity/complementarity analyses to identify different types of friend dyads and explore their implications for adolescent adjustment is a particularly promising approach for future research.

Friendship Quality

Along with studies of peer popularity, research on the quality of adolescent friendships has been plentiful in recent years. Many of these investigators have employed one of three standard measures of quality: the Friendship Quality Scale (FQS; Bukowski, Hoza, & Boivin, 1994), the Friendship Quality Questionnaire (FQQ; Parker & Asher, 1993), or the Network of Relationships Inventory (NRI; Furman & Buhrmester, 1985), but some studies feature observational assessments or self-report measures of more specific aspects of relationship quality. Along with efforts to sketch basic features of friendship quality, investigators have been concerned with both the antecedents and the correlates or consequences of friendship quality, and occasionally with ways in which it moderates associations between other variables and adolescent adjustment.

Basic Features

The nature of gender differences has preoccupied some researchers, with the general expectation that female adolescents manifest higher quality, more intimate relationships than males (e.g., Radmacher & Azmitia, 2006). For example, Brendgen, Markiewicz, Doyle, and Bukowski (2002) found more positive (and fewer negative) friendship features among Canadian adolescent girls than boys, using both self-reports (FQS) and observer ratings (which were substantially correlated with each other). Curiously, boys self-disclosed primarily to their best friend, whereas girls self-disclosed rather evenly across their friend network.

Ethnicity has also been a basic issue in research on friendship quality. In a short-term (6-month) longitudinal study of middle-class Canadian youth from various ethnic backgrounds, Schneider, Dixon, and Udvari (2007) found that interethnic relationships were less stable than ethnically homogeneous friendships. Only 45% of interethnic relationships continued at both measurement points, compared to nearly 70% of ethnically homogeneous alliances. Interethnic relationships were also rated (by participants) as lower in positive qualities, more competitive, and more conflictual at both time points. The authors speculated that coethnic friendships may be advantageous at this age period because they facilitate ethnic identity development and allow for consistency and maintenance of cultural beliefs. Nguyen and Brown (in press) reached a similar conclusion in their study of immigrant Hmong teenagers in the United States.

Occasionally, investigators consider more specific characteristics than the general features tapped by friendship quality measures. Updegraff et al. (2004) explored perceptions of control in friendships among European American, lower- to middle-class, rural youth in the United States. Generally, adolescents with unequal distributions of control did not report less positive experiences than peers in more balanced friendships. However, those who felt more controlling in their friendships did report moderately higher levels of conflict. Also, there was some consistency in control levels across relationships: Perceived control in sibling relationships was associated with perceived control in friendships, and boys' reported level of control in their friendships corresponded to their fathers' reports of control in their spousal relationship.

Antecedents of Friendship Quality

An important objective of researchers is to identify factors that contribute to the quality of adolescent friendships. As in studies of popularity, aggression has received considerable attention in this regard. Cillessen, Jiang, West, and Laszkowski (2005) identified same-sex friendship dyads (reciprocal nomination as close friends) within a sample of working- to lower-middle-class high school students, then applied the actor–partner interdependence model to data from the dyads to get more accurate estimates of the effects of aggression on friendship quality (measured with the FQS). Adolescents in this sample who rated themselves high in overt aggression depicted their friendship as high in conflict; both they and their partner tended to view the relationship as low in closeness and support. Adolescents who rated themselves high in relational aggression also portrayed their friendship as high in conflict and low in positive qualities, but their partner did not concur with this assessment. By contrast, adolescents who rated themselves high in prosocial behavior had friendships that both partners viewed as high in positive qualities. In a less sophisticated analysis of a demographically similar but younger sample, Rose, Swenson, and Carlson (2004) also found that overt aggression (rated by peers) was associated with lower friendship quality and higher rates of conflict with one's friend. Curiously, however, the more that adolescents were rated as high in relational aggression, the more positive their own ratings of friendship quality were. Most associations in this study, however, represented very small effects.

One other interesting study of antecedents of friendship quality examined Internet usage in a sample of European American adolescents (grades 9–11; Blais, et al., 2007). Across time, they found that using instant messaging was positively associated with friendship quality (FQQ), whereas use of chat rooms or gaming and other entertainment features of the Internet was negatively associated with friendship quality. Internet usage predicted (later) friendship quality, but the reverse was not true. The implication is that young people establish interpersonal patterns in their Internet use that affect the kinds of relationships that they can build with peers. As Internet usage grows among adolescents, the need for more careful research of its effects increases (see also chapter 9, this volume).

Correlates and Consequences of Friendship Quality

Like Cillessen et al. (2005), Burk and Laursen (2005) employed the actor–partner interdependence model to obtain more accurate estimates of the effects of friendship quality on academic and psychological adjustment in an ethnically diverse, middle-class sample of early and middle adolescents. Comparing reports of respondents and their best same-sex friend (using the NRI and measures of interpersonal conflict), the investigators first affirmed that these reports were more similar than those of random pairs of subjects, indicating that the data reflected something more than simply a general portrait of the friendship relationship. They then discovered that perceptions of positive features of friendship were not as clearly correlated with outcome measures as reports of negative features, which were associated with poor psychological adjustment and lower grade point average. Especially among males, perceived conflict in the relationship also predicted poor outcomes.

Aikins, Bierman, and Parker (2005) followed a sample of middle-class European American youth across the middle school transition and found that pre-transition friendship quality (measured by the FQQ) predicted students' school adjustment, but only among those who retained their friendship across the transition. Nearly two-thirds of the sample named a new peer as their best friend in the posttransition interview, although 80% included their pretransition best friend in their list of close friends, posttransition.

Summary

Studies of friendship quality represent an important advance over previous research on friendship. Investigators have now ceased relying upon one adolescent to report their partner's as well as their own attitudes about or actions in the relationship. Moreover, they have derived new methodologies to coordinate data from both partners. These techniques provide better estimates of the compatibility of partners' perspectives, as well as the effects of relationship characteristics on individual adjustment.

Despite the expanding work on this topic, however, it is difficult to discern the common threads that unite much of the research. It would be helpful to see friendship quality probed more systematically, with reference to a common set of theoretically derived issues that could help to integrate findings across different studies and procedures. A stronger conceptual framework also might help scholars to integrate additional important variables in their designs, such as the duration or intensity (frequency of interaction) of the relationship. More work is needed on whether friendship quality serves as a moderator of other relationship patterns and effects. For example, can high-quality relationships buffer the effects of sociometric popularity (or its absence) on psychological adjustment?

Another task is to extend research on friendship features to important subgroups of the adolescent population. Diamond and Lucas (2004), for example, provided a provocative comparison of friendships among sexual minority and heterosexual adolescents. Their analyses focused more on network size and friendship stability than friendship quality, but the findings suggested that younger sexual-minority teenagers and those who were not yet open with associates about their orientation allowed few peers into their circle of intimate relationships, compared to older, open sexual-minority peers or heterosexual teenagers. However, older, open sexual minority respondents encountered greater loss of friends and fears about friendships than did other portions of the sample. Findings can be explained in terms of discrimination that sexual minority adolescents often encounter, but they leave open the question of the quality of relationships in this specific group and how quality affects their psychological well-being.

Antagonistic Relationships

Expanding research on friendships of sexual minority teens is just one way of diversifying the literature on adolescent peer relations. Researchers are beginning to recognize that, in addition to positive affiliations, many adolescents encounter more antagonistic relationships with peers. Growing attention to bullying and victimization should prompt scholars to look more carefully at bully–victim relationships, as well as other kinds of antagonistic alliances. Despite our call for more work on this topic (in the last edition of this *Handbook*), little has been forthcoming. In a review of the literature, Abecassis (2003) listed numerous forms of mutual antipathies, including former friends, bully–victim dyads, competitiors, and peers who simply dislike each other; former romantic partners might be added to this list. She also pointed to the need to clarify criteria and measurement strategies for identifying different forms of these relationships, as well as more understanding on the part of internal review boards about the importance of asking young people about such relationships. Methodological issues related to this domain of research are challenging (Hartup, 2003), especially until researchers settle on definitions of these relationships and ways to reliably identify them.

At this point there are some glimpses of the kind of research to come on this topic. A problem in studying the effects of mutual antipathies is separating the effects of the relationship from the effects of simply being rejected (disliked) by a peer. Witkow, Bellmore, Nishina, Juvonen, and Graham (2005) examined levels of internalized distress among adolescents who had a mutual antipathy (identified via sociometric data). Without controlling for rates of peer rejection, it appeared as if having a mutual antagonist was associated with higher internalizing symptoms, but when analyses were limited to respondents who had some level of peer rejection (i.e., whether in

the context of a mutual antipathy or not), having the antagonistic relationship actually was correlated with some positive outcomes, such as peer nominations of being "cool." This suggests that, despite the drawbacks of mutual antipathies, there may be some advantages for youth who suffer rejection from peers.

Veenstra et al. (2007) explored basic features of individuals involved in bully–victim dyads within a sample of Dutch preadolescents and early adolescents. Qualifying dyads were identified from sociometric procedures that asked respondents to name the peers whom they bully or by whom they were bullied. Not surprisingly, bullies picked on peers who were rejected by others and could be harassed with impunity. Bullies (but not victims) were more often male. But like other research on bullying, this investigation stopped short of scrutinizing the *relationship* forged by bully–victim pairs. Do bullies build sustained relationships with their targets? Do they focus on the same peer over a period of time, and if so, does that relationship evolve through phases, as do other dyadic peer relationships? How stable are interaction patterns in these relationships? Is there more of a tendency for the relationship to be interrupted by others (e.g., peers coming to the rescue of the victim or peers joining in the bully's attacks)? What characteristics of the bully or victim serve to interrupt, redirect, or terminate the association?

Such questions are relevant to a variety of antagonistic relationships, including group level antagonistic interactions that may occur between rival friendship groups, gangs, or peer crowds. Investigators must overcome the inclination to approach these relationships strictly in terms of the characteristics or behaviors of individual participants. Effective interventions concerning bullying and other forms of antagonistic relationships require a better understanding of the relational features of these phenomena.

Peer Group Relationships

As significant as friendships and other dyadic relationships are to adolescents, much of a teenager's time with peers in most societies is spent interacting together in larger groups. Over the past five years, efforts to explore the features of interaction based groups—friendship cliques, gangs, and the like—have stalled, as we could find few recent reports devoted to this topic. In the past, some of the most insightful work on peer group structures and functioning has been derived from ethnographic investigations. These, too, have been in short supply over the last decade. A modest exception is a report on perceptions of gangs among 77 Latino adolescents from low-income immigrant families (Lopez, Wishard, Gallimore, & Rivera, 2006). Through individual interviews, the researchers queried adolescents about their perceptions of gangs in their neighborhood. Adolescents distinguished between gangs and "crews," describing crews as more loosely organized, short-term, informal collectives, engaged in delinquent activities similar to that of gangs, but lacking the gang's initiation rituals or extremely violent activities. The higher the respondent's achievement level, the less likely he or she was to interact with gangs or crews or to be well acquainted with group members. Most of the sample perceived gangs in more negative terms than crews.

The difficulties of doing research on antisocial groups such as gangs are obvious, as young people fear recriminations for sharing information about groups that engage in deviant, sometimes violent, behavior. There are challenges in examining more prosocial peer groups as well, mostly in identifying group members, gaining access to the group, and winning group members' trust. Statistical programs capable of delineating groups often require high participation rates among members of a peer social system in order to define each person's position accurately. These are not new problems, however. Researchers simply need to pursue group-level peer phenomena in adolescence with renewed vigor, focusing especially on the long-neglected dynamics of friendship groups in middle adolescence.

One exemplar of the research needed is Kiuru, Aunola, Vuori, and Nurmi's (2007) assessment of the role of peer groups in adolescents' educational expectations. The researchers gathered data from 400 ninth graders in Finland, the year before Finnish students are tracked into different types of schools. Friendship nominations were used to identify groups within each participating school, differentiating between cliques, loose groups, and dyads. Each of these groups was characterized by the average level of members' educational expectations and academic achievement. Through multilevel modeling, done separately by gender, the authors discerned that the average level of adjustment in girls' groups predicted the group's level of short-term and long-term educational expectations. In boys' groups, by contrast, only the mean level of problem behavior of group members predicted group level educational expectations. Using the group as the unit of analysis is an important first step in understanding group dynamics that may influence individual members' behavior.

At the same time as research on interaction-based groups has slowed, there has been a modest resurgence of interest in the other level of adolescent peer groups: reputation-based crowds. Horn (2006) explored how adolescents' crowd affiliation affected decisions about allocating limited resources and justifications for their decision. Students self-identified as members of particular crowds, whose status had been ascertained in previous steps of the research, then responded to hypothetical scenarios about giving positions, privileges, or opportunities to someone associated with a high- or low-status crowd. Respondents claiming membership in high-status groups or no crowd allocated resources to high-status crowd members more often than low-status crowd members. High-status crowd members were more likely to appeal to social convention in justifying their decision, whereas low-status crowd members more often employed moral arguments. High-status crowd members also used stereotypes more often than individuals who claimed membership in no crowd. The findings suggest that crowd membership shapes not only members' actions but also their attitudes toward allocation of resources.

Garner, Bootcheck, Lorr, and Rauch (2006) employed a variety of techniques to discern the structure of peer crowds in five different schools in a metropolitan region. Techniques included self-report surveys from students attending the school, participant observations conducted over a semester, content analysis of school yearbooks, or insights from parents-as-researchers. In each school, the researchers attempted to ascertain the social climate of the peer system, noting stark contrasts among the schools. One school featured what might be regarded as a conventional peer structure, labeled by these researchers as the "pyramid of prep dominance." Groups were organized into a clear status structure, with jocks and preps at the apex and groups toward the bottom of the hierarchy feeling marginalized. In another school, the climate was one of "oppositional takeover," in which crowds such as the "gangstas" or "stoners" challenged the authority of both high-status crowds and adult authorities. The climate in the third school was described as "fragmentation," in which no crowd dominated, nor did the crowds (or students) seem to focus much attention on the school itself; indeed, students did not care enough about school to be interested in peer status structures. The lack of systematic and consistent measurement techniques raises questions about the credibility of these data. Differences in the size, location, ethnic composition, and degree of ethnic and socioeconomic diversity of schools also complicate interpretations of findings. Nevertheless, this portrait of radical differences in the organization of peer crowd systems does underscore the need to attend to larger group structures in seeking to understand individual and dyadic level facets of adolescent peer culture. One wonders, for example, what sort of structure existed in the school that Horn (2006) examined, and

how a different structure might yield different patterns of resource allocation.

PEER RELATIONSHIP PROCESSES

As evidence accumulates that adolescents with certain types of peer relationships (e.g., stable friendships, mutual antipathies, specific crowd affiliations) or relationships with specific features (e.g., high quality, conflict laden) are more prone to certain outcomes, the question looming large is precisely how peer relationships or relationship features contribute to those outcomes. There have been some sophisticated efforts to estimate the magnitude of peer effects. Kindermann (2007), for example, used social–cognitive mapping techniques to locate an almost complete 6th-grade cohort from one town into peer groups, then followed the students over time to tease out three possible sources of change in their levels of school engagement and achievement (group selection, group socialization, and similar treatment by members outside of their group). He was able to estimate with confidence how much of students' change in school behaviors was due to their peer group associates, but still not able to specify the mechanism of influence. What happens within peer relationships to facilitate changes in individuals? What are the processes by which certain outcomes are affected? What patterns of interaction facilitate adaptive or maladaptive behaviors? How do peers influence adolescents?

Kindermann acknowledges that these are very difficult questions to answer, requiring direct observation of social interactions, preferably in naturally occurring environments. Such observations are time consuming and logistically challenging, but researchers are making some headway.

Exemplary Studies

A recent but now classic example of new approaches is Granic and Dishion's (2003) careful analysis of conversation patterns in friend dyads. The investigators noted how antisocial youth tended to guide conversations in the way they react to partners' utterances. Through nonverbal cues (e.g., attention or inattention) and verbal responses (e.g., laughing or extending the topic with their own commentary), antisocially oriented pairs would selectively attend to deviant talk, thereby reinforcing a norm of antisocial behavior. Equally important was the fact that these adolescents were generally nonresponsive when friends introduced conversation about normative activities. Nondeviant friends responded very differently to similar utterances.

In more recent work, Dishion and colleagues have looked more carefully at conversation patterns among youth with different records of antisocial activity. They attend not only to the content of conversations and response patterns but also the level of organization in conversations—whether or not there is a flow of topics that is easy to follow. Comparing interaction patterns at ages 14, 16, and 18 in a sample of antisocial boys and their friends to conversations among a well-adjusted comparison group, Dishion, Nelson, and Winter (2004) noticed that the deviant group's conversations were more disorganized and unpredictable than the comparison group. However, the more organized antisocial adolescents' conversations were, the more likely they were to continue their deviant activity into adulthood. In other words, when conversations were sufficiently patterned to allow partners to reinforce antisocial utterances, the antisocial behavior was more likely to persist. A subsequent study indicated that these conversation dynamics applied to girls as well as boys (Piehler & Dishion, 2007).

Although the conversations of Dishion's respondents took place in a university laboratory, they seemed to approximate interchanges the young people were likely to have in actual daily encounters. Other investigators have attempted to approximate "real world" contexts in clever designs of more controlled laboratory experiments. For example, Gardner and Steinberg (2005) had samples of middle adolescents, late adolescents, and adults play

a computer game that involved driving a car across the screen. The further they drove, the more points they would earn, but also the more likely it was that they would encounter a stoplight and lose all of their points. Some participants played the game alone, whereas others played in the company of two peers, who were free to call out advice on what the player should do. Although individuals, on average, took more risks in the company of peers, the differences between behavior in the peer versus solo conditions were much more substantial (and significant) for late and, especially, middle adolescents than for adults. The age X condition effects were more pronounced for non-White than White respondents.

In an effort to determine how adolescents are influenced by peers during an effort to "break in" to an interaction-based group, Cohen and Prinstein (2006) involved a sample of American high school males of average social status in what they were led to believe was a chat room encounter with e-confederates who appeared to be either high or low in social status. The researchers used previous information collected on students in the school to construct groups of e-confederates whose identity (though not revealed) the subjects could infer. The e-confederates displayed aggressive and health-risk behaviors, and the experimenters tracked the degree to which subjects conformed to confederates' behavior. Subjects modeled this behavior when it emanated from ostensibly high-status peers, but actually rejected the same behavior when it came from what appeared to be low-status peers.

Peer Influence Processes

All three of the aforementioned studies are clever attempts to create controlled environments that can capture the types of behaviors adolescents would manifest in peer interactions in natural settings. Like their predecessors from decades ago (Costanzo & Shaw, 1966; Sheriff, 1961), these studies provide important insights into the processes that underlie peer group influences. Curiously, however, each study probes a different mechanism of peer influence. Dishion's work focuses on how a friend's response to an adolescent's utterances *reinforces* certain attitudes or behaviors and not others. Gardner and Steinberg focus more on situations in which peers *encourage* or perhaps even *pressure* an adolescent to behave in certain ways, and Cohen and Prinstein's electronic chat room allows (ostensible) peers to *display behaviors* that adolescents can model (or choose to scrupulously avoid).

Still missing, then, is a comprehensive framework of peer influence processes that would serve to tie together findings across these various studies. One effort to provide such a framework stipulates five different modes of peer influence, along with a series of personal and situational factors that can explain how and when these modes are enacted and responded to by adolescents (Brown, Bakken, et al., 2008). In addition to three of the modes of influence already mentioned (reinforcement, peer pressure, and behavioral display), the investigators refer to two others: *structuring opportunities*, a frequently overlooked mode in which peers provide occasions or contexts for the pursuit of particular behaviors, and *antagonistic behavior*, such as occurs in many bullying interactions. Other strategies could be added to this list. For example, it may be prudent to differentiate peer pressure, which involves a direct, overt, and express attempt to prescribe certain attitudes or activities and proscribe others, from peer encouragement, a less forceful effort to support certain behaviors. Obstruction—direct but not necessarily intentional interference with a course of action—is another often neglected form of influence. An example of obstruction would be when a peer asks a girl out whom another teenager was planning to pursue, thereby obstructing the teenager's opportunity to pursue a romantic relationship with the girl.

Brown, Bakken, et al.'s (2008) model stipulates further, however, that peer influences can vary in timing, intensity, and consistency as well as mode. That is, in responding a particular way, adolescents may be reacting to an immediate encounter with peer influence, such as the drivers in Gardner and Steinberg's experiment, or their recall of something that occurred in previous peer encounters, such as subjects' disinclination to model their behavior after low-status peers in Cohen and Prinstein's study (assuming that their decision to distance themselves from these peers stems from their recall of how they were derided at some point in the past). Brown and colleagues also argue that peer influence can vary in intensity and consistency. Not all of one's friends would necessarily laugh at one's accounting of deviant activities, or ignore talk about more normative events.

The model further suggests that responses to peer influence are conditioned by the target adolescent's openness to influence, the salience of the influencers, the nature of the relationship the target has with the influencer, and the target's ability and opportunity to be responsive to the influence. These details are reflected in some recent research relevant to peer influence processes. Ellis and Zarbatany (2007) found that short-term (3-month) effects of group membership on behaviors of Canadian early adolescents depended upon the group's position within the peer social system. Using a modified social cognitive mapping method to identify cliques, the investigators found that group level of deviance predicted individual change in deviance, but only among those who belonged to groups who were low in social preference (e.g., whose members were generally disliked by peers). Prosocial behaviors increased among respondents belonging to groups high in centrality (i.e., forming the core of the peer social system), but decreased among those in groups that were low in centrality. Adolescents' commitment to the peer group also seems to be an important factor. Verkooijen, et al. (2007) reported that strong identification with one of the risk-prone crowds in a sample of Danish 16- to 20-year-olds was associated with higher rates of substance use.

No single study can be expected to attend fully to Brown, Bakken, et al. (2008)'s model, or similar conceptualizations by others (e.g., Bukowski, Velasquez, & Brendgen, 2008). However, such conceptual frameworks can be used in planning studies so that results can be compared and integrated more easily across research programs.

Other Process Issues

Although most aspects of peer interaction can be thought of in terms of peer influence, it is not necessarily wise to do so. For example, there is a small cadre of studies that conceives of certain peer alliances in terms of attachment relationships (e.g., Freeman & Brown, 2001; Furman & Simon, 2006; Marsh et al., 2006); this is most common with reference to romantic issues (see chapter 4, this volume). Studies of attachment to friends or lovers, or investigations of how working models or attachment state of mind affects the course of peer relationships, are important to pursue.

Research on friendship quality as a general feature of the relationship may mask more specific interaction processes that affect the stability of the relationship. Schneider, Woodburn, Soteras del Toro, and Udvari (2005) added a scale assessing competition within the friendship to a more general measure of friendship quality. In a cross-national sample of early adolescents, they found that hypercompetitiveness was linked to conflict and often led to termination of the relationship, whereas, in some social contexts, friendlier social competition actually enhanced the closeness of male friends. Observational studies of such specific friendship processes would provide a better sense of what happens when one friend "crosses the line" and engages in behavior that damages, rather than enhances, the relationship. Little is known about the specific relationship repair mechanisms that adolescents enact to allow relationships to continue after conflicts, although there has been some effort in self-report studies to explore common conflict resolution strategies

that adolescents employ (Thayer, Updegraff, & Delgado, 2008).

There has been some effort to explore interaction patterns within friendship cliques. Most of this work is ethnographic and focuses on early adolescent girls (e.g., Finders, 1997). Until investigators accumulate a broader corpus of evidence about interaction among a wider array of adolescent groups, it is difficult to determine the role that such interactions play in adolescents' peer relations or their psychological and social development.

CONTEXTUAL INFLUENCES ON ADOLESCENT PEER RELATIONS

Over the past 2 decades, most North American investigators have ventured well beyond samples of middle class, European American youth, which dominated studies of peer relations through most of the previous century. In seeking more diverse samples, scholars often encounter instances in which cultural factors outside of the social world of adolescence shape the nature of peer interactions. Dealing with cultural issues is a challenge, even when samples are sufficiently large to consider the moderating role of culture or ethnicity on the issues being studied. Likewise, when investigators transfer their sampling frame from school- to community-based populations, or when they observe adolescent peer interactions in a specific activity context, they confront context-specific factors that can alter the nature of peer social dynamics significantly. Recall, for example, the different peer group structures that seemed to be present in different schools that Garner et al. (2006) observed. Although adolescents often attempt to escape the attention of adults and engage in peer interactions away from major social contexts, the truth is that peer relationships always proceed within a broader social context. Many investigators have intentionally explored the effects of contextual forces on adolescent peer relationships. We highlight some of this work to illustrate the numerous ways in which context should be considered in peer relations research.

Culture and Ethnicity

Although we have attended primarily to research on samples of North American youth in this review, there is a sizable literature on adolescent peer relations in other nations, particularly in Europe. The organization of everyday life for teenagers can vary dramatically among nations as a function of differences in such things as school organization, school attendance patterns, access to part-time employment and organized leisure activities, ethnic or cultural diversity within the country, and, consequently, in normative expectations about relationship processes. Within this diversity it can be challenging to ascertain which factors are most relevant for peer interactions.

Some investigators have focused on the general distinction between individualistic and collectivistic cultures as a factor that may shape peer relationships. For example, French, Pidada, and Victor (2005) compared the quality of friendship (using the FQQ) among early adolescents in the U.S. (virtually all were European American) with the same age group in Indonesia, a more collectivist culture that emphasizes harmonious group relations more than dyadic alliances. The researchers expected U.S. youth to be more focused on and affected by friendships than their Indonesian peers, and to some extent this was borne out in findings. Students in the United States rated their friendships as comparatively more intimate and more influential in enhancing self-worth, whereas Indonesian youth reported higher rates of conflict and use of friends for instrumental aid. A second study, involving college students in the two nations, indicated that Indonesian students engaged in more frequent and longer interactions with peers than U.S. college students, saw a wider variety of peer associates, and were more inclined to include others in interactions with close friends. In other words, friendships and peer relations appeared to be very important to youth in both nations, but the quality or character of relationships differed in accordance with distinctive norms of the two societies. It is noteworthy than French and

colleagues decided to standardize scores within each country because of cultural differences in response patterns (U.S. students showing greater inclination to select extreme values on a response scale). Attentiveness to this sort of measurement issue is important in cross-national research.

Of course, there often is cultural diversity within one nation that can play out in peer relations within a given community or school setting. Hamm, Brown, and Heck (2005) compared rates of cross-ethnic friendship nominations among youth from various ethnic backgrounds in multiethnic U.S. high schools. Controlling for school ethnic composition, which would affect the simple chances of selecting someone of another ethnicity as a friend, the investigators found that cross-ethnic friendships occurred at significantly lower rates than one would expect by chance (e.g., if adolescents selected friends randomly from available peers), especially for European American teenagers. The specific variables correlated with propensity to nominate cross-ethnic peers as friends differed among major ethnic groups. A strong academic orientation was an important factor for African American students, whereas high achievement level among Asian American youth was associated with *lower* likelihood of cross-ethnic friendships. Length of time living in the United States was a significant factor for Latino youth.

Ethnicity played a different role in Bellmore, Witkow, Graham, & Juvonen's (2004) intriguing study of peer victimization in multiethnic middle schools. Appealing to principles of person–context fit theory, the investigators speculated that victimization might have stronger negative effects on adolescents in contexts in which the behavior deviated more from norms of the predominant group in the context. Consistent with this expectation, the effects of victimization on social anxiety and loneliness were stronger as a function of the number of ethnic peers in the classroom. When victims had few peers in the setting, they could attribute their victimization to racial or ethnic prejudice, but if they were surrounded by ethnic peers, it was difficult to escape the conclusion that their plight was a function of some personal short-coming. The implication of this study is that ethnicity or cultural background may affect social relationships not simply through the way that individuals internalize cultural norms but also in the extent to which such norms dominate a specific social context. These are important factors to consider in research on populations diverse in terms of any characteristic (race, culture, gender, socioeconomic status, sexual orientation) that could affect values and expectations about peer relations.

Family Influences

One hallmark of adolescent peer relations is that, to a greater extent than in childhood, they occur out of range of immediate parental oversight. This does not mean, however, that parents and family have little impact on peer interactions. Investigators have probed numerous ways in which family impact can be felt in adolescents' social interactions with age-mates.

One factor is the way in which families shape the social orientations of their children. Sharabany, Eschel, and Hakim (2008) linked the friendship patterns of Arab youth in Israel to their perceptions of parenting style. They found that level of intimacy with same-sex friends correlated positively with maternal authoritativeness and also with fathers' parenting styles, but differently for each gender. Boys' level of intimacy with friends correlated positively with paternal authoritativeness and negatively with fathers' permissiveness, whereas friendship intimacy among girls correlated positively with paternal permissiveness and authoritativeness. These patterns probably reflect gender role expectations for youth in Arab society, as well as the distinctive child-rearing roles of mothers and fathers.

Families also may, in effect, launch a child on a trajectory toward a certain pattern of behavior, which then is either continued or deflected through relationships with peers. Past research indicates that problematic parenting or troubled parent–child relations in childhood can lead children to associate with deviant peers, which in turn promotes their own engagement in anti-social activities. In a recent illustration of this principle, Beyers and Seiffge-Krenke (2007) found that youth from three different family types, based on parenting practices and the quality of parent–child relationships, had distinctive rates of internalizing and externalizing behavior. However, these associations were significantly attenuated when the quality of peer relations was introduced as a mediating factor. The best outcomes were observed among females from individuated families, who seemed to launch their daughters on a pathway toward high psychosocial adjustment, which was reinforced through high-quality relationships with friends and romantic partners.

Researchers have also observed interactions between family and peer factors. In some cases, the quality of peer relationships can attenuate or exacerbate the ill effects of family characteristics on adolescent outcomes (Lansford, Criss, Pettit, Dodge, & Bates, 2003). In other cases, family functioning serves to moderate associations between peer experiences and adolescent adjustment. Both pathways emphasize the interconnectedness that continues to exist between family and peer settings over the course of adolescence. It is likely that the degree of interconnectedness depends to some extent on cultural factors, such as the cultural norms for peer relations that were observed in comparisons of U.S. and Indonesian society by French and colleagues. To date, however, the literature is not systematic and extensive enough to consider these higher order contingencies.

New Social Contexts for Peer Interaction: Internet Studies

The common assumption is that, for the most part, adolescent peer relations are carried out through face-to-face interactions in various physical contexts in the community—especially the school, extracurricular activity contexts, venues for leisure pursuits, and, to a diminishing extent, adolescents' homes. Although this is still likely to be true, another context is emerging as a major locus of peer interaction, namely, the world of electronic media: text messaging, Internet web pages, and other portions of cyberspace. Researchers are just beginning to explore these new media as social contexts. Much of the work to date has been devoted to simply cataloging the extent and type of interactions that adolescents pursue on electronic media.

Electronic media have the capacity to alter the nature of peer interactions dramatically. Adolescents are no longer confined to developing relationships with age-mates whom they physically encounter in three-dimensional space. Through web sites and chat rooms they can link up with other adolescents thousands of miles away. They can carry on extensive conversations with strangers about whom they have only the most rudimentary information (whatever appears in a person's comments in a chat room). They can adopt fictitious personae and pursue relationships with other individuals on the basis of a completely false identity. Alternatively, they can employ electronic media to extend interactions with peers whom they regularly meet face to face. They can even use electronic media to replace face-to-face interactions, as when two teenagers "text" each other from across the room, or in the midst of a school class.

Adults often worry that the flexibility of electronic media to create new social environments will draw adolescents away from "real-world" interactions that are an essential component of "normal" life in a culture. So, one important question to be pursued is whether adolescents use media to replace or simply augment more normative peer interactions. However, for adolescents who are anxious and insecure in their face-to-face interactions with peers, the Internet might offer an alternative way to pursue relationships in an environment that the young person can control more easily. Yet again, the potential anonymity of the Internet could make it an ideal venue

for aggressive behaviors; young people could engage in relational aggression toward specific peers with little worry that they will be caught and somehow punished for their behavior.

Valkenburg and Peter (2007) attempted to address some of these concerns in a survey of how a sample of Dutch youth aged 10–16 used the Internet. They found an association between Internet use and closeness to peers. For respondents who used the Internet primarily to communicate with existing friends, online communication increased their closeness to friends. Socially anxious youth were less likely to use the Internet, but when they did, they emphasized the opportunities it afforded to broaden their communication with others. This suggested that some young people find the Internet to be a viable alternative to face-to-face interactions, especially if they become anxious in pursuing such interactions.

Blais et al., (2008) found similar results in a short-term longitudinal study of Canadian high school students. The authors noted improvements over a one-year period in the quality of close friendships and romantic relationships among young people who used the Internet to communicate with existing associates (e.g., instant messaging), but declines among those who frequented chat rooms or gaming sites, where they interacted primarily with strangers. These findings emphasize that certain Internet modalities facilitate existing, face-to-face relationships, whereas other modalities interfere with them. These other modalities may be important in compensating for deficiencies in adolescents' existing social networks, although Blais et al.'s findings are not consistent with this speculation.

Concerns that the Internet may exacerbate rates of bullying or victimization have been addressed by several scholars. Juvonen and Gross (2008) conducted an anonymous survey with a sample of convenience (whoever wished to respond to the survey, which was posted online) about their experiences of being bullied online. Not surprisingly, most of the respondents had experienced bullying, both at school at through electronic media. Two-thirds of those who reported electronic bullying said they knew the perpetrator. Very few indicated that they reported their peers' aggressive behavior to adults. Both in-school and online victimization contributed independently to social anxiety levels.

These formative studies underscore the need for more systematic research on how electronic media are becoming an important context for peer interactions. They suggest that no single pattern of media use dominates, so the task before researchers is to sketch the various motivations and patterns of peer-related media usage that occurs, then carefully explore each pattern's effect on the quality and character of peer relationships, as well as the effects on social and psychological adjustment. Existing research on face-to-face interactions will serve as a blueprint for much of this work, but researchers must be open to the possibility that peer relationships and interactions are transformed, rather than simply extended, by electronic media.

FINAL COMMENTS

At this stage in its history, research on adolescent peer relations has grown remarkably diverse. No longer can the field be easily captured by a handful of key issues or dominant theories and research paradigms. This is both a blessing and a curse. Researchers are documenting the variety of ways in which peer relations help to mold the character and course of adolescent development. At the same time, without the guiding lights of previous decades it is very difficult to connect insights gleaned from one study to the next. There also seems to be a real danger that as the focus shifts to individual trees—very specific aspects of adolescents' encounters with peers—the research community will miss the forest by losing sight of peer relations in general and the way that these relations mesh with other aspects of young people's lives.

It is especially important that investigators maintain some awareness that most adolescents venture through several peer contexts within any given day, sometimes encountering them simultaneously. Encounters with aggressive peers occur immediately preceding or following, or perhaps even in the midst of, interactions with friends, and during these encounters adolescents must respond not only to the immediate situation but maintain an awareness of how it affects their perceived and sociometric popularity in the broader peer group. Most adolescents belong to more than one clique or friendship group; sometimes their various groups will intersect different crowds (Kindermann, 2007), forcing them to switch normative frames of reference as they shift from one set of interaction partners to the next. The advent of electronic media makes it difficult for adolescents to escape from peers, even when the peers are no longer physically present. As researchers carefully dissect the peer context to pursue studies of various specific aspects, they should not ignore opportunities to occasionally integrate information across research programs and issues, and to keep the big picture in mind.

This challenge is more easily accomplished when researchers work under the guidance of an integrative conceptual framework and the rigors of specific theories. Much of the current work in the field strikes us as relatively atheoretical, or based on conceptual frameworks too specific to a given research question to allow integration with a broader corpus of work. In preparing this review we have been reminded of Hartup's (2005) basic dictum that peer interactions are largely a matter of (1) individuals (2) in relationships (3) in social contexts. Although simple, this formula serves as a litmus test for researchers. If their efforts cannot easily be placed within this framework, and if connections cannot be easily made to other research at other levels of analysis, they need to refine the issue they are addressing or the way they are addressing it.

In the previous edition of this *Handbook*, we ended the chapter on peer relations by challenging researchers to unravel the complexities of this domain. Over the past 5 years that has been done, with a vengeance, and the task must continue. The new challenge is to pursue these complexities in a way that allows for a more coordinated, integrative understanding of how adolescents encounter peers and weave these encounters into the fabric of their daily lives.

REFERENCES

Abecassis, M. (2003). I hate you just the way you are: Exploring the formation, maintenance, and need for enemies. *New Directions for Child and Adolescent Development, 102,* 5–22.

Adler, P. A., & Adler, P. (1998). *Peer power: Preadolescent culture and identity.* New Brunswick, NJ: Rutgers University Press.

Aikins, J. W., Bierman, K. L., & Parker, J. G. (2005). Navigating the transition to junior high school: The influence of pre-transition friendship and self-system characteristics. *Social Development, 14,* 42–60.

Becker, B. E., & Luthar, S. S. (2007). Peer-perceived admiration and social preference: Contextual correlates of positive peer regard among suburban and urban adolescents. *Journal of Research on Adolescence, 17*(1), 117–144.

Bellmore, A. D., Nishina, A., Witkow, M. R., Graham, S., & Juvonen, J. (2007). The influence of classroom ethnic composition on same- and other-ethnicity peer nominations in middle school. *Social Development, 16*(4), 720–740.

Bellmore, A. D., Witkow, M. R., Graham, S., & Juvonen, J. (2004). Beyond the individual: The impact of ethnic context and classroom behavioral norms on victims' adjustment. *Developmental Psychology, 40*(6), 1159–1172.

Berndt, T. J., & Murphy, L. M. (2002). Influences of friends and friendships: Myths, truths, and research recommendations. In R. V. Kail (Ed.), *Advances in child development and behavior,* vol. 30 (pp. 275–310). San Diego, CA: Academic Press.

Beyers, W., & Seiffge-Krenke, I. (2007). Are friends and romantic partners the "best medicine?" How the quality of other close relations mediates the impact of changing family relationships on adjustment. *International Journal of Behavioral Development, 31,* 559–568.

Bigelow, B. J., & LaGaipa, J. J. (1980). The development of friendship values and choice. In H. C. Foot, A. J. Chapman, & J. R. Smith (Eds.), *Friendship and social relations in children* (pp. 15–44). New York: John Wiley & Sons.

Blais, J. J., Craig, W. M., Pepler, D., & Connolly, J. (2008). Adolescents online: The importance of Internet activity choices to salient relationships. *Journal of Youth and Adolescence, 37,* 522–536.

Brendgen, M., Markiewicz, D., Doyle, A. B., & Bukowski, W. M. (2002). The relations between friendship quality, ranked-friendship preference, and adolescents' behavior with their friends. *Merrill-Palmer Quarterly, 47,* 395–415.

Brown, B. B. (1990). Peer groups and peer cultures. In S. S. Feldman and G. R. Elliott (Eds.), *At the threshold: The developing adolescent* (pp. 171–196). Cambridge, MA: Harvard University Press.

Brown, B. B., Bakken, J. P., Ameringer, S. W., & Mahon, S. D. (2008). A comprehensive conceptualization of the peer influence process in adolescence. In M. J. Prinstein & K. Dodge (Eds.), *Understanding peer influence in children and adolescents* (pp. 17–44). New York: Guilford Press.

Brown, B. B., Herman, M., Hamm, J. V., & Heck, D. (2008). Ethnicity and image: Correlates of minority adolescents' affiliation with individual-based versus ethnically defined peer crowds. *Child Development, 79,* 529–546.

Brown, B. B., Mory, M., & Kinney, D. A. (1994). Casting adolescent crowds in relational perspective: Caricature, channel, and context. In R. Montemayor, G. R. Adams, & T. P. Gullotta (Eds.), *Advances in adolescent development,* vol. 6: *Personal relationships during adolescence* (pp. 123–167). Newbury Park, CA: Sage.

Brown, B. B., Von Bank, H., & Steinberg, L. (2008). Smoke in the looking glass: Effects of discordance between self- and peer rated crowd affiliation on adolescent anxiety, depression and self-feeling. *Journal of Youth and Adolescence, 37,* 1163–1177.

Bukowski, W. M., & Adams, R. (2005). Peer relationships and psychopathology: Markers, moderators, mediators, mechanisms, and meanings. *Journal of Clinical Child and Adolescent Psychology, 34,* 3–10.

Bukowski, W. M., Hoza, B., & Boivin, M. (1994). Measuring friendship quality during pre- and early adolescence: The development and psychometric properties of the Friendship Qualities Scale. *Journal of Social and Personal Relationships, 11,* 471–484.

Bukowski, W. M., Velasquez, A. M., & Brendgen, M. (2008). Variation in patterns of peer influence: Considerations of self and other. In M. J. Prinstein & K. Dodge (Eds.), *Understanding peer influence in children and adolescents* (pp. 125–140). New York: Guilford Press.

Burk, W. J., & Laursen, B. (2005). Adolescent perceptions of friendship and their associations with individual adjustment. *International Journal of Behavioral Development, 29,* 156–164.

Cairns, R. B., Leung, M.-C., & Buchanan, L. (1995). Friendships and social networks in childhood and adolescence: Fluidity, reliability, and interrelations. *Child Development, 66,* 1330–1345.

Card, N. A., & Hodges E. V. E. (2006). Shared targets for aggression by early adolescent friends. *Developmental Psychology, 42*(6), 1327–1338.

Cillessen, A. H. N., & Borch, C. (2006). Developmental trajectories of adolescent popularity: A growth curve modeling analysis. *Journal of Adolescence, 29,* 935–959.

Cillessen, A. H. N., Bukowski, W. M., & Haselager, G. J. T. (2000). Stability of sociometric categories. In A. H. N. Cillessen & W. M. Bukowski (Eds.), *Recent advances in the measurement of acceptance and rejection in the peer system. New direction for child and adolescent development* (no. 88; pp. 75–93). San Francisco: Jossey-Bass.

Cillessen, A. H. N., Jiang, X. L., West, T. V., & Laszkowski, D. K. (2005). Predictors of dyadic friendship quality in adolescence. *International Journal of Behavioral Development, 29,* 165–172.

Cillessen, A. H. N., & Mayeux, L. (2004a). From censure to reinforcement: Developmental changes in the association between aggression and social status. *Child Development, 76,* 147–163.

Cillessen, A. H. N., & Mayeux, L. (2004b). Sociometric status and peer group behavior: Previous findings and current directions. In J. B. Kupersmidt & K. A. Dodge (Eds.), *Children's peer relations: From development to intervention* (pp. 3–20). Washington, DC: American Psychological Association.

Cillessen, A. H. N., & Rose, A. J. (2005). Understanding popularity in the peer system. *Current Directions in Psychological Science, 14,* 102–105.

Cohen, G. L., & Prinstein, M. J. (2006). Peer contagion of aggression and health risk behavior among adolescent males: An experimental investigation of effects on public conduct and private attitudes. *Child Development, 77,* 967–983.

Cohen, J. M. (1977). Sources of peer group homogeneity. *Sociology of Education, 50,* 227–241.

Connolly, J., Furman, W., & Konarski, R. (2000). The role of peers in the emergence of heterosexual romantic relationships in adolescence. *Child Development, 71,* 1395–1408.

Costanzo, P. R., & Shaw, M. E. (1966). Conformity as a function of age level. *Child Development, 37,* 967–975.

Crain, M. M., Finch, C. L., & Foster, S. L. (2005). The relevance of the social information processing model for understanding relational aggression in girls. *Merrill-Palmer Quarterly, 51,* 213–249.

Daddis, C. (2008). Similarity between early and middle adolescent close friends' beliefs about personal jurisdiction. *Social Development, 17*, 1019–1038.

de Bruyn, E. H., & Cillessen, A. H. N. (2006a). Heterogeneity of girls' consensual popularity: Academic and interpersonal behavioral profiles. *Journal of Youth and Adolescence, 35*, 435–445.

de Bruyn, E. H., & Cillessen, A. H. N. (2006b). Popularity in early adolescence: Prosocial and antisocial subtypes. *Journal of Adolescent Research, 21*, 607–627.

Delsing, M. J. M. H., ter Bogt, T. F. M., Engels, R. C. M. E., & Meeus, W. H. J. (2007). Adolescents' peer crowd identification in the Netherlands: Structure and associations with problem behaviors. *Journal of Research on Adolescence, 17*, 467–480.

Diamond, L. M., & Lucas, S. (2004). Sexual-minority and heterosexual youths' peer relationships: Experiences, expectations, and implications for well-being. *Journal of Research on Adolescence, 14*, 313–340.

Dishion, T. J., Nelson, S. E., & Winter, C. E. (2004). Adolescent friendship as a dynamic system: Entropy and deviance in the etiology and course of male antisocial behavior. *Journal of Abnormal Child Psychology, 32*, 651–663.

Dunphy, D. C. (1969). *Cliques, crowds, and gangs.* Melbourne, Australia: Cheshire.

Eckert, P. (1989). *Jocks and burnouts: Social categories and identity in the high school.* New York: Teachers College Press.

Finders, M. J. (1997). *Just girls: Hidden literacies and life in junior high.* New York: Teachers College Press.

Freeman, H., & Brown, B. B. (2001). Primary attachment to parents and peers during adolescence: Differences by attachment style. *Journal of Youth and Adolescence, 30*, 653–674.

French, D. C., Bae, A., & Pidada, S. (2006). Friendships of Indonesian, South Korean, and U.S. college students. *Personal Relationships, 13*, 69–81.

French, D. C., Jansen, E. A., & Pidada, S. (2002). United States and Indonesian children's and adolescents' reports of relational aggression by disliked peers. *Child Development, 73*, 1143–1150.

French, D. C., Pidada, S., & Victor, A. (2005). Friendships of Indonesian and United States youth. *International Journal of Behavioral Development, 29*, 304–313.

Furman, W., & Buhrmester, D. (1985). Children's perceptions of the personal relationships in their social networks. *Developmental Psychology, 21*, 1016–1024.

Furman, W., & Simon, V. A. (2006). Actor and partner effects of adolescents' romantic working models and styles on interactions with romantic partners. *Child Development, 77*, 588–604.

Gardner, M., & Steinberg, L. (2005). Peer influence on risk taking, risk preference, and risky decision making in adolescence and adulthood: An experimental study. *Developmental Psychology, 41*, 625–635.

Garner, R., Bootcheck, J., Lorr, M., & Rauch, K. (2006). The adolescent society revisited: Cultures, crowds, climates, and status structures in seven secondary schools. *Journal of Youth and Adolescence, 35*, 1023–1035.

Gini, G. (2008). Association among overt and relational victimization and adolescents' satisfaction with friends: The moderating role of the need for affective relationships with friends. *Journal of Youth and Adolescence, 37*, 812–820.

Giordano, P. C., Longmore, M. A., & Manning, W. D. (2006). Gender and the meanings of adolescent romantic relationships: A focus on boys. *American Sociological Review, 71*, 260–287.

Goldstein, S. E., Young, A., & Boyd, C. (2007). Relational aggression at school: Associations with school safety and social climate. *Journal of Youth and Adolescence*, original paper.

Granic, I., & Dishion, T. J. (2003). Deviant talk in adolescent friendships: A step toward measuring a pathogenic attractor process. *Social Development, 12*, 314–334.

Gummerum, M., & Keller, M. (2008). Affection, virtue, pleasure, and profit: Developing an understanding of friendship closeness and intimacy in western and Asian societies. *International Journal of Behavioral Development, 32*, 218–231.

Guroglu, B., van Lieshout, C. F. M., Haselager, G. J. T., & Scholte, R. H. J. (2007). Similarity and complementarity of behavioral profiles of friendship types and types of friends: Friendships and psychosocial adjustment. *Journal of Research on Adolescence, 17*, 357–386.

Hamm, J. V., Brown, B. B., & Heck, D. J. (2005). Bridging the ethnic divide: Student and school characteristics in African American, Asian-descent, Latino, and White adolescents' cross-ethnic friend nominations. *Journal of Research on Adolescence, 15*, 21–46.

Hartup, W. W. (1999). Peer experience and its developmental significance. In Bennett, M. (Ed.), *Developmental psychology: Achievements and prospects* (pp. 106–125). New York: Psychology Press.

Hartup, W. W. (2003). Toward understanding mutual antipathies in childhood and adolescence. *New Directions for Child and Adolescent Development, 102,* 111–123.

Hartup, W. W. (2005). Peer interaction: What causes what? *Journal of Abnormal Child Psychology, 33,* 387–394.

Heaven, P. L., Ciarrochi, J., Vialle, W., & Cechavicuite, I. (2005). Adolescent peer crowd self-identification, attributional style, and perceptions of parenting. *Journal of Community and Applied Psychology, 15,* 313–318.

Horn, S. S. (2006). Group status, group bias, and adolescents' reasoning about the treatment of others in school contexts. *International Journal of Behavioral Development, 30,* 208–218.

Horn, S. S. (2007). Adolescents' acceptance of same-sex peers based on sexual orientation and gender expression. *Journal of Youth and Adolescence, 3,* 363–371.

Jiang, X. L., & Cillessen, A. H. N. (2005). Stability of continuous measures of sociometric status: A meta-analysis. *Developmental Review, 25,* 1–25.

Juvonen, J., & Gross, E. F. (2008). Extending the school grounds? Bullying experiences in cyberspace. *Journal of School Health, 78,* 496–505.

Kandel, D. B. (1978). Homophily, selection, and socialization in adolescent friendships. *American Journal of Sociology, 84,* 427–436.

Kandel, D. B., & Andrews, K. (1987). Processes of adolescent socialization by parents and peers. *International Journal of the Addictions, 22,* 319–342.

Kao, G., & Joyner, K. (2004). Do race and ethnicity matter among friends? Activities among interracial, interethnic, and intraethnic adolescent friends. *Sociological Quarterly, 45,* 557–573.

Killen, M., Henning, A., Kelly, M. C., Crystal, D., & Ruck, M. (2007). Evaluations of interracial peer encounters by majority and minority U.S. children and adolescents. *International Journal of Behavioral Development, 31,* 491–500.

Kindermann, T. A. (2007). Effects of naturally existing peer groups on changes in academic engagement in a cohort of sixth graders. *Child Development, 78,* 1186–1203.

Kinney, D. (1993). From "nerds" to "normals": Adolescent identity recovery within a changing social system. *Sociology of Education, 66,* 21–40.

Kiuru, N., Aunola, K., Vuori, J., & Nurmi, J.-E. (2007). The role of peer groups in adolescents' educational expectations and adjustment. *Journal of Youth and Adolescence, 36,* 995–1009.

Lansford, J. E., Criss, M. M., Pettit, G. S., Dodge, K. A., & Bates, J. E. (2003). Friendship quality, peer group affiliation, and peer antisocial behavior as moderators of the link between negative parenting and adolescent externalizing behavior. *Journal of Research on Adolescence, 13,* 161–184.

Lopez, E. M., Wishard, A., Gallimore, R., & Rivera, W. (2006). Latino high school students' perceptions of gangs and crews. *Journal of Adolescent Research, 21,* 299–318.

Marsh, P., Allen, J. P., Ho, M., Porter, M., & McFarland, F. C. (2006). The changing nature of adolescent friendships: Longitudinal links with early adolescent ego development. *Journal of Early Adolescence, 24,* 55–62.

Mayeux, L., Sandstorm, M. J., & Cillessen, A. H. N. (2008). Is being popular a risky proposition? *Journal of Research on Adolescence, 18,* 49–74.

Nguyen, J., & Brown, B. B. (in press). Making meanings, meaning identity: Hmong adolescent perceptions and use of language and style as identity symbols. *Journal of Research on Adolescence.*

Noakes, M. A., & Rinaldi, C. M. (2006). Age and gender differences in peer conflict. *Journal of Youth and Adolescence, 35,* 881–891.

Parker, J. G., & Asher, S. R. (1993). Friendship and friendship quality in middle childhood: Links with peer group acceptance and feelings of loneliness and social dissatisfaction. *Developmental Psychology, 29,* 611–621.

Parker, J. G., Low, C. M., Walker, A. R., & Gamm, B. K. (2005). Friendship jealousy in young adolescents: Individual differences and links to sex, self-esteem, aggression, and social adjustment. *Developmental Psychology, 41,* 235–250.

Peshkin, A. (1991). *The color of strangers, the color of friends.* Chicago: University of Chicago Press.

Piehler, T. F., & Dishion, T. J. (2007). Interpersonal dynamics within adolescent friendships: Dyadic mutuality, deviant talk, and patterns of antisocial behavior. *Child Development, 78,* 1611–1624.

Prinstein, M. J. (2007). Assessment of adolescents' preference- and reputation-based peer status using sociometric experts. *Merrill-Palmer Quarterly, 53,* 243–261.

Prinstein, M. J. (2007). Moderators of peer contagion: A longitudinal examination of depression socialization between adolescents and their best friends. *Journal of Clinical Child and Adolescent Psychology, 36,* 159–170.

Prinstein, M. J., & La Greca, A. M. (2002). Peer crowd affiliation and internalizing distress in childhood and adolescence: A longitudinal follow-back study. *Journal of Research on Adolescence, 12,* 325–351.

Prinstein, M. J., & Wang, S. S. (2005). False consensus and adolescent peer contagion: Examining discrepancies between perceptions and actual reported levels of friends' deviant and health risk behaviors. *Journal of Abnormal Child Psychology, 33,* 293–306.

Radmacher, K., & Azmitia, M. (2006). Are there gendered pathways to intimacy in early adolescents' and emerging adults' friendships? *Journal of Adolescent Research, 21,* 415–448.

Rose, A. J., Swenson, L. P., & Carlson, W. (2004). Friendships of aggressive youth: Considering the influences of being disliked and of being perceived as popular. *Journal of Experimental Child Psychology, 88,* 25–45.

Rose, A. J., Swenson, L. P., & Waller, E. M. (2004). Overt and relational aggression and perceived popularity: Developmental differences in concurrent and prospective relations. *Developmental Psychology, 40,* 378–387.

Rubin, K. H., Bukowski, W. M., & Parker, J. G. (2006). Peer interactions, relationships, and groups. In N. Eisenberg, W. Damon, & R. M. Lerner (Eds.), *Handbook of child psychology,* vol. *3: Social, emotional, and personality development* (6th ed.; pp. 571–645). Hoboken, NJ: John Wiley & Sons.

Sandstrom, M. J., & Cillessen, A. H. N. (2006). Likeable versus popular: Distinct implications for adolescent adjustment. *International Journal of Behavioral Development, 30,* 305–314.

Savin-Williams, R. C. (1980). Dominance hierarchies in groups of middle and late adolescent males. *Journal of Youth and Adolescence, 9,* 75–85.

Savin-Williams, R. C., & Berndt, T. J. (1990). Friendship and peer relations. In S. S. Feldman & G. R. Elliott (Eds.), *At the threshold: The developing adolescent* (pp. 277–307). Cambridge, MA: Harvard University Press.

Schneider, B. H., Woodburn, S., Soteras del Toro, M. P., & Udvari, S. (2005). Cultural and gender differences in the implications of competition for early adolescent friendship. *Merrill-Palmer Quarterly, 51,* 163–191.

Schneider, B. H., Dixon, K., & Udvari, S. (2007). Closeness and competition in the inter-ethnic and co-ethnic friendships of early adolescents in Toronto and Montreal. *Journal of Early Adolescence, 27,* 115–138.

Schwartz, D., Gorman, A. H., Nakamoto, J., & McKay, T. (2006). Popularity, social acceptance, and aggression in adolescent peer groups: Links with academic performance and school attendance. *Developmental Psychology, 42,* 1116–1127.

Sharabany, R., Eschel, Y., & Hakim, C. (2008). Boyfriend, girlfriend in a traditional society: Parenting styles and development of intimate friendships among Arabs in school, *International Journal of Behavioural Development, 32,* 66–75.

Sheriff, M. (1961). *Intergroup conflict and cooperation: The Robbers Cave experiment.* Norman, OK: University Book Exchange.

Simmons, R. (2003). *Odd girl out: The hidden culture of aggression in girls.* New York: Harcourt Trade.

Stone, M. R., Barber, B. L., & Eccles, J. S. (2008). We knew them when: Sixth grade characteristics that predict adolescent high school social identities. *Journal of Early Adolescence, 28,* 304–328.

Storch, E. A., & Masia-Warner, C. (2004). The relationship of peer victimization to social anxiety and loneliness in adolescent females. *Journal of Adolescence, 27,* 351–362.

Thayer, S. M., Updegraff, K. A., & Delgado, M. Y. (2008). Conflict resolution in Mexican American adolescents' friendships: Links with culture, gender, and friendship quality. *Journal of Youth and Adolescence, 37,* 783–797.

Updegraff, K. A., Helms, H. A., McHale, S. M., Crouter, A. C., Thayer, S. M., & Sales, L. H. (2004). Who's the boss? Patterns of perceived control in adolescents' friendships. *Journal of Youth and Adolescence, 33,* 403–420.

Valkenburg, P. M., & Peter, J. (2007). Preadolescents' and adolescents' online communication and their closeness to friends. *Developmental Psychology, 43,* 491–508.

Veenstra, R., Lindenberg, S., Zijlstra, B. J. H., De Winter, A. F., Verhulst, F. C., & Ormel, J. (2007). The dyadic nature of bullying and victimization: Testing a dual-perspective theory. *Child Development, 78,* 1843–1854.

Way, N., & Greene, M. L. (2006). Trajectories of perceived friendship quality during adolescence: Patterns and contextual predictors. *Journal of Research on Adolescence, 16,* 293–320.

Wiseman, R. (2002). *Queen bees and wannabes: Helping your daughter survive cliques, gossip, boyfriends, and other realities of adolescence.* New York: Crown.

Witkow, M. R., Bellmore, A. D., Nishina, A. D., Juvonen, J., & Grahamm, S. (2005). Mutual antipathies during early adolescence: More than just rejection. *International Journal of Behavioral Development, 29,* 209–218.

CHAPTER 4

Romantic Relationships in Adolescence

JENNIFER A. CONNOLLY AND CAROLINE McISAAC

A central feature of social development in adolescence is the emergence of romantic relationships. These relationships strike new ground for young people, representing a heretofore never experienced integration of passionate attraction and sexuality into the voluntary and mutual relationships that characterize the world of peers. It is the awakening of sexuality and intense feelings of love that distinguish the adolescent experience from those of the preceding childhood years. Although children can direct passionate feelings toward a peer (Carlson & Rose, 2007; Hatfield, Schmitz, Cornelius, & Rapson, 1988), it is not until the onset of puberty that such feelings become linked to sexual desire and thus channeled toward interaction with a potential partner. Our description of adolescent romance as the initial union of sexuality and passion in a peer relationship does not depend on the gender of the partners, applying equally well to same- and opposite-sex pairs (see chapter 14, vol. 1 of this *Handbook*). Regardless of an adolescent's gender, sexual orientation, or cultural background, we consider romantic interactions to be an important learning context and training ground for their future close relationships. Adolescent romantic experiences are the initial steps on a journey toward the loving and committed partner relationships that characterize the adult world.

HISTORICAL PERSPECTIVE

We begin our discussion of adolescent romantic relationships with a look backward at the history of "dating," as this social experience is very much linked to the modern world, especially in the industrialized West. For much of history, cross-gendered interactions have been viewed as part of a courtship process during which a young man and a young woman might get to know one another with the intent of entering into marriage. Courtship partners were selected by the family, based on patterns of kinship or economic advantage, and not considered the free choice of the young people themselves (Cate & Lloyd, 1992). Parental influence on partner selection began to wane during the time of the Industrial Revolution, when young people were increasingly provided with economic opportunities outside of the home. As marriage became less tied to familial and economic considerations, there was a complementary increase in viewing romantic love as the basis for selecting a lifetime partner. This shift in focus empowered adolescents to take a more direct role in the courtship process. Although parents in the Victorian Era supervised the cross-sex interactions of their adolescent children and ensured the marriage suitability of their partners, the youth themselves chose whom they courted based on romantic feelings (Cate & Lloyd, 1992; Sears, 2008).

Youth-directed courtship accelerated during the early decades of the twentieth century when dating emerged as an important social activity of the adolescent and young adulthood years (Bailey, 1988). During this period of history, dating referred to the social appointments that one kept with a person of romantic and sexual interest, for example, attending a dance or going to the movies. These dates took place outside of the family home, meaning that the formal restrictions imposed by parental supervision were replaced by the relatively less constrained mores of the community. Scholars have attributed the historical emergence of dating to the prevailing social and intellectual trends of the time (Bailey, 1988; Murstein, 1974). The first of these trends was the identification of adolescence as a distinct period of development. G. Stanley Hall, who has been credited with this theoretical advancement, conceptualized adolescence as the period of delay between the onset of reproductive capacity and its actual activation, highlighting the important role of cross-gender socialization in bridging this gap (Arnett, 2006; Sears, 2008). The second of these social trends was the introduction of compulsory secondary education. Extending the years of schooling to the end of the adolescent period effectively brought young people into extended contact with a wide variety of potential dating partners from diverse socioeconomic backgrounds. The third trend was the rise of a popular teenage culture, communicated via radio, magazines, and then television, which led to the creation of a shared set of rules that promoted dating and romance. Finally, the emergence of dating as an important social phenomenon was supported by the shift from rural to urban living and the widespread use of the automobile, both of which made dating in a community context generally more accessible to a wider group of adolescents. Yet despite the changing social landscape and the increasing acceptability of dating, romantic activities in the early to mid-twentieth century were nonetheless courtship based and expected to result in marriage (Bailey, 1988).

The detachment of dating from courtship, or the understanding that adolescent romantic relationships may be temporary and occur without the expectation of marriage, can be traced back to the latter half of the twentieth century (Fields, 2003; Sears, 2008). This conceptual shift may be attributed to the social and political climate of America during the 1960s and 1970s. The feminist movement and the sexual revolution, coupled with scientific advancements in reproductive contraception, empowered both girls and boys to become more active participants in *dating*, as opposed to courtship. Alongside the increasing numbers of young people choosing to pursue post-secondary education, these significant societal trends delayed the age at which most young people entered into marriage as well as gave pause to a number of youth as to whether or not they would even make such a formal commitment. The social landmarks of the 1960s and 1970s paved the way for the currently held view that adolescents in the industrialized West are "free agents" when it comes to their romantic relationships. Although parents may set guidelines and age restrictions around the dating activities of their children, today's adolescents are generally at liberty to choose their partners and move in and out of dating relationships at will. This altered mind-set has given adolescents an extended period of time in which experimentation is possible, thus stimulating the functional value of romantic relationships for individual development. As such, rather than the fulfillment of familial, economic, or societal contracts, contemporary romantic relationships are increasingly available to adolescents as a context for the mastery of psychosocial tasks and the achievement of social and emotional well-being (Furman, Brown, & Feiring, 1999).

DEFINING ROMANTIC RELATIONSHIPS IN ADOLESCENCE

A special challenge for contemporary researchers is to operationalize the phenomenon of adolescent romance in a way that corresponds to youth's actual experiences and to use language that is consistent with their understanding of romantic relationships (Furman & Shaffer, 2003). Most researchers use terms such as *boyfriend/girlfriend* or *romantic relationship* when soliciting information from adolescents about whether or not they are part of a couple. One may question the salience of these terms to adolescents since the language they themselves use to describe their romantic partner status is often colloquial and linked to an ever-changing popular culture. While arguments can be made in favor of using more everyday language, in order to better connect with adolescents, there is a risk to this practice in that teen language is highly localized to a community context. Using specific forms of slang terminology would likely hinder the generalizability of findings across studies. Hence, we support the use of language that has a common understanding across sectors of a community, even though these terms may not be the ones used by youth themselves when talking about their romantic relationships. Our preference is for the use of the term *boyfriend* or *girlfriend* to identify adolescents' romantic relationship status, that is, whether or not they have experienced a current or past romantic relationship.

Relationships Versus Activities

In addition to clearly establishing an adolescent's romantic status, an equally important definitional challenge is distinguishing between romantic activities and romantic relationships. Sometimes these activities, such as going to movies, restaurants or other venues, are solely couple based. Other times, a couple's romantic activities happen in a broader social context, such as when they spend time with other romantic pairs or with their peer group. Further complicating the distinction between romantic activities and relationships, many adolescents without a boyfriend or girlfriend participate in cross-gender group activities with other teens to whom they are romantically attracted. Romantic activities of this nature are important for researchers to take note of because they can be the prelude to formalizing a romantic relationship. We believe that it is important to separate activities from relationships when the research goal is to

identify the romantic status of a young person. If researchers ask about a specific romantic or dating activity with the intention of gathering information about romantic status, there may be less reliable information from youth because a positive response could be provided by adolescents both with and without a partner. In this chapter, we refer to romantic relationship status when the focus is on the connection between the two partners, and dating or romantic activities when the focus is on the content of their interactions. We refer to dating when the focus is on the activities and the status is less certain.

Sexual activities may also occur in both romantic and nonromantic relationships and researchers need to be mindful of this possibility when asking about romantic experiences. Recent research suggests that a significant minority of teens have had sex with someone other than their current boyfriend or girlfriend. About half of the time, this occurs as a single encounter with an acquaintance or a former romantic partner. Adolescents refer to these "one-time" experiences as "hook-ups" (Furman & Shaffer, 2003; Manning, Giordano, & Longmore, 2006) and, given their short-term duration, these interactions are unlikely to be confused with a romantic relationship. That being said, *friends with benefits* (FWBs), a term that adolescents use to denote an ongoing sexual relationship with a friend who is not a romantic partner, is a more challenging phenomenon for adolescent researchers. These FWB relationships are enduring and have multiple meanings for boys and girls (Hughes, Morrison, & Asada, 2005; Puentes, Knox, & Zusman, 2008). Many adolescents hope that these relationships will become romantic ones and, for some, it is clear that FWBs have been a route to the formalization of a romantic relationship (Manning et al., 2006). Other adolescent FWBs do not blossom into a stable romantic partnership, and this may be a source of distress for young people, especially girls. Taken as a whole, the complexities surrounding FWBs may motivate some adolescents to report a relationship as romantic, even if it is not acknowledged as such by both parties. Researchers need to be mindful of this possibility and use terms in their research that allow adolescents to respond differently to romantic relationships and FWBs.

Platonic Cross-Sex Relationships

When outlining the definitional terrain of adolescents' romantic relationships, it is important to note that adolescents' social experiences also include platonic relationships with cross-sex peers (Bukowski, Sippola, & Hoza, 1999; Connolly, Craig, Goldberg, & Pepler, 1999; Feiring, 1999a; Kuttler & La Greca, 2004). Platonic relationships are normative during the teenage years and, in fact, a key feature of this life stage is an expansion in the number of cross-sex friends that adolescents report in their social networks (Blyth, Hill, & Thiel, 1982; Connolly, Furman, & Konarski, 2000; Poulin & Pederson, 2007). One may wonder whether young people can indeed separate platonic and romantic relationships. Evidence overwhelmingly suggests that they can and do make this distinction, based on the presence or absence of passion or romantic attraction (Connolly et al., 1999; Johnson, 2004). Platonic friendships have many important functions for adolescents' romantic development, including insights into the ways of the other gender and access to potential romantic partners. Outlining their contributions, however, is beyond the scope of this chapter.

The definitional distinctions that we have been making are important from a methodological perspective if we are to be accurate and consistent in our measurement of romantic relationships. Yet, in the real world, there is considerable fluidity in the boundaries between adolescents' romantic and nonromantic activities and relationships. For example, cross-sex platonic friendships or FWBs may turn into a romantic relationship at some later point given that the sharing of positive experiences is a common route to feelings of attraction. Social activities can also be fluid and ambiguous in romantic intent. A group outing to a movie

may be experienced by some adolescents as purely platonic, by others as an opportunity to interact with someone they are romantically attracted to, and still by others as a date with their boyfriend or girlfriend. Further complicating the picture, adolescents' romantic attractions may or may not be reciprocated by the target of their affections. Cross-gender friendships, both platonic and "beneficial" ones, may be imbued with far more passion and longing by one person than by the other. According to Baumeister and Wotman (1992), almost all young adults have had at least one experience with unrequited love. Given the nascent character of adolescents' romantic relationships, it is not surprising that "crushes," infatuations, and unrequited romance are part of our cultural understanding of the teenage experience. How these one-sided romances play into adolescents' understanding of when they are in or not in a relationship, has yet to be elucidated. Taken as a whole, the fluidity, ambiguity, and uncertainty of romance at this stage in the life cycle creates definitional challenges that need to be kept in mind when studying adolescents' romantic relationships.

PREVALENCE AND PATTERNS OF ROMANTIC RELATIONSHIPS

Our documentation of the prevalence of romantic relationships during the teenage years has been greatly aided by data gathered as part of the Add Health Longitudinal Survey, which is a large-scale nationally representative study of youth in the United States. Utilizing the question, *"Have you had a special romantic relationship with anyone in the past 18 months,"* the Add Health data show that romantic relationships are common during adolescence and that their frequency steadily increases with age (Carver, Joyner, & Udry, 2003). Approximately 25% of 12-year-olds, 50% of 15-year-olds, and 70% of 18-year-olds report a romantic relationship in an 18-month time frame. The Add Health Survey also addresses many of the aforementioned definitional challenges by posing important follow-up questions to those adolescents who do *not* report a positive romantic status. These questions ask noncoupled adolescents about sexual behaviors (e.g., holding hands, kissing) and feelings (e.g., liking, loving) that they may have experienced outside the context of a special romantic relationship. Researchers who utilize the Add Health data set label the co-occurrence of these behaviors and feelings *liked relationships* and note that they are reported by approximately 10% of youth (Carver et al., 2003). Although some studies combine these "liked" relationships with "special relationships" (e.g., Joyner & Udry, 2000), we recommend that they be analyzed separately, given that youth may understand these experiences as quite unique.

Relationship Duration

The Add Health data set also points to the time-limited nature of adolescent romantic relationships, a finding consistent with other research (Carver et al., 2003). Youth under the age of 14 years typically report relationships of a few weeks' duration, and rarely report durations of longer than 4 months (Carver et al., 2003; Connolly & Johnson, 1996; Feiring, 1996; Shulman & Scharf, 2000). Romantic relationships become more enduring with age. Sixteen-year-olds typically report that their relationships last for 6 months, and 18-year-olds typically report that their relationships endure for 1 year or more. These duration changes may be due to differing capacities for maintaining an intimate relationship, with older adolescents more equipped to sustain dyadic connections than their younger counterparts (Connolly & Johnson, 1996). Duration differences may also relate to challenges tracking the "official" beginnings of relationships, especially in the younger years (Carver et al., 2003). The relationships of younger adolescents are highly embedded in the peer network (Connolly, Furman, et al., 2000), and, as we have noted previously, there is much fluidity between romantic partners and friends. Thus, the shorter durations reported by younger

adolescents may also stem from the fact that they have fuzzier boundaries between romantic and nonromantic relationships than researchers are inclined to see.

Prevalence of Romantic Dissolutions

In contrast to the substantial database that is now accumulating on the prevalence of romantic relationships in adolescence, there is relatively little information on the occurrence of romantic dissolutions. Yet the relatively short duration of adolescents' relationships strongly suggests that breakups are both common and frequent during this life stage. Barber (2006), reporting on the Michigan Study of Adolescent Life Transitions, found that more than half of 10th-grade students had experienced a breakup in the last 6 months. Drawing on data from a large Canadian sample, Connolly and McIsaac (2008, in press) also found that relationship terminations occur frequently across the adolescent years. Paralleling the age-related increase in romantic relationships, these authors found that the number of youth who reported a breakup also increases with age. Whereas less than half of 11- to 13-year-olds reported the termination of a romantic relationship, almost all 20- to 25-year olds did so. Conversely, the likelihood of reporting a recent breakup (i.e., within the last 12 months) decreased with age. The less frequently occurring romantic dissolutions of older adolescents likely reflects their increased skill in sustaining a relationship, as well as selecting more compatible romantic partners with whom the relationship is more likely to endure. Finally, Connolly and McIsaac's data show that adolescents generally consider themselves to be in control of their relationship terminations, as most youth report that they initiated the breakup, either on their own or jointly with their partner. Adolescents' tendency to assume control of the termination process is perhaps central to their recovery from the heartache of a romantic breakup. Later, we return to this point, when we consider the adjustment impact of romantic relationships on adolescents.

Gender and Prevalence

Although boys and girls generally report comparable frequencies of romantic relationships, there are some notable differences between them. For instance, in early adolescence, more boys than girls report having a current romantic relationship (Connolly, Craig, Goldberg, & Pepler, 2004; Darling, Dowdy, Van Horne, & Caldwell, 1999; Longmore, Manning, & Giordano, 2001). That being said, those girls who do report a romantic relationship indicate a longer duration than the boys, a pattern that continues across the adolescent years (Carver et al., 2003; Shulman & Sharf, 2000). There is also evidence to suggest that parenting practices differentially influence the romantic experiences of early adolescents. Girls, relative to boys, are more intensely supervised, and this restricts their participation in romantic activities at this age (Kan, McHale, & Crouter, 2008). New patterns of gendered romance take shape in mid- to later adolescence. At this stage, girls become more likely than boys to report a romantic relationship (Carver et al., 2003; Davies & Windle, 2000). Although the reason for this trend is unknown, it is possible that girls' relational focus is more able to come to the fore as the suppressive effect of parental supervision declines (Feldman & Rosenthal, 1991). The pairing of a younger female with an older male partner also becomes the norm during mid- to later adolescence (Carver et al., 2003). This pattern, which has been extensively documented among adults, continues across the life span and is thought to have its roots in evolutionary pressures for reproductive success (Kenrick, Gabrielidis, Keefe, & Cornelius, 1996).

Culture and Prevalence

Descriptive information about adolescents' romantic relationships comes almost exclusively from North America. Very little is known about the prevalence and patterns of these relationships in non-Western countries, and this is a significant limitation of the field since cultural values likely influence the onset, frequency, and timing of romantic relationships (Coates, 1999; Feldman & Rosenthal, 1990; 1991). As the adolescent experience becomes increasingly globalized, youth of different backgrounds connect more and more, underscoring the need for a culturally sensitive understanding of romantic relationships during this stage of life (Brown, Larson, & Saraswathi, 2002). Research findings may play an important role in facilitating greater tolerance across cultures by clarifying both the differences and similarities that adolescents experience in their romantic relationships.

Although we have virtually no data that can speak to adolescents' romantic experiences outside of the industrialized West, we do have information about the romantic relationships of adolescents from different ethnocultural groups who are living in North America, as well as from other Western countries. Focusing first on the American context, adolescents of Asian descent living in Canada and the United States are significantly less likely to report a romantic partner than are youth of other ethnic backgrounds (Carver et al., 2003; Connolly et al., 2004). Although the Add Health data set does not reveal similar levels of nonparticipation for Hispanic youth, other studies suggest that there may be quantitative differences in the timing of romantic experiences between Whites and Latinos. A recent qualitative study of Latina college women found that these youth recalled a later start to dating due to considerable restrictions placed on them by their parents (Raffaelli, 2005). In contrast, North American adolescents of African and Caribbean descent report similar rates of romantic involvement as Whites (Connolly et al., 2004; Giordano, Manning, & Longmore, 2005). Black adolescents, however, report more durable relationships than any other ethnic group residing in North America (Carver et al., 2003; Giordano et al., 2005).

We also have data about the romantic experiences of youth living in industrialized countries outside of North America. Recent studies of European, Israeli, and Australian youth provide evidence that romantic relationships are common in these regions as well (Menesini & Nocentini, 2008; Shulman & Sharf, 2000, Zimmer-Gembeck & Petherick, 2006). Indeed, there is some indication that European adolescents are more likely to enter into romantic relationships in early adolescence than their North American counterparts. Whereas 20% of young adolescents report romantic relationships in North America (Carver et al., 2003; Connolly et al., 2004), 40% of young adolescents in Germany report having a romantic partner (Seiffge-Krenke, 2006). Similarly, 80% of 14-year-old Israeli youth report some kind of dating experience (Shulman & Scharf, 2000), while the comparable rate among North American youth is closer to 50% (Carver et al., 2003). These cultural differences seem less apparent in the late adolescent period, as similar romantic status and duration rates are reported by European, Israeli, Australian, and North American youth (Carver et al., 2003; Menesini & Nocentini, 2008; Seiffge-Krenke, Shulman, & Klessinger, 2001). Considering the aforementioned definitional challenges that accompany the study of adolescent romantic relationships, it is not clear whether these patterns are due to actual differences between the youth in these countries or to differences in the way the terms used to capture adolescent dating and romance are interpreted. Clarity of this issue awaits cross-national studies that employ common terms and methods of inquiry.

Sexual Minority Youth

It is important to acknowledge that the patterns of dating and romantic relationships that we have described are for opposite-gender relationships. Yet roughly 5% of adolescents report same-sex romantic attractions, or nonheterosexual orientations (Carver et al., 2003; Russell & Consolacion, 2003; Williams, Connolly, Pepler, & Craig, 2003), and there is emerging evidence that these youth participate in romantic relationships during their adolescence (Carver et al., 2003; Diamond & Lucas,

2004; Dubé & Savin-Williams, 1999; Elze, 2002; Russell & Consolacion, 2003; Williams et al., 2003). Furthermore, it appears that sexual-minority youth have as many romantic experiences as their heterosexual peers. In a recent study of 16-year-old adolescents in the Add Health data set, 75% of youth with same-sex attractions reported a romantic relationship within the past 18 months (Russell & Consolacion, 2003). Researchers have recently noted that the target of romantic attractions for these youth can be quite fluid because of the emergent process of establishing a sexual-minority identity (Diamond, 1998, 2008; Savin-Williams & Ream, 2007). Consistent with this emergent status, adolescents with same-sex attractions more often report dating partners of the opposite sex than of the same sex (Russell & Consolacion, 2003).

THEORIES OF ROMANTIC RELATIONSHIPS

Having traced the historical roots of adolescent dating and outlined the prevalence of romantic involvement during this life stage, we now turn our attention to describing the theories that have been articulated to account for the emergence of romantic relationships. Two broad frameworks have guided much of the research on adolescent romantic relationships, namely, attachment theories and development-contextual theories. These theoretical perspectives differ in their relative emphasis on the inner life of the individual or the ecological contexts in which they live as explanatory mechanisms in romantic development. Attachment theories favor an understanding of adolescents' internal representations of close relationships and contextual theories concentrate more on the dynamic between individuals and their social contexts. Both theoretical perspectives have a common interest in understanding how adolescents accomplish key developmental tasks and rich research findings are accumulating within both traditions. We first outline the positions that these theories have taken with respect to romantic relationship development in adolescence, then we review the theories of adolescent romance that have been influenced by these perspectives, and finally we consider the supporting empirical findings that address important questions from each of these frameworks.

Romantic Attachment Theory

Hazan and Shaver (1987) were the first to extend the attachment perspective from parent–child interactions to include relationships in the romantic domain. Focusing specifically on adult couples, they argued that mature romantic relationships provide the attachment functions that individuals first experience in a parent–child relationship, namely, safe haven, proximity seeking, and secure base. These authors, as well as others (Collins & Sroufe, 1999; Furman & Simon, 1999; Furman & Wehner, 1994), noted that the adolescent period is normally the time when the attachment functions begin to transition from figures in the family to a romantic partner. The transfer of attachment figures is thought to be motivated by adolescents' emerging sexuality, as well as their increased capacity for experiencing intimacy with same-aged peers. As in their relationships with parents, adolescents are thought to differ in the style of attachment they display with their romantic partners, be it secure or insecure (Collins & Sroufe, 1999; Hazan & Shaver, 1987). Securely attached adolescents are comfortable in their relationship and trust that their partner will support them in times of stress. Insecurely attached adolescents are, conversely, uncomfortable in turning to their partners for support. This discomfort may be manifested as an avoidance or withdrawal from the partner, coupled with a general disinterest in the emotional dimensions of the relationship. Discomfort may also be expressed as a preoccupation with the partner's availability to meet their needs and an anxious overinvestment in the emotional dynamics of the relationship. Traditionally, these secure and insecure styles have been thought to remain stable as adolescents transition their attachment from

parents to romantic partners (Collins & Sroufe, 1999; Hazan & Shaver, 1987). More recently, it has been suggested that adolescents' romantic attachments may not be shaped solely by their prior interactions within the family, but also respond to ongoing experiences with romantic partners (Furman & Simon, 1999). Adolescents are thought to integrate present and past experiences with attachment figures to form working models of romantic relationships. This transactional process may introduce some degree of instability and change in adolescents' romantic attachment development.

Development-Contextual Theory of Romantic Relationships

Development-contextual theories shift the lens of inquiry to the interpersonal systems within which adolescents develop and consider how these systems contribute to the attainment of multiple developmentally important tasks. Building on Bronfenbrenner's (1979) seminal idea of nested ecological contexts, development-contextual models suggest that romantic relationships are multilayered as they both provide a context for individual development, and at the same time, they are themselves shaped by dynamics that occur in the micro- and macrosystems within which they are encompassed (Brown, 1999; Connolly & Goldberg, 1999; Lerner & Simi, 2000). Microsystem influences on romantic development include the peer group and the family. Peers are thought to dictate romantic norms and facilitate opportunities for romantic interaction. Families are thought to provide models of intimate connections and regulate the pace at which adolescents become involved in romantic relationships. Macrosystems are much broader in scope. Included in these systems are ethnocultural beliefs about the value of romantic love, appropriate timetables for romantic engagement, and the roles of males and females in a romantic relationship. Community resources such as schools, access to health care, and employment opportunities also contribute to the macro context within which adolescents' relationships develop. Contextual models of romantic development ultimately propose that it is the transaction among the systemic and individual levels that leads to the resolution of developmental tasks within this context. These tasks have been broadly conceptualized as those that define how adolescents connect with others, namely intimacy and sexuality, and those that define how adolescents achieve an independent sense of themselves, namely identity and autonomy (Collins & Steinberg, 2006). Intimacy is a complex construct that entails feelings of warmth and closeness to another person (Camarena, Sarigiani, & Petersen, 1990), as well as the behaviors that support these feelings such as affiliation and self-disclosure (Sharabany, Gershoni, & Hoffman, 1981). Like intimacy, sexuality also has an affective component, with feelings of passion, desire, and attraction being as central to adolescent romance as the sexual behaviors in which youth may potentially engage. Whereas sexuality and intimacy bring the romantic dyad together, identity and autonomy processes support the existence of two distinct individuals within the same relationship. *Identity* refers to the sense of having stable and consistent self-attributes, and *autonomy* refers to the confidence one feels in maintaining a separate identity while relating to close others, and at the same time respecting the unique identity of one's relationship partners (Noom, Dekovic, & Meeus 2001; Nurmi, 2004).

Impact of Sullivan, Erikson, and Dunphy on Romantic Theories

Although not specifically theories of romantic development, the theories of Sullivan (1953), Erikson (1968), and Dunphy (1963) should be noted, as they have been influential in understanding romantic relationships. Erikson and Sullivan first oriented the field to the importance of romantic relationships for the mastery of psychosocial tasks, especially intimacy and identity. According to Sullivan (1953), adolescent relationships are profoundly shaped by the emerging need for sexual expression within the context of a close peer relationship. These latter relationships emerge in the preadolescent period and these special "chumships," or dyadic bonds with a same-sex friend, allow for the first expression of intimacy outside of the family. With the onset of puberty, adolescents experience new feelings of sexuality alongside their desire for intimacy with age-mates and they begin to look to romantic partners to fulfill both needs. Thus, from a Sullivanian perspective, romantic relationships represent two distinct developmental milestones: the transition from same-sex to cross-sex intimacy and the integration of intimacy with sexuality. Sullivan suggested that intimacy with a romantic partner helps adolescents to come to know and understand themselves, which is the foundation for identity.

In contrast to Sullivan's position, Erikson (1968) did not consider romantic relationships to be central to the adolescent life stage. Instead, in his articulation of the psychosocial stages of development, Erikson positioned romantic relationships in the period of early adulthood. Locating these relationships in this life stage stems from his argument that intimacy development follows, rather than precedes, identity formation. In Erikson's view, psychosexual identity is the critical achievement of the adolescent years, and its resolution supports intimacy in relationships later in the life span. The interplay between intimacy and identity, expressed in the theories of Erikson and Sullivan, is an important theme in contemporary theories of adolescent romantic relationships.

The work of Dunphy (1963) first oriented the field to the importance of social context on adolescents' romantic development. Dunphy was particularly focused on the peer group, and he argued that the central function of the peer crowd was to solidify adolescents' heterosexual role. Using ethnographic methods, Dunphy studied the clique and crowd stages of peer group formation throughout adolescence. According to Dunphy, mixed-gender peer crowds, which are formed by the coalescence of same-gender cliques, bring adolescent boys and girls together in unstructured situations that allow for the possibility of romantic activity. Peer crowds are held together by high-status leaders of both genders whose popularity and prestige is linked to their advanced heterosocial development. These popular youth lead the way in forging romantic relationships, and they encourage the romantic involvement of their group members. By documenting the changing gender composition and hierarchical structure of adolescent peer groups, Dunphy's work provided a valuable starting point for the investigation of romantic development. His attention to the peer context is considered to be a landmark contribution, and many contemporary theories draw on his ideas in their formulations of adolescent romance.

Stage Theories of Romantic Development

Theories of adolescent romantic relationships, be they attachment or development contextual, must confront the reality that, at any one point in time, many adolescents do not have boyfriends or girlfriends. This fact is made abundantly clear by the Add Health findings, which indicate that 65% of 12-year-olds, 40% of 15-year-olds, and 18% of 18-year-olds have not had a romantic relationship within the past 18 months (Carver et al., 2003). That being said, it would be erroneous to conclude that the presence or absence of a romantic relationship is the central indicator of romantic development in adolescence. Irrespective of their romantic relationship status, adolescents are known to be preoccupied with romantic concerns (Eder, 1993) and participate in mixed-sex interactions (Richards, Crowe, Larson, & Swarr, 1998). These are important facets of adolescent romance and pose challenges for the simplistic view that romantic development in adolescence is an on/off phenomenon. Instead, a more comprehensive view would consider a developmental progression of activities that lead to romantic relationships, as well as fluidity in dating patterns and romantic relationships. Modeling these facets

and their interactions is of central concern to theories of romantic development, all of which try to account for the progression of romantic experiences through phases or stages of development. In accounting for patterns of romantic development, theories also address psychosocial tasks as well as the inner processes that influence their development.

Early Stage Theories

Feinstein and Ardon (1973) outlined one of the first stage theories of romantic development. Focusing largely on dating activities, they used a neo-Freudian theory of object relations to account for the developmental progression that begins with an awakening of sexual interest and ends with the adult outcome of investment in a permanent love object. Central to their theory is the notion that forming a romantic relationship is part of the stormy process of individuation from parents, which these authors conceptualized as having the ultimate goal of finding an appropriate object for libidinal drives. Feinstein and Ardon identified a four-stage model of romantic development, spanning the ages of 13–25 years, with each stage specifying particular dating activities that are central to the task of adolescent ego development and identity formation.

Extending this focus on psychosexual development, McCabe (1984) outlined a theory of dating in which she conceptualized adolescent romantic relationships as central to the resolution of a sexual identity. Rather than specific stages, McCabe described an adolescent pathway in which biological and societal influences contribute to the sexual and affectional components of dating involvement. These pathways are highly gendered, as McCabe perceived boys to be motivated by sexual goals, and girls to be more oriented to achieving a relationship with a stable partner. The theories of Feinstein and Ardon (1973) and McCabe (1984) are important to the field because they move beyond simple descriptions of dating activities and try to account for the psychosocial functions of dating and romantic activities. That being said, their ideas were not elaborated upon at the time, perhaps because adolescents' romantic relationships were not treated with much seriousness by the research community (Collins, 2003). Two decades passed before researchers came to see romantic relationships as meaningful contexts that support adolescent development.

Contemporary Stage Theories

In 1994, Furman and Wehner outlined the first contemporary theory of adolescent romantic development. Unlike their predecessors (i.e., Feinstein & Ardon, 1973; McCabe, 1984), these authors shifted the focus from the resolution of identity to intimacy. Furman and Wehner accomplished this intimacy focus by integrating romantic attachment theory with the social needs articulated by Sullivan. In particular, they expanded upon the connectedness focus of both perspectives to describe a series of stages that allowed for the full realization of intimate functions, namely, affiliation, attachement, sexuality, and caretaking. Although the majority of these functions had been previously linked to romantic relationships, the affiliative function of adolescent romance had never before been highlighted and is considered to be a novel contribution of Furman and his colleagues (Furman & Simon, 1999; Furman, Simon, Shaffer, & Bouchey, 2002; Furman & Wehner 1994). Companionship and the sharing of pleasurable time with age-mates is the crux of affiliation, and Furman and Wehner extend this central peer function to the romantic domain and articulate its role in the progressive integration of a mature romantic attachment. Proceeding from a stage of *simple interchanges* between opposite-sex peers that is motivated by pubertal maturation, young adolescents quickly move to a stage of *casual dating*, which fulfills their needs for affiliation as well as sexuality. Adolescents then proceed to *stable relationships,* in which attachment needs emerge

alongside sexuality and affiliation. In late adolescence and early adulthood, the stage of *committed relationships* emerges as young people are increasingly able to provide caretaking functions to their partner. Furman and Wehner (1994) use the term *behavioral system* to showcase the role of the relationship context, in driving adolescents' progression through the romantic stages. Their theory is also the first to explicate the potential for developmental continuity between romantic relationships and other relationship systems. Continuity is hypothesized to be carried by views of relationships, both conscious and unconscious, that adolescents form through their interactions and experiences in both present and past relationships with parents, friends, and previous romantic partners.

Brown (1999), expanding upon Dunphy's (1963) focus on peer crowds, outlined a development-contextual theory in which identity, rather than intimacy, is presented as the key psychosocial task that is supported by romantic development. By focusing on identity, Brown's model echoes those of the early romantic stage theorists (i.e., Feinstein & Ardon; 1973; McCabe, 1984). Brown argues that a central challenge of adolescence is to create an integrated self-image, which includes a representation of the self as a romantic partner. The romantic self-image first emerges as a group-based identity, and this component facilitates the adoption of the romantic norms of a peer crowd. Once a group identity has been solidified, a self-based identity component is able to emerge in which adolescents define their own particular romantic interests as distinct from those of their group. The group and self components of romantic self-image emerge in four developmental stages. Pubertal maturation triggers the first or *initiation phase,* as well as the changes that occur in the gender composition of the peer group. Peers provide norms for romantic relationships, censure inappropriate behavior, and safely constrain the initiations and endings of romantic involvements. Brown's second stage, termed the *status phase*, distinguishes his theory from the work of other stage theorists. In this phase of romantic development, social status in the peer group is highly linked to having romantic involvements. Reinforcing the formation of a group identity, romantic partners are thought to be selected primarily for their ability to enhance one's social position in the peer group. Low-status peers are avoided as potential partners, even when an attraction might be present, because of the fear of social rejection. Certain peer crowds, such as the "populars" and "jocks," are thought to be especially affected by peer evaluation because membership in these groups is highly linked to romantic expertise. In the *affection phase* of romantic development, adolescents become more open to the individual expression of affectionate needs and are less tied to group values. Having established a sense of group identity, and having gained confidence in their romantic competencies, adolescents begin to have relationships that enhance the self components of their identity. At the end of adolescence and the start of emerging adulthood, Brown's theory points to the possibility of the *bonding phase* of romantic development. Identity needs are fused with those of intimacy at this stage, and young people select partners who complement their personalities and future goals, as well as satisfy their affectional needs.

Connolly and colleagues (Connolly, Craig, Goldberg, & Pepler, 2004; Connolly, Furman, & Konarski, 2000; Connolly & Goldberg, 1999) have also proposed a development-contextual theory of romantic development in which the social–emotional tasks that underlie youth's growing participation in romantic relationships are articulated. These authors argue that the inner drive to accomplish critical tasks is the impetus toward romantic relationships, and, as such, romantic participation provides a context for adolescents to advance developmentally. The essence of these tasks is the interplay between intimacy and autonomy needs and this dynamic shapes the developmental sequencing of dating and romantic

relationships in Connolly's model. Drawing on Sullivan (1953), the fundamental desire to form intimate connections outside of the family is the primary motivator for romantic relationships in adolescence. In this way, the desire for romantic relationships is a component of adolescents' expanding ways of intimate relating within the peer world. Unique, however, from peers and friendships, romantic relationships are also thought to be motivated by sexual and passionate forms of intimate expression. Connolly and Goldberg (1999) conceptualized passion as the intense feelings of love and attraction that are at the core of romantic relationships. Passionate feelings catalyze romantic interest and spark adolescents' desire to participate in romantic relationships. These authors suggest that, in early adolescence, passionate feelings do not have to be acted upon in order for romantic development to begin. In fact, passion, unaccompanied by actual romantic contact, is the central property of the first stage of romantic development, termed the *infatuation stage*. Rather than communicated directly to a partner, these initial infatuations are given voice within the peer group as friends share in this emerging interest and support its expression. In the ensuing *affiliative stage* of romantic development, the supportive role of friends expands to include interactions with potential partners within mixed-gender peer groups. Whereas Furman and Wehner's (1994) interest is in the affiliative functions of the romantic dyad, and Brown's theory (1999) is concerned with peer group's provision of a romantic identity, the framework proposed by Connolly and colleagues highlights affiliation among friends, cliques, and crowds as it naturally occurs within the peer context. "Dating in groups" is thought to provide access to new partners and models of romantic interactions, thereby creating a supportive context for exploring romantic involvements. Group dating is important to the development of romantic intimacy as it regulates the pace of involvement and prevents overinvestment in romantic dyads before the skills for negotiating sexuality and intimacy are established. This type of romantic involvement is a normative path that leads to the couple relationships that become the focus of the *intimacy stage* of romantic development. Rather than being based in a group, these romantic relationships are essentially dyadic, and have a life outside of the peer network. This newfound comfort with romantic partners encourages emotional forms of intimacy based on mutual disclosure and shared trust, both of which are integrated with affiliative and passionate needs. Once adolescents have gained experience with deeper forms of intimacy, the developmental challenge turns to questions of autonomy, as articulated by Connolly and Goldberg (1999) in the final *committed stage* of romantic relationships. Maintaining a separate self outside of the relationship, while simultaneously remaining intimate, becomes the central challenge for romantic partners. Extracurricular involvements and nonromantic interests are seen as important facets of the individual that need to be maintained outside of the relationship. Unlike other theories in which the importance of the peer group wanes at this stage of development, Connolly and Goldberg (1999) highlight the continued involved of the peer group as friends facilitate the negotiation of the intimacy–autonomy dynamic by providing an outlet for these other social interests. Adolescents in the committed stage have an eye on the future and begin to reflect on how the partnership mirrors their own values and future goals, increasingly utilizing the romantic relationship as a means of self-discovery and identity formation.

Although each contemporary stage theory makes a distinct contribution, with Furman focused on the intimacy provisions of romantic couples, Brown on the peer status ramifications of partner choice, and Connolly on the developmental functions of the peer context, many consistent themes are evident across these perspectives. The first of these consistencies is the catalyzing role played by pubertal maturation and sexual need fulfillment. Second, each theorist connects the development of

romantic relationships to individuation from the family and to increasing connectedness to peers. Third, the need to achieve mature forms of intimacy, attachment, sexuality, identity, and autonomy are seen by theorists as important developmental motivators of romantic relationships. Fourth, romantic participation is commonly thought to increase an individual's capacity for mature relationships, thus allowing for progression to more advanced stages of romance. The final consistency among these theorists is the stage-model framework itself. Furman, Brown, and Connolly all conceptualize romantic relationships within a series of developmental stages that progressively move the adolescent along a continuum from nascent longings and initial forays into romantic exchanges, to dyadic relationships that are similar to those of adults in their emotional maturity. Capitalizing on the commonalities of these theories, we believe that three stages of romantic development can be articulated. The first of these describes the entry into romantic relationships, the second highlights the exploratory functions of dating, and the third culminates in the consolidation of dyadic relationships. We now turn to a description of these three broad stages, focusing on their characteristics, age ranges, and developmental context, with reference to supporting empirical evidence.

EMPIRICAL SUPPORT FOR THE STAGES OF ROMANTIC DEVELOPMENT

Stage 1: Entry Into Romantic Attractions and Affiliations in Early Adolescence

Empirical data confirm that the first stage of romantic development is triggered by pubertal maturation, both of the individual and of the adolescents in his or her peer group (Dornbusch et al., 1981; Friedlander, Connolly, Pepler, & Craig, 2007; Graber, Brooks-Gunn, & Warren, 1995; Smolak, Levine, & Gralen, 1993). During the age range of 11–13 years, adolescents become intensely interested in matters of romance and evidence suggests that this topic dominates conversations among friends at this stage (Eder, 1993). Crushes on individuals and shared infatuations become new ways of joining with same-sex friends, even if there is little actual interaction with the loved objects. A majority of adolescents at this age report having been in love many times, despite limited or even no romantic contact with the object of their affections (Montgomery & Sorell, 1998). These findings support the irony highlighted by Connolly and Goldberg's (1999) infatuation stage in that adolescents' developing interest in cross-sex romantic relationships first affects their same-sex friendships before any impact on other-sex relationships is realized. This pubertally mediated interest in romance and love moves adolescents away from the exclusively same-sex contexts of childhood and into mixed-gender groups, where there is an opportunity for affiliating with cross-sex peers (Connolly et al., 2004; Darling et al., 1999; Pellegrini & Long, 2007; Poulin & Pedersen, 2007; Richards et al., 1998). These cross-sex affiliative contacts include diverse social activities, both inside and outside of school time. Movies, sporting events, school dances, and parties are popular at this age, and a recent study suggests that 80% of middle school students participate in at least some of these activities over the course of a school year (Connolly et al., 2004). These activities gently advance romantic development because they bring both genders into social situations in which romantic attractions are possible but not obligatory. Despite the motivating role of passionate attraction, however, youth's initial cross-gender affiliations may be dictated more by status concerns than by personal chemistry. Consistent with Brown's theory (1999), although perhaps somewhat sooner than he would have predicted, the early adolescent years usher in the guiding function of social status in romantic interactions as youth who are popular with their same-sex peers socialize with popular youth of the opposite gender (Bukowski, Sippola,

& Hoza, 1999) and also are the first among their peers to start to have romantic relationships (Carlson & Rose, 2007).

Stage 2: Exploring Romantic Relationships in Middle Adolescence

Two forms of involvement are evident in the second stage of romantic development, roughly spanning the middle adolescent period of 14–16 years of age. First, as proposed by Furman and his colleagues (Furman & Simon, 1999; Furman & Wehner, 1994), casual dating emerges as an important form of romantic involvement as dyadic connections arise between pairs of adolescents who are mutually attracted to one another. Casual dating connections are quite short lived, lasting only a few months at best, and often enduring for no more than a few weeks (Feiring, 1996; Nieder & Seiffge-Krenke, 2001; Seiffge-Krenke, 2003). At this stage, many adolescents report having more than one such casual dating relationship over the course of a year (Zimmer-Gembeck, 1999). The second form of romantic involvement is "dating in groups," which speaks to Connolly and Goldberg's (1999) notion that many of the casual dyadic relationships that youth develop are themselves embedded in a peer context. Several lines of empirical data confirm the existence of group dating (Connolly, Furman, et al., 2000; Kuttler, La Greca, & Prinstein, 1999; Nieder & Seiffge-Krenke, 2001), essentially describing the phenomenon whereby mixed-gender peer networks become increasingly populated by pairs of teens who have formed a "special relationship" with each other. Yet at this time dating activities complement, rather than replace, time spent with same-sex friends because group affiliations enable adolescents to maintain these ties (Zimmer-Gembeck, 1999). Friends are often the "brokers" of dating, serving as third-party facilitators of a potential romantic relationship by conveying their friend's romantic attraction and confirming whether this is reciprocated (Tolman, Spencer, Harmon, Rosen-Reynoso, & Striepe, 2004). As predicted by Brown (1999), romantic participation in middle adolescence is heavily linked to social status in the peer group. Adolescents who are members of popular groups more often view themselves in romantically relevant terms, such as being physically attractive and socially connected (Youniss, McLennan, & Strauss, 1994). Alongside these self-perceptions, high-status youth are more likely to be involved in dating activities than their lower status classmates (Franzoi, Davis, & Vasquez-Suson, 1994). Among these adolescents, the most frequent daters are those whose high status is "controversial," meaning that more of their classmates say that they would be unlikely to spend time with them, even though there are many who say that they would be likely to do so. These findings suggest that high school dating and popularity are linked and that this association is not without its costs, as high-status dating can create boundaries between popular adolescents and their less romantically active peers.

Stage 3: Consolidating Dyadic Romantic Bonds in Late Adolescence

The final stage of romantic involvement typically occurs at the end of the high school years and concerns the formation of dyadic romantic relationships. The theories of Brown (1999) and Furman (Furman & Simon, 1999; Furman & Wehner, 1994) have been particularly linked to this stage of development (Seiffge-Krenke, 2003). Consistent with their ideas, consolidated romantic relationships have been shown to be rooted in strong emotional bonds, more closely resembling the couple relationships of adulthood than those of younger adolescents. These bonds are stable and enduring, often lasting for 1 year or more (Carver et al., 2003; Connolly & Johnson, 1996; Seiffge-Krenke, 2003). Adolescents describe these relationships as serious, exclusive, and highly supportive on an emotional as well as an affiliative level (Connolly & Johnson, 1996; Furman & Buhrmester, 1992; Seiffge-Krenke, 2003; Shulman & Scharf, 2000; Zimmer-Gembeck, 1999). These qualitative changes in romantic relationships coincide

with adolescents' decreasing level of involvement in larger peer structures (Kuttler & La Greca, 2004). Adolescents in consolidated relationships derive more emotional support from their romantic partners than they do from their friends and also spend more of their leisure time with their romantic partner than they do in their friendship networks (Furman & Buhrmester, 1992; Zimmer-Gembeck, 1999). Yet, as proposed by Connolly and Goldberg (1999), increasing involvement with a romantic partner begins to challenge adolescents' need to maintain a separate sense of self. According to Seiffge-Krenke and colleagues (2001), 17-year-olds with highly connected romantic relationships simultaneously struggle with questions of self-identity. Thus the challenge of the dyadic bonds stage is to balance intimacy and autonomy within the romantic relationship.

Gender and Romantic Stages

It is of interest to note that boys and girls do not differ much in the trajectories of their romantic experiences (Carver et al., 2003; Connolly & McIsaac, 2008; Furman & Shaffer, 2003). Once the transition from same-sex to mixed-sex social contexts has been made, boys and girls follow very similar pathways to romantic relationships. This gender similarity speaks to the strength of romantic staging models, which at their core presuppose that the genders will come together in the same developmental space to jointly embark on the social transition to a romantic relationship (Maccoby, 1998). Nonetheless, there may be qualitative differences in the roles adopted by boys and girls at different stages in the developmental trajectory that advance the romantic maturation of both genders. Girls, in the early adolescent years, take the lead in creating the social settings for romantic interests to flourish (Pellegrini & Long, 2007). They do this by initiating the cross-gender contacts that eventually lead to the creation of larger mixed-gender peer groups, contexts that are instrumental in the transition to romantic relationships (Connolly et al., 2000; Feiring, 1999a; Poulin & Pedersen, 2007). Once these mixed-gender groups have been created by the girls, boys then become highly active and take the lead in connecting with girls in more directly romantic ways (Pellegrini & Long, 2007). Boys are the ones who initiate "dates" with girls—a role that both genders agree is their responsibility (Jackson, Jacob, Landman-Peeters, & Lanting, 2001). Once dates have been initiated, girls' greater intimacy skills may again put them at an advantage in terms of shaping the quality of the relationship. Girls' relatively greater capacity for self-disclosure and mutual support is reflected by the more intimate relationships that they can sustain with their same-sex friends (Camarena et al., 1990; Leaper & Anderson, 1997; Rose & Rudolph, 2006; Sharabany et al., 1981). According to gender socialization theory (Maccoby, 1998; Leaper & Anderson, 1997), previous experience in same-sex friendships creates a domain of considerable strength for girls when they transition into romantic relationships, and this expertise likely enables them to shape the emotional tone of the relationship. Indirectly supporting this notion, boys' cross-sex relationships are more intimate than their same-sex friendships, whereas girls' relationships with same- and cross-sex friends are comparable in terms of intimacy (Sharabany et al., 1981).

Intraindividual Differences in Romantic Stages

Stage theories present a picture of romantic development in which the changes in the romantic activities that define a particular stage are closely linked to chronological age. This age-based perspective offers a developmental view of the normative romantic progression for typical youth, most of the time. However, by focusing on the romantic activities that are shared by members of a particular age range, this perspective may obscure important changes that occur at the individual level. Two intraindividual romantic trajectories warrant discussion. First, an individual adolescent may engage in a varied set of romantic experiences at any one age period.

Although individual adolescents may predominantly be involved with the romantic activities that characterize their particular age-based stage, they may also sporadically experiment with forms of romance from different stages. These relatively fluid explorations of other romantic activities may occur simultaneously or cyclically. Connolly and colleagues (2004) found that, over short periods of time, adolescents often cycle between the adjacent stages of mixed-gender affiliation, dating in groups, and dyadic relationships. Some adolescents reported moving from affiliative to group dating, others from group dating to a romantic relationship, and still others from a dyadic relationship back to group dating. Although not explored by Connolly and her colleagues (2004), cycling of romantic activities can also occur within the course of an ongoing relationship, and we consider the developmental progression of a specific romantic attraction to be the second source of intraindividual variation. Davies and Windle (2000) found evidence to support this shift in their 1-year longitudinal study of middle-adolescent romantic relationships. Sixteen-year-olds who participated in an enduring romantic relationship became progressively less embedded in their friendships groups over the course of a year, demonstrating a shift from peer- to couple-based relationships. Intraindividual changes within a relationship have also been uncovered in a narrative study of sexual-minority youth of African American descent (Eyre, Milbrath, & Peacock, 2007). These youth reported a common trajectory in which their romantic relationships emerged out of attractions that were initiated in peer groups and progressively led to more dyadic encounters. Aside from these studies, the extent to which relationships mature and evolve over their life cycle has not been well explored in adolescence.

Interindividual Differences in Romantic Stages

Although the stage distinctions that were outlined above provide a useful rubric for mapping prototypical developmental patterns, researchers acknowledge that participation in romantic activities can vary among individuals of the same age (Collins, 2003). This interindividual variation has been conceptualized in terms of the developmental timing of romantic activity, as well as the type of activity in which adolescent daters engage (Welsh, Grello, & Harper, 2003). Young adolescents who form romantic partnerships in advance of their age-mates are known as *early starters* (Neemann, Hubbard, & Masten, 1995; Thornton, 1990; Zimmer-Gembeck, Siebenbruner, & Collins, 2001). On the opposite end of the spectrum, the term *late bloomers* is often used to describe those young people for whom entry into committed dyadic relationships does not occur until the adult years (Caspi, Elder, & Bem, 1988). Early entry into dating and romantic relationships has been the focus of much research, especially among girls, because of the putative risks to psychosocial adjustment associated with this form of off-time involvement. This risk stems from the fact that adolescents who experience transitions at earlier ages are less likely to have acquired the intra- and interpersonal skills necessary to successfully navigate the psychosocial demands of these contexts. Conversely, there has been almost no exploration of late bloomers, even though from the development-contextual perspective of task attainment, this off-time pattern may be equally problematic. We will return to a discussion of the adjustment implications of early or delayed timing in a later section. Here, we consider the evidence that early- and later starting adolescents can be distinguished on the basis of individual, familial, and cultural factors.

Early Starters

As previously discussed, the most typical romantic activity for early adolescents is dating in a group setting. Nonetheless, approximately 15%–20% of youth between the ages of 11 and 13 years report a current romantic relationship, and up to 35% of youth in this age range report having some previous experience in a romantic partnership (Carver et al., 2003; Connolly et al., 2004). Consistent with this accelerated trend, early starting youth experience a larger number of romantic dissolutions and more frequent partner turnover than their relatively on-time counterparts (Zimmer-Gembeck et al., 2001). The romantic relationships of early starters tend to be quite intense, both emotionally and sexually (Thornton, 1990). There is also some evidence that early entry into relationships places adolescents on a trajectory of continuous, rather than episodic, romantic involvement. Neemann and colleagues (1995) report that youth who have a romantic partner in the early adolescent years are more likely than their nonpaired counterparts to have a boyfriend or girlfriend later in adolescence. Also demonstrating this trend of continuous involvement, Raley and colleagues (2007) found that youth who are engaged in serious romantic relationships during their adolescent years are more likely to marry or cohabit prior to age 25, a relatively early age in contemporary Western society (Fields, 2003). Perhaps such an ongoing focus with intimate relationships over the course of adolescence interferes with adolescents' ability to adequately form a separate sense of identity that would help them balance their intimacy needs with achievement in other domains, much as suggested by Erikson (1968).

Precocious dating is most consistently predicted by early pubertal maturation (Aro & Taipale, 1987; Ellis & Garber, 2000; Friedlanders et al., 2007; Magnusson, Stattin, & Allen, 1985; Phinney, Jensen, Olsen, & Cundick, 1990). These data refer especially to adolescent girls, as the links between puberty and early dating have been less consistent for boys, with some studies reporting a positive association (Kim & Smith, 1999; Lam, Shi, Ho, Stewart, & Fan, 2002), and other studies, no association at all (Susman et al., 1985). Other predictors of early dating concern the functioning and structure of the family. Insecure attachment to parents is one such factor linked to early dating (Cooper, Shaver, & Collins, 1998). Parental monitoring is another important feature of family dynamics as adolescents who report that their parents are relatively unaware of their social or leisure activities are more likely to be advanced in their romantic development (Friedlander et al., 2007). The marital status of an adolescent's parents has also been linked to early dating. Youth from divorced families tend to become involved in romantic relationships at younger ages than do youth from intact family structures (Chase-Lansdale, Cherlin, & Kiernan, 1995; Tasker & Richards, 1994). Links with parental divorce may be indirect, as some evidence shows that this association is mediated by the degree of conflict in the parent–adolescent relationship. Youth from divorced families who report a high degree of conflict with their parents are most likely to report dating in early adolescence (Veprinska & Connolly, 2007). Finally, peer group dynamics may give rise to early dating. Associating with older peers is a risk for precocious romantic relationships, likely because these peers model more advanced forms of dating involvement (Billy, Rodgers, & Udry, 1984; Friedlander et al., 2007; Stattin & Magnusson, 1990). We will return later in the chapter to the possibility that these associated factors may operate concurrently to compound the negative impact of early dating on adjustment.

Late Bloomers

Turning to the other end of the romantic continuum, approximately 10% of late adolescents report no experience in either romantic activities or relationships (Connolly & McIsaac, 2008) and an additional 15% do not participate in relationships that endure beyond four months (Carver et al., 2003). Although very little is known about the romantic trajectories of late-blooming youth, documenting whether their eventual entrance into romantic relationships is a gradual or direct process may be particularly important. Late bloomers who commence their romantic involvement by directly entering into a couple relationship may be quite challenged by the intimacy

expectations of these unions since their cross-sex intimacy skills are less honed and their ideas of what is acceptable in a relationship are less validated by the peer group. Because of this, late-blooming youth may be more vulnerable to affective and behavioral fluctuations in their romantic relationships than adolescents who have been scaffolded by their prior experiences with casual dating—an idea we will return to in our section on adjustment.

The predictors of this off-time pathway have not been well articulated. Some evidence suggests that late bloomers are less embedded in their peer networks and that they lack intimacy in their relationships with friends (Connolly & Johnson, 1996; Davies & Windle, 2000). This peer isolation may be reflective of the personality of late-blooming adolescents. Shy adolescents, for example, have been characterized as late bloomers because they are less likely to have a romantic partner in adolescence or marry when they reach adulthood (Caspi et al., 1988). In addition to temperamental factors, delayed entry into romantic relationships may be due to differences in physical appearance, especially when these features bear on the attainment of culturally desirable images. A recent study of diversity in body weight among young adolescent girls demonstrated that even small variations in weight can lead to different romantic trajectories (Halpern, King, Oslak, & Udry, 2005). Nonobese adolescents with above-average body fat were far less likely to be romantically involved than girls who were at, or below, the mean body fat percentage of their peer group. Along a similar vein, adolescents who have a physical illness, such as juvenile diabetes, have fewer romantic relationships than their healthier peers (Seiffge-Krenke, 1997, 2000). Explanations as to why temperamentally or physically different adolescents would have fewer romantic experiences than other adolescents are often rooted in the friendship network. It may be that these special populations of adolescents have difficulty finding acceptance in their same-sex peer groups, which may in turn restrict their access to mixed-gender romantic activities and impede their progress to romantic relationships.

Culture and Timing

A later-than-average age of entry into romantic involvements should be considered within a cultural context. Asian cultures normatively delay the onset of cross-gender activities to the middle adolescent years and the formation of romantic relationships, until high school has been completed (Coates, 1999). There is a strong focus on family interdependency in Asian cultures, and this may contribute to parents' reluctance to encourage their children's entry into activities that pull them away from the home (Feldman & Rosenthal, 1990; Stevenson & Zusho, 2002). Adolescents whose later start is part of the cultural norm may have qualitatively different experiences from those youth whose off-time trajectories were created by individual characteristics. Because culturally prescribed romantic delays do not necessarily limit access to peers, the normative sequencing of developmental stages is unlikely to be altered. Rather, it is quite possible that the overall shape of the trajectory will be intact, but that it will begin to unfold somewhat later in time. In support of this idea, studies focusing on Canadian and American adolescents of Asian descent have found that there is a later start to romantic activities among Asian adolescents in the early and middle adolescent years and less serious relationships later on (Connolly et al., 2004; Regan, Durvasula, Howell, Ureño, & Rea, 2004). That being said, it appears that once these young Asians begin to engage in romantic activities, they follow a similar sequence of stages as their North American peers (Connolly et al., 2004). It is unclear whether the late starters of other minority groups will follow the same gradual progression of romantic involvement noted for Asian youth. Some evidence suggests that this may not be the case and that a more abrupt transition from no involvement to dyadic relationships may occur. This possibility

is highlighted in a retrospective interview study of Latino college students who were asked to reflect on their high school romantic experiences (Rafaelli, 2005). These students reported a delayed onset of dating during their high school years but noted that when dating did emerge, it was couple based from the start, rather than progressing through a prior group stage. This pattern was particularly evident for girls. Studies that address the issue of romantic stages in non-Western cultures are relatively few in number and we believe that this is an important area for future inquiry.

NORMS AND EXPECTATIONS OF ROMANTIC RELATIONSHIPS

Having reviewed the progression of romantic activities that support relationship development, we now turn to a consideration of the norms and personal expectations that color adolescents' approach to interactions with a romantic partner. Adolescents' entry into romantic activities is guided by their global understanding of culturally sanctioned feelings and behaviors, as well as the roles of adult men and women in heterosexual relationships (Feiring, 1999b). Given that adolescents do not have an established sense of their own identity in romantic interactions, from a developmental perspective, they tend to rely on the gendered and stereotypic images that are portrayed in the popular media to inform their beliefs about what constitutes an appropriate relationship (Feiring, 1999b). As highlighted in our review of the historical context of adolescent dating, the popular culture promotes a set of norms that position idealized notions of passionate love as the basis of all romantic relationships.

Norms of Passionate Love

At least among Western cultures, adolescents' relationship views center on the all-encompassing importance of romantic love and the belief that a passionate connection with one's partner is a necessary and achievable state of being that is sustainable over the short and long term (Hatfield, 1988). Feelings of passionate love refer to the intense and special connection that one has to a romantic partner, and the idealization of this experience begins in middle childhood and persists virtually unchanged into the adolescent years (Connolly et al., 1999; Hatfield et al., 1988). Within this overarching mind-set, there are prescriptive norms that specify the "correct" way of attracting and maintaining a partner. A study of romantic beliefs conducted by Simon, Eder, and Evans (1992) found that adolescent girls could articulate several rules that dictate the expression of romantic feelings, not the least of which was the requirement for one to be in a constant state of love. Also included among these rules were exclusivity, monogamy, and maintaining loving feelings regardless of a partner's actions.

Yet coexisting alongside the norm of passionate love, there are also competing norms that advocate for the restraint of romantic expression. "Playing it cool" by not allowing romantic attractions to become a preoccupation, at least in the eyes of one's peers, is a form of behavioral restraint that is valued by both boys and girls (Simon et al., 1992; Tolman et al., 2004). The requirement of restraint also finds extensive voice in the norm of "compulsory heterosexuality." Passionate love is restricted to cross-sex attractions, and same-sex love is highly censured (Simon et al., 1992; Striepe & Tolman, 2003; Tolman et al., 2004). The heterosexual norm places additional restrictions on the behaviors of each gender. Girls are required to focus on pleasing their boyfriends at the expense of themselves, particularly in the sexual arena. A girl who violates this norm by taking too many liberties with her sexuality is often subject to negative labeling by society at large. For boys, the heterosexual norm carries with it the expectation that they will be sexually aggressive with their girlfriends and focus their efforts on sexual, rather than relational, forms of intimacy (Striepe & Tolman, 2003). Although acceptance of these restraints may be questioned by some adolescents and rebelled against by others, they nonetheless inform adolescents' views of appropriate romantic interactions and shape their behaviors accordingly.

Same-Sex Peer Groups as Enforcers of Norms

Same-sex peers make a significant contribution to the interpretation, communication, and regulation of romantic norms. Yet the processes through which this normative information is transmitted tend to be quite different for groups of boys and groups of girls. Groups of girls frequently discuss romantic feelings, and these exchanges are the primary means of translating the broader cultural messages into scripts that are meaningful for their daily experiences (Cavanagh, 2007; Eder, 1993; Simon et al., 1992). Gossip about other adolescents' relationships is a prominent form of romantic dialogue among girls, as is teasing each other about the appropriateness of their romantic attractions and dating behaviors (Eder, 1993; O'Sullivan & Meyer-Bahlburg, 2003; Simon et al., 1992). Romantic norm violations are typically handled by excluding the offending girl from the friendship group. Fear of rejection is quite salient for adolescent girls, and, as such, the technique of social ostracism is effective in regulating romantic feelings and behaviors. A recent study by O'Sullivan and Meyer-Bahlburg (2003) suggests that a domain in which girls are particularly vigilant is sexual expression. They report that groups of girls permit sexual activity only when it is accompanied by feelings of intimacy. That being said, the allowable level of sexual expression is closely tied to the level romantic involvement, as sexual intercourse is seen as more acceptable in longer term relationships than it is in relationships that are of shorter duration. Girls who are sexually active outside of intimate or stable relationships are typically condemned by their same-sex peers and labeled with such terms as *slut* or *ho*. As a result, these offending girls experience a decrease in their social standing.

Rather than teasing or social exclusion, boys reinforce romantic norms through more directly aggressive means, especially bullying and sexual harassment (McMaster, Connolly, Pepler, & Craig, 2002). For boys, the most stringently enforced norm concerns the unacceptability of same-sex attraction and behavior (Tolman et al., 2004). Homophobic slurs are the most common method of same-sex verbal harassment among adolescent boys, and these remarks clearly convey the heterosexual norm. In support of this, adolescent boys who experience same-sex attractions or who question their sexual orientation report higher levels of victimization and sexual harassment from their same-sex peers (Williams et al., 2003). Groups of boys also foster mutual adherence to the stereotype of heightened masculinity and sexuality. Adolescent boys encourage each other to actively pursue purely sexual encounters with girls (Tolman et al., 2004). This norm is often communicated in the context of group discussions wherein boys jockey with each other for positions of increasing social status. For both genders, then, peer group interactions function to promote the development of romantic views that are consistent with those of the broader culture.

Personal Goals and Motives

Aside from the universal norms that are supported by the peer group, adolescents also have their own personal motives for engaging in romantic relationships. It is interesting to note that adolescents' personal views do not always mirror the norms as outlined above. When researchers invite individual adolescents to reflect on the particular elements that they are seeking in a romantic relationship, they tend to receive less stereotyped responses than when they obtain information about romantic expectations through discussions in a group setting. The use of individually focused methodologies brings into the forefront adolescents' desire for closeness and intimacy in their romantic relationships (Connolly et al., 1999; Feiring, 1996; Roscoe, Diana, & Brooks, 1987; Shulman &

Kipnis, 2001; Shulman & Scharf, 2000; Smiler, 2008). Although adolescents' intimacy goals are broadly consistent with the cultural norm of passionate love, they also reflect concern about the degree to which they are *personally* satisfied with the level of closeness in their relationships.

The ways in which adolescents expect to connect with their close romantic partners changes with age. In the early years of adolescence, romantic expectations and goals pertain more to affiliative and recreational ways of aligning with a partner (Connolly et al., 1999; Feiring, 1999a; Roscoe et al., 1987; Shulman & Kipnis, 2001; Shulman & Scharf, 2000). These intimacy goals appear to be in harmony with the group-based nature of romantic interactions in the early adolescent period. Older adolescents, in contrast, are more likely to describe their relationship goals in terms of emotional intimacy and reciprocal caretaking, expectations that blend well with the later romantic stage of consolidated dyadic relationships. Taken as a whole, the differing intimacy goals of younger and older adolescents seem to overlap well with the particular relationship structures that predominate at each stage of development.

There are also differences between the relationship motives of boys and girls. Relative to girls, boys place more value on physical attractiveness, sexuality, and game playing, and this is particularly the case in the early adolescent years (Feiring, 1996; Roscoe et al., 1987; Shulman & Scharf, 2000). Girls, however, tend to emphasize emotional intimacy and attachment more so than boys (Feiring, 1996; Roscoe et al., 1987; Shulman & Scharf, 2000). Despite these differences, there are many ways in which boys and girls think similarly about their romantic relationships. Boys and girls equally value the affiliative functions of romance (Connolly et al., 1999; Feiring, 1996), and both genders look for positive personality traits in their partners (Regan & Joshi, 2003). Also speaking to the issue of gender similarity, an interesting set of findings by Smiler (2008) suggests that adolescent boys may be more oriented toward intimacy goals in their relationships than previously believed. His data show that middle adolescent boys are more motivated to pursue romantic relationships because of loving feelings and a desire for closeness than the possibility of sexual behaviors. These patterns likely reflect the methods employed by Smiler (2008) as he invited boys to report on both "stereotypically male" motivations for dating as well as those that allowed for a more nuanced understanding. As previously noted, our ability to document the ways in which young people pursue both cultural norms and personal goals in their romantic relationships is inherently tied to the methods that we employ to ask about these varied sets of expectations. Moving forward, we suggest that researchers consider romantic values at the level of the community, peer group, and individual.

Culture and Norms

A noticeable gap in our understanding of adolescent romantic norms is the assessment of cross-cultural differences. Additional investigation of this issue is likely to be quite revealing, given that romantic values and expectations are largely socially constructed and, as such, reflect cultural beliefs about the roles of men and women in relationships. The limited data that are available do suggest that Black and White adolescents living in the United States have somewhat different romantic and sexual expectations. O'Sullivan and Meyer-Bahlburg (2003) found that American girls of African descent experience culturally specific pressures to engage in high levels of sexuality within their romantic relationships. This pattern was echoed in a recent study using the Add Health data set in which African American boys and girls were reported to have more sexualized conceptions of romantic relationships than their White counterparts (Cavanagh, 2007). The findings of these two studies support the contention that African American culture is relatively accepting of sexual behaviors that occur outside of the

context of idealized romance (O'Sullivan & Meyer-Bahlburg, 2003). Philbrick and Stones (1988a, 1988b) have also conducted studies that support the idea that African and Western cultures differ in their emphasis on the overriding importance of romantic love. Using a South African data set, these authors found that both Black and White adolescents considered romantic power, or the belief that romance has a potent influence on a person's life, to be a more salient relationship norm than passionate love. Despite our limited understanding of cross-cultural norms, the evidence reviewed in this section generally supports the ecological perspective of Bronfenbrenner (1979). That is, the appropriate expression of romantic intimacy is first conveyed by the broader culture, then interpreted and regulated by the peer group, and, finally, internalized by the individual within the context of his or her romantic relationship.

Negative Expectations of Romance

Consistent with the general desirability of romantic relationships, there is little to suggest that adolescents have many negative views of romance. When negative expectations do surface, they tend to focus on problems maintaining independence rather than creating sufficient levels of closeness or intimacy. In support of this, Feiring (1996) found that the largest disadvantage to romantic participation, as conceptualized by 16-year-old boys and girls, was that it might require too much commitment. Other disadvantages focused on the potential for negativity in the couples' interaction with each other, particularly conflict. It is of interest to note that only 10% of the adolescents in Feiring's (1996) study were able to identify a single disadvantage of having a romantic relationship. That being said, adolescents who do not adhere to cultural scripts of romantic love may be more likely to have negatively colored perceptions. Sexual-minority youth, who by definition do not conform to the norm of heterosexuality, express fewer positive expectations about romantic relationships (Diamond &

Lucas, 2004). These youth are most anxious about their prospects of finding a romantic partner, as well as their likelihood of maintaining a relationship once it begins.

Adolescents' ideas about the negative features of romance may become more apparent when they reflect upon specific relationships that are troubled or have dissolved. One commonly occurring relationship problem during the adolescent years, despite the cultural norm of monogamy, is infidelity. Feldman and Cauffman (1999a) report that over 60% of late adolescents have been in a relationship where some degree of sexual betrayal has occurred, whether perpetrated by the self, the partner, or both parties. Studies that have asked late adolescents to describe the negative relationship features that would justify cheating have often pointed to a loss of passionate love or the presence of jealousy or insecurity in the relationship (Feldman & Cauffman 1999b; Feldman, Cauffman, Arnett Jensen, & Arnett, 2000; Roscoe, Cavanaugh, & Kennedy, 1988). These justifications suggest an absence of closeness between the partners, which, in turn, echoes the intimacy attributes that adolescents expect to find in their relationships. Other popular explanations for infidelity relate to adolescents' wariness about making a romantic commitment, including the desire to experiment with a number of different partners (Feldman & Cauffman 1999b, Feldman et al., 2000; Roscoe et al. 1988).

Asking adolescents to account for why a particular relationship came to an end may also elicit valuable information about their negative expectations of romance. Connolly and McIsaac (in press, 2008) have taken this approach in their investigation of adolescent breakups. Similar to the reasons offered for infidelity, adolescents' relationships dissolve because of dissatisfaction with the level of intimacy or closeness between the partners, be it expressed as a lack of affiliation, trust, open communication, or romantic feelings. Unlike infidelity, the desire for freedom or experimentation is rarely used to account for

relationship endings. Thus, adolescents' attributions for dissolution seem better able to provide a window onto the expectations that youth have about the positive qualities that maintain relationships rather than the disadvantages of having a boyfriend or girlfriend. This logic resonates with our overall point that adolescents are rather blind to the potential for problems in their romantic encounters, a cognitive filter which may contribute to their naïve enthusiasm for these relationships, as well as their relative instability. Adolescents' neglect of the more negative facets of romantic relationships may also cause them to react more strongly to relationship problems when they do occur, perhaps accounting for the emotional lability that accompanies romantic involvements during this stage of life (Larson, Clore, & Wood, 1999).

ROMANTIC RELATIONSHIP PROCESSES

Having considered adolescents' concepts of romance and their various motives for wanting a relationship, we now explore whether the qualities of their romantic interactions are consistent with their expectations. Researchers have primarily investigated the qualitative features of adolescents' romantic relationships by documenting the many support, conflict, and power processes that are contained within their couple interactions. Romantic support has typically been conceptualized as a positive process because these features are desired by adolescents and also affirming of their involvement in the relationship (Shulman & Scharf, 2000). Conflict processes are more complex in their relational valence. Often, they are viewed as negative features that impede and detract from the relationship. Yet other times it is thought that successful negotiation of conflict is positive in that it enhances the couple's satisfaction and investment (Collins, Laursen, Mortensen, Luebker, & Ferreria, 1997; Shulman, 2003). Power processes are most often cast in a negative light because lack of equity tends to destabilize close romantic relationships

(Banister & Jakubec, 2004). In the coming sections, we outline support, conflict, and power processes in adolescents' romantic interactions and argue that these relational attributes contribute to adolescents' management of critical developmental tasks.

Support Processes
Adolescents consider their romantic relationships to be among the most supportive and caring of all their personal connections (Adams, Laursen, & Wilder, 2001; Connolly & Johnson, 1996; Laursen & Williams, 1997; Seiffge-Krenke, 2000; 2003; Shulman & Sharf, 2000, Werebe, 1987). The support offered by a romantic partner has both behavioral and affective dimensions. Common behavioral demonstrations of support include spending time together, exchanging gifts, and acknowledging the couple status to others (Carver et al., 2003; O'Sullivan, Mantsun, Harris, & Brooks-Gunn, 2007). More affectionate ways of showing support include disclosing personal feelings, developing a sense of caretaking and trust, and communicating loving sentiments (Connolly et al., 2000; Connolly & Johnson, 1996; Seiffge-Krenke, 2000, 2003). By the end of the adolescent years, boyfriends and girlfriends ascend to the top of the hierarchy of close relationships, surpassing both parents and friends in terms of their perceived level of support (Furman & Buhrmester, 1992). Older adolescents, relative to their younger counterparts, consistently spend more time with romantic partners, as well as note more trust, communication, and feelings of love in their romantic relationships (Adams et al., 2001; Carver et al., 2003; Connolly, Furman, et al., 2000; Laursen & Williams, 1997; Meeus, Branje, van der Valk, & de Wiede, 2007; Seiffge-Krenke, 2000). The developmental link between age and romantic support is mediated by adolescents' growing skill in maintaining longer term relationships (Connolly & Johnson, 1996), as well as the increasing salience of romantic partnerships in their own lives and in the lives of their peers (Meeus et al., 2007).

As with age, the support processes of romantic relationships can also vary with gender and cultural context. Girls and boys have been shown to be similar in their reporting of the behavioral dimensions of romantic support, such as spending time together as a couple (Carver et al., 2003; Connolly, Furman, et al., 2000, Connolly & Johnson, 1996; Seiffge-Krenke, 2000, 2003). Yet there is a marked gender difference in terms of the emotional support that is perceived. Consistent with their greater focus on relationship dynamics, girls generally view their romantic relationships as more nurturing, caring, and affectionate than boys (Connolly & Johnson, 1996). This pattern suggests that girls and boys experience their relationships quite differently, even though the time they spend together is comparable. Ethnicity also moderates the degree of support expressed in a romantic relationship. Giordano and colleagues (2005) found that African American youth describe their romantic relationships in less supportive and caring terms than White adolescents. These authors attribute this difference to the strong family values of the African American culture. In this context, extensive connections with a large kin network are quite valued, leaving relatively fewer personal resources to devote to the deepening of a specific relationship (Giordano et al., 2005).

Support Processes and Developmental Tasks
Romantic support processes have most often been linked to the achievement of intimacy, sexuality, and attachment to a partner. Yet disentangling the links between support processes and the interdependence tasks that they are thought to promote is often methodologically and conceptually challenging. Methodological problems are most evident in the links between support processes and intimacy attainment because intimacy has been framed as both a process and an outcome in studies of adolescent romance. Furthermore, the "process" and "task" aspects of intimacy are typically

measured at the same time, using similar instrumentation, making conclusions about an adolescent's capacity for intimacy isomorphic with the assessment of the quality of his or her interaction with a romantic partner. A study by Montgomery (2005) has addressed this methodological limitation by examining the intimacy task from an Eriksonian, rather than an interpersonal, perspective. She assessed adolescents' impressions of their capacity for intimacy and then connected this to their dating history and quality, ultimately noting that youth with more extensive love experiences expressed more confidence in their capacity to attain a high degree of intimacy in their close relationships. Another way in which the task and process components of intimacy may be separated is through the use of a longitudinal design. Focusing on Brown's (1999) notion of *bonded love*, Seiffge-Krenke and colleagues (2001, 2003) found that this attainment in young adulthood was predicted by the support processes that characterized their romantic relationships at the age of 17 years. Additional longitudinal studies within the adolescent period would be helpful in confirming the causal pathway between positive processes and the resolution of intimacy.

In contrast to intimacy, the links between romantic support and sexuality suffer from more of a conceptual silence. Although many romantic theorists (Connolly & Goldberg, 1999; Furman & Wehner, 1994; Sullivan, 1963) have suggested that sexuality should be integrated with romantic feelings, the essential components of sexual maturity are not entirely clear. Is the task of sexuality relatively behavioral, concerning adolescents' increasing participation in sexual activity with a romantic partner? Or is the task of sexual development more consistent with identity formation in that a sexual aspect of the self must be uncovered and integrated alongside other aspects of one's personal definition? Or, finally, is sexuality relatively biological in that the task concerns fulfilling reproductive potential in a stable and committed relationship? As the research fields

of adolescent sexuality and romance become more collaborative, these questions will no doubt be addressed, likely revealing the multifaceted aspects of sexual development that may occur in the context of a relationship. The data that we currently have speaks to the link between support processes and sexual behaviors. For example, a positive association has been found between relationship support and light sexual behaviors, such as hand holding, kissing, and fondling, among late adolescent couples (Rostosky, Galliher, Welsh, & Kawaguchi, 2000). This connection has yet to be established longitudinally, meaning that it is equally possible for the achievement of sexuality to increase the level of support and intimacy in a relationship.

Attachment research may be better positioned to avoid these pitfalls because the conceptualization and measurement of specific attachment styles is more clearly differentiated from the underlying support processes that promote romantic security. That being said, there is unfortunately a dearth of research that directly examines the links between supportive romantic qualities and attachment to a romantic partner. A recent study by Furman and Simon (2006) made an important step in filling this gap. These authors evaluated the cross-sectional links between romantic relationship processes and working models of romantic attachment among middle adolescents in stable romantic dyads. Youth who reported that their relationships were characterized by open communication and expressions of caring were more likely to be categorized as securely attached to their partner than were youth whose relationships were lacking in these qualities. Furman and Wehner's (1994) notion that positive processes will carry forward from one relationship to another, thus facilitating secure romantic attachments at a later time in adolescence, remains unexplored.

Psychosocial achievements that concern adolescents' growing sense of self, including the formation of a romantic self-concept, sex-role identity, and maintaining autonomy with a romantic partner, are also thought to be aided by romantic support processes (Connolly & Goldberg, 1999; Feiring, 1999b; Furman & Shaffer, 2003). Research findings, though not voluminous, generally attest to a link between positive relationship processes and independence tasks. Dating and romantic status, for example, have been linked to romantic self-concept, namely, the belief that one can attract and maintain a romantic partner (Connolly & Konarski, 1994; Kuttler, LaGreca, & Prinstein, 1999). Speaking more directly to the issue of relationship processes, when adolescents view their couple relationships as supportive, satisfying, and enduring they feel more competent in the romantic domain (Bouchey, 2007; Laursen, Furman, & Mooney, 2006) and are more settled in their sex-role identity (Zimmer-Gembeck & Petherick, 2006). Similar links have been found for romantic autonomy. Adolescents who are in supportive relationships are more able to set boundaries and maintain a separate sense of self relative to those youth whose relationships are less close (Shulman & Knafo, 1997; Taradash, Connolly, Pepler, Craig, & Costa, 2001).

Conflict Processes

Conflict does occur in adolescents' relationships with their romantic partners, although far less frequently than with other members of their social network (Furman & Buhrmester, 1992; Shute & Charlton, 2006). Adolescent romantic partners most commonly argue about issues that relate to the functioning of the dyad, including jealousy, trust, neglect, and betrayal (McIsaac, Connolly, McKenney, Pepler, & Craig, 2008). External factors, such as selecting social activities or responding to pressure from peers, are seldom reported by adolescents as issues that spark a conflict with their romantic partner (McIsaac et al., in press). Similar to the trajectory of support processes, romantic partner conflicts also increase across the adolescent years (Furman & Buhrmester, 1992; Shulman & Tuval-Mashiach, 2006). This overlap is unlikely to be a coincidence. Conflict

can occur only between partners who are sufficiently close to become aware of incompatibilities. As well, relationship partners must have cultivated enough emotional investment in the relationship to enter into the conflict, rather than taking the easier path of letting the relationship dissolve without a struggle (Collins, Laursen et al., 1994; Shulman, 2003).

Conflict can be detrimental or beneficial to a relationship, depending on the way in which it is handled (Laursen, Finkelstein, & Betts, 2000). Hence, there has been considerable effort made to understand how adolescents respond to conflict with their romantic partner. According to adolescents' self-reports, the most common conflict negotiation strategy used with a romantic partner is compromise. This includes such behaviors as listening to one's partner, expressing personal feelings, and proposing mutually satisfying solutions (Feldman & Gowen, 1998). The reported use of compromising strategies increases with age. Somewhat less often, adolescents report using distraction to avoid addressing the problem altogether, employing such tactics as telling jokes, or engaging in a different activity. Other romantic conflict strategies include seeking support from friends and using overt expressions of anger, although these are less often reported by adolescent romantic couples (Feldman & Gowen, 1998).

Boys and girls report similar rates of conflict with their romantic partners (Furman & Buhrmester, 1992). That being said, there are quite clear gender differences in the most frequent type of conflict strategy utilized, with girls reporting more compromise and boys reporting more distraction (Feldman & Gowen, 1998). There is also some data to suggest that, in their romantic partner interactions, boys and girls are inclined to adopt a conflict approach that is characteristic of the other gender. In particular, Shute and Charlton (2006) found that adolescent boys and girls report conflict strategies with a romantic partner that are somewhat similar to the strategies used by the other gender in their conflicts with a same-sex best friend. Relative to their peer disagreements, with their romantic partners, girls are more likely to report the use of overt anger and boys are more likely to report the use of compromise. Shute and Charlton's (2006) data thus lend support to Maccoby's (1998) view that the imitation of opposite-gender interaction styles may be an attempt by adolescent dating partners to accommodate to the novel behaviors of the other, as well as their willingness to engage in unfamiliar strategies for the sake of relationship maintenance.

Observations of adolescents' conflict processes paint a somewhat different picture than the one based on self-reports. In contrast to the self-reported use of compromise, the most commonly observed strategy employed by adolescents is actually to disown the conflict by *downplaying* its significance or impact on the relationship (Tuval-Mashiach & Shulman, 2006).

While not generally viewed as relationship enhancing, downplaying may nonetheless serve a useful function to adolescents in that relationships that are characterized by this style are quite enduring, at least over a 1-year period (Shulman, Tuval-Mashiach, Levran, & Anbar, 2006). Far less often than downplaying, adolescents use an *integrative* strategy in which they sincerely engage with the conflict and try to negotiate a solution that will enhance mutual understanding in the relationship (Shulman et al., 2006). The integrative style only emerges as typical in the young adult years and the relative maturity of this style is evident in its link with relationship durations of 2 years or more (Shulman et al., 2006). In contrast to these more adaptive techniques, a minority of adolescents approach disagreement in a coercive manner, using *conflictive* strategies that escalate the interaction into a negative confrontation which fails to resolve the issue. Unsurprisingly, conflictive strategies do not resolve the disagreement, but rather, they contribute to the further destabilization of the couple, leading to the rapid termination

of the relationship (Shulman et al., 2006). Conflictive strategies also have the potential to escalate the argument to the point of physical aggression (Capaldi & Gorman-Smith, 2003; Connolly & Josephson, 2007; O'Leary & Slep, 2003). Adolescent dating violence is an important issue however, further discussion of the theory and evidence for this phenomenon is beyond the scope of this chapter.

Observations of romantic conflict suggest that, in real life, adolescents are less able to use the compromising and collaborative strategies that they indicate in their own reports. It is likely that adolescents' desire to compromise with their partners is not matched by their actual negotiation skills in the emergent context of a romantic relationship. Boys, in particular, rarely acknowledge the use of any negative conflict resolution strategies with their girlfriends (Feldman & Gowen, 1998). Girls, however, seem more able to acknowledge their use of angry or coercive strategies from time to time. It cannot presently be determined whether there are consistent differences in the observed strategies of boys and girls because the majority of observational studies position the couple as the unit of the analysis, rather than the individual partners (e.g., Tuval-Mashiach & Shulman, 2006). Given the small number of observational studies of conflict resolution, further work on the gendered ways of negotiating a disagreement is clearly in order.

Conflict Processes and Developmental Tasks

Researchers have considered whether the process of resolving a conflict is linked to the attainment of developmental tasks. Autonomy has been a particular focus because successful negotiation of a conflict necessitates behaviors that aid the establishment of a sense of independence in the relationship, such as the expression of individual opinions and points of view (Collins et al., 1997). This connection was examined in a recent observational study of conflict management and autonomy in adolescent romantic couples (McIsaac et al., 2008). Data obtained from this study suggest that when adolescents enable the negotiation of conflict by using compromise, active listening, and reciprocal turn taking, both boys and girls show more autonomy. Conversely, when adolescents obstruct the negotiation process by refusing to talk about the problem, using distraction or verbally attacking the other, lower levels of autonomy are expressed. McIsaac and colleagues (2008) thus support the notion that conflict is complex and its function in supporting developmental tasks is dependent on the strategies adopted by the adolescents. This study also uncovered an interesting pattern of gender dynamics. Girls who employed enabling conflict management styles enhanced the autonomous functioning of their boyfriends, as well as themselves. However, similarly skilled boys did not influence their girlfriends' autonomy. As we have previously discussed, girls appear to take on a "managerial" role in their interactions with a boyfriend, echoing their interpersonal strengths in the dyadic context (Leaper & Anderson, 1997; Maccoby, 1998; Underwood, 2007).

Similar to autonomy, the links between conflict processes and attachment representations have a clear conceptual base (Creasey, Kershaw, & Boston, 1999). Because conflict threatens the stability of a relationship, arguments are thought to provide a salient context for the activation of attachment representations. Romantic conflicts may be particularly challenging for adolescents with anxious attachments because they tap into their fears about relationship loss and rejection. The fragility of anxious youth has been documented by Creasey and his colleagues (Creasey & Hesson-McInnis, 2001; Creasey et al., 1999). Relative to late adolescents who are securely oriented toward their close relationships, anxious youth report lower confidence in their ability to manage negative affect during a conflict situation. Creasey and Ladd (2004) recently suggested that high negative mood expectancy underlies the perception of escalating conflict for

anxiously attached youth. Yet this expectation seems to primarily color their internal experience of the conflict, rather than their actual negotiation, as Creasey and Ladd (2004) did not observe any strategy differences between anxiously attached and securely attached youth during a romantic conflict interaction task. In support of the notion of an "inner struggle," Campbell and colleagues (2005) found that anxious adolescents describe their romantic relationships as conflictual, even though these high ratings are not corroborated by their partners. Yet, in contrast to Creasey and Ladd (2004), Campbell and colleagues (2005) also observed anxious youth to escalate their conflicts by overreacting to their romantic partner, as well as by being unresponsive to their partner's attempts to calm and refocus the discussion. The somewhat different picture painted by these two studies may reflect the locus of attachment that was measured, with Creasey and Ladd (2004) tapping into late adolescents' *general* representations of close relationships and Campbell and colleagues (2005) tapping into *specific* attachment to a romantic partner. As such, the latter study may have been better positioned to reveal links between attachment representations and adolescents' *actual* negotiation of the romantic conflict. Although most attachment-based studies of conflict negotiation have focused on anxious youth, there is some data to suggest that avoidant youth are also ineffective managers of their romantic conflicts. Avoidant youth are more likely than anxious or secure youth to use such strategies as withdrawal, inattention, and defensiveness during a conflict (Creasey et al., 1999; Creasey & Ladd, 2004), behaviors which highlight their disconnectedness from the emotional needs of their partners. The theoretically intriguing links that we have presented between conflict processes and attachment representations await replication in samples of early and middle adolescents.

Conflict processes have also been linked to the achievement of romantic intimacy (Collins & Laursen, 1994; Shulman, 2003). Late adolescents, in particular, seem to recognize that some level of conflict is not only expectable in their relationships, but also valuable in terms of improving communication and understanding between the partners (Simon, Kobielski, & Martin, 2008). Such constructive beliefs about the utility of conflict have been associated with the self-reported level of emotional intimacy in the romantic relationship. Adolescent boys and girls who believe that conflict can be a healthy way of resolving differences report more positive conflict negotiation strategies and more intimacy in their romantic relationships than youth who believe that conflicts should be avoided because of the threats they pose to couple stability (Simon et al., 2008). Complementary findings about the intimacy functions of conflict have been found using video-recall methods of late adolescents' couple interactions (Galliher, Welsh, Rostosky, & Kawaguchi, 2004). Adolescent girls who rated their boyfriends as less angry in their interactions also reported more closeness in the relationship. Boys, in contrast, were less affected by the presence of frustration as their satisfaction with the relationship was unlinked to conflict, even though they reported that it occurred at the same level as did their girl friends'. Rather than attending to the more negative aspects of the conflict, boys' satisfaction with the relationship was linked to their beliefs about their own ability to incorporate their girl friends' points of view into decisions about the relationship. These observational findings suggest intriguing gendered links between intimacy and conflict such that boys and girls may be sensitive to different aspects of the conflict dynamic in their close romantic partnerships.

In the same way that adaptive methods of solving a conflict can support emotional forms of intimacy, one might argue that such conflict processes would also support the expression of healthy sexuality between romantic partners. At present, there is little data available to assess the links between conflict negotiation strategies and sexual development. Data obtained in a study of late adolescent couples (Rostosky et al., 2000), however, support

the idea that conflict dynamics and sexuality are connected. Boys and girls who describe their romantic interactions as highly argumentative report having more frequent sexual intercourse than couples who do not regularly engage with their partner in conflict. The authors suggest that this counterintuitive finding may be explained by positioning sexual intercourse as a proxy for the stability of the couples' investment in the relationship, which in turn creates a safe atmosphere for them to air their grievances with each other. However, because conflictual processes were not simultaneously associated with more affectionate forms of sexual behaviour, such as hand holding or kissing, it may also be that high levels of conflict impede normative trajectories of sexual development by launching adolescents into sexually intense relationships before they are able to manage these dynamics. Further work on the links between conflict and sexuality are needed to clarify these, and other, possibilities.

Imbalance of Power

The Western notion of romantic love embraces the concept of equity between partners because of the high value placed on individual choice in this cultural context (Chung, 2005; Felmlee, 1994). Despite this cultural norm, studies of young adults show that women generally do not perceive their relationships to be balanced in decision making, emotional investment, or the amount of personal resources committed to the relationship (Felmlee, 1994). Unlike adults, it could be argued that adolescents should not experience power imbalance in their romantic relationships because developmentally, these unions are lower in the emotional, financial, and day-to-day commitments that often spark perceptions of inequity. Consistent with this, many adolescents report that power in their romantic relationships is shared (Furman & Buhrmester, 1992). This finding is stable across the adolescent years and does not differ between boys and girls. It may be premature, however, to conclude that power dynamics are not present in adolescent couples' interactions with each other. In contrast to self-report findings, interviews with youth and observational studies of couple interactions suggest that power imbalances are a central theme in adolescents' romantic relationships. Adolescent girls' discussions about their dating relationships highlight problems with equity and suggest that they perceive themselves to hold inferior power relative to their boyfriends (Banister & Jakubec 2004; Chung, 2005). Girls nonetheless want to believe that their relationships conform to the romantic ideal of equity and so to accomplish this, they take charge of the "emotional work" of the relationship (Chung, 2005). By casting their boyfriends as emotionally incompetent, girls use their interpersonal strengths to reclaim a sense of power. This way of framing power is also evident in a recent study of adolescent girls and their boyfriends (Bentley, Galliher, & Fergusen, 2007). Girlfriends who acknowledge a power imbalance in decision making are nonetheless satisfied with their romantic relationship as long as they feel in control of the discussion that led to the decision.

Power and Developmental Tasks

Negotiating power in a relationship would appear to be central to the developmental tasks of independence. In theory, the achievement of equity would necessitate the kind of self-expression and active listening skills that are compatible with a strong sense of self, and an ability to maintain this separateness while interacting with romantic partners instead of suppressing one's perspective. However, the links between power, identity, and autonomy have not yet been explored in the context of adolescent romance. Intimacy, in contrast, has been connected to power processes. Adams, Laursen, and Wilder (2001) found that intimacy in a romantic relationship was associated with reciprocal interactions in which both adolescents perceived the authority to be shared between themselves and their partner. Although not yet explored, other developmental tasks may also be influenced by power

dynamics in the relationship. Adolescents with anxious attachments, for example, may be particularly vulnerable to feelings of powerlessness because it may affirm their own insecurities about their worthiness as a romantic equal. Power imbalances in a romantic relationship may also encourage some girls to use their sexuality as a means to regain a sense of control, much as they are thought to seek control by managing the emotional tone of the interaction (e.g., Chung, 2005). Taken as a whole, studies of romantic power suggest that this dynamic is more central to the adolescent period than originally thought. Rather than a pattern of discontinuity with the romantic relationships of adults, issues of power imbalance are evident in adolescent relationships and are not dependent on high levels of emotional or financial commitment for their surfacing. Moreover, there is emerging evidence that power processes are linked to the manner in which developmental tasks are resolved, reinforcing the relevance of a better understanding of this relationship dimension in adolescence.

LINKS WITH PARENT AND FRIEND RELATIONSHIPS

Romantic relationships do not occur in isolation but are connected to adolescents' relationships with their families and their friends. Having reviewed the processes of romantic relationships and the developmental tasks that they facilitate, a key question is how other relationships contribute to romantic functioning. Both attachment and developmental-contextual perspectives have guided researchers' efforts to address this question. Attachment theory is fundamentally concerned with the continuity of working models and relationship processes from parents to other close relationships. As previously noted, adolescence is a key transitional period when attachments migrate from parents to friends and then to romantic partners (Collins & Sroufe, 1999; Collins & van Dulmen, 2006; Furman & Simon, 2006; Furman & Wehner,

1994; Hazan & Shaver, 1987). The developmental-contextual approach focuses more on the patterns of influence that exist within the nested contexts of parents, peers, and romantic partners (Conger, Cui, Bryant, & Elder, 2000; Connolly & Goldberg, 1999; Ford & Lerner, 1992; Gray & Steinberg, 1999). Within this perspective, parents and friends are thought to create overlapping social contexts within which adolescents develop the skills and personal attributes that are then directed toward their romantic relationships. Both the attachment and developmental-contextual traditions examine outcomes that bear on negative and positive transmission. Drawing on these perspectives, we summarize what is known about the independent and joint contributions of parents and friends to romantic relationships.

Continuity with Parental Relationships

Consistent with both attachment and developmental-contextual views, there is evidence of a significant overlap in positive processes between parental and romantic relationships. Emotional closeness and support with a parent are predictive of similar expressions of these processes in adolescents' romantic relationships, both concurrently and over time (Laursen, Furman, & Mooney, 2006; Seiffge-Krenke et al., 2001; Smetana & Gettman, 2006). Processes that promote independence in relationships also are connected. Adolescents who openly express their opinions with their parents are similarly comfortable having open discussions with their boyfriends and girlfriends (Taradash et al., 2001). These linkages may be due to the positive views of relationships engendered by secure attachment to parents. Indeed, two longitudinal studies examining romantic development find that secure parental attachment in late adolescence is predictive of mutual caring, emotional investment, trust, and intimacy with a romantic partner in emerging adulthood (Mayseless & Scharf, 2007; Roisman, Madsen, Hennighausen, Sroufe, & Collins, 2001).

Romantic conflict processes also reflect parental interactions. Several studies have shown that adolescents tend to use the same strategies that they employ in their parental conflicts, be they integrative, avoidant, or coercive, to manage the disagreements that they have with their romantic partners (Martin, 1990; Reese-Weber & Bartle-Haring, 1998; Reese-Weber & Khan, 2005). The overlap of conflict processes can also be seen at the level of the marital interaction. When parents experience antagonistic relationships with each other, the romantic relationships of their children are often marked by similar levels of hostility (Scharf & Mayseless, 2001; Stocker & Richmond, 2007). Research conducted by Steinberg, Davila, and Fincham (2006) suggests that an important mediator of the connection between interparental conflict and adolescent romantic outcomes is the working model of close relationships held by the young person. In their study of early adolescent girls, these authors found that girls who were sensitive to themes of hostility and rejection in their parents' arguments with each other also tended to have insecure working models of relationships—a style of attachment that in turn set the stage for their participation in risky romantic and sexual activities. Reese-Weber and colleagues (1998, 2005) have also highlighted the importance of the parent–adolescent dynamic to account for the link between marital discord and adolescent romantic behavior. These researchers have shown that parent–adolescent conflict mediates the link between adolescents' perceptions of interparental friction and the strategies that they themselves use when arguing with their romantic partners. The same indirect path held for adolescents from divorced as well as intact families (Reese-Weber & Khan, 2005). Although family structure does not appear to shape conflict negotiation in the romantic domain, family dissolutions have been shown to cast a shadow on other aspects of adolescent romance. Adolescents from divorced families hold less favorable views about committed romantic relationships and marriage than do youth whose families are still intact, and they also experience lower levels of intimacy with their romantic partners (Guiliani, Lafrate & Rosnati, 1998; van Schaick & Stolberg, 2001).

Identifying the parenting practices that lead to healthy romantic relationships is a matter of importance for researchers and parents alike. An important debate concerns whether parents should encourage the romantic involvements of their teenagers, restrict their cross-sex interactions, or find some middle ground of encouragement with careful monitoring. Studies are beginning to address this particular question. Examining family decision making and conflict among dating and nondating adolescents, Dowdy and Kliewer (1998) found that frequent dating was associated with teens' perceptions of greater autonomy in making decisions about their social and romantic activities. This level of autonomy seemed to come at a cost, however, as the frequent daters also reported conflictual interactions with their parents. However, having too little input into family decision making may also be problematic for romantic development. Youth in more restrictive family environments report negative interactions with their romantic partners, even when this high level of restraint is tempered by family warmth (Smetana & Gettman, 2006). It is likely that moderate levels of adolescent autonomy are optimal, especially when embedded in supportive family dynamics. This balanced line of thinking is affirmed in a recent longitudinal study of parents' concerns and practices around the romantic activities of their children (Kan, McHale, & Crouter, 2008). The results of this study demonstrate that when active monitoring is imbedded in positive parental relationships, adolescents are particularly likely to experience high-quality interactions with their romantic partner and to have a strong sense of their romantic competence.

Continuity with Friendships

In light of the substantial role that peers have in shaping adolescent romantic involvement, it is not surprising that considerable overlap between friend and romantic quality has been found. Adolescents' closeness, trust, and openness with their friends are all mirrored by comparable qualities in their romantic relationships (Connolly & Johnson, 1996; Kuttler & Greca, 2004; Laursen et al., 2006; Seiffge-Krenke, 2000; Shulman & Sharf, 2000). Autonomy with friends also generalizes as adolescents who feel confident expressing their differing views with their friends do this with their romantic partner as well (Taradash et al., 2001).

A similar pattern of continuity is apparent for the more negative aspects of friendships and romantic relationships. Levels of argumentativeness, hostility, and annoyance are all correlated between friends and romantic partners (Furman et al., 2002; Kuttler & LaGreca, 2004; Stocker & Richmond, 2007). For some youth, these negative peer tendencies may crystallize into stable patterns of bullying and this too can be carried over into their romantic relationships (Connolly, Pepler, Craig, & Taradash, 2000). Consistent with this, a study of young adolescents found that the romantic relationships of youth who bully are characterized by little affection and support, as well as gross imbalances of power, favoring themselves. Negative feelings may also be engendered between friends when they begin to participate romantic relationships. Roth and Parker (2001) studied the reactions of adolescents to the romantic involvement of their best friends. Their results suggest that when adolescents start to date, their friends may feel excluded from the new relationship and this may lead to feelings of jealousy. Clearly, an important task for adolescents is learning to balance the competing demands of friends and romantic partners in ways that promote harmony and agreement in the two social contexts.

Joint Contributions of Parents, Friends, and Romantic Partners

Although parent and peer influences can be studied independently, from a developmental-contextual view, these relational contexts are thought to be both linked and mutually influential on romantic development. In essence, independent consideration of the contributions of parents and friends to romantic quality belies the more accurate reality that these relationships create overlapping contexts of social experience within which romantic development occurs. Two such patterns of overlapping influence are apparent in the literature, namely conjoint effects and primacy effects, and we will consider how both of these patterns in turn create an interface between the worlds of families, peers, and romantic partners.

Conjoint effects on romantic processes are obtained via the shared contribution of parents and friends. In essence, these effects suggest that both families and peers compliment the influence of the other, thereby enhancing the overall outcome. An example of conjoint effects can be found in Laursen and colleagues' (2006) study of romantic self-concept in middle adolescence. These researchers found that adolescents could be clustered into groups based on the level of support that they experienced in their mother, best-friend, and romantic relationships. The adolescents who indicated high support in all three domains saw themselves as highly competent in their romantic relationships. Highlighting the importance of nested contexts in development, conjoint effects have also been noted for the relationship process of romantic autonomy. Taradash and colleagues (2001) found that autonomy with mothers and best friends was conjointly associated with this attribute in romantic partnerships. As with positive processes, conjoint negative influences can also be seen. Hostility with family members and with friends has been shown to jointly contribute to patterns of conflict that exist between adolescent couples (Stocker & Richmond, 2007).

By primacy effects, we are referring to those that showcase the supremacy of one relationship context over that of the other, such that the presence of the more dominant agent overshadows any direct links attributed to the other party. In terms of adolescent romance, peers and friends may hold a position of primary influence relative to parents. Such an effect is evident in a recent study conducted by Furman and his colleagues (2002). These authors examined the links among working models of parent, best friend, and romantic attachments in middle adolescence. Supporting the primacy of the friend–romantic link, parent attachments were unrelated to working models of romantic relationships once peer connections were considered. That being said, their data did show strong connections between friend and parent attachment, thus supporting the notion that adolescent friends function as transitional attachment figures between parents and romantic partners (Hazan & Shaver, 1987; Furman & Wehner, 1994). Similar primacy effects can be seen in romantic intimacy processes, for which all available evidence suggests that support from friends overrides the contribution of parental support in predicting the level of closeness between boyfriends and girlfriends (Shulman & Scharf, 2000; Taradash et al., 2001). The primacy of friends' influence on adolescent romance should be placed in a developmental context, however, and tempered by the likelihood that parental attachments are more primary at other points in development. Supporting the long-term importance of parents on romantic functioning, secure attachment in infancy has been shown to carry forward into positive romantic interactions in the late adolescent years (Simpson, Collins, Tran, & Haydon, 2007). Yet, also reinforcing the role of friends, the parent–romantic association reported in this study was partially mediated by the quality of attachments to friends in middle adolescence. One may speculate that, in the early years of adulthood when young people may no longer require the transitional attachment functions of friends, the link between parent and romantic attachment may once again become more direct.

ROMANTIC RELATIONSHIPS AND PSYCHOSOCIAL ADJUSTMENT

Intense feelings of love uniquely characterize romantic relationships. This state of high arousal elicits strong physiological, cognitive, and emotional responses from adolescents. Young people in love report frequent mood swings, sleep loss, and an inability to concentrate on day-to-day tasks because of obsessive thoughts of their beloved (Brand et al., 2007). Dealing with these strong reactions can be challenging, not only because of the novelty of this relational context, but also because adolescents are less likely to have developed the skills that are necessary to cope with these new romantic situations (Larson et al., 1999). Although romantic relationships are normative and developmentally beneficial, from the point of view of the adolescent, they can also be a significant source of stress (Grover & Nangle, 2003; Nieder & Seiffge-Krenke, 2001; Seiffge-Krenke, 2003; Steinberg & Morris, 2001). Theories of adolescent coping indicate that when stress levels move beyond the psychosocial resources that are available to the adolescent, his or her adjustment is likely to suffer (Compas, 1998). Indeed, it appears that romantic relationships may at times overwhelm adolescents' coping resources as romantic involvement has been linked to depression (Davila, 2008), anxiety (e.g., LaGreca & Mackey, 2007), poor academic performance (e.g., Doyle, Brendgen, Markiewicz, & Kamkar, 2003), and delinquency (e.g., Davies & Windle, 2000). A review of the findings linking romantic relationships to mental health problems suggests that this overlap may be viewed as operating at three levels. At the level of the individual, we argue that deviations from normative romantic trajectories and negative cognitions about relationships both contribute to poor adjustment with romantic stress. At the level of the dyad, we note that poor-quality romantic processes can compromise a young person's adjustment. Finally, at the contextual level, we consider how romantic stress can be amplified by unsupportive peer and family connections. Both internalizing and externalizing symptoms may result from dysfunction at each of these levels and so we organize our discussion of romantic relationships and

adjustment to account for these differing patterns of symptoms.

Individual Factors and Adjustment

Timing of Relationships

Returning to the issue of individual differences in romantic timing, there is a substantial literature attesting to the psychosocial risks of being an "early starter" on the romantic trajectory. According to the developmental appropriateness hypothesis (Graber & Brooks-Gunn, 1996; Welsh et al., 2003; Williams, Connolly & Cribbie, 2008), adolescents who experience transitions at an earlier age than their peers are less likely to have acquired the skills necessary to successfully navigate these changing social contexts, thereby conferring risk for maladjustment. Because early starters are also out of step with the romantic progress of their age-mates, they may look to older peers for romantic companionship. However, their younger age makes them less likely to be accepted by a normative group of older peers, resulting in their romantic socialization with more deviant youth (Stattin & Magnusson, 1990; Young & d'Arcy, 2005). If involvement with marginalized older peers does occur, the stage is set for the development of antisocial behaviors and externalizing problems. Although the mediating role of older peers has not been fully supported (Friedlander et al., 2007), there is substantial evidence connecting early romantic relationships to externalizing problems. Higher rates of delinquency, aggression, bullying, school problems, risky sexual behavior, alcohol use, and substance abuse have all been associated with precocity in the romantic domain (Brendgen, Vitaro, Doyle, Markiewicz, & Bukowski, 2002; Connolly, Pepler, et al., 2000; Friedlander et al., 2007; Neeman, Hubbard, & Masten, 1995; Tubman, Windle, & Windle, 1996; Zimmer-Gembeck et al., 2001 2004). These externalizing problems are more pronounced among girls, although the patterns do generalize to boys as well. Early-starting girls have also been noted to experience body dissatisfaction, dieting, and problematic eating behaviors (Cauffman & Steinberg, 1996; Compian, Gowen & Hayward, 2004). Internalizing symptoms are also common for early-starting girls, most notably depression and lower self-esteem (Compian, et al., 2004; Doyle et al., 2003; McDonald & McKinney, 1994; Zimmer-Gembeck et al., 2001). The problems associated with early starting may place youth on developmental trajectories that continue to have adverse effects over the course of adolescence, ultimately setting the stage for a troubled transition to young adulthood (Rutter, 1996; Zimmer-Gembeck & Collins, 2008). Yet whether these psychological problems are due only to the early timing of their romantic trajectory is not entirely clear. Other predisposing factors located in the family, peer group, or community may well be implicated in channeling the adjustment consequences of early dating. We report on what is known of these moderating factors in subsequent sections of this discussion.

A different nonnormative trajectory, which we have previously labeled as "late bloomers," might also be associated with adjustment difficulties. Adolescents who encounter social transitions at older ages than their peers are thought to have significantly less experience in the very contexts that support the mastery of critical skills (Sullivan, 1953). Underdeveloped proficiency in age-related tasks, such as the formation of intimate bonds with persons outside the family, may place these late-developing youth at risk for psychological distress (Allen et al., 2006; Sullivan, 1953). There is virtually no research directed to this question. However, a recent study by La Greca and Mackey (2007) found that older adolescents who had never had a romantic relationship reported higher levels of dating anxiety than their more romantically experienced age-mates. From these findings we may infer that, at some point in adolescence, the absence of dating creates anxiety for young people who may see themselves as less competent or attractive than their peers. La Greca and Mackey's (2007) data also raises the possibility that preexisting emotional symptoms, personality traits, or cognitive biases may inhibit some adolescents from forming age-appropriate relationships with peers and romantic partners. Likely, preexisting factors and a lack of peer experience combine to set adolescents on a course of later maturity in the romantic domain, however, how these interactive effects might unfold is not currently known.

Relationship Cognitions

A controversial finding from the Add Health data set, published by Joyner and Udry (2000), indicates that having a romantic partner in the last 18 months is associated with depressive symptoms. Because this finding runs counter to the idealized notion that romantic love makes people happy, developmental researchers have been motivated to search for an explanation to this link (Davila, 2008). A major focus of this research has been to identify the relationship cognitions that underlie depression in the face of romantic involvement. From an attachment perspective, insecure working models have been hypothesized to be one such relationship cognition. The thought is that insecure attachment styles color adolescents' interpretations of their romantic interactions in negative and stress-inducing ways, thereby leading to adjustment problems (Cooper, Shaver, & Collins, 1998). In support of this claim, insecure romantic attachment has been linked to depressive symptoms in early and late adolescent girls, especially for those with a preoccupied style (Davila, Steinberg, Kachadourian, Cobb, & Fincham, 2004). Relative to other forms of insecurity, preoccupied attachments are thought to be especially risky as youth with this style of attachment are intensely drawn to relationships, but soon after they enter into them, experience significant distress because they are unable to fully trust their partners or view themselves as worthy of love (Davila et al., 2004). The repercussions of anxious attachments appear to go beyond depressive symptoms as romantically involved boys and girls with these working models report substance abuse, delinquency, truancy, hostility, and risky sexuality (Cooper et al., 1998; Margolese, Markiewicz, & Doyle, 2005).

Rejection sensitivity is another relationship cognition that puts adolescents at risk for maladjustment when they begin dating. The construct of rejection sensitivity refers to the anxious expectation of rejection in close relationships, which, in turn, causes adolescents who are high on this attribute to emotionally overreact when instances of rejection are experienced (Downey, Bonica, & Rincón, 1999). Rejection sensitivity develops early in life by way of negative messages about acceptance and rejection communicated by parents or other significant figures. Youth who receive such messages are thought to become hypersensitive to rejection, a state that ironically makes them behave in ways that increase the likelihood that rejection will actually occur. Evidence suggests that adolescents who are rejection sensitive experience challenges in their romantic relationships. These youth do not trust their romantic partners and are hostile towards them, yet are willing to engage in antisocial or self-silencing behaviors to maintain the relationship (Harper, Dickson & Welsh, 2006; Purdie & Downey, 2000). In terms of adjustment, being overly sensitive to romantic rejection has been linked to depression for both adolescent boys and girls (Harper et al., 2006), reinforcing the value of this cognitive bias for understanding the link between romantic relationships and psychological symptomatology.

Dyadic Factors and Adjustment

Couple Processes

Shifting focus from the individual to the dyad, negative romantic interactions are also thought to underlie the psychosocial difficulties of adolescent partners (Tabares & Gottman, 2003). Similar to adult romantic relationships, it has been suggested that adolescent couples can develop repetitive patterns of criticism, contempt, defensiveness, and withdrawal in their interactions with each other. These coercive patterns stifle communication and create distress for both partners. Although less studied than individual factors, there is evidence that relationship dynamics are linked to adjustment. Reflecting the ideas of Tabares and Gottman (2003), depression, anxiety, and low self-esteem have been reported by adolescents whose relationships are characterized by high levels of conflict and criticism, low levels of support, and an imbalance of power between the partners (Galliher et al., 1999; La Greca & Harrison, 2005; La Greca & Mackey, 2007; Reese-Weber & Marchand, 2002; Rizzo Daley, & Gunderson, 2006; Welsh et al., 1999; Williams, Connolly & Segal, 2001). The volatile and unstable nature of these relationships likely pushes them toward dissolution, which in and of itself, can compound the effects of negative processes.

Dissolutions

Romantic relationship dissolutions are considered to be highly stressful by researchers, clinicians, and adolescents alike. Relationship endings can constitute a significant interpersonal loss for young people, engendering feelings of worthlessness, abandonment, and despair about their romantic future (Weber, 1998). When such negative feelings persist, romantic loss may go beyond adolescents' ability to cope, resulting in significant mental health problems, and in particular, depression (Hankin & Abramson, 2001; Joyner & Udry, 2000). A large-scale, prospective study of adolescent depressive disorders affirms this connection (Monroe, Rohde, Seeley, & Lewinsohn, 1999). Of the adolescent boys and girls who developed a major depressive disorder over the course of the study, half of them reported having had a romantic breakup in the preceding 12 months. Given that this severe outcome did *not* befall all of the youth who experienced a breakup, it stands to reason that individual differences may moderate the impact of romantic loss on adolescent adjustment. Although work on this topic is at an early stage, some important moderators have already been noted. Individual differences in interpersonal sensitivity to rejection have been shown to be important. Rizzo and colleagues (2006) found that highly sensitive girls were most likely to report clinical depression following the experience of a romantic dissolution. The number of breakups that an adolescent has experienced may be another important moderator of psychological distress. Youth who report a large number of relationship turnovers likely experience accumulating feelings of loss that eventually overwhelm their coping resources. Consistent with this, youth identified as having a persistent pattern of multiple relationship start-ups and terminations report more depression than other adolescents, as well as other problem behaviors such as binge drinking and minor delinquency (Barber, 2006; Davies & Windle, 2000). Moderators of the negative consequences of romantic dissolutions have also been identified at the level of the dyad. In particular, it is important to know which partner initiated the demise of the relationship. Adolescents who ascribe the breakup to their partner's dissatisfaction report more depressive symptoms than those who indicate that they initiated the breakup themselves (McIsaac & Connolly, 2004). These initial studies are useful in identifying individuals who are at risk for serious problems following a romantic dissolution, yet further work in this area is warranted to better understand when a normative event, such as a breakup, can become a precipitant for depression and other mental health concerns.

Contextual Factors and Adjustment
Peers

We have previously discussed the important role of peers in creating a context for finding romantic partners, transmitting romantic norms, facilitating relationship activities, and modeling social skills. Extending this perspective to adolescents' adjustment, we might expect that peer networks and close friends will help adolescents manage the stresses that are inherent to the emergent character of their romantic relationships. By the same token, we might expect that adolescents who move into romantic activities in the absence of a supportive peer context will be vulnerable to adjustment problems. Evidence to support this association can be found in La Greca and Mackey's (2007) study of dating anxiety in adolescence. Young people who do not belong to a cross-gender peer network, or who have conflictual relationships with their same-sex best friends, are more likely than other youth to report dating anxiety. The moderating effects of peer context can also be seen in a recent investigation of early-dating adolescents (Brendgen et al., 2002). In this study, early dyadic dating was linked to lower self-esteem, antisocial behaviors, and academic problems, but only for adolescents who were unpopular with their same-sex peers. Thus, it appears that a positive peer group can reverse the impact of otherwise negative events.

The links between peer groups, romantic relationships, and adjustment are, perhaps, not as straightforward as the previous set of findings would suggest. This is because peer groups have many overlapping functions that at times, may seem to work at cross-purposes. For instance, although frequent contact with peers can facilitate romantic development, it can also influence youth to engage in minor deviancy or health risk behaviors (Dishion & Piehler, 2007). When these two functions converge, adolescents' romantic activities are likely to include group-based deviant or risky behaviors. In support of these dual functions, adolescents with multiple or steady romantic partners report more alcohol use and minor deviancy than other youth (Davies & Windle, 2000). These romantically involved youth also report belonging to peer groups that are composed of heavy drinkers. The processes that connect these converging peer functions may relate to how social status is defined. Many adolescent groups endorse alcohol use and minor misbehavior, as well as confer high status to those who participate in romantic relationships (Brown, 1999, 2004; Prinstein, 2008). Adolescents, on the whole, may be prone to conforming to these norms in order to fit in with their peers, and so they engage in dating and delinquency to achieve status on both fronts. That being said, these dual pressures may be more salient for some peer groups than others (Allen, 2008; Prinstein, 2008). Adolescents who are in status-focused groups may be influenced by the overlapping norms of dating and deviancy more so than adolescents who are in groups with less stringent rules about peer popularity. Understanding these co-occurring peer influences on adolescents' romantic development is an important task for future research.

Parents

Very little is known about how specific family processes may moderate the adjustment implications of adolescent dating. Rather, family effects have typically been conceptualized as distal influences that impact adjustment by shaping adolescents' internal views of relationships, as discussed earlier in this section (e.g., Davila et al., 2004). It is possible, however, that family processes play a role in adolescents' responses to romantic involvement. Some evidence suggests that such moderating effects may indeed be present, especially when adolescents make the transition to romantic relationships. In particular, marital conflict has been shown to moderate the link between early dating and adjustment in girls (Doyle et al., 2003). Early-dating girls in families with high marital conflict report low self-esteem, whereas in families with low conflict, early daters do not differ from nondaters. As with positive peer associations (i.e., Brendgen et al., 2002), it appears that family dynamics can also minimize the risk associated with early dyadic dating. Whether other family practices, such as high parental monitoring in the face of young adolescent dating, mitigate the risks of early involvement awaits future study.

SUMMARY AND FUTURE DIRECTIONS

Developmental research on adolescent romantic relationships has come a long way. From a rather uninformed starting point a decade ago, a substantial literature on this topic has emerged. Spurred by the seminal publication of Furman, Brown and Feiring, (1999), and the groundbreaking Society for Research on Adolescence (SRA) presidential address of Collins (2003), we now have compelling theoretical frameworks that help us understand the developmental significance of this relationship. Our understanding of adolescent romance has improved in several key areas. These include defining the unique attributes of this relationship; mapping patterns and prevalence in multiple contexts; charting developmental progressions in structure and quality; describing normative pressures; linking relationship processes and developmental tasks; connecting romance with other key relationships; and exploring the ramifications for psychosocial adjustment. These many advances lead us to better appreciate adolescents' romantic relationships as a pivotal bridge between the relationship contexts of childhood and those of the adult years. A foundation is now in place for further meaningful examination of adolescent romantic relationships. We outline several directions for future research that would expand current knowledge and fill gaps in our developmental understanding of romantic relationships. We organize our discussion of these future directions around the organizational themes of this chapter.

Definitions and Patterns of Relationships

As researchers, we often impose definitions and boundaries on adolescents' romantic relationships, but these may not always fit well with their lived experiences. Adolescents' relationships are very much "in progress" and the fuzzy boundaries that separate one type of cross-gender relationship from another may be difficult to document with the romantic status–oriented questions that are in common use. This fluidity in adolescents' minds about different relationships may introduce an element of error into traditional self-report methodologies as researchers may not be consistently capturing the same group of daters from one study to another. One useful direction to redress this issue would be to use qualitative methodologies to gain a richer understanding of relationship boundaries and validate our definitions of the romantic landscape. In elaborating our definitions of romantic relationships, we note that there is an equally urgent need to use categories that reflect the experiences of youth in a broader social context than is currently the case. Our present knowledge is highly confined to the experiences of Western youth in White, middle-class families. Whether youth in different neighborhoods, communities, cultures, and countries live with similarly fluid boundaries in their romantic experiences is unknown. Addressing these issues will be central to moving forward an agenda of more inclusive and ecologically valid research.

Stages of Romantic Development

The definitional restrictions noted above reflect, at least in part, the silence of our current theories to adequately address diversity of developmental experiences in romance. Our theories need to be broadened to account for varying trajectories of development that come from different baseline experiences. A particular issue that comes to mind is the fact that mixed-gender peer experiences are the starting points of all contemporary romantic theories. Yet these peer experiences can have very different meanings for some of our youth, suggesting that peer groups may not operate in the same way for all individuals. Sexual-minority adolescents surely have romantic relationships, but it is doubtful that their mixed-gender peer experiences play the same role as they do for heterosexual youth. Sexual-minority youth are, in general, understudied from a romantic perspective. While we might believe that patterns of development are invariant across

sexual orientation, it could well be that these youth follow different pathways and timetables to healthy and harmonious relationships. Returning to the role of mixed-gender peer groups as romantic catalysts, our theories also do not speak to those youth who lack cross-gender friendships, whether due to social rejection, poor mental or physical health, or cultural prohibitions. How such youth initiate relationships outside of natural peer contexts needs to be incorporated into our theories. Perhaps to commence our charting of trajectories that do not begin with typical peer experiences, we need to devote more consideration to passionate attraction as the primary root for relationship formation and study what alternative behavioral strategies these feelings may lead to when peer groups are absent.

Turning to another gap in the literature, theorized romantic pathways have been tested in segmented ways, focusing on either the early or later years of adolescence. Longitudinally studying romantic pathways across the full course of adolescence would allow us to better understand the links between romantic stages, especially the period of exploratory romantic relationships in the middle adolescent years. This stage of romantic activity is rather understudied, in comparison to the formation and dyadic stages of a relationship, and a trajectory approach would address this gap. Such an approach would also bring to light nonnormative romantic pathways, in addition to that of early starters. Late bloomers have largely been ignored in the current literature and the conditions that set them on this pathway are unknown. As we have already noted, later involvement might pose a long-term challenge to youth as they have not had the opportunity to acquire or practice necessary romantic skills. However, delaying romantic entry until the emerging adult years may be beneficial to some youth who choose to focus their energies on school, elite sports, or volunteer activities. There may also be alternative routes to mature and fulfilling romantic relationships, which are not described in our current theories or empirical studies.

Romantic Norms and Cultural Variation

Romantic norms are critical to examine cross-culturally if we are to appreciate which aspects of the human need for love and belonging are expressed universally and which are unique to specific ecological contexts. Although researchers in many different countries are studying adolescent romantic relationships, a direct comparison of the norms and values of youth in different cultures has yet to be made. Yet such work is essential if we are to understand romantic values and ideals that differ from Western ones, and also, how such norms shape romantic behavior in these different cultural contexts. A related issue to consider is the impact of Western media images on the norms and values of youth who live in other countries. The idealization of passionate love that is popularized in the Western media is now available to a diverse audience of youth by way of the Internet. This romantic norm may conflict with the expectations of kin-based cultures and how adolescents resolve this clash of values in their romantic and family relationships would be valuable to learn.

A related issue concerns the ways in which adolescents interpret the norms within their own cultures and how they integrate this understanding into their own behavior. Here, we are thinking especially about adolescent boys in Western cultures. We have noted what we are beginning to learn about how boys interpret the norms of masculinity and how they integrate these status-oriented values into their search for romantic intimacy and companionship. We know more about these issues with girls, and the information that we have acquired about the ways in which they resolve competing tensions between idealized relationships, peer norms, and personal desires has lead to innovative approaches to help them successfully navigate romantic relationships (e.g., Banister & Begoray, 2004; Banister & Jakubec, 2004). Comparable efforts directed to boys would likely lead to similarly fruitful outcomes.

Romantic Processes

Broadening our views of trajectories, it would be important to consider relationship processes within the developmental cycle of an individual relationship. Currently, researchers are inclined to study romantic relationship processes at one point in the cycle, either at formation or later, once the couple has been established. A much neglected point in the life cycle of a relationship is its termination. Romantic dissolutions can have a powerful impact on adolescents and understanding how this event connects to earlier points in the relationship trajectory needs to be better understood. Extending this dyadic focus, mapping the course of a relationship from its formation to its conclusion would allow for a better understanding of how the processes of support, conflict, and power evolve, and how these transformations may either further the growth of the individual partners and strengthen the relationship, or conversely, lead to its termination. A relationship cycle approach would also focus research attention on the dyadic level and push us to explore more carefully how couple processes may deepen or change as partners adjust to the needs and cues of each other. This might be especially important for our understanding of conflict processes and of how particular negotiation strategies may be most useful at different points in the relationship. Another consequence of this approach would be to bring to the forefront the question of reciprocal influence. Current studies most typically focus on one member of the couple relationship. Learning more about the partner and how that person's attitudes and behaviors influence the individual adolescent is a critical issue for future research. And, finally, we note that this approach will help to address how gender differentially shapes these partner effects. As we have discussed, gendered socialization patterns create challenges for adolescents when they start to connect with opposite-sex partners. Yet these connections also create opportunities for learning new skills and ways of relating for both boys and girls. A vital task for researchers is to articulate more clearly how adolescents of each gender confront the challenges of adapting to the new interaction cues of their romantic partners.

To date, adolescent romantic relationships have largely been framed as a context for intimacy and later attachments. Far less attention has been paid to their role in facilitating other developmental landmarks. To advance our thinking about how romantic relationships promote identity, autonomy, or sexuality, there is a need to better conceptualize these developmental tasks within a romantic framework. For example, autonomy with a romantic partner is likely different from its expression with parents or peers. A clear conceptualization of romantic autonomy would also contribute to a better understanding of the optimal balance between this task and romantic intimacy. Balancing relatedness with autonomy is a key marker of healthy adult relationships and so it is incumbent upon researchers to start to explore the trajectory of this dynamic in the adolescent years. Similar arguments can be made for the tasks of sexuality and identity. As we have noted in this chapter, refinement of the meaning of these tasks in the romantic context is essential if we are to advance our understanding of the connections between romance and sexuality, as well as with the many facets of identity formation.

Peer and Family Links

Implicit in the developmental contextual view that romantic relationships are embedded in a broader set of peer and family connections is the notion of reciprocal and bidirectional influences. At present, most research has examined the influence of families, peers, and friends on romantic development. Yet how an adolescent's romantic experiences might influence other relational contexts warrants further consideration. For example, how do romantic relationships alter the nature of the parent–child interaction, especially around issues of autonomy and independence? Likewise, we need to examine the renegotiations that occur

in a close friendship once one friend enters into a serious romantic partnership. Although there is some evidence that this transition can be negative, creating jealousies and feelings of exclusion, the potential for positive outcomes should also be explored. Having a romantic relationship might assist friendships in many ways, including for example, enabling a socially excluded youth to find his or her way into a group of peers that he or she would not otherwise have access to.

Romantic Relationships and Adjustment

Current research makes clear that romantic relationships are problematic for some youth, contributing to symptoms of anxiety and depression, or alternatively, encouraging various forms of misbehavior. Clinical implications of these findings suggest that it would be important to incorporate some aspects of romantic relationship functioning into the clinical assessments of young people presenting with mental health issues. This domain of adolescents' lives is frequently overlooked in clinical contexts, yet our data suggest that romantic stresses are quite significant in precipitating their visits to mental health treatment centers. Incorporating healthy romantic functioning into interventions for anxiety, depression, and problem behaviors would also be an important direction to pursue. Currently, the dialogue between researchers and clinicians on this front is minimal. Yet adolescents would no doubt benefit from the combined efforts of researchers and clinicians in designing interventions that would take them off of at-risk romantic trajectories and put them on a path toward healthy romantic involvement.

Despite their possible challenges to adjustment, we conclude by commenting that we think of romantic relationships as a developmental asset. When romantic experiences are paced with the competencies of the adolescent, and embedded in a social context that both supports and regulates appropriate involvement, romantic relationships are healthy and beneficial. This view is consistent with current interest in positive youth development. As we move away from a "deficits" view of adolescence, it is critical for researchers to share what we know about positive romantic development with the youth themselves and, also, with the adults who support them in multiple contexts. Translating research findings into policy and practice would contribute to positive youth development on a broader scale and in a way that is most beneficial to the social and romantic functioning of adolescents.

REFERENCES

Adams, R. E., Laursen, B., & Wilder, D. (2001). Characteristics of closeness in adolescent romantic relationships. *Journal of Adolescence. Special Issue: Adolescent romance: From experiences to relationships, 24,* 353–363.

Allen, J. P., Insabella, G., Porter, M. R., Smith, F. D., Land, D., & Phillips, N. (2006). A social-interactional model of the development of depressive symptoms in adolescence. *Journal of Consulting and Clinical Psychology, 74,* 55–65.

Arnett, J. J. (2006). G. Stanley Hall's adolescence: Brilliance and nonsense. *History of Psychology, 9,* 186–197.

Aro, H., & Taipale, V. (1987). The impact of timing of puberty on psychosomatic symptoms among fourteen- to sixteen-year-old Finnish girls. *Child Development, 58,* 261–268.

Bailey, B. L. (1988). *From front porch to back seat: Courtship in twentieth-century America.* Baltimore, MD: Johns Hopkins University Press.

Banister, E., & Begoray, D. L. (2004). Beyond talking groups: Strategies for improving adolescent health education. *Health Care for Women International, 25,* 481–488.

Banister, E., & Jakubec, S. (2004). "I'm stuck as far as relationships go": Dilemmas of voice in girls' dating relationships. *Child & Youth Services, 26,* 33–52.

Barber, B. (2006). To have loved and have lost: Adolescent romantic relationships and rejection. In A. C. Crouter & A. Booth (Eds.), *Romance and sex in adolescence and emerging adulthood: Risks and opportunities. The Penn State University family issues symposia series* (pp. 29–40). Mahwah, NJ: Lawrence Erlbaum.

Baumeister, R. F., & Wotman, S. R. (1992). *Breaking hearts: The two sides of unrequited love. Emotions and social behavior.* New York: Guilford Press.

Bentley, C. G., Galliher, R. V., & Fergusen, T. J. (2007). Association among aspects of interpersonal power and relationship functioning in adolescent romantic couples. *Sex Roles, 57,* 483–495.

Billy, J. O., Rodgers, J. L., & Udry, J. R. (1984). Adolescent sexual behavior and friendship choice. *Social Forces, 62,* 653–678.

Blyth, D. A., Hill, J. P., & Thiel, K. S. (1982). Early adolescents' significant others: Grade and gender differences in perceived relationships with familial and nonfamilial adults and young people. *Journal of Youth and Adolescence, 11,* 425–450.

Bouchey, H. A. (2007). Perceived romantic competence, importance of romantic domains, and psychosocial adjustment. *Journal of Clinical Child and Adolescent Psychology, 36,* 503–514.

Brand, S., Luethi, M., von Planta, A., Hatzinger, M., Holsboer-Trachsler, E. (2007). Romantic love, hypomania, and sleep pattern in adolescents. *Journal of Adolescent Health, 41,* 69–76.

Brendgen, M., Vitaro, F., Doyle, A. B., Markiewicz, D., & Bukowski, W. M. (2002). Same-sex peer relations and romantic relationships during adolescence: Interactive links to emotional, behavioral, and academic adjustment. *Merrill-Palmer Quarterly, 48,* 77–103.

Bronfenbrenner, U. (1979). *The ecology of human development.* Cambridge, MA: Harvard University Press.

Brown, B. (2004). Adolescents' relationships with peers. In R. Lerner & L. Steinberg (Eds.), *Handbook of adolescent psychology* (2nd ed., pp. 363–394). Hoboken, NJ: John Wiley & Sons.

Brown, B. B. (1999). "You're going out with who?" Peer group influences on adolescent romantic relationships. In W. Furman, B. B. Brown, & C. Feiring (Eds.), *The development of romantic relationships in adolescence* (pp. 291–329). New York: Cambridge University Press.

Brown, B. B., Larson, R. W., & Saraswathi, T. S. (2002). *The world's youth: Adolescents in eight regions of the globe.* New York: Cambridge University Press.

Bukowski, W. M., Sippola, L. K., & Hoza, B. (1999). Same and other: Interdependency between participation in same- and other-sex friendships. *Journal of Youth and Adolescence, 28,* 439–459.

Camarena, P. M., Sarigiani, P. A., & Petersen, A. C. (1990). Gender-specific pathways to intimacy in early adolescence. *Journal of Youth and Adolescence, 19,* 19–32.

Campbell, L., Simpson, J. A., Boldry, J., & Kashy, D. A. (2005). Perceptions of conflict and support in romantic relationships: The role of attachment anxiety. *Journal of Personality and Social Psychology, 88,* 510–531.

Capaldi, D., & Gorman-Smith, D. (2003). The development of aggression in young male/female couples. In P. Florsheim (Ed.) *Adolescent romantic relations and sexual behavior: Theory, research and practical implications* (pp. 243–278). Mahwah, NJ: Lawrence Erlbaum.

Carlson, W., & Rose, A. J. (2007). The role of reciprocity in romantic relationships in middle childhood and early adolescence. *Merrill-Palmer Quarterly, 53,* 262–290.

Carver, K., Joyner, K., & Udry, J. R. (2003). National estimates of adolescent romantic relationships. In P. Florsheim (Ed.), *Adolescent romantic relations and sexual behavior: Theory, research, and practical implications* (pp. 23–56). Mahwah, NJ: Lawrence Erlbaum.

Caspi, A., Elder, G. H., & Bem, D. J. (1988). Moving away from the world: Life-course patterns of shy children. *Developmental Psychology, 24,* 824–831.

Cate, R. M., & Lloyd, S. A. (1992). *Courtship.* Newbury Park, CA: Sage.

Cauffman, E., & Steinberg, L. (1996). Interactive effects of menarcheal status and dating on dieting and disordered eating among adolescent girls. *Developmental Psychology, 32,* 631–635.

Cavanagh, S. E. (2007). The social construction of romantic relationships in adolescence: Examining the role of peer networks, gender, and race. *Sociological Inquiry, 77,* 572–600.

Cawley, J. (2001). Body weight and the dating and sexual behaviors of young adolescents. In R. T. Michael (Ed.), *Social awakening: Adolescent behavior as adulthood approaches* (pp. 174–198). New York: Russell Sage Foundation.

Chase-Lansdale, P. L., Cherlin, A. J., & Kiernan, K. K. (1995). The long-term effects of parental divorce on the mental health of young adults: A developmental perspective. *Child Development, 66,* 1614–1634.

Chung, D. (2005). Violence, control, romance and gender equality: Young women and heterosexual relationships. *Women's Studies International Forum, 28,* 445–455.

Coates, D. L. (1999). The cultured and culturing aspects of romantic experience in adolescence. In W. Furman, B. B. Brown, & C. Feiring (Eds.), *The development of romantic relationships in adolescence* (pp. 330–363). New York: Cambridge University Press.

Collins, W. A. (2003). More than myth: The developmental significance of romantic relationships during adolescence. *Journal of Research on Adolescence, 13,* 1–24.

Collins, W. A., Laursen, B., Mortensen, N., Luebker, C., & Ferreria, M. (1997). Conflict processes and transitions in parent and peer relationships: Implications for autonomy and regulation. *Journal of Adolescent Research, 12,* 178–198.

Collins, W. A., & Sroufe, L. A. (1999). Capacity for intimate relationships: A developmental construction. In W. Furman, B. B. Brown, & C. Feiring (Eds.), *The development of romantic relationships in adolescence* (pp. 125–147). New York: Cambridge University Press.

Collins, W. A., & Steinberg, L. (2006). Adolescent development in interpersonal context. In N. Eisenberg, W. Damon, & R. M. Lerner (Eds.), *Handbook of child psychology*, vol. 3: *Social, emotional, and personality development* (6th ed., pp. 1003–1067). Hoboken, NJ: John Wiley & Sons.

Collins, W. A., & van Dulmen, M. (2006). "The course of true love(s) …": Origins and pathways in the development of romantic relationships. In A. C. Crouter & A. Booth (Eds.), *Romance and sex in emerging adulthood: Risks and opportunities. The Penn State University family issues symposia series* (pp. 63–86). Mahwah, NJ: Lawrence Erlbaum.

Compas, B. E. (1998). An agenda for coping research and theory: Basic and applied developmental issues. *International Journal of Behavioral Development, 22,* 231–237.

Compian, L., Gowen, L. K., & Hayward, C. (2004). Peripubertal girls' romantic and platonic involvement with boys: Associations with body image and depression symptoms. *Journal of Research on Adolescence, 14,* 23–47.

Conger, R. D., Cui, M., Bryant, C. M., & Elder, G. H., Jr. (2000). Competence in early adult romantic relationships: A developmental perspective on family influences. *Journal of Personality and Social Psychology, 79,* 224–237.

Connolly, J., Craig, W., Goldberg, A., & Pepler, D. (1999). Conceptions of cross-sex friendships and romantic relationships in early adolescence. *Journal of Youth and Adolescence, 28,* 481–494.

Connolly, J., Craig, W., Goldberg, A., & Pepler, D. (2004). Mixed-gender groups, dating, and romantic relationships in early adolescence. *Journal of Research on Adolescence, 14,* 185–207.

Connolly, J., Furman, W., & Konarski, R. (2000). The role of peers in the emergence of heterosexual romantic relationships in adolescence. *Child Development, 71,* 1395–1408.

Connolly, J., Pepler, D., Craig, W., & Taradash, A. (2000). Dating experiences of bullies in early adolescence. *Child Maltreatment, 5,* 299–310.

Connolly, J. A., & Goldberg, A. (1999). Romantic relationships in adolescence: The role of friends and peers in their emergence and development. In W. Furman, B. B. Brown, & C. Feiring (Eds.), *The development of romantic relationships in adolescence* (pp. 266–290). New York: Cambridge University Press.

Connolly, J. A., & Johnson, A. M. (1996). Adolescents' romantic relationships and the structure and quality of their close interpersonal ties. *Personal Relationships, 3,* 185–195.

Connolly, J. A., & Josephson, W. (2007). Aggression in adolescent dating relationships: Predictors and prevention. *Prevention Researcher, 14,* 3–5.

Connolly, J. A., & Konarski, R. (1994). Peer self-concept in adolescence: Analysis of factor structure and of associations with peer experience. *Journal of Research on Adolescence, 4,* 385–403.

Connolly, J. A., & McIsaac, C. (in press). Adolescents' explanations for romantic dissolutions: A developmental perspective *Journal of Adolescence.*

Connolly, J. A., & McIsaac, C. (2008). Adolescent romantic relationships: Beginnings, endings and psychosocial challenges. *International Society for Behavioral Development Newsletter, 53,* 1–5.

Cooper, M. L., Shaver, P. R., & Collins, N. L. (1998). Attachment styles, emotion regulation, and adjustment in adolescence. *Journal of Personality and Social Psychology, 74,* 1380–1397.

Creasey, G., & Hesson-McInnis, M. (2001). Affective responses, cognitive appraisals, and conflict tactics in late adolescent romantic relationships: Associations with attachment orientations. *Journal of Counseling Psychology, 48,* 85–96.

Creasey, G., Kershaw, K., & Boston, A. (1999). Conflict management with friends and romantic partners: The role of attachment and negative mood regulation expectancies. *Journal of Youth and Adolescence, 28,* 523–543.

Creasey, G., & Ladd, A. (2004). Negative mood regulation expectancies and conflict behaviors in late adolescent college student romantic relationships: The moderating role of generalized attachment representations. *Journal of Research on Adolescence, 14,* 235–255.

Darling, N., Dowdy, B. B., Van Horn, M. L., & Caldwell, L. L. (1999). Mixed-sex settings and the perception of competence. *Journal of Youth and Adolescence, 28,* 461–480.

Davies, P. T., & Windle, M. (2000). Middle adolescents' dating pathways and psychosocial adjustment. *Merrill-Palmer Quarterly, 46,* 90–118.

Davila, J. (2008). Depressive symptoms and adolescent romance: Theory, research, and implications. *Child Development Perspectives, 2,* 26–31.

Davila, J., Steinberg, S. J., Kachadourian, L., Cobb, R., & Fincham, F. (2004). Romantic involvement and depressive symptoms in early and late adolescence: The role of a preoccupied relational style. *Personal Relationships, 11,* 161–178.

Diamond, L. M. (1998). Development of sexual orientation among adolescent and young adult women. *Developmental Psychology, 34,* 1085–1095.

Diamond, L. M. (2008). Female bisexuality from adolescence to adulthood: Results from a 10-year longitudinal study. *Developmental Psychology, 44,* 5–14.

Diamond, L., & Lucas, S. (2004). Sexual-minority and heterosexual youth' peer relationships: Experiences, expectations, and implications for well-being. *Journal of Research on Adolescence, 14,* 313–340.

Dishion, T. J., & Piehler, T. F. (2007). Peer dynamics in the development and change of child and adolescent problem behavior. In A. S. Masten (Ed.), *Multilevel dynamics in developmental psychopathology: Pathways to the future* (pp. 151–180). Mahwah, NJ: Lawrence Erlbaum.

Dornbusch, S. M., Carlsmith, M., Gross, R. T., Martin, J. A., Jennings, D., Rosenberg, A., et al. (1981). Sexual development, age, and dating: A comparison of biological and social influences upon one set of behaviors. *Child Development, 52,* 179–185.

Dowdy, B. B., & Kliewer, W. (1998). Dating, parent-adolescent conflict, and behavioral autonomy. *Journal of Youth and Adolescence, 27,* 473–492.

Downey, G., Bonica, C., & Rincón, C. (1999). Rejection sensitivity and adolescent romantic relationships. In W. Furman, B. Brown, & C. Feiring (Eds.), *The development of romantic relationships in adolescence* (pp. 148–174). New York: Cambridge University Press.

Doyle, A. B., Brendgen, M., Markiewicz, D., & Kamkar, K. (2003). Family relationships as moderators of the association between romantic relationships and adjustment in early adolescence. *Journal of Early Adolescence, 23,* 316–340.

Dubé, E. M., & Savin-Williams, R. C. (1999). Sexual identity development among ethnic sexual-minority male youth. *Developmental Psychology, 35,* 1389–1398.

Dunphy, D. C. (1963). The social structure of urban adolescent peer groups. *Sociometry, 26,* 230–246.

Eder, D. (1993). "Go get ya a French!": Romantic and sexual teasing among adolescent girls. In D. Tannen (Ed.), *Gender and conversational interaction. Oxford studies in sociolinguistics* (pp. 17–31). New York: Oxford University Press.

Ellis, B. J., & Garber, J. (2000). Psychosocial antecedents of variation in girls' pubertal timing: Maternal depression, stepfather presence, and marital and family stress. *Child Development, 71,* 485–501.

Elze, D. E. (2002). Against all odds: The dating experiences of adolescent lesbians and bisexual women. *Journal of Lesbian Studies, 6,* 17–29.

Erikson, E. H. (1968). *Identity, youth, and crisis.* New York: W. W. Norton.

Eyre, S. L., Milbrath, C., & Peacock, B. (2007). Romantic relationships trajectories of African American gay/bisexual adolescents. *Journal of Adolescent Research, 22,* 107–131.

Feinstein, S. C., & Ardon, M. J. (1973). Trends in dating patterns and adolescent development. *Journal of Youth and Adolescence, 2,* 157–166.

Feiring, C. (1996). Concepts of romance in 15-year-old adolescents. *Journal of Research on Adolescence, 6,* 181–200.

Feiring, C. (1999a). Other-sex friendship networks and the development of romantic relationships in adolescence. *Journal of Youth and Adolescence, 28,* 495–512.

Feiring, C. (1999b). Gender identity and the development of romantic relationships in adolescence. In W. Furman, B. Brown, & C. Feiring (Eds.), *The development of romantic relationships in adolescence* (pp. 211–232). New York: Cambridge University Press.

Feldman, S. S., & Cauffman, E. (1999a). Sexual betrayal among late adolescents: Perspectives of the perpetrator and the aggrieved. *Journal of Youth and Adolescence, 28,* 235–258.

Feldman, S. S., & Cauffman, E. (1999b). Your cheatin' heart: Attitudes, behaviors, & correlates of sexual betrayal in late adolescents. *Journal of Research on Adolescence, 9,* 227–252.

Feldman, S. S., Cauffman, E., Arnett Jensen, L., & Arnett, J. J. (2000). The (un)acceptability of betrayal: A study of college students' evaluations of sexual betrayal by a romantic partner and betrayal of a friends' confidence. *Journal of Youth and Adolescence, 29,* 499–523.

Feldman, S. S., & Gowen, L. K. (1998). Conflict negotiation tactics in romantic relationships in high school students. *Journal of Youth and Adolescence, 27,* 691–717.

Feldman, S. S., & Rosenthal, D. A. (1990). The acculturation of autonomy expectations in Chinese high schoolers residing in two Western nations. *International Journal of Psychology, 25,* 259–281.

Feldman, S. S., & Rosenthal, D. A. (1991). Age expectations of behavioral autonomy in Hong Kong, Australian and American youth: The influence of family variables and adolescents' values. *International Journal of Psychology, 26,* 1–23.

Felmlee, D. H. (1994). Who's on top? Power in romantic relationships. *Sex Roles, 31,* 275–295.

Fields, J. (2003). *America's family and living arrangements.* Washington, DC: U.S. Bureau of the Census.

Ford, D. H., & Lerner, R. M. (1992). *Developmental systems theory: An integrative approach.* Newbury Park, CA: Sage.

Franzoi, S. L., Davis, M. H., & Vasquez-Suson, K. A. (1994). Two social worlds: Social correlates and stability of adolescent status groups. *Journal of Personality and Social Psychology, 67,* 462–473.

Friedlander, L. J., Connolly, J. A., Pepler, D. J., & Craig, W. M. (2007). Biological, familial, and peer influences on dating in early adolescence. *Archives of Sexual Behavior, 36,* 821–830.

Furman, W., Brown, B. B., & Feiring, C. (Eds.). (1999). *The development of romantic relationships in adolescence.* New York: Cambridge University Press.

Furman, W., & Buhrmester, D. (1992). Age and sex differences in perceptions of networks of personal relationships. *Child Development, 63,* 103–115.

Furman, W., & Shaffer, L. (2003). The role of romantic relationships in adolescent development. In P. Florsheim (Ed.), *Adolescent romantic relations and sexual behaviors: Theory, research, and practical implications* (pp. 3–22). Mahwah, NJ: Lawrence Erlbaum.

Furman, W., & Simon, V. A. (1999). Cognitive representations of adolescent romantic relationships. In W. Furman, B. B. Brown, &

C. Feiring (Eds.), *The development of romantic relationships in adolescence* (pp. 74–98). New York: Cambridge University Press.

Furman, W., & Simon, V. A. (2006). Actor and partner effects on adolescents' romantic working models and styles on interactions with romantic partners. *Child Development, 77,* 588–604.

Furman, W., Simon, V. A., Shaffer, L., & Bouchey, H. A. (2002). Adolescents' working models and styles for relationships with parents, friends, and romantic partners. *Child Development, 73,* 241–255.

Furman, W., & Wehner, E. (1994). Romantic views: Toward a theory of adolescent romantic relationships. In R. Montemayor, G. R. Adams, & T. P. Gullotta (Eds.), *Personal relationships during adolescence,* vol. 6 (pp. 168–195). Thousand Oaks, CA: Sage.

Galliher, R.V., Rostosky, S. S., Welsh, D. P., & Kawaguchi, M. C. (1999). Power and psychological well-being in late adolescent relationships. *Sex Roles, 40,* 689–710.

Galliher, R. V., Welsh, D. P. Rostosky, S. S., & Kawaguchi, M. C. (2004). Interaction and relationship quality in late adolescent romantic couples. *Journal of Social and Personal Relationships, 21,* 203–216.

Giordano, P. C., Longmore, M. A., & Manning, W. D. (2006). Gender and the meanings of adolescent romantic relationships: A focus on boys. *American Sociological Review, 71,* 260–287.

Giordano, P. C., Manning, W. D., & Longmore, M. A. (2005). The romantic relationships of African-American and White adolescents. *Sociological Quarterly, 46,* 545–568.

Graber, J. A., & Brooks-Gunn, J. (1996). Transitions and turning points: Navigating the passage from childhood through adolescence. *Developmental Psychology, 32,* 768–776.

Graber, J. A., Brooks-Gunn, J., & Warren, M. P. (1995). The antecedents of menarcheal age: Heredity, family environment, and stressful life events. *Child Development, 66,* 346–359.

Gray, M. R., & Steinberg, L. (1999). Adolescent romance and the parent–child relationship: A contextual perspective. In W. Furman, B. B., Brown, & C. Feiring (Eds.), *The development of romantic relationships in adolescence* (pp. 235–265). New York: Cambridge University Press.

Grover, R. L., & Nangle, D. W. (2003). Adolescent perceptions of problematic heterosocial situations: A focus group study. *Journal of Youth and Adolescence, 32,* 129–139.

Halpern, C. T., King, R. B., Oslak, S. G., & Udry, J. R. (2005). Body mass index, dieting, romance, and sexual activity in adolescent girls: Relationships over time. *Journal of Research on Adolescence, 15,* 535–559.

Hankin, B. L., & Abramson, L. Y. (2001). Development of gender differences in depression: An elaborated cognitive vulnerability–transactional stress theory. *Psychological Bulletin, 127,* 773–796.

Harper, M. S., Dickson, J. W., & Welsh, D. P. (2006). Self-silencing and rejection sensitivity in adolescent romantic relationships. *Journal of Youth and Adolescence, 35,* 459–467.

Harper, M. S., & Welsh, D. P. (2007). Keeping quiet: Self-silencing and its association with relational and individual functioning among adolescent romantic couples. *Journal of Social and Personal Relationships, 24,* 99–116.

Hatfield, T. (1988). Passionate and companionate love. In R. J. Sternberg & M. L. Barnes (Eds.), *The psychology of love* (pp. 191–217). New Haven, CT: Yale University Press.

Hatfield, E., Schmitz, E., Cornelius, J., & Rapson, R. L. (1988). Passionate love: How early does it begin? *Journal of Psychology & Human Sexuality, 1,* 35–51.

Hazan, C., & Shaver, P. (1987). Romantic love conceptualized as an attachment process. *Journal of Personality and Social Psychology, 52,* 511–524.

Hughes, M., Morrison, K., Asada, K. J. K. (2005). What's love got to do with it? Exploring the impact of maintenance rules, love attitudes, and network support on friends with benefits relationships. *Western Journal of Communication, 69,* 49–66.

Jackson, S., Jacob, M. N., Landman-Peeters, K., & Lanting, A. (2001). Cognitive strategies employed in trying to arrange a first date. *Journal of Adolescence, 24,* 267–279.

Johnson, H. D. (2004). Gender, grade and relationship differences in emotional closeness within adolescent friendships. *Adolescence, 39,* 243–255.

Joyner, K., & Udry, J. R. (2000). You don't bring me anything but down: Adolescent romance and depression. *Journal of Health and Social Behavior, 41,* 369–391.

Kan, M. L., McHale, S. M., & Crouter, A. C. (2008). Parental involvement in adolescent romantic relationships: Patterns and correlates. *Journal of Youth and Adolescence, 37,* 168–179.

Kenrick, D. T., Gabrielidis, C., Keefe, R. C., & Cornelius, J. S. (1996). Adolescents' age preferences for dating partners: Support for an evolutionary model of life-history strategies. *Child Development, 67,* 1499–1511.

Kim, K., & Smith, P. K. (1999). Family relations in early childhood and reproductive development. *Journal of Reproductive and Infant Psychology, 17,* 133–148.

Kuttler, A. F., & La Greca, A. M. (2004). Linkages among adolescent girls' romantic relationships, best friendships, and peer networks. *Journal of Adolescence, 27,* 395–414.

Kuttler, A. F., La Greca, A. M., & Prinstein, M. J. (1999). Friendship qualities and social–emotional functioning of adolescents with close, cross-sex friendships. *Journal for Research on Adolescence, 9,* 339–366.

La Greca, A. M., & Harrison, H. M. (2005). Adolescent peer relations, friendships, and romantic relationships: Do they predict social anxiety and depression? *Journal of Clinical Child and Adolescent Psychology, 34,* 49–61.

La Greca, A. M., & Mackey, E. R. (2007). Adolescents' anxiety in dating situations: The potential role of friends and romantic partners. *Journal of Clinical Child and Adolescent Psychology, 36,* 522–533.

Lam, T. H., Shi, H. J., Ho, L. M., Stewart, S. M., & Fan, S. (2002). Timing of pubertal maturation and heterosexual behavior among Hong Kong Chinese adolescents. *Archives of Sexual Behavior, 31,* 359–366.

Larson, R. W., Clore, G. L., & Wood, G. A. (1999). The emotions of romantic relationships: Do they wreck havoc on adolescents? In W. Furman, B. B. Brown, & C. Feiring (Eds.), *The development of romantic relationships in adolescence* (pp. 19–49). New York: Cambridge University Press.

Laursen, B., & Collins, W. (1994). Interpersonal conflict during adolescence. *Psychological Bulletin, 115,* 197–209.

Laursen, B., Finkelstein, B., & Betts, N. (2001). A developmental meta-analysis of peer conflict resolution. *Developmental Review, 21,* 423–449.

Laursen, B., Furman, W., & Mooney, K. S. (2006). Predicting interpersonal competence and self-worth from adolescent relationships and relationship networks: Variable-centered and person-centered perspectives. *Merrill-Palmer Quarterly, 52,* 572–600.

Laursen, B., & Williams, V. A. (1997). Perceptions of interdependence and closeness in family and peer relationships among adolescents with and without romantic partners. In S. Shulman & W. A. Collins (Eds.), *Romantic relationships in adolescence: Developmental perspectives* (pp. 3–20). San Francisco, CA: Jossey-Bass.

Leaper, C., & Anderson, K. J. (1997). Gender development and heterosexual romantic relationships during adolescence. In S. Shulman & W. A. Collins (Eds.), *Romantic relationships in adolescence: Developmental perspectives. New directions for child development* (no. 78; pp. 85–103). San Francisco, CA: Jossey-Bass.

Lerner, R. M., & Simi, N. L. (2000). A holistic, integrated model of risk and protection in adolescence: A developmental contextual perspective about research, programs, and policies. In L. R. Bergman, R. B. Cairns, L. Nilsson, & L. Nystedt (Eds.), *Developmental science and the holistic approach* (pp. 421–443). Mahwah, NJ: Lawrence Erlbaum.

Longmore, M. A., Manning, W. D., & Giordano, P. C. (2001). Preadolescent parenting strategies and teens' dating and sexual initiation: A longitudinal analysis. *Journal of Marriage and the Family, 63,* 322–335.

Maccoby, E. E. (1998). *The two sexes: Growing up apart, coming together.* Cambridge, MA: Harvard University Press.

Magnusson, D., Stattin, H., & Allen, V. L. (1985). Biological maturation and social development: A longitudinal study of some adjustment processes from mid-adolescence to adulthood. *Journal of Youth and Adolescence, 14,* 267–283.

Manning, W. D., Giordano, P. C., & Longmore, M. A. (2006). Hooking up: The relationship contexts of "nonrelationship" sex. *Journal of Adolescent Research, 21,* 459–483.

Margolese, S. K., Markiewicz, D., & Doyle, A. B. (2005). Attachment to parents, best friend, and romantic partner: Predicting different pathways to depression in adolescence. *Journal of Youth and Adolescence, 34,* 637–650.

Martin, B. (1990). The transmission of relationship difficulties from one generation to the next. *Journal of Youth and Adolescence, 19,* 181–200.

Mayseless, O., & Scharf, M. (2007). Adolescents' attachment representations and their capacity for intimacy in close relationships. *Journal of Research on Adolescence, 17,* 23–50.

McCabe, M. P. (1984). Toward a theory of adolescent dating. *Adolescence, 19,* 159–170.

McDonald, D. L., & McKinney, J. P. (1994). Steady dating and self-esteem in high school students. *Journal of Adolescence, 17,* 557–564.

McIsaac, C., Connolly, J. A., McKenney, K. S., Pepler, D., & Craig, W. (in press). Observational study of the actor and partner effects of conflict negotiation on autonomy in adolescent boyfriends and girlfriends, *Journal of Adolescence, 31,* 691–707.

McIsaac, C., & Connolly, J. A. (2004). Attributions for romantic dissolution and depressive problems in adolescence. In V. A. Simon & L. Shaffer Hand (Chairs), *The interface of romantic experience and development.* Paper symposium presented at the biennial meeting of the Society for Research on Adolescence, Baltimore, MD.

McMaster, L. E., Connolly, J., Pepler, D., & Craig, W. M. (2002). Peer to peer sexual harassment in early adolescence: A developmental perspective. *Development and Psychopathology, 10,* 25–56.

Meeus, W. H. J., Branje, S. J. T., van der Valk, I., & de Wiede, M. (2007). Relationships with intimate partner, best friend, and parents in adolescence and early adulthood: A study of the saliency of the intimate partnership. *International Journal of Behavioral Development, 31,* 569–580.

Menesini, E. & Nocentini, A. (2008). Comportamenti aggressive nelle prime esperienze sentimentali in adolescenza (Aggression in dating relationship). *Giornale Italiano di Psicologia,* 407–434.

Monroe, S. M., Rohde, P., Seeley, J. R., & Lewinsohn, P. M. (1999). Life events and depression in adolescence: Relationship loss as a prospective risk factor for first onset of major depressive disorder. *Journal of Abnormal Psychology, 108,* 606–614.

Montgomery, M. J. (2005). Psychosocial intimacy and identity: From early adolescence to emerging adulthood. *Journal of Adolescent Research, 20,* 346–374.

Montgomery, M. J., & Sorell, G. T. (1998). Love and dating experience in early and middle adolescence: Grade and gender comparisons. *Journal of Adolescence, 21,* 677–689.

Murstein, B. I. (1974). *Love, sex, and marriage through the ages.* New York: Springer.

Neemann, J., Hubbard, J., & Masten, A. S. (1995). The changing importance of romantic relationship involvement to competence from late childhood to late adolescence. *Development and Psychopathology, 7,* 727–750.

Newcomer, S., & Udry, J. R. (1987). Parental marital status effects on adolescent sexual behavior. *Journal of Marriage and the Family, 49,* 235–240.

Nieder, T., & Seiffge-Krenke, I. (2001). Coping with stress in different phases of romantic development. *Journal of Adolescence, 24,* 297–311.

Noom, J., Dekovic, M., & Meeus, W. (2001). Conceptual analysis and measurement of adolescent autonomy. *Journal of Youth and Adolescence, 30,* 577–595.

Nurmi, J. (2004). Socialization and self-development: Channeling, selection, adjustment and reflection. In R. M. Lerner & L. Steinberg (Eds.), *Handbook of adolescent psychology* (2nd ed., pp. 85–124). Hoboken, NJ: John Wiley & Sons.

O'Leary, K. D., & Slep, A. M. S. (2003). A dyadic longitudinal model of adolescent dating aggression. *Journal of Clinical Child and Adolescent Psychology, 32,* 314–327.

O'Sullivan, L. F., Mantsun, M., Harris, K. M., & Brooks-Gunn, J. (2007). I wanna hold your hand: The progression of social, romantic and sexual events in adolescent relationships. *Perspectives on Sexual and Reproductive Health, 39,* 100–107.

O'Sullivan, L. F., & Meyer-Bahlburg, H. F. L. (2003). African American and Latina inner-city girls' reports of romantic and sexual development. *Journal of Social and Personal Relationships, 20,* 221–238.

Pellegrini, A. D., & Long, J. D. (2007). An observational study of early heterosexual interaction at middle school dances. *Journal of Research on Adolescence, 17*(4), 613–638.

Philbrick, J. L., & Stones, C. R. (1988a). Love attitudes in black South Africa: A comparison of school and university students. *Psychological Record, 38,* 249–251.

Philbrick, J. L., & Stones, C. R. (1988b). Love-attitudes of white South African adolescents. *Psychological Reports, 62,* 17–18.

Phinney, V. G., Jensen, L. C., Olsen, J. A., & Cundick, B. (1990). The relationship between early development and psychosexual behaviors in adolescent females. *Adolescence, 25,* 321–332.

Poulin, F., & Pedersen, S. (2007). Developmental changes in gender composition of friendship networks in adolescent girls and boys. *Developmental Psychology, 43,* 1484–1496.

Prinstein, M. J. (2008). Developmental trends in the associations among adolescents peer acceptance/rejection, peer perceived popularity and alcohol use. In J. P. Allen (Chair), *Where peer relationships ultimately lead: Longitudinal predictions of social functioning and problem behaviors.* Paper presented at the biennial meeting of the Society for Research on Adolescence, Chicago, IL.

Puentes, J., Knox, D., & Zusman, M. E. (2008). Participants in "friends with benefits" relationships. *College Student Journal, 42,* 176–180.

Purdie, V., & Downey, G. (2000). Rejection sensitivity and adolescent girls' vulnerability to relationship-centered difficulties. *Child Maltreatment, 5,* 338–349.

Raffaelli, M. (2005). Adolescent dating experiences described by Latino college students. *Journal of Adolescence, 28,* 559–572.

Raley, R. K., Crissey, S., Muller, C. (2007). Of sex and romance: Late adolescent relationships and young adult union formation. *Journal of Marriage and Family, 69,* 1210–1226.

Reese-Weber, M., & Bartle-Haring, S. (1998). Conflict resolution styles in family subsystems and adolescent romantic relationships. *Journal of Youth & Adolescence, 27,* 735–752.

Reese-Weber, M., & Khan, J. H. (2005). Familial predictors of sibling and romantic-partner conflict resolution: Comparing late adolescents from intact and divorced families. *Journal of Adolescence, 28,* 479–493.

Reese-Weber, M., & Marchand, J. F. (2002). Family and individual predictors of late adolescents' romantic relationships. *Journal of Youth and Adolescence, 31,* 197–206.

Regan, P. C., Durvasula, R., Howell, L., Ureño, O., & Rea, M. (2004). Gender, ethnicity, and the developmental timing of first sexual and romantic experiences. *Social Behavior and Personality, 32,* 667–676.

Regan, P. C., & Joshi, A. (2003). Ideal partner preferences among adolescents. *Social Behavior and Personality, 31,* 13–20.

Richards, M. H., Crowe, P. A., Larson, R., & Swarr, A. (1998). Developmental patterns and gender differences in the experience of peer companionship during adolescence. *Child Development, 69,* 154–163.

Rizzo, C. J., Daley, S. E., & Gunderson, B. H. (2006). Interpersonal sensitivity, romantic stress, and the prediction of depression: A study of inner-city, minority adolescent girls. *Journal of Youth and Adolescence, 35,* 469–478.

Roisman, G. I., Madsen, S. D., Hennighausen, K. H., Sroufe, L. A., & Collins, W. A. (2001). The coherence of dyadic behavior across parent-child and romantic relationships as mediated by the internalized representation of experience. *Attachment and Human Development, 3,* 156–172.

Roscoe, B., Cavanaugh, L. E., & Kennedy, D. R. (1988). Dating infidelity: Behaviors, reasons and consequence. *Adolescence, 23,* 35–43.

Roscoe, B., Diana, M. S., & Brooks, R. H. (1987). Early, middle, and late adolescents' views on dating and factors influencing partner selection. *Adolescence, 22,* 59–68.

Rose, A., & Rudolph, K. (2006). A review of sex differences in peer relationships processes: Potential trade-offs for the emotional and behavioural development of girls and boys. *Psychological Bulletin, 132,* 98–131.

Rostosky, S. S., Galliher, R. V., Welsh, D. P., & Kawaguchi, M. C. (2000) Sexual behaviors and relationship qualities in late adolescent couples. *Journal of Adolescence, 23,* 583–597.

Roth, M. A., & Parker, J. G. (2001). Affective and behavioral responses to friends who neglect their friends for dating partners: Influences of gender, jealousy and perspective. *Journal of Adolescence, 24,* 281–296.

Russell, S. T., Consolacion, T. B. (2003). Adolescent romance and emotional health in the United States: Beyond binaries. *Journal of Clinical Child and Adolescent Psychology, 32,* 499–508.

Savin-Williams, R. C., & Ream, G. L. (2007). Prevalence and stability of sexual orientation components during adolescence and young adulthood. *Archives of Sexual Behavior, 36,* 385–394.

Scharf, M., & Mayseless, O. (2001). The capacity for romantic intimacy: Exploring the contribution of best friend and marital and parental relationships. *Journal of Adolescence, 24,* 379–399.

Sears, J. T. (Ed.). (2008). *The Greenwood encyclopedia of love, courtship, and sexuality through history,* vol. 6: *The modern world.* Westport, CT: Greenwood Press.

Seiffge-Krenke, I. (1997). The capacity to balance intimacy and conflict: Differences in romantic relationships between healthy and diabetic adolescents. In S. Shulman & W. A. Collins (Eds.), *Romantic relationships in adolescence: Developmental perspectives* (pp. 53–67). San Francisco, CA: Jossey-Bass.

Seiffge-Krenke, I. (2000). Diversity in romantic relations of adolescents with varying health status: Links to intimacy in close friendships. *Journal of Adolescent Research, 15,* 611–636.

Seiffge-Krenke, I. (2003). Testing theories of romantic development from adolescence to young adulthood: Evidence of a developmental sequence. *International Journal of Behavioral Development, 27,* 519–531.

Seiffge-Krenke, I. (2006). Coping with relationship stressors: The impact of different working models of attachment and links to adaptation. *Journal of Youth and Adolescence, 35,* 25–39.

Seiffge-Krenke, I., Shulman, S., & Klessinger, N. (2001). Adolescent precursors of romantic relationships in young adulthood. *Journal of Social and Personal Relationships, 18,* 327–346.

Sharabany, R., Gershoni, R., & Hofman, J. E. (1981). Girlfriend, boyfriend: Age and sex differences in intimate friendships. *Developmental Psychology, 17,* 800–808.

Shulman, S. (2003). Conflict and negotiation in adolescent romantic relationships. In P. Florsheim (Ed.), *Adolescent romantic relations and sexual behavior: Theory, research, and practical implications* (pp. 109–135). Mahwah, NJ: Lawrence Erlbaum.

Shulman, S., & Kipnis, O. (2001). Adolescent romantic relationships: A look from the future. *Journal of Adolescence, 24,* 337–351.

Shulman, S., & Knafo, D. (1997). Balancing closeness and individuality in adolescent close relationships. *International Journal of Behavioral Development, 21,* 687–702.

Shulman, S., & Scharf, M. (2000). Adolescent romantic behaviors and perceptions: Age- and gender-related differences, and links with family and peer relationships. *Journal of Research on Adolescence, 10,* 99–118.

Shulman, S. Tuval-Mashiach, R., Levran, E., & Anbar, S. (2006). Conflict resolution patterns and longevity of adolescent romantic couples: A 2-year follow-up study. *Journal of Adolescence, 29,* 575–588.

Shute, R., & Charlton, K. (2006). Anger or compromise? Adolescents' conflict resolution strategies in relation to gender and type of peer relationship. *International Journal of Adolescence and Youth, 13,* 55–69.

Simon, R. W., Eder, D., & Evans, C. (1992). The development of feeling norms underlying romantic love among adolescent females. *Social Psychology Quarterly, 55,* 29–46.

Simon, V. A., Kobielski, S. J., & Martin, S. (2008). Conflict beliefs, goals, and behavior in romantic relationships during late adolescence. *Journal of Youth and Adolescence, 37,* 324–355.

Simpson, J. A., Collins, W. A., Tran, S., & Haydon, K. C. (2007). Attachment and the experience and expression of emotions in romantic relationships: A developmental perspective. *Journal of Personality and Social Psychology, 92,* 355–367.

Smetana, J. G., & Gettman, D. C. (2006). Autonomy and relatedness with parents and romantic development in African American adolescents. *Developmental Psychology, 42,* 1347–1351.

Smiler, A. P. (2008). "I wanted to get to know her better": Adolescent boys' dating motives, masculinity ideology, and sexual behaviour. *Journal of Adolescence, 31,* 17–32.

Smolak, L., Levine, M. P., & Gralen, S. (1993). The impact of puberty and dating on eating problems among middle school girls. *Journal of Youth and Adolescence, 22,* 355–368.

Stattin, H., & Magnusson, D. (1990). *Pubertal maturation in female development. Paths through life,* vol. 2. Hillsdale, NJ: Lawrence Erlbaum.

Steinberg, L., & Morris, A. S. (2001). Adolescent development. *Annual Review of Psychology, 52,* 83–110.

Steinberg, S. J., Davila, J., & Fincham, F. (2006). Adolescent marital expectations and romantic experiences: Associations with perceptions about parental conflict and adolescent attachment security. *Journal of Youth and Adolescence, 35,* 333–348.

Stevenson, H. W., & Zusho, A. (2002). Adolescence in China and Japan: Adapting to a changing environment. In B. B. Brown, R. Larson, & T. Saraswathi (Eds.), *The world's youth: Adolescence in eight regions of the globe* (pp. 141–171). New York: Cambridge University Press.

Stocker, C. M., & Richmond, M. K. (2007). Longitudinal associations between hostility in adolescents' family relationships and friendships and hostility in their romantic relationships. *Journal of Family Psychology, 21,* 490–497.

Striepe, M. I., & Tolman, D. L. (2003). Mom, dad, I'm straight: The coming out of gender ideologies in adolescent sexual-identity development. *Journal of Clinical Child and Adolescent Psychology, 32,* 523–530.

Sullivan, H. S. (1953). *The interpersonal theory of psychiatry.* New York: W. W. Norton.

Susman, E. J., Nottelmann, E. D., Inoff, G. E., Dorn, L. D., Cutler, G. B., Jr., Loriaux, D. L., et al. (1985). The relation of hormone levels and physical development and social–emotional behavior in young adolescents. *Journal of Youth and Adolescence, 14,* 245–252.

Tabares, A., & Gottman, J. (2003). A marital process perspective of adolescent romantic relationships. In P. Florsheim (Ed.), *Adolescent romantic relations and sexual behavior: Theory, research, and practical implications* (pp. 337–354). Mahwah, NJ: Lawrence Erlbaum.

Taradash, A., Connolly, J., Pepler, D., Craig, W., & Costa, M. (2001). The interpersonal context of romantic autonomy in adolescence. *Journal of Adolescence, 24,* 365–377.

Tasker, F. L., & Richards, M. P. M. (1994). Adolescents' attitudes toward marriage and marital prospects after parental divorce: A review. *Journal of Adolescent Research, 9,* 340–362.

Thornton, A. (1990). The courtship process and adolescent sexuality. *Journal of Family Issues 11,* 239–273.

Tolman, D. L., Spencer, R., Harmon, T., Rosen-Reynoso, M., & Striepe, M. (2004). Getting close, staying cool: Early adolescent boys' experiences with romantic relationships. In N. Way & J. Y. Chu (Eds.), *Adolescent boys: Exploring the diverse cultures of boyhood* (pp. 235–255). New York: New York University Press.

Tubman, J., Windle, M., & Windle, R. (1996). Cumulative sexual intercourse patterns among middle adolescents: Problem behavior precursors and concurrent health risk behaviors. *Journal of Adolescent Health, 18,* 182–191.

Tuval-Mashiach, R., & Shulman, S. (2006). Resolution of disagreements between romantic partners, among adolescents, and young adults: Qualitative analysis of interaction discourses. *Journal of Research on Adolescence, 16,* 561–588.

Underwood, M. K. (2007). Girlfriends and boyfriends diverging in middle childhood and coming together in romantic relationships. *Merrill-Palmer Quarterly, 53,* 520–526.

van Schaick, K., & Stolberg, A. L. (2001). The impact of paternal involvement and parental divorce on young adults' intimate relationships. *Journal of Divorce & Remarriage, 36,* 99–122.

Veprinska, M., & Connolly, J. (2007). *Family divorce and romantic relationships in early adolescence.* Poster presented at the 68th Canadian Psychological Association Annual Convention, Ottawa.

Weber, A. L. (1998). Loving, losing, and letting go: Coping with nonmarital break-ups. In B. H. Spitzberg & W. R. Cupach (Eds.), *The dark side of close relationships* (pp. 267–306). Mahwah, NJ: Lawrence Erlbaum.

Welsh, D., Grello, C. M., & Harper, M. S. (2003). When love hurts: Depression and adolescent romantic relationships. In P. Florsheim (Ed.), *Adolescent romantic relations and sexual behavior: Theory, research, and practical implications* (pp. 185–211). Mahwah, NJ: Lawrence Erlbaum.

Welsh, D. P., Galliher, R. V., Kawaguchi, M. C., & Rostosky, S. S. (1999). Discrepancies in adolescent romantic couples' and observers' perceptions of couple interaction and their relationships to depressive symptoms. *Journal of Youth and Adolescence, 28,* 645–666.

Werebe, M. G. (1987). Friendship and dating relationships among French adolescents. *Journal of Adolescence, 10,* 269–289.

Williams, S., Connolly, J., & Segal, Z. V. (2001). Intimacy in relationships and cognitive vulnerability to depression in adolescent girls. *Cognitive Therapy and Research, 25,* 477–496.

Williams, T., Connolly, J. A., & Cribbie, R. (2008). Light and heavy heterosexual activities of young Canadian adolescents: Normative patterns and differential predictors. *Journal of Research on Adolescence, 18,* 145–172.

Williams, T., Connolly, J. A., Pepler, D., & Craig, W. (2003). Questioning and sexual minority adolescents: High school experiences of bullying, sexual harassment and physical abuse. *Canadian Journal of Community Mental Health, 22,* 47–58.

Young, A. M., & d'Arcy, H. (2005). Older boyfriends of adolescent girls: The cause or a sign of the problem? *Journal of Adolescent Mental Health, 36,* 410–419.

Youniss, J., McLellan, J. A., & Strouse, D. (1994). "We're popular, but we're not snobs": Adolescents describe their crowds. In R. Montemayor, G. R. Adams, & T. P. Gullotta (Eds.), *Personal relationships during adolescence. Advances in adolescent development: An annual book series,* vol. 6 (pp. 101–122). Thousand Oaks, CA: Sage.

Zimmer-Gembeck, M. J. (1999). Stability, change and individual differences in involvement with friends and romantic partners among adolescent females. *Journal of Youth and Adolescence, 28,* 419–438.

Zimmer-Gembeck, M. J., & Collins, W. A. (2008). Gender, mature appearance, alcohol use, and dating as correlates of sexual partner accumulation from ages 16–26 years. *Journal of Adolescent Health, 42,* 564–572.

Zimmer-Gembeck, M. J., & Petherick, J. (2006). Intimacy dating goals and relationship satisfaction during adolescence and emerging adulthood: Identity formation, age and sex as mod-erators. *International Journal of Behavioral Development, 30,* 167–177.

Zimmer-Gembeck, M. J., Siebenbruner, J., & Collins, W. A. (2001). Diverse aspects of dating: Associations with psychosocial functioning from early to middle adolescence. *Journal of Adolescence, 24,* 313–336.

Zimmer-Gembeck, M. J., Siebenbruner, J., & Collins, W. A. (2004). A prospective study of intraindividual and peer influences on adolescents' heterosexual romantic and sexual behavior. *Archives of Sexual Behavior, 33,* 381–394.

CHAPTER 5

Mentoring in Adolescence

JEAN E. RHODES AND SARAH R. LOWE

I know in my heart that I would not be the same person without Josh and Big Brothers Big Sisters. . . .
I don't believe there are bad kids, just kids with potential who need opportunities.
—Darius Murray (Barrett, Annis, & Riffey, 2004, p. 36)

Youth who have achieved positive developmental outcomes despite difficult circumstances often attribute their success to the influence of a caring adult. Such attributions have been corroborated by a growing body of literature, which has underscored the positive influence of volunteer mentors, coaches, teachers, and others in the lives of adolescents. Despite the promise of mentoring, as well as the recent rapid growth of volunteer programs across the United States, many questions remain concerning the nature and effects of mentor relationships. In this chapter we provide an overview of the research literature on youth mentoring and discuss a theoretical model of the processes through which mentoring is likely to promote positive development for adolescents. Implications for future research and preventative intervention are discussed.

An estimated 3 million youth are in formal one-to-one mentoring relationships in the United States, and funding and growth imperatives continue to fuel program expansion. Even larger numbers of youth report experiencing mentoring relationships outside of these types of programs (Beam, Chen, & Greenberger, 2002; Zimmerman, Bingenhimer, & Notaro, 2002). Such relationships appear to be a particularly important asset in the lives of today's youth.

In a national survey of youth, the Minnesota-based Search Institute found that the greater the number of such developmental assets present in a youth's life, the lower the rate of risk-taking behaviors. These researchers created a list of 40 assets that are conducive to adolescents' healthy development, including "support from three or more other adults" and "adult role models." More recently, Theokas and Lerner (2006) identified the presence of mentors (both natural and through programs) was the most import asset for positive youth development in communities.

DOES MENTORING PROMOTE POSITIVE OUTCOMES?

What do we know about the effectiveness of youth mentoring? A better understanding of the research evidence for youth mentoring, including findings from the reviews, evaluations, and meta-analyses that have been conducted in recent years, provides the rationale for taking a more informed, practically applicable approach to strengthening youth mentoring interventions.

Evidence from Literature Reviews

Several comprehensive reviews of the literature have emerged from the United States, Canada, and United Kingdom in recent years (see Table 5.1). These surveys of the literature have the advantage of moving readers beyond the more piecemeal approach of individual studies. Reviews can also locate gaps in the knowledge base and guide decision making. Yet there are problems with encompassing reviews. Mentoring programs can vary on a multitude of dimensions, including their duration, intensity, integration with other services, target populations, and approaches in ways that complicate global assessments of effectiveness. Similarly, although high-quality

TABLE 5.1   Summary of Mentoring Literature Reviews

Review	Affiliation(s)	Number of Studies Reviewed*	# Peer-Reviewed	Examples of Overall Tone
Hansen, K. (2007). One-to-one mentoring: Literature review. Philadelphia: Big Brothers Big Sisters of America.	Big Brothers Big Sisters of America	61	35	"The studies consistently find a broad range of positive outcomes from both community-based and school/site-biased mentoring. Outcome areas include attitudes, academic and socio-emotional behaviours with various youth populations. The literature continues to explore the extent and depth of these outcomes, though it is clear that programs using identifiable positive program practices regularly yield higher outcomes in the youth than programs that are not well-run" (3).
Phillip, K., & Spratt, J. (2007). *A synthesis of published research on mentoring and befriending for The Mentoring and Befriending Foundation.* University of Aberdeen: The Rowan Group.	The Rowan Group, University of Aberdeen	24	3	"While it is clear that youth mentoring and befriending have minimal impact on offending behaviour and attitudes to this, research to date has pointed to the very different ways in which mentoring in particular, has been delivered within programmes. . . . Questions of dosage, duration and intensity demand more intensive scrutiny. In particular, more requires to be learned about why matches fail and what the implications are for those young people who do not "stay the course"" (41).
Roberts, H., Liabo, K., Lucas, P., DuBois, D., & Sheldon, T. A. (2004). Mentoring to reduce antisocial behavior in childhood. British Medical Journal, 328, 512–514.	Institute of Health Sciences, City University, London School of Public Health, University of Illinois at Chicago Department of Health Sciences, University of York	6	3	"Rolling out national programmes based on inadequate evidence can, however, do more harm than good. We use the example of mentoring for young people with, or at risk of, antisocial behaviour problems to show the potential dangers of running ahead of the evidence" (512). "On the basis of these findings, we concluded that non-directive mentoring programmes delivered by volunteers cannot be recommended as an effective intervention for young people at risk of or already involved in antisocial behaviour or criminal activities. . . . We are not suggesting that mentoring cannot work. There are many different kinds of mentoring, and some show better evidence of effect than others. Our current state of knowledge on the effectiveness of mentoring is similar to that of a new drug that shows promise but remains in need of further research" (513).

TABLE 5.1   (*Continued*)

Review	Affiliation(s)	Number of Studies Reviewed*	# Peer-Reviewed	Examples of Overall Tone
Liabo, K., & Lucas, P. (2006). *One-to-one mentoring programmes and problem behaviour in adolescence. What Works for Children Group: Evidence Nugget.* Economic & Social Research Council.	Evidence Network, Economic & Social Research Council City University, London Barnardo's NHS Health Development Agency University of York	15	8	"We currently do not know whether mentoring is an overall positive intervention. Mentoring therefore needs to be evaluated in a randomised controlled trial."
Brady, B., Dolan, P., O'Brien, M., & Canavan, J. (2005). *Big Brothers Big Sisters Ireland youth mentoring programme: Evaluation report.* Galway Child & Family Resarch & Policy Unit.	Child & Family Research and Policy Unit; Health Service Executive Western Region Department of Political Science and Sociology, National University of Ireland, Galway	17	8	"A range of research highlights that mentoring can have positive outcomes with young people. The best outcomes from mentoring are achieved when strong relationships develop and where young people experience environmental risk and disadvantage. Positive outcomes are more likely to accrue when 'best practice' procedures are in place— including screening of volunteers, supervision, training, ongoing support and group activities. Where such practices are neglected, there is potential for programmes to have negative effects on youth" (29).
Hall, J. C. (2003). *Mentoring and young people: A literature review.* The SCRE Centre: University of Glasgow.	The SCRE Centre, University of Glasgow	35	20	"The US studies indicate that mentoring can have a significant impact on a number of measures, but that this impact may not be large. . . . The best US evidence is that mentoring may have some impact on problem or high-risk behaviours, academic/educational outcomes, and career/employment outcomes" (15). "There is evidence of positive outcomes from mentoring (though the effects are not large); and there are definite features associated with successful — and unsuccessful — mentoring schemes (33).
Jekielek, S., Moore, K. A., & Hair, E. C. (2002). *Mentoring programs and youth development.* Washington, DC: Child Trends.	Child Trends Edna McConnell Clark Foundation	19	6	"A number of well-designed program evaluations indicate that mentoring programs are beneficial to at-risk youth. Given accumulating evidence about the effectiveness of these programs, and widespread interest in initiating these programs, further research would be helpful to those who seek to implement mentoring programs" (35).

TABLE 5.1   (*Continued*)

Review	Affiliation(s)	Number of Studies Reviewed*	# Peer-Reviewed	Examples of Overall Tone
Sipe, C. L. (2002). Mentoring programs for adolescents: A research summary. *Journal of Adolescent Health, 31,* 251–260.	Public/Private Ventures	20	4	"First and foremost, the field now has definitive evidence of the positive benefits mentoring can produce for the youth being served by these programs. We have also learned that unrelated youth and adults can come together to form meaningful and satisfactory relationships but not without time and the right attitude" (259). "In the wake of the positive effects that mentoring can have for youth, at a time when few youth programs have been able to report success, practitioners across the country are jumping on the mentoring bandwagon. But many of these programs are implementing mentoring models that have not been adequately researched" (259).

* Does not include meta-analyses or review papers.

work is often included, many of the reviews also contain a discouraging mix of flawed studies. It is not uncommon, for example, to see rigorously, peer-reviewed research placed on relatively equal footing with unpublished in-house reports. Moreover, as apparent in Table 5.1, reviews of overlapping bodies of work sometimes draw dramatically different conclusions.

For example, Big Brothers Big Sisters of America's review (Hansen, 2007) recently concluded that, "studies consistently find a broad range of positive outcomes from both community-based and school/site-based mentoring." A survey of some of the same studies, however, led researchers (Roberts, Liabo, Lucas, DuBois, & Sheldon, 2004) to conclude in the *British Medical Journal* (BMJ) that, "mentoring programmes as currently implemented may fail to deliver on their promises." This difference of opinion stems, in no small part, from how and what evidence is considered. For example, the BMJ review and others (e.g., Hall, 2003; Liabo & Lucas, 2006; Philip & Spratt, 2007; Roberts, 2005) placed considerable

stock in the DuBois et al. (2002) meta-analysis, a study that distilled 55 evaluations. By contrast, Hansen (2007) put more weight on the evaluation of Big Brothers Big Sisters of America, which has been interpreted quite positively. A more general concern regarding review articles is that they tend to differentially highlight potential iatrogenic effects and set different standards for including studies (i.e., strict evaluation versus a mix of evaluations, secondary analyses, and more qualitative program descriptions).

Review articles and chapters in special issues of journals and academic handbooks, which summarize the literature as it bears on particular topics (gender, special needs, etc.), can also be quite helpful to programs and decision makers. Yet, like comprehensive reviews, they are only as strong as the research and evaluations on which they stake their claims. More generally, although both comprehensive and more circumscribed reviews are sometimes presented as objective accounts of available evidence, biases can affect how evidence is weighed (Pawson, 2006).

Recent Program Evaluations

A growing number of program evaluations, which have been conducted since the DuBois et al. (2002) meta-analysis also shed light on the field (see Table 5.2). These studies vary in their ability to rule out confounds, and there exists a constant tension between the real and the ideal. The quality and fidelity of experimental designs can easily fall prey to the vicissitudes of meager, short-term funding streams and glitches in program implementation. And, when effects are found, their implications are not always clear. With a large enough sample, small differences can show statistical significance, whereas large differences can be obscured by small samples. Moreover, important outcomes of mentoring may go unmeasured, or remain undetectable within short intervals. An over-reliance on randomized controlled studies as the "gold standard" for mentoring evaluation has, in some cases, come at the expense of a more nuanced, triangulated understanding of group variation and a full appreciation of

developmental trajectories (Lerner & Overton, in press). Other problems with the available evaluations of youth mentoring include unspecified program inputs, heavy reliance on self-reports, the use of psychometrically unsound instruments, high attrition, absence of control or comparison groups, inconsistent sampling procedures, and the collection of data at a compressed or single time point. In addition, a publication bias that favors the selection of studies with significant effects over those showing no effect makes it nearly impossible for practitioners to learn the lessons of unsuccessful programs and approaches.

Even when well implemented, evaluations of mentoring programs have not been particularly encouraging. Findings from the few evaluations conducted since the DuBois et al. (2002) meta-analysis that collected follow-up assessments do not suggest the strong effects on young people that are central to arguments offered for investment in mentoring initiatives. In some instances, negative or

TABLE 5.2   Selected Mentoring Program Evaluations

Evaluation	Sample*	Design	Main Outcomes
Herrera, C., Grossman, J.B., Kauh, T.J., Feldman, A.F., & McMaken, J. (with Jucovy, L.Z.). (2007). Making a difference in schools: The Big Brothers Big Sisters school-based mentoring impact study. Philadelphia, PA: Public/Private Ventures.	1,139; 4th-9th grade; 37% White, 23% Hispanic or Latino, 18% Black or African American, 6% Native American, 1% Asian or Pacific Islander, 13% Multiracial, 3% Other; Approx. 80% were receiving free or reduced-price lunch; 77% were having difficulties with 1 or more assessed areas of risk (academic performance, school behavior, relationships, misconduct)	Randomized control group; 9 and 15 months between pre-posttests; Looked at match length and closeness as moderators	At 9 months, mentored group had been matched for an average of 5.3 months. Mentored group had improvements in academic attitudes (e.g. scholastic efficacy), performance (e.g. overall performance and in science and written and oral language specifically) and behaviors (e.g. fewer unexcused absences) compared to the control group. Mentored group was also more likley to report a supportive non-parental adult in their life. No benefits found for drug and alcohol use, misconduct outside of school, relationships with parents and peers, and self-esteem. At 15 month follow-up, only 52% of youth were still receiving mentoring. Few benefits of mentoring were sustained: mentored youth remained less likely to skip school, more likely to report a

TABLE 5.2   (*Continued*)

Evaluation	Sample*	Design	Main Outcomes
			supportive non-parental adult, and reported greater confidence that they would attend and finish college than controls. Both match length and closeness were associated with stronger impacts for mentored youth.
Barnoski, R. (2006). *Recidivism findings for the Juvenile Rehabilitation Administration's mentoring program: Final report.* Olympia, WA: Washington State Institute for Public Policy.	$N = 156$; Mean age: 16.3 years; 39.7% African American, 9% Native American, 51% White; Youth returning from juvenile rehabilitation (JRA) facilities.	Matched comparison group, pre-/posttest, 12, 24, and 36 months.	Mentored group had lower rates of total, violent felony, and felony recidivism at 12 months, with differences between the mentored and control group approaching significance for violent felony and felony recidivism. No significant differences in any category of recidivism at 24 or 36 months.
Dappen, L., & Isernhagen, J. C. (2006). Urban and nonurban schools: Examination of a statewide student mentoring program. *Urban Education, 41,* 151–168.	$N = 511$; 6th–12th grade; urban schools: White, 26% minority; nonurban schools: 76% White, 24% minority.	Two groups of mentored youth (urban and nonurban), posttest only.	Urban students reported fewer behavior changes than those of nonurban students. Compared to total urban and nonurban student population, urban students were underrepresented in mentoring pairs.
DeWit, D. J., Lipman, E., Manzano-Munguia, M., Bisanz, J., Graham, K., Offord, D. R., et al. (2006). Feasibility of a randomized controlled trial for evaluating the effectiveness of the Big Brothers Big Sisters community match program at the national level. *Children and Youth Services Review, 29,* 383–404.	$N = 59$; 7–14 years; mean = 9.96 years; 3.8% African-Canadian or aboriginal; 76.9% White European; 19.2% other (e.g., Hispanic, Asian, Arab, Jewish); 77% from single-parent families; 51% with gross household income of less than $20,000.	Randomized control group, pre-/posttest, 12 months. There was nonequivalence between groups and nonrandom attrition.	Significant improvements for experimental group in child self-reported emotional problems, social anxiety, generalized social anxiety and distress, teacher social support, and social skills and self-control.

TABLE 5.2   (*Continued*)

Evaluation	Sample*	Design	Main Outcomes
Osterling, K. L., & Hines, A. M. (2006). Mentoring adolescent foster youth: Promoting resilience during developmental transitions. *Child and Family Social Work,* *11*, 242-253.	*N* = 52; mean = 16.3 years; (SD = 1.1 years) 38.0% White, 36.0% Mexican American/Other Latino; foster-care youth.	Descriptive.	66.7% of youth reported that their relationship with their advocate was like a friend. The majority of youth also reported positive feelings toward their advocate (e.g., confidence in advocate's helping ability, importance of relationship, a good connection). In qualitative interviews, youth and advocates tended to report positive changes related to emotional gains and ability to complete concrete tasks.
Clayden, J., & Stein, M. (2005). *Mentoring young people leaving care.* York, UK: Joseph Roundtree Foundation.	*N* = 181; 15–23 years; 76% White, 9% Black African, 6% Mixed heritage, 5% Other Black, 2% Black Caribbean, 2% Asian; youth "leaving care."	Descriptive. Included data from 13 mentoring programs. Variability in the extent and quality of data collection across different programs. Qualitative.	93% of relationships had some positive outcome. 76% achieved goal stated at the beginning of the relationship; 52% achieved goals that emerged during the relationship. Half the relationships had some negative outcome. 37% had unplanned endings, often because of youth missing appointments. Longer relationships were associated with greater goal achievement and positive outcomes.
Karcher, M. J. (2008). The Study of Mentoring in the Learning Environment (SMILE): A randomized evaluation of the effectiveness of school-based mentoring. *Prevention Science.*	*N* = 516; aged 10–18, primarily Latino students who attended urban public schools.	Random assignment to (1) supportive services alone or (2) supportive services plus school-based mentoring; controlled for mentor/mentee attendance.	Brief duration of school-based mentoring (avg. 8 meetings). Small positive main effects of mentoring on self-reported connectedness to peers, self-esteem, and social support from friends. No effects on grades or social skills. Elementary school boys and high school girls benefitted the most from mentoring.
Portwood, S. G., Ayers, P. M., Kinnison, K. E., Waris, R. G., & Wise, D. L. (2005). YouthFriends: Outcomes from a school-based mentoring program. *Journal of Primary Prevention, 26,* 129–145.	*N* = 170; 4th–12th grade; 152 listed ethnicity: 72.3% White, 16.4% African American, 4.6% American Indian, 1.3% Native Hawaiian or Pacific Islander, 0.6% Asian American, 4.6% other; for full sample, 7% Hispanic.	Matched comparison group, pre-/posttest, Approximately 9 months (full school year); pretest measures completed after group assignment.	Mentored group had significantly higher sense of school membership at posttest. Mentored boys had significant improvements in attitudes toward drug use item and in self-esteem. At-risk mentored youth had significant improvement on community connectedness and goal setting. Among students with GPAs below 2.0 at baseline, mentored youth had significant improvement, whereas controls did not.

(Continued)

TABLE 5.2   *(Continued)*

Evaluation	Sample*	Design	Main Outcomes
Shiner, M., Young, T., Newburn, T., & Groben, S. (2004). *Mentoring disaffected young people: An evaluation of Mentoring Plus.* York, UK: Joseph Roundtree Foundation.	*N* = 102; 12–19 years; of original sample (*n* = 428), 43% White, 41% Black African/Caribbean, 2% Asian, 14% Mixed race/dual heritage; targeted at-risk youth; Many referred by Youth Offending Teams, Educational Welfare Services, and schools.	Comparison group, pre-/posttest, 10–12 months, and 16–18 months. Comparison group *not* included in second follow-up assessment; did not utilize tests of statistical significance.	70% of mentored youth considered their mentors fairly or very helpful. Mentored group had substantial increases in engagement in education, training and work, whereas comparison group did not. Levels of offending decreased for both mentored and comparison groups.
Maxfield, M., Schrim, A., & Rodriguez-Planas, N. (2003). *The Quantum Opportunity Project demonstration: Implementation and short-term impacts.* Washington, DC: Mathematic Policy Research.	*N* = 1069; 9th grade; from high schools with 40% or more dropout rate; GPA below 67th percentile of students meeting other requirements.	Randomized control group, posttests only, 4 years, and 7–10 months later. QOP included case management, mentoring, supplemental education, development activities, community service, supportive services, and financial incentives.	QOP group had significantly higher graduation and enrollment in postsecondary education or training than control group. QOP did not significantly improve performance in high school or reduce risky behaviors. QOP participants were significantly more likely to report that they participated in a program that helps students stay in school get good grades, stay away from illegal drugs, prepare for work or college, and make good decisions in life. Program impact varied substantially by site.
Keating, L. M., Tomashina, M. A., Foster, S., & Allesandri, M. (2002). The effects of a mentoring program on at-risk youth. *Adolescence, 37*, 717–734.	*N* = 68, 10–17 years; mean = 13.02; 32% White, 24% African American, 37% Latino, 3% Asian, 3% Other; referred by professionals (e.g., school counselor, agency personal); "At risk" (e.g., due to poor grades, behavioral problems).	Matched comparison group, pre-/posttest, 6 months. Pretest measures completed after group assignment. Mentored group reported significantly fewer delinquent acts at baseline.	Teacher and parent reports of significant decreases in internalizing and externalizing behaviors in mentored group. 54% of intervention group listed their mentor as a supportive person.
Aseltine, R. H., Dupre, M., & Lamlein, P. (2000). Mentoring as a drug prevention strategy: An evaluation of Across Ages. *Adolescent and Family Health, 1*, 11–20.	*N* = 400 (approx); 6th grade; participants from MA district with 72% racial minorities, low-income.	Random assignment; pre-/posttest, 6 months after program completion; 3 groups: (1) mentoring, life-skills curriculum, and community service, (2) life-skills curriculum and community service only, (3) control group.	Compared to control group, mentored group had significantly lower levels of problem behavior and alcohol use; significantly higher self-control, cooperation, attachment to school and family, school absences, and attitudes toward the elderly and helping. Compared to both groups, mentored group had significantly higher levels of self-control and school bonding. At 6-month follow-up, program effects only for cooperation and initiation of marijuana use.

(Continued)

TABLE 5.2   (*Continued*)

Evaluation	Sample*	Design	Main Outcomes
Blechman, E. A., Maurice, A., Buecker, B., & Helberg, C. (2000). Can mentoring or skill training reduce recidivism? Observational study with propensity analysis. *Prevention Science, 1,* 139–155.	$N = 255$; at time of intake arrest: 10.82–18.44 years; mean = 15.25; 76.7% White, 17.1% Latino, 6.1% Black, Asian, Native American or multiethnic; juvenile offenders.	Propensity analysis of assignment to juvenile diversion (JD), JD plus skills training (ST), and JD plus mentoring (MEN); 2.06–3.41 years; mean = 2.62 years.	Significant differences between ST and MEN groups in externalizing and internalizing problems, prosocial coping, age at earliest arrest and at intake, with ST participants consistently having more favorable scores. MEN group had significant more posttreatment arrests than ST group, but this decreased to borderline significance using propensity blocking. Time to first rearrest was significant longer for ST group than MEN and JD groups, with group differences especially pronounced in the first year after intake arrest. With propensity stratification, differences between ST and MEN groups, and ST and JD groups were not significant.
Cavell, T. A., & Hughes, J. N. (2000). Secondary prevention as context for assessing change processes in aggressive children. *Journal of School Psychology, 38,* 199–235.	$N = 60$; 2nd–3rd grade; 48.3% African American, 36.7% White, 11.7% Hispanic; identified by teachers as exhibiting aggressive behaviors; 41.7% from single-parent households.	Randomized control group, pre-/posttest at 16 and 28 months; PrimeTime included therapeutic mentoring (18 hrs. mentor training), teacher/ parent consultation, and problem-solving skills training (PSST); Compared with Standard Mentoring by mentors who had been trained for 1 hour.	No differences between groups at posttreatment or follow-up. At posttreatment, both groups had significant declines in aggression as rated by parents and teachers, and significant gains in teacher-rated acceptance. At follow-up, both groups had significant declines from pretreatment in parent and peer-rated aggression. In addition, children had significant improvement in perceived competence and social acceptance, and social support. Study also looked at social cognitions about aggression, mentor relationship quality, parents' history of maternal rejection, and peer-rated narcissism. Notably, mentee-rated relationship quality predicted lower parent-reported aggression for children in the PrimeTime condition only. Mentor-rated relationship quality was associated with lower teacher-rated aggression. For PrimeTime group, low pre-PSST.

TABLE 5.2   *(Continued)*

Evaluation	Sample*	Design	Main Outcomes
Dennison, S. (2000). A win-win peer mentoring and tutoring program: A collaborative model. *Journal of Primary Prevention, 20*, 161–174.	25, 3rd–4th grade, not specified, identified by teachers as being at risk of becoming high school dropouts; at least 1 years behind on reading and math subject areas.	Single group, pre-/posttest; approximately 9 months (full school year).	Teachers noted improvement in academic areas in which mentors provided tutoring.
Grossman, J. B., & Tierney, J. P. (1998). Does mentoring work? An impact study of the Big Brothers Big Sisters program. *Evaluation Review, 22*, 403–426.	*N* = 959; 10–16 years; 55% racial minorities; of those, 71% African American, 18% Hispanic, 5% biracial, 3% Native American, 3% other; Almost all from single-parent households; many from low-income households, or households with a prior history of family violence or substance abuse.	Randomized control group, pre-posttest; 18 months.	78% of youth in treatment group were matched by the end of the study. Compared to controls, youth matched with mentors: were less likely to initiate drug or alcohol use; were less likely to hit someone; skipped fewer classes, felt more competent about schoolwork, and showed modest gains in their GPA; had higher quality parental relationships at the end of the study, primarily due to increased trust; had improvements in their peer relationships. Some notable gender and racial differences.
LoSciuto, L., Rajala, A., Townsend, T. N., & Taylor, A. S. (1996). An outcome evaluation of Across Ages: An intergenerational mentoring approach to drug prevention. *Journal of Adolescent Research, 11*, 116–129.	*N* = 526; 6th grade; 52.2% African American, 15.8% White, 9.1% Asian American, 9.0% Hispanic, 13.9% other; from Philadelphia's "most stressed" neighborhoods.	Random assignment; pre-/posttest; 12 months; 3 groups: (1) mentoring, life skills curriculum, community service, and parent workshops; (2) life skills curriculum, community service, and parent workshops; (3) control group.	Compared to control group, mentored group had significantly greater knowledge about older people; improved reactions to situations involving drug use; greater levels of community service; and greater school attendance. Compared to both groups, mentored group had significantly greater improvement in attitudes toward school, the future, and elders. Significant differences between marginal, average, and exceptional mentoring involvement groups on school attendance, with greater levels of involvement associated lower numbers of absences. Significant difference between marginal or average mentoring involvement and exceptional mentoring involvement (all favoring exceptional mentoring involvement) on attitudes towards school, the future and elders; attidues toward older people; reactions to situations involving drugs; and knowledge about drug use.

* Includes youth only (i.e., not mentors, parents, or program personnel). For studies looking at changes over time, includes subjects who completed all assessments.

no effects have been found (e.g., Blechman, Maurice, Buecker, & Helberg, 2000), or effects have eroded to nonsignificance within only a few months of program participation (Aseltine, Dupre, & Lamlein, 2000). In fact, only one mentoring program, "Across Ages," has achieved the status of "model program" on the Substance Abuse and Mental Health Services Administration (SAMHSA) Registry of Evidence-Based Programs and Practices (NREPP), an online registry of independently reviewed and rated interventions.

Big Brothers Big Sisters of America (BBBSA) was listed on this registry as an "effective program," a designation that stemmed, in part, from the landmark study of BBBSA community-based mentoring (CBM) programs (Grossman & Tierney, 1998). The evaluators traced the experiences of youth given access to the program, as well as a control group, over time. Several widely cited, statistically significant differences in behavior and academic functioning between the mentored youth and the control group were uncovered after 18 months. But, as mentioned above, statistical significance does not necessarily indicate practical significance and, in that regard, standardized effect sizes are considered a more useful metric of evaluation (Flay et al., 2005). In statistical terms, effect size represents the degree to which two groups differ (in this case, the mentoring group versus the wait-listed control group). Although promising the standardized effect size across all outcomes in the BBBSA CBM study was relatively small ($r = 0.06$) (Herrera, Grossman, Kauh, Feldman, & McMaken, 2007). DuBois et al. (2002) remarked that this effect size was "not necessarily consistent with the manner in which results of the large-scale evaluation frequently have been cited by the media as demonstrating a large impact for mentoring relationships."

This inconsistency can be understood when we consider that *all* of the youth, including those who had mentors, showed gradual increases in problems over time, with the treatment group showing slightly fewer problems. Characterizations of the cost–benefit ratios

that were derived from these data were also reported in optimistic terms. For instance, researchers recently noted that BBBS yielded a "net monetary benefit" (Aos, Lieb, Mayfield, Miller, & Pennucci, 2005, p. 131), when, in fact, the benefits exceeded costs by only the narrowest of margins when including both taxpayer and other costs (estimate of $1.01 benefit for each $1.00 of cost). When calculated only in terms of taxpayer cost (i.e., excluding volunteer and in-kind contributions), the benefit per dollar was $3.28.

More recently, a large randomized evaluation of BBBSA's new, school-based mentoring program (SBM) (Herrera et al., 2007) yielded the same effect size ($r = 0.06$) as found in the CBM study. In SBM, interactions between youth and mentors typically are confined to the school setting and the 1-year minimum commitment of mentors is shortened to the 9-month school year. Because SBM is linked to the academic calendar, the relationships tend to be less enduring than those forged through CBM. Indeed, the average length of the relationships in the SBM evaluation was just 5.3 months (compared to 11.4 months in the CBM evaluation), and nearly half (48%) of the relationships did not continue into the following school year. Overall, findings were mixed. At the end of the first school year, youth assigned to receive mentoring showed significant improvements in their academic performance, perceived scholastic efficacy, school misconduct, and attendance relative to a control group of nonmentored youth. These effects, generally small in magnitude, varied by which outcome was assessed: for school-related outcomes, the overall effect size was 0.09, and for non-school-related outcomes (e.g., behavioral and psychosocial outcomes), effect sizes ranged from 0.02 to 0.18. These effects did not persist over time, however, and, when youth were reassessed a few months into the following school year, most differences were no longer statistically significant.

Despite these somewhat discouraging trends, the group differences that have been uncovered in both national evaluations do give grounds for cautious optimism about the potential viability of mentoring interventions. In light of the vast continuum in the quality and duration that existed in the mentoring relationships, however, it would have been unrealistic to expect a relatively loosely structured social program to produce dramatic, across-the-board reversals of the negative trajectories that are typical of adolescence. Indeed, matches vary considerably in their effectiveness, depending on the characteristics of the individuals involved and the quality of the relationships they form, in ways that affect outcomes. Indeed, secondary analyses of the SBM evaluation data revealed that mentees who experienced longer, higher quality relationships received bigger benefits than those in shorter or weaker relationships (Herrera et al., 2007). And in year 2, those involved in weaker, shorter relationships actually showed declines relative to their nonmentored peers. The same patterns have been found in CBM when Grossman and Rhodes (2002) reanalyzed the BBBSA CBM data, taking the quality and length of relationships into account, and detected wide variations in program effects. When all relationships are combined, as was the case in the analyses conducted for national evaluations, positive outcomes are easily masked by the neutral and even negative outcomes associated with less effective mentoring relationships. The challenge is to identify those program inputs and factors that can facilitate the formation of close, enduring, and, ultimately, effective mentor–youth ties, a task for which meta-analysis is well suited.

Meta-Analyses

A series of meta-analyses (see Table 5.3) have permitted researchers to empirically summarize the results of mentoring across multiple studies and to statistically determine the strength of program-related effects. Comparisons across studies have revealed important patterns and gaps in the literature. Meta-analysis permits researchers to empirically summarize results on a single topic across multiple studies and to statistically determine the strength

of program-related effects. Notably, meta-analyses are not without problems. For example, the method does not typically control for the design flaws of the studies that are included, and researchers' ability to code studies on various dimensions (e.g., program approach, relationship quality and length) is constrained by whatever information is provided in the original study (see Cooper & Hedges, 1994; Durlak, Meerson, & Foster, 2002; Lipsey & Wilson, 2001). Nonetheless, meta-analysis does have several advantages. Comparisons across studies can reveal important patterns and gaps in the literature, sources of bias can be controlled, and power is increased when samples are combined (Lipsey & Wilson, 2001).

In the most comprehensive meta-analysis on youth mentoring to date, DuBois et al. (2002) began by identifying all of the relevant studies on the topic. To be included in the analyses, studies had to meet several criteria. First, the evaluated program needed to include a one-to-one relationship in which an older, more experienced mentor was paired with a younger (under 19) mentee. Second, the study had to examine empirically the effects of participation in a mentoring program, by pre-program versus post-program comparisons of the same group of youth or by comparisons between one group of youth receiving mentoring and another group not receiving mentoring. After identifying relevant studies, the researchers summarized the results of each study and then calculated effect sizes across the entire group of studies. The favorable effects of mentoring programs were found to hold true across relatively diverse types of program samples, including programs in which mentoring was provided alone or in conjunction with other services. Positive effects were found both in programs that had general goals and in those with more focused goals, and held up for youth of varying backgrounds and demographic characteristics. Among the small number of studies included follow-up assessments, the benefits of mentoring appeared to extend a year or more beyond the end of a youth's participation in the program.

TABLE 5.3 Summary of Mentoring Meta-Analyses

Author, Year	# of Studies (# of Samples)	Average Effect Size	Effect Size – Range	Moderators Associated with Larger Effect Size	Overall Conclusion About Effectiveness of Mentoring
Eby et al., in press	(40)	—	0.03 – 0.14 (Absolute value)	Meta-analysis of three major areas of mentoring: (1) youth, (2) academic, and (3) workplace. Type of mentoring—smaller effect sizes for youth mentoring, compared to academic and workplace mentoring.	"This pattern seems to suggest that generally speaking academic mentoring has stronger effects than does youth mentoring and that workplace mentoring is somewhere in between . . . youth who are mentored commonly face numerous challenges (e.g., academic problems, parental conflict, unhealthy peer relationships) that may be difficult to overcome with mentoring alone" (16).
Jolliffe & Farrington, 2007[1]	16 (18)	0.079	–0.244 –1.271	Study reported characteristics of mentoring interventions with larger effect sizes (i.e., did not use moderator analyses). Longer duration of each meeting. Greater frequency of each meeting—meeting once a week or more (vs. less often or frequency unspecified). Mentoring as part of a multimodal treatment (vs. mentoring as sole intervention). Youth apprehended by police (vs. at risk because of "social situation," during probation, or on parole). Lower quality of methodology. Smaller sample size.	"Mentoring is a promising, but not proven intervention. Mentoring programmes where mentoring was combined with other interventions and where mentors and mentees met at least weekly and spent a longer time together per meeting (e.g., five or more hours) were more successful in their impact on reoffending as long as the mentoring continued" (9).
Tolan, 2005[2]	—	—	—		
Delinquency	18	0.32	–0.18 – 1.73		"Potentially substantial benefit for delinquency."
Aggression	5	0.22	–0.05 – 0.44		"Promising findings for aggression."
Drug Use	5	0.08	0.13 – 0.19		"Not likely effective for drug use."
Academics	14	0.23	–0.15 – 1.45		"Moderate effect for academic achievement."

Smith, 2002—Overall[3]	43	0.20	−0.80 – 1.65	Review process—peer-reviewed studies (vs. non-peer-reviewed); non-peer-reviewed studies (vs. dissertations/theses). Non-experimental (vs. experimental) design. Lower treatment fidelity—"not reported/low" (vs. "medium") fidelity; "medium" (vs. "high") fidelity. Source of outcome data—"youth and other" (vs. "youth only" and "other only"). Youth age—"high school" and "mixed" (vs. "middle school"). Youth gender—primarily female (vs. primarily male or mixed) samples. Youth ethnicity—primarily African American (vs. mixed) samples. Risk criteria—"academic problems" (vs. "behavioral problems" or "other"). Natural (vs. formal) mentoring. Frequency of contact—"biweekly" or "more than once a week" (vs. "once a week"). Less time per visit—"less than 1 hour" (vs. "1–2 hours" or "more than 2 hours"). Matching of mentor dyads—"systematic matching" (vs. "mentors choosing mentee" and "matching by common interests"). Additional treatment (vs. mentoring only).	"Despite the relatively small size of mentoring effects, these findings hold potential value when viewed in light of the cost effectiveness of using volunteers as direct service providers. Additionally, when the sheer volume of mentored youth is considered, even a small effect size can produce beneficial outcomes across a large number of children" (57).
Smith, 2002—Academic/Career[3]	31	0.27	−0.44 – 0.99	Review process—dissertations/theses and peer-reviewed (vs. non-peer-reviewed). Nonexperimental (vs. experimental) design. Source of outcome data—"youth and other" (vs. "youth only" and "other only").	—

(Continued)

TABLE 5.3 (Continued)

Author, Year	# of Studies (# of Samples)	Average Effect Size	Effect Size – Range	Moderators Associated with Larger Effect Size	Overall Conclusion about Effectiveness of Mentoring
				Youth age—"high school" (vs. "middle school").	
				Youth gender—primarily female (vs. primarily male or mixed) samples.	
				Youth ethnicity—primarily African American (vs. mixed) samples.	
				Risk criteria—"academic problems" (vs. "behavioral problems," "both academic and behavioral problems," and "other").	
				Natural (vs. formal) mentoring.	
				Lower frequency of contact— "biweekly" (vs. "weekly" or "more than weekly").	
				Mentor training/supervision—"both trained and supervised" (vs. "trained only" and "neither").	
				Additional treatment (vs. mentoring only).	
				Mentor gender—mixed (vs. primarily male).	
Smith, 2002—Social/ Emotional Adjustment[3]	27	0.15	−0.80–1.01	Nonexperimental (vs. experimental) design.	—
				Youth gender—primarily female (vs. primarily male or mixed) samples.	
				Natural (vs. formal) mentoring.	
				Matching of mentor dyads— "matching by sex and/or ethnicity" and "no matching" (vs. "mentor choice").	
				Mentor ethnicity—African American mentors (vs. Caucasian mentor).	

Study	N	Effect size	Effect size range	Moderators	Comments
Smith, 2002—*Drug & Alcohol Use*[3]	7	0.17	0.07–0.54	Nonexperimental (vs. experimental) design. Youth gender—primarily female (vs. primarily male or mixed) samples.	—
Smith, 2002—*Aggression/ Delinquency*[3]	15	0.14	-0.56–1.65	Review process—dissertations/theses (vs. non-peer-reviewed). Shorter length of relationship—"less than 3 months" (vs. "12 months or longer"). Less time per visit—"less than 1 hour" (vs. "1–2 hours" and "2 or more hours"). Mentor training / supervision – "trained only" (vs. "trained and supervised"). Basis for mentor selection—"school personnel" (vs. "college/high school student").	
Dubois et al., 2002[4]	55 (59)	0.14	-0.51–1.90	More recent year of report (approaching significance). Use of nonequivalent control group (approaching significance). Smaller sample size. Nonschool setting for mentoring activities (e.g., workplace or community). Reported monitoring of implementation. Mentor background in a helping role or profession. Ongoing training of mentors. Structured activities for mentors. Parent support/involvement. Expectations about frequent of contact. Low socioeconomic status. At-risk status—"individual and environmental risk" and "environmental risk" (vs. "individual risk").	"Results further indicate, however, that it may be most appropriate to expect the typical youth participating in a mentoring program to receive benefits that are quite modest in terms of absolute magnitude. . . . This aspect of findings is seemingly inconsistent with the widespread and largely unquestioned support that mentoring initiatives have enjoyed in recent years" (187).

[1] Looked specifically at studies of mentoring interventions to reduce youth's risk of reoffending. Average effect size listed assumes fixed effects; study also reported average effect size assuming random effects (d = 0.208).

[2] For all Tolan results, effect sizes with studies equally weighted are reported. The author also gives sample size weighted, and sample size and design quality weighted effect sizes.

[3] Includes 7 studies of natural mentors. Effect sizes reported here do not include statistical outliers (two of the 15 effect sizes in the Aggression / Delinquency outcome domain). Moderators are for full sample of studies; author also reported moderators for "trimmed" sample, excluding two studies with particularly large sample sizes.

[4] Average effect size and moderators listed assume fixed effects. Study also reported average effect size assuming random effects (d = 0.18). See reference for moderator relationships assuming random effects. Study did not find type of outcome to be a significant moderator of effect size. Under fixed effects, average effect size for each outcome category were as follows: emotional/psychological – d = .09; problem/high-risk behavior – d = 0.19; social competence – d = 0.16; academic/educational – d = 0.13; and career/employment – d = 0.19.

As DuBois et al. (2002) note, however, the magnitude of these effects on the average youth participating in a mentoring program was quite modest. Although there was considerable variation across studies, the average effect size across the samples was relatively small ($r = 0.14$), particularly in comparison to the effect sizes that have been found in meta-analyses of other prevention programs for children and adolescents. For example, a meta-analysis of 177 prevention studies found effects ranging from 0.24 to 0.93, depending on program type and target population (Durlak & Wells, 1997). Meta-analyses of youth psychotherapy, encompassing hundreds of studies, have reported even stronger mean effects, ranging from 0.71 to 0.88 depending on the age of the children being treated (Weisz, Sandler, Durlak, & Anton, 2005). But, importantly, while the overall effect size of mentoring programs was modest, substantial variation in the effectiveness of different programs emerged across these studies. More structured programs, in which there were clear expectations, a focus on instrumental goals, and the ongoing support to volunteer mentors yielded notably strongest effects (see Table 5.3). Interestingly, a similar pattern emerged in meta-analyses of youth psychotherapy. Indeed, Weisz et al. (2005) note that, in studies of "treatment as usual in settings in which therapists were able to use their clinical judgment to deliver treatment as they saw fit, not constrained by evidence-based interventions or manuals, and in which there was a comparison of their treatment to a control condition," effect sizes were close to zero (see, e.g., Weisz, Donenberg, Han, & Weiss, 1995), indicating no treatment benefit.

More recently, Tolan, Henry, Shoen, and Bass (2005) conducted a meta-analysis of 31 youth mentoring programs. Focusing on a more limited array of outcomes, the researchers found effect sizes ranging from 0.24 to 0.28 for delinquent and aggressive outcomes, respectively, while effect sizes for drug use (0.08) and academic outcomes (0.16) were somewhat smaller. The authors concluded that additional evaluations that include random assignment and growth measurement over time were needed. Jolliffe and Farington (2007) explored the effects of youth mentoring on recidivism among juvenile offenders. Their analyses, which were based on 18 evaluations, revealed a combined fixed effect of only 0.08. Again, significant variation emerged across studies; seven studies showed significant positive impacts on reoffending while an equal number showed negative (but not statistically significant) impact. Programs that combined mentoring with other interventions, required weekly meetings for longer periods of time per meeting, and had more enduring relationships had the most positive effects on reoffending. Looking at a broader range of outcomes, Eby, Allen, Evans, Ng, and DuBois (in press) conducted a meta-analysis of 40 youth mentoring evaluations, comparing them to 53 adult workplace mentoring and 23 college-level academic mentoring evaluations. Again, the effect sizes were generally small, with mentoring more highly related to some outcomes (school attitudes) than others (psychological distress). Interestingly, effect sizes were found to vary across the three types of mentoring, ranging from only 0.03 to 0.14 in youth mentoring to 0.11 to 0.36 and 0.03 to 0.19 in academic and workplace mentoring, respectively. This relative ranking is consistent with the previous meta-analysis and makes sense when one considers the greater challenges facing youth and the fact that academic and workplace mentoring includes a mix of assigned and natural mentors. Nonetheless, the authors conclude that "we believe the results underscore the need to temper what are sometimes seemingly unrealistic expectations about what mentoring can offer to protégés, institutions, and society at large." Finally, in an unpublished dissertation, Smith (2002) reports an effect size of just 0.20 across 43 studies. Similar to Tolan et al. (2005), effect sizes varied depending on the outcome assessed.

Although less thoroughly explored than in the DuBois et al. (2002) study, the findings of the more recent meta-analyses suggest that the effects are likely to vary depending on an array of youth, mentor, and program characteristics as well as the quality of the evaluation methodology. Given this variation, it is unfortunate that only two of the meta-analyses (DuBois et al.; Smith, 2002) have conducted formal tests for moderators of program effects. A study that includes a systematic, up-to-date meta-analytic review of the current literature and a thorough test of the moderators would thus represent a significant contribution to the literature.

Nonexperimental Research

Secondary analyses, longitudinal developmental studies, and qualitative studies have suggested a host of factors that can account for variation in the closeness and effectiveness of mentoring relationships. For example, studies of both informal and formal mentoring have highlighted the importance of relationship intensity, indicated by how often mentors and youth spend time together (Blakely, Menon, & Jones, 1995; DuBois & Neville, 1997; DuBois, Neville, Parra, & Pugh-Lilly, 2002; DuBois & Silverthorn, 2005a; Freedman, 1988; Herrera, Sipe & McClanahan, 2000; McLearn, Colasanto, & Schoen, 1998; Parra, DuBois, Neville, Pugh-Lilly, & Povinelli, 2002). Regular contact can lead to the engagement beneficial activities (Parra et al., 2002), the provision of emotional and instrumental support (Herrera et al., 2000), and a deeper involvement of the adult in the youth's social network (DuBois, Neville, et al., 2002). This involvement, in turn, may enhance the mentee's feelings of security and attachment in interpersonal relationships (Keller, 2005; Rhodes, 2005). Relationship duration represents another key determinant of effectiveness. As mentioned previously, for example, Grossman and Rhodes (2002) found that positive effects on youth outcomes became progressively stronger as relationships persisted for longer periods of time in the reanalysis of the data of the BBBSA CBM program. Relative to controls, youth whose relationships terminated within a year appeared to derive the fewest benefits, and those in short matches (i.e., terminating within the first 3–6 months) actually suffered declines

in reported levels of feelings of self-worth and perceived scholastic competence. For youth who were in matches that lasted more than a year, however, positive effects were evident on levels of self-worth, perceived social acceptance and scholastic competence, parental relationship quality, school value, and levels of both drug and alcohol use. Spencer (2007) has underscored the emotional closeness and deep psychological connections that are sometimes forged in male's youth mentoring relationships over time. Natural relationships that endure for multiple years (DuBois & Silverthorn, 2005b; Klaw, Fitzgerald, & Rhodes, 2003; McLearn, et al., 1998; Werner, 1995) have also shown the strongest effects.

Several additional factors associated with better outcomes include the background characteristics of the mentor and the effectiveness of the mentor in addressing the developmental needs of the child. For example, close, effective mentoring relationships seem to be facilitated when adults possess certain skills and attributes. These include prior experience in helping roles or occupations (DuBois et al., 2002), an ability to demonstrate appreciation of salient socioeconomic and cultural influences in the youth's life (Hirsch, 2005), and a sense of efficacy for being able to mentor young people (DuBois, Neville, et al., 2002; Hirsch, 2005; Karcher, Nakkula, & Harris, 2005; Parra et al., 2002). Other researchers have noted the importance of shared experiences, difficulties, or disabilities (Veith, Sherman, & Pellino, 2006). The ability to model relevant behaviors, such as skills required for job performance in the work setting, appears to be of further benefit (Hamilton & Hamilton, 2005) as does refraining from actions (e.g., substance use) that may encourage youth to adopt unhealthy behaviors (Beam, Gil-Rivas, Greenberger, & Chen, 2002).

Moreover, relationships that are youth centered (sometimes also referred to as developmental) in their orientation, as opposed to being driven primarily by the interests or expectations of the mentor (sometimes also referred to as prescriptive), have been found to predict greater relationship quality and duration

(Herrera et al., 2000; Morrow & Styles, 1995; Styles & Morrow, 1992) as well as improvements in how youth experience their relationships with other adults (Karcher, Roy-Carlson, Benne, Gil-Hernandez, Allen, & Gomez, 2006). A youth-driven approach, however, needs to be balanced with structure and goals. Langhout, Rhodes, and Osborne (2004), for example, found that outcomes were most favorable when youth reported experiencing both structure and support from their mentors. By contrast, no benefits were evident for an unconditional support relationship type, thus suggesting a need for mentors to be more than simply "good friends." Helping youth to set and work toward goals that are important to their development appears to be beneficial (Balcazar, Davies, Viggers, & Tranter, 2006; Balcazar, Keys, & Garate, 1995; Davidson & Redner, 1988 Hamilton & Hamilton, 2005), especially if the mentor and youth agree upon goals in accordance with the youth-centered approach described above (Larose, Chaloux, Monaghan, & Tarabulsy, 2006). Acceptance and attunement to the needs and interests of the youth and the ability to adapt his or her approach accordingly (Pryce, 2006; Spencer, 2006) are thus important indicators of relationship effectiveness. Of course, researchers have also noted that close youth–adult mentoring relationships are not immune from conflict and other negative emotional experiences (e.g., disappointment) and that these may have an adverse impact on youth, as well as the sustainability of the relationship (Grossman & Rhodes, 2002 Rhodes, Reddy, Roffman, & Grossman, 2005).

Although other factors, such as similarity in the ethnic or racial backgrounds or the age of the volunteer mentor, have not emerged as a significant factors in predicting closeness or outcomes (Rhodes, Reddy, Grossman, & Lee, 2003; Sanchez & Colon, 2005), additional research on these and related variables is warranted. Research that delves into the relative impact of mentoring on different populations of youth with varying profiles of and outcomes would be particularly useful in this regard.

A Model of Youth Mentoring

The preceding review of the mentoring literature suggests that mentoring relationships have the potential to benefit youth in a wide range of important areas and sheds light upon the conditions under which mentoring relationships are likely to be beneficial. A remaining question is *how* mentoring relationships impact youth. Based on empirical and theoretical literature, Rhodes (2005) has proposed a model that delineates several processes and conditions presumed to be important for understanding the effects of mentoring relationships on youth (see Figure 5.1).

First and foremost, beneficial effects are expected only to the extent that the mentor and youth manage to forge a strong connection that is characterized by mutuality, trust, and empathy (component a in Figure 5.1). As Levinson (1979) observed, "Mentoring is not a simple, all-or-none matter" (p. 100), and if a bond does not form, youth and mentors may disengage from the match before the relationship lasts long enough to have a positive impact on youth. Theoretically, a meaningful connection becomes possible only to the extent that the mentee is willing to share his or her feelings and self-perceptions and is actively engaged in the relationship (Csiksilzentmihalyi & Rathunde, 1998). Dworkin, Larson, and Hansen (2003) have described this process in terms of both motivation and concentration, wherein the youth is "involved in actively constructing personal change" (p. 17). This focus on empathy and engagement does not imply that every moment needs to be packed with profundity and personal growth. It seems more likely that successful mentoring of youth is more often characterized by a series of small wins that emerge sporadically over time. Yet these mundane moments, which might be laced with boredom, humor, and even frustration, can help to forge a connection from which the mentee may draw strength in moments of vulnerability or share triumph in moments of accomplishment.

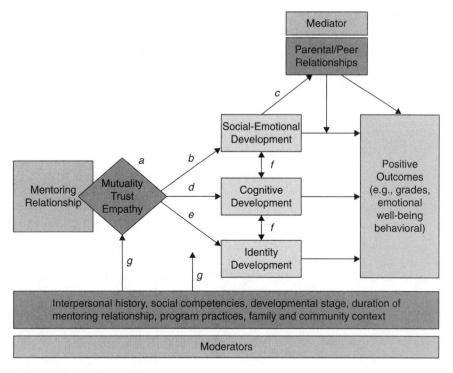

FIGURE 5.1   A Model of Youth Mentoring

Research has indicated the benefits of attunement in adult–youth relationships (Pianta, 1999). Allen et al. (2003), for example, found that more empathic and supportive parenting was predictive of attachment security among adolescents. Such parents appeared to be better able to provide the sort of safe haven that youth needed to take on challenges and cope with emotional stress. By the same token, mentors who are attuned to their mentees are likely to be in a better position to handle discussions around vulnerable topics without undermining the youngsters' sense of self-confidence. After examining survey data on more than 600 mentoring pairs in community- and school-based programs, Herrera et al. (2000) concluded, "at the crux of the mentoring relationship is the bond that forms between the youth and mentor" (p. 72).

In addition, for a truly meaningful bond to arise, mentors and youth are likely to need to spend time together on a consistent basis over some significant period of time (Rhodes &

DuBois, 2006). Only then may youth derive significant benefits. For example, as noted earlier, in an evaluation of the BBBSA program, positive effects on youth outcomes became progressively stronger as relationships persisted for longer periods of time, whereas youth whose mentoring relationships prematurely terminated showed declines in functioning relative to controls (Grossman & Rhodes, 2002). Beyond issues of time, research indicates that the extent to which mentors and youth establish a strong connection is influenced by the dynamics of their interactions with each other (Rhodes & DuBois, 2006). In general, close and enduring ties are fostered when mentors adopt a flexible, youth-centered style in which the young person's interests and preferences are emphasized rather than focusing predominantly on their own agendas or expectations for the relationship. Thus, although it is clear that a structured or goal-oriented dimension to a mentor's activities with a young person can be beneficial, these advantages may be compromised if the overall approach is not sufficiently collaborative in its orientation.

Youth Outcomes

As shown in Figure 5.1, well-established mentoring relationships may contribute to positive youth outcomes through three interacting developmental processes: social–emotional, cognitive, and identity-related.

Social–Emotional Development There are several ways in which the social–emotional development of children and adolescents may be furthered through mentoring (Figure 5.1, path b). By modeling caring and providing support, for example, mentors can both challenge negative views that some youth may hold of themselves and demonstrate that positive relationships with adults are possible. In this way, a mentoring relationship may become a "corrective experience" for youth who have experienced unsatisfactory relationships with parents or other caregivers.

The basis for expecting that positive mentoring relationships can modify youth perceptions of other relationships is derived largely from attachment theory (Bowlby, 1988). According to attachment theorists, children construct cognitive representations of relationships through their early experiences with primary caregivers (Bretherton & Waters, 1985). These experience-based expectations, or working models, are believed to be incorporated into the personality structure and to influence behavior in interpersonal relationships throughout and beyond childhood (Ainsworth, 1989; Bowlby, 1988). Working models are considered to be relatively stable over time, yet flexible to modification in response to changing life circumstances, such as engagement in unconditionally supportive relationships (Belsky & Cassidy, 1994; Sroufe, 1995). By serving as a sounding board and providing a model of effective adult communication, mentors also may help youth to become better able to understand, express, and regulate their emotions (Pianta, 1999). Gottman (2001) has referred to "emotion coaching," in which adults model and teach

strategies for managing feelings. Mentors who openly display positive emotions, particularly under difficult circumstances, actively model the process of using positive emotions constructively (Denham & Kochanoff, 2002). In doing so, mentors may facilitate youth coping and help them to approach even negative experiences as opportunities for intimacy, growth, and learning.

In some cases, connections with mentors also may function as alternative or secondary attachment figures, providing a secure base from which youth can achieve crucial social and cognitive competencies. In other cases, the relationship might have a positive impact by simply alleviating some of the relationship tensions and conflicts that arise throughout adolescence. Closely related to the above discussion, the model further assumes that positive social–emotional experiences with mentors can generalize, enabling youth to interact with others more effectively (Figure 5.1, path c). When there has been a history of unsatisfactory ties, mentors can precipitate fundamental shifts in children's and adolescents' abilities to form and sustain beneficial connections to others. Among youth with generally healthy relationships, mentoring relationships may ease difficulties in everyday interactions by promoting improved communication and emotional regulation.

Preliminary research support has emerged for the potential of positive relationships with mentors to strengthen or modify the social–emotional development of youth. Mentoring relationships formed through community- and school-based programs have been linked to improvements in children's and adolescents' perceptions of their parental relationships, including levels of intimacy, communication, and trust (Karcher, Davis, & Powell, 2002; Rhodes, Grossman, & Resch, 2000). These improvements, in turn, have been found to be associated with positive changes in a wide array of areas, such as overall feelings of self-worth, perceived scholastic competence, and grades (Rhodes et al., 2000); spelling achievement

(Karcher et al., 2002); and substance use (Rhodes, Reddy, & Grossman, 2005). Additional research has linked mentoring relationships to significant improvements in youth' perceptions of their parental relationships as well as their relationships with peers and other adults in their social networks (e.g., DuBois, Neville, et al., 2002; Rhodes, Haight, & Briggs, 1999; Rhodes, Grossman, & Resch, 2000).

Cognitive Development   Mentoring relationships similarly may affect a range of cognitive developmental processes (Figure 5.1, path d). As children develop, they experience improvements in basic cognitive processes, such as information processing, abstract and relativistic thinking, and self-monitoring (Steinberg, 2005). The field of cognitive neuroscience has mapped the ways in which relationships interact with the developing brain to shape mental processes and perception (Johnson & Munakata, 2006). Similarly, Vygotsky (1978) described a "zone of proximal development" in which learning takes place: beyond what a child or adolescent can attain when problem solving independently but within the range of what he or she can do while working under adult guidance or with more capable peers. When children's or adolescents' interactions with caring adults stretch them into this zone, this is assumed to facilitate cognitive and intellectual growth. Along similar lines, children and adolescents, through interactions with mentors, may acquire and refine new thinking skills and may become more receptive to adult values, advice, and perspectives (Rogoff, 1990). Meaningful, youth-relevant conversations between mentors and mentees may be one important mechanism through which such benefits accrue (DuBois, Neville, et al., 2002; Hamilton & Darling, 1996).

Research on the role of social support in fostering cognitive development underscores the social nature of learning and, specifically, the potential contributions of adults in mentoring roles. Feelings of closeness with teachers, for example, have been associated with more positive academic adjustment for children and adolescents (e.g., Connell & Wellborn, 1991; Roeser & Eccles, 1998). In particular, consistent associations have been documented between perceptions of teacher-student relationships and increases in student motivation, academic competence and achievement, school engagement, school value, and behavioral adjustment (Reddy, Rhodes, & Mulhall, 2003; Roeser & Eccles, 1998; Ryan & Grolnick, 1986). Several studies also have revealed improvements in academic outcomes for youth in the context of close and enduring ties with natural and assigned mentors (Klaw, Fitzgerald, & Rhodes, 2003; Lee & Cramond, 1999; Slicker & Palmer, 1995).

Identity Development   As noted, mentoring relationships also may facilitate identity development (Figure 5.1, path e). Illustratively, mentors may help shift youth conceptions of both their current and future identities. Freud (1914) described an identification process in which people internalize the attitudes, behaviors, and traits of individuals they wish to emulate. Similarly, Kohut (1984) theorized that children and adolescents attach themselves to an idealized parental *imago* whose qualities they incorporate into their own personalities. As they identify with their mentors and view them as role models, children's and adolescents' early internalizations may begin to change, causing shifts in their sense of identity and social roles. This process is related to what Cooley (1902) described as the *looking-glass self*, wherein significant people in children's and adolescents' lives can become social mirrors into which the young people look to form opinions of themselves. The opinions that they see reflected back at them then become integrated into their sense of self. Mead (1934) similarly posited that individuals can incorporate the *reflected appraisal* of others' views of them, imagining how they are perceived by significant people in their lives.

As the mentor's perceived positive appraisal becomes incorporated into the mentee's sense of self, it may modify the way the youth thinks that parents, peers, teachers, and others see him or her. Through this process of reflected appraisals, mentors may help shift children and adolescents' conceptions of both their current and future identities. Along similar lines, Markus and Nurius (1986) also have referred to *possible selves*: individuals' ideas of what they might become, what they would like to become, and what they fear becoming. Such possibilities, which often emerge as youth observe and compare the adults they know, can inform current decisions and behavior. Indeed, many lower-income youth have limited contact with positive role models outside the immediate family and believe that their opportunities for success are restricted. Nonparent adults can provide opportunities for youth to reflect on the consequences of both positive and negative behaviors (Sanchez, Reyes, & Singh, 2006). Even among middle-income youth, adult occupations and skills can seem obscure and out of reach (Larson, 2000). Still other youth have unrealistic expectations and little knowledge about the levels of education that are needed for their chosen professions or how to set goals. This situation is exemplified in a description of the role that a basketball coach took in shaping the life course of a youth:

> When I first met [basketball coach] Steve, I was the product of the housing projects, a product of a single-parent home looking for guidance and attention. I was in and out of trouble. One day Steve took me aside and said, "Do you know what the word *goal* means?" I knew what a goal was in hockey or soccer and I knew what a field goal was in basketball, but when he started talking about setting goals and trying achieve goals, it was like he was speaking Chinese . . . it was just one conversation, one afternoon on the baseketball court, but it opened a door in my life.
>
> —Socrates De La Cruz, a
> criminal defense attorney

More generally, relationships with adults can provide both social and cultural capital in the form of knowledge (Dubas & Snider, 1993), helping youth to make use of community resources and recreation programs and opening doors to educational or occupational opportunities (Darling, Hamilton, Toyokawa, & Matsuda, 2002). Participation in such new opportunities also can facilitate identity development by providing experiences on which children and adolescents can draw to construct their sense of self (Erikson, 1964; Yates & Youniss, 1996). Indeed, Waterman (1982) has proposed that activities provide opportunities for discovering special talents and abilities and are thus a primary source through which identity is formed. Beyond this function, participation in prosocial activities and settings may expose youth to more socially desirable or high-achieving peer groups with whom they can identify.

The empirical literature supports the possibility that mentors can affect change in youth behaviors relating to their identity development. Children and adolescents with natural and volunteer mentors have been found to be less likely to take part in delinquent problem behaviors (Aseltine, Dupre, & Lamlein, 2000; Davidson & Redner, 1988; Grossman & Tierney, 1998) and more likely to graduate from high school (Klaw et al., 2003), both of which suggest the presence of a more positive future orientation in the identities of mentored youth. In a study of future perceptions, Hellenga, Rhodes, and Aber (2002) empirically distinguished between adolescents with and without discrepancies between their vocational aspirations and expectations for the future. Having a career mentor was associated with a match (as opposed to a gap) between adolescents' aspirations and expectations (Hellenga et al., 2002). However, it should be noted that the direction of the preceding types of linkages is not yet fully established. It also is plausible in this regard, for example, that being prosocial, academically successful, and future oriented increases the likelihood that natural mentors will emerge in the lives of such youth.

Bidirectional Pathways

The social–emotional, cognitive, and identity processes described in the preceding sections are assumed to work in concert with one another over time (see Figure 5.1, f arrows). For example, the use of a mentor as a role model and the ability to entertain multiple possible selves may be fostered by the ability of youth to make more nuanced comparisons across relationships and a growing capacity to understand the world from the perspective of others (Keating, 1990).

Growth in these cognitive abilities, in turn, can enhance the capacity of youth to regulate complicated emotions (Diamond & Aspinwall, 2003) and to select institutions and relationships that best match their goals, values, and abilities (Clausen, 1991). Similarly, adolescents' striving for autonomy and their intensifying desire for connection to others and involvement in the larger social context provide opportunities for the revision of working models of attachment (Allen & Land, 1999; Main, Kaplan, & Cassidy, 1985), as well as openings for role models and other forms of social capital.

Moderating Processes

This model further proposes that both the strength of the mentoring relationship's foundation in trust, empathy, and mutuality and the pathways linking model components to youth outcomes may be conditioned by a range of individual, family, and contextual influences (Figure 5.1, g arrows).

Child's Interpersonal History Children and adolescents who have enjoyed healthy relationships with their parents may more easily be drawn to adults as role models and confidants. In such cases, the relationship may focus more on the acquisition of skills and the advancement of critical thinking than on emotional issues (Hamilton & Darling, 1996). Indeed, Rhodes, Contreras, and Mangelsdorf (1994) found that, compared with those who did not report having a natural mentor, adolescents with natural mentors recalled early relationships with their mothers as more accepting. More recently, Soucy and Larose (2000) found evidence that the positive effects of mentors were stronger among those youth who reported having higher levels of security in their relationships with their mothers. This suggests that mentors may not entirely compensate for insecure family bonds. Instead, they may be beneficial as long as there is already a minimum level of support from at least one parent.

However, those who have experienced unsatisfactory or difficult parental ties may initially resist the overtures of a caring adult, but over time develop more intense bonds with their mentors that help to satisfy their social and emotional needs. Mentoring relationships also may serve to compensate for absent relationships. Immigrant youth, for example, many of whom have suffered long separations from their parents, may gravitate to mentors for compensatory emotional support. Mentors may provide these youth with a safe haven for learning new cultural norms and practices, as well as with information that is vital to success in school (Roffman, Suarez-Orozco, & Rhodes, 2002; Stanton-Salazar & Spina, 2003). The same holds true for youth in foster homes, many of whom have suffered child abuse and neglect. Rhodes et al. (1999) found that foster youth derived greater interpersonal benefits (i.e., improvements in peer relationships, heightened trust and comfort in interactions with others) than nonfoster youth.

Social Competencies As mentioned earlier, youth who are better able to regulate their emotions and who have positive temperaments and/or other engaging attributes may be primed for higher levels of involvement with adults than are peers who lack these attributes. Werner and Smith (1982), for example, observed that youth who had thrived despite adversity tend to have hobbies or other interests and a capacity to connect with adults through those activities. More generally, youth with higher levels of social competence tend to be held in higher regard by their peers and teachers (Morison & Masten, 1991). The research on mentoring bears this out: Adolescents who are overwhelmed by social or behavioral problems tend to be less likely to benefit from mentoring (DuBois, Holloway, Valentine, & Cooper., 2002; Grossman & Johnson, 1998). Grossman and Rhodes (2002), for example, found that mentoring relationships with adolescents who had been referred for psychological treatment or who had sustained emotional, sexual, or physical abuse were less likely to remain intact. Such youth appear to have more difficulties trusting adults and may have little experience with behaviors that establish and maintain closeness and support (Lynch & Cicchetti, 1997).

Developmental Stage   The mentee's age may also affect the nature and course of a mentoring relationship. For example, whereas early adolescents who are beginning to struggle with identity issues may wish to engage in abstract conversations with their mentors, children whose levels of cognitive sophistication are less advanced may benefit more from structured activities (Keating, 1990). In addition, adolescents on the brink of adulthood may be less interested in establishing emotional ties with mentors, instead gravitating to peers and vocational skill-building activities. Older adolescents tend to be more peer-oriented than their younger counterparts and less likely to sustain their involvement in structured mentoring programs. Indeed, researchers have found that relationships with older adolescents are characterized by lower levels of closeness (Herrera et al., 2000), heightened risk for termination during any given month (Grossman & Rhodes, 2002), and shorter duration than those with younger youth (Bauldry & Hartmann, 2004). A mentor who is attuned to his or her mentee's developmental stage and adjusts to it accordingly can create an optimal stage-environment fit (see chapter 12, vol. 1 of this *Handbook*) and is better positioned to meet the child's developmental needs.

Relationship Duration   As noted previously, the benefits of mentoring appear to

accrue over a relatively long period of time. Evidence for the importance of relationship duration has emerged from the BBBSA studies of CBM and SBM programs cited previously (Grossman & Rhodes, 2002; Herrera et al., 2007). These findings are consistent with other studies (Lee & Cramond, 1999), as well as the meta-analysis by DuBois et al. (2002).

Program Practices   Programs that offer adequate infrastructure increase the likelihood that relationships can endure difficult periods (DuBois et al., 2002; Rhodes, 2002). In fact, program practices that support the mentor and relationship (i.e., training for mentors, offering structured activities for mentors and youth, having high expectations for frequency of contact, and monitoring of overall program implementation) produce stronger positive effects (DuBois et al., 2002). These practices, which speak to a program's ability to not only match mentors and youth but also sustain those matches, converge with the beneficial practices identified by other researchers (Herrera et al., 2000). Unfortunately, moving youth off long wait lists can sometimes take priority over creating high-quality matches. Even among the growing number of programs with careful recruitment, screening, and matching, a relatively smaller proportion devote themselves to in-depth training of volunteers or ongoing support to the mentors (DuBois et al., 2002; Rhodes, 2002; Sipe & Roder, 1999). Cost, combined with a general reluctance to make demands on volunteers, is the primary obstacle to providing more sustained involvement and infrastructure beyond the initial match (DuBois et al., 2002).

Family Context   The likelihood of a child's or adolescent's forming strong ties with mentors may be affected by a range of processes in the family, including the encouragement and opportunities that parents provide for the development of such ties. Families characterized by sensitivity to others' ideas and needs and open expression of views are more likely to encourage adolescents to become involved in positive relationships outside the family (Cooper, Grotevant, & Condon, 1983). With specific relevance to mentoring, children and adolescents with more supportive parental relationships and higher levels of shared family decision making have been found to be more likely to report natural mentors (Zimmerman, et al., 2002). Parents who actively cultivate connections and channel their children to community-based recreational and social programs also may increase the likelihood that their children will form beneficial relationships with adults beyond the nuclear family (Zimmerman et al., 2002). Mentoring programs that reach out to parents tend to have greater success in shaping youth outcomes. Other family-related factors, including stability and mobility, can facilitate or hinder the establishment and maintenance of strong ties (DuBois et al., 2002; Rhodes, 2002).

Neighborhood Ecology   Researchers have observed that extracurricular activities and supportive relationships with adults tend to be more beneficial to adolescents raised in urban poverty than to lower risk youth who encounter more supportive adults in their everyday lives (DuBois et al., 2002 Grossman & Johnson, 1998). Indeed, neighborhood characteristics and norms (i.e., neighborhood effects) can influence the availability of caring, informal adult ties as well as the willingness of volunteers to genuinely connect with children and adolescents (see Leventhal & Brooks-Gunn, this *Handbook*). Changing family and marital patterns, crowded schools, and less cohesive communities have dramatically reduced the availability of caring adults in the lives of youth (Putnam, 2000). Even when they are available, however, fewer American adults are willing to offer support and guidance to unrelated youth. Parents have come to be considered solely responsible for their children, so the involvement of other adults is often met with suspicion and discomfort (Scales, 2003). Indeed, words like *clergy, uncles,* and even *neighbors* no longer simply conjure images of

front-porch warmth and goodwill; they also evoke parental anxiety and confusion about the boundaries of trust and safety. Similarly, as mentoring programs increasingly accommodate volunteers' busy schedules, they have eased requirements for relationship commitment and intensity. The result in some cases has been the formation of perfunctory ties that resemble, but share little in common with, the long-term community-based relationships from which they have evolved (Rhodes, 2002). In essence, changing family and neighborhood configurations, busy schedules, and shifting norms regarding adult involvement in the lives of youth have limited the likelihood that youth will engage in the sorts of caring relationships with mentors that can lead to developmental change.

Summary of the Model

Overall, the model presented here suggests that a close mentoring relationship characterized by mutuality, trust, and empathy can serve as a catalyst for several intertwined developmental processes pertaining to the social–emotional, cognitive, and identity development of youth. These developmental gains, in turn, contribute to positive outcomes for youth, mediated at least in part by their contributions to positive growth in other significant relationships in their lives. The extent to which foundational qualities (e.g., trust) are established, as well as how, and in what sequence, the various model pathways are activated, is presumed to be governed, at least in part, by the length of the relationship, as well as the youth, family, and contextual characteristics. Research to date provides support for the model's key assumptions. However, this research is limited in scope and has not addressed the nature and extent of several of the specific processes that are posited in the model. At the same time, there has been heightened interest in longstanding organizations like the YMCA, 4-H, Boys and Girls Clubs of America, and Big Brothers Big Sisters of America, in which youth can find more protected opportunities for intergenerational ties (Hirsch & Deutsch, 2005; Lerner, Lerner, Almerigi, Theokas, Phelps, Gestsdottir, et al., 2005).

WHAT ARE THE IMPLICATIONS FOR MENTORING PRACTICE, RESEARCH, AND POLICY?

As the preceding literature review and proposed theoretical model suggest, mentoring programs should be conceptualized, designed, and implemented effectively in order to produce consistent and positive outcomes (Weissberg, Caplan, & Sivo, 1989). Yet standards for identifying effective programs and policies are in short supply. Evaluations that employ sound measures and rigorous methods are needed to determine the efficacy of the various approaches to mentoring (Flay et al., 2005). Several high-quality random assignment evaluations of community-based programs— Friends of the Children (Grossman, in press); National Guard Challenge program, (Brock, in press) and school based mentoring (Peer Mentoring Program (Karcher, in press); U.S. Department, of Education Student Mentoring Program (Bernstein & Hunt, in press)—are currently under way. Their findings will fall on fertile soil and provide grist for subsequent meta- and secondary analyses. Once identified, the most efficacious approaches should be carefully disseminated through manuals appropriate for training, and supported through ample, ongoing supervision (Flay et al., 2005). In the meantime, the findings compiled here suggest a range of strategies for researchers, practitioners, and policy makers that could significantly advance the field.

Implications for Research

The literature to date on youth mentoring, as well as the proposed theoretical model, point to several implications for improving and prioritizing research in the field. The following suggestions would lead the field toward establishing evidence-based practices for mentoring programs, and a better understanding of the processes the underlie high-quality mentoring relationships. Furthermore, they would shed light on characteristics of children and mentors, mentoring relationships, and programs that facilitate benefits to youth.

Adhere to Established Standards of Evidence

First, mentoring fits within the broader field of prevention science and, as such, should more directly align itself with the field's standards of evidence. In particular, prevention scientists have developed a set of criteria for evaluating prevention programs and policies. Although beyond the scope of this review, the criteria involve first establishing and conducting rigorous trials, similar to those that have been completed (Herrera et al., 2007) or are under way (Bernstein & Hunt, in press; Brock, in press; Grossman, in press; Karcher, in press), and showing "consistent positive effects (without serious iatrogenic effects) and reporting at least significant long-term effect." Although the jury is still out regarding the latter stipulations, this new crop of high quality evaluations are likely to significantly advance the field. Assuming effectiveness, however, mentoring interventions should meet several additional criteria. These include having manuals, training, and technical support, evidence of the ability to "go to scale," clear cost information, and monitoring and evaluation tools so that effectiveness can be tested in various settings. The field of mentoring has made notable strides in many of these areas, but a more systematic approach to establishing effectiveness and disseminating interventions would better align youth mentoring with the broader field of prevention science.

To this end, there is also a need for greater involvement of prevention researchers in all phases of the process of designing, piloting, implementing, evaluating, and disseminating interventions in the area of youth mentoring (DuBois et al., in press). New mentoring initiatives should have well-developed evaluation systems in place *prior to* implementation. To date, the role of research has been predominantly to evaluate programs once they have been developed, often only after they have been widely dispatched to the field. Instead, researchers and practitioners should work together to specify the goals and procedures of the mentoring program. Where possible, experimental designs should be employed and data from multiple sources and methods should be collected.

Understand Variation or Diversity

Even the best models are likely to be more helpful in some contexts than others, and for some groups than others. Systematic comparison of practices of differing type and intensity are needed within all relevant program areas, including recruitment, training, matching, supervision and mentor/mentee activities and across various settings. Also necessary is information regarding the core elements of successful mentoring relationships and how these might vary as a function of the needs and characteristics of particular youth. Such information has become increasingly important, particularly as programs are encouraged to serve specialized populations or are implemented in new settings.

There is growing evidence, for example, that boys and girls experience and benefit from the mentoring process in different ways, with girls experiencing more troubled maternal relationships at baseline and being more reactive to relationship length (Rhodes, Lowe, Litchfield, & Walsh-Samp, in press). The same may hold true for younger versus older youth, an assumption that is supported the by research on mentee age as related to quality and durations of mentoring relationships cited previously (Bauldry & Hartmann, 2004; Grossman & Rhodes, 2002; Herrera et al., 2000; Keating, 1990). Future research should also explore the impact of mentoring relationships for youth of differing ethnic backgrounds. For example, although mentors with a similar racial and ethnic background may be better equipped to understand the social and psychological conflicts of minorityyouth (Sanchez et al., 2006), it is also clear that effective relationships can develop despite such differences (Rhodes, Reddy, Grossman, & Lee, 2003).

Of course, as mentoring programs serve a growing number of immigrant children, issues of race and language are likely to be more salient. Mentors, particularly those who share similar backgrounds with their mentees, may be better positioned as role models in the challenging process of developing a bicultural identity. They can exemplify the ways in which the youth can preserve and celebrate elements of their ethnic identity while still incorporating features of the more mainstream culture of the United States (Roffman et al., 2002).

As previously indicated, gender is another important area that deserves consideration. Surprisingly few studies have focused on how gender might shape youth mentoring relationships. Studies examining gender differences in outcomes among program participants have been mixed (DuBois, Holloway, Valentine, Cooper, 2002; Tierney, Grossman, & Resch, 1995), and few studies have looked at differences in relationship quality or length. Yet, findings from diverse disciplinary perspectives suggest that gender might affect adult–youth mentoring relationships, including their duration and perceived importance and helpfulness (Kram, 1984). In a recent study, Rhodes, Lowe, Litchfield, & Walsh-Samp (in press) examined the role of gender in youth mentoring relationships. Prior to being matched with mentors, girls reported significantly lower levels of parental trust and higher levels of alienation from their parents than boys. Nonetheless, girls' mentoring relationships lasted significantly longer than those of boys. Particularly in light of the heightened mistrust and alienation from parents at baseline, and the role of improved parent relationships in mediating the effects of mentoring, the protective aspect of longer lasting mentoring relationships may be particularly salient for girls.

Still other young people served by mentoring programs have special needs. They may be in foster care, have learning or physical disabilities, or have a parent who is incarcerated, and so on. Research should investigate factors that facilitate supportive mentoring relationships for these groups. Screening tools that permit greater specification of baseline risk, strengths, and circumstances of children and families are also likely to be particularly helpful in this regard.

Understanding the Impact of Quality and Duration

Although policy makers are increasingly calling for quality mentoring programs, exactly how quality is defined and measured remains somewhat unclear. Assessing program quality across a range of relationships (youth–volunteer, youth–staff, volunteer–staff, staff–administration) and relating these to outcomes can provide an empirical rationale for supporting enhancements in mentoring programs. Moreover, research to date has focused predominantly on the effects of mentoring over a relatively short period of time. The more substantial benefits that may be associated with longer term relationships have yet to be examined. Another important consideration may be whether relationships are continued for the full duration of whatever expectations were established, even if for only a short period of time (De Ayala & Perry, 2005; Larose, Tarabulsy, & Cyrenne, 2005). Research on the role of duration and intensity, including the minimum required dosage to achieve various outcomes, the role of expectations, and the effects of long wait lists is needed (see chapter 7, this volume).

In addition, previous research sheds little light onto the subtle dynamics and vulnerabilities affecting existing matches. Mentors and youth often experience difficulties and disappointment, particularly during the first few months of the match, which may forecast premature terminations (Rhodes, 2002). A series of exploratory interviews with volunteers and youth in successful and terminated relationships (Spencer, 2006) revealed that unfulfilled expectations, pragmatic concerns, and frustration often emerge in the early, vulnerable stages. Research (Kalbfleisch, 2002; Grossman

& Rhodes, 2002) has further suggested that difficulties often arise from such failings as the misuse of power (e.g., exploitation, political or religious proselytizing), inappropriate boundaries (e.g., breaching confidentiality, improper disclosures), and communication breakdowns (e.g., breaking commitments). The growing body of research on volunteer and employee recruitment and retention (e.g., Branhan, 2006; Stukas, Snyder, & Clary, 1999; Stukas, Daly & Clary, 2006; Stukas, Snyder, & Clary, 1999) as well as ongoing qualitative inquiry into the factors underlying mentor attrition (Philip, 2003; Spencer, 2006) should be brought to bear on this issue. Research on the motivation of mentors, the benefits that they derive, and the qualities of enduring and effective matches are also likely to be beneficial in this regard (Stukas et al., 2006). Within this context, it will be important to explore optimal strategies for balancing the needs of children for intensity with the time constraints and interests of volunteers. Studies that enable programs to separate the absolutely necessary inputs from the merely recommended will foster better decision making in this regard. With better attention to retention, volunteers are likely to reap more benefits (Grimm, Spring, & Dietz, 2007) and programs will be relieved of some of the pressure to recruit new volunteers.

Assess the Underlying Effects of Mentoring

During program conceptualization, program developers should articulate the goals and the theoretical models of change that guide their approach, including the processes that are thought to mediate outcome and their temporal ordering. Indeed, although a relationship between a caring adult and a young person lies at the heart of mentoring, little is known about how such relationships actually influence youth outcomes. By more thoroughly examining relationship processes, researchers can help mentoring programs develop more effective strategies for training and supervising mentors. Researchers examining these models should investigate relationship processes from both the mentors' and mentees' perspectives, with attention to the broader influences of families, schools, and communities. Qualitative research, which provides in-depth descriptions of how relationships develop and why they sometimes fail, as well as longitudinal studies of outcomes, have a vital role to play in theory development.

There is a marked lack of theoretical models to guide researchers as they explore the development of mentoring relationships. The model presented in this chapter represents a step toward a deeper understanding of the mentoring process, which programs can utilize to more effectively capitalize on the potential for positively influencing a range of developmental outcomes. However, the model described in this chapter should be further tested and refined through additional research. For example, it will be important to examine the ways in which mentoring relationships operate within and depart from the emotional frameworks developed through parent–child relationships. Longitudinal investigations should be conducted whenever possible to help clarify directions of effect and long-term magnitude of impact of different types of model effects. Again, it will be essential to explore how youth characteristics, such as age, gender, ethnicity, sexual orientation, disability, and interpersonal and social histories, moderate the applicability of the theoretical model. Finally, a better understanding of relationship processes, from both the mentors' and mentees' perspectives, could contribute to a deeper understanding of the processes in the proposed model.

Examine Processes Across Different Types of Relationships and Programmatic Contexts

There is also a need for systematic comparisons of the relationships that are forged in natural versus assigned relationships and in programs that vary in type, intensity, supervision, training, matching, and length. The relative effectiveness and cost of approaches such as group

mentoring, peer mentoring, and e-mentoring need to be gauged carefully, using, if possible, randomized, controlled studies. In essence, relationships, programs, and practices need to be evaluated for their ability to produce enduring, positive outcomes that generalize across multiple areas of functioning.

Once a close mentoring relationship is forged, the pathways to developmental change appear to vary on the bases of both individual and contextual influences. Given this diversity, it is promising that mentoring programs are in the process of expanding into a wide array of program strategies, including mentoring in groups, at schools and work settings, and even over the Internet. At the same time, it would be shortsighted to assume that all of these newer types of relationships will offer the same benefits as the well-run, community-based, one-to-one mentoring programs that have been studied most intensively. Pending this type of research, one promising strategy for practitioners is to critically examine the extent to which different mentoring program strategies are likely to address the mediating processes emphasized in the model proposed in this chapter.

Furthermore, mentoring has been increasingly included as part of larger youth development programs that have several different components. Researchers thus need to compare stand-alone mentoring programs to those that integrate it with other services, and examine the extent to which mentoring adds to the effectiveness of programs with multiple components (e.g., Blechman et al., 2000; Taylor, LoScuito, Fox, Hilbert, & Sonkowsky, 1999). Indeed, there is some evidence that volunteer mentoring relationships are more effective when they are integrated into a larger network of youth services (Smith & Smoll, 2002).

IMPLICATIONS FOR PRACTICE

The preceding review and theoretical model also yield several implications for practitioners, some closely paralleling those for researchers. These implications therefore suggests ways in which practitioners and researchers could collaborate in their efforts to develop high-quality mentoring programs—for example, by developing and empirically testing training manuals, evaluating initiatives to reduce volunteer attrition and engage parents, and investigating the effectiveness of mentoring when housed within alternative programmatic contexts, such as in an after-school programs, summer camps, and sports teams. Even in the absence of such collaborations, the following suggestions illustrate ways in which practitioners could shape their interventions to maximally benefit youth and their mentors, and lead to satisfying and supportive mentoring relationships.

Develop and Empirically Test Training Protocols

As described in this chapter, a strong program infrastructure that promotes the development and maturation of close positive relationships between youth and their mentors is likely to be critical to the formation of close relationships and, ultimately, the effectiveness of the newer forms of mentoring. No matter how well a mentoring program is designed and conceptualized, it will not achieve its potential benefits if implementers lack the training and organizational support to carry them out with fidelity (Durlak & Wells, 1997). As mentoring continues to expand, it will be important to incorporate evidence-based practices into training and replication manuals, which specify the content and sequencing of various components.

Careful documentation of the implementation will enable practitioners to know what shortcomings to address if interventions fail to achieve desired outcomes. This training should be informed by observations and research, with a particular eye toward what constitutes high-quality mentoring relationships. Prematch and ongoing training should include coverage of such topics as the importance of consistency, handling terminations, ethical quandaries, advocacy on behalf the child, gifts and money, working with the child's family/school, and diversity issues. Attention to training other

relevant parties (i.e., the caseworkers, mentees) and guidance around the kind of relationships that agencies and program staff should establish with parents is also needed. Several important considerations, including a well-delineated, guiding conceptual framework, a user-friendly interface, and well-coordinated links to national-practice networks would help to ensure widespread and consistent utilization of training materials. Along these lines, programs should more effectively capitalize on the Internet as a portal for initial and ongoing training and evaluation. The flexibility, convenience, and interactive nature of this medium, particularly with a volunteer effort that is inherently decentralized, have yet to be fully realized.

Reduce Volunteer Attrition

A lack of systematic standards for training and support might help to explain the growing difficulties with volunteer retention, a particularly troubling trend given the adverse effects associated with breakdowns of relationships (Grossman & Rhodes, 2002). Indeed, high rates of volunteer attrition represent a major drain on staff and financial resources in mentoring programs, particularly given the effort involved in recruiting, screening, training, and matching volunteers. Given the evidence of an important moderating effect of relationship duration in the formation of close relationships, efforts should be made to recruit and retain mentors who are willing to stick with their mentees through thick and thin. To reduce attrition, programs should set reasonable goals regarding the number of youth they intend to serve, adhere to fidelity guidelines, and seek out technical assistance when needed. Recruitment efforts should also describe both the benefits a volunteer can expect and the commitment that is required. Program personnel who are sensitive to any circumstances and characteristics that might put volunteers at risk for early termination should carefully screen recruited volunteers.

It might also be helpful to tap into pools of volunteers who are at lower risk for termination.

Some programs have recognized the enormous volunteer potential that exists among retired adults. Older adults have more time to devote to this pursuit and are ideally positioned to provide the level of personal attention and emotional support that many youth need (Taylor & Bressler, 2001). At the same time, efforts should be made to facilitate the volunteer efforts of working parents and other adults. It also should not be overlooked that these pools of volunteers may include individuals whose backgrounds and abilities make them well prepared to enhance processes (e.g., role modeling, advocacy) that are discussed in this chapter as mediating positive effects of relationships on outcomes.

Connect Mentoring with Other Youth Settings

Caring adult–youth relationships have never been the sole province of mentoring programs. After-school programs, summer camps, competitive sports teams, church youth groups, and other positive youth development programs represent rich contexts for the formation of strong intergenerational ties (Foster-Bey, Dietz, & Grimm, 2006; Lerner, Brittain, & Fey, 2007). Adults in these settings are often afforded ongoing opportunities to engage youth in the sorts of informal conversations and enjoyable activities that can give rise to close bonds (Rhodes, 2004). Other settings can also be a rich source of adult support and guidance for youth. Religious communities often provide ongoing encouragement and mentoring through youth outreach and services. Walker and Freedman (2002) have argued that since social policies in general, and mentoring programs in particular, often do not reach or support the most severely disadvantaged youth, churches often play a critical support role. This is particularly true in urban, Black churches, which tend to be socially active in their communities and participate in a wide range of community programs.

Vulnerable youth often come in contact with publicly funded service systems, such as welfare, juvenile justice, housing, and teen-parenting programs. Adolescents entering these systems are less likely than others to gain access to mentoring or other youth development programs. Although many such youth would benefit from the support of adults, these systems rarely capitalize on this caring potential. The programs are often inaccessible, disconnected from each other, and staffed with professionals who are burdened with large caseloads. With more deliberate planning, such settings could be made more responsive to the needs of youth (Steinberg, Chung, & Little, 2004).

Meaningful relationships between adults and adolescents can occur in many contexts, ranging from youth development programs to the more spontaneous, yet influential, ties that sometimes arise with cherished aunts and uncles, teachers, or clergy. Although it is tempting to argue for a more caring society that would render arranged one-on-one mentoring relationships unnecessary, it is a mistake to be anything less than vigilant in supporting a full array of resources for caring relationships with adults. Changes in families, work demands, and communities have left many adolescents bereft of the adult supports that were available just a few decades ago, while presenting them with increasingly complex challenges. No one institution—whether families, schools, church, or positive youth development programs—can completely compensate for the social isolation that many children and adolescents experience, and each institution is stretched by the limitations of the others. Different youth derive benefits from different resources, and mentoring and other youth programs can protect them against negative choices and support their healthy development.

Developing and evaluating strategies that facilitate skillful, intentional mentoring and determining how to encourage youth to recruit adults represent promising new directions for policy with potentially far-reaching implications (Clary & Rhodes, 2006; Larson, 2006; Smith & Smoll, 2002). We can also learn from the strategies and lessons that have emerged in other youth settings. For example, approaches to assessing program characteristics, youth–adult engagement and implementation issues related to implementation have appeared in the after-school literature (see Birmingham, Pechman, Russell, & Mielke, 2005; Vandell, Schumow, & Posner, 2005; www.youth.highscope.org) and could be incorporated into the mentoring assessment and training.

Involve and Engage Parents and Families

An assumption of the proposed theoretical model with direct practical application is that the positive effects of mentoring relationships can reverberate back, ultimately drawing adolescents and their parents closer together. Although mentoring programs have not always involved parents and families in a comfortable or coherent manner, program personnel should remain aware of the ways that successful mentoring relationships can improve family dynamics, and they should take steps to capitalize on that possibility. If parents feel involved in—as opposed to shut out by—the process that brings other adults into their children's lives, they may be more likely to reinforce mentors' positive influences (DuBois et al., 2002).

IMPLICATIONS FOR POLICY

Policy makers, advocacy organizations, and funders have a critically important role to play in holding all youth-serving programs, organizations, and institutions to a high standard in their efforts to make high-quality mentoring relationships available to young people. A shared vision of excellence, along with a commitment to scientifically informed guidance and support, will be needed to achieve this goal and thus ensure that advances in the practice of mentoring truly improve the lives of our nation's youth. To this end, the contents of this chapter also have implications for policy.

Promote Evidence-Based Innovation

As this chapter makes clear, policies that demand greater adherence to evidence-based practice and the use of rigorous evaluations are needed to ensure quality receives as much attention as does quantity as the practice of youth mentoring continues to expand. Models of successful program replication can help guide such growth. Most replicated programs do not retain the original effectiveness, but there are a few examples, including two that involve mentoring components: the Nurse-Family Partnership (Olds, 2006) and the Across Ages Mentoring Program (Taylor, LoSciuto, & Porcellini, 2005). These programs have successfully identified the critical elements of the program, assessed the new "market," and provided ongoing supervision and monitoring to ensure that the new programs retained all the critical components (Racine, 2004). So, even as Across Ages expanded to over 30 sites in 17 states, it continues to boast relatively low volunteer attrition; match durations that greatly exceed national averages; and positive behavioral, academic, and psychosocial outcomes.

Promote Rigorous Evaluation, Replication, and Dissemination

In addition, policy makers should encourage mentoring programs to adhere to well-developed evaluation systems in place prior to implementation. This has not been the case to date. There are encouraging signs of change, however. These include the Mentoring Initiative for System Involved Youth, sponsored by the Office of Juvenile Justice and Delinquency Prevention (OJJDP). This initiative will be launched in only four demonstration sites and rigorously evaluated within a research-oriented framework (OJJDP, 2006), a marked contrast to its predecessor, the Juvenile Mentoring Program (JUMP). Several large-scale random-assignment evaluations of school-based mentoring are also under way that promise to shed important light on this program model. Funding that extends these evaluations and leverages the initial investment through secondary analysis could further illuminate mentoring processes and outcomes. Policy makers should also promote the evaluation of intentional mentoring relationships in other youth settings, such as after-school programs and competitive sports teams. As mentioned above, these are settings in which relationships between adults and youth historically have developed naturally, and policy makers should encourage evaluation of more intentional mentoring relationships in these contexts.

Reward Sustainability and Quality

In addition, policymakers should consider developing methods to reward mentoring programs for high levels of sustainability and quality. One option would be to develop clearly stipulated standards to which programs seeking external funds would seek to adhere. Involving researchers and evaluators in this process could help to ensure that evidence-based practices are efficiently disseminated to the field. Research that identifies how youth and mentor characteristics shape the match, and which matches are most vulnerable to early termination would be particularly helpful in this regard.

Improve Dialogue Among Constituents

To facilitate movement toward the above goals, channels of communication between researchers, practitioners, and policy makers must be improved. Many practitioners have neither the technical savvy nor the time to decipher the scientific merits and limitations of research findings. And, because academic journals remain largely inaccessible, these constituencies are left to accept abstracted summaries and handed-down interpretations of findings. As described, more easily accessed information often exaggerates the benefits of mentoring, and abstracted summaries have had a way of incorporating inaccuracies as they branch from the original source.

Moreover, although scholars are reasonably adept at writing for each other, technical jargon and esoteric statistics can render their work virtually incomprehensible to practitioners. Even when clear and relevant, it can be difficult to actually put findings into practice. A review by University of St. Andrew's Research Unit for Research Utilization (RURU) (Walter, Nutley, & Davies, 2003, p. 11) concluded that "Simply providing research information is unlikely to lead to changes in behaviour. Users need to adapt and re-negotiate findings from research to their practice or policy contexts." This suggests the potential value of translating research findings and offering ongoing workshops to increase practitioners' skills and knowledge in applying evidence-based practice (Stevens, Liabo, Frost, & Roberts, 2005). A good model for such dissemination is the Cochrane Library, a quarterly subscription service that provides reliable and comprehensible information to medical practitioners about health care effects. Working groups of researchers, practitioners, and policy makers, and research staff positions within agencies, would foster more collaborative engagement among the various constituents.

CONCLUSIONS

The enthusiasm for and growth of mentoring programs speaks volumes about the faith our society places in one-to-one relationships between vulnerable young people and unrelated but caring adults. And with good cause. The success of human services initiatives often rests on the quality of relationships that are forged among participants. By putting relationships at center stage, mentoring programs can deliver this healing in full potency. Moreover, as discussed in this chapter, a growing body of research provides an encouraging base of evidence for the benefits of high-quality mentoring relationships and by implication the programs and settings that are able to establish and support these types of relationships. Although much remains to be done to understand the complexities of mentoring relationships and to determine the circumstances under which mentoring programs make a difference in the lives of youth, at this stage, we can safely say that mentoring is, by and large, a modestly effective intervention. In some cases, it can do more harm than good; in others, it can have extraordinarily influential effects. The balance can and should be tipped toward the latter. A deeper understanding of mentoring relationships, combined with high-quality programs, enriched settings, and a better integration of research, practice, and policy will better position programs to harness the full potential of youth mentoring.

REFERENCES

Ainsworth, M. (1989). Attachments beyond infancy. *American Psychologist, 44,* 709–716.

Allen, J. P., & Land, D. (1999). Attachment in adolescence. In J. Cassidy, P. R. Shaver, et al., (Eds.), *Handbook of attachment: Theory, research, and clinical applications* (pp. 319–335). New York: Guilford Press.

Allen, J. P., McElhaney, K. B., Land, D. J., Kuperminc, G. P., Moore, C. W., O'Beirne-Kelly, H., et al. (2003). A secure base in adolescence: Markers of attachment security in mother–adolescent relationship. *Child Development. 74,* 292–307.

Anderson, E. (1999). *Code of the street: Decency, violence, and the moral life of the inner city.* New York: W. W. Norton.

Aos, S., Lieb, R., Mayfield, J., Miller, M., & Pennucci, A. (2004). *Benefits and costs of prevention and early intervention programs for youth.* Report to the Washington State Legislature. Olympia, WA: Washington State Institute for Public Policy. Retrieved April 18, 2005, from www.wsipp.wa.gov.

Aseltine, R. H., Dupre, M., & Lamlein, P. (2000). Mentoring as a drug prevention strategy: An evaluation of Across Ages. *Adolescent and Family Health, 1,* 11–20.

Balcazar, F. E., Davies, G. L., Viggers, D., & Tranter, D. (2006). Goal attainment scaling as an effective strategy to assess the outcomes of mentoring programs for troubled youth. *International Journal of School Disaffection, 4,* 43–52.

Balcazar, F. E., Keys, C. B., & Garate, J. (1995). Learning to recruit assistance to attain transition goals: A program for adjudicated youth with disabilities. *Remedial and Special Education, 16,* 237–246.

Barnoski, R. (2006). *Recidivism findings for the Juvenile Rehabilitation Administration's mentoring program: Final report.* Olympia, WA: Washington State Institute for Public Policy.

Bauldry, S., & Hartmann, T. A. (2004). *The promise and challenge of mentoring high-risk youth. Findings from the national faith-based initiative.* Philadelphia: Public/Private Ventures.

Beam, M. R., Chen, C., & Greenberger, E. (2002). The nature of the relationships between adolescents and their "very important" nonparental adults. *American Journal of Community Psychology, 30,* 305–325.

Beam, M. R., Gil-Rivas, V., Greenberger, E., & Chen, C. (2002). Adolescent problem behavior and depressed mood: Risk and protection within and across social contexts. *Journal of Youth and Adolescence, 31,* 343–357.

Belsky, J., & Cassidy, J. (1994). Attachment: Theory and evidence. In M. Rutter & D. F. Hay (Eds.), *Development through life: A handbook for clinicians* (pp. 373–402). Oxford, UK: Blackwell Science.

Bernstein, L., & Hunt, D. (in press). *An evaluation of the U.S. Department of Education.* Cambridge, MA: Abt Associates.

Birmingham, J., Pechman, Russell, C. A., Mielke, M. (2005). Shared features of high performing after-school programs: A follow-up to the TASC Evaluation. Retrieved March 20, 2007, from hwww.sedl.org/pubs/fam107/fam107.pdf.

Blakely, C. H., Menon, R., & Jones, D. C. (1995). *Project BELONG: Final report.* College Station, TX: Texas A&M University, Public Policy Research Institute.

Blechman, E. A., Maurice, A., Buecker, B., & Helberg, C. (2000). Can mentoring or skill training reduce recidivism? Observational study with propensity analysis. *Prevention Science, 1,* 139–155.

Bowlby, J. (1988). *A secure base: Parent–child attachment and healthy human development.* New York: Basic Books.

Brady, B., Dolan, P., O'Brien, M., & Canavan, J. (2005). *Big Brothers Big Sisters Ireland youth mentoring programme: Evaluation report.* Galway Child & Family Resarch & Policy Unit.

Branham, L. (2006). *The 7 hidden reasons employees leave: How to recognize the subtle signs and act before it's too late.* New York: AMACOM.

Bretherton, I., & Waters, E. (Eds.). (1985). Growing points of attachment theory and research. *Monograph of the Society for Research in Child Development 50*(1–2, serial no. 209).

Brock, T. (in press). *Evaluation of National Guard Youth Challenge Program.* New York: MDRC.

Cavell, T. A., & Hughes, J. N. (2000). Secondary prevention as context for assessing change processes in aggressive children. *Journal of School Psychology, 38,* 199–235.

Clary, G., & Rhodes, J. E. (2006). Mobilizing the village: Adult volunteerism and child welfare. In G. Clary & J. Rhodes (Eds.), *Mobilizing adults for positive youth development: Lessons from the behavioral sciences on promoting socially valued activities* (Peter Benson, Series Ed.). Minneapolis, MN: Search Institute.

Clausen, J. A. (1991). Adolescent competence and the life course: Or why one social psychologist needed a concept of personality. *Social Psychology Quarterly, 54,* 4–14.

Clayden, J., & Stein, M. (2005). *Mentoring young people leaving care.* York, UK: Joseph Roundtree Foundation.

Cohen, J. (1988). *Statistical power analysis for the behavioral sciences.* Hillsdale, NJ: Lawrence Erlbaum.

Connell, J. P., & Wellborn, J. G. (1991). Competence, autonomy and relatedness: A motivational analysis of self-system processes. In M. R. Gunnar & L. A. Sroufe (Eds.), *Minnesota symposium on child psychology,* vol. 23: *Self-processes in development* (pp. 43–77). Hillsdale, NJ: Lawrence Erlbaum.

Cooley, C. H. (1902). *Human nature and the social order.* New York: Scribner.

Cooper, C. R., Grotevant, H. D., & Condon, S. M. (1983). Individuality and connectedness both foster adolescent identity formation and role taking skills. In H. D Grotevant & C. R. Cooper (Eds.), *Adolescent development in the family: New directions for child development, 22,* 43–59. San Francisco: Jossey-Bass.

Cooper, H., & Hedges, L. (Eds.). (1994). *Handbook for research synthesis.* New York: Russell Sage Foundation.

Csiksilzentmihalyi, M., & Rathunde, K. (1998). The development of person: An experiential perspective on the ontogenesis of psychological complexity. In R. M. Lerner (Ed.), *The handbook of child development,* vol. 1: *Theoretical models of human development* (5th ed.; pp. 635–684). New York: John Wiley & Sons.

Dappen, L., & Isernhagen, J. C. (2006). Urban and nonurban schools: Examination of a statewide student mentoring program. *Urban Education, 41,* 151–168.

Darling, N., Hamilton, S. F., Toyokawa, T., & Matsuda, S. (2002). Naturally occurring mentoring in Japan and the United States: Social roles and correlates. *American Journal of Community Psychology 30:* 245–270.

Davidson, W. S., & Redner, R. (1988). The prevention of juvenile delinquency: Diversion from the juvenile justice system. In R. H. Price, E. L. Cowen, R. P. Lorion, & E. J. Ramos-McKay (Eds.), *Fourteen ounces of prevention: Theory, research, and prevention* (pp. 123–137). New York: Pergamon Press.

De Ayala, R. J., & Perry, C. M. (2005, April). *The effects of a mentoring program on eating behavior, physical activity, and self-efficacy in overweight upper-elementary students.* Paper presented at the American Alliance for Health, Physical Education, Recreation and Dance National Convention and Exposition, Chicago, IL.

Denham, S., & Kochanoff, A. T. (2002). Parental contributions to preschoolers' understanding of emotion. *Marriage & Family Review, 34,* 311–343.

Dennison, S. (2000). A win-win peer mentoring and tutoring program: A collaborative model. *Journal of Primary Prevention, 20,* 161–174.

DeWit, D. J., Lipman, E., Manzano-Munguia, M., Bisanz, J., Graham, K., Offord, D. R., O'Neill, E., Pepler, D., & Shaver, K. (2006). Feasibility of a randomized controlled trial for evaluating the effectiveness of the Big Brothers Big Sisters community match program at the national level. *Children and Youth Services Review, 29,* 383–404.

Diamond, L. M., & Aspinwall, L. G. (2003). Emotion regulation across the life span: An integrative perspective emphasizing self-regulation, positive affect, and dyadic processes. *Motivation and Emotion. 27,* 125–156.

Dubas, J. S., & Snider, B. A. (1993). The role of community-based youth groups in enhancing learning and achievement through non-formal education. In R. M. Lerner (Ed.), *Early adolescence: Perspectives on research, policy, and intervention* (pp. 150–174). Hillsdale, NJ: Lawrence Erlbaum.

DuBois, D. L., Holloway, B. E., Valentine, J. C., & Cooper, H. (2002). Effectiveness of mentoring programs: A meta-analytical review. *American Journal of Community Psychology, 30,* 157–197.

DuBois, D. L., & Neville, H. A. (1997). Youth mentoring: Investigation of relationship characteristics and perceived benefits. *Journal of Community Psychology, 25,* 227–234.

DuBois, D. L., Neville, H. A., Parra, G. R., & Pugh-Lilly, A. O. (2002). Testing a new model of mentoring. *New Directions for Youth Development, 93,* 21–57.

DuBois, D. L., & Rhodes, J.E. (2006). Youth mentoring: Bridging science with practice. *Journal of Community Psychology, 34,* 547–565.

DuBois, D. L., & Silverthorn, N. (2005a). Characteristics of natural mentoring relationships and adolescent adjustment: Evidence from a national study. *Journal of Primary Prevention, 26,* 69–92.

DuBois, D. L., & Silverthorn, N. (2005b). Natural mentoring relationships and adolescent health: Evidence from a national study. *American Journal of Public Health, 95,* 518–524.

Durlak, J. A., Meerson, I., & Foster, C. J. E. (2003). Meta-analysis. In J. C. Thomas & M. Hersen (Eds.), *Understanding research in clinical and counseling psychology* (pp. 243–267). Mahwah, NJ: Lawrence Erlbaum.

Durlak, J. A., & Wells, A. M. (1997). Primary prevention mental health programs for children and adolescents: A meta-analytic review. *American Journal of Community Psychology, 25,* 115–152.

Dworkin, J. B., Larson, R., & Hansen, D. (2003). Adolescents' accounts of growth experiences in youth activities. *Journal of Youth and Adolescence, 32,* 17–26.

Eby, L. T., Allen, T. D., Evans, S. C., Ng, T. W. H., & DuBois, D. (in press). Does mentoring matter? A multidisciplinary meta-analysis comparing mentored and non-mentored individuals. *Journal of Vocational Behavior.*

Erikson, E. H. (1964). *Identity and the life cycle.* New York: W. W. Norton.

Flay, B. R., Biglan, A., Boruch, R. F., Castro, F. G., Gottfredson, D., Kellam, S., et al. (2005). Standards of evidence: Criteria for efficacy, effectiveness and dissemination. *Prevention Science, 6*(3), 151–175.

Foster-Bey, J., Dietz, N., & Grimm, R. (2006). *Volunteers mentoring youth: Implications for closing the mentoring gap.* Washington, DC: Corporation for National & Community Service.

Freedman, M. (1988). *Partners in growth: Elder mentors and at risk youth.* Philadelphia: Public Private Ventures.

Freud, S. (1914). On narcissism: An introduction. In J. Strachey (Ed.), *Standard edition of the complete psychological works of Sigmund Freud, 14,* 73–102.

Gottman, J. M. (2001). Meta-emotion, children's emotional intelligence, and buffering children from marital conflict. In C. D. Ryff & B. H. Singer (Eds.), *Emotion, social relationships, and health* (pp. 23–39). New York: Oxford University Press.

Grimm, R., Jr., Spring, K., & Dietz, N. (2007). *The health benefits of volunteering: A review of recent research.* Washington, DC: Corporation for National and Community Service, Office of Research and Policy Development.

Grossman, J. B. (in press). *Evaluation of friends of the children.* Philadelphia: Public/Private Ventures.

Grossman, J. B., & Johnson, A. (1998). Assessing the effectiveness of mentoring programs. In J. B. Grossman (Ed.), *Contemporary issues in mentoring* (pp. 25–47). Philadelphia: Public/Private Ventures.

Grossman, J. B., & Rhodes, J. E. (2002). The test of time: Predictors and effects of duration in youth mentoring relationships. *American Journal of Community Psychology, 30,* 199–219.

Grossman, J. B., & Tierney, J. P. (1998). Does mentoring work? An impact study of the Big Brothers Big Sisters program. *Evaluation Review, 22,* 403–426.

Hall, J. C. (2003). *Mentoring and young people: A literature review.* Glasgow: University of Glasgow, SCRE Centre.

Hamilton, S. F., & Darling, N. (1996). Mentors in adolescents' lives. In K. Hurrelmann & S. F. Hamilton (Eds.), *Social problems and social contexts in adolescence: Perspectives across boundaries* (pp. 199–215). New York: Pergamon Press.

Hamilton, M. A., & Hamilton, S. F. (2005). Work and service-learning. In D. L. DuBois & M. J. Karcher (Eds.), *Handbook of youth mentoring* (pp. 348–363). Thousand Oaks, CA: Sage.

Hansen, K. (2007). *One-to-one mentoring: Literature review.* Philadelphia: Big Brothers Big Sisters of America.

Hellenga, K., Rhodes, J. E., & Aber, M. S. (2002). African American adolescent mothers' vocational aspiration–expectation gap: Individual, social and environmental influences. *Psychology of Women Quarterly, 26,* 200–212.

Herrera, C., Grossman, J. B., Kauh, T. J., Feldman, A. F., & McMaken, J. (with Jucovy, L. Z.). (2007). *Making a difference in schools: The Big Brothers Big Sisters school-based mentoring impact study.* Philadelphia: Public/Private Ventures.

Herrera, C., Sipe, C. L., & McClanahan, W. S. (2000). *Mentoring school-age children: Relationship development in community-based and school-based programs.* Philadelphia: Public/Private Ventures. (Published in collaboration with MENTOR/National Mentoring Partnership, Alexandria, VA).

Hirsch, B. J. (2005). *A place to call home: After-school programs for urban youth.* Washington, DC: American Psychological Association/New York: Teachers College Press.

Jekielek, S., Moore, K. A., & Hair, E. C. (2002). *Mentoring programs and youth development.* Washington, DC: Child Trends.

Johnson, M. H., & Munakata, Y. (2005). Processes of change in brain and cognitive development. *Trends in Cognitive Sciences, 9,* 152–158.

Jolliffe, D., & Farington, D. P. (2007). *A rapid evidence assessment of the impact of mentoring on re-offending: A summary.* Cambridge University: Home Office Online Report 11/07. Retrieved May 8, 2007, from www.crimereduction.gov.uk/workingoffenders/workingoffenders069.htm.

Kalbfleisch, P. J. (2002). Communication in mentoring relationships: A theory for enactment. *Communication Theory, 12,* 63–69.

Karcher, M. (in press). *Study of mentoring in the learning environment (SMILE).* San Antonio: University of Texas, San Antonio.

Karcher, M. J. (2008). *No fooling around: The role of play, activities, and pressure to succeed academically in SBM outcomes.* Maryland Mentoring Conference, Maryland Mentoring Partnership. Baltimore, MD.

Karcher, M. J. (2005). The effects of developmental mentoring and high school mentors' attendance on their younger mentees' self-esteem, social skills, and connectedness. *Psychology in the Schools, 42,* 65–77.

Karcher, M. J., Davis, C., & Powell, B. (2002). The effects of developmental mentoring on connectedness and academic achievement. *School Community Journal, 12*(2), 35–50.

Karcher, M. J., Nakkula, M. J., & Harris, J. T. (2005). Developmental mentoring match characteristics: Correspondence between mentors' and mentees' assessments of relationship quality. *Journal of Primary Prevention, 26,* 93–110.

Karcher, M. J., Roy-Carlson, L., Benne, K., Gil-Hernandez, D., Allen, C., & Gomez, M. (2006). A mixed methods approach to identifying factors that influenced Latino mentees' changes in connectedness after mentoring. In C. M. Buchanan (Chair), *The impact of mentoring of Latino youth: Academic outcomes and other developmental assets.* Symposium presented at the Biennial Meeting of the Society for Research on Adolescence, San Francisco, CA.

Keating, D. P. (1990). Adolescent thinking. In S. S. Feldman & G. R. Elliott (Eds.), *At the threshold: The developing adolescent* (pp. 54–89). Cambridge, MA: Harvard University Press.

Keating, L. M., Tomashina, M. A., Foster, S., & Allesandri, M. (2002). The effects of a mentoring program on at-risk youth. *Adolescence, 37,* 717–734.

Keller, T. E. (2005). The stages and development of mentoring relationships. In D. L. DuBois & M. J. Karcher (Eds.), *Handbook of youth mentoring* (pp. 82–99). Thousand Oaks, CA: Sage.

Klaw, E. L., Fitzgerald, L. F., & Rhodes, J. E. (2003). Natural mentors in the lives of African American adolescent mothers: Tracking relationships over time. *Journal of Youth and Adolescence, 32,* 322–332.

Kohut, H. (1984). *How does analysis cure?* Chicago: University of Chicago Press.

Langhout, R. D., Rhodes, J. E., & Osborne, L. N. (2004). An exploratory study of youth mentoring in an urban context: Adolescents' perceptions of relationship styles. *Journal of Youth and Adolescence, 33,* 293–306.

Larose, S., Chaloux, N., Monaghan, D., & Tarabulsy, G. M. (2006). *Working alliance as a moderator of the impact of mentoring relationships among academically at-risk students.* Manuscript submitted for publication.

Larose, S., Tarabulsy, G., & Cyrenne, D. (2005). Perceived autonomy and relatedness as moderating the impact of teacher–student mentoring relationships on student academic adjustment. *Journal of Primary Prevention, 26,* 111–128.

Larson, R. (2006). Positive youth development, willful adolescents, and mentoring. *Journal of Community Psychology, 34,* 677–689.

Larson, W. (2000). Toward a psychology of positive youth development. *American Psychologist, 55,* 170–183.

Lee, J., & Cramond, B. (1999). The positive effects of mentoring economically disadvantaged students. *Professional School Counseling, 2,* 172–178.

Lerner, R. M., Brittian, A. S., & Fay, K. E. (2007). Mentoring: A key resource for promoting positive youth development. In J. E. Rhodes (Ed.), *Research in action.* Alexandria, VA: National Mentoring Partnership.

Lerner, R. M., Lerner, J. V., Almerigi, J., Theokas, C., Phelps, E., Gestsdottir, S., et al. (2005). Positive youth development, participation in community youth development programs, and community contributions of fifth grade adolescents: Findings from the first wave of the 4–H Study of Positive Youth Development. *Journal of Early Adolescence, 25,* 17–71,

Lerner, R. M., & Overton, W. F. (in press). Exemplifying the integrations of the relational developmental system. *Journal of Adolescent Research.*

Levinson, D. J. (1979). *The seasons of a man's life.* New York: Ballantine Books.

Liabo, K., & Lucas, P. (2006). *One-to-one mentoring programmes and problem behaviour in adolescence. What works for children group: Evidence nugget.* Economic & Social Research Council.

Lipsey, M. W., & Wilson, D. B. (2001). *Practical meta-analysis.* Thousand Oaks, CA: Sage.

LoScuito, L., Rajala, A., Townsend, T. N., & Taylor, A. S. (1996). An outcome evaluation of Across Ages: An intergenerational mentoring approach to drug prevention. *Journal of Adolescent Research, 11,* 116–129.

Lynch, M., & Cicchetti, D. (1997). Children's relationships with adults and peers: An examination of elementary and junior high school students. *Journal of School Psychology, 35,* 81–100.

Main, M., Kaplan, N., & Cassidy, J. (1985). Security in infancy, childhood, and adulthood: A move to the level of representation. In I. Bretherton, & E. Waters (Eds.), *Growing points of attachment theory and research. Monographs of the Society for Research in Child Development, 50*(1–2, serial no. 209, 66–104).

Markus, H., & Nurius, P. (1986). Possible selves. *American Psychologist, 41,* 954–969.

Maxfield, M., Schrim, A., & Rodriguez-Planas, N. (2003). *The Quantum Opportunity Project demonstration: Implementation and short-term impacts.* Washington, DC: Mathematic Policy Research.

McLearn, K. T., Colasanto, D., & Schoen, C. (1998). Mentoring makes a difference: Findings from the Commonwealth Fund 1998 Survey of Adults Mentoring Youth People. New York: The Commonwealth Fund. Retrieved July 18, 2004, from www.cmwf.org/programs/child/mclea277.asp.

Mead, G. H. (1934). *Mind, self, and society from the standpoint of a social behaviorist.* Chicago: University of Chicago Press.

MENTOR. (2006). *The National Agenda for Action: How to close America's mentoring gap.* Retrieved May, 15, 2006, from www.mentoring.org/leaders/files/nationalagenda.pdf.

Morison, P., & Masten, A. S. (1991). Peer reputation in middle childhood as a predictor of adaptation in adolescence. A seven-year follow-up. *Child Development, 62,* 991–1007.

Morrow, K. V., & Styles, M. B. (1995). *Building relationships with youth in program settings: A study of Big Brothers/Big Sisters.* Philadelphia: Public/Private Ventures.

Office of Juvenile Justice and Delinquency Prevention (OJJDP). (2006). Mentoring initiative for system-involved youth. Retrieved May 21, 2006, from http://ojjdp.ncjrs.org/grants/solicitations/06mentoringinitiative.pdf.

Olds, D. (2006). The nurse–family partnership: An evidence-based preventive intervention. *Infant Mental Health Journal, 27,* 5–25.

Osterling, K. L., & Hines, A. M. (2006). Mentoring adolescent foster youth: Promoting resilience during developmental transitions. *Child and Family Social Work, 11,* 242–253.

Parra, G. R., DuBois, D. L., Neville, H. A., Pugh-Lilly, A. O., & Povinelli, N. (2002). Mentoring relationships for youth: Investigation of a process-oriented model. *Journal of Community Psychology, 30,* 367–388.

Pawson, R. (2006). Digging for nuggets: How "bad" research can yield "good" evidence. *International Journal of Research Methodology, 9,* 127–142.

Philip, K. (2003). Youth mentoring: The American dream comes to the UK? *British Journal of Guidance & Counseling, 31,* 101–112.

Phillip, K., & Spratt, J. (2007). *A synthesis of published research on mentoring and befriending for the Mentoring and Befriending Foundation.* Aberdeen: University of Aberdeen, The Rowan Group.

Pianta, R. C. (1999). *Enhancing relationships between children and teachers.* Washington, DC: American Psychological Association.

Portwood, S. G., Ayers, P. M., Kinnison, K. E., Waris, R. G., & Wise, D. L. (2005). YouthFriends: Outcomes from a school-based mentoring program. *Journal of Primary Prevention, 26,* 129–145.

Pryce, J. M. (2006). *Up-close and personal: A view of school-based mentoring relationships.* Doctoral dissertation, University of Chicago.

Putnam, R. D. (2000). *Bowling alone: The collapse and revival of American community.* New York: Simon & Schuster.

Racine, D. (2004). *Capturing the essential elements*. Philadelphia: Public/Private Ventures.

Reddy, R., Rhodes, J., & Mulhall, P. (2003). The influence of teacher support on student adjustment in the middle school years: A latent growth curve study. *Development and Psychopathology, 15,* 119–138.

Rhodes, J. E. (2002). *Stand by me: The risks and rewards of mentoring today's youth*. Cambridge, MA: Harvard University Press.

Rhodes, J. E. (2004). The critical ingredient: Caring youth–staff relationships in after-school settings. In G. Noam (Ed.), *Afterschool worlds: Creating a new social space for development and learning* (pp. 145–161). San Francisco: Jossey-Bass.

Rhodes, J. E. (2005). A model of youth mentoring. In D. L. DuBois & M. J. Karcher (Eds.), *Handbook of youth mentoring* (pp. 30–43). Thousand Oaks, CA: Sage.

Rhodes, J. E., Contreras, J. M., & Mangelsdorf, S. C. (1994). Natural mentor relationships among Latina adolescent mothers: Psychological adjustment, moderating processes, and the role of early parental acceptance. *American Journal of Community Psychology, 22,* 211–228.

Rhodes, J., & DuBois, D. (2006). Understanding and facilitating the youth mentoring movement. *Social Policy Report, XX,* 3–19.

Rhodes, J. E., Grossman, J. B., & Resch, N. R. (2000). Agents of change: Pathways through which mentoring relationships influence adolescents' academic adjustment. *Child Development, 71,* 1662–1671.

Rhodes, J. E., Haight, W. L., & Briggs, E. (1999). The influence of mentoring on the peer relationships of foster youth in relative and nonrelative care. *Journal of Research on Adolescence, 9,* 185–201.

Rhodes, J., Lowe, S. R., Litchfield, L., & Walsh-Samp, K. (in press). The role of gender in youth mentoring relationship formation and duration. *Journal of Vocational Behavior*.

Rhodes, J. E., Reddy, R., & Grossman, J. (2005). The protective influence of mentoring on adolescents' substance abuse: Direct and indirect pathways. *Applied Developmental Science, 9,* 31–47.

Rhodes, J. E., Reddy, R., Grossman, J. B., & Lee, J. M. (2003). Same versus cross-race matches in mentoring programs: A comparison. *Journal of Applied Social Psychology, 32,* 2114–2133.

Rhodes, J. E., Reddy, R., Roffman, J., & Grossman, J. B. (2005). Promoting successful youth mentoring relationships: A preliminary screening questionnaire. *Journal of Primary Prevention, 26,* 146–167.

Ripple, C. H., & Zigler, E. (2003). Research, policy, and the federal role in prevention initiatives for children. *American Psychologist, 58,* 482–490.

Roberts, H., Liabo, K., Lucas, P., DuBois, D., & Sheldon, T. A. (2004). Mentoring to reduce antisocial behavior in childhood. *British Medical Journal, 328,* 512–514.

Roeser, R. W., & Eccles, J. S. (1998). Adolescents' perceptions of middle school: Relation to longitudinal changes in academic and psychological adjustment. *Journal of Research on Adolescence, 8*(1), 123–158.

Roffman, J. G., Suarez-Orozco, C., & Rhodes, J. E. (2002). Facilitating positive development in immigrant youth: The role of mentors and community organizers. In D. F. Perkins, L. M. Borden, J. G. Keith, & F. A. Villarruel (Eds.), *Positive youth development: Creating a positive tomorrow*. New York: Kluwer Academic Press.

Rogoff, B. (1990). *Apprenticeship in thinking: Cognitive development in social context*. New York: Oxford University Press.

Ryan, R. M., & Grolnick, W. S. (1986). Origins and pawns in the classroom: Self-report and projective assessments of individual differences in children's perceptions. *Journal of Personality and Social Psychology, 50,* 550–558.

Sanchez, B., & Colon, Y. (2005). Race, ethnicity, and culture in mentoring relationships. In D. L. DuBois & M. J. Karcher (Eds.), *Handbook of youth mentoring* (pp. 191–204). Thousand Oaks, CA: Sage.

Sánchez, B., Reyes, O., & Singh, J. (2006). A qualitative examination of the relationships that play a mentoring function for Mexican American older adolescents. *Cultural Diversity and Ethnic Minority Psychology, 12,* 615–631.

Scales, P. C. (2003). *Other people's kids: Social expectation and American adults' involvement with children and adolescents*. New York: Kluwer Academic Press.

Shiner, M., Young, T., Newburn, T., & Groben, S. (2004). *Mentoring disaffected young people: An evaluation of Mentoring Plus*. York, UK: Joseph Roundtree Foundation.

Sipe, C. L. (2002). Mentoring programs for adolescents: A research summary. *Journal of Adolescent Health, 31,* 251–260.

Sipe, C. L., & Roder, A. E. (1999). *Mentoring school-age children: A classification of programs*. Philadelphia: Public/Private Ventures. (Published in collaboration with MENTOR/ National Mentoring Partnership, Alexandria, VA).

Slicker, E. K., & Palmer, D. J. (1993). Mentoring at-risk high school students: Evaluation of a school-based program. *The School Counselor, 40,* 327–333.

Smith, A. (2002). Does mentoring really work? A meta-analysis of mentoring programs for at-risk youth (Doctoral dissertation, Texas A&M University, 2002). *Dissertation Abstracts International, 63,* 5537.

Smith, R. E., & Smoll, F. L. (2002). Youth sports as a behavior setting for psychosocial interventions. In J. L. Van Raalte & B. W. Brewer (Eds.), *Exploring sport and exercise psychology* (2nd ed., pp. 341–371). Washington, DC: American Psychological Association.

Soucy, N., & Larose, S. (2000). Attachment and control in family and mentoring contexts as determinants of adolescent adjustment at college. *Journal of Family Psychology, 14,* 125–143.

Spencer, R. (2006). Understanding the mentoring process between adolescents and adults. *Youth Society, 37,* 287–315.

Sroufe, A. L. (1995). Contribution of attachment theory to developmental psychopathology. In E. A. Carlson, & A. L. Sroufe (Eds.), *Developmental psychopathology*, vol. 1: *Theory and methods* (pp. 581–617). New York: Plenum Press.

Stanton-Salazar, R. D., & Spina, S. U. (2003). Informal mentors and role models in the lives of urban Mexican-origin adolescents. *Anthropology & Education Quarterly, 34,* 231–254.

Steinberg, L. (2005). Cognitive and affective development in adolescence. *Trends in Cognitive Sciences, 9,* 69–74.

Steinberg, L., Chung, H., & Little, M. (2004). Reentry of young offenders from the justice system: A developmental perspective. *Youth Violence and Juvenile Justice, 1,* 21–38.

Stevens, M., Liabo, K., Frost, S., & Roberts, H. (2005). Using research in practice: A research information service for social care practitioners. *Child and Family Social Work, 10,* 67–75.

Stukas, A., Snyder, M., & Clary, E. (1999). The effects of "mandatory volunteerism": Satisfaction, intentions, and motivations to volunteer. *Psychological Science, 10,* 59–64.

Stukas, A. A., Daly, M., & Clary, E. G. (2006). Lessons from research on volunteering for mobilizing adults to volunteer for positive youth development. In E. G. Clary & J. E. Rhodes (Eds.), *Mobilizing adults for positive youth development: Strategies for closing the gap between beliefs and behaviors* (pp. 65–82). New York: Springer.

Styles, M. B., & Morrow, K. V. (1992). *Understanding how youth and elders form relationships: A study of four Linking Lifetimes programs*. Philadelphia: Public/Private Ventures.

Taylor, A., LoSciuto, L., & Porcellini, L. (2005). Intergenerational mentoring. In D. L. DuBois & M. J. Karcher (Eds.), *Handbook of youth mentoring* (pp. 2–11). Thousand Oaks, CA: Sage.

Taylor, A. S., & Bressler, J. (2001). *Mentoring across generations: Partnerships for positive youth development*. New York: Kluwer Academic Press.

Taylor, A. S., LoSciuto, L., & Fox, M., Hilbert, S. M., & Sonkowsky, M. (1999). The mentoring factor: Evaluation of the across ages' intergenerational approach to drug abuse prevention. *Child and Youth Services, 20,* 77–99.

Theokas, C., & Lerner, R. M. (2006). Promoting positive development in adolescence: The role of ecological assets in families, schools, and neighborhoods. *Applied Developmental Science, 10,* 61–74.

Tolan, P., Henry, D., Shoen, M., & Bass, A. (2005). *What we know about what mentoring can and might do for youth crime.* Presented at The Fifth Annual Jerry Lee Crime Prevention Symposium: Systematic Evidence on What Works in Crime and Justice: Raising Questions and Presenting Findings, May 3, 2005.

Vandell, D. L, Schumow, L., & Posner, J. (2005). Extracurricular activities, after-school and community programs. In J. L. Mahoney, R. Larson, & J. S. Eccles (Eds.), *Organized activities as contexts of development* (pp. 437–456). Mahwah, NJ: Lawrence Erlbaum.

Veith, E. M., Sherman, J. E., Pellino, T. A. Yasui, T. Y. (2006). Qualitative analysis of the peermentoring relationship among individuals with spinal cord injury, *Rehabilitation Psychology, 51,* 289–298

Vygotsky, S. (1978). *Mind in society.* Cambridge, MA: Harvard University Press.

Walter, I., Nutley, S. M. & Davies, H. T. O. (2003). *Research impact: A cross-sector review.* Research Unit for Research Utilisation, University of St. Andrew.

Waterman, A. S. (1982). Identity development from adolescence to adulthood: An extension of theory and a review of research. *Developmental Psychology, 18,* 341–358.

Weissberg, R. P., Caplan, M., & Sivo, P. J. (1989). A new conceptual framework for establishing school-based social competence promotion programs. In L. A. Bond & B. E. Compas (Eds.), *Primary prevention and promotion in the schools* (pp. 255–296). Newbury Park, CA: Sage.

Weisz, J., Donenberg, G., Han, S., & Weiss, B. (1995). Bridging the gap between lab and clinic in child and adolescent psychotherapy. *Journal of Consulting and Clinical Psychology, 63,* 688–701.

Weisz, J. R., Sandler, I. N., Durlak, J. A., & Anton, B. S. (2005). Promoting and protecting youth mental health through evidence-based prevention and treatment. *American Psychologist, 60,* 628–648.

Werner, E. E. (1995). Resilience in development. *Current Directions in Psychological Science, 4,* 81–85.

Werner, E. E., & Smith, E. S. (1982). *Vulnerable but invincible: A study of resilient children.* New York: McGraw-Hill.

Yates, M., & Youniss, J. (1966). Community service and political–moral identity in adolescents. *Journal of Research on Adolescence, 6,* 271–284.

Zimmerman, M. A., Bingenheimer, J. B., & Notaro, P. C. (2002). atural mentors and adolescent resiliency: A study with urban youth. *American Journal of Community Psychology, 30,* 221–243.

PART II

Institutional Influences

CHAPTER 6

Schooling Adolescents

RICHARD F. ELMORE

"I learned the truth at seventeen . . . "
—Janis Ian, "At Seventeen" (1975)

"Let us make ourselves clear as to what the first task of education is. The child must learn to control his instincts. It is impossible to give him liberty to carry out all his impulses without restriction. To do so would be a very instructive experiment for the child psychologist; but life would be impossible for the parents and the children themselves would suffer grave damage. . . . Accordingly, education must inhibit, forbid, suppress, and this has abundantly been seen to in all periods of history. But we have learnt from analysis that precisely this suppression of instincts involves the risk of neurotic illness. . . .Thus, education has to find its way between the Scylla of non-interference and the Charybdis of frustration."
—Sigmund Freud, *The Complete Introductory Lectures on Psychoanalysis* (1933/1966)

"The most effective rule is invisible and appears to be inevitable."
—Anne Norton, *95 Theses on Politics, Culture, and Method* (2004)

SCHOOL IN THE LIFE OF ADOLESCENTS

One hundred eighty days a year, 6 hours a day, over the course of 13 years, not counting homework, disciplinary detention, remediation, test preparation, and extracurricular activities—roughly *14,000 hours*—this is the claim that schools make on children in our society. About half of this claim occurs between the ages of 11 and 18, a period roughly defined as adolescence, give or take a year or two on either end. One would think that a society that requires its children to spend half their growing years in the confines of a single institution would have a clear developmental theory of what this claim on the lives of children is intended to accomplish. One would think so. But one would be wrong.

School as a social institution lives by its own logic, which only occasionally and often incidentally intersects with our most powerful ideas about the cognitive, social, emotional, and moral development of children and adolescents. In order to succeed in school, students (which is what we call young people when they are under the institutional control of the school) and their families must master the logic of the institution, apart from their own views about what is appropriate or meaningful in their own lives or the lives of their children. In the early years of school, the claims of the institution on the lives of children appear more benign, both because the stakes attached to doing well in school appear to be lower and because the espoused ideology of schooling in the primary

I would like to express my deepest appreciation to Nathan and Toby Elmore, and to Kirsten Olson, Lily, Sam, Cole, and Henry Lanier, who have taught me most of what I know about adolescence and schooling.

grades is more nurturing. Beginning in the middle grades, with the onset of adolescence, what the sociologist Mary Metz (1978) has called "real school" begins with a vengeance. This is the world of large backpacks full of heavy textbooks, of weekly planners with homework assignments penciled in, of complex class schedules and movement from one classroom to another, of more distant relationships with teachers, of serious and consequential tests and grades, of frontal teaching and note-taking. It is a world in which adults speak casually about not "babying" students anymore, as elementary schools are alleged to do, and of teaching students "personal responsibility" for the consequences of their actions and choices, which in school means being responsible for complying with adult expectations. It is a world in which adult approval in school begins to have serious, material consequences for students' later academic success. And, for most adolescents, it is a world in which school begins to define individual identity in ways that it has not before.

Students become known among adults and peers increasingly for what they have accomplished, and less for who they are, or, to put it more accurately, what they have accomplished increasingly *becomes* who they are. Schools begin to call attention with increasing explicitness to winners and losers in the world of academic work. Schools begin to monopolize extracurricular activities, especially in athletics and music, in ways that ration access to the scarce resource of adult attention, recognition, and status within the school and the community. Most students' first experience of unqualified, public failure—academic failure, failure to make the team, failure to make friendships with the most popular group of peers, and so on—occurs in the middle grades. Peer groups begin to differentiate according to complex status codes, in part driven by the codes of school, in part in reaction to them. The differences between the chosen and the unchosen become more evident in the daily life of schools.

In adolescence, then, the institutional code of schooling begins to dictate many consequences for the present and future lives of young people. (For a review of institutional theory applied to schools, see Bidwell & Yasumoto, 1999; Myer & Rowan, 1978; and Rowan, 1990.) The success of adolescents in school depends increasingly on students' capacity to decode and master the often inscrutable rules of the institution and to adjust their behavior, if not their attitudes and beliefs, to the institutional culture of schools. Success requires adolescents to learn how to gain the approval of adults in many situations that they may regard as pointless and arbitrary, and for which the institution itself often provides no explicit rationale other than its own order. Some adolescents make this transition more or less smoothly.

Many adolescents find this transition deeply problematic. Most adults, including virtually all those who work in schools, find the failure of adolescents to adapt to the institutional code of schooling to be highly problematic. Failure in school on any dimension—cognitive, social, or emotional—carries a heavy penumbra of moral shame in our society; it leaves emotional scars that persist into adulthood; it can cause perfectly functional adults to questions their own intelligence and competence in daily life. The labels that schools apply to people in adolescence often persist long into adulthood. Even success in school, while it carries many emotional and material rewards, often carries the cost of self-doubt, which happens when young people are rewarded for what they do, rather than who they are and how diligently they apply themselves (Dweck, 1999, 2006). Many thoughtful high school seniors leave school wondering why they succeeded while others, whom they regard as equally competent in the world, but less attuned to adult approval, are marked with various forms of failure. A primary social function of schools during the period of adolescence is to allocate status as if it were a scarce good. Scarcity *requires* that some young people succeed and others don't. Some students and their parents understand how the complex and inscrutable code of schooling works, while others do not. This is the central principle of status competition: some do, some don't; those who do succeed in the terms dictated by the institution; those who don't, don't.

It is now more or less conventional wisdom to speak of all stages of human development, from infancy through senility, as liminal. In our current understanding of human development, one does not develop *from* childhood *into* adolescence, and then *into* adulthood, at which point one stops developing and starts living. Now everything is liminal; everything is transitional; each stage of development has its own peculiar patterns and problems. But development never stops. The boundaries among stages are porous and ill defined; people progress and regress; social conditions change our understanding of what it means to be at one stage of development or another. In this context, the challenges of defining adolescence as a developmental stage in relation to the institution of schooling are significant. It seems advisable to avoid simple temporal definitions of adolescence—say, from the ages of 11 to 18—even though this is the primary way schools define adolescence for themselves. A more promising approach would be to define adolescence functionally as, say, the onset of puberty, accompanied by increasing social pressure over time for individuals to assume greater control over multiple dimensions of their lives, concluding with the transition into some form of adult autonomy. This definition sets only very broad temporal limits on adolescence and allows us to see institutions, like schools, not just as places where adolescents happen to be during a certain stage of development, but also in terms of their influence on the developmental course of adolescents, allowing for the possibility that schools themselves may shape the very meaning of the period we call adolescence.

If all developmental stages are liminal, adolescence is arguably the most liminal. Liminality

carries the central meaning of being in transition, of being neither here nor there; of ambiguity, openness, and indeterminacy in one's personal understanding of the world, and one's identity in that world; the possibility of living in more than one identity simultaneously, moving back and forth as circumstances dictate; the emerging idea of risk and uncertainty in the consequences of one's personal choices; and the deepening of the idea of human agency, or the capacity to act on the world as an individual and accept the consequences of one's actions. Adolescence is also about attachment and differentiation. It is about learning to form intimate and sustained attachments with peers and adults outside one's immediate family circle. It is about learning how one is different from one's parents and other adults who have been significant in one's childhood years. It is about searching for peer attachments that have meaning, but it is also about discovering how one is different from one's peers. It is about having views and opinions on matters that were previously considered someone else's province. And it is about a growing capacity to reflect on and begin to exercise influence over one's own developmental course.

In an ideal world, adolescence would be a period in which young people could move in and out of various activities and commitments, testing their interests and aptitudes against their understanding of the world outside their immediate family and peer group. It would be a period in which adults in various settings—schools, voluntary organizations, and performance venues—would coach young people in the development of their interests and competencies and provide them with the maximum range of opportunities to succeed, fail, and try again. It would be a forgiving period in which failure would be taken as a mark of the courage to take risks, rather than as a sign of moral inadequacy. It would be a period in which young people would be allowed the possibility of surprising themselves by their capacities to do things they thought they might not be able to do. It would be a period in which peers and adults would be tolerant of the possibility that identity—social, political, and sexual preferences, for example—would be a malleable quality that could be actively chosen and rejected, rather than a fixed attribute. In an ideal world, in other words, adolescence would be a period of nurtured growth on multiple dimensions in multiple domains, accompanied by the gradual transfer of agency over life's choices from adults to young people. Adolescence would be a period of possibility, choice, nurture, support and, ultimately, autonomy and responsibility.

It is hard to imagine a less promising place for this ideal world to occur than within the confines of the institution of schooling. This chapter is about how the institution called *school* constructs the developmental period called *adolescence*. It is about the relationship between individual young people and the adults they encounter in school. It is about how this relationship is determined by the structures, rules, norms, and policies that define what schooling is in the middle and upper grades. And it is about the consequences of schooling for the transition from adolescence to adulthood.

THE MIDDLE GRADES: WELCOME TO "REAL SCHOOL"

This section discusses the institutional realities of the middle grades, focusing on these grades as sorting institutions. The issued of quality and structure in the middle grades is reviewed, and the possibility of "reform" of middle grades schooling in the United States is considered. In addition, student performance and the ways in which the institutional structure and the culture of schooling relate to the process of adolescent development are discussed.

The Institutional Realities of the Middle Grades

If you spend a lot of time in schools, as I do, the middle grades—say, from about 5th to 9th grade, or from roughly 11 to 15 years of age— are an astonishing place. In the lower grades, one gets used to the idea of the self-contained classroom—a single teacher with more or less complete dominion over a single group of students for an entire day, teaching multiple subjects across more or less well-defined parts of the day. Children in the lower grades, with certain rare exceptions, seem to internalize adult authority in the classroom, whether they understand how to comply with it or not. Regardless of how engaging the teaching is, students seem to understand that they are rewarded for sitting still when they are supposed to and for at least appearing to be engaged in learning most of the time.

The astonishing thing about the middle grades is the extraordinary variety and heterogeneity of young people. Some students, typically boys, look like they could be two or more years younger than they are. Some, typically girls, look like they could be two or more years older than they are. Students in the same classroom could be at all stages of physical development from well into puberty to, apparently, not having yet entered it. In urban schools, many of the boys and girls look like adults, often because they are, in fact, older than their grade-level peers, as a consequence of their previous experience in school. Their adult-like appearance makes them physically problematic and threatening for adults in schools. It is common for middle-grades teachers to speak of feeling threatened by the sheer physical size of their students. If you observe classrooms, as I often do, you notice that students come to school with widely varying social skills and widely varying propensities to engage in the kind of behavior that adults associate with being a "good" student. Some students clearly understand how to get adult attention and approval, some seem indifferent and detached, some move in and out of engagement with adults in a more or less random way. Another common characteristic of middle-grades classrooms is a more or less constant struggle with the construction of adult authority. Students actively test the rules of decorum and classroom routines, often for no apparent reason other than to demonstrate that they can. Middle-grade classrooms—even "well-managed" ones—are much more likely to dissolve into chaos than elementary classrooms. The most common pattern of disruption is when one or two students more or less deliberately decide not cooperate in the current order of work and manage to disrupt the work of everyone else while the teacher tries to figure out what to do about it. Since order is the *sine qua non* of secondary school, such violations are considered to be among the most serious. Not surprisingly, middle-grade teachers and administrators typically cite "discipline" and "engagement" as their major problems, almost always before the quality of academic learning or teaching.

Middle-grade corridors are places where students find their place in an increasingly explicit, highly differentiated, and hierarchical social order. Groups form, and affiliation with peer groups is a major source of social identity. Identity is increasingly expressed in dress and physical appearance as young people begin to exercise increasing control over their own presence in the world. Peer attachments begin to substitute for adult approval as a source of positive reinforcement, with a concomitant attenuation of adult authority in classrooms and corridors. The typical adult response in the middle grades to the attenuation of adult authority is to rely increasingly on rules, sanctions, and enforcement, rather than persuasion, as a means of social control, which, of course, reinforces the sense of separation between peer culture and adult culture in schools.

The other astonishing thing about one's first impression of middle-grades schools is that they typically seem *very* large and *very* impersonal relative to the elementary schools from which their students come. It is not unusual for a student to move from an elementary school of 300–500 to a middle-grades school of 700–1,000 or more students. The national average school size increases from around 400 at the elementary level, to around 600 in the middle grades, to more than 750 in high schools. In all states, the school size increases by a ratio of about 1.2 to 1.5 as you move from one level to the next. Florida (1,069), California (904), Georgia (834), Maryland (785), and New York (770) have the highest middle-grades average enrollments (NCES, 2006). The experience of students in the middle grades is typically very different from their experience in elementary school. The buildings are complex. The hallways are labyrinthine. The presence of adult authority is apparent, in the form of disciplinary staff, security staff, and, in many settings, metal detectors and screening devices. Because middle-grades schools are so large, the impedimenta of discipline and security are very evident. Adults cruise the hallways with walkie-talkies blaring staticky messages. Students are routinely stopped and questioned by adults about what they are doing and why. Depending on the size of the school, there may be as few as one (never fewer) or as many as four or five adults whose sole responsibility is the maintenance of order and the administration of discipline in classrooms and corridors.

The middle grades are where students first begin to experience, in an explicit way, school as a formal hierarchy for allocating social status. Teachers typically specialize by content, so students move from teacher to teacher, and the currency of exchange between teachers and students revolves around the students' ability to convince the teacher that they have mastered a specific body of content. The ability of teachers to know the multiple aptitudes and competencies of their students is limited by this specialized structure and by teacher caseloads, which typically vary between 80 and 120 students. Even if teachers were motivated to know students across multiple dimensions, they would face serious organizational challenges doing so. With this type of organization comes increased routinization—students' learning and engagement in school is increasingly measured and described in terms of assignments completed, results on quizzes and tests, and teachers' judgments of classroom engagement and decorum.

In the middle grades, explicit distinctions in the assignment of students to different academic levels become more legitimate and visible. While it is now unfashionable to use the term *tracking* to describe these distinctions, they are nonetheless still common in virtually all middle grades schools. Students are assigned to different levels of curriculum—as few as two, as many as four or five—based on teachers' and administrators' assessment of students' "ability." The most explicit distinctions are made in mathematics, where teachers have very clear preconceptions about what constitutes ability and prior knowledge. Decisions about the placement of students as early as 5th grade can determine the level of mathematics they are allowed to take in high school. Distinctions are less explicit in language arts and social studies, but are still present in many schools (Loveless, 1999; Oakes, 2005). And in most middle-grades schools, there is some form of "gifted and talented" program, sometimes self-contained, where students identified as gifted and talented take the same courses together, or, more likely now, special supplementary periods where students are grouped into activities that are considered to be more academically challenging than are appropriate for their less talented peers. Likewise, differentiation on the lower end of academic performance becomes more structurally explicit in the middle grades. Students are more likely to be placed in separate settings with other students of similar status for special remedial attention for all or part of the day.

It is important to note that the increasing use of school structures to allocate status is taken for granted as a legitimate function of schools by adults, both inside and outside schools. It is not unusual for adults to contest the placement of their child in a *particular* class or track in a school, *if* the parents are knowledgeable enough about the organizational code of the school to even recognize that their child is being tracked. It is *very* unusual for adults to contest the *practice* of tracking, in general, in their children's schools. Adults, inside or outside of schools, generally take the assignment of status by schools as a legitimate function. Students quickly internalize the codes by which schools allocate status, even if they don't entirely understand why or how those codes are constructed or how they work. Differences among students in their academic standing in school quickly translate, both positively and negatively depending on peer culture, into status distinctions that are accepted and reified by students.

The Middle Grades as Sorting Institutions

By the time students enter the middle grades, their differences around academic learning are more apparent to adults and to each other. The structure of the middle grades amplifies preexisting differences among students. Relatively minor and apparently tractable differences in the early grades around students' mastery and fluency of academic learning become the basis for relatively major distinctions among students in the middle grades. Relatively major differences in learning in the early grades become even more major in the middle grades. Differences among students tend to be interpreted by adults, both educators and parents, as relatively fixed *attributes* of individual students, rather than as failures of previous instruction in school or as challenges to conventional ideas about children's aptitudes, learning patterns, and development. The language that adults use to describe the unique characteristics of particular children are heavily laden with attributions, often carrying heavy overtones of moral judgment—children are judged to be "smart," "average," or "slow," either overall or in particular areas; children are judged to be highly motivated or lazy; children are praised and rewarded for demonstrating that they have characteristics that adults approve of, rather than for being some authentic version of who they are; children are rewarded, often in very visible ways, in assemblies and in hallway displays, for being fluent and accurate in responding to adult expectations. Differences among students are interpreted as evidence of growing disparities in talent, rather than as occasions that challenge adult judgment and expertise. Adults in school are charged with making these distinctions, more clearly and explicitly in the middle grades than in the elementary grades, and they do so based on their *existing* ideas and knowledge about intelligence, learning, and competence, rather than interpreting differences among children as an occasion for questioning their own knowledge, competence, or judgment.

In the American system, these patterns in the construction of adult authority and in the assignment of status distinctions among students are present to varying degrees in all but a tiny fraction of middle-grades schools, but they are amplified several-fold in urban schools, where the populations are disproportionately poor, racial, ethnic, or linguistic minorities. In the "typical" urban middle-grades school (if there is such a thing), the number of home language groups might be as low as 2 or 3 (never lower) and as high as 10 or 12. Students' reading levels in these schools typically vary from a minimum of two grade levels below their current placement to two grade levels above. Students may come from intact families, they may come from single-parent families, they may be in the care of a family member other than a biological parent, or they may be in foster homes. Students may have spent their previous years in the United States, or they may be new entrants. Residential instability is a fact of life among the urban poor. Students may have been in a single elementary school prior to their entry, or they may have been in several. They may stay in their present school throughout their time in the middle grades, or they may change schools. Turnover rates of 30% or more among middle-grades students in urban schools are not unusual; students may have been in as many as four or five schools between the 5th and 9th grades (Heinlein & Shinn, 2000.)

The differences between urban middle-grades schools and their suburban and exurban counterparts are substantial. Middle-grades schools are typically large; urban schools tend to be even larger. Middle-grades schools include students across a wide range of developmental levels, cognitively, physically, emotionally, and socially, with concomitant differences in their willingness of adapt to the academic structure. In urban schools, because of their social context, the range of developmental levels is likely to be even larger. Middle-grades schools begin the explicit process of differentiating among students based on adults' assessments of the their academic and social competence; urban middle schools, because they deal with more diverse developmental levels, tend to create even more differentiation. Whatever the general patterns of institutional practice in middle-grades schools, they are more extreme in their urban counterparts.

Quality and Structure in the Middle Grades

In terms of conventional measures of school quality and performance, the middle grades in the United States are highly problematic. Middle-grades schools have the highest proportions of teachers teaching outside their certified areas of expertise—somewhere between a quarter and a third of teachers in the middle grades. Middle-grades teachers tend to be less experienced, are less likely to participate in professional development, and are more likely to manifest negative attitudes toward professional development than their elementary or high school peers. About one-third of middle-grades school administrators say they have significant difficulty recruiting and retaining teachers, about twice the proportion of elementary schools. Teachers in middle- and upper-level schools are less likely than elementary school teachers to say that they are included in important decisions about their work, that they receive adequate parental support, and that the expectations under which they work are clearly stated. Middle-grades teachers report lower

levels of satisfaction with the level of intellec-
tual challenge in their work than elementary
teachers. The proportion of teachers reporting
problems of serious physical conflict is higher
in the middle grades (11%) than either the elementary grades (7%) or upper grades (8%). In
general, middle-grades principals rate the seriousness of problems in their schools lower than
the teachers in their schools (NCES, 2000)

Thus far, I have spoken of middle-grades
schools as if they were a homogeneous institutional structure. In fact, there are at least
three distinct institutional structures in U.S.
middle-grades schools, with significant variations around these patterns. One is the kindergarten–8th-grade structure (K–8), another is
the middle school structure (6–8), and a third
is the junior high school structure (7–9). The
national *School and Staffing Survey* (SASS)
in 1993–1994 (1996) found that 60% of students were enrolled in schools with at least one
grade below the 5th, and no grade higher than
8th (which the survey defines as "elementary,"
but which includes K–8 schools), about 14%
were enrolled in schools with no grade lower
than 5th nor higher than 8th (which the survey
defines as "middle schools"), and about 21%
were enrolled in schools with no grade lower
than 7th nor higher than 9th (which the survey defines as "secondary schools," but which
corresponds to the conventional definition of
junior high school). The remaining number
of schools in the sample were either non-
graded or had grade configurations other than
those in the study framework (NCES, 2000).
More recent studies show that the middle
school configuration (6–8) has been growing
substantially in both number and proportion,
from about 1,600 schools in the 1970s to more
than 8,000 schools in 2000 (Banks, 2004).

Among middle-grades educators the middle
school structure offers the most explicit philo-
sophical orientation and network of professional affiliations in the field. The National
Middle School Association is a high-visibility
organization with its own journal and a significant national membership. The association

has been the center of discourse about the
purpose and practices of middle schools and
takes a detailed and relatively clear philo-
sophical stance. Among its core beliefs is that
teachers, while retaining their disciplinary subject matter orientation, should be organized
in cross-subject teams with responsibility for
smaller groups of students. Schools should
employ an "integrative curriculum" that connects academic subject matter around current,
engaging topics, flexible scheduling, assessment practices that support continuous learning for all students, intensive advisory and
counseling functions, and explicit strategies
for engaging parents and community members in the schools. A number of middle school
exponents also sponsor the idea of integrating
student learning into community service projects (Andrews, Caskey, & Anfara, 2007; Reed &
Rossi, 2007).

The "Reform" of Middle-Grades Schooling in the United States

The reform of middle-grades education in the
United States has been a subject of active advocacy and debate since the 1950s. The Carnegie
Council on Adolescent Development's landmark
reports, *Turning Points: Preparing American
Youth for the 21st Century* (1989) and *Turning
Points 2000: Educating Adolescents in the
21st Century* (2000), set a broad agenda for
strengthening the connection between young
people and schools, focusing on bringing
curriculum and teaching into alignment with
student interests and real-world problems;
improving the quality of the teaching force in
the middle grades through recruitment, professional development, and greater involvement
of staff in school decisions; and creating a school
environment that reinforces caring and support
for students.

The Center for the Study of the Social
Organization of Schools (CSOS) at Johns
Hopkins University has created a knowledge
base that diagnoses the sources of academic
success and failure in the middle grades and
proposes a model intervention, the Talent

Development Program, which addresses these issues in organization and practice. Their research suggests, not surprisingly, given the institutional structures and rules that govern middle-grades schools, that four factors reliably predict the likelihood of student success in the middle grades: poor attendance, poor marks for behavior in school, failing grades in English, or failing grades in mathematics. Talent Development is designed to improve the quality of instructional practice in core academic subjects and to assist teachers and administrators in expanding the repertoire of curriculum and teaching to promote the engagement of students. Well-implemented versions of Talent Development seem to have positive effects relative to control schools (MacIver et al., 2004).

Analyses of the relative effectiveness of different grade structures for middle-grades schools, while they are not extensive, generally conclude that K–8 structures are more conducive to student engagement and learning than are middle schools or junior highs. Offenberg found in a study of middle schools and K–8s in Philadelphia that well-established K–8s significantly outperformed middle schools, on average, and that newly established K–8s also outperformed middle schools, but not by as much (Offenberg, 2001). Evidence on the effects of middle schools is generally mixed, with considerable variation in performance across different sites, and different treatment-comparison effects across different academic content areas (e.g., Backes, Ralston, & Ingwalson, 1999; Byrnes & Ruby, n.d.).

If you visit K–8 schools, as I do on a regular basis, it becomes apparent why they might have some advantage over other grade configurations for student learning. The most obvious reason is that the structure, by itself, dictates that the size of the middle-grades population will virtually always be smaller than in other grade configurations. Sixth through 8th grades comprise less than a third of the total student population of the typical K–8 school. Another possibility is that the presence of younger children in the same physical

setting seems to have a definite effect on the climate of adult–student relations. Students see teachers routinely that they have had in earlier elementary grades. Teachers in the middle grades are routinely exposed in the corridors to younger students, and usually to the younger siblings of their own students. The climate of student–adult hostility that develops in many middle-grades schools is moderated, but not necessarily eliminated, by the presence of younger children. Notice that I haven't said anything about the advantages of cross-grade coherence in teaching practice and adult expectations in K–8 schools. My own experience working in these setting suggests that middle-grades teachers and students more often than not regard themselves as operating in a separate world from elementary teachers and students. In virtually all K–8 schools, the middle grades are structurally isolated from the elementary grades—often on the top floor of a multistory building, or in a separate wing of a single-level building—and the middle-grades teachers have virtually nothing to do with the elementary grades teachers in their daily practice. Instruction in the middle grades in K–8 schools often looks very much like instruction in single-purpose middle-grades schools. And one can see, as I have seen many, many times in K–8 schools, students being asked to do work in the middle grades that is lower level and more routine than the work they were asked to do in the same school a few years earlier in the elementary grades. This phenomenon could occur only in a situation in which the adults don't actually talk to each other about what students are capable of doing. So it is wise not to draw strong conclusions from structural factors. The K–8 structure may *enable* certain things to happen that might not otherwise happen in different structures, but whether those things do happen is a matter of institutional culture more than structure.

The general thrust of middle-grades reform proposals, since the 1950s, has been to try to break the institutional pattern of traditional schools by softening the boundaries between traditional academic content areas, by trying to create more flexible and responsive curricula and teaching strategies, by finding ways to strengthen adult–student interactions in schools, and by focusing increasing attention on the swift remediation of preexisting learning deficits in core academic areas like reading and mathematics. The effects of middle-grades reforms follow a more general pattern of reforms in American education: When the reforms are well- and deeply implemented— that is, when teachers and administrators internalize the ideas and practices of the reforms in the structure and operation of their organizations and in their own behavior—the results are often promising. Overall, though, reforms are never implemented consistently with this level of commitment and focus. So what typically results is a pattern in which the average or median effect of the reforms at a broad scale is zero or negligibly positive, while the variability in performance across schools that are nominally doing the same reforms is so large as to swamp any main effect (see Elmore 2005; Vernez et al. 2006). Reformers like to call attention to their greatest successes, not surprisingly, because they want practitioners to know what good practice can do when it is done well and consistently. Reformers almost never call attention to the wide range of variability in the effects of their ideas and their relatively negligible impact on overall practice and performance.

What this pattern of effects reveals is the strength and resilience of the default culture that is embedded in the existing institutional structure. What reformers fail to acknowledge is that the structures and practices they are trying to overthrow exist for a *reason*. They exist because they are highly functional in sustaining an existing equilibrium in the definition of roles and responsibilities in organizations, and in legitimating the institution itself. They exist because they reinforce dominant patterns in the allocation of privilege and status in the society at large. And, perhaps most importantly, they exist because they are largely, if

not totally, *invisible* to the people who work in the institutions in their daily lives. Middle-grades reforms, like most educational reforms, have modest-to-negligible effects because they attempt to disturb a deeply rooted institutional structure and code that promotes and supports a largely unequal social structure in the broader society. Students begin to be excluded from access to academic content that is associated with high achievement in the middle grades because middle-grades schools have taken on the primary functions of social control—managing the troublesome behavior of adolescents for the broader society—and, more importantly, allocating status through differential access to academic content. Most educators would deny that these are the primary functions of middle-grades education, but, unfortunately, the data on student learning in the middle years say otherwise.

Student Performance in the Middle Grades

On the National Assessment of Educational Progress (NAEP), the nationally constructed assessment of student performance, 4th-grade reading scores have improved steadily, but modestly, over the period 1992–2007, and the minority–White achievement gap in reading has narrowed modestly over that same period. There is a persistent and significant male–female gap in reading achievement, favoring girls, over this period. Still, two-thirds of 4th graders in the United States scored either below basic or basic on the reading measure, while about one-quarter scored at proficient and only 7% scored at the advanced level. For 8th graders, reading performance has been relative static over the 1992–2007 period, with roughly 70% scoring at the basic or below-basic level, a little over one-quarter scoring at the proficient level, and 2% scoring at the advanced level. The minority–White achievement gap is about the same as the gap in grade 4, but it has been more or less constant over the 1992–2007 period. The male–female gap is significantly larger in the 8th grade than in the 4th grade. In the NAEP framework, "basic" means essentially literal comprehension of text, "proficient" means literal comprehension plus the ability to draw simple inferences and connections to one's own experience, and "advanced" means all the previous abilities plus the ability to extract themes and draw evidence from text to support arguments. In brief, roughly two-thirds to three-quarters of American students are functioning at or below the lowest level of reading performance necessary to be functional in society, about a quarter are functional, and a relatively small proportion, from 2% to 7%, are operating fluently. The persistence of minority–White and male–female achievement gaps in reading suggests that little is happening between the 4th and 8th grades to address inequalities in access to text (NAEP, 2007a).

Interestingly, the evidence in NAEP math scores is somewhat different. There have been substantial increases in students' math performance over the period of 1992–2007 in both 4th and 8th grades. Minority–White math achievement differences have declined significantly, although the size of the current score gap mirrors the current gap in reading. The male–female gap in math started small and has remained so over the period of 1992–2007. Still, about two-thirds of both 4th graders and 8th graders score at the basic and below-basic levels, about one-quarter score at the proficient level, and between 5% and 7% score at the advanced level. Students who score at the basic level and below demonstrate basic understanding of the application of math algorithms appropriate to their grade level and a minimum competency in the handling calculators, rulers, and geometric shapes to solve math problems. Students who score at the proficient level can demonstrate accuracy and fluency in the application of math algorithms and are capable of accurate and complex explanations of their work and its results. Students who score at the advanced level demonstrate the ability to draw inferences from their mathematical work and to choose appropriate solutions to nonroutine

problems. In brief, while mathematics performance has improved at both the 4th- and 8th-grade levels, according to NAEP, the overall level of performance in math mirrors that in reading. Somewhere between two-thirds and three-quarters of 4th and 8th graders are functioning at or below the minimal level necessary to operate in society, and about a quarter are operating at or above, while less than 10% can demonstrate fluency (NAEP, 2007b).

These results mirror those of international assessments of student performance in reading and math. The Program for International Student Assessment (PISA) is based on a probability sample across the 42 member countries of the Organization for Economic Cooperation and Development (OECD) and selected other nonmember countries that have chosen to participate. The PISA assessment focuses on reading, mathematics, and science. It analyzes student performance across six levels, instead of NAEP's three, and it is considered to be a much higher level assessment at the high end than NAEP. In other words, while the kinds of skills that might qualify a student as "basic" in PISA might be similar to NAEP, the kinds of skills at the proficient and advanced levels of PISA allow for students to demonstrate much higher levels of understanding and fluency in the application of knowledge. The PISA assessment items also typically take their point of departure from practical, real-world problems and provide students with progressively more challenging levels of complexity. In general, American 15-year-olds score in the bottom quarter or third of students in the PISA sample, and the distinctive pattern of performance that occurs in NAEP is also present in PISA. That is, something like two-thirds of American students score in the lowest two levels of the PISA framework—factual recall and procedural accuracy—or below, a quarter to a third score around the middle levels of proficiency, and a minuscule proportion score at the highest levels. These patterns hold thus far for both reading and mathematics. The countries that score at higher levels in the PISA sample that the United States might compare itself to—Canada and Australia, for example—have very different distributions of performance on the PISA assessment, with relatively small proportions scoring at the below-basic and basic levels, relatively large proportions at proficient and above, and significant proportions in the advanced categories.

Inequality of student performance among 15-year-olds is relatively high in the United States, according to the PISA results, but not the highest among the countries in the PISA sample. The PISA analysis does suggest, however, that the socioeconomic and racial composition of schools in the United States has a significant impact on students' demonstrated performance (PISA, 2003).

The Third International Mathematics and Science Study (TIMSS), a precursor to PISA, took a detailed look at actual instructional practice inside schools in the participating countries. The TIMSS analysis of U.S. mathematics and science classrooms provides a revealing portrait of the patterns of instructional that produce the type of performance seen in NAEP and PISA. American mathematics classrooms focus primarily on procedural mastery of math facts and algorithms, rather than problem-solving and inferential activities. American teachers spend on the order of two to three times as much classroom time on review and reteaching as their counterparts in higher performing countries. Science classrooms tend to be somewhat more focused on higher level inferential tasks, but the level of review and reteaching is similar. Curriculum in U.S. schools, according to the TIMMS analysis, consists of textbook-driven problems that focus on routine mastery on computation skills. Review of homework consumes a significantly larger proportion of classroom time in American schools than in other, higher performing countries. And there is relatively little integration of content across grade levels, according to some overall conceptual design of what students ought to be able to do at a given level. In general, the pedagogical practice in

"higher level" math and science classes in the United States does not differ significantly from that in "lower level" classes, which would account for the relatively low level of performance of U.S. students—even those who have had high-level content—in higher level conceptual tasks on international assessments (Schmidt et al., 1999).

The TIMSS analysts have offered seven explanations for the relatively weak and variable performance of American students in math and science:

1. They argue that there are multiple visions of what good curriculum and teaching practice should look like, and these visions do not get resolved before they enter the classroom, resulting a lack of clarity and coherence in the enacted curriculum.

2. The official curriculum is "a mile wide and an inch deep." That is, the typical curriculum and textbook adoptions contain a multitude of topics presented in a disjointed and incoherent fashion.

3. The American curriculum is textbook driven, not knowledge and competency driven, and because textbooks must cater to the adoption standards of a handful of states—notably Texas and California, which have statewide textbook adoption policies and account for more than half the total textbook adoptions in the United State—they reflected a broad, inclusive, and watered-down view of content that works against focus and deep understanding.

4. Classroom instruction reflects the incoherence of the curriculum. Content coverage is stressed over depth of understanding, and routine knowledge suffices as a demonstration of academic learning.

5. Because there is little overall design or coherence to the enacted curriculum, teaching tends to be repetitive. American teachers spend more time in review and reteaching, and there is more repetition across basic content from one year to the next than in any other industrialized country in the world.

6. The incoherence of the curriculum—the number of topics covered, the lack of coherence and continuity across topics, and the level of review and reteaching—increases significantly in the middle grades, meaning that there a more topics competing for scarce time and less opportunity to assess what students actually understand.

7. American teachers, especially in the middle and upper grades, are more likely to attribute student learning and performance to the inherent characteristics of students—native ability, motivation, and so on—than they are to sustained practice and multiple opportunities to learn in different ways. Hence, teachers tend to take students' initial performance as the mark of their ability and to calibrate their teaching to that expectation, rather than to focus on devising multiple opportunities for students to master high-level content (Schmidt et al., 1999).

The Code

With this profile of the middle grades in U.S. schools, we begin to get a picture of the ways in which the institutional structure and culture of schooling—the code—relate to the process of adolescent development. The middle grades, for most young people, are the beginning of serious acculturation to school as an institutional structure for allocating status among students and their families. American schools construct status as a scarce good, allocated according to a code that is largely invisible to those who live and work in the institution. Distinctions among students in terms of their levels of academic performance and their capacity to secure adult approval become more explicit and consequential in the middle grades. Schools begin to monopolize more and more of students' lives, with an increase in the level of academic work in school, expectations for homework outside of school, and the general tendency of extracurricular opportunities to be determined by competition for available slots in school-sponsored activities. At the same time, the evidence on quality and performance suggests that school is not a particularly interesting, challenging, or stimulating place for adolescents to live their lives. Most of the work that students are asked to do, and most of the learning they demonstrate as a consequence of having done that work, is of a basic, routine nature. This narrowing of options for self-expression and identity development, the accompanying socialization to a status hierarchy based on a largely inscrutable code, and emphasis on low-level cognitive work as a demonstration of success sends a powerful message to adolescents: Learn to do what adults expect, no matter how engaging it is, no matter what its consequences for your personal identity, and you will do well in school.

Life is difficult in school for students who have not internalized this code. Adults are more sensitive to and less forgiving of behavioral infractions and more intimidated by the physical presence of adolescent students who seem not to have mastered the code. The relatively narrow, less forgiving code of academic performance in the middle grades doesn't match with the huge range of developmental stages present in the student population. The heavy emphasis on low-level work does not create a range of opportunities for students to pursue their interests beyond what is offered in textbooks and the enacted curriculum. One would predict, based on this scenario, that students who were least able to master the code would have the lowest attachment to school as an institution, and would be most at risk of exercising their default option of simply leaving the institution. This turns out to be the case for a very large number and proportion of adolescents, as we shall see. The question is not *whether* certain students will choose to give up on the institution of schooling as a place to grow and develop; rather, the question is *how many, of what type, and with what consequences for later life will do this?*

Middle-grades reformers, from the 1950s forward, have shared this diagnosis of the problems of the middle grades. But the reforms have had little overall impact on the life of adolescents in school. One possibility that reformers might consider is that the reason their best ideas haven't worked is that they share a misconception about the purpose of middle-grades education—that it is to provide a healthy developmental environment for young people—socially, emotionally, and cognitively. Actually, the primary purpose of middle-grades schooling—a purpose it accomplishes quite well—is to begin the complex institutional process of sorting students and allocating status—to prepare students for the next stage of schooling, which is organized around the attainment structure of high schools. Reforms of middle-grades schools are not likely to succeed until the purposes of schooling at that level are exposed to public scrutiny and a larger debate ensues around whether the institutional code by which schools operate is equal to the task of supporting and sustaining the development of adolescents.

ACCOUNTABILITY: A BRIEF DIGRESSION

The single most important change in the institutional environment of American schools in the past 20 years has been the emergence of performance-based accountability. Beginning in the early 1980s, states began taking a more aggressive role in attempting to regulate the quality and performance of schools. Led by an entrepreneurial group of governors, primarily from the South, including then-governor of Arkansas, Bill Clinton, and his future secretary of education, Richard Riley, from South Carolina, states began to introduce statewide performance tests, to tighten state curriculum standards, and to increase teacher qualifications. By the mid-1990s, all but a handful of states had instituted various forms of statewide testing and some form of reporting of school-level student results. Some states worked at the frontiers of assessment practice—Vermont, for example, introduced a statewide portfolio assessment system, in which each student's academic progress was assessed according to a diverse body of work by teachers operating as independent judges; Maryland introduced an ambitious new performance-based assessment that involved very ambitious open-response test items. Most states, however, worked closely with large commercial testing companies to adapt existing, largely multiple choice, assessments to their specific contexts.

The advent of the No Child Left Behind Act of 2001 (NCLB) essentially federalized what had been, up to that point, a primarily state-driven, but national, reform movement. The law mandated testing for every student in grades 3–8 in reading and math, with expansion into the upper grades and other subjects in the late 2000s. It set a nationwide definition of satisfactory student performance—adequate yearly progress (AYP)—that requires states to set a standard of proficiency against which all students would be assessed and to regulate school performance in such a way that all students will meet the proficiency target by the year 2013. States are allowed to set their own standards for what constitutes AYP in any given year, and their own targets for proficiency. NCLB sets in place very explicit requirements on reporting of performance: Students are grouped by categories (race, ethnicity, family income, special education status, etc.) and individual schools are required to meet not just overall performance targets for the whole school, but also specific targets for each student subpopulation. Schools that fail to meet performance targets are subject to a regime of increasingly stringent, federally mandated sanctions, including offering parents in failing schools the choice to move to other more successful schools and ultimately school closing and reconstitution.

The primary effect of NCLB has been to standardize what had been a relatively diverse—some would say unnecessarily so—collection of state accountability systems into a single, federalized system with significant leeway for states to set their own standards and decide on their own testing systems. Not surprisingly, the annual testing requirement substantially narrowed the type of assessments states use, pushing them away from innovative but more expensive to administer tests that could not be given to every student every year. The proficiency-by-2013 requirement, again, not surprisingly, introduced very strong incentives for states to play a variety of games with standard-setting, including making it easy to achieve AYP in the short run and pushing off major gains in performance to what seemed in 2001 like an indefinite future. Some states solved the problem of proficiency, as we shall see, by simply choosing a low standard.

The basic idea behind performance-based accountability is a plausible one in the current political culture that emphasizes economic productivity as a primary goal of schooling. Schools are public institutions, the argument goes, and they spend large amounts of public money. They should be accountable in some way for their performance, which should be measured against some agreed-upon set of metrics and goals, and the public and parents should have access to a regular supply of information on the performance and quality of the schools they are paying for. Furthermore, the argument goes, if education is to be a primary engine of economic growth, the level of knowledge and skills that students are expected to master should have something to do with the level that is required to be competitive in a global economy. Schools that fail to meet the public's performance expectations, the argument concludes, should either improve or make way for more successful schools to take their place.

The debate on the impact of NCLB is complex and, at this point, indeterminate—also, beyond the scope of this chapter. The evidence from the NAEP, discussed in the previous section (NAEP 2007a, 2007b), constitutes the only national assessment of changes in student learning over time. These data suggest that there have been no dramatic effects of NCLB on student performance—it is hard to discern a specific shift in student performance attributable to NCLB, post 2001, from the longer term secular trends that have occurred since

the early 1990s. The existence of NAEP data, however, has exposed a deeper, systemic problem with performance-based accountability systems. Overall performance on state tests, not surprisingly, has increased steadily since the advent of NCLB—not surprisingly, because states have very strong incentives under the law to promulgate standards and tests that demonstrate gains.

However, something like twice the proportion of state-tested students are judged "proficient" as are judged proficient on NAEP. Comparisons of performance on state tests with NAEP performance show that the gap between NAEP performance and state performance has increased over time, suggesting that the system of performance incentives put in place by NCLB is pushing states further away from, rather than closer to, national agreement on what constitutes student proficiency. Wide variability in the level and content of state curriculum standards means that some states with extremely low standards—Mississippi, for example—are showing higher proportions of student attaining proficiency than states with much higher standards—Massachusetts, for example.

In urban settings, there is crisis brewing around the AYP requirement. The number of schools moving *into* various stages of sanctions under AYP in most urban areas is considerably greater than the number of schools moving *out of* sanctions. What this means is that there is a growing backlog of schools that, under NCLB, require states and localities to provide specific, intensive remedial interventions. The interventions are obviously not working with the degree of success required to reduce the backlog, and the result is that districts are faced with increasing sanctions under the law and a limited capacity to deal with the consequences of those sanctions. States seem to be progressively distancing themselves from this problem by pushing more and more of the responsibility for remediation of failing schools down to the local level and assuming a monitoring posture toward local districts. The federal government has no apparent interest in or incentive to deal with the problem because federal policymakers benefit no matter what the result is. If an increasing number of urban schools are seen to be failing, federal policy makers can take credit for exposing the terrible state of urban education and taking a tough posture toward school performance. If urban schools are seen to be improving, federal policy makers can take credit for the improvement. Accountability, it seems, applies less to policy makers than it does to people who work in and attend schools.

For purposes of this analysis, the important fact about performance-based accountability is that, for the first time in the history of American education, there is an explicit, policy-driven incentive structure under which schools are expected to work. The political and cultural symbolism of this fact is incredibly important. Performance-based accountability, at least from the perspective of policy makers, is designed to shift the logic of confidence between schools and their publics from one of *implicit* agreement that schools are doing the right thing for children to one in which schools are expected to provide *explicit* evidence of their impact on student learning. This shift has had a significant impact on the way schools are organized and managed in many jurisdictions, especially urban schools. The most important effect of this shift in the logic of confidence is that it creates the broad-scale impression that the main purpose of schools is to produce *performance*, by whatever metric that is measured. Before the advent of performance-based accountability, schools exercised considerable latitude over their choice of goals—social adjustment, nurture and care, inculcation of religious and social values, preparation for citizenship, and the like were all equally plausible goals and ends for schooling in addition to students' measured cognitive performance. With the advent of performance-based accountability, public discourse has shifted toward measured performance as the primary goal of schooling and the proxy for other valuable things that children are supposed to know.

As with most social and political movements in the United States, performance-based accountability has been couched in anodyne rhetoric of social equity. Indeed, the phrase "No Child Left Behind" was appropriated (without permission) directly from the masthead of an organization, the Children's Defense Fund, founded by a person, Marion Wright Edelman, with a lifelong commitment to social equality for children of color and poor children. The phrase came to characterize, in the early stages of the law's history, a broad, bipartisan commitment to improved results for all children, but especially for children most at risk. The rhetoric of social equality still permeates the performance-based accountability movement.

HIGH SCHOOL: WELCOME TO THE ATTAINMENT STRUCTURE

This section reviews two competing accountability systems in high school—performance and attainment—and discusses meliorist versus institutionalist views of the problem of dropping out. Issues pertinent to the quality of academic work in high schools are considered, the ideas about high schools as settings for the private practice of teaching are forwarded. The section includes also a discussion of the "transition" from high school to college.

Two Competing Accountability Systems: Performance and Attainment

The institutional realities of the education sector, however, paint a different picture of how accountability works, especially in high schools. The political rhetoric of performance-based accountability suggests that NCLB and its state-level progeny are, in fact, *the* accountability system for education in the United States. In fact, schools, especially secondary schools, and especially high schools, do *not* operate in a single accountability system. They operate in *multiple* accountability systems in different social settings, for different groups of students, addressed to different purposes of schooling. Because high school is where the

American education system reaches it highest level of differentiation, this is where the difference among these accountability systems become more visible, more problematic, and much more consequential for adolescents. Advocates of performance-based accountability systems have an interest in promoting the belief that *all* schools are judged by a common (read equal) metric of performance, and that holding all schools to the same regime of performance means that all students will have an equal opportunity to achieve. In fact, only schools with high proportions of minority, poor, and language minority students are *actually* subject to the most rigorous version of performance-based accountability. Middle- and upper-middle-class schools treat performance-based accountability as a more or less prophylactic measure. These schools have to make sure that they do not embarrass themselves or their publics with low test scores, but the *real* accountability system within which they work is a quite different one from the one that more diverse schools work in. Their accountability system focuses only incidentally on *performance*, as measured by the official accountability system, but much more intensively on *attainment*, which is the coin of the realm in their communities and in the American economy at large.

Residential property values and academic reputations in middle- and upper-middle-class high schools are not driven primarily by their scores on state-mandated tests; they are driven by college enrollment rates and, more importantly, by *which* colleges and universities their graduates attend. Since social class strongly predicts performance on standardized tests, and secondary schools are heavily segregated by social class, which is in turn driven by residential patterns, higher socioeconomic schools have the advantage of being able to *choose* which accountability system they wish to operate in. They can, on alternate weeks or days, take credit for their test scores on the state accountability assessment (which is largely determined not by teaching, but by social class)

and then shift the discourse to what their clients think is really important, which is attainment. Schools in lower socioeconomic areas have no such choice. They have to focus first on performance accountability, and, if they understand that there is such a thing—which many don't—they *then* can focus on attainment.

This distinction between *performance* and *attainment* is central to understanding the institutional logic of the American high school, and, hence, the institutional world in which American adolescents and their families have to operate. Performance, as noted above, has to do with actual measured mastery within a specific cognitive domain—reading, mathematics, science, and so on. Attainment has a broader, more complex meaning that includes measured performance but also takes note of the mastery of complex institutional codes and structures. Attainment is best defined as the ability to achieve status within an established social hierarchy according to the codes and structures of that system. Attainment in high school, for example, includes not just performance on tests of cognitive mastery, it also includes a myriad of other markers that gain a student status within the institution called high school—for example, the courses a student has taken within a structure that has a clearly defined hierarchy of status and the grades achieved in those courses; the external validation that students acquire by taking optional tests, like advanced placement examinations in specific content areas or specific subject matter assessments in the Scholastic Achievement Test (the so-called SAT-2); access to specialized tutoring to remediate low test score performance or low performance in courses; community volunteer activities that students undertake to demonstrate "breadth" in their interests; travel and cultural experiences that demonstrate "breadth" of exposure to people and places outside their home communities; extracurricular achievements in athletics, music, drama, and demonstrations of extra performance in, say, science and mathematics; and, perhaps most importantly, relationships with adults other than family members that students can rely on as references for future academic pursuits. Successful high school students and their families understand, however implicitly, that (1) there *is* an attainment structure that determines the student's position in a competitive status hierarchy, and (2) operating successfully in that attainment structure requires the mastery of a complex, ever-changing set of institutional rules and structures that are designed to ration access to the scarce benefits that accrue to attainment.

It turns out, as we shall see, that attainment is a much more powerful predictor of future economic and social well-being than is performance, and that, while performance is, as we have seen above, still heavily influenced by race, ethnicity, and social class, attainment is even more heavily influenced by these factors. For middle-class and upper-middle-class students and their families, whether they understand it explicitly or not, attainment is the *real* accountability system for high schools in America, *not* performance. Urban high schools may labor under the misconception that if they get their students' test scores up on federally mandated, state-administered tests, then good things will happen to their students in their future lives. In the current institutional structure, this is a sucker's bet. Attention to performance, without equal or greater attention to attainment, will not lead to better results for low-income, minority students.

Two important factors are central to understanding the way attainment operates in American high schools. The first is the idea of *status competition*, introduced earlier in the analysis of middle-grades schools. The basic idea here is that status is a scarce resource that has to be allocated differentially, based on criteria that are socially defensible. We begin the process of differentially allocating status in the middle grades by the ways in which we group students and the ways in which we define what "success" in schools means for official purposes. In the middle grades, the criteria for differential allocation of status are strategically vague,

and, as we have seen, they are often based on nativist ideas about inherent attributes like "giftedness," "intelligence," "cooperation," and "adaptability." In high schools, the institutional code becomes much more explicit, the differentiation process becomes much more systematic, and the dominant criteria for status competition become very powerful, if not always very explicitly defined or widely understood.

The main criterion is, and has been since the end of World War II in the United States, something called *merit*. The essential idea behind merit is the notion that status is *earned*, by virtue of objective criteria, such as academic performance, rather than *granted* by virtue of privileges, like social class. It is closely connected to the fundamental American cultural belief that *anyone* who applies him-or herself and behaves consistently with society's expectations not only *can*, but *will* succeed, because the American social system rewards application, effort, persistence, and talent over wealth and inherited privilege. As Nicholas Lemann has demonstrated in his history of meritocracy and the testing industry in the United States, the growth of the idea of merit was coterminous with the growth of the field of psychometrics, and the belief of Americans that talent could be objectively measured and rewarded. In Lemann's account, the leaders of the testing movement in the transition from secondary school to college viewed themselves as ambitious social reformers, engaged in a broad social agenda of freeing access to college and university education from outmoded principles of inherited privilege and replacing it with principles based on the inherent talent of the individual (Lemann, 1999). It was out of this movement that our present system of precollegiate testing, notably the Scholastic Achievement Test, arose. This idea of merit has wide social currency, and it exercises a powerful grip on the way Americans, especially American high school educators and the parents of high-attainment students, think about the purposes of schooling (Baez, 2006).

The second idea that is central to understanding the attainment structure is the idea of *social capital*. Social capital is both an individual and a collective phenomenon. At the individual level, it comprises the personal influence and control one exercises over one's life by virtue of one's associations with others in the workplace, the community, and the professional world. At the collective level, it comprises the social networks that form around individuals and institutions to provide the benefits of collective, as opposed to purely individual, actions. Attainment depends on the accumulation and use of social capital. It depends on knowledge, often implicit, about the rules and structures that determine success— knowledge that can be acquired *only* by actively engaging the institutions that embody attainment. And it depends on the predisposition to *exercise agency and control* over one's actions in a complex social environment. Much has been written about the alleged decline of social capital in American society—the so-called bowling alone problem, or the atrophy of voluntary associations that are supposed to provide the social connective tissue for more formal social and political affiliations. Whatever the status of social capital in society at large, it is alive and well in the attainment structure. Moving a student successfully through the status hierarchy of the American high school requires an increasingly formidable knowledge and command of social networks and their value.

The first thing to note about attainment is that it carries a heavy economic premium when it works and a heavy individual and social cost when it doesn't. The most recent data suggest that high school dropouts have an average annual income of about $17,000, those with a high school diploma have an income of only about $27,000, those with an associate's degree or equivalent have an income of about $37,000 and those with a bachelor's degree

have an income of about $53,000. Another way of measuring the benefits of attainment is the proportional earnings differentials among people with different levels of education. In 2002, male college graduates earned 75% more than high school graduates, and those with more than 4 years of higher education earned 99.6% more. Females earned 64% more with 4 years of college and 73% more with more than 4 years (Alliance for Excellent Education, 2007; Murnane & Levy, 1999; U.S. Bureau of the Census, 2006;). Failures in the attainment structure carry a correspondingly heavy social cost. One estimate is that each high school dropout costs society in social benefits about $260,000, which aggregates at the current high school dropout rate to about $12 trillion over the next decade (Rouse, 2005)

One would assume, given the high stakes attached to attainment, that secondary schools would focus a great deal of energy on keeping students in school and creating conditions that allow them to succeed, until they had at least successfully graduated from high school. The evidence suggests otherwise.

According to the U.S. Department of Education, among the states reporting dropout data (13 of 50 states were either disqualified for providing inadequate data or were unable to provide it at all), the annual number of officially defined dropouts[1] nationally rises from about 16,000 in the 7th grade, to 25,000 in the 8th, to 125,000 in the 9th, to 139,000 in the 10th, back to 125,000 in the 11th, to 150,000 in the 12th, on an enrollment base of between 3 and 4 million students per year. The data from specific urban areas, which we will review in a moment, suggests that these figures may considerably underestimate the scale of the problem. The raw data also tell an interesting story about progression in school. Enrollment figures nationally are around 3 million students per grade in the 7th and 8th grades. They

---

[1]The official definition of what constitutes a dropout is a student who was present in the preceding school, absent in the current year, has not officially graduated or transferred to another school (NCES, 2007, p. 2).

balloon to over 4 million in the 9th grade, and then settle back to 3.6 million in the 10th grade, dropping to 3.3 million in the 11th, and about 3 million in the 12th. Anyone familiar with the institutional structure of secondary schools, and with current accountability policy, would immediately be able to explain the enrollment bulge in 9th grade. In most states, the 10th grade is the primary high school testing grade, in which students are given the test that most often is used to determine whether they will graduate from high school and to identify schools for sanctions under NCLB. In this incentive structure, there are very strong incentives for schools and school systems to hold back students in the 9th grade whom they think will fail the state accountability test in the 10th grade, producing ballooning enrollments in the 9th grade that gradually show up as increased dropouts in the 10th–12th grades (NCES, 2007, Table B1, p. B10)

Another measure of attainment is the "promoting power" of high schools, defined as the ratio of entering students in the 9th or 10th grades who are present in their senior year 3 or 4 years later. About 2,000 high schools in the United States (from a base of about 10,000), enrolling about 2.6 million students, have at least 60% fewer seniors than they have entering students in the same age cohort. The number of schools with the lowest promoting power has increased somewhere between 60% and 75% in the past 15 years, while the number of high schools in general has increased about 8%. Schools with low promoting power (losing 60% or more of a cohort) enroll a majority of the total school population of minority, low-income students. Among high schools with 90% or more White student populations, about 1% fall into the category of lowest promoting power. Nearly half of the country's African American students, about 40% of its Latino students, and only 11% of White students attend high schools with the lowest promoting power. Among high schools that enroll 90% or more minority students, two-thirds fall into the category of lowest promoting power.

Interestingly, only about 13% of all high schools have promoting power greater than 90%; the modal number for all high schools is about 80%, which suggests that, under the best of circumstances, about 20% of students who enter high school overall do not show up on time as seniors. Ten cities— including New York, Los Angeles, Chicago, Houston, Cleveland, and Philadelphia—contain 29% of the high schools with the lowest promoting power. In New York alone, 81% of the high schools have less than 60% of their entering students present in their senior year. While the majority of schools with low promoting power are predictably located in urban areas with the highest concentrations of low-income, minority students, it is worth noting that 20% of high schools with the lowest promoting power are located in the suburbs and 13% in rural areas (Balfanz & Legters, 2004).

Most studies that attempt to quantify the dropout problem suffer from the fact that schools, school systems, and states are not required to keep uniform and consistent records on student progression in school. Hence, dropout studies are always qualified with caveats about the fallibility of measures and the limits of existing databases. Any time a study attempts to report dropout data for a particular level of schooling or a particular jurisdiction, someone with official responsibility in that jurisdiction responds by saying that the data don't represent the "real" conditions on the ground—which are always alleged to be better, never worse, than the data suggest. Virtually all school systems keep detailed student records of grades, standardized test scores, attendance, school location, and disciplinary status, organized according to a unique student identification number. For at least the past 10 years or so, these records have been computerized in most districts. Yet virtually all the research on dropouts is conducted using purpose-built data sets, because most school systems claim that they cannot produce routine administrative data that accurately measure their dropout rates. The best analogy to the state of drop-out measurement in the U.S. education sector would be a health care system that is unable to keep consistent records on morbidity and mortality, and in which you couldn't get a straight answer to the lowest level health status questions about, for example, how many people died in a given hospital in a given year. Another analogy might be when the Bureau of Labor Statistics reports the monthly unemployment rate, the official in charge would say, "It seems like there are a lot of unemployed people, but we don't really know how many, or whether it's a large or small proportion of the labor force." Educators offer elaborate and largely unconvincing arguments for why it is so difficult to track the progress of students through their systems, but when they are required to report enrollment data on a particular date in order to receive funding under state school finance systems, they somehow always manage to say precisely how many students are enrolled. This gnashing of teeth around the measurement of dropouts has been going on for at least 30 years, and education professionals, and the systems they run, have yet to take responsibility for measuring and reporting the most basic facts about progression in school in a common metric that can be used across jurisdictions. One begins to understand that the explanation for this failure might have less to do with the technical difficulties of measuring dropouts than with the institutional codes and processes of the system—it is easier to explain away that which isn't measured. We measure what we care about.

More fine-grained studies of progression and attainment provide a detailed picture of what it means to be at risk of failure in secondary school. Melissa Roderick and Eric Camburn (1999) focused on risk factors in the transition from elementary school to high school in Chicago, finding that failure in core academic courses in students' early secondary school experience varied by gender (boys were more likely than girls to experience initial failure), by race and ethnicity (Latinos were more likely to experience failure, even controlling for prior academic achievement, than African American students), and, somewhat surprisingly to those who believe that being in school is a good thing, school attendance had a weak effect on the likelihood of failure. The average 9th-grade student in Chicago had a 24% likelihood of failing 50% or more of core academic subjects in the first semester. Being a year over age on entry to the 9th grade carried a 26% likelihood of failing 50% or more core subjects. Being 2 years below grade level carried a 28% probability of failure. They found that the likelihood of failure varied significantly by school, controlling for student characteristics, and that school effects on academic failure were significantly greater for Latino students than for African American students. And they also found that the effects of academic failure are cumulative—failing a core academic subject in the first semester significantly increases the likelihood not just of failing another course in subsequent semesters, but of failing *more* courses subsequently. Failing one core course in the first semester of 9th grade means that you have about a 37% likelihood of failing at least one course in the second semester, but failing 50%–75% of first-semester courses increases the likelihood that you will fail 50% or more courses in the second semester to 70%. Academic failure is cumulative and costly (Roderick & Camburn, 1999, Tables 5 and 8, pp. 323, 331). The data also suggest, most importantly, that initial failure does not trigger any particularly effective remedial process inside schools that is designed to reduce the likelihood of future failure. In fact, it suggests that initial failure creates a self-fulfilling process inside the school that *increases* the likelihood of future failure. This is the sort of effect one would expect in an attainment structure organized around the principle that some students must fail in order for other students to succeed. One thing secondary schools are good at, it appears, is producing failure.

These results have been corroborated by later work in Philadelphia. The annual dropout rate in the 2003–2004 school year in Philadelphia secondary schools was about 10%—about 6% could be determined to have left school, and the other 4% were officially enrolled in school but did not attend more than half the time (called "near dropouts" in the study). This amounts to about 13,000 students. Two-thirds of the dropouts were in 10th grade or lower, and one-third were in 9th grade or lower. One-third of the dropout population was in the 11th and 12th grades. About 20% of Latino students, 18% of African American students, 15% of White students, and 12% of Asian students in Philadelphia secondary schools were dropouts in the 2003–2004 school year. In six cohorts of students moving through Philadelphia secondary schools in the 2000–2005 school years, no racial or ethnic group had an on-time graduation rate of more that 71%. Using a school-completion target of 6 years, in the 2000 through 2003 cohorts, about 40% of Latino students successfully competed high school in 6 years or less, about 50% of African American and White males finished, and about two-thirds of Asian males finished. Females did slightly better: Slightly more that half of Latino females finished in six years, about two-thirds of African American and white females, and about three-quarters of Asian females. As in the Chicago study, failure in core academic subjects predicts and compounds the likelihood of failure in later subjects and dropping out. Among 8th graders who failed either math or English or both, 77% subsequently dropped out. Students who were *not* judged by their academic performance or attendance to be at risk of dropping out in the 8th grade could become at risk of dropping out in the 9th grade. Those students who were successful in the 8th grade but had just one of three risk factors in the 9th grade (attendance of less than 70%, deficiencies in academic credit, or failure to be promoted to the 10th grade) had a 75% likelihood of dropping out in subsequent years. The Philadelphia study concluded that about 80% of students who later dropped out could be identified as early as 8th or 9th grade using a small number of risk factors focused on attendance and academic progress. Given the powerful incentives operating on schools to hold students out of the 10th grade testing population for accountability purposes, by not promoting them from the 9th grade, one can see how the institutional code works dramatically against success in school for urban students.

Meliorist Versus Institutionalist Views of the Problem

The evidence on attainment of at-risk adolescents paints a grim picture of the conflict between the institutional incentives that drive behavior in public schools and the healthy development of young people in secondary schools. Overall, it is fairly clear that secondary schools simply don't know what to do with a substantial proportion of the urban adolescent population. The scope of this problem is not just serious—it's epidemic. It is symptomatic of a major institutional failure. The evidence also makes it clear that a very large proportion of the adolescent population—urban and nonurban—are very weakly attached to the institution called school, despite the fact that persistence in school carries substantial economic and social rewards. Most educators read the data on attainment and dropping out, if they know about it at all, as evidence that there is a knowledge gap and practice gap in secondary schools around how to remediate academic failure. This is what one might call a meliorist view: We all have good intentions, we're all trying as hard as we can, we just need to do better and get smarter and things will get better. This meliorist impulse is at the basis of most, if not all, current reform proposals for the middle and upper grades: We need to humanize secondary schools, make them more accessible and congenial to students of all types, especially at-risk students, by making them smaller, more congenial, more academically challenging places for adolescents to be.

There is an alternative to the meliorist position that rarely gets discussed among education reformers. That alternative view is that secondary schools operate the way they do because they are designed to operate that way, and they represent a deeply rooted institutional culture that is isomorphic with a broader social structure, organized around race and class, that is much more powerful and enduring than any idea a school reformer might have, no matter how well intentioned or well designed. When you put the evidence on attainment and dropping out with the earlier evidence on students' cognitive performance and the actual content of teaching and learning in the secondary grades, it is possible to conclude that adolescents' weak attachment to school probably is an entirely rational act. If you are a middle- or upper-middle-class teenager with a mental model of how the attainment structure works, and a well-organized network of social capital to protect you against obvious academic failure, you might be willing to endure the low-level instruction and behavior control in most secondary schools because you enjoy school as a social setting, because your extracurricular life is organized around school, and because you are surrounded by adults who give you constant reinforcement and tell you that there are very strong economic and social payoffs at the end of what might seem to be a largely boring, pointless, and inscrutable enterprise.

If you are a low-income, minority student with very limited social capital in the traditional sense, and you are surrounded by a more or less steady barrage of adult disapproval in the form of bad grades, low test scores, and disciplinary action, coupled with a setting in which it is obvious to you on a daily basis that the adults don't know what to do when you are struggling academically, it takes a fairly heroic act of faith to believe that there are going to be big payoffs, of whatever sort, for *you personally* in persisting in an environment where the academic tasks are low level and unengaging. You might decide, on an entirely rational basis,

that, since the system seems to be stacked against you anyway, you might as well choose to organize your life around things other than school. At least in that environment you might exercise some agency or control over your own life. It is common for adults who work in secondary schools to remark on how present-oriented adolescents are and how, particularly among at-risk students, it is very difficult to convince them to invest effort in the short term for the longer term payoffs of staying in school. It is just possible that the kids know the institution better than the adults do.

The Quality of Academic Work in High Schools

But surely high schools must work well for some adolescents. And they do, but not always in the ways that their supporters think they do. Secondary schools are, if nothing else, very good at adapting in symbolic ways to the ambient signals they get from their social and political environments, without at the same time actually changing their fundamental practices. The most provocative recent evidence of this is the National Center on Education Statistics' High School Transcript Study (2007b), which examined a nationally representative sample of 26,000 transcripts (from the roughly 2.5 million) 2005 high school graduates, including 17,400 students who took the 12th grade NAEP math and science assessment.[2]

In general, it is clear that high schools are reading the signals that attainment—defined as higher level course taking in core academic subjects coupled with good grades—is the primary business of high schools. Substantially more students are taking more academic subjects at higher levels than 15 years earlier. The average high school student is taking the equivalent of about three additional Carnegie Units more, which is the equivalent of an

---

[2]It is important to note, as does NCES, that high school dropouts were *not*, by definition, included in the transcript study, so none of the evidence on course taking, grades, or performance that follow can be generalized to that population from this study.

additional 360 hours more of core academic work (the average high school graduate takes about 33 Carnegie Units, which is the equivalent of about 1,000 hours of instructional time per year). Grade point averages (GPAs) are up by nearly one-third overall over 1990. The proportion of minority students completing at least mid-level high school courses has increased and the course-taking gap between White and minority students has narrowed, although minority students are still substantially less likely to take the highest level courses than Whites. More females than males are taking higher level or mid-level courses, but there is no difference between the number of males and females taking mid-level and below courses. As we previously saw in the Chicago and Philadelphia studies, how well you do in the 8th and 9th grades largely determines what courses you will take and how well you will do in them in later grades. Failing to take algebra by the 9th grade effectively precludes higher level math courses in subsequent years that will make you competitive for college admission. In general, it is clear that high schools are responding to the message that attainment is important and that there is modest impact of this movement on equity between minority and White students (NCES, 2007b).

Virtually all the growth in academic course taking has occurred in "standard" (lowest level) or mid-level courses. The proportion of students completing the highest level courses has stayed constant at about 10% since 1998, up from 5% in 1990. Among those who say they do not plan to go on to college, more than three-quarters take a less-than-standard or standard curriculum. Among those who say they do expect to go to college, about 40% are taking a standard or less-than-standard curriculum, 47% are taking a mid-level curriculum, and the remaining 12%-plus are taking the highest level curriculum. The standard curriculum includes at least 13 units of English, social studies, math, and science, but it does *not* include geometry or algebra I and II, which are considered entry-level math requirements

for even modestly selective colleges. The mid-level curriculum includes 14 units of English, social studies, mathematics, science, and foreign language, including geometry, algebra, and at least two science courses. This would be a threshold-level transcript for a modestly competitive college. The rigorous curriculum includes 17 units, including one more unit of math than the mid-level curriculum (precalculus or above), three science courses, and three foreign language courses. This curriculum would be competitive at a relatively selective college. Thus, in essence, what the transcript study says is that, while academic course taking has indeed increased, the movement has largely been out of the below-standard into the standard, and very marginally out of the standard into the mid-level curriculum, which actually makes fairly modest cognitive demands on students. After 1998 there were no gains in the proportion of students taking the highest level curriculum (NCES, 2007b, Figure 6, p. 9). So, while academic course taking and grades have increased significantly, the *level* of academic work that high school students are doing is generally very low. The institutional adaptation of high schools to external pressure has been to enroll more students in courses with academic titles, and give them higher grades, but to keep the level of academic work low. This result would be consistent with the NAEP, PISA, and TIMSS data showing low-level instructional practice and relatively low performance of American secondary school students.

Even more telling than the course-taking data is the evidence on the relationship between NAEP scores and course taking. Students taking the rigorous curriculum had significantly higher scores on the NAEP math and science assessment than students in the other curricula, but the average score for students in the rigorous curriculum was at the bottom of the "proficient" range, just above "basic." Those taking the mid-level curriculum scored at the bottom of the "basic" range, and those taking the standard and below-standard curricula, scored well below basic (NCES, 2007b, Figures 12 and 13, p. 16). In general, the transcript study concluded that, while there were significant gains in academic course taking, GPAs, and minority student access to higher level courses, there was no evidence of increased student performance in math and science. The report suggests, gently and diplomatically, in an afterthought, that this result might have to do with lack of student motivation to do well on the assessment, the fact that the test has low stakes, and the fact that high school seniors have taken a number of higher-stakes tests before they take the NAEP. The authors also suggest that the result might have something to do with the level of content and instruction in the courses. They conclude that "more in-depth analyses of these data are needed" (NCES, 2007b, p. 34).

The most interesting feature of the performance data, however, is that, in terms of the distribution of student performance across levels of cognitive demand, and the distribution of student access to academic content, the results are completely congruent with the international data from TIMSS and PISA discussed earlier. The general pattern of American student performance in those studies was that our highest performing students score below the most challenging levels and the vast majority of students score at the basic and below-basic levels.

Results like those of the transcript study suggest that increases in nominal attainment measures, like course taking and GPAs, may be mostly about institutional signaling between high schools, their authorizing agencies, and their more alert clients, not much about actual student engagement in serious, interesting, and meaningful academic work, and not much at all about the learning that results from it. The distribution of student course taking revealed by the transcript study suggests that American students aren't exactly stretching the limits of their cognitive capacities in their course taking. About half of the 2005 graduates were taking either the standard, or below-standard, high school curriculum, which, on its face, would not prepare them to do the sort of work

required to perform at higher levels on the NAEP or the international assessments, much less to do well in highly challenging postsecondary institutions (NCES, 2007b, Figure 16, p. 21). But while the content that the typical high school student is exposed to in the United States is mediocre or below, it seems to work in signaling seriousness and rigor to the schools' external clientele.

High Schools as Settings for the Private Practice of Teaching

The social structure of secondary schools in the United States, and of high schools in particular, explains a great deal about why they operate as they do and what the prospects might be for getting them to operate differently. American secondary schools are distinctive among industrialized countries in their degree of internal atomization around instructional practice and student learning. Empirical studies of high schools find consistently that instructional decisions about what gets taught to whom are made largely at the classroom and departmental levels, and that school-level organizational factors have little or no influence on the content and pedagogy in the classroom (Bidwell & Yasumoto, 1999; Siskin, 1994). These studies also demonstrate that departments have widely different cultures around student learning, manifested in their course structures, tracking practices, curriculum choices, teaching practices and assumptions about student learning. These content- and departmentally based differences are reinforced by external institutional arrangements—curriculum standards, professional networks, textbook adoptions, and the like—that reinforce the internal cultures of departments. Not surprisingly, then, among industrialized countries, the United States has the highest proportion of variance in student learning explained by factors at the classroom level.

In essence, this means that teaching practice and student learning varies more among classrooms than it does among schools, and that the size of this variance is much larger in the United States than in other industrialized countries (Schmidt et al., pp. 163–183). The implications of this research for our purposes are twofold: First, since the standards, expectations, and practices that attach to academic work in secondary schools vary considerably from teacher to teacher and from department to department, cracking the attainment code for any student in any given school is a complicated undertaking requiring considerable sophistication in reading and interpreting different, often conflicting, signals from adults about what constitutes acceptable work and behavior. This kind of complexity, of course, rewards high social capital.

The American high school works better organizationally for those who understand its peculiar internal structure and culture, and for those who have the resources—access to private tutoring, adult guidance, and peer networks—that make the institutional code understandable and negotiable. Attainment and course-taking data suggest that a large proportion of high school students find this code inscrutable, impenetrable, or simply not worth learning. Since the main effect of atomization in secondary schools is to separate adults from one another, and since young people are relatively accomplished at constructing multiple peer cultures within schools, it is usually the case that students who are willing to invest the effort know considerably more about how high schools actually operate, at the classroom level, and across classrooms within schools, than the adults do. Students directly experience the high degree of variability in instructional practice and expectations in their daily lives. If they are skilled at reading the organizational code, they adjust successfully to the highly variable practices and expectations of adults and learn how to provide adults with the reinforcement they require to treat students positively. Adults, however, typically experience only what goes on in their own classrooms.

The second implication of this atomization of secondary schools is that one cannot depend on schools to operate as *organizations* when they are given a collective task like, for example, changing the way they treat adolescents. High schools are not organizations in the usual sense of the term—that is, collectivities that are capable of making decisions that are binding on their members, and capable of producing collective results. High schools are more accurately characterized as collections of individuals, organized into subject-matter specialties, who engage largely in the private practice of teaching with public money. Their coherence and legitimacy as institutions inheres in the fact that they produce a socially valued (but dysfunctional) good, called attainment, that does not require them to act purposefully as organizations but only to do what they do. Most high school reformers have discovered the hard way that reforms that require high levels of adult agreement and commitment to an organized mission are doomed to fail within the existing attainment structure.

The "Transition" from High School to College: Self-Interested Institutions Determine Public Ends

As noted earlier, the organizing ideology of the attainment structure is merit, which, in principle, means that people advance in society based on their demonstrated knowledge, skill, persistence, and effort, rather than on their social position. There is ample documentation now that the transition from high school to college in the United States, while still ideologically wrapped in the idea of merit, is more or less deliberately designed to reinforce privilege and social class.

Aggregate attainment measures have shown a modest, steady increase over the past 2 decades. High school graduation rates in the population aged 25 or older have increased from about 75% in 1986 to about 82% in 1996 to their present level of about 85%. The proportion of the population 25 and older who have earned a bachelor's degree or higher has also increased from 19% in 1986 to 24% in 1996 to its present level of 28%. Current African American high school graduation rates in the over-25 population are at about 80%, and bachelors-or-higher rates are about 18%; Latino high school graduation rates are at about 59%, and bachelors or higher are about 12% (NCES, 2006, Table 8). Attrition rates among students entering postsecondary institutions are relatively high. Among so-called traditional students, defined as students who enter directly from high school and are not financially independent, annual attrition rates for the 1989–1990 cohort were 10%–15% per year. Among nontraditional students, defined as students have delayed enrollment after high school, are financially independent, are a single parent, have other nonspouse dependents, or who work more than 35 hours per week, attrition rates are between 15% and 30% per year for the same cohort. Of the traditional students who left postsecondary education, 40% took a "downward transfer" from a 4- to a 2-year institution or from a degree program to a certificate program, about 30% said they were "stopping out," and about 30% left without return. For the nontraditional students, nearly half left without return and the remaining were equally split between stopping out and downward transfers (NCES, 2002). Clearly, moving successfully from high school to postsecondary education is a far-from-predictable course into the economic and social benefits of the attainment structure. Recall that the income premiums attached to 4-year college completion are extremely high—75% for men and 64% for women.

Explorations of the connections and gaps between secondary and postsecondary education suggest that there are two main problems. The first is, not surprisingly, that the institutional links between high schools and postsecondary institutions are extremely weak and disarticulated. That is, high schools don't prepare students very well for what they will confront in college, and colleges don't have a clear way of communicating their academic expectations to high school students and their families. The second problem is that the formal institutional mechanisms by which

students are selected out of high school into postsecondary institutions reward institutional knowledge and social capital, not academic prowess. The college admissions process has grown to Byzantine complexity as status competition within the high school attainment structure has become more intense. Byzantine processes reward people who have the social and economic resources to negotiate them, and they penalize those who either don't have the resources or don't understand that the processes exist.

A study of student knowledge of college admission processes in California found that 9th- and 11th-grade students had highly variable and often inaccurate ideas about the basic requirements for admission to California public higher education institutions, and that, not surprisingly, students in higher attainment high schools had greater, more accurate knowledge than those in lower attainment high schools, which translated into racial, ethnic, and economic biases in attainment. Only about one-third of students in the sample could state all six of the curricular entry requirements of the California system. Less than 1% of the students' parents knew what the requirements were (Kirst & Bracco, 2004, Table 2.10, pp. 62, 71). This pattern was played out with modest variations in other states.

As the NCES transcript study indicates, the majority of students are enrolled in standard or below-standard high school curriculum, which does not equip them to succeed in a more demanding higher education environment. With the exception of the highest academic levels—exemplified by the national advanced placement examination system—there is no explicit articulation of secondary and postsecondary curricula. The same can be said about assessments. Students take multiple state- and district-level assessments over their course of time in secondary school. None of these assessments are actually used by higher education institutions to evaluate students' learning or academic performance. In some states, these assessments are used to determine whether students graduate from high school, but those assessments and the standards on which they are based are not explicitly articulated with postsecondary entry requirements.

It is understandable that a student or parent might be confused when the state test scores come home showing a decent level of performance, but that information has no bearing on the student's prospects for college admission. The college admission testing system is entirely separate from the state and local assessment system, and it requires a great deal more sophistication to navigate. A student who is contemplating application to a modestly competitive postsecondary institution must begin the process of preparing for tests no later than the 10th grade. The Scholastic Achievement Test (SAT) is administered to 11th and 12th graders, but the preparatory test that serves as both a practice test and a diagnostic for the "real" test—the Preliminary Scholastic Achievement Test (PSAT)—must be taken well in advance in order to be useful. In the past few years, the Education Testing Service (ETS) the testing arm of the College Board, has introduced subject-matter tests, the SAT-2, in core academic areas—English, mathematics, sciences, and so on—that are now being used to screen students in more competitive postsecondary institutions.

College advisors routinely counsel parents that their students must take two to three SAT-2s in addition to taking, and retaking, the main SAT. Parents who understand something about the attainment structure, or who have the economic resources to hire people who do, usually pay for SAT preparation courses. The SAT-2 sets up a strategic problem for high school juniors and seniors. The SAT-2s are subject matter specific. Therefore, it matters what the proximity is between the completion of a subject matter course in high school and the actual date that the test will be administered. If you don't know how to articulate these two logistical requirements, your student will be taking a subject-matter test over content that he or she studied last year.

On top of the SAT system is another entire testing regime in the advanced placement (AP) system, which is also, not surprisingly, run by the ETS and the College Board. The AP system is the main device that is used to discriminate among students at the very top of the high school attainment structure. With steadily increasing GPAs, and high school curricula that label courses in ways that college admissions officers have learned to suspect, acquiring AP course credit and test scores on top of the all the other assessments is the main way to distinguish a relatively high level student from his or her peers.

The AP system is unique in the United States in that it carries a fairly well specified course curriculum and a nationally administered and scored examination system. The original rationale for the AP was to allow high school students to study college-level content and, upon successfully completing the AP examination, to gain a head start in college with college credit. Most competitive colleges and universities are now quite cautious about granting college credit for AP courses, and most do not allow AP credit to count against overall credit requirements for college graduation. Currently, there are 34 AP examinations available, covering subjects as diverse as calculus, chemistry, Chinese language and culture, environmental science, Latin, music theory, statistics, and studio art. In order for students to have access to the AP, the high school has to offer the courses. AP courses typically have lower enrollments than "regular" courses, are therefore more resource intensive, and tend to drive the staffing levels and schedules of courses across the entire school. Hence, the AP not only sets another level of complexity in the attainment structure, it also allocates resources differentially away from other students who are positioned differently in the attainment structure.

If you are the parent of a high school–aged son or daughter, and you are interested in making the attainment structure work to maximum advantage, the information costs and economic costs can be substantial. The best test preparation courses typically cost in the thousands of dollars. Many parents with aspirations for their children to attend highly competitive institutions employ private professional college counselors, who charge a minimum of $3,000 to $5,000 for the basic service of providing a list of possible colleges, some assistance in writing college essays, and some hand holding through the process of filling out and filing applications. Testing costs are in the hundreds to thousands of dollars, depending on how many tests and how often students have to retake them. And the cost of time in overseeing and monitoring the application process is considerable. This all precedes the privilege of paying $40,000 to $50,000 per year for attending the institution.

The important thing to acknowledge about the transition from high school to postsecondary education is that it is highly complex, extremely costly, highly incoherent, and completely unaccountable institutional structure. The costs of not knowing what the intricacies of the attainment structure are and how it works are potentially very high for parents and their children. The system itself is not really a system, it is a set of institutions, each with its own interests, incentives, and clients that are locked together in a mutual benefit relationship, but which are not coherent at the level of the student. The representation of the "public" interest in this set of institutional relationships is ambiguous at best, and it is a by-product of the self-interested behavior of largely private, largely unregulated institutions.

Public secondary schools operate in their own world, supplying students into a structure of postsecondary institutions, and the two sets of institutions, which operate largely in the public domain, do not have an agreed-upon set of expectations for what constitutes adequate preparation. Dropout rates in the secondary school sector and attrition rates in the postsecondary sector are considered to be frictional costs to the system, and the dramatic economic and social costs of these institutional

failures are never reckoned in the budgets or the mandates of the institutions themselves. The testing system that, to a very large degree, influences which students are chosen for the most competitive postsecondary institutions is a private, nominally not-for-profit institution, the College Board and ETS, that runs a massively "profitable" testing business, and is accountable to no public authority for the consequences of its actions. This is the way we, as a society, manage the progress of adolescents through schooling.

THE WAY FORWARD

There is no shortage of promising ideas for how to reform the schooling of adolescents in our society. Nor is there any shortage of ideas about what a developmentally powerful environment would be for adolescents in school or evidence that these ideas in practice can change the lives of students. The problem is not the availability of good ideas. The problem is the deeply chronic and pathological relationship between the institutions we have created to "school" adolescents and the society in which these institutions operate. Earlier, I referred to the meliorist view of reform in the secondary school sector, in which we put our best ideas forward, test them with a relatively small group of students, demonstrate that they address the most fundamental problems of schooling for adolescents, and then predictably fail to operationalize them on a scale that has any significant consequences for the most pressing problems in the population of adolescents at large. It is important to have existence proofs that demonstrate that we can do better with adolescents in school than we are currently doing. But we should acknowledge that these ideas exist in an institutional environment that, in its basic incentives, structures, and processes, is designed to insure their failure. It will not help to continue to supply new ideas if we don't confront the institutional structure that subverts them.

Here are five basic ideas about how to begin the process of opening up the secondary school sector to ideas that support the development of adolescents:

1. Attainment is a public good, not a private good, and public institutions, and the people who work in them, should have to bear the costs of failing to produce an equitable distribution of attainment.

    Educational attainment, defined as sustained engagement with and progress in school accompanied by cognitive, social, and emotional growth, coupled with advancement in a status hierarchy, is a classic example of a public good that has been converted into a private good through the neglect of public responsibility by public officials and public institutions. The individual costs of attainment failures in secondary schooling are high. But the public costs are extraordinarily high, not just in terms of the direct costs of social services to compensate for systemic failures but, more importantly, in the indirect costs of economic productivity that accrue to society as a whole as a consequence of having a large portion of its population more or less deliberately excluded from schooling by the incompetence and neglect of public institutions. The institutional problem is that schools and schools systems do not have to internalize the costs of their incompetence—they move their failures out of the system and they pass them along to other institutions through the attainment structure. Dropout figures should carry similar economic costs to secondary schools that medical error rates carry for hospitals. They should be publicized, they should carry substantial financial penalties to the individuals, not just to the institutions, and they should carry the same, or greater importance, in accountability systems that measure student performance carries. Every child who enters the 6th grade should carry a case number, and that child should be followed through every contact with the institution called school, and every individual who comes in contact with that child should be required to account for the time that the child spends with that individual. When the child disappears from the system, a public authority should be responsible for finding that child and reinitiating contact with some form of educational opportunity. And the public institution should bear the responsibility and cost of remediating its failures.

    Directly addressing the attainment structure will trigger predictable political and social backlash from the primary beneficiaries of the existing system, cloaked in the language of merit and lax standards. But it will be difficult for any of the good ideas about how schools can support the development of adolescents to work if the students aren't there and if the adults and the institutions in which they work aren't taking responsibility for keeping them there and keeping them engaged. The current accountability system sends different messages to high- and low-attainment secondary schools. We hold low-attainment schools accountable for performance, with an incentive structure that encourages them to shift enrollments by grade level and to bury their educational failures in their dropout rates, rather than directly addressing the pathologies of the environments they have created for young people. High-attainment schools, no matter the mediocrity of their academic programs, are not required to take performance accountability seriously after they meet a threshold and operate in an environment where they are held accountable for results that are largely produced by the socioeconomic status of their clients, not by themselves. Accountability systems should shed the same light on quality of academic instruction and attainment as they shed on test score performance, and the test score performance of high socioeconomic schools should be adjusted for the effect of social class in comparison with low socioeconomic schools. Dropping out of school and failing to progress in school are, and should be acknowledged to be, completely rational acts for a large proportion of students in secondary school. More students would probably drop out than are currently doing so, if they were authorized to do so by the adults in their lives. The problem is that school is not a particularly engaging place to be for a large proportion of the population, and this should be made a central concern of the accountability system.

2. Cognitive, social, and emotional growth of adolescents are all equally important and mutually reinforcing goals for schooling, and they should all be included in systems of public accountability.

    The current preoccupation with measured cognitive performance as the main index for students' school success has created a massively complex, largely inscrutable, disarticulated metastasizing test-based system that is driven by the ideology of merit, but in fact rewards primarily those with economic resources and social capital to play the game. States and localities are not directly accountable to families and children for the level of testing they do. ETS and the College Board, and the institutions that support them by requiring the that parents and students purchase their products, are not accountable for the costs they impose on parents and students through the testing system. School systems and postsecondary institutions are not accountable for the inconsistencies, discontinuities, and gaps in the expectations they have for what constitutes real learning and adequate academic progress. In a world in which tests are a more or less a free good to those who create them and require them to produce, and in which the main costs of the testing system are borne by the people who take them, we can only predict that the testing system

will become even more complex, intrusive, and Byzantine than it already is.

Again, this is public good's problem. No one is making the creators of the testing system bear the actual costs of what they do and to internalize these costs in their decisions about how they operate. The College Board is more or less free to increase the complexity and cost of the testing regime required for college entry, and to distort the indices for determining attainment, because there is no countervailing discipline that forces it to internalize that costs of its actions. Furthermore, making the attainment structure more complex and difficult to decode helps substantially in making the idea of merit legitimate, when the main determinants of success are actually income and social capital.

One partial solution to this problem is to begin to broaden the scope of accountability systems and to require schools to produce information on multiple dimensions of students' experience in school, rather than just test-based cognitive performance. In Australia and Canada, for example, educators are routinely required to participate in 360-degree evaluations, in which teachers, students, parents, and community members are asked to assess their experience in schools on a regular basis, and educators are required to provide responses to the data they receive.

Another partial solution is to make the economic and social costs of testing and the complexity of the attainment structure part of the policy discourse about the performance of public educational institutions. Why does the most influential institution in the country in determining attainment—the College Board—operate in an environment in which it is accountable to no public authority (other than possibly the Internal Revenue Service, which polices the proportion of its income it has to spend on it nominally not-for-profit activities)? Who is responsible for reckoning the individual and social costs of complexity and failure in a nominally market-based system of attainment? And who is responsible for deciding how those costs should be distributed?

3. Quality and access to academic work should be of equal importance with measured academic performance in evaluating individuals and institutions.

The underlying problems of secondary schools in the United States are deeper than the multiple failures of accountability. In fact, one could argue, based on the evidence, that secondary schools have adapted quite successfully to the performance-based accountability regime by relabeling low-level content as "academic," by increasing graduates' GPAs, and by continuing to do what they do best, which is to teach low-level content and to act as society's primary institution for social stratification. They have succeeded in doing what they have always done and calling it something else.

The evidence clearly suggests that, despite the aspirations of secondary school reformers, secondary school educators do not have a developmental view of their work. Their underlying model of professional practice, translated into institutional structures, curricula, and classroom practices, is one in which the student is divided into pieces based on traditionally defined subject matter domains, and each piece of the organization, without consulting with any other piece of the organization, proceeds to teach and evaluate students according to its particular view of what students should know and be able to do. Not surprisingly, this model doesn't produce a coherent or powerful developmental environment for adolescents. There is nothing novel about this diagnosis; it has been the basis of secondary school reform proposals

for a century. The underlying problem is that secondary school educators don't acquire a developmental view of their work because they are not required to do so as a condition of professional practice, and because they are not required to have a developmental theory of their practice in order to function effectively in the organizations in which they work. People are generally rational. They do what they are required to do; they produce what they are required to produce. Reform proposals that require adults in secondary school to function as if they were experts in adolescent development and learning are essentially pushing on a string. People will exercise a developmental view of their practice when they are required to have that knowledge and skill as a condition of being able to practice and when they are held accountable for having that knowledge and skill in their daily practice.

It is a profound misconception, in part resulting from a misinterpretation of the middle school reform movement, that cognitive development is somehow separate from social and emotional development and that focusing on the social and emotional somehow precludes focusing on the cognitive. Current research on cognition and learning reinforce the powerful and complex relationships among domains. Further, the most powerful current research on learning in subject matter areas is *developmental* research, that is, it examines how young people make meaning in the context of content, how the conditions under which they learn affect their development, and how their relationships with the world affect their capacity to acquire and use cognitive skills. It is not unreasonable, given the mediocre level of student learning manifested in current assessments, to expect that all educators become experts in research on cognitive, social, and emotional development.

The current, pathological situation in secondary schools will persist as long as the institutions and the individuals who work in them are not held accountable for developing the knowledge and skill required to engage students in high-level cognitive work and to make that engagement a worthwhile developmental activity in the lives of adolescents. This means that schools should be held equally accountable for the quality of experience they provide and for their capacity to engage adolescents in that experience in a sustained, continuous way, as they are for measured performance and attainment. This shift requires movement away from the idea that secondary schools exist to determine access to scarce positions in a competitive attainment structure, and toward a view that they job of secondary schools to—hold your breath—provide a high-level, supportive environment for the cognitive, social, and emotional development of adolescents.

4. Equal investments must be made in capability and performance.

   Major changes in institutional purpose and competence do not occur solely as a result of changes in accountability. If people are required to do their work differently, they have to learn how to do it differently in addition to being rewarded or penalized for doing it differently. The evidence is clear that U.S. secondary schools, in their basic institutional structure, do not provide adults with the opportunity to learn to their work differently or to examine the purposes of their work and its collective impact on students in any systematic way. It is highly unlikely that the institutional incentive structure that drives American secondary schools will change if the adults in them aren't exposed to a different way of thinking about and doing their work. As with most problems of performance in education, improvement is a human investment enterprise, and the costs of improvement are always underestimated because there is a weak understanding at all levels about the knowledge and skill requirements of high-level developmental work in school. Just as cognitive, emotional, and social development should be equally weighted in the assessments of school performance, and just as the quality of the environment should be equally weighted with its performance, so too should the capability—investments in knowledge, skill, and practice—be equally weighted with performance in the evaluation of schools.

   Just as there are strong incentives for school systems to bury their failures to provide opportunities for student engagement in rhetoric about how difficult it is to measure dropout rates, there are equally powerful incentives for states and school systems not to recognize the true costs of increasing adult capability to provide a high quality development environment for adolescents. Just as dropouts have to bear the social stigma and costs of their failures to engage in a dysfunctional system, so, too, do adults have to pretend that they are prepared to do work that they are manifestly not capable of doing. Part of the solution is to acknowledge that we have a crisis of huge proportions in secondary schools and that that crisis is a function of the failure of the institutions and the adults who work in them to engage students in productive, healthy ways, and to say, simply and flatly, that in order to address that crisis, adults will have to know things they currently do not know and will have to practice in ways they currently do not practice, and that the costs of developing these new capabilities will be borne publicly.

5. Provide multiple attainment opportunities for students whom the system has failed.

Accountability rhetoric to the contrary, in the current social structure attainment matters much more than performance. A middle-class student who stays in school and takes a substandard, unchallenging curriculum and manages to negotiate the complex process of getting into college will make considerably more money in the current social structure than a minority, low-income student who has received equally mediocre instruction but who has experienced school as a constant barrage of negative feedback about his or her inadequacies as a student and been the subject of a more or less intentional process of cooling out his or her expectation for further academic progress. Mediocrity, it is important to say, is the standard of academic content in *both* environments; it is just that in the former mediocrity leads to good economic results and in the latter it leads to bad results.

The first step in addressing this situation is to acknowledge that, for the vast majority of secondary students at risk, *dropping out or disengaging from school is a rational choice developmentally, if not economically.* No healthy, self-actualizing, autonomous adult would willingly choose to stay in a social environment in which he or she deliberately, systematically, and repeatedly experienced failure as the normal circumstance. If you internalize the purpose of secondary school as being to tell you that you will not succeed in as many ways as possible, you will eventually either accept that verdict or, if you are a healthy individual, decide to take yourself out of that environment. This is the situation of a very large proportion of students in U.S. secondary schools.

In the short term, it should be a more or less routine public function to provide places for dropouts and pushouts in settings where they can experience academic success and where they can be adolescents, rather than young people with adult responsibilities in the world. These settings will be, of necessity in the short term, outside the established secondary school structure, since there is little evidence that established secondary schools are actually capable of providing a safe and supportive environment for these students. Academic success in these settings should carry the same formal attainment value as success in regular secondary schools—they should grant regular high school diplomas and carry regular academic credit, not "alternative" forms of certification—and these settings should be deliberately rewarded for measures of engagement, persistence in school, and attainment, as much or more than academic performance. Students at risk of academic failure should have the same access to the value of attainment as middle-class students taking mediocre courses in "regular" high schools.

CONCLUSIONS

Measures such as I have discussed have the potential of reducing the economic premium attached to the established attainment structure and creating a major bottleneck in the transition from secondary to postsecondary education. They will be predictably criticized by traditional educators and conservative commentators as "diluting" the quality of the system. In fact, it would be difficult to dilute the quality of the system much more than it is already diluted.

All these measures do is equalize the benefits of mediocrity. They will not function to improve the overall capability of high school and college graduates unless they are accompanied by major changes in the institutional culture and incentives of the secondary school sector in general.

REFERENCES

Alliance for Excellent Education. (2007, October). *The high cost of high school dropouts: What the nation pays for inadequate high schools.* Washington, DC: Author.

Andrews, P. G., Caskey, M. M., & Anfara, V. A., Jr. (2007). *Research summary: Characteristics of exemplary schools for young adolescents.* www.nmsa.org/Research/ResearchSummaries/ Exemplary Schools/tabid/256/Default.aspx.

Backes, J., Ralston, A., & Ingwalson, G. (1999). Middle level reform: The impact on student achievement. *Research in Middle Level Education Quarterly, 22,* 43–57.

Baez, B. (2006). Merit and difference. *Teachers College Record, 108,* 996–1016.

Balfanz, R., Herzog, L., & MacIver, D. J. (2007). Preventing student disengagement and keeping students on the graduation path in urban middle-grades schools: Early identification and effective interventions. *Educational Psychologist, 42,* 223–235.

Balfanz, R., & Legters, N. (2004, June). *Locating the dropout crisis: Which high schools produce the nation's dropouts? Where are they located? Who attends them?* Baltimore: Center for Social Organization of Schools, Johns Hopkins University.

Bidwell, C., & Yasumoto, J. (1999). The collegial focus: Teaching fields, collegial relationships, and instructional practice in American high schools. *Sociology of Education, 72,* 234–256.

Byrnes, V., & Ruby, A. (n.d.). *Comparing K-8 and middle schools: A large-scale empirical study.* Baltimore: Center for Social Organization of Schools.

The Carnegie Council on Adolescent Development. (1989). *Turning points: Preparing American youth for the 21st century.* New York: Carnegie Corporation.

The Carnegie Council on Adolescent Development. (2000). *Turning points 2000: Educating adolescents in the 21st century.* New York: Carnegie Corporation.

Dweck, C. (1999). *Self-theories: Their role in motivation and personality development.* Philadelphia: Psychology Press.

Dweck, C. (2006). *Mindset: The new psychology of success.* New York: Random House.

Freud, S. (1933/1966). *The complete introductory lectures on psychoanalysis.* New York: W. W. Norton.

Georgia State Department of Education. (1998). Statewide evaluation of Georgia's middle grades educational program: Phase I report.

Heinlein, L. M., & Shinn, M. (2000). School mobility and student achievement in an urban setting. *Psychology in the Schools, 37,* 349–357.

Ian, J. (1975). "Seventeen," from her recording, Between the Lines. Columbia Records.

Kirst, M., & Bracco, K. R. (2004). Bridging the great divide: How the K–12 and postsecondary split hurts students, and what can be done about it. In M. Kirst & A. Venezia (Eds.), *From high school to college: Improving opportunities in postsecondary* education. San Francisco: Jossey-Bass.

Lemann, N. (1999). *The big test: The secret history of the American meritocracy.* New York: Farrar, Strauss, and Giroux.

Loveless, T. (1999). *The tracking wars: State reform meets school policy.* Washington, DC: Brookings Institution.

Metz, M. (1978). Classrooms and corridors: The crisis of authority in desegregated secondary schools. Berkeley: University of California Press.

Murnane, R., & Levy, F. (1999). *The new division of labor: How computers are creating the next job market.* Princeton, NJ: Princeton University Press.

Myer, J., & Rowan, B. (1978). The structure of educational organizations. In M. Meyer (Ed.), *Environment and organizations* (pp. 78–110). San Francisco: Jossey-Bass.

National Assessment of Educational Progress (NAEP). (2007a). *The nation's report card: Reading 2007.* Washington, DC: U.S. Department of Education.

National Assessment of Educational Progress (NAEP). (2007b). *The nation's report card: Mathematics 2007.* Washington, DC: U.S. Department of Education.

National Center for Educational Statistics (NCES). (2000, July). *In the middle: Characteristics of public schools with a focus on middle schools.* washington, DC: U.S. Department of Education, Office of Educational Research and Improvement. NCES Rpt. #: 2000–312.

National Center for Educational Statistics (NCES). (2006). *Digest of educational statistics.* washington, DC: U.S. Department of Education, Office of Educational Research and Improvement.

National Center for Educational Statistics (NCES). (2007). *Common core of data: State-level public use data file on public school dropouts: School year 2004–2005.* Washington, DC: U.S. Department of Education.

Norton, A. (2004). *95 theses on politics, culture, and method.* New Haven, CT: Yale University Press.

Oakes, J. (2005). *Keeping track: How schools structure inequality.* New Haven, CT: Yale University Press.

Offenberg, R. M. (2001). The efficacy of Philadelphia's K-to-8 schools compared to middle grades schools. *Middle School Journal, 32,* 23–29.

Program on International Student Achievement (PISA). (2003). *Learning for tomorrow's world: First results from PISA 2003.* Paris: Organization for Economic Cooperation and Development (OECD).

Rouse, C. E. (2005, October). *Labor market consequences of an inadequate education.* Paper prepared for the symposium on the Social Costs of Inadequate Education, Teachers College, Columbia University.

Rowan, B. (1990). Commitment and control. *Review of Educational Research, 16,* 359–389.

Schmidt, W., et al. (1999). *Facing the consequences: Using TIMSS for a closer look at U.S. mathematics and science education.* Dordrecht, Netherlands: Kluwer.

School and Staffing Survey. (1996). *SASS by state, 1993–94.* Washington, DC: Institute for Educational Sciences, U.S. Department of Education.

Siskin, L. (1994). *Realms of knowledge: Academic departments in secondary schools.* Washington, DC: Falmer.

U.S. Bureau of the Census. (2006). *Income in 2005 by educational attainment of the population 18 years and over* (Table 8). Washington, DC: U.S. Government Printing Office. Retrieved from www.census.gov/population/www/socdemo/education/ cps2006.html.

Vernez, G., Karam, R., Mariano, L. T., & DeMartini, C. (2006). *Evaluating comprehensive school reform models at scale: Focus on implementation.* Santa Monica, CA: RAND.

CHAPTER 7

Adolescent Out-of-School Activities

JOSEPH L. MAHONEY, DEBORAH LOWE VANDELL, SANDRA SIMPKINS, AND NICOLE ZARRETT

This is the first edition of the *Handbook of Adolescent Psychology* to include a chapter focused on out-of-school activities. The inclusion signifies new awareness that, along with settings common to adolescent research (i.e., the school, family, and peer group), out-of-school activities also represent important contexts of youth development. Considerable research is now available to show that the out-of-school activities in which youth participate significantly affect their social, educational, civic, and physical development (e.g., Durlak & Weissberg, 2007; Feldman & Matjasko, 2005; Mahoney, Larson, & Eccles, 2005; National Research Council and Institute of Medicine [NRC-IOM], 2002; Vandell, Pierce, & Dadisman, 2005). Along with the rapid expansion of empirical research, theoretical perspectives on adolescence and positive youth development have been revamped to impart greater significance to out-of-school activities (e.g., Larson, 2000; Lerner, 2007; Vandell & Posner, 1999), and policy discussions at the local and national levels have focused increasingly on the significance of out-of-school activities for youth (e.g., Lerner, 2006; Mahoney & Zigler, 2006).

Rather than provide a comprehensive review of this literature, the purpose of our chapter is to highlight central issues and emerging areas of research conducted over the past three decades that has been concerned with adolescents' (ages 12–18) out-of-school activities and development. Elucidating those areas where research is especially rich or exemplary, where limited empirical knowledge exists, and where new knowledge is sorely needed are broad goals of the chapter. An additional goal is to consider how the developmental significance of participating in out-of-school activities may vary according to differences in individual characteristics, activity features, and the broader ecologies in which youth and activities are situated. Finally, we consider how the research can inform practical and policy decision making concerning out-of-school activities and youth development.

The chapter is divided into five main sections. Following this introduction, the second section discusses implications of a bioecological perspective for conceptualizing the role of out-of-school activities in adolescent development. The third section addresses the issue of whether adolescent involvement in

---

This chapter is concerned with adolescent involvement in activities that take place outside of the formal schoolday, including afternoons, evenings, weekends, holidays, and summertime. Two categories of these out-of-school activities have received the greatest amount of attention from researchers and are the focus of this chapter: (1) activities that lack adult supervision and tend not to be highly structured (e.g., self-care, hanging out with peers); and (2) organized activities that are supervised by adults, structured, and goal oriented (e.g., extracurricular activities, after-school programs, and community-based organizations).

unsupervised out-of-school activities promotes competence or poses a risk for the healthy development of young people. The final two sections focus on the predictors and adjustment processes connected to youth participation in organized out-of-school activities, respectively.

A BIOECOLOGICAL PERSPECTIVE TO OUT-OF-SCHOOL ACTIVITIES

School-aged youth in the United States and other Western nations average 40%–50% of their waking hours in discretionary activities outside of school (Larson & Verma, 1999). Researchers, policy makers, practitioners, and individual families have become increasingly interested in the opportunities and risks associated with how youth spend this time. Understanding what types of out-of-school activities are available, desirable, and apt to facilitate the healthy development of youth from different backgrounds is of particular interest. We begin to address this issue by outlining some basic assumptions about the developmental process that follow from a bioecological perspective. This perspective has been helpful to conceptualizing developmental consequences of youth involvement in a variety of contexts (e.g., family, school, neighborhood), including out-of-school activities (e.g., Jelicic, Bobek, Phelps, Lerner, & Lerner, 2007; Mahoney, Parente, & Zigler, in press; Vandell & Posner, 1999).

Key Tenets of a Bioecological Perspective to Development

Most modern theories of human development share a basic proposition: Development occurs as part of a complex process involving a system of interactions within the individual and between the individual and the environmental contexts in which he or she is one part, over time (e.g., Lerner, 2002; Magnusson & Stattin, 1998). A direct implication of this proposition is that understanding adolescent development requires that the network of relations between

characteristics of the individual and the ecologies in which he or she develops must be studied in an integrated and temporal manner (e.g., Lerner, Theokas, & Bobek, 2005).

In his seminal work, Bronfenbrenner (1979) described the child's ecology in terms of a set of nested levels. He labeled ecologies where face-to-face interactions between the child and the environment take place the *microsystem*. An adolescent's direct involvement in the school classroom, an out-of-school activity, peer group, family, and neighborhood are examples of microsystems. The combinations of microsystems that encapsulate the child's direct experiences across settings were referred to as the *mesosystem*. At the level of the mesosystem, the developmental consequences associated with involvement in any one microsystem (e.g., the school) are seen as relative to the child's experience in other microsystems (e.g., the family, the peer group). In other words, these proximal ecologies are assumed to have reciprocal and synergistic influence on the developmental process such that the impact of one setting can only be understood with reference to the others. At a more distal level, the term *exosystem* refers to ecologies that youth may not be involved in directly but, nonetheless, may influence their development indirectly by affecting the conditions of the microsystems (e.g., conditions at the parent's workplace could influence the family microsystem). Finally, the term *macrosystem* represents the broadest level of influence in this framework and encompasses aspects such as culture or federal policy that both affect and are affected by the combinations of ecologies described previously.

Although Bronfenbrenner's earlier work specified that development involves a dynamic interplay within and across levels of the individual's ecologies, attention to the biological contributions and the child's own role in the developmental process was limited. However, more recent versions of the bioecological theory of human development emphasize that all characteristics of the individual—biological, psychological, social, and emotional—must be considered to understand the developmental process (e.g., Bronfenbrenner & Morris, 2006). In this more recent view, the child is seen as an active and purposeful agent in the developmental process; characteristics of the whole child both affect and are affected by the interactions that occur within and across the nested levels of ecologies in a reciprocal fashion across development. This underscores the general assumption guiding most modern developmental theories: Development "happens" through a process of systemic interactions within and between the individual and the environment, over time (cf. Cairns, Elder, & Costello, 1996; Magnusson & Stattin, 1998).

Bronfenbrenner and Morris (2006) noted that person-context interactions occurring at the microsystem level were of special importance. Although more distal ecologies influence the type and quality of interactions that occur within the microsystem, development is directly influenced by the moment-to-moment pattern of exchange between the individual and his or her surroundings. Whether, and to what extent, these proximal exchanges facilitate development in a positive direction depends partly on what scholars have referred to as "stage–environment fit" (e.g., Eccles & Midgley, 1989; Eccles & Roeser, this volume). According to stage–environment fit theory, the development of any given behavior or attribute depends on the degree of match between a child's existing abilities, characteristics, and interests and the opportunities afforded to him or her in the immediate social environment. Fit is optimal when the environmental features experienced are structured according to the child's current needs and developmental level (cf. Vygotsky's 1978 conceptualization of the "zone of proximal development"). A mismatch in fit reflects asynchrony between the type or amount of stimulation in the environment and the adolescent's existing abilities or motivations. One implication of this theory is that simultaneous attention to the developmental trajectory of the adolescent and the structure,

stimulation, and opportunities in the environment are needed to understand how any microsystem affects development. A second implication is that to maintain a good stage–environment, fit parameters of microecologies must be adjusted over time to reflect the adolescent's increasing maturity and changing needs and interests.

Implications for Out-of-School Activities and Adolescent Development

The bioecological perspective helps to frame the role of out-of-school activities in adolescent development. Four general implications of this perspective for conceptualizing out-of-school activities as contexts of adolescent development are highlighted below. These implications also serve as orienting themes from which to organize and discuss the literature for the remainder of this chapter.

First, *the selection of out-of-school activities is influenced by a combination of person and context factors.* Adolescent participation in out-of-school activities is not a random affair. The type of activity chosen, time spent in the activity setting, and social-contextual features of the activity setting are each affected by factors operating at the person and environmental levels (e.g., characteristics and interests of the adolescent; social support from peers and adults; family economy; parent work schedules; and the types, costs, and proximities of activity offerings in the surrounding community; e.g., Bouffard et al., 2006). These factors are often functionally correlated and operate in a synergistic fashion. As a result, involvement in various out-of-school activities will differ as a function of the youth and environments considered. While some adolescents will have considerable opportunities, means, and social supports available to facilitate their participation in a diversity of out-of-school activities, multiple and coeffecting constraints will restrict the out-of-school activity prospects available to other youth (e.g., Lareau, 2003; NRC-IOM, 2002).

Second, *the developmental consequences of participating in an out-of-school activity depend on the proximal processes within the activity context.* Whether participation in out-of-school activities facilitates, maintains, or impedes the healthy development of adolescents depends on the type, frequency, and quality of interchanges in the activity context. The nature of these interchanges should be relative to:

- Characteristics of the individual, including the competencies, cultural and economic background, and developmental needs that youth bring to the activity context.
- Characteristics of the activity context that affect the content and quality of offerings including structural (e.g., activity-based physical, social, and material resources) and process dimensions (e.g., the cognitive and affective content of peer-to-peer and youth-to-adult interchanges that take place during the activity).
- The degree to which there is a match between the activity-based opportunities and the characteristics, interests, and needs of the developing adolescent (i.e., the person–stage–environment fit).

In addition, because activity participation is not random, the composition of youth (and adults) selecting (or recruited) into a given activity will have in common those characteristics driving the selection process. These selection-based characteristics are also likely to shape the proximal processes that take place in the activity.

Third, *proximal processes occurring within an out-of-school activity both affect and are affected by adolescent experiences in linked ecologies, including other out-of-school contexts.* The bioecological perspective specifies that the multiple ecologies in which development occurs are interdependent and have reciprocal influences on one another. This suggests that a youth's experiences in an out-of-school activity are apt to affect and be affected

by her or his experiences in other developmental contexts such as the family, peer group, school, and neighborhood (NRC-IOM, 2002). Recent studies suggest this is the case. For example, parental support and value of organized activities predict that youth will subsequently choose to participate in supervised and structured out-of-school activities (e.g., Fredericks & Eccles, 2006a; Simpkins, Davis-Kean, & Eccles, 2005) the types out-of-school activities in which youth participate affect the development of peer relationships and status in the school classroom (e.g., Brown, 1990; Eder & Kinney, 1995; Sandstrom & Coie, 1999), and the associated consequences of how young people spend their out-of-school time depend on the neighborhood conditions in which youth and activities are situated (e.g., Fauth, Roth, & Brooks-Gunn, 2007; Lord & Mahoney, 2007). These relations have two critical implications: (1) A complete understanding of adolescent development necessitates careful study of out-of-school activities; and (2) understanding how out-of-school activities contribute to adolescent development requires that interrelations between multiple contexts be studied concomitantly across time.

With reference to cross-contextual influence, relations between different out-of-school contexts are also important to consider. Youth are often involved in several different out-of-school activities during the course of a week or even a single day (Capizzano, Tout, & Adams, 2000; Mahoney, Lord, & Carryl, 2005b; Vandell & Posner, 1999). All out-of-school activities are not created equal in terms of their potential to facilitate positive youth development. For example, consider the opportunities for adolescents to develop social, academic, or physical competencies while they participate in an organized team sport, attend an after-school homework program, visit a drop-in youth center, "hang out" at a shopping mall with peers, or watch television alone at home. Because an adolescent could pursue several or all of these activities, relations across these different activities is likely to be important. For instance, in terms of development toward a particular competency or orientation (e.g., civic-mindedness), cross-contextual influences could be parallel, complementary, partially conflicting, or fully opposing across different out-of-school activities. Accordingly, understanding the role of a particular out-of-school activity may be best understood with reference to the broader out-of-school ecology in which the adolescent is involved. Figure 7.1 depicts common contexts in the out-of-school ecology of adolescents and highlights basic parameters of the settings (i.e., physical and social characteristics, types of opportunities provided, and aspects of participation; cf. Vandell & Posner, 1999).

Fourth, *adolescents and out-of-school activities are changing and dynamic entities requiring that research take a developmental approach.* The bioecological perspective is a developmental theory. From this perspective, persons and contexts need to be studied in tandem and over time. With respect to out-of-school activities, one implication is that as youth develop toward adulthood, their interest in out-of-school activities will change. Activities that help youth develop marketable skills,

allow them to participate in community- and service-learning activities, become involved in the paid labor force, and provide for greater autonomy and increasing opportunities to take leadership roles become increasingly important across adolescence (e.g., Larson, Walker, & Pearce, 2005; Lauver, Little, & Weiss, 2004; NRC-IOM, 2002). Accordingly, maintaining a good person–stage–environment fit requires that out-of-school offerings keep pace with these changing skills and interests and remain developmentally appropriate to the population of youth considered. In addition, the fact that activities are themselves changing and developing entities needs to be taken into account. For example, the goals, personnel, participants, and resources for a given out-of-school activity often change in the space of months or even weeks, particularly for activities and youth programs at the early stages of development (Mahoney & Zigler, 2006). This suggests that the features, offerings, and quality of out-of-school activities will also be dynamic and fluid over time. As a result, longitudinal study is needed to understand the bidirectional influence occurring between the developing

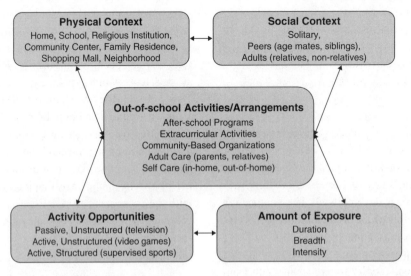

FIGURE 7.1   Key parameters in the ecology of out-of-school activities. Youth may be involved in one or several activities that can vary with respect physical location, social context and supervision, amount of exposure, activity level, and opportunities for skill building. Relations between these aspects are assumed critical for understanding how activity participation influences adolescent development.

adolescent and evolving out-of-school contexts in which he/she is involved.

Finally, *when situated in a life-course perspective* (e.g., Elder & Shanahan, 2006), *the bioecological model also underscores the significance of macro-time and timing.* Conclusions regarding both the prevalence and significance of adolescent participation in out-of-school activities may be relative to when and how often youth are involved in such activities. For example, very basic events such as the yearly changes of seasons can affect both the types and amounts of time that youth spend in different out-of-school activities. Indeed, transitions between the school year and summertime (the largest consecutive period of out-of-school time) may affect a range of adolescent activities, including sleep/wake patterns, amounts of discretionary time, hours spent without adult supervision, and opportunities for involvement in supervised endeavors such as paid employment and organized activities (e.g., Apel, Paternoster, Bushway, & Brame, 2006; Capizzano, Adelman, & Stagner, 2002). This seasonal impact on activity availability and participation is nested further in the historical and social–political zeitgeist (e.g., Halpern, 2002). For instance, recent historical changes in the perceived need for, and interest in, out-of-school activities have markedly impacted the funding for, and availability of, supervised out-of-school activities for young people (e.g., Mahoney et al., in press).

Summary

In summary, the bioecological perspective provides a general framework from which to delineate broad theoretical issues that help to guide the study of out-of-school activities and adolescent development. The perspective calls attention to the need to study dynamics between persons, contexts, processes, and time occurring within and across different types of out-of-school activity settings, for youth from different backgrounds and developmental levels, all in relation to other developmental contexts of adolescence. From this vantage point,

we now consider research pertaining to adolescent involvement in the first of two broad categories of out-of-school activities, namely, activities that lack adult supervision and tend not be highly structured.

OUT-OF-SCHOOL ACTIVITIES THAT LACK ADULT SUPERVISION

Developmental consequences for youth whose out-of-school activities lack direct supervision from adults has been of interest to researchers, policy makers, and families for decades (e.g., Riley & Steinberg, 2004; Stewart, 2001; Woods, 1972). Prior to the mid-1980s, youth in this arrangement were often referred to as *latchkey children* because of the house key they wore around their necks (e.g., Long & Long, 1982). However, some considered this term to have negative connotations (Rodman, Pratto, & Smith Nelson, 1985), and descriptors such as *self-care* and *nonadult care* have become increasingly common replacements. The changing terms coincide with an ongoing debate over the consequences of this arrangement for the healthy development of young people. The potential positive consequences of self-care for youth (e.g., greater responsibility, independence, self-reliance) and parents (e.g., facilitation of work) have been contrasted with the presumed negative impacts for youth (e.g., fear, exposure to crime, involvement with deviant peers, victimization, injury) and parents (e.g., worry, guilt; e.g., Galambos & Dixon, 1984; Riley & Steinberg, 2004).

In this section we begin by providing some descriptive information on the prevalence of self-care and review research on factors associated with its use. We then discuss theoretical perspectives and investigations concerned with the consequences of self-care for adolescents. In each case, main points of agreement, controversy, and areas for needed research are identified.

Prevalence and Predictors of Self-Care

The prevalence of self-care has risen markedly over the past 60 years. Changes in family and labor-force participation are the main explanation for this increase. The rise in women's participation in the paid labor force first became substantive during World War II, when fathers were away and maternal employment outside of the home expanded. By 1955, 38% of mothers with children aged 6–17 were employed (U.S. Department of Labor, 2000). Until recent years, the percentage has increased steadily, with 46%, 55%, 70%, and 74% of mothers employed in 1965, 1975, 1985, and 1995, respectively. In 2006, 73% of mothers with children aged 6–17 were working (U.S. Department of Labor, 2007). These changes in labor-force participation were driven by several factors, including economic necessity and the rise in single-parent families.

Three factors are quite consistently linked to the prevalence of self-care, namely, child age, maternal employment, and family structure. Figure 7.2 illustrates relations for two of these factors—child age and maternal employment—using data from 2002 Survey of Income and Program Participation (SIPP) (Overturf Johnson, 2005). Self-care becomes more common across middle childhood and early adolescence with approximately 40% of 12- to 14-year-olds regularly spending time in self-care during a typical week. This is a consistent finding across studies (e.g., Cain & Hofferth, 1989; Casper & Smith, 2002). Nonetheless, it is noteworthy that these studies did not consider self-care beyond the age of 14 or past grade 9. As a result, we know very little about such relations for older adolescents (Stewart, 2001).

Self-care is also higher for youth whose mothers are working, and some research points to a positive, linear relationship between the amount of self-care that youth experience and the number of hours their mothers are employed (e.g., Brandon, 1999; Rodman & Pratto, 1987). However, Cain and Hofferth's (1989) analysis of the 1984 Current Population Survey (CPS) indicated that although maternal employment predicts the use of nonparental care in general, it does not predict the specific type of nonparental care (e.g., self-care, sibling care, relative care).

Finally, with regard to family structure, studies tend to report that among families where the mother is employed, early adolescents from single-parent families are more likely to experience self-care relative to those living in intact, two-parent households (e.g., Dwyer et al., 1990; Overturf Johnson, 2005). The availability of nonparental adults, such as a grandmother, that are nearby and able to "check in" on unsupervised youth as well as the presence of older siblings in the home make self-care more likely (e.g., Brandon, 1999; Cain & Hofferth, 1989).

Some demographic predictors of self-care are less intuitive. For example, despite popular perceptions that poor, inner-city youth from

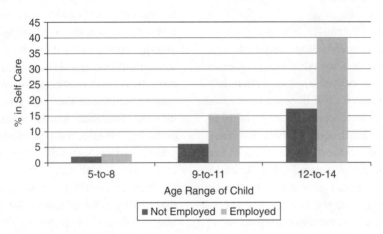

FIGURE 7.2 Percentage of youth in self-care according to age of child and employment status of mother.

traditionally defined minority groups are most apt to experience self-care, the data reveal this belief to be largely unfounded. Indeed, a consensus of findings from national, regional, and local investigations shows that the adolescents most likely to be in self-care tend to be White (vs. Black or Hispanic), reside in higher-income areas, and come from middle-class or higher-income families with a mother who tends to hold a bachelor's degree or has completed a higher level of education (e.g., Casper & Smith, 2002; Dwyer et al., 1990; Overturf Johnson, 2005). Two exceptions deserve comment. First, although self-care is more common for White youth, Casper and Smith's (2002) analysis of the 1995 SIPP data found that Black youth were more likely to experience intensive amounts (10+ hours/week) of self-care. Second, in a sample of impoverished 10- to 14-year-olds, Levine Coley, Morris, and Hernandez (2004) found that out-of-home unsupervised care was associated with greater socioeconomic disadvantage. The latter finding is troubling insofar as it suggests that, among poor families, those youth living in the deepest poverty may be less apt to be supervised after school. Efforts to replicate the finding should be undertaken, and additional research is needed to know whether this owes to a lack of available and affordable supervised alternatives for families living in poverty and those residing in extreme disadvantage.

Beyond demographics, comparatively less is known about the psychosocial aspects of adolescents or their parents that make out-of-school self-care likely. For example, Belle's (1997) qualitative study of children and early adolescents showed that whether parents rely on self-care depends on child/adolescent characteristics such as level of maturity, ability to follow rules, and lack of disruptive and anxiety problems. With respect to parents, studies have found that youth in self-care tend to have parents who are relatively poor monitors of their behavior (Levine Coley et al., 2004; Pettit et al., 1999), permissive in their parenting style (Steinberg, 1986), and more likely to smoke

and drink (Richardson, Dwyer, McGuigan et al., 1989). However, it is difficult to sort out directionality in these studies because person characteristics have typically been assessed in tandem with the self-care experience and relegated to control variables. Considerably more work is needed to understand the "effects of causes" through longitudinal studies that focus on the selection of self-care as an important person–context process itself.

Several additional areas of study would elucidate which youth are likely to experience self-care and why. First, as noted earlier, most of what is known about predictors of youth self-care comes from studies of early adolescents. Examining how various demographic and person factors relate to self-care across the full period of adolescence is called for. Second, although several studies show racial/ethnic-related differences in the use of self-care, the explanations for the differences are not clear. The differences could relate to family income or parental education levels or to cultural differences concerning the use of extended family members as care providers. These possibilities need to be examined more directly in future research. Third, for decades scholars have identified the need to understand how neighborhood factors such as levels of disadvantage and crime affect the use of self-care (Galambos & Dixon, 1984; Riley & Steinberg, 2004; Stewart, 2001). Although neighborhood factors have begun to be examined in relation to outcomes associated with self-care (see below), few studies have considered which neighborhood conditions are most apt to affect adolescents' out-of-school activities. It would be particularly interesting to know whether and how particular neighborhood conditions might interface with other known demographic predictors of out-of-school activities such as age, gender, or family structure (e.g., Fauth et al., 2007; Lord & Mahoney, 2007).

Finally, it should be noted that considerable discrepancy exists across studies in terms of how self-care has been defined and operationalized. This includes differences in intensity and duration of self-care, directness of adult supervision, presence/absence of siblings or peers, location, time of day and season, age of youth, whether it is voluntary or required, and whether time in other out-of-school activities is considered (e.g., Riley & Steinberg, 2004; Stewart, 2001). Over recent decades a variety of definitions have been offered. For instance, Rodman and Cole (1987) defined self-care as a youth " . . . between the ages of approximately 6 and 13 who spends time at home alone or with a younger sibling on a periodic basis." Although this definition could be apt in very general terms, it is inadequate to capture the full complexity of the phenomenon (e.g., Belle, 1997; Coleman, Rowland, & Robinson, 1989, 1990; Steinberg, 1988). It is probably less important that scholars spend time finding a single definition that will satisfy all investigations and investigators and more important to be clear on theoretical and empirical bases for including or excluding the various parameters under study.

Consequences Associated with Self-Care

The available literature on whether and to what extent self-care has consequences for adolescent development contains mixed findings. A majority of studies have found that youth who experience self-care on a regular basis show relatively poor adjustment in areas ranging from substance use (e.g., Levine Coley et al., 2004; Mott, Crowe, Richardson, & Flay, 1999; Richardson, Radziszewska, Dent, & Flay, 1993), aggression, deviance, and misconduct (e.g., Galambos & Maggs, 1991; Levine Coley et al., 2004; Marshall et al., 1997; Pettit et al., 1999), fear and anxiety (e.g., Long & Long, 1982; Shulman, Kedern, Kaplan, Sever, & Braja, 1998), to low academic performance and school attendance (e.g., Dwyer et al., 1990; Pettit et al., 1997; Posner & Vandell, 1999). However, a partially overlapping set of studies reports that self-care has no significant relation to either psychosocial behavior problems (e.g., Galambos & Dixon, 1984; Rodman et al.,

1985; Shulman et al., 1998) or low academic performance (e.g., Dwyer et al., 1990; Vandell & Ramanan, 1991).

Why the discrepant findings across studies and outcomes? From a bioecological perspective, the associations should depend on both social-contextual features of the self-care environment and characteristics of the youth considered. With respect to context, Routine Activity Theory (e.g., Osgood et al., 1996) emphasizes several basic elements of out-of-school activities that may affect the development of problem behaviors during adolescence. In this view, antisocial behaviors common to adolescence are partly a function of opportunity. Opportunities for deviance may be highest when youth lack adult supervision, are involved in unstructured settings without an agenda, and are in the company of peers (Osgood & Anderson, 2004). This circumstance characterizes the out-of-school experience of many youth and could help to account for the fact that juvenile violence peaks during the hours following school dismissal (Newman, Fox, Flynn, & Christenson, 2000) and is highest during the summer months (U.S. Department of Justice, 2004).

Consistent with this proposal, across adolescence, time with peers increases, and peer interactions tend to take place further from the home and occur in longer intervals without direct parental supervision (e.g., NRC-IOM, 2003; Osgood, Anderson, & Shaffer, 2005). These trends are correlated with the growth of criminal offending that emerges during early adolescence and resonate with studies linking unstructured and unsupervised out-of-school time with adolescent antisocial behavior (e.g., Dodge, Dishion, & Lansford, 2006; Dwyer et al., 1990; Mahoney, Stattin, & Magnusson, 2001). Moreover, evidence suggests that a lack of adult supervision presents a significant associated risk for adolescents primarily when the self-care environment is away from the home rather than inside the home (e.g., Steinberg, 1986).

Parenting styles and behaviors also clarify the link between self-care and adolescent adjustment. For example, permissive parenting is associated with low levels of parental monitoring and related knowledge about the whereabouts, activities, and peer involvement of youth. This lack of knowledge, in turn, predicts adolescent susceptibility to peer pressure and substance use, particularly for youth whose self-care environment extends outside of the home (e.g., Mott et al., 1999; Richardson et al., 1993; Steinberg, 1986). In contrast, authoritative parenting styles characterized by a combination of warmth/support, clear expectations/rules, and consequences has been linked to a lessening of negative consequences associated with adolescent out-of-home self care (e.g., Mott et al., 1999). Identifying the mechanisms behind this association requires further study. However, it has been suggested that authoritative parents are particularly effective in establishing a relationship of trust and communication with their adolescent children. The nature of this relationship, and the adolescent's desire to maintain it, is thought to allow authoritatively parented youth greater ease in resisting peer pressures toward deviance that occur in the absence of adult supervision (e.g., Riley & Steinberg, 2004; Stattin & Kerr, 2000; but see Levine Coley et al., 2004).

Similarly, the neighborhood in which self-care occurs contributes to the associated impact of self-care on adolescent adjustment. Consistent with Routine Activity Theory, youth who are unsupervised and in the midst of dangerous and poorly organized neighborhoods are presumed to encounter more opportunities for deviance and experience fewer controls to interfere with or redirect such opportunities compared to youth who are supervised and/or remain at home (e.g., Lord & Mahoney, 2007; Vandell & Ramanan, 1991). Research tends to support this notion. For instance, early studies reporting negative consequences of self-care tended to be conducted with samples of youth residing in the inner city rather than rural or suburban areas (e.g., Galambos & Dixon, 1984; Robinson, Coleman, & Rowland, 1986). More recent work shows that features of urban

neighborhoods such as low levels of perceived safety and collective efficacy appear to intensify the risk of antisocial behavior for youth experiencing out-of-home self-care and low parental monitoring (e.g., Levine Coley et al., 2004; Pettit et al., 1999).

Person-level factors may also affect the extent to which self-care relates to problem behaviors during adolescence. Gender is one such factor. Although problem behaviors can characterize both boys and girls in self-care, adverse outcomes such as peer pressure, deviant peer affiliations, and substance use are more apparent for girls than for boys (e.g., Galambos & Maggs, 1991; Richardson et al., 1993; Steinberg, 1986). This gender difference is most evident when girls perceive their parents' lack knowledge of their whereabouts and activities (Richardson et al., 1993) and when their relationship with parents is high in conflict and control and low in acceptance (e.g., Galambos & Maggs, 1991).

Preexisting behavior problems is a second person-level factor. Both Pettit and colleagues (1999) and Levine Coley and colleagues (2004) found that the antisocial behavior and misconduct associated with self-care was particularly marked if the adolescents had a history of behavior problems. Richardson and colleagues (1989) offer one explanation. Self-care could facilitate youth's perception of maturity and promote decision making in the absence of adults. This may be viewed in positive terms for some youth. However, the sense of maturity and independence may render adolescents with established behavior problems susceptible to the influence of like-minded and deviant peers and to become involved in risky situations when they lack adult supervision.

Finally, time and timing are important elements of the bioecological model and shed additional light on consequences associated with adolescent self-care. Although studies have often operationalized self-care dichotomously (e.g., youth ever experiences self-care, self-care is the youth's primary out-of-school arrangement), a few have examined amount of time that adolescents spend in self-care (e.g., hours per week). In general, behavior problems are more likely for youth who spend several hours/week in self-care. This relationship seems to hold for adolescent smoking (Mott et al., 1999), externalizing behavior problems (Pettit et al., 1999), and substance use and depression (Richardson et al., 1989, 1993). For example, net of controls, Richardson and colleagues (1989) found that substance use was twice as high for youth who spent 11 or more hours/week in self-care compared to those not experiencing self-care. Richardson and colleagues (1993) also noted that the association between time in self-care and adjustment can vary by outcome. For instance, the largest associated increase for substance use occurred around 4 or more hours/week of self-care, whereas the most sizable increase in depression occurred around 10 or more hours/week of self-care. Limited evidence also suggests that the onset and stability of self-care is important when interpreting links to adolescent adjustment. Among adolescents experiencing self-care, Dwyer and colleagues (1990) found that early adolescents' use of cigarettes, alcohol, and marijuana was significantly higher when self-care began in childhood and continued into adolescence.

Summary

Debate concerning whether self-care facilitates psychosocial problems or facilitates independence and solitary competence has generated a sizable literature over recent decades. The ensuing debate over self-care was originally centered on childhood. However, recognition that adolescents who were not monitored by adults during the out-of-school hours may also be at risk for developing psychosocial and antisocial behavior problems provided impetus for studies of early and middle adolescence. Overall, it appears that under some conditions self-care does represent a risk for compromising the healthy development of adolescents. Specifically, psychosocial behavior problems are more likely when the

self-care experience (1) occurs increasingly further from the home, (2) involves permissive parenting and low monitoring, (3) takes place in dangerous and disorganized neighborhoods, (4) occurs for youth with preexisting behavior problems, and (5) is intensive and persistent.

Conclusions and Future Directions

Although considerable advances have been made in understanding predictors and associated consequences of adolescent self-care, the literature review points to areas where more research is needed. First, advocates of self-care propose that the arrangement can foster independence, self-reliance, and responsibility while facilitating parent work and peace of mind during the out-of-school hours. Very few studies of self-care have been designed to assess whether these potential positives might apply to some subgroups of youth.

Second, as noted earlier, the majority of research on self-care has been directed toward childhood and early adolescence. We know very little about the significance of time spent without adult supervision for older adolescents. As youth mature, they are expected to become increasingly autonomous, independent, and responsible in the absence of adults. This would suggest that direct adult supervision should ordinarily lessen and that self-care may, overall, be less indicative of adjustment in later adolescence. However, it is also the case that some problem behaviors connected with self-care (e.g., substance use, crime, depression) continue or augment across adolescence. As such, the extent to which self-care remains a risk factor for continuing or initiating problem behaviors in late adolescence remains an open question.

Third, the bulk of knowledge on adolescent self-care comes from single-time-point, cross-sectional studies. A limited number of short-term longitudinal studies have also been employed. In general, these studies have included only a small number of known selection factors identified in the first part of this section. Furthermore, only the longitudinal studies are able to account for youth adjustment in the selection process. As a result, there remains doubt about the directionality of associations reported. This is true despite the consistency of findings across studies following different designs and including different controls. Moreover, because there is a limited amount of longitudinal research, precious little is known about the processes by which self-care translates into adjustment outcomes over time or whether such processes may operate differently across the period of adolescence.

Finally, interpreting the consequences of any out-of-school activity or arrangements can depend on the comparison activity considered (e.g., Mahoney, Lord, & Carryl, 2005b). With some notable exceptions (e.g., Galambos & Maggs, 1991; Levine Coley et al., 2004; Mott et al., 1999), studies of adolescent self-care have been vague concerning which types of supervised arrangements are serving as the reference comparison. As we discuss in the next section, supervised activities involve their own selection processes, and failing to account for these factors clouds the interpretation of findings. In addition, those studies that have compared self-care to specific alternative activities have tended to conduct analyses as if youth experience only one out-of-school activity. This denies the reality that youth are often involved in several different activities in a given week such that self-care can be part of a patchwork of out-of-school experiences (e.g., Lord & Mahoney, 2007; Polatnick, 2002). Furthermore, the combination of arrangements experienced can be expected to change across adolescence.

Because the experience and consequences of self-care can depend on these other activities (e.g., Pettit et al., 1997), analytic approaches that identify and compare patterns of adolescent activities seem promising (e.g., Mahoney et al., 2005b; Pedersen, 2005). However, a more complete accounting will depend on the success of dynamic modeling approaches that are able to simultaneously map behavioral changes with changes in individual patterns of out-of-school activities over time.

ADOLESCENT PARTICIPATION IN ORGANIZED ACTIVITIES

Although rates of self-care increase across middle childhood and adolescence, most youth participate in one or more structured out-of-school activities in the presence of supervising adults. Indeed, the risks associated with adolescent self-care have contributed to growing interest in supervised out-of-school activities (Mahoney et al., in press; Vandell et al., 2005). Participation in two main types of structured and supervised adolescent out-of-school activities have received that largest amount of attention from researchers, namely: (1) organized activities such as formal sports teams, arts, civic, religion, and mentoring programs commonly offered through school-based extracurricular activities or community-based organizations; and (2) formal and informal paid employment. As noted at the outset, the focus of this chapter is organized out-of-school activities and, more specifically, adolescent participation in sports, arts, and youth clubs. Readers interested in adolescent employment are directed to chapter 8 (this volume). Moreover, although some attention is given to participation in civic and mentoring activities, chapters 5 and 11 (this volume) provide more comprehensive coverage of these activity types, respectively.

This section is divided into two main parts. The first part is concerned with research on the factors that influence whether youth will participate in organized activities. The second part considers research on the associated consequences of organized activity participation for adolescent development.

Who Participates in Organized Activities and Why?

This subsection considers research into the factors affecting why youth do and do not participate in organized activities. We begin with definitional and measurement issues related to the construct of participation. Next, we consider descriptive information that is concerned with rates of youth participation in organized activities. Finally, the respective roles of demographic, psychosocial, and contextual factors as predictors of adolescent participation in organized activities are discussed.

Participation as a Multifaceted Construct

The term participation has been used to represent the time adolescents spend at an activity and what they do there. The most common indicators of participation include enrollment, attendance, breadth, and engagement. Although many of these indicators are positively associated (e.g., Busseri, Rose-Krasnor, Willoughby, & Chalmers, 2006; Marsh & Kleitman, 2002; Simpkins, O'Donnell, & Becnel, 2007), they are conceptually distinct and uniquely predict outcomes. These indicators address the temporal progression of participation and the type of activity.

Several of the indictors of participation relate to one another in a temporal progression. For example, adolescents must enroll in an activity before they can attend. The intensity/frequency of adolescents' attendance in activities (e.g., once a month or four times a week) precedes duration and engagement. Duration is an indicator of the longevity of attendance, such as the number of years one has attended the same program. Engagement captures adolescents' degree of involvement (e.g., interest, effort, and enjoyment) in the activity. Duration and engagement have been viewed as reciprocal processes that support one another across time (Pearce & Larson, 2006).

The second distinction in participation addresses the type of activity. Although there may be some common affordances across all high-quality organized activities (e.g., safety, positive social interactions), opportunities also depend on the types of activity. For example, participating in the school band builds music skills, whereas participating on a school sports team or the swim team at the local YMCA builds athletic skills. Even though the two athletic activities in the example are similar in terms of the skills they address, they are different in regard to where they are offered (i.e., school vs. community). This may have different implications for the social capital and related value systems to which the adolescent participant is exposed (Patrick, Ryan, Alfeld-Liro et al., 1999). Accordingly, researchers have begun to conceptualize activity type with reference to both content (e.g., music, sport, service) and location (e.g., school, community center, religious setting).

An additional consideration in defining participation is the fact that adolescents vary in whether they devote all of their time to one type of activity, such as sports, or multiple activity types, such as sports and student government. Researchers have labeled the variety of adolescents' participation across different activity types as activity breadth (e.g., Eccles & Barber, 1999). Approximately 70% of adolescents simultaneously participate in multiple activities (Larson, Hansen, & Moneta, 2006). In response to findings that suggest different types of activities provide different learning experiences and skill mastery (e.g., Barber, Eccles, & Stone, 2001; Larson et al., 2006), some researchers have also begun to examine the different combinations of activities in which youth participate (e.g., frequent participation in combinations of sports and school clubs compared to frequent participation in sports and volunteering) to provide a more complete understanding of individual variation in the out-of-school ecologies of young people (e.g., Bartko & Eccles, 2003; Pedersen, 2005; Zarrett et al., 2007).

Measuring Participation

Participation can be measured quantitatively and qualitatively through individual reports (e.g., self/parent/peer-report) and observations. The majority of the literature incorporates quantitative procedures drawing on individual reports of participation. A variety of procedures and data sources have been employed, including yearbooks, time diaries, experience sampling, questionnaires, and checklists. School yearbooks are unique from the other measures because they enable researchers to collect indicators of school-based activities without burdening respondents and to collect information on participants after a study has ended (e.g., Mahoney & Cairns, 1997). The other measures are all options researchers can use to measure activity participation in an ongoing study.

Time diaries have been used for decades to measure how people spend time. In time diaries, people are asked to report the starting and ending times of every activity during a specified time frame, such as the past 24 hours. Researchers have also employed a modified time diary in which people report their primary activity during specified intervals, such as 15-minute intervals after school (e.g., NICHD Early Childcare Network, 2004; Posner & Vandell, 1999). This methodology is more useful in providing detailed information on activities that occur daily, such as television viewing, than activities that occur seasonally or infrequently (e.g., once per week).

The experience sampling method is another method that has been used to collect detailed information on participation. This method emerged from research on engagement and experiences during activities (Larson, 1989). During a set period, such as 2 weeks, adolescents are signaled to answer questions about what they are doing and their experiences when they are signaled via a communication device (e.g., pager, watch, phone, etc.). This method allows researchers to capture adolescent experience in vivo rather than in retrospect.

Researchers have often used stylized questions to capture aspects of participation. In contrast to the previous two methods, stylized questions allow a researcher to collect the same information on a variety of activities that occur throughout the year for each participant. In this method, adolescents typically report how often they attend a particular activity with a Likert response scale that measures time on a monthly or weekly basis (e.g., once per month, twice per week, less than 1 hour per week, 5–6 hours per week). Data from these stylized questions can be recoded to capture enrollment, attendance, duration, and breadth. Furthermore, stylized questions can be used to collect information on level of engagement or one's experiences during the activity (e.g., Hansen, Larson, & Dworkin, 2003; Rosenthal & Vandell, 1996).

A common method to quickly capture adolescents' participation in a wide range of activities is a checklist. This method is often used to measure adolescents' participation in school-based clubs and activities for the entire school year. For example, in the Study of Adolescent Health, respondents marked which school clubs and activities they participated in, or planned to participate in, during the current school year from a list of 31 possible activities. Researchers have made use of these checklists to develop a better understanding of indicators of enrollment, duration, and breadth.

Predictors of Participation

Participation in organized activities is a common developmental experience. Although most youth participate in at least one organized activity during adolescence, this is not true for all youth (e.g., Mahoney, Harris, & Eccles, 2006). Moreover, there is considerable variability in the timing, duration, and type of involvement among participants (e.g., Darling, 2005; Pedersen, 2005). Researchers are beginning to study the individual and contextual factors that predict whether youth will participate in organized activities. It appears that a variety of individual and contextual factors affect activity participation. For example, demographic factors such as age, socioeconomic status (SES), and race/ethnicity can affect the overall availability of activities and/or the types of activities chosen. Similarly, individual competencies, interests, and motivations are central determinants of participation. Finally, these demographic and person-level factors are supported by the immediate contexts in which individuals develop, including peer groups, families, schools, neighborhoods, and the activities themselves.

Demographic Characteristics Demographic characteristics are among the most common predictors of organized activity participation that have been studied in recent decades. Aspects such as age, SES, and race/ethnicity affect the availability, affordability, and types of activities available to youth, as well their interest and ability to participate.

Age Activity participation significantly changes during the adolescent period. For example, on the one hand, adolescents' participation in community-based programs, such as religious and service activities, is generally low but declines further still during adolescence (Furstenberg, Cook, Eccles, Elder, & Sameroff, 1999). Research suggests that some of these declines begin in elementary school (e.g., Simpkins, Ripke, et al., 2005). On the other hand, children's participation in school-based activities generally increases through elementary school and peaks in adolescence (e.g., Darling, 2005; Gauvain & Perez, 2005; Mahoney & Cairns, 1997; Simpkins, Ripke, et al., 2005). The timing of the peak depends, in part, on the type of the activity. For instance, participation in athletic and performing arts activities has been found to peak in middle school, whereas participation in government or other school clubs seems to peak in late high school (e.g., Cooley, Henriksen, Nelson, & Thompson, 1995; Darling, 2005; Darling, Caldwell, & Smith, 2005).

These age-graded shifts emerge for several reasons. First, in comparison to childhood, adolescents have new demands on their time, such as formal employment, which lessen the potential time they have to spend on other activities (e.g., Borden, Perkins, Villarruel, & Stone, 2005; Halpern, Barker, & Mollard, 2000; Jordan & Nettles, 2000). Second, adolescents may also need to spend a substantial amount of time on homework or contributing to the family through chores (e.g., Borden et al., 2005; Halpern et al., 2000). Third, adolescents are likely to spend their time with friends or unsupervised due, in part, to increasing autonomy. Fourth, adolescents have more activity options

than children because there are typically activities for adolescents available at schools in addition to the community. Fifth, competitive standards of activities increase from childhood to adolescence such that skill level increasingly determines access to (or exclusion from) an activity (e.g., McNeal, 1998).

Finally, in some cases there has been failure of activities and programs to match adolescents' interests, skill level, and developmental needs. Consistent with the notion of person–stage–environment fit, scholars have suggested that to maintain youth attendance programs need to operate in a manner consistent with the developmental status and interests of the participants (e.g., Larson, Walker, & Pearce, 2005; Lauver et al., 2004). This work suggests that organized activities may be more attractive to adolescents when they offer flexible schedules that acknowledge youth are likely to have competing interests during the out-of-school hours; provide a diversity of activities that both differ from the school-day and resonate with adolescents' interest in developing marketable skills; allow for participation in community- and service-learning activities and to become involved in the paid labor force; provide for greater autonomy and increasing opportunities to take leadership roles as they mature; and ensure that staff are able to relate well to the youth served.

Socioeconomic Status One of the most consistent findings is that adolescents from high SES families are more likely to participate in organized activities than adolescents from low SES families (e.g., Fredricks & Eccles, 2006a; Marsh & Kleitman, 2002; Simpkins, Ripke et al., 2005; Theokas & Bloch, 2006). These differences tend to be pronounced in activities that require high investments, such as sports and lessons (Bouffard et al., 2006; Simpkins, Ripke, et al., 2005). For example, only 3% of children aged 6–14 living in poor families participated in organized sports, compared to 14% of children in more affluent families (Smith, 2002).

The different rates of participation associated with SES likely represent numerous processes at the individual and contextual levels. Adolescents from low-income families typically have lower academic achievement and psychosocial adjustment than their more affluent counterparts, which predicts lower participation. For example, adolescents with low academic achievement may have more difficulty meeting grade point average (GPA) requirements for activities. At the family level, parents may have fewer monetary resources to afford the luxury of activities and/or more constraints in terms of transportation and time to devote to activities (e.g., Halpern et al., 2000; Shann, 2001). Adolescents from low-income families often reside in neighborhoods and attend schools that are of lower quality (e.g., Leventhal & Brooks-Gunn, 2000), which may limit activity options, particularly high-quality activities (e.g., Quiroz, 2000; Shann, 2001). Furthermore, concerns about neighborhood safety may drive parents to restrict adolescents' participation (e.g., Furstenberg et al., 1999; Shann, 2001).

The barriers to participation for poor adolescent youth are significant. Researchers have found that factors placing an adolescent at risk for maladjustment predicted lower participation for more affluent adolescents, but not for poor adolescents (Wimer et al., in press). It seems that, for low-income adolescents, the barriers that are related to income are so pervasive that risk factors that normally predict lower participation are no longer significant factors.

Race/Ethnicity   The findings concerning race and ethnicity are mixed. Some researchers have found that African Americans have higher participation than European Americans (e.g., Bouffard et al., 2006; Mahoney & Cairns, 1997; Marsh & Kleitman, 2002). However, other studies report the opposite results (e.g., Darling, 2005; Larson, Richards, Sims, & Dworkin, 2001; Theokas & Bloch, 2006). The different rates of participation may depend on the types of activities studied. For instance, African Americans were higher in sports but lower in government than European American students (Mahoney & Cairns, 1997). Moreover, overall rates of participation are also important to consider. For example, although Shann (2001) did not find racial differences, most of the adolescents in this study (77%) were not involved organized activities.

The majority of work has focused on African- and European American adolescents. Less is known about other ethnic groups. Emerging evidence suggests that Asian Americans are less likely to participate in sports than all other ethnic groups (Darling et al., 2005; Shann, 2001). In addition, studies are beginning to converge on the finding that Latinos are often least likely of all ethnic groups to participate (e.g., Darling, 2005; Davalos, Chavez, & Guardiola, 1999).

Like adolescent self-care, little research has attempted to examine the mechanisms underlying the ethnic differences in participation. It likely involves a confluence of factors including SES, culture, and the process of immigration. Generational status and acculturation of Latino youth is associated with participation and reasons to participate (Borden et al., 2005; Davalos et al., 1999; Gauvain & Perez, 2005). The differences in activity participation across racial and ethnic groups as well as within these groups appear to be explained, in part, by SES and generational status. It is important for future research to address the origins of differences *between* groups as well as variation *within* groups.

Psychosocial and Contextual Factors   The bioecological perspective to development recognizes that youth are active, purposeful agents in the developmental process. The extent to which individual differences in adolescents' competencies, motivations, values, and social relationships with peers and adults relate to their involvement in organized activities has received increasing amounts of attention from researchers in recent years.

Competence   Researchers have found that adolescents' overall adjustment (Busseri et al., 2006) as well as their academic achievement (Jordan & Nettles, 2000; Marsh & Kleitman, 2002; Quiroz, 2000) and social competences (Mahoney, Cairns, & Farmer, 2003; Marsh & Kleitman, 2002; Persson, Kerr, & Stattin, 2007) are positive predictors of activity participation. In addition, previous participation during middle childhood and adolescence predicts subsequent participation (Busseri et al., 2006; Jordan & Nettles, 2000; Mahoney, Cairns, & Farmer, 2003). It seems plausible that previous participation builds the necessary skills and internal motivation to sustain participation even when activities become competitive in high school (Quiroz, 2000; Simpkins, Ripke, et al., 2005).

Interest and Motivation   One of the main reasons adolescents enroll in organized activities and continue to participate is due to interest (e.g., Luthar, Shoum, & Brown, 2006; Mahoney, Harris, & Eccles, 2006). Indeed, motivation theories suggest that the strongest predictors of activity participation should be adolescents' beliefs about their abilities and interest in an activity (Ryan & Deci, 2000; Eccles, 1993). Over the past 20 years, Eccles and colleagues (Eccles, 1983; Simpkins, Davis-Kean, & Eccles, 2006; Simpkins, Fredricks, et al., 2006) have developed and tested a model of motivational factors that influence achievement behaviors and goals, including both educational choices and recreational activity participation. The model explains activity-related choices as directly linked to whether the individual attaches importance/value to the activity and if he or she feels competent and expects future success in the activity. These self-beliefs are not only powerful predictors of individual differences in voluntary participation in an activity but also predict persistence in participation over time.

An important feature of this model is that adolescents' activity- and achievement-related decisions are often made in the context of a wide range of choices and related consequences. These choices are often made between options requiring that youth weigh the trade-offs among several possible ways to spend their leisure time. For example, deciding to join the basketball team might be weighed against the chance to volunteer at the local hospital, take on a part-time job, or just spend more time "hanging out" with friends. As a result, adolescents who regularly spend time participating in organized activities are ordinarily fueled by a strong internal motivation and interest in the particular activity (e.g., Mahoney, Harris, & Eccles, 2006).

It should be noted that not all adolescents enroll in an activity due to internal motivating factors such as interest. External motivators are also important for some youth and these include: requirements (Pearce & Larson, 2006), desire to increase marketability and skills for employment opportunities or college admissions (Quiroz, 2000), and encouragement and support from others (e.g., friends, parents; Loder & Hirsch, 2003). However, even when adolescents' report enrolling for external reasons, some research suggests that external motivations evolve into internal motivations over time (Pearce & Larson, 2006). Importantly, the different types of motivation (e.g., individual interest, encouragement from friends) are predictive of adolescents' experiences during the activity. For example, Hansen and Larson (2007) found that adolescents whose motivations to participate in organized activities included interest or wanting to pursue future goals also reported having more developmental growth experiences as a result of such participation.

Friends and Peers   Spending time with friends is one of the central motivating factors driving adolescents to join, stay, and leave activities (Borden et al., 2005; Loder & Hirsch, 2003; Patrick et al., 1999; Persson et al., 2007). Spending time with friends during an activity increases adolescents' enjoyment and likelihood of sustaining their participation (Patrick et al., 1999). One of the reasons adolescents cease participation is that the activity is not attended or valued by their friends. This is has been shown for community-based activities and other specific types of activities such as music/art.

Theoretical and empirical work suggests that one's friends influence the type of activity in which an adolescent participates (e.g., Hartup & Stevens, 1997). The peer homophily literature has consistently shown that adolescents are likely to be friends with persons who are similar to themselves (e.g., Kandel, 1978). Research suggests that adolescents in the same crowd are likely to participate in similar organized activities, such as sports in the case of the jock crowd (Eccles & Barber, 1999; Luthar, Shoum, & Brown, 2006). More broadly, adolescents who have more friends that are a positive influence (e.g., friends who value school, don't disobey their parents) are more likely to participate in a wider variety of activities (Simpkins, Eccles, & Becnel, 2007). In summary, the characteristics and interests of one's friends appear to affect both whether an adolescents participates in organized activities and, if so, the type of activity chosen.

Parents   Empirical studies have begun to examine the link between parents, parenting, and youth's organized activity participation. Overall, parents appear to both directly and indirectly influence adolescents' activity participation. For example, parents determine the neighborhoods in which the adolescent resides and the schools he or she attends (Parke et al., 2003). These contexts, in turn, determine the proximity and variety of organized activities most available to adolescents. Related, youth participation in organized activities often requires parental permission and investment in terms of money, time, and/or transportation. To be sure, the extents to which parents are able and willing to support and encourage, rather than limit, their adolescents' participation is tied to family resources. However, such decisions also seem relative to the ecology in

which the family resides and the gender of the youth. For instance, some studies find that parents are more apt to impose restrictions on organized activity participation for females than males when concerns about neighborhood safety are high (e.g., Borden et al., 2005; Halpern et al., 2000; Shann, 2001).

Parenting styles and behaviors are also positive indicators of adolescent activity participation and related adjustment. For example, participation in organized activities tends to be high for youth whose parents adopt an authoritative parenting style (e.g., warmth coupled with clear rules and expectations) and for those whose parents are themselves participants in community activities (e.g., Fletcher, Elder, & Mekos, 2000; Mahoney & Magnusson, 2001; Persson et al., 2007; Simpkins et al., in press; Wimer et al., in press). These parenting behaviors are presumed to positively impact participation rates, in part, by promoting adolescents' socioemotional adjustment and academic achievement. Research on this process is limited but consistent with this notion. For instance, Fletcher et al. (2000) studied 451 9th–10th graders living in rural areas of the United States. Results from a path analysis supported a process of parental warmth and reinforcement predicting activity participation. However, the process was apparent only for youth whose parents' own community involvement was low. This suggests the need to consider parents' activity involvement as a moderating factor to youth involvement and related outcomes (e.g., Mahoney & Magnusson, 2001).

Theories of motivation suggest that parenting behaviors geared toward a particular activity, such as encouragement and provision of activity-related materials, should promote initiation and continuity of activity participation by increasing adolescents' intrinsic interest (Eccles, 1993). On this score, quantitative evidence from cross-sectional and longitudinal studies shows that parents' activity-specific behaviors, interests, and values do predict adolescents' participation in activities in middle childhood, adolescence, and across these age periods (e.g., Anderson, Funk, Elliot, & Smith, 2003; Huebner & Mancini, 2003; Simpkins, Fredricks, et al., 2006).

In kind, qualitative research suggests the importance of parental messages concerning the activity participation process. Shannon's (2006) study of high school seniors involved youth reports of parental messages received about organized activity participation. Common themes that parents emphasized to their adolescents included the importance and value of activity participation for physical and psychosocial well-being, special opportunities to develop leadership and teamwork skills, the possibility of opening up windows of opportunity for one's future (more often from fathers), and/or developing friendships (more often from mothers). Work by Larson and colleagues (Dworkin, Larson, & Hansen, 2003; Larson, Pearce, Sullivan, & Jarrett, 2007) confirms that organized activities are often rich sources for teamwork, promoting family connectedness, and developing relationships with nonrelated adults (e.g., activity leaders, coaches). Such activities also appear to facilitate a healthy and natural process of increasing autonomy between youth and parents across adolescence (Larson et al., 2007).

Schools and Neighborhoods The school and neighborhood are important contexts of youth development that can both directly and indirectly influence adolescent adjustment by the affecting proximal processes in other nested settings (e.g., family, peer groups; Bronfenbrenner, 1979). They are particularly critical in predicting participation, as these are two contexts in which organized activities are offered. These contexts may impact adolescents' activity participation in two regards. First, schools and neighborhoods vary in terms of activity access. Participation rates are lower at large schools, in part because the ratio of open slots to the student population is more favorable in a small school than a large school (e.g., Barker & Gump, 1964; Jordan & Nettles,

2000; Marsh & Kleitman, 2002). Second, features of the school environment seem to affect participation rates. For instance, McNeal's (1999) analysis of schools in the High School and Beyond (HSB) study showed that higher pupil-to-teacher ratios, greater proportions of antisocial students, and schools with a stronger achievement emphasis tended to have lower levels of participation in extracurricular activities. School-level SES was only modestly linked to participation. The results held in a multilevel model that included race/ethnicity, gender, age, family SES, school track, hours of work, and urban/rural residence.

Third, school or neighborhood qualities, such as safety, may impact adolescent participation. For example, parents in neighborhoods they consider unsafe often engage in higher management behaviors that restrict their adolescents' activities (Furstenberg et al., 1999; Shann, 2001). However, consistent with bioecological theory, school and neighborhood risk factors tend to be weaker predictors of participation when compared to proximal factors at the individual and family levels (Wimer et al., in press).

Activity Features Compared to childhood, adolescents typically have greater options and autonomy concerning how they will spend their out-of-school time. Indeed, youth can often "vote with their feet" when it comes to participating in organized activities. Although limited, research on the linkages between features of organized activity settings and adolescents' involvement is available. This work is beginning to elucidate the sorts of activities that are and are not appealing to young people.

Structural and Process Parameters Much of the work on how aspects of the activity context lead to participation is based on theory and qualitative work. One of adolescents' basic needs is that they want a place where they are physically safe and where it is safe to share their ideas (e.g., Borden et al., 2005; Lauver & Little, 2005; Loder & Hirsch, 2003; Pearce & Larson,

2006). Another common attribute adolescents seek in an activity is that it is fun and interesting (e.g., Loder & Hirsch, 2003; Mahoney, Harris, & Eccles, 2006). Clearly, the type of activity (e.g., sports, performing arts) has differential appeal to adolescents, which is likely to be critical during enrollment.

Other aspects of the activity, such as relationships with staff and learning experiences influence adolescents' continued interest (Pearce & Larson, 2006). Staff who exhibit interaction styles akin to the authoritative parenting style is associated with higher adolescent interest in the activity (Cumming, Smith, & Smoll, 2006; Pearce & Larson, 2006; Smith, Smoll, & Barnett, 1995). In fact, coaches' behavior has been shown to be more important for young adolescents' enjoyment of sports than their team's win–loss record (Cumming, Smoll, Smith, & Grossbard, 2007). In addition, activities that are appropriate in terms of the skill level and adolescent needs (e.g., opportunities for leadership) promote participation (e.g., Borden et al., 2005; Lauver & Little, 2005) by optimizing adolescent learning and motivation (Ryan & Deci, 2000; Rogoff, 2003). Activities that provide supportive relationships and appropriate offerings are likely to increase adolescents' interest and decrease their negative reactions to the environment (e.g., unhappiness, stress) are also associated with continued participation (Barnett et al., 2005; Scanlan, Babkes, & scanlan, 2005; Smith et al., 2005).

Activity Type Participation varies across different types of activities and, for American youth, sports are the most common type of organized activity. The National Center for Education Statistics (2005) reported that 39% of high school seniors participated on a school sports team and 67% of high school seniors participated in sports, athletics, or physical exercise outside of school at least once a week in 2001. However, it should be noted that American youth report spending considerably more time in athletics than do adolescents in

postindustrial European and Asian countries (e.g., Larson & Verma, 1999).

Participation in activities other than sports is also common and, for some activities, has increased in recent decades. For example, the percentage of adolescents participating in music and other performing arts activities increased between 1990 and 2001 and follow sports as the second most common school-sponsored organized activity (25%) and after-school activity (44%) among U.S. high school seniors. The percentage of high school seniors who participated in community service and other volunteer activities at least once or twice month also increased from 24% in 1980 to 34% in 2001. Participation rates for academic clubs (15%), student council/government (11%), and newspaper/yearbook (10%) make them among the common extracurricular activities that youth reported participating in during 2001. Information from other national datasets corroborates the commonality of organized activity participation during adolescence. For instance, the National Survey of Families (NASF, 1997) indicated that among youth aged 12 to 17, 57% participated on a sports team, 60% participated in clubs or organizations and 29% participated in lessons after school or on weekends during the previous year.

CONSEQUENCES OF ORGANIZED ACTIVITY PARTICIPATION

Research on the consequences of youth participation in organized activities has expanded in recent decades. There is now an increasing awareness that how adolescents spend their out-of-school time has important implications for their social, educational, cognitive, physical, and civic development. In this section we consider research on whether, to what extent, and how and why participation in organized activities may affect the development of young people. We assume that framing and interpreting these questions from a bioecological systems perspective is important (e.g., Mahoney, Lord, & Carryl, 2005b; Marshall et al., 1997; Vandell & Posner, 1999). Accordingly, when possible, the findings from research on consequences associated with organized activity participation are discussed in terms of interactions between person, program, and contextual factors.

As a starting point, consider Holland and Andre's landmark review of organized activities published in 1987. This review involved 30 studies published between 1964 and 1984 that focused on outcomes associated with extracurricular activity participation during secondary school. The bulk of studies reviewed reported that activity participants showed more favorable outcomes than nonparticipants in terms of relatively high self-esteem, academic achievement, educational attainment, and relatively low antisocial and delinquent behaviors. However, Holland and Andre noted that most of the existing studies were methodologically weak in that most failed to account for any selection factors in the analyses and only one of the studies followed a prospective, longitudinal design. In addition, studies attempting to the identify mechanisms by which participation may affect adolescent development was nearly absent. A final limitation shared by many of these early studies was the absence of a guiding theoretical framework to formulate specific research questions and/or guide the interpretation of findings.

Since the time of Holland and Andre's review, we suggest that the field of research on the consequences of organized activity participation for adolescent development has evolved in at least five ways, namely:

1. Theoretical frameworks have been developed and/or adapted from other fields of inquiry to help guide the study of out-of-school activity participation and youth adjustment.
2. Activities types have been studied in greater depth and breadth across diverse populations of young people.
3. Large scale longitudinal studies of out-of-school activities involving local, regional, and national samples have become commonplace.

4. Much greater attention has been given to understanding and accounting for the selection process surrounding out-of-school activity participation, and this owes, in part, to more sophisticated analytic strategies such as multilevel and latent growth modeling and pattern-based analyses.
5. Developmental research considering moderating factors and mediating processes and mechanisms that help to explain the conditions under which activity participation is linked to adolescent development are emerging.

The remainder of this section discusses advancements in these areas.

Conceptual Frameworks

In addition to the general bioecological framework described earlier in this chapter, several theoretical frameworks from developmental and clinical psychology, sociology, criminology, and education have been used to inform research on organized activities. These include *social control theory, person–stage–environment fit theory, flow theory,* and *positive youth development.* Although these frameworks were typically not developed to guide research on organized activities per se, they have been of value and have influenced the direction of research in this field over the past 20 years.

Social Control Theory

Social control theory (Hirshi, 1969; Sampson & Laub, 1992) posits that the strength of ties between youth and social institutions affects behavioral development. Informal social controls provided through attachments with family, peer groups, and school (and the social capital therein) are salient during adolescence. Such attachments are believed to regulate the development of desired principles and conventional values that translate into behavioral outcomes. Positive ties to these social institutions may both diminish the likelihood of deviant behaviors and facilitate social–academic competence while a lack of such ties could increase social–educational adjustment problems.

Social control theory further proposes that conditions of socioeconomic disadvantage reduce opportunities for youth to develop positive attachments with these social institutions for a number of reasons (e.g., neighborhood disorganization, restricted and/or transient social capital from adults, stress related to single-parent families, poor-quality educational institutions, paucity of safe out-of-home environments) (e.g., Jencks & Mayer, 1990; Leventhal & Brooks-Gunn, 2000). Moreover, from a bioecological perspective, key microsystems involved in the regulation of youth behavior (school, home, peer group) are interdependent and have synergistic influence on development over time. In this view, the developmental impact of social institution ties could become more diverse, intertwined, and powerful from childhood through adolescence.

Organized activity participation is positively associated with connections to key social institutions that social control theory identifies for adolescents. For example, research consistent with this perspective shows that organized activity participation is related to positive parent–adolescent relationships, including more frequent parent–adolescent discussions and shared activities (e.g., Mahoney, Harris, & Eccles, 2006), higher parental knowledge about youth out-of-home activities (Mahoney & Stattin, 2000), increased school connectedness (Brown & Evans, 2002), less substance use (Gottfredson, Gerstenblith, Soulé, Wormer, & Lu, 2004), and higher educational attainment (McNeal, 1995; 1999). In addition, organized activities help to structure adolescent peer groups. Activity-based peer relationships often involve youth who are less deviant, more school oriented, and less apt to experience peer rejection than peer relationships not involving activity participants (e.g., Mahoney, Lord, & Carryl, 2005a; Sandstrom & Coie, 1999). These relationships, in turn, appear to mediate or moderate activity-related gains in social–academic competence (Gottfredson et al., 2004; Mahoney, 2000).

Similarly, organized activity participants often form close relationships with adult activity leaders, who can serve as mentors. These mentoring relationships appear to positively influence emotional, behavioral, and academic outcomes of participants (e.g., Rhodes, this volume). Such activity-based relationships may be particularly important for high risk and disadvantaged youth (Rhodes & DuBois, 2006). Finally, organized activity participation has been linked to both increased school/community engagement and attachment (e.g., Larson, 1994; Youniss, McLellan, & Yates, 1997) that may facilitate adolescent educational success (e.g., Mahoney & Cairns, 1997).

Person–Stage–Environment Fit

The person–stage–environmental fit perspective developed by Eccles and her colleagues has been influential in research on organized activities and other out-of-school contexts. This perspective holds that the *fit* between an individual's developmental stage and the social environment in which he/she is a part affects developmental outcomes (e.g., Eccles & Roeser, vol. 1; Eccles & Midgley, 1989). A good fit reflects environmental demands that are appropriate to the adolescent's physical, psychosocial, emotional, and cognitive needs and is anticipated to facilitate positive developmental outcomes. In contrast, a poor person–context fit is apt to increase risks for negative developmental outcomes.

In early work following the person–stage–environment fit perspective, Eccles and colleagues focused on the school setting. This work suggested there was sometimes a mismatch between the operation and capacities of middle schools and developmental needs of the students they served. Although adolescents are seeking chances to gain autonomy, independence, leadership, and make decisions, the middle school experience often presented them with few such opportunities. It seems that the middle school practice of changing classrooms every period constrained opportunities for youth to develop meaningful school-based relationship with adults which, in turn, increased risks for developing adjustment problems. Thus, problematic behaviors that can characterize the period of adolescence are not necessarily a reflection of being adolescent but rather concern a poor fit between the needs of youth and the environments in which they develop.

Eccles's more recent research on the person–stage–environment theory has included out-of-school contexts (e.g., Eccles, 1999; in press). Importantly, organized activities have the potential to provide youth with greater amounts of choice and autonomy than do traditional schools. As a result, the developmental interests and needs of youth may be well (perhaps uniquely) served through participation in organized out-of-school settings. Indeed, emerging research focusing on the reports of adolescent activity participants suggests that organized activities do often represent a better fit than some other developmental contexts. For example, Larson and colleagues (Dworkin, Larson, & Hansen, 2003; Hansen & Larson, 2007; Larson, Hansen, & Moneta, 2006) showed that organized activities were particularly effective in providing developmental experiences that can promote adolescent's initiative, self-regulation, and social and group skills. The combination of growth experiences provided in organized activities was not typically found in other youth contexts (e.g., the school classroom, peer group, watching TV, employment) (Larson, 2000).

Flow Theory

The theoretical notion of flow (Csikszentmihalyi, 1990) enhances understanding of the psychological components of person–stage–environment theory. Flow experiences are intrinsically motivating and reported by youth to be deeply involving and enjoyable while at the same time absorbing their concentration. Pursuits that provide a balance between challenges/demands of the environment and the skills/resources of the individual are conducive to flow. This combination of psychological experiences is particularly well suited for learning, growth, and skill acquisition. As such flow experiences are proposed to be particularly effective in facilitating the developmental process.

Larson's (2000) research on organized out-of-school settings suggests that, relative to other settings, organized activities are effective in fostering experiences conducive to flow. Specifically, adolescents reported psychological states at school, at home, and during structured voluntary activities. Voluntary structured activities were the contexts in which youth tended to report high levels of intrinsic motivation *and* high levels of effort and concentration (i.e., the flow experience). Larson has posited that this combination of high effort, concentration, and intrinsic motivation fosters positive youth development, particularly the development of *initiative*, defined as motivation from within to initiate and sustain effort towards a challenging goal over time.

This view is consistent with the research of Vandell and colleagues (2005). Findings from a sample of low-income middle school students whose experiences were sampled 35 times/week in the fall and spring showed adolescents' activities, feeling states, and motivation differed markedly when they attended organized after-school programs versus other settings. Among other things, students in organized after-school programs reported greater levels of engagement, higher concentration and effort, and also cared about their activities at programs more than elsewhere.

Positive Youth Development

In contrast to a long-standing view of adolescence as a developmental period characterized by the increasing number and severity of problem behaviors (e.g., school failure, substance use, crime, risky sexual behavior), more recently scholars have begun to view youth as resources to be developed (e.g., Lerner, Lerner, Almerigi, et al., 2005). This positive youth development (PYD) perspective is concerned with adjustment beyond the absence of problems including the attainment of developmental assets, morality, civic engagement, initiative, and thriving (e.g., Bensen, 2004; chapter 15, vol. 1 of this *Handbook*). As a result, the traditional "deficit model" approach to youth development has been broadened in recent years by theoretical, methodological, and empirical studies focused on PYD (e.g., Benson, Scales, Hamilton, & Sesma, 2006).

In addition to preventing problems, youth development programs and many other organized activities focus on skill and competency development (Roth, Brooks-Gunn, Murray, & Foster, 1998). As a result, organized activity participation allows youth to practice social, physical, and cognitive skills that are useful in multiple settings; contribute to the well-being of their community; belong to a group of interconnected members with positive social norms; try on new roles/identities in a safe environment; receive support from caring adults and peers; experience and navigate intra- and interpersonal challenges and goals; and foster positive connections between family, school, and community (e.g., Eccles, Barber, Stone, & Hunt, 2003; Morrisey & Werner-Wilson, 2005; NRC-IOM, 2002). In this view, organized activity participation represents a developmental context that should be effective in both problem reduction and PYD (Mahoney, Eccles, Larson, & Lord, 2005).

Emerging research following a PYD perspective suggests that organized activity participation is an important developmental context. For example, in their review of one important type of organized activity—youth programs—Roth and colleagues (1998) concluded that participation was linked to both a reduction in problem behaviors (e.g., involvement in the juvenile justice system) and promoted some competencies (e.g., improved peer relations). Positive outcomes were most apt to be observed for participants attending programs with full and consistent implementation, sustained service and frequent/durable participation, and those fostering links with other contexts of youth development (e.g., home, school).

Similarly, Lerner and colleagues (Jelicic, Bobek, Phelps, et al., 2007; Lerner et al., 2005) have proposed that participation in youth development programs provide rich opportunities for youth to develop the "Five Cs"—Competence, Confidence, Connection, Character, and Caring. Findings from the first two waves of data from the 4-H Study of Youth Development suggest that youth development program participation and the Five Cs predict youth' subsequent contribution to their communities (i.e., leadership, service, helping). However, additional work is needed to know whether the presumed, full longitudinal process (i.e., youth development program participation predicts increased PYD that, in turn, predicts increased contribution) is accurate.

Finally, research from the 8-Waves and 15-Years longitudinal investigation Michigan Study of Adolescent Life Transitions (MSALT; see Eccles, Barber, Stone, & Hunt, 2003, for a review) has followed a PYD framework. Findings from MSALT suggest that adolescent participation in organized activities may both reduce problems and promote competence. However, this long-term investigation also indicates that whether and to what extent participation is beneficial may depend on the activities and outcomes considered. For example, net of multiple controls for selection bias (i.e., prior activity involvement, gender, maternal education, verbal and math aptitude), adolescent participation in prosocial activities such as volunteer and community service was predictive both of a reduction in problem behaviors (drinking, drug use, and skipping school) and an increase in positive behaviors (higher GPA, more academic friends). In contrast, youth participating in team sports showed an *increase* in one problem behavior (e.g., they drank alcohol and got drunk more often in high school) but also an increase in many positive outcomes (i.e., school liking, GPA, tertiary education, obtaining a job that offered a better future and more autonomy). Thus, with regard to PYD, all activities may not be equal. We return to this issue in more detail later.

Organized Activity Participation and Adolescent Adjustment

Studies concerned with the link between adolescent participation in organized activities and adjustment have increased over the past 30 years with the most rapid growth over the past decade. The bulk of this research has focused on three broad areas of adjustment; namely:

1. Academic and educational outcomes such as academic performance (e.g., GPA, achievement tests), educational attainment (e.g., school completion/dropout, college attendance), and related occupational/career success during young adulthood
2. Antisocial behaviors such as substance use, norm breaking, and criminal offending
3. Psychosocial functioning including self and identity development

Research in each of these areas has been informed by an increasing interest in moderating factors and meditational processes. This includes attention to the significance of activity type and quality in understanding adolescent outcomes associated with participation. A discussion of research in these areas follows.

Academic and Educational Outcomes

Several studies have examined associations between participation in organized activities (most often school-based extracurricular activities) and academic and educational outcomes. Most of the recent research indicates that participation in organized activities is positively associated with indicators of academic success (e.g., GPA, achievement test peformance) when comparisons are made between participants and nonparticipants and/or among participants who vary in the extent to which they participate (e.g., Cooper, Valentine, Nye, & Lindsay, 1999; Darling, 2005; Eccles, Barber, et al., 2003). This tends to hold also for studies that are longitudinal and include multiple controls that help to account for concerns about selection factors differentiating students according to their participation status.

Similarly, studies of activity participation and educational attainment tend to report that activity participants are both less likely to drop out of secondary school (e.g., Mahoney & Cairns, 1997; McNeal, 1995) and more likely to attend and complete college (e.g., Barber et al., 2001; Mahoney, Cairns, & Farmer, 2003; Zaff, Moore, Papillo, & Williams, 2003).

Some of the associated achievement and educational benefits could be the result of gains in academic knowledge. This would be particularly true of activities where the content is directly linked to the schoolday curriculum (e.g., math team, French club, Quiz Bowl). More often, however, academic/educational success related to activity participation is explained by virtue of other psychosocial processes. Specifically, relative to nonparticipants, activity participants have been to found to have greater access to teachers, counselors, and other supportive adults (e.g., Eccles et al., 2003; Grossman & Bulle, 2006; Hansen et al., 2003), heightened school satisfaction and connectedness (e.g., Brown & Evans, 2002; Gilman, 2001), opportunities to develop and gain social support for an achievement-oriented identity (e.g., Barber et al., 2001), and positive developmental growth experiences including interpersonal competence and teamwork, developing initiative, and gaining insights and preparation for one's future (e.g., Hansen & Larson, 2007; Larson et al., 2006; Mahoney et al., 2003).

Person and context factors can moderate the general associations between organized activity participation and achievement and educational success. For example, there is some evidence that students who are at risk for school failure due to behavior problems and economic disadvantage may benefit most from activity participation (e.g., Mahoney, 2000; Mahoney & Cairns, 1997). This likely owes to greater significance of academic-related resources for such youth (see above). Race/ethnicity may also affect the association in complex ways. For instance, Mahoney, Harris, and Eccles' (2006) analysis of the Panel Study of Income Dynamics–Child Developmental Supplement found that, at high amounts of participation, reading achievement gains associated with organized activity participation were more apparent for African American youth than their European American counterparts. This finding held after controlling for gender, parental education, family income, and family structure.

In contrast, Gerber's (1996) investigation using the National Educational Longitudinal Study of 1988 (NELS 88) data found that, net of gender and SES, 8th graders' extracurricular activity involvement predicted higher achievement, especially for European Americans in the area of math. Finally, Brown and Evans (2002) found that activity-related increases in school connectedness were especially apparent for Hispanic youth. The reasons for such racial/ethnic differences are not well understood. Much more theoretical and empirical work is required before conclusions can be made about potential racial/ethnic differences in the benefits of activity participation (Feldman & Matjasko, 2005).

Finally, stability of participation also modifies the general association between activity participation and increased academic/educational success. For example, in a 3-year longitudinal study of high school students' stability and change in activity participation, results from Darling's (2005) multilevel analysis showed, first, that individual participation in activities varied significantly over time and, second, that academic-related gains (e.g., higher GPA) were evident for students primarily during participation years and greatest for those with consistent year-to-year participation. Similarly, an analysis of the NELS 88 by Zaff et al. (2003) found that, net of controls (e.g., SES, race/ethnicity, gender, family composition, reading/math achievement, emotional or other disability), consistent participation across adolescence was strongly linked to an increased likelihood of college attendance. An 8-year analysis of data from the Carolina Longitudinal Study (Mahoney et al., 2003) also found stability of participation an important predictor of educational attainment, especially for youth with low interpersonal competence during early adolescence.

This general finding is consistent with the emerging research on after-school program participation and academic success for children (e.g., Mahoney et al., in press). Theoretically, it is also anticipated by propositions of bioecological theory. Proximal interchanges that are direct, sustained, and stimulating are ordinarily most influential in the developmental process (Bronfenbrenner & Morris, 2006).

Self and Identity

Research suggests that activity participation contributes to several aspects of the developing of self. For example, longitudinal research conducted by Barber and colleagues (Barber et al., 2001, 2005; Eccles et al., 2003) shows that adolescent identity is often associated with types of activities in which youth participate. Crowd-based identities (i.e., jock, brain, princess, criminal, and basket case) are, in turn, predictive of subsequent adjustment during both adolescence and young adulthood. For example, identifying oneself as belonging to the "jock" crowd predicts relative high rates of alcohol use during adolescence for males, but low levels of depression during young adulthood. Identifying oneself as part of the "criminal" crowd predicts high alcohol and marijuana use for adolescent males and low rates of college completion at young adulthood. Finally, "brains" show low levels of substance use during adolescence and low depression and high rates of college completion during young adulthood. Other aspects of adolescent identity, such as civic-mindedness, are also associated with activity participation during adolescence (e.g., Hirsch, 2005; Kleiber & Kirshnit, 1991; Youniss, McLellan, & Yates, 1999).

In a series of studies, Larson and colleagues (e.g., Dworkin et al., 2003; Hansen & Larson et al., 2007; Larson et al., 2006) also show that the growth and developmental experiences provided by organized activities relate positively to adolescent identity and self-knowledge of limits and abilities. In addition, these studies find that activity participation can facilitate youth's capacity for both self-regulation (e.g., controlling emotions, managing stress, using positive emotions constructively) and initiative (e.g., learning to set realistic goals, sustaining effort and perseverance to reach desired objectives, learning to manage one's time and responsibilities).

Perhaps ironically, the developing sense of self connected to activity participation is likely to be facilitated, in part, by the social relationships with peers and adults in the activity context. For instance, activity-based processes that develop the Five Cs are certain to depend on youth' knowing that they belong to a social organization and that they matter to others in that setting (Lerner et al., 2005; Morrisey & Werner-Wilson, 2005; NRC-IOM, 2002). Activity-based relationships with peers and adult activity leaders have also been shown to mediate individual emotions and psychological adjustment, including depressed mood (e.g., Fredricks & Eccles, 2006b; Mahoney, Schweder, & Stattin, 2002). In addition, relations with parents and, in particular, the process of autonomy granting that surrounds adolescent activity participation appears to promote skills such as self-reliance, independence, and leadership (Larson et al., 2007; Shannon, 2006). Finally, among other things, relationships with activity leaders can help to facilitate participants' self-esteem (e.g., Hirsch, 2005; McLaughlin, 2000; chapter 5, this volume).

Antisocial Behaviors

The most common types of antisocial behaviors linked to organized activity participation are substance use and crime. Net of a variety of demographic and behavioral controls, the bulk of evidence from cross-sectional (e.g., Borden, Donnemeyer, & Scheer, 2001; Mahoney, Harris, & Eccles, 2006; Shilts, 1991), quasi-experimental longitudinal (e.g., Darling, 2005; Fredricks & Eccles, 2006b; Mahoney, 2000), and experimental longitudinal (e.g.,

Gottfredson et al., 2004) studies is available to show that youth who participate in organized activities engage in less substance use (smoking, alcohol consumption, marijuana use) and delinquency during adolescence and criminal offending during young adulthood than youth who do not participate.

Because peer group dynamics are known to influence the development of deviant behaviors (e.g., Borden et al., 2001; Cairns, Cairns, Neckerman, Gest, & Gariépy, 1988; Dodge, Dishion, & Lansford, 2006), it is perhaps not surprising that peer relations have been found to moderate or mediate the association between activity participation and antisocial behavior. For example, among adolescents with multiple-risk profiles, Mahoney (2000) found that activity-related reductions in dropping out of school or criminal offending were evident only when both youth and the majority of his or her peer social network participated in organized activities. In addition, Gottfredsen and colleagues (2004) found that after-school program participation diminished substance use and that this relation was mediated by intentions not to use drugs and more positive peer associations for program participants. Similarly, under some conditions, the peer culture surrounding organized team sports appears to augment alcohol consumption during adolescence (e.g., Eccles et al., 2003; Hoffman, 2006). We discuss this finding in greater detail later.

Finally, Mahoney and colleagues (e.g., 2001, 2004) found that peer group dynamics in activity settings may also promote antisocial behavior when the activity is of poor quality. Specifically, Swedish adolescents who became involved in youth centers that were low in structure and adult supervision showed marked increases in antisocial and criminal behavior compared to similar adolescents who did not participate in the centers. This finding was primarily observed among youth centers that served a high proportion of antisocial youth. Taken together, these studies suggest that the peer relations surrounding adolescent organized activity participation are a critical aspect of whether participation might diminish or promote antisocial behavior.

Activity Types

Approaching research on organized activities from a bioecological perspective presupposes that the different settings in which individuals are nested (e.g., school, neighborhood, family) provide distinct learning environments and developmental opportunities (e.g., Bronfenbrenner, 1979; Lerner, 2002). Researchers assert that different activities that take place in different contexts (e.g., school, community, religious institution) provide unique normative systems and expectations, goals, relationships with a network of adults and peers, and opportunities for growth (e.g., Hansen et al., 2003; Rogoff, Baker-Sennet, Lacasa, & Goldsmith, 1995; Youniss, McLellan, & Yates, 1997). In support of this premise, when researchers have examined whether different types of organized activities relate to different types of youth outcomes, they have almost always found this to be the case (e.g., Barber et al., 1999; Broh, 2002; Fredricks & Eccles, 2006b; Larson et al., 2006).

Sports

Among organized activities, sports have received the greatest amount of attention from researchers. There are several reasons for this attention. First, sports remain the most ubiquitous organized activity among American youth (National Center for Education Statistics, 2005) and ordinarily consume somewhat more time than other activity types during adolescence (e.g., Mahoney, Harris, & Eccles, 2006). Second, decades of research show that sports (or athletics) tend to be high-status activities that influence adolescent peer culture. This includes the formation and composition of peer groups and crowds as well as affecting social trends (e.g., dress/appearance) and behaviors that are "in" and valued for males and females (e.g., Brown, 1990; Coleman, 1961; Eder & Kinney, 1995). Finally, as discussed below, participation in

sports is connected to adolescent psychosocial and academic development.

In comparison to nonparticipants, youth who participate in organized sports tend to have a higher GPA in high school, a greater likelihood of attending college, and report greater autonomy and satisfaction in their first job (Barber, Eccles, & Stone, 2001). Participation in sports is also linked to lower use of cigarettes, marijuana, cocaine, and "other drugs" (e.g., Fredricks & Eccles, 2006b), lower rates of depression, and lower incidence of suicidal behavior (Barber et al., 2001; Gore Farrell, & Gordon, 2001). In addition, female athletes report lower rates of sexual activity and/or early sexual intercourse, net of the influence of race, age, SES, quality of family relations, and participation in other extracurricular activities (e.g., Miller, Sabo, Farrell, Barnes, & Melnick, 1998).

Researchers have asserted that sports facilitate positive developmental trajectories because youth who participate learn skills associated with initiative (i.e., sustaining effort, setting goals) and develop values such as responsibility, conformity, persistence, resistance to risk-taking, courage, and self-control (e.g., Hansen & Larson, 2007; Kleiber & Kirshnit, 1991). For instance, Larson and colleagues' (2006) study of 2,300 eleventh graders compared developmental experiences across multiple types of organized activities. Results from a multilevel model that adjusted for amount of participation, gender, ethnicity, and SES revealed that, in comparison to other activities, sports participants were high in initiative, emotional regulation, and teamwork. This was particularly true when compared to the experiences in alternative out-of-school contexts (e.g., academic class, hanging out with friends, employment). The associated benefits from sports participation may reflect greater opportunities to learn to manage excitement and disappointments following sports competitions and performances, collaborate with team members toward shared goals, and develop and carryout plans to increase the skills and success of the team. The associated emotional benefits also appear to be mediated by numbers of supportive and prosocial peers (e.g., Fredricks & Eccles, 2006b).

Although participation in team sports tends to predict multiple indicators of positive youth development, this is not always the case. For example, very intense sports participation has been linked to engagement in risky behaviors including greater use of smokeless tobacco, steroids, alcohol, and adolescents' binge drinking and getting drunk (e.g., Eccles & Barber, 1999; Garry & Morrisey, 2000; Winnail, Valois, & Dowda, 1997), as well as greater exposure to risk-taking peers (e.g., Eccles & Barber, 1999) and, at times, to possible impediments in prosocial and identity development (e.g., Larson et al., 2006; Shields & Bredemeier, 2001). However, follow-up studies indicate that such negative associations tend not to be evident post high school. In addition, some studies have linked adolescents' participation in competitive sports to relatively high levels of stress (e.g., Danish, Kleiber, & Hall, 1987; Scanlan, Babkes, & Scanlan, 2005). Particularly for elite athletes, this may owe to the achievement elements of highly competitive sports that include public demonstration, testing, and evaluation of adolescents' abilities.

Finally, although very few studies have compared different types of sporting activities, a recent 3-year longitudinal study of early adolescent boys showed that participating in "power sports" (kickboxing, weightlifting, wrestling) was linked to marked increases in violence and other antisocial behaviors (Endressen & Olweus, 2005). Similarly, Fauth and colleagues' (2007) multilevel analysis of data from the Project on Human Development in Chicago Neighborhoods revealed that sports participation was indicative of high average scores on delinquency and growth in substance use. Thus, breaking down adolescent sports participation by intensity, type, and neighborhood context may refine how differences within this largest category of organized activities relate to adolescent adjustment.

Arts

Performing and fine arts include activities such as music, dance, drama, art and drawing clubs, and photography. There has been relatively little systematic research examining youth experiences in the arts and how it compares to youth experiences in other types of activities. Although most studies find beneficial outcomes, the findings are mixed. Some research on participation in the arts suggests that this activity may help adolescents develop initiative and interpersonal skills (e.g., Heath, 2001; Larson et al., 2006) and is related to identity development (e.g., Hansen et al., 2003; O'Neill, 2005). Participation in the performing arts has also been shown to predict high GPAs (e.g., Eccles et al., 2003), lower rates of school dropout (e.g., McNeal, 1995), and, for adolescent males, high levels of educational attainment as measured by the total years of education completed by age 25 (e.g., Barber et al., 2001). Youth participating in performing arts have also been found to have fewer risky friends and more academic friends (e.g., Eccles et al., 2003).

However, in comparison to other organized activities, participation in the arts has also been linked to low levels of positive relationship experiences, teamwork, and experiences with adult networks (Larson et al., 2006). There are also conflicting results about the association between participation in the arts and substance use. For instance, across activity types, Barber and colleagues (2001) found performance arts related to the steepest increase in drinking and to high and increasing marijuana use into young adulthood. In contrast, Fauth and colleagues (2007) found arts participation indicative of low rates of substance use for Black and Latino youth. Further research is required to understand the reasons for these differences.

School-Based Clubs

Academic clubs include an array of school-based activities that have a focus on either education (e.g., computer club); leadership (e.g., school government); or cultural, social, or honorary experiences (e.g., pep squad). Overall, participation in school-based clubs has been linked to high levels of academic engagement and achievement. For example, Eccles and colleagues (2003) found that students who participated in school clubs in 10th grade had a higher GPA at high school graduation and more years of tertiary education at age 21 than the average adolescent participating in other activities. Similarly, Marsh and Kleitman (2002) found that youth who participated in school clubs in early high school had higher academic performance in 12th grade and a greater likelihood of college completion.

Similarly, in a multiyear study of a sample of mostly African American youth, Fredricks and Eccles (2006b) found that, controlling for parental educational attainment, child motivation/need for achievement, and baseline adjustment, participation in clubs was positively related to GPA, educational aspirations, and post–high school educational attainment. This study also found clubs related to lower internalizing behavior problems for African American youth and lower alcohol and marijuana use for boys. Qualitative examinations of youth experiences in academic clubs indicate that these activities primarily provide developmental experiences in the academic domain (e.g., Hansen et al., 2003; Larson et al., 2006). However, a broad array of activities falls under the general category of "clubs," and a limited number of specific clubs have been examined in depth.

Community Programs

Some examples of nationally funded community programs include 4-H Clubs, Boys and Girls Clubs, Boy Scouts and Girl Scouts, Big Brothers Big Sisters, Future Business Leaders of America, and FFA (formerly known as Future Farmers of America). Most of these community-based activity programs share a central mission of providing highly safe and structured environments where youth can build relationships with adult mentors and peers and form connections to local institutions and employers. Moreover, many community programs focus on promoting their own unique overarching goals. For example, 4-H is a "community of young people across America who are learning leadership, citizenship and life skills" (National 4-H Council, 2006), and the Boys and Girls Clubs focus on "promoting and enhancing the development of boys and girls by instilling a sense of competence, usefulness, belonging and influence" (Boys and Girls Clubs website, 2006). Participation in community programs has been linked to the development of leadership skills, prosocial norms, and opportunities to establish positive adult connections (e.g., Larson et al., 2006; Lerner, 2004; Marsh & Kleitman, 2002).

Service Activities

Service activities, including volunteer activities, are associated with interpersonal and civic-related development during and beyond adolescence. For example, participation in such activities has been linked to the development of altruism, social responsibility, and moral and political identity (e.g., Yates & Youniss, 1996). Moreover, longitudinal research shows that service activities predict continued political activity (e.g., voting) and commitment to civic service (e.g., volunteering) into young adulthood (e.g., Flanagan, 2004; Glanville, 1999; Zaff et al., 2003).

Another example of the effectiveness of service learning components for adolescents comes from the experimental evaluation of the Teen Outreach Program (TOP; Allen, Philliber, Herrling, & Kuperminc, 1997). TOP provided supervised community service opportunities and classroom-based discussions of the service activities to high school students. Over time, students participating in TOP had significantly lower rates of school suspension and course failure, and female participants had lower rates of teenage pregnancy compared to control group students who did not participate in TOP. (For a detailed review of service and civic activities, see chapter 11, this volume).

Faith-Based Activities

Research shows that religion is an important and positive part of life for many adolescents (e.g., Benson, 2004; McKinney, 1999). However, precious little research has focused specifically on the benefits of participation in religious youth groups. Studies examining the associated influence of religious youth groups suggest that they integrate young people into a community of adults and peers (e.g., Regnerus, 2000; Smith, 2003). At least one study (Larson et al., 2006) found that, in comparison with other organized activities, participation in religious activities was linked to high levels of identity work, emotional regulation, positive relationships, and experiences with adult networks. However, contrary to what might be expected, faith-based youth groups were similar to other activities in the extent to which youth report negative experiences (e.g., social exclusion, negative peer influence). Clearly, more work is needed in this area.

Activity Quality and Experiences

An additional feature of organized activities that helps to explain associated adjustment for youth participants is quality. Activity quality has proven useful in elucidating why organized activities are sometimes associated with positive developmental outcomes, sometimes with negative developmental outcomes, and sometimes have no discernable effects. For example, poorly monitored and disorganized activities in conjunction with low support from adult leaders are associated with adolescent antisocial behavior and deviant peer relations (Mahoney & Stattin, 2000; Mahoney, Stattin, & Lord, 2004). In contrast, after-school programs characterized by supportive relations with adult leaders and peers, appropriate levels of support (not chaotic, but not rigidly controlled), and skill-building opportunities have been linked to gains in work habits and reductions in misconduct over the course of a school year (Vandell & Reisner, 2006).

McLaughlin's (2000) longitudinal study of exemplary community-based programs provides a rich description of intentional learning environments in which adults made ongoing efforts to make activities accessible and challenging for all attendees. Adult leaders embedded opportunities to build academic competences and life skills within the program activities to deepen skills and competence through engagement in a specific area. Many activities were organized around culminating events such as a performance, a product such as a book or newspaper, or a big game. Materials were adapted to the interests and strengths of the youth, and adolescents contributed to the design, content, and conduct of the activities.

However, the quality of many organized activities is not as high. For example, through both on-site visits and participant surveys, Gambone and Arbreton (1997) found that many youth programs fail to meet the participants' needs in several areas. Thirty-six percent of those surveyed reported feeling less safe at the program than elsewhere, 39% felt never or almost never valued, 35% felt there were no adults at the program to whom they could turn, and 40% reported never or almost never having input in program activities. It seems unlikely that these programs would have the same effects as those in which youth feel valued, have input in program activities, and are connected to adults.

Drawing on the work of McLaughlin (2000) and other scholars (i.e., NRC-IOM, 2002), eight features of out-of-school activities that are linked to PYD have been named:

1. Supportive relationships with adults and peers
2. Appropriate structure
3. Opportunity for skill building
4. Support for efficacy and mattering
5. Opportunities for belonging
6. Physical and psychological safety
7. Positive social norms
8. Integration of family, school, and community efforts

Other, more recent work (e.g., Blum, 2003; Roth & Brooks-Gunn, 2003) has provided further empirical support for three of these dimensions: (1) sustained and positive youth–adult relationships; (2) activities that build youth's life skills; and (3) opportunities for participation and leadership in valued community activities. Lerner (2004, 2007) named these attributes the "Big 3." In addition, other researchers (e.g., Larson, 2000) have emphasized the importance of quality parameters such as voluntary engagement and sustained effort in out-of-school activities.

A number of research and evaluation tools have been developed to measure program quality. These measurement tools include surveys completed by youth (Rosenthal & Vandell, 1996; Study of Promising Afterschool Programs, 2005), interviews and surveys completed by program directors or activity leaders (Study of Promising Afterschool Programs, 2005), and observations. A recent compilation by Yohalem and Wilson-Ahlstrom (2007) provides a description and comparison of nine observational measures that assess program quality, namely:

1. *Afterschool Program Assessment System* (National Institute on Out-of-School Time, 2008)
2. *Out-of-School Time Observation* (Policy Studies Associates, 2005)
3. *Program Observation Tool* (National Afterschool Association)
4. *Program Quality Observation* (Vandell & Pierce, 1998)
5. *Promising Practices Rating Scale* (Vandell, Reisner, Brown,Dadisman, Pierce, Lee, & Pechman, 2005)
6. *Quality Assurance System* (Foundations Inc., 2007)
7. *Program Quality Self-Assessment* (New York State Afterschool Network, 2005)
8. *School-Age Care Environment Rating Scale* (Harms, Jacobs, & White, 1996)
9. *Youth Program Quality Assessment* (Smith & Hohmann, 2005)

Collectively, these evaluation tools use a variety of measurement strategies, including qualitative ratings, checklists, time samples, and spot samples. Some of the measures were designed primarily for continuous improvement efforts designed for use by program staff, and others were developed for purposes of research and/or program evaluation. However, consistent with the aforementioned list of program features that promote PYD, most include assessments of the quality of social interactions and relationships, aspects of the physical environment, levels of student engagement, social/behavioral norms, skill-building opportunities, and routines.

Investigators have called for an examination of how program features may be differentially associated with developmental outcomes (e.g., Granger, Durlak, Yohalem, & Reisner, 2007; Mahoney et al., in press; Pierce, Bolt, & Vandell, in press). Although some quality evaluation tools have focused on one or a few components of program quality in relation to both program participation and developmental outcomes, further research is needed to determine whether various program features represent unique or distinct components of program quality. In the text that follows, we consider some evidence in this area.

Supportive Relationships with Adults

Attachment theory (Bowlby, 1969; Pianta, 1999) has highlighted the central role of supportive relationships with parents and teachers as a secure base from which young people learn and develop. Supportive relationships with activity leaders, coaches, and mentors are emerging as essential elements in out-of-school activities as well.

The quality of these relationships with staff has been assessed by surveys completed by the youth and by program observations. The After-School Environment Scale (ASES; Rosenthal & Vandell, 1996) is a 36-item survey that assesses emotional support from staff, peer affiliation, and autonomy/privacy. Rosenthal and Vandell (1996) observed that adults appeared more negative and hostile toward youth when student–staff ratios and group sizes were larger. Youth, in turn, reported that less emotional support in these larger programs in which staff were more negative and hostile. In programs with more highly educated and trained staff, adults used more positive behavior management strategies and were less harsh. Youth reported more emotional support in those programs (Rosenthal & Vandell, 1986). In addition, Mahoney and colleagues (2002) found that students reported less depressed mood when they attended programs where they perceived high support from the activity leader. Youth also reported that they learned more in programs when they perceived staff as positive and supportive (Grossman, Campbell, & Raley, 2007).

Peer Affiliations and Interactions

The significance of relationships with peers and peer networks plays a critical role in the development of young people, for good or for ill (Brown, 2004; Hartup, 1996). Although peer relations have traditionally been studied in the school context, it is increasingly apparent that peer networks in- and out-of-school contexts can affect the development of young people. For example, Eccles and colleagues (Barber, Eccles, & Stone, 2001; Eccles & Barber, 1999) have shown that participation in extracurricular activities are connected to both peer group characteristics and identity development during adolescence. Depending on the activity in which youth participate, differences were observed in the proportion of one's friends perceived to have an academic orientation, to have skipped school, or used drugs. Those youth who participated in prosocial activities were apt to view themselves and their peer group as academically oriented and unlikely to engage in risky behaviors. Such affiliations were, in turn, linked to relatively high academic achievement and long-term educational attainment.

Aspects of peer acceptance are also linked out-of-school activity participation. For instance, cross-sectional work by Sandstrom and Coie (1999) found that rejected children who regularly attended programs became less rejected over time, a change that was not observed in rejected children who did not attend programs. Mahoney and colleagues (2005a) found similar results in a longitudinal study of ethnically diverse, disadvantaged children. The investigators speculated that the programs offered these young people opportunities to improve their social standing through the development of competence in activity-related skills that are valued in the peer group and through interaction with competent peers who model appropriate social behavior (Brown, 1990; Coleman, 1961).

However, the presence of friends and frequent interactions with those friends in out-of-school activities does not ensure that the peer context is supportive of positive developmental outcomes. For example, Catterall (1987) found that bonds that formed among low-achieving high school students appeared to augment their feelings of alienation at school. Similarly, Dishion and colleagues (e.g., Dishion, McCord, & Poulin, 1999) showed that high-risk youth can reinforce each other's problem behaviors. Deviant youth who participated in an intervention program that included peer-based activities were less likely to show reductions in problem behaviors compared to similar youth who experienced a family-based intervention. Accordingly, the challenge for high quality out-of-school activities is to foster the development of positive peer networks that support societal norms and expectations. One of the features of exemplary programs identified in the Study of Promising After School Programs (Vandell, Reisner, et al., 2005) is that positive, supportive peer relationships were observed in conjunction with positive, supportive relationships with adult staff.

Appropriate Structure and Opportunities for Skill Building

A recent meta-analysis of 66 different program evaluations, Durlak and Weissberg (2007) found that high-quality implementation of program activities was associated with improvements in students' feelings about self and attitudes toward school, social adjustment, and school performance, whereas less structured approaches to activity implementation were not associated with youth outcomes. In this analysis, program quality was measured with four criteria; namely: (1) the extent to which activities were sequenced to achieve skill objectives (sequenced); (2) whether learning was active (active); (3) whether at least one program component was focused on developing personal or social skills (focus); and (4) whether specific personal or social skills was targeted (explicit).

Youth who attended programs that met all four criteria demonstrated positive results on all seven of the outcome categories (improved feelings of self-confidence and self-esteem, school bonding, positive social behaviors, school grades and achievement test scores, together with reduced problem behaviors and drug use). In contrast, youth who attended programs that were less intentional did not produce positive results in any category. The authors concluded that youth' personal and social skills are promoted by programs that are SAFE—sequenced, active, focused, and explicit.

Engagement and Opportunities to Follow One's Own Passions

In a series of studies, Larson and colleagues (e.g, Larson, 2000) examined adolescents' psychological states at school, at home, and when they were engaged in structured voluntary activities at randomly sampled moments. During classwork and homework, adolescents reported high levels of concentration and challenge, but low levels of intrinsic motivation. While watching television and while hanging out with friends, students reported low concentration and effort but high intrinsic motivation. However, experiences in which youth combine effort, concentration, and choice were high when participating in quality organized activities. This combination of psychological

experience is thought to foster the development of initiative, defined as motivation from within to initiate and sustain effort toward a challenging goal over time, and represents a significant developmental asset for young people.

This is consistent with the work of Shernoff and Vandell (2007), who examined the quality of adolescents' experiences in particular activities at after-school programs. Experiences of concentrated effort and engagement were higher during sports and arts activities than homework and socializing. While doing homework, youth reported lower intrinsic motivation, positive affect, and overall engagement, while reporting higher apathy. Moreover, in a study of low-income, ethnically diverse middle school students (Pierce, Bolt, & Vandell, in press; Shernoff & Vandell, 2007; Vandell, Shumow, & Posner, 2005), youth were given logbooks and watches that are programmed to signal at random times. When signaled, the adolescents recorded where they were, what they were doing, whom they were with, and how they were feeling. Engagement and motivation were assessed in a series of additional questions that reflected three factors: concerted effort (challenge, skills, and concentration), intrinsic motivation (enjoyment, choice, and interest), and importance (a stand-alone item). Youth also rated 11 emotional states (happy, proud, excited, relaxed, sad, angry, worried, scared, stressed, bored, and lonely).

There were substantial differences in activities, feeling states, and motivation when the youth were at after-school programs or other organized activities versus when these same youth were elsewhere (other settings such as home or transit). Specifically, when involved in organized activities, youth were almost twice as likely to experience high choice in combination with concentrated effort (40% of their experiences versus 21% of their experiences elsewhere). High choice in conjunction with high concentrated effort is consistent with the feeling states that Larson (2000) theorized would support the development of initiative and positive youth development. While at programs, youth also experience more intrinsic motivation, put forth more concerted effort, and feel less apathetic, underscoring the potential of after-school programs as a positive developmental context for youth. Overall, it appears that quality organized activities provide youth with substantially different experiences than they are exposed to elsewhere outside of school hours.

Summary

The knowledge base on adolescent participation in organized activities has both broadened and deepened over the past three decades. Advances have occurred in several areas and begin to fill the knowledge gaps that characterized much of the research prior to 1980. First, the construct of participation has been refined. Whereas the early work on organized activities relied on a dichotomous measure of overall participation, the more recent studies have been concerned with amount, duration, and breadth of participation across different types of activities.

Second, investigations into the reasons why young people do and do not participate have emerged rapidly. Whether and to what extent youth participate in organized activities is not a random affair. Consistent with a bioecological framework, participation depends on characteristics, interests, and motivations of the individual and opportunities, resources, and social supports across the multiple ecologies in which he or she is a part (e.g., peers, family, school, and neighborhood). This knowledge has been useful in accounting for possible selection influences, and we now have many studies that have controlled for obvious selection factors at several levels. In combination with advances in statistical analysis (e.g., multilevel modeling, pattern analysis) and the increasing numbers of longitudinal studies, conclusions about the consequences of organized activity participation now rest on far more rigorous designs than was true three (or even two) decades ago.

Finally, with respect to activity participation and adolescent development, the general domains of adjustment studied in recent

decades have not been dramatically different from those studied prior to 1980 (i.e., academic performance and educational attainment, antisocial behaviors, and self and identity). However, in addition to the enhanced rigor and longevity of the study designs, recent research is beginning to examine processes and mechanisms of change within these domains. This is evident in work on bidirectional relations between individual differences in selection and participation processes over time, the mediating role between activity participation and peers in the reduction of risk behaviors, or the linkages between participation, PYD, and adolescents' contribution to the community. Similarly, research into the developmental and growth experiences connected to activity participation has provided greater insight into the mechanisms by which participation affects adolescent development.

CONCLUSIONS AND FUTURE DIRECTIONS

It is evident that research on organized activity and adolescent development has taken marked strides forward. The advances have occurred in multiple areas including theory, operationalization of constructs, research designs, and attention to mechanisms and processes. However, much more needs to be known about adolescent out-of-school activities. The existing knowledge base points to several areas where additional and/or new research is needed.

First, although research has shown that several aspects of the participation construct (e.g., amount, duration, and breadth) are important for adolescent development, little is known about how these facets relate—theoretically or empirically—and/or how they vary across activity types. Moreover, activity participation is now understood to be dynamic. Because much of the research in this area has been conducted on one occasion, information on the developmental dynamics of short- and long-term participation across different types of activities is needed.

Second, basic selection influences (e.g., SES) are now routinely accounted for in research on organized activities. However, most of the existing research has considered predictors of participation as "noise" to be controlled rather than as a part of the process that can inform our understanding of the consequences of participation. Indeed, the tendency to control for "selection factors" (e.g., SES, race/ethnicity, gender, family structure, and school/neighborhood characteristics) to isolate "activity effects" often means that the opportunity to understand how person and contextual features interact in the adjustment process is lost. On this score, Barber, Stone, and Eccles (2005) assert that separating out selection influences from the influence of social experience is "a futile effort in naturalistic, longitudinal studies" (p. 204). In line with Cairns's (1996) notion of sociogenesis (a transactional process in which individuals and their social environments collaborate to effect continuity and change in development), Barber and colleagues (2005) explain that "selection and social experience work together as a fluid synergistic system to influence developmental trajectories," and thus, an examination of "the net influence of either selection or socialization is meaningless" (p. 204).

The implication is that participation in organized activities and the development of adolescent competence are coeffecting aspects in the developmental process. Thus, where research suggests that youth with a variety of positive assets at the community, family, and individual level are also likely to be involved in positive out-of-school activities, it is just as likely that activity involvement helped to foster some of these assets (e.g., Zarrett, 2007). Overall, the bioecological perspective suggests that failing to account for person-in-context dynamics can lead to conclusions about the developmental process that are misleading or wrong. Thus, theoretical and empirical research that marries the selection, participation, and adjustment processes is needed.

Third, important aspects of youth development continue to be understudied. For example, many organized activities have the capacity to promote adolescent physical health and fitness. The few studies that have been concerned with the physical development of youth have shown that activity participation is linked to heightened physical activity, increased strength/endurance, and decreased body mass index and clinical obesity (e.g., Elkins, Cohen, Koralewicz, & Taylor, 2004; Pabayo, O'Loughlin, Gauvin, et al., 2006). For example, in a multi-wave longitudinal study, Mahoney and colleagues (2005a) found that disadvantaged children who were obese tended to be unpopular and were not desired by their classmates. However, net of several selection influences including early assessment of body mass index, obese children who became regular participants in after-school programs showed both a significant reduction in measures of obesity and improvements in measures of peer acceptance over time as assessed by ratings from their classmates and teachers.

Finally, little is known about the processes that occur within the activity setting or how these processes facilitate youth engagement and development (Posner & Vandell, 1999; Vandell, Shumow, & Posner, 2005). To better realize the potentials of activity programs we need more in-depth qualitative and longitudinal research that evaluates the mediating processes both within and between categories of activities (Larson et al., 2006), as well as more dynamic models that account for the synergistic relations between the characteristics of youth; their environments, including community- and neighborhood-level influences; and activities.

In summary, given the limited historical attention to the role of organized activities in adolescent development it is exciting to highlight some of the advances in activity-related theories and research over the past 3 decades. It is clear that organized activities have an important place in the lives of adolescents and are consequential for their development. It is equally clear that many questions remain unanswered. Researchers are only beginning to understand the significance of organized activities from a bioecological perspective. This perspective calls for knowledge of the interactions between persons, contexts, processes, and time. Continued investment in these types of studies is needed to advance the knowledge on organized activity participation and adolescent development.

REFERENCES

Allen, J. P., Philliber, S., Herrling, S., & Kuperminc, G. P. (1997). Preventing teen pregnancy and academic failure: Experimental evaluation of a developmentally based approach. *Child Development, 64,* 729–724.

Anderson, J. C., Funk, J. B., Elliot, R., & Smith, P. H. (2003). Parental support and pressure and children's extracurricular activities: Relationships with amount of involvement and affective experience of participation. *Journal of Applied Developmental Psychology, 4,* 241–257.

Apel, R., Paternoster, R., Bushway, S. D., & Brame, R. (2006). A job isn't just a job: The differential impact of formal versus informal work on adolescent problem behavior. *Crime & Delinquency, 52,* 333–369.

Barber, B. L., Eccles, J. S., & Stone, M. R. (2001). Whatever happened to the jock, the brain, and the princess? Young adult pathways linked to adolescent activity involvement and social identity. *Journal of Adolescent Research, 16,* 429–455.

Barber, B. L., Stone, M. R., & Eccles, J. S. (2005). Adolescent participation in organized activities. In K. A. Moore & L. Lippman (Eds.), *What do children need to flourish? Conceptualizing and measuring indicators of postitive development* (pp. 133–146). New York: Springer.

Barker, R., & Gump, V. (1964). *Big school, small school: High school size and student behavior.* Stanford, CA: Stanford University Press.

Barnett, L. A. (2005). Measuring the ABCs of leisure experience: Awareness, boredom, challenge, distress. *Leisure Sciences, 27,* 131–155.

Bartko, T. W., & Eccles, J. S. (2003). Adolescent participation in structured and unstructured activities: A person-oriented analysis. *Journal of Youth and Adolescence, 32,* 233–241.

Belle, D. (1997). Varieties of self-care: A qualitative look at children's experiences in the after-school hours. *Merrill-Palmer Quarterly, 43,* 478–496.

Benson, P. (2004). Emerging themes in research on adolescent spiritual and religious development. *Applied Developmental Science, 8,* 47–50.

Benson, P. L., Scales, P. C., Hamilton, S. F., & Sesma, A., Jr. (2006). Positive youth development: Theory, research and application. In R. M. Lerner (Ed.), *Handbook of child psychology* (6th ed.), vol. 1: *Theoretical models of human development.* (pp. 894–941). Editors-in-chief: W. Damon & R. M. Lerner. Hoboken, NJ: John Wiley & Sons.

Blum, R. W. (2003). Positive youth development: A strategy for improving health. In F. Jacobs, D. Wertlieb, & R. M. Lerner (Eds.), *Handbook of applied developmental science,* vol. 2: *Promoting positive child, adolescent, and family development through research, policies, and programs* (pp. 237–252). Thousand Oaks, CA: Sage.

Borden, L. M., Donnermeyer, J. F., & Scheer, S. D. (2001). The influence of extra-curricular activities and peer influence on substance use. *Adolescent and Family Health, 2,* 12–19.

Borden, L. M., Perkins, D. F., Villarruel, F. A., & Stone, M. R. (2005). To participate or not to participate: That is the question. In G. G. Noam (Ed.), H. B. Weiss, P. M. D. Little, &

S. M. Bouffard (Issue Eds.), *New Directions for Youth Development, 105: Participation in youth programs: Enrollment, attendance, and engagement,* 33–50.

Bouffard, S., Wimer, C., Caronongan, P., Little, P., Dearing, E., & Simpkins, S. D. (2006). Demographic differences in patterns of youth out-of-school time activity participation. *Journal of Youth Development, 1*(1). www.nae4ha.org/directory/jyd/index.html.

Bowlby, J. (1969). *Attachment and loss.* New York: Basic Books.

Boys and Girls Club of America. (2006). *Our mission.* Retrieved September 9, 2006, from www.bgca.org/whoweare/mission.asp.

Brandon, P. D. (1999). Determinants of self-care arrangements among school-age children. *Children and Youth Services Review, 21,* 497–520.

Broh, B. A. (2002). Linking extracurricular programming to academic achievement: Who benefits and why? *Sociology of Education, 75,* 69–91.

Bronfenbrenner, U. (1979). *The ecology of human development: Experiments by nature and design.* Cambridge, MA: Harvard University Press.

Bronfenbrenner, U., & Morris, P. (2006). The bioecological model of human development. In W. Daman & R. M. Lerner (Editors-in-Chief), and R. M. Lerner (Volume Ed.), *Handbook of child psychology, vol 1: Theoretical models of human development* (pp. 793–828). Hoboken, NJ: John Wiley & Sons.

Brown, B. B. (1990). Peer groups and peer cultures. In S. S. Feldman & G. R. Elliott (Eds.), *At the threshold: The developing adolescent* (pp. 171–196). Cambridge, MA: Harvard University Press.

Brown, B. B. (2004). Adolescents' relationships with peers. In R. M. Lerner & L. Steinberg (Eds.), *Handbook of adolescent psychology* (2nd ed., pp. 363–394). Hoboken, NJ: John Wiley & Sons.

Brown, R., & Evans, W. P. (2002). Extracurricular activity and ethnicity: Creating greater school connection among diverse student populations. *Urban Education, 37,* 41–58.

Busseri, M. A., Rose-Krasnor, L., Willoughby, T., & Chalmers, H. (2006). A longitudinal examination of breadth and intensity of youth activity involvement and successful development. *Developmental Psychology, 42,* 1313–1326.

Cain, V. S., & Hofferth, S. L. (1989). Parental choice of self-care for school-age children. *Journal of Marriage and the Family, 51,* 65–77.

Cairns, R. B. (1996). Socialization and sociogenesis. In D. Magnusson (Ed.), *The life-span development of individuals: A synthesis of biological and psychosocial perspectives* (pp. 277–295). New York: Cambridge University Press.

Cairns, R. B., Cairns, B. D., Neckerman, H. J., Gest, S. D., & Gariépy, J-L. (1988). Social networks and aggressive behavior: Peer support or peer rejection? *Developmental Psychology, 24,* 815–823.

Cairns, R. B., Elder, G. H., Jr., & Costello, E. J. (Eds.) (1996). *Developmental science.* Cambridge: Cambridge University Press.

Capizzano, J., Adelman, S., & Stagner, M. (2002). *What happens when the school year is over? The use and costs of child care for school-age children during the summer months.* Assessing the New Federalism. Occasional paper no. 58. Washington, DC: Urban Institute.

Capizzano, J., Tout, K., & Adams, G., (2000). *Child care patterns of school-age children with employed mothers.* Washington, DC: Urban Institute.

Casper, L. M., & Smith, K. E. (2002). Dispelling the myths: Self-care, class, and race. *Journal of Family Issues, 23,* 716–727.

Catterall, J. S. (1987). An intensive group counseling drop-out prevention intervention: Some cautions on isolating at-risk adolescents within high schools. *American Educational Research Journal, 24,* 521–540.

Coleman, J. S. (1961). *The adolescent society: The social life of the teenager and its impact on education.* New York: Free Press of Glencoe.

Coleman, M., Rowland, B., & Robinson, B. (1989). Latchkey children and school-age child care: A review of programming needs. *Child and Youth Quarterly, 18,* 39–48.

Cooley, V. E., Henriksen, L. W., Nelson, C. V., & Thompson, J. C. (1995). A study to determine the effect of extracurricular participation on student alcohol and drug use in secondary schools. *Journal of Alcohol and Drug Education, 40,* 71–87.

Cooper, H., Valentine, J. C., Nye, B., & Lindsay, J. J (1999). Relationships between five after-school activities and academic achievement. *Journal of Educational Psychology, 91,* 369–378.

Csikszentmihalyi, M. (1990). *Flow.* New York: Harper & Row.

Cumming, S. P., Smith, R. E., & Smoll, F. L. (2006). Athlete-perceived coaching behaviors: Relating two measurement traditions. *Journal of Sport and Exercise Psychology, 28,* 205–213.

Cumming, S. P., Smoll, F. L., Smith, R. E., & Grossbard, J. R. (2007). Is winning everything? The relative contributions of motivational climate and won-lost percentage in youth sports. *Journal of Applied Sport Psychology, 19,* 322–336.

Danish, S., Kleiber, D., & Hall, H. (1987). Developmental intervention and motivation enhancement in the context of sport. In M. L. Maehr & D. A. Kleiber (Eds.), *Advances in motivation and achievement: A research annual* (pp. 211–235). Greenwich, CT: JAI Press.

Darling, N. (2005). Participation in extracurricular activities and adolescent adjustment: Cross-sectional and longitudinal findings. *Journal of Youth and Adolescence, 34,* 493–505.

Darling, N., Caldwell, L. L., & Smith, R. (2005). Participation in school-based extracurricular activities and adolescent adjustment. *Journal of Leisure Research, 37,* 51–76.

Davalos, D. B., Chavez, E. L., & Guardiola, R. J. (1999). The effects of extracurricular activity, ethnic identification, and perception of school on student dropout rates. *Hispanic Journal of Behavioral Sciences, 21,* 61–77.

Dishion, T. J., McCord, J., & Poulin, F. (1999). When interventions harm: Peer groups and problem behavior. *American Psychologist, 54,* 755–764.

Dodge, K. A., Dishion, T. J., & Lansford, J. E. (2006). Deviant peer influences in intervention and public policy for youth. *Social Policy Report, 20,* 1–20.

Durlak, J. A, & Weissberg, R. P. (2007). *The impact of after-school programs that promote personal and social skills.* Chicago: Collaborative for Academic, Social, and Emotional Learning.

Dworkin, J. B., Larson, R. W., Hansen, D. (2003). Adolescents' accounts of growth experiences in youth activities. *Journal of Youth and Adolescence, 32,* 17–26.

Dwyer, K. M., Richardson, J. L., Danley, K. L., Hansen, W. B., Sussman, S. Y., Brannon, B., et al. (1990). Characteristics of eighth-grade students who initiate self-care in elementary and junior high school. *Pediatrics, 86,* 448–454.

Eccles, J. S. (1983). Expectancies, values, and academic behaviors. In J. Spence (Ed.), *Achievement and achievement motivation* (pp. 75–146). San Francisco: Freeman.

Eccles, J. S. (1993). School and family effects on the ontogeny of children's interests, self-perceptions, and activity choice. In J. Jacobs (Ed.), *Nebraska symposium on motivation, 1992: Developmental perspectives on motivation* (pp. 145–208). Lincoln: University of Nebraska Press.

Eccles, J. S., & Barber, B. (1999). Student council, volunteering, basketball, or marching band: What kind of extracurricular participation matters? *Journal of Adolescent Research, 14,* 10–43.

Eccles, J. S., Barber, B. L., Stone, M., & Hunt, J. (2003). Extracurricular activities and adolescent development. *Journal of Social Issues, 59,* 10–43.

Eccles, J. S., & Midgley, C. (1989). Stage/environment fit: Developmentally appropriate classrooms for early adolescents. In R. E. Ames & C. Ames (Eds.), *Research on motivation in education,* vol. 3 (pp. 139–186). San Diego, CA: Academic Press.

Eder, D., & Kinney, D. A. (1995). The effects of middle school extracurricular activities on adolescents' popularity and peer status. *Youth & Society, 26,* 298–324.

Elder, G. H., Jr., & Shanahan, M. J. (2006). The life course and human development. In Richard M. Lerner (Ed.), *Handbook of child psychology* (6th ed.), vol. 1: *Theoretical models of human development* chapter 12, pp. 665–715), William Damon (Series Ed.). Hoboken, NJ: John Wiley & Sons.

Elkins, W. L., Cohen, D. A., Koralewicz, L. M., & Taylor, S. N. (2004). After school activities, overweight, and obesity among inner city youth. *Journal of Adolescence, 27,* 181–189.

Endressen, I. M., & Olweus, D. (2005). Participation in power sports and antisocial involvement in preadolescent and adolescent boys. *Journal of Child Psychology and Psychiatry, 46,* 468–478.

Fauth, R. C., Roth, J. L., & Brooks-Gunn, J. (2007). Does the neighborhood context alter the link between youth's after-school time activities and developmental outcomes? A multilevel analysis. *Developmental Psychology, 43,* 760–777.

Feldman, A. F., & Matjasko, J. L. (2005). The role of school-based extracurricular activities in adolescent development: A comprehensive review and future directions. *Review of Educational Research, 75,* 159–210.

Flanagan, C. (2004). Volunteerism, leadership, political socialization, and civic engagement. In R. Lerner & L. Steinberg (Eds.), *Handbook of adolescent psychology* (2nd ed., pp. 721–745). Hoboken, NJ: John Wiley & Sons.

Fletcher, A. C., Elder, G. H., Jr., & Mekos, D. (2000). Parental influences on adolescent involvement in community activities. *Journal of Research on Adolescence, 10,* 29–48.

Foundations, Inc. (2007). *Quality assurance system.* Retrieved May 13, 2007, from http://qas.foundationsinc.org.

Fredricks, J. A., & Eccles, J. S. (2006a). Extracurricular involvement and adolescent adjustment: Impact of duration, number of activities, and breadth of participation. *Applied Developmental Science, 10,* 132–146.

Fredricks, J. A., & Eccles, J. S. (2006b). Is extracurricular participation associated with beneficial outcomes? Concurrent and longitudinal relations. *Developmental Psychology, 42,* 698–713.

Furstenberg, F. F., Cook, T. D., Eccles, J. S., Elder, G. H., & Sameroff, A. (1999). *Managing to make it: Urban families and adolescent success.* Chicago: University of Chicago Press.

Galambos, N. L., & Dixon, R. A. (1984). Toward understanding and caring for latchkey children. *Child Care Quarterly, 13,* 116–125.

Galambos, N. L., & Maggs, J. L. (1991). Out-of-school care of young adolescents and self-reported behavior. *Developmental Psychology, 27,* 644–655.

Gambone, M. A., & Arbreton, A. J. A. (1997). *Safe havens: The contribution of youth organization to healthy adolescent development.* Philadelphia: Public/Private Ventures.

Garry, J. P., & Morrisey, S. L. (2000). Team sports participation and risk-taking behaviors among a biracial middle school population. *Clinical Journal of Sports Medicine, 10,* 185–190.

Gauvain, M., & Perez, S. M. (2005). Parent–child participation in planning children's activities outside of school in European American and Latino families. *Child Development, 76,* 371–383.

Gerber, S. B. (1996). Extracurricular activities and academic achievement. *Journal of Research and Development in Education, 30,* 42–50.

Gilman, R. (2001). The relationship between life satisfaction, social interest, and frequency of extracurricular activity among adolescent students. *Journal of Youth and Adolescence, 30,* 749–767.

Glanville, J. L. (1999). Political socialization or selection? Adolescent extracurricular participation and political activity in early adulthood. *Social Science Quarterly, 80,* 279–290.

Gore, S., Farrell, F., & Gordon, J. (2001). Sports involvement as protection against depressed mood. *Journal of Research on Adolescence, 11,* 119–130.

Gottfredson, D. C., Gerstenblith, S. A., Soulé, D. A., Worner, S. C., & Lu, S. (2004). Do after school programs reduce delinquency? *Prevention Science, 5,* 253–266.

Granger, R., Durlak, J. A., Yohalem, N., & Reisner, E. (2007). *Improving after-school program quality.* New York: William T. Grant Foundation.

Grossman, J. B., & Bulle, M. J. (2006). Review of what youth programs do to increase the connectedness of youth with adults. *Journal of Adolescent Health, 39,* 788–799.

Guest, A., & Schneider, B. (2003). Adolescents' extracurricular participation in context: The mediating effects of schools, communities, and identity. *Sociology of Education, 76,* 89–109.

Halpern, R. (2002). A different kind of child development institution: the history of after-school programs for the low-income children. *Teachers College Record, 104,* 178–211.

Halpern, R., Barker, G., & Mollard, W. (2000). Youth programs as alternative spaces to be: A study of neighborhood youth programs in Chicago's West Town. *Youth & Society, 31,* 469–506.

Hansen, D. M., & Larson, R. W. (2007). Amplifiers of developmental and negative experiences in organized activities: Dosage, motivation, lead roles, and adult-youth ratios. *Journal of Applied Developmental Psychology, 28,* 360–374.

Hansen, D. M., Larson, R. W., & Dworkin, J. B. (2003). What adolescents learn in organized youth activities: A survey of self-reported developmental experiences. *Journal of Research on Adolescence, 13,* 25–55.

Harms, T., Jacobs, E., & White, D. (1996). *School Age Care Environment Rating Scale.* New York: Teachers College Press.

Hartup, W. W. (1996). The company they keep: Friendships and their developmental significance. *Child Development, 67,* 1–13.

Hartup, W. W., & Stevens, N. (1997). Friendships and adaptation in the life course. *Psychological Bulletin, 121,* 355–370.

Heath, S. B. (2001). Three's not a crowd: Plans, roles, and focus in the arts. *Educational Researcher, 30,* 10–17.

Hirsch, B. J. (2005). *A place to call home: After-school programs for urban youth.* Washington, DC: American Psychological Association.

Hirshi, T. (1969). *Causes of delinquency.* Berkeley: University of California Press.

Hoffman, J. P. (2006). Extracurricular activities, athletic participation, and adolescent alcohol use: Gender-differentiated and school-contextual effects. *Journal of Health and Social Behavior, 47,* 275–290.

Holland, A., & Andre, T. (1987). Participation in extracurricular activities in secondary school: What is known, what needs to be known? *Review of Educational Research, 57,* 437–466.

Huebner, A. J. & Mancini, J. A. (2003). Shaping structured out-of-school time use among youth: The effects of self, family, and friend systems. *Journal of Youth and Adolescence, 32,* 453–463.

Jelicic, H., Bobek, D. L., Phelps, E., Lerner, R. M., & Lerner, J. V. (2007). Using positive youth development to predict contribution and risk behaviors in early adolescence: Findings from the first two-waves of the 4-H Study of Positive Youth Development. *International Journal of Behavioral Development, 31,* 263–273.

Jencks, C., & Mayer, S. E. (1990). The social consequences of growing up in a poor neighborhood. In L. E. Lynn, Jr. & M. F. H. McGeary (Eds.), *Inner-city poverty in the United States* (pp. 111–186). Washington, DC: National Academy Press.

Jordan, W. J., & Nettles, S. M. (2000). How students invest their time outside of school: Effects on school-related outcomes. *Social Psychology of Education, 3,* 217–243.

Kandel, D. B. (1978). Homophily, selection, and socialization in adolescent friendships. *American Journal of Sociology, 84,* 427–436.

Kleiber, D. A. & Kirshnit, C. E. (1991). Sport involvement and identity formation. In Diamant, L. (Ed.), *Mind–body maturity: Psychological approaches to sports, exercise, and fitness* (pp. 193–211). Washington, DC: Hemisphere.

Lareau, A. (2003). *Unequal childhoods: Class, race, and family life.* Berkeley: University of California Press.

Larson, R. (1989) Beeping children and adolescents: A method for studying time use and daily experience. *Journal of Youth and Adolescence, 18,* 511–530.

Larson, R. (1994). Youth organizations, hobbies, and sports as developmental contexts. In E. R. K.. Silberiesen & E. Todt (Eds.), *Adolescence in context: The interplay of family, school, peers, and work in adjustment* (pp. 46–65). New York: Springer-Verlag.

Larson, R. W. (2000). Toward a psychology of positive youth development. *American Psychologist, 55,* 170–183.

Larson, R. W., Hansen, D. M., & Moneta, G. (2006). Differing profiles of developmental experiences across types of organized youth activities. *Developmental Psychology, 42,* 849–863.

Larson, R. W., Pearce, N., Sullivan, P. J., & Jarrett, R. L. (2007). Participation in youth programs as a catalyst for negotiation of family autonomy with connection. *Journal of Youth and Adolescence, 36,* 31–45.

Larson, R., W., Richards, M. H., Sims, B., & Dworkin, J. (2001). How urban African American young adolescents spend their time: Time budgets for locations, activities, and companionship. *American Journal of Community Psychology, 29,* 565–597.

Larson, R. W., & Verma, S. (1999). How children and adolescents spend time across the world: Work, play, and developmental opportunities. *Psychological Bulletin, 125,* 701–736.

Larson, R., Walker, K., & Pearce, N. (2005). Youth-driven and adult-driven youth development programs: Contrasting models of youth-adult relationships. *Journal of Community Psychology, 33,* 57–74.

Lauver, S., & Little, P. M. D. (2005). Recruitment and retention strategies for out-of-school time programs. In G. G. Noam (Ed.), H. B. Weiss, P. M. D. Little, and S. M. Bouffard (Issue Eds.), *New Directions for Youth Development, 105: Participation in youth programs: Enrollment, attendance, and engagement,* 71–89.

Lauver, S., Little, P. M. D., & Weiss, H. (2004). *Moving beyond the barriers: Attracting and sustaining youth participation in out-of-school time programs.* Retrieved June 13, 2008, from www.hfrp.org/content/download/1098/48603/file/issuebrief6.pdf.

Lerner, R. M. (2002). *Concepts and theories of human development* (3rd ed.). Mahwah, NJ: Lawrence Erlbaum.

Lerner, R. M. (2004). *Liberty: Thriving and civic engagement among America's youth.* Thousand Oaks, CA: Sage.

Lerner, R. M. (2006). Developmental science, developmental systems, and contemporary theories of human development. In R. M. Lerner (Ed.), *Handbook of child psychology* (6th ed.), vol. 1: *Theoretical models of human development.* Editors-in-chief: W. Damon & R. M. Lerner. Hoboken, NJ: John Wiley & Sons.

Lerner, R. M. (2007). *The good teen: Rescuing adolescents from the myths of the storm and stress years.* New York: Crown.

Lerner, R. M., Lerner, J. V., Almerigi, J. B., Theokas, C., Phelps, E., Gestsdottir, S., et al. (2005). Positive youth development, participation in youth development programs, and community contributions of fifth-grade adolescents: Findings from the first wave of the 4-H Study of Positive Youth Development. *Journal of Early Adolescence, 25,* 17–71.

Lerner, R. M., Theokas, C., & Bobek, D. L. (2005). Concepts and theories of human development: Historical and contemporary dimensions. In M. H. Bornstein & M. E. Lamb (Eds.), *Developmental science: An advanced textbook* (5th ed.; (pp. 3–44). Mahwah, NJ: Lawrence Erlbaum.

Leventhal, T., & Brooks-Gunn, J. (2000). The neighborhoods they live in: The effects of neighborhood residence upon child and adolescent outcomes. *Psychological Bulletin, 126,* 309–337.

Levine Coley, R., Morris, J. E., & Hernandez, D. (2004). Out-of-school care and problem behavior trajectories among low-income adolescents: Individual, family, and neighborhood characteristics as added risk. *Child Development, 75,* 948–965.

Loder, T. L., & Hirsch, B. J. (2003). Inner-city youth development organizations: The salience of peer ties among early adolescent girls. *Applied Developmental Science, 7,* 2–12.

Long, T. J., & Long, L. (1982). *Latchkey children: The child's view of self care.* Unpublished manuscript. Catholic University of America.

Lord, H., & Mahoney, J. L. (2007). Neighborhood crime and self care: Risks for aggression and lower academic performance. *Developmental Psychology, 43,* 1321–1333.

Luthar, S. S., Shoum, K. A. & Brown, P. J. (2006). Extracurricular involvement among affluent youth: A scapegoat for "ubiquitous achievement pressures"? *Developmental Psychology, 42,* 583–597.

Magnusson, D., & Stattin, H. (1998). Person–context interaction theories. In W. Damon (Series Ed.) and R. M. Lerner (Vol. Ed.), *Handbook of child psychology.* vol. 1: *Theory* (pp. 685–760). New York: John Wiley & Sons.

Mahoney, J. L. (2000). Participation in school extracurricular activities as a moderator in the development of antisocial patterns. *Child Development, 71,* 502–516.

Mahoney, J. L., & Cairns, R. B. (1997). Do extracurricular activities protect against early school dropout? *Developmental Psychology, 33,* 241–253.

Mahoney, J. L., Cairns, B. D., & Farmer, T. W. (2003). Promoting interpersonal competence and educational success through extracurricular activity participation. *Journal of Educational Psychology, 95,* 409–418.

Mahoney, J. L., Harris, A. L., & Eccles, J. S. (2006). Organized activity participation, positive youth development, and the over-scheduling hypothesis. *SRCD Social Policy Report, 20,* 1–31.

Mahoney, J. L., Larson, R. W., & Eccles, J. S. (Eds.). (2005). *Organized activities as contexts of development: Extracurricular activities, after-school and community programs.* Mahwah, NJ: Lawrence Erlbaum.

Mahoney, J. L., Lord, H., & Carryl, E. (2005a). Afterschool program participation and the development of child obesity and peer acceptance. *Applied Developmental Science, 9,* 202–215.

Mahoney, J. L., Lord, H., & Carryl, E. (2005b). An ecological analysis of after-school program participation and the development of academic performance and motivational attributes for disadvantaged children. *Child Development, 76,* 811–825.

Mahoney, J. L., & Magnusson, D. (2001). Parent participation in community activities and the persistence of criminality. *Development and Psychopathology, 13,* 123–139.

Mahoney, J. L., Parente, M. E., & Zigler, E. F. (in press). *Afterschool program participation and children's development.* To appear in J. Meece & J. Eccles (Eds.), *Handbook on schools, schooling, and human development.*

Mahoney, J. L., Schweder, A. E., & Stattin, H. (2002). Structured after-school activities as moderator of depressed mood for adolescents with detached relations to their parents. *Journal of Community Psychology, 30,* 69–86.

Mahoney, J. L., & Stattin, H. (2000). Leisure activities and adolescent antisocial behavior: The role of structure and social context. *Journal of Adolescence, 23,* 113–127.

Mahoney, J. L., Stattin, H., & Lord, H. (2004). Participation in unstructured youth recreation centers and the development of antisocial behavior: Selection processes and the moderating role of deviant peers. *International Journal of Behavioral Development, 28,* 553–560.

Mahoney, J. L., Stattin, H., & Magnusson, D. (2001). Youth recreation center participation and criminal offending: A 20-year longitudinal study of Swedish boys. *International Journal of Behavioral Development, 25,* 509–520.

Mahoney, J. L. & Zigler, E. F. (2006). Translating science-to-policy under the No Child Left Behind Act of 2001: Lessons from the national evaluation of the 21st-Century Community Learning Centers. *Journal of Applied Developmental Psychology, 27,* 282–294.

Marsh, H. W., & Kleitman, S. (2002). Extracurricular school activities: The good, the bad, and the nonlinear. *Educational Review, 72,* 464–514.

Marshall, N. L., Coll, C. G., Marx, F., McCartney, K., Keefe, N., & Ruh, J. (1997). After-school time and children's behavioral adjustment. *Merrill-Palmer Quarterly, 43,* 497–514.

McKinney, J. P. (Ed.). (1999). Adolescents and religion: A view from the millennium. *Journal of Adolescence, 22,* 185.

McLaughlin, M. W. (2000). *Community counts: How youth organizations matter for youth development.* Washington, DC: Public Education Network.

McNeal, R. B., Jr. (1995). Extracurricular activities and high school dropouts. *Sociology of Education, 68,* 62–81.

McNeal, R. B., Jr. (1998). High school extracurricular activities: "Closed" structures and stratifying patterns of participation. *Journal of Educational Research, 91,* 183–191.

McNeal, R. B., Jr. (1999). Participation in high school extracurricular activities: Investigating school effects. *Social Science Quarterly, 80,* 291–309.

Miller, K. E., Sabo, D. F., Farrell, M. P., Barnes, G. M., & Melnick, M. J. (1998). Athletic participation and sexual behavior in adolescents: The different worlds of boys and girls. *Journal of Health and Social Behavior, 39,* 108–123.

Morrisey, K. M., & Werner-Wilson, R. J. (2005). The relationship between out-of-school activities and positive youth development: An investigation of the influences of communities and families. *Adolescence, 40,* 67–85.

Mott, J. A., Crowe, P. A., Richardson, J., & Flay, B. (1999). After-school supervision and adolescent cigarette smoking: Contributions of the setting and intensity of after-school self care. *Journal of Behavioral Medicine, 22,* 35–58.

National Center for Education Statistics (NCES) (2005). *Youth indicators, 2005: Trends in the well-being of American youth.* Washington, DC: U.S. Government Printing Office.

National 4-H Council (2006). 4-H homepage. Retrieved June 13, 2008, from www.fourhcouncil.edu/default.aspx.

National Institute on Out-of-School Time (2008). *The Afterschool Program Assessment System (APAS).* Retrieved on June 6, 2008, from www.niost.org/publications/APAS%20brochure_Jan_25_08.pdf.

National Research Council and Institute of Medicine (NRC-IOM). (2002). *Community programs to promote youth development.* Washington, DC: National Academy Press.

New York State Afterschool Network. (2005). *Program quality self-assessment tool.* Retrieved May 13, 2007, from www.nysan.org.

Newman, S. A., Fox, J. A., Flynn, E. A., & Christenson, W. (2000). *The prime time for juvenile crime or youth enrichment and achievement.* Washington, DC: Fight Crime Invest in Kids.

NICHD Early Child Care Network. (2004). Are child developmental outcomes related to before- and after-school care arrangements? Results from the NICHD Study of Early Child Care. *Child Development, 75,* 280–295.

O'Neill, S. A. (2005). Youth music engagement in formal and informal contexts. In J. L. Mahoney, R. W. Larson, & J. S. Eccles (Eds.), *Organized activities as contexts of development: Extracurricular activities, after-school and community programs* (pp. 255–274). Mahwah, NJ: Lawrence Erlbaum.

Osgood, D. W., & Anderson, A. L. (2004). Unstructured socializing and rates of delinquency. *Criminology, 42,* 519–549.

Osgood, D. W., Anderson, A. L., & Shaffer, J. N. (2005). Unstructured leisure in the after-school hours. In J. L. Mahoney, R. W. Larson, & J. S. Eccles (Eds.), *Organized activities as contexts of development: Extracurricular activities, after-school and community programs* (pp. 45–64). Mahwah, NJ: Lawrence Erlbaum.

Osgood, D. W., Wilson, J. K., Bachman, J. G., O'Malley, P. M., & Johnston, L. D. (1996). Routine activities and individual deviant behavior. *American Sociological Review, 61,* 635–655.

Overturf Johnson, J. (2005). *Who's minding the kids? Child care arrangements.* Current Population Reports. Washington, DC: U.S. Bureau of the Census.

Pabayo, R., O'Loughlin J., Gauvin, L., Paradis, G., & Gray-Donald, K. (2006). Effect of a ban on extracurricular sports by secondary school teachers on physical activity levels of adolescents: A multilevel analysis. *Health Education and Behavior, 33,* 690–702.

Parke, R. D., Killian, C., Dennis, J., Flyr, M., McDowell, D. J., Simpkins, S. D., et al. (2003). Managing the external environment: The parent as active agent in the system. In L. Kuczynski (Ed.), *Handbook of dynamic in parent–child relations* (pp. 247–270). Thousand Oaks, CA: Sage.

Patrick, H., Ryan, M. A., Alfeld-Liro, C., Fredricks, J. A., Hruda, L. Z., & Eccles, J. S. (1999). Adolescent' commitment to developing talent in adolescence: The role of peers in continuing motivation for sports and the arts. *Journal of Youth and Adolescence, 28,* 741–763.

Pearce, N. J., & Larson, R. W. (2006). How teens become engaged in youth development programs: The process of motivational change in a civic activism organization. *Applied Developmental Science, 10,* 121–131.

Pedersen, S. (2005). Urban adolescents' out-of-school activity profiles: Associations with youth, family, and school transition characteristics. *Applied Developmental Science, 9,* 107–124.

Persson, A., Kerr, M., & Stattin, H. (2007). Staying in or moving away from structured activities: Explanations involving parents and peers. *Developmental Psychology, 43,* 197–207.

Pettit, G. S., Bates, J. E., Dodge, K. A., & Meece, D. W. (1999). The impact of after-school peer contact on early adolescent externalizing problems is moderated by parental monitoring, perceived neighborhood safety, and prior adjustment. *Child Development, 70,* 768–778.

Pianta, R. C. (1999). *Enhancing relationships between children and teachers.* Washington, DC: American Psychological Association.

Pierce, K. M., Bolt, D. M., & Vandell, D. L. (in press). Features of after-school program quality: Differential associations with children's functioning in middle childhood. *American Journal of Community Psychology.*

Polatnick, M. R. (2002). Too old for child care? Too young for self-care? Negotiating after-school arrangements for middle school. *Journal of Family Issues, 23,* 728–747.

Policy Studies Associates, Inc. (2005). Out of school time observation instrument. Retrieved May 13, 2007, from www.afterschoolresources.org/kernel/images/psaost.pdf.

Posner, J. K., & Vandell, D. L. (1999). After-school activities and the development of low-income urban children: A longitudinal study. *Developmental Psychology, 35,* 868–879.

Quiroz, P. (2000). A comparison of the organizational and cultural contexts of extracurricular participation and sponsorship in two high schools. *Educational Studies, 31,* 249–275.

Regnerus, M. D. (2000). Shaping schooling success: Religious socialization and educational outcomes in metropolitan public schools. *Journal for the Scientific Study of Religion, 39,* 363–370.

Rhodes, J. E., & DuBois, D. L. (2006). Understanding and facilitating the youth mentoring movement. *SRCD Social Policy Report, 20,* 1–19.

Richardson, J. L., Dwyer, K., McGuigan, K., et al. (1989). Substance use among eight-grade students who take care of themselves after school. *Pediatrics, 84,* 556–566.

Richardson J. L., Radziszewska, B., Dent, C. W., & Flay, B. R. (1993). Relationship between after-school care of adolescents and substance use, risk taking, depressed, and academic achievement. *Pediatrics, 92,* 32–38.

Riley, D. & Steinberg, J. (2004). Four popular stereotypes about children in self-care: Implications for family life educators. *Family Relations, 53,* 95–101.

Robinson, B. E., Coleman, M., & Rowland, B. H. (1986). The after-school ecologies of latchkey children. *Children's Environments Quarterly, 3,* 4–8.

Rodman, H. & Cole, C. (1987). Latchkey children: A review of policy and resources. *Family Relations, 36,* 101–105.

Rodman, H., & Pratto, D. J. (1987). Child's age and mother's employment in relation to greater use of self-care arrangements for children. *Journal of Marriage and the Family, 49,* 573–578.

Rodman, H., Pratto, D. J., & Smith Nelson, R. (1985). Child care arrangements and children's functioning: A comparison of self-care and adult-care children. *Developmental Psychology, 21,* 413–418.

Rogoff, B. (2003). *The cultural nature of human development.* Oxford: Oxford University Press.

Rogoff, B., Baker-Sennet, J., Lacasa, P., & Goldsmith, D. (1995). Development through participation in sociocultural activity. In J. J. Goodnow, P. J. Miller, & F. Kessel (Eds.), *Cultural practices as contexts for development: New directions for child development,* vol. 67 (pp. 45–65). Hoboken, NJ: Jossey-Bass.

Rosenthal, R., & Vandell, D. L. (1996). Quality of care at school aged-child-care programs: Regulatable features, observed experiences, child perspectives, and parent perspectives. *Child Development, 67,* 2434–2445.

Roth, J. L., & Brooks-Gunn, J. (2003). What is a youth development program? Identification and defining principles. In F. Jacobs, D. Wertlieb, & R. M. Lerner (Eds.), *Handbook of applied developmental science: Promoting positive child, adolescent, and family development through research policies, and program,* vol. 2: *Enhancing the life chances of youth and families: Public service systems and public policy perspectives* (pp. 197–223). Thousand Oaks, CA: Sage.

Roth, J. L., Brooks-Gunn, J., Murray, L., & Foster, W. (1998). Promoting healthy adolescents: Synthesis of youth development program evaluations. *Journal of Research on Adolescence, 8,* 423–459.

Ryan, R. M., & Deci, E. L. (2000). Self-determination theory and the facilitation of intrinsic motivation, social development, and well-being. *American Psychologist, 55,* 68–78.

Sampson, R. J., & Laub, J. H. (1992). *Crime in the making: Pathways and turning points through life.* Cambridge, MA: Harvard University Press.

Sandstrom, M. J., & Coie, J. D. (1999). A developmental perspective on peer rejection: Mechanisms of stability and change. *Child Development, 70,* 955–966.

Scanlan, T. K., Babkes, M. L., & Scanlan, L. A. (2005). Participation in sport: A developmental glimpse at emotion. In J. L. Mahoney, R. W. Larson, & J. S. Eccles (Eds.), *Organized activities as contexts of development: Extracurricular activities, after-school and community programs* (pp. 275–310). Mahwah, NJ: Lawrence Erlbaum.

Shann, M. H. (2001). Students' use of time outside of school: A case for after school programs for urban middle school youth. *Urban Review, 33,* 339–356.

Shannon, C. S. (2006). Parents' messages about the role of extracurricular and unstructured leisure activities: Adolescents' perceptions. *Journal of Leisure Research, 38,* 398–420.

Shernoff, D. J., & Vandell, D. L. (2007). Engagement in after-school program activities: Quality of experience from the perspective of participants. *Journal of Youth and Adolescence, 36,* 891–903.

Shields, D. L., & Bredemeier, B. L. (2001). Moral development and behavior in sport. In R. N. Singer, H. A. Hausenblas, & C. M. Janell (Eds.), *Handbook of sport psychology* (pp. 585–603). New York: John Wiley & Sons.

Shilts, L. (1991). The relationship of early adolescent substance use to extracurricular activities, peer influence, and personal attitudes. *Adolescence, 103,* 613–617.

Shulman, S., Kedern, P., Kaplan, K. J., Sever, I., & Braja, M. (1998). Latchkey children: Potential sources of support. *Journal of Community Psychology, 26,* 185–197.

Simpkins, S. D., Bouffard, S., Dearing, E., Wimer, C., Caronongan, P., & Weiss, H. B. (in press). Adolescent adjustment and patterns of parents' behaviors in early and middle adolescence. *Journal of Research on Adolescence.*

Simpkins, S. D., Davis-Kean, P. E., & Eccles, J. S. (2005). Parents' socializing behavior and children's participation in math, science, and computer out-of-school activities. *Applied Developmental Science, 9,* 14–30.

Simpkins, S. D., Davis-Kean, P. E., & Eccles, J. S. (2006). Math and science motivation: A longitudinal examination of the links between choices and beliefs. *Developmental Psychology, 42,* 70–83.

Simpkins, S. D., Eccles, J. S., & Becnel, J. (2007). *The role of breadth in activity participation and friends in adolescents' adjustment.* Manuscript submitted for publication.

Simpkins, S. D., Fredricks, J., Davis-Kean, P., & Eccles, J. S. (2006). Healthy minds, healthy habits: The influence of activity involvement in middle childhood. In A. Huston & M. Ripke (Eds.), *Developmental contexts in middle childhood: Bridges to adolescence and adulthood* (pp. 283–302). New York: Cambridge University Press.

Simpkins, S. D., Ripke, M., Huston, A. C., & Eccles, J. S. (2005). Predicting participation and outcomes in out-of-school activities: Similarities and differences across social ecologies. In G. G. Noam (Ed.), H. B. Weiss, P. M. D. Little, and S. M. Bouffard (Issue Eds.), *New Directions for Youth Development, 105: Participation in youth programs: Enrollment, attendance, and engagement,* 51–70.

Smith, C. (2003). Religious participation and network closure among American adolescents. *Journal for the Scientific Study of Religion, 42,* 259–267.

Smith, K. (2002). Who's minding the kids? Child care arrangements: Spring 1997. *Current Population Reports, P70–86.* Washington, DC: U.S. Bureau of the Census.

Smith, C., & Hohmann, C. (2005). Full findings from the Youth PQA validation study. *High/Scope Educational Research Foundation.* Retrieved May 13, 2007, from www.highscope .org/file/EducationalPrograms/Adolescent/ResearchEvidence/ WebFinalYouthPQATechReport.pdf.

Smith, R. E., Smoll, F. L., & Barnett, N. P. (1995). Reduction of children's sport performance anxiety through social support and stress-reduction training for coaches. *Journal of Applied Developmental Psychology, 16,* 125–142.

Stattin, H., & Kerr, M. (2000). Parental monitoring: A reinterpretation. *Child Development, 71,* 1072–1085.

Steinberg, L. (1986). Latchkey children and susceptibility to peer pressure: An ecological analysis. *Developmental Psychology, 22,* 433–439.

Steinberg, L. (1988). Simple solutions to a complex problem: A response to Rodman, Pratto, and Nelson (1988). *Developmental Psychology, 24,* 295–296.

Stewart, R. (2001). Adolescent self-care: Reviewing the risks. *Families in Society: Journal of Contemporary Human Services, 82,* 119–126.

Theokas, C., & Bloch, M. (2006). *Out-of-school time is critical for children: Who participates in programs?* Washington, DC: Child Trends.

U.S. Department of Labor. (2000). *Report on the youth labor force.* Available at www.bls.gov/opub/rylf/rylfhome.htm.

U.S. Department of Labor. (2007). *Employee characteristics of families in 2006.* Available at www.bls.gov/opub/rylf/rylfhome .htm; www.bls.gov/news.release/pdf/famee.pdf.

Vandell, D. L., & Pierce, K. M. (1998). *Measures used in the study of after-school care.* Unpublished glossary, University of Wisconsin–Madison.

Vandell, D. L., Pierce, K. M., & Dadisman, K. (2005). Out-of-school settings as a developmental context for children and youth. In R. V. Kail (Ed.), *Advances in child development and behavior,* vol. 33, pp. 43–77). New York: Academic Press.

Vandell, D. L., & Posner, J. K. (1999). Conceptualization and measurement of children's after-school environments. In S. L. Friedman & T. Wachs (Eds.), *Measuring environments across the lifespan: Emerging methods and concepts* (pp. 167–196). Washington, DC: American Psychological Association.

Vandell, D. L., & Ramanan, J. (1991). Children of the National Longitudinal Survey of Youth: Choices in after-school care and child development. *Developmental Psychology, 27,* 637–643.

Vandell, D. L., & Reisner, E. R. (2006, March). Developmental outcomes associated with the after-school contexts of low-income children and youth. In H. B. Weiss (Chair), *Critical issues in adolescent participation in out-of-school time activities.* Symposium conducted at the biennial meeting of the Society for Research in Adolescence, San Francisco, CA.

Vandell, D. L., Reisner, E. R., Brown, B. B., Dadisman, K., Pierce, K. M., Lee, D., et al. (2005, March). *The Study of Promising After-School Programs: Examinations of intermediate outcomes in year 2.* Report to the Charles Steward Mott Foundation. Retrieved May 16, 2007, from www.wcer.wisc. edu/childcare/pdf/pp/year_2_report_final.pdf.

Vandell, D. L., Shernoff, D. J., Pierce, K. M., Bolt, D. M., Dadisman, K., & Brown, B. B. (2005). Activities, engagement, and emotion in after-school programs. In H. B. Weiss, P. M. D. Little, & S. M. Bouffard (Issue Eds.), G. G. Noam (Editor-in-Chief), *New directions in youth development,* vol. 105: *Participation in youth programs: Enrollment, attendance, and engagement* (pp. 121–129). San Francisco: Jossey-Bass.

Vandell, D. L, Shumow, L., & Posner, J. (2005). After-school programs for low-income children: Differences in program quality. In J. L. Mahoney, R. W. Larson, & J. S. Eccles (Eds.), *Organized activities as contexts of development: Extracurricular activities, after-school and community programs* (pp. 437–456). Mahwah, NJ: Lawrence Erlbaum.

Vygotsky, L. S. (1978). *Mind and society: The development of higher mental processes.* Cambridge, MA: Harvard University Press.

Wimer, C., Simpkins, S. D., Dearing, E., Caronongan, P., Bouffard, S., & Weiss, H. B. (in press). Predicting youth out-of-school time participation: Multiple risks and developmental differences. *Merrill-Palmer Quarterly.*

Winnail, S. D., Valois, R. F., & Dowda, M. (1997). Athletics and substance use among public high school students in a southern state. *American Journal of Health Studies, 13,* 187–194.

Woods, M. B. (1972). The unsupervised child of the working mother. *Developmental Psychology, 6,* 14–25.

Yates, M., & Youniss, J. (1996). Community service and political–moral identity in adolescents. *Journal of Research on Adolescence, 6,* 271–284.

Yohalem, N., & Wilson-Ahlstrom, A. (2007). Measuring youth program quality: A guide to assessment tools. Retrieved May 13, 2006, from www.forumfyi.org/files/Measuring_Youth_ Program_Quality.pdf.

Youniss, J., McLellan, J. A., & Yates, M. (1997). What we know about engendering civic identity. *American Behavioral Scientist, 40,* 619–630.

Youniss, J., McLellan, J. A., & Yates, M. (1999). The role of community service in identity development: Normative, unconventional, and deviant orientations. *Journal of Adolescent Research, 14,* 248–261.

Zaff, J. S., Moore, K. A., Papillo, A. R., & Williams, S. (2003). Implications of extracurricular activity participation during adolescence on positive outcomes. *Journal of Adolescent Research, 18,* 599–630.

Zarrett, N. R. (2007). The dynamic relation between out-of-school activities and adolescent development. Doctoral dissertation, University of Michigan, 2006. *Dissertation Abstracts International, 67,* 6100B.

Zarrett, N., Lerner, R. M., Carrano, J., Fay, K., Peltz, J. S., & Li, Y. (2007). Variations in adolescent engagement in sports and its influence on positive youth development. In N. L. Holt (Ed.), *Positive youth development and sport.* Oxford: Routledge.

CHAPTER 8

Adolescents and the World of Work

JEREMY STAFF, EMILY E. MESSERSMITH, AND JOHN E. SCHULENBERG

It was a brainless job, being the guy at the end of the automatic carwash. I had three moves—holding my
hand up to tell the driver not to go yet, then waving them forward after the pin rolling the front tires cleared,
and then waving goodbye as they drove off (now there is a light machine to do all that). It took about 2 minutes to learn what I had to do on the job, and then another 2 seconds to decide that this sort of job was not my
future. The hardest part was fighting off boredom, and we would get creative about how to do this, usually
while getting high. But it was an important experience—I saw what it was like to work, got more independent, and made some friends I still know. The money helped me get my first car and first real girlfriend.
> —Middle-aged geologist reflecting on his first "real job" during high school.

Among the more vivid memories of one's
own adolescence, it is likely that paid work
experiences loom large, though not always
for positive reasons. First "real jobs" constitute packages of new experiences that include
new skills and social relations, a burst of
independence, and an official entry into the
worker role. Typically, the jobs are entry level,
and rarely do they provide experiences directly
relevant to the young person's eventual occupation. Nonetheless, such jobs can provide
developmental benefits, offering new contexts
for demonstrating competencies and signaling
greater independence. Of course, there are also
potential developmental drawbacks associated
with adolescent jobs, in terms of health risks,
problem behaviors, and time and energy trade-
offs. The field has provided ample evidence

about such associations, though the causal
connections underlying these associations are
far from being clear.

Within the study of adolescent development,
career development is the little-known sibling
of paid work. For reasons we discuss later in this
chapter, how career interests develop during
adolescence and how adolescents make career
decisions are topics that are often ignored in
the adolescent development literature. This is
unfortunate, as such topics can offer important
windows into, for example, adolescent identity development, decision making, family and
peer relations, and educational motivations
and goals. How career development relates
to paid work experiences in adolescence is
understudied. Such oversights, however, are
fixable, and there is important new research

We thank Jeylan T. Mortimer, Matthew Nelson, Erik Porfeli, and Fred Vondracek for helpful advice and comments on an earlier draft of this paper, and Kathryn Johnson for editorial assistance. This paper builds upon
a chapter titled "Work and Leisure in Adolescence" that appeared in the second edition of the *Handbook of
Adolescent Psychology,* by Jeremy Staff, Jeylan T. Mortimer, and Christopher Uggen. The first author gratefully
acknowledges support from a Mentored Research Scientist Development Award in Population Research from
the National Institute of Child Health and Human Development (K01 HD054467). This chapter highlights findings from the Monitoring the Future study, which is supported by a grant from the National Institute on Drug
Abuse (R01 DA01411).

on adolescent career development and how it intersects with early work experiences (see Mortimer & Zimmer-Gembeck, 2007; Zimmer-Gembeck & Mortimer, 2006, for reviews).

In this chapter, our goals are to provide a review of the literature relevant to the topics of early work experiences and career development during adolescence, to draw connections among these two and other related topics in order to provide a fuller picture of adolescent development, and to offer some direction for future research. Out of both necessity and preference, we draw from several different disciplines, particularly including developmental, educational, and counseling psychology, and sociology. Throughout the chapter, we also draw upon nationally representative data from the Monitoring the Future (MTF) study to provide some descriptive statistics on youth employment. Beginning in 1976, the MTF project has collected data on large (approximately 17,000 students per grade) samples of middle and high school students in the United States each year (Johnston, O'Malley, Bachman, & Schulenberg, 2007a, 2007b).

We begin with a brief historical and theoretical overview about the study of adolescent work and career development, considering conceptual interrelations between the two, and embedding both within the broader context of adolescent development. We then provide a review of the literature on early work experiences, organizing the literature in terms of the key themes of potential costs and benefits of part-time work as well as of causal and spurious relations. Next, we consider the career development literature, focusing our review on important constructs and how they develop and interrelate across adolescence. We conclude with a summary of key points, a discussion of theoretical and practical implications, and a consideration of future directions to advance our understanding of adolescent work and career development and how both relate to other aspects of adolescence and life course development.

WORK AND ADOLESCENT DEVELOPMENT

The recognition of adolescence as a distinct period in the life course in the United States was partly a function of separating young people from the workforce at the beginning of the twentieth century. Then, for several decades in this country (and as is still the case in most other developed countries), a key inclusionary criterion for defining someone as an adolescent was not a member of the paid workforce. This status has some important advantages. At a fundamental level, adolescence is a time of preparation for adulthood (and much more than that). Keeping youth out of the paid workforce enables them to emphasize education and gain more developmentally appropriate experiences and competencies. It also permits more paid work opportunities for adults. At the same time, complete disconnection from the world of work is likely to carry some developmental disadvantages for young people in terms of limited career-relevant experiences for skill development, exploration, and decision making, as well as starker school-to-work transitions.

The somewhat haphazard system we currently have in the United States, where the vast majority of adolescents find some way to combine full-time school with part-time work during their high school years, also has important benefits and drawbacks. Ideally, early paid work experiences provide opportunities, for example, to gain responsibility, to test skills and develop new ones, to develop a sense of those aspects of work that are more or less important or aversive, and to get a sense of the extent to which initial career goals represent a good pathway. Drawbacks are many, particularly in terms of possible negative health and risky behavior outcomes and the typical lack of connection between most jobs in adolescence and career-track jobs that are more common during adulthood.

The study of both paid work and career development during adolescence—topics that have not received extensive attention from researchers who focus on adolescent development—are nonetheless important for the larger field of adolescent development. Both provide unique vantage points and unifying themes for understanding adolescence, and more broadly the study of human development. In this section, we briefly consider the history and broader significance of the study of these two topics. To set the appropriate stage for understanding work and career development influences, we begin with a brief overview of our theoretical orientation.

Developmental Conceptualizations

Our perspective on development draws from a broad interdisciplinary developmental science framework that emphasizes multidimensional and multidirectional developmental change across life, characterized by successive mutual selection and accommodation of individuals and their contexts (Baltes, Lindenberger, & Staudinger, 2006; Cairns, 2000; Elder & Shanahan, 2006; Lerner, 2006; Sameroff, 2000). Through a process of niche selection, individuals select available environments and activities based on personal characteristics, beliefs, interests, and competencies; selected ecological niches then provide various opportunities for continued socialization and further selection. For instance, career aspirations, reflecting the young person's perceived talents and future potential, guide various educational decisions; in turn, these educational experiences contribute to refinement or alteration of aspirations and help shape the duration and character of school, work, and family trajectories. This progressive accommodation suggests the qualities of coherence and continuity in development. However, given dynamic person–context interactions and multidirectional change, development does not necessarily follow a smooth and progressive function. New experiences and contexts can shift ongoing developmental trajectories (e.g., Cairns, 2000; Cicchetti & Rogosch, 2002; Laub & Sampson, 2003; Lewis, 1999; Schulenberg & Zarrett, 2006). From a systems perspective (Sameroff,

2000), development is viewed as a function of strong person–context interactions with a temporal course given to fits and starts that correspond, at least in part, to shifts in the individual, contexts, and the interaction between the two (Schulenberg, Maggs, & O'Malley, 2003). A key question for us is how paid work experiences during adolescence can alter and/or help solidify ongoing trajectories related to career development and entry, as well as health and adjustment, family formation behaviors, and socioeconomic attainment.

Consistent with an ecological perspective on adolescent development (Bronfenbrenner & Morris, 2006), involvement in paid work represents a unique and consequential microsystem during adolescence. The first such paid work experience reflects an ecological transition, offering the young person a "brand new" context, and offering scientists opportunities to consider key questions concerning broader issues of selection, socialization, self-regulation, and bidirectional influences (Schulenberg, 2006). Much of the impact of paid work experiences depends on the interconnections—the mesosystems—of this microsystem with others including family, school, and peer networks. Thus, another key question is the extent to which there is consistency in promoted values and norms between school and work microsystems. Similarly, drawing from life-course theory, we note the importance of linked lives in understanding the type and meaning of paid work experiences and career opportunities and trajectories (Elder & Shanahan, 2006).

Furthermore, in line with broad cultural and historical influences (Bronfenbrenner & Morris, 2006; Elder & Shanahan, 2006; Lerner, 2006), the meaning and function of part-time work and career development during adolescence draw from the overarching cultural and subcultural context and can shift historically. This theoretical framework assumes that individual trajectories are shaped by major events, such as war, economic depression, and migrations, as well as other circumstances of the historical period in which life transitions occur. In particular, such forces as rapid technological change and the lengthening of the life course contribute to changes in the course and content of career development, very likely moving many of the more concrete aspects of career decision making out of adolescence and into early adulthood for many young people. The lengthening of the period between adolescence and adulthood, sometimes referred to as emerging adulthood (Arnett, 2004), contributes to delays in assuming the full-time worker role, which in turn highlights the importance of early work experiences to ease (and sometimes delay) the transition into full-time employment. Thus, all that we cover in this chapter reflects dynamic relations that shift along with cultural and technological changes.

The Context of Adolescent Paid Work

As mentioned earlier, combining school and part-time work during adolescence is a recent (past 4 to 5 decades) and uniquely American (though this is changing) phenomenon. It is likely that this phenomenon has arisen due to many aspects of the American culture, including capitalism, consumerism, and independence. Teenage paid work has become a necessary component of the economy, both in terms of needing inexperienced workers willing to work part-time at low pay as well as needing young people with an abundance of disposable income. Typically, young people want to work, and their parents are supportive of part-time work. For instance, only 5% of 8th graders in a 2006 MTF survey who were not employed indicated that they had no current desire to work (and less than 1% of employed 8th graders wished they did not have to work). These statistics are not surprising. Young people seek paid work for many reasons: to gain some autonomy from parental supervision and other authority figures, to save money for future education or other purposes, to support their families, or to assert themselves as more "adult-like" in the eyes of parents, teachers, and peers. Most often, young people seek employment because they want money to buy things (e.g., clothes, music, video games, fast food) and to spend on friends and social activities, contributing to what has been called "premature affluence" (Bachman, 1983).

In addition, parents support their children's entry (and sometimes push them) into paid work partly because most parents believe that work helps young people become more responsible, independent, and hardworking (Phillips & Sandstrom, 1990). In 2006, for example, only 10% of 8th graders in the MTF study believed that their parents did not want them to work (see also Bachman, Safron, Sy, & Schulenberg, 2003). Parents of adolescents of high socioeconomic status (SES) have especially favorable attitudes toward youth employment, and adolescents from more advantaged backgrounds report working at younger ages than those from low SES origins (Mortimer, Finch, Owens, & Shanahan, 1990). Consistent with these ideas, in the 1970s, many high-level government panels recommended part-time work for young people, mentioning the many assumed virtues of working for young people in terms of responsibility, independence, and experience (Coleman et al., 1974).

It was not until the groundbreaking research of Greenberger and Steinberg during the early 1980s—showing some of the negative correlates of adolescent involvement in paid work in terms of health risks, time sacrifices in terms of school and activities, and exposure to unethical business practices—that the downside of part-time work started becoming a concern (e.g., Greenberger & Steinberg, 1986; Steinberg & Dornbusch, 1991; Steinberg, Fegley, & Dornbusch, 1993). Following the research of Greenberger and Steinberg, as well as the extensive research by Mortimer and colleagues following a cohort of young people longitudinally (Mortimer, 2003), part-time work has become an increasingly common topic of research among those studying adolescence. As discussed in more depth later, the research on this topic has followed an interesting path, with initial research focusing on global costs and benefits of part-time work and more recent research starting to focus on more nuanced effects to address questions regarding for whom and under what conditions work contributes to positive and negative outcomes. Clearly, a major issue has become the extent to which part-time work contributes to any harmful or beneficial outcomes, as opposed to simply reflecting selection effects. The study of work has become an interdisciplinary topic, of interest to developmental and educational psychologists, sociologists, and, more recently, criminologists.

Adolescent Career Development

As mentioned earlier, the topic of career development has not had a central role in the understanding of adolescence. Clearly, career development strongly relates to many central aspects of adolescent development and is a topic of keen interest to many young people and their parents. For example, career development during adolescence relates to cognitive development in terms of career-related decision making and how thoughts of careers and one's skills, interests, and aspirations change as a function of cognitive growth; to cognitive and identity development in terms of thinking about possible selves and future orientation; to identity in terms of a way to organize information about the self and providing a more concrete foothold to identity questions; to family relations and school context influences in terms of stimulating and restricting various career interests and options; to educational goals and achievement, which are often in service of broader future career goals; and to self-regulation given that persons rather than organizations are becoming more responsible for constructing and maintaining careers in the modern economy (Porfeli & Vondracek, in press). Career development is an organizing schema for much of what young people are preparing and planning (Vondracek, Lerner, & Schulenberg, 1986).

It is instructive to briefly consider why career development has not played a more central role in the adolescent literature. Part

of the reason derives from graduate training (Vondracek, 2001). Developmental and social psychology programs that focus on adolescence do not typically involve training and research on career development (there are important exceptions, of course). Among sociologists, the beginning of the occupational career is typically viewed as occurring after the completion of school, so most sociologists assume a "socioeconomic life cycle" in which the first full-time job after the completion of school marks the beginning of the career. Teenage work experiences and vocational development are given very little attention in these sociological models (again, there are important exceptions). Instead, most of the research on career development comes out of counseling and educational psychology programs, in which adolescent development is typically not a major emphasis, and in which research tends to be more applied rather than basic. Similarly, much of the literature on adolescent career development is published in vocational and counseling journals, and not in developmental or adolescent journals.

Career development is often viewed as an applied topic, but this is unlikely a reason why it is not more central in the adolescent development literature, because much of the emphasis in this field, especially recently, is on applied topics. There are questions about how to study career development during adolescence given that career decisions are usually not an immediate adolescent matter. There are also questions about what constructs to study (we discuss this in more detail later in this chapter). Perhaps part of the reason career development is not given more attention is that it is viewed as the purview of identity research, but career development has not recently been a particularly salient topic among identity researchers. Finally, perhaps the laissez-faire approach the United States takes in terms of guiding young people's career development (Hamilton, 1990) drifts into research priorities in the adolescent development field.

Nonetheless, it is clear that adolescent career development has played a marginal role in developmental research. As we review in the next section, adolescent involvement in paid work has received much more research attention.

PAID WORK IN ADOLESCENCE

Social scientists more often than not measure career entry as the "first" full-time (at least 35 hours of work per week) civilian occupation held after leaving school for the last time. Unfortunately, this conception of career entry ignores work experiences that occur prior to school completion, as youth today often combine paid work with school (Arum & Hout, 1998; Kerckhoff, 2000, 2002). For instance, the vast majority of high school students are employed at some point during the school year, and over half of full-time postsecondary students and almost all part-time students work for pay (U.S. Department of Labor, 2000, 2006). This "sharing" of work and school roles begins as early as age 12 (Entwisle, Alexander, & Olson, 2000) and continues during the high school years through college (Hotz, Xu, Tienda, & Ahituv, 2002; Schulenberg, O'Malley, Bachman, & Johnston, 2005; Staff & Mortimer, 2007). Furthermore, as postsecondary students are becoming increasingly older in the United States (44% of students currently enrolled in degree-granting institutions are over 25 years of age; U.S. Department of Education, 2007), young people can accumulate a substantial amount of labor market experience prior to school completion. On average, high school students graduate with approximately 1,500 hours of work experience, and college students graduate with nearly 5,000 hours in paid work (Light, 2001).

Psychologists, sociologists, economists, and criminologists have debated whether the sharing of work and school roles, especially in adolescence, adversely affects long-term socioeconomic attainment and social development (Mortimer, 2003). Thus far, four contrasting perspectives have emerged. According to the first view, early investments in paid work may disrupt academic performance and promote behaviors and orientations that interfere with school achievement, positive adjustment, and career development (Steinberg & Cauffman, 1995). Employed adolescents may have less time for extracurricular activities as well as less time for activities that take place in the contexts of the school, the family, and the community. In addition, young workers will spend less time doing homework and will be more likely to come to school tired and unprepared for learning than other students (Greenberger & Steinberg, 1986). Furthermore, if adolescents become less attached to school, they may become less likely to engage in activities that are organized by the school and monitored by adults for the benefit of young people, such as playing sports, participating in various clubs and organizations, and attending school-sponsored events and functions. Working youth may then become more attracted to unstructured leisure activities, such as going to parties with friends, using drugs and alcohol, and cruising around in cars, because these activities may be more compatible with their work schedules than are adult-sponsored and school-related leisure activities (Osgood, 1999). Considerable research shows that those youth who work more than 20 hours per week are more likely to engage in delinquency, substance use, and sexual activity (Bachman & Schulenberg, 1993; Bozick, 2006; Greenberger & Steinberg, 1986; Ku, Sonenstein, & Pleck, 1993; McMorris & Uggen, 2000; Mortimer & Johnson, 1998b; Steinberg & Dornbusch, 1991; Steinberg et al., 1993).

The second view challenges the zero-sum logic that employed adolescents cannot have a well-rounded lifestyle including successful work, family, and school roles. Research shows that when adolescents limit the hours they spend in paid work, they are able to balance their multiple commitments to school, family, and their jobs (Mortimer, 2003). Furthermore, these early work experiences may help youth navigate the largely unstructured school-to-work transition in the United States (Rosenbaum, 2001). This labor market experience may be especially important for recent cohorts of youth given the increasing difficulty young people have in making occupational choices (Rindfuss, Cooksey, & Sutterlin, 1999; Schneider & Stevenson, 1999). In addition, early workforce involvement may benefit later employability, earnings, and occupational standing through on-the-job training and skill development. It may also foster "soft skills" such as dependability, responsibility, trustworthiness, and good work habits (Ruhm, 1997; Stern & Nakata, 1989).

A third line of research suggests the apparent effects of early work involvement may be spurious correlates of preexisting individual differences in school performance, problem behaviors, orientations toward work and school, SES, and academic achievement and motivation (Apel et al., 2007; Bachman et al., 2003, 2008; Hotz et al., 2002; Paternoster, Bushway, Brame, & Apel, 2003; Rothstein, 2007; Schoenhals, Tienda, & Schneider, 1998; Warren, LePore, & Mare, 2000). Young people who have less involvement, interest, and success in conventional adolescent activities—such as going to school and participating in extracurricular sports, clubs, and organizations—may be more likely to invest themselves in paid work and to prefer work to school-related activities. Moreover, prior engagement in substance use and minor deviance may predispose some youth to enter work environments that offer fewer social constraints on these behaviors than do school and family (Newcomb & Bentler, 1988). These factors may coalesce in a pattern of "precocious maturity" characterized by long work hours, school disengagement, low academic achievement, and continued involvement in heavy drinking, substance use, and delinquency.

Finally, because the decision about whether to work, and how much to work, reflects the young person's background and prospects for the future, some research suggests that the effects of teenage work hours may be conditioned by gender, race, and SES. For instance, long work hours may not be as harmful for those youth who come from more disadvantaged backgrounds, who are also probably more likely to need to work more hours to help support their families; to pay for educational expenses such as field trips, transportation, and lab fees; or for personal expenses (Entwisle et al., 2000; Newman, 1999). Furthermore, whereas many youth in poor urban neighborhoods face a restricted and competitive job market (Newman, 1999; Sullivan, 1989), youth in more prosperous areas may find a labor market characterized by an abundance of low-level retail and service jobs. Early work experiences may mean little for high-SES youth who have the resources and opportunities to lose and regain jobs.

In this section, we elaborate on these four views on the precursors and consequences of adolescent paid work for educational investment, vocational development, deviance and substance use, educational attainment, and the acquisition of full-time work in early adulthood. Before we turn to these issues, however, we first briefly document the scope of adolescent involvement in paid work in the United States.

Scope of Teenage Employment in the United States

Most young people in America today hold paid jobs as teenagers. In recent years, an estimated 80 to 90 percent are formally employed at some point during the high school period (Hirschman & Voloshin, 2007; U.S. Department of Labor, 2000). The likelihood of employment, as well as the "intensity" of paid work (i.e., average hours), increases each year during high school. Figure 8.1 displays the percentage of 8th, 10th, and 12th graders who work during the school year, as well as the average number of hours worked per week. These results are based on a pooled cross-sectional data set of approximately 750,000 middle and high school students from the 1991 to 2006 MTF surveys. As shown in Figure 8.1, during 8th and 10th grades, the majority of students

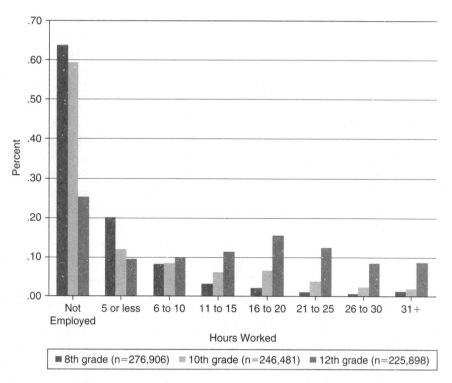

FIGURE 8.1 Percentage of employed students and number of hours worked during the school year by 8th, 10th, and 12th grade (combined 1991 to 2006 Monitoring the Future cohorts).

do not work in paid jobs during the school year (65 percent and 60 percent, respectively), whereas in 12th grade only one-quarter are not employed during the school year. In 8th grade, intensive work hours are relatively uncommon; only a small percentage of middle school students spend more than 10 hours per week in paid work. By 12th grade, however, the majority of employed students work more than 16 hours per week. Furthermore, nearly 1 in 10 employed 12th graders averages more than 30 hours of work per week during the school year (compared to just 1% of employed 8th graders). Though most prior research focuses on paid work involvement during the school year, it is important to note that adolescents average more hours of work during the months of summer vacation (National Research Council, 1998, pp. 38–39).

Research shows that the percentage of employed students and the number of hours

they work has changed very little in the past 40 years (Ruhm, 1997). Figure 8.2 shows the distribution of workers and the number of hours worked during the school year for 12th graders in 1976, 1986, 1996, and 2006. These descriptive statistics are also based on nationally representative samples of youth from the MTF study, although we limit the analyses to 12th graders because 8th and 10th graders in the MTF study were not surveyed prior to 1991. As shown in Figure 8.2, the number of nonworking 12th graders in 2006 is slightly higher than in 1976, including approximately one-quarter of the students. The distributions of hours worked among employed youth during the school year, however, are nearly identical across the four cohorts.

Gender, race and ethnicity, and SES influence the onset, intensity, duration, and earnings of paid workers during adolescence (Pabilonia, 2001). Girls tend to work at an

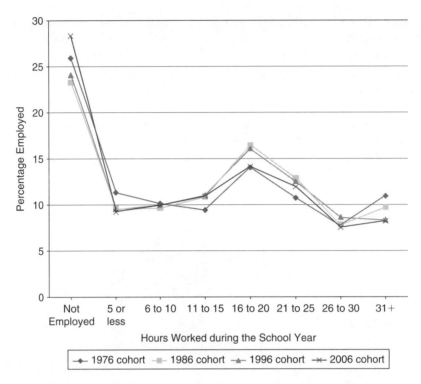

FIGURE 8.2 Percentage of employed students and number of hours worked during the school year (1976, 1986, 1996, and 2006 12th-grade Monitoring the Future cohorts).

earlier age than boys, but boys typically average more hours of paid work than girls, especially in the later years of high school. White youth are nearly twice as likely as African American and Hispanic youth to work during the school year, although African American and Hispanic teenagers average three to five additional hours of employment during the school year when they are employed (U.S. Department of Labor, 2000). Family socioeconomic background influences the age of labor market entry and the average hours of employment. Youth in lower income households are less likely to hold jobs at younger ages. In 1999, only 15% of 15- to 17-year-olds were employed in families reporting incomes of less than $27,300 in the previous year, almost half the rate of employment for teenagers in families reporting higher household incomes (U.S. Department of Labor, 2000). Although

low SES youth are less likely to be employed, recent research shows that disadvantaged youth average greater hours when they are employed than their high SES counterparts (Entwisle et al., 2000; Hirschman & Voloshin, 2007; Mortimer, 2003; Mortimer, Staff, & Oesterle, 2003; Staff & Mortimer, 2008).

In recent years, employed adolescents have become concentrated in the retail sector of the economy (up from 48 percent in 1977 to 62 percent; see the U.S. Department of Labor, 2000). In contrast, the percentage of youth employed in the agriculture and mining/construction/manufacturing industries declined by 25% and 49%, respectively, during the past 30 years. Hirschman and Voloshin (2007), using data from the 2005 Current Population Survey, show that over three-quarters of youth aged 16–19 are currently employed in food service (primarily food preparation and serving), sales, and office administration. The MTF data set contains detailed information on the types of jobs youth work in during the school year. Figures 8.3a, b, and c display the percentage of employed youth by job type for 8th, 10th, and 12th graders, respectively, during the school year (combined 1995 to 2006 MTF cohorts). In 8th grade (Figure 8.3a), the majority of youth workers are employed informally during the school year as babysitters (41%), yard workers (21%), newspaper delivery (2%), and in odd jobs (5%). By 10th grade (Figure 8.3b), increasing numbers of working youth are employed in restaurants (16%), though 41% of youth still work in informal jobs. Store clerk and fast-food worker are the most common jobs held by 10th graders (7% each of workers). By 12th grade, less than 10% of youth

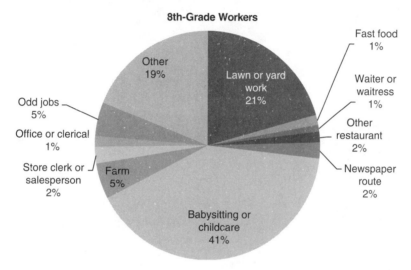

FIGURE 8.3a   Percentage of employed 8th-grade students by job type during the school year (combined 1995 to 2006 Monitoring the Future cohorts; approximate weighted sample size = 117,269 students).

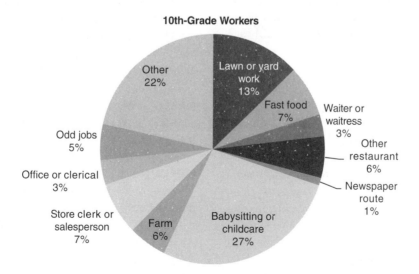

FIGURE 8.3b   Percentage of employed 10th-grade students by job type during the school year (combined 1995 to 2006 Monitoring the Future cohorts; approximate weighted sample size = 110,387).

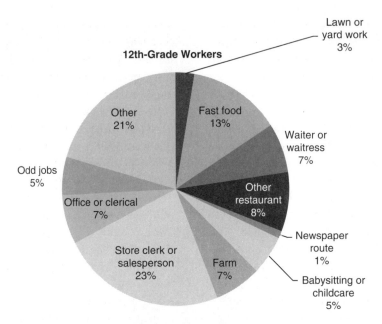

FIGURE 8.3c Percentage of employed 12th-grade students by job type during the school year (1995 to 2006 Monitoring the Future cohorts; approximate weighted sample size = 43,540 students).

work in informal jobs. Instead, one-quarter are employed as clerks and 28% work in restaurants. The 20% of youth employed in "other" jobs during the 8th, 10th, and 12th grades suggests considerable diversity in the early work experiences of contemporary teenagers (see also U.S. Department of Labor, 2000).

In summary, for many young people in the United States, paid work begins at an early age and involves a considerable time commitment during the school year. Participation in the workforce increases with age, but differs by gender, race and ethnicity, and SES.

FOUR VIEWS ON PAID WORK IN ADOLESCENCE

In this section, we summarize recent research on adolescent work into four general viewpoints. Though adolescent work activities occur in various contexts—home, school, and volunteer settings—we focus on paid jobs because the majority of adolescents are employed outside the family setting and most of these jobs lack clear ties to the school.

Early Work Experiences May Be Harmful

Whereas prior generations of youth were often employed in factories, farms, shops, and mills, under the supervision and guidance of family, friends, and relatives, it is argued that contemporary cohorts of youth work in low-quality jobs with supervisors who are approximately the same age as their subordinates. Greenberger and Steinberg's (1986) classic text, *When Teenagers Work: The Psychological and Social Costs of Adolescent Employment*, argued that the very contexts of paid work had changed across cohorts of youth. For example, they contend that: (1) the majority of teenage jobs no longer provide skills and workplace knowledge as preparation for adult work (the educational context); (2) most teenagers work for discretionary income rather than to provide for the financial needs of the family or for future educational expenses (the economic context); and (3) most teenagers work in age-segregated jobs with few opportunities for meaningful interaction with adults (the social context).

In such workplace settings, paid employment during adolescence may provide few benefits and impose "opportunity costs" that jeopardize a successful transition to adulthood.

Extracurricular activities in the arts, sports, and various academic clubs and organizations provide important opportunities for young people to explore their potential interests and values (Csikszentmihalyi & Schneider, 2000). Engagement in these activities fosters positive adjustment in high school and young adulthood (Barber, Eccles, & Stone, 2001; Eccles & Barber, 1999). By this logic, paid work may constrain adolescents from participation in these activities with their friends and in school, and it may potentially jeopardize the moratorium adolescents need from the demands and constraints of the adult world (Erikson, 1964). Indeed, empirical evidence has shown the inverse relationship between work hours and participation in extracurricular sports (Osgood, 1999); declining participation in extracurricular athletics may potentially undermine a healthy lifestyle, even though sports may offer little protection from alcohol and drug use (e.g., Crosnoe, 2002; Hoffmann, 2006; Peck, Vida, & Eccles, 2008). Consistent with this point of view, Bachman and Schulenberg (1993) and Safron, Bachman, and Schulenberg (2001) find that long hours of work are associated with less sleep and exercise and a greater frequency of skipping breakfast.

Paid work in adolescence may also jeopardize longer term socioeconomic attainment if early work experiences limit time for school-related activities and disrupt academic performance (Steinberg & Cauffman, 1995). Working youth may come to school unprepared and fatigued when they work during the week, making learning and examinations difficult. Paid employment may also detract from time spent getting help from teachers, completing homework, and studying for examinations. Although empirical research has generally found little difference in school performance between working and nonworking

adolescents (Mortimer & Finch, 1986; Steinberg, Greenberger, Garduque, Ruggiero, & Vaux, 1982; Warren et al., 2000), intensive work hours (more than 20 hours per week) are found to be associated with lower academic success in high school (Carr, Wright, & Brody, 1996; D'Amico, 1984; Greenberger & Steinberg, 1986; Marsh & Kleitman, 2005; Mortimer & Finch, 1986; Steinberg et al., 1982), increased school absences (Schoenhals, Tienda, & Schneider, 1998), and the probability of school dropout (Lee & Staff, 2007; McNeal, 1997; Warren & Lee, 2003). Research also shows that intensive involvement in paid labor during high school shapes subsequent educational investment and acquisition of full-time work after high school. Heavy involvement in paid work during adolescence (more than 20 hours per week throughout high school) is associated with a reduced likelihood of obtaining a 4-year college degree (Carr et al., 1996; Mortimer, 2003; Staff & Mortimer, 2007). Moreover, adolescents who pursue intensive work hours obtain fewer months of higher education than do their nonworking or moderately working peers (Mortimer et al., 2003).

Employed adolescents who work long hours may also have less flexibility in their work schedules relative to those who work fewer hours. Such work not only constrains the time available to engage in sports and other extracurricular activities, but youth may also become more attracted to less structured, unsupervised, and potentially deviant activities outside the workplace (Osgood, 1999; Safron et al., 2001). Osgood (1999) speculated that employment may also provide teenagers financial resources (e.g., money for gas and car payments) and autonomy from parental supervision (e.g., employment requiring late hours away from home) that enable more unstructured socializing. Youth who spend long hours on the job are more likely to go to parties and bars and to ride around in cars for fun, all of which are activities that increase the likelihood of delinquency and substance use (Osgood, Wilson, O'Malley, Bachman,

& Johnston, 1996). Indeed, much evidence suggests that those students who work more than 20 hours per week are more likely to engage in delinquency and substance use (Greenberger & Steinberg, 1986; McMorris & Uggen, 2000; Mortimer & Johnson, 1998a; Steinberg & Dornbusch, 1991; Steinberg et al., 1993), especially among those employed in informal jobs (Apel et al. 2006).

Furthermore, the absence of adult supervisors in the employment setting may foster deviance both within and outside the workplace, especially activities linked to defiance of adult authority and violation of workplace rules (such as giving products or services to friends for free, fabricating hours on time cards, or lying about reasons for being absent or tardy). Adolescents who are employed alongside delinquent coworkers tend to commit more workplace crime (Wright & Cullen, 2000) as well as demonstrate more general deviance than do those who do not work with delinquent peers (Ploeger, 1997). Paid jobs may also weaken the informal social controls of the school and family in restraining these activities. Social control theory (Hirschi, 1969; Kornhauser, 1978) emphasizes the importance of social bonds, which facilitate socialization and restrain deviant behavior. In adolescence, involvement in school and family activities, as well as attachment and commitment to home and school, are key components of the bond to society. Adolescents who reject the authority of parents and school are less likely to be controlled by them and more likely to commit delinquent acts. By providing an alternative arena for status and success—specifically income, autonomy, and peer status (Staff & Uggen, 2003)—early work roles may loosen conventional social controls during adolescence.

Intensive teenage work hours do not appear to increase adult criminality and substance use, despite the positive association between work hours and problem behaviors during adolescence (Mihalic & Elliott, 1997, did find, however, that total years of adolescent work—not work hours—predicted higher rates of alcohol and marijuana use at ages 27 and 28). The preponderance of evidence indicates that college attendance rather than adolescent work hours predicts high rates of alcohol use in young adulthood (Bachman et al., 2002; McMorris & Uggen, 2000). Though the higher rates of delinquency and substance use associated with early work roles do not continue into young adulthood, these early problem behaviors may still compromise long-term attainment and career development. According to Newcomb and Bentler (1988), drug use in adolescence hastens other markers of adult status, such as leaving school and acquiring a full-time job, establishing a residence away from the parental home, and engaging in premarital cohabitation. However, this foreshortening of a critical developmental period during late adolescence is considered detrimental to successful adjustment in young adulthood. Although early drug use accelerates a pseudomaturity that is admired by peers, the adolescent is socially and developmentally unprepared to deal with these new adult-like responsibilities and is thus more likely to fail at these roles over time. Newcomb and Bentler (1988) found that adolescent drug use (a latent measure of the frequency of alcohol, cannabis, and hard-drug use) decreased job stability and college matriculation in young adulthood. Teenage cannabis and hard-drug use in particular were associated with several indicators of maladjustment in young adulthood, including unemployment, criminal activities, loneliness, and marital problems. (Alcohol use did not predict these deleterious outcomes.)

However, teenage drug use (especially cannabis and hard-drug use) increased income in young adulthood, which is consistent with findings from other studies (Gill & Michaels, 1992; Kaestner, 1991). Newcomb and Bentler (1988) attribute the positive effects of early drug use on attainment to the economic returns of work experience. Thus, such activities, which are common accompaniments to early work roles, can have positive short-term economic correlates in the passage to adult status.

The short-term gains from an early transition may be fleeting, however. If early drug use diminishes educational attainment, future trajectories of earnings and job prestige may be compromised. Furthermore, young drug users tend to work in jobs that offer high initial wages but limited potential for wage growth (Kandel, Chen, & Gill, 1995). Thus, early transitions and problem behaviors may be beneficial to early career attainment, but they may be detrimental to long-term occupational trajectories and educational attainment.

In summary, there is considerable evidence that *intensive* involvement in paid work during adolescence is associated with poor school performance, limited involvement in extracurricular activities, increased use of alcohol and illegal substances, minor delinquency, and reduced educational attainment in young adulthood. In the next section, we highlight studies that show short- and longer term benefits of *moderate* work involvement during the high school years.

Early Work Experiences May Be Beneficial

In 1974, the Panel on Youth of the President's Science Advisory Committee gathered to discuss institutions that would help young people become better adults. Headed by James Coleman, the panel advocated a stronger connection between work and school, thus encouraging young people to acquire paid jobs. It was believed that early work experiences would facilitate "closer personal relations between adults and youth" (Coleman et al., 1974, p. 160). The Panel on Youth report suggested that working adults could mentor youth in preparing for future careers, teach them responsibility and independence, and limit their leisure time. In particular, the committee believed that paid jobs would limit the leisure activities characteristic of the generally antiadult "adolescent society." Furthermore, work was thought to complement the student role because work experiences were expected

to impress students with the practical importance of what they were learning in school.

Consistent with this more positive view, evidence suggests that moderate involvement in paid jobs may not constrain time for beneficial leisure and school activities. Using data from the Youth Development Study (YDS), Shanahan and Flaherty (2001) explored time use patterns indicated by the number of hours youth spent in paid work, homework, extracurricular activities, volunteer work, household work, and leisure time with friends. Although several patterns of time use emerged from a person-centered cluster analysis involving various work and leisure roles, teenagers in the two most prevalent groups (comprising approximately 55% of the total sample) spent almost equal amounts of time doing homework, household chores, volunteer work, and extracurricular activities. However, those in the first group did not work (20% of the 12th-grade sample), whereas those in the second group (35% of the 12th-grade sample) spent considerable time in paid work (averaging approximately 20 hours per week in the 12th grade).

Shanahan and Flaherty's analysis suggests that many employed adolescents make time for beneficial leisure activities as well as for household, school, and volunteer work. For these young people, paid work did not diminish hours of homework or extracurricular activities. Other studies indicate that paid jobs in adolescence may actually support the student role. Limited employment during adolescence (20 hours or less per week during high school) is associated with reduced high school dropout rates (D'Amico, 1984), increased involvement in school activities (Mihalic & Elliott, 1997), and higher grade point averages (Mortimer & Johnson, 1998b). Moreover, some evidence suggests that working moderate hours during high school does not reduce class rank, nor does it limit time for homework and reading outside of class (D'Amico, 1984; Schoenhals et al., 1998). In fact, analyses of the National Education Longitudinal Survey and the MTF study suggest that time spent watching television is reduced when young people work more hours (Bachman et al., 2003; Osgood, 1999; Schoenhals et al., 1998). Note that in Shanahan and Flaherty's analysis (2001), time spent with friends in nonstructured leisure activities, considered by other investigators such as Safron and colleagues (2001) to be the most likely to foster delinquency and substance use, is remarkably consistent for the various groups of workers and nonworkers (averaging 6–9 hours per week).

Research shows that early and more limited work is beneficial for the transition to adulthood; these benefits are evident in a diverse set of life domains. For example, early work experiences may help adolescents gain a sense of responsibility, independence, and self-confidence (Aronson, Mortimer, Zierman, & Hacker, 1996; Elder & Rockwell, 1979; Greenberger, 1988; Greenberger & Steinberg, 1986; Phillips & Sandstrom, 1990). Further developmental advantages include exposing teenagers to new challenges, promoting valuable coping skills, building status among peers, and helping young people solidify their occupational values (Mortimer, 2003; Mortimer, Finch, Ryu, Shanahan, & Call, 1996; Mortimer & Shanahan, 1991, 1994). This crystallization of work values may be especially beneficial, given the difficulty many young people have in preparing for their future occupations (Rindfuss et al., 1999; Schneider & Stevenson, 1999). In some historical circumstances, work at an early age may be especially valuable for future development. Elder's (1974) study of youth in the Depression era found that early work experiences were associated with more positive mental health and achievement. In this era of economic hardship and stress, young people gained confidence and self-esteem as they contributed to their families through paid jobs and household labor (Elder & Rockwell, 1979).

Shanahan and Flaherty (2001) found that teenagers who balanced paid jobs, schoolwork, and extracurricular activities were more likely to attend college after their senior year of high school. Other research shows that moderate work hours over the duration of high school increase the likelihood of a 4-year college degree, especially for youth who display limited educational promise at the onset of high school (Mortimer, 2003; Staff & Mortimer, 2007). In addition, the minor delinquency and substance use associated with a balanced pattern of work appears to have little consequence for future socioeconomic attainment. For example, Jessor, Donovan, and Costa (1991) found that adolescent problem behaviors (as measured by general deviance and by cigarette, alcohol, marijuana, and illicit drug use) had little effect on occupational prestige, educational attainment, political participation, general health, life satisfaction, self-esteem, or alienation. There was no spillover effect of early problem behavior on young adult occupational or educational attainment, although youth in this sample had moderate rates of problem behaviors and were mostly from middle-class social origins. In a recent study using the MTF data set, Bachman and colleagues (2008) found that alcohol and drug use during the high school years had little effect on longer term educational attainment after controlling for educational aspirations and academic success in middle school. Similarly, using longitudinal data from the National Education Longitudinal Study, Siennick and Staff (2008) also found that delinquency and substance use had little effect on college matriculation and completion once accounting for differences between delinquents and nondelinquents in educational expectations and school effort. However, it is likely that more intensive and ongoing drug use and other problem behaviors do show long-term consequences (Schulenberg et al., 2003; Schuster, O'Malley, Bachman, Johnston, & Schulenberg, 2001).

These studies, as well as others, find that many employed adolescents do not substitute delinquency and substance use for school-related leisure and work activities. Those who limit their hours of work (especially to 20 hours per week or less) make time for school-related leisure and work activities, and they tend to have higher educational attainment than their peers who work intensively or not at all. However, some research shows that even intensive work roles in adolescence can benefit occupational attainment, at least in the short term. Intensive work patterns during adolescence have been found to reduce unemployment and increase wages in the years immediately following high school (Stern & Nakata, 1989). Similarly, Carr et al. (1996) found that teenage work has a positive effect on occupational outcomes. Intensive work hours during high school increased wages and employment 10 years later but decreased college attendance, especially the completion of 4 or more years of college. Carr et al. (1996) concluded, ". . . the positive direct effect of teenage work on earnings greatly exceeded its negative indirect effect through educational attainment" in the early career (p. 79). Moreover, teenagers with a lengthy work history (total years employed) have "greater employability" in young adulthood (Mihalic & Elliott, 1997). In the YDS, those teenagers who worked over 20 hours per week throughout most of their high school years averaged the most months of full-time work, as well as the highest wages, in the years immediately following high school (Mortimer et al., 2003; Staff & Mortimer, 2008). Thus, it appears that even long hours of work during adolescence can have positive short-term effects on income and employability.

Certain types of jobs may be beneficial in reducing substance use and delinquency, even at high levels of work intensity. For instance, Staff and Uggen (2003) found that workplace conditions that fostered a balance between work and school and provided opportunities to learn useful skills reduced the likelihood of school-related deviance, substance use, and arrest in the 12th grade. Jobs that do not compromise the student role appear to inhibit deviance, net of work hours, prior deviance, and self-selection processes. Similarly, Schulenberg and Bachman (1993) found that

when early work experiences were connected to future careers and provided opportunities to learn new skills, adolescents were less likely to use drugs and alcohol. Indeed, when examining the possible benefits (and detriments) of paid work during adolescence, it is likely that the quality of the work experience moderates the impact of hours worked on outcomes. There has been surprisingly little research on this topic, suggesting, as we discuss later in this chapter, an important direction for future research.

Early Work Experiences May Not Matter

A third view is that preexisting characteristics of the individual explain the findings described earlier. While working students may receive lower grades because they have less time to devote to homework and studying than non-working students (the zero-sum hypothesis), the relationship between early work experiences and achievement may alternatively be spurious. Students with little interest in school and poor achievement may choose to invest more time in employment than those who have greater success in school (National Research Council, 1998). In a study by Bachman and Schulenberg (1993), poor school performance, low educational aspirations, and prior delinquency increased the likelihood of intensive work hours during high school. Youth with limited ability and lack of early opportunities for success in school may avoid both work and school during the teenage years, as low achievement scores and limited reading skills in adolescence predict school dropout and poor labor market outcomes in young adulthood (Caspi, Wright, Moffitt, & Silva, 1998). Youth with high motivation may invest in both school and work during the transition to adulthood, thereby maximizing their human capital acquisition through schooling, on-the-job training, and other workplace knowledge. Studies using data from the National Education Longitudinal Study (NELS 88) found little evidence of a relationship between paid work hours and school performance once they accounted for prior differences between individuals (Schoenhals et al., 1998; Warren et al., 2000). Hotz and colleagues (2002) report that unobserved differences between students explained why those who were employed at some point during adolescence earned higher wages in young adulthood than those who did not work.

Paid work and engagement in health risk behaviors may also constitute a syndrome of precocious adultlike identity formation (Bachman & Schulenberg, 1993; Newcomb & Bentler, 1988). Some youth prematurely enter adult roles, such as school completion, the acquisition of full-time employment, economic and residential independence, family formation, and intimate cohabitation or marriage, before they are developmentally and socially mature enough for the responsibilities of adulthood. The various manifestations of this process have been referred to as adolescent transition proneness (Jessor & Jessor, 1977), precocious development (Newcomb & Bentler, 1988), hurried adolescence (Safron et al., 2001), and pseudomaturity (Greenberger & Steinberg, 1986). Each of these concepts suggests a coalescence of more adult-like leisure and work activities influenced by the prior orientations, attitudes, and SES of the young person.

Precocious development theory suggests that prior engagement in delinquency and substance use influences the propensity for paid work in adolescence. According to this theory (Newcomb & Bentler, 1988), early drug use hastens the transition to adulthood. Early drug use is incompatible with the preadult stage of adolescence, as schools and parents attempt to restrain problem behaviors. Adolescent drug users thus have a higher probability of selecting into adult-like situations that are more compatible with substance use, such as moving into their own apartments, quitting school, and acquiring full-time jobs. According to Newcomb and Bentler, ". . . early drug use may increase interest in self-sufficiency and independence, as afforded by a job" (1988, p. 169). Although the pseudomaturity is reinforced through the admiration of peers in certain contexts, who perceive the adolescent as more mature and streetwise (Newcomb & Bentler, 1988), these premature adult roles do not provide adequate social control. Drug use and deviance subsequently increase for these precocious youth in young adulthood (Krohn, Lizotte, & Perez, 1997).

Newcomb and Bentler (1988) found that teenage drug use increased the odds of early family formation (marriage and children) as well as more adult-like work roles. Other studies (Bachman & Schulenberg, 1993) have found a similar relationship between alcohol use and adolescent work hours. Binge drinking during high school is associated with a syndrome of adult-like behaviors such as intensive work hours, limited involvement in adolescent-centered activities, inadequate sleep, and poor diet. Evidence from the YDS also suggests that 9th graders with higher rates of substance use, school-related deviance, and law violations worked more hours in subsequent years of high school (Mortimer, 2003; Staff & Uggen, 2003). Thus, the negative effect of paid work on substance use and deviance may arise from an endogenous or reciprocal process because prior engagement in these behaviors influences the decision to work.

Other theories suggest that precocious work roles may simply be a common correlate of problem behaviors such as delinquency, heavy drinking, and substance use because both signify adult-like status. According to problem behavior theory (Jessor & Jessor, 1977), the problem behaviors associated with an early transition to adulthood, such as marijuana use, sexual activity, heavy drinking, and general deviance, reflect transition proneness, or the desire to act like an adult. Alcohol use, smoking, drug use, and sexual activity assume symbolic significance as claims to adult status. Using a longitudinal sample of middle school students as well as college students from the early 1970s, the Jessors found significant interrelations among marijuana use, sexual intercourse, drinking, heavy drinking, and general deviance. These behaviors were negatively correlated with conventional behaviors (e.g., school achievement and church attendance). Jessor and Jessor (1977) concluded that these various transition behaviors represented a syndrome of adult-like activities that were often incompatible with more age-appropriate activities.

While prior involvement in delinquency and substance use encourages early adult-like work patterns, prior orientations toward work and school also influence the motivation to work in adolescence. Students who have less success in school and extracurricular activities are likely to invest themselves in paid work and to prefer work to school. Moreover, prior engagement in delinquency, such as drinking, having sex, using drugs, and misbehaving in school, may predispose some adolescents to enter work environments that offer fewer social constraints on these behaviors than do school and family (Newcomb & Bentler, 1988). This perspective contends that delinquency precedes involvement in work and any observed associations between paid work and deviance are spuriously related to preexisting differences between individuals. Evidence based on the annual MTF surveys suggests that an early desire for youth work (measured before the youth obtained jobs) predates both intensive work hours and problem behaviors in later adolescence (Bachman et al., 2003). Once these individual differences are considered, recent analyses find that the effects of intensive work hours on substance use, delinquency, and school-related misconduct diminish to statistical nonsignificance (Apel et al., 2007).

In summary, these studies suggest that paid work has little effect on short- and long-term achievement and social development during the transition to adulthood once preexisting and unobserved differences between students in their motivation, ability, and effort are taken into account. In the next section, we review research that also highlights the importance of selection into early work roles. However, this research suggests that paid work experiences *do* matter for achievement and adjustment, but these effects are conditioned by preexisting individual characteristics.

Early Work Experiences May Matter for Some Youth More Than Others

As mentioned before, gender, race and ethnicity, and SES affect whether teenagers work, what kinds of jobs they hold, and how much they work. Boys and youth in lower income households are less likely to hold jobs at younger ages than girls and youth from more advantaged backgrounds. However, boys typically average more hours of paid work than girls, African American and Hispanic teenagers average longer hours of employment during the school year when they are employed than White teenagers, and low SES adolescents average more hours when they are employed than their more advantaged peers do. Youth from low SES families are likely to enter the labor force at a younger age, work more hours, and have less connection to the educational system than their more advantaged peers (Kerckhoff, 2002).

The short- and long-term effects of paid work may depend on the opportunities available to young people. Although poor youth tend to work more hours than nonpoor youth when they are employed, many youth in poor urban neighborhoods face a limited and competitive job market (Entwisle et al., 2000; Newman, 1999). In contrast, youth in more prosperous neighborhoods find what is called a "youth labor market" characterized by an abundance of low-level retail and service jobs, as well as schools with numerous opportunities for extracurricular leisure activities. Thus, without many of these opportunities, early work may be a positive experience for adolescent in poor neighborhoods. Alternatively, the premature affluence (Bachman, 1983) associated with work for high SES youth may intensify delinquency and substance use and thereby limit participation in the many school-related activities that are available. In addition, the abundance of jobs in more prosperous neighborhoods can sometimes foster more negative work attitudes and misbehaviors in young people, such as tardiness, absenteeism, and giving away of goods and services, because youth in these neighborhoods may have ample opportunities to lose and regain work. Thus, the structural opportunities of the young person may influence involvement in paid jobs as well as both beneficial and harmful leisure activities.

For low SES teenagers who are more likely to select into intensive work roles in adolescence (Mortimer et al., 2003), the early workplace may be a viable source of human and social capital. Among a sample of delinquent teenagers in New York, paid work during early adolescence led to higher quality employment opportunities in subsequent years (Sullivan, 1989). Among a sample of mostly lower SES youth in Baltimore, Entwisle and colleagues (2000) found that early work involvement increased the skill level of the occupation held in later adolescence; they speculated that early employment (e.g., during middle school) allowed youth with less interest in school an alternative source of social and human capital for future employment. Consistent with this notion, teenagers in the YDS who engaged in a more continuous and intensive employment pattern during high school reported more work-related learning opportunities than did those who limited their hours (Mortimer, 2003).

In regard to socioeconomic attainment, D'Amico (1984) found that intensive work in the 10th grade increased the probability of dropping out only for white males, whereas in the 11th grade, the association between work hours and dropout was only statistically significant for females. Marsh (1991) found that work intensity did not have an effect on school performance among students who were working to save money for college. Furthermore, long work hours may not be as harmful for adolescents who come from more disadvantaged backgrounds (who are also probably more

likely to need to work more hours). For young, economically disadvantaged males, paid work actually increased their chances of high school completion (Entwisle, Alexander, & Olson, 2005). Analyses of summer employment programs by Farkas and colleagues (Farkas, Olsen, & Stromsdorfer, 1981; Farkas, Smith, & Stromsdorfer, 1983) report similar benefits of employment for the school enrollment of youth in low-income households. Lee and Staff (2007), using propensity score methods to control for observable differences between individuals, found that long hours on the job do not encourage high school dropout among youth who had especially high or low probabilities of intensive work. Thus, the effect of teenage work on school dropout is conditional on the young person's propensity to work long hours on the job. The differential effects of work hours extend beyond just achievement-related outcomes. Johnson (2004) found that the effects of long work hours did not increase the alcohol and substance use of Africans American and Hispanic youth.

Some adolescent jobs actually decrease the unstructured leisure about which critics of youth work warn; this may be especially likely when adolescents are employed in contexts that connect them to family and school—as in family businesses, on farms, or in school-supervised employment (Hansen, Mortimer, & Krueger, 2001). But even employment in fast-food restaurants or other common teenage jobs may reduce illegal and otherwise problematic leisure activities for low SES youth. For example, Newman (1999), through her participant observation of more than 150 fast-food workers in Harlem, found that fast-food jobs provided a way for many teenagers to avoid the danger of street violence and participation in the drug trade. Sullivan (1989), in his ethnographic analysis of teenagers in New York, also observed that poor adolescents in urban areas may gain greater exposure to conventional, prosocial adults and other young people in their jobs, reducing their risk for future delinquency.

Recent work by Staff and Mortimer (2007) suggests that employment patterns during the high school years can help disadvantaged youth establish strategies of time management that persist in young adulthood and facilitate higher educational attainment. Using data from the YDS, the authors found that youth from more advantaged backgrounds were likely to pursue a steady work pattern of low-intensity and high-duration work during high school, followed by a similar pattern of part-time work combined with schooling in the years immediately following high school graduation. The inclusion of accumulated months of postsecondary "school and part-time work" mediated the benefits of the steady high school work pattern on subsequent receipt of a bachelor's degree. By contrast, youth from disadvantaged backgrounds were likely to pursue more intensive work patterns (high average work hours and high employment duration), followed by full-time work immediately after the scheduled date of high school graduation. These more intensive workers had little likelihood of acquiring 4-year college degrees, and they were more likely to feel they were in "career" jobs during the years following high school (Mortimer, Vuolo, Staff, Wakefield, & Xie, 2008). When disadvantaged low SES youth followed a steady work pattern during high school, their educational attainment and longer term wages were especially enhanced (Staff & Mortimer, 2008).

In summary, it is difficult to discern whether paid jobs in adolescence cause adjustment and achievement problems, whether they encourage well-rounded combinations of both work and school that benefit youth long term during the transition to adulthood, or whether the purported effects of paid work reflect unobserved differences between students or are common constituents of broader syndromes or configurations of adult-like behaviors. Each proposition reviewed, positing a different relationship between paid work and social development, is supported to some extent by empirical research. Further complicating the picture, paid work

may matter for some youth and not for others, as prior orientations, leisure involvements, and demographic background features influence the decision to work—as well as to engage in school—in adolescence. In the conclusion section, we address some of these issues and suggest future research directions to assess the short- and longer term consequences of adolescent paid work. We now turn to the adolescent career development literature.

CAREER DEVELOPMENT

Career development, or the process through which individuals regulate and structure their working lives, unfolds across a large portion of the life span. It includes several subprocesses that are often conceptualized to be distinct and progressive, but which are in reality overlapping and discontinuous. These subprocesses include gaining an understanding of oneself and the world of work, exploring career options, making career-related decisions, implementing decisions, and evaluating those decisions. Individuals who effectively engage in the career development process tend to be more satisfied with their jobs and less likely to be unemployed than those who do not engage in these processes. However, this general trend hides nuances in structure, process, and outcomes; these nuances will be addressed below.

There are several different theoretical perspectives concerning career development and decision making, but they are rarely juxtaposed, so there is not the same rivalry of perspectives as was just discussed concerning paid work during adolescence. Thus, we structure this section differently. We first briefly review several theories of work and career that have influenced our view of career development in adolescence. Then we describe salient concepts in career development and their application to the study of adolescents. Finally, we conclude this section by outlining a few proposals for the advancement of career development research.

Theories of Career Development

The 1940s through the 1970s saw a burst of activity in terms of career development theory, revealing connections to the broader field of psychology in terms of emphasis on personality traits, developmental progressions, and social learning. Over the past few decades, broader multidimensional, context-based, and life-span theoretical frameworks have been offered. We briefly describe a few key theories that have shaped the field of career development, both in terms of counseling practice and research. We focus particularly on theories that explicitly discuss adolescence.

Much early work in the field of vocational choice was devoted to fitting people into jobs on the basis of their interests, aptitudes, and abilities—testing to place men in appropriate jobs within the Army, for instance—and was rooted in the notion of incremental and sequential maturation (Osipow & Fitzgerald, 1996). The impetus of these theories, including trait and factor theory (Parsons, 1909), personality theory of career choice (Roe, 1947), and career typology theory (Holland, 1973) was to understand and facilitate person–job fit by defining types of people and types of jobs, and to establish a maturational continuum. When development was considered, it was often discussed in terms of childhood antecedents to adult outcomes, as in Roe's personality theory of career choice.

Adolescence is explicitly discussed as an important period in the process of career development by several stage development theories. In such theories, the adolescent years are a stage of exploration of career options; young adulthood is a time of commitment or implementation of a career choice. Examples of stage approaches to career development include theories by Ginzberg, Ginsberg, Axelrad, and Herma (1951) and Super (1954). Another important stage model is that of Erikson (1964). Rather than being a career development theory, Erikson's theory is concerned with socialization and identity. Work, as a central activity of adulthood, plays a

significant role in this theory. The stage of adolescence is concerned with identity formation, and occupational identity is a large portion of one's overall identity. During childhood, individuals are concerned with developing a sense of being an industrious worker, which promotes the establishment of an occupational identity during adolescence. Adolescents need to create an identity, including a sense of oneself as a productive worker, in order to become well-functioning adults. Erikson's perspective was primarily concerned with the process of career development within the individual. In this view, healthy adolescents develop through personal exploration and decision making that result in a commitment to an occupational trajectory. Recent work continues to examine adolescents' occupational or vocational identity and decision making, though contextual influences are increasingly considered as well.

In recent years, popular career development theories focused on individuals as agents in their own development. Social cognitive career theory (SCCT; Lent, Brown, & Hackett, 1994), social learning theory of career selection (Krumboltz, Mitchell, & Jones, 1976), and other social–cognitive perspectives focus primarily on individuals' beliefs about themselves and the world of work. Adolescents' previous experiences, social observations, and physiological arousal influence their self-efficacy beliefs and outcome expectancies. In turn, these beliefs largely determine career development, including how career interests are formed, how educational and career goals are chosen, and how those choices are pursued (i.e., the success of the pursuit).

The social and interactive nature of career development is also salient in action theory (Young & Valach, 1994). In this perspective, the individual creates his or her career identity and makes career decisions through interactions with significant others such as parents and peers. Finally, life-span developmental theory (Vondracek et al., 1986) is another key perspective that integrates theory about contexts with individual development. In all of these theories, beliefs, attitudes, and affect play a central role in individuals' career pathways and are generally the point of entry for most research questions. Skills and interests remain important components (which makes these theories similar to the personality theories), but the individuals' interpretation of these is also key.

In summary, career development theories commonly view adolescence as a time of exploration and increasing refinement of career choices. Ideal career development is presumed to conform to a normative maturational model leading from increasing one's knowledge of oneself and the world of work to a job choice that "fits" with one's personal characteristics. Actual career choice tends to occur in late adolescence or early adulthood, and sometimes continues across adulthood depending on social and occupational constraints and opportunities (Vondracek et al., 1986). Career development theories still tend to focus on personality traits, interests, and beliefs, but acknowledge that these are largely formed by individuals' experiences and opportunities in social contexts.

Aspects of Career Development

As discussed earlier, research and theory regarding part-time employment during adolescence focuses on work as a context that can have negative and positive implications for other domains that are typically of more interest to many developmental researchers (such as school and family relationships). In the career development literature, research remains focused primarily on the individual and internal processes of cognitive and identity growth and decision making, without giving much attention to contextual influences. Context is increasingly considered, but is largely viewed from the individual perspective rather than at an institutional or structural level.

In this section, we summarize the recent research concerning the salient components of career development during adolescence. These salient components—related to the success

and desirability of career outcomes—are common aspects of the career development of many, though not necessarily all, young people. We begin with a description of the content of career development, that is, the individual beliefs, attitudes, and interests that influence individuals' career outcomes (e.g., competency beliefs, career interests). Then we discuss contextual influences on career development, including both social (familial and educational) and sociodemographic contexts (i.e., race, gender, and SES). Finally, we describe the outcomes of career development in terms of processes and changes over time. Because the educational experiences of adolescents are directly related to their career interests and prospects, we also incorporate some career-related research on school settings.

Competency Beliefs

In agentic perspectives of career development, an individual's sense of personal competence is often a central component. Self-efficacy beliefs are one way of assessing or conceptualizing competence beliefs, and are well researched in part because of the centrality of this construct in SCCT (Lent et al., 1994). Self-efficacy is the perception of one's ability to master or successfully complete a task or a set of related tasks, or to influence events (Bandura, 2001). Competency beliefs are also central in other theories that have been applied to career choice and development, such as expectancy-value (Eccles et al., 1983) and self-determination theories (Gagné & Deci, 2005). In studies that are grounded in these perspectives, alternative measures of competency beliefs (such as expectancies of success or self-concepts) may be used instead of self-efficacy. Although there are theoretical distinctions between these constructs, they function similarly during the career development process. Overall, competency beliefs allow individuals to discriminate between careers for which they can assume a likelihood of success and careers for which they are not well suited.

Competency beliefs can be formed and revised in several ways. Often, they are drawn from experiences that occur in academic and workplace settings. Individuals use successes and failures as indications of their abilities, talents, and skills. When students experience success with a task (i.e., perform well on homework assignments, tests, or across a whole course), they come to believe that they are capable at that task and that they can replicate their success in the future (Schunk & Pajares, 2002). In contrast, when coursework is difficult or failures occur, students develop lower perceptions of their competence.

Previous successes and failures also influence individuals' perceptions of their ability on tasks that are similar, but not identical to the original. For instance, students' self-efficacy in mathematics courses predicts their self-efficacy for mathematics careers (Correll, 2001). Likewise, perceived academic self-efficacy predicts perceived self-efficacy for occupations that require a significant amount of postsecondary education, such as those in science, technology, medicine, and education (Bandura, Barbaranelli, Caprara, & Pastorelli, 2001). Competency beliefs are also influenced by perceptions of competence in nonsimilar domains. This can occur when internal comparisons between two unequal abilities lead individuals to increase their self-efficacy in one domain and decrease their self-efficacy in the opposing domain. For instance, achievement in mathematics predicts lower self-efficacy in biology for male students (Nagy, Trautwein, Baumert, Koller, & Garrett, 2006). Perceived self-efficacy for certain occupations both positively predicts young adolescents' choices for related careers and negatively predicts their choice of unrelated careers (Bandura et al., 2001). Additional influences on competency beliefs are described in following sections.

Perceived self-efficacy predicts adolescents' career choices (Bandura et al., 2001). For instance, self-efficacy in mathematics and science is positively related to intentions to study or pursue a career in math and science (Navarro, Flores, & Worthington, 2007). High self-efficacy is also related to more successful school-to-work transitions (Pinquart, Juang, & Silbereisen, 2003). In times of social change, self-efficacy predicts resilience in adapting to the labor market and holding higher career aspirations (Pinquart et al., 2003; Pinquart, Juang, & Silbereisen, 2004).

Much of the research on competency beliefs has focused on competence for particular academic domains or job tasks. In addition to these domains, career decision making is also examined in terms of adolescents' perceptions of their competence. Career decision-making self-efficacy is theorized to be an important component of successful career development, as it indicates that adolescents believe they can make a career choice that will suit them. O'Brien and colleagues (2000) showed that Upward Bound, a career intervention program, was related to an increase in students' career decision-making self-efficacy.

Outcome Expectations

In addition to competency beliefs, outcome expectancies play a large role in SCCT. Outcome expectancies are the anticipated consequences of a behavior. Empirical studies have generally supported the theorized influences on outcome expectancies, which include prior experiences, social learning and mentoring, and parental support (Ferry, Fouad, & Smith, 2000; Martino, Collins, Ellickson, Schell, & McCaffrey, 2006). Self-efficacy is also theorized to contribute to outcome expectations (Lent et al., 1994). However, empirical evidence for the link between self-efficacy and outcome expectations is usually examined in cross-sectional studies (see Navarro et al., 2007).

Why are outcome expectancies meaningful to career development? Adolescents are more likely to choose a career field if they hold positive outcome expectancies for entering that career. In tandem with competency beliefs, outcome expectancies in particular disciplines or career fields predict interest in those and related fields (Quimby, Wolfson, & Seyala, 2007).

Career Interests

Competency beliefs and outcome expectancies can be viewed as rational and cognitive components in many models of career decision making. The more affective component of career decision making is interest. Holland's (1997) Realistic, Investigative, Artistic, Social, Enterprising, Conventional (RIASEC) typology has been a particularly influential theory regarding occupational interests. In this perspective, career interests and job characteristics can both be measured along six dimensions. Other interest inventories (see Rottinghaus, Coon, Gaffey, & Zytowski, 2007) divide interests along different category lines or separate them into more specific components. Career interests are typically the basis for school-based career testing.

Interest in a career field is derived in part from one's self-efficacy for the skills that are utilized in that career field (Lent, Brown, Nota, & Soresi, 2003; Turner & Lapan, 2002). Theoretically, adolescents are more interested in careers in which they expect to be successful. For instance, investigative self-efficacy is related to interest in environmental science (Quimby et al., 2007). Mathematics self-efficacy and outcome expectations predict young adolescents' interest in math- and science-related careers (Turner, Steward, & Lapan, 2004). The apparent relation between self-efficacies and interests is not just an artifact of a relation between actual abilities and interests; indeed, some research has found no relation between the two (Tracey, Robbins, & Hofsess, 2005).

Despite the primacy of self-efficacy in determining career interests in many studies, other aspects of career development and occupational identity have been related to interests as well. For instance, valuing social relationships is related to higher social and artistic interests, whereas valuing independence is related to higher enterprising and conventional career interests (Rees, Luzzo, Gridley, & Doyle, 2007). As with competency beliefs, prior experiences and achievement in the domain, and in different domains, also appear to have direct effects on interests (Nagy et al., 2006). Specifically, achievement in mathematics negatively predicts interest in biology, but prior achievement in biology positively predicts interest in biology.

Aspirations and Expectations

Career aspirations are individuals' ideal career choices, while career expectations are individuals' anticipated career choices. In some studies, aspirations may also refer to the level of social prestige one desires, regardless of the anticipated career field (see Flores & O'Brien, 2002). Adolescents' aspirations are necessarily future oriented, though the time horizon for the realization of one's career aspirations may become shorter as individuals enter the transition into adulthood.

Working during the transition to adulthood appears to be related to more volatility in occupational aspirations than attending college—while college students' aspirations remain stable, the aspirations of their nonstudent peers exhibit more change (Rojewski & Kim, 2003). However, even among the group of young adults who change their aspirations over time, the social prestige of their aspirations does not appear to change substantially.

If adolescents believe that they can successfully perform a job, they will be more likely to think of that job as a potential career option. Therefore, self-efficacy beliefs regarding job tasks, activities, and training are related to adolescents' career aspirations (Flores, Spanierman, Armstrong, & Velez, 2006). Aspirations are also theorized to arise from outcome expectations and interests (Diegelman & Subich, 2001; Flores, Spanierman, et al., 2006).

Work Values

Work values may be thought of as individuals' evaluations of their affective regard for various job characteristics. Extrinsic values, such as earning a high salary, and intrinsic values, such as being able to learn on the job, are the most commonly studied work values during adolescence (see Johnson, 2005; Leong, Hardin, & Gaylor, 2005). Other work value classifications also exist, such as social values, leisure values, values for job security, and safety (Johnson, 2002; Sinisalo, 2004), though some researchers consider these subcomponents of the broader intrinsic and extrinsic sets of values.

How are work values related to career development? During adolescence, work values become more stable as career decision making progresses (e.g., Schulenberg, Vondracek, & Kim, 1993). Over time, work values predict career interests (Rottinghaus & Zytowski, 2006) and career choice, including specialties within a single broad career field (medicine) (Leong et al., 2005). They also appear to be related to decisions about work–life balance. Adolescents with high extrinsic values are more likely to marry and become parents during their 20s, while adolescents with high intrinsic work values are less likely to adopt these social roles during young adulthood (Johnson, 2005).

Social Context

So far, we have discussed ways that individuals' experiences, beliefs, attitudes, and interests influence and are influenced by the career development process. In recent decades, career development theories have increasingly paid attention to contexts, and empirical research is beginning to contribute meaningfully to our understanding of the ways that social and structural institutions can influence career pathways. Below, we discuss several of the most salient social contexts in adolescents' lives.

One important source of social support is the family, which influences adolescents' and young adults' career development in a myriad of ways (Otto, 2000; Schulenberg, Vondracek, & Crouter, 1984; Whiston & Keller, 2004). One of these ways is through providing a positive and secure socioemotional climate (Roisman, Bahadur, & Oster, 2000). Child-centered parenting practices are related to higher levels of career exploration (Kracke, 2002). Receiving emotional support from one's family is related

to career planning and certainty in one's career choice (Constantine, Wallace, & Kindaichi, 2005; Hargrove, Inman, & Crane, 2005). Parental encouragement for specific career pathways in math and science predict adolescents' self-efficacy for those careers (Turner & Lapan, 2002; Turner et al., 2004). General social support from parents also predicts math and science self-efficacy (Navarro et al., 2007).

Parents also influence their adolescent children's views of work through their explicit and implicit messages of the role of work in one's life and the role of men and women in the workplace (Bryant, Zvonkovic, & Reynolds, 2006). Receiving advice about life plans from one's father is related to higher certainty in one's career choice (Tucker, Barber, & Eccles, 2001). Active engagement between parents and their adolescent children centering on "personal projects," or career-related tasks, encourages adolescents' career maturity (Young, Ball, Valach, Turkel, & Wong, 2003; Young et al., 2001, 2006).

In the past, the institution of the family provided almost all necessary economic socialization for children. More recently, parents still communicate messages and values about work (Ryu & Mortimer, 1996), but they may not be able to provide guidance for unfamiliar career pathways (Skorikov & Vondracek, 2007). This is especially true in rapidly changing sectors of the economy, such as information technology. In the place of families, schools and colleges provide career guidance, planning opportunities, and training. Classroom-based career interventions can have an influence on students' career decision-making self-efficacy beliefs (O'Brien et al., 2000).

Social support and encouragement can also come from other sources. Capability by peers or adults with whom an adolescent identifies can also influence self-efficacy by illustrating the possibility of success. For example, encounters with adults who discuss or demonstrate their occupational skills increase students' vocational self-efficacies (Kolodinsky et al., 2006). Having mentors who provide inspiration and role modeling in a particular type of career predicts college students' likelihood of considering that type of career (Quimby & DeSantis, 2006). Discussions with peers about careers also facilitate career exploration (Kracke, 2002).

Gender

Structural forces in society affect career development through individuals' perceptions of occupational barriers and support systems (Lent et al., 1994). Low representation of women (as well as minorities) in some careers can be one indication of potential barriers to entering those careers. Discrimination in school, early work settings, or during other experiences can also contribute to adolescents' perceptions of occupational barriers.

One way that perceived occupational barriers could influence career development is through the processes of circumscription and compromise in career choice (Gottfredson, 1981, 2005). Compromise is the process whereby less desirable career options become preferred over more desirable but less likely career options. Circumscription is the process through which individuals narrow occupational possibilities through consideration of their own personal characteristics, such as gender. Sex typing in career possibilities and preferences begins during childhood (see Hartung, Porfeli, & Vondracek, 2005 for a review). Gottfredson suggests that sex typing is the least likely aspect of one's career choice to be subject to compromise; adolescents are more likely to prefer careers that are gender appropriate than careers that are personally interesting but not gender appropriate. A convergence of scholarly interest in sex typing and science, technology, engineering, and mathematics (STEM) careers has led to several studies that examine choice for male-dominated career fields (Meece, 2006).

The extent to which young adolescents perceive careers to be sex typed predicts their self-efficacies and interests in those careers (i.e., adolescents are drawn to careers that are perceived to be more typed to their gender) (Ji, Lapan, & Tate, 2004; Turner & Lapan, 2002). Because mathematics is a male-dominated field, gender typing on the part of the adolescent (i.e., identifying oneself as feminine or masculine) predicts math self-efficacy and math outcome expectations (Turner et al., 2004). In addition, women may be wary of entering male-dominated fields because they anticipate experiencing workplace discrimination and harassment (Messersmith, Garrett, Davis-Kean, Malanchuk, & Eccles, 2008). Nevertheless, although career interests during adolescence tend to follow along stereotypical gender lines, gender effects are often moderated by such characteristics as parental SES, educational aspirations, and career certainty (Schulenberg, Goldstein, & Vondracek, 1991).

There tend to be gender differences in work values as well, but such differences are not consistent, suggesting that some differences are sample and measurement dependent, given to historical variation, or moderated by other demographic and social context characteristics. In one study, adolescent girls valued achievement and flexibility more than boys, while boys valued creativity, independence, and income more than girls (Rottinghaus & Zytowski, 2006). In another study, boys valued extrinsic work rewards more than girls, while girls valued nondemanding and safe work more than boys (Sinisalo, 2004). And in a study of seniors in high school, young women were found to value intrinsic, altruistic, and social aspects of work more strongly than young men, but there were no gender differences in extrinsic work values (Marini, Fan, Finley, & Beutel, 1996).

Another issue in the career development of males and females is that young women are more likely to value family over work than are young men (Cinamon & Rich, 2002). Valuing other aspects of one's life more than work can result in less effort devoted to the process of career development. In one study, boys generated more career-focused possible selves than girls (Knox, Funk, Elliott, & Bush, 2000), indicating that the boys had engaged in more consideration of their future careers.

Finally, one's social context may interact with gender to influence different career-related outcomes. For instance, the specific types of parental support that are most strongly related to vocational self-efficacies differ for male and female adolescents (Alliman-Brissett, Turner, & Skovholt, 2004). Adolescent girls tend to report more influence from other females (mothers, female friends, and female teachers) on their career expectations than do boys (Paa & McWhirter, 2000). Given the intergenerational transmission of values (Otto, 2000), receiving advice from members of one's own gender more than receiving cross-gender career advice could be another mechanism that preserves gendered preferences in career choices.

Race and Ethnicity

Over the past several decades, there has been an increase in the percentage of articles related to racial/ethnic minorities published in work/career-related journals (Flores, Berkel, et al., 2006). However, it is not clear whether this trend has also occurred in the career development articles focusing on adolescence. Furthermore, although several theories attend to race/ethnicity, gender, and social class as contextual or structural influences in the lives of adolescents, these variables are often treated as individual differences in empirical studies of adolescent career development.

Ethnic differences may arise as a function of the perception of access to certain careers for members of one's racial or ethnic group. For instance, there are ethnic differences in adolescents' interests in careers such as medical science and protective services (Turner & Lapan, 2003). Racial and ethnic differences in the workforce may promote perceived occupational barriers, which are especially prevalent among minority youth. Perceived barriers are related to higher career indecision (Constantine et al., 2005; Patton, Creed, & Watson, 2003) and lower prestige of career

aspirations (Jackson, Kacanski, Rust, & Beck, 2006). However, among a sample of urban adolescents, being aware of potential barriers was positively related to clearer vocational identities, career choice commitment, and the importance of work (Diemer & Blustein, 2006).

Since its inception, Holland's (1997) six-factor interest theory has garnered empirical support and is widely used in career counseling. Recently, more attention has been paid to sociocultural differences in the factor structure of these interests (Turner & Lapan, 2003). The underlying theoretical assumptions and the measures used to assess interests along the RIASEC dimensions may not work well for some populations, including minorities (for Mexican Americans, see Flores, Spanierman, et al., 2006).

Although there are apparent racial/ethnic differences in both self-efficacy and interests, there is limited evidence that these extend to adolescents' career aspirations or expectations. In fact, several studies have found no evidence of such differences (Chang, Chen, Greenberger, Dooley, & Heckhausen, 2006; Csikszentmihalyi & Schneider, 2000; Phinney, Baumann, & Blanton, 2001). Chang and colleagues (2006) suggested that studies finding racial/ethnic differences in career expectations may confound ethnicity with SES.

Finally, race/ethnicity and gender may also have interacting effects on adolescents' career development. Among female Mexican Americans, acculturation is related to the traditionality of their career aspirations, such that more acculturated females have a stronger preference for career fields in which the majority of workers are female (Flores & O'Brien, 2002). There does not appear to be a similar connection between acculturation and career choice traditionality among Mexican American males (Flores, Navarro, Smith, & Ploszaj, 2006).

Socioeconomic Status

SES has been examined as a context of career development to an even lesser extent than race/

ethnicity and gender. We do know that SES predicts career aspirations, such that adolescents with lower SES tend to aspire to careers with lower social prestige (Majoribanks, 1997; Rojewski & Kim, 2003; Schulenberg et al., 1984). High school students whose parents have higher levels of education report lower evaluations of extrinsic rewards and security, but higher evaluations of influence (Johnson, 2002). Interestingly, some research has shown that adolescents in divorced families are more certain and optimistic about their occupational aspirations than adolescents in intact families (Tucker et al., 2001). As mentioned earlier, many of the apparent racial and ethnic differences in adolescents' career development may actually be artifacts of SES (Chang et al., 2006).

The Process of Career Development

Career development is a complex process that spans the life course; its outcomes are multiple and varied. Because much of it extends past adolescence, the outcomes of study during adolescence and young adulthood are often thought of as necessary precursors of continued healthy career development in adulthood. These outcomes include the degree of adolescents' career exploration, career maturity, and clarity of occupational identity.

Career exploration consists of an examination of various career options. It can occur through intentionally thinking about possible careers, but it can also happen less intentionally during experiences in part-time work and leisure activities. Marcia (1994) described the theoretical benefits to exploration before committing to a particular identity (i.e., having an "achieved" identity status). Indeed, career exploration and indecision are related to more general identity exploration and indecision during adolescence (Vondracek, Schulenberg, Skorikov, Gillespie, & Wahlheim, 1995). Yet career exploration during high school does not necessarily predict the extent of career establishment in mid-adulthood (Jepsen & Dickson, 2003). That is not to say that career exploration is not important for adolescents; in fact,

exploring career options can reduce career indecision (Baker, 2002). As many of the more concrete aspects of career decision making get pushed further into early adulthood, the experiences and functions of career exploration during adolescence may shift and become broader and more diffuse (see Patton & Porfeli, 2007; Porfeli, in press).

Another common marker of career development during adolescence is career maturity (sometimes referred to as career preparedness) (Hartung, Porfeli, & Vondracek, 2005). Career maturity refers to awareness of the career development process itself, as well as knowing how to seek information about the world of work and understanding the steps that will lead to successful career entry. Not surprisingly, career maturity during high school predicts more postsecondary education involvement and higher occupational status during the post–high school transition (Patton, Creed, & Muller, 2002). Occasionally, career maturity is conceptualized as the degree of certainty in one's career choice. As with other forms of career maturity, choice certainty during adolescence predicts job advancement and organizational fit during adulthood (Jepsen & Dickson, 2003). But it is likely that career uncertainty (sometimes referred to as career indecision) is functional for many young people, given the complexity of many occupations requiring more time and information for successful decision making (Arnett, 2006).

The subprocesses that compose career development also assist in vocational or occupational identity development. Occupational identity is the clarity, coherence, and stability of one's conception of self in relation to the context of work (Skorikov & Vondracek, 2007). Occupational identity is also sometimes measured by content, such as the "possible selves" that an adolescent hopes for or fears for their vocational futures (Unemori, Omoregie, & Markus, 2004). Occupational identity is a particularly salient aspect of identity development during adolescence and is often among the first aspects of identity to become clarified

(Danielsen, Lorem, & Kroger, 2000; Skorikov & Vondracek, 1998; 2007). However, when adolescents struggle with other identity development tasks (such as developing a sense of oneself as a sexual minority), occupational identity development may be slower (Schmidt & Nilsson, 2006).

Marcia (1966, 1993) conceptualized identity development in a model of four stages characterized by the degree to which individuals have committed to an identity and explored an identity. An important consideration for the occupational domain of identity in particular is the occurrence of cyclical fluctuations in identity status between moratorium (the active process of exploration) and achievement (having a committed identity). This conceptualization of occupational identity development acknowledges continued development throughout adulthood, which provides a more flexible approach to understanding career transitions and unstable occupational pathways.

Early work experiences contribute to the occupational identity and career development of adolescents and young adults (Cohen-Scali, 2003; Mortimer & Zimmer-Gembeck, 2007). Working is related to greater certainty in one's career choices (Creed, Prideaux, & Patton, 2005), and adolescents' experiences at work are related to changes in their work values and their goals for future work (Mortimer, Pimentel, Ryu, Shanahan, & Call, 1996; Mortimer & Zimmer-Gembeck, 2007; Skorikov & Vondracek, 1997). Furthermore, learning more about oneself and the world of work, in addition to planning for one's occupational future, facilitates the school-to-work transition during young adulthood (Nurmi, Salmela-Aro, & Koivisto, 2002; Savickas, 1999). We cover the broader point of the interconnection between early work experience in adolescence and career development in the concluding section.

Career Development Across Adolescence

As a summary of the normative progress of career development, we provide a general timeline below. Despite differences in the content of adolescents' career exploration and choices (i.e., career interests, competencies, beliefs, and aspirations), there appears to be some consistency across individuals in the process of career development, progressing (though not always in linear ways) toward increasing realism about and integration of individual talents and preferences.

Early in adolescence, many individuals can identify specific career aspirations. Often at this age, their aspirations appear sex typed; Gottfredson (1981, 2005) suggested that attention to gender stereotypes and gender roles occurs during mid-childhood, although this aspect continues to be considered throughout adolescence and beyond (Vondracek et al., 1986). During late childhood, social status tends to be an important consideration in children's career aspirations (Gottfredson, 1981, 2005), so by early adolescence career aspirations also tend to be highly prestigious. As they grow older, adolescents get more realistic and begin to abandon fantasy aspirations and match their unique interests and values to various job characteristics (Blanchard & Lichtenberg, 2003; Hartung, Porfeli, & Vondracek, 2005; Helwig, 2001); consideration of interests (Helwig, 2001) and exploration (Hirschi & Läge, 2007) aid in this process.

Tracey and colleagues (2005) found that interests become more aligned with adolescents' career choices between 8th and 10th grades, but become less aligned with career choices between 10th and 12th grades. This is an unexpected trend given theoretical notions of career development as a general progression toward person–job fit. Tracey et al. suggest that their college-bound sample might enter into a new period of fluctuation before their post–high school transitions. This explanation is also provided by Kalakoski and Nurmi (1998), who found that adolescents engaged in more career exploration prior to an educational transition (in this case, the transition from secondary school to a vocational or senior high school in Finland). Other research has shown the more expected progression of congruence between career expectations and aspirations as individuals prepare to leave secondary education and enter the workforce (Heckhausen & Tomasik, 2002). A broader point here is that career interests, typically the basis for vocational testing in schools, are not necessarily stable or traitlike during adolescence or even early adulthood, but instead are given to developmental and situational variation (e.g., Schulenberg, Vondracek, & Nesselroade, 1988; Vondracek, 2001; Vondracek et al.,1986).

Increasing realism in career aspirations over time is also due to an increased knowledge of the world of work. During the high school period (approximately ages 14–18), adolescents' work values for current part-time jobs and future careers become more similar (Porfeli, 2007). Older adolescents' work values also become increasingly differentiated such that they have clearer preferences for some work values over others (Johnson, 2005). Both of these findings regarding the longitudinal nature of work values suggest that adolescents become better at discriminating between different aspects of jobs and identifying the aspects of their current experiences that are most important to themselves and their future job satisfaction. In the years after high school, career interests appear to be relatively stable (Rees et al., 2007). However, new roles (such as marriage and parenthood) can bring about changes in work values (Johnson, 2005).

In summary, the field of career development has made important empirical steps over the past decade. Career development research is moving away from static, personality- and trait-focused theories and toward perspectives that highlight the agency of an individual to influence his or her career trajectory. Increasingly, researchers are paying attention to synergies and transactional relationships between individuals and their parents, peers, teachers, and other members of their social networks. Career development theories have been calling for such research for many decades (see Vondracek et al., 1986), but it

has been slow to emerge. Building on these changes, in the conclusion of this chapter we offer several potentially fruitful directions for future research in career development during adolescence.

FUTURE RESEARCH

Paid work and career development during adolescence have not received extensive attention from researchers, but as we have argued in this chapter, they are nonetheless critical for the larger field of adolescent development. Early work experiences and adolescent career development provide unique vantage points and unifying themes for advancing our collective understanding of adolescent social functioning and decision making, as well as our understanding of the contexts that influence, and are influenced by, adolescents. To understand how adolescent work experiences and career explorations shape development more generally, we drew upon an interdisciplinary framework that emphasizes developmental change across the life span, characterized by successive mutual selection and accommodation of individuals and their contexts.

Paid Work and Career Development Linkages

An interesting aspect of the relevant literature is that there has been little consideration of how part-time work and career development are interlinked. But of course, they are connected. Teenage work provides crucial real-life experience, which supplies feedback about career goals. "Good" jobs may provide opportunities to develop new skills, gain a sense of responsibility and dependability, learn how to balance the demands of work and school, and establish positive vocational identities and work values; such paid work experiences in adolescence may also involve a supportive supervisor who helps guide the young person to appropriate postsecondary degree programs that match their own interests and capacities. These qualities of work may be especially important for youth whose own parents lack work experience and career resources, or youth who have less interest or success in school (Staff & Mortimer, 2008). Even experiences in "bad" jobs during adolescence may give the young person a sense of the extent to which initial career aspirations represent a good pathway.

Of course, early work experiences are likely to vary with respect to important job qualities including the degree of supervisory support, learning opportunities, and skill development; and different types of jobs are likely to be more or less relevant to future career goals. Among adults, it is clear that bad jobs typically involve low pay and limited benefits, and entail non-standard work arrangements that are part-time and temporary (Kalleberg, Reskin, & Hudson, 2000). In a recent study, Hirschman and Voloshin (2007) consider employment as lifeguards, athletic coaches, tutors, office clerks, or receptionists as "good jobs" in adolescence because those who work in these types of jobs earn high wages and often moderate the number of hours they work per week. Yet the conditions of youth work appear to vary substantially across other important dimensions, such as provision of intrinsic rewards, stressful features, and compatibility with school (Mortimer, 2003).

To assess whether teenage work experiences influence career goals, it is important to identify the differences between "good" and "bad" teenage jobs. To address what types of jobs constitute good employment experiences during the teenage years, we again draw upon measures of work quality among employed 12th graders in the MTF data set. Figure 8.4 shows mean levels of job quality across different types of jobs based on a combined data set of thirteen 12th-grade cohorts (includes approximately 20,000 employed youth from 1991 to 2003). The self-reported measures of job quality indicate the extent to which 12th graders' current job: (1) causes stress and tension; (2) interferes with education, family, or social life; (3) uses their skills and abilities, makes good use of their special skills at

work, and provides them opportunities to learn new skills; (4) provides them with a young supervisor; (5) provides them with coworkers who are similar in age to the respondent; and (6) provides them a job that is "career-like" (i.e., is a career job, a "stepping-stone," not something done just for the money). We display each of these variables as z-scores to ease interpretation. We then coded job type into seven categories:

1. Informal jobs (e.g., babysitting, newspaper delivery, yard maintenance, and odd jobs)
2. Fast-food jobs
3. Restaurant jobs (e.g., waiters and waitresses, cooks, other restaurant workers)
4. Farm and agriculture jobs
5. Sales and retail jobs
6. Office or clerical positions
7. Other jobs

Figure 8.4 also shows the percentage of 12th-grade workers in each occupational category.

As shown in Figure 8.4, of the seven job types, fast-food workers (14% of employed 12th graders) rate poorly across the work-quality dimensions. For instance, fast-food workers report the highest levels of job stress and job incompatibility with school, family, and friends. Adolescents in fast-food settings also work with young coworkers and supervisors and are unlikely to indicate that their job provides skills or is a "career-like" job. Adolescents employed as store clerks and in sales positions, which are the most typical among young workers, report similar problems. The most desirable jobs appear to be office and clerical positions (8% of workers), as adolescents in these jobs report low job stress, older coworkers and supervisors, little interference with school and family roles, and ample opportunities to learn new skills or build a career. Given these patterns, an obvious recommendation for future research is to attend

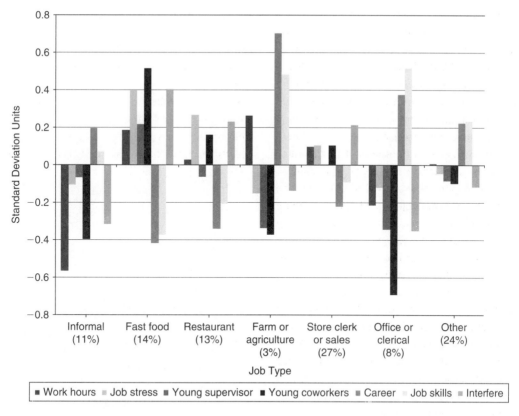

FIGURE 8.4 Subjective work quality measures (z-scores) in the 12th grade by job type: MTF 12th graders (combined 1991–2003 cohorts; approximately 19,804 students).

to type and quality of work experiences when examining the possible positive and negative effects of paid work on career development, and more generally, adolescent development.

Another way that paid work and career development are interlinked is that paid work experiences in adolescence and during the transition to adulthood can fill the void that delayed career development creates. It is clear that, among recent cohorts of young people, the timing and sequencing of school, work, and family roles during the transition to adulthood is increasingly delayed (Shanahan, 2000) as cohabitation has become more normative, teenage fertility has declined, and more and more young people are continuing their education into young adulthood. Arnett (2004) describes these demographic trends as a new

formative period of "emerging adulthood" in which young people today explore possible life directions and gradually arrive at more enduring choices in intimate relationships, work, and worldview. As previously mentioned, most young people today balance school and work during the transition to young adulthood and often accumulate a substantial amount of work experience prior to school completion (i.e., before they enter into "careers"). Emerging adults can occupy "adolescent" roles by continuing school, residing with their parents, and remaining childless, but they can show movement toward adulthood through career development or cohabitation, and yet still not attain the traditional markers of adulthood (e.g., parenthood, marriage, career acquisition, and school completion). Emerging adults are "in-between" adolescence and adulthood as they are "no longer adolescent but not yet fully adult" (Arnett, 2006, p. 114). In short, emerging adulthood is in some ways prolonged—and perhaps delayed—career development.

Prolonged role exploration in school, work, and relationships may benefit longer term socioeconomic and career success if it helps to ensure that good choices are made. Arnett (2006) contends that:

> . . . for emerging adults their choice of work is now primarily identity-based. . . . Today emerging adults wish to find a job that is an expression of their identity, not just a way to make money but an activity that is personally fulfilling and enjoyable. (p. 118)

For instance, recent cohorts of youth have been shown to have considerable difficulty in deciding on future occupations (Rindfuss et al., 1999; Savickas, 2005). If experimentation with different types of jobs or fields of study during emerging adulthood leads to more enduring careers in young adulthood, as Arnett predicts, then longer term attainment and career acquisition is likely to be enhanced. Likewise, as Bynner (2005) notes, independent role exploration in work and school may also lead to the accumulation of workplace experiences, job skills, and employer contacts that would similarly benefit wage attainments.

Yet, for many young people in the United States, delayed transitions to adulthood entail prolonged schooling without the acquisition of a postsecondary degree and nonstandard work arrangements in low-quality jobs. Research shows that young people who complete high school in the United States do not have clear institutional bridges to the occupational world because clear pathways from school to work are lacking (Kerckhoff, 1998). It is plausible that the observed instability in work and school roles among emerging adults is not a reflection of role exploration but instead indicates "floundering" in the labor market (Kerckhoff, 2003), especially among the 42%

of youth who initially enter 4-year colleges but do not earn degrees. Young people comprising this growing "sub-baccalaureate" labor market (Kerckhoff, 2002), lacking the career placement services provided by most colleges, often move from job to job in the secondary labor market (Kalleberg et al., 2000). In these circumstances, young people may find themselves in part-time jobs that are similar to the ones they held in adolescence. Research attending to how part-time work during adolescence and emerging adulthood promotes or interferes with positive career development is needed.

Additional Future Directions

Though the connection between work in adolescence and career development has not been a strong one in the literature, these examples illustrate some important ways developmental and other social scientists can draw stronger connections in future research. In addition, four important issues regarding adolescent paid work and career development deserve further attention.

Niche Selection

Young people make choices and compromises with respect to paid work and future careers based on the opportunities and constraints of their circumstances and their own interests and competencies. Yet prior research on paid work and career development rarely considers the young person's orientations toward work or even their desire to hold a job. Although it is clear that adolescents with little interest or success in school tend to work more hours during adolescence (Bachman & Schulenberg, 1993; Warren, 2002), some of these adolescents may also have weak orientations toward employment or may not want to work. Furthermore, the young person's desire to work may change because of family dissolution, local labor market conditions, parental expectations, discrimination, family obligations, compulsory school attendance, or legislation limiting the hours and type of employment. For this reason, it is important for researchers to distinguish adolescents who have a strong desire to work from those who do not. Bachman and colleagues (2003) found that an early desire for youth work (measured before the youth obtained jobs) predates both intensive work hours and problem behaviors in later adolescence. Future research should address whether the desire for work, as well as the individual and contextual contributions to the desire to work (e.g., Porfeli & Vondracek, in press), irrespective of the actual investment in paid work, affects the young person's career aspirations and development, school achievement, and longer term socioeconomic attainment.

With respect to career development, most prior research assumes that paid work will play a meaningful role in all adolescents' future lives. Yet work can be viewed as one manifestation of individuals' sense of purpose. For instance, some workers may use their work as an outlet for their sense of self and meaning, but not all individuals do so. For some youth, paid work may be secondary in importance to volunteer or unpaid employment, sports and extracurricular activities, or even unstructured leisure activities. Indeed, research shows that some individuals choose not to work for a large portion of their adult lives; this choice is not always acknowledged or modeled in studies of career development. Because work may fulfill different objectives in individuals' lives, we think it would be beneficial to expand on traditional measures of job success. When distal outcomes of adolescent career development are considered, they are often limited to job prestige, security, or satisfaction. Additional outcomes might include measures of whether the job fills the expected role in one's life, or whether work is an expression of one's purpose.

Research in educational psychology and related fields has illustrated the importance of "school readiness," or young children's cognitive and behavioral self-regulation skills that are beneficial to academic achievement and adjustment in school settings (McClelland

et al., 2007; Snow, 2007). Similarly, in the career development field, there has been some emphasis on the notion of "readiness for career choices" as a concept (e.g., Phillips & Blustein, 1994). Building on this concept as well as the recent work that has illustrated the effects of workplace stress on adolescents' well-being and their subsequent functioning (Mortimer & Staff, 2004), as well as research that has highlighted the importance of conceptualizing work quality as having opportunities to learn new skills (Stone & Mortimer, 1998), we see an area for rich new longitudinal research illustrating the importance of certain skills for early workplace success and for actively engaging the career development process. Such a view of "career readiness" would build on current conceptualizations of career maturity or preparedness, but would focus on the developmental readiness of adolescents for engaging in career development within various work settings. In particular, career readiness studies could target adolescents before they enter paid employment, following them through their first (or several first) jobs, ultimately identifying the characteristics and skills that facilitate early job adjustment, job satisfaction, and career development. Given the differences between adolescent employment and adult employment we discussed above, it is likely that adolescents need, and may not consistently have, different vocational skills than those needed and possessed by adults.

Moreover, the assumption that adolescents have the same degree of choice with respect to early work experiences and future careers is also questionable. It is clear that age, gender, race and ethnicity, and SES influence the onset, intensity, and duration of paid work during adolescence. Against this backdrop, it is important to specify the conditions under which the effects of teenage work on career and social development vary by gender, race and ethnicity, and SES. Not only could the meaning of intensive vs. moderate work hours be different for more or less advantaged youth, the effects of the quality of these early work experiences, as well as the notion of whether the work is career-like, may also differ. For example, although fast-food work, on average, is associated with poor work quality, youth in poor neighborhoods face a restricted and very competitive labor market, and work in fast-food restaurants can link teenagers with older adults in the community and foster positive social development (Newman, 1999). By contrast, youth in more prosperous areas may find a labor market characterized by an abundance of jobs and may have little stake in even office or clerical positions with the numerous opportunities to lose and regain work.

One should not assume that adolescents have the same degree of choice with respect to career development either (Blustein et al., 2002). In middle- and upper-class groups, most adolescents engage in exploration of various work-related options, think about what kinds of careers they may like to have, and use their unique skills, values, and interests as guides for this thought process. Yet career development is not an essential aspect of growing up or being human; it is a convention of modernity and the pursuit of individuality and autonomous choice. Even though the focus is on personal agency, the process itself is a creation of these social realities and forces. Thus, new conceptualizations of career development will need to address cultural, historic, and structural influences on individuals' career pathways. Future research should document whether youth from more or less advantaged backgrounds follow distinct work careers (involving movement between different types of jobs and hours of work) during adolescence, as well as the consequences of these experiences for longer term career outcomes.

Context

The notion that individuals select available environments and activities suggests some continuity in development. Yet, as our review illustrates, career development does not necessarily follow a smooth and progressive function, and more proximal experiences and contexts can shift ongoing developmental trajectories. Involvement in paid work during adolescence and career development may be viewed as a function of strong person–context interactions with a temporal course given to fits and starts that correspond, at least in part, to shifts in the individual, the context, and the interaction between the two.

Most prior research on teenage employment has given insufficient attention to the context of these experiences. For instance, past studies overwhelmingly focus on the hours of work and devote very little attention to different types of jobs and qualities of work experience. The National Research Council, in its 1998 report, *Protecting Youth at Work*, called for "longitudinal studies of how individuals who have worked in their youth function as adolescents and adults and how various outcomes are associated with the quality of the work experiences" (1998, p. 15). Mortimer and her colleagues have shown the importance of considering the context of adolescents' and young adults' work experiences and work history. For instance, Mortimer, Harley, and Staff (2002) examined the relation between the quality of adolescents' work experiences and their well-being and depression during 12th grade. Being satisfied with one's wages and believing that working was not interfering with school achievement were both positively related to well-being and negatively related to depression. Furthermore, finding congruence between school and work was negatively related to depressed mood, and experiencing work-related stress was related to higher depressive scores. In another investigation of the effects of work stressors, experiencing work stress during the sophomore, junior, and/ or senior year of high school was positively related to depressed mood, negatively related to self-esteem, and negatively related to self-efficacy during the senior year (Mortimer & Staff, 2004). These effects of contemporaneous work stress on mental health appeared during young adulthood as well. However, work experiences during adolescence also primed individuals for later work experiences. Experiencing work stressors during adolescence mitigated the undesirable effects of work stress experienced during young adulthood.

Research on adolescent work and career development can also inform the field of developmental science and theory about the role of context in individual development. A developmental science framework calls for an interdisciplinary examination of the influences of biology, social interactions, and dynamic systems on ontogeny (see Cairns, 2000). Thus far, little research on adolescent work and career development considers biological and social contexts meaningfully. Yet the act of working and work environments may prove to be mediators of the linkage between biological development and deviancy.

Historical Time and Place

When documenting cohort variation in these early work experiences, as well as their potential short- and longer term effects on career development, it is necessary to control for changing trends in the school-to-work transition, family formation behaviors, and occupational structures. For instance, some scholars suggest that recent cohorts of young people are prolonging their school-to-work transition and establishing a period of emerging adulthood (Arnett, 2004). In fact, almost all of high school seniors now plan to go to college (Schneider & Stevenson, 1999) and 70 percent of them do enter 4-year colleges. Moreover, among recent cohorts of young people, marriage is increasingly delayed (Ventura & Bachrach, 2000), cohabitation is more normative (Bumpass & Lu, 2000), rates of teenage fertility have declined (Furstenberg, 2003), and women are more likely to be in the labor force (Spain & Bianchi, 1996). The occupational structure has also changed in recent years with the decline in the demand for unskilled labor and the rise in high-skill labor markets (Murphy & Welch, 1993). Increasingly, careers are malleable (Hamori, 2006). Adults rarely remain in one job until retirement, and they tend to

switch careers. Very likely, this malleable and changing aspect of adult career trajectories will continue as today's adolescents enter the workforce. Furthermore, career opportunities themselves will change: New careers exist today that did not exist in the middle of the last century (such as those in the computer industry), and other careers no longer exist (such as a tinker, see Vondracek et al., 1986, p. 113).

These may sound like simple propositions to those who study adolescent work and career development, but they are not explicitly acknowledged in many theories, nor are they modeled empirically. In many research projects, adolescents are asked to provide only one career aspiration or expected career. Career choice and choice certainty are considered to be desirable outcomes during adolescence. Such conceptualizations may be appropriate for some studies, but if researchers want to understand the meaning or impact of career development for later occupational outcomes, then more nuanced measures of career aspirations and career development are necessary. Knowing what we do about the nature of work in adulthood, researchers should consider what optimal career development might look like during adolescence, and whether adolescents who are highly career developed in the traditional sense are truly prepared to deal with the complexities of the modern economy. According to Osipow and Fitzgerald (1996), vocational maturity is assessed normatively; it is "congruence between an individual's vocational behavior and the expected vocational behavior at that age" (p. 115). That definition seems accurate— unfortunately, measures often do not appropriately capture "expected" vocational behavior; we measure what we as researchers grounded in a traditional worldview of work stability would measure, rather than what employers of the future workforce might choose to measure.

Future research should also address whether the adolescent workplace is different than in years past. The types of jobs adolescents currently work in are indeed different; adolescents have become concentrated in the retail sector of the economy and fewer adolescents work in the agriculture, mining/construction/manufacturing, and service industries. According to the U.S. Department of Labor (2000), more and more adolescents are employed in eating and drinking establishments. Notwithstanding these broad changes in the distribution of employed teenagers across industries, little research addresses whether the nature of teenage work has indeed changed across the educational, economic, and social context. Do fewer teenagers report that their jobs provide skills for future work than in years past? Are contemporary cohorts of youth less likely to use at least part of their earnings for their family or educational expenses than earlier cohorts? Has the teenage workplace become more age segregated?

If so, these changes in the workplace may yield distinct cohort effects of teenage employment on adjustment and achievement. Bacolod and Hotz (2006) found cohort effects of early work and school experiences on wage attainments using two sets of birth cohorts from the National Longitudinal Surveys. The authors found that the transition from school to work during the 1970s contrasts with the experience of youth who entered adulthood during the 1980s. Not only did the younger birth cohort accumulate more years of school and work experience before reaching full-time work at a later age, they also experienced greater returns in wages from these early investments. Other analyses, using data from MTF, find that the relationship between hours of work and substance use varies across class cohorts (Brown, Schulenberg, Bachman, O'Malley, & Johnston, 2001). These studies illustrate some distinct cohort effects of work hours, but we still know very little about the changing adolescent work experience (across the aforementioned dimensions) and whether it has short- and longer term consequences for career development and a successful transition to adulthood.

Family and Peers

Finally, the study of part-time work represents a key and unique microsystem during adolescence,

and we argue that much of its impact may depend on the interconnections with others including family, school, and peers. Furthermore, career exploration and decision making are heavily influenced by within- and between-microsystem—mesosystem—processes.

For example, part-time work and career development are exceptionally useful domains in which to examine intergenerational transmission of values and beliefs and family socialization processes. In some domains, such as school, adolescents may feel as though they have as much relevant knowledge as their parents, if not more. Work is different; even older adolescents rarely have as much employment experience or knowledge of the world of work as their parents. Thus, work is a domain in which parental advice may be more readily accepted by adolescents. In addition, discussions about work and careers may provide a venue for the transmission of other values and beliefs. Young and colleagues (2003) demonstrated that career-related discussions with parents can create not only a jointly constructed career choice, but can also facilitate adolescents' connection to their cultural heritage. Research by Young and colleagues also highlights the fact that family socialization processes can be bidirectional.

In addition, future research should consider how paid work in adolescence affects family formation behaviors, such as pregnancy, residential independence, cohabitation, marital status, and childbearing. The concern that teenage employment engenders a precocious maturity, however, is based primarily on analyses of paid work and substance use. Consistent with the precocious maturity thesis, more adult-like work roles could affect family formation behaviors. For example, young women may increase their chances of pregnancy if they are employed with older workers or if their work schedule facilitates unstructured and unsupervised socializing. Alternatively, it is possible that early work experiences might discourage family formation behaviors, especially for young female workers. For instance, research on adult females suggests that rising employment has coincided with reduced rates of fertility. Analyses of young women from the 1979 National Longitudinal Survey of Youth finds that employment reduces the likelihood of pregnancy, especially for women who are working and attending school (Budig, 2003). The effect of paid work on family formation behaviors may also depend on the quality of the job. For example, low wages may prevent some adolesents from establishing residential independence from their parents. Young workers in career-like jobs may delay family formation so as not to disrupt their vocational development. As in Budig's study, when addressing the relationship between paid work and the timing of family formation, it is important to consider changing orientations toward work as well as school. It is plausible that, for adolescents who have a strong desire to spend long hours on the job, their orientation to work and not their actual work investments per se would predict both work and family roles.

CONCLUSION

Work experiences—especially during the teenage years—should be studied in the context of changing family and school roles during the transition to adulthood. Adolescents change jobs relatively frequently; each entry into or departure from a work setting represents a transition. In each of these transitions, young people have the ability to influence their contexts and choose niches that suit them or that provide opportunities for personal growth. Furthermore, work transitions can act as turning points when they lead to significant change in adolescents' developmental trajectories. The continuity and change in work roles is assumed to be consequential for trajectories of family and school involvement, as well as social and behavioral development. Because the decision about whether to work, and how much to work, reflects the young person's background and prospects for the future—defined by gender, race, and SES—it is important to document how sociodemographic characteristics affect whether teenagers work, what kinds of jobs they hold, and how much they work. Age, historical timing, economic conditions, and locality also influence these choices.

As we come to know more about the positive and negative consequences of employment during high school and the importance of these early work experiences for the process of career development, it is clear that work plays a key role in adolescents' lives. Recently, large-scale studies of adolescents have begun to include more variables that tap into a wider range of adolescent experiences. Measures of the quantity, and sometimes the quality, of early experiences in paid work are among these variables. The inclusion of work and career development variables in large-scale and longitudinal studies will prove to be a significant benefit to the scientific community. Further consideration of work and career development has the potential to broaden the field of adolescent development in general, facilitating connections between work and other aspects of adolescent development, and locating adolescence more clearly within the total life course.

REFERENCES

Alliman-Brissett, A. E., Turner, S. L., & Skovholt, T. M. (2004). Parent support and African American adolescents' career self-efficacy. *Professional School Counseling, 7*, 124–132.

Apel, R., Bushway, S., Brame, R., Haviland, A., Nagin, D., & Paternoster, R. (2007). Unpacking the relationship between adolescent employment and antisocial behavior: A matched samples comparison. *Criminology, 45*, 67–97.

Apel, R., Paternoster, R., Bushway, S., & Brame, R. (2006). A job isn't just a job: The differential impact of formal versus informal work on adolescent problem behavior. *Crime and Delinquency, 52*, 333–369.

Arnett, J. J. (2004). *Emerging adulthood: The winding road from the late teens through the twenties.* Oxford: Oxford University Press.

Arnett, J. J. (2006). Emerging adulthood in Europe: A response to Bynner. *Journal of Youth Studies, 9*, 11–123.

Aronson, P. J., Mortimer, J. T., Zierman, C., & Hacker, M. (1996). Generational differences in early work experiences and evaluations. In J. T. Mortimer & M. D. Finch (Eds.), *Adolescents, work, and family: An intergenerational developmental analysis* (pp. 25–62). Newbury Park, CA: Sage.

Arum, R., & Hout, M. (1998). The early returns: The transition from school to work in the United States. In Y. Shavit & W. Müller (Eds.), *From school to work: A comparative study of educational qualifications and occupational destinations* (pp. 471–510). Oxford: Clarendon Press.

Bachman, J. G. (1983). Premature affluence: Do high school students earn too much money? *Economic Outlook USA, 10*, 64–67.

Bachman, J. G., O'Malley, P. M., Schulenberg, J. E., Johnston, L. D., Bryant, A. L., & Merline, A. C. (2002). *The decline of substance use in young adulthood: Changes in social activities, roles, and beliefs*. Mahwah, NJ: Lawrence Erlbaum.

Bachman, J. G., O'Malley, P. M., Schulenberg, J. E., Johnston, L. D., Freedman-Doan, P., & Messersmith, E. E. (2008). *The education–drug use connection: How successes and failures in school relate to adolescent smoking, drinking, drug use, and delinquency*. New York: Lawrence Erlbaum/Taylor & Francis.

Bachman, J. G., Safron, D. J., Sy, S. R., & Schulenberg, J. E. (2003). Wishing to work: New perspectives on how adolescents' part-time work intensity is linked with educational disengagement, drug use, and other problem behaviours. *International Journal of Behavioral Development, 27*, 301–315.

Bachman, J. G., & Schulenberg, J. E. (1993). How part-time work intensity relates to drug use, problem behavior, time use, and satisfaction among high school seniors: Are these consequences or merely correlates? *Developmental Psychology, 29*, 220–235.

Bacolod, M., & Hotz, V. J. (2006). Cohort changes in the transition from school to work: Evidence from three NLS surveys. *Economic Education Review, 25*, 351–373.

Baker, H. E. (2002). Reducing adolescent career indecision: The ASVAB Career Exploration Program. *Career Development Quarterly, 50*, 359–370.

Baltes, P. B., Lindenberger, U., & Staudinger, U. M. (2006). Life span theory in developmental psychology. In R. M. Lerner & W. Damon (Eds.), *Handbook of child psychology* (6th ed.), vol. 1: *Theoretical models of human development* (pp. 569–664). Hoboken, NJ: John Wiley & Sons.

Bandura, A. (2001). Social cognitive theory: An agentic perspective. *Annual Review of Psychology, 52*, 1–26.

Bandura, A., Barbaranelli, C., Caprara, G. V., & Pastorelli, C. (2001). Self-efficacy beliefs as shapers of children's aspirations and career trajectories. *Child Development, 72*, 187–206.

Barber, B. L., Eccles, J. S., & Stone, M. R. (2001). Whatever happened to the jock, the brain, and the princess? Young adult pathways linked to adolescent activity involvement and social identity. *Journal of Adolescent Research, 16*, 429–455.

Blanchard, C. A., & Lichtenberg, J. W. (2003). Compromise in career decision making: A test of Gottfredson's theory. *Journal of Vocational Behavior, 62*, 250–271.

Blustein, D. L., Chaves, A. P., Diemer, M. A., Gallagher, L. A., Marshall, K. G., Sirin, S., et al. (2002). Voices of the forgotten half: The role of social class in the school-to-work transition. *Journal of Counseling Psychology, 49*, 311–323.

Bozick, R. (2006). Precocious behaviors in early adolescence: Employment and the transition to first sexual intercourse. *Journal of Early Adolescence, 26*, 60–86.

Bronfenbrenner, U., & Morris, P. A. (2006). The bioecological model of human development. In R. M. Lerner & W. Damon (Eds.), *Handbook of child psychology* (6th ed.), vol. 1: *Theoretical models of human development* (pp. 793–828). Hoboken, NJ: John Wiley & Sons.

Brown, T. N., Schulenberg, J. E., Bachman, J. G., O'Malley, P. M., & Johnston, L. D. (2001). Are risk and protective factors for substance use consistent across historical time? National data from the high school classes of 1976–1997. *Prevention Science, 2*, 29–43.

Bryant, B. K., Zvonkovic, A. M., & Reynolds, P. (2006). Parenting in relation to child and adolescent vocational development. *Journal of Vocational Behavior, 69*, 149–175.

Budig, M. J. (2003). Are women's employment and fertility histories interdependent? An examination of causal order using event history analysis. *Social Science Research, 32*, 376–401.

Bumpass, L., & Lu, H. (2000). Trends in cohabitation and implications for children's family contexts in the United States. *Population Studies, 54*, 29–41.

Bynner, J. (2005). Rethinking the youth phase of the life-course: The case for emerging adulthood? *Journal of Youth Studies, 8*, 367–384.

Cairns, R. B. (2000). Developmental science: Three audacious implications. In L. R. Bergman, R. B. Cairns, L.-G. Nilsson, & L. Nystedt (Eds.), *Developmental science and the holistic approach* (pp. 49–62). Mahwah, NJ: Lawrence Erlbaum.

Carr, R., Wright, J., & Brody, C. (1996). Effects of high school work experience a decade later: Evidence from the National Longitudinal Study. *Sociology of Education, 69*, 66–81.

Caspi, A., Wright, B. R., Moffitt, T. E., & Silva, P. (1998). Childhood predictors of unemployment in early adulthood. *American Sociological Review, 63*, 424–451.

Chang, E. S., Chen, C., Greenberger, E., Dooley, D., & Heckhausen, J. (2006). What do they want in life? The life goals of a multi-ethnic, multi-generational sample of high school seniors. *Journal of Youth and Adolescence, 35*, 321–332.

Cicchetti, D., & Rogosch, F. A. (2002). A developmental psychopathology perspective on adolescence. *Journal of Consulting and Clinical Psychology, 70*, 6–20.

Cinamon, R. G., & Rich, Y. (2002). Gender difference in the importance of work and family roles: Implications for work-family conflict. *Sex Roles, 47*, 531–541.

Cohen-Scali, V. (2003). The influence of family, social, and work socialization on the construction of professional identity of young adults. *Journal of Career Development, 29*, 237–249.

Coleman, J., Bremner, R., Clark, B., Davis, J., Eichorn, D., Griliches, Z., et al. (1974). *Youth: Transition to adulthood*. Chicago: University of Chicago Press.

Constantine, M. G., Wallace, B. C., & Kindaichi, M. M. (2005). Examining contextual factors in the career decision status of African American adolescents. *Journal of Career Assessment, 13*, 307–319.

Correll, S. J. (2001). Gender and the career choice process: The role of biased self-assessments. *American Journal of Sociology, 106*, 1691–1730.

Creed, P. A., Prideaux, L., & Patton, W. (2005). Antecedents and consequences of career decisional states in adolescence. *Journal of Vocational Behavior, 67*, 397–412.

Crosnoe, R. (2002). Academic and health-related trajectories in adolescence: The intersection of gender and athletics. *Journal of Health and Social Behavior, 43*, 317–335.

Csikszentmihalyi, M., & Schneider, B. (2000). *Becoming adult: How teenagers prepare for the world of work*. New York: Basic Books.

D'Amico, R. (1984). Does employment during high school impair academic progress? *Sociology of Education, 57*, 152–164.

Danielsen, L. M., Lorem, A. E., & Kroger, J. (2000). The impact of social context on the identity-formation process of Norweigian late adolescents. *Youth & Society, 31*, 332–362.

Diegelman, N. M., & Subich, L. M. (2001). Academic and vocational interests as a function of outcome expectancies in social cognitive career theory. *Journal of Vocational Behavior, 59*, 394–405.

Diemer, M. A., & Blustein, D. L. (2006). Critical consciousness and career development among urban youth. *Journal of Vocational Behavior, 68*, 220–232.

Eccles, J. S., Adler, T. F., Futterman, R., Goff, S. B., Kaczala, C. M., Meece, J. L., et al. (1983). Expectancies, values, and academic behaviors. In J. T. Spence (Ed.), *Achievement and achievement motivation* (pp. 75–146). San Francisco: W. H. Freeman.

Eccles, J. S., & Barber, B. (1999). Student council, volunteering, basketball, and marching band: What kind of extracurricular involvement matters? *Journal of Adolescent Research, 14*, 10–43.

Elder, G. H., Jr. (1974). *Children of the great depression*. Chicago: University of Chicago Press.

Elder, G. H., Jr., & Rockwell, R. C. (1979). Economic depression and postwar opportunity in men's lives: A study of life patterns and health. In R. G. Simmons (Ed.), *Research in community and mental health* (pp. 249–303). Greenwich, CT: JAI Press.

Elder, G. H., Jr., & Shanahan, M. J. (2006). The life course and human development. In R. M. Lerner & W. Damon (Eds.),

Handbook of child psychology (6th ed.), vol. 1: *Theoretical models of human development* (pp. 665–715). Hoboken, NJ: John Wiley & Sons.

Entwisle, D. R., Alexander, K. L., & Olson, L. S. (2000). Early work histories of urban youth. *American Sociological Review, 65,* 279–297.

Entwisle, D. R., Alexander, K. L., & Olson, L. S. (2005). Urban teenagers: Work and dropout. *Youth and Society, 37,* 3–32.

Erikson, E. H. (1964). *Childhood and society.* New York: W. W. Norton.

Farkas, G., Olsen, R. J., & Stromsdorfer, E. W. (1981). Youth labor supply during the summer: Evidence for youths from low-income households. *Research in Labor Economics, 4,* 151–190.

Farkas, G., Smith, D. A., & Stromsdorfer, E. W. (1983). The youth entitlement demonstration: Subsidized employment with a schooling requirement. *Journal of Human Resources, 18,* 557–573.

Ferry, T. R., Fouad, N. A., & Smith, P. L. (2000). The role of family context in a social cognitive model for career-related choice behavior: A math and science perspective. *Journal of Vocational Behavior, 57,* 348–364.

Flores, L. Y., Berkel, L. A., Nilsson, J. E., Ojeda, L., Jordan, S. E., Lynn, G. L., et al. (2006). Racial/ethnic minority vocational research: A content and trend analysis across 36 years. *Career Development Quarterly, 55,* 2–21.

Flores, L. Y., Navarro, R. L., Smith, J. L., & Ploszaj, A. M. (2006). Testing a model of nontraditional career choice goals with Mexican American adolescent men. *Journal of Career Assessment, 14,* 214–234.

Flores, L. Y., & O'Brien, K. M. (2002). The career development of Mexican American adolescent women: A test of social cognitive career theory. *Journal of Counseling Psychology, 49,* 14–27.

Flores, L. Y., Spanierman, L. B., Armstrong, P. I., & Velez, A. D. (2006). Validity of the Strong Interest Inventory and Skills Confidence Inventory with Mexican American high school students. *Journal of Career Assessment, 14,* 183–202.

Furstenberg, F. F., Jr. (2003). Teenage childbearing as a public issue and private concern. *Annual Review of Sociology, 29,* 23–39.

Gagné, M., & Deci, E. L. (2005). Self-determination theory and work motivation. *Journal of Organizational Behavior, 26,* 331–362.

Gill, A. M., & Michaels, R. J. (1992). Does drug use lower wages? *Industrial and Labor Relations Review, 45,* 419–434.

Ginzberg, E., Ginsberg, S. W., Axelrad, S., & Herma, J. L. (1951). *Occupational choice: An approach to a general theory.* New York: Columbia University Press.

Gottfredson, L. S. (1981). Circumscription and compromise: A developmental theory of occupational aspirations. *Journal of Counseling Psychology, 28,* 545–579.

Gottfredson, L. S. (2005). Applying Gottfredson's theory of circumscription and compromise in career guidance and counseling. In S. D. Brown & R. W. Lent (Eds.), *Career development and counseling: Putting theory and research to work* (pp. 71–100). Hoboken, NJ: John Wiley & Sons.

Greenberger, E. (1988). Working in teenage America. In J. T. Mortimer & K. M. Borman (Eds.), *Work experience and psychological development through the life span* (pp. 21–50). Boulder, CO: Westview.

Greenberger, E., & Steinberg, L. D. (1986). *When teenagers work: The psychological and social costs of teenage employment.* New York: Basic Books.

Hamilton, S. F. (1990). *Apprenticeship for adulthood: Preparing youth for the future.* New York: Free Press.

Hamori, M. (2006). Executive career advancement in career moves across employers: The role of organization-level predictors. *International Journal of Human Resource Management, 17,* 1129–1151.

Hansen, D., Mortimer, J. T., & Krueger, H. (2001). Adolescent part-time employment in the United States and Germany: Diverse

outcomes, contexts, and pathways. In C. Pole, P. Mizen, & A. Bolton (Eds.), *Hidden hands: International perspectives on children's work and labor* (pp. 121–138). London: Routledge Falmer Press.

Hargrove, B. K., Inman, A. G., & Crane, R. L. (2005). Family interaction patterns, career planning attitudes, and vocational identity of high school adolescents. *Journal of Career Development, 31,* 263–278.

Hartung, P. J., Porfeli, E. J., & Vondracek, F. W. (2005). Child vocational development: A review and reconsideration. *Journal of Vocational Behavior, 66,* 385–419.

Heckhausen, J., & Tomasik, M. J. (2002). Get an apprenticeship before school is out: How German adolescents adjust vocational aspirations when getting close to a developmental deadline. *Journal of Vocational Behavior, 60,* 199–219.

Helwig, A. A. (2001). A test of Gottfredson's theory using a ten-year longitudinal study. *Journal of Career Development, 28,* 77–95.

Hirschi, A., & Läge, D. (2007). Holland's secondary constructs of vocational interests and career choice readiness of secondary students: Measures for related but different constructs. *Journal of Individual Differences, 28,* 205–218.

Hirschi, T. (1969). *Causes of delinquency.* New Brunswick, NJ: Transaction Publishers.

Hirschman, C., & Voloshin, I. (2007). The structure of teenage employment: Social background and the jobs held by high school seniors. *Research in Social Stratification and Mobility, 25,* 189–203.

Hoffmann, J. P. (2006). Extracurricular activities, athletic participation, and adolescent alcohol use: Gender-differentiated and school contextual effects. *Journal of Health and Social Behavior, 47,* 275–290.

Holland, J. L. (1973). Applying an occupational classification to a representative sample of work histories. *Journal of Applied Psychology, 58,* 34–41.

Holland, J. L. (1997). *Making vocational choices: A theory of vocational personalities and work environments* (3rd ed.). Odessa, FL: Psychological Assessment Resources.

Hotz, V. J., Xu, L. C., Tienda, M., & Ahituv, A. (2002). Are there returns to the wages of young men from working while in school? *Review of Economics and Statistics, 84,* 221–236.

Jackson, M. A., Kacanski, J. M., Rust, J. P., & Beck, S. E. (2006). Constructively challenging diverse inner-city youth's beliefs about educational and career barriers and supports. *Journal of Career Development, 32,* 203–218.

Jepsen, D. A., & Dickson, G. L. (2003). Continuity in life-span career development: Career exploration as a precursor to career establishment. *Career Development Quarterly, 51,* 217–233.

Jessor, R., Donovan, J. E., & Costa, F. M. (1991). *Beyond adolescence: Problem behavior and young adult development.* New York: Cambridge University Press.

Jessor, R., & Jessor, S. (1977). *Problem behavior and psychosocial development: A longitudinal study of youth.* New York: Academic Press.

Ji, P. Y., Lapan, R. T., & Tate, K. (2004). Vocational interests and career efficacy expectations in relation to occupational sex-typing beliefs for eighth grade students. *Journal of Career Development, 31,* 143–154.

Johnson, M. K. (2002). Social origins, adolescent experiences, and work value trajectories during the transition to adulthood. *Social Forces, 80,* 1307–1341.

Johnson, M. K. (2004). Further evidence on adolescent employment and substance use: Differences by race and ethnicity. *Journal of Health and Social Behavior, 45,* 187–197.

Johnson, M. K. (2005). Family roles and work values: Processes of selection and change. *Journal of Marriage and Family, 67,* 352–369.

Johnston, L. D., O'Malley, P. M., Bachman, J. G., & Schulenberg, J. E. (2007a). *Monitoring the Future national survey results on drug use, 1975–2006,* vol. I: *Secondary school students* (NIH

Publication No. 07-6205). Bethesda, MD: National Institute on Drug Abuse.

Johnston, L. D., O'Malley, P. M., Bachman, J. G., & Schulenberg, J. E. (2007b). *Monitoring the Future national survey results on drug use, 1975–2006,* vol. II: *College students and adults ages 19–45* (NIH Publication No. 07-6206). Bethesda, MD: National Institute on Drug Abuse.

Kaestner, R. (1991). The effect of illicit drug use on the wages of young adults. *Journal of Labor Economics, 9,* 381–412.

Kalakoski, V., & Nurmi, J. E. (1998). Identity and educational transitions: Age differences in adolescent exploration and commitment related to education, occupation, and family. *Journal of Research on Adolescence, 8,* 29–47.

Kalleberg, A. L., Reskin, B. F., & Hudson, K. (2000). Bad jobs in America: Standard and nonstandard employment relations and job quality in the United States. *American Sociological Review, 65,* 256–278.

Kandel, D., Chen, K., & Gill, A. (1995). The impact of drug use on earnings: A life-span perspective. *Social Forces, 74,* 243–270.

Kerckhoff, A. C. (2000). Transition from school to work in comparative perspective. In M. T. Hallinan (Ed.), *Handbook of the sociology of education* (pp. 453–474). New York: Kluwer Academic/Plenum.

Kerckhoff, A. C. (2002). The transition from school to work. In J. T. Mortimer & R. W. Larson (Eds.), *The changing adolescent experience: Societal trends and the transition to adulthood* (pp. 52–87). New York: Cambridge University Press.

Kerckhoff, A. C. (2003). From student to worker. In J. T. Mortimer & M. Shanahan (Eds.), *Handbook of the life course* (pp. 251–267). Kluwer Academic/Plenum Publishers.

Knox, M., Funk, J., Elliott, R., & Bush, E. G. (2000). Gender differences in adolescents' possible selves. *Youth and Society, 31,* 287–309.

Kolodinsky, P., Schroder, V., Montopoli, G., McLean, S., Mangan, P. A., & Pederson, W. (2006). The career fair as a vehicle for enhancing occupational self-efficacy. *Professional School Counseling, 10,* 161–167.

Kornhauser, R. R. (1978). *Social sources of delinquency: An appraisal of analytic models.* Chicago: University of Chicago Press.

Kracke, B. (2002). The role of personality, parents and peers in adolescents career exploration. *Journal of Adolescence, 25,* 19–30.

Krohn, M. D., Lizotte, A. J., & Perez, C. M. (1997). The interrelationship between substance use and precocious transitions to adult statuses. *Journal of Health and Social Behavior, 38,* 87–103.

Krumboltz, J. D., Mitchell, A. M., & Jones, G. B. (1976). A social learning theory of career selection. *Counseling Psychologist, 61,* 71–81.

Ku, L., Sonenstein, F. L., & Pleck, J. H. (1993). Neighborhood, family, and work: Influences on the premarital behaviors of adolescent males. *Social Forces, 72,* 479–503.

Laub, J. H., & Sampson, R. J. (2003). *Shared beginnings, divergent lives: Delinquent boys to age 70.* Cambridge, MA: Harvard University Press.

Lee, J. C., & Staff, J. (2007). When work matters: The varying impact of adolescent work intensity on high school drop-out. *Sociology of Education, 80,* 158–178.

Lent, R. W., Brown, S. D., & Hackett, G. (1994). Toward a unifying social cognitive theory of career and academic interest, choice, and performance. *Journal of Vocational Behavior, 45,* 79–122.

Lent, R. W., Brown, S. D., Nota, L., & Soresi, S. (2003). Testing social cognitive interest and choice hypotheses across Holland types in Italian high school students. *Journal of Vocational Behavior, 62,* 101–118.

Leong, F. T. L., Hardin, E. E., & Gaylor, M. (2005). Career specialty choice: A combined research-intervention project. *Journal of Vocational Behavior, 67,* 69–86.

Lerner, R. M. (2006). Developmental science, developmental systems, and contemporary theories of human development. In R. M. Lerner & W. Damon (Eds.), *Handbook of child psychology* (6th ed.), vol. 1: *Theoretical models of human development.* Hoboken, NJ: John Wiley & Sons.

Lewis, M. (1999). Contextualism and the issue of continuity. *Infant Behavior & Development, 22,* 431–444.

Light, A. (2001). In-school work experience and the returns to schooling. *Journal of Labor Economics, 19,* 65–93.

Majoribanks, K. (1997). Family background, social and academic capital, and adolescents' aspirations: A mediational analysis. *Social Psychology of Education, 2,* 177–197.

Marcia, J. E. (1966). Development and validation of ego identity status. *Journal of Personality and Social Psychology, 5,* 551–558.

Marcia, J. E. (1993). The ego identity status approach to ego identity. In J. E. Marcia, A. S. Waterman, D. R. Matteson, S. L. Archer, & J. L. Orlofsky (Eds.), *Ego identity: A handbook for psychosocial research* (pp. 1–21). New York: Springer-Verlag.

Marcia, J. E. (1994). The empirical study of ego identity. In H. A. Bosma, T. L. Graafsma, H. D. Grotevant, & D. J. de Levita (Eds.), *Identity and development: An interdisciplinary approach* (pp. 67–80). Thousand Oaks, CA: Sage.

Marini, M. M., Fan, P.-L., Finley, E., & Beutel, A. M. (1996). Gender and job values. *Sociology of Education, 69,* 49–65.

Marsh, H. W. (1991). Employment during high school: Character building or subversion of academic goals? *Sociology of Education, 64,* 172–189.

Marsh, H. W., & Kleitman, S. (2005). Consequences of employment during high school: Character building, subversion of academic goals, or a threshold? *American Educational Research Journal, 42,* 331–369.

Martino, S. C., Collins, R. L., Ellickson, P. L., Schell, T. L., & McCaffrey, D. (2006). Socio-environmental influences on adolescents' alcohol outcome expectancies: A prospective analysis. *Addiction, 101,* 971–983.

McClelland, M. M., Cameron, C. E., Connor, C. M., Farris, C. L., Jewkes, A. M., & Morrison, F. J. (2007). Links between behavioral regulation and preschoolers' literacy, vocabulary, and math skills. *Developmental Psychology, 43,* 947–959.

McMorris, B., & Uggen, C. (2000). Alcohol and employment in the transition to adulthood. *Journal of Health and Social Behavior, 41,* 276–294.

McNeal, R. B. (1997). Are students being pulled out of high school? The effect of adolescent employment on dropping out. *Sociology of Education, 70,* 206–220.

Meece, J. L. (2006). Introduction: Trends in women's employment in the early 21st century. *Educational Research and Evaluation, 12,* 297–303.

Messersmith, E. E., Garrett, J. L., Davis-Kean, P. E., Malanchuk, O., & Eccles, J. S. (2008). Career development from adolescence through emerging adulthood. *Journal of Research on Adolescence, 23,* 206–227.

Mihalic, S. W., & Elliott, D. S. (1997). Short- and long-term consequences of adolescent work. *Youth and Society, 28*(4), 464–498.

Mortimer, J. T. (2003). *Working and growing up in America.* Cambridge, MA: Harvard University Press.

Mortimer, J. T., & Finch, M. D. (1986). The effects of part-time work on self-concept and achievement. In K. Borman & J. Reisman (Eds.), *Becoming a worker* (pp. 66–89). Norwood, NJ: Ablex.

Mortimer, J. T., Finch, M. D., Owens, T. J., & Shanahan, M. (1990). Gender and work in adolescence. *Youth and Society, 22,* 201–224.

Mortimer, J. T., Finch, M. D., Ryu, S., Shanahan, M., & Call, K. (1996). The effects of work intensity on adolescent mental health, achievement, and behavioral adjustment: New evidence from a prospective study. *Child Development, 67,* 1243–1261.

Mortimer, J. T., Harley, C., & Staff, J. (2002). Adolescent work quality and mental health. *Work and Occupations, 29,* 166–197.

Mortimer, J. T., & Johnson, M. (1998a). Adolescent part-time work and educational achievement. In K. Borman & B. Schneider (Eds.), *The adolescent years: Social influences and educational challenges* (pp. 183–206). Chicago: National Society for the Study of Education.

Mortimer, J. T., & Johnson, M. (1998b). New perspectives on adolescent work and the transition to adulthood. In R. Jessor (Ed.), *New perspectives on adolescent risk behavior* (pp. 425–496). New York: Cambridge University Press.

Mortimer, J. T., Pimentel, E., Ryu, S., Shanahan, M., & Call, K. T. (1996). The effects of work intensity on adolescent mental health, achievement, and behavioral adjustment: New evidence from a prospective study. *Child Development, 67,* 1243–1261.

Mortimer, J. T., & Shanahan, M. J. (1991, August). *Adolescent work experience and relations with peers.* Paper presented at the annual meeting of the American Sociological Association, Cincinnati, OH.

Mortimer, J. T., & Shanahan, M. J. (1994). Adolescent work experience and family relationships. *Work and Occupations, 21,* 369–384.

Mortimer, J. T., & Staff, J. (2004). Early work as a source of developmental discontinuity during the transition to adulthood. *Development and Psychopathology, 16,* 1047–1070.

Mortimer, J. T., Staff, J., & Oesterle, S. (2003). Strategic patterns of adolescent work and early socioeconomic attainment. In J. T. Mortimer & M. Shanahan (Eds.), *Handbook of the life course* (pp. 437–464). Kluwer Academic/Plenum Publishers.

Mortimer, J. T., Vuolo, M., Staff, J., Wakefield, S. & Xie, W. (2008). Tracing the timing of 'career' acquisition in a contemporary youth cohort. *Work and Occupations, 35,* 44–84.

Mortimer, J. T., & Zimmer-Gembeck, M. (2007). Adolescent paid work and career development. In V. Skorikov & W. Patton (Eds.), *Career development in childhood and adolescence* (pp. 255–275). Rotterdam, The Netherlands: Sense Publishers.

Murphy, K. M., & Welch, F. (1993). Occupational change and the demand for skill, 1940–1990. *American Economic Review, 83,* 122–126.

Nagy, G., Trautwein, U., Baumert, J., Koller, O., & Garrett, J. (2006). Gender and course selection in upper secondary education: Effects of academic self-concept and intrinsic value. *Educational Research and Evaluation, 12,* 323–345.

National Research Council. (1998). *Protecting youth at work: Health, safety, and development of working children and adolescents in the United States.* Committee on the Health and Safety Implications of Child Labor. Washington, DC: National Academy Press.

Navarro, R. L., Flores, L. Y., & Worthington, R. L. (2007). Mexican American middle school students' goal intentions in mathematics and science: A test of social cognitive career theory. *Journal of Counseling Psychology, 54,* 320–335.

Newcomb, M. D., & Bentler, P. M. (1988). *Consequences of adolescent drug use: Impact on the lives of young adults.* Newbury Park, CA: Sage.

Newman, K. S. (1999). *No shame in my game: The working poor in the inner city.* New York: Alfred A. Knopf, Inc. and the Russell Sage Foundation.

Nurmi, J.-E., Salmela-Aro, K., & Koivisto, P. (2002). Goal importance and related achievement beliefs and emotions during the transition from vocation school to work: Antecedents and consequences. *Journal of Vocational Behavior, 60,* 241–261.

O'Brien, K. M., Bikos, L. H., Epstein, K. L., Flores, L. Y., Dukstein, R. D., & Kamatuka, N. A. (2000). Enhancing the career decision-making self-efficacy of upward bound students. *Journal of Career Development, 26,* 277–293.

Osgood, D. W. (1999). Having the time of their lives: All work and no play? In A. Booth, A. C. Crouter, & M. J. Shanahan (Eds.), *Transitions to adulthood in a changing economy: No work, no family, no future?* (pp. 176–186). Westport, CT: Praeger.

Osgood, D. W., Wilson, J. K., O'Malley, P. M., Bachman, J. G., & Johnston, L. D. (1996). Routine activities and individual deviant behavior. *American Sociological Review, 61,* 635–655.

Osipow, S. H., & Fitzgerald, L. F. (1996). *Theories of career development* (4th ed.). Boston: Allyn & Bacon.

Otto, L. B. (2000). Youth perspectives on parental career influence. *Journal of Career Development, 27,* 111–118.

Paa, H. K., & McWhirter, E. H. (2000). Perceived influences on high school students' current career expectations. *Career Development Quarterly, 49,* 29–44.

Pabilonia, S. W. (2001). Evidence on youth employment, earnings, and parental transfers in the National Longitudinal Survey of Youth 1997. *Journal of Human Resources, 4,* 795–822.

Parsons, F. (1909). *Choosing a vocation.* Boston: Houghton Mifflin.

Paternoster, R., Bushway, S., Brame, R., & Apel, R. (2003). The effect of teenage employment on delinquency and problem behaviors. *Social Forces, 82,* 297–336.

Patton, W., Creed, P. A., & Muller, J. (2002). Career maturity and well-being as determinants of occupational status of recent school leavers: A brief report of an Australian study. *Journal of Adolescent Research, 17,* 425–435.

Patton, W., Creed, P. A., & Watson, M. (2003). Perceived work related and non-work related barriers in the career development of Australian and South African adolescents. *Australian Journal of Psychology, 55,* 74–82.

Patton, W., & Porfeli, E. J. (2007). Career exploration. In V. B. Skorikov & W. Patton (Eds.), *Career development in childhood and adolescence* (pp. 47–70). Rotterdam, the Netherlands: Sense Publishers.

Peck, S. C., Vida, M., & Eccles, J. S. (2008). Adolescent pathways to adulthood drinking: Sport activity involvement is not necessarily risky or protective. *Addiction, 103,* 69–83.

Phillips, S. D., & Blustein, D. L. (1994). Readiness for career choices: Planning, exploring, and deciding. *Special Issue: From vocational guidance to career counseling: Essays to honor Donald E. Super, 43,* 63–73.

Phillips, S., & Sandstrom, K. L. (1990). Parental attitudes towards youth work. *Youth and Society, 22,* 160–183.

Phinney, J. S., Baumann, K., & Blanton, S. (2001). Life goals and attributions for expected outcomes among adolescents from five ethnic groups. *Hispanic Journal of Behavioral Sciences, 23,* 363–377.

Pinquart, M., Juang, L. P., & Silbereisen, R. K. (2003). Self-efficacy and successful school-to-work transition: A longitudinal study. *Journal of Vocational Behavior, 63,* 329–346.

Pinquart, M., Juang, L. P., & Silbereisen, R. K. (2004). The role of self-efficacy, academic abilities, and parental education in the change in career decisions of adolescents facing German unification. *Journal of Career Development, 31,* 125-142.

Ploeger, M. (1997). Youth employment and delinquency: Reconsidering a problematic relationship. *Criminology, 35,* 659–675.

Porfeli, E. J. (in press). Career exploration. In F. T. L. Leong (Ed.), *Career and vocational counseling,* vol. 3. Thousand Oaks, CA: Sage.

Porfeli, E. J. (2007). Work values system development during adolescence. *Journal of Vocational Behavior, 70,* 42–60.

Porfeli, E. J., & Vondracek, F. W. (in press). Career development, work, and occupational success. In M. C. Smith & T. G. Reio (Eds.), *Handbook of research on adult development and learning.* Mahwah, NJ: Lawrence Erlbaum.

Quimby, J. L. & DeSantis, A. M. (2006). The influence of role models on women's career choices. *Career Development Quarterly, 54,* 297–306.

Quimby, J. L., Wolfson, J. L., & Seyala, N. D. (2007). Social cognitive predictors of African American adolescents' career interests. *Journal of Career Development, 33,* 376–394.

Rees, A. M., Luzzo, D. A., Gridley, B. E., & Doyle, C. (2007). Relational personality theory and Holland's typology among women: An exploratory investigation. *Career Development Quarterly, 55,* 194–205.

Rindfuss, R. R., Cooksey, E. C., & Sutterlin, R. L. (1999). Young adult occupational achievement: Early expectations versus behavioral reality. *Work and Occupations, 26,* 220–263.

Roe, A. (1947). Personality and vocation. *Transactions of the New York Academy of Sciences, 9,* 257–267.

Roisman, G. I., Bahadur, M. A., & Oster, H. (2000). Infant attachment security as a discriminant predictor of career development in late adolescence. *Journal of Adolescent Research, 15,* 531–545.

Rojewski, J. W., & Kim, H. (2003). Career choice patterns and behavior of work-bound youth during early adolescence. *Journal of Career Development, 30,* 89–108.

Rosenbaum, J. E. (2001). *Beyond college for all: Career paths for the forgotten half.* New York: Russell Sage Foundation.

Rothstein, D. S. (2007). High school employment and youths' academic achievement. *Journal of Human Resources, 42,* 194–213.

Rottinghaus, P. J., Coon, K. L., Gaffey, A. R., & Zytowski, D. G. (2007). Thirty-year stability and predictive validity of vocational interests. *Journal of Career Assessment, 15,* 5–22.

Rottinghaus, P. J., & Zytowski, D. G. (2006). Commonalities between adolescents' work values and interests. *Measurement and Evaluation in Counseling and Development, 38,* 211–221.

Ruhm, C. (1997). Is high school employment consumption or investment? *Journal of Labor Economics 15,* 735–776.

Ryu, S., & Mortimer, J. T. (1996). The "occupational linkage hypothesis" applied to occupational value formation in adolescence. In J. T. Mortimer & M. D. Finch (Eds.) *Adolescents, work, and family: An intergenerational developmental analysis* (pp. 167–190). Newbury Park, CA: Sage.

Safron, D., Bachman, J. G., & Schulenberg, J. E. (2001). Part-time work and hurried adolescence: The links among work intensity, social activities, health behaviors, and substance use. *Journal of Health and Social Behavior, 42,* 425–449.

Sameroff, A. J. (2000). Developmental systems and psychopathology. *Development and Psychopathology, 12,* 297–312.

Savickas, M. L. (1999). The transition from school to work: A developmental perspective. *Career Development Quarterly, 47,* 326–336.

Savickas, M. L. (2005). The theory and practice of career construction. In R. W. Lent & S. D. Brown (Eds.), *Career development and counseling: Putting theory and research to work* (pp. 42–70). Hoboken, NJ: John Wiley & Sons.

Schmidt, C. K., & Nilsson, J. E. (2006). The effects of simultaneous developmental processes: Factors relating to the career development of lesbian, gay, and bisexual youth. *Career Development Quarterly, 55,* 22–37.

Schneider, B., & Stevenson, D. (1999). *The ambitious generation: America's teenagers, motivated but directionless.* New Haven, CT/London: Yale University Press.

Schoenhals, M., Tienda, M., & Schneider, B. (1998). The educational and personal consequences of adolescent employment. *Social Forces, 77,* 723–762.

Schulenberg, J. E. (2006). Understanding the multiple contexts of adolescent risky behavior and positive development: Advances and future directions. *Applied Developmental Science, 10,* 107–113.

Schulenberg, J. E., & Bachman, J. G. (1993, March). *Long hours on the job? Not so bad for some types of jobs: The quality of work and substance use, affect and stress.* Paper presented at the Biennial Meeting of the Society for Research on Child Development, New Orleans, LA.

Schulenberg, J., Goldstein, A., & Vondracek, F. W. (1991). Gender differences in adolescents' career interests: Beyond main effects. *Journal of Research on Adolescence, 1,* 41–65.

Schulenberg, J. E., Maggs, J. M., & O'Malley, P. M. (2003). How and why the understanding of developmental continuity and discontinuity is important: The sample case of long-term consequences of adolescent substance use. In J. T. Mortimer &

M. J. Shanahan (Eds.), *Handbook of the life course* (pp. 413–436). New York: Plenum.

Schulenberg, J. E., O'Malley, P. M., Bachman, J. G., & Johnston, L. D. (2005). Early adult transitions and their relation to well-being and substance use. In R. A. Settersten, Jr., F. F. Furstenberg, Jr., & R. G. Rumbaut (Eds.), *On the frontier of adulthood: Theory, research, and public policy* (MacArthur network edited volume, pp. 417–453). Chicago: University of Chicago Press.

Schulenberg, J. E., Vondracek, F. W., & Crouter, A. C. (1984). The influence of the family on vocational development. *Journal of Marriage and the Family, 46,* 129–143.

Schulenberg, J. E., Vondracek, F. W., & Kim, J. R. (1993). Career certainty and short-term changes in work values during adolescence. *Career Development Quarterly, 41,* 268–284.

Schulenberg, J. E., Vondracek, F. W., & Nesselroade, J. R. (1988). Patterns of short-term changes in individual's work values: P-technique factor analyses of intra-individual variability. *Multivariate Behavioral Research, 23,* 377–395.

Schulenberg, J. E., & Zarrett, N. R. (2006). Mental health during emerging adulthood: Continuity and discontinuity in courses, causes, and functions. in J. J. Arnett & J. L. Tanner (Eds.), *Emerging adults in America: Coming of age in the 21st century* (pp. 135–172). Washington, DC: American Psychological Association.

Schunk, D. H., & Pajares, F. (2002). The development of academic self-efficacy. In A. Wigfield & J. S. Eccles (Eds.), *Development of achievement motivation* (pp. 15–31). San Diego, CA: Academic Press.

Schuster, C., O'Malley, P. M., Bachman, J. G., Johnston, L. D., & Schulenberg, J. E. (2001). Adolescent marijuana use and adult occupational attainment: A longitudinal study from age 18 to 28. *Substance Use and Misuse, 36,* 997–1014.

Shanahan, M. J. (2000). Pathways to adulthood in changing societies: Variability and mechanisms in life course perspective. *Annual Review of Sociology, 26,* 667–692.

Shanahan, M. J., & Flaherty, B. P. (2001). Dynamic patterns of time use in adolescence. *Child Development, 72,* 385–401.

Siennick, S. E., & Staff, J. (2008). Explaining the educational deficits of delinquent youths. *Criminology, 46,* 609–636.

Sinisalo, P. (2004). Changing work values and expressed educational plans of adolescents: A cross-sectional follow-up of three cohorts in Finland. *European Journal of Psychology of Education, 19,* 227–236.

Skorikov, V. B., & Vondracek, F. W. (1997). Longitudinal relationships between part-time work and career development in adolescents. *The Career Development Quarterly, 45,* 221–235.

Skorikov, V. B., & Vondracek, F. W. (1998). Vocational identity development: Its relation to other identity domains and to overall identity development. *Journal of Career Assessment, 6,* 13–35.

Skorikov, V. B., & Vondracek, F. W. (2007). Vocational identity. In V. B. Skorikov & W. Patton (Eds.), *Career development in childhood and adolescence* (pp. 143–168). Rotterdam, Netherlands: Sense Publishers.

Snow, K. L. (2007). Integrative views of the domains of child function: Unifying school readiness. In R. C. Pianta, M. J. Cox, & K. L. Snow (Eds.), *School readiness and the transition to kindergarten in the era of accountability* (pp. 197–216). Baltimore: Paul H. Brooks Publishing.

Spain, D., & Bianchi, S. M. (1996). *Balancing act: Motherhood, marriage, and employment among American women.* New York: Russell Sage Foundation.

Staff, J., & Mortimer, J. T. (2007). Educational and work strategies from adolescence to early adulthood: Consequences for educational attainment. *Social Forces, 85,* 1169–1194.

Staff, J., & Mortimer, J. T. (2008). Social class background and the "school to work" transition. *New Directions for Child and Adolescent Development, 119,* 55–69.

Staff, J., & Uggen, C. (2003). The fruits of good work: Early work experiences and adolescent deviance. *Journal of Research in Crime and Delinquency, 40,* 263–290.

Steinberg, L. D., & Cauffman, E. (1995). The impact of employment on adolescent development. *Annals of Child Development, 11,* 131–166.

Steinberg, L. D., & Dornbusch, S. M. (1991). Negative correlates of part-time employment during adolescence: Replication and elaboration. *Developmental Psychology, 27,* 304–313.

Steinberg, L. D., Fegley, S., & Dornbusch, S. M. (1993). Negative impact of part-time work on adolescent adjustment: Evidence from a longitudinal study. *Developmental Psychology, 29,* 171–180.

Steinberg, L. D., Greenberger, E., Garduque, L., Ruggiero, M., & Vaux, A. (1982). Effects of working on adolescent development. *Developmental Psychology, 18,* 385–395.

Stern, D., & Nakata, Y. (1989). Characteristics of high school students' paid jobs, and employment experience after graduation. In D. Stern & D. Eichorn (Eds.), *Adolescence and work: Influences of social structure, labor markets, and culture* (pp. 189–233). Hillsdale, NJ: Lawrence Erlbaum.

Stone, J. R., & Mortimer, J. T. (1998). The effect of adolescent employment on vocational development: Public and educational policy implications. *Journal of Vocational Behavior, 53,* 184–214.

Sullivan, M. L. (1989). *Getting paid: Youth crime and work in the inner city.* Ithaca, NY: Cornell University Press.

Super, D. E. (1954). *The psychology of careers.* New York: John Wiley & Sons.

Tracey, T. J. G., Robbins, S. B., & Hofsess, C. D. (2005). Stability and change in interests: A longitudinal study of adolescents from grades 8 through 12. *Journal of Vocational Behavior, 66,* 1–25.

Tucker, C. J., Barber, B. L., & Eccles, J. S. (2001). Advice about life plans from mothers, fathers, and siblings in always-married and divorced families during late adolescence. *Journal of Youth and Adolescence, 30,* 729–747.

Turner, S., & Lapan, R. T. (2002). Career self-efficacy and perceptions of parent support in adolescent career development. *Career Development Quarterly, 51,* 44–55.

Turner, S. L., & Lapan, R. T. (2003). The measurement of career interests among at-risk inner-city and middle-class suburban adolescents. *Journal of Career Assessment, 11,* 405–420.

Turner, S. L., Steward, J. C., & Lapan, R. T. (2004). Family factors associated with sixth-grade adolescents' math and science career interests. *Career Development Quarterly, 53,* 41–52.

Unemori, P., Omoregie, H., & Markus, H. R. (2004). Self-portraits: Possible selves in European-American, Chilean, Japanese and Japanese-American cultural contexts. *Self and Identity, 3,* 321–338.

U.S. Department of Education. (2007). *Digest of education statistics, 2006.* Washington, DC: U.S. Government Printing Office.

U.S. Department of Labor. (2000). *Report on the youth labor force.* Washington, DC: U.S. Government Printing Office.

U.S. Department of Labor. (2006). *College enrollment and work activity of 2005 high school graduates.* Washington, DC: Bureau of Labor Statistics.

Ventura, S. J., & Bachrach, C. A. (2000). Nonmarital childbearing in the United States, 1940–1999. *National Vital Statistics Reports, 48*(16). Hyattsville, MD: National Center for Health Statistics.

Vondracek, F. W. (2001). The developmental perspective in vocational psychology. *Journal of Vocational Behavior, 59,* 252–261.

Vondracek, F. W., Lerner, R. M., & Schulenberg, J. E. (1986). *Career development: A life-span developmental approach.* Hillsdale, NJ: Lawrence Erlbaum.

Vondracek, F. W., Schulenberg, J., Skorikov, V., Gillespie, L. K., & Wahlheim, C. (1995). The relationship of identity status to career indecision during adolescence. *Journal of Adolescence, 18,* 17–29.

Warren, J. R. (2002). Reconsidering the relationship between student employment and academic outcomes: A new theory and better data. *Youth and Society, 33,* 366–393.

Warren, J. R., & Lee, J. C. (2003). The impact of adolescent employment on high school dropout: Differences by individual and labor-market characteristics. *Social Science Research, 32,* 98–128.

Warren, J. R., LePore, P. C., & Mare, R. D. (2000). Employment during high school: Consequences for students' grades in academic courses. *American Educational Research Journal, 37,* 943–969.

Whiston, S. C., & Keller, B. K. (2004). The influences of the family of origin on career development: A review and analysis. *Counseling Psychologist, 32,* 493–568.

Wright, J. P., & Cullen, F. T. (2000). Juvenile involvement in occupational delinquency. *Criminology, 38,* 863–896.

Young, R. A., Ball, J., Valach, L., Turkel, H., & Wong, Y. S. (2003). The family career development project in Chinese Canadian families. *Journal of Vocational Behavior, 62,* 287–304.

Young, R. A., Marshall, S., Domene, J. F., Arato-Bolivar, J., Hayoun, R., Marshall, E., et al. (2006). Relationships, communication, and career in the parent-adolescent projects of families with and without challenges. *Journal of Vocational Behavior, 68,* 1–23.

Young, R. A., & Valach, L. (1994). Evaluation of career development programs from an action perspective. *Canadian Journal of Counseling, 28,* 299–307.

Young, R. A., Valach, L., Ball, J., Paseluikho, M. A., Wong, Y. S., DeVries, R. J., et al. (2001). Career development in adolescence as a family project. *Journal of Counseling Psychology, 48,* 190–202.

Zimmer-Gembeck, M. J., & Mortimer, J. T. (2006). Adolescent work, vocational development, and education. *Review of Educational Research, 76,* 537–566.

CHAPTER 9

Adolescence, Adolescents, and Media

DONALD F. ROBERTS, LISA HENRIKSEN, AND ULLA G. FOEHR

"I multi-task every single second I am on line. At this very moment I am watching TV, checking my e-mail every two minutes, reading a news-group about who shot JFK, burning some music to a CD and writing this message."

—A 17-year-old (cited in Lenhart, Rainie, & Lewis, 2001, p. 10)

To the extent that the young man quoted above is typical—and he certainly is not atypical—he lives in a home saturated with media. He is also likely to be alone, in his bedroom, because he has his own television, computer, radio, and cell phone. Before day's end, he will spend more than 6 hours using media, and because of media multitasking (i.e., using several media concurrently), he will be exposed to more than 8 hours of media messages (Roberts & Foehr, 2008; Roberts, Foehr, & Rideout, 2005). Either directly or incidentally, those messages describe, depict, and/or comment on the important and the trivial: gods and devils, violence and altruism, friendship and enmity, politics, professions, sex, drugs, beauty, baseball, body odor, Britney Spears—indeed, almost any dimension of human concern imaginable. More and more, those messages emanate from channels designed primarily, if not exclusively, for young people, and they are largely framed by an incessant hymn to consumerism (Christenson, Roberts, Strange, & Wild, 2004; Pecora, 1998).

Concern with what, if any, effect all those hours of exposure to messages from "outside" the family and local community have on our youth has a long history (Comstock & Scharrer, 2007; Roberts, 2003; Starker, 1989).

Apprehension about potentially harmful effects of media messages on youth extends back at least to Plato's banning of storytellers from *The Republic* and has reappeared with the emergence of each new communication technology, most recently in the controversy associated with attempts to control the Internet (e.g., the Communications Decency Act; the Child Online Protection Act). Given such a history, it is surprising that researchers concerned with adolescence have paid relatively little attention to mass media. The first edition of this *Handbook* (Adelson, 1980) ignored media, and until recently few textbooks on adolescent development devoted much attention to the role of media in adolescents' lives.

This chapter surveys a widely scattered empirical literature on media and adolescents. It focuses on youth from roughly 10 through 20 years old, and covers research on leisure time exposure to television, music, movies, print, and the new digital communication media. We begin with a summary of research on media use, then turn to several theories that have dominated much of the work on media effects. Finally, we briefly summarize research on media effects in topic areas of particular relevance to adolescence: violence and aggression, sex, substance use, and body image.

PATTERNS OF ADOLESCENT MEDIA USE

Amount of Media Use and Exposure

The second decade of life witnesses significant changes in young people's media use—changes in time devoted to media, in how that time is allocated among media, in the social contexts within which media are consumed, in the motivations for using media, and in the messages to which young viewers are exposed. The distinction between use and exposure is important, albeit seldom made prior to 1999 (Roberts, Foehr, Rideout, & Brodie, 1999). Measures of *media exposure* typically sum estimated time spent with various media (i.e., TV time + radio time + print time). Estimates of *media use*, however, adjust exposure time to account for concurrent use of several media, a common and rapidly growing phenomenon. Thus, for example, a teenager who spends an hour playing video games while simultaneously listening to music *uses* media for 1 hour, but is *exposed* to 2 hours of media messages. Media multitasking has probably occurred since the early twentieth century (e.g., reading while listening to a radio), but has grown as digital technology and miniaturized media have become more available (Roberts & Foehr, 2008). Indeed, one of the most noteworthy recent findings is that there was an hour increase in total daily media exposure from 1999 (7:29) to 2004 (8:33), but no change in amount of media use (6:19 vs. 6:21)—a difference that goes hand in hand with a concomitant increase in media multitasking (Roberts & Foehr, 2008; Roberts, et al., 2005).

Media exposure begins early; 0- to 1-year-olds average 1¾ hours of exposure daily (Rideout & Hammel, 2006). Exposure increases fairly rapidly until around 12 or 13 years, when it reaches about 8 hours daily. Exposure to screen media (television, videotapes, movies) decreases as adolescents' age increases, but overall media exposure continues to climb to nearly 8¾ hours daily during late adolescence (Roberts et al., 2005). Media use—person hours devoted to media of any kind—follows much the same pattern: 8- to 10-year-olds report just under 6 hours per day, and older adolescents report just over 6½ hours per day. In other words, approximately 25% of the time that U.S. adolescents use media, they use two or more media concurrently. This represents an 8% increase in the proportion of adolescents engaged in media multitasking since 1999 (Roberts et al., 1999, 2005). As noted earlier, most of the increase in overall media exposure is accounted for by increases in time spent with computers and video games, and we suspect that the associated rise in media multitasking largely explains the recent growth in overall exposure during later adolescence.

In spite of recent attention to young people's fascination with various interactive media, television continues to dominate their overall media exposure even in late adolescence, and when time devoted to viewing videotapes and movies is folded in, screen media exposure accounts for the largest part of the overall media budget throughout adolescence (Brown et al., 1990; Roberts & Foehr, 2003; Roberts, Foehr & Rideout, 2005). Screen media currently account for 55% of total media exposure among 8- to 10-year-olds and 39% among 15- to 18-year-olds (Roberts, Foehr & Rideout, 2005). Among other things, the substantial amount of time adolescents devote to screen media (particularly television) probably reflects the fact that two-thirds of U.S. 8- to 18-year-olds have a television in their bedroom (Roberts, 2000; Roberts & Foehr, 2003; Roberts, Foehr & Rideout, 2005; Wartella, Heintz, Aidman, & Mazzarella, 1990), and that much television exposure consists of "monitoring" rather than attentive viewing (Comstock & Scharrer, 2007). That said, it is important to note that screen media exposure declines across the adolescent years; 15- to 18-year-olds view a full hour less than 8- to 10-year-olds, likely reflecting increased time that older adolescents devote to activities outside the home (e.g., school, work, social engagements).

Several contrasting, age-related patterns in exposure to other media emerge. One is a steady and substantial increase in the time adolescents spend with audio media—radio, recordings, digital streaming—which for them are largely synonymous with music media (Christenson & Roberts, 1998). Music exposure climbs from about an hour daily among 8- to 10-year-olds to almost 2½ hours by late adolescence, ultimately challenging television as older teens' medium of choice. Indeed, several researchers argue that music media rank as the most important during late adolescence (Christenson & Roberts, 1998; Larson, Kubey, & Colletti; 1989; Roberts & Henriksen, 1990; Roe, 1987).

The likelihood of engaging in leisure reading on any given day is unrelated to age, a change from a decade ago when there was a significant decline from early to late adolescence in leisure reading time (Roberts et al., 1999). From 8 through 18 years, about 70% of youth report spending at least 5 minutes daily reading a newspaper, magazine, or book, and average print exposure hovers around 40 minutes daily across age. There is, however, a drop in the proportion of older teens devoting at least 30 minutes daily to leisure reading, with most of the decrease occurring for books (Roberts et al., 2005), a decline we suspect is related to increased school-related reading required of older teens. Remarkably, we have located no research on the time youth spend reading online.

Video game time (handheld and console games) declines steadily with age, from just over 1 hour daily among 8- to 10-year-olds to just over one-half hour among 15- to 18-year-olds, primarily because a large proportion of adolescents cease to engage in video gaming as they grow older. For example, in 2004, 58% of 8- to 14-year-olds spent at least 5 minutes video gaming on any given day; among 15- to 18-year-olds, the proportion was 39% (age-related declines also occur in the proportions spending an hour or more daily with video games—from 27% among 8- to 10-year-olds

to 15% among 15- to 18-year-olds). That said, the time young people spend with video games has increased from an average of 26 minutes daily in 1999 to 49 minutes in 2004, partly a result of widespread availability of handheld games (Roberts, Foehr, & Rideout, 2005).

Adolescent computer use has also increased substantially. By 2000, most adolescents had used a computer (Kaiser Family Foundation, 2001), and their time spent with computers more than doubled between 1999 (27 minutes daily) and 2004 (62 minutes daily) (Roberts et al., 2005). Computer time also increases with age, more than doubling between 8 to 10 years and 15 to 18 years (see Table 9.1). Similarly, the proportion of 12- to 17-year-olds using the Internet "at least occasionally" increased from 73% in 2000 (Lenhart, Rainie, & Lewis, 2001) to 93% in 2007 (Lenhart, Madden, Macgill, & Smith, 2007). The growing appeal among adolescents of computers and the Internet access they provide seems largely attributable to the technology's increasing ability to serve multiple functions simultaneously—functions of particular importance to teenagers. First, computers are assuming many of the functions of older media, rapidly becoming a primary music and audiovisual channel (i.e., streaming music, television, and motion picture content) and a means to play DVDs, CDs, and stored MP3 files. Second, computers provide fingertip access to information, and more than three quarters of 12- to 17-year-olds report using them to obtain information about news, current events, entertainment or sports, and so forth (Pew Internet & American Life Project, 2006). Third, and perhaps most important for adolescents, computers (and "smart phones"—cell phones that function like computers) simultaneously provide an increasingly important venue for social interaction (Hoffner, 2008; Lenhart, Rainie, & Lewis, 2001), blurring the boundaries between mass and interpersonal communication and enabling young people both to interact with others and to produce and comment about, as well as consume, media content. It is small wonder

TABLE 9.1. Average Daily U.S. Adolescent Leisure-Time Media Exposure by Age in 2004

	8-18 years	8-10 years	11-14 years	15-18 years
Television	3:04	3:17	3:16	2:36
Videos/DVDs/movies	1:11	1:24	1:09	1:05
Audio (radio, CDs, tapes)	1:44	:59	1:42	2:24
Print media	:43	:44	:41	:45
Video games	:49	1:05	:52	:33
Computer	1:02	:37	1:02	1:22
Total media exposure	*8:33*	*8:05*	*8:41*	*8:44*
Total media use	*6:21*	*5:52*	*6:33*	*6:31*

Note: Cell entries are means (hh:mm). Adapted from Roberts, Foehr, & Rideout (2005).

that more and more adolescents nominate computers as their preferred medium (Knowledge Networks, 2002).

Predictors of Media Use

Adolescent media exposure varies with a number of background characteristics, although the pattern of relationships is beginning to change from what it was just a few years ago. Two decades ago adolescent girls devoted more time than did boys to both television and radio (Brown, Childers, Bauman, & Koch, 1990). Recent data, however, reveal no gender differences in television exposure, although girls continue to spend substantially more time than boys listening to music (Roberts & Foehr, 2003; Roberts, et al., 2005). Boys play video games more than girls, and there are differences in the specific computer activities that boys and girls prefer. However the gender gap in overall computer time reported some years ago seems to have closed (Lenhart, et al., 2007; Roberts & Foehr, 2003; Roberts, et al., 2005).

Traditionally, indicators of family socioeconomic status (SES) such as household income and parent education were correlated negatively with young people's television viewing and positively with print exposure (e.g., Schramm, Lyle, & Parker, 1961; Lyle & Hoffman, 1972;

Comstock & Scharrer, 2007) and computer use (e.g., Roberts, et al., 1999). These patterns, however, may be changing. The Kaiser Family Foundation's most recent national survey of young people's media use found no relationship between household income and either print exposure or time spent with computers, although level of parent education remains a strong predictor of both. Perhaps most surprising, the negative relationships between screen exposure and both family income and parent education have dissipated; that is, no relationship emerged between two of the most common measures of SES and screen time (Roberts, et al., 2005). Comstock and Scharrer (2007) urge caution on the basis of a single study, but speculate that perhaps television has "become so ubiquitous as to overshadow any previously distinguishing socioeconomic differences" (p. 16). Youth from single-parent homes also spend more time with media in general and television in particular, probably because, lacking the energy and/or economic resources to provide alternative activities, single parents are less likely to control media use (Brown et al., 1990; Medrich, Roizen, Rubin, & Buckley, 1982; Roberts & Foehr, 2003). Finally, race and ethnicity remain strong predictors of media exposure (Roberts & Foehr, 2003; Roberts et al., 2005). Overall media exposure among African American 8- to 18-year-olds averages 10:10 daily; Hispanic youth average 8:52, and White youth report 7:58. Most of the racial/ethnic differences in overall exposure are accounted for by screen media; African American youth report substantially more viewing of television, prerecorded videos, and movies in theaters (5:53 daily), followed by Hispanic youth (4:37), then White youth (3:47). Moreover, these relationships largely withstand controls for SES, supporting Comstock's observation, now nearly 2 decades old, that television "occupies a particularly prominent place in the lives of young persons in black households" (1991, p. 71).

Comstock (1991) noted that "household television centrality" substantially increases the likelihood that children and adolescents are heavy television viewers. Indicators of television centrality include a household television that operates during most waking hours, norms that permit viewing at all hours and occasions, absence of rules regulating viewing, and high levels of viewing among adults. Although each of the various indicators tends to occur more frequently in lower socioeconomic households and in African American households, they are by no means limited to these groups. Even when such factors as race or household socioeconomic status are controlled, adolescents from homes in which television plays a "central" role view significantly more of it (Medrich et al., 1982; Roberts & Foehr, 2003; Roberts, et al., 2005). Moreover, subsequent to leaving home for college, a setting in which time to view television is presumably limited, youth from homes where television had been central continue to view more (Kenny, 1985, reported in Comstock & Scharrer, 1999). In short, household television centrality during childhood and adolescence appears to cultivate lifelong viewing habits.

Averages, of course, conceal a great deal of information. For any given medium on any given day, an adolescent's exposure may range from 0 to well over 5 hours. Since personal computers have not yet reached saturation levels (85% of 8- to 18-year-olds live in households with a personal computer), it is not surprising that almost 40% of U.S. 8- to 18-year-olds report no computer use on a given day as opposed to 28% reporting more than 1 hour daily (32% report less than an hour). However, given that the typical U.S. household contains three television sets, and U.S. youth average more than 3 hours of TV viewing daily, it may be a bit more unexpected that on any given day almost 20% report *no* television exposure. At the other extreme, 20% of all youth report in excess of 5 hours daily television viewing—some claiming as much as 8 or 9 hours (Roberts et al., 2005).

Furthermore, it appears that media use begets media use. When youth classified as light, moderate, or heavy users of one medium are compared on exposure to other media (e.g., when light and heavy television viewers' use of all media *except* television is examined), those classified as heavy users of one medium report from 2 to 3 hours more exposure to the remaining media than those classified as light or moderate users. For example, youth who spend between 1 and 5 hours daily watching television spend slightly more than 5 hours with other media, while those who report 5 or more hours of daily television viewing spend 7½ hours with other media. Similarly, youth classed as heavy computer users (more than 2 hours daily) report 3 hours more daily use of all other media than those classed as low or moderate computer users (Roberts, et al., 2005; Roberts & Foehr, 2003).

Finally, studies consistently find greater than average amounts of reading among teenagers who watched above average amounts of television (California Assessment Program, 1980; Morgan, 1980; Roberts et al., 2005). Morgan speculates that high television use and high print use may go hand in hand because heavy users are more interested in media in general. The phenomenon may also derive from greater use of "escapist" reading material by adolescents who watch a lot of TV, material of the sort that may be compatible with viewing television while reading (Comstock & Scharrer, 1999). The value judgment implicit in the term *escapist* gives pause, but the idea that reading and viewing occur at the same time has merit.

Media Multitasking

Differences in media exposure between heavy and moderate users of various individual media, particularly computers, offer further evidence of the growing frequency of media multitasking among adolescents. Value judgments about the nature of the content aside, more than any other medium, the computer facilitates use of several channels simultaneously. Adolescents surf the Web as they stream music, play video games, and/or watch television. Indeed, it strains credulity to think that the remarkably high amounts of overall media exposure reported by some adolescents could be achieved were it not for such media multitasking.

Foehr's (2006) examination of media multitasking supports such reasoning. Thirty percent or more of 7th- through 12th-grade youth report using other media "most of the time" when they watch TV, use computers, or listen to music (another 30% media multitask "some of the time"). Conversely, about one-fifth of teens say they typically do not engage in concurrent media use. Moreover, young people who report more exposure to media also report more media multitasking—arguably two sides of the same coin. Additionally, youth classified as high sensation seekers report multitasking more often than their low-sensation-seeking counterparts, possibly an indication of stimulation-seeking behavior (Foehr, 2006).

Environmental factors strongly influence media multitasking. For example, young people from homes containing a computer, from homes in which the TV can be seen from the computer, and from homes in which the television plays a central role are more likely to multitask. Indeed, the computer plays a central role in much media multitasking. When adolescents engage in any particular computer activity, they are likely also concurrently

engaged in a secondary activity, other media activities dominate as secondary activities, and another computer activity is most likely to be paired with the primary computer activity (e.g., instant messaging is often paired with doing homework on the computer). The proportion of shared time associated with various computer activities ranges from 60% of time spent doing homework on a computer to 83% of time spent sending/receiving e-mail. Indeed, as we will see below, much of the impetus for recent increases in media multitasking arguably derives from the growing use by adolescents of digital media for social communication.

Given the relative newness of research on media multitasking, an important issue remaining to be examined is whether and how such multitasking influences young people's information processing, comprehension, and communication behavior—both as receivers and senders of messages.

Contexts of Media Use

Historical and age-related changes in the social context of adolescent media use have implications both for the functions that media serve and for their possible consequences. As adolescents grow older, increasingly more of their media consumption occurs without adult supervision or guidance—that is, either in the presence of peers or siblings or while alone (Roberts & Foehr, 2003).

Television is sometimes described as the most family-oriented medium, and the decline in adolescents' television viewing has been characterized as an indicator of young people's attempts to establish independence from, or at least to renegotiate, parental controls (Kubey & Csikszentmihalyi, 1990; Larson, 1995; Larson & Kubey, 1983; Larson et al., 1990). However, such characterizations are based on data gathered in the 1980s or earlier, when three major networks competed for a family audience and the bulk of viewing typically occurred around a single household television. The situation today is quite different. The proliferation of television sets within

U.S. households, their migration to young people's bedrooms (Roberts, 2000; Roberts et al., 2005), and industry recognition of adolescents' purchasing power (Pecora, 1998; Teen spending, 2006; Teenage Research Unlimited, 2004) has led to niche programming aimed at young audiences, undermining the notion of television as a family medium. Television may remain the medium most likely to be shared with family, but by the beginning of adolescence, parent–child coviewing is more the exception than the rule. Family sharing of music, movies and video, digital media, and print appears to be even less common.

Sheer time spent with age-mates identifies the peer group as an important context for adolescent behavior, including media behavior. From 12 years onward, more than one-third of adolescents watch television "mainly" in the presence of friends or siblings; almost 60% are mainly with friends or siblings when watching movies or videotapes (Roberts & Foehr, 2003). Group viewing of videotapes is the norm for 9th and 10th graders with access to a VCR (Greenberg & Heeter, 1987), who are more likely to watch television and rented movies (frequently R-rated) with a girlfriend, boyfriend, or other peers than with parents or alone. Similarly, music listening often occurs in the company of friends—at parties, concerts, and dances, as a background to interaction, and as grist for the conversation mill (Christenson & Roberts, 1998); Roe (1985) characterizes popular music listening as "essentially a group phenomenon" (p. 355).

By mid-adolescence, however, the most typical context for media consumption appears to be in the solitude of adolescents' bedrooms. Reading has always been a solitary pastime, but adolescents more and more engage most other media while alone. Over 60% of 7th–12th graders claim to be alone when they use computers or play video games. By late adolescence more than one-third state they are "mainly alone" when they watch television, and diary data indicate that over 40% of all viewing time transpires in solitude (Roberts et al., 1999). Although music listening may be a "group phenomenon" in that it serves various social functions, most adolescent exposure to radio and recordings tends to be solitary and personal (Christenson, 1994; Christenson & Roberts, 1998; Larson & Kubey, 1983).

In short, as youth progress through adolescence, television viewing decreases, music listening and computer use increase, and media usage tends to migrate to adolescents' bedrooms. Media exposure increasingly occurs in the company of friends or siblings or while alone, another indicator of increasing adolescent independence from family and the importance of both peer groups and solitude as contexts for adolescent development (Christenson & Roberts, 1998; Harris, 1998; Kubey & Csikszentmihalyi, 1990; Larson, 1995; Sang, Schmitz, & Tasche, 1992).

DIGITALLY MEDIATED SOCIAL INTERACTION

A substantial part of the appeal of digital media (i.e., computers, smart phones) to adolescents derives from their facilitation of interpersonal connectivity concurrent with their use as more traditional channels of media content. Indeed, some argue that for many young people, social communication has become the primary function of the new communication technologies (e.g., Boyd, 2008; Boyd & Ellison, 2007), although Lenhart and her colleagues (2007) find that information gathering continues to trump social communication on the Internet. Subrahmanyam and Greenfield (2008) list 11 forms of online activities that constitute social communication and that are currently engaged in by large numbers of adolescents: e-mail, instant messaging, text messaging, chat rooms, bulletin boards, blogs, social networking sites (SNSs), video sharing, photo sharing, massively multiplayer online computer games (MMOGs), and virtual worlds. Although most of these began as computer-based activities, several are now also supported by cell phones (i.e., smart phones, which are rapidly becoming handheld versions of laptop computers), personal digital assistants, and/or cameras with wireless capabilities, all of which enhance the convenience and appeal of digitally mediated social interaction.

The Internet, of course, forms the backbone of digital social communication. The Pew Internet & American Life Project (2006) reports that 93% of U.S. 12- to 17-year-olds use the Internet "at least occasionally" (61% report daily use), and that it is increasingly treated as a venue for social communication. Similarly, the mobile phone is fast emerging as essential teenage equipment (Batista, 2003; Tobin, 2005). In 2006, 63% of 12- to 17-year-olds reported having their own cell phone (up from 45% in 2004), and 60% said they use it to talk to friends "at least several times a week" (39% reported daily conversations) (Pew Internet & American Life Project, 2006). In addition, 9 of 10 teens with cell phones have text messaging capabilities, and two-thirds claim to text message daily (Subrahmanyam & Greenfield, 2008), a means of social communication that, along with instant messaging, seems rapidly to be replacing adolescents' e-mail activity. Lenhart and colleagues (2007) classify 28% of U.S. adolescents as "multichannel teens"—that is, teens who have mobile phones and Internet access, send text messages and instant messages, and use social network sites (SNS)—stating that they are "notable for the intensity with which they use connective technologies" (p. 19).

Another indicator of the growing presence and importance of online social communication is the number of teens who engage in some form of online content creation, arguably activities that to a greater or lesser degree constitute social interaction (i.e., to create and share a photograph, story, or journal entry is an act of social communication) (Jenkins, 2006; Lenhart et al., 2007). Fully 59% of U.S. 12- to 17-year-olds (64% of online teens) have engaged in at least one of the following forms of online content creation: sharing personal artistic creations (photos, stories, artwork, videos); creating Web pages or blogs for others; creating their own online journal or blog; maintaining a personal Web page; or remixing online content into new creations. In addition, 55% of U.S. 12- to 17-year-olds report having created a profile on a social networking site (Lenhart et al., 2007) and 44% have posted photos (Pew Internet, & American Life Project, 2006), proportions that lead Lenhart and her colleagues to conclude that "participatory culture" is blossoming among young people largely because social networking applications (e.g., Facebook, MySpace) provide a means to display content created elsewhere in a centralized location (Lenhart et al., 2007, pp. 2–3). The result is the growing importance in adolescent life of "participatory media" and "participatory culture" (Jenkins, 2006), both of which operate to encourage artistic creation and sharing. Nevertheless, it is also interesting to note that teens most involved in such content creation are equally or more likely than other teens to participate in a variety of offline activities (e.g., participating in school-affiliated extracurricular activities, in a sports club activity not affiliated with school, holding a part-time job; Lenhart et al. 2007).

Although content creation and sharing is important to adolescents, the word *social* remains the operant term in social networking. It is the ability to initiate and maintain social contact that drives connective technology's popularity with so many young people. Over 80% of networking teens use SNSs to keep in touch with friends they infrequently see, and 91% say they use SNSs to stay in touch with friends they frequently see in person. Indeed, fears that digital connectivity may displace face-to-face contact seem unwarranted. Over 30% of all teens spend face-to-face time with their friends on a daily basis, another 34% spend such time several times per week, and 24% at least once a week. Perhaps more interesting, the proportion of teens reporting daily in-person time with friends increases slightly among digitally connected teens (e.g., 38% of teens who use SNSs report daily face-to-face contact with friends). Similarly, neither the computer nor the cell phone has replaced landline telephones; 39% of all teens and 41% of teens with cell phones report daily use of landline telephones (Lenhart et al., 2007). It appears, then, that much in the same way that adolescents have adopted new media alongside rather than in place of older media (resulting in substantial increases in media multitasking), so too are they combining connective technologies with more traditional forms of interpersonal interaction (resulting in multichannel, social communicators), expanding rather than substituting channels for social interaction. In other words, today's teens continue to engage in high levels of face-to-face communication even as they are flocking to digital channels, text messaging, and SNSs. And while it is true that communication patterns vary across subpopulations that engage in different forms of digital connectivity (i.e., cell phone users vs. SNS users), those who engage in more digital social communication tend also to engage in more social communication of any kind.

The merging of digital connectivity with more traditional types of social interaction (i.e., face-to-face, landline telephones, handwritten notes) raises a number of issues concerning whether and how these new channels and forms of social communication may affect adolescents' relationships with others: families, friends, peers, strangers, and so on. Subrahmanyam and Greenfield (2008) offer an extensive and perceptive examination of these questions within a framework of some of the key developmental tasks of adolescence: identity, autonomy, intimacy, sexuality (e.g., Hill, 1983).

Subrahmanyam and Greenfield (2008) posit a number of possible consequences of online social communication, both positive and negative. For example, they address concerns about such things as increased contact with strangers, a prospect that brings with it the very real threat of young people's encountering harassment, hate speech, and unwanted sexual solicitation. The ease with which people can maintain anonymity makes the potential for negative consequences quite real, particularly among younger users or more troubled adolescents, who might be at risk for reasons unrelated to digital connectivity (e.g., depression, feelings of isolation or inadequacy, or family conflict; Wolak, Mitchell, & Finkelhor, 2003). For example, although between 2000 and 2005, the *incidence* of adolescents experiencing unwanted sexual solicitation and harassment on line declined, possibly as a result of more effective law enforcement and better education that same period also witnessed increases in the *proportion* of adolescents reporting online exposure to harassment and to unwanted sexual materials (Wolak, Mitchell, & Finkelhor, 2007). That said, it also appears that as some of the dangers inherent in digital connectivity have become more widely recognized, particularly among young people, and as various controls have been established (e.g., privacy measures, restrictions on access, registration requirements), a substantial majority of adolescents seem to be exercising some caution and using many of the available controls (Hindaju & Patchin, 2008; Lenhart et al., 2007; Subrahmanyam & Greenfield, 2008).

Additionally, there are several possible positive consequences of online contact with strangers. For example, one survey has found that online communication with unknown others helps to relieve feelings of loneliness or social anxiety (Gross, Juvnen, & Gable, 2002), and one of the few experimental studies to look at digital social communication demonstrated that interaction with unknown peers can help teens recover from the sting of social rejection (Gross, 2007). Similarly, adolescents seek and obtain information from strangers by accessing numerous discussion groups and bulletin boards covering a wide variety of youth-relevant topics, ranging from music, sports, and pop culture to health issues, interpersonal relations, and sexuality (e.g., Suzuki & Beale, 2006; Suzuki & Calzo, 2004). There are several reasons that teenagers like to obtain information from online interaction with strangers.

A minimal list includes the anonymity of such communication (making it easier to ask sensitive questions), the opportunity to obtain information passively (looking at responses to other people's questions), the breadth of such responses (information from a much wider and diverse array of sources than just one's immediate circle of family and friends), and convenience (information is available on demand, 24 hours daily) (Subrahmanyam & Greenfield, 2008).

Other issues related to the consequences of adolescents' heavy use of online social communication include whether digital connectivity harms or enhances family relations, peer relations, romantic relations, school performance, and identity development. In each instance, Subrahmanyam and Greenfield (2008) cite evidence supporting both outcomes, but generally conclude that the positives outweigh the negatives, and generally dispute the notion that these new forms of social communication cause the problems most often discussed. Rather, they argue the evidence seems to indicate that negative behaviors that have long existed are "simply being transferred to a new stage—from offline to online" (Brooks-Gunn & Donahue, 2008, p. 6).

Research concerned with online social communication is in its infancy. Both the forms of online social interaction and teenagers' adoption of the social activities they make available continue to change quite rapidly. For example, the proportion of adolescents from homes with Internet access went from 47% in 1999 to 74% in 2004; the proportion of U.S. teenagers with cell phones went from a trivial number at the end of the twentieth century to almost two-thirds by 2006; text messaging, although ubiquitous, is a relatively new phenomenon among U.S. youth; and this year's most popular social networking site runs a good chance of being obsolete before today's high school freshman graduates (*Washington Post,* 2007). Moreover, the empirical data relevant to young people's online social communication consists almost entirely of correlational studies (many

of which suffer from the bias of using online samples) or of analyses of various forms of social content (e.g., the content of bulletin boards, lurking in chat rooms). Causal inferences about many of the relationships noted above are simply not warranted. It is clear, however, that online social communication has become an integral part of adolescents' lives, and that, given its potential to play a role in key developmental tasks, a good deal more research is most definitely warranted.

MEDIA AND ADOLESCENT DEVELOPMENT

Attempts to integrate developmental theory with research on media use and effects generally proceed from either or both of two fundamental notions. One concerns the importance of an array of tasks or issues that adolescents engage on their way to adulthood. The second views adolescence as a period of psychological fragmentation associated with, among other things, exploration of a variety of potential "selves." Ultimately, more or less consciously, adolescents construct their own evolving worldviews and an assortment of attitudes, beliefs, and behaviors that define each individual.

Theories of adolescent development typically recognize a number of tasks or issues that adolescents must resolve (Conger & Peterson, 1985; Feldman & Elliot, 1990; Violato & Holden, 1987) and that may come into focus at different times for different youth (Coleman, 1993). Regardless of when adolescents confront a particular developmental issue, uncertainty associated with the task engenders a need for relevant information. Intense focus on an issue and "lived experience" (i.e., a construct that encompasses the ways in which background variables, developmental status, and other factors "differentiate one person's experience of day-to-day occurrences from that of another"; Brown, 2000, p. 36) interact to influence how any particular message is interpreted. Thus, depending on the issue, two teenagers may derive quite different meanings and gratifications from the same television program. For example, adolescent girls interpreted and responded to sexual media content differently depending on whether they had yet to confront, were confronting, or had already confronted the issue of sex and sexuality (Brown, White, & Nikopoulou, 1993).

A central adolescent task is identity formation—that is, defining the self in terms of attributes displayed across multiple roles or personae (e.g., academic, athletic, romantic, sexual; identity in relation to parents, peers, community; etc.; Brown, 2000; Harter, 1990a, 1990b; Larson, 1995; Markus & Nuriuis, 1986). Each of the myriad decisions adolescents face (e.g., how to behave on a date, whether to study, to take drugs, to go to college) adds to their continually evolving "lived experience" (Brown, 2000), and contributes to values, beliefs, and goals that guide future behaviors (Harter, 1999; Marcia, 1980). All of this points to adolescence as a period of rapid change and attendant uncertainty, conditions long associated with increased information seeking (Berlyne, 1965). The uncertainty inherent in adolescence emerges just when parental controls on information seeking in general and media use in particular begin to weaken. Therefore, adolescents increasingly take control of their own information and media choices. Finally, contemporary media often address highly salient topics (i.e., sex, drugs, and the many facets of pop culture) that parents and other adults are likely to ignore, avoid, or know relatively little about. Thus, media emerge, almost by default, as potentially powerful sources of information for adolescents who are self-socializing to the adult world (Arnett, 1995; Brown, 2000; Christenson & Roberts, 1998; Larson, 1995; Roberts, 1993).

As youth construct their identity, they may use media to relieve anxiety about developmental changes, explore alternative solutions to problems, reinforce the choices they make, or perhaps most important, reflect on who they are and who they may become. Most exploration of potential selves occurs in solitude, when adolescents explore their private selves. Given that much of contemporary Western adolescents' private (solitary) time occurs in the context of mass media, and because media content frequently touches on important adolescent issues and depicts a wide array of potential roles and personae, media are arguably increasingly important socialization agents for contemporary youth (Arnett, 1995; Bandy, 2006; Brown, 2000; Larson, 1995; Markus & Nuriuis, 1986; Roberts, 1993; Steele & Brown, 1995; Strouse & Fabes, 1985).

Motivations for Media Use

Teens use media for various reasons: entertainment, tension relief, staying current with popular culture, learning about the world, sensation seeking, escape from loneliness, and many others (for reviews, see Christenson & Roberts, 1998; Dominick, 1996; Rubin, 2002). One distillation of the literature suggests five, superordinate categories of uses and gratifications (Dominick, 1996):

1. *Diversion:* seeking pleasure, relaxation, escape from boredom or worries, mood management. This is frequently labeled the "entertainment" function, and tends to dominate adolescents' stated reasons for using media.

2. *Cognition:* seeking or acquiring information, ranging from monitoring current events via news media, to learning the alphabet from Sesame Street or norms for various aspects of human behavior from entertainment content. It is important to note that much of the information acquired is *incidental*—neither intentionally sought nor produced to teach or inform (e.g., screen portrayals of violence; "thin ideal" depictions of women).

3. *Social utility:* facilitating relationships with family, friends, or desired social groups; a social lubricant; a source of "conversational

currency" (Dominick, 1996); for "parasocial interaction" (i.e., establishing vicarious social relationships with media and people in the media; Horton & Wohl, 1956; Rubin, Perse, & Powell, 1985).

4. *Withdrawal:* establishing barriers between the self and others, whether to avoid conflict, ensure uninterrupted attention and focus, or simply obtain solitude.

5. *Personal identity:* assisting in establishing a sense of self through the "auditioning" of potential roles and identities; building self-confidence; seeking moral guidance, social acceptance, or status. Although this final category might be distributed across the first four, its clear relevance to the developmental tasks of adolescence argues for keeping it separate (Brown, 2000; Christenson & Roberts, 1998; McQuail, Blumler, & Brown, 1972).

The propensity for different media to gratify these needs and the factors that influence individual media choices vary substantially. Moreover, gratifications obtained are not always those that are sought. Although youth may turn on the television simply to have fun or to escape boredom, often they incidentally learn about the latest fashion, confirm or disconfirm existing beliefs or values, experience a change in mood, and so forth. When asked directly, adolescents typically say that they use media for pleasure; to fill time or relieve boredom and loneliness; and to create, change, or maintain certain moods (Arnett, 1995; Christenson & Roberts, 1998; Wells, 1990). The social uses and meanings that media offer also provide an important key to understanding their role in the lives of adolescents. Media in general, and music media in particular, serve "quasi-social" functions for adolescents when used to relieve feelings of loneliness by invoking or replacing absent peers (Gantz, Gartenberg, Pearson, & Schiller, 1978; Larson, et al., 1989; Roe, 1984). In addition, solitary listening may provide social capital helpful in earning status with peers; for example, pop

music "experts" tend to have more friends and enjoy enhanced social status (Adoni, 1978; Brown & O'Leary, 1971).

Theoretical Approaches to Media Effects

Three theoretical approaches most frequently applied to media effects research are cultivation theory (Gerbner, Gross, Morgan, Signorelli, & Shanahan, 2002), social cognitive theory, particularly as it applies to observational learning (Bandura, 1986, 2002), and various conceptualizations of schematic information processing (Berkowitz, 1990; Berkowitz & Rogers, 1986; Fiske & Taylor, 1991; Schank & Abelson, 1977; Shrum, 2002; Zillmann, 2002).

Cultivation theory posits (1) that mass media systems in general and television in particular present highly uniform pictures of the world that tend to conceal their biased and selective nature (e.g., television's world is more violent and more male dominated than the real world); (2) that most people consume media nonselectively; and (3) that high exposure "cultivates" acceptance of the media's view of the world (Gerbner et al., 2002; Morgan, 1988). Cultivation research is dominated by correlational studies relating amount of television exposure to beliefs and attitudes characteristic of the television view of the world. For example, subsequent to documenting that television portrays the world as a mean and scary place, Gerbner and associates found that adolescents who viewed a lot of television were substantially more likely than light viewers to report being afraid to walk alone in the city at night. Heavy viewers also overestimated both the percentage of people involved in violence and the frequency with which police use violence (Gerbner, Gross, Signorielli, Morgan, & Jackson-Beeck, 1979).

Fundamental questions regarding the legitimacy of many of the causal inferences drawn from cultivation studies have been raised (e.g., Comstock, 1991; Hirsch, 1980, 1981; Potter, 1993; Shrum, 1995, 1998). Nevertheless, numerous cultivation studies indicate a strong association between amount of exposure and acceptance of television's worldview even when relevant third variables are controlled, and identify a variety of moderating conditions that influence these consequences (Gerbner, Gross, Morgan, & Signorielli, 1980; Hawkins & Pingree, 1980; Shanahan & Morgan, 1999; Signorielli & Morgan, 1990).

Media research employing social cognitive theory's conceptualization of observational learning focuses on cognitive and psychological processes as they relate to how media portrayals influence learning and/or performance of observed behavior. According to social cognitive theory, when people pay attention to and think about information from others or from media, they acquire new or modify existing mental representations. What is observed, learned, or performed depends on both characteristics of the modeled display (e.g., is the behavior rewarded? performed by an attractive model?) and characteristics of the observer (e.g., age, gender, preexisting beliefs and attitudes). Learned symbolic representations (i.e., mental constructs) serve to guide subsequent behavior depending on such factors as feelings of self-efficacy, opportunity, perceived appropriateness, expectations of reinforcement, and the like (Bandura, 1986, 2002). Thus, for example, relative to youth who see a model punished for aggressive behavior, those who see aggression either rewarded or eliciting no consequences subsequently behave more aggressively (Bandura, Ross, & Ross, 1963b).

Various approaches to schematic information processing implicate (1) how the mental representations (schemas, scripts, etc.) people store in memory influence social judgments (Fiske & Taylor, 1991; Schank & Abelson, 1977), (2) factors influencing schema accessibility, (Berkowitz, 1990; Higgins, 1996; Sanbonmatsu & Fazio, 1991), and (3) factors implicated in the development of schema, with some recent attention to the role played by media (Roskos-Ewoldsen, Roskos-Ewoldsen, & Carpentier, 2002; Shrum, 2002; Zillmann, 2002). Media scholars have long held that to some degree one's prior mental representation of the world influences interpretation of new information (e.g., Boulding, 1966; Roberts, 1971; Schramm, 1971). Schema theories predict which mental constructs are brought to mind. The degree to which those constructs influence interpretation and judgment (i.e., are primed or activated) depends on the nature of the portrayal in relation to individual and contextual factors. For example, for one person, a fight scene might elicit thoughts primarily associated with violence or aggression, ranging from shouting matches to gunfights to riots. For another, or for the same person under different conditions, the portrayed fight might elicit primarily thoughts of pain, fear, flight, and the nature of victims. Interpretation of the portrayal varies depending on which schema have been primed—that is, brought into focal awareness and used to interpret the scene. Additionally, the act of attending and interpreting influences subsequent accessibility of whatever schema a portrayal implicates. Thus, individuals who see a fight scene are more likely than those who do not to interpret a subsequent, ambiguous scene or event as aggressive or as fearful. To the extent that schema are primed, judgments about media content are affected; to the extent that media content is attended to, schemas are primed and accessibility of associated schemas is affected (Roskos-Ewoldsen et al., 2002).

Although not exclusively, and not always explicitly, these three general theoretical approaches underlie much of the research concerned with media effects on adolescents' perceptions, attitudes, and behaviors.

MEDIA EFFECTS ON ADOLESCENTS

The following review briefly summarizes research examining media influences on adolescents in the realms of violence and aggression, sexual beliefs and behavior, body image, and substance use—topics chosen because they represent areas of public concern and bodies of empirical research.

Violence and Aggression

Although criticisms of analyses of violent media content abound (Potter, 2002), there is little question that portrayals of violence are a mainstay of media content, particularly for television and film (e.g., Gerbner & Gross, 1976; Gerbner, et al., 1979; Gerbner, Gross, Morgan, & Signorielli, 1980) and video games (Dietz, 1998; Smith, Lachlan, & Tamborini, 2003). An examination of 3 years (1994–1997) of U.S. television based on approximately 2,700 hours of material each year, found that over 60% of entertainment programs portray some violence, with almost a third portraying nine or more violent interactions (Smith et al., 1998). More important, violence is largely portrayed in ways that experimental research has demonstrated are likely to increase viewers' learning of, desensitization to, and/or fear of aggressive behavior. For example, television violence is seldom punished, frequently justified, and often performed by attractive characters—all contextual variables that increase learning, desensitization, or fear in potentially undesirable ways (Smith et al., 1998; Strasburger, Wilson, & Jordan, 2009).

Concern with effects of media violence on youth dates at least from early twentieth-century criticisms of pulp fiction, penny westerns, and silent films (Starker, 1989). Some of the first empirical research on media effects of any sort examined young adolescents' responses to violent motion pictures (Charters, 1933; Peterson & Thurston, 1933). Not until the early 1960s, however, did two seminal experiments demonstrate that exposure to audiovisual violence increased children's (Bandura, Ross, & Ross, 1963a) and adolescents' (Berkowitz & Rawlings, 1963) aggressive responses. These studies stimulated a torrent of empirical research on youth and media violence (for reviews, see Comstock & Scharrer, 2007; Gentile, 2003; Kirsh, 2006; Potter, 2002; Strasburger, Wilson, & Jordan, 2009). Numerous laboratory experiments have documented a short-term, causal relationship between young people's exposure to media violence and subsequent aggressiveness, as well as desensitization and fear (Cline, Croft, & Courrier, 1973; Linz, Donnerstein, & Penrod, 1984, 1988). Additionally, correlational research has consistently shown positive associations between amount of violence viewing and both aggressive attitudes and behaviors (e.g., Belson, 1978; McIntyre & Teevan, 1972) and perceptions of a "mean and scary world" (Gerbner et al., 1979). Although such synchronous correlations preclude causal inferences, several longitudinal studies, at least one of which spanned more than 20 years (Heusmann, 1986; Heusmann & Eron, 1986; Heusmann & Miller, 1994), have demonstrated that heavy viewing of television violence during the early years predicts subsequent aggressiveness—even criminal behavior—in the adolescent and early adult years. Finally, meta-analyses that estimate an effect size from numerous studies report causal links between violence viewing and subsequent aggression accounting for as much as 10% of the variance in aggression (Bushman & Anderson, 2001; Hearold, 1986; Paik & Comstock, 1994).

Meta-analyses indicate that violence viewing produces more pronounced and measurable effects among young children than adolescents (Comstock & Scharrer, 2007), probably because older youth are more socialized to avoid aggression and have better impulse control. Nevertheless, numerous studies find that exposure to symbolic violence increases adolescents' aggressive beliefs, attitudes, and behaviors. These include experimental demonstrations that exposure to violent music videos decreased adolescents' disapproval of violence (Greeson & Williams, 1986; Hansen & Hansen, 1990; Johnson, Jackson, & Gatto, 1995) and that watching a brutal beating portrayed as vengeful increased college students' willingness to administer shocks to another student (Berkowitz & Alioto, 1973), as well as cross-sectional and longitudinal surveys that yield consistently positive associations between adolescents' violence viewing and serious aggressive behavior (Belson, 1978; Huesmann, Eron, Lefkowitz, & Wilder, 1984).

Extensive reviews of the literally hundreds of empirical studies of youth and media violence (Comstock & Scharrer, 2007; Kirsch, 2007; Potter, 2002) point to three major generalizations about young people's responses to symbolic violence. First, media depictions of violence affect behavior by influencing the development of cognitive schema that serve as rough guides to action depending on cues operating in some subsequent situation. Second, susceptibility to a given portrayal varies dramatically as a function of individual experiences, abilities, needs, interests, emotional states and so forth—a constellation of variables similar to Brown's concept of "lived experience" (Brown, 2002; Steele & Brown, 1995). Third, various message characteristics affect individual interpretations of a given depiction. Comstock (1991) characterizes them as affecting the degree to which a behavior is perceived as efficacious (e.g., is the act rewarded or punished, successful, useful?), normative (e.g., is the act justified or congruent with accepted social norms?), or pertinent (e.g., is the act familiar, useful, important to the viewer, or relevant to conditions the viewer is likely to encounter?).

Recently, violent electronic games have received attention, particularly the highly realistic and graphic games of the past decade (for reviews, see Anderson & Bushman, 2001; Gentile & Anderson, 2003; Kirsch, 2006). Although electronic games share many of the same attributes as other forms of audiovisual violence, there are several important differences. One is the potential to engage players deeply, possibly to the point that immersion in electronic games leads to altered states during which rational thought is suspended and highly arousing aggressive scripts are increasingly likely to be learned (Gentile & Anderson, 2003; Glickson & Avnon, 1997; Moneta & Csikszentmihalyi, 1996). Another is the extent

to which rewards for violent behavior in video games are experienced directly rather than vicariously. That is, television viewers witness on-screen characters receive reinforcements for their actions, but game players "win points" (i.e., are directly rewarded) contingent on their actions (Provenzo, 1991).

Studies of effects of electronic games yield mixed results. Correlational evidence suggests that adolescents with more violent electronic game experience produce more aggressive responses than youngsters with less experience (Cohen, 1995). Surveys also find that high use of electronic games is related to more delinquent behavior and more aggressive personality styles (Anderson & Dill, 2000), and that game players receive higher teacher ratings of aggressiveness (Fling et al., 1992). Experiments have not demonstrated increased aggressive behavior subsequent to playing violent games, but there is evidence that violent games engender increased feelings of aggression and hostility (Anderson & Bushman, 2001; Dill & Dill, 1998) and decreases in empathy and stronger pro-violence attitudes (Funk, Buchman, Schimming, & Hagen, 1998). From their comprehensive meta-analysis, Anderson and Bushman (2001) conclude that "playing violent video games increases aggression in males and females, in children and adults, in experimental and non-experimental settings" (p. 358), although Kirsch's (2007) recent examination of the data on youth and video games urges caution in generalizing too far.

Several recent reviews of research on the impact of media violence on youth draw chilling conclusions. Taken together, hundreds of relevant studies, representing different assumptions, different approaches, and different weaknesses and strengths, offer strong evidence of a causal link between exposure to media violence and various antisocial outcomes (i.e., increased aggressiveness, increased acceptance of violence, decreased sensitivity to others' suffering; see Comstock & Scharrer, 2007). The connection is as strong for serious delinquent behavior (e.g., violent assault) as for milder acts (e.g., hostile questionnaire responses) (Comstock, 1991). Indeed, Bushman and Anderson (2001) show that the strength of the media violence–aggression linkage is almost as strong as that between smoking and cancer, and it is stronger than for such largely unquestioned causal linkages as those between condom use and decreased risk of HIV, or between amount of homework and academic achievement. In short, although media violence is only one of several contributors to adolescent antisocial behavior, there is solid evidence that for some adolescents under some conditions, exposure to symbolic violence plays a significant causal role.

Sexual Beliefs and Behavior

Because one of the major developmental tasks of adolescence is adjusting to a sexually maturing body and sexual feelings (Simpson, 2001), it is not surprising that sexual exploration is a hallmark of the period (LeVay & Valente, 2003). Because the sensitive nature of the topic of sex often diminishes open communication between adolescents and parents or other adults, the potential for media influence may be magnified during this period of heightened sensitivity to sexual information. Indeed, youth's unprecedented access to media featuring abundant, widely varied, on-demand information about sex and sexual behavior would seem to make incidental and intentional learning about sex from media virtually inevitable.

The sheer quantity of sexual content in media frequently consumed by adolescents is noteworthy (Cope, 1998; Pardun, L'Engle, & Brown, 2005; Kunkel, Eyal, Finnerty, Biely, & Donnerstein, 2005; Walsh-Childers, Gotthoffer, & Lepre, 2002). Recent analyses of television find that some type of sexual content, ranging from "talk about sex" (the most common sexual content), through passionate kissing and intimate touching, to strongly implied or explicit sexual intercourse (in 12%–14% of programs), occurs in roughly two-thirds of all TV programs (Kunkel, Biely, Eyal, Cope-Farrar,

Donnerstein, & Fandrich, 2003; Kunkel, Cope, Farinola, Biely, Rollin, & Donnerstein, 1999; Kunkel, Cope-Farrar, Biely, Farinola, & Donnerstein, 2001; Kunkel, et al., 2005). Heavy doses of sexual content have also been reported for music lyrics and music videos (Christenson & Roberts, 1998), movies (Pardun, et al., 2005; Greenberg, 1994), and magazines (Evans, Rutberg, Sather & Turner, 1991; Walsh-Childers et al., 2002). Finally, although few data describing Internet content are available, there is ample reason to believe that sexual content is abundant. Cooper (1998) suggests that sex is the most searched topic on the Internet, and in a Kaiser Family Foundation study (2001), 70% of 15- to 17-year-old computer users reported inadvertently encountering pornographic online content.

The amount of sexual content in media seems to be rising. The past several decades have witnessed an increase in the sexual content in magazines (Walsh-Childers, et al., 2002), magazine ads (Reichert, 1999), music (Christenson & Roberts, 1998), and television programs, although from 2002 to 2005 there was a decline in depictions of sexual intercourse in the "Top 20 Teen Programs" (Kunkel, et al., 2005). Sexual content also varies within and across media. For example, the proportion of recent television shows portraying sexual behaviors ranges from 5% of reality shows and 10% of news magazines, to 39% of comedies, 61% of soap operas, and 79% of movies (Kunkel, 2005). Pardun, L'Engle, and Brown (2005), using a procedure that roughly equates units of comparison across media (e.g., a continuous shot in TV or film; a magazine paragraph; a song lyric verse), found the highest proportion of sexual content in music (40% of verses), followed by movies (12% of shots), then television (11% of shots), magazines (8% of paragraphs), and Internet sites (6%).

How sexual content is portrayed is important. Generally, television portrays sex as pleasurable and carefree, rarely referring to associated risks, responsibilities, or consequences (Greenberg & Buselle, 1996; Greenberg &

Woods, 1999; Kunkel et al., 2005). Popular teen television shows are more likely than others to portray risks and consequences associated with sexual activity (Kunkel et al., 2005), but those are far more likely to be emotional or social consequences (e.g., humiliation, disappointment, guilt) than physical consequences (e.g., unwanted pregnancy, STDs; Aubrey, 2002). Negative consequences accrue more often to female characters than to males. Sex most often occurs between unmarried partners (Kunkel et al., 2005; Sapolsky & Tabarlet, 1991). About half of characters engaging in sexual contact have an established romantic relationship with each other, 20% know each other but have no romantic relationship, and 15% have just met (Kunkel, et al.). Most characters engaging in intercourse are over age 25; 1 in 10 are teens or young adults (18–24), down from 1 in 4 in 1998 (Kunkel et al.).

Clearly, when using media, incidental exposure to substantial amounts of information about sex often occurs. Adolescents also rank media among their most important sources (along with school health classes, peers, and parents) when intentionally seeking sexual information (Sutton, Brown, Wilson, & Klein, 2002). Adolescents search for sexual information from television (Brown et al., 1993; Greenberg & Linsangan 1993; Kaiser Family Foundation, MTV, & Teen People, 1999; Kaiser Family Foundation & *YM* Magazine, 1996; Sutton et al., 2002), magazines (Kaiser Family Foundation & *YM* Magazine, 1998), and the Internet (Kaiser Family Foundation, 2001). Not only do they use the Internet to find information about sex, some adolescent girls use their personal homepages as tools for sexual self-expression (Stern, 2002). Finally, some adolescents are exposed to pornographic content acquired through alternative channels Buerkel-Rothfuss, Strouse, Pettey, & Shatzer, 1993; Kaiser Family Foundation, 2001). In short, a growing body of research shows that sexual content is readily available in media messages, and that adolescents encounter those messages both incidentally and intentionally.

The question, then, is whether and how such exposure affects beliefs and behavior.

Research generally links adolescents' exposure to various kinds of sexual portrayals to more lenient views of sex and sexuality. In one experiment, 13- and 14-year-olds who watched 15 hours of prime-time television shows depicting sexual relations between unmarried partners rated sexual improprieties as significantly less objectionable than did viewers of sexual portrayals between married partners or viewers of nonsexual relationships (Bryant & Rockwell, 1994). Exposure to sexual content is also related to more permissive attitudes toward premarital sex (Greeson & Williams, 1986; Strouse, Buerkel-Rothfuss, & Long, 1995), more "recreational attitudes" toward sex (Ward, 2002; Ward & Rivadeneyra, 1999), and more negative attitudes toward remaining a virgin (Courtright & Baran, 1980). There is also evidence that television exposure is related to expectations of higher frequency of sexual behaviors in the real world (Buerkel-Rothfuss & Strouse, 1993; Ward & Rivadeneyra, 1999), and in some cases to decreased sexual satisfaction (Baran, 1976). Studies examining the effects of exposure to somewhat more sexually explicit films report similar results: greater acceptance of sexual infidelity and promiscuity (Zillman, 1994), reduced disapproval of rape (Brown, Childers, & Waszak, 1990; Zillman & Bryant, 1982), and less satisfaction with intimate partners (Zillman & Bryant, 1988). Finally, research on responses to pornographic content, primarily conducted with college students (over 18 years old) has found serious negative consequences of exposure to sexually explicit content. Zillmann (2000) explored the influence of extended exposure to sexually explicit material and cited such effects as habituation, distorted perceptions of sexual activity in the populace, diminished trust in intimate partners, and evaluation of promiscuity as the natural state. Finally, several studies have found a positive relationship between teens' viewing of sexual content in music videos and soap operas and self-reported sexual activity (Strouse & Burkel-Rothfuss, 1987; Strouse et al., 1995), and another found that teens who watched more sexual television content were more likely than those who watched less to have had sexual intercourse (Brown & Newcomer, 1991).

The issue here, of course, is whether viewing sexual content leads to sexual activity or sexual activity engenders viewing of sexual content, or whether some unidentified third variable mediates both. Recently, several highly sophisticated, longitudinal studies have reported strong, positive relationships between exposure to sexual television and music lyric content and adolescents' sexual behavior (Collins 2005; Collins et al., 2004; Martino, et al., 2006; Martino, Collins, Kanouse, Elliott, & Berry, 2005). These studies employed large, representative samples of 12- to 17-year-olds and gathered data on exposure to sexual content in television and music, adolescents' sexual behavior, and a wide variety of potentially related variables (e.g., religiosity, parental monitoring, etc.) at 1- and 2-year intervals. Using procedures that enabled controls for as many as 18 variables that might have influenced the relationship, the studies report highly similar results: Early exposure to sexual content, whether on television or in music, leads a higher probability that young viewers/listeners will engage in coitus in the ensuing year and a higher probability of reporting more sexual activity on a noncoital scale ranging from kissing to oral sex.

It appears, then, that media may play an important role in shaping adolescents' sexual beliefs, attitudes, and behaviors. When all media are considered, the amount and variety of content related to sex (broadly defined) easily equals (and may surpass) the amount related to violence. Moreover, virtually every adolescent experiences a period when he or she is likely to be intensely focused on information about sex. Arguably, the sensitive nature of the issue and ensuing reluctance of many adults to discuss sex with adolescents, in combination with the ubiquitous and private nature of sexual content available in media, have given media an important role in sexual socialization— almost by default.

Body Image

As with other areas in which social concerns have fueled studies of media influence on adolescents, the issue of body image gained attention because of its importance to adolescents' physical and emotional health and because of the quantity and nature of relevant information to be found in mainstream media. Most of the research in this area focuses on young women, because they exhibit higher rates of body dissatisfaction and eating disorders than do young men (van Hoeken, Lucas, & Hoek, 1998; Levchuck, Kosek, & Drohan, 2000). However, popular media also convey stereotypes of the ideal male body, with similarly negative consequences for adolescent males (Labre, 2002).

The media complicate adolescents' task of developing and maintaining a positive body image by normalizing excessive thinness. Content analyses of the ad and editorial contents of beauty and fashion magazines confirm the extent to which thinness and weight loss are highly rewarded (Owen & Laurel-Seller, 2000; Saraceni & Russell-Mayhew, 2007; Wiseman, Gray, Mosimann, & Ahrens, 1992). This thin ideal also dominates television, where underweight women are overrepresented in comparison to the general population (Fouts & Burggraff, 1999, 2000), and a preponderance of commercials tout the benefits of weight loss and beauty aids (Downs & Harrison, 1985). Even children's cartoons convey the stereotype that "thin is in and stout is out" (Klein & Shiffman, 2005).

No fewer than 50 experiments have examined the effects of exposure to ideal-body images on psychological responses, such as negative affect, distorted perceptions of body size, and other indicators of body dissatisfaction (for review, see Levine & Harrison, 2004). A meta-analysis of 25 such studies demonstrated a small but relatively consistent effect on girls and women, indicating lower body satisfaction after viewing thin media images than after viewing images of average-size models, plus-size models, or inanimate objects (Groesz, Levine, & Murnen, 2002). Effects were greater among younger women (not yet in college) and among those with initially low levels of body satisfaction. In some cases, the impact of acute exposure to thin-ideal media persisted for at least a short period of time (e.g., Hausenblaus, Janelle, & Gardner 2004). One field experiment randomly assigned girls to a 15-month subscription for *Seventeen* magazine or a no-subscription control group (Stice, Spangler, & Agras, 2001). The magazine increased body dissatisfaction, dieting behaviors, and bulimic symptoms, but only among girls who also lacked adequate social support.

Cross-sectional surveys demonstrate positive but small or moderate correlations between teenagers' media use and their concerns about weight and body image (for review, see British Medical Association, 2000; Harrison & Hefner, 2008). For example, body dissatisfaction is greater among girls who watch comparatively more soap operas and music videos (Tiggemann & Pickering, 1996), watch television programs featuring thin main characters (Botta, 1999; Harrison, 2001), read magazines at least twice a week (Field et al., 1999), and read magazines that feature thin models and dieting information (Harrison & Cantor, 1997). However, the few longitudinal studies that test whether media exposure predicts subsequent change in body image or related outcomes corroborate cross-sectional evidence for television viewing but not for magazine reading. Among girls aged 7–12, baseline exposure to television, but not magazines, predicted preferences for a thinner adult body and higher scores on a measure of disordered eating one year later (Harrison & Hefner, 2006). In girls as young as 5 to 8 years old, exposure to appearance-focused television programs, but not magazines, predicted decreased satisfaction with appearance 1 year later (Dohnt

& Tiggemann, 2006). Among high school girls, no media variables predicted change in body satisfaction, perhaps because body satisfaction is firmly established by that age (Tiggemann, 2006).

A comparison of two samples of adolescent girls surveyed 1 month and 3 years after the introduction of television to Fiji provides further information about the impact of prolonged exposure to television on body-image disturbance and eating pathology (Becker, 1995; Becker, Burwell, Herzog, Hamburg, & Gilman, 2002). The proportion of teen girls with abnormally high scores on a questionnaire about disordered eating more than doubled in the 3 years after the introduction of television, and girls who lived in households with a television were three times more likely to have abnormally high scores than girls without such access (Becker, 1995; Becker et al. 2002). In stark contrast to the pretelevision norm that endorsed a robust appetite and body size, 74% of girls reported feeling "too big or fat" and 69% said they had dieted to lose weight subsequent to television's introduction. The prevalence of vomiting to control weight, which was nonexistent at baseline, increased to 11%. In Fiji, then, exposure to television appeared to create body-image disturbance and symptoms of eating disorders where little potential for such outcomes existed previously. In other cultural contexts, mass media are thought to affect body image directly and indirectly, through acceptance of socially defined standards of weight and beauty and excessive appearance comparison (Cash & Pruzinsky, 2002).

Various measures of thin-ideal internalization assess the extent to which individuals wish to look like fashion models or media celebrities, compare their own body to media figures, and use the media to learn about what is attractive (Cusamano & Thompson, 2001; Heinberg, Thompson, & Stormer, 1995; Thompson & Stice, 2001). In a large prospective study of girls and boys (ages 9–14), wanting to look like people in the media was among the strongest predictors of becoming very concerned about weight (Field et al., 2001). In some cases, the effects of exposure to thin-ideal media may be greatest for (or limited to) women who most aspire to be thin (Dittmar & Howard, 2004) or women for whom appearance-related information is more salient (Brown & Dittmar, 2005).

Presumptions about media influence on others may contribute additional pressures to conform to a thin ideal. Young women who perceived a greater prevalence of the thin ideal in popular media believed that others (women and men) were more influenced by exposure to these messages and thus overestimated the extent to which others preferred thin body types (Park, 2005). Notably, this effect was independent of a direct effect of exposure to beauty and fashion magazines on the desire to be thin. Thus, interventions are needed to address not only how media influence adolescents' body image, but also how media influence what adolescents think others think about ideal body image.

Media literacy education, which increases skepticism about thin-ideal depictions, has been effective in reducing thin-ideal internalization (Irving & Berel, 2001) and in mitigating the impact of media images on body dissatisfaction (Posavac, Posavac, & Weigel, 2001). Future research should consider how media literacy curricula could be tailored to suit the needs of different age, gender, and ethnic groups. One experiment suggests that the use of average-sized rather ultrathin models does not detract from advertising effectiveness (Halliwell & Dittmar, 2004). Additional research is needed to persuade advertisers that more responsible advertising strategies may benefit adolescents without compromising product evaluations.

Tobacco, Alcohol, and Illicit Drug Use

Much of the research on media influence on adolescent substance use addresses public concern about widespread promotion of tobacco and alcohol. In 2001, the most recent year for which comparative data are available, the tobacco industry spent $214 million (of $11.2 billion total) on print, outdoor and Internet advertising (Federal Trade Commission, 2007); the alcohol industry spent $1.6. billion (of nearly $5 billion total) on traditional advertising (television, radio, print, and outdoor; Institute of Medicine, 2004). Not included in these expenditures are the costs to feature products, logos, or signs in movies, television programs, and music videos, which is forbidden for cigarette companies, but commonplace for the alcohol industry. In a single year, for example, the alcohol industry arranged product placements in 233 movies and 181 television series, including 8 of the 15 shows most popular with teens (FTC, 1999).

Although the tobacco and alcohol industries deny targeting consumers who are too young to buy their products, advertising makes smoking and drinking more appealing to youth (for reviews, see U.S. Department of Health and Human Services, 1994; Strasburger, 2002). Advertising associates cigarettes and alcohol with the same qualities and traits—sex appeal, rebelliousness, sophistication—that adolescents admire (Jackson, Hastings, Wheeler, Eadie, & Mackintosh, 2000; Shadel, Niaura, & Abrams, 2002). Clothing, personal accessories, and other promotional items that feature alcohol or cigarette brand names offer opportunities to "try on" the images of a drinker or smoker (McClure Dalcin, Gibson, & Sargent, 2006; Feighery, Borzekowski, Schooler, & Flora, 1998). Event sponsorships also represent alcohol and cigarette brands as part of the entertainment and sporting cultures of adolescence (Casswell, 2004; Hafez & Ling, 2006). Advertising is estimated to account for 34% of adolescents' experimentation with cigarettes (Pierce, Gilpin, & Choi, 1999) and 10%–30% of adolescents' alcohol use (Atkin, 1993; Gerbner, 1990).

A growing number of prospective studies corroborate and extend the volume of cross-sectional correlations between advertising exposure and the uptake of smoking (for review, see Lovato, Linn, Stead, & Best, 2003;

Wakefield, Flay, Nichter, & Giovino, 2003). For example, adolescents (ages 12–15) who had never smoked, who named a favorite cigarette brand and owned a promotional item for cigarettes at baseline were more than twice as likely as other peers to be identified as established smokers 4 years later (Biener & Siegel, 2000). Indeed, several researchers suggest that tobacco advertising exerts greater influence on adolescent smoking than does smoking by peers or family members (Evans, Farkas, Gilpin, Berry, & Pierce, 1995; Pierce et al., 1998; Sargent et al., 2000).

Movies are the primary focus of research and advocacy concerned with the role of media in glamorizing tobacco use. Tobacco appeared in 68% of the most popular movies of all time (Gunaskera, Chapman, & Campbell, 2005) and in 56% of G-rated, animated features (Goldstein, Sobel, & Newman, 1999). Several prospective studies conclude that exposure to smoking in movies promotes adolescent smoking (for review, see National Cancer Institute, in press). Although Black adolescents report comparatively higher exposure to smoking in movies, there is no evidence that its impact is more detrimental for this group. In fact, one study concluded that watching R-rated movies and having a bedroom television predicted smoking initiation among White adolescents, but not among Black adolescents (Jackson, Brown, & L'Engle, 2007).

Evidence of advertising effects on adolescent drinking is much weaker than it is for adolescent smoking. Only a few longitudinal surveys identify exposure to alcohol advertising on television (Collins et al., 2007; Stacy, Zogg, Unger, & Dent, 2004), ownership of alcohol-branded items (Collins et al., 2007; Fisher et al., 2007), and ad recognition or recall (Connolly, Casswell, Zhang, & Silva, 1994; Henriksen, Feighery, Schleicher, & Fortmann, 2008) as risk factors for alcohol use. Some evidence for a dose response relationship between advertising exposure and drinking exists. For example, advertising expenditures in media markets and the amount of advertising adolescents'

recalled predicted both the quantity of alcohol they consumed and greater increases in consumption over time (Snyder, Milici, Slater, Sun, & Strizhakova, 2006). Although the longitudinal studies of this topic control for several known predictors of adolescent alcohol use, the small to moderate effect sizes may be attributed to other unmeasured confounders.

Alcohol is even more prevalent than tobacco in popular media fare, although fewer studies address the influence of such portrayals on youth (see for review, Grube & Waiters, 2005). Alcohol appeared in 94% of R-rated, 97% of PG-13, and 76% of G- or PG-rated movies (Roberts, Henriksen, & Christianson, 1999). Approximately 70% of 80 top-rated prime-time situation comedies and serial dramas depicted alcohol use; 42% portrayed major characters at a place or event where alcohol was present, and 22% were set in a bar, club, or restaurant where alcohol was served (Christenson, Henriksen, & Roberts, 2000). The presence of alcohol in music videos has increased with the popularity of rap music, a genre in which references to luxury brands of champagne and brandy as status symbols are particularly common (Roberts, Christenson, Henriksen, & Bandy, 2002). Longitudinal research that examines the role of these popular media in the onset of alcohol use is sparse. Among 9th graders, both hours of television and music video viewing increased the odds of first alcohol use within 18 months, but did not predict continued alcohol use (Robinson, Chen, & Killen, 1998). Among children (ages 10–14) who had never tried alcohol, those who reported higher levels of exposure to drinking in movies were more likely than their peers to try alcohol within 1–2 years (Sargent, Mills, Stoolmiller, Gibson, & Gibbons, 2006). Adolescents who reported more frequent television and music video viewing at baseline reported greater alcohol consumption at follow-up, and these associations (albeit small) were equivalent in magnitude to those of drinking with smoking status and pubertal development (van den Bulck & Beullens, 2005). Additional research is needed to explain how media effects occur, to identify the individual differences that predict which adolescents "see" and "hear" substance use references in popular media, and to examine how adolescents' interpretations of these portrayals affect their attitudes and behaviors regarding tobacco and alcohol.

In spite of the growing concern that mass media glamorize illicit drug use, few empirical studies address this topic. Illicit drugs appeared in 22% of the 200 most popular video rentals in 1996 and 1997—in 20% of R-rated and 17% of PG-13 movies (Roberts, Henriksen, et al., 1999). Prime-time television more often talks about than shows illicit drugs; they were mentioned in 21% and seen in 4% of the situation comedies and serial dramas most popular with adolescents (Christenson et al., 2000). Compared to drug users in the U.S. population, drug users on TV were more likely to be minority than White (Long, O'Connor, Geroner & Canto, 2002).

What little is known about the relationship between illicit drug use and media exposure focuses on adolescent preferences for different types of popular music. The perception that some music subcultures promote drug use dates back at least as far the association of jazz and cocaine in the 1920s (Berridge, 1988). Marijuana was mentioned in 14% of the 200 most popular songs of 2005, but more so in rap than in any other genre (Primack, Dalton, Carroll, Agarwal, & Fine, 2008). Illicit drugs were mentioned in 63% of rap lyrics and in about 10% of lyrics from other popular music genres in 1997–1998 (Roberts, Henriksen, et al., 1999). Notably, a companion study of music videos found that mainstream and modern rock videos were more likely to show illicit drug use than rap/hip-hop or other videos (Roberts et al., 2002).

Correlational studies confirm disproportionately higher rates of self-reported drug use among fans of rap (Chen, Miller, Grube, & Waiters, 2006), heavy metal (Arnett, 1991; King 1988; Martin, Clarke, & Pearce, 1993), and techno/rave music (Forsyth, Barnard, &

McKeganey, 1997; Pedersen & Skrondal, 1999). Longitudinal research is needed to identify the individual differences and underlying mechanisms that may explain why adolescents who favor particular types of music are also more likely to use illicit drugs. Roe (1995) coined the term *media delinquency* to refer to adolescents' affinity for what he calls "disvalued" media and other forms of delinquency, including illicit drug use. Other researchers emphasize the role of sensation seeking, a preference for exciting experiences and stimuli (Arnett, 1991; Litle & Zuckerman, 1986). Future research should examine how myriad aspects of involvement with music—lyric comprehension, concert attendance, magazine subscriptions, and celebrity identification—inform adolescents' attitudes and behaviors regarding illicit drug use.

RETROSPECT AND PROSPECT

Empirical evidence describing both media content and patterns of adolescent media exposure far outweighs data on the consequences of such exposure. There is a growing body of research on how different characteristics of the adolescent audience (i.e., Brown's "lived experience"; Brown, 2000) influence interpretations of media content. However, other than a few studies that use age as a proxy for developmental status, and even fewer that use sexual attitudes and/or experience to infer the status of adolescent sexual development (e.g., Bandy, 2006; Brown et al., 1993; Thompson, Walsh-Childers, & Brown, 1993), research looks primarily at social and demographic variables (e.g., gender, race, parent–child relations) rather than developmental status. In short, research concerning media effects on adolescents consists largely of studies conducted *with* adolescents, either because of public concern over media influence on youth (typically, negative influence) or because compulsory education renders school-age youth a readily available subject population. Rarely does this work investigate adolescence per se.

The "problem orientation" of most studies of adolescents and media is also noteworthy (Roberts & Bachen, 1981). That is, research typically begins with an area of social behavior perceived to be problematic, then looks for theoretical models that can be applied to examine whether and how media influence relevant cognitive, attitudinal, or behavioral outcomes (see, e.g., Comstock, 1991; Comstock et al., 1978; Strasburger et al., 2009). Thus, public perceptions (and/or empirical evidence) of increases in youth violence, sexual activity, substance use, and so on, raise questions about the media's role in such behavior, stimulating systematic examination of media content and of how such content affects beliefs and behavior. Hence, there exist many more studies of potentially harmful or antisocial behavior than of helpful or prosocial behavior.

For the most part, research on adolescents and media falls under one of three general headings: content analyses, media use studies, and effects studies. A large number of content analyses of most media are relevant to adolescents and most media. Most content analyses document the quantity and nature of media messages that are particularly germane to adolescent audiences—that is, studies emphasizing perceived and/or real social problems. Such research has documented how much media portray various "problem" issues and related behaviors and how such portrayals are framed, identifying the prevalence of numerous message-related variables that have been documented to influence learning and acceptance of any kind of message. One glaring exception is a dearth of systematic information about content available on the World Wide Web.

In addition to content analyses, a large research literature indicates that adolescents spend substantial time exposed to media messages. Surveys have examined the relationship between various demographic and social variables and media consumption, documenting important age-related and individual differences in the amount, type, and content of media

adolescents consume. Three recent trends are important to understanding the potential consequences of adolescent media use. First, the preponderance of adolescent media use occurs in solitude, increasing from early to late adolescence. Second, the past decade has witnessed a substantial increase in media channels and content aimed particularly at adolescents, largely due to recognition that adolescents constitute a valuable market for advertisers. Third, media multitasking is an increasingly important phenomenon among teenagers.

Finally, effects studies shed light on factors that mediate learning from media exposure. Research has identified an extensive list of message-related and audience-related variables that influence reception and interpretation of media messages, as well as conditions influencing subsequent display of what has been learned from media content. Many of the findings apply to children, adolescents, and adults alike. However, to the extent that adolescent development influences or is influenced by media exposure, a great many holes in our knowledge remain. Much media effects research relies on either correlational data obtained from surveys or short-term experiments. Comfort levels with both the external validity of and causal inferences from many of the cited studies would be greatly enhanced by more long-term, longitudinal, and observational research.

Unlike research concerned with young children, developmental theory has seldom guided research on media effects and adolescents. Indeed, most of our knowledge about media and adolescence exists because studies of relevant social issues have been conducted with adolescents. However, adolescence denotes a much richer concept than the age criterion for research subjects. It is a period of rapid change and attendant uncertainty, during which youth confront an array of developmental tasks that mark the transition to adulthood (e.g., establishing self-identity, sexual identity, independence). One characterization of adolescent development points to a kind of psychological fragmentation, a process by which young people differentiate a public from a private self, and possibly many private selves from each other (Larson, 1995). During such fragmentation, adolescents confront identity formation by "trying on" an array of potential selves. Moreover, it appears that the disequilibrium inherent in confronting a given developmental task likely triggers a need for information about that task and simultaneously implicates related schema or cognitive categories that serve as frameworks within which new information is processed. In such instances, the same media content may be mainly construed in terms of sexual behavior or independence from authority, depending on which issue a given adolescent confronts.

This view of adolescent development, considered in relation to findings from research on media and adolescents, points to the importance of bridging the gap between the two literatures. Psychological fragmentation may, as Larson (1995) argues, occur largely in "solitude." However, it is largely solitude from "live" sources of information—parents, siblings, peers—not from mediated sources. Today's adolescents withdraw to rooms filled with media offering an array of messages designed to appeal particularly to their age group. To the extent that they confront developmental tasks and explore various potential selves during such private time, media potentially play a central role in adolescent socialization. Media provide content about issues central to development just when adolescents are most likely to be seeking that information. Focus on a given issue increases accessibility of issue-related schema. These, in turn, influence how media content is interpreted, what view of the world is cultivated, what specific beliefs and behaviors are learned, and to some extent, what view of the emerging self is constructed. In other words, media speak to the unique needs of adolescents when they are highly susceptible to influence from any messages.

Research that integrates theories of adolescent development with theories of media processes and effects is needed. Such integration offers the promise of increasing understanding of how adolescent development affects uses of and responses to media content, and perhaps more important, how media content influences adolescent socialization.

REFERENCES

Adelson, J. (Ed.) (1980). *Handbook of adolescent psychology*. New York: John Wiley & Sons.

Adoni, H. (1978). The functions of mass media in the political socialization of adolescents. *Communication Research, 6*, 84–106.

Anderson, C. A., & Bushman, B. J. (2001). Effects of violent video games on aggressive behavior, aggressive cognition, aggressive affect, physiological arousal, and prosocial behavior: A meta-analytic review of the scientific literature. *Psychological Science, 12*, 353–359.

Anderson, C. A., & Dill, K. E. (2000). Video games and aggressive thoughts, feelings, and behavior in the laboratory and in life. *Journal of Personality and Social Psychology, 78*, 772–790.

Arnett, J. J. (1991). Adolescents and heavy metal music: From the mouths of metalheads. *Youth & Society, 23*, 76–98.

Arnett, J. J. (1992). Reckless behavior in adolescence: A developmental perspective. *Developmental Review, 12*, 339–373.

Arnett, J. J. (1995). Adolescents' uses of media for self-socialization. *Journal of Youth and Adolescence, 24*, 519–533.

Atkin, C. K. (1993). Effects of media alcohol messages on adolescent audiences. *Adolescent Medicine: State of the Art Reviews, 4*, 527–542.

Atkin, C., Hocking, J., & Block, M. (1984). Teenage drinking: Does advertising make a difference? *Journal of Communication, 34*, 157–167.

Aubrey, J. S. (2002). *The sexual double standard in teen-oriented programming: A content analysis*. Paper presented at the Society for Research on Adolescence, New Orleans, LA.

Austin, E. W., & Knaus, C. (2000). Predicting the potential for risky behavior among those "too young" to drink as the result of appealing advertising. *Journal of Health Communication, 5*, 13–27.

Bandura, A. (1986). *Social foundations of thought and action: A social cognitive theory*. Englewood Cliffs, NJ: Prentice Hall.

Bandura, A. (2002). Social cognitive theory of mass communication. In J. Bryant & D. Zillmann (Eds.), *Media effects: Advances in theory and research* (2nd ed.; pp.121–153). Mahwah, NJ: Lawrence Erlbaum.

Bandura, A., Ross, D., & Ross, S. A. (1963a). Imitation of film-mediated aggressive models. *Journal of Abnormal and Social Psychology, 66*, 3–11.

Bandura, A., Ross, D., & Ross, S. A. (1963b). Vicarious reinforcement and imitative learning. *Journal of Abnormal and Social Psychology, 67*, 601–607.

Bandy, E. A. (2006). *Growing up with Buffy: How adolescent female fans use the program in their everyday lives*. Unpublished Ph.D. dissertation. ProQuest Dissertations database (Publication No. ATT 3242518).

Baran, S. (1976). Sex on TV and adolescent sexual self-image. *Journal of Broadcasting, 20*, 61–68.

Barker, D. (1994). Changes in the cigarette brand preferences of adolescent smokers—United States 1989–1993. *Morbidity and Mortality Weekly Report, 43*, 577–581.

Batista, E. (2003, April). She's gotta have it: Cell phones. *Wired*. www.wired.com/print/culture/lifestyle/news/2003/05/58861 (accessed 4/25/08).

Baxter, R. L., De Riemer, C., Landini, A., Leslie, L., & Singletary, M. W. (1985). A content analysis of music videos. *Journal of Broadcasting and Electronic Media, 29*, 333–340.

Becker, A. E. (1995). *Body, self, and society: The view from Fiji.* Philadelphia: University of Pennsylvania Press.

Becker, A. E., Burwell, R. A., Herzog, D. B., Hamburg, P., & Gilman, S. E. (2002). Eating behaviours and attitudes following prolonged exposure to television among ethnic Fijian adolescent girls. *British Journal of Psychiatry, 180,* 509–514.

Belson, W. A. (1978). *Television violence and the adolescent boy.* Westmead, UK: Saxon House, Teakfield Limited.

Berkowitz, L. (1990). On the formation and regulation of anger and aggression: A cognitive–neoassociationist analysis. *American Psychologist, 45,* 494–503.

Berkowitz, L., & Alioto, J. T. (1973). The meaning of an observed event as a determinant of aggressive consequences. *Journal of Personality and Social Psychology, 28,* 206–217.

Berkowitz, L., & Rawlings, E. (1963). Effects of film violence on inhibitions against subsequent aggression. *Journal of Abnormal and Social Psychology, 66,* 405–412.

Berkowitz, L., & Rogers, K. H. (1986). A priming effect analysis of media influence. In J. Bryant & D. Zillmann (Eds.), *Perspectives on media effects* (pp. 57–81). Hillsdale, NJ: Lawrence Erlbaum.

Berlyne, D. (1965). *Structure and direction in thinking.* New York: John Wiley & Sons.

Berridge, V. (1988). The origins of the English drug "scene," 1890–1930. *Medical History, 32,* 51–64.

Biener, L., & Siegel, M. (2000). Tobacco marketing and adolescent smoking: more support for a causal inference. *American Journal of Public Health, 90,* 407–411.

Botta, R. A. (1999). Television images and adolescent girls' body image disturbance. *Journal of Communication, 49,* 22–41.

Boyd, D. (2008). Why youth (heart) social network sites: The role of networked publics in teenage social life. In D. Buckingham (Ed.), *Youth, identity, and digital media* (pp. 119–142). Cambridge, MA: MIT Press.

Boyd, D., & Ellison, N. B. (2007). Social network sites: Definition, history, and scholarship. *Journal of Computer-Mediated Communication, 13*(1), article 11. (http://jcmc.indiana.edu/vol13/Issue1/boyd.ellison.html).

Brooks-Gunn, J., & Donahue, E. H. (2008). Introducing the issue. *The Future of Children, 18,* 3–10.

Broughton, J. M. (1981). The divided self in adolescence. *Human Development, 24,* 13–32.

Brown, A., & Dittmar, H. (2005). Think "thin" and feel bad: The role of appearance schema activation, attention level, and think-ideal internalization of young women's responses to ultra-thin media ideals. *Journal of Social and Clinical Psychology, 24,* 1088–1113.

Brown, J. D. (1993). Theoretical overview. In B. S. Greenberg, J. D. Brown, & N. L. Buerkel-Rothfuss (Eds.), *Media, sex and the adolescent* (pp. 19–25). Creskill, NJ: Hampton Press.

Brown, J. D. (2000). Adolescents' sexual media diets. *Journal of Adolescent Health, 24,* 25–40.

Brown, J. D., & Newcomer, S. F. (1991). Television viewing and adolescents' sexual behavior. *Journal of Homosexuality, 21,* 77–91.

Brown, J. D., Childers, K., Bauman, K., & Koch, G. (1990). The influence of new media and family structure on young adolescents' television and radio use. *Communication Research, 17,* 65–82.

Brown, J. D., Childers, K. W., & Waszak, C. S. (1990). Television and adolescent sexuality. *Journal of Adolescent Health Care, 11,* 62–70.

Brown, J. D., White, A. B., & Nikopoulou, L. (1993). Disinterest, intrigue, resistance: Early adolescent girls' use of sexual media content. In B. S. Greenberg, J. D. Brown, & N. L. Buerkel-Rothfuss (Eds.), *Media, sex and the adolescent* (pp. 177–195). Creskill, NJ: Hampton Press.

Brown, R., & O'Leary, M. (1971). Pop music in an English secondary school system. *American Behavioral Scientist, 14,* 401–413.

Bryant, J., & Rockwell, S. C. (1994). Effects of massive exposure to sexually oriented prime-time television programming on adolescents' moral judgment. In D. Zillman, J. Bryant, & A. C. Huston (Eds.), *Media, children, and the family: Social scientific, psychodynamic, and clinical perspectives* (pp. 183–195). Hillsdale NJ: Lawrence Erlbaum.

Buerkel-Rothfuss, N. L. (1993). Background: What prior research shows. In B. S. Greenberg, J. D. Brown, & N. L. Buerkel-Rothfuss (Eds.), *Media, sex and the adolescent* (pp. 5–18). Creskill, NJ: Hampton Press.

Buerkel-Rothfuss, N. L., & Strouse, J. S. (1993). Media exposure and perceptions of sexual behaviors: The cultivation hypothesis moves to the bedroom. In B. S. Greenberg, J. D. Brown, & N. L. Buerkel-Rothfuss (Eds.), *Media, sex and the adolescent* (pp. 225–247). Creskill, NJ: Hampton Press.

Buerkel-Rothfuss, N. L., Strouse, J. S., Pettey, G., & Shatzer, M. (1993). Adolescents' and young adults' exposure to sexually oriented and sexually explicit media. In B. S. Greenberg, J. D. Brown, & N. L. Buerkel-Rothfuss (Eds.), *Media, sex and the adolescent* (pp. 99–113). Creskill, NJ: Hampton Press.

Bushman, B. J., & Anderson, C. A. (2001). Media violence and the American public: Scientific fact versus media misinformation. *American Psychologist, 56,* 477–489.

California Assessment Program. (1980). *Student achievement in California schools. 1979–1980 annual report: Television and student achievement.* Sacramento: California State Department of Education.

Carey, J. (1969). Changing courtship patterns in the popular song. *American Journal of Sociology, 4,* 720–731.

Cash, T. F., & Pruzinsky, T. (2002). *Body image: A handbook of theory, research, and clinical practice.* New York: Guilford Press.

Casswell, S. (2004). Alcohol brands in young people's everyday lives: New developments in marketing. *Alcohol & Alcoholism, 39,* 471–476.

Casswell, S., & Zhang, J. F. (1998). Impact of liking for advertising and brand allegiance on drinking and alcohol-related aggression: A longitudinal study. *Addiction, 93,* 1209–1217.

Charters, W. W. (1933). *Motion pictures and youth: A summary.* New York: Macmillan.

Chen, M. J., Miller, B. A., Grube, J. W., & Waiters, E. D. (2006). Music, substance use, and aggression. *Journal of Studies on Alcohol, 67,* 373–381.

Christenson, P. G. (1994). Childhood patterns of music use and preferences. *Communication Reports, 7,* 136–144.

Christenson, P. G., Henriksen, L., & Roberts, D. F. (2000). *Substance use in popular prime-time television.* Washington, DC: U.S. Office of National Drug Control Policy.

Christenson, P. G., & Roberts, D. F. (1998). *It's not only rock and roll: Popular music in the lives of adolescents.* Cresskill, NJ: Hampton Press.

Cline, V. B., Croft, R. G., & Courrier, S. (1973). Desensitization of children to television violence. *Journal of Personality and Social Psychology, 27,* 360–365.

Cohen, L. B. (1995). Violent video games: Aggression, arousal, and desensitization in young adolescent boys. Doctoral dissertation, University of Southern California, 1995). *Dissertation Abstracts International, 57,* 1463. University Microfilms No. 9616947.

Coleman, J. (1993). Adolescence in a changing world. In S. Jackson & H. Rodrigues-Tome (Eds.), *Adolescence and its social worlds* (pp. 251–268). Hove, UK: Lawrence Erlbaum.

Collins, R. L. (2005). Sex on television and its impact on American youth: Background and results from the RAND television and adolescent sexuality study. *Child and Adolescent Psychiatric Clinics of North America, 14,* 371–385.

Collins, R. L., Ellickson, P. L., McCaffrey, D., & Hambarsoomians, K. (2007). Adolescent exposure to alcohol advertising and its relationship to underage drinking. *Journal of Adolescent Health, 40,* 527–534.

Collins, R. L., Elliott, M. N., Berry, S. H., Kanouse, D. E., Kunkel, D., Hunter, S. B., et al. (2004). Watching sex on television predicts adolescent initiation of sexual behavior. *Pediatrics, 114,* 280–289.

Comstock, G. (1991). *Television and the American child.* San Diego, CA: Academic Press.

Comstock, G., Chaffee, S., Katzman, N., McCombs, M., & Roberts, D. F. (1978). *Television and human behavior.* New York: Columbia University Press.

Comstock, G., & Scharrer, E. (1999). *Television: What's on, who's watching, and what it means.* San Diego, CA: Academic Press.

Comstock, G., & Scharrer, E. (2007). *Media and the American child.* Boston, MA: Academic Press.

Conger, J., & Peterson, A. (1984). *Adolescence and youth: Psychological development in a changing world* (3rd ed.). New York: Harper & Row.

Connolly, G. M., Casswell, S., Zhang, J. F., & Silva, P. A. (1994). Alcohol in the mass media and drinking by adolescents: A longitudinal study. *Addiction, 89,* 1255–1263.

Cooper, A. (1998). Sexuality and the Internet: Surfing into the new millennium. *CyberPsychology & Behavior, 1,* 181–187.

Cope-Farrar, K., & Kunkel, D. (2002). Sexual messages in teens' favorite prime-time television programs. In J. D. Brown, J. R. Steele, & K. Walsh-Childers (Eds.), *Sexual teens, sexual media* (pp. 59–75). Mahwah, NJ: Lawrence Erlbaum.

Courtright, J. A., & Baran, S. J. (1980). The acquisition of sexual information by young people. *Journalism Quarterly, 57,* 107–114.

Cusumano, D. L., & Thompson, J. K. (2001). Media influence and body image in 8–11-year-old boys and girls: A preliminary report on Multidimensional Media Influence Scale. *International Journal of Eating Disorders, 29,* 37–44.

Dietz, T. L. (1999). An examination of violence and gender role portrayals in videogames: Implications for gender role socialization and aggressive behavior. *Sex Roles, 38,* 425–442.

Dill, K. E., & Dill, J. C. (1998). Video game violence: A review of the empirical literature. *Aggression and Violent Behavior, 3,* 407–428.

Dittmar, H., & Howard, S. (2004). Ideal-body internalization and social comparison tendency as moderators of thin media models' impact on women's body-focused anxiety. *Journal of Social and Clinical Psychology, 23,* 747–770.

Dohnt, H., & Tiggemann, M. (2006). The contribution of peer and media influences to the development of body satisfaction and self-esteem in young girls: A prospective study. *Developmental Psychology, 42,* 929–936.

Dominick, J. (1974). The portable friend: Peer group membership and radio usage. *Journal of Broadcasting, 18,* 164–169.

Dominick, J. (1996). *The dynamics of mass communication* (5th ed.). New York: McGraw-Hill.

Downs, A. C., & Harrison, S. K. (1985). Embarrassing age spots or just plain ugly? Physical attractiveness stereotyping as an instrument of sexism on American television commercials. *Sex Roles, 13,* 9–19.

Evans, N., Farkas, F., Gilpin, E., Berry, C., & Pierce, J. (1995). Influence of tobacco marketing and exposure to smokers on adolescent susceptibility to smoking. *Journal of the National Cancer Institute, 87,* 1538–1545.

Faber, R., Brown, J., & McLeod, J. (1979). Coming of age in the global village: Television and adolescence. In E. Wartella (Ed.), *Children communicating: Media, and the development of thought, speech, understanding* (pp. 215–249). Beverly Hills, CA: Sage.

Federal Trade Commission. (1999). *Self-regulation in the alcohol industry: A review of industry efforts to avoid promoting alcohol to underage consumers.* Washington, DC: Author.

Federal Trade Commission. (2000). *Marketing violent entertainment to children: A review of self-regulation and industry practices in the motion picture, music recording & electronic game industries.* Washington, DC: Author.

Federal Trade Commission. (2007). *Cigarette report for 2004 and 2005.* Washington, DC: Author.

Fedler, F., Hall, J., & Tanzi, L. A. (1982). Popular songs emphasize sex, de-emphasize romance. *Mass Communication Review, 9,* 10–15.

Feighery, E. C., Borzekowski, D., Schooler, C., & Flora, J. (1998). Seeing, wanting, owning: The relationship between youth receptivity to tobacco marketing and smoking susceptibility. *Tobacco Control, 7,* 123–128.

Feldman, S. S., & Elliott, G. R. (Eds.). (1990). *At the threshold: The developing adolescent.* Cambridge, MA: Harvard University Press.

Field, A. E., Camargo, C. A., Jr., Taylor, C. B., Berkey, C. S., Roberts, S. B., & Colditz, G. A. (2001). Peer, parent, and media influences on the development of weight concerns and frequent dieting among preadolescent and adolescent girls and boys. *Pediatrics, 107,* 54–60.

Field, A. E., Cheung, L., Wolf, A. M., Herzog, D. B., Gortmaker, S. L., & Colditz, G. A. (1999). Exposure to the mass media and weight concerns among girls. *Pediatrics, 103,* E36.

Fisher, L. B., Miles, I. W., Austin, S. B., Camargo, C.A., & Colditz, G. A. (2007). Predictors of initiation of alcohol use among U.S. adolescents. *Archives of Pediatric and Adolescent Medicine, 151,* 959–966.

Fiske, S. T., & Taylor, S. E. (1991). *Social cognition* (2nd ed). New York: McGraw-Hill.

Fling, S., Smith, L., Rodriguez, T., Thornton, D., Atkins, E., & Nixon, K. (1992). Videogames, aggression, and self-esteem: A survey. *Social Behavior and Personality, 20,* 39–46.

Foehr, U. G. (2006). *Media among American youth: Prevalence, predictors and pairings.* Menlo Park, CA: Henry J. Kaiser Family Foundation.

Forsyth, A. J., Barnard, M., & McKeganey, N. P. (1997). Musical preference as an indicator of adolescent drug use. *Addiction, 92,* 1317–1325.

Fouts, G., & Burggraf, K. (1999). Television situation comedies: Female body images and verbal reinforcements. *Sex Roles, 40,* 473–481.

Fouts, G., & Burggraf, K. (2000). Television situation comedies: Female weight, male negative comments, and audience reactions. *Sex Roles, 42,* 925–932.

Funk, J. B., Buchman, D. D., Schimming, J. L., & Hagen, J. D. (1998, August). *Attitudes towards violence, empathy, and violent electronic games.* Paper presented at the annual meeting of the American Psychological Association, Washington, DC.

Gantz, W., Gartenberg, H., Pearson, M., & Schiller, S. (1978). Gratifications and expectations associated with popular music among adolescents. *Popular Music and Society, 6,* 81–89.

Gentile, D. A. (Ed.) (2003). *Media violence and children: A complete guide for parents and professionals.* Westport, CT: Praeger.

Gentile, D. A., & Anderson, C. A. (2003). Violent video games: The newest media violence hazard. In D. A. Gentile (Ed.), *Media violence and children: A complete guide for parents and professionals* (pp. 131–152). Westport, CT: Praeger.

Gerbner, G. (1990). Stories that hurt: Tobacco, alcohol, and other drugs in the mass media. In H. Resnik (Ed.), *Youth and drugs: Society's mixed messages* (pp. 53–129). Rockville, MD: Office for Substance Use Prevention.

Gerbner, G., & Gross, L. (1976). Living with television: The violence profile. *Journal of Communication, 26*(2), 172–199.

Gerbner, G., Gross, L., Morgan, M., & Signorielli, N. (1980). The "mainstreaming" of America: Violence profile No. 11. *Journal of Communication, 30,* 10–29.

Gerbner, G., Gross, L., Morgan, M., Signorielli, N., & Shanahan, J. (2002). Growing up with television: Cultivation processes. In J. Bryant & D. Zillman (Eds.), *Media effects: Advances in theory and research* (2nd ed.; pp. 43–67). Mahwah, NJ: Lawrence Erlbaum.

Gerbner, G., Gross, L. Signorielli, N., Morgan, M., & Jackson-Beeck, M. (1979). The demonstration of power: Violence profile no. 10. *Journal of Communication, 29,* 177–201.

Gidwani, P. P., Sobol, A., DeJong, W., Perrin, J. M., Gortmaker, S. L. (2002). Television viewing and initiation of smoking among youth. *Pediatrics, 110,* 505–508.

Glickson, J., & Avnon, M. (1997). Exploration in virtual reality: Absorption, cognition, and altered state of consciousness. *Imagination, Cognition, and Personality, 17,* 141–151.

Goldstein, A. O., Sobel, R. A., & Newman, G. R. (1999). Tobacco and alcohol use in G-rated children's animated films. *Journal of the American Medical Association, 281,* 1131–1136.

Greenberg, B. S. (1993). Race differences in television and movie behaviors. In B. S. Greenberg, J. D. Brown, & N. L. Buerkel-Rothfuss (Eds.), *Media, sex and the adolescent* (pp. 145–152). Creskill, NJ: Hampton Press.

Greenberg, B. S., & Buselle, R. (1996). Soap operas and sexual activity: A decade later. *Journal of Communication, 46,* 153–160.

Greenberg, B. S., Graef, D., Fernandez-Collado, C., Korzenny, F., & Atkin, C. K. (1980). Sexual intimacy on commercial TV during prime time. *Journalism Quarterly, 57,* 211–215.

Greenberg, B., & Heeter, C. (1987). VCRs and young people. *American Behavioral Scientist, 30,* 509–521.

Greenberg, B., & Linsangan, R. (1993). Gender differences in adolescents' media use, exposure to sexual content and parental mediation. In B. S. Greenberg, J. D. Brown, & N. L. Buerkel-Rothfuss (Eds.), *Media, sex and the adolescent* (pp. 134–144). Creskill, NJ: Hampton Press.

Greenberg, B. S., Perry, K. L., & Covert, A. M. (1983). The body human: Sex education, politics and television. *Family Relations, 32,* 419–425.

Greenberg, B. S., Sherry, J. L., Busselle, R. W., Hnilo, L. R., & Smith, S. W. (1997). Daytime television talk shows: Guests, content and interactions. *Journal of Broadcasting and Electronic Media, 41,* 412–426.

Greenberg, B. S., Siemicki, M., Dorfman, S., Heeter, C., Stanley, C., Soderman, A., et al. (1993). Sex content in R-rated films viewed by adolescents. In B. S. Greenberg, J. D. Brown, & N. L. Buerkel-Rothfuss (Eds.), *Media, sex and the adolescent* (pp. 45–58). Creskill, NJ: Hampton Press.

Greenberg, B. S., & Woods, M. G. (1999). The soaps: Their sex, gratifications, and outcomes. *Journal of Sex Research, 36,* 250–257.

Greeson, L., & Williams, R. A. (1986). Social implications of music videos for youth: An analysis of the content and effects of MTV. *Youth and Society, 18,* 177–189.

Groesz, L. M., Levine, M. P., & Murnen, S. K. (2002). The effect of experimental presentation of thin media images on body satisfaction: A meta-analytic review. *International Journal of Eating Disorders, 31,* 1–16.

Gross, E. (2007). Logging on, bouncing back: An experimental investigation of online communication following social exclusion. University of California–Los Angeles. Cited in Subrahmanyam, K., & Greenfield, P. (2008).

Gross, E., Juvonen, J., & Gable, S. (2002). Internet use and well-being in adolescence. *Journal of Social Issues, 58,* 75–90.

Grube, J. W., & Waiters, E. D. (2005) Alcohol in the media: Effects on drinking beliefs and behaviors among youth. *Adolescent Medicine Clinics, 16,* 327–343.

Gunaskera, H., Chapman, S., & Campbell, S. (2005). Sex and drugs in popular movies: An analysis of the top 200 films. *Journal of the Royal Society of Medicine, 98,* 464–470.

Hafez, N., & Ling, P. M. (2006). Finding the Kool Mixx: How Brown & Williamson used music marketing to sell cigarettes. *Tobacco Control, 15,* 359–366.

Halliwell, E., & Dittmar, H. (2004). Does size matter? The impact of model's body size on advertising effectiveness and women's

body-focused anxiety. *Journal of Social and Clinical Psychology, 23,* 105–132.

Hansen, C. H., & Hansen, R. D. (1990). Rock music videos and antisocial behavior. *Basic and Applied Social Psychology, 11,* 357–369.

Harris, J. R. (1998). *The nurture assumption: Why children turn out the way they do.* New York: Free Press.

Harrison, K. (2001). Ourselves, our bodies: Thin-ideal media, self-discrepancies, and eating disorder symptomatology in adolescents. *Journal of Social & Clinical Psychology, 20,* 289–323.

Harrison, K., & Cantor, J. (1997). The relationship between media consumption and eating disorders. *Journal of Communication, 47,* 40–67.

Harrison, K., & Hefner, V. (2006). Media exposure, current and future body ideals, disordered eating among preadolescent girls: A longitudinal panel study. *Journal of Youth and Adolescence, 35,* 153–163.

Harrison, K., & Hefner, V. (2008). Media, body image, and eating disorders. In S. L. Calvert & B. J. Wilson (Eds.), *The handbook of children, media, and development* (pp. 381–406). Oxford: Wiley-Blackwell.

Harter, S. (1990a). Processes underlying adolescent self-concept formation. In R. Montemayor, G. Adams, & T. Gullotta (Eds.), *From childhood to adolescence: A transitional period?* (pp. 205–239). Newbury Park, CA: Sage.

Harter, S. (1990b). Self and identity development. In S. Feldman & G. Elliott (Eds.), *At the threshold: The developing adolescent* (pp. 352–387). Cambridge, MA: Harvard University Press.

Harter, S. (1999). *The construction of the self: A developmental perspective.* New York: Guilford Press.

Hausenblaus, H. A., Janelle, C. M., & Gardner, R. E. (2004). Viewing physique slides: Affective responses of women at high and low drive for thinness. *Journal of Social and Clinical Psychology, 23,* 45–60.

Hawkins, R. P., & Pingree, S. (1980). Some processes in the cultivation effect. *Communication Research, 7,* 193–226.

Hearold, S. (1986). A synthesis of 1043 effects of television on social behavior. In G. Comstock (Ed.), *Public communication and behavior,* vol. 1 (pp. 65–133). New York: Academic Press.

Heinberg, L. J., Thompson, J. K., & Stormer, S. (1995). Development and validation of the Sociocultural Attitudes Towards Appearance Questionnaire (SATAQ). *International Journal of Eating Disorders, 17,* 81–89.

Henriksen, L., Feighery, E. C., Schleicher, N. C., Fortmann, S. P. (2008). Receptivity to alcohol marketing predicts initiation of alcohol use. *Journal of Adolescent Health, 42,* 28–35.

Hill, J. (1983). Early adolescence: A framework. *Journal of Early Adolescence, 3,* 1–21.

Hindaju, S. & Patchin, J.W. (2008). Personal information of adolescents on the Internet. *Journal of Adolescence, 31,* 125–146.

Hirsch, P. (1980). The "scary world" of the nonviewer and other anomalies: A reanalysis of Gerbner et al. Findings on cultivation analysis, part I. *Communication Research, 7,* 403–456.

Hirsch, P. (1981). On not learning from one's own mistakes: A reanalysis of Gerbner et al. Finding on cultivation analysis, part II. *Communication Research, 8,* 3–38.

Hoffner, C. (2008). Parasocial and online social relationships. In S. L. Calvert & B. J. Wilson (Eds.), *The handbook of children, media, and development* (pp. 309–333). Malden, MA: Blackwell.

Horton, D., & Wohl, R. R. (1956). Mass communication and parasocial interaction. *Psychiatry, 19,* 215–229.

Huesmann, L. R. (1986). Psychological processes promoting the relation between media violence and aggressive behavior by the viewer. *Journal of Social Issues, 42,* 125–139.

Huesmann, L. R., & Eron, L. D. (Eds.). (1986). *Television and the aggressive child: A cross-national comparison.* Hillsdale, NJ: Lawrence Erlbaum.

Huesmann, L. R., Eron, L. D., Lefkowitz, M. M., & Wilder, L. O. (1984). The stability of aggression over time and generations. *Developmental Psychology, 20,* 1120–1134.

Huesman, L. R., & Miller, L. S. (1994). Long-term effects of repeated exposure to media violence in childhood. In L. R. Huesmann (Ed.), *Aggressive behavior: Current perspectives* (pp. 153–186). New York: Plenum Press.

Institute of Medicine. (2004). *Reducing underage drinking: A collective responsibility.* Washington, DC: National Academies Press.

Irving L. M., & Berel, S. R. (2001). Comparison of media-literacy programs to strengthen college women's resistance to media images. *Psychology of Women Quarterly, 25,*103–111.

Jackson, C., Brown, J. D., & L'Engle, K. (2007). R-rated movies, bedroom televisions, and initiation of smoking by white and black adolescents. *Archives of Pediatric and Adolescent Medicine, 161,* 260–268.

Jenkins, H. (2006, October). Confronting the challenges of participatory culture: Media education for the 21st century (part one). www.henryjenkins.org/2006/10/confronting_the_challenges_of.html. (Cited in Lenhart et al., 2007).

Johnson, J. D., Jackson, L. A., & Gatto, L. (1995). Violent attitudes and deferred academic aspriations: Deleterious effects of exposure to rap music. *Basic and Applied Social Psychology, 16,* 27–41.

Kaiser Family Foundation. (2001). *Generation Rx.com: How young people use the Internet for health information.* Menlo Park, CA: Author.

Kaiser Family Foundation, MTV, & Teen People. (1999). *What teens know and don't (but should) about sexually transmitted diseases.* Menlo Park, CA: Authors.

Kaiser Family Foundation & *YM* Magazine. (1996). *Kaiser Family Foundation survey on teens and sex.* Menlo Park, CA: Authors.

Kaiser Family Foundation & *YM* Magazine. (1998). *Teens talk about dating, intimacy and their sexual experiences.* Menlo Park, CA: Authors.

Kenny, J. F. (1985). *The family as mediator of television use and the cultivation phenomenon among college students.* Unpublished doctoral dissertation, Syracuse University, Syracuse, NY.

King, P. (1988). Heavy metal music and drug abuse in adolescents. *Postgraduate Medicine, 83,* 295–304.

Kirsh, S. J. (2006). *Children, adolescents, and media violence: A critical look at the research.* Thousand Oaks, CA: Sage.

Klein, H., & Shiffman, K. S. (2005). Thin is "in" and stout is "out": What animated cartoons tell viewers about body weight. *Eating and Weight Disorders, 10,* 107–116.

Klein, J. D., Brown, J. D., Childers, K. W., Oliveri, J., & Porter, C. (1993). Adolescents' risky behavior and mass media use. *Pediatrics, 92,* 24–31.

Knowledge Networks. (2002, April). More kids say Internet is the medium they can't live without (press release). Westfield, NJ/Menlo Park, CA: Author.

Kubey, R., & Czikszentmihalyi, M. (1990). *Television and the quality of life: How viewing shapes everyday experience.* Hillsdale, NJ: Lawrence Erlbaum.

Kunkel, D., Cope, K. M., & Colvin, C. (1996). *Sexual messages on family hour television: Content and context.* Menlo Park, CA: Children Now/Kaiser Family Foundation.

Kunkel, D., Cope, K. M., Farinola, W. M., Biely, E., Rollin, E., & Donnerstein, E. (1999). *Sex on TV.* Menlo Park, CA: Kaiser Family Foundation.

Labre, M. P. (2002). Adolescent boys and the muscular male body ideal. *Journal of Adolescent Health, 30,* 233–242.

Larson, R. (1995). Secrets in the bedroom: Adolescents' private use of media. *Journal of Youth and Adolescence, 24,* 535–550.

Larson, R., & Kubey, R. (1983). Television and music: Contrasting media in adolescent life. *Youth and Society, 15,* 13–31.

Larson, R., Kubey, R., & Colletti, J. (1989). Changing channels: Early adolescent media choices and shifting investments in family and friends. *Journal of Youth and Adolescence, 18,* 583–599.

Lavay, S., & Valente, S. (2003). *Human sexuality.* Sunderland, MA: Sinauer Associates.

Lavine, H., Sweeney, D., & Wagner, S. H. (1999). Depicting women as sex objects in television advertising: Effects on body dissatisfaction. *Personality & Social Psychology Bulletin, 25,* 1049–1058.

Lenhart, A., Madden, M., Macgill, A. R., & Smith, A. (2007). *Teens and social media.* Washington, DC: Pew Internet and American Life Project. (www.pewInternet.org/pdfs/PIP_Social_Media_Final.pdf. (accessed 6/22/08).

Lenhart, A., Rainie, L., & Lewis, O. (2001). *Teenage life online: The rise of the instant-message generation and the Internet's impact on friendships and family relationships.* Washington, DC: Pew Internet and American Life Project. (www.pewInternet.org/reports/toc.asp?Report=36)

Levine, M. P., & Harrison, K. (2004). Media's role in the perpetuation and prevention of negative body image and disordered eating. In J. K. Thompson (Ed.), *Handbook of eating disorders and obesity* (pp. 695–771). Hoboken, NJ: John Wiley & Sons.

Linz, D., Donnerstein, E., & Penrod, S. (1984). The effects of multiple exposures to filmed violence against women. *Journal of Communication, 34,* 130–147.

Linz, D., Donnerstein, E., & Penrod, S. (1988). Effects of long-term exposure to violent and sexually degrading depictions of women. *Journal of Personality and Social Psychology, 55,* 758–768.

Litle, P., & Zuckerman, M. (1986). Sensation seeking and music preferences. *Personality and Individual Differences, 7,* 575–577.

Long, J. A., O'Connor, P. G., Gerbner, G., & Concato, J. (2002). Use of alcohol, illicit drugs, and tobacco among characters on prime-time television. *Substance Abuse, 23,* 95–103.

Lovato, C., Linn, G., Stead, L. F., & Best, A. (2003). Impact of tobacco advertising and promotion on increasing adolescent smoking behaviours. *Cochrane Database of Systematic Reviews, 3,* Art No: CD003439.

Marcia, J. (1980). Identity in adolescence. In J. Adelson (Ed.), *Handbook of adolescent psychology* (pp. 159–187). New York: John Wiley & Sons.

Markus, H. & Nuriuis, P. (1986). Possible selves. *American Psychologist, 41,* 954–969.

Martin, G., Clarke, M., & Pearce, C. (1993). Adolescent suicide: Music preference as an indicator of vulnerability. *Journal of the American Academy of Child and Adolescent Psychiatry, 32,* 530–535.

Martino, S. C., Collins, R. L., Elliott, M. N., Strachman, A., Kanouse, D.E., & Berry, S. H. (2006). Exposure to degrading versus nondegrading music lyrics and sexual behavior among youth. *Pediatrics, 118,* 430–441.

Martino, S. C., Collins, R. L., Kanouse, D. E., Elliott, M., & Berry, S. H. (2005). Social cognitive processes mediating the relationship between exposure to television's sexual content and adolescents' sexual behavior. *Journal of Personality and Social Psychology, 89,* 914–924.

McClure, A. C., Dal Cin, S., Gibson, J., & Sargent, J. D. (2006). Ownership of alcohol-branded merchandise and initiation of teen drinking. *American Journal of Preventive Medicine, 30,* 277–283.

McIntyre, J. J., & Teevan, J. J., Jr. (1972). Television violence and deviant behavior. In G. A. Comstock & E. A. Rubinstein (Eds.), *Television and social behavior,* vol. 3: *Television and adolescent aggressiveness* (pp. 239–313). Washington, DC: U.S. Government Printing Office.

McQuail, D., Blumler, J. G., & Brown, J. R. (1972). The television audience: A revised perspective. In D. McQuail (Ed.), *Sociology of mass communications* (pp. 135–165). Harmondsworth, UK: Penguin.

Medrich, E. A., Roizen, J. A., Rubin, V., & Buckley, S. (1982). *The serious business of growing up: A study of children's lives outside school.* Berkeley: University of California Press.

Mitchell, K. J., Wolak, J., & Finkelhor, D. (2007). Trends in youth reports of sexual solicitations, harassment and unwanted exposure to pornography on the Internet. *Journal of Adolescent Health, 40,* 116ç126.

Moneta, G. B., & Csikszentmihalyi, M. (1996). The effect of perceived challenges and skills on the quality of subjective experience. *Journal of Personality, 64,* 275–310.

Morgan, M. (1980). Television viewing and reading: Does more equal better? *Journal of Communication, 30,* 159–165.

Morgan, M. (1988). Cultivation analysis. In E. Barnouw (Ed.), *International encyclopedia of communication* (vol. 1, pp. 430–433). New York: Oxford University Press.

National Cancer Institute. (in press). *Use of the media to promote and discourage tobacco use.* Smoking and Tobacco Control Monograph No. 20. Bethesda, MA: U. S. Department of Health and Human Services, National Institutes of Health, National Cancer Institute.

Neumann, S. B. (1995). *Literacy in the television age* (2nd ed). Norwood, NJ: Ablex.

Owen, P. R., & Laurel-Seller, E. (2000). Weight and shape ideals: Thin is dangerously in. *Journal of Applied Social Psychology, 30,* 979–990.

Paik, H., & Comstock, G. (1994). The effects of television violence on antisocial behavior: A meta-analysis. *Communication Research, 21,* 516–546.

Park, S. (2005). The influence of presumed media influence on women's desire to be thin. *Communication Research, 32,* 594–614.

Paxton, S. J., Wertheim, E. H., Gibbons, K., Szmukler, G. I., Hillier, L., & Petrovich, J. L. (1991). Body image satisfaction, dieting beliefs, and weight loss behaviors in adolescent girls and boys. *Journal of Youth & Adolescence, 20,* 361–379.

Pecora, N. O. (1998). *The business of children's entertainment.* New York: Guilford Press.

Pedersen, W., & Skrondal, A. (1999). Ecstasy and new patterns of drug use: A normal population study. *Addiction, 94,* 1695–1706.

Peterson, R.C., & Thurston, L.L. (1933). *Motion pictures and the social attitudes of children.* New York: Macmillan.

Pew Internet & American Life Project (2006, October-November). *Survey of parents and teens.* (www.pewInternet.org/pdfs/PIAL%Parents%20&%20Teens%2006%Final%20Topline.doc) (accessed 1/28/08).

Pierce, J., Choi, W., Gilpin, E., Farkas, A., & Berry, C. (1998). Tobacco industry promotion of cigarettes and adolescent smoking. *Journal of the American Medical Association, 279,* 511–515.

Pierce, J. P., Gilpin, E. A., & Choi, W. S. (1999). Sharing the blame: Smoking experimentation and future smoking-attributable mortality due to Joe Camel and Marlboro advertising and promotions. *Tobacco Control, 8,* 37–44.

Posavac, H. D., Posavac, S. S., & Weigel, R. G. (2001). Reducing the impact of media images on women at risk for body image disturbance: Three targeted interventions. *Journal of Social & Clinical Psychology, 20,* 324–340.

Potter, W. J. (1993). Cultivation theory and research: A conceptual critique. *Human Communication Research, 19,* 564–601.

Potter, W. J. (2002). *The 11 myths of media violence.* Thousand Oaks, CA: Sage.

Primack, B. A., Dalton, M. A., Carroll, M. V., Agarwal, A. A., Fine, M. J. (2008). Content analysis of tobacco, alcohol, and other drugs in popular music. *Archives of Pediatric and Adolescent Medicine, 162,* 169–175.

Provenzo, E. F. (1991). *Video kids: Making sense of Nintendo.* Cambridge, MA: Harvard University Press.

Roberts, D. F. (1971). The nature of human communication effects. In W. Schramm & D. F. Roberts (Eds.), *The process and effects of mass communication* (pp. 349–387). Urbane: University of Illinois Press.

Roberts, D. F. (1993). Adolescents and the mass media: From *Leave It to Beaver* to *Beverly Hills 90210. Teachers College Record, 94,* 629–644.

Roberts, D. F. (2000). Media and youth: Access, exposure and privatization. *Journal of Adolescent Health, 24,* 8–14.

Roberts, D. F. (2003). From Plato's Republic to Hillary's village: Children and the changing media environment. In R. Weissberg, H. Walberg, M. O'Brien & C. Kuster (Eds.), *Trends in the well-being of children and youth: Issues in children's and families' lives* (pp. 255–276). Washington, DC: Child Welfare League of America Press.

Roberts, D. F., & Bachen, C. M. (1981). Mass communication effects. In M. R. Rozenzweig & L. W. Porter (Eds.), *Annual Review of Psychology,* vol. 32 (pp. 307–356). Palo Alto, CA: Annual Reviews.

Roberts, D. F., Christenson, P., Henriksen, L., & Bandy, E. (2002). *Substance use in popular music videos.* Washington, DC: Office of National Drug Control Policy.

Roberts, D. F., & Foehr, U. G. (2004). *Kids and media in America.* New York: Cambridge University Press.

Roberts, D. F., & Foehr, U. G. (2008). Trends in media use. *The Future of Children, 18,* 11–37.

Roberts, D. F., Foehr, U. G., Rideout, V. J., & Brodie, M. (1999). *Kids and media at the new millennium.* Menlo Park, CA: Henry J. Kaiser Family Foundation.

Roberts, D. F., & Henriksen, L. (1990, June). *Music listening vs. television viewing among older adolescents.* Paper presented at the annual meetings of the International Communication Association, Dublin, Ireland.

Roberts, D. F., Henriksen, L., & Christenson, P. (1999). *Substance use in popular movies and music* (No. BKD305). Rockville, MD: National Clearinghouse for Alcohol and Drug Information.

Robinson, T. N., Chen, H. L., & Killen, J. D. (1998). Television and music video exposure and risk of adolescent alcohol use. *Pediatrics, 102,* E54.

Roe, K. (1984, August). *Youth and music in Sweden: Results from a longitudinal study of teenagers' music use.* Paper presented at the annual meeting of the International Association of Mass Communication Research, Prague.

Roe, K. (1985). Swedish youth and music: Listening patterns and motivations. *Communication Research, 12,* 353–362.

Roe, K. (1987). The school and music in adolescent socialization. In J. Lull (Ed.), *Popular music and communication* (pp. 212–230). Beverly Hills, CA: Sage.

Roskos-Ewoldsen, D. R., Roskos-Ewoldsen, B., & Carpentier, F. R. D (2002). Media priming: A synthesis. In J. Bryant & D. Zillmann (Eds.), *Media effects: Advances in theory and research* (2nd ed.; pp. 97–120). Mahwah, NJ: Lawrence Erlbaum.

Rubin, A. M. (2002). The uses-and-gratifications perspective of media effects. In J. Bryant & D. Zillmann (Eds.), *Media effects: Advances in theory and research* (2nd ed.; 525–548). Mahwah, NJ: Lawrence Erlbaum.

Rubin, A. M., Perse, E. M., & Powell, R. A. (1985). Loneliness, parasocial interaction, and local television news viewing. *Human Communication Research, 12,* 155–180.

Sang, F., Schmitz, B., & Tasche, K. (1992). Individuation and television coviewing in the family: Developmental trends in the viewing behavior of adolescents. *Journal of Broadcasting and Electronic Media, 36,* 427–441.

Sapolsky, B. S., & Tabarlet, J. O. (1991). Sex in primetime television: 1979 versus 1989. *Journal of Broadcasting and Electronic Media, 35,* 505–516.

Saraceni, R., & Russell-Mayhew, S. (2007). Cultural expectations of thinness in women: A partial replication and update of magazine content. *Eating and Weight Disorders, 12,* e68–e74.

Sargent, J. D., Dalton, M., Beach, M., Bernhardt, A., Heatherton, T., & Stevens, M. (2000). Effect of cigarette promotions on smoking uptake among adolescents. *Preventive Medicine, 30,* 320–327.

Sargent, J. D., Wills, T. A., Stoolmiller, M., Gibson, J., & Gibbons F. X. (2006). Alcohol use in motion pictures and its relation with early-onset teen drinking. *Journal of Studies on Alcohol, 67,* 54–65.

Schank, R. C., & Abelson, R. P. (1977). *Scripts, plans, goals, and understanding: An inquiry into human knowledge structures.* Hillsdale, NJ: Lawrence Erlbaum.

Schramm, W. (1971). The nature of communication between humans. In W. Schramm & D.F. Roberts, (Eds.), *The process and effects of mass communication* (pp. 3–53). Urbana: University of Illinois Press.

Shanahan, J., & Morgan, M. (1999). *Television and its viewers: Cultivation theory and research.* Cambridge: Cambridge University Press.

Sherman, B. L., & Dominick, J. R. (1986). Violence and sex in music videos: TV and rock 'n' roll. *Journal of Communication, 36*(1), 79–93.

Shrum, L. J. (1995). Assessing the social influence of television: A social cognition perspective on cultivation effects. *Communication Research 22,* 402–429.

Shrum, L. J. (2002). Media consumption and perceptions of social reality: Effects and underlying processes. In J. Bryand & D. Zillmann (Eds.), *Media effects: Advances in theory and research* (2nd ed.; pp. 69–95). Mahwah, NJ: Lawrence Erlbaum.

Shrum, L. J., Wyer, R. S., Jr., & O'Guinn, T. C. (1998). The effects of television consumption on social perceptions: The use of priming procedures to investigate psychological processes. *Journal of Consumer Research, 24*(4): 447–458.

Signorielli, N., & Morgan, M. (Eds.). (1990). *Cultivation analysis: New directions in media effects research.* Newbury Park, CA: Sage.

Simpson, A. R. (2001). *Raising teens: A synthesis of research and a foundation for action.* Boston, MA: Harvard School of Public Health.

Smith, S. L., Lachlan, K., & Tamborini, R. (2003). Popular video games: Quantifying the presentation of violence and its context. *Journal of Broadcasting & Electronic Media, 47,* 58–76.

Smith, S. L., Wilson, B. J., Kunkel, D., Linz, D., Potter, W. J., Colvin, C., et al. (1998). Violence in television programming overall: University of California, Santa Barbara study. In *National television violence study,* vol. 3 (pp. 5–220). Newbury Park, CA: Sage.

Snyder, L. B., Milici, F. F., Slater, M., Sun, H., & Strizhakova, Y. (2006). Effects of alcohol advertising exposure on drinking among youth. *Archives of Pediatrics & Adolescent Medicine, 160,* 18–24.

Stacy, A. W., Zogg, J. B., Unger, J. B., & Dent, C. W. (2004). Exposure to televised alcohol ads and subsequent adolescent alcohol use. *American Journal of Health Behavior, 28,* 498–509.

Starker, S. (1989). *Evil influences: Crusades against the mass media.* New Brunswick, CT: Transaction Publishers.

Steele, J. R., & Brown, J. D. (1995). Adolescent room culture: Studying media in the context of everyday life. *Journal of Youth and Adolescence, 24,* 551–576.

Stern, S. (2002). Sexual selves on the World Wide Web: Adolescent girls' home pages as sites for sexual self-expression. In J. D. Brown, J. R. Steele, & K. Walsh-Childers (Eds.), *Sexual teens, sexual media* (pp. 265–285). Mahwah, NJ: Lawrence Erlbaum.

Stice E., Schupak-Neuberg E., Shaw, H. E., & Stein, R. I. (1994). Relation of media exposure to eating disorder symptomatology: An examination of mediating mechanisms. *Journal of Abnormal Psychology, 103,* 836–840.

Stice, E., Spangler, D., & Agras, W. S. (2001). Exposure to media-portrayed thin-ideal images adversely affects vulnerable girls: A longitudinal experiment. *Journal of Social and Clinical Psychology, 20,* 270–288.

Strasburger, V. C. (2002). Alcohol advertising and adolescents. *Pediatric Clinics of North America, 49,* 353–376.

Strasburger, V. C., Wilson, B. J., & Jordan, A. B. (2009). *Children, adolescents, & the media* (2nd ed.). Thousand Oaks, CA: Sage.

Strouse, J. S., & Buerkel-Rothfuss, N. L. (1987). Media exposure and the sexual attitudes and behaviors of college students. *Journal of Sex Education and Therapy, 13,* 43–51.

Strouse, J. S., Buerkel-Rothfuss, N., & Long, E. C. (1995). Gender and family as moderators of the relationship between music video exposure and adolescent sexual permissiveness. *Adolescence, 30,* 505–521.

Strouse, J. S., & Fabes, R. A. (1985). Formal vs. informal sources of sex education: Competing forces in the sexual socialization process. *Adolescence, 78,* 251–263.

Subrahmanyham, K., & Greenfield, P. (2008). Online communication and adolescent relationships. *The Future of Children, 18*(1), 119–146.

Sutton, M. J., Brown, J. D., Wison, K. M., & Klein, J. D. (2002). Shaking the tree of knowledge for forbidden fruit: Where adolescents learn about sexuality and contraception. In J. D. Brown, J. R. Steele, & K. Walsh-Childers (Eds.), *Sexual teens, sexual media* (pp. 25–55). Mahwah, NJ: Lawrence Erlbaum.

Taylor, C. B., Sharpe, T., Shisslak, C., Bryson, S., Estes, L. S., Gray, N., et al. (1998). Factors associated with weight concerns in adolescent girls. *International Journal of Eating Disorders, 24*(1), 31–42.

Teen spending estimated to top 190 billion by 2006 (2006). (www.marketresearchworldnet/index.php?option=content&task=view&id=65&Itemid=).

Teenage Research Unlimited. (2004, January). Teens spend $175 billion in 2003 (press release; www.teenresearch.com/Prview.cfm?edit_id=168), (accessed 2/3/08).

Thompson, J. K., & Stice, E. (2001). Thin-ideal internalization: Mounting evidence for a new risk factor for body-image disturbance and eating pathology. *Current Directions in Psychological Science, 10*(5), 181–183.

Thompson, M., Walsh-Childers, K., & Brown, J. D. (1993). The influence of family communication patterns and sexual experience on processing of a movie video. In B. S. Greenberg, J. D. Brown, & N. L. Buerkel-Rothfuss (Eds.), *Media, sex and the adolescent* (pp. 248–263). Creskill, NJ: Hampton Press.

Tiggemann, M., & Pickering, A. S. (1996). Role of television in adolescent women's body dissatisfaction and drive for thinness. *International Journal of Eating Disorders, 20*(2), 199–203.

Tiggemmann, M. (2006). The role of media exposure in adolescent girls' body dissatisfaction and drive for thinness: Prospective results. *Journal of Social and Clinical Psychology, 25,* 523–541.

Tobin, D. (2005, March). Teens and cell phones. Ezine. http://ezinearticles.com/?Teens-And-Cell-Phones&id=24519&opt=print (accessed 4/25/08).

Took, K. J., & Weiss, D. S. (1994). The relationship between heavy metal and rap music and adolescent turmoil: Real or artifact? *Adolescence, 29*(115), 613–621.

Unger, J. B., Johnson, C. A., & Rohrbach, L. A. (1995). Recognition and liking of tobacco and alcohol advertisements among adolescents: Relationships with susceptibility to substance use. *Preventive Medicine, 24,* 461–466.

van den Bulck, J., & Beullens, K. (2005). Television and music video exposure and adolescent alcohol use while going out. *Alcohol and Alcoholism, 40,* 249–253.

van Hoeken, D., Lucas, A. R., & Hoek, H. W. (1998). Epidemiology. In H. W. Hoek, J. L. Treasure, & M. A. Katzman (Eds.), *Neurobiology in the treatment of eating disorders* (pp. 97–126). New York: John Wiley & Sons.

Violato, C., & Holden, W. (1987). A confirmatory factory analysis of a four-factory model of adolescent concerns. *Journal of Youth and Adolescence, 17,* 101–113.

Wakefield, M., Flay, B., Nichter, M., & Giovino, G. (2003). Role of the media in influencing trajectories of youth smoking. *Addiction, 98,* 79–103.

Walsh-Childers, K., Gotthoffer, A., & Lepre, C.R. (2002). From "Just the Facts" to "Downright Salacious": Teens' and women's magazine coverage of sex and sexual health. In J. D. Brown, J. R. Steele, & K. Walsh-Childers (Eds.), *Sexual teens, sexual media* (pp. 153–171). Mahwah, NJ: Lawrence Erlbaum.

Ward, L. M. (1995). Talking about sex: Common themes about sexuality in the prime-time television programs children and adolescents view most. *Journal of Youth and Adolescence, 24,* 595–615.

Ward, L. M. (2002). Does television exposure affect emerging adults' attitudes and assumptions about sexual relationships? Correlational and experimental confirmation. *Journal of Youth and Adolescence, 31,* 1–15.

Ward, L. M., & Rivadeneyra, R. (1999). Contribution of entertainment television to adolescents' sexual attitudes and expectations: The role of viewing amount versus viewer involvement. *Journal of Sex Research, 36,* 237–249.

Wartella, E., Heintz, K., Aidman, A., & Mazzarella, S. (1990). Television and beyond: Children's video media in one community. *Communication Research, 17,* 45–64.

Washington Post (2006, October 29). In teens' web world, MySpace is so last year, p. A-1.

Wells, A. (1990). Popular music: Emotional use and management. *Journal of Popular Culture, 24*(1), 105–117.

Wilks, J., Vardanega, A. T., & Callan, V. J. (1992). Effect of television advertising of alcohol on alcohol consumption and intentions to drive. *Drug and Alcohol Review, 11*(1), 15–21.

Wiseman, C. V., Gray, J. J., Mosimann, J. E., & Ahrens, A. H. (1992). Cultural expectations of thinness in women: An update. *International Journal of Eating Disorders, 11*(1), 85–89.

Wolak, J., Mitchell, K. J., & Finkelhor, D. (2003). Escaping or connecting? Characteristics of youth who form close online relationships. *Journal of Adolescence, 26,* 105–119.

Wolak, J., Mitchell, K. J., & Finkelhor, D. (2007). Online victimization of youth: Five years later. *National Center for Missing and Exploited Children Bulletin.* (www.unh.edu/ccrc/pdf/CV138.pdf (accessed 6/21/08).

Zillmann, D. (1994). Erotica and family values. In D. Zillmann & J. Bryant (Eds.), *Media, children, and the family: Social scientific, psychodynamic, and clinical perspectives* (pp. 199–213). Hillsdale, NJ: Lawrence Erlbaum.

Zillmann, D. (2000). Influence of unrestrained access to erotica on adolescents' and young adults' disporitions toward sexuality. *Journal of Adolescent Health, 27,* 41–44.

Zillmann, D. (2002). Exemplification theory of media influence. In J. Bryant & D. Zillmann (Eds.), *Media effects: Advances in theory and research* (2nd ed.; pp. 19–41). Mahwah, NJ: Lawrence Erlbaum.

Zillmann, D. & Bryant, J. (1982). Pornography, sexual callousness, and the trivialization of rape. *Journal of Communication, 32*(4), 10–21.

Zillmann, D. & Bryant, J. (1988). Pornography's impact on sexual satisfaction. *Journal of Applied Social Psychology, 18,* 438–453.

CHAPTER 10

The Legal Regulation
of Adolescence

JENNIFER L. WOOLARD AND ELIZABETH SCOTT

The scientific view of the boundaries between childhood and adulthood recognizes adolescence as a discrete developmental period "beginning in biology and ending in society," (Lerner & Galambos, 1998, p. 414). Scientists generally divide the span of adolescence into early (ages 11 to 14), middle (ages 15–18) and late (ages 18–21) periods (Steinberg, 2008). Few believe that development in all domains tracks these phases with stagelike consistency, but instead considers adolescent development as a series of transitions to maturity, the pace of which varies among adolescents and across domains within an individual (Steinberg, 2008). Biological, cognitive, and social transitions affect adolescents' capacities to respond to their environment and elicit changing expectations and reactions from the larger social world (Lerner & Galambos, 1998; Steinberg, 2008).

To what extent does legal regulation recognize the developmental reality of adolescence as a discrete stage and distinguish between adolescents and children (and between adolescents and adults)? The answer is, not very much at all. Generally, policymakers ignore this transitional developmental stage, classifying adolescents legally either as children or as adults, depending on the issue at hand. Lawmakers have quite a clear image of childhood, and legal regulation is based on this image (Scott, 2000). Children are assumed to be vulnerable and dependent and to lack the capacity to

make competent decisions. Thus, not surprisingly, they are not held legally accountable for their choices or behavior. Children also are not accorded most of the legal rights and privileges that adults enjoy, such as voting, driving, drinking, and making their own medical decisions. Finally, children are assumed to be vulnerable and unable to care for themselves, and thus their parents and the government are obligated to provide the care, support, and education that allow them to develop into healthy adults. Once children cross the line to legal adulthood, they are considered autonomous citizens responsible for their own conduct, entitled to legal rights and privileges, and no longer entitled to protections.

The simple binary classification of legal "childhood" and legal "adulthood" in fact is more complex than it seems because the boundary between childhood and adulthood varies depending on the policy purpose. For example, for most purposes, children become legal adults on their 18th birthday, which is the modern "age of majority" in most states. However, 20-year-old college students are legally prohibited from drinking alcohol, while youth in elementary school can be subject to the adult justice system when they are charged with crimes. Thus, although legal regulation offers a clear account of the attributes of children that indicate the need for treating them differently from adults under the

This chapter draws on Elizabeth Scott, "The Legal Construction of Adolescence," *Hofstra Law Review* 29: 547–98 (2000).

law, children's legal status is complicated by the shifting boundary between childhood and adulthood.

For most purposes, adolescents are described in legal rhetoric as though they were indistinguishable from young children, and are subject to paternalistic policies based on assumptions of dependence, vulnerability, and incompetence. For other purposes, teenagers are treated as fully mature adults, who are competent to make decisions, accountable for their choices and entitled to no special accommodation. The variation is due mostly to the fact that different policy goals are important in different context, rather than to efforts to attend to variations in developmental maturity in different domains. For example, although many of the same cognitive and psychosocial capacities affect decision making both behind the wheel and in a bar, allowing 16-year-olds to drive gives young persons independence and mobility, while restricting the privilege to buy alcoholic beverages until age 21 protects youth (and the rest of us) from the costs of immature judgment.

Is there a cost to a legal approach that ignores the developmental realities of adolescence? In our view, the binary classification of childhood and adulthood works quite well for most purposes. It has the advantage of simplicity and administrative efficiency, and arguably it promotes parental responsibility by linking parents' support obligation to their children's general status as dependents. Moreover, because adult rights and duties are extended at different ages for different purposes, the transition to adulthood takes place gradually, even without an intermediate stage of legal adolescence. Adolescents may benefit if they are allowed to make some adult decisions, but not others. To return to our example, 16-year-olds acquire experience in the adult domain of driving long before they are legally authorized to make other adult choices, such as drinking. Thus, even though the crude legal categories distort developmental reality, for the most part, the binary classification system

is not harmful to the welfare of adolescents or to general social welfare. In fact, in some areas in which legal regulation subjects adolescents to special treatment (different from adults or children), youth would be better served by the standard approach. As we will discuss, regulation of adolescent abortion is such a case.

In some contexts, however, binary categorical assumptions that ignore the transitional stage of adolescence can lead to harmful outcomes. Juvenile justice policy provides a stark example of a failure of the binary approach. This is an arena in which the boundary of childhood shifted dramatically over the course of the twentieth century, and strikingly different accounts of young offenders have been deployed in service of the different policy agendas. The juvenile justice system was established at the end of the nineteenth century with the purpose of providing rehabilitation to young offenders instead of punishment in the criminal justice system. The Progressive reformers who founded the juvenile court were very committed (in their rhetoric, at least) to describing and dealing with young offenders as children (Van Waters, 1926). In recent years, a major law reform movement has transformed this system, such that today even preadolescents can be tried as adults for serious crimes in many states (Snyder & Sickmund, 2006). Developmental research indicates both portraits (i.e., adolescents as children and adolescents as adults) are largely fictional; developmental reality is much more complex. Moreover, in our view, both the romanticized vision of youth offered by the early Progressive founders and the harsh account of modern conservatives have been the basis of unsatisfactory policies. In contrast to many other areas of legal regulation, binary classification in the juvenile justice sphere imposes significant costs on both young offenders and society. In this context, effective legal regulation requires a realistic account of adolescence based on developmental theory and empirical research.

For over 30 years, social scientists and legal scholars have argued for the need for developmental research on adolescence to inform legal policy and practice (Grisso & Lovinguth, 1982; Melton, 1981; Reppucci, Weithorn, Mulvey, & Monahan, 1984; Wald, 1976). In this chapter we describe and evaluate the extent to which legal regulation recognizes the developmental reality of adolescence and differences between adolescents and either children or adults. First, we present the legal account of childhood, sketching the traits that are assumed to distinguish children from adults, and the absence of any clear vision of adolescence. Next, we describe how the legal boundary between childhood and adulthood is determined, and we show that the judgment is determined by policy (and politics) as much as science. Our analysis includes a description of the forces that led to the passage of the 26th Amendment, which extended voting rights to 18-year-olds—an enactment that led states to lower the age of majority for many other purposes. We then examine medical decision making and abortion rights; the latter is an issue that clarifies the difficulties in creating a special legal status for adolescence. Finally, we examine juvenile justice policy, and explain why binary classification has not worked well in this context. We describe recent research that supports the conclusion that a justice policy that treats adolescence as a distinct legal category not only will promote youth welfare, but will also help reduce the costs of youth crime.

LEGAL ASSUMPTIONS ABOUT CHILDHOOD

Several assumptions undergird the legal regulation of children. Because children are assumed to be incapable of looking out for themselves, they need adult care and protection. Specifically, three interrelated dimensions of immaturity guide legal policy. First, children are dependent beings, and must rely on adults to meet their basic needs for survival—food, shelter, clothing—and for education and care to allow them to mature into healthy, productive adults. Children are also presumed to be incapable of making sound decisions, due

to cognitive immaturity that limits youthful understanding and reasoning, and psychosocial immaturity that may lead to poor judgment and harmful or risky choices (Scott, 1992; Zimring, 1982). Finally, children are presumed to be malleable, making them susceptible to influence and vulnerable to harm from others (Van Waters, 1926).

These assumptions about childhood justify the need for adult control over children's lives and clarify why the legal rights, privileges, and duties assigned to adults are not extended to children. The law accords parents the primary authority and responsibility for rearing children and caring for their needs. Parents have authority to make decisions about all aspects of children's lives, from medical care and education to the most mundane aspects of daily living. In turn, the law charges parents with safeguarding children's welfare and protecting them from harm. The U.S. Supreme Court elaborated on the basis of parents' legal and constitutional authority in *Parham v. J.R* (1979), an opinion that dealt with the commitment of children to state psychiatric hospitals:

> The law's concept of a family rests on a presumption that parents possess what children lack in maturity, experience, and capacity for judgment required to make life's difficult decisions. More importantly, historically it has recognized that natural bonds of affection lead parents to act in the best interests of their children. (p. 602)

Parents do not have blanket authority in making child-rearing decisions, however. When parents fail to fulfill their duties, the consequences redound to the child and to a society interested in a healthy, productive citizenry. When parents abuse or neglect their children, the state intervenes on children's behalf under its *parens patriae* authority to protect the welfare of minors (Rendleman, 1971). The state also preempts parental authority categorically on some matters. Thus, parents' decisions about their children's behavior are subject to child labor and compulsory school attendance laws that remove discretion on these matters (*Prince v. Massachusetts*, 1944).

The unique legal status of children is revealed in several distinct aspects of legal regulation. First, the rights and privileges of children are more restricted than are those of adults. For example, concerns about juvenile crime and victimization led to curfew laws that restrict minors' nighttime freedom in ways that would clearly be unconstitutional if applied adults (*Schleifer v. City of Charlottesville*, 1997). Limitations on free speech (such as censorship of school newspapers) are imposed on youth because of their presumed vulnerability (*Hazelwood School District v. Kuhlmeier*, 1988; *Morse v. Frederick*, 2007). Minors are not permitted to vote, drink alcohol, drive a vehicle, or give consent to their own medical treatment.

Second, children are not held accountable for their choices or responsible for their behavior to the same extent as adults because of assumptions about their cognitive and social immaturity and vulnerability to influence. For example, under the infancy doctrine in contract law, minors can avoid liability on their contracts, presumably because they cannot be expected to exercise adult-like judgment or to resist a seller's influence when considering a purchase (Scott & Kraus, 2007). Also, youth (traditionally, at least) have not been held to adult standards for their criminal conduct. The juvenile court was created in part on the premise that youthful misconduct is in part a product of immaturity and that young offenders are less culpable than their adult counterparts (Arenella, 1992; Scott & Steinberg, 2003).

Third, children are accorded special legal protections and entitlements because of their dependency. Parents are required by law to provide the necessities of food, shelter, clothing, and care for their children and the government subsidizes the provision of these services when parents who are financially unable to do so themselves. The public education system guarantees a free education to children in all states. Civil and criminal child maltreatment laws encourage parents to care for their children; failure to do so can result in coercive interventions ranging from parenting assistance to termination of parental rights and/or criminal conviction.

In summary, assumptions about the vulnerability, incompetence, and dependency of children result in a complex set of regulations that accord children a unique status in law. Minors are provided special legal protections and entitlements, held less accountable for their actions, and accorded fewer rights and privileges than adults. Policy makers have multiple goals of protecting children, promoting parental responsibility, and ensuring that children mature into productive adults, all of which are grounded in a set of shared assumptions about what it means to be a child.

DRAWING THE LINE BETWEEN LEGAL CHILDHOOD AND ADULTHOOD

Although the law sets varying age boundaries depending on the domain of interest, the presumptive boundary between childhood and adulthood is the legal age of majority, which currently is age 18. To some extent, this line tracks developmental knowledge; late adolescents are more similar to adults than children in their physical and cognitive development (Gardner, Scherer, & Tester, 1989; Siegler & Alibali, 2004). However, childhood has multiple legal boundaries that are reflected in a complex system of age grading. Deviations from the age of majority can be explained in part as justified because different decision-making domains require different maturity levels. For example, greater maturity is required to serve as president than to drive a motor vehicle. However, although assumptions about maturity and immaturity play a role in the legal judgment about when children become adults for different purposes, other considerations factor into the age grading scheme. Lawmakers balance the competing goals of promoting youth welfare, protecting parental authority, and considering societal benefit. Administrative efficiency also plays a role, as does political controversy and compromise, as is seen most clearly in the debate over minors' access to abortion. In this section, we examine the categorical approach of the age of majority, and then turn to medical decision making and abortion access to illustrate the complexity of domain-specific variation in the legal view of adolescence. Both of these latter issues have generated interest among researchers interested in evaluating the legal standard guiding boundary drawing by comparing adolescent and adult capacities.

The Age of Majority: The Legal Invisibility of Adolescence

The age of majority functions as the threshold to legal adulthood for many purposes. Upon attaining the age of 18, adolescents are no longer subject to parental authority; parents are no longer responsible for their children, and the state withdraws the services and protections available under its *parens patriae* powers. Eighteen-year-olds have the legal authority to consent to medical treatment, to execute contracts, deeds and leases, to vote, and to serve on juries (e.g., *Va. Code Ann.* §1-13.42). They are considered responsible, autonomous individuals who bear the consequences, both good and bad, of their actions and choices.

The legal age of majority represents a crude judgment that late adolescents are mature enough to function in society as adults, but it is not tailored to recognize any specific developmental milestone. Life-span research confirms that development is by no means complete at age 18; indeed, some have suggested that young adulthood should constitute a new post-adolescence phase of development (Arnett, 2000; Arnett & Tanner, 2006). Differences between late adolescents and adults are a matter of degree rather than kind, yet as with most phases of development individuals vary widely in their capacities (Scott, Reppucci, & Woolard, 1995; Steinberg & Cauffman, 1996).

The categorical age of majority ignores variation among individuals as well as varying maturity demands in different decision domains, but extending legal childhood into late adolescence has some advantages, even though adult privileges and rights likely are often withheld from competent youth (Melton, 1983a). An extended dependency period assures that youth receive protections and support, both from their parents and from the government, and it may reinforce parental responsibility (Scott & Scott, 1995). A bright line rule creates certainty regarding expectations for the relationship between youth, parents, and the state. Domain- or decision-specific assessments of adolescents' capacities would undermine that certainty, creating a complex, inefficient, and costly process prone to error. Moreover, for most purposes postponement of adult status imposes few costs on adolescents. Thus, even though it sacrifices developmentally accuracy, the categorical approach embodied in the current operationalization of the age of majority meets most of the legal system's needs with minimal developmental cost to adolescents.

The right to vote has long been a defining marker of legal adulthood, and it has historically been linked to the age of majority. A cornerstone of participatory democracy, the right to vote is withheld from minors because they are presumed less capable of exercising the right through educated, informed understanding (Cultice, 1992). Thus, the question of when individuals are capable of exercising this right is a consideration in the judgment of when the right should be extended. In the 1960s, research suggested that adolescents possess some of the capacities that are important to political participation. For example, abstract understanding of rights, a sense of community, and conception of the individual as part of the larger social contract develop throughout adolescence into adulthood (Adelson & O'Neil, 1966; Torney-Purta, 1992). Moreover, recent research that separates understanding of rights, civil liberties, and democracy from hypothetical situations that place rights in conflict with other moral principles, even young children evince more sophisticated understanding that previously thought (Helwig & Turiel, 2002; chapter 7, vol.1, this *Handbook*).

Most of that early work on "political socialization" focused on attitudes and perceptions of children and adolescents, rather than their underlying cognitive capacities. More recent work examines the development of political socialization and cognitive representations of the social order and political system (e.g., Helwig & Turiel, 2002; but empirical data on age differences between adolescents and adults or developmental trajectories are quite limited (see chapter 7, vol. 1 of this *Handbook*). Although some reviews of political socialization research suggest that there is no particular point when persons learn about politics or develop civic engagement (Dudley & Gitelson, 2002; Flanagan & Sherrod, 1998; Sherrod, Flanagan, & Youniss, 2002), recent theoretical and empirical research supports the importance of civically motivated behavior during adolescence as a predictor of civic engagement, including voting behavior, in adulthood (Campbell, 2006).

Although adolescents may possess the necessary capacities to engage in informed voting behavior, only rarely in our history has attention focused on the age at which the right to vote is extended, and for the most part, few objections have been expressed over withholding this right from minors—in contrast to protest over withholding other constitutionally protected rights, such as the right to make abortion decisions. This probably reflects recognition that it would be costly to identify those individual adolescents who are capable of making informed voting decisions. Lawmakers may also assume that adolescents (and society) incur little harm by postponing the exercise of voting rights until age 18.

In the 1960s, these factors were overcome by a substantial and ultimately successful effort to lower the voting age from 21 to 18. The historical record of this important reform, which is embodied in the 26th Amendment to the U.S. Constitution, highlights the importance of the social and political factors in defining adult status, and underscores that developmental maturity may not be the core consideration (Cultice, 1992). During the Vietnam War, legal minors, who were not permitted to vote or exercise other adult rights, were being drafted into military service and sent into battle. Moreover, college students were actively engaged in political participation, protesting against the Vietnam War and in support of civil rights. Noting these political facts, the Senate committee that considered the proposal to lower the voting age also documented in its report that this age group already engaged in a number of adult roles as employees, taxpayers, and citizens subject to criminal laws and punishments (S. Rep. No. 92-26, 1971). The report emphasized that, for most purposes, psychological maturity is achieved by age 18.

The passage of the 26th Amendment offers an interesting account of the forces that influence judgments about when children become legal adults. First, social and political forces in large measure propelled the initiative to shift the boundary of childhood, but legislators also felt it was important to ground their proposal in substantive developmental claims about the cognitive and psychosocial maturity of 18-year-olds. Another interesting theme is that, in defining the boundary of adult status, lawmakers thought that parity should exist between rights and responsibilities. On this view, 18-year-olds were recast from children into adults with the most important right of citizenship because they were required to bear the most onerous civic responsibility—military service.

Because the right to vote has always been the marker of legal adulthood, the age of majority was lowered to age 18 for most purposes after the passage of the 26th Amendment. This took place through sweeping legislative and judicial action at both the state and federal level that lowered the age of adult status in domains as disparate as medical decision making, contracting, and entitlement to support.

Medical Decision Making: Special Legal Status for Adolescents

In contrast to the sparse empirical foundation for the extension of voting rights to late adolescents, a substantial body of research has focused on adolescents' capacity to consent to medical treatment. Although in general, adolescents are subject to their parents' authority in this realm, the law has granted adolescents the authority to consent to certain types of treatment without involving their parents. Moreover, a complex regulatory scheme governs adolescent decisions to obtain abortion; in this domain lawmakers have adopted the unusual approach of treating adolescents as a category distinct from childhood and adulthood. Although the capacities to consent to different medical procedures may develop comparably, different social and political considerations have shaped legal policies in these various contexts. Thus, the broad domain of medical decision making offers an interesting case study in how factors other than maturity may determine the boundary between childhood and adulthood.

Medical Treatment: Informed Consent and Mature Minors

Adolescents do not have the legal authority to consent to most medical treatments until they reach the age of majority. Presumed to lack the necessary capacities, they are subject to the decision-making authority of their parents, who are presumed to act in their children's best interests. The basis for parental authority in this area is relatively straightforward. Medical treatment must be based on competent informed consent—otherwise, the treatment provider commits a battery on the patient (e.g., *Younts v. St. Francis Hospital*, 1970). For consent to be informed, it must be knowing, rational, and voluntary (Meisel, Roth, & Lidz, 1977). In general, these legal concepts have been translated to mean that an individual must have a factual understanding of the information provided, utilize a rational process to assimilate information, and make a decision that

is not simply the result of coercion or deference to another. Legal regulation gives parents authority to give informed consent to their children's (including adolescents') medical treatment, in part because lawmakers assume that children and adolescents are not competent to do so themselves.

Thus, an interesting threshold question is whether this assumption about adolescents' incompetence is valid. Competence is a legal construct that may differ depending on the context; a finding of competence to consent to one form of medical treatment does not necessarily indicate a generalized "competence to consent" to all treatments. Nonetheless, basic cognitive capacities known to develop during childhood and adolescence underlie the ability to provide informed consent, regardless of the specific context. Grisso and Vierling (1978) map the legal terms of *knowing, intelligent,* and *voluntary consent* onto relevant psychological concepts and developmental considerations. Using their framework, we summarize what is known about adolescents' capacities generally, providing detail from a recent review (Miller, Drotar, & Kodish, 2004) and empirical studies of informed consent.

Grisso and Vierling (1978) define *knowing* consent as the match between the meaning of the information provided to the patient and the meaning attached by the patient to that information; this implicates understanding of specific terms as well as ethical and legal concepts such as rights and confidentiality. Research on children's knowledge of rights reports an age-based progression from concrete thinking about what rights can do for an individual to more abstract appraisals of rights and moral implications, typically emerging in adolescence (Melton, 1980, 1983b; Melton & Limber, 1992), although concrete thinking about rights still persists in adolescence (e.g., Ruck, Keating, Abramovitch & Koegl, 1998).

Intelligent consent refers to the capacity for assimilating and processing the information in a rational manner to reach a decision. Such a process implicates a wide range of abilities for abstract reasoning and logical thinking. Recent reviews conclude that these basic cognitive capacities have developed sufficiently by about mid-adolescence, although variations exist among individuals and within individuals across decision domains (Steinberg & Cauffman, 1996). In one study, for example, Weithorn and Campbell (1982) presented 9-, 14-, 18-, and 21-year-olds with hypothetical dilemmas regarding alternative treatments for two medical conditions (diabetes and epilepsy) and two psychological conditions (depression and enuresis). The 14-year-olds performed comparably to the two adult groups on outcome scores for evidence of choice, reasonableness of outcome (as judged by experts in the field), rationality of reasons, and understanding on three of four dilemmas. In the epilepsy dilemma, however, a higher percentage of adolescents rejected the reasonable treatment, which occasionally had physical side effects that might affect attractiveness. Although able to express a reasonable treatment choice, the 9-year-olds clearly demonstrated poorer capacities than adolescents and adults to understand and reason about the information provided.

Voluntary consent is given freely, not as a product of coercion or deference to others. Scherer and colleagues (Scherer, 1991; Scherer & Reppucci, 1998) presented groups of children, adolescents, and adults with three hypothetical treatment dilemmas in which the degree of parental influence varied. Most participants in all groups deferred to parental authority for less serious treatment decisions, but adolescents and young adults were less likely than children to go along with parental wishes regarding a kidney transplant. Developmental aspects of deference to the authority of medical personnel are less well known. In this realm, research on consent to treatment is sparse; once treatment decisions have been made, however, adolescents are generally less compliant than adults but rates vary by the type of treatment and related factors such as complexity of regime (Cromer & Tarnowski, 1989).

The research literatures on consent to treatment are limited by their reliance on samples of white, middle class youth responding to hypothetical vignette, but it indicates that, by age 14, most adolescents have developed the capacities to meet the threshold requirements for informed consent to medical and mental health treatment. Thus, empirical evidence largely contradicts the legal presumption of minors' incompetence to consent to treatment.

Even if many adolescents are competent to make medical decisions, giving parents legal authority may be a sensible policy for most medical treatments. It obviates the need and cost of individual competence assessments and it encourages parents to provide for their children's welfare—and to pay their medical bills. Moreover, although adolescents may be competent to make medical decisions within the informed consent framework, psychosocial influences on decision making may lead them to make choices that reflect immature judgment. For example, as mentioned, Weithorn and Campbell (1982) found adolescents more reluctant than adults to choose a beneficial treatment with untoward effects on physical appearance, perhaps due to greater youthful sensitivity to peer approval. In general, it seems likely that children and their parents do not have a conflict of interest about most treatment decisions, so the standard approach of giving parents authority generally functions satisfactorily to protect children's interests in this realm.

Most exceptions to the general rule that parents have authority to make medical decisions for their children arise in contexts in which minors' welfare and the general social welfare would be compromised if parental consent were required. The traditional mature minor doctrine allows older competent minors to consent to routine beneficial treatment or treatment in emergency situations when parents would likely consent or are unavailable (Wadlington, 1973). More interesting are statutes in many states that give minors the authority to consent to specific types of medical treatments. These typically include treatment for sexually transmitted diseases, substance abuse, mental health problems, and contraception and pregnancy (e.g., *Va. Code Ann.* §44.1-2969).

These minor consent statutes presume that adolescents are competent to consent to the designated medical treatments, but not on the basis of a judgment about adolescent maturity. Instead, minors are allowed to seek treatment without involving their parents out of concern that the standard requirement of parental consent may expose vulnerable youth to harm. The harm may come from two sources. First, lawmakers may rightly be concerned that for the kinds of treatments targeted by minors' consent statutes, parents, in fact, may have a conflict of interest with their children; if so, the traditional presumption that parents will generally act to promote their children's welfare may not hold. For example, parents may be angry when they learn of their children's sexual activity or drug use. Just as important, adolescents' fears about the anticipated parental reaction, whether accurate or not, might deter some adolescents from seeking needed treatment. Removing the parental consent barrier to treatment benefits the adolescents themselves as well by encouraging them to seek treatment; it also may reduce the prevalence of harmful and costly conditions (e.g., drug addiction, unwanted pregnancy), and thus benefit social welfare as well.

Access to Abortion: Competing Ideologies and Developmental Capacities

Of the issues in which lawmakers have departed from the standard legal treatment of adolescence, none has generated more controversy than the question of when and if legal minors should have access to abortion. This debate has brought into stark relief conflicting perspectives on adolescents and their capacities. Conservatives depict pregnant teens as children who should be subject to their parents' authority, while advocates for youthful

self-determination describe them as adults who should have the freedom to make their own decisions about abortions. Moreover, both sides are concerned not only with the developmental capacities and rights of minors, but also with the larger contest over abortion rights, regardless of age (Gorney, 1998; Rubin, 1998). Developed against the background of this intense controversy, the resulting legal framework is a complex product of judicial and political compromise. Thus, in many states, lawmakers regulating abortion have rejected the conventional binary classification and created a separate legal category for adolescents, in which teens are subject to judicial proceedings to determine whether they will be authorized to make their own decisions about abortion. We argue that this costly regulatory scheme harms the interests of pregnant teens and offers little in the way of social benefit.

Advocates of adolescent self-determination argue that adolescents should be accorded adult status in this context because the decision to terminate a pregnancy differs in many ways from other types of medical treatment. Because this choice is grounded in constitutionally based privacy and autonomy rights, lawmakers cannot ignore evidence that adolescents have the developmental maturity to make this decision. In the last 2 decades, researchers have struggled to investigate adolescent decision making about abortion in ecologically valid ways. Social scientists have examined many dimensions of the abortion decision, including moral and personal dimensions of reasoning (e.g., Smetana, 1981), patterns of consultation with others (e.g., Finken & Jacobs, 1996; Resnick, Bearlinger, Stark, & Blum, 1994), and the medical and mental health sequelae (Pope, Adler, & Tschann, 2001; Quinton, Major, & Richards, 2001).

The few studies that have focused on this decision context have found few significant differences between the capacities of older adolescents and adults to meet the legal requirements for informed consent to abortion. Lewis (1980) interviewed 42 adolescents and adults about their pregnancy decisions, and found no age-based differences in decision-making strategy or abstract reasoning. Adolescents did view their decisions as more externally compelled (through pressure from parents) than adults, indirectly implicating the voluntariness prong of competence. Ambuel and Rappaport (1992) interviewed young adolescents (ages 15 and under), older adolescents (ages 16–17), and adults (ages 18–21) awaiting pregnancy test results at a medical clinic. Responses were scored according to four criteria relevant to legal competence: volition of choice, global quality of reasoning, consequences, and richness of reasoning. Overall, these researchers found no age differences in any dimensions of competence. Young adolescents who reported they would not consider abortion as an option scored significantly worse than adults on volition, consequences, and global quality of reasoning. Although limited, these studies are consistent with more general research on decision making in their conclusion that mid- to late adolescents have developed the basic cognitive capacities required to provide valid informed consent.

Those who argue that adolescents should be classified as adults for purposes of abortion decision making do not rely solely on developmental claims or on the constitutional importance of the decision. After all, minors may be competent to exercise constitutional rights in other domains (e.g., voting, jury service) but are not granted the right to do so, in part because no great harm results from postponement. A distinguishing feature of the childbearing decision is that it cannot be postponed and that it has enormous consequences for the individual, often for the course of her future life. Moreover, pregnancy and childbirth pose substantial health risks for teens—and for their children—as well as negative consequences for the future welfare of both young mothers and their children (Furstenburg, Brooks-Gunn, & Chase-Lansdale, 1989). For these reasons, advocates who have little interest in adolescent self-determination per se might well support

adolescent access to abortion on paternalistic grounds (Scott, 1992).

The rationale for allowing adolescents to make decisions about abortion without involving their parents is similar in many regards to that which supports the minor consent statutes, discussed earlier. As with treatment for substance abuse, contraception, and sexually transmitted diseases, the decision about abortion is one on which parents' interests may not be consonant with their children. Parents' moral or religious views about abortion or teenage sexual behavior may trump concerns for the health or welfare of their pregnant adolescents. Although substantial research documents parental attitudes, behaviors, and influence on adolescent sexual behavior (Brooks-Gunn & Furstenburg, 1989; Meschke, Bartholomae, & Zentall, 2002), only a few studies have examined parental views or decision making in the abortion context (Henshaw & Kost, 1992; Resnick et al., 1994; Torres, Forrest, & Eisman, 1980).

Abortion is similar to treatments targeted by minor consent statutes in another way. Even if parents would be supportive of the choices their daughters make, teens might postpone dealing with the pregnancy because they fear their parents' reactions—a consequence with potentially even greater consequences that postponing other treatments. Approximately one-half to two-thirds of all adolescents do consult their parents about pregnancy; younger adolescents, who may be most in need of parental support and advice, are more likely than older girls to talk to their parents (Adler, Ozer & Tschann, 2003). Indeed, most adolescents who obtain an abortion consult parents or another adult (Resnick et al., 1994). In a nationally representative sample of unmarried minors having an abortion, 61% had told their parents; the most common reasons for nondisclosure were desires to preserve the relationship with parents (e.g., they might be hurt, disappointed, or angry), to prevent interference with relationships (e.g., parents might prevent the continuation of a relationship with the sexual partner), and to protect parents from additional problems (e.g., parents already had enough stress; Henshaw & Kost, 1992). In a study of women obtaining an elective, first-trimester abortion, adolescents scored significantly higher than adults on perceptions that having an abortion conflicts with how thier parents viewed them (Quinton et al., 2001). At 1 month postabortion, adolescents reported fewer benefits and greater harm from the abortion than adults, a difference that was explained in part by the significant age difference in parental conflict. Some observers have suggested that adolescents have unrealistically negative views of potential parental reaction to sex-related issues (Newcomer & Udry, 1985), but in large measure the accuracy of their beliefs is less relevant than the impact of those beliefs and concerns on adolescent behavior. In the Henshaw and Kost (1992) study, a substantial proportion of adolescents who did not tell their parents about their abortions reported as the reasons that they had experienced family violence, feared domestic violence, or thought they might be kicked out of the house if their parents found out about the abortion. Five of 26 Massachusetts young women who pursued a judicial bypass to parental consent requirements (i.e., a provision under the state's law that permits an adolescent to act without her parents' involvement if a judge agrees that the minor is mature enough to make the decision herself or that this course of action is in her best interests under the circumstances) did so out of fear of parental reaction; each of them described prior threatened or actual harm (Ehrlich, 2006). One-fourth of minors seeking judicial bypass under Minnesota's two-parent notification law brought one parent with them in the quest to legally bypass notification of the other parent (O'Keefe & Jones, 1990). Thus, standard legal requirements of parental consent to minors' medical treatment may pose a threat to the welfare of pregnant teens.

In one way, abortion is different from the treatments targeted by minors' consent statutes, but the difference itself arguably points in the direction of adolescent self-determination in this context. Unlike other procedures for which adolescents can provide consent without their parents' involvement, abortion involves a highly contested moral choice. Few dispute that the "right" choice for adolescents with a drug problem is treatment. However, no consensus exists about the "right" choice for a pregnant adolescent. Thus, a core issue in classifying pregnant teens as children or as adults is whether parents (or courts) should have the authority to impose their values on a pregnant adolescent or whether her values should determine whether she ends the pregnancy or has a child.

The legal regulation of adolescent access to abortion varies in different states. Some states (e.g., Connecticut, Washington) have shifted the boundary of childhood downward and classified pregnant teens as adults for abortion decisions, adopting the approach of the minor consent statutes. Others have maximized the reach of parental authority to the extent that it is constitutionally permitted, within limits set by the U.S. Supreme Court in a series of decisions have defined the parameters of state regulation. These decisions permit restrictions that would be unconstitutional for adults while simultaneously preventing states from subjecting adolescents to conventional parental authority over their children. Parental consent cannot be required of mature minors, but states can require that the determination of "maturity" be the subject of a judicial proceeding (*Bellotti v. Baird*, 1979). Under Supreme Court doctrine, if a minor is found to be immature, the court, exercising the state's *parens patriae* authority, must determine whether an abortion without parental involvement is in her best interest (*Bellotti v. Baird*, 1979; *City of Akron v. Akron Center for Reproductive Health*, 1983). Although parents are not granted veto power over an adolescent's abortion (*Bellotti v. Baird*, 1979; *City of Akron v. Akron Center for Reproductive Health*, 1983; *Planned Parenthood of Central Missouri v. Danforth*, 1976), states can require that parents must be notified of their daughter's intent to obtain an abortion (*H.L. v. Matheson*, 1981; *Hodgson v. Minnesota*, 1990; *Ohio v. Akron Center for*

Reproductive Health, 1990; *Ayotte v. Planned Parenthood of Northern New England*, 2006). Indeed, the Court upheld a parental requirement that *both* parents be notified, even if they are divorced (*Hodgson v. Minnesota*, 1990).

A substantial majority of states have responded to Supreme Court's pronouncements by passing laws requiring parental involvement in minors' abortion decisions, either through consent or notification, unless the pregnant minor demonstrates that she is "mature and well enough informed" to make her own abortion decision in a judicial bypass hearing (Alan Guttmacher Institute, 2008; *Bellotti v. Baird*, 1979, p. 647). The Court has provided no further guidance to judges making these determinations, and studies and judicial opinions confirm that the indeterminacy of such a standard results in wide variability of bypass hearing outcomes. In some states, virtually all petitions are granted using justifications that appear paternalistic rather than autonomy focused (Mnookin, 1985). In Massachusetts, 1,000 hearings per year resulted in just 13 denials over a 10-year period (Mnookin, 1985). Similarly, only 9 minors were deemed immature out of 477 Ohio bypass hearings that lasted an average of 12 minutes (Yates & Pliner, 1988). However, some states grant few petitions, and advocates recommended that adolescents go to nearby states to seek an abortion (Lewin, 1992). The capacities of those adolescents seeking abortion via judicial bypass (as a distinct subgroup of adolescents seeking abortion) have not been systematically studied (but see Ehrlich, 2006, for results of extensive interviews); nonetheless, it is highly unlikely that the extreme variation in the outcomes of bypass hearings (i.e., virtually all young women in one state are competent to consent, whereas all in another state are not) are a function of neutral competence assessments, particularly given the hearings' limited duration. Much more likely is that the attitudes of courts about abortion, teen pregnancy, and parental authority play an important role in judges' evaluations of "maturity."

The legal framework endorsed by the Supreme Court can be understood as an effort to find an acceptable resolution to a highly contested dispute about the boundary of childhood—a dispute that has more to do with conflicting attitudes about abortion itself than with views on the maturity or autonomy interests and capacities of adolescents. In a legal framework that predicates the minor's exercise of her constitutional right of choice on her ability to persuade a court of her maturity, even mature teens are subject to greater regulation than their adult counterparts. At the same time, however, states are precluded from treating pregnant adolescents as children subject to their parents' authority, solely because they are minors. This regulatory scheme eschews the standard binary classification of childhood and adulthood in favor of a special intermediate status for adolescents, albeit through a costly, time-consuming procedure of individualized maturity determinations.

On its face, this exception to the bright line rule is consistent with recognition of adolescence as a unique developmental period. However, it appears that this regulatory framework that treats adolescence as an intermediate category can be understood as the result of political and moral compromise, rather than as an expression of developmentally based legal theory. Although this compromise may remove the controversy from the politically charged legislative arena to the more deliberative setting of the courtroom, the regulatory scheme has little to recommend it. Empirical research has yet to examine the impact of participation in bypass hearings on health and developmental outcomes, but this procedural hurdle may lead pregnant teens to delays that can increase the health risks of abortion. Moreover, there is little reason to believe that the assessment of maturity that is the function of bypass hearings serves any useful purpose. Few studies examine the factors that predict judicial decision making. In some jurisdictions minimal variability in the outcome measure precludes meaningful statistical analysis; in others, judicial attitudes about abortion or teen pregnancy may trump adolescent capacities as an outcome predictor (Ehrlich, 2006). Some courts even refuse to conduct bypass hearings. (Silverstein, 2007). The upshot is that the creation of an intermediate category of adolescence in this context apparently does little to promote the health of adolescents and the welfare of society, and has no obvious advantage over the binary classification found in minors' consent statutes under which adolescents are simply treated as legal adults.

The experience with abortion regulation reinforces the theme with which we began. Although psychologists recognize adolescence as a distinct developmental period, for the most part, the law's tendency to ignore this transitional stage does not seem to have harmful effects. The rather simplistic approach of binary classification, under which the transition to adulthood is effected through a series of bright line legal rules, seems to serve the collective purpose of facilitating young citizens' development to healthy adulthood. Adolescents can drive at age 16, and vote and execute contracts at age 18, but they remain children until age 21 for the purposes of purchasing alcohol and (in some states) receiving child support while they attend college. The societal and developmental costs of delaying these rights and responsibilities do not appear to outweigh the benefits of such an approach.

RECOGNIZING ADOLESCENCE IN JUVENILE JUSTICE POLICY

There is one context in which policies that recognize the unique developmental status of adolescence would serve to promote both the interests of youth and of society. In juvenile justice policy, lawmakers have followed the conventional approach, treating young offenders either as children or as adults during different historical periods. As the following account will suggest, neither of these approaches has worked satisfactorily. Scientific knowledge about adolescence can serve as the basis of a legal regime that is fair to young offenders

and at the same time promotes social welfare (Scott & Steinberg, 2008).

Contrasting Portraits of Adolescent Offenders

The Era of Wayward Children— The Traditional Juvenile Court

The establishment of the juvenile court at the turn of the twentieth century was part of a broader Progressive reform agenda that expanded the boundaries of childhood, and dramatically reshaped the relationship between families and the state (Kett, 1977; Levine & Levine, 1970; Tiffin, 1982). With the creation of compulsory school attendance laws, the prohibition of child labor, and the establishment of a child welfare system, government assumed a far more active role in the supervision and even preemption of parental authority in the upbringing of children. Progressive reformers pursued a fundamental objective of improving the experience of childhood and expanding its boundaries, with a goal of shaping youth into productive citizens. In the rhetoric of this era, adolescents were described as children who required the care and protection of their parents, or of the state if parents were not up to the task. A reformer and juvenile court judge, Miriam Van Waters (1926) described the underlying theory of the new juvenile court, which was a core component of the Progressive program, in the following terms:

> [T]he child of the proper age to be under the jurisdiction of the juvenile court is encircled by the arm of the state, which, as a sheltering, wise parent, assumes guardianship and has power to shield the child from the rigors of the common law and from the neglect and depravity of adults. (p. 9)

In an era in which teens often assumed adult roles and responsibilities, reformers used several strategies to create a new image of adolescents. First, as the statement by Waters suggests, advocates described the youth who would benefit from Progressive policies in terms that emphasized their vulnerability, innocence and dependence. For example, dramatic stories of horrendous working conditions in factories bolstered the arguments for the need for protection through compulsory school attendance and child labor laws (Bremner, 1974). The solution to exploitation of children was a government ready to intervene to provide what the Progressives thought parents failed to provide—firm guidance and benevolent protection from harm.

The paternalistic rhetoric and protectionist agenda was readily accepted as applied to children who were subject to parental maltreatment, but reshaping the image of delinquent youth was more of a challenge. An important focus of Progressive reform was the establishment of a separate court that would respond to the needs of children who were subject to abuse and neglect by their parents and would also deal with juvenile offenders up to 16 or 18 years of age. Young offenders would not be subject to criminal punishment, but instead would receive rehabilitative treatment that would guide them on the path to productive adulthood. A second rhetorical "strategy" employed by the reformers was to downplay distinctions between young offenders and child victims of parental abuse, by arguing that abuse, neglect, and delinquency were *all* manifestations of inadequate parenting (Fox, 1967). Thus, young offenders were portrayed as children whose parents had failed them, and the state's role in both delinquency and maltreatment cases was "to intervene in the spirit of a wise parent" (Van Waters, 1926, p. 11) to provide care and rehabilitation. Advocates and judges related stories of young offenders—boys and girls, younger and older teens, committing minor and more serious offenses—who came before the juvenile court and responded favorably to paternalistic interventions designed only to promote their welfare (Lindsey & O'Higgins, 1909).

Although the child labor and school attendance reforms effectively shifted the boundary of childhood, the Progressive efforts in the area of juvenile justice were less successful. The romanticized accounts of young offenders as innocent children wronged by their parents ignored the crucial distinction between delinquents and maltreated children—that criminal conduct causes harm to others. Thus, the system's pretense that delinquency proceedings were solely to promote the welfare of the child before the court ignored the state's legitimate interest in protecting society from crime. Moreover, acceptance of the rehabilitative model was likely always premised on the success of rehabilitative interventions in reforming young offenders and protecting society, and over time, confidence in the effectiveness of rehabilitation waned.

Criticism of the juvenile court came from those who thought the system failed to control juvenile crime, but it also came from liberals who cared about the welfare of young offenders. Advocates for youth became disenchanted, because young offenders were not receiving treatment and yet they were processed without the procedural protections and guarantees that were provided to adults in criminal court (Allen, 1964). In 1967, the U.S. Supreme Court agreed a landmark opinion holding that juveniles facing the deprivation of their liberty in delinquency proceedings were entitled to many of the rights accorded to adult criminal defendants under the Due Process Clause of the Constitution—most importantly, the right to an attorney (*In re Gault*, 1967).

In the view of many observers, *Gault* marked the beginning of the end of the traditional juvenile court. Although it was at least 2 more decades before the idea that juvenile offenders should be subject to more lenient treatment in the juvenile system was seriously challenged, *Gault* dealt a severe blow to the already faltering rehabilitative model. More importantly, perhaps, although thoughtful reforms were proposed in the 1970s and 1980s, no coherent contemporary rationale for maintaining a separate juvenile justice system took hold (American Bar Association, 1982; Zimring, 1978). Youth continued to be processed in the juvenile system, but it was not clear what its purposes should be or how it should differ from the adult system.

Contemporary Reform and Young Criminals

Conservative critics ridiculed the leniency of the juvenile justice system and, as violent juvenile crime rates rose in 1980s and early 1990s, they intensified their attacks. In sharp contrast to the Progressive depiction of young offenders as children, these punitive reformers argued that youth who commit serious crimes should be tried and punished as adults. This modern reform movement has led to sweeping statutory changes over the past decade or so (Torbet & Szymanski, 1998). The explicit goals of this crusade were public safety and punishment, and little concern was expressed about the welfare of young wrongdoers or hope for their reform. The historical depiction of delinquents as wayward children has been replaced by a modern archetype of the savvy young criminal who is a serious threat to society. Modern advocates of tough policies have denied any psychological distinctions between youth and adults that are relevant to criminal responsibility; the mantra of the movement is "adult time for adult crime" (Ellis, 1993; Regnery, 1985).

Contemporary reformers have accomplished the transformation of children charged with crimes into legal adults through several legislative strategies. First, the age at which juveniles can be transferred to adult court has been lowered for many crimes (Torbet, Gable, Hurst, Montgomery, Szymanski, & Thomas, 1997). The juvenile court has always used transfer to adult court as a safety valve for those juveniles ill suited to its jurisdiction. Traditionally, transfer required a judicial inquiry into a juvenile's appropriateness for juvenile court that considered a broad set of criteria, including the youth's maturity and development. Recent reforms have not only lowered the age of transfer and expanded the range of crimes that can trigger a transfer hearing, they have also narrowed the scope of the

transfer inquiry to focus only on offense seriousness and prior record (Wagman, 2000). In combination, these changes facilitate the transfer of greater numbers of juveniles.

Moreover, reliance on judicial hearings in which transfer decisions are made on a case-by-case basis by judges has yielded in many states to other avenues to criminal court adjudication and punishment of juveniles. Legislative waiver categorically excludes from juvenile court jurisdiction large classes of young offenders, usually defined by age and offense category. Thus, a 13-year-old charged with armed robbery may be statutorily defined as an adult and simply not eligible for juvenile court treatment at all. Moreover, "direct file" statutes confer discretion on prosecutors to charge youth as juveniles or as adults for certain crimes (Snyder & Sickmund, 2006). In addition, youth sentenced in juvenile court under blended sentencing schemes serve time in adult facilities once they exceed the age of juvenile corrections jurisdiction. Through these mechanisms, the modern reformers have transformed the legal landscape by lowering the age of adult prosecution and punishment for a broad range of juvenile offenders. Although no national statistics exist, researchers estimate that over 200,000 youth are tried annually as adults (Sickmund, Snyder, and Poe-Yamagata, 1997).

The reforms have resulted in more punitive treatment of youth in the juvenile system as well. Incarceration plays a much larger role in the disposition of juveniles today as a result of the "get-tough" reforms of the 1990s. A study in Washington State found that confinement rates in that state's juvenile system increased by 40% during the 1990s—period when serious crime rates fell by 50%. In the late 1980s, out of each 1,000 Washington youth, 2.5 youth were confined in juvenile facilities; a decade later the confinement rate had increased to 3.5 youth per 1,000 (Aos, Phipps, Barnoski, & Lieb, 2001). Two changes have led to increased confinement of juveniles across the country. First, juveniles who would have received community sanctions in an earlier era are sent to secure facilities today. Moreover, incarceration periods are much longer than they once were.

On one level, these reforms are consistent with some other policies that have lowered the age boundary to define adolescents as adults. Advocates for minors' consent statutes and alcohol restrictions, for example, argue that these policies respond to harmful conduct by adolescents in ways that promote social welfare. Unlike these other policies, however, the modern juvenile justice reforms make little pretense that punishing young offenders as adults will benefit the juveniles themselves. Their advocacy rests solely on a claim that punitive policies will reduce the social costs of youth crime and promote social welfare. In its lack of regard for the welfare of young persons, juvenile justice policy is unique and anomalous in the legal regime of youth regulation. Shortly, we will review the growing research base that challenges this claim and argue that social welfare and youth welfare are undermined by modern juvenile justice reforms.

Enthusiasm for punishing young criminals seems to have abated in recent years as policy makers and the public are having second thoughts about a justice system in which age and immaturity often are ignored in calculating criminal punishment. Rates of violent juvenile crime decreased steadily beginning for since the mid-1990s (Snyder, 2005; Torbet & Szymanski, 1998), and legislatures have begun to realize that harsh sanctions are costly to taxpayers. In several states, punitive statutes adopted in the 1990s are being moderated or repealed (National Juvenile Defender Center, 2007). There is also evidence that public support for harsh policies is weaker than conventional wisdom presumed (Nagin et al., 2005). Courts and legislatures are beginning to pay attention to arguments by critics of contemporary policies that holding young offenders fully responsible for their crimes violates well-accepted principles that define just punishment in the criminal law (Scott & Steinberg, 2003; Steinberg & Scott, 2003). In this calmer climate, many observers argue that a reexamination of punitive justice policies is in order (Scott & Steinberg, 2008; Zimring, 1998).

A Developmental Model of Juvenile Justice Policy

Both the history of the traditional juvenile court and the account of contemporary justice policies under which youth often are classified as adults suggest that the standard approach to legal regulation of adolescence—binary classification as either children or adults—has not worked well in the context of crime policy. Instead, a system that treats adolescence as an intermediate legal category between childhood and adulthood and that is based on scientific knowledge about this developmental stage is likely to be more satisfactory than either the traditional or the contemporary approach. Juvenile crime regulation based on developmental knowledge has two important advantages over the alternatives. First, it is more compatible with principles of fairness that shape the constitutional contours of criminal punishment and procedures. Second, a system based on scientific knowledge of adolescence is more likely to promote social welfare by reducing the social costs of juvenile crime (Scott & Steinberg, 2008).

Traditional juvenile justice policy, although its tone was benign, did more harm than good. Even assuming that the Progressive reformers had pure intentions (an assumption that some have challenged; Platt, 1977), the myth of offenders as vulnerable children was implausible when applied to older youth charged with serious crimes. It undermined the credibility of the system, leading many to believe that public safety and accountability did not get adequate attention (Feld, 1999). Moreover, as the Court recognized in *Gault*, young offenders themselves were harmed because the juvenile court operated without the procedural constraints that protect adult criminal defendants, whose interest was always understood to be in conflict with that of the state. Further, because the ostensible purpose of intervention was to rehabilitate rather than punish the child, the court and correctional system had virtually unbridled discretion in fashioning dispositions, unconstrained by the principles limiting criminal punishment (Allen, 1964; Scott & Steinberg, 2003). Thus, because punishment and public protection were important but hidden forces at work in the disposition of young offenders, the reality of the juvenile justice system was that many youth got little rehabilitation in prison-like correctional facilities. A return to traditional juvenile justice policy is not the solution to the excesses of the recent punitive reforms.

Modern reformers make several empirical assumptions in justifying punitive policies—assumptions that the scientific evidence does not support. First, they assume that adolescents are not different from adults in any way that is important to criminal responsibility and thus deserve the same punishment for their offenses as their adult counterparts. Second, they assume that youth who are tried in criminal proceedings are as capable as adults of functioning adequately as defendants and meet the constitutional mandate that criminal defendants must be competent to stand trial (*Pate v. Robinson,* 1966). Finally, conservative reformers also assume (and argue) that punishing young offenders as adults is essential to protect society from juvenile crime. The empirical evidence from developmental psychology challenges all of these assumptions.

First, the evidence indicates that adolescent psychosocial immaturity distinguishes young lawbreakers from adults in ways that are very likely to affect their understanding and judgment in making criminal choices. Thus, holding them fully accountable for their crimes violates the principle of proportionality, which defines fair criminal punishment. Second, research shows that younger teens are likely to be less capable than adults of functioning competently in the trial setting, raising questions about whether they meet the constitutional mandate of trial competence (Grisso, et. al., 2003; Scott & Grisso, 2005). Finally, the claim that harsh punishment promotes social welfare does not stand up to empirical scrutiny.

Research comparing youth retained in juvenile court with those prosecuted as adults indicates that harsh policies may aggravate recidivism rates (Bishop & Frazier, 2000; Fagan, 1996). Moreover, recent research on developmental pathways indicates that the most adolescent offenders desist from offending as part of their life course development and are not likely to become career criminals unless the justice system pushes them in that direction (Moffitt, 1993; Piquero, Farrington, & Blumstein, 2003). This, together with research showing the importance of social context for the accomplishment of critical developmental tasks, suggests that correctional interventions can play an important role in the whether young offenders continue in lives of crime or become productive (or at least noncriminal) adults (Steinberg, Chung & Little, 2004). Thus, policies based on utilitarian goals must consider the long-term consequences of punishment in addition to the direct costs of juvenile crime.

Criminal Responsibility in Adolescence

The criminal law assumes that most offenders make rational autonomous choices to commit crimes, and that the legitimacy of punishment is undermined if the criminal decision is coerced, irrational, or based on a lack of understanding about the meaning of the choice (Bonnie, Coughlin, Jeffries, & Low, 2004). Punishment must be proportionate to blameworthiness, which is mitigated if the individual's decision-making capacity is seriously compromised.

Historically, developmental immaturity has been deemed irrelevant to criminal responsibility because juveniles were processed in a separate court and correctional system that ostensibly did not impose punishment at all (Scott & Steinberg, 2003; Walkover, 1984). Thus, the question of how the criminal law should take immaturity into account in deciding fair punishment got little attention. Recently, the role of immaturity in the determination of criminal responsibility has become important, as younger and younger offenders are processed in adult court. There is a pressing need for theory and research regarding how developmental immaturity should be considered in determining criminal responsibility and punishment.

Psychological research supports the hypothesis that developmental factors influence youthful judgment and (ultimately) decision making in ways that could be relevant to criminal choices. Several authors have reviewed how aspects of adolescent cognitive and, particularly, psychosocial development might implicate youth's capacities as defendants (e.g., Scott et al., 1995; Scott & Steinberg, 2008; Scott & Grisso, 1997; Cauffman & Steinberg, 2000; Steinberg & Cauffman, 1996; Woolard, 2002).

Capacities for reasoning and understanding improve significantly from late childhood into adolescence, and by mid-adolescence, most teens are close to adults in their ability to reason and to process information (what might be called pure cognitive capacities), at least in the abstract (Keating, 2004). The reality, however, is that adolescents are likely less capable than adults are in *using* these cognitive capacities in making real-world choices partly because of lack of experience and partly because teens do not tend to learn from experience as effectively as adults (Reyna & Farley, 2006; Ward & Overton, 1990).

Psychosocial maturation lags behind cognitive development, however, and psychosocial immaturity may contribute to decisions about involvement in criminal activity, in several ways. First, adolescents are more responsive to peer influence than are adults. Peer conformity and compliance are powerful influences on adolescent behavior and likely play an important role in delinquent conduct as well (Berndt, 1979; Costanzo & Shaw, 1966; Gardner & Steinberg, 2005). In contrast to adult offending, most juvenile crime occurs in groups, and peer influence may be an important motivating factor (Reiss & Farrington, 1991). Adolescents also generally have a foreshortened temporal perspective; they tend to identify and focus on short-term consequences more readily than those in the future (Nurmi, 1991; Greene, 1986;

Steinberg et al., in press). Developmental differences in future orientation may be linked to differences in risk preferences: it is well documented that youth tend to engage in risky behaviors more often than adults. They also appear to calculate and weigh risks and benefits somewhat differently than adults, tending to focus more on rewards and less on risks than do adults (Reyna & Farley, 2006; Steinberg, 2004; Byrnes, 1998; Furby & Beyth-Marom, 1992; Gardner, 1992). Adolescents' capacities for risk *perception* are almost as good as adults in laboratory studies, but teens' abilities are diminished in social contexts where emotion, experience, willingness, and opportunity for risk behavior interact (Reyna & Farley, 2006; Steinberg, 2004). Finally, the limited research that exists suggests that adolescents are more impulsive than adults, that they tend to be subject to more rapid and extreme mood changes, and that they may be more reactive to environmental cues and temptations—although the relationship between impulsivity and moodiness is unclear (Reyna & Farley, 2006; Steinberg & Cauffman, 1996).

These psychosocial attributes of adolescence may be linked to neurological development. Recent studies of adolescent brain development show that important structural change takes place during this stage in the frontal lobes of the brain, most importantly in the prefrontal cortex. This region is central to "executive functions" and self-regulation—advanced thinking processes that are employed in planning, regulating emotions, the anticipation of future consequences, and weighing the costs and benefits of decisions before acting (Dahl, 2004; Giedd, 2004; Spear, 2000). Researchers believe that the prefrontal cortex does not fully develop until one's early 20s. Thus, the immature judgment of teens to some extent may be a function of hard wiring that creates a disjunction between heightened sensitivity to reward and regulatory capacity (Steinberg, 2004).

Adolescents, due to their psychological immaturity, are less blameworthy than adult offenders for another reason. The criminal law presumes that a criminal act reflects the actor's bad character. Thus, offenders who can show that their criminal conduct was out of character (by offering evidence that they generally are persons of good character) may be able to get a reduced sentence. This source of mitigation applies to adolescents as well, not because they can demonstrate good character, but because their characters are unformed. As psychologists since Erik Erikson have observed, an important developmental task of adolescence is the formation of personal identity (Erikson, 1968). During this stage, identity is fluid; values, plans, attitudes, and beliefs are likely to be tentative as teens struggle to figure out who they are. This process involves a lot of experimentation, which for many adolescents means engaging in risky activities, including crime. Research supports that much juvenile crime stems from experimentation typical of this developmental stage rather than moral deficiencies reflecting bad character. Thus, it is not surprising that 17-year-olds commit more crimes than any other age group and that the rate declines steeply thereafter (Piquero et al., 2003).

Developmental research is consistent with theories about cognitive and psychosocial differences between adolescent offenders and adults, but only a few empirical studies exist that deal even indirectly with decision making about criminal activity. (That little research deals *directly* with these matters is easy to understand.) Fried and Reppucci (2001) evaluated the influence of several psychosocial factors on criminal decision making using videotaped vignettes of a series of decisions resulting in a crime. Age-based differences in psychosocial capacities followed a U-shaped function with mid-adolescents (ages 15–16) scoring lower on maturity than their younger (ages 12–14) and older (ages 17–18) counterparts. A possible explanation for this pattern is that the responses of younger teens, who have not yet undergone individuation, may reflect their parents' values. Cauffman and Steinberg (2000) examined age differences between adolescents and adults on a series of hypothetical

vignettes describing various criminal behaviors. They also found age differences in psychosocial factors, which in turn predicted decision outcomes. Higher psychosocial maturity was associated with more socially responsible decisions in the vignettes. Age did not remain a significant predictor once psychosocial maturity was taken into account.

Although limited in scope, this research provides initial support for the hypothesis that developmental factors contribute to immature judgment in ways that may differentiate adolescent criminal decision making from that of adults. These studies provide the impetus for continued research into developmental capacities that are relevant to legal assessments of culpability. The findings are consistent with the notion that adolescent offenders should be considered less blameworthy than adults but not blameless, as an insane defendant or a child might be. In short, developmental arguments support adoption of a mitigation model in the regulation of juvenile crime—a model that recognizes the adolescents generally are less culpable than adults (Scott & Steinberg, 2008; Steinberg & Scott, 2003).

The U.S. Supreme Court has recognized that adolescent immaturity mitigates culpability in a landmark case holding that imposing the death penalty for crimes committed by juveniles is a violation of the Constitutional prohibition against cruel and unusual punishment (*Roper v. Simmons*, 2005). Adopting the mitigation framework offered by Scott and Steinberg in an *American Psychologist* article (Steinberg & Scott, 2003), the Court pointed to the diminished decision-making capacity of adolescents, which leads them to make "impetuous and ill-considered decisions," and also to youthful vulnerability to peer pressure. Justice Kennedy, writing for the majority, also emphasized transient nature of the traits that contribute to youthful criminal conduct. He opined that the unformed nature of adolescent character make it "less supportable to conclude that even a heinous crime [by an adolescent] was evidence of an irretrievably depraved character" (p. 570).

Adolescent Competence as Criminal Defendants

The punitive juvenile justice policies of the past generation implicate another issue of constitutional importance. The Supreme Court has held that under the Due Process Clause of the 14th Amendment to the Constitution, criminal defendants cannot be subject to criminal adjudication unless they are competent to stand trial. The competence standard that is applied to criminal trials focuses on the defendant's "rational as well as factual" understanding of the proceedings against him and his capacity to assist his attorney in his defense (*Dusky v. United States,* 1960). This requirement was developed to ensure that mentally disabled (adult) defendants are dealt with fairly in the justice system; fundamental fairness requires that an individual facing the deprivation of his or her liberty in a criminal proceeding must understand the purposes and consequences of the trial and be capable of participating effectively. Only recently have courts and legislatures begun to recognize that the competence requirement also applies to defendants whose competence may be questionable due to developmental immaturity (National Juvenile Defender Center, 2007; Scott & Grisso, 2005). As increasing numbers of juveniles are transferred to the adult system and subject to criminal prosecution, the question arises of whether they are competent under the standards applied to adult criminal defendants. The concern, of course, is particularly great for younger teens, who today are eligible for adult treatment for a broad range of crimes. A second concern relates to the standard of trial competence to be applied in delinquency proceedings.

As the boundaries between the adult and juvenile justice systems became more porous in the 1990s, the need for a comprehensive study comparing the capacities of juveniles and adults to function as trial defendants became apparent. The MacArthur Adjudicative Competence Study was conducted in response to that need (Grisso et. al., 2003). Conducted in four sites and involving almost 1,400 participants

between the ages of 11 and 24 from the community and from the justice system, this study aimed to examine whether and how adolescent immaturity affected abilities that are important in the trial setting. The study employed several measures, including an instrument that had been developed and validated independently to measure reasoning and understanding relevant to the trial context: the MacArthur Competence Assessment Tool–Criminal Adjudication (MacCAT-CA) (Poythress et al., 2002). A cutoff score denoting significant impairment was derived by administering the test to thousands of defendants, including a large group that had been found incompetent to stand trial. The researchers also used an instrument developed for the study to assess psychosocial capacities as they affect judgment in decision making in the trial context: the MacArthur Judgment Evaluation instrument (MacJEN).

The study confirmed that competence-related abilities improve with age during adolescence. On average, youth aged 11–13 performed significantly more poorly than adults on the competence measures. The performance of approximately one-third of this age group evidenced significant impairment, comparable to adults found incompetent to stand trial. Approximately 20% of youth ages 14 and 15 showed substantial impairment. Adolescents aged 16 and 17 performed comparably to adults. Younger youth also performed less well on the measures of psychosocial maturity. For example, 11- to 13-year-olds were much more inclined to waive their constitutional rights and admit their crimes than were older participants, suggesting that they are more vulnerable to coercion by adult authority figures (e.g., the police). They also were less inclined to consider the future consequences of their decisions (regarding interrogation and accepting a plea agreement) than older participants.

This study raises a significant constitutional challenge to the adjudication of younger teens as adults and supports the conclusion that, at a minimum, competence should be evaluated whenever younger teens are transferred (and perhaps that trying young teens as adults generally risks unfairness and inefficiency) and implications for remediation be considered (see Viljoen & Grisso, 2007). Just as importantly, the study raises a question of what the standard for competence should be in *juvenile* delinquency proceedings. Courts have recognized that the requirement of trial competence applies to these proceedings, but have been uncertain about whether the adult (*Dusky*) standard applies (*People v. Carey*, 2000). The MacArthur study suggests that a more relaxed standard should be applied—to avoid a large number of younger youth being found incompetent to be tried in *any* court. Under constitutional Due Process principles, however, a more relaxed competence standard is acceptable only if the stakes that juveniles face in delinquency proceedings are substantially different from sentences imposed by criminal courts. This suggests a need to rethink the trend toward sanctions in the juvenile system that is similar to adult punishment (Scott & Grisso, 2005).

Adolescent Development and the Social Costs of Crime

In reality, although the scientific evidence of adolescent immaturity is compelling, principle alone will not dictate juvenile crime policy, any more than it has dictated policy governing minors' access to abortion. Ultimately, the most compelling argument for a separate, less punitive, system for dealing with young criminals rests on utilitarian grounds. In this section, we draw on developmental and criminological research to challenge the claim offered by proponents of the recent reforms that punitive policies are the best means to achieve public protection and minimize the social cost of youth crime. These ends can better be served by policies that attend to the developmental needs of young offenders as adolescents.

The utilitarian argument for tough sanctions has a superficial appeal; after all, youth who are in prison cannot be on the street committing crimes. It seems likely, indeed, that the expanded use of incarceration has contributed to the decline in juvenile crime through incapacitation, at least in the short term. But researchers directly examining the impact of statutory change have not found that reform laws have a deterrent effect. For example, a few researchers have studied the effect of automatic transfer statutes, either by comparing two similar states with different laws, or by examining crime rates in a single state before and after a legislative reform (Singer & McDowell, 1988; Jensen & Metsger, 1994). These studies have found that punitive reforms have little effect on youth crime. Only one substantial study has found that crime rates appear to decline under harsh statutes (and the methodology of that study has been sharply criticized) (Doob & Webster, 2003; Levitt, 1998). Interview studies find that many incarcerated youth express intentions to avoid harsh penalties in the future, but the extent to which these intentions result in behavior change is unclear (Schneider & Ervin, 1990).

More importantly, supporters of tough policies ignore what are likely to be substantial long-term costs of punitive policies, in light of existing knowledge about the developmental patterns of antisocial behavior in adolescence. Rather than reducing crime, prosecuting and sentencing youth as adults and subjecting them to long periods of incarceration may have iatrogenic effects that increase the costs of offending both for individual offenders and for society. Interventions in the juvenile system, however, both in facilities and in community programs, potentially can facilitate the transition of delinquent youth to conventional adult roles.

Developmental knowledge underscores the risks associated with the recent trend toward widespread processing and punishing of adolescents as adults. A major flaw of these policies from a social welfare perspective is that they expand the net of social control well beyond the relatively small proportion of juvenile offenders that research indicates are on long-term offending trajectories. Many youth engage in some form of delinquency during adolescence, but desist as adulthood approaches (Piquero et al., 2003; Farrington, 1986; Jessor & Jessor, 1977). Indeed, most teenage males participate in some delinquent behavior as part of the experimentation that contributes to identity formation, described earlier. This reality has led Terrie Moffitt, a developmental psychologist, to conclude that delinquent behavior is "a normal part of teen life" (Moffitt, 1993). These youth are not headed toward lives of crime, unless the correctional system pushes them in that direction. Thus, based on her research on developmental trajectories, Moffitt labels most youthful criminal conduct "adolescence-limited" behavior. Her research, which is supported by many other studies, identifies a relatively small percentage of youthful offenders who are at high risk of becoming career criminals, (D'Unger, Land, McCall, & Nagin, 1998; Moffitt, 1993). A number of factors predict the likelihood of belonging to the group that Moffitt has labeled "life-course persistent offenders," most importantly, a pattern of antisocial conduct that often begins in early childhood, but differentiating them from more typical adolescent offenders in a cross-sectional sample of same-aged offenders is an uncertain business and prone to error. Transfer policies driven by age and offense type cannot distinguish serious persistent offenders from those likely to desist with maturity.

The likelihood that typical adolescent offenders will accomplish the transition to adulthood successfully may depend in part on the state's response to their criminal conduct. A policy of imposing adult criminal penalties on young offenders may increase the probability that they will become career criminals, or it may delay desistence. At a minimum, criminal punishment is likely to undermine their future educational and employment prospects and general social productivity as members of society.

Research evidence supports this concern. Prosecution and incarceration in the adult system appear to increase recidivism and limit prospects for a productive future. Young offenders in Florida described the criminal court process in very different terms than their youthful counterparts in juvenile court (Bishop and Frazier, 2000; Bishop, Frazier, Lanza-Kaduce, & White, 1998). Offenders perceived juvenile court in relatively favorable terms, describing the court process and resulting punishment as well intentioned and fair. Transferred offenders, in contrast, felt court officials (including some defense counsel) were disengaged or hostile to their interests; they found the process confusing and the outcomes unfair. Transferred juveniles felt physically and emotionally threatened by staff and other inmates. They also reported learning about crime from other inmates. Although one might reasonably expect that inmates would view incarceration as a negative experience, the distinctions drawn between the inmates in the juvenile and criminal justice systems may be important to the extent that the effectiveness of punishment in reducing recidivism depends in part on perceptions of its legitimacy (Bishop & Frazier, 2000).

Studies also indicate that adult punishment may increase recidivism rates for most offense categories. Studies in Florida (Bishop et al., 1998; Johnson, Lanza-Kaduce, & Woolard, in press; Winner, Lanza-Kaduce, Bishop, & Frazier, 1997) and New York and New Jersey (Fagan, 1996) compared youth adjudicated as adults with those retained in juvenile court for comparable offenses. Both sets of studies used multiple measures of recidivism over short-term and long-term (4–7 years) follow-up periods. Fagan's research found that transfer was associated with higher rearrest and reincarceration among robbery offenders, although not among burglary offenders. Using a matching procedure that paired transferred youth and juvenile system youth on demographic and offense variables, the Florida studies found that transferred youth were more likely to reoffend in five of the seven offense categories studied, and were rearrested more often and more rapidly than their juvenile court counterparts. Recent analyses of matched pairs of transferred and retained youth suggest that transfer may aggravate recidivism because it "leapfrogs" over a system of graduated sanctions often found in juvenile court (Johnson et al., in press). Repeat offenders in the juvenile justice system who received graduated sanctions had lower recidivism as adults than those in the juvenile justice system who did not receive graduated sanctions (and proceeded directly to incarceration) and those who were transferred to the adult criminal justice system. Transfer status failed to predict recidivism when measures of correctional histories, including graduated sanctions, were included in the analysis.

Higher recidivism rates are not the only potential social cost of transfer; criminal conviction also harms young offenders' future prospects for productive lives upon release. The research on transfer's effects is scanty at present, but it challenges the claim that punitive legal policies are the optimal response to juvenile offending.

Developmental knowledge reinforces this conclusion. Adolescence is a critical developmental stage during which teens acquire competencies, skills, and experiences essential to success in adult roles (Steinberg et al., 2004). Acquiring necessary skills is a process of interaction between the individual and her social environment, which can enhance or impede healthy development. Correctional facilities and programs constitute this environment for youth in the justice system. If a youth's experience in the correctional system disrupts educational and social development severely, it may irreversibly undermine prospects for gainful employment, successful family formation, and engaged citizenship, and directly or indirectly contribute to reoffending.

The differences between the juvenile and adult systems have blurred a bit in recent years, but, even today, juvenile facilities and programs are far more likely to provide an adequate context for development than adult prison. Prisons are aversive developmental settings. They are generally large institutions with staff whose function is custodial and who generally relate to prisoners as adversaries; educational and counseling programs are sparse, and older prisoners are often mentors in crime or abusive to incarcerated youth (Bishop & Frazier, 2000). The juvenile system, although far from optimal, operates in many states on the basis of policies that recognize that offenders are adolescents with developmental needs. Facilities are less institutional than prisons; staff–offender ratio is higher; staff attitudes are more therapeutic and more programs are available (Forst, Fagan, & Vivona, 1989). A substantial body of research produced over the past 15 years show that many juvenile programs, in both community and institutional settings, have a substantial crime-reduction effect; for the most promising programs that effect is in the range of 20%–30% (Aos et al., 2001; Lipsey, 1995). In general, successful programs are those that attend to the lessons of developmental psychology.

The success of rehabilitative programs does not mean that we should return to the traditional rehabilitative model of juvenile justice, however; punishment is an appropriate purpose when society responds to juvenile crime. Both adult prisons and juvenile correctional programs impose punishment, however, and the juvenile system is better situated to invest in the human capital of young offenders and facilitate the transition to conventional adult roles, a realistic goal for youth who are adolescent-limited offenders. In reality, the future prospects of juveniles in the justice system are not as bright as those of other adolescents. But developmental knowledge reinforces a growing body of empirical research indicating that juvenile offenders more likely to desist from criminal activity and to become noncriminal adults if they are not dealt with as adults, but rather are sanctioned as juveniles in a separate system that is attendant to the needs of adolescents as a special class of offenders.

CONCLUSION

Over the course of the last century, lawmakers have tended to ignore adolescence as a distinctive age period, preferring instead to categorize individuals in this developmental stage as either children or adults depending on the policy context and goals. Presumptions about dependency, vulnerability, and incompetence to make decisions are used to justify a bright line demarcation between childhood and adulthood. In general, this approach has functioned well, providing adolescents with societal protections at relatively low cost to their developmental autonomy. However, in juvenile justice policy, the binary approach has been a failure. Cast alternately as innocent, wayward children or as fully mature predators, juvenile delinquents have been subject to policy initiatives that fail to protect their interests or those of society. A policy approach grounded in a realistic account of adolescence would maximize the likelihood that juvenile offenders could desist from crime and reintegrate successfully into the community.

The twenty-first century may see policy makers paying attention to this transitional stage in other areas. Although, as we have suggested, this move can be costly and should be taken only when binary categories are inadequate, in some contexts, adolescents might benefit from a probationary period in which adult skills can be acquired, with protection from the costs of inexperienced choices. Some states have recently adopted this approach in changing laws governing driving, authorizing adolescents to drive motor vehicles, but imposing restrictions (e.g., no night driving) that do not apply to adults (*California Vehicle Code* §12814.6). On issues as varied as liability for contracts and the weight accorded to teens' preferences in divorce custody disputes, lawmakers have recently taken tentative steps toward recognizing the uniqueness of this developmental stage (Scott, 2000). Developmental research underscores the notion that adolescents resemble both children and adults in many ways, depending on the context and circumstances. The developmental realities of adolescence alone will never dictate legal regulation, but developmental research and theory can provide the empirical foundation for policies that promote a healthy and productive transition from childhood to adulthood.

REFERENCES

Adelson, J., & O'Neil, R. (1966). The growth of political ideas in adolescence: The sense of community. *Journal of Personality and Social Psychology, 4,* 295–306.

Adler, N. E., Ozer, E. J., & Tschann, J. M. (2003). Abortion among adolescents. *American Psychologist, 58,* 214–234.

Alan Guttmacher Institute. (2008). Parental involvement in minors' abortions. *State policies in brief as of May 1, 2008.* New York: Author.

Allen, F. (1964). *The borderland of criminal justice.* Chicago: University of Chicago Press.

Ambuel, B., & Rappaport, J. (1992). Developmental trends in adolescents' psychological and legal competence to consent to abortion. *Law & Human Behavior, 16,* 129–153.

American Bar Association. (1982). Standards relating to dispositions. *Institute of Judicial Administration/American Bar Association Juvenile Justice Standards.* Washington, DC: Author.

Aos, S., Phipps, P., Barnoski, R. & Lieb, R. (2001). *The comparative costs and benefits of programs to reduce crime.* Olympia: Washington State Institute for Public Policy.

Arenella, P. (1992). Convicting the morally blameless. *UCLA Law Review, 39,* 1511–1622.

Arnett, J. J. (2000). Emerging adulthood: A theory of development from the late teens through the twenties. *American Psychologist, 55,* 469–480.

Arnett, J. J., & Tanner, J. L. (Eds.). (2006). *Emerging adults in America: Coming of age in the 21st century.* Washington, DC: American Psychological Association.

Ayotte v. Planned Parenthood of Northern New England, 546 U.S. 320 (2006).

Bellotti v. Baird, 443 U.S. 622 (1979).

Berndt, T. J. (1979). Developmental changes in conformity to peers and parents. *Developmental Psychology, 15,* 608–616.

Bishop, D. M., & Frazier, C. E. (2000). Consequences of transfer. In J. Fagan & F. Zimring (Eds.), *The changing borders of juvenile justice: Transfer of adolescents to the criminal court* (pp. 227–276). Chicago: University of Chicago Press.

Bishop, D. M., Frazier, C. E., Lanza-Kaduce, L., & White, H. G. (1998). *Juvenile transfers to criminal court study: Phase I final report.* Washington, DC: Office of Juvenile Justice and Delinquency Prevention.

Bonnie, R., Coughlin, A., Jeffries, J, & Low, P. (2004). *Criminal law* (2nd ed.). New York: Foundation Press.

Bremner, R. H. (Ed.). (1974). *Children and youth in America: A documentary history,* vol. 4. Cambridge, MA: Harvard University Press.

Brooks-Gunn, J., & Furstenburg, F., Jr. (1989). Adolescent sexual behavior. *American Psychologist, 44,* 249–257.

Byrnes, J.P. (1998). *The nature and development of decision making.* Mahwah, NJ: Lawrence Erlbaum.

California Vehicle Code § 12814.6 (2000).

Campbell, D. E. (2006). *Why we vote: How schools and communities shape our civic life.* Princeton, NJ: Princeton University Press.

Cauffman, E., & Steinberg, L. (2000). (Im)maturity of judgment in adolescence: Why adolescents may be less culpable than adults. *Behavioral Sciences and the Law, 18,* 741–760.

City of Akron v. Akron Center for Reproductive Health, 462 U.S. 416 (1983).

Costanzo, P. R., & Shaw, M. E. (1966). Conformity as a function of age level. *Child Development, 37,* 967–975.

Cromer, B. A., & Tarnowski, K. J. (1989). Noncompliance in adolescents: A review. *Journal of Developmental and Behavioral Pediatrics, 10,* 207–215.

Cultice, W. (1992). *Youth's battle for the ballot: A history of the voting age in America.* Westport, CT: Greenwood Press.

Dahl, R. (2004). Adolescent brain development: A period of vulnerabilities and opportunities. *Annals of the New York Academy of Sciences, 1021,* 1–22.

Doob, A., & Webster, C. (2003). Sentencing severity and crime: Accepting the null hypothesis. In M. Tonry (Ed.), *Crime and Justice, 30,* 143–195. Chicago: University of Chicago Press.

Dudley, R. L. & Gitelson. A. R. (2002). Political literacy, civic education, and civic engagement: A return to political socialization? *Applied Developmental Science, 6,* 175–182.

D'Unger, A. V., Land, K. C., McCall, P. L., & Nagin, D. S. (1998). How many latent classes of delinquent/criminal careers? Results from mixed Poisson regression analyses. *American Journal of Sociology, 103,* 1593–1630.

Dusky v. United States, 362 U.S. 402 (1960).

Ehrlich, J. S. (2006). *Who decides? The abortion rights of teens.* Westport, CT: Praeger.

Ellis, E. (1993, January 15). Lungren to seek lower age for trial as adult. *Los Angeles Times,* p. A3.

Erikson, E. H. (1968). *Identity: Youth and crisis.* New York: W. W. Norton.

Fagan, J. (1996). The comparative advantages of juvenile versus criminal court sanction on recidivism among adolescent felony offenders. *Law and Policy, 18,* 77–112.

Farrington, D. (1986). Age and crime. In M. Tonry & N. Morris (Eds.), *Crime and justice: An annual review of research* (pp. 189–250). Chicago: University of Chicago Press.

Feld, B. (1999). *Bad kids: Race and transformation of the juvenile court.* New York: Oxford University Press.

Finken, L. L., & Jacobs, J. E. (1996). Consultant choice across decision contexts: Are abortion decisions different? *Journal of Adolescent Research, 11,* 235–260.

Flanagan, C. A., & Sherrod, L. R. (1998). Youth political development: An introduction. *Journal of Social Issues, 54,* 447–450.

Forst, M., Fagan, J., & Vivona, T. (1989). Youths in prisons and training schools: Perceptions and consequences of the treatment–custody dichotomy. *Juvenile & Family Court Journal, 40,* 1–14.

Fox, S. (1967). *The juvenile court: Its context, problems and opportunities.* Washington DC: President's Commission on Law Enforcement and Administration of Justice.

Fried, C., & Reppucci, N.D. (2001). Criminal decision making: The development of adolescent judgment, criminal responsibility, and culpability. *Law and Human Behavior, 25,* 45–61.

Furby, L., & Beyth-Marom, R. (1992). Risk taking in adolescence: A decision-making perspective. *Developmental Review, 12,* 1–44.

Furstenburg, F. F., Brooks-Gunn, J., & Chase-Lansdale, L. (1989). Teenaged pregnancy and childbearing. *American Psychologist, 44,* 313–320.

Gardner, M., & Steinberg, L. (2005). Peer influence on risk-taking, risk preference, and risky decision-making in adolescence and adulthood: An experimental study. *Developmental Psychology, 41,* 625–635.

Gardner, W. (1992). A life span theory of risk taking. In N. Bell & R. W. Bell (Eds.), *Adolescent and adult risk taking: The 8th Texas symposium on interfaces in psychology* (pp. 66–83). Thousand Oaks, CA: Sage.

Gardner, W., Scherer, D., & Tester, M. (1989). Asserting scientific authority: Cognitive development and adolescent legal rights. *American Psychologist, 44,* 895–902.

Giedd, J.N. (2004). Structural magnetic resonance imaging of the adolescent brain. *Annals of the New York Academy of Sciences, 1021,* 77–85.

Goldberg, E. (2001). *The executive brain: Frontal lobes and the civilized mind.* New York: Oxford University Press.

Gorney, C. (1998). *Articles of faith: A frontline history of the abortion wars.* New York: Simon and Schuster.

Greene, A. L. (1986). Future-time perspective in adolescence: The present of things future revisited. *Journal of Youth and Adolescence, 15,* 99–113.

Griffin-Carlson, M. S., & Mackin, K. J. (1993). Parental consent: Factors influencing adolescent disclosure regarding abortion. *Adolescence, 28,* 1–11.

Grisso, T., & Lovinguth, T. (1982). Lawyers and child clients: A call for research. In J. Henning (Ed.). *Children and the law.* Springfield, IL: Charles C. Thomas.

Grisso, T., Steinberg, L., Woolard, J. L., Cauffman, E., Scott, E., Graham, S., et al. (2003). Juveniles' competence to stand trial: A comparison of adolescents' and adults' capacities as trial defendants. *Law and Human Behavior, 27,* 333–364.

Grisso, T., & Vierling, L. (1978). Minors' consent to treatment: A developmental perspective. *Professional Psychology, 9,* 412–426.

H.L. v. Matheson, 450 U.S. 398 (1981).

Hazelwood School Dist. v. Kuhlmeier, 484 U.S. 260 (1988).

Helwig, C. C., & Turiel, E. (2002). Civil liberties, autonomy, and democracy: Children's perspectives. *International Journal of Law and Psychiatry, 25,* 253–270.

Henggeler, S., Melton, G., & Smith, L. (1992). Family preservation using multisystemic therapy: An effective alternative to incarcerating serious juvenile offenders. *Journal of Consulting and Clinical Psychology, 60,* 953–961.

Henshaw, S. K., & Kost, K. (1992). Parental involvement in minors' abortion decisions. *Family Planning Perspectives, 21,* 85–88.

Hodgson v. Minnesota, 497 U.S. 417 (1990).

In re Gault, 387 U.S. 1 (1967).

Jensen, E., & Metsger, L. (1994). A test of the deterrent effect of legislative waiver on violent juvenile crime. *Crime and Delinquency, 40,* 96–104.

Jessor, R., & Jessor, S. L. (1977). *Problem behavior and psychosocial development: A longitudinal study of youth.* New York: Academic Press.

Johnson, K., Lanza-Kaduce, L., & Woolard, J. L. (in press). Disregarding graduated treatment: Why transfer aggravates recidivism. *Crime and Delinquency.*

Keating, D. (2004). Cognitive and brain development. In R. Lerner & L. Steinberg (Eds.), *Handbook of adolescent psychology,* (2nd ed., pp. 45–84). Hoboken, NJ: John Wiley & Sons.

Kett, J. (1977). *Rites of passage: Adolescence in America 1790 to the present.* New York: Basic Books.

Lerner, R. M., & Galambos, N. L. (1998). Adolescent development: Challenges and opportunities for research, programs, and policies. *Annual Review of Psychology, 49,* 413–446.

Levine, M., & Levine, A. (1970). *A social history of helping services: Clinic, court, school and community.* New York: Appleton-Century-Crofts.

Levitt, S. (1998). Juvenile crime and punishment. *Journal of Political Economy, 106,* 1158–1185.

Lewin, T. (1992, May 28). Parental consent to abortion: How enforcement can vary. *New York Times,* p. A1.

Lewis, C. C. (1980). A comparison of minors' and adults' pregnancy decisions. *American Journal of Psychiatry, 50,* 446–453.

Lindsey, B. B., & O'Higgins, H. J. (1909). *The beast.* Seattle: University of Washington Press.

Lipsey, M. (1995). What do we learn from 400 research studies on the effectiveness of treatment with juvenile delinquents? In J. McGuire (Ed.), *What works? Reducing reoffending guidelines from research and practice* (pp. 63–78). New York: John Wiley & Sons.

Meisel, A., Roth, L. H., & Lidz, C. W. (1977). Toward a model of the legal doctrine of informed consent. *American Journal of Psychiatry, 134,* 285–289.

Melton, G. B. (1980). Children's concepts of their rights. *Journal of Clinical Child Psychology, 9,* 186–190.

Melton, G. (1981). Psycholegal issues in juveniles' competency to waive their rights. *Journal of Clinical Child Psychology, 10,* 59–62.

Melton, G. B. (1983a). Toward "personhood" for adolescents: Autonomy and privacy as values in public policy. *American Psychologist, 38,* 99–103.

Melton, G. B. (1983b). *Child advocacy: Psycholegal issues and interventions.* New York: Plenum Press.

Melton, G. B., & Limber, S. (1992). What children's rights mean to children: Children's own views. In M. Freeman & P. Veerman (Eds.), *Ideologies of children's rights* (pp. 167–187). Dordrecht, Netherlands: Martinus Nijhoff.

Meschke, L. L., Bartholomae, S., & Zentall, S. R. (2002). Adolescent sexuality and parent-adolescent processes: Promoting health teen choices. *Journal of Adolescent Health, 31,* 264–279.

Miller, V. A., Drotar, D., & Kodish, E. (2004). Children's competence for assent and consent: A review of empirical findings. *Ethics and Behavior, 14,* 255–295.

Mnookin, R. (1985). *Bellotti v. Baird:* A hard case. In R. H. Mnookin (Ed.), *In the interest of children: Advocacy, law reform and public policy* (pp. 150–264). New York: W. H. Freeman.

Moffitt, T. E. (1993). Life-course-persistent and adolescence-limited antisocial behavior: A developmental taxonomy. *Psychological Review, 100,* 674–701.

Morse v. Frederick, 127 S. Ct. 2618 (2007).

National Juvenile Defender Center. (2007). *2006 State juvenile justice legislation.* Washington, DC: Author.

Newcomer, S. F., & Udry, J. R. (1985). Parent–child communication and adolescent sexual behavior. *Family Planning Perspectives, 17,* 169–174.

Nurmi, J. (1991). How do adolescents see their future: A review of the development of future orientation and planning. *Developmental Review, 11,* 1–59.

Ohio v. Akron Center for Reproductive Health, 497 U.S. 502 (1990).

O'Keefe, J., & Jones, J. M. (1990). Easing restrictions on minors' abortion rights. *Issues in Science and Technology, 7,* 74–80.

Parham v. J.R., 442 U.S. 584 (1979).

Pate v. Robinson, 383 U.S. 375 (1966).

People v. Carey, 615 N.W.2d 742 (Mich. Ct. App. 2000)

Piquero, A., Farrington, D., & Blumstein, A. (2003). The criminal career paradigm. *Crime and Justice: An Annual Review of Research, 30,* 359–506.

Planned Parenthood of Central Missouri v. Danforth, 428 U.S. 52 (1976).

Platt, A. (1977). *The child savers: The invention of delinquency* (2nd ed.). Chicago: University of Chicago Press.

Pope, L. M., Adler, N. E., & Tschann, J. M. (2001). Postabortion psychological adjustment: Are minors at increased risk? *Journal of Adolescent Health, 29,* 2–11.

Poythress, N. G., Bonnie, R. J., Monahan, J., Otto, R., & Hoge, S. K. (2002). *Adjudicative competence: The MacArthur studies.* New York: Springer.

Prince v. Massachusetts, 321 U.S. 158 (1944).

Quinton, W. J., Major, B., & Richards, C. (2001). Adolescents and adjustment to abortion: Are minors at greater risk? *Psychology, Public Policy, and Law, 7,* 491–514.

Regnery, A. S. (1985). Getting away with murder: Why the juvenile justice system needs an overhaul. *Policy Review, 34,* 65–72.

Reiss, A., Jr., & Farrington, D. (1991). Advancing knowledge about co-offending: Results from a prospective longitudinal survey of London males. *Journal of Criminal Law and Criminology, 82,* 360–395.

Rendleman, D.R. (1971). *Parens patriae:* From chancery to the juvenile court, *South Carolina Law Review, 23,* 205–259.

Reppucci, N. D., Wiethorn, L. A., Mulvey, E. P., & Monahan, J. (Eds.) (1984). *Children, mental health, and the law.* Beverly Hills, CA: Sage.

Resnick, M. D., Bearinger, L. H., Stark, P., & Blum, R. W. (1994). Patterns of consultation among adolescent minors obtaining an abortion. *American Journal of Orthopsychiatry, 64,* 310–316.

Reyna, V. F., & Farley, F. (2006). Risk and rationality in adolescent decision making: Implications for theory, practice, and public policy. *Psychological Science in the Public Interest, 7,* 1–44.

Roper v. Simmons, 543 U.S. 551 (2005).

Rubin, E. R. (Ed.). (1998). *The abortion controversy: A documentary history.* Westport, CT: Praeger.

Ruck, M. D., Keating, D. P., Abramovitch, R., & Koegl, C. J. (1998). Adolescents' and children's knowledge about rights: Some evidence for how young people view rights in their own lives. *Journal of Adolescence, 21,* 275–289.

S. Rep. No. 92–26 (1971).

Scherer, D. G. (1991). The capacities of minors to exercise voluntariness in medical treatment decisions. *Law and Human Behavior, 15,* 431–449.

Scherer, D. G., & Reppucci, N. D. (1988). Adolescents' capacities to provide voluntary informed consent: The effects of parental influence on medical dilemmas. *Law and Human Behavior, 12,* 123–141.

Schleifer v. City of Charlottesville, 963 F. Supp. 534 (W.D. Va. 1997), *aff'd* 159 F. 3d 843 (4th Cir. 1998).

Schneider, A., & Ervin, L. (1990). Specific deterrence, rational choice and decision heuristics: Applications in juvenile justice, *Social Science Quarterly, 71,* 585–601.

Scott, E. (1992). Judgment and reasoning in adolescent decision making. *Villanova Law Review, 37,* 1607–1669.

Scott, E. (2000). Criminal responsibility in adolescence: Some lessons from developmental psychology. In T. Grisso & B. Schwartz (Eds.), *Youth on trial* (pp. 291–324). Chicago: University of Chicago Press.

Scott, E., & Grisso, T. (2005). Developmental incompetence, due process, and juvenile justice policy. *North Carolina Law Review, 83,* 793–845.

Scott, E., & Kraus, J. S. (2007). *Contract law and theory* (4th ed.). Newark, NJ: Lexis Nexis.

Scott, E. S., Reppucci, N. D., & Woolard, J. L. (1995). Adolescent decision making in legal contexts. *Law and Human Behavior, 19,* 221–244.

Scott, E., & Scott, R. (1995). Parents as fiduciaries. *Virginia Law Review, 81,* 2401–2476.

Scott, E., & Steinberg, L. (2003). Blaming youth. *Texas Law Review, 81,* 799–40.

Scott, E., & Steinberg, L. (2008). *Rethinking juvenile justice.* Cambridge, MA: Harvard University Press.

Sherrod, L. R., Flanagan, C., & Youniss, J. A. (2002). Editors' introduction. *Applied Developmental Science, 6,* 173–174.

Sickmund, M., Snyder, H. N., & Poe-Yamagata, E. (1997). *Juvenile offenders and victims: 1997 update on violence.* Washington, DC: U.S. Department of Justice, Office of Juvenile Justice and Delinquency Prevention.

Siegler, R. S., & Alibali, M. W. (2004). *Children's thinking* (4th ed.). Englewood Cliffs, NJ: Prentice Hall.

Silverstein, H. (2007). *Girls on the stand: How courts fail pregnant minors.* New York: New York University Press.

Singer, S., & McDowell, D. (1988). Criminalizing delinquency: The deterrent effects of the New York juvenile offender law. *Law and Society Review, 22,* 521–535.

Smetana, J. G. (1981). Reasoning in the personal and moral domains: Adolescent and young adult women's decision-making regarding abortion. *Journal of Applied Developmental Psychology, 2,* 211–226.

Snyder, H. (2005). OJJDP Bulletin: Juvenile arrests 2004, www .ncjrs.gov.

Snyder, H., & Sickmund, M. (2006). *Juvenile offenders and victims: 2006 national report*. Washington, DC: Office of Juvenile Justice and Delinquency Prevention, U.S. Department of Justice.

Spear, L. P. (2000). The adolescent brain and age-related behavioral manifestations. *Neuroscience and Biobehavioral Reviews, 24,* 417–463.

Steinberg, L. (2004). Risk-taking in adolescence: What changes, and why? *Annals of the New York Academy of Sciences, 1021,* 51–58.

Steinberg, L. (2008). *Adolescence* (8th ed.). New York: McGraw-Hill.

Steinberg, L., & Cauffman, E. (1996). Maturity of judgment in adolescence: Psychosocial factors in adolescent decision making. *Law and Human Behavior, 20,* 249–272.

Steinberg, L., & Cauffman, E. S. (1999). The elephant in the courtroom: A developmental perspective on the adjudication of youthful offenders. *Virginia Journal of Social Policy and Law, 6,* 389–417.

Steinberg, L., Chung, H., & Little, M. (2004). Reentry of young offenders from the justice system: A developmental perspective. *Youth Violence and Juvenile Justice, 2,* 21–38.

Steinberg, L., Dahl, R., Keating, D., Kupfer, D. J., Masten, A. S., & Pine, D. (2006). The study of developmental psychopathology in adolescence: Integrating affective neuroscience with the study of context. In D. Cohen & D. Cicchetti (Eds.), *Developmental psychology,* vol. 2: *Developmental neuroscience* (2nd ed.; pp. 710–741). Hoboken, NJ: John Wiley & Sons.

Steinberg, L., Graham, S., O'Brien, L., Woolard, J., Cauffman, E., & Banich, M. (in press). Age differences in future orientation and delay discounting. *Child Development*.

Steinberg, L., & Scott, E. (2003). Less guilty by reason of adolescence: Developmental immaturity, diminished responsibility, and the juvenile death penalty. *American Psychologist, 58,* 1009–1018.

Tiffin, S. (1982). *In whose best interest? Child welfare reform in the progressive era*. Westport, CT: Greenwood Press.

Torbet, P., Gable, R., Hurst, H., IV, Montgomery, I., Szymanski, L, & Thomas, D. (1997). *State reponses to serious and violent juvenile crime*. Washington DC: Office of Juvenile Justice and Delinquency Prevention, U.S. Department of Justice.

Torbet, P., & Szymanski, L. (1998). *State legislative responses to violent juvenile crime: 1996–1997 update*. Washington, DC: Office of Juvenile Justice and Delinquency Prevention, U.S. Department of Justice.

Torney-Purta, J. (1992). Cognitive representations of the political system in adolescents: The continuum from pre-novice to expert. In H. Haste & J. Torney-Purta (Eds.), *The development of political understanding: A new perspective* (pp. 11–25). San Francisco: Jossey-Bass.

Torres, A., Forrest, J. D., & Eisman, S. (1980). Telling parents: Clinic policies and adolescents' use of family planning and abortion services. *Family Planning Perspectives, 12,* 284–292.

Van Waters, M. (1926). *Youth in conflict*. New York: Republic.

Viljoen, J. L., & Grisso, T. (2007). Prospects for remediating juveniles' adjudicative incompetence. *Psychology, Public Policy, and Law, 13,* 87–114.

Virginia Code Annotated 1-13.42 (Michie 2000).

Virginia Code Annotated 44.1-2969 (Michie 1999).

Wadlington, W. (1973). Minors and health care: The age of consent. *Osgoode Hall Law Journal, 11,* 115–125.

Wagman, M. (2000). Innocence lost in the wake of green: The trend is clear—If you are old enough to do the crime you are old enough to do the time. *Catholic University Law Review, 11,* 643–677.

Wald, M. (1976). Legal policies affecting children: A lawyer's request for aid. *Child Development, 46,* 1–5.

Ward, S. L., & Overton, W. F. (1990). Semantic familiarity, relevance, and the development of deductive reasoning. *Developmental Psychology, 26,* 488–493.

Walkover, A. (1984). The infancy defense in the new juvenile court. *UCLA Law Review, 31,* 503–562.

Weithorn, L. A., & Campbell, S. B. (1982). The competence of children and adolescents to make informed treatment decisions. *Child Development, 53,* 1589–1598.

Winner, L., Lanza-Kaduce, L., Bishop, D.M., & Frazier, C.E. (1997). The transfer of juveniles to criminal court: Reexamining recidivism over the long term. *Crime and Delinquency, 43,* 548–563.

Woolard, J. L. (2002). Capacity, competence, and the juvenile defendant: Implications for research and policy. In B. L. Bottoms, M. B. Kovera., & B. D. McAuliff (Eds.), *Children and the law: Social science and policy* (pp. 270–298). New York: Cambridge University Press.

Yates, S., & Pliner, A. J. (1988). Judging maturity in the courts: The Massachusetts consent statute. *American Journal of Public Health, 78,* 646–649.

Younts v. St. Francis Hospital and School of Nursing, Inc., 469 P.2d 300 (Kan. 1970).

Zabin, L. S., Hirsch, M. B., & Emerson, M. R. (1989). When urban adolescents choose abortion: Effects on education, psychological status, and subsequent pregnancy. *Family Planning Perspectives, 21,* 248–255.

Zimring, F. E. (1978). *Confronting youth crime: Report of the Twentieth Century Fund Task Force on sentencing policy toward young offenders*. New York: Holmes and Meier Publishers.

Zimring, F. E. (1982). *The changing legal world of adolescence*. New York: Free Press.

Zimring, F. E. (1998). *American youth violence*. New York: Oxford University Press.

CHAPTER 11

The Development of Citizenship

LONNIE R. SHERROD AND JAMES LAUCKHARDT

Civic engagement is a critically important topic in that a democracy requires engaged citizens in order to survive. Unfortunately, this topic has not, however, generated the amount of research seen for other areas of child and youth development. Furthermore, it has not enjoyed extensive policy or program attention. Civics education has, for example, probably been deemphasized as a result of the No Child Left Behind legislation. In this chapter, we make the case for increased research and policy attention to the development of citizenship.

We begin by addressing the importance of civic engagement and exploring its possible definitions. We review research on the development of civic engagement and examine the socialization factors that have been shown to contribute to its development. We then address the importance of investigating this topic across today's diverse youth. We conclude by providing a model that attempts to integrate the different definitional issues and developmental factors.

THE CRITICAL IMPORTANCE OF CIVIC ENGAGEMENT

The United States is a democracy, as are most industrialized countries throughout the world. Alexis de Tocqueville visited the United States in the 1830s and was impressed with our involvement in a myriad of civic associations (de Tocqueville, 1966). Since publication of his *Democracy in America,* the United States has come to represent the embodiment

of democracy (Putnam, 1996), and the United States has a history of promoting democracy throughout the world. The Vietnam War in the 1960s and the War in Iraq in the mid-2000s are only two examples.

De Tocqueville emphasized the importance of civic engagement. For a democracy to survive, it must have informed, involved citizens who take an active part in their democracy. Putnam (1996), in fact, cites the results of his own 20-year quasi-experimental longitudinal study in Italy to demonstrate empirically the impact of civic engagement on the performance of representative government. Hence, citizenship is as important a domain of adult responsibility as work or family. And its development from childhood into adulthood should be of paramount importance to researchers interested in development, and social programs and policies should keenly attend to its promotion across development. Unfortunately, civic engagement has been the subject of far less research and even less social policy or program attention than have areas such as cognitive development as preparation for work or social development as preparation for family formation. The development of citizenship is, for example, almost never covered in child development texts. In addition, educational policies such as No Child Left Behind emphasize math, reading, and science over social studies and civics (Porter & Polikof, 2007).

Fortunately, interest in the development of citizenship is enjoying somewhat of a renaissance, fueled in part by the writings of Robert

Putnam (1996, 2000), who argues that we face a crisis in this country today because of historically low levels of civic engagement. He argues and presents data that civic participation has been declining and is at an all-time low. The crisis is especially serious for young people who have the lowest level of civic engagement of all groups, as represented by voting, for example. Like de Tocqueville, Putnam sees declining civic participation as critically important to democracy. Hence, declining levels of civic engagement are seen to constitute a crisis. Putnam's argument is controversial and we will consider it later in the paper, but the point here is that Putnam, like de Tocqueville, has revitalized our attention to civic engagement and its role in democracy. In this chapter, we examine past and current research on the development of civic engagement and review what we know about social mechanisms that exist to promote it.

HISTORY OF RESEARCH ON CIVIC ENGAGEMENT

There have been two major periods of research on the development of civic engagement in this century, the 1950s and the 1970s (Flanagan & Sherrod, 1998; McLeod, 2000). In the 1950s, developmental research emphasized the importance of early development, before school age, and focused on the role of socialization, especially within the family. This period of work viewed children to be rather passive recipients of socialization. This orientation to developmental research was also reflected in attention to the development of civic engagement. Early parental socialization was viewed to be the main influence on later civic engagement, and general orientation and interest were seen to be cemented early in development.

Research during the 1970s resulted in part from the social movements at the time and those that had preceded it, for example, the anti–Vietnam war protests and the civil rights movement. There was quite a bit of research on social movements (e.g., McAdam, 1988) and civic engagement was therefore examined

from this perspective. Because youth were among the main participants, attention did focus on youth. Scholars argued that this time of life provided an opportunity to explore values without responsibility (Newcomb, Koenig, Flacks, & Warwick, 1967). However, since most research was with college students, age could not be separated from college setting, which offers the same benefits. There was nonetheless a strong generational orientation to this work with reference to Mannheim's (1952) ideas about the importance of this time of life. And there were follow-up studies indicating that views and experiences during the transition to adulthood lasted into midlife (Marwell, Aiken, & Demareth, 1987, McAdam, 1988).

Ideas and methods from life-span research that arose in the 1970s continued to promote this longitudinal view of research on development from childhood into adulthood. Life-span ideas promoting lifelong plasticity, a view of development allowing for a plurality of developmental paths and outcomes, the importance of social–political context, the role of historical factors in development, and the promotion of longitudinal cohort–sequential research using multiple methods offered a means of continuing genuine developmental research throughout the life span (Hetherington, Lerner & Perlmutter, 1988). Research on civic engagement is, by its nature, multidisciplinary. It is a topic that crosses the boundaries of several developmental periods. Hence, these life-span ideas provided tools for the research on civic engagement that begin to emerge in the mid-1990s, thereby adding further impetus to its growth.

Nonetheless, research on the development of civic engagement has remained limited. A survey of 1,000 articles during 1982–1987 found only 14 on political socialization (Flanagan & Gallay, 1995; Sears, 1990). Putnam's (1996, 2000) argument that we face a crisis in terms of low levels of civic engagement has fueled a new wave of research during the past decade.

This new wave of research benefits from a new approach to research and policy on youth development which arose in the 1990s: positive youth development (PYD). Generally, PYD is an approach, not an actual construct, similar to a life-span approach to developmental research (Sherrod, Busch, & Fisher, 2004). As an approach it offers a model of applied research and has important implications for policy that affects young people, and it is especially relevant to civic engagement because political participation can be seen as both an example of and an outcome of PYD.

PYD argues that development is promoted by assets, both internal and external. There is variability in the assets individuals bring to their contexts of growth and development, and these contexts of families, schools, communities, and societies or nations vary in the qualities that promote the development of these assets (Benson, 2004; Benson, Leffert, Scales, & Blyth, 1998; Benson, Scales, Hamilton, & Semsa, 2006). This approach offers guidance for policy and programs as well as research. Following decades of unsuccessful research and policy to eliminate risk and prevent negative outcomes, PYD advocates for examining the strengths youth have—rather than their risks—and for designing policies and programs oriented to promoting positive outcomes—rather than preventing negative ones (Sherrod, 2006). Recent research has continued to examine and define the specific nature of assets (Theokas et al., 2005). Nonetheless, the PYD approach clearly highlights the need for development of youth policy to promote development based on the resources available to them in their families, schools and communities, and this need is especially critical in regard to the development of civic engagement. It emphasizes empowerment as an important ingredient to successfully engaging youth in their communities (Cargo, Grams, Ottoson, Ward, & Green, 2003). The PYD approach offers tools both for the conceptualization of civic engagement and for measurement of it so that its timely entry into research on youth promotes attention to the development of civic engagement.

CONCEPTUALIZING AND DEFINING CIVIC ENGAGEMENT

The brief history of research attention to the topic summarized above illustrates the diversity in approaches to conceptualization or definition of civic engagement. It is difficult for new research to proceed without sufficient conceptual attention to the topic. The lack of a clear definition of civic engagement challenges measurement and contributes to conflicting findings across studies even in regard to assessing its prevalence. As a result, we devote considerable attention to examining what constitutes civic engagement.

The *American Heritage Dictionary* defines *citizenship* as the status of a citizen with its duties, right, and privileges (Hyman, 2002). This definition is useful mainly in terms of pointing out that citizenship involves rights and responsibilities, so that in assessing views of citizenship, one can ask how much of a balance is seen between these. Walzer (1989) defines a *citizen* as "most simply, a member of a political community, entitled to whatever prerogatives and encumbered with whatever responsibilities are attached to membership." The word *citizen* comes to us from the Latin *civis*; the Greek equivalent is *polites*, member of the polis, from which comes our politics. Membership, rights, and obligations are characteristics across all these definitions.

In fact, research on political engagement generally has increasingly included a broader concern with what is considered political. Early studies that were not concerned with development focused mainly on voting and campaigning (Augemberg, 2007). At most, these early studies considered only three or four activities, adding donating money and contacting a politician to voting and campaigning (Augemberg, 2007: Brady, Verba, & Schlozman, 1995; Conway, 1991; Verba, Schlozman, & Brady 1995). In 1969, Barber wrote:

> Political participation is an abstract phrase too gross to catch the lively and varied ways citizens act their political parts. Voting is the baseline, but talking, writing, petitioning, demonstrating

and a wide range of other organized and individual activities are significant forms of participation (p. 1).

More recent studies have adhered to this view and have included up to 35 activities in their assessment of political engagement. For example, Brady et al. (1995) include in their Citizen Participation Study the above-mentioned electoral activities, but also attending rallies and involvement in community affairs such as local board meetings and school affairs (Augemberg, 2007).

As these studies—mostly in political science and social psychology—show, citizenship clearly involves some allegiance to, commitment or loyalty to, and participation in one's nation state. Examples of behaviors that can result from this allegiance include obeying laws, voting, or following current events. Behaviors that represent taking an interest in and being involved in the larger, national interest or polity are considered to be civic engagement. They constitute the electoral activities traditionally measured in research on political participation.

However, since children are rarely given the opportunity to participate in electoral activities, developmental research has typically employed a much broader definition. This is reasonable since the nation state is not the only social institution to which citizens can show allegiance. One can be involved in one's community or devoted to a school or church and express some of those same behaviors but oriented to an institution other than the nation state. Furthermore, concern for others and altruism is also frequently viewed as a component of citizenship. Yet one can be quite selfish and oriented entirely to one's own material or occupational success and still be involved with and committed to the nation state, in regard to voting, campaigning, following news, and so on. Tolerance and sensitivity to diversity is also often cited as a component of good citizenship. Yet one can be quite bigoted and still vote, express patriotism and participate as a citizen. Hence, citizenship is certainly multi-faceted, if not a quite complex domain. Barber (1991) and others in that tradition recognized this complexity. As a result, our preference is to follow the trend of more recent research in political science and related fields by examining attitudes and behaviors that may constitute components of civic engagement. We view each of these to be necessary, but no single one is sufficient for the expression of civic engagement. Then, research and assessment can simply outline which components are present without debating if this is really civic engagement or not.

Attitudes and their relationship to knowledge and behavior are clearly related to civic engagement and may constitute components. There is a long history of research in fields such as social psychology and political science on social attitudes and their relationship to behavior. As a result, we begin our consideration of conceptualization with a review of this research.

Attitudes, Knowledge, and Behavior

Involvement in politics or one's community, concern for others, and tolerance each involve attitudes, knowledge, and behavior. Furthermore, the formation of attitudes about political issues such as poverty or defense and about ideas of what citizenship involves is at the core of development into citizenship. They drive political behaviors such as voting as well as interest in one's community.

The Social Psychology of Attitudes

Three issues have been researched in the developmental, social psychological, and political science literatures on the relationship between attitudes and behavior: the function of attitudes, the impact of social structure or social group membership on attitudes, and the circumstances under which attitudes impact behavior (Herek, 1987; Kiecolt, 1988). Allport (1935) was one of the first to propose that attitudes served as guides to behavior; although early research did not support this thesis, subsequent studies have shown a stronger relationship between attitudes and behavior. The issue is when and under what conditions attitudes impact behavior, as well as the nature of the impact. Studies of functions and of social group impact have provided a means of examining the relationship between attitudes and behavior.

The Function of Attitudes

One way that attitudes relate to behavior is through their functions. Four functions have been proposed for attitudes: (1) value expressive, in which attitudes serve the self-concept; (2) social adjustive, in which attitudes serve membership in a social group; (3) defensive, for minimizing anxiety about the self; and (4) utilitarian, where attitudes guide behavior to increase rewards and minimize punishment (Herek, 1986; Katz, 1960; Shavitt, 1990). A given attitude can serve one or all four of these functions. The function also affects the extent to which an attitude may impact behavior; for example, if membership in a social group is tenuous, an attitude may surface to serve a social adjustive function and increase comfort in the group by showing shared attitudes. Research has also shown that attitudes are more likely to affect behavior when they are strong, stable, specific, relevant to the behavior, and easily accessible (Ajzen & Sexton, 1999; Eagly & Chaiken, 1993, 1998; Fazio, 1995; Fazio & Towles-Schwen, 1999). Knowledge has also been shown to link attitudes and behavior in the political sphere in that civic knowledge relates to voting behavior (Niemi & Junn, 2000; Torney-Purta, 2002).

Values and Attitudes: Typologies

Values are the guiding principles behind attitudes and provide the individual with a sense of right and wrong; they help with the establishment of goals regarding the individual's role in society. Values thus provide a means for attitudes to impact behavior. However, there is less research on values than on attitudes, perhaps because they are more abstract. Values are first mentioned in research in Talcott Parsons's

(1939) *The Structure of Social Action*. Rokeach (1968, 1973) gave guidance to research by defining a value as: ". . . an enduring belief that a specific mode of conduct or end-state of existence is personally or sociably preferable to an opposite or converse mode of conduct or end-state of existence" (p. 5). Rokeach (1973) operationalized this definition of values in his Value Survey (Augemberg, 2007). "The most important distinction of values from attitudes is that values are abstract and generalized guides of conduct, transcendent of specific situations and objects, whereas attitudes are very specific judgments focused on a single object or situation" (Augemberg, 2007 p. 8). Thus, values are more limited in number than attitudes, and much research has been devoted to articulating a typology of values or focusing on values systems.

For example, in one large cross-cultural study of values, Schwartz (1992) found that teachers' ratings of 56 values generated 9 value types. These 9 types represented four dimensions: openness to change, self-enhancement, conservation, and self-transcendence.

Values and Civic Engagement

Understandably, most research examining the relationship between values and civic engagement focuses on political attitudes. Political attitudes might, for example, be considered to be one instance of values, since attitudes are the overarching category to values. And research has shown relationships between values and political party affiliation and conservatism versus liberalism, for example (Augemberg, 2007; Devos, Spini, & Schwartz 2002; Feather, 1977; Feldman, 2003). Rokeach (1973) suggested that values are part of political ideology, which consists of two dimensions: freedom and equality (Augemberg, 2007).

There is not a lot of developmental research focusing on values. Most developmental studies have been concerned either with moral development or values such as trust. The moral roots of citizenship have, for example, been explored in research on moral development (Carr, 2006).

The more limited research focusing on associations between values and political behavior, as opposed to attitudes, has centered on voting (Augemberg, 2007; Caprara et al., 2006). Unlike other research on voting behavior, these studies examine the relationship between values and how people vote, not whether they vote (Augemberg, 2007). For example, Schwartz's dimensions correlated with political behavior; individuals showing openness to change, for example, were more likely to endorse liberal political candidates (Schwartz, 1996) and to participate in a rally supporting equal rights (Rokeach, 1980). When behaviors are categorized as instrumental (i.e., taking action) versus psychological (e.g., interest in and concern for politics), values relate more to instrumental political behaviors than to psychological ones (Augemberg, 2007). This result is somewhat at odds with the bulk of research showing that values relate more to political attitudes than to behaviors.

Again, developmental research is limited. Interpersonal trust has been shown to predict civic orientation in middle and high school students (Crystal & DeBell, 2002). Beliefs about the causes of social problems such as poverty

predict teens' political views about solutions (Flanagan & Tucker, 1999).

Attitudes and behaviors are what constitute civic engagement, so it is necessary to understand their functioning. However, civic engagement consists of specific examples of each, and these constitute the components of civic engagement around which measurement should be structured.

THE MULTIFACETED NATURE OF CIVIC ENGAGEMENT

The preceding discussion has highlighted what a complex and multifaceted phenomenon civic engagement is. We propose that research on civic engagement should attend to its three key ingredients: knowledge, attitudes, and behaviors (Sherrod, 2003). Knowledge involves both the civic knowledge that one gets in civic courses as well as awareness of current events. General attitudes drive both instrumental and psychological political behaviors as well as general political ideology such as party affiliation. This approach has driven our research program focusing on political knowledge, attitudes, and behavior or participation. Figure 11.1 illustrates specific ways in which

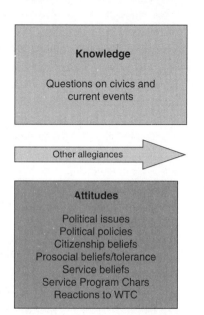

FIGURE 11.1   Knowledge, attitudes, and behaviors as aspects of civic engagement to be studied

we have pursued this orientation to research on youth civic engagement.

Knowledge, attitudes, and behaviors must, however, be applied to domains. Hence, we must also consider what are the domains of civic engagement. We argue that there are several domains. Certainly, one domain in which one may study the attitudes, behavior, and knowledge of civic engagement is politics and civics.

Civic Versus Political

Clearly, political behaviors and involvement in politics is one domain of civic engagement. However, the most contentious issue in defining civic engagement is whether it must involve political behaviors such as voting or can also consist just of community involvement such as doing service. That is, politics is clearly sufficient for defining civic engagement, but is it also necessary?

Borrowing from Walzer's definition, Flanagan and Faison (2001) distinguish *civic,* from the Latin *civis*, from *political,* from the Greek *polites*. Although the two terms have different historical roots, they have similar meaning, denoting a member of the polity. But Flanagan and Faison argue that *political* has come to mean more specifically affairs of the state or the business of government. *Civic* maintains the broader meaning associated with being a member of the polity. Hence, they choose to use *civic* as the broader version. They then differentiate *civic literacy* as knowledge of community affairs and political issues, *civic skills* as competencies in achieving group goals, and *civic attachment* as a feeling or belief that you matter. They argue and present evidence that social relations, opportunities for practice, and the values and behaviors communicated by adults and social institutions determine youth's civic development in these three areas. It is their differentiation of literacy, skills, and attachment that is most useful because these focus on processes inherent to the individual (i.e., skills and attachments) rather than factors that are outside the person such as politics or community.

It seems clear that involvement in community or civic affairs is as important as political participation. Indeed, the very label *civic engagement* implies this to be the case. Furthermore, adolescents see the responsibilities of citizenship to consist of politically oriented ones such as voting and civic-oriented ones such as serving one's community (Bogard & Sherrod, in press). Hence, both political and civic can be considered to be aspects of civic engagement. We therefore need to consider both in some form when we assess the civic engagement of youth. Concern for other people and tolerance of diversity are also often considered, especially by youth, to be aspects of civic engagement.

Concern for Others and Tolerance of Diversity

Concern for others and tolerance are two components that also demand attention because they can underline either civic or political involvement. Prosocial behavior, empathy, and moral cognition are all aspects of concern for others. There has been considerable developmental research on each of these concepts.

Behaviors involving cooperation, sharing, and emotions such as empathy may relate rather straightforwardly to later development of concern for social justice, to the development of a concern for others. The development of extraordinary moral commitment has also been studied, and typically becomes part of identity in young adulthood (Colby & Damon, 1995). Hart, Atkins, and Ford (1998) define moral identity as self-conscious commitment to lines of action benefiting others and propose a model of its development involving social attitudes, self-conceptions, and opportunities for practice. Analyses of the National Longitudinal Survey of Youth provide support for their model.

Eisenberg-Berg and Hand (1979) propose that prosocial behaviors that involve a cost are more other oriented than everyday helping behaviors that have little cost; this is an important distinction that has not always been considered, and there has been little developmental research on it.

Empathy and prosocial behavior clearly relate to certain forms of civic involvement such as volunteering or community service. Political behavior can be motivated by empathy or prosocial behavior, but it is not clearly a prerequisite; but the same is true for behaviors such as community service that also may be done for self-serving reasons (Lerner, 2004; Sherrod, 2008).

Moral cognition refers to competency in reasoning about moral issues. Higher stages of moral reasoning have been described to relate to a generalized concern for others, but it is not clear if this level of reasoning contributes to moral behavior (Colby et al., 1983). Verbogt (1996) finds that level of moral reasoning relates to a cultural dimension of political beliefs, but not to an economic dimension. Unlike previous research that had related higher levels of moral reasoning to progressive political ideas, he shows that the relation is to cultural aspects irrespective of liberalism versus conservatism.

Social group membership in terms of gender, social economic class, race or ethnicity, religion, and sexual orientation defines one form of diversity across populations in this country and others. Tolerance must apply across all these dimensions of diversity. Erikson (1968) argued that tolerance and interdependence were essential parts of a democratic identity (Flanagan & Gallay, 1995). Research has shown that social group membership has an important effect on attitudes toward other groups. One of the earliest and now classic studies of the impact of social norms on attitudes showed that Bennington college students became increasingly liberal during their undergraduate years of study as a result of contact with the liberal faculty and advanced undergraduates; these liberal attitudes were retained throughout adulthood (Alwin, Cohen, & Newcomb, 1991; Newcomb, 1943; Newcomb et al, 1967).

Membership in a group of college undergraduates is quickly acquired as a result of enrollment in the school. Individuals are socialized into membership in most naturally occurring social groups related to race or citizenship and acquire norms as a part of this socialization process. Tolerance relates to appreciation of differences across different social groups and the lack of stereotypes or prejudices toward other groups. Tolerance of diversity is important to civic engagement because it promotes positive intergroup relations. A democracy cannot survive if its citizens are constantly at odds with each other.

The groups that constitute these different categories of people must get along with each other if society is to function smoothly, so tolerance is as important to the survival of a democracy as is voting. Tolerance becomes increasingly important as our society becomes more diverse (Hernandez, 1993).

SOCIAL AND HUMAN CAPITAL

Human capital has traditionally been defined as the tools, skills, knowledge, and the like an individual possesses that contributes to his or her productivity, which is defined mainly in economic terms. It might be considered to consist of three of the Cs of PYD: competence, confidence, and character. It results from education and socialization. Putnam (1996) uses the idea of social capital, defined as the social networks, norms, and social trust that relate to concern for and participation in the larger common good. Social capital relates directly to the domains of civic engagement. In Putnam's view, it is social capital that facilitates civic engagement, and civic engagement has declined because social capital has declined.

Portes (1998) has suggested that this view of social capital is a simplification. He cites Bourdieu's (1985) definition of *social capital* as "the aggregate of the actual or potential resources which are linked to possession of a durable network of more or less institutionalized relationships of mutual acquaintance and recognition." Hence, he emphasizes resources as much as relationships. Hyman (2002) suggests that social capital has two parts: relationships that give one access to resources, and the amount and quality of the available resources. He defines *social capital* as "an asset representing actionable resources that are contained in and accessible through a system of relationships." Social capital is not a form of civic engagement; it is a precursor to it. Each of the domains we have described for civic engagement result from and reflect social capital.

Accordingly, building social capital is one means of promoting civic engagement. This idea of social capital provides a rationale for a broader conceptualization of civic engagement than just political behavior.

THE CIVIC STATUS OF TODAY'S YOUTH

There has been quite a bit of concern about the civic engagement, or lack thereof, of today's young people, certainly fueled by Putnam (1996, 2000). However, there have been numerous attempts to assess the involvement of youth. Having agreement on the ingredients that constitute civic engagement and on its domains allows a clearer evaluation of these efforts. Because of its impact, we begin with a detailed description of Putnam's thesis and then review the more recent surveys that have attempted to assess the civic involvement of today's youth.

Putnam (1996) observes that voting turnout declined by about 25% from the 1960s to the 1990s. He also cites statistics from the Roper Organization, which surveyed national samples 10 times a year from 1973 to 1993. The number of Americans attending a public, town, or school affairs meetings dropped by one-third. Similar or greater declines are seen in attending a political rally or speech, serving on a committee of a local organization, and working for a political party. At the same time, the number of Americans who report feeling trust for the government has more than doubled during the same period (Putnam, 1996).

The General Social Survey repeated 14 times during the decades of the 1970s and 1980's reports that church-related groups are the most common type of organization joined by Americans. At the same time, church attendance has declined. Participation in labor unions, PTAs, and League of Women Voters has shown similar declines, as has volunteering for Boy Scouts and the Red Cross. In fact, volunteering overall declined by one-sixth over the 2 decades in question. Participation in fraternal organizations such as Lions, Elks, Shriners, and Jaycees also declined from 12% to 4%. The one social behavior that increased across these decades was bowling—hence the title of his article, "Bowling Alone" (Putnam, 1996).

Putnam (1996) does note that there have been increases in participation in organizations such as Sierra Club, National Organization for Women, and American Association of Retired Persons. However, he considers these to be tertiary organizations because they can involve only paying dues and do not involve social connectedness. Support groups such as Alcoholics Anonymous have also grown, but he does not consider that they play the same role as traditional civic associations. This is the aspect of Putnam's argument that has been most criticized. Critics argue that civic engagement has not declined; it has simply changed so that the traditional indicators cited by Putnam are no longer relevant. Again, the definition of *civic engagement* becomes relevant. The issue is what impact such changes have had on social capital and hence on the contribution of citizens.

Putnam does not singly address youth, although they are included in his statistics. Nonetheless, other work indicates that youth political participation seems to have indeed dropped precipitously (Delli Carpini, 2000). Voter turnout, as one among many criteria of participation, averaged 37%, in the age 18- to 24-year-old category in the past three presidential elections; this was 21% lower than among all citizens. This level compares unfavorably with three earlier elections, 1972–1980, when the 19- to 24-year-old age group averaged 44% and was 17% below that of all citizens, respectively (McLeod, 2000). This raises the issue of what is it, exactly, that is causing this change, and there is very little research that addresses this question. Putnam (1996, 2000) blames television and the media as likely contributors. Another that has been proposed is the segregation of youth from adults and their relative lack of opportunity for engaging in truly responsible behavior (Camino & Zeldin, 2002). It has furthermore been proposed that large numbers of youth relative to adults in communities leads to decreased civic engagement in youth, although this effect would explain differences across regions (or countries) more than the social change (Hart, Atkins, Markey, & Youniss, 2004).

The concern about youth civic engagement is not limited to the United States; it has been, for example, argued that social policies in the United Kingdom assume that young people lack citizenship and need interventions to develop it (Smith, Lister, Middleton, & Cox, 2005). Focus groups as well as surveys have also been used to explore young people's involvement or lack thereof; this qualitative research reports that young adults' views are nuanced and therefore challenge quantification, perhaps raising questions about the validity of the surveys that report low levels of civic involvement (Andolina, Jenkins, Keeter, & Zulkin, 2003). Such research does, however, contribute to political debates about the nature of citizenship (Haste & Hogan, 2006).

The Center for Information and Research for Civic Learning and Engagement (CIRCLE) is an important resource and clearinghouse that focuses specifically on youth civic engagement. It has provided the most recent and most detailed view of the civic status of today's youth, based on surveys. In 2006, CIRCLE completed the National Civic and Political Health Study (CPHS). A nationally representative sample of 1,700 youth aged 15–25 years was surveyed, as were 550 adults over 26

years of age. The sample is representative of the population in the United States except that various ethnic groups were oversampled for strategic reasons. There were 19 core measures of civic engagement; the measure employed in this study was based on a scale used by Keeter, Sukin, Andolina, and Jenkins (2002). This study provides one of the best views available of the civic attitudes and behaviors of today's young people.

The report of the study demonstrates that there is considerable variability in youth civic engagement across individuals and across forms of civic engagement. Some forms of engagement are quite widespread in many youth, but substantial numbers of young people are not at all involved in either politics or community life. And some forms of civic engagement, notably the important behavior of voting, are quite low.

Some notable results include: 72% say that at least some of the time they follow what's going on in government and public affairs; 36% have volunteered within the last year; 35% participate in political discussions; 30% have boycotted a product because of the conditions under which it was made or the values of the company that made it; 26% of those aged 20–25 years say that they "always" vote.

The report suggests that a small number of young people are intensely involved. Thirteen percent engage in at least two different forms of both community engagement and political participation. Seven percent are even more involved and report 10 or more different kinds of civic participation. Those who are highly involved show a particular demographic profile: more likely to be Democratic (or leaning toward the Democrats), liberal, urban, from a family with parents who volunteer, a current student (in college or high school), and from college-educated homes. They are also more likely to regularly attend church, and these are more likely to be African American. These findings generally replicate previous research (Bogard & Sherrod, in press; Flanagan & Tucker, 1999) and provide important clues for how to promote civic engagement in youth (Sherrod & Lauckhardt, 2008).

A lot of young people (58%) are not involved at all, failing to report as few as two forms of civic or political engagement. The report describes these youth as "disengaged." Of these disengaged young people, 28% report doing not even one of the 19 forms of civic engagement measured in this survey. One reason for their disengagement is that they have much less confidence in their ability to make a difference than does the highly engaged group. Demographically, they are less likely to have college-educated parents or to have parents who volunteer. They themselves are also less likely to have any college experience. They do not align with either political party and are more likely to be Latinos or immigrants (Sherrod & Lauckhardt, 2008). Other research does show that disengagement relates to cynicism (Bynner & Ashford, 1994). Later in this chapter, we discuss diversity because these views held by this segment of the population are not totally unfounded given their status in the United States.

The fact that more than half of our young people are not at all involved is a statistic about which to be concerned. Whether this represents a social change is less important than the fact that it now exists and that as a democracy we are going to be in trouble unless we address this lack of involvement in civic engagement. The two mechanisms available for addressing youth political inactivity and disinterest is research on the development of civic engagement that may help us understand the individual variability in participation and the causes thereof, and the study of programs and policies to promote civic engagement in young people.

THE DEVELOPMENT OF CIVIC ENGAGEMENT

The transition to adulthood in areas other than citizenship, for example, work and family life, is a bit clearer than it is for citizenship. Schooling, school achievement, job training,

apprenticeships, and other preparatory efforts are the main trajectory into work. Family life is preceded by dating, one or more serious social/sexual relationships, perhaps cohabitation, and marriage. And one can consider the skills involved in such trajectories: for example, cognitive and communication skills for work and capacity for intimacy and parenting skills for family life.

The same is not true for civic engagement. One does not typically participate as a citizen until adulthood. Hence, the development of citizenship clearly shows developmental discontinuity (Brim & Kagan, 1980). This makes developmental research challenging because one must look to different early illustrations of the behavior than those that constitute the outcome of interest. Furthermore, the different aspects and domains we have described for civic engagement follow different developmental paths, and developmental discontinuity applies mostly to explicitly political activities. Young people have numerous opportunities to be civically engaged, usually through community service. Concern for others and tolerance can be witnessed, perhaps in different forms across development. Another clear aspect of civic engagement is some form of loyalty, allegiance, or connectedness to some social institution. For political behavior, this group is, of course, the nation. Socialization into various groups such as the family, the community, one's race, or religion begins early in life.

Reflecting its developmental discontinuity, a number of childhood precursors have been shown to relate to civic engagement and political involvement in adulthood—or citizenship. In one symposium on the topic, for example, a speaker listed working in the civil rights movement, college campus civil disobedience, working in a soup kitchen, doing service learning such as tutoring younger children, extracurricular school activities, and participating in a local community based organization in the same paragraph. There has been research demonstrating the relevance of all of these. Youth activism, doing volunteer work such as community service, extracurricular activities in high school, and civics courses have all been shown to relate to some form of adult political involvement (Jennings & Niemi, 1974; Verba et al., 1995). Yet, surely, working for civil rights and working for the high school yearbook are quite different behaviors with different developmental histories and different consequences. They all have been shown to relate to adult civic engagement because we have included an equally diverse array of adult behaviors under the citizenship rubric. We need to be much clearer about the adult behavior(s) we wish to explain and about the possible precursors of those specific behaviors. Describing civic engagement in terms of components such as attitudes and behaviors and domains such as politics and concern for others facilitates this attention to the processes that link earlier activities to later behaviors.

Research needs to be more attentive to mechanisms, so that we can understand how earlier behaviors relate to later ones. Although mechanisms have been proposed to relate youth behaviors to adult civic engagement, it has not been explained how working as an activist might have different causes and consequences than high school extracurricular activities, for example. It may well be that each simply represents a different developmental path to the same outcome, but we need to be clear about which developmental path works for which youth. The variability in civic engagement across today's youth, as indicated in the CIRCLE survey, implies there may be different developmental paths. Focusing on the components and domains of civic engagement provides one with the means of directing our attention to development and the early precursors of citizenship, and it begins to help generate a concern for mechanisms by which precursors are related to later behaviors. That is, we expand the options for developmental study, especially for ages earlier than adolescence and youth. As a result, we review the development of civic engagement in terms of three domains or aspects: Political interests

and activities, concern for others and tolerance, and allegiances or connectedness to one or more group. We earlier reviewed research on more general components such as knowledge, attitudes and behaviors.

Political or Active Citizenship

The political side of civic engagement is the component that shows most discontinuity. One does not typically engage in behaviors that one would define as active citizenship until adulthood. Eighteen years is the legal voting age, for example; it was formerly 21 years. Hence, the developmental progression to the behaviors that are explicitly defined as citizenship must involve earlier different forms of civic engagement. Research, then, should focus on the socialization process that leads to participation as a citizen.

Research has generally focused on other forms of participation and generally shows that active children and youth become active adults. That is, one clear precursor of political involvement is participation in those activities and organizations that are available to different age groups. Involvement in youth organizations relates to later civic engagement—from extracurricular school activities including sports to involvement in youth serving organizations such as 4-H and Boys/Girls clubs and doing community service during school (Barber & Eccles, 1997; Jennings & Niemi, 1974; Verba et al. 1995). This makes sense because it represents youth involvement in those organizations and activities that are available to them as young people. Participation in youth organizations also generally promotes PYD (Larson, 2000), which may be one mechanism by which it relates to civic engagement. For both reasons—relation to civic engagement and promotion of positive development—we need to expand the range of activities available to youth and the responsibility inherent in such participation (Zeldin, Camino, & Calvert, 2003).

Hence, there are clear precursors in adolescence that have been shown to predict later political interest and involvement. The issue is what precursors might exist before adolescence. Understandably, most research has focused on adolescence and youth since they are on the verge of exercising their citizenship, but we need now to look for earlier precursors. Aspects of early childhood play have, for example, been found to relate to later civic involvement (Astuto & Ruck, in press).

Concern for Others and Tolerance

Development of a concern for social justice and for the welfare of others is one domain of citizenship that clearly relates to prosocial and/ or moral development. There is long history of outstanding developmental research on moral development, although it has not explicitly addressed its relevance to civic engagement. Concern for others has at least two components that have been studied: prosocial behavior and moral cognition. These, of course, relate to our concern for attitudes and behaviors.

Prosocial Behavior

Even quite young children show forms of prosocial behaviors and empathy, which may be precursors of a generalized concern for others, for the welfare of other people. Hence, early behaviors involving cooperation, sharing, and emotions such as empathy may relate rather straightforwardly to later development of concern for social justice or to the development of a concern for others. In fact, Eisenberg et al. (1999) reported consistency from preschool (4–5 years) to young adulthood (21–24 years) in prosocial orientation. Actual prosocial behaviors such as sharing in preschool predicted prosocial behavior, cognitions, and empathy-related responding in young adulthood. The development of extraordinary moral commitment has also been studied, and typically becomes part of identity in young adulthood (Colby & Damon, 1995). Hart, Atkins, and Ford (1998) define moral identity as self-conscious commitment to lines of action benefiting others and propose a model of its development involving social attitudes,

self-conceptions, and opportunities for practice. Analyses of the National Longitudinal Survey of Youth provide support for their model. Eisenberg-Berg and Hand (1979) propose that preschool prosocial behaviors that involve a cost to the child are more other oriented than is everyday helping behavior that has little cost; this is an important distinction that has not always been considered, and there has been little developmental research. None of this research has explored interactions with civic engagement.

Moral Cognition

There has also been considerable research on moral cognition. The development of moral reasoning follows a developmental path that mirrors that for cognition more generally, proceeding from concrete and literal to abstract (Kohlberg, 1984; Ruck, Abramovitch & Keating, 1998). Higher stages of moral reasoning have been described to relate to a generalized concern for others, but it is not clear if this level of reasoning contributes to moral behavior (Colby et al., 1983). Verbogt (1996) finds that level of moral reasoning relates to a cultural dimension of political beliefs, but not to an economic dimension. Unlike previous research that had related higher levels of moral reasoning to progressive political ideas, he shows that the relation is to cultural aspects irrespective of liberalism versus conservatism.

In summary, there is less developmental discontinuity in this component of citizenship than there is for political participation. The issue is how distinct it is from political participation. That is, is development of a concern for social justice as one component of citizenship different from prosocial and/or moral development? And what is the relationship, if any, to political behavior?

THE SOCIALIZATION INTO CITIZENSHIP

Because citizenship is a behavior that is inherently tied to social institutions, it is not a behavior that naturally develops like cognition, emotions, or personality. The development of group allegiance or connectedness should relate to the direct socialization of the child or at least to socialization experiences such as the experience of racial discrimination or involvement with a religious group or church. Children and youth, of course, differ in the extent to which they experience a strong directive socialization experience. It is not clear how children become attached to a particular social institution when their socialization does not direct them to one institution over another. One reason for the perceived lack of civic engagement of youth may be that many young people do not experience any such explicit socialization to community or national interests. Bogard and Sherrod (in press) show that across race, class, and immigrant status youth do show different allegiances to family, school, and community, and these allegiances relate to their views of the rights and responsibilities of citizenship.

Socialization, although perhaps more directly related to allegiances, can also relate to other aspects of civic engagement. In fact, a variety of different socialization influences have been shown to relate to several domains of civic engagement, at least for some youth. Civics education, community service, school activities, and youth programs of course relate rather explicitly to citizenship and the extent to which it involves civic versus political involvement. Community service, however, also relates to prosocial behavior and concern for others. Family influences, the media, and religion can relate to all three domains. In this section, we review the various socialization mechanisms that have been shown to influence the development of civic engagement.

Family Influences

Our review of the history of research on civic engagement highlights that studies in the 1950s saw the family as the most important influence on the development of political interests and values. One prime example of

this work is Hyman's (1959) study of political socialization; he reports that parents are the main vehicle of political socialization. These results mainly reported similarities between parental and child political values and activities. Research continues to show that children and youth politically resemble their parents; politically active children tend to have politically active parents (Flanagan & Tucker, 1999; Niemi & Junn, 2000).

Jennings and Niemi (1968), Acock and Bengston (1978), and Connell (1972) argue that sampling biases and use of single item measures led to overestimation of the role of parents in children's political socialization in this early research. Certainly, all such research is correlational. One cannot ascertain why children and parents resemble each other. There are indications that socialization or modeling of parents by children is at work, but it cannot be concluded with certainty.

More recent research has emphasized the diversity of influences of which family is only one, the interaction between the family and other factors such as socioeconomic status (SES), and finally changes in the nature of the family (Dalhouse & Frideres, 1996; Wray-Lake & Flanagan, 2008). Jennings and Niemi (1974) furthermore report that families have little impact on youth political beliefs, compared to other influences. Certainly, family influence generally seems to have mediated rather than direct effects on the political socialization of children. Families are viewed as only one of many possible influences. Furthermore, it is not just a family's political activity that influences the child's civic interest; the gender of the active parent, SES, and family type are also important (Dalhouse & Friederes, 1996, Ichilov, 1988). For example, Jankowski (1992) finds that parents do encourage or discourage particular types of political behaviors and beliefs, but there are important class differences. Middle-class parents discouraged activities that might interfere with success, whereas lower-class parents warned youth against activities that might lead to harm.

In addition, families are important to civic engagement because they socialize children and youth into different degrees of connectedness to the family. Certain cultures, particularly Hispanic and Asian groups, tend to promote loyalty to the family (Fuligni, Tseng, & Lam, 1999). Asian and Latino high school youth show stronger values and greater expectations regarding their duty to assist, respect, and support their families than do youth of European backgrounds. We do not know how family loyalty may relate to civic involvement.

Clearly, family is an important institution for youth in regard to their socialization, but it can, like other social institutions, vary as to where it directs the young person's allegiance. The relationship to political development is not clear from available research.

Civics Education

Education is an important influence on the development of civic engagement. However, education certainly builds on what children bring from their families in regard to values and civic orientation (Halstead & Taylor, 2000). Furthermore, civics education or civics classes are the most direct educational tools to relate to civic engagement, but they are not the only educational influence. Other more general characteristics of schools and education are also influential. For example, factors such as school climate and teacher behavior have been shown to predict later civic participation (Flanagan & Tucker, 1999; Niemi & Junn, 2000). Classes that encourage open discussion of issues promote higher levels of understanding of civics materials; deliberative learning and interactive curricula play an important role (Flanagan & Tucker, 1999; McDevitt & Kiousis, 2006). Moral and character education programs also contribute to the civic involvement of young people (Althof & Berkowitz, 2006).

A large international study recently examined the civic education of 14,000 fourteen-year-olds across 28 countries (Torney-Purta, Lehmann, Oswald, & Schultz, 2001). This was the Civic Education Study of the International Association for the Evaluation of Educational Achievement (IEA). This study examined teens' understanding of democracy, of the governments in their country, and of their rights and responsibilities as citizens. It allowed comparative research across 28 countries including the United States. This 2001 study acquired nationally representative samples totaling 90,000 students across the 28 countries. In the United States, nearly 2,800 students and their teachers were surveyed. Finally, in 2000, a follow-up sample of 50,000 seventeen- to 19-year-olds was examined in 16 of the 28 (Sherrod & Lauckhardt, 2008).

Two book-length publications report initial findings on the 90,000 fourteen-year-olds tested in 1999 in 28 countries (Torney-Purta, et al., 2001) and also on the 50,000 seventeen-to 19-year-olds tested in 2000 in 16 countries (Amadeo, Torney-Purta, Lehmann, Husfeldt, & Nikolova, 2002). These publications can be obtained from the project's Web page: www .wam.umd.edu/~iea.

The initial findings confirm that there was little variability from nation to nation in teen levels of civic knowledge, and overall civic knowledge was not very high. The investigators argue that teens' knowledge of political processes and political concepts was not sufficient to allow them to participate fully and effectively as adult citizens in their respective countries. For example, teens thought democracy was the only form of representative government. Niemi, Sanders, and Whittington (2005) report not only that knowledge is low in the higher high school grades, but also that there has been a decline in knowledge across the past quarter-century. Seniors answered questions in 1998 only a little better than 8th graders in the mid-1970s. As previous research has consistently shown, having a higher level of civic knowledge was associated an increased tendency to vote—with an expectation that they would vote since these were 14-year-olds. Increased knowledge has also been found to relate to decreased fearfulness in U.S. youth following the September 11, 2001, tragedy in New York City and Washington, D.C. (Sherrod, Quinones, & Davila, 2004). Otherwise, knowledge has not been found to relate to any other form of participation such as volunteer activities or protest actions (Sherrod, 2003; Torney-Purta, 2005). Furthermore, there are many other forms of civic engagement, and there are predictors other than knowledge of these other forms so that is important not to focus exclusively on knowledge (Torney-Purta, Barber, & Wikenfeld, 2007). Nonetheless, research, especially in political science, has emphasized knowledge because of its association with voting, and there is growing concern that knowledge is inadequate and seems to be declining. If democracy is to work, citizens need to participate, and voting is one of the most important forms of adult participation (Torney-Purta, 2002).

The IEA study was a massive undertaking, but there have been numerous other studies of civics knowledge. Research understandably has shown that the content of civics textbooks is important to students' views of citizenship. Content that focuses directly on democracy seems to lead students to adopt nonextremist views (Slomczynski & Shabad, 1998). Analyses of U.S. texts have shown that texts emphasize rights over obligations, and students' views in turn focus on rights (Bos et al., 2007). College may, however, provide an opportunity to broaden students' views leading to an appreciation of not only civil rights but also for political responsibility (Flanagan, 1998). But, generally, research shows that both the nature and content of civics education matters.

Analyses of the IEA data have identified several other predictors of civic engagement related to education. One predictor is the extent to which students are encouraged to get together to deal with school organization, functioning, and problems (Torney-Purta, 2002, Torney-Purta & Richardson, 2004), that is, to participate as citizens in their schools. School culture is another educational variable that relates to fostering engagement and activism (Flanagan & Tucker, 1999; Torney-Purta &

Barber, 2007). Teacher behavior is yet another variable. Teachers who treat students fairly foster just behavior in their students (Flanagan & Tucker, 1999). Hence, a number of aspects of students' educational experience other than classes in civics are also important to later civic engagement. All these variables need attention in the context of policies relating to civics education (Sherrod & Lauckhart, 2008).

Because of their relationship to economic productivity, math and science have long been valued. However, if democracy is to survive, thereby allowing economic freedom, youth need to understand how their government works, what their role can and should be, how they can influence government through voting as well as other means, and when it is important to take more drastic action to change things for the better and how to do so. Civics education, broadly defined, should be of the same national priority as math and science; it is as important to functioning as an adult in society as are math and science, and it is equally important to the functioning and economic viability of the country (Sherrod, 2003; Sherrod & Lauckhardt, 2008). Nonetheless, the current U.S. No Child Left Behind legislation (NCLB) is being implemented to focus entirely on achievement in reading and math. Although a variety of school-based character education programs have been funded through NCLB, there has been little attention to civics achievement or outcomes. In fact, a number of schools and school districts are abandoning their social studies curriculum, including civics, because of the need to focus on achievement testing in other areas. Furthermore, the types of analyses of NAEP data for math are not even possible for civics because of the way that data is collected (Torney-Purta, Barber, & Richardson, 2004).

Community Service and Service Learning

Community service has now been recognized in this country as an important experience for young people, and service learning has been created to combine the social or prosocial aspects of service with academics (Andersen, 1998; McPherson & Zimmerman, 2002; Sax & Astin, 1997). Service has, in fact, received a disproportionate amount of attention, especially in terms of promoting participation by young people (Walker, 2002; Yates & Youniss, 1996). Regrettably, this explosion of attention has not carried with it an explosion of research, and available research is not sufficient to support this level of social promotion. However, research on political socialization has shown a relationship between service and later civic engagement, and this result is one datum promoting this heightened level of attention to service in this country (Verba, et al., 1995; Youniss et al., 2002).

Thomas Jefferson emphasized the importance of community service for young people, and John Dewey described the pedagological benefits of service learning (Blanchard, n.d.). It just seems like a good thing to do. Another reason for its popularity is that service has indeed been found to relate to a host of positive outcomes, of which increased civic engagement is only one desirable goal (Andersen, 1998; Myers-Lipton, 1994).

Perhaps for this reason, attention has been programmatic as well as being researched. For example, there is the 1990 National and Community Service Act and the 1993 National Service Trust Act, which funded President Clinton's Americorps program and created the Corporation for National Service. This legislation gave states the money to turn student volunteering into service learning by tying it to the curriculum (Blanchard, n.d.). And several states (e.g., Maryland) and cities (e.g., St. Louis and Detroit) now require service as part of education (Stukas, Clary, & Synder, 1999), and there was a Grantmaker Forum on Service. Generally, service has been recognized as a valuable experience for all people, but particularly for youth.

Community Service and Positive Development

Service has been found to relate to a variety of positive qualities. Service has been found to increase prosocial skills, to relate to positive self-esteem, to promote identity development, to relate to career choice, and to promote civic engagement (Andersen, 1998; Austin, Vogelgesang, Ikeda, & Yee, 2000; Markus, Howard, & King, 1993; Schmidt, Shumow, & Kackar, 2007; Stukas et al., 1999; Yates & Youniss, 1996; Youniss & Yates, 1999). Service also relates to future service (McAdam, 1988) and enhances moral development (Leming, 2001; Lerner, Dowling, & Anderson, 2003). Although most research on service is nonexperimental, there have been a few experimental studies that have reported similar findings to those from correlational studies (Andersen, 1998).

Community service and service learning have been shown in several studies to relate positively to later civic enagement (Andersen, 1998; Austin, et al., 2000; Billig, Root, & Jesse, 2005; Hart, Atkins, & Ford, 1998; Markus, et al., 1993; Reinders & Youniss, 2006; Stukas, et al., 1999; Tierney & Branch, 1992; Walker, 2002; Yates & Youniss, 1996; Youniss & Yates, 1997, 1999). This relationship is a large part of the reason for increased attention to service. However, we know little about how different types of service relate to particular aspects of later civic engagement, and we know that the nature of the program is more important than the amount of service (Buchanan et al., 2008). Furthermore, participation in community programs also relates to later political behaviors (Larson, 2000) as do school activities (Barber & Eccles, 1997), so that service does not provide a magic bullet to promote civic engagement. And we are not close to understanding the relationship between service and civic engagement.

Service may be a precursor to later civic engagement. However, as a potential precursor, we do not know if service is just another form of youth activity, like working for the yearbook, that serves to prepare youth for adult responsibilities including citizenship or if it is specifically tied to civic engagement by, for example, relating to youth's beliefs about equality and social justice. Billig, et al., (2005) differentiate indirect service (e.g., fundraising), direct service (e.g., tutoring or helping the elderly), and civic action (e.g., petitioning, community organizing); the importance of each to civic engagement followed the order listed.

Service may also be considered to be an actual form of civic engagement rather than a precursor. It is somewhat controversial whether civic engagement has to involve the political or whether community work such as service can be considered to be an actual form of political participation (Flanagan & Faison, 2001; Sherrod, Flanagan, & Youniss, 2002). Youth may also do service as a substitute for political participation, because they are cynical about politics or prefer activities where they see immediate, direct impact of their activities (Walker, 2002).

Hence, although a relationship between community service and later civic engagement is a good reason for promoting service, we need to understand this relationship much more fully before we can effectively link the two.

Service Learning
Service has also been found to relate to academic gains (Markus et al., 1993). As attention to educational gains has increased over past years, a more pronounced movement to combine service and learning has emerged. The term *service learning* was first coined in 1967 as a result of a credit-based internship program for students working on community-based projects with the Southern Regional Economic Board. The practice of service learning, however, was limited to a small number of participants until the mid-1980s, but the 1990s saw great growth in service-learning initiatives. Service learning is, in fact, now regarded as an educational movement (Billing, et al., 2000; Markus, et al., 1993; Reinders & Youniss, 2006; Scales, Blyth, Berkas, & Kielsmeier et al., 2000; Yates & Youniss, 1996).

Service and service-learning programs differ in a number of respects, such as length of service, populations served, types of activity or service (e.g., tutoring young children versus working in a soup kitchen), whether voluntary or mandatory, opportunities for reflection, and the organization or school department that organizes the service (Stukas, et al., 1999; Yates & Youniss, 1996).

Research has shown that the characteristics of service programs relate to their effects (Austin et al., 2000; Markus, et al., 1993; Stukas et al., 1999; Waterman, 1997; Yates & Youniss, 1996). Service programs that are voluntary versus mandatory and that offer an opportunity to reflect on one's experience with a mentor have the most impact; furthermore, different types of service, that is, the activity actually done as service, carry different consequences (Reinders & Youniss, 2006; Yates & Youniss, 1996, Youniss, 2005).

Since service and service-learning programs differ in a number of respects, one might expect them to represent different experiences for youth. Different program characteristics are likely to lead to a different personal experience of service, and one would expect how the young people experience service to influence its personal consequences. Research, however, has not examined how service and service-learning programs differ for the young participants. Most research compares students in one form of service to ones who do not do service. The greatest shortcoming in service research is failure to examine possible relationships between different qualities of service and outcomes. Service is by no means a monolithic experience, and it is not clear if we are lumping under the same rubric what are quite different experiences for youth. Research is needed on the differences between different forms of service, especially between service and service learning.

There have been a few studies that examined differences in service. Leming (2001) describes two different types of community service. The first type includes a structured ethical reasoning component. Students are given a chance to ethically reflect on the work they do. The second type incorporates limited reflection on the ethics of the service. Students who participated in the ethical expression form of service had a stronger sense of social responsibility within their school. Also, these students focused less on personal pleasure and more on responsibility and helping others than did those who did not have the expression component. That is, both identity formation and ethical consideration were shown to be enhanced by the ethical expression component of the community service.

Hence, although community service and service-learning programs are being promoted because it is believed that they lead to civic engagement and prosocial behaviors, these relationships are by no means clear, and much more research is needed to understand how different forms of service relate to different forms of civic engagement. We need to ask how and why.

Extracurricular Activities and Youth Programs

Participation in school government, clubs, publications, athletics, and other extracurricular activities is in many ways similar to participation in politics later in life. It is not surprising that participation in high school extracurricular activities relates to later civic involvement (Barber & Eccles, 1997; Eccles & Barber, 1999; Holland & Andre, 1987). These activities offer opportunities for involvement in the larger community; the difference with political involvement is that extracurricular activities support the person's school rather than his or her country. It is therefore to be expected that teens who participate in these school activities are more likely to participate in civic and political activities later in life. What is perhaps more surprising is that activity involvement predicted citizenship activity and volunteering 10–15 years later (Obradovic & Masten, 2007).

We do not know, however, the origins of participation in these activities. Not all young people participate. Participation may relate to connectedness to school, but available research does not address this question. We also need research that connects specific activities to later specific civic behaviors. For example, participation in school government would seem to be more relevant than participation in an arts club.

Those youth who do not participate in extracurricular activities frequently do participate in various community-based programs for youth. Many of these can also serve to prepare young people for citizenship. There are a number of relevant programs today including the 4-H, Boys and Girls Clubs, and YouthBuild.

YouthBuild gives youth an opportunity to serve but goes far beyond community service. It started with a few youth in East Harlem in New York City and has now spread across the country. It has benefited from the large amount of federal and private funds that have gone into community service across the past decades. But it has also benefited tremendously from its founder, Dorothy Stoneman, who for at least 2 decades has tried to give young people a constructive opportunity to use their tremendous energy. It is unique and highly successful because it involves youth in project creation, gives them responsibilities and authority over their own activities, and provides an opportunity for youth to engage in issue-based advocacy. It offers training in a variety of skills and leadership opportunities mainly for unemployed out-of-school youth. One of YouthBuild's main activities is to rehabilitate housing in low-income areas. YouthBuild connects youth to meaningful experiences, allows them do something to help their communities, provides opportunities to develop relationships with building supervisors and peers, and at the same time, the participants learn practical and social skills. Many of the youth later move into more management-level-type positions within the program, demonstrating its success in contributing to human development. There is a strong connectedness to the program among the participants, providing evidence of the importance of connectedness as a feature of civic engagement. YouthBuild participants feel about YouthBuild just as we hope citizens feel toward their country (Stoneman, 2002; Tolan, Sherrod, Gorman-Smith, & Henry, 2003).

The 4-H has been associated with clubs that relate to agricultural activities such as growing corn, tomatoes, pigs, or other livestock. It was created for the educational development of youth, and it has sought to tap the creativity and energy through the programs it has organized. Despite its reputation for agricultural-type activities, it has recently redirected its attention to urban youth. A variety of activities are designed to attract such youth, one of which is that 4-H is one of the first youth organizations to add young people as voting members of its board of directors.

Another example of a new activity with urban youth is the Metro Youth Art Force. This program recognizes youth's need for support for their artistic activities (Tolan et al., 2003). Various activities, such as weekend workshops, are organized from the perspective of promoting positive youth development, which then relates to civic engagement. It promotes artistic expression as a form of involvement. This is an innovative approach to promoting involvement, which then might be related to civic engagement.

Common Cents is a New York City–based program that collects pennies from individuals, organizations, and businesses. This organization has raised hundreds of thousands of dollars. The funds raised by collecting pennies are used to set up small school-based foundations that are run by youth and offer small grants for youth-designed and run projects. Youth review applications for funding and establish priorities (Tolan et al., 2003). As is true for YouthBuild, participants see how their involvement has an impact. They play a role in their schools by funding projects that can benefit the school and all its students.

After-school programs are an increasingly popular form of youth programs (Granger, 2008).

There has been very little research asking how participation in after-school programs relates to later civic engagement. One preliminary study shows that after-school programs do not show a strong relationship to adolescents' views of citizenship (Hoxie & Sherrod, 2008; Sherrod & Hoxie, 2007). However, this may result from the fact that many programs emphasize academics and offer activities such as homework help. Programs that attend to civics by discussing political issues do relate to views of citizenship (Sherrod & Hoxie, 2007). Hence, after-school programs may represent a vehicle for promoting civic engagement that has yet to be tapped for this purpose.

PROGRAMS DESIGNED TO PROMOTE CIVIC ENGAGEMENT

Because research has found an association between media use and civic activity (Pasek, Kenski, Romer, & Hall-Jamieson, 2006), a number of school-based interventions devoted to enhancing civic involvement have a media component. For example, the Student Voices project piloted by the Annenberg School of Communication at the University of Pennsylvania suggests that Web-based information gathering and interactions can increase high school students' knowledge of and interest and engagement in local elections (Delli Carpini, 2000). In this program, the main goal was to actively engage students in the learning process through interactive exercises. The Student Voices Project encourages the civic engagement of young people by bringing the study of local government, policy issues, and political campaigns into the classroom. Working with school districts throughout the country, Student Voices makes the study of government relevant and exciting for high school students by helping them examine how issues they consider important are played out in their own governments and election campaigns. Each class formulates a Youth Issues Agenda, reflecting the issues that are of most concern to students in the class and their communities. These issues provide the focus for students through the rest of the course, ensuring that they research and act on issues that concern them. Students use the interactive Student Voices web site to find information on issues and candidates and discuss policy issues online. Through classroom visits and forums, students raise their concerns directly to political candidates and public officials and hear what can be done to address them. Finally, students communicate their concerns to the general public by making their voices heard in the news media" (Annenberg Public Policy Center, 2007). In an evaluation of this program, Flanagan, Syvertsen, Mitra, Oliver, and Sethuraman, (2005) found it to have an impact; there was an increased overall use of media to obtain political information as well as an increase in use of specific forms of media such as radio, newspaper, and the Internet to access information about political affairs and current events. Research has also reported long-term effects of the program (Pasek, Feldman, Romer, & Jamieson, 2008).

Another school-based intervention called *Kids Voting, USA* produced similar results to the Student Voices program. *Kids Voting, USA* gets students involved and ready to be educated, engaged citizens through a combination of classroom activities, an authentic voting experience, and family dialogue. The creators of the program claim that their "high-quality instructional materials provide K–12 teachers with valuable civic learning tools to be used throughout the school year, every year. In addition to classroom activities about voting and elections, students also explore the right to vote, democracy and citizenship" (McDevitt & Chaffee, 2000). In an evaluation of the *Kids Voting, USA* curriculum, McDevitt and Chaffee (2000) found that this school-based curriculum prompted student–parent discussion at home and that there was an increase in student's newspaper reading, TV news viewing, attention to campaign news, and election knowledge.

Not only do programs like these foster knowledge within the students, but they can also have an impact on the family. McDevitt and Chafee (2000) found that because of the student–parent discussion component of the curriculum, parents were significantly more likely to watch television news and become interested in current events after their students were involved in the curriculum as opposed to before. Hence, school-based curricula show a potential to benefit students involved in the program as well as members of their family.

Media

The media, and in particular the increasingly diverse forms of electronic media, are clearly an important influence on youth civic engagement. Media consumption has both direct and indirect effects on youth' political attitudes, but does relate to democratic values (Johansson, 1991). Pasek et al. (2006), in fact, report that media use is associated with greater involvement in civic activities and higher levels of political awareness. This report was based on an aggregate scale of media use, and as a whole, media use was positively related to civic activities. McLeod (2000) found that in terms of political learning among adolescents, newspaper and news magazine use has positive effects that are stronger than the negative effects of television time. Content makes a difference within television use. Watching news has beneficial effects, whereas watching entertainment has a negative influence on civic knowledge.

The growing availability of the Internet implies that this form of information dissemination should have an impact on society, and this impact may disproportionately involve youth since they are heavy users (McLeod, 2000). Youth, for example, are conscious participants in blogs, chat rooms, and meetings organized through the Internet and use these media vehicles to participate in political campaigns (Levine & Lopez, 2004). It does not seem however that youth between the ages of 18 and 24 years are using the Internet to compensate for inattention to newspapers and television news sources (Keeter et al., 2002). In fact, the Internet is not a more popular source among those aged 15–25 years than it is for those 26 and older. The frequency of use of the Internet for news information is comparable across these two age groups; the older generation may, in fact, use the Internet more than the younger one (Lopez Leviner, Dautric, Yalof, 2007).

McDevitt and Chaffee (2002) found that when children reach adolescence, newspaper use becomes a strong predictor of further progress toward political competence. While this information is important, we also need to figure out how we can get adolescents to become consistent consumers of information. Atkin (1981) regards adolescent media use as a cost-benefit trade-off in which the child weighs various gratifications against expenditures such as mental effort. The implication of this theory is that it is necessary to make news media consumption more gratifying for children so that they are more willing to devote the mental effort necessary to process the information they are receiving. McDevitt and Chaffee (2002) found that news attention is more likely when children perceive that the media provides useful information for conversations or school assignments.

The media have also been proposed to be the reason for declining civic engagement especially in youth. Putnam reviews a long list of possible contributors to the decline he describes, such as the increasing divorce rate, and concludes that the media are, particularly television, the main reason for the decline in civic engagement (Putnam, 1996, 2000). There is a public perception that entertainment media rarely addresses serious societal issues and instead may be used as an outlet to escape serious issues as politics or current events. Meyrowitz (1985) argued that one effect of the electronic media is the reduction of trust in formal institutions, such as the government.

Sociopolitical Context

A life-span approach is very relevant to research on civic engagement, because civic involvement is a behavior that occurs in a broad social political context and is likely to reflect that context. There have, in fact, been a number of studies that have examined the impact of major social political factors (e.g., collapse of communism in eastern Europe, the fall of apartheid in South Africa, and the ongoing religious strife in Northern Ireland) on young people's political attitudes and behaviors. The most ambitious of these studies examined adolescents' civic commitments in seven countries. The countries were divided into three stable democracies and four that were in the midst of social change. Overall, this study examined public interest as a life goal of adolescents and asked how it was influenced by volunteering, by school climate, and by family values. A family ethic that emphasized social responsibility influenced public interest as a life goal across both gender and type of country. In addition, volunteering and developing a sense of solidarity at school related to this life goal. Another major finding was significant differences between boys and girls in five of the countries; girls' families encouraged more social responsibility, and they volunteered more than boys (Flanagan Johnsson, Csapo, & Sheblanova, 1998). Hence, proximal factors seemed to be more important than the larger context.

Another study examined adolescents' perceptions of economic changes occurring in three countries undergoing social change in eastern Europe—Hungary, Bulgaria, and the Czech Republic. Perceptions of the justice of the newly emerging social contract were also examined. Older adolescents and girls were more likely to observe that economic disparities were increasing due to social change; as a result, they were cynical about the value of working hard. There were also differences across countries with high school students in the Czech Republic, the least cynical, and those in Bulgaria, the most cynical (Macek et al., 1998).

South Africa is another country that underwent massive social changes in the 1990s, and since the changes were clearly of a political nature, researchers were keen to examine the influence on youth civic engagement. Racial segregation in the form of apartheid was eliminated, a democratic government was put in place for all citizens, and the first elections were held. A study by Finchilescu and Dawes (1998) examined high school students' reactions to these changes. All had grown up in an era of racially segregated communities, not unlike what the first author experienced as a teen in the Southeastern United States in the early 1960s. All adolescents were concerned about the future in the midst of this change. However, White adolescents felt alienation, whereas Black Africans were generally positive. Indian teens and those of mixed racial descent fell in the middle. Age was not an important influence on views (Finchilescu & Dawes, 1998).

Northern Ireland is a country where politics and religion loom large in citizens' daily lives, even though it is not undergoing current social change. A study of adolescents in Belfast, Ireland, found that national identity was important to their perceptions of the fairness of the current political system. Teens who saw themselves as Irish or British were more likely to rate politics higher than those who saw themselves as Catholic or Protestant (Whyte, 1998).

Research about the influence of the World Trade Center attacks in New York City on September 11, 2001, provides an example in this country. Teenagers' political views influenced their reactions. For example, youth showing a concern for others worried about impact on prejudice to Arab Americans, whereas youth more self-focused thought we should retaliate. Furthermore, it had a powerful impact on current political views, reinforcing the importance of protecting us from terrorism over issues like poverty and education (Sherrod, et al., 2004).

Overall, these studies show that sociopolitical context does make a contribution but not more than the other factors such as gender and families. In fact, it may operate through these more proximal variables.

Religion/Spirituality

There is an increasing amount of attention to youth religiosity, which has been shown to relate to a host of positive outcomes for youth, including civic engagement. For a long while, religion and spirituality were considered inappropriate for research—or too difficult to research. In recent years, however, research has grown (King & Boyatzis, 2004).

Research has first documented in a demographic way the religious experiences of today's teens. One study used three national surveys of teens to ask about their religious participation: Monitoring the Future (1996), Survey of Adolescent Health (1995), and Survey of Parents and Youth (1998). This study asked about religious affiliation, religious service attendance, and involvement in youth church groups. The majority of American youth affiliate with some religious group. The number of Christian youth has been declining. Half of American youth regularly attend some type of church services. Participation in religion, however, declines with age (Granqvist, 2002; King, Furrow, & Roth, 2002). Girls tend to participate in religious activities more than boys. African Americans participate in religion more than other ethnic groups, and youth from the southern states were more active religiously than youth from other parts of the country (Smith & Lundquist-Denton, 2002).

Research has also shown that religion serves as a protective factor against anxiety, maladaptive adjustment, and other stress and psychological problems (Ball, Armistead, & Austin, 2003: Cook, 2000; Davis, Kerr, & Kurpius, 2003) and from involvement in problem behaviors such as substance use and early sexuality (Hardy & Raffaelli, 2003; King, Furrow, & Roth, 2002; Nonnemaker, McNeely, & Blum, 2003). Religiosity also relates to several positive qualities: physical and psychological health (Martin, Kirkcaldy & Siefen, 2003), positive family and peer relations (King, Furrow, & Roth, 2002), conscientiousness as a personality characteristic (McCullough, Tsang, & Brion, 2003), and thriving in youth (Dowling, Gestsdottir, & Anderson, 2003; Lerner, 2004). Religiously active youth also show higher levels of moral behavior (King, 2001). Finally, religion has been shown to relate to participation in community service, with religious youth being more likely to participate (Youniss, McLellan, & Yates, 1999). Hence, it is not clear if religion has a direct effect on civic engagement or influences it indirectly through its relationship to factors such as service (Sherrod & Spiewak, in press).

Perhaps the most direct contribution of religion to civic engagement is through the socialization of the individual into the beliefs and practices of the particular religion. Conservative religious groups such as Orthodox Jews or the Amish indoctrinate their young into group connectedness to their religion. However, other religious training may promote a concern for one's fellow man rather than allegiance to a particular set of beliefs; the Jesuit tradition of Catholicism, for example, follows this course. Fordham University's motto is "men and women for others." While the Catholic church, like all organized religions, has a particular dogma to promote, advocating allegiance to the church, the Jesuit version promotes more of a generalized concern for others. Quakers also promote both a particular type of group loyalty and concern for others. Most religions would advocate for a primary allegiance to the set of values represented in that religion. Concern for others might be part of that value system, as can loyalty to nation (and, for example, willingness to fight in wars), but national loyalty may not be a component of the religious values.

Religion and religiosity involves following the rules and regulations and beliefs of a particular organized religion; hence, it can be considered similar to civic engagement, which relates to following the rules and regulations of one's country. One question, therefore, is whether religiosity promotes civic engagement or is a substitute for it. Since participation in service relates to later civic engagement, examining the relationship between religiosity and participation in service allows one to address the question of whether religion

promotes or replaces civic engagement. Does religion promote service because it involves helping people or do religious youth participate in service just because the religion promotes that it is important? Examining young people's reasons for participating in service, which has not been studied to any great degree (Sherrod & Spiewak, in press), allows one to explore the relationship between religiosity and service. Understanding more fully the relationship between religiosity and service then also allows one to consider the relationship between religion and civic engagement.

Religiosity is usually used to mean participation in an organized religion including beliefs in deities such as God and/or in an afterlife. Youth also can show a sense of spirituality, which can involve a sense of other worldliness as well as a sense of spirit or existence above and beyond mundane daily reality (Sherrod & Spiewak, in press). One question is whether religiosity and spirituality coexist, or do youth show one form or another? And do both or only one relate to participation in service and civic engagement? That is, do each relate to different reasons for doing service; or do both show similar relationships with service and also with civic engagement?

INDIVIDUAL DIFFERENCES IN THE SOCIALIZATION INTO CITIZENSHIP

Today's population of youth is quite heterogeneous, and it is becoming more so. There are several dimensions that constitute this heterogeneity. Ethnicity and immigrant status are two important dimensions by which youth vary, and the youth population in the United States is becoming increasingly diverse across these dimensions. Soon, populations that are now considered minority will be in the majority (Flanagan & Gallay, 1995; Hernandez, 1993). Gender and social class are two dimensions in addition to ethnicity and immigrant status that are important dimensions of individual variability, although population demographic changes are not occurring as is true for ethnicity and immigrant status.

The contexts of socialization vary across these demographic characteristics of youth, and to the extent that these socialization experiences influence civic engagement, we would expect civic engagement to also vary across these dimensions of individual variability. Diverse youth grow up in differing contexts and ecologies. As a result, their connectedness to different social institutions is likely to vary. Diverse youth, such as immigrants or ethnic minorities, develop connectedness to institutions such as family, school, and communities, and these may be more salient to them than their affiliation to the nation-state (Bogard & Sherrod, in press; Fuligni, Tseng, & Lam, 1999; Larson, Richards, Sims, & Dworkin, 2001; Metzger & Smetana, 2008; Sherrod et al. 2002; Tseng, 2004). Research also indicates that gender and social class influence the allegiances of youth to social institutions (Bogard & Sherrod, in press).

Gender

One of the most important issues across which civic engagement and its development differs is gender. Boys and girls, men and women, show a variety of differences in political orientation. Girls, for example, tend to be more prosocial and do more community service, which research shows to be one precursor of later civic engagement. We review these differences below. As is true for many gender differences, it is difficult to determine the source of the difference, but in this case they are likely to result from socialization.

Gender Differences in Adult Political Orientation

A number of gender differences have been described for political behavior and political orientation. Voting is, of course, one especially important political behavior, and a gender gap has been described for voting behavior (Trevor, 1999). A gender-congeniality effect has been described to explain this difference. Each sex seems to vote for the candidate that supports issues endorsed by their own sex. Three experiments showed this effect in Republican and independent men and women in the United States. It was not found in Democrats because Democratic men and women seemed to favor the same issues (Eagly Diekman, Schneider, & Kulesa, 2003). Women also tend to express their political opinions less than men. The National Election Study in the United States asked respondents about likes and dislikes of candidates, political parties, and policies. Women express fewer strong likes and dislikes than men and are more likely to respond "don't know." The authors suggest that this difference has existed for 50 years in the United States (Atkeson & Rapoport, 2003). Also, generally, women tend to be more supportive of government programs in the United States, relating to perceived differences in opportunity and perceived efficacy of the programs. These differences are found in regard to a government role in medical care, long-term care, substance abuse treatment, public education, and housing (Schlesinger & Heldman, 2001). There is also evidence that these differences relate to women being more prosocial in their orientation to political issues, supporting increased government support for issues that, for example, help the poor; these differences have been reported since 1960 in the United States and seem to have increased during the 1970s (Shapiro & Mahajan, 1986).

Equally distinctive gender differences have been found internationally. The World Values Survey examined cross-national political outlook and participation, attitudes toward religion, views on women's roles, and existence of social movements. There was a commonality in both the young and old on these attitudes across countries. Although age and nationality interacted across different attitudes, gender emerged as one of the most powerful dimensions of individual differences in attitudes, as influential as age (Tilley, 2002). Gender differences have also been found to be as influential as race and partisanship (Schlesinger & Heldman, 2001).

Hence, research has found gender differences in the basis of voting behavior, in expression of political opinions, in support for government programs and in general political outlook. Gender seems to be as powerful a dimension of individual variability as race, class, and age. Research has also asked about gender differences in political socialization and about when these gender differences might emerge developmentally.

Gender Differences in Youth Political Orientation

Adolescence is likely to be an important time for the emergence of gender differences in politics. Developmentally, it is a period of intense change. Teens acquire Piagetian formal operations, which is the ability to examine the alternative solutions to a problem (Piaget & Inhelder, 1956). They also begin to search for a personal identity (Erikson, 1968). In addition, the socialization pressure for gender-typical behavior intensifies (Hill & Lynch, 1983). Although teens experience an array of other changes, such as puberty, these three developmental achievements are the ones most relevant to the emergence of gender differences in politics.

It had been expected that girls were less political than boys, but it is now clear that they are just different politically (Jacobi & Harrow, 1995). One recent study of almost 15,000 children and youth across 20 states in the United States, in fact, reports that girls surpass boys in political interest and activity, and this sex difference persists from children to adolescence (Alozie, Simon, & Merrill, et al., 2003). A very important way that girls and boys, differ is that girls are more prosocial in orientation than boys, and this flavors their political orientation. The egalitarian or prosocial political orientation of girls has been demonstrated internationally (Flanagan et al., 1998; Gille, 2000; Kuhn, 2004).

As previously discussed, a number of correlates have been identified between childhood or youth experiences and later adult civic engagement; school activities, civic education and community service are three important ones, for example (Eccles & Barber, 1999; Jennings, 2002; Torney-Purta et al., 2001; Verba et al., 1995; Youniss & Yates, 1997). To the extent that these vary across gender, they may help explain gender differences in civic engagement, but in fact few sex differences have been found in such experiences. For example, an international study of civic education in 28 countries found no gender differences in 27 of the 28 countries (Torney-Purta et al., 2001; Torney-Purta, 2002). Hence, it is not clear that childhood socialization experiences that promote adult civic engagement are in themselves responsible for adult gender differences in politics. The developmental origins of the gender difference in prosocial orientation are not clear, but researchers of moral reasoning (e.g., Gilligan, 1982) argue that it does result from gender specific socialization.

Hence, girls seem to be more prosocial than boys, but this is not a difference that is specific to politics. Nonetheless, one needs to ask about the relationship between this gender difference and age as it impacts political views. In addition, it is not clear whether girls experience different socialization pressures that would promote a different political orientation, but we need to ask if there are gender differences in the relationship of these socialization factors to political views. Research has found that gender differences in participation in social movements are related to differences in socialization, for example (Sherkat & Blocker, 1994).

Ethnicity

Minority groups in the United States face discrimination, which can vary according to whether they are voluntary or involuntary minorities (Ogbu, 1991). Some racial groups believe that due to experienced discrimination, one must develop an allegiance to one's race, and parents socialize their children to achieve this end (Hughes & Chen, 1997; Stevenson, 1994). Distress following experienced discrimination is also a powerful contributor to the development of political attitudes and a sense of group membership (Fisher, Wallace, & Fenton, 2000; Jankowski, 1992). Fisher et al. (2000) report that racial discrimination seems to be a pervasive stressor in the daily lives of teens. Spencer (1999) suggests that racial issues substantially influence adolescents' attitudes and behavior, especially in regard to self; discrimination may lead to negative self-evaluations, which then affects beliefs and behavior. Prejudice can also lead to stereotypic feelings about certain behaviors such as test taking (Steele & Aronson, 1995). Research on attitudes has shown that such direct experiences have a powerful impact on the formation of attitudes (Regan & Fazio, 1977). Hence, one would expect ethnicity to relate to political attitudes and behaviors.

Some minority parents try to prepare youth for discrimination; parental preparation for discrimination and prejudice is related to level of experienced discrimination and its stressfulness (Fisher et al., 2000). Some minority parents also socialize their children to identify with their race and take pride in their racial heritage as one form of protection against discrimination, and this seems to lead to healthy racial identity (Hughes & Chen, 1997; Spencer, 1999). Other families, particularly those that are voluntary minorities or immigrants, socialize their children to develop loyalty to family rather than to race (Fuligni et al., 1999; Ogbu, 1991). Thus, differences in connectedness to race, acquired through direct socialization or experience of that race, may relate to civic engagement.

Research shows that young people from different ethnic background develop differences in political orientation at an early age. Middle school Anglo students have at least rudimentary information about government and politics, practice democratic skills, and have positive political values compared to other ethnicities. Among minority young people, Native Americans have the least knowledge and the fewest opportunities to practice democracy; they also show the most negative

values (Fridkin, Kenney, & Crittenden, 2006). However, discourse analyses of urban minority youth "political texts" show that they feel empowered in regard to dealing with issues that affect their lives such as AIDS, drugs, and violence (Starr, 1998). Ethnicity does, therefore, seem to influence the civic engagement of youth, but it is not a matter of minorities simply showing less (Metzger & Smetana, 2008).

Social-Class Influences

A critical issue in attention to class is its confounding with race. Johnson (2000) expands Boykin's (1986) triple quandary theory of race by adding a class component. The initial model deals with minority versus majority experience, and these two are related to culture, a third domain; Johnson adds class experience as a fourth important realm. The four domains overlap, but the degree of overlap varies by race as well as class. In no case does one domain become isomorphic with another. This model provides a means of trying to disentangle race and class experiences. And research shows that class is an important influence on civic engagement.

Some youth, perhaps particularly ones from more affluent families, may develop allegiance mainly to the pursuit of financial success and wealth (Kasser & Ryan, 1993). Middle-class parents emphasize academic orientation and how it leads to material success in their advice about political beliefs and behaviors (Jankowski, 1992; Sanchez-Jankowski, 2002). Lower-class youth frequently have unrealistic ideas about opportunities for success (Fisher et al., 2000). In a capitalist world dominated by the pursuit of material possessions, youth orientation to occupational and material success must be an important ingredient in the development of their allegiances and political ideas. This aspect interacts in complex ways with the person's concern for others; it can lead to selfishness and lack of concern or to pursuit of more altruistic goals. But the point is that youth differ in the extent to which they receive socialization experiences that promote the pursuit of wealth and success versus goals related to prosocial concerns or to citizenship. There is some evidence that the circumstances of poor youth may, under certain circumstances, orient them to the goals of wealth and success (Kasser & Ryan, 1993).

There are important differences across SES in youth' beliefs about political issues such as social mobility and equality of opportunity. Lower-class youth are more likely to have unrealistic views (Goodman, Amick, & Rezendes, 2000). Youth from different classes also have different views about the causes of social problems such as poverty (Flanagan & Tucker, 1999). One must conclude that SES can have a powerful influence on the development of civic engagement; more research is needed that allows examination of the separate effects of race and class.

Race and Class Differences in the Development of Citizenship

Since race and class are confounded in this country, it is important to explore their combined influence on civic engagement. That is, it is important to examine the mechanisms by which poor and minority youth may feel some social group membership in terms of the nation-state. It is also imperative that we make clear distinctions about the areas (e.g., knowledge, attitudes, and behaviors) and the domains of components of citizenship (political and civic, concern for others, and connectedness) when attending to the development of citizenship in poor and in minority youth; the ways in which citizenship is expressed may differ in these youth.

Poor and minority youth have different opportunities to practice citizenship in the form of behaviors such as extracurricular school activities. We know, for example, that they are less likely to engage in extracurricular activities and other avenues for group involvement that relate to volunteering for service and the development of civic engagement. They may

be less likely to develop concern for others or a sense of group membership outside their own race or community because of the constraints imposed by being poor or being a minority that may face prejudice and discrimination (Fisher et al., 2000; Hughes & Chen, 1997; McLoyd & Steinberg, 1998; Spencer, 1999).

A variety of differences in the development of citizenship have been noted for poor youth and racial minority youth. Poor and minority youth are less likely to vote. They are less likely to do community service, to participate in extracurricular activities, and to show other behaviors shown to relate to adult civic engagement (Hart, Atkins, & Ford,1998); Hart et al. (1998), in fact, argue that poor inner-city youth, who are also minority, do not have the opportunity to practice moral self-concept.

Poor and minority youth also tend to have more conservative views of why people are poor and of the role of government programs; they typically state that people are poor due to their own shortcomings rather than due to social constraints and that government programs promote dependency (Flanagan & Tucker, 1999). A number of authors have argued that youth feel alienated and disconnected (Putnam, 2000); such feelings are especially true for poor and minority youth.

Hence, while we as a nation may be ignoring the civic development of our youth, this is especially true for poor and minority youth. They are not typically given opportunities to practice citizenship-type behaviors. They are not afforded chances to explore their own morality in order to develop concerns for others. And they may be pushed to develop concern for their own self-interest and material success (which research has shown does not contribute to well-being) rather than to develop attachments to other targets of social group membership (Kasser & Ryan, 1993). This does not mean, however, that they are lost to citizenship; instead, we need to explore the aspects of their development that may provide opportunities for engaging them in civic-related areas.

Immigrant Youth

The United States today has the largest number of immigrants it has ever had. Immigrant youth are the fastest growing sector of the population; roughly 1 out of 5 young people lives in an immigrant-headed household (Stepick, 2008; Suarez-Orozco & Suarez-Orozco, 2001). Furthermore, today's immigrant youth are also frequently young people of color, so they are distinguished both by ethnicity and being an immigrant. Generally, research has not differentiated youth who are themselves immigrants from youth whose parents were immigrants (Bogard & Sherrod, in press; Stepick & Stepick, 2002). Recent research does show that assimilation is not a single path to a single destination; immigrants often must struggle to acquire the rights of citizenship and they also must accommodate to the major U.S. ethnic group to which they belong (Stepick & Stepick, 2002).

Children of immigrants tend to be more politically active than their parents, but most research has focused singly on voting (Stepick & Stepick, 2002). Most other research on civic engagement cannot determine whether it is being an immigrant or being an ethnic minority that accounts for the behavior or attitudes; for example, there was quite a bit of political awareness and activity around Proposition 187 in California, but U.S.-born Latinos were not differentiated from recent immigrants (Bedolla, 2000).

Generally, immigrant youth Americanize rather quickly; what is not clear is whether this extends to civic engagement as it does to language and instances of culture such as music and clothes (Portes & Rumbaut, 2001). Schools provide an ideal environment for fostering civic engagement in youth; immigrant youth have the opportunity in school for civics classes, extracurricular activities, and community service, all of which relate to later civic engagement (Stepick & Stepick, 2002). However, most immigrants also maintain ties to their country of origin, so that it is often not clear where their major connectedness lies (Morawska, 2001). Generally, addressing the civic engagement of immigrant youth raises more questions than answers: Research is sorely needed (Stepick, 2008; Stepick & Stepick, 2002).

Sexual-Minority Youth

Sexual-minority youth are particularly at risk because they face the multiple challenges of adolescence as well as the prejudice and discrimination associated with being gay, lesbian, bisexual, or transgendered (LGBT). The fact that coming out often occurs in adolescence further complicates the developmental challenges facing these youth. However, the current generation of youth is the first to grow up in an era where LGBT issues are part of public consciousness (Russell, 2002; Russell & Laub, 2008).

Plummer (1995) has coined the term *intimate citizenship* to denote this new openness that allows LGBT youth to tell their stories; Richardson (2000) has described sexual-minority youth as "partial citizens" because they are denied certain rights such as to marry and excluded from certain responsibilities of citizenship (e.g., the military's "don't ask, don't tell" policy) (Russell, 2002). As a result, they may be more cynical and feel more disenfranchised than other youth. Often, their families may also have difficulty accepting their sexual orientation. And social institutions such as schools and religions also do not offer safe havens. As a result, it is not clear to what social institution sexual minority youth can connect.

However, the LGBT civil rights movement and the emergence of groups such as Gay Straight Alliances in schools and communities have offered new opportunities for civic engagement (Russell & Laub, 2008). The new electronic media with public spaces through the Internet have provided new forums for discussion and involvement and new categories of connectedness. Research is needed on these new opportunities for sexual-minority youth and for how they may contribute to the development of civic engagement.

In all cases, the development of a sense of connectedness and social group membership can relate to the direct socialization of the child or at least to socialization experiences such as the experience of racial discrimination or pursuit of wealth and success. Other aspects of civic engagement such as concern for others and tolerance and even involvement in politics and civics are also strongly influenced by the child's socialization. Children and youth, of course, differ in the extent to which they experience a strong directive socialization experience. It is not clear how children become attached to a particular social institution or develop a concern for others or an interest in politics when their socialization does not direct them in at least one of these directions. One reason for the perceived lack of civic engagement of youth may be that many young people do not experience any such explicit socialization that orients them to community or national interests.

CONCLUSIONS: A CONCEPTUALIZATION OF CIVIC ENGAGEMENT

For research on the development of citizenship to progress, it must be based on a clear conceptualization of the phenomenon. We have proposed in this chapter that we need to differentiate knowledge and understanding, participation and behaviors, and attitudes and beliefs as important ingredients of civic engagement (Sherrod, 2003). These three distinctions are similar respectively to Flanagan and Faison's civic literacy, skills, and attachment (2001). These three categories represent distinctions of processes that would apply to any overall conceptualization of civic engagement (2001). We also propose that civic engagement consists of three domains or components that focus on the political, concern for others including tolerance, and connectedness.

This model of civic engagement proposing three domains or components is illustrated in Figure 11.2. The first component is "active citizenship" or the person's involvement in what

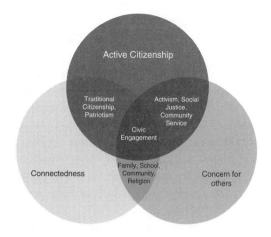

FIGURE 11.2   Components of Civic Engagement

Flanagan and Faison define as political as well as civic activities that are not explicitly political. However, this component also represents the person's knowledge about, involvement in and commitment to politics, government, or country; it includes both instrumental or active political participation (i.e., behavior) and passive or psychological political participation (i.e., interest in and concern for politics). This is what is typically studied as civic engagement in both adults and youth, but civic activity as well as traditional patriotism would fall here. To study civic engagement developmentally, we argue that one must also consider two other components. One is concern for others, an interest in contributing to the general social good as well as helping one's neighbors. This is a type of altruism or prosocial behavior; however, altruism must be further differentiated as to whether it requires self-sacrifice. It is far easier to be concerned about one's neighbor and interested in helping others if it doesn't cost you anything. Tolerance would also fall here in terms of respecting others. Of course, one can also be concerned with self and oriented to self without tolerance for people who are different. This component represents where the individual falls along a spectrum of concern for others, from self-centered to altruistic. Finally, there is a sense of group connectedness. To whom or what does one's loyalty lie; to whom or what is the person most attached.

This can be to one's self, to one's race, to the family, to the community or neighborhood or some institution therein such as the church, to one's nation or country, and/or to one's fellow man. These three components—active or typical citizenship, concern for others, and group connectedness—follow somewhat different developmental trajectories, so their development must be studied separately. By developmentally following these three domains, we may uncover new information about the emergence of civic engagement.

The PYD approach is very relevant here because it promotes the existence of 5 Cs that constitute positive development: confidence, character, competence, caring, and connection. A sixth C—contribution—emerges from these 5 Cs. Although there may be other forms of contribution, civic engagement is certainly an important form of contribution. These Cs are clearly relevant to the three components of civic engagement we have described; contribution is active citizenship, caring is concern for others, and connection is group connectedness. Confidence, competence, and character, the other three Cs, contribute to all three of these first Cs, and relate to social and human capital, which relate to civic engagement.

All three components must be present for the young person to show civic engagement in the form we desire for our citizens. Overlaps between two components represent some of the aspects of civic engagement we have reviewed. Connectedness and active citizenship is the traditional citizen who obeys laws, votes, and shows patriotism, for example. Concern for others and active citizenship generate the activist who is concerned with social justice. Concern for others and connectedness generate community service or some other behavior to help one's community. Involvement in religion or a strong involvement with family might also be expressed as a result of these two overlapping components.

The challenge for programs and policies, and for the nation, is not only to develop each component, but also contribute to their overlap

so truly civically engaged citizens result. The challenge is to assess which one or two components the young person has and then to consider how we may develop the remaining component(s) in order to move them to true civic engagement, to becoming the type of citizen a healthy democracy needs.

REFERENCES

Acock, A. C., & Bengston, V. L. (1980). Socialization and attribution processes: Actual versus perceived similarity among parents and youth. *Journal of Marriage and the Family, 42,* 501–515.

Ajzen, I., & Sexton, J. (1999). Depth of processing, belief congruence, and attitude behavior correspondence. In S. Chaiken & Y. Trope (Eds.), *Dual-process theories in social psychology* (pp. 117–138). New York: Guilford Press.

Allport, G. W. (1935). Attitudes. In C. Murchison (Ed.), *Handbook of social psychology* (pp. 789–844). Worcester, MA: Clark University Press.

Alozie, N. O., Simon, J., & Merrill, B. D. (2003). Gender and political orientation in childhood. *Social Science Journal, 40,* 1–18.

Althof, W., & Berkowitz, M. W. (2006). Moral education and character education: Their relationship and roles in citizenship education. *Journal of Moral Education, 35,* 495–518.

Alwin, D. F., Cohen, R. L, & Newcomb, T. M. (1991). *Political attitudes over the life span: The Bennington women after fifty years.* Madison: University of Wisconsin Press.

Amadeo, J.-A., Torney-Purta, J., Lehmann, R., Husfeldt, V. & Nikolova, R. (2002). *Civic knowledge and engagement: An IEA study of upper secondary students in sixteen countries.* Amsterdam: IEA.

Andersen, S. (1998). *Service learning: A national strategy for youth development.* Position paper prepared for Education Policy Task Force, George Washington University. Retrieved March 25, 2008, from www.gwu.edu-ccps/pops/svc.html.

Andolina, M., Jenkins, K., Zukin, C., & Keeter, S. (2003). Habits from home, lessons from school: Influences on youth civic engagement. *PS: Political Science and Politics, 36,* 275–280.

Annenberg Public Policy Center (2007). *About student voices.* Retrieved March 26, 2008, from http://student-voices.org/about/index.php?SiteID=10.

Astuto, J., & Ruck, M. (in press). Creating a foundation for civic engagement in early childhood. In L. Sherrod, J. Torney-Purta, & C. Flanagan (Eds.), *Handbook of research on civic engagement in youth.*

Atkeson, L. R., & Rapoport, R. B. (2003). The more things change the more they stay the same: Examining gender differences in political attitude expression. *Public Opinion Quarterly, 67,* 495–521.

Atkin, C. (1981). Communication and political socialization. In D. Nimmo & K. Sanders (Eds.), *Handbook of political communication* (pp. 299–328). Beverly Hills, CA: Sage.

Augemberg, C. (2007). *Values and politics: Value priorities as predictors of psychological and instrumental political engagement.* Unpublished doctoral dissertation, Fordham University, Rose Hill.

Austin, A., Vogelgesang, L., Ikeda, E., & Yee, J. (2000). *How service learning affects students.* Paper prepared for High Education Research Institute, UCLA.

Ball, J., Armistead, L., & Austin, B. (2003). The relationship between religiosity and adjustment among African-American, female, urban adolescents. *Journal of Adolescence, 26,* 431–446.

Barber, B. R. (1991). A mandate for liberty: Requiring education-based community service. *Responsive Community, 1,* 46–55.

Barber, B., & Eccles, J. (1997). *Student council, volunteering, basketball, or marching band: What kind of extracurricular involvement matters?* Presentation at meeting of Society for Research in Child Development, April, Washington D.C.

Barber, J. D. (1969). *Readings in citizen politics.* Chicago: Markham.

Bedolla, L. G. (2000). They and we: Identity, gender, and politics among Latino youth in Los Angeles. *Social Science Quarterly, 81,* 106–122.

Benson, P. (2004). *Developmental assets and human development.* Paper presented at International conference on Applied Developmental Scien ce, University of Jena, Germany, October 7–9, 2004.

Benson, P., Leffert, N., Scales, P., & Blyth, D. (1998). Beyond the village rhetoric: Creating healthy communities for children and adolescents. *Applied Developmental Science, 2,* 138–159.

Benson, P. L., Scales, P. C., Hamilton, S. F., & Semsa, A., Jr. (2006). Positive youth development: Theory, research, and applications. In R. M. Lerner (Ed.), *Handbook of child psychology* (6th ed.), vol. *1: Theoretical models of human development.* (Editors-in-chief: W. Damon & R. M. Lerner). Hoboken, NJ: John Wiley & Sons.

Billig, S., Root, S., & Jesse, D. (2005). *The impact of participation in service learning on high school students' civic engagement.* Center for Information and Research on Civic Learning & Engagement, Working Paper 33. Available at www.civicyouth.org/?page_id=152.

Blanchard, D. (n.d.). *Academics service learning: The reflection component.* Center on Philanthropy, Indiana University. Prepared for Council of Michigan Foundation, Learning to Give.

Bogard, K., & Sherrod, L. (in press). The influence of discrimination distress and parent socialization on civic attitudes among youth of color. *Journal of Cultural Diversity and Ethnic Minority Psychology.*

Bos, A., Williamson, L., Sullivan, J., Gonzales, M. H., & Avery, P. (2007). The price of rights: High school students' civic values and behaviors. *Journal of Applied Social Psychology, 37,* 1265–1284.

Bourdieu, P. (1985). The social space and the genesis of groups. *Social Science Information, 24,* 195–220.

Boykin, A. (1986). Triple quandary and the schooling of Afro-American children. In N. Neisser (Ed.), *The school achievement of minority children.* Hillsdale, NJ: Lawrence Erlbaum.

Brady, H. E., Verba, S., & Schlozman, K. L. (1995). Beyond SES: A resource model of political participation. *The American Political Science Review, 89,* 271–294.

Brim, O. G., Jr., & Kagan, J. (Eds.), (1980). *Constancy and change in human development.* Cambridge, MA: Harvard University Press.

Buchanan, C., Jahrami, P., Kourmanova, R., Smith, C., Austin, A., Kennedy, S., et al. (2008, March 6). *Service experiences and the development of civic values and intentions among high school students required to do service.* Paper presented at Biennial meeting of Society for Research on Adolescence, Chicago, IL.

Bynner, J., & Ashford, S. (1994). Politics and participation: Some antecedents of young people's attitudes to the political system and political activity. *European Journal of Social Psychology, 24,* 223–236.

Camino, L., & Sheldon, S. (2002). From periphery to center: pathways for youth civic engagement in the day-to-day life of communities. *Applied Developmental Science, 4,* 213–220.

Caprara, G. V., Schwartz, S. H., Capanna, C., Vecchione, M., & Barbaranelli, C. (2006). Personality and politics: values, traits, and political choice. *Political Psychology, 27,* 1–28.

Cargo, M., Grams, G. D., Ottoson, J. M., Ward, P., & Green, L. W. (2003). Empowerment as fostering positive youth development and citizenship. *American Journal of Health Behavior, 27,* s66–s79.

Carr, D. (2006). The moral roots of citizenship: reconciling principle and character in citizenship education. *Journal of Moral Education, 35,* 445–456.

Colby, A., & Damon, W. (1995). The development of extraordinary moral commitment. In M. Killen & D. Hart (Eds.), *Morality in everyday life: Developmental perspectives* (pp. 342–370). New York: Cambridge University Press.

Colby, A., Kohlberg, L., Gibbs, J., & Lieberman, M. (1983). A longitudinal study of moral judgement. *Monographs of the Society for Research in Child Development, 48*(1–2).

Connell, R. W. (1972). Political socialization in the American family: The evidence re-examined. *The Public Opinion Quarterly, 36,* 323–333.

Conway, M. M. (1991). *Political participation in the United States* (2nd edition). Washington, DC: A Division of Congressional Quarterly.

Cook, K. (2000). "You have to have somebody watching your back, and if that's God, then that's mighty big": The church's role in the resilience of inner-city youth. *Adolescence, 35,* 717–730.

Crystal, D., & DeBell, M. (2002). Sources of civic orientation among American youth: Trust, religious valuation, and attributions of responsibility. *Political Psychology, 23,* 113–132.

Dalhouse, M., & Frideres, J. S. (1996). Intergenerational congruency. *Journal of Family Issues, 17,* 227–248.

Davis, T. L., Kerr, B. A., & Kurpius, S. E. (2003). Meaning, purpose, and religiosity in at-risk youth: The relationship between anxiety and spirituality. *Journal of Psychology & Theology, 31,* 356–365.

de Tocqueville, A. (1848/1966). *Democracy in America.* New York: Harper & Row.

Delli Carpini, M. X. (2000). GenCom: Youth, civic engagement, and the new information environment. *Political Communication, 17,* 341–349.

Devos, T., Spini, D., & Schwartz, S. H. (2002). Conflicts among human values and trust in institutions. *British Journal of Psychology, 41,* 481–494.

Dowling, E. M., Gestsdottir, S., & Anderson, P. M. (2003). Spirituality, religiosity, and thriving among adolescents: Identification and confirmation of factor structures. *Applied Developmental Science, 7,* 253–260.

Eagly, A. H., & Chaiken, S. (1993). *The psychology of attitudes.* Fort Worth, TX: Harcourt, Brace Jovanovich College.

Eagly, A. H., & Chaiken, S. (1998). Attitude structure and function. In D. Gilbert, S. Fiske, & G. Lindzey (Eds.), *Handbook of social psychology,* Vol. 1 (pp. 269–322). New York: McGraw-Hill.

Eagly, A. H., Diekman, A. B., Schneider, M. C., & Kulesa, P. (2003). Experimental tests of an attitudinal theory of the gender gap in voting. *Personality & Social Psychology Bulletin, 29,* 1245–1258.

Eccles, J., & Barber, B. (1999). Student council, volunteering, basketball, or marching band: What kind of extracurricular involvement matters? *Journal of Adolescent Research, 14,* 10–43.

Eisenberg, N., Guthrie, I., Murphy, B., Shepard, S., Cumberland, A., & Carlo, G. (1999). Consistency and development of prosocial dispositions: A longitudinal analysis. *Child Development, 70,* 1360–1372.

Eisenberg-Berg, N., & Hand, M. (1979). The relationship of preschooler's reasoning about prosocial moral conflicts to prosocial behavior. *Child Development, 50,* 356–363.

Erikson, E. (1968). *Identity: Youth and crisis.* New York: W. W. Norton.

Fazio, R. H. (1995). Attitudes as object-evaluation associations: Determinants, consequences, and correlates of attitude accessibility. In R. E. Petty & J. A. Krosnick (Eds.), *Attitude strength: Antecedents and consequences* (pp. 247–282). Mahwah, NJ: Lawrence Erlbaum.

Fazio, R. H., & Towles-Schwen, T. (1999). The MODE model of attitude behavior processes. In S. Chaiken & Y. Trope (Eds.), *Dual-process theories in social psychology* (pp. 97–116). New York: Guilford Press.

Feather, N. T. (1977). Value importance, conservatism, and age. *European Journal of Social Psychology, 7,* 241–245.

Feldman, S. (2003). Values, ideology, and the structure of political attitudes. In D. O. Sears, L. Huddy, & R. Jervis (Eds.), *Oxford handbook of political psychology* (pp. 477–510). New York: Oxford University Press.

Finchilescu, G., & Dawes, A., (1998). Catapulted into democracy: South African adolescents' sociopolitical orientations following rapid social change. *Journal of Social Issues, 54,* 563–583.

Fisher, C., Wallace, S., & Fenton, R. (2000). Discrimination distress during adolescence. *Journal of Youth and Adolescence, 29,* 679–695.

Flanagan, C., & Faison, N. (2001). Youth civic development: Implications of research for social policy and programs. *Social Policy Reports, 1,* 2001.

Flanagan, C., & Gallay, L. (1995). Reframing the meaning of "political" in research with adolescents. *Perspective on Political Science, 24,* 34–41.

Flanagan, C., Johnsson, B., Csapo, B., Sheblanova, E. (1998). Ties that bind: Correlates of adolescents' civic commitments in seven countries. *Journal of Social Issues, 54,* 457–475.

Flanagan, C., & Tucker, C. (1999). Adolescents' explanations for political issues: Concordance with their views of self and society. *Developmental Psychology, 35,* 1198–1209.

Flanagan, C., & Sherrod, L. R. (1998). Youth political development: An introduction. Political development: Growing up in a global community. *Journal of Social Issues, 54,* 447–456.

Flanagan, C. A., Syvertsen, A. K., Mitra, D., Oliver, M. B., & Sethuraman, S. S. (2005). *Randomized field design of implementation of Student Voices in Pennsylvania schools: A final report.* Philadelphia: Annenberg Public Policy Center.

Fridkin, K. L., Kenney, P. J., & Crittenden, J. (2006). On the margins of democratic life: The impact of race and ethnicity on the political engagement of young people. *American Politics Research, 34,* 605–626.

Fuligni, A. J., Tseng, V., & Lam, M. (1999). Attitudes toward family obligations among American adolescents from Asian, Latin American, and European backgrounds. *Child Development, 70,* 1030–1044.

Gille, M. (2000). Werte, Rollenbilder und soziale Orientierung. In M. Gille & W. Kruger (Eds.). *Unzufriedene demokraten: Politische orientierungen der 16- bis 29 jahrigen im vereingten Deutschland* (pp. 143–203). Opladen: Leske+Budrich.

Gilligan, C. (1982). *In a different voice: Psychological theory and women's development.* Cambridge, MA: Haravard University Press.

Goodman, E., Amick, B. C., & Rezendes, M. O. (2000). Adolescents' understanding of social class: A comparison of white upper middle class and working class youth. *Journal of Adolescent Health, 27,* 80–83.

Granger, R. (2008). After-school programs and academics: Implications for policy, practice, and research. *Social Policy Report, 12,* 3–19.

Granqvist, P. (2002). Attachment and religiosity in adolescence: Cross-sectional and longitudinal evaluations. *Personality and Social Psychology Bulletin, 28,* 260–270.

Halstead, M. G., & Taylor, M. J. (2000). Learning and teaching about values: A review of recent research. *Cambridge Journal of Education, 30,* 169–204.

Hardy, S. A., & Raffaelli, M. (2003). Adolescent religiosity and sexuality: An investigation of reciprocal influences. *Journal of Adolescence, 26,* 731–739.

Hart, D., Atkins, R., & Ford, D. (1998). Urban America as a context for the development of moral identity in adolescence. *Journal of Social Issues, 54,* 513–530.

Hart, D., Atkins, R., Markey, P., & Youniss, J. (2004). Youth bulges in communities: The effect of age structure on adolescent civic knowledge and civic participation. *Psychological Science, 15,* 591–597.

Haste, H., & Hogan, A. (2004). Beyond conventional civic participation, beyond the moral–political divide: Young people and contemporary debates about citizenship. *Journal of Moral Education, 4,* 473–498.

Herek, G. (1986). The instrumentality of attitudes: Toward a neo-functional theory. *Journal of Social Issues, 42,* 99–114.

Herek, G. (1987). Can functions be measured? A new perspective on the functional approach to attitudes. *Social Psychology Quarterly, 50,* 285–303.

Hernandez, D. (1993). *America's children: Resources from family, government, and the economy.* New York: Russell Sage Foundation.

Hetherington, E., Lerner, R., & Perlmutter, M. (1988). *Child development in life span perspective.* Hillsdale, NJ: Lawrence Erlbaum.

Hill, J. P., & Lynch, M. E. (1983). The intensification of gender-related role expectations during early adolescence. In J. Brooks-Gunn & A. C. Petersen (Eds.), *Girls at puberty: Biological and psychosocial perspectives* (pp. 201–228). New York: Academic Press.

Holland, A., & Andre, T. (1987). Participation in extracurricular activities in secondary school: What is known, what needs to be known. *Review of Educational Research, 57,* 437–466.

Hoxie, A. M., & Sherrod, L. (2008, March 8). *Experiences in after-school programs associated with youth civic development.* Poster presented at biennial meeting of Society for Research on Adolescence, Chicago, IL.

Hughes, D., & Chen, L. (1997). When and what parents tell children about race: An examination of race related socialization among African-American families. *Applied Developmental Science, 1,* 200–214.

Hyman, H. (1959). *Political socialization.* New York: Free Press.

Hyman, J. B. (2002). Exploring social capital and civic engagement to create a framework for community building. *Applied Developmental Science, 6,* 196–202.

Ichilov, O. (1988). Family politicization and adolescents' citizenship orientations. *Political Psychology, 9,* 431–444.

Jacobi, J., & Harrow, J. (Trans.). (1995). Are girls less political than boys? Research strategies and concepts for gender studies on 9- to 12-year-olds. *Individuation in Childhood and Adolescence,* 117–128.

Jankowski, M. (1992). Ethnic identity and political consciousness in different social orders. *New directions for child development, 56,* 79–93.

Jennings, M. K. (2002). Generation units and the student protest movement in the United States: An intra- and intergenerational analysis. *Political Psychology, 23,* 303–324.

Jennings, M. K., & Niemi, R. G. (1968). The transmission of political values from parent to child. *American Political Science Review, 62,* 169–184.

Jennings, M., & Niemi, R. (1974). *The political character of adolescence.* Princeton, NJ: Princeton University Press.

Johansson, O. (1991). Youth and mass media: On the co-variation between mass media use and democratic values. *Politics & the Individual, 1,* 49–65.

Johnson, D. (2000). Disentangling race and poverty. *Applied Developmental Science, 4,* 55–67.

Kasser, T., & Ryan, R. (1993). A dark side of the American dream: Correlates of financial success as a central life aspiration. *Journal of Personality and Social Psychology, 65,* 410–422.

Katz, D. (1960). The functional approach to the study of attitudes. *Public Opinion Quarterly, 24,* 163–204.

Keeter, S., Sukin, C., Andolina, M., & Jenkins, K. (2002). *The civic and political health of the nation: A generational portrait* [Report]. New Brunswick, NJ: Center for Information and Research on Civic Learning and Engagement.

Kiecolt, K. (1988). Recent developments in attitudes and social structure. *Annual Review of Sociology, 14,* 381–403.

King, P. E. (2001). Adolescent religiousness and moral behavior: A proposed model of social capital resources and moral outcomes. *Dissertation Abstracts International Section A: Humanities and Social Sciences, 62,* 1228.

King, P. E., & Boyatzis, C. J. (2004). Exploring adolescent spiritual and religious development: Current and future theoretical and empirical perspectives. *Applied Developmental Science, 81,* 2–6.

King, P. E., Furrow, J. L., & Roth, N. (2002). The influence of families and ppers on adolescent religiousness. *Journal of Psychology and Christianity, 21,* 109–120.

Kohlberg, L. (1976). Moral stage and moralization: The cognitive–developmental approach. In T. Lickona (Ed.), *Moral development and behavior: Theory, research and social issues* (pp. 84–107). New York: Holt, Rinehart, & Winston.

Kuhn, H. P. (2004). Explaining gender differences in adolescent political and civic identity. The impact of self concept of political competence and value orientations. In A. Sliwka, M. Diedrich, & M. Hofter (Eds.), *Citizenship Education: Theory, Research, and Practice,* (pp. 59–72).

Larson, R. (2000). Toward a psychology of positive youth development. *American Psychologist, 55,* 170–183.

Larson, R. W., Richards, M. H., & Sims, B. (2001). How urban African American young adolescents spend their time: Time budgets for locations, activities, and companionship. *American Journal of Community Psychology, 29,* 565–597.

Leming, J. (2001). Integrating a structure ethical reflection curriculum into high school community service experiences: Impact on students' sociomoral development. *Journal of Research on Adolescence, 36,* 33–45.

Lerner, R. (2004). *Liberty: Thriving and civic engagement among America's youth.* Thousand Oaks, CA: Sage.

Lerner, R., Dowling, E., & Anderson, P. (2003). Positive youth development: Thriving as the basis of personhood and civil society. *Applied Developmental Science, 7,* 172–180.

Levine, P., & Lopez, M. H. (2004). Young people and political campaigning on the internet. CIRCLE fact sheet. Available at www.civicyouth.org/?page_id=154#2

Lopez, M. H., Levine, P., Dautric, K., & Yalof, D. (2007). *Schools, education policy, and the future of the first amendment.* CIRCLE working paper 56. Available at www.civicyouth.org/?page_id=152

Macek, P., Flanagan, C., Gallay, L., Kostron, L., Botcheva, L., & Csapo, B. (1998). Postcommunist societies in times of transition: Perceptions of change among adolescents in central and eastern Europe. *Journal of Social Issues, 54,* 547–561.

Mannheim, K. (1952). *Essays in the sociology of knowledge.* London: Routledge and Kegan Paul.

Markus, G., Howard, J., & King, D. (1993). Integrating community service and classroom instruction enhances learning: Results from an experiment. *Educational Evaluation and Policy Analysis, 15,* 410–419.

Martin, T., Kirkcaldy, B., & Siefen, G. (2003). Antecedents of adult wellbeing: Adolescent religiosity and health. *Journal of Managerial Psychology, 18,* 453–470.

Marwell, G., Aiken, M. T., & Demareth. N. J. (1987). The persistence of political attitudes among 1960s civil rights activists. *Public Opinion Quarterly, 51,* 359–375.

McAdam, D. (1988). *Freedom summer.* New York: Oxford University Press.

McCullough, M. E., Tsang, J., & Brion, S. (2003). Personality traits in adolescence as predictors of religiousness in early adulthood: Findings from the Terman longitudinal study. *Personality and Social Psychology Bulletin, 29,* 980–991.

McDevitt, M., & Chaffee, S. (2000). Closing gaps in political communication and knowledge: Effects of a school intervention. *Communication Research, 27*(3), 259–292.

McDevitt, M., & Kiousis, S. (2006). Deliberative learning: An evaluative approach to interactive civic education. *Communication Education, 55,* 247–264.

McLeod, J. (2000). Media and civic socialization of youth. *Journal of Adolescent Health, 27,* 45–51.

McLoyd, V., & Steinberg, L. (1998). *Studying minority adolescents.* Hillsdale, NJ: Lawrence Erlbaum.

McPherson, P., & Zimmerman, D. (2002). Real-world practical learning: developing a comprehensive model in the new land-grant tradition. In M. Kenny, L. A. Simon, K. Kiley-Brabeck & R. Lerner (Eds.), *Learning to serve: Promoting civil society through service learning* (pp. 209–224). Boston: Kluwer Academic.

Metzger, A., & Smetana, J. G. (2008 March). Civic beliefs and behavior in diverse American youth. In L. Sherrod, *Paths to Citizenship in Diverse Youth.* Symposium conducted at the meeting of the Society for Research on Adolescence, Chicago, IL.

Meyrowitz, J. (1985). *No sense of place: The impact of electronic media on social behavior.* New York: Oxford University Press.

Morawska, E. (2001). Gappy immigration controls, resourceful migrants, and *pendel* communities: East–west European travelers. In E. Morawska (Ed.), *Controlling a new migration world* (pp. 173–199). New York: Rutledge.

Myers-Lipton, S. (1994). *The effects of service-learning on college students' attitudes toward civic responsibility, international understanding and racial prejudice.* Ph.D. Dissertation: Abstract and discussion of results. University of Colorado, Boulder, CO.

Newcomb, T. M. (1943). *Personality and social change.* New York: Dryden Press.

Newcomb, T. L., Koenig, K. E., Flacks, R., & Warwick, D. P. (1967). *Persistence and change: Bennington College and its students after 25 years.* New York: John Wiley & Sons.

Niemi, R. & Junn, J. (2000) *Civic education: What makes students learn.* New Haven, CT: Yale University Press.

Niemi, R., Sanders, M., & Whittington, D. (2005). Civic knowledge of elementary and secondary school students, 1933–1998. *Theory and Research in Social Education, 33,* 172–199.

Nonnemaker, J. M., McNeely, C. A., & Blum, R. W. (2003). Public and private domains of religiosity and adolescent health risk behaviors: Evidence from the National Longitudinal Study of Adolescent Health. *Social Science & Medicine, 57,* 2049–2054.

Obradovic, J., & Masten, A. (2007). Developmental antecedents of young adult civic engagement. *Applied Developmental Science, 11,* 2–19.

Ogbu, J.U. (1991). Minority coping responses and school experience. *Journal of Pyschohistory, 18,* 433–456.

Parsons, T. (1939). The professions and social structure. *Social Forces, 17,* 457–467.

Pasek, J., Kenski, K., Romer, D., & Hall-Jamieson, K. (2006). America's youth and community engagement: How use of mass media is related to civic activity and political awareness in 14- to 22-year-olds. *Communication Research, 33,* 115–135.

Piaget, J., & Inhelder, B. (1956). *The early growth of logic in the child.* New York: W. W. Norton.

Plummer, K. (1995). *Telling sexual stories: Power, change, and social worlds.* London: Routledge.

Porter, A. C., & Polikoff, M. S. (2007). NCLB: State interpretations, early effects, and suggestions for reauthorization. *Social Policy Report, 21,* 3–9.

Portes, A. (1998). Social capital and its origins and applications in modern sociology. *Annual Review of Sociology, 24,* 1–24.

Portes, A., & Rumbaut, R. G. (2001). Legacies. *The story of the immigrant second generation.* Berkeley: University of California Press.

Putnam, R. (1996). The strange disappearance of civic America. *American Prospect,* 34–48.

Putnam, R. (2000). *Bowling alone: The collapse and revival of American community.* New York: Simon & Schuster.

Regan, D. T., & Fazio, R. (1977). On the consistency between attitudes and behavior: Look to the method of attitude formation. *Journal of Experimental Social Psychology, 13,* 28–45.

Reinders, H., & Youniss, J. (2006). School-based required community service and civic development in adolescents. *Applied Developmental Science, 10,* 2–12.

Rokeach, M. (1968). The role of values in public opinion research. *Public Opinion Quarterly, 32,* 547–559.

Rokeach, M. (1973). *The nature of human values*. New York: Free Press.

Rokeach, M. (1980). Some unresolved issues in theories of beliefs, attitudes and values. In M. Page (Ed.), *1979 Nebraska symposium on motivation*. Lincoln: University of Nebraska Press.

Ruck, M. D., Abramovitch, R., & Keating, D. (1998) Children's and adolescents' understanding of rights: Balancing nurturance and self determination. *Child Development, 64*, 404–417.

Russell, S. T. (2002). Queer in America: Citizenship for sexual minority youth. *Applied Developmetal Science, 6*, 258–263.

Russell, S. T., & Laub, C. (2008, March 7). *LGBT politics, youth activism, and civic engagement*. Paper presented at biennial meeting of Society for Research on Adolescence, Chicago, IL.

Sanchez-Jankowski, M. (2002) Minority youth and civic engagement: The impact of group relations. *Applied Developmental Science, 6*, 237–245.

Sax, L., & Astin, A. (1997). The benefits of service: Evidence from undergraduates. *Educational Record, 78*, 25–32.

Scales, P., Blyth, D., Berkas, T., & Kielsmeier, J. (2000). The effects of service learning on middle school students' social responsibility and academic success. *Journal of Early Adolescence, 20*, 332–358.

Schlesinger, M., & Heldman, C. (2001). Gender gap or gender gaps? New perspectives on support for government action and policies. *Journal of politics, 63*, 59–92.

Schmidt, J., Shumow, L., & Kackar, H. (2007). Adolescents' participation in service activities and its impact on academic, behavioral, and civic outcomes. *Journal of Youth and Adolescence, 36*, 127–140.

Schwartz, S. (1992). Universals in the content and structure of values: Theoretical advances and empirical tests in 20 countries. *Advances in Social Psychology, 25*, 1–65.

Schwartz, S. H. (1996). Value priorities and behavior: Applying a theory of integrated value systems. In C. Seligman, J.M. Olson, & M.P. Zanna (Eds.), *The psychology of values: The Ontario symposium*, vol. 8 (pp. 1–24). Hillsdale, NJ: Lawrence Erlbaum.

Sears, D. O. (1990). Whither political socialization research? The question of persistence. In O. Ichilov (Ed.), *Political socialization, citizenship education, and democracy*. New York: Columbia University Teachers College Press.

Shapiro, R. Y., & Mahajan, H. (1986). Gender differences in policy preferences: A summary of trends from the 1960's to the 1980's. *Public Opinion Quarterly, 50*, 42–61.

Shavitt, S. (1990). The role of attitude objects in attitude functions. *Journal of Experimental Social Psychology, 26*, 124–148.

Sherkat, D. E., Blocker, T. J. (1994). The political development of sixties' activists: Identifying the influence of class, gender, and socialization on protest participation. *Social Forces, 73*, 821–842.

Sherrod, L. R. (2003, April). Promoting the development of citizenship in diverse youth. *PS: Political Science and Politics*, 287–292.

Sherrod, L. R. (2006). Promoting citizenship and activism in today's youth. In S. Ginwright & Watts, R. (Eds.), *Beyond resistance! Youth activism and community change: New democratic possibilities for practice and policy for America's children*. New York: Rutledge.

Sherrod, L. R., & Baskir, L. R. (2008). *Youth's participation in community service: Individual differences in service experience and its relationship to civic engagement*. Unpublished manuscript.

Sherrod, L. R., & Hoxie, A. M. (2007, March). *The civic mission of after school*. Paper presented at the biennial meeting of the Society for Reasearch in Child Development, Boston, MA.

Sherrod, L. R., Busch, N., & Fisher, C. (2004). Applying developmental science: Methods, visions, and values. In R. Lerner & L. Steinberg (Eds.), *Handbook of adolescent psychology* (pp. 747–780). New York: John Wiley & Sons.

Sherrod, L. R., Flanagan, C., & Youniss, J. (2002). Dimensions of citizenship and opportunities for youth development: The what, why when, where and who of citizenship development. *Applied Developmental Science, 6*, 264–272.

Sherrod, L. R., & Lauckhardt, J. (2008). Cultivating civic engagement. In J. Rettew (Ed.), *Positive psychology: The science of human flourishing*, vol 4. Westport: Greenwood Publishing Group.

Sherrod, L. R., Quinones, O., & Davila, C. (2004). Youth's political views and their experience of September 11, 2001. *Applied Developmental Psychology, 25*, 149–170.

Sherrod, L. R., & Spiewak, G. (in press). Possible interrelationships between civic engagement, positive youth development, and spirituality/religiosity. In R. Roeser, R. Lerner, & E. Phelps (Eds.), *On the study of spirituality and development during adolescence*.

Slomczynski, K., & Shabad, G. (1998). Can support for democracy and the market be learned in school? A natural experiment in post-communist Poland. *Political Psychology, 19*, 749–799.

Smith, C., & Lundquist-Denton, M. L. (2002). Mapping American adolescent religious participation. *Journal for the Scientific Study of Religion, 41*, 597–612.

Smith, M., Lister, R., Middleton, S., & Cox, L. (2005). Young people as real citizens: Towards an inclusionary understanding of citizenship. *Journal of Youth Studies, 8*, 425–443.

Spencer, M. (1999). Social and cultural influences on school adjustment: The application of an identity-focused cultural ecological perspective. *Educational Psychology, 34*, 43–57.

Starr, A. (1998). "Safe places to go and things to do": Political texts from urban youth of color. *Journal of Sociology and Social Welfare, 25*, 75–90.

Steele, C. M., & Aronson, J. (1995). Stereotype threat and the intellectual test performance of African Americans. *Journal of Personality and Social Psychology, 69*, 797–811.

Stepick, A. (2008, March 7). *Immigrant youth civic engagement*. Paper presented at biennial meeting of Society for Research on Adolescence, Chicago, IL.

Stepick, A., & Stepick, C. D. (2002). Becoming American, constructing ethnicity: Immigrant youth and civic engagement. *Applied Developmental Science, 6*, 246–257.

Stevenson, H. (1994). Validation of the scale of racial socialization for African American adolescents: Steps towards multidimensionality. *Journal of Black Psychology, 20*: 445–468.

Stoneman, D. (2002). The role of youth programming in the development of civic engagement. *Applied Developmental Science, 6*, 221–226.

Stukas, A., Clary, E. G., & Snyder, M. (1999). Service learning: Who benefits and why. *Social Policy Report: Society for Research in Child Development, 8*, 1–19.

Suarez-Orozco, C., & Suarez-Orozco, M. M. (2001). *Children of immigration*. Cambridge, MA: Harvard University Press.

Theokas, C., Almerigi, J., Lerner, R., Dowling, E., Benson, P., Scales, P., et al. (2005). Conceptualizing and modeling individual and ecological asset components of thriving in early adolescence. *Journal of Early Adolescence, 25*, 113–143.

Tierney, J. P., & Branch, A. Y. (1992). *College students as mentors for at-risk youth*. Philadelphia: Public/Private Ventures.

Tilley, J. (2002). Is youth a better predictor of sociopolitical values than is nationality? *Annals of the American Academy of Political and Social Science, 580*, 226–256.

Tolan, P. H., Sherrod, L. R., Gorman-Smith, D., & Henry, D. (2003). Building protection, support, and opportunity for inner-city children and youth and their families. In K. Maton, C. Schellenbach, & B. Leadbeater (Eds.), *Fostering resilient children, youth, families and communities: Strength-based research and policy*. Washington, DC: APA Press.

Torney-Purta, J. (2002). The school's role in developing civic engagement: A study of adolescents in twenty-eight countries. *Applied Developmental Science, 6*(4), 202–211.

Torney-Purta, J. (2005). IEA Civic Education Study. In L. Sherrod, C. Flanagan, R. Kassimir, & A. Syvelsten (Eds.), *Youth activism: An international encyclopedia* (pp. 324–329). New York: Greenwood.

Torney-Purta, J., Barber, C. H., & Richardson, W. R. (2004). Trust in government-related institutions and political engagement among adolescents in six countries. *Acta Politica, 39,* 380–406.

Torney-Purta, J., Barber, C. H., & Wikenfeld, B. (2007). Latino adolescents' civic development in the United States: Research results from the IEA Civic Education Study. *Journal of Adolescence, 36,* 111–125.

Torney-Purta, J., Lehmann, R., Oswald, H., & Schultz, W. (2001). *Citizenship and education in 28 countries: Civic knowledge and engagement at age fourteen.* Amsterdam: IEA.

Torney-Purta, J., & Richardson, W. K. (2004). Anticipated political engagement among adolescents in Australia, England, Norway and the United States. In J. Demaine (Ed.), *Citizenship and political education today.* London: Palgrave.

Trevor, M. C. (1999). Political socialization, party identification, and the gender gap. *Public Opinion Quarterly, 63,* 62–89.

Tseng, V. (2004). Family interdependence and academic adjustment in college: Youth from immigrant and U.S.-born families. *Child Development, 75,* 966–983.

Verba, S., Schlozman, L., & Brady, H. (1995). *Voice and equality: Civic voluntarism in American life.* Cambridge, MA: Harvard University Press.

Verbogt, T. (1996). *Moral reasoning and political beliefs in adolescents.* Paper presented at meeting of International Society for the Study of Behavior Development, August, Quebec City.

Walker, T. (2002). Service as a pathway to political participation: What research tells us. *Applied Developmental Science, 6,* 183–188.

Walzer, M. (1989). *Citizenship.* New York: Cambridge University Press.

Waterman, A. (Ed.). (1997). *Service learning applications from the research.* Mahwah, NJ: Lawrence Erlbaum.

Whyte, J. (1998). Young citizens in changing times: Catholics and Protestants in northern Ireland. *Journal of Social Issues, 54,* 603–620.

Wray-Lake, L., & Flanagan, C. (2008, March 6). *The development of adolescents' civic values and the role of family value messages.* Paper presented at Biennial meeting of Society for Research on Adolescence, Chicago, IL.

Yates, M., & Youniss, J. (1996). A developmental perspective on community service in adolescence. *Social Development,* 1–26.

Youniss, J. (2005). G. Stanley Hall: Neither psychology alone nor basic research is sufficient. *Journal of Research on Adolescence, 15,* 357–366.

Youniss, J., Bales, S., Christmas-Best, V., Diversi, M., McLaughlin, M., & Silbereisen, R. (2002). Youth civic engagement in the twenty-first century. *Journal of Research on Adolescence, 12,* 121–148.

Youniss, J., McLellan, J. A., & Yates, M. (1999). Religion, community service, and identity in American youth. *Journal of Adolescence, 22,* 243–253.

Youniss, J., & Yates, M. (1997). What we know about engendering civic identity. *American Behavioral Scientist, 40,* 620–631.

Youniss, J., & Yates, M. (1999). Youth service and moral-civic identity: A case for everyday morality. *Educational Psychology Review, 11,* 361–376.

Zeldin, S., Camino, L., & Calvert, M. (2003). Toward an understanding of youth in community governance: Policy priorities and research directions. *Social Policy Report, 17,* 3–20.

PART III

The Broader Context of Adolescence

CHAPTER 12

Neighborhood Influences on Adolescent Development

TAMA LEVENTHAL, VÉRONIQUE DUPÉRÉ, AND JEANNE BROOKS-GUNN

Social contexts, particularly beyond the family, exert increasing influence on development during the second decade of life (Booth & Crouter, 2001; Bronfenbrenner, 1979; Steinberg & Morris, 2001). The growing need for autonomy during the adolescent years implies that adolescents spend more time outside of the home, typically with peers. Neighborhoods are thought to be one of the primary contexts for adolescents' out-of-home time. They provide not only the physical space in which youth frequently operate but also the social space in which a wide array of interactions occur.

In the United States, attention to neighborhoods as a social context for adolescent development dates back at least to the nineteenth century. Demographic changes at that time, including increasing industrialization, urbanization, and immigration led to social concerns about youth growing up in urban centers. Progressive Era reforms, such as the formation of juvenile courts, are a reflection of this movement (Kamerman & Kahn, 2001). It was not until almost a century later, however, that social scientists attempted to document links between neighborhood residence and adolescents' development (Sampson & Morenoff, 1997; Sampson, Morenoff, & Gannon-Rowley, 2002).

The focus continued to remain on urban youth and their involvement in risky behaviors such as crime and delinquency (Park, 1916; Shaw & McKay, 1942). Like the early research, contemporary interest in neighborhoods as a context for adolescent development was also fueled by demographic circumstances (Hernandez, 1993; Massey & Denton, 1993; Wilson, 1987, 1996). The loss of industrial jobs in favor of service and technology jobs, coupled with rising concentrations of poverty and unemployment in urban centers served to reignite scientific and policy interest in urban youth and their problematic behaviors (e.g., Bursik, 1988; Kornhauser, 1978; Sampson, 1992; Sampson & Groves, 1989; see also Sampson & Morenoff, 1997, for a review). Contemporary research on adolescent development in neighborhood context, much of it emanating from developmental scientists, although interested in risky behavior, has taken a broader lens in terms of outcomes of interest and types of neighborhoods studied (Leventhal & Brooks-Gunn, 2000).

The goal of this chapter is to review methodological, empirical, and theoretical advances in studying neighborhood contexts and adolescent development. The first section summarizes approaches to studying neighborhood

The authors would like to thank the William T. Grant Foundation for its support. Additional support was provided by grant R40 MC 07845 from the Maternal and Child Health Bureau (Title V, Social Security Act), Health Resources and Services Administration, Department of Health and Human Services. The second author was supported by a fellowship from the Canadian Institutes of Health Research (CIHR). We are also grateful to Rachel Crimmel and Andrea Wysocki for their research assistance.

influences, focusing on measurement and study designs. The following section reviews current research findings on neighborhood socioeconomic effects on adolescent development by domain—achievement (education and employment), emotional and social well-being (mental health, crime, delinquency, and substance use), and sexual activity and childbearing. The third section considers a taxonomy we developed for addressing the potential pathways through which neighborhood effects might operate on these outcomes (i.e., indirect pathways). The proposed theoretical models include institutional resources (characteristics and range of community resources), norms and collective efficacy (community social structure, peers, and physical threats), and relationships and ties (parenting, home environment, and support networks). Processes most relevant to adolescents are highlighted. The fourth section highlights emerging trends in neighborhood research on adolescent development and unresolved issues in the field. Finally, future directions for research on neighborhood contexts and adolescence and policy implications are summarized.

METHODOLOGICAL ISSUES IN STUDYING ADOLESCENT DEVELOPMENT IN NEIGHBORHOOD CONTEXTS

This section presents a brief review of key methodological issues confronting the study of adolescent development in neighborhood contexts, including definitions of neighborhoods, identification and measurement of neighborhood dimensions, study designs, and selection problems. This overview is intended to provide a backdrop for the remaining sections in this chapter.

Neighborhood Definitions

An important question to consider when studying adolescent development in neighborhood contexts is, *"What is a neighborhood?"* Alternative strategies have been used to define the neighborhood unit of analysis. The most frequent approach is to employ data collected from the U.S. Decennial Census compiled from the census forms completed on the first of April during the first year of every decade. A neighborhood is then typically defined as a census tract; tracts contain approximately 3,000 to 8,000 individuals and are identified with the advice of local communities working under Census Bureau guidelines to reflect prominent physical and social features that signify neighborhoods, such as major streets, railroads, ethnic divisions, and the like. Another common, but somewhat smaller unit is the block group (census tracts contain one to four block groups), which contains approximately 600 to 3,000 people. Some researchers have combined two to three adjacent or relatively homogenous tracts or block groups into neighborhood clusters (e.g., Brody et al., 2001; Sampson, Raudenbush, & Earls, 1997). The smallest neighborhood unit used is the street- or face-block, which includes the two sides of the street facing a person's home. In contrast, most studies do not specify neighborhood boundaries when participant reports of neighborhood conditions are gathered; however, residents' reports of neighborhood boundaries appear to approximate census tracts (or clusters of tracts; Coulton, Korbin, Chan, & Su, 2001; Sampson, 1997).

Neighborhood Dimensions

A critical distinction to make in defining neighborhood dimensions is between neighborhood structure and neighborhood processes. Neighborhood structure entails compositional or sociodemographic attributes, such as median income, employment rate, and racial composition. Neighborhood processes include aspects such as social organization and institutional resources. Although it is thought to be a function of neighborhood structure, neighborhood social organization describes the capacity of residents to work together toward common goals and values and to establish institutions that promote and enforce these goals by regulating behavior (especially that of youth; Sampson et al., 2002; Shaw & McKay, 1942).

Institutional resources involve the presence of services and organizations that promote health, well-being, and general social welfare.

Given the accessibility of census data, census-based measures of neighborhood structural characteristics are employed in a majority of studies (Jencks & Mayer, 1990; Leventhal & Brooks-Gunn, 2000). Neighborhood income or socioeconomic status (SES)—a combination of social and economic indicators—is the most commonly studied structural dimension. Researchers often separate measures of neighborhood SES into high-SES/affluence (e.g., indexing percent high-income residents, percent professionals, and percent college-educated) and low SES/poverty (e.g., assessing percent poor, percent female-headed households, percent on public assistance, and percent unemployed). This distinction is made because the presence of poor and affluent neighbors may have differential associations with adolescent outcomes (Brooks-Gunn, Duncan, Klebanov, & Sealand, 1993; Jencks & Mayer, 1990). Other structural characteristics frequently considered are racial and ethnic diversity (e.g., percent Black, percent Latino, and percent foreign-born) and residential instability (e.g., percent moved in last 5 years, percent households in current home less than 10 years, and percent homeowners; Brooks-Gunn, Duncan, & Aber, 1997; Sampson et al., 1997). Despite general consistency across studies, specific definitions of these structural dimensions differ somewhat.

Neighborhood social organizational features commonly examined include informal social control, which depicts the degree to which residents monitor the behavior of others in accordance with socially accepted practices; and social cohesion, which refers to the extent of social connections within the neighborhood (measures of informal control and cohesion have been combined to assess what has been called, "collective efficacy"; Elliot et al., 1996; Sampson et al., 1997). Other organizational features that may result from the content and consensus of values include physical and social disorder, which describes physical conditions (e.g., abandoned housing and graffiti) and social interactions (e.g., public drinking and prostitution) in the neighborhood (Ross & Jang, 2000; Sampson & Raudenbush, 1999). Institutional resources include the quantity and quality of services, schools, health care facilities, and recreational programs. The census does not directly evaluate neighborhood organization or resources, which are necessary for testing theoretical models (as we subsequently describe). Thus, much research has relied upon individual parents' or youth's ratings to capture neighborhood processes; these ratings are problematic for several reasons. First, they are often confounded with outcome measures also obtained by means of participant ratings, leading to problems of shared method variance. Second, the reliability of such measures may be questionable because in most cases it relies on individual rather than ecological data and corresponding methods for handling data. Raudenbush and Sampson (1999) lay out a compelling argument for "ecometric" standards of gathering data from multiple reporters (preferably independent of study families) to enhance reliability of neighborhood measures and to use appropriate statistical tools to generate neighborhood-level reliability indices.

Alternative methodologies are required to measure the neighborhood processes described, including systematic social observations, community surveys, neighborhood expert surveys, and administrative data. Systematic social observations or windshield surveys involve trained observers using a structured format to characterize neighborhoods through video-taping, rater checklists, or audiotaping (Barnes McGuire, 1997; Kohen, Brooks-Gunn, Leventhal, & Hertzman, 2002; Raudenbush & Sampson, 1999; Sampson & Raudenbush, 2004; Spencer, McDermott, Burton, & Kochman, 1997; Taylor, Gottfredson, & Brower, 1984). Community surveys entail interviewing nonparticipants in the study about their neighborhoods, yielding measures of neighborhoods that are independent from those obtained by study participants (Sampson, 1997; Sampson et al., 1997). Moreover, as noted, interviewing multiple residents per neighborhood increases the reliability in neighborhood measurement. Neighborhood expert surveys require interviewing key community leaders such as prominent religious, political, business, and social leaders in the community about their neighborhoods (Sampson & Raudenbush, 2004). Finally, alternative administrative data sources are available from city, state, and federal agencies and include vital statistics from health departments, crime reports from police departments, school records from education departments, and child abuse and neglect records from human and social service agencies (Coulton & Korbin, 2007).

Study Designs

Researchers interested in understanding neighborhood effects on adolescent development have used nonexperimental and experimental approaches; each is reviewed in turn.

Nonexperimental Approaches

The earliest set of neighborhood studies used census-based measures of neighborhood structural characteristics in conjunction with data collected on youth and their families to examine associations among neighborhood residence and adolescent outcomes. This early nonexperimental research was based on two general classes of studies. The first set was large national data set, such as the Panel Study of Income Dynamics (PSID; Hill, 1991) and the National Longitudinal Survey of Youth–Child Supplement (NLSY-CS; Baker & Mott, 1989). These studies typically had large variation in neighborhood (and family) types and permitted estimation of neighborhood effects based on few adolescents per neighborhood. The second set was samples of youth drawn from single-city or regional samples in which the range of sampled neighborhoods as well as neighborhood types varied across studies. These city and regional samples were often comprised of primarily urban, low-income

neighborhoods. Well-known examples of these types of studies include the Pittsburgh Youth Study (Loeber & Wikström, 1993), the Beginning School Study in Baltimore (Entwisle, Alexander, & Olson, 1994), and the Chicago Youth Development Study (Gorman-Smith, Tolan, Zelli, & Huesmann, 1996).

Many of the earlier nonexperimental studies with appended census data were cross-sectional and were primarily useful for documenting associations between neighborhood residence and adolescent outcomes; however, they did not yield much information about the dynamic relationship between adolescents over the course of development and the neighborhoods in which they live, which may change over time through a variety of internal or external means. The next phase of neighborhood research, which incorporated neighborhoods into the study design, took on this challenge. In these neighborhood-based studies, a wide range of neighborhood types may be examined (e.g., neighborhoods from a variety of sociodemographic make-ups), or specific types of neighborhoods may be sampled (e.g., low- and moderate-poverty neighborhoods). Sampling is also conducted to ensure an adequate number of adolescents per neighborhood (e.g., at least 15–30 study participants per neighborhood; Duncan & Raudenbush, 1999) to conduct multilevel, longitudinal analyses. Multilevel analyses provide estimates of variation in outcomes both within and between neighborhoods, yielding more reliable estimates of neighborhood effects on adolescent outcomes. One well-known example of a neighborhood-based study is the Project on Human Development in Chicago Neighborhoods (PHDCN) in which census data were used to define two stratification variables—SES (three levels) and racial–ethnic composition (seven levels)—that were cross-classified, and then a stratified probability sample of 80 neighborhood clusters was selected for the longitudinal component of the study (Leventhal & Brooks-Gunn, 2003c). Finally, children and youth falling within seven age cohorts spanning from birth through

18 years of age were sampled from these 80 neighborhoods; approximately 75 children per neighborhood cluster were interviewed. In addition, PHDCN included an independent community survey component, in which neighborhood residents were interviewed regarding the social processes at play within their neighborhoods, as well as systematic social observations.

Experimental Approaches

Experimental and quasi-experimental studies that randomly assign families to live in certain types of neighborhoods have been conducted in the context of housing programs for low-income families. Because programs cannot serve all eligible or interested families, selection of neighborhoods is often random, based on housing availability (i.e., quasi-random), or both. In these studies, a subset of families is typically provided assistance in relocating from public housing located in high-poverty areas to less poor neighborhoods (e.g., families may receive vouchers to rent housing in private market or be offered public housing built in nonpoor neighborhoods).

The oldest quasi-experimental study is the Gautreaux Program, enacted following a 1976 court order to desegregate Chicago's public housing. Families were given vouchers to move, and assignment was based on housing availability (Rubinowitz & Rosenbaum, 2000). The most well known experimental study, the Moving to Opportunity for Fair Housing (MTO) demonstration program, was launched by the U.S. Department of Housing and Urban Development in 1994 partially in response to positive findings reported in the Gautreaux Program. Approximately 4,600 families across five cities were randomly assigned vouchers to move out of public housing in high-poverty neighborhoods into private housing of their choice or into private housing in low-poverty neighborhoods (with special assistance); by design, a subset of families remained in public housing (Goering & Feins, 2003).

Another type of experimental study that is relatively new is the use of natural experiments

in which some exogenous or external shift occurs that affects residents over time or differentially impacts neighborhoods (Fauth & Brooks-Gunn, 2008). Although few of these studies focus on neighborhoods per se, several have examined the impact of changes in environmental regulations on children's health at either the county or zip code level (Chay & Greenstone, 2003; Currie & Neidell, 2005). For example, Chay and Greenstone (2003) demonstrated how declines in county pollution levels were associated with declines in infant mortality. To our knowledge, this approach has not been employed in studies of adolescents, but provides a promising avenue for future research to explore.

Selection

Selection or omitted variable bias is the major criticism of nonexperimental designs used to study "neighborhood effects" and represents a potential threat to the validity of most existing neighborhood studies. Selection refers to the fact that families have some choice as to the neighborhoods in which they live, and some omitted (or unmeasured) variable associated with choice of neighborhood residence might account for any observed neighborhood effects (Duncan, Connell, & Klebanov, 1997; Manski, 1993; Tienda, 1991). A common strategy used to minimize selection as a problem is to account for child (e.g., sex and age) and family (e.g., income, parent education, family structure) demographic characteristics in analytic models. Although this approach is preferable (and, in our opinion, essential) because neighborhood characteristics are defined by family composition, it does not fully overcome the problem of selection. Moreover, many hypothesized omitted variables such as parental depression or motivation are not included in most studies, nor is the direction of bias resulting from the omission of these variables clear. For example, adolescents' parents who have poor mental health may be more likely to stay in disadvantaged neighborhoods than are parents with superior health. Conversely, more organized parents may be more likely to stay in disadvantaged neighborhoods to conserve funds for recreational activities for their adolescents than are less organized parents. Despite potential selection problems due to unobserved variables, a recent study examining the factors influencing neighborhood selection among PHDCN families found that omitted variables hypothesized to represent potential threats of selection bias in neighborhood studies, such as those mentioned, had little impact on neighborhood selection over time (Sampson & Sharkey, 2008). Rather, family socioeconomic characteristics routinely controlled for in neighborhood studies, including race/ethnicity, income and education, were the most potent factors associated with residential stratification. Thus, controlling for these key family characteristics, as suggested earlier, might be sufficient for achieving reasonable estimates of neighborhood effects.

Researchers also have used various analytic strategies to address selection issues. These approaches include comparisons of siblings or first cousins, which hold family characteristics constant (Aaronson, 1997); instrumental variable analyses, which minimize unmeasured correlations between neighborhood characteristics and adolescent outcomes (Foster & McLanahan, 1996); behavior genetics models, which differentiate between genetic and environmental influences (Caspi, Taylor, Moffitt, & Plomin, 2000; Cleveland, 2003); and propensity score methods, which match adolescents who do and do not live in certain types of neighborhoods (Harding, 2003). However, only experimental designs can fully overcome the selection problem in neighborhood research (although other selection problems may arise).

A REVIEW OF NEIGHBORHOOD STRUCTURAL EFFECTS ON ADOLESCENT DEVELOPMENT

This review builds on previous summaries of published neighborhood research conducted during the 1990s (Leventhal & Brooks-Gunn, 2000, 2003a, 2004a). The field has continued to proliferate in the twenty-first century (Entwisle, 2007; Sampson et al., 2002). To incorporate these recent developments, reviews of relevant databases were conducted following similar procedures as those used previously (Leventhal & Brooks-Gunn, 2000, 2003a, 2004a). In these reviews, we focused on the three structural dimensions (assessed by the census) most frequently examined: income/SES (affluence/high SES and poverty/low SES), racial/ethnic diversity, and residential instability. Our reviews yielded few and somewhat inconsistent findings for racial/ethnic diversity and residential instability, thus, only findings for SES are summarized here. Other neighborhood dimensions are considered in the subsequent section. In both sections, only studies that accounted for individual and family characteristics such as child sex, age, and race-ethnicity; family income and composition; and maternal education, age, and the like in the analysis were included due to potential selection issues.

Three domains of well-being are considered in turn: (1) educational and occupational achievement (test scores, grade failure, high school dropout status, college attendance, years of completed schooling, employment, and earnings), (2) emotional and social well-being (mental health, crime, delinquency, and substance use), and (3) sexual activity (age of initiation, number of partners, and contraception use) and childbearing. Whenever possible, we discriminate between findings for early adolescents (11–15 years old) and late adolescents (16–19 years old) because neighborhoods may have differential effects on outcomes during each developmental period (Aber, Gephart, Brooks-Gunn, & Connell, 1997). For instance, neighborhood influences may increase during late adolescence, when youth are often granted more autonomy than they are at younger ages, resulting in greater exposure to extrafamilial influences, including neighborhoods (Elliot et al., 1996).

Achievement

Across the studies reviewed, the strongest evidence was found for the association between neighborhood high SES and adolescent achievement outcomes (after accounting for child and family background characteristics). Living in a neighborhood with more high SES residents was beneficial for both younger and older adolescents' achievement. This pattern of findings was supported in nonexperimental research using a variety of analytic techniques, and to a lesser extent by experimental research.

Early research on neighborhood SES effects on young adolescents' achievement drew primarily upon nonexperimental city and regional samples with appended census data (Connell & Halpern-Felsher, 1997; Dornbusch, Ritter, & Steinberg, 1991; Entwisle et al., 1994; Halpern-Felsher et al., 1997). In general, these studies documented a positive association between neighborhood high SES/income and various indicators of adolescents' achievement (math achievement, basic skills tests, grade point average, and educational risk score). This pattern of findings was confirmed more recently in two longitudinal neighborhood-based studies of children who ranged in age from 4 to 16 years old and a multisite study of youth aged 9–17. The first neighborhood-based study, drawing on a diverse sample of Chicago children, found that the presence of managers/professionals in the neighborhood was positively associated with children's average verbal ability over 6 years (Leventhal, Xue, & Brooks-Gunn, 2006). The second neighborhood-based study drew on a representative study of Ontario children and reported that a measure of neighborhood affluence during late childhood through adolescence was associated with young adult educational attainment, particularly among youth from nonpoor families (Boyle, Georgiades, Racine, & Mustard, 2007). Finally, a multisite, cross-sectional study of geographically diverse, primarily European American adolescents documented a positive association between neighborhood median income and adolescents' verbal ability, but in this case the association was strongest among youth from lower income families (Gordon et al., 2003).

Additional findings on young adolescents' achievement from city and regional studies entail links between neighborhood low SES and related measures (e.g., male joblessness and female-headed households) and poor educational outcomes (Connell & Halpern-Felsher, 1997; Halpern-Felsher et al., 1997). Several of the studies reviewed also found that neighborhood SES may have more pronounced effects on young adolescent boys' achievement than on girls' achievement (Entwisle et al., 1994; Halpern-Felsher et al., 1997).

Studies of older adolescents have relied primarily on national data sets. A number of studies based on the PSID reported associations between neighborhood high SES/affluence and youth's educational attainment (high school graduation, college attendance, and years of completed schooling; Brooks-Gunn et al., 1993; Duncan, 1994; Halpern-Felsher et al., 1997); these associations were more salient among European American than among African American youth. However, one city-based study of African American adolescents found that the presence of managerial and professional neighbors was positively associated with boys' educational attainment (Ensminger, Lambkin, & Jacobson, 1996). In addition, a nonlinear association between this SES measure and youth's chances of completing high school was found in the Public Use Microdata Sample (PUMS), such that when the percentage of professional or managerial workers fell to five percent or fewer (or reached a tipping point), neighborhood effects were more pronounced, especially among African American males (Crane, 1991).

Findings from a quasi-experimental study in which low-income, minority youth residing in public housing in poor urban neighborhoods moved to the more affluent suburbs concur with the results of the nonexperimental literature. In a 10-year follow-up of the Gautreaux Program, youth who moved to the suburbs were found to be more likely to graduate from high school, take college preparatory classes, attend college, be employed, and earn higher wages than were their peers who remained in the city (Rubinowitz & Rosenbaum, 2000). More recently, however, no achievement effects were reported in HUD's 5-year evaluation of the MTO program, which used a true experimental design (Leventhal, Fauth, & Brooks-Gunn, 2005; Sanbonmatsu, Kling, Duncan, & Brooks-Gunn, 2006).

The MTO findings must be understood in the context of a social experiment. Because social experiments occur in the real world and not in a laboratory with highly controlled conditions, several important features of MTO impact our interpretation of the "neighborhood effects" reported. Only approximately 50 percent of families offered vouchers used them to move to new neighborhoods. Many low-poverty families who relocated typically moved to poorer neighborhoods after the first year in which they were required to be in low-poverty neighborhoods. Moving is disruptive to youth's social networks and may offset benefits associated with more advantaged neighborhoods (Adam, 2004; Adam & Chase-Lansdale, 2002; Pribesh & Downey, 1999). Finally, and specific to education, because many families in MTO who moved remained in urban areas, children continued to attend highly disadvantaged urban public schools. In contrast, children in the Gautreaux study attended schools in advantaged suburban school districts. More in line with MTO, a 7-year follow-up of another quasi-experimental study of a desegregation effort in Yonkers, New York, in which all families remained in public housing within the same city and school district found that older adolescents who moved to middle-income neighborhoods reported poorer school performance than youth who remained in high-poverty neighborhoods (Fauth, Leventhal, & Brooks-Gunn, 2007).

Two recent nonexperimental studies with the PSID have focused on neighborhood low SES and its association with dropping out of high school (Crowder & South, 2003; Harding, 2003). In contrast to neighborhood high SES/affluence, neighborhood low SES had more pronounced effects on African Americans' odds of dropping out of high school than European Americans', particularly among African American boys (Crowder & South, 2003). Of note is that the magnitude of the association between neighborhood disadvantage and African Americans' high school disruption increased over time from 1970 to 1990, the 1980s being the period on which much of the earlier neighborhood work with this sample was based (Brooks-Gunn et al., 1997). Finally, one study using another national data set indicates that neighborhood poverty during adolescence may have long-run associations with adult unemployment, particularly among males (Holloway & Mulherin, 2004). However, a quasi-experimental study of Canadian adolescents, which did not have the confounding of neighborhood and relocation like MTO, found that older adolescents who lived in public housing in poor neighborhoods did not differ in their earnings, employment, or welfare receipt at age 30 compared with peers from public housing in middle-income neighborhoods (Oreopoulos, 2003).

Other measures of neighborhood SES, such as the high school completion rate, percentage of female-headed households, and female employment rate, were found to be associated with educational attainment as well. Almost all of these studies were based on the PSID or other large, national studies (Aaronson, 1997; Brooks-Gunn et al., 1993; Duncan, 1994; Ensminger et al., 1996; Foster & McLanahan, 1996; Garner & Raudenbush, 1991). In a number of these studies, neighborhood SES effects on adolescent achievement were reported when techniques were used to address problems of selection bias or advanced statistical approaches were employed, including sibling analyses (Aaronson, 1997; Plotnick & Hoffman, 1999), instrumental variable analyses (Foster & McLanahan, 1996; cf. Evans, Oates, & Schwab, 1992), multilevel models (Garner & Raudenbush, 1991), and propensity score matching (Harding, 2003).

Behavioral and Emotional Outcomes

Growing evidence from well-designed studies supports the conclusion that neighborhood SES is associated with adolescent behavioral and emotional outcomes after accounting for background characteristics. Most notable are links between low SES neighborhoods and criminal, delinquent, and violent behavior among both younger and older adolescents.

Similar to studies of achievement, earlier studies examining neighborhood SES effects during young adolescence primarily drew from city and regional samples with appended census data. For example, in a rural Iowa sample of European American 8th and 9th graders, neighborhood low SES was positively associated with boys' psychological distress, and the percentage of single-parent families was positively associated with girls' conduct problems (Simons, Johnson, Beaman, Conger, & Whitbeck, 1996). Likewise, among 13- and 16-year-old boys in the Pittsburgh Youth Study, living in low-SES or "underclass" neighborhoods (characterized by poverty, unemployment, male joblessness, female headship, nonmarital childbearing, African American presence, and welfare receipt) was positively associated with youth engaging in delinquent and criminal behavior, and effects were more pronounced among younger than older adolescents, as well as among impulsive adolescents (Loeber & Wikström, 1993; Lynam et al., 2000; Peeples & Loeber, 1994; see also Beyers, Loeber, Wikström, & Stouthamer-Loeber, 2001).

Several recent multisite, neighborhood-based studies also find links between neighborhood SES and young adolescents' engagement in a range of problem behaviors. Results from the Family and Community Health Study (FACHS), which originally sampled 10- to 12- year-old African American children and their families in Georgia and Iowa living in a wide variety of neighborhood settings (i.e., not just urban central city neighborhoods), demonstrated an association between neighborhood low SES and affiliation with deviant peers (especially among early maturers) and girls'

(but not boys') substance use (Brody et al., 2001; Ge, Brody, Conger, Simons, & Murry, 2002; Gibbons et al., 2004). A related finding from the PHDCN study reveals that living in a low SES neighborhood was associated with violent behavior among adolescent girls (13–17 years old) who experienced early menarche (Obeidallah, Brennan, Brooks-Gunn, & Earls, 2004). Finally, another multilevel study conducted in three cities found that low levels of concentrated affluence were associated with young adolescent boys' greater externalizing of problems (Beyers, Bates, Pettit, & Dodge, 2003).

A number of recent studies have used data from the National Longitudinal Study of Adolescent Health (Add Health), a nationally representative, longitudinal study of middle and high school students, to explore aspects of neighborhood SES associated with adolescents' behavior and emotional outcomes. Most of this work has used a multilevel analytic framework. Research focusing on violent behavior reported that the proportion of single-parent families in the neighborhood, an indicator of low SES, was associated with adolescents' self-reported violent behavior (Knoester & Haynie, 2005), while another investigation found that neighborhood socioeconomic disadvantage was associated with this outcome (Haynie, Silver, & Teasdale, 2006). Two additional studies with this sample demonstrate associations between community disadvantage and adolescents' depressive symptoms (Wickrama & Bryant, 2003; Wickrama, Merten, & Elder, 2005).

Nonexperimental research focusing on older adolescence documents associations between neighborhood low SES and a range of problem behaviors, too. Two studies using data from a British national study found adverse associations between residence in low SES neighborhoods and adolescents' participation in crime and delinquency (Sampson & Groves, 1989; Veysey & Messner, 1999). Along these same lines, a national study of U.S. 10th graders found that the male joblessness rate was positively associated with drug use; however, the poverty rate was negatively associated with drug use among these same youth (Hoffman, 2002). A neighborhood-based study in Chicago, however, found links between the presence of few managers and professionals in the neighborhood and older adolescents' self-reported violent behavior (Sampson, Morenoff, & Raudenbush, 2005).

Finally, Aneshensel and Sucoff (1996) examined the effect of neighborhood SES and racial-ethnic diversity simultaneously on the mental health outcomes of 12- to 17-year-olds in Los Angeles. Their results indicated that the prevalence of conduct disorder was highest among adolescents in low SES, African American neighborhoods and lowest among adolescents in low SES, Latino neighborhoods. The prevalence of oppositional defiant disorder, however, was highest among adolescents in middle SES communities with high concentrations of European Americans and Latinos and lowest among adolescents in low SES, African American neighborhoods. Latinos displayed more depressive symptoms than did European American and African American youth, except in low SES neighborhoods with high concentrations of Latinos.

In line with the nonexperimental literature revealing links between low-SES neighborhoods and older adolescents' social, emotional, and behavioral outcomes are experimental findings from the MTO program 5-year evaluation (Kling, Liebman, & Katz, 2007). Adolescent girls who moved to low-poverty neighborhoods reported less psychological distress, anxiety, and substance use and were less likely to be arrested (for both violent and property crimes) than girls who remained in public housing in high-poverty neighborhoods. Unfortunately, such benefits of moving to low-poverty neighborhoods were not seen among adolescent boys, who demonstrated some negative outcomes after moving. Interestingly, a 7-year evaluation of a quasi-experimental study of housing desegregation in Yonkers, New York, also found some negative effects,

especially among older adolescents. In this study, older adolescents who relocated to more advantaged neighborhoods reported more behavior problems and substance use than peers who remained in impoverished neighborhoods (Fauth, Leventhal, et al., 2007). In these experimental studies, it is likely that the disruptive effects of moving on social networks were more harmful among boys than girls in the case of MTO and among older than younger adolescents in the case of Yonkers.

Sexual Activity and Childbearing

Converging evidence from numerous national data sets as well as multilevel studies points to associations between neighborhood SES—especially low SES—and adolescents' sexual behavior and fertility (controlling for individual and family characteristics). This pattern holds among both younger and older adolescents. In addition, neighborhood employment measures appear to be associated with these outcomes, but the direction of effects is mixed.

Recently, increased attention in the neighborhood literature has focused on younger adolescents' sexual initiation. One study based on a Canadian national sample reported that among 12- to 15- year-olds, neighborhood disadvantage was associated with adolescent girls' sexual initiation overall and both girls' and boys' sexual initiation among those with a history of conduct problems (Dupéré, Lacourse, Willms, Leventhal, & Tremblay, 2008). Using multilevel data from the PHDCN, Browning and colleagues demonstrated in a series of studies a link between neighborhood concentrated poverty and sexual onset among youth 11–16 years of age (Browning, Burrington, Leventhal, & Brooks-Gunn, 2008; Browning, Leventhal, & Brooks-Gunn, 2004, 2005).

Studies using six different national data sets (National Survey of Adolescent Males [NSAM], National Survey of Children [NSC], National Survey of Family Growth [NSFG-III], PSID, PUMS, and Add Health) reported that indicators of neighborhood SES were associated with predominately older adolescents' sexual activity. Across these studies, the presence of advantaged socioeconomic conditions such as affluent or professional neighbors was associated with a decreased risk of female adolescents' nonmarital childbearing (Billy & Moore, 1992; Brooks-Gunn et al., 1993; Crane, 1991; South & Crowder, 1999; c.f. Cubbin, Santelli, Brindis, & Braveman, 2005), whereas the absence of such resources, including high poverty and low housing values, was adversely associated with both boys' and girls' initiation of sexual intercourse, frequency of intercourse, number of partners, contraceptive use, pregnancy outcomes, and overall sexual risk behavior (Baumer & South, 2001; Cleveland & Gilson, 2004; Cubbin et al., 2005; Ku, Sonenstein, & Pleck, 1993; Ramirez-Valles, Zimmerman, & Juarez, 2002; Ramirez-Valles, Zimmerman, & Newcomb, 1998; South & Baumer, 2001; South & Crowder, 1999). Moreover, two studies found nonlinear associations, such that the odds of female youth bearing children increased when community disadvantage reached an extreme threshold (Crane, 1991; South & Crowder, 1999). Finally, the association between neighborhood poverty and adolescent girls' odds of nonmarital childbearing were confirmed in propensity score models (Harding, 2003).

Employment indicators were associated with adolescent sexual and fertility outcomes, although the pattern of results was inconsistent. Among adolescent males 15–19 years of age in the NSAM, a high unemployment rate was positively associated with impregnating someone and fathering a child (Ku et al., 1993), and among middle school and high school students in Add Health, the proportion of idle youth was associated with boys' sexual initiation (Cubbin et al., 2005). Likewise, among females in the NSFG-III and Add Health, unemployment and joblessness were positively associated with sexual initiation, frequency of intercourse, contraceptive use, and nonmarital childbearing (Billy, Brewster, & Grady, 1994; Billy & Moore, 1992; Cubbin et al., 2005). However, among these same young women in the

NSFG-III, but not Add Health, the percentage of women employed in the neighborhood was positively associated with timing of first intercourse and risk of premarital sex (Billy et al., 1994; Brewster, 1994b). In addition, among female youth aged 14–20 in the NSFG-III, female labor force participation was positively associated with noncontracepted first intercourse among African American, urban young women and with contracepted first intercourse among European American young women (Brewster, 1994a; Brewster, Billy, & Grady, 1993). Findings related to female employment may be related to the monitoring and supervision of youth as opposed to socioeconomic resources.

A FRAMEWORK FOR UNDERSTANDING POTENTIAL PATHWAYS OF NEIGHBORHOOD EFFECTS ON ADOLESCENT OUTCOMES

The research presented in the previous section documents associations between neighborhood structure and adolescent outcomes; however, it does not address the potential pathways through which these neighborhood effects are transmitted to youth. A widely held view among researchers is that neighborhood influences are indirect (or mediated), operating through various processes such as community social organizations, families, peers, and schools. In addition, neighborhood effects are thought to condition (or interact with) other contextual influences—particularly the family environment—in shaping adolescent development. Despite such expectations, much more theoretical than empirical work has explored mediated and moderated neighborhood effects on adolescent outcomes. Empirical investigations of underlying mechanisms of neighborhood influences have been hindered by the lack of a coherent framework outlined by outcome, age of child, and specific pathways, as well as by methodological limitations—particularly, adequate study designs and neighborhood measures. However, over the past several years emerging empirical support concurs with expectations, indicating that neighborhood effects are largely indirect, operating through individual-, family-, and community-level processes.

In this section, three theoretical models for conceptualizing how neighborhoods might influence adolescent development are presented, (Leventhal & Brooks-Gunn, 2000, 2001). The first model, *institutional resources*, posits that the quality, quantity, and diversity of community resources mediate neighborhood effects. The second model, *norms and collective efficacy*, speculates that the extent of community formal and informal institutions present to monitor residents' behavior (especially peer groups) and physical threats to residents accounts for neighborhood effects. The final model, *relationships and ties*, hypothesizes that parental attributes, social networks, and behavior as well as home environment characteristics transmit neighborhood influences. These theoretical frames were developed based on a review and analysis of neighborhood studies by Jencks and Mayer (1990), the literature on economic hardship and unemployment (Conger, Ge, Elder, Lorenz, & Simons, 1994; McLoyd, 1990), and work on social disorganization theory (Sampson, 1992; Sampson et al., 1997; Shaw & McKay, 1942; see Sampson & Morenoff, 1997, for a review)

These theoretical models are intended to be complementary rather than conflicting. For instance, institutional resource mechanisms may be most salient when studying high SES–achievement links, norms and collective efficacy processes may be most relevant for examining low-SES–delinquency associations, and relationship pathways may be most useful for examining SES–sexual outcome links. In terms of developmental differences, relationship mechanisms might be more relevant for younger than older adolescents because families may exert a greater influence during this period, whereas community norms and processes may be more salient for older than for younger adolescents because of the

growing influence of peers during this period. Community institutional resources may play an equally important role both earlier and later in adolescence, but the specific resource of most relevance may differ for the two age groups. Accordingly, the present review of the theoretical models highlights aspects of each model that are most relevant to adolescents.

Institutional Resources

Economic resource perspectives, focusing typically on the family context, identify resources or opportunities to which children and youth theoretically have access (Becker, 1981; Brooks-Gunn, Klebanov, Liaw, & Duncan, 1995; Haveman & Wolfe, 1994). Extrapolating this model to neighborhoods, community resources include the quantity, quality, diversity, and affordability of several types of resources in the community pertinent to adolescents—schools, health and social services, recreational and social programs, and employment—that could influence well-being (Leventhal & Brooks-Gunn, 2000; Neuman & Celano, 2001).

For adolescents, schools are a primary vehicle through which neighborhood effects may operate on adolescents' achievement in particular. Relevant aspects of schools include quality, climate, norms, and demographic makeup. Living in a disadvantaged neighborhood is adversely associated with these school attributes as well as with adolescents' educational outcomes (Card & Payne, 2002; Jencks & Mayer, 1990). Several studies have looked at the intersection of neighborhood context and school norms regarding risky behavior. Findings indicate that neighborhood structure is associated with school norms, which in turn may be associated with adolescents' sexual initiation and their substance use (Eitle & McNulty Eitle, 2004; Ennett, Flewelling, Lindrooth, & Norton, 1997; Teitler & Weiss, 2000; see School Versus Neighborhood Influences section for additional details).

The availability, quality, and affordability of medical and social services in the community may be a potential pathway of neighborhood influences, notably on mental and physical health (including sexual risk behavior and pregnancy). Although work examining this resource is scant, access, quality, and variety of health services vary as a function of family SES, with high income generally conferring beneficial effects (Newacheck, Hughes, & Stoddard, 1996; Newacheck, Stoddard, & McManus, 1993). Differences in health care services availability relevant to adolescents have been show to vary as a function of neighborhood SES. Results based on Add Health indicate that high schools located in lower SES communities are less likely to offer school-based health services than schools in more advantaged communities (Billy et al., 2000). However, reduced availability of health services in disadvantaged communities does not necessarily explain differences in adolescent health behaviors or attitudes. For instance, several studies of adolescent sexual behavior found that the availability of family planning and abortion providers in the community was not associated with adolescents' sexual activity, fertility outcomes, or attitudes toward contraceptive use (accounting for neighborhood structure, Brewster et al., 1993; Hughes, Furstenberg, & Teitler, 1995). In contrast, another nationally representative study found that although availability of family planning clinics in the county of residence was not associated with adolescents' sexual activity, it was predictive of contraceptive use among sexually active adolescent girls (Averett, Rees, & Argys, 2002).

Another possible mechanism of neighborhood effects—particularly on physical and social development—is the presence of social and recreational activities such as parks, sports programs, art and theater programs, and community centers. Generally, studies of youth programs and after-school care point to these programs as having beneficial effects on adjustment, particularly among low-income youth (Eccles & Gootman, 2002). In the same manner, enrollment in these activities could be especially beneficial for adolescents living in disadvantaged neighborhoods. For example,

participation in organized activities was found to be most protective against cigarette smoking among adolescents exposed to higher levels of neighborhood risks in terms of SES and racial composition (Xue, Zimmerman, & Howard Caldwell, 2007; see also Coley, Morris, & Hernandez, 2004; and Pettit, Bates, Dodge, & Meece, 1999), and among low- and moderate-income African American youth, participation in locally based organized activities promoted affiliation with neighborhood prosocial peers (Quane & Rankin, 2006; see also Rankin & Quane, 2002). However, it is important to note that involvement in activities, such as community-based clubs, might have negative effects on adolescent adjustment in highly violent communities, possibly because it could increase exposure to violence (Fauth, Roth, & Brooks-Gunn, 2007).

In spite of the potential benefits associated with activity participation, adolescents living in low SES neighborhoods might have limited access to organized recreational activities as compared to their peers in more affluent communities. A neighborhood-based study of adolescent development in low- to middle-income neighborhoods found that the extent of prosocial activities varied across neighborhoods and was linked to problem behavior (Furstenberg, Cook, Eccles, Elder, & Sameroff, 1999; see also Furstenberg, 2001). Meanwhile, research on youth from affluent communities also points to the need for more after-school programs (or at least participation in such programs) to prevent youth from engaging in problem behaviors (Luthar, 2003). In addition, a recent review of the environmental correlates of youth's physical activity indicated that higher neighborhood crime levels were associated with lower participation in physical activities, although evidence was mixed regarding a direct link between availability of sports facilities and programs in the community and youth's physical activity (Ferreira et al., 2006). Two reasons might explain why availability is not consistently associated with participation. First, qualitative and quantitative research on families in disadvantaged neighborhoods indicates that when social and recreational programs are not available in families' own communities, parents access resources from the larger surrounding community (Elder, Eccles, Ardelt, & Lord, 1995; Jarrett, 1997). Second, the link between availability and participation appears to vary as a function of neighborhood characteristics, with youth living in disadvantaged communities more likely to participate in neighborhood-based organized activities when offered the chance (Quane & Rankin, 2006).

The last institutional resource most relevant to achievement outcomes and possibly problem behaviors entails the supply of employment opportunities, access to jobs (including transportation), and adolescents' own expectations about available opportunities. Although studies have not examined neighborhood–employment links on adolescent development (most studies focus on young adults), we draw upon research on family-level SES differences in the consequences of adolescent employment (Bachman & Schulenberg, 1993; Gleason & Cain, 2004; Leventhal, Graber, & Brooks-Gunn, 2001; Mortimer, Finch, Ryu, Shanahan, & Call, 1996; Newman, 1999; Steinberg, Fegley, & Dornbusch, 1993; Sullivan, 1989). Specifically, the impact of adolescent employment (and available opportunities) on subsequent outcomes may be moderated by neighborhood SES, such that in disadvantaged neighborhoods, the effects of employment may be beneficial because fewer developmentally enhancing outlets beyond employment may exist. In contrast, in more affluent neighborhoods, where learning and social activities may provide more enriching alternatives to employment, the effects of employment may be more detrimental. A related finding supporting this view comes from a recent study that found that the association between longer work hours during middle and late adolescence and adolescents' heavy episodic drinking was moderated by community context, specifically rates of adolescent drinking; longer hours were more detrimental in lower risk counties (i.e., those

with low levels of adolescent alcohol use; Breslin & Adlaf, 2005).

At the individual level, adolescents' expectations about employment opportunities available to them are likely affected by their neighborhoods (including presence of working role models). These expectations as well as related feelings of hopelessness may be associated with adolescent outcomes, including educational attainment, substance use, crime, sexual activity, and childbearing (Billy et al., 1994; Bolland, 2003; Bolland, Lian, & Formichella, 2005; Willis, 1977).

Norms and Collective Efficacy

The norms and collective efficacy model draws heavily from social organization theory and its more recent formulations, particularly collective efficacy theory (Sampson, 1992; Sampson et al., 1997; Shaw & McKay, 1942). According to these perspectives, collective efficacy—defined as the extent of community-level social connections including mutual trust, shared values among residents, and residents' willingness to intervene on behalf of community—controls the ability of communities to monitor residents' behavior in line with social norms and to maintain public order (Sampson, Morenoff, & Earls, 1999; Sampson et al., 1997). Formal and informal community institutions are thought to act as regulatory mechanisms, and the capacity of these institutions to monitor residents' behavior—especially peer groups and physical threats, in turn—is hypothesized to be a function of specific community structural characteristics, including low SES, racial/ethnic diversity, residential instability, and single parenthood (Coulton, Korbin, Su, & Chow, 1995; Sampson, 1992; Sampson & Groves, 1989). For instance, in poor, residentially unstable, racially/ethnically diverse neighborhoods with many single parents, social organization is often low, resulting in the promulgation of adolescent problem behaviors such as crime and vandalism. In contrast, when social organization is high, adolescents are less likely to engage in these negative behaviors and may display more prosocial behaviors such as school engagement and civic participation. Over the past decade, a number of researchers studying adolescents have tested various components of this model, and much of the work has focused on problem behaviors—delinquency, crime, violence, and substance use—and to a lesser extent sexual activity. This section reviews research on the different model components.

An important distinction to make is that the social connections described under the norms and collective efficacy model are more diffuse than the social networks discussed under the relationships model (see next section) and operate primarily at the community level (see Sampson, 1999, for further discussion of this distinction). In PHDCN, collective efficacy and social control (measured by a community survey) were found to be negatively associated with neighborhood socioeconomic disadvantage, level of crime and violence, and observations of physical and social disorder (Raudenbush & Sampson, 1999; Sampson et al., 1999; Sampson et al., 1997; see also Pattillo, 1998). Such links have also been reported in studies of adolescents. For example, in a study based on a nationally representative sample (Add Health) and two other studies with city-based samples of at-risk minority adolescent boys (juvenile offenders and adolescent boys from disadvantaged inner-city neighborhoods), structural characteristics were associated with parents' and youth's perceptions of community social organization (Chung & Steinberg, 2006; Tolan, Gorman-Smith, & Henry, 2003; Wickrama & Bryant, 2003); neighborhood social organization, in turn, was associated with adolescent adjustment. At both the neighborhood and individual levels, community social control of youth is negatively associated with a number of adolescent externalizing (delinquency and violence, affiliation with deviant peers, and carrying a concealed weapon) and internalizing (depressive symptoms) outcomes (after accounting for neighborhood structure; Brody et al., 2001; Chung & Steinberg, 2006;

Elliot et al., 1996; Molnar, Miller, Azrael, & Buka, 2004; Sampson, 1997; Sampson et al., 2005; Tolan et al., 2003; Wickrama & Bryant, 2003). Moreover, collective efficacy is associated with more private adolescent behaviors including delayed sexual onset and a lower number of sexual partners (Browning et al., 2008; Browning et al., 2004).

Peer group behavior and norms are central pathways through which neighborhood structure is anticipated to influence adolescent outcomes, especially social and emotional outcomes. Peer effects are generally hypothesized to be adverse because potential negative peer group influences are exacerbated when community institutions and norms fail to regulate their behavior. In disadvantaged contexts, neighborhood peers represent a significant proportion of adolescents' peer networks (Dolcini, Harper, Watson, Catania, & Ellen, 2005), and living in a socially disadvantaged neighborhood is positively associated with adolescents' affiliation with deviant peers as well as exposure to violent and unconventional peers (Brody et al., 2001; Dupéré, Lacourse, Willms, Vitaro, & Tremblay, 2007; Ge et al., 2002; Harding, 2007; Haynie et al., 2006; Quane & Rankin, 1998). Thus, affiliation with deviant peers may be facilitated in disadvantaged neighborhoods through increased opportunities to do so.

Accumulating research supports the notion that deviant peer affiliation is an important mediator of neighborhood structural and social organizational effects on adolescent behavior problems, such as delinquency and substance use (Chuang, Ennett, Bauman, & Foshee, 2005; Chung & Steinberg, 2006; Haynie et al., 2006; Meyers & Miller, 2004; Simons et al., 1996). For instance, a lack of formal and informal institutions present to supervise adolescent peer group activities has been found to mediate the association between neighborhood SES (and related characteristics) and adolescents' delinquent, criminal, and prosocial behavior (Sampson & Groves, 1989; Shaw & McKay, 1942; Veysey & Messner, 1999).

In addition, emerging empirical and ethnographic evidence suggests that peer characteristics, notably involvement with deviant and older peers, are potential mediators of neighborhood effects on adolescent sexuality and childbearing (Dupéré et al., 2008; Harding, 2005; South & Baumer, 2000). Other work has shown that peer interactions moderate neighborhood effects on adolescents' antisocial behavior, substance use, and school achievement, such that in high-risk neighborhoods, peer influences have more negative effects, whereas in low-risk neighborhoods, peer effects are more beneficial (Dubow, Edwards, & Ippolito, 1997; Gonzales, Cauce, Friedman, & Mason, 1996; Pettit et al., 1999).

Physical threats, including the extent of violence, the availability of harmful and illegal substances, and other general threats to well-being, are hypothesized to be associated with community mechanisms of control and subsequent adolescent outcomes, especially physical and socioemotional development. Two housing programs in which low-income families moved from public housing in high-poverty neighborhoods to less poor neighborhoods found that parents reported that getting away from drugs and gangs was their primary motivation for wanting to move (Briggs, 1997; Goering & Feins, 2003). In fact, initial and longer term follow-ups of these programs have found that children and youth who moved to more advantaged neighborhoods were less likely to be exposed to violence and danger than were peers who remained in poor neighborhoods (Fauth, 2004; Fauth, Leventhal, & Brooks-Gunn, 2005; Fauth et al., 2008; Katz, Kling, & Liebman, 2001; Kling et al., 2007). In nonexperimental work, youth from poor, urban neighborhoods who are exposed to high levels of community violence display internalizing and externalizing problems as well as physical and psychiatric symptoms (Cooley-Quille, Boyd, Frantz, & Walsh, 2001; Gorman-Smith, Henry, & Tolan, 2004; Gorman-Smith & Tolan, 1998; Haynie et al., 2006). In addition, several studies have found that neighborhood danger

accounted for links between neighborhood low SES and adolescent outcomes, including emotional problems and timing of first intercourse (Aneshensel & Sucoff, 1996; Pettit et al., 1999; Upchurch, Aneshensel, Sucoff, & Levy-Storms, 1999).

Access to illegal and harmful substances has been shown to vary as a function of neighborhood characteristics, with low-income/SES neighborhoods and those with high proportions of African Americans providing adolescents with greater access to alcohol, cigarettes, and cocaine than do higher income/SES neighborhoods or predominately European American neighborhoods (Duncan, Duncan, & Strycker, 2002; Fauth et al., 2005; Freisthler, Lascala, Gruenewald, & Treno, 2005; Landrine, Klonoff, & Alcaraz, 1997). Studies of disadvantaged youth found that adolescents' reports of drug availability in their neighborhoods were adversely linked with their substance use, offending behavior, and likelihood of gang affiliation (Chung, Hill, Hawkins, Gilchrist, & Nagin, 2002; Hill, Howell, Hawkins, & Battin-Pearson, 1999; Lambert, Brown, Phillips, & Ialongo, 2004). In addition, levels of drug activity in the neighborhood are positively associated with school rates of cigarette smoking (Ennett et al., 1997).

Relationships and Ties

According to the relationships and ties model, parental relationships are hypothesized to be a potential pathway of neighborhood effects on adolescent development, especially social and emotional well-being. This framework draws heavily from the family stress model developed from research on economic hardship and unemployment, in which links between family low income and adolescent outcomes are accounted for by parents' sense of financial strain, depression, and resultant parenting (Conger et al., 1994; Conger, Wallace, Sun, Simons, McLoyd, & Brodie, 2002; McLoyd, 1990). Parental relationships and support networks are thought to mediate and moderate associations between parents' (and possibly youth's) well-being and their behavior. We broaden this model of family economic hardship to neighborhood disadvantage such that neighborhood disadvantage may affect parental well-being and subsequent adolescent outcomes through parental behavior and the home environment (see Figure 12.1). Beyond looking at aspects of neighborhood structure, such as poverty, that may serve as sources of disadvantage, more recently researchers have expanded disadvantage to include social features of neighborhoods that may pose challenges to parents, such as low collective efficacy, disorder, and violence (e.g., Simons, Simons, Burt, Brody, & Cutrona, 2005). We review research exploring whether these proposed individual and family mechanisms transmit neighborhood influences to adolescents as well as relevant work on the different components of the model.

Aspects of parental well-being thought to be associated with neighborhood residence include physical and mental health, efficacy, coping skills, and irritability. At both the individual and neighborhood levels, compelling evidence exists for links between adults' physical and mental health and neighborhood structural conditions, particularly SES (e.g., Cubbin, LeClere, & Smith, 2000; Diez-Roux, 2001; Hill, Ross, & Angel, 2005; Ross, 2000).

For example, experimental work indicates that low-income parents who moved from high- to low-poverty neighborhoods reported superior mental and physical health compared with parents who remained in high-poverty neighborhoods (Fauth et al., 2008; Kling et al., 2007). Another study based on adolescent reports found that neighborhood disadvantage was positively associated with family stress (after accounting for family SES; Allison et al., 1999). Neighborhood structural characteristics, and parental well-being have also been linked with parenting practices and adolescent outcomes. Among families in disadvantaged neighborhoods, parental efficacy mediated the use of family management strategies employed with adolescents among African American parents but not European American parents (Elder et al., 1995). In addition, maternal self-esteem was found to moderate the positive association between the neighborhood drop-out rate and adolescent risk-taking behavior, such that this association was enhanced among youth with mothers with low self-esteem (Kowaleski-Jones, 2000). Finally, a study examining the family stress model within a sample of African American adolescent boys found that neighborhood poverty indirectly

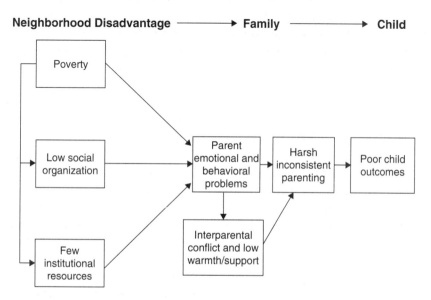

FIGURE 12.1 Model of Neighborhood Disadvantage

affected violent behavior by means of family stress and conflict and by means of adolescents' own feelings of self-worth (however, analyses did not control for individual and family background characteristics; Paschall & Hubbard, 1998).

Support networks, including access to friends and family and connections within neighborhood, may intervene between neighborhood economic resources and adolescent well-being (Cook, Shagle, & Degirmencioglu, 1997). These support networks may buffer parents from the stressors of neighborhood poverty, violence, and disorder and in so doing may diminish the adverse effects of low parental functioning on adolescent development (Conger et al., 1994; Elder et al., 1995; McLoyd, 1990; Ross & Jang, 2000). It is unclear whether the density of support networks varies by neighborhood SES and racial/ethnic diversity; support may be strongest in middle-income neighborhoods (compared with low- and middle-income neighborhoods) as well as in those with high concentrations of immigrants, particularly Latino populations (Klebanov, Brooks-Gunn, & Duncan, 1994; Molnar, Buka, Brennan, Holton, & Earls, 2003; Rosenbaum, Popkin, Kaufman, & Rusin, 1991). For parents, social connections within the community appear to be particularly useful for job referral networks and for assisting with monitoring and caring for children (Coleman, 1988; Jones, Forehand, O'Connell, Armistead, & Brody, 2005; Logan & Spitze, 1994). With respect to adolescents' own relationships and ties, in a sample of adolescents receiving social services, adolescents received support from family and peers appeared to buffer the positive association between reported neighborhood problems and their mental health, especially internalizing problems (Stiffman, Hadley-Ives, Elze, Johnson, & Doré, 1999).

Neighborhood conditions—notably poverty, violence, and danger—are hypothesized to be associated with several parenting behaviors—warmth, harshness, and supervision and monitoring—and subsequent adolescent development. Both quantitative and qualitative work on family economic hardship reveals that parental stress and anxiety may have the largest impact on harsh parenting (Conger et al., 1994; McLoyd, 1990). In a quasi-experimental study, both younger and older adolescents who moved from poor to less poor neighborhoods reported receiving less harsh parenting than did youth who remained in poor neighborhoods (Fauth, Leventhal et al., 2007; c.f., Leventhal & Brooks-Gunn, 2005). Along these lines, in poor and dangerous neighborhoods, parent–child relationships have been shown to be marked by low warmth and high aggression (Earls, McGuire, & Shay, 1994; Klebanov et al., 1994; Taylor, 2000), which may be linked to adolescent problem behavior (Beyers et al., 2001). In fact, two studies report that involved parenting and close parent–child relationships buffered adolescents' development (peer deviance and number of sexual partners) from the adverse consequences of neighborhood disadvantage (Brody et al., 2001; Cleveland & Gilson, 2004), while others have found that such parenting behaviors lost their effectiveness in highly disadvantaged neighborhoods (Gorman-Smith, Tolan, & Henry, 2000; Knoester & Haynie, 2005; Wickrama & Bryant, 2003). Yet other research demonstrates that the beneficial effects of parental involvement on sexual risk behavior were amplified in more advantaged neighborhood settings (Cleveland & Gilson, 2004; Roche et al., 2005), or that the adverse effects of uninvolved parenting on adolescent delinquency were exacerbated in more disadvantaged neighborhoods (Roche, Ensminger, & Cherlin, 2007).

A number of well-designed, multilevel studies have also explicitly tested mediation models, and most have focused on social organizational features of neighborhood rather than poverty and other aspects of structural disadvantage (though all account for neighborhood structure). For example, a longitudinal study based on the FACHS data set found that increases in neighborhood collective efficacy over time were associated with increased authoritative (warm and firm) parenting, and that increases in authoritative parenting, in turn, were associated with decreases in adolescent delinquency and affiliation with deviant peers (Simons et al., 2005). Two cross-sectional studies, also focusing on neighborhood organization, provide further support for indirect neighborhood effects. The first study, based on a sample of male juvenile offenders, reported that ineffective parenting (a composite of low warmth, limited knowledge, and lax monitoring) partially mediated the association between neighborhood disorder and adolescents' reported peer deviance (Chung & Steinberg, 2006). The second study, using data from Add Health, found that parental acceptance and involvement accounted for the association between neighborhood collective socialization and adolescent depressive symptoms (Wickrama & Bryant, 2003). Finally, another study found that quality of parenting (monitoring, warmth/ support, inductive reasoning, harsh discipline, hostility, and communication), assessed through videotaped parent–child interactions, mediated the positive association between community disadvantage and adolescents' problem behavior (Simons et al., 1996).

In the field of neighborhood research, parental supervision and monitoring are thought to be particularly important during the adolescent years by modulating adolescents' exposure to community influences (Beyers et al., 2003; Browning et al., 2005; Gorman-Smith et al., 2004). Along these lines, a number of ethnographic researchers have observed that parents in dangerous and impoverished neighborhoods may use restrictive monitoring techniques to limit their adolescents' exposure to negative community influences (Anderson, 1999; Burton, 1990; Burton & Jarrett, 2000; Furstenberg, 1993; Jarrett, 1997). One quasi-experimental study of moving from low- to middle-income neighborhoods supports this finding; parents who moved to advantaged neighborhoods reported less stringent monitoring than did parents who remained in low-income neighborhoods (Fauth, Leventhal, et al.,

2007). In terms of links with adolescent outcomes, parental monitoring of early dating behavior was found to mediate the positive association between neighborhood low SES and teenage childbearing (Hogan & Kitagawa, 1985; c.f. Baumer & South, 2001; South & Baumer, 2000).

Accumulating research has focused on how the intersections between neighborhood contexts and parental monitoring, supervision, and control are associated with adolescent outcomes; much of this work draws from neighborhood-based studies. For instance, in the PHDCN sample, neighborhood collective efficacy was associated with delaying sexual onset only among youth who experienced low levels of parental monitoring (Browning et al., 2005). In contrast, within a sample of low- to moderate-income African American families, also in Chicago, the beneficial effects of parental monitoring on promoting competency and deterring problem behavior were enhanced when collective efficacy was low (Rankin & Quane, 2002). Similar findings regarding the importance of monitoring and control for protecting youth against negative outcomes in more disadvantaged neighborhoods have been reported by others as well (Beyers et al., 2003; Roche et al., 2005), particularly when high levels of monitoring are used in combination with high levels of emotional support (Brody et al., 2001; Gorman-Smith et al., 2000). In contrast, additional research demonstrates that the deterrent effects of parental control on young adolescents' conduct problems are less effective in communities marked by danger and disorder (Simons et al., 2002), while another study of low-income, minority families found that permissive and disengaged parenting were associated with adolescent boys engaging in more delinquency in the most dangerous and socially disorganized neighborhoods (Roche et al., 2007).

Several characteristics of the home environment may act as vehicles of neighborhood influences on youth—physical home environment, presence of routines and structure, and exposure to violence. The physical home environment may be most salient for adolescents' health. Neighborhood low income (compared with middle income) is negatively associated with quality of physical home environments (after controlling for family SES; Klebanov et al., 1994). Nonexperimental evidence reveals that children and adolescents living in poor neighborhoods may be at risk for injury and asthma (e.g., Borrell et al., 2002; Soubhi, Raina, & Kohen, 2004; Wright & Fisher, 2003). This situation is probably in part due to quality of the physical home environment.

The presence of family routines and structure, such as regular mealtimes and homework times, are thought to be significant for adolescents' social development (Boyce, Jensen, James, & Peacock, 1983; Bradley, 1995). At the theoretical level, it has been hypothesized that such routines may be weak in neighborhoods characterized by high poverty and unemployment, marked violence, and low social cohesion (Leventhal & Brooks-Gunn, 2000; Wilson, 1987, 1991). Two experimental studies found no effect of moving from poor to less poor neighborhoods on family routines; however, this hypothesis remains to be further tested (Fauth et al., 2005; Leventhal & Brooks-Gunn, 2005).

Finally, exposure to violence (as a witness or a victim) may be a potential mechanism for neighborhood effects on adolescents' physical and emotional health in particular (Wright, 1998). Living in a poor neighborhood is associated with children's exposure to violence in the community and in the home (Coulton, Korbin, & Su, 1999; Coulton et al., 1995; Martinez & Richters, 1993; Richters & Martinez, 1993). As noted before (see the section on Norms and Collective Efficacy), findings suggest that exposure to violence in the community is associated with adolescent adjustment (e.g., Gorman-Smith et al., 2004; Gorman-Smith & Tolan, 1998; Haynie et al., 2006); however, it is unclear if exposure to community violence has an independent association with child and adolescent well-being beyond co-occuring

exposure to violence in the home (see Buka, Stichick, Birdthistle, & Earls, 2001 for a review). Additional research is needed to elucidate how the intersection of exposure to violence in the home and the community affects adolescent development.

EMERGING TRENDS AND UNRESOLVED ISSUES

In this section, we review some emerging trends in the neighborhood literature that have been alluded to in our review thus far. Specifically, we review findings on individual characteristics that appear to modify neighborhood effects and explore potential explanations. In addition, we discuss some unresolved issues that bear on the theoretical and empirical significance of neighborhood influences on adolescent development including whether adolescence is a salient time for neighborhood influences and the relative importance of neighborhood context as compared with school context.

Modifiers of Neighborhood Effects

Our review of the literature on neighborhood structural effects on adolescents' development suggests that associations among neighborhood SES and adolescent outcomes vary as a function of key individual characteristics, notably, gender, race/ethnicity, and possibly pubertal timing and personality traits. Perhaps the most compelling evidence exists for gender differences in neighborhood SES effects on adolescent development, although the findings to date have been mixed across the nonexperimental and experimental literature. In the nonexperimental literature, the strongest support for gender differences is seen with respect to achievement, with boys benefiting more from affluent/high SES neighborhoods and being hindered more by poverty/low SES, especially African American boys in the case of poverty/low SES (Connell, Halpern-Felsher, Clifford, Crichlow, & Usinger, 1995; Crane, 1991; Crowder & South, 2003; Ensminger et al., 1996; Entwisle et al., 1994; but see Ceballo,

McLoyd, & Toyokawa, 2004). Although fewer studies of social and emotional outcomes have explored gender differences in neighborhood SES effects, the studies reviewed earlier suggest that the association between low SES and this class of outcomes is more pronounced among boys than girls, which may be a function in part of the lower prevalence of risky behaviors displayed by girls as compared with boys. A similar conclusion indicating stronger effects among boys was reached in another recent review looking at gender differences in neighborhood effects on conduct problems and delinquency (Kroneman, Loeber, & Hipwell, 2004). This review also concluded that boys and girls tended to be differentially influenced by specific neighborhood characteristics, with girls being especially sensitive to the proportion of single-parent families and the presence of affluent neighbors. Finally, gender differences in neighborhood effects on adolescents' sexual behavior in the studies reviewed varied as a function of the specific outcome under study (i.e., childbearing/impregnating someone versus age at sexual initiation), but also according to other defining individual characteristics such as race/ethnicity.

Although findings from early MTO site-specific evaluations, which used experimental designs, were consistent with patterns seen in the nonexperimental literature, the recent 5-year results, as reviewed previously, have not been. Specifically, 2–3 years into the program, low-income children and adolescents who moved to low-poverty neighborhoods had higher educational achievement, superior mental health, and fewer arrests for violent crime than their peers who remained in high-poverty neighborhoods, with effects largely restricted to boys (Goering & Feins, 2003; Katz et al., 2001; Leventhal & Brooks-Gunn, 2003b, 2004b; Ludwig, Duncan, & Hirschfield, 2001). Despite these early positive program effects on boys, a more recent cross-site, 5-year follow-up evaluation found that adolescent girls who moved to low-poverty neighborhoods were faring better than their peers who remained in

high-poverty neighborhoods in most of these domains and that boys in low-poverty neighborhoods experienced minimal if not negative outcomes compared with peers in high-poverty neighborhoods (Kling et al., 2007; Kling, Ludwig, & Katz, 2005).

Although the results from the nonexperimental and experimental literature on gender differences in neighborhood effects appear to be at odds, potential explanations for such gender differences reconcile some of the discrepancies when considered in the larger context of MTO as discussed earlier (see section on Achievement). First, only a handful of studies, primarily emanating from sociology, have considered how neighborhoods might contribute to gender differences in adolescent outcomes. These researchers have speculated that family socialization practices largely account for gender differences in neighborhood SES effects. Specifically, parents may provide less supervision and regulation of boys' activities relative to girls', resulting in boys' greater exposure or susceptibility to neighborhood influences (Ensminger et al., 1996; Entwisle et al., 1994; Hagan, Simpson, & Gillis, 1987; Kroneman et al., 2004). Thus, for boys, neighborhood influences may operate more through processes outside of the home, especially through interactions with peers; whereas, for girls, neighborhood influences may operate more through processes inside the home, especially via parent–child interactions (Clampet-Lundquist, Duncan, Edin, & Kling, 2006; Kroneman et al., 2004). If neighborhood conditions are advantageous, exposure may benefit boys more than girls unless it results in contact with more deviant peers (for example, as might have been the case in MTO). In contrast, in disadvantaged neighborhoods, lower levels of exposure may protect girls from adverse outcomes, particularly in the case of a supportive home environment.

Findings on gender differences also point to the salience of race–ethnicity as a potential moderator of neighborhood influences. Minority youth are more likely than their nonminority peers to reside in poor, segregated neighborhoods (Kahn, Kaplowitz, Goodman, & Emans, 2002; Klebanov et al., 1994; Massey & Denton, 1993). In addition, these neighborhoods are often marked by pervasive crime and violence, low social cohesion, delinquent peer groups, and low-quality schools (Jencks & Mayer, 1990; Sampson, 1997; Sampson & Raudenbush, 1999). African American families' neighborhoods are also more likely than European American families' neighborhoods to be disadvantaged in terms of their embeddedness in larger spatial areas of structural and social disadvantage (Morenoff, Sampson, & Raudenbush, 2001; Sampson et al., 1999). Not only are African American neighborhoods objectively more disadvantaged than comparable European American neighborhoods, but they are also more likely to be perceived as more disordered by residents of all races (Sampson & Raudenbush, 2004). The consequence of this difference in the larger environments in which European American and African American youth live is that the influence of neighborhood advantage, such as high SES, may have less impact on the well-being of African American adolescents than on that of European American adolescents and, conversely, that low SES may have more adverse consequences for African American than European American youth (e.g., Crowder & South, 2003).

Despite the apparent threats to well-being accrued to African American youth in predominantly poor and/or African American neighborhoods, research with Latinos suggests that high concentrations of immigrants and/or Latinos may be protective for adolescents, especially Latino youth (Aneshensel & Sucoff, 1996; Browning et al., 2008; Sampson et al., 2005). In ethnic enclaves, more traditional norms may prevail that prohibit youth from engaging in problematic behavior, and such communities may be socially cohesive, which is also protective (Garcia Coll & Szalacha, 2004; Portes & Rumbaut, 1996). Thus, the intersection of race/ethnicity and neighborhood structure may have a complex association with adolescent development.

In addition to gender and race/ethnicity, an emerging literature focusing on risky behaviors suggests that other individual characteristics, specifically, pubertal timing and personality traits related to conduct problems and antisocial behavior, are also likely to moderate the impact of neighborhood SES on adolescent outcomes. Generally, these studies indicate that neighborhood disadvantage amplifies the impact of these individual-level risk factors. In other words, the combination of individual and neighborhood risks seems to be especially problematic. For example, early physical maturation appears to increase the chances that adolescent girls in disadvantaged neighborhoods will engage in problem behaviors such as violence and substance use (Foshee et al., 2007; Ge et al., 2002; Obeidallah et al., 2004). Among boys in the Pittsburgh Youth Study, an interaction effect revealed that the link between impulsivity and delinquency was amplified in disadvantaged neighborhoods (Lynam et al., 2000), although this result was not replicated in the Add Health sample (Vazsonyi, Cleveland, & Wiebe, 2006). Moreover, other results obtained in a Canadian national sample indicated that a history of conduct disorder and related personality traits accentuated the threats posed by disadvantaged neighborhoods to youth gang affiliation and early sexual initiation (Dupéré et al., 2008; Dupéré et al., 2007). Explanations for these amplification effects usually revolve around differential peer and family processes as a function of neighborhood context. For instance, Dupéré et al. (2008) found that affiliation with deviant and older peers partly explained why vulnerable adolescent girls living in a disadvantaged neighborhood were more likely to experience early sexual initiation. Similarly, neighborhood disadvantage and related conditions may further strain parent-adolescent relationships already challenged by other circumstances such as early maturation or difficult personality traits (Obeidallah et al., 2004).

Timing of Neighborhood Influences

Theoretically oriented work suggests that the impact of neighborhoods increases during adolescence compared with earlier childhood because parents may begin to grant their older children greater autonomy, resulting in more exposure to extrafamilial influences (Bronfenbrenner, 1979; Maccoby & Martin, 1983; Paikoff & Brooks-Gunn, 1991; Steinberg & Morris, 2001). Given general restrictions on adolescents' mobility, neighborhoods provide as well as organize opportunities for social interactions and out-of-school activities. Early and middle adolescence also entail significant changes in physical maturation brought on by puberty, advanced cognitive capacities (e.g., ability to think more abstractly), shifts in school climate and organization with the move from elementary to middle school and then high school (e.g., less personal, more restrictive, and more competitive), and alterations in salient relationships in the family and peer group (Feldman & Elliott, 1990; Graber, Brooks-Gunn, & Petersen, 1996; Steinberg & Morris, 2001). Each of these challenges has implications for the prominence of neighborhood influences during adolescence (compared with earlier childhood). However, somewhat surprisingly, almost no research has explored this essential premise regarding the salience of adolescence as a developmental period for heightened neighborhood influences.

In contrast to research on neighborhood income and SES, research on family economic status has explicitly tested whether the association between economic conditions and developmental outcomes varies across developmental periods—early childhood, middle childhood, early adolescence, middle adolescence, and young adulthood. This shortcoming in the neighborhood literature results in large part from the fact that a majority of the existing work is cross-sectional, based on neighborhood residence at a single point in time, or both. A study by Wheaton and Clarke (2003) using longitudinal data on children followed from early to middle childhood into late adolescence found that neighborhood SES during early to middle childhood had more pronounced effects on mental health in late adolescence than neighborhood conditions during middle or late adolescence (see also Leventhal & Brooks-Gunn, 2001). Consistent with these findings is the work on family income and poverty, which indicates that family economic resources during early childhood, as opposed to other developmental periods, are most salient for late adolescent outcomes, notably educational attainment (Duncan & Brooks-Gunn, 1997). Together, this evidence may challenge the notion that adolescence is an especially significant period for neighborhood influences, at least as far as socioeconomic conditions are concerned. We caution any firm conclusions at this time until more research is available to contribute to this debate.

School Versus Neighborhood Influences

School and neighborhood represent two primary extrafamilial contexts for adolescent development where youth spend substantial amounts of time (Gershoff & Lawrence, 2006). The extent of exposure suggests that both contexts could exert pronounced influence on development during adolescence, but distinguishing school and neighborhood effects and their relative significance is a difficult task given the nonnegligible overlap between these two contexts. This situation is due in part to the fact that neighborhood characteristics affect school resources and school choice, indicating that school could be a powerful mediator of neighborhood effects (Lauen, 2007; Leventhal & Brooks-Gunn, 2000; Waanders, Mendez, & Downer, 2007). Yet, school characteristics such as composition and achievement also impact neighborhood conditions, such as property values (Bogart & Cromwell, 2000). Peers also serve as a source of overlap between the two contexts, with large portions of adolescent peer networks comprised of school- and neighborhood-based friendships (Dishion, Andrews, & Crosby, 1995; Dolcini et al., 2005; DuBois &

Hirsch, 1990). Further, ethnographic evidence suggests that among inner-city youth, significant peer conflict occurring at school often originates in the neighborhood, and vice versa (Mateu-Gelabert & Lune, 2003). For these reasons, and because limited research, particularly methodologically rigorous work, has considered simultaneous associations between neighborhood and school characteristics with individual adolescent outcomes (as opposed to aggregated school or neighborhood outcomes; Eitle & McNulty Eitle, 2004; Ennett et al., 1997), it is very difficult to disentangle neighborhood from school effects or to assess the relative influence of each.

Somewhat surprisingly, nonexperimental studies focusing on achievement appear to find that neighborhood effects were equivalent to or stronger than school effects (Bowen & Bowen, 1999; Card & Rothstein, 2007; Eamon, 2005; Garner & Raudenbush, 1991; Raudenbush, 1993). For example, multilevel studies of Scottish adolescents found more variation in educational attainment at the neighborhood than at the school level and that neighborhood deprivation was negatively associated with attainment, even after controlling for school characteristics (Garner & Raudenbush, 1991; Raudenbush, 1993). In addition, Card and Rothstein (2007), using a sample of roughly one-third of SAT test takers in the 1998–2001 high school graduation classes, found that when both neighborhood and school segregation were examined simultaneously, only neighborhood segregation was associated with the city-level Black–White gap in test scores.

In contrast to the nonexperimental work on achievement, research on behavioral outcomes tends to find that neighborhoods and schools have comparable effects, or that schools are more significant (Cook, Herman, Phillips, & Settersen, 2002; Duncan, Boisjoly, & Harris, 2001; Teitler & Weiss, 2000). For instance, a multilevel study (students nested in schools and in neighborhoods) examining sexual initiation among Philadelphia youth aged 14–18

found that there was more between-school than between-neighborhood variation in youth's sexual activity, and that when the two contexts were considered simultaneously, only school variation remained significant (Teitler & Weiss, 2000). Another study used Add Health to look at various contextual influences on achievement and delinquency by comparing correlations between pairs of siblings within a family, between best friends, between grade-mates within a school, and between schoolmates living in the same neighborhood (Duncan et al., 2001). Results indicated that family and peer contexts were more strongly associated with adolescent outcomes than school and neighborhood contexts, which both yielded similarly weak associations.

Findings from the experimental literature also bear on the neighborhood vs. school debate. These studies suggest that as far as achievement is concerned, schools are an integral part of "neighborhood effects" in the context of housing mobility programs. As discussed earlier, in the Gautreax Program where children changed neighborhoods and school districts by moving from the city to the affluent suburbs, youth demonstrated achievement benefits (Rubinowitz & Rosenbaum, 2000). In contrast, in the MTO and Yonkers studies, where neighborhood change was not necessarily accompanied by a change in school and/or school district, such benefits were not evident (Deluca, 2007; Fauth, Leventhal et al., 2007; Leventhal & Brooks-Gunn, 2005; Sanbonmatsu et al., 2006).

Taken together, the nonexperimental and experimental studies suggest that both neighborhood and schools matter for adolescent development, but that their relative influence may depend on the outcome under investigation. For achievement, results from experimental studies suggest that neighborhood advantage without corresponding school advantage may not generate benefits for adolescent outcomes, indicating that schools may be a vehicle through which neighborhood effects operate (although results from limited nonexperimental studies are mixed on this score).

For behavioral outcomes, the relative strength of school versus neighborhoods influences suggests that schools may not serve as an indirect route for neighborhood effects for these outcomes. They also point to the potential importance of peer interactions, which occur in both contexts but apparently most consistently at school (Dolcini et al., 2005).

POLICY IMPLICATIONS AND FUTURE DIRECTIONS

Adolescence is a period marked by expanding social interactions. Therefore, the goal of this chapter was to examine the influence of one social context on adolescent development—neighborhoods. We took as our starting point that neighborhoods likely play an important role during this phase of the life course (though we also note that the premise regarding adolescence as a uniquely susceptible period remains to be tested). The empirical evidence was reviewed to this end, followed by specification of a framework for studying the pathways of neighborhood influences on developmental outcomes. An overview of methodological issues was also provided along with some emerging trends and debates in the field. In conclusion, an integration of the empirical, theoretical, and methodological findings is presented in this section, along with policy implications and directions for future research.

Findings from our review of the literature revealed growing support for neighborhood SES effects on adolescent development. These effects were not restricted to a particular domain; however, the specific aspect of SES that mattered most varied by outcome. Neighborhood high SES was positively associated with adolescents' educational achievement, and neighborhood low SES was adversely associated with their behavioral and social well-being and with sexual and fertility outcomes. Findings were generally consistent with respect to both older and younger adolescents, particularly in the nonexperimental studies that drew on neighborhood-based studies or national samples.

Despite consistent patterns of results, the overall size of neighborhood structural effects reported in nonexperimental studies has been small to modest, accounting for approximately 5%–10% of the variance in adolescent outcomes (after adjusting for child and family background characteristics; see also Entwisle, 2007; and Sampson et al., 2002). In most studies, other factors, such as family characteristics including income and parent education, appear to matter more than neighborhood residence characteristics. In comparison to nonexperimental studies, the limited experimental work suggests somewhat larger neighborhood income/poverty effects on adolescent development, at least when low-income youth and their families were given the opportunity to move from poor to less poor neighborhoods; however, these effects were both positive and negative. Together, these findings suggest that neighborhood influences contribute to adolescents' developmental outcomes and should be incorporated into research on this phase of the life course.

To understand the observed associations between neighborhood structure and adolescent development requires drawing upon our theoretical models—institutional resources, norms and collective efficacy and relationships and ties. The models proposed within this framework highlight different underlying mechanisms (individual, family, school, peer, and community), with the utility of each model dependent on the outcome under investigation and the age group studied. Accordingly, we use these models to interpret the findings from descriptive studies of neighborhood effects in conjunction with relevant research findings examining processes of influence.

The association between neighborhood high SES and achievement is best understood in accordance with the institutional resource model. Affluent neighborhoods may have higher quality schools as well as students with more achievement-oriented norms than do less advantaged communities. Economically advantaged neighborhoods also may have more resources that promote learning, such as libraries and educational programs, than do more disadvantaged communities. As reviewed, some empirical support exists for the premise regarding school quality. Alternatively, family relationships may be at work. High SES neighborhoods may be conducive to the maintenance of home environments with structure and routines that foster educational attainment; however, little work has examined this hypothesis.

The associations among exposure to low SES neighbors and mental health problems, delinquency, crime, sexual activity, and childbearing are best understood within the rubric of the norms and collective efficacy model. In economically and socially disadvantaged neighborhoods, community-level supervision of youth may be lax, resulting in fewer institutions that regulate adolescent peer group behavior. Compelling evidence, as reviewed, exists to support this argument for a range of risky behaviors. In addition, according to the institutional resource framework, low SES neighborhoods may lack social and recreational resources such as after-school and youth programs, which in turn, adversely affects adolescents' adjustment. Again, research indicates this situation to be the case. Adolescents in low SES neighborhoods also may have low expectations about the opportunities available to them, resulting in a disincentive to avoid problem behavior; very little empirical work addresses this hypothesis. Finally, although findings are quite mixed, growing research points to relationship mechanisms, often in response to or in conjunction with neighborhood low SES and other forms of social disadvantage, as contributing to links between low SES and adolescent problem behavior, particularly parental supervision and monitoring of youth and involved and supportive parenting.

One can use the theoretical models described in this chapter to interpret the results of the literature review, but much more work remains to be done in conceptually oriented neighborhood research on adolescents. As we have described, an increasing number of researchers are beginning to approach this challenge. Both the norms and collective efficacy and relationships and ties models have been most widely tested, particularly with respect to problem behavior. Researchers have even begun to test these models jointly, moving the field another big step forward.

In many ways, conceptually focused neighborhood research has been hampered by methodological limitations. Specifically, studies that are not designed to study neighborhood effects often lack variation within and between neighborhoods to test theoretical models, nor do these studies measure (or at least measure reliably) the neighborhood processes necessary for examining theoretical models, such as social control and school norms, or family mechanisms, such as parental supervision.

To assess the neighborhood processes discussed under the institutional resource and norms and collective efficacy models, which appear to be especially important for understanding neighborhood influences on adolescent development, alternative methodologies are required. The strategies reviewed and recommended include community surveys, systematic social observations, and alternative administrative data sources. The advantage of these approaches is that they provide measures of neighborhood dimensions (beyond structure) obtained from independent sources (as opposed to participant ratings, which are often subject to threats of nonindependence of measurement). An important corollary is that measurement and analytic models accommodate multilevel structures (i.e., raters or participants nested within neighborhoods). Aside from neighborhood-based studies, which typically address these design and measurement limitations, experimental studies are advocated because they overcome problems of selection or omitted variable bias present in nonexperimental neighborhood research.

Testing theoretical models permits the identification of specific underlying mechanisms of neighborhood influences, which is necessary for drawing policy recommendations. The findings presented in this chapter suggest that the aspect of neighborhood most sensibly targeted by policy makers and practitioners depends on the outcome under consideration. If adolescents' educational attainment is the primary outcome of interest, focusing on potential pathways of high SES, such as school quality, would be recommended. Alternatively, if adolescent delinquent, violent, and sexual behaviors are the target, then building community mechanisms of control would be recommended, as well as providing recreational and social programs for youth. In addition, another strategy would be to work with families to help parents successfully monitor children and to foster close parent–child relations. Moreover, altering these potential pathways of neighborhood influences can be achieved through a variety of mechanisms. As we have noted, current policy efforts that have relocated families out of high-poverty neighborhoods into nonpoor neighborhoods have met with mixed success, as have community-based efforts to alter the economic and social conditions of existing neighborhoods where families (typically those who are poor) live (Kubisch et al., 2002).

In summary, neighborhoods appear to matter for adolescent development; however, *how* they matter is only beginning to be elucidated. Process-oriented research is needed to design effective neighborhood-focused programs and policies aimed at enhancing the lives of adolescents and their families.

REFERENCES

Aaronson, D. (1997). Sibling estimates of neighborhood effects. In J. Brooks-Gunn, G. J. Duncan, & J. L. Aber (Eds.), *Neighborhood poverty: Policy implications in studying neighborhoods, vol. 2* (pp. 80–93). New York: Russell Sage Foundation Press.

Aber, J. L., Gephart, M., Brooks-Gunn, J., & Connell, J. P. (1997). Development in context: Implications for studying neighborhood effects. In J. Brooks-Gunn, G. J. Duncan, & J. L. Aber (Eds.), *Neighborhood poverty: Context and consequences for children, vol. 1* (pp. 44–61). New York: Russell Sage Foundation.

Adam, E. K. (2004). Beyond quality: Parental and residential stability and children's adjustment. *Current Directions in Psychological Science, 13,* 210–213.

Adam, E. K., & Chase-Lansdale, P. L. (2002). Home, sweet home(s): Parental separations, residential moves, and adjustment problems in low income adolescent girls. *Developmental Psychology, 38,* 792–805.

Allison, K. W., Burton, L. M., Marshall, S., Perez-Febles, A., Yarrington, J., Kirsh, L. B., et al. (1999). Life experiences among urban adolescents: Examining the role of context. *Child Development, 70,* 1017–1029.

Anderson, E. (1999). *The code of the street: Decency, violence, and the moral life of the inner city.* New York: W. W. Norton.

Aneshensel, C. S., & Sucoff, C. A. (1996). The neighborhood context of adolescent mental health. *Journal of Health and Social Behavior, 37,* 293–310.

Averett, S. L., Rees, D. I., & Argys, L. M. (2002). The impact of government policies and neighborhood characteristics on teenage sexual activity and contraceptive use. *American Journal of Public Health, 92,* 1771–1778.

Bachman, J. G., & Schulenberg, J. (1993). How part-time work intensity relates to drug use, problem behavior, time use, and satisfaction among high school seniors: Are these consequences or merely correlates? *Developmental Psychology, 29,* 220–235.

Baker, P. C., & Mott, F. L. (1989). *NLSY child handbook 1989: A guide and resource document for the National Longitudinal Survey of Youth 1986 Child Data.* Columbus, OH: Center for Human Resources Research, Ohio State University.

Barnes McGuire, J. (1997). The reliability and validity of a questionnaire describing neighborhood characteristics relevant to families and young children living in urban areas. *Journal of Community Psychology, 25,* 551–566.

Baumer, E. P., & South, S. J. (2001). Community effects on youth sexual activity. *Journal of Marriage and Family, 63,* 540–554.

Becker, G. S. (1981). *A treatise on the family* (2nd ed.). Cambridge, MA: Harvard University Press.

Beyers, J. M., Bates, J. E., Pettit, G. S., & Dodge, K. A. (2003). Neighborhood structure, parenting processes, and the development of youth's externalizing behavior: A multilevel analysis. *American Journal of Community Psychology, 31,* 35–53.

Beyers, J. M., Loeber, R., Wikström, P. H., & Stouthamer-Loeber, M. (2001). What predicts adolescent violence in better-off neighborhoods? *Journal of Abnormal Child Psychology, 29,* 369–338.

Billy, J. O., Brewster, K. L., & Grady, W. R. (1994). Contextual effects on the sexual behavior of adolescent women. *Journal of Marriage and Family, 56,* 387–404.

Billy, J. O., & Moore, D. E. (1992). A multilevel analysis of marital and non-marital fertility in the U.S. *Social Forces, 70,* 977–1011.

Billy, J. O. G., Grady, W. R., Wenzlow, A. T., Brener, N. D., Collins, J. L., & Kann, L. (2000). Contextual influences on school provision of health services. *Journal of Adolescent Health, 27,* 12–24.

Bogart, W. T., & Cromwell, B. A. (2000). How much is a neighborhood school worth? *Journal of Urban Economics, 47,* 280–305.

Bolland, J. M. (2003). Hopelessness and risk behaviour among adolescents living in high-poverty inner-city neighbourhoods. *Journal of Adolescence, 26,* 145–158.

Bolland, J. M., Lian, B. E., & Formichella, C. M. (2005). The origins of hopelessness among inner-city African-American adolescents. *American Journal of Community Psychology, 36,* 293–305.

Booth, A., & Crouter, A. C. (2001). *Does it take a village? Community effects on children, adolescents, and families.* Mahwah, NJ: Lawrence Erlbaum.

Borrell, C., Rodriguez, M., Ferrando, J., Brugal, M. T., Pasarin, M. I., Martinez, V., et al. (2002). Role of individual and contextual effects in injury mortality: New evidence from small area analysis. *Injury Prevention, 8,* 297–302.

Bowen, N. K., & Bowen, G. L. (1999). Effects of crime and violence in neighborhoods and schools on the school behavior and performance of adolescents. *Journal of Adolescent Research, 14,* 319–342.

Boyce, W. T., Jensen, E. W., James, S. A., & Peacock, J. L. (1983). The Family Routines Inventory: Theoretical origins. *Social Science and Medicine, 17,* 193–200.

Boyle, M. H., Georgiades, K., Racine, Y., & Mustard, C. (2007). Neighborhood and family influences on educational attainment: Results from the Ontario Child Health Study follow-up 2001. *Child Development, 78,* 168–189.

Bradley, R. H. (1995). Environment and parenting. In M. H. Bornstein (Ed.), *Handbook of parenting, vol. 2: Biology and ecology of parenting* (pp. 235–261). Mahwah, NJ: Lawrence Erlbaum.

Breslin, F. C., & Adlaf, E. M. (2005). Part-time work and adolescent heavy episodic drinking: The influence of family and community context. *Journal of Studies on Alcohol, 66,* 784–794.

Brewster, K. L. (1994a). Neighborhood context and the transition to sexual activity among young Black women. *Demography, 31,* 603–614.

Brewster, K. L. (1994b). Race differences in sexual activity among adolescent women: The role of neighborhood characteristics. *American Sociologial Review, 59,* 408–424.

Brewster, K. L., Billy, J. O. G., & Grady, W. R. (1993). Social context and adolescent behavior: The impact of community on the transition to sexual activity. *Social Forces, 71,* 713–740.

Briggs, X. S. (1997). Moving up versus moving out: Neighborhood effects in housing mobility programs. *Housing Policy Debate, 8,* 195–234.

Brody, G. H., Ge, X., Conger, R. D., Gibbons, F. X., Murry, V. M., Gerrard, M., et al. (2001). The influence of neighborhood disadvantage, collective socialization, and parenting on African American children's affiliation with deviant peers. *Child Development, 72,* 1231–1246.

Bronfenbrenner, U. (1979). *The ecology of human development.* Cambridge, MA: Harvard University Press.

Brooks-Gunn, J., Duncan, G. J., & Aber, J. L. (1997). *Neighborhood poverty, vol. 1: Context and consequences for children.* New York: Russell Sage Foundation Press.

Brooks-Gunn, J., Duncan, G. J., Klebanov, P. K., & Sealand, N. (1993). Do neighborhoods influence child and adolescent development? *American Journal of Sociology, 99,* 353–395.

Brooks-Gunn, J., Klebanov, P., Liaw, F., & Duncan, G. J. (1995). Toward an understanding of the effects of poverty upon children. In H. E. Fitzgerald, B. M. Lester & B. S. Zuckerman (Eds.), *Children of poverty: Research, health, and policy issues, vol. 23* (pp. 3–41). New York: Garland.

Browning, C. R., Burrington, L. A., Leventhal, T., & Brooks-Gunn, J. (2008). Neighborhood structural inequality, collective efficacy, and sexual risk behavior among urban youth. *Journal of Health and Social Behavior, 49,* 269–85.

Browning, C. R., Leventhal, T., & Brooks-Gunn, J. (2004). Neighborhood context and racial differences in early adolescent sexual activity. *Demography, 41,* 697–720.

Browning, C. R., Leventhal, T., & Brooks-Gunn, J. (2005). Sexual initiation in early adolescence: The nexus of parental and community control. *American Sociologial Review, 70,* 758–778.

Buka, S. L., Stichick, T. L., Birdthistle, I., & Earls, F. J. (2001). Youth exposure to violence: Prevalence, risks, and consequences. *American Journal of Orthopsychiatry, 71,* 298–310.

Bursik, R. J. (1988). Social disorganization and theories of crime and delinquency: Problems and prospects. *Criminology, 26,* 515–552.

Burton, L. M. (1990). Teenage childbearing as an alternative life-course strategy in multigenerational black families. *Human Nature, 1,* 123–143.

Burton, L. M., & Jarrett, R. L. (2000). In the mix, yet on the margins: The place of families in urban neighborhood and child development research. *Journal of Marriage and Family, 62,* 1114–1135.

Card, D., & Payne, A. A. (2002). School finance reform, the distribution of school spending, and the distribution of student test scores. *Journal of Public Economics, 83,* 49–82.

Card, D., & Rothstein, J. (2007). Racial segregation and the black-white test score gap. *Journal of Public Economics, 91,* 2158–2184.

Caspi, A., Taylor, A., Moffitt, T. E., & Plomin, R. (2000). Neighborhood deprivation affects children's mental health: Environmental risks identified in a genetic design. *Psychological Science, 11,* 338–342.

Ceballo, R., McLoyd, V. C., & Toyokawa, T. (2004). The influence of neighborhood quality on adolescents' educational values and school effort. *Journal of Adolescent Research, 19,* 716–739.

Chay, K. Y., & Greenstone, M. (2003). The impact of air pollution on infant mortality: Evidence from geographic variation in pollution shocks induced by a recession. *Quarterly Journal of Economics, 118,* 1121–1167.

Chuang, Y., Ennett, S. T., Bauman, K. E., & Foshee, V. A. (2005). Neighborhood influences on adolescent cigarette and alcohol use: Mediating effects through parent and peer behaviors. *Journal of Health and Social Behavior, 46,* 187–204.

Chung, H. L., & Steinberg, L. (2006). Relations between neighborhood factors, parenting behaviors, peer deviance, and delinquency among serious juvenile offenders. *Developmental Psychology, 42,* 319–331.

Chung, I., Hill, K. G., Hawkins, J. D., Gilchrist, L. D., & Nagin, D. S. (2002). Childhood predictors of offense trajectories. *Journal of Research in Crime and Delinquency, 39,* 60–90.

Clampet-Lundquist, S., Duncan, J., Edin, K., & Kling, J. (2006). *Moving at-risk teenagers out of high-risk neighborhoods: Why girls fare better than boys.* Princeton, NJ: Princeton University, Department of Economics, Industrial Relations Section.

Cleveland, H. H. (2003). Disadvantaged neighborhoods and adolescent aggression: Behavioral genetic evidence of contextual effects. *Journal of Research on Adolescence, 13,* 211–238.

Cleveland, H. H., & Gilson, M. (2004). The effects of neighborhood proportion of single-parent families and mother-adolescent relationships on adolescents' number of sexual partners. *Journal of Youth and Adolescence, 33,* 319–329.

Coleman, J. S. (1988). Social capital in the creation of human capital. *American Journal of Sociology, 94,* S95–S120.

Coley, R. L., Morris, J. E., & Hernandez, D. (2004). Out-of-school care and problem behavior trajectories among low-income adolescent: Individual, family and neighborhood characteristics as added risks. *Child Development, 75,* 948–965.

Conger, R. D., Ge, X., Elder, G. H., Jr, Lorenz, F. O., & Simons, R. L. (1994). Economic stress, coercive family process, and developmental problems of adolescent. *Child Development, 65,* 541–561.

Conger, R. D., Wallace, L. E., Sun, Y., Simons, R. L., McLoyd, V. C., & Brody, G. H. (2002). Economic pressure in African American families: A replication and extension of the family stress model. *Developmental Psychology, 38,* 179–193.

Connell, J. P., & Halpern-Felsher, B. L. (1997). How neighborhoods affect educational outcomes in middle childhood and adolescence: Conceptual issues and empirical examples. In J. Brooks-Gunn, C. Duncan, & J. L. Aber (Eds.), *Neighborhood poverty: Context and consequences for children, vol. 1* (pp. 174–199). New York: Russell Sage Foundation.

Connell, J. P., Halpern-Felsher, B. L., Clifford, E., Crichlow, W., & Usinger, P. (1995). Hanging in there: Behavioral, psychological, and contextual factors affecting whether African-American adolescents stay in school. *Journal of Adolescent Research, 10,* 41–63.

Cook, T. D., Herman, M. R., Phillips, M., & Settersen, R. A., Jr. (2002). Some ways in which neighborhoods, nuclear families, friendship groups, and schools jointly affect changes in early adolescent development. *Child Development, 73,* 1283–1309.

Cook, T. D., Shagle, S. C., & Degirmencioglu, S. M. (1997). Capturing social process for testing mediational models of neighborhood effects. In J. Brooks-Gunn, G. J. Duncan, & J. L. Aber (Eds.), *Neighborhood poverty, vol. 2: Policy implications in studying neighborhoods* (pp. 94–119). New York: Russell Sage Foundation.

Cooley-Quille, M., Boyd, R. C., Frantz, E., & Walsh, J. (2001). Emotional and behavioral impact of exposure to community violence in inner-city adolescents. *Journal of Clinical Child Psychology, 30,* 199–206.

Coulton, C. J., & Korbin, J. E. (2007). Indicators of child well-being through a neighborhood lens. *Social Indicators Research, 84,* 349–361.

Coulton, C. J., Korbin, J., Chan, T., & Su, M. (2001). Mapping residents' perceptions of neighborhood boundaries: A methodological note. *American Journal of Community Psychology, 29,* 371–383.

Coulton, C. J., Korbin, J. E., & Su, M. (1999). Neighborhoods and child maltreatment: A multi-level study. *Child Abuse and Neglect, 23,* 1019–1040.

Coulton, C. J., Korbin, J. E., Su, M., & Chow, J. (1995). Community level factors and child maltreatment rates. *Child Development, 66,* 1262–1276.

Crane, J. (1991). The epidemic theory of ghettos and neighborhood effects on dropping out and teenage childbearing. *American Journal of Sociology, 96,* 1126–1159.

Crowder, K. D., & South, S. J. (2003). Neighborhood distress and school dropout: The variable significance of community context. *Social Science Research, 32,* 659–698.

Cubbin, C., LeClere, F. B., & Smith, G. S. (2000). Socioeconomic status and injury mortality: Individual and neighborhood determinants. *Journal of Epidemiology & Community Health, 54,* 517–524.

Cubbin, C., Santelli, J., Brindis, C. D., & Braveman, P. (2005). Neighborhood context and sexual behaviors among adolescents: Findings from the National Longitudinal Study of Adolescent Health. *Perspectives on Sexual and Reproductive Health, 37,* 125–134.

Currie, J., & Neidell, M. (2005). Air pollution and infant health: What can we learn from California's recent experience? *Quarterly Journal of Economics, 120,* 1003–1030.

Deluca, S. (2007). All over the map: Explaining educational outcomes of the Moving to Opportunity program. *Education Next, 7,* 29–36.

Diez-Roux, A. V. (2001). Investigating neighborhood and area effects on health. *American Journal of Public Health, 91,* 1783–1789.

Dishion, T. J., Andrews, D. W., & Crosby, L. (1995). Antisocial boys and their friends in early adolescence: Relationship characteristics, quality, and interactional process. *Child Development, 66,* 139–151.

Dolcini, M. M., Harper, G. W., Watson, S. E., Catania, J. A., & Ellen, J. M. (2005). Friends in the 'hood: Should peer-based health promotion programs target nonschool friendship networks? *Journal of Adolescent Health, 36,* 267.e6–267.e15.

Dornbusch, S. M., Ritter, L. P., & Steinberg, L. (1991). Community influences on the relation of family status to adolescent school performance: Differences between African Americans and non-Hispanic whites. *American Journal of Education, 38,* 543–567.

DuBois, D. L., & Hirsch, B. J. (1990). School and neighborhood friendship patterns of Blacks and Whites in early adolescence. *Child Development, 61,* 524–536.

Dubow, E. F., Edwards, S., & Ippolito, M. F. (1997). Life stressors, neighborhood disadvantages, and resources: A focus on inner-city children's adjustment. *Journal of Clinical Child Psychology, 26,* 130–144.

Duncan, G. J. (1994). Families and neighbors as sources of disadvantage in the schooling decisions of White and Black adolescents. *American Journal of Education, 103,* 20–53.

Duncan, G. J., Boisjoly, J., & Harris, K. M. (2001). Sibling, peer, neighbor and schoolmate correlations as indicators of the importance of context for adolescent development. *Demography, 38,* 437–447.

Duncan, G. J., & Brooks-Gunn, J. (1997). *Consequences of growing up poor.* New York: Russell Sage Foundation Press.

Duncan, G. J., Connell, J. P., & Klebanov, P. K. (1997). Conceptual and methodological issues in estimating causal effects of neighborhood and family conditions on individual development. In J. Brooks-Gunn, G. J. Duncan, & J. L. Aber (Eds.), *Neighborhood poverty: Context and consequences for children, vol. 1* (pp. 219–250). New York: Russell Sage Foundation Press.

Duncan, G. J., & Raudenbush, S. W. (1999). Assessing the effects of context in studies of child and youth development. *Educational Psychologist, 34,* 29–41.

Duncan, S. C., Duncan, T. E., & Strycker, L. A. (2002). A multilevel analysis of neighborhood context and youth alcohol and drug problems. *Prevention Science, 3,* 125–133.

Dupéré, V., Lacourse, E., Willms, J. D., Leventhal, T., & Tremblay, R. E. (2008). Neighborhood poverty and early transition to sexual activity in young adolescents: A developmental ecological approach. *Child Development, 79,* 1463–1476.

Dupéré, V., Lacourse, E., Willms, J. D., Vitaro, F., & Tremblay, R. E. (2007). Affiliation to youth gangs during adolescence: The interaction between childhood psychopathic tendencies and neighborhood disadvantage. *Journal of Abnormal Child Psychology, 35,* 1035–1045.

Eamon, M. K. (2005). Social-demographic, school, neighborhood, and parenting influences on the academic achievement of Latino young adolescents. *Journal of Youth and Adolescence, 34,* 163–174.

Earls, F., McGuire, J., & Shay, S. (1994). Evaluating a community intervention to reduce the risk of child abuse: Methodological strategies in conducting neighborhood surveys. *Child Abuse & Neglect, 18,* 473–485.

Eccles, J., & Gootman, J. A. (2002). *Community programs to promote youth development.* Washington, DC: National Academic Press.

Eitle, D. J., & McNulty Eitle, T. (2004). School and county characteristics as predictors of school rates of drug, alcohol, and tobacco offenses. *Journal of Health and Social Behavior, 45,* 408–421.

Elder, G. H., Eccles, J. S., Ardelt, M., & Lord, S. (1995). Inner-city parents under economic pressure: Perspectives on the strategies of parenting. *Journal of Marriage and the Family, 57,* 771–784.

Elliot, D. S., Wilson, W. J., Huizinga, D., Sampson, R. J., Elliot, A., & Rankin, B. (1996). The effects of neighborhood disadvantage on adolescent development. *Journal of Research in Crime and Delinquency, 33,* 389–426.

Ennett, S. T., Flewelling, R. L., Lindrooth, R. C., & Norton, E. C. (1997). School and neighborhood characteristics associated with school rates of alcohol, cigarette, and marijuana use. *Journal of Health and Social Behavior, 38,* 55–71.

Ensminger, M. E., Lambkin, R. P., & Jacobson, N. (1996). School leaving: A longitudinal perspective including neighborhood effects. *Child Development, 67,* 2400–2416.

Entwisle, B. (2007). Putting people into place. *Demography, 44,* 687–704.

Entwisle, D. R., Alexander, K. L., & Olson, L. S. (1994). The gender gap in math: Its possible origins in neighborhood effects. *American Sociological Review, 59,* 822–838.

Evans, W. N., Oates, W. E., & Schwab, R. M. (1992). Measuring peer group effects: A study of teenage behavior. *Journal of Political Economy, 100,* 966–991.

Fauth, R. C. (2004). Short-term effects of moving from public housing in poor to middle-class neighborhoods on low-income, minority adults' outcomes. *Social Science and Medicine, 59,* 2271–2284.

Fauth, R. C., Leventhal, T., & Brooks-Gunn, J. (2005). Early impacts of moving from poor to middle-class neighborhoods on low-income youth. *Journal of Applied Developmental Psychology, 26,* 415–439.

Fauth, R. C., Leventhal, T., & Brooks-Gunn, J. (2007). Welcome to the neighborhood? Long-term impacts of moving to low-poverty neighborhoods on poor children's and adolescents' outcomes. *Journal of Research on Adolescence, 17,* 249–284.

Fauth, R. C., Leventhal, T., & Brooks-Gunn, J. (2008). Seven years later: Effects of a neighborhood mobility program on poor Black and Latino adults' well-being. *Journal of Health and Social Behavior, 49,* 119–130.

Fauth, R. C., Roth, J. L., & Brooks-Gunn, J. (2007). Does the neighborhood context alter the link between youth's after-school time activities and developmental outcomes? A multilevel analysis. *Developmental Psychology, 43,* 760–777.

Fauth, R. C., & Brooks-Gunn, J. (2008). Are some neighborhoods better for child health than others? In R. F. Schoenir, J. S. House, G. A. Kaplan, & H. Pollack (Eds.), *Making Americans healthier: Social and economic policy as health policy.* NY: Russell Sage Foundation.

Feldman, S. S., & Elliott, G. R. (1990). *At the threshold: The developing adolescent.* Cambridge, MA: Harvard University Press.

Ferreira, I., van der Horst, K., Wendel-Vos, W., Kremers, S., van Lenthe, F. J., & Brug, J. (2006). Environmental correlates of physical activity in youth: A review and update. *Obesity Reviews, 58,* 129–154.

Foshee, V. A., Ennett, S. T., Bauman, K. E., Granger, D. A., Benefield, T., Suchindran, C., et al. (2007). A test of biosocial models of adolescent cigarette and alcohol involvement. *Journal of Early Adolescence, 27,* 4–39.

Foster, E. M., & McLanahan, S. (1996). An illustration of the use of instrumental variables: Do neighborhood conditions affect a young person's chance of finishing high school? *Psychological Methods, 1,* 249–260.

Freisthler, B., Lascala, E. A., Gruenewald, P. J., & Treno, A. J. (2005). An examination of drug activity: Effects of neighborhood social organization on the development of drug distribution systems. *Substance Use and Misuse, 40,* 671–686.

Furstenberg, F. F., Jr. (1993). How families manage risk and opportunity in dangerous neighborhoods. In W. J. Wilson (Ed.), *Sociology and the public agenda* (pp. 231–238). Newbury Park, CA: Sage.

Furstenberg, F. F., Jr. (2001). Managing to make it: Afterthoughts. *Journal of Family Issues, 22,* 150–162.

Furstenberg, F. F., Jr., Cook, T. D., Eccles, J., Elder, G. H., & Sameroff, A. (Eds.). (1999). *Managing to make it: Urban families and adolescent success.* Chicago: University of Chicago Press.

Garcia Coll, C. G., & Szalacha, L. A. (2004). The multiple contexts of middle childhood. *The Future of Children, 14,* 81–97.

Garner, C. L., & Raudenbush, S. W. (1991). Neighborhood effects on educational attainment: A multilevel analysis. *Sociology of Education, 64,* 251–262.

Ge, X., Brody, G. H., Conger, R. D., Simons, R. L., & Murry, V. M. (2002). Contextual amplification of pubertal transition effects on deviant peer affiliation and externalizing behavior among African-American children. *Developmental Psychology, 38,* 42–54.

Gershoff, E. T., & Lawrence, A. J. (2006). Neighborhoods and schools: Contexts and consequences for the mental health and risk behaviors of children and youth. In L. Balter & C. S. Tamis-LeMonda (Eds.), *Child psychology: A handbook of contemporary issues* (2nd ed.). New York, NY: Psychology Press.

Gibbons, F. X., Gerrard, M., Lune, L. S. V., Wills, T. A., Brody, G., & Conger, R. D. (2004). Context and cognitions: Environmental risk, social influence, and adolescent substance use. *Personality and Social Psychology Bulletin, 30,* 1048–1061.

Gleason, P. M., & Cain, G. G. (2004). Earnings of Black and White youth and its relation to poverty. In C. M. Henry (Ed.), *Race, poverty, and domestic policy.* New Haven, CT: Yale University Press.

Goering, J., & Feins, J. D. (Eds.). (2003). *Choosing a better life? Evaluating the Moving to Opportunity social experiment.* Washington, DC: Urban Institute Press.

Gonzales, N. A., Cauce, A. M., Friedman, R. J., & Mason, C. A. (1996). Family, peer, and neighborhood influences on academic achievement among African-American adolescents: One-year prospective effects. *American Journal of Community Psychology, 24,* 365–387.

Gordon, R. A., Savage, C., Lahey, B. B., Goodman, S. H., Jensen, P. S., Rubio-Stipec, M., et al. (2003). Family and neighborhood income: Additive and multiplicative associations with youth' well-being. *Social Science Research, 32,* 191–219.

Gorman-Smith, D., Henry, D. B., & Tolan, P. H. (2004). Exposure to community violence and violence perpetration: The protective effects of family functioning. *Journal of Clinical Child and Adolescent Psychology, 33,* 439–449.

Gorman-Smith, D., & Tolan, P. (1998). The role of exposure to community violence and developmental problems among inner-city youth. *Development and Psychopathology, 10,* 101–116.

Gorman-Smith, D., Tolan, P. H., & Henry, D. B. (2000). A developmental-ecological model of the relation of family functioning to patterns of delinquency. *Journal of Quantitative Criminology, 16,* 169–198.

Gorman-Smith, D., Tolan, P. H., Zelli, A., & Huesmann, L. R. (1996). The relation of family functioning to violence among inner-city minority youth. *Journal of Family Psychology, 10,* 115–129.

Graber, J. A., Brooks-Gunn, J., & Petersen, A. C. (1996). *Transitions through adolescence: Interpersonal domains and context.* Mahwah, NJ: Lawrence Erlbaum.

Hagan, J., Simpson, J., & Gillis, A. R. (1987). Class in the household: A power-control theory of gender and delinquency. *American Journal of Sociology, 92,* 788–816.

Halpern-Felsher, B. L., Connell, J. P., Spencer, M. B., Aber, J. L., Duncan, G. J., Clifford, E., et al. (1997). Neighborhood and family factors predicting educational risk and attainment in African American and White children. In J. Brooks-Gunn, G. J. Duncan, & J. L. Aber (Eds.), *Neighborhood poverty: Context and consequences for children, vol. 1,* pp. 146–173). New York: Russell Sage Foundation.

Harding, D. J. (2003). Counterfactual models of neighborhood effects: The effect of neighborhood poverty on dropping out and teenage pregnancy. *American Journal of Sociology, 109,* 676–719.

Harding, D. J. (2005). *Neighborhood violence and the age structure of peer networks: Socialization of adolescent boys in disadvantaged neighborhoods.* Ann Arbor, MI: Population Studies Center Research Report No. 05–586.

Harding, D. J. (2007). Cultural context, sexual behavior, and romantic relationships in disadvantaged neighborhoods. *American Sociologial Review, 72,* 341–364.

Haveman, R., & Wolfe, B. (1994). *Succeeding generations: On the effects of investments in children.* New York: Russell Sage Foundation.

Haynie, D. L., Silver, E., & Teasdale, B. (2006). Neighborhood characteristics, peer influence, and adolescent violence. *Journal of Quantitative Criminology, 22,* 147–169.

Hernandez, D. J. (1993). *America's children: Resources from family, government, and the economy.* New York: Russell Sage Foundation Press.

Hill, K. G., Howell, J. C., Hawkins, J. D., & Battin-Pearson, S. R. (1999). Childhood risk factors for adolescent gang membership: Results from the Seattle Social Development Project. *Journal of Research in Crime and Delinquency, 36,* 300–322.

Hill, M. (1991). *The Panel Study of Income Dynamics: The Sage series guides to major social science data bases, vol. 2.* Newbury Park, CA: Sage.

Hill, T. D., Ross, C. E., & Angel, R. J. (2005). Neighborhood disorder, psychophysiological distress, and health. *Journal of Health and Social Behavior, 46,* 170–186.

Hoffman, J. P. (2002). The community context of family structure and adolescent drug use. *Journal of Marriage and the Family, 64,* 314–330.

Hogan, D. P., & Kitagawa, E. M. (1985). The impact of social status, family structure, and neighborhood on the fertility of Black adolescents. *American Journal of Sociology, 90,* 825–855.

Holloway, S. R., & Mulherin, S. (2004). The effect of adolescent neighborhood poverty on adult employment. *Journal of Urban Affairs, 26,* 427–454.

Hughes, M. E., Furstenberg, F. F., & Teitler, J. O. (1995). The impact of an increase in family planning services on the teenage population of Philadelphia. *Family Planning Perspectives, 27,* 60–65.

Jarrett, R. L. (1997). Bringing families back in: Neighborhood effects on child development. In J. Brooks-Gunn, G. J. Duncan, & J. L. Aber (Eds.), *Neighborhood poverty: Policy implications in studying neighborhoods, vol. 2* (pp. 48–64). New York: Russell Sage Foundation.

Jencks, C., & Mayer, S. (1990). The social consequences of growing up in a poor neighborhood. In L. Lynn & M. McGeary (Eds.), *Inner-city poverty in the United States* (pp. 111–186). Washington, DC: National Academy Press.

Jones, D. J., Forehand, R., O'Connell, C., Armistead, L., & Brody, G. (2005). Mothers' perceptions of neighborhood violence and mother-reported monitoring of African American children: An examination of the moderating role of perceived support. *Behavior Therapy, 36*, 25–34.

Kahn, J. A., Kaplowitz, R. A., Goodman, E., & Emans, S. J. (2002). The association between impulsiveness and sexual risk behaviors in adolescent and young adult women. *Journal of Adolescent Health, 30*, 229–232.

Kamerman, S. B., & Kahn, A. J. (2001). Child and family policies in the United States at the opening of the twenty-first century. *Social Policy and Administration, 35*, 69–84.

Katz, L. F., Kling, J., & Liebman, J. B. (2001). Moving to Opportunity in Boston: Early results of a randomized mobility experiment. *Quarterly Journal of Economics, 116*, 607–654.

Klebanov, P. K., Brooks-Gunn, J., & Duncan, G. J. (1994). Does neighborhood and family poverty affect mothers' parenting, mental health, and social support? *Journal of Marriage and the Family, 56*, 441–455.

Kling, J. R., Liebman, J. B., & Katz, L. F. (2007). Experimental analysis of neighborhood effects. *Econometrica, 75*, 83–119.

Kling, J. R., Ludwig, J., & Katz, L. F. (2005, February). Neighborhood effects on crime for female and male youth: Evidence from a randomized housing voucher experiment. *Quarterly Journal of Economics, 120*, 87–130.

Knoester, C., & Haynie, D. L. (2005). Community context, social integration into family, and youth violence. *Journal of Marriage and Family, 67*, 767–780.

Kohen, D. E., Brooks-Gunn, J., Leventhal, T., & Hertzman, C. (2002). Neighborhood income and physical and social disorder in Canada: Associations with young children's competencies. *Child Development, 73*, 1844–1860.

Kornhauser, R. (1978). *Social sources of delinquency*. Chicago: University of Chicago Press.

Kowaleski-Jones, L. (2000). Staying out of trouble: Community resources and problem behavior among high-risk adolescents. *Journal of Marriage and the Family, 62*, 449–464.

Kroneman, L., Loeber, R., & Hipwell, A. E. (2004). Is neighborhood context differently related to externalizing problems and delinquency for girls compared with boys? *Clinical Child and Family Psychology Review, 7*, 109–122.

Ku, L., Sonenstein, F. L., & Pleck, J. H. (1993). Neighborhood, family and work: Influences on the premarital behaviors of adolescent males. *Social Forces, 72*, 479–503.

Kubisch, A. C., Auspos, P., Brown, P., Chaskin, R., Fulbright-Anderson, K., & Hamilton, R. (2002). *Voices from the field II: Reflections on comprehensive community change*. Washington, DC: Aspen Institute.

Lambert, S. F., Brown, T., Phillips, C. M., & Ialongo, N. S. (2004). The relationship between perceptions of neighborhood characteristics and substance use among urban African American adolescents. *American Journal of Community Psychology, 34*, 205–218.

Landrine, H., Klonoff, E. A., & Alcaraz, R. (1997). Racial discrimination in minors' access to tobacco. *Journal of Black Psychology, 23*, 135–147.

Lauen, D. L. (2007). Contextual explanations of school choice. *Sociology of Education, 80*, 179–209.

Leventhal, T., & Brooks-Gunn, J. (2000). The neighborhoods they live in: The effects of neighborhood residence on child and adolescent outcomes. *Psychological Bulletin, 126*, 309–337.

Leventhal, T., & Brooks-Gunn, J. (2001). Changing neighborhoods and child well-being: Understanding how children may be affected in the coming century. *Advances in Life Course Research, 6*, 263–301.

Leventhal, T., & Brooks-Gunn, J. (2003a). Children and youth in neighborhood contexts. *Current Directions in Psychological Science, 12*, 27–31.

Leventhal, T., & Brooks-Gunn, J. (2003b). Moving to Opportunity: An experimental study of neighborhood effects on mental health. *American Journal of Public Health, 93*, 1576–1582.

Leventhal, T., & Brooks-Gunn, J. (2003c). Neighborhood-based initiatives. In J. Brooks-Gunn, A. S. Fuligni, & L. J. Berlin (Eds.), *Early child development in the 21st century: Profiles of current research initiatives*. New York: Teachers College Press.

Leventhal, T., & Brooks-Gunn, J. (2004a). Diversity in developmental trajectories across adolescence: Neighborhood influences. In R. M. Lerner & L. Steinberg (Eds.), *Handbook of adolescent psychology* (2nd ed.; pp. 451–486). Hoboken, NJ: John Wiley & Sons.

Leventhal, T., & Brooks-Gunn, J. (2004b). A randomized study of neighborhood effects on low income children's educational outcomes. *Developmental Psychology, 40*, 488–507.

Leventhal, T., & Brooks-Gunn, J. (2005). Neighborhood and gender effects on family processes: Results from the Moving to Opportunity program. *Family Relations, 54*, 633–643.

Leventhal, T., Fauth, R. C., & Brooks-Gunn, J. (2005). Neighborhood poverty and public policy: A five-year follow-up of children's educational outcomes in the New York City Moving to Opportunity demonstration. *Developmental Psychology, 41*, 933–952.

Leventhal, T., Graber, J. A., & Brooks-Gunn, J. (2001). Adolescent transitions into employment: When a job is not just a job. *Journal of Research on Adolescence, 11*, 297–323.

Leventhal, T., Xue, Y., & Brooks-Gunn, J. (2006). Immigrant differences in school-age children's verbal trajectories: A look at four racial/ethnic groups. *Child Development, 77*, 1359–1374.

Loeber, R., & Wikström, P.-O. H. (1993). Individual pathways to crime in different types of neighborhoods. In D. P. Farrington, R. J. Sampson & P.-O. H. Wikström (Eds.), *Integrating individual and ecological aspects of crime* (pp. 169–204). Stockholm, Sweden: National Council for Crime Prevention.

Logan, J. R., & Spitze, G. D. (1994). Family neighbors. *American Journal of Sociology, 100*, 453–476.

Ludwig, J., Duncan, G. J., & Hirschfield, P. (2001). Urban poverty and juvenile crime: Evidence from a randomized housing-mobility experiment. *Quarterly Journal of Economics, 116*, 655–679.

Luthar, S. S. (2003). The culture of affluence: Psychological costs of material well-being. *Child Development, 74*, 1581–1593.

Lynam, D. R., Caspi, A., Moffitt, T. E., Wikström, P. H., Loeber, R., & Novak, S. P. (2000). The interaction between impulsivity and neighborhood context on offending: The effects of impulsivity are stronger in poorer neighborhoods. *Journal of Abnormal Psychology, 109*, 563–574.

Maccoby, E. E., & Martin, J. A. (1983). Socialization in the context of the family: Parent-child interaction. In E. M. Hetherington (Ed.), *Handbook of child psychology, Vol. 4: Socialization, personality and social development*, (4th ed.; pp. 1–102). New York: John Wiley & Sons.

Manski, C. (1993). Identification of endogenous social effects: The reflection problem. *Review of Economic Studies, 60*, 531–542.

Martinez, P., & Richters, J. E. (1993). The NIMH Community Violence Project: II. Children's distress symptoms associated with violence exposure. *Psychiatry, 56*, 22–35.

Massey, D. S., & Denton, N. (1993). *American apartheid: Segregation and the making of the underclass*. Cambridge, MA: Harvard University Press.

Mateu-Gelabert, P., & Lune, H. (2003). School violence: The bidirectional conflict flow between neighborhood and school. *City & Community, 2*, 353–368.

McLoyd, V. C. (1990). The impact of economic hardship on black families and children: Psychological distress, parenting, and socioemotional development. *Child Development, 61*, 311–346.

Meyers, S. A., & Miller, C. (2004). Direct, mediated, moderated, and cumulative relations between neighborhood characteristics and adolescent outcomes. *Adolescence, 39*, 121–144.

Molnar, B. E., Buka, S. L., Brennan, R. T., Holton, J. K., & Earls, F. (2003). A multilevel study of neighborhoods and parent-to-child physical aggression: Results from the Project on Human Development in Chicago Neighborhoods. *Child Maltreatment, 8*, 84–97.

Molnar, B. E., Miller, M. J., Azrael, D., & Buka, S. L. (2004). Neighborhood predictors of concealed firearm carrying among children and adolescents: Results from the Project on Human Development in Chicago Neighborhoods. *Archives of Pediatrics and Adolescent Medicine, 158,* 657–664.

Morenoff, J. D., Sampson, R. J., & Raudenbush, S. W. (2001). Neighborhood inequality, collective efficacy, and the spatial dynamics of urban violence. *Criminology, 39,* 517–559.

Mortimer, J. T., Finch, M. D., Ryu, S., Shanahan, M. J., & Call, K. T. (1996). The effects of work intensity on adolescent mental health, achievement, and behavioral adjustment: New evidence from a prospective study. *Child Development, 67,* 1243–1261.

Neuman, S. B., & Celano, D. (2001). Access to print in low-income and middle-income communities: An ecological study of four neighborhoods. *Reading Research Quarterly, 36,* 8–26.

Newacheck, P. W., Hughes, D. C., & Stoddard, J. J. (1996). Children's access to primary care: Differences by race, income, and insurance status. *Pediatrics, 97,* 26–32.

Newacheck, P. W., Stoddard, J. J., & McManus, M. (1993). Ethnocultural variations in the prevalence and impact of childhood chronic conditions. *Pediatrics, 91,* 1031–1038.

Newman, K. S. (1999). *No shame in my game: The working poor in the inner city.* New York: Knopf and Russell Sage Foundation.

Obeidallah, D., Brennan, R. T., Brooks-Gunn, J., & Earls, F. (2004). Links between pubertal timing and neighborhood contexts: Implications for girls' violent behavior. *Journal of the American Academy of Child and Adolescent Psychiatry, 43,* 1460–1468.

Oreopoulos, P. (2003). The long-run consequences of living in a poor neighborhood. *The Quarterly Journal of Economics, 118,* 1533–1575.

Paikoff, R., & Brooks-Gunn, J. (1991). Do parent-child relationships change during puberty? *Psychological Bulletin, 110,* 47–66.

Park, R. (1916). Suggestions for the investigations of human behavior in the urban environment. *American Journal of Sociology, 20,* 577–612.

Paschall, M. J., & Hubbard, M. L. (1998). Effects of neighborhood and family stressors on African-American male adolescents' self-worth and propensity for violent behavior. *Journal of Consulting and Clinical Psychology, 66,* 825–831.

Pattillo, M. E. (1998). Sweet mothers and gangbangers: Managing crime in a black middle-class neighborhood. *Social Forces, 76,* 747–774.

Peeples, F., & Loeber, R. (1994). Do individual and neighborhood context explain ethnic differences in juvenile delinquency? *Journal of Quantitative Criminology, 10,* 141–157.

Pettit, G. S., Bates, J. E., Dodge, K. A., & Meece, D. W. (1999). The impact of after-school peer contact on early adolescent external- izing problems is moderated by parental monitoring, perceived neighborhood safety, and prior adjustment. *Child Development, 70,* 768–778.

Plotnick, R. D., & Hoffman, S. D. (1999). The effect of neighborhood characteristics on young adult outcomes: Alternative estimates. *Social Science Quarterly, 80,* 1–18.

Portes, A., & Rumbaut, R. G. (1996). *Immigrant America: A portrait* (2nd ed.). Berkeley: University of California Press.

Pribesh, S., & Downey, D. B. (1999). Why are residential and school moves associated with poor school performance? *Demography, 36,* 521–534.

Quane, J. M., & Rankin, B. H. (1998). Neighborhood poverty, family characteristics, and commitment to mainstream goals: The case of African American adolescents in the inner city. *Journal of Family Issues, 19,* 769–794.

Quane, J. M., & Rankin, B. H. (2006). Does it pay to participate? Neighborhood-based organizations and the social development of urban adolescents. *Children and Youth Services Review, 28,* 1229–1250.

Ramirez-Valles, J., Zimmerman, M. A., & Juarez, L. (2002). Gender differences of neighborhood and social control process: A study of the timing of first intercourse among low-achieving, urban, African American youth. *Youth and Society, 33,* 418–441.

Ramirez-Valles, J., Zimmerman, M. A., & Newcomb, M. (1998). Sexual risk behavior among youth: Modeling the influence of prosocial activities and socioeconomic factors. *Journal of Health and Social Behavior, 39,* 237–253.

Rankin, B. H., & Quane, J. M. (2002). Social contexts and urban adolescent outcomes: The interrelated effects of neighbor- hoods, families, and peers on African-American youth. *Social Problems, 49,* 79–100.

Raudenbush, S. W. (1993). A crossed random effects model for unbalanced data with applications in cross-sectional and longitu- dinal research. *Journal of Educational Statistics, 18,* 321–349.

Raudenbush, S. W., & Sampson, R. J. (1999). Ecometrics: Toward a science of assessing ecological settings, with application to the systematical observation of neighborhoods. *Sociological Methodology, 29,* 1–41.

Richters, J. E., & Martinez, P. (1993). The NIMH Community Violence Project: I. Children as victims of and witnesses to vio- lence. *Psychiatry, 56,* 7–21.

Roche, K. M., Ensminger, M. E., & Cherlin, A. J. (2007). Variations in parenting and adolescent outcomes among African American and Latino families living in low-income, urban areas. *Journal of Family Issues, 28,* 882–909.

Roche, K. M., Mekos, D., Alexander, C. S., Astone, N. M., Bandeen- Roche, K., & Ensminger, M. E. (2005). Parenting influences on early sex initiation among adolescents: How neighborhood matters. *Journal of Family Issues, 26,* 32–54.

Rosenbaum, J. E., Popkin, S. J., Kaufman, J. E., & Rusin, J. (1991). Social integration of low-income black adults in middle-class white suburbs. *Social Problems, 38,* 448–461.

Ross, C. E. (2000). Neighborhood disadvantage and adult depression. *Journal of Health and Social Behavior, 41,* 177–187.

Ross, C. E., & Jang, S. J. (2000). Neighborhood disorder, fear, and mistrust: The buffering role of social ties with neighbors. *American Journal of Community Psychology, 28,* 401–420.

Rubinowitz, L. S., & Rosenbaum, J. E. (2000). *Crossing the class and color lines: From public housing to White suburbia.* Chicago: University of Chicago Press.

Sampson, R. J. (1992). Family management and child development: Insights from social disorganization theory. In J. McCord (Ed.), *Facts, frameworks, and forecasts: Advances in criminological theory, vol. 3* (pp. 63–93). New Brunswick, NJ: Transaction Books.

Sampson, R. J. (1997). Collective regulation of adolescent misbe- havior: Validation results from eighty Chicago neighborhoods. *Journal of Adolescent Research, 12,* 227–244.

Sampson, R. J. (1999). What 'community' supplies. In R. F. Ferguson & W. T. Dickens (Eds.), *Urban problems and commu- nity development* (pp. 241–292). Washington, DC: Brookings Institution Press.

Sampson, R. J., & Groves, W. B. (1989). Community structure and crime: Testing social-disorganization theory. *American Journal of Sociology, 94,* 774–780.

Sampson, R. J., & Morenoff, J. D. (1997). Ecological perspec- tives on the neighborhood context of urban poverty: Past and present. In J. Brooks-Gunn, G. J. Duncan, & J. L. Aber (Eds.), *Neighborhood poverty. Policy implications in study- ing neighborhoods, vol. 2* (pp. 1–22). New York: Russell Sage Foundation.

Sampson, R. J., Morenoff, J. D., & Earls, F. (1999). Beyond social capital: Spatial dynamics of collective efficacy for children. *American Sociological Review, 64,* 633–660.

Sampson, R. J., Morenoff, J. D., & Gannon-Rowley, T. (2002). Assessing "neighborhood effects": Social processes and new directions in research. *Annual Review of Sociology, 28,* 442–478.

Sampson, R. J., Morenoff, J. D., & Raudenbush, S. (2005). Social anatomy of racial and ethnic disparities in violence. *American Journal of Public Health, 95,* 224–236.

Sampson, R. J., & Raudenbush, S. W. (1999). Systematic social observation of public spaces: A new look at disorder in urban neighborhoods. *American Journal of Sociology, 105,* 603–651.

Sampson, R. J., & Raudenbush, S. W. (2004). Seeing disorder: Neighborhood stigma and the social construction of "Broken Windows." *Social Psychology Quarterly, 67,* 319.

Sampson, R. J., Raudenbush, S. W., & Earls, F. (1997). Neighborhoods and violent crime: A multilevel study of collective efficacy. *Science, 277,* 918–924.

Sampson, R. J., & Sharkey, P. (2008). Neighborhood selection and the social reproduction of concentrated racial inequality. *Demography, 45,* 1–29.

Sanbonmatsu, L., Kling, J. R., Duncan, G. J., & Brooks-Gunn, J. (2006). Neighborhoods and academic achievement: Results from the Moving to Opportunity experiment. *Journal of Human Resources, 41,* 649–691.

Shaw, C., & McKay, H. (1942). *Juvenile delinquency and urban areas.* Chicago: Chicago University Press.

Simons, R. L., Johnson, C., Beaman, J., Conger, R. D., & Whitbeck, L. B. (1996). Parents and peer group as mediators of the effect of community structure on adolescent problem behavior. *American Journal of Community Psychology, 24,* 145–171.

Simons, R. L., Lin, K. H., Gordon, L. C., Brody, G. H., Murry, V., & Conger, R. D. (2002). Community differences in the association between parenting practices and child conduct problems. *Journal of Marriage and the Family, 64,* 331–345.

Simons, R. L., Simons, L. G., Burt, C. H., Brody, G. H., & Cutrona, C. (2005). Collective efficacy, authoritative parenting and delinquency: A longitudinal test of a model integrating community- and family-level processes. *Criminology, 43,* 989–1029.

Soubhi, H., Raina, P., & Kohen, D. (2004). Neighborhood, family and child predictors of childhood injury in Canada. *American Journal of Health Behavior, 28,* 397–409.

South, S. J., & Baumer, E. P. (2000). Deciphering community and race effects on adolescent premarital childbearing. *Social Forces, 78,* 1379–1408.

South, S. J., & Baumer, E. P. (2001). Community effects on the resolution of adolescent premarital pregnancy. *Journal of Family Issues, 22,* 1025–1043.

South, S. J., & Crowder, K. D. (1999). Neighborhood effects on family formation: Concentrated poverty and beyond. *American Sociological Review, 64,* 113–132.

Spencer, M. B., McDermott, P. A., Burton, L. M., & Kochman, T. J. (1997). An alternative approach to assessing neighborhood effects on early adolescent achievement and problem behavior. In J. Brooks-Gunn, G. J. Duncan, & J. L. Aber (Eds.), *Neighborhood poverty, vol. 2: Policy implications in studying neighborhoods* (pp. 145–163). New York: Russell Sage Foundation.

Steinberg, L., Fegley, S., & Dornbusch, S. M. (1993). Negative impact of part-time work on adolescent adjustment: Evidence from a longitudinal study. *Developmental Psychology, 29,* 171–180.

Steinberg, L., & Morris, A. S. (2001). Adolescent development. *Annual Review of Psychology, 52,* 83–110.

Stiffman, A. R., Hadley-Ives, E., Elze, D., Johnson, S., & Doré, P. (1999). Impact of environment on adolescent mental health and behavior: Structural equation modeling. *American Journal of Orthopsychiatry, 69,* 73–86.

Sullivan, M. L. (1989). *Getting paid: Youth crime and work in the inner city.* Ithaca, NY: Cornell University Press.

Taylor, R. B., Gottfredson, S., & Brower, S. (1984). Block crime and fear: Defensible space, local social ties, and territorial functioning. *Journal of Research in Crime and Delinquency, 21,* 303–331.

Taylor, R. D. (2000). An examination of the association of African American mothers' perceptions of their neighborhoods with their parenting and adolescent adjustment. *Journal of Black Psychology, 26,* 267–287.

Teitler, J. O., & Weiss, C. C. (2000). Effects of neighborhood and school environments on transitions to first sexual intercourse. *Sociology of Education, 73,* 112–132.

Tienda, M. (1991). Poor people and poor places: Deciphering neighborhood effects on poverty outcomes. In J. Huber (Ed.), *Macro-micro linkages in sociology* (pp. 244–262). Newbury Park, CA: Sage.

Tolan, P. H., Gorman-Smith, D., & Henry, D. B. (2003). The developmental ecology of urban males' youth violence. *Developmental Psychology, 39,* 274–291.

Upchurch, D. M., Aneshensel, C. S., Sucoff, C. A., & Levy-Storms, L. (1999). Neighborhood and family contexts of adolescent sexual activity. *Journal of Marriage and the Family, 61,* 920.

Vazsonyi, A. T., Cleveland, H. H., & Wiebe, R. P. (2006). Does the effect of impulsivity on delinquency vary by level of neighborhood disadvantage? *Criminal Justice and Behavior, 33,* 511–541.

Veysey, B. M., & Messner, S. F. (1999). Further testing of social disorganization theory: An elaboration of Sampson and Groves's "community structure and crime." *Journal of Research in Crime and Delinquency, 36,* 156–174.

Waanders, C., Mendez, J. L., & Downer, J. T. (2007). Parent characteristics, economic stress and neighborhood context as predictors of parent involvement in preschool children's education. *Journal of School Psychology, 45,* 619–636.

Wheaton, B., & Clarke, P. (2003). Space meets time: Integrating temporal and contextual influences on mental health in early adulthood. *American Sociological Review, 68,* 680–706.

Wickrama, K. A. S., & Bryant, C. (2003). Community context of social resources and adolescent mental health. *Journal of Marriage and Family, 65,* 850–866.

Wickrama, K. A. S., Merten, M. J., & Elder, G. H., Jr. (2005). Community influence on precocious transitions to adulthood: Racial differences and mental health consequences. *Journal of Community Psychology, 33,* 639–653.

Willis, P. (1977). *Learning to labor: How working-class kids get working-class jobs.* New York: Columbia.

Wilson, W. J. (1987). *The truly disadvantaged: The inner city, the underclass, and public policy.* Chicago: University of Chicago Press.

Wilson, W. J. (1991, February). Studying inner-city social dislocations: The challenge of public agenda research. *American Sociological Review, 56,* 1–14.

Wilson, W. J. (1996). *When work disappears: The world of the new urban poor.* New York: Vintage Books.

Wright, R. J. (1998). Exposure to violence. from www.macses.usf.edu/Research/Psychosocial/notebook/violence.html.

Wright, R. J., & Fisher, E. B. (2003). Putting asthma into context: Community influences on risk, behavior, and intervention. In I. Kawachi & L. F. Berkman (Eds.), *Neighborhoods and health* (pp. 233–264). New York: Oxford University Press.

Xue, Y., Zimmerman, M. A., & Howard Caldwell, C. (2007). Neighborhood residence and cigarette smoking among urban youth: The protective role of prosocial activities. *American Journal of Public Health, 97,* 1865–1872.

CHAPTER 13

Poverty and Socioeconomic Disadvantage in Adolescence

VONNIE C. McLOYD, RACHEL KAPLAN, KELLY M. PURTELL, ERIKA BAGLEY,
CECILY R. HARDAWAY, AND CIARA SMALLS

The 1990s witnessed an outpouring of research linking poverty and economic stress to child and adolescent functioning, precipitated in part by the sharp rise in childhood (birth to 17 years of age) poverty during the early 1980s and persistently high rates of childhood poverty through the late 1990s. Taken as a whole, research published in the past two decades about poverty, economic stress, and child development differs in critical ways from the equally abundant research published during the 1960s and early 1970s about the development of poor children. The recent generation of research is distinguished by its rigorous differentiation of income poverty from low socioeconomic status (SES), more precise measurement of degrees of income poverty and affluence as reflected in the widespread use of income-need ratios, direct tests of the processes through which poverty has its effects, and assessments of the contexts of poverty (McLoyd, 1998).

Moreover, rather than conceptualizing economic disadvantage as a static phenomenon, contemporary scholars have focused on the dynamics of childhood poverty, raising questions, for example, about the consequences of the duration of poverty for development. This shift in focus was prompted in large measure by evidence from national survey research published in the 1980s documenting the volatility of income in American families (Duncan, 1984). Finally, whereas much of the early research posited cultural deprivation

as a major factor underlying differences in the behavior and competencies of poor and nonpoor children and their parents, poverty research conducted during the past 2 decades has emphasized ecological influences at the home, school, and community levels and their links to social structural forces as explanatory variables (McLoyd, Aikens, & Burton, 2006).

These fresh perspectives, in combination with sophisticated research designs, yielded a trove of new and important insights. We learned, for example, that (1) most children who are poor are only temporarily poor, (2) persistent poverty compromises children's cognitive and psychosocial functioning to a much greater degree than does transitory or occasional poverty, (3) ethnic disparities in persistent poverty are much larger than ethnic disparities in poverty at single points in time, and (4) African American children who are poor are much more likely than European American children who are poor to live in poor neighborhoods (Bolger, Patterson, & Thompson, 1995; Duncan, 1991; Duncan & Brooks-Gunn, 1997; Duncan, Brooks-Gunn, & Klebanov, 1994; Duncan & Rodgers, 1988; McLeod & Shanahan, 1996).

A large proportion of the research on poverty, socioeconomic disadvantage, and child functioning published during and subsequent to the 1990s, especially studies concerned with cognitive functioning and school achievement, focused on children in early and middle

444

childhood. This pattern reflects, in part, the venerable and widespread belief in the primacy of early experience (Smith, Brooks-Gunn, & Klebanov, 1997; Zigler & Berman, 1983). A major cornerstone of Head Start (Zigler & Berman, 1983), this notion was popularized during the 1960s by Bloom's (1964) influential treatise in which he argued that the effects of the environment on intelligence and other human characteristics are greatest during the early and most rapid periods of development of the characteristics and that intervention should occur as early in life as possible to ameliorate the effects of environmental deprivation.

Another factor that likely promoted greater attention to poverty during early and middle childhood than during adolescence is the higher rates of poverty among young children as compared to adolescents. Adolescents are at lower risk of being poor than are children under 6 years of age, largely because their parents are older and command higher wages as a result of more work experience (Fass & Cauthen, 2007). For example, in 2006, 15% of 12- to 17-year-olds lived in families with income below the poverty threshold, as compared to 20% of children under age 6. A similar age disparity is evident when the income threshold is set at twice the federal poverty level, viewed by many as a better approximation of the average minimum income families need to make ends meet. Families with incomes below this level are considered "low-income." In 2006, 35% of 12- to 17-year-olds lived in low-income families, as compared to about 43% of children under age 6 (Douglas-Hall & Chau, 2007).

Although the recent generation of poverty-related research has given comparatively less attention to adolescents, as compared to children in early and middle childhood, we have learned a great deal from this work about the association of poverty and socioeconomic disadvantage with adolescent functioning and about factors that mediate and moderate these links. This chapter presents a selective review

and analysis of this research, encompassing studies that focus on *poverty* and *low-income status* (as defined by income-to-need ratios), *economic loss* (i.e., adverse changes in family economic circumstances), and *low SES*.

The distinct, but overlapping nature of these socioeconomic constructs has been discussed extensively elsewhere (McLoyd, 1998). Suffice it to say that poverty is not a unitary variable or distinct event. Rather, it is a conglomerate of stressful conditions and events, many of which are outside personal control, especially if the poverty is chronic. Individuals who are poor are confronted with an unremitting succession of negative life events (e.g., eviction, physical illness, criminal assault) in the context of adverse life conditions such as inadequate housing and dangerous neighborhoods that together increase the exigencies of day-to-day existence. In addition, they are exposed to a daunting array of aversive physical conditions (e.g., proximity to toxic waste dumps, elevated levels of exposure to lead, pesticides, ambient air pollution, radon, etc.) (Evans, 2004). Because of limited financial resources, negative life events often precipitate additional crises. Problems in one domain can exacerbate or create problems in another domain. Because of this high contagion of stressors, chronic poverty is a pervasive, rather than bounded, crisis. It restricts choices in virtually all domains of life (e.g., choice of neighborhood, school, educational and recreational activities) and renders the person more subject to control by others (DuBois, Felner, Meares, & Krier, 1994; Makosky, 1982; McLoyd, 1990).

The stressors associated with living in chronic poverty are more extensive than those resulting from economic loss, that is, adverse changes in economic circumstances such as a reduction in wages, being fired or laid off, or suffering a financial loss in business. Economic loss does not necessarily push families into poverty, but it can result in economic circumstances and related stressors similar to those that chronically poor families experience, including low per capita income, unmet material needs (e.g., adequate housing, clothing, food, medical care), and difficulty paying bills (Conger et al., 2002; Elder, 1974). Low SES, although associated with economic deprivation, is distinct from poverty, low-income status, and economic loss in that it signifies an individual's, family's, or group's low ranking in a hierarchy based on access to or control over some combination of valued commodities such as wealth, power, and social status. It is a multidimensional concept, and when applied to families, is typically denoted by low family income, low levels of parental education, and low parental occupational status (McLoyd, 1998). Throughout the chapter, we attempt to maintain distinctions among poverty, low-income status, economic loss, and low SES, using the term that most closely approximates the indicator employed in the particular investigation. For ease of discussion, however, we use the term *socioeconomic disadvantage* when referring to poverty, low-income status, economic loss, and low SES in a collective sense.

The chapter consists of seven major sections. It begins with a discussion of changes that occur as children move from childhood into and through adolescence and how these development-related changes potentially modify the meaning and influence of socioeconomic disadvantage. We then turn our attention to linkages between socioeconomic disadvantage and four major domains of adolescent functioning—mental health, educational achievement, future orientation, and delinquency. Each of these domains is discussed separately, although we note similarities across domains in mediating and moderating processes. In the sixth section of the chapter, we examine the antecedents and correlates of a unique experience that bridges between the institutional realms of education and work, namely adolescent employment. Although adolescent employment is not a domain of functioning in the traditional sense, its antecedents and correlates among adolescents who are socioeconomically

disadvantaged cut across multiple domains of functioning. To the extent that relevant research permits, we consider multilevel influences (e.g., parents, peers, neighborhoods, schools) on each of the five outcomes. We end the chapter with a discussion of major gaps in our knowledge about linkages between socioeconomic disadvantage and adolescent development and suggestions for future research.

Throughout the chapter, we highlight what little is known about processes that contribute to resilience among adolescents from socioeconomically disadvantaged backgrounds. There is a dearth of research about contributors to positive adaptation in the context of socioeconomic disadvantage. This limitation, combined with the disproportionate attention paid to problem behaviors among adolescents generally, has prompted calls for more holistic representations of adolescent development and more work focusing on competence among economically diverse adolescents (Mahoney & Bergman, 2002; Seidman & Pedersen, 2003). The past decade witnessed burgeoning interest in positive youth development as a framework for understanding how both economically disadvantaged and affluent adolescents develop in healthy ways and for delineating the kinds of supports and opportunities adolescents need to successfully transition to healthy and productive adulthood. Guided by the notion that "problem-free is not fully prepared" (Pittman, Irby, & Ferber, 2001), this perspective moves beyond the focus on reduction and prevention of risk and expands the concept of adolescent health to include "the skills, prosocial behaviors, and competencies needed to succeed in employment, education, and civic life" (Benson, Mannes, Pittman, & Ferber, 2004, p. 783). Despite strong scholarly interest in understanding positive youth development and finding ways to promote it, empirical work on these issues specifically in relation to youth who are poor or from low SES backgrounds is very sparse (Lerner, Almerigi, Theokas, & Lerner, 2005; Roth, Murray, Brooks-Gunn, & Foster, 1999).

SITUATING SOCIOECONOMIC DISADVANTAGE WITHIN THE CONTEXT OF ADOLESCENT DEVELOPMENT: A LIFE COURSE PERSPECTIVE

Questions about whether the effects of socio-economic disadvantage depend on the developmental period during which socioeconomic disadvantage is experienced go to the heart of developmental issues, and hence, provide an important backdrop for the contents of this chapter. Life-course theory and event-history models provide conceptual tools especially useful for framing these issues. These models view causal processes as time-variant and prompt questions such as (1) "Is a spell of poverty or economic hardship that occurs in early life more damaging than one that occurs during adolescence?" (2) "What factors mediate and moderate the effects of poverty and economic hardship on development?" and (3) "Do causal processes and moderating influences differ as a function of the child's developmental status (e.g., childhood versus adolescence)?" (Elder, 1997). A rich body of research exists about (2), but remarkably few studies have assessed the comparative effects of economic disadvantage during childhood versus economic disadvantage during adolescence or investigated whether mediating and moderating influences vary across different developmental periods. This is likely a consequence of the methodological complexities involved in adequately addressing these issues and the tendency of scholars in child development to focus their research efforts within, rather than across, developmental periods.

In the remainder of this section, we discuss changes that occur as children move from childhood into and through adolescence and how these changes potentially modify the meaning and consequences of socioeconomic disadvantage, pathways of influence, and the extent to which particular factors mitigate risks associated with socioeconomic disadvantage. We also highlight findings from the few studies that directly investigate the comparative effects of poverty during adolescence versus poverty during the years prior to adolescence. In the case of persistent poverty that encompasses early and middle childhood as well as adolescence, the critical question is whether poverty during adolescence exerts unique effects on development or whether links between adolescent functioning and poverty during adolescence, if found, are due solely to developmental continuities resulting from poverty experienced prior to adolescence. Although existing research is insufficient to draw firm conclusions, this question merits careful attention because of its relevance for theory (e.g., notions about early critical periods) and social policy.

Changes in Psychological Characteristics, Contexts, and Time Use

As children move from childhood into and through adolescence, myriad psychological and social changes occur that likely have implications for how family- and neighborhood-level socioeconomic disadvantage influence adjustment. These changes argue against facile extrapolation of findings across different developmental periods. Early childhood, middle childhood, and adolescence are distinct developmental periods across which the meaning and consequences of socioeconomic disadvantage, pathways of influence, and moderating influences may change. Moreover, some outcomes linked to socioeconomic disadvantage arguably are of greater consequence during adolescence than earlier developmental periods. For example, future orientation during adolescence (Bigler, Averhart, & Liben, 2003; Cook et al., 1996; Flanagan, 1990; MacLeod, 1987) in all likelihood is more consequential than it is during childhood because of the planning and decision making that occur during adolescence that ultimately can alter an individual's life course (Nurmi, 1991; Trommsdorff, 1986).

Adolescence marks growth in abstract thought, cognitive processing skills, social perspective-taking abilities, and the ability to integrate one's own experiences and the experiences of others. This means, among other things, that children's awareness of their socioeconomic disadvantage is greater during adolescence than childhood and, hence, that their own sense of financial strain is probably more important in linking objective poverty to psychosocial adjustment during adolescence than during childhood (McLoyd, Jayaratne, Ceballo, & Borquet, 1994; Wadsworth & Compas, 2002). Moreover, cognitive growth during adolescence undoubtedly results in increased awareness of the social meaning of being disadvantaged socioeconomically—a development that often prompts efforts to mask one's disadvantage. A prosaic, yet poignant example is displayed during lunch periods in schools across the country. Unlike elementary school children, middle-school children have an aversion to subsidized lunches provided in schools because they comprehend the stigma attached to this subsidy. Because of this increased awareness, combined with heightened sensitivity to peer evaluations during adolescence, the percentage of eligible students who take advantage of federally subsidized meal programs in schools plummets when children reach middle school. Many middle school students who are poor, if they do not bring lunches from home, decide to go hungry rather than be seen with a subsidized meal. As one student said, lunchtime "is the best time to impress your peers" and being seen with a subsidized meal "lowers your status" (Pogash, 2008, p. 1).

Other changes that occur as children navigate adolescence are growing needs for autonomy and differentiation and increased exposure to diverse social contexts (e.g., increased contact with extrafamilial persons and societal agents, greater geographic mobility) (McKown, 2004; Quintana, 1998; Simons et al., 2002; Steinberg & Silk, 2002). Compared to preadolescent children, adolescents spend less time at home, fewer of their waking hours with family members, and more time with opposite sex peers (Larson & Verma, 1999). These developmental shifts and

changes in ecology can forge realignments of various kinds. For example, they may modify the effects of parenting in high crime, poor neighborhoods. Evidence exists that the protective effect of restrictive parenting in impoverished neighborhoods on children's academic performance found during early and middle childhood wanes as children progress through adolescence—likely a function of increasing needs for autonomy (Dearing, 2004; Gutman, Friedel, & Hitt, 2003). The consequences of living in a poor neighborhood on children's experiences and development may also differ depending on developmental stage. As Bradley and Corwyn (2002) point out, for preschool children who are poor, living in an economically depressed, deteriorated neighborhood may mean less access to stimulating resources and well-appointed recreational facilities, whereas for adolescents who are poor, the same neighborhood may mean increased exposure to deviant peers.

Employment is another stage-dependent experience that has implications for how poverty and socioeconomic disadvantage influence children's adjustment. Entry into part-time paid employment typically occurs during mid- to late adolescence, with most adolescents in the United States working at some point during high school (Larson & Verma, 1999; Mortimer, 2003; Steinberg & Cauffman, 1995). This experience may lessen the psychological costs of economic hardship for adolescents, as compared to younger children, in part, by decreasing time spent at home, and hence, reducing exposure to punitive, inconsistent parenting brought on by economic stress. Elder, Foster, and Ardelt's (1984) pioneering studies of families of the Great Depression found evidence of this age effect, accounted for in part, by the older boys' employment experiences.

Poverty and Low Income During Adolescence: Unique Effects or Continuity of Effects?

Duncan and colleagues (Duncan & Brooks-Gunn, 1997; Duncan, Yeung, Brooks-Gunn, &

Smith, 1998) found evidence pointing to the preschool years as a period of heightened vulnerability to the negative impact of poverty and low income on cognitive functioning and school achievement. A major source of the evidence for this conclusion is the replication analyses that Duncan and Brooks-Gunn (1997) coordinated across a diverse set of child development studies. Collating the findings in relation to effect sizes and the developmental stage in which income was measured, they found that poverty and low-income status during early and middle childhood had much stronger links to cognitive ability and school achievement than did poverty and low-income status during adolescence.

Guo (1998) raised several important caveats about these analyses, however. Duncan and Brooks-Gunn's estimates of income effects on early cognitive outcomes are based on numerous measures from a variety of samples, whereas income effects on cognitive outcomes during adolescence are based on fewer measures from fewer samples. Moreover, the estimates are not based on the same set of children across developmental periods. That is, income effects on early outcomes are estimated from one set of children, whereas income effects on later outcomes are estimated from another set of children. Hence, as Guo points out, the observed differences between the two sets of children may not be due to differences in timing alone, but to other differences between the two groups.

Duncan and colleagues (Duncan & Brooks-Gunn, 1997; Duncan et al., 1998) speculated that the timing of poverty effect may reflect the influence of school readiness, and in turn, teachers' affective responses and expectancies, both of which predict later school achievement (Alexander et al., 1987; Brooks-Gunn, Guo, & Furstenberg, 1993; Rist, 1970). Their findings and interpretations are consistent with the school of thought emphasizing early childhood as a critical period when the child must be exposed to certain growth-enhancing experiences (e.g., cognitively stimulating

home environment), without which lasting damage will be done to the child's cognitive development. However, there is a competing school of thought—of special relevance to adolescence—emphasizing environmental influences on learning that become more important to an older child's educational and cognitive outcomes because of their increased understanding of the broader world around them. For example, the latter may result in disillusionment about the real worth of education, internalization of negative stereotypes about the poor, and a fuller understanding of societal messages that he or she receives from an impoverished environment, all of which can undermine academic effort. This school of thought argues that persistent poverty that continues into adolescence will continue to have a strong and unique effect on older children's educational and cognitive outcomes, but for reasons more related to motivational and opportunity factors than cognitive ability (Guo, 1998).

Addressing this issue adequately requires a longitudinal research design in which the *same* sets of children are measured repeatedly throughout childhood and adolescence, in terms of both their functioning and family income. Guo satisfied these criteria, using data from the National Longitudinal Study of Youth. Absent of such a design, it is not possible to determine, among other things, if living in poverty during adolescence has unique effects on a particular outcome over and above the effects of living in poverty during earlier developmental periods. It is conceivable that an association between poverty and school achievement among adolescents who have been poor since birth is due solely to developmental continuities resulting from poverty experienced during early childhood.

Guo distinguished between *cognitive ability* and *school achievement*, arguing that the school of thought that emphasizes early childhood as a critical period is speaking more to the question of ability. In contrast, the second school of thought is speaking more to the question of school achievement, an outcome influenced by not only ability, but motivation and opportunity as well. Guo predicted that poverty experienced in childhood would be more damaging to cognitive ability (as measured by the Picture Peabody Vocabulary Test, Digit Span subscale of the Wechsler Intelligence Scale for Children) than poverty experienced in early adolescence, whereas poverty experienced in early adolescence would have a larger impact on achievement (as measured by the Peabody Individual Achievement Test) than poverty experienced in childhood. Guo found that long-term poverty had substantial influences on both ability and achievement as measured in childhood (5th–8th year of life) and early adolescence (11th–14th year of life), but the time patterns of these influences were distinctly different. As he predicted, poverty cumulated during childhood (birth to the 5th–8th year of life) had a much stronger link to cognitive ability than poverty experienced in early adolescence or poverty cumulated from birth to early adolescence, a pattern suggesting that poverty experienced after early to mid-childhood does not have an additional adverse influence on cognitive ability. In contrast and consistent with Guo's prediction, poverty experienced in early adolescence was more strongly associated with achievement than poverty experienced during childhood. Guo's research illustrates the kind of conceptual analyses and empirical investigations needed to advance our understanding of the consequences of the timing of poverty and socioeconomic disadvantage. In the next four sections of the chapter, we give focused attention to the current state of knowledge about links between socioeconomic disadvantages and domain of adolescent functioning.

MENTAL HEALTH

Numerous studies conducted by researchers in public health, psychology, and sociology have found that children in early, mid-, and late adolescence who are "officially poor," from low SES backgrounds, receive federally mandated free or reduced price school, and/or experience economic strain (e.g., not enough money to pay bills, purchase preferred foods and clothing), are at an increased risk of mental health problems (e.g., depressive symptomatology, hostility, difficulties in peer relations, low self-esteem, drug use) than are more socioeconomically advantaged counterparts (Bolger, Patterson, & Thompson, 1995; Brooks-Gunn & Furstenberg, 1989; Currie & Lin, 2007; Elder, Nguyen, & Caspi, 1985; Goodman, 1999; Goosby, 2007; Strohschein, 2005; Wadsworth, Ravir, Compas, & Connor-Smith, 2005). Moreover, studies indicate that longer duration of poverty is positively associated with increased peer difficulties, externalizing problems, social withdrawal, depressive symptoms, and anxiety in early adolescence (Bolger et al., 1995; Goosby, 2007).

Direct associations between economic disadvantage (e.g., low income-to-need ratio, economic strain) and adolescent mental health are most commonly found when mothers, teachers, clinicians, and peers are informants about the adolescent's adjustment. However, when adolescents report on their own mental health, usually only indirect associations, mediated though the actions of parents, are found (e.g., Conger, Conger, & Elder 1997; McLoyd et al., 1994; Conger et al., 1994). Reliance on maternal reports of adolescents' psychological adjustment is problematic because mothers' mental health may influence how they perceive their children. Hence, associations between family economic disadvantage and maternal reports of adolescents' psychological adjustment may be inflated, reflecting to some degree associations between economic disadvantage and mothers' psychological distress (Conger et al., 1997). In the sections that follow, we discuss conceptual frameworks that have been used to account for these links. These frameworks center around either concepts of stress or social evaluation processes.

Stress Models

Scholars have proposed several models to explain the relationship between socioeconomic disadvantage and adolescent mental health.

Because of the myriad stressors attendant to low-income status and poverty discussed at the beginning of this chapter, it is not surprising that stress is a salient construct in models linking disadvantage and adolescent mental health. These models differ in their sensitivity to developmental issues. Some focus on or accommodate processes unique to adolescence as a developmental period. Others are largely nondevelopmental, presuming that the child's developmental status does not moderate or complicate the hypothesized processes. In addition, the models differ in terms of whether they focus on specific mental health diagnoses or adjustment problems thought to be precursors to mental health disorders.

Family Stress Model

The family stress model is one of the most widely examined explanations for the association between family economic disadvantage and mental health outcomes in children and adolescents. The core assumption of this model is that economic hardship adversely affects children's psychological adjustment indirectly through its impact on the parent's behavior toward the child. This model derives from Elder's seminal studies of the effects of parental job and income loss on European American families during the Great Depression (Elder, 1974; Elder, et al., 1985). In these studies, Elder and colleagues found few direct effects of economic hardship on children's behavior and psychological functioning. Rather, the adverse effect of economic hardship was produced indirectly, through negative effects on fathers' psychological functioning and parenting behaviors. Fathers who sustained heavy financial loss became more irritable, tense, and explosive, which increased their tendency to be punitive, rejecting, and inconsistent in disciplining their children. In turn, these negative fathering behaviors were predictive of several emotional difficulties in children.

Studies of contemporary families have generated robust support for this model. These studies document associations between economic stress and psychological distress in parents (e.g., more depressive symptoms, lower sense of mastery). Moreover, they demonstrate that parental psychological distress and family processes such as spousal relations, parenting behaviors, and parent–child relations mediate the relation between economic hardship and psychosocial outcomes such as internalizing and externalizing behavior in early adolescents and preadolescents and that these relations generally hold across ethnicity, socioeconomic background, and geographic context (i.e., rural, urban) (e.g., Bolger et al., 1995; Brody, Stoneman, Flor, McCrary, Hastings, & Conyers, 1994; Conger, Conger, Elder, et al., 1992; Conger, Ge, et al., 1994; Conger, et al., 2002; Goosby, 2007; Gutman, McLoyd, & Tokoyawa, 2005; McLoyd et al., 1994; Mistry, Vandewater, Huston, McLoyd, 2002; Taylor, Rodriquez, Seaton, & Dominguez, 2004). Researchers have not produced and tested variants of this model that accommodate different developmental periods (e.g., increased influence of peers during adolescence, adolescent employment). This is surprising, in part, because Elder's research focusing on families during the Depression, which gave rise to the family stress model, reflected a strong developmental perspective.

In Elder's study, economic loss adversely affected the psychosocial adjustment of boys who were one year old or less at the beginning of the Depression. Severe income loss increased the frequency of temper tantrums and the tendency toward quarrelsome, negativistic, and explosive behavior 5–10 years later, mediated through the father's increasingly arbitrary and harsh discipline. In contrast, economic loss did not compromise the psychosocial adjustment of boys who were 8–9 years old at the beginning of the Depression. Rather, as these boys progressed through adolescence and the Depression lingered, they showed a pattern of resilience and ego strength. Older boys were less vulnerable than younger boys partly because many found employment outside the home and consequently were less exposed to marital conflict and fathers' harsh, inconsistent discipline. Their exposure to economic hardship was also shorter in duration than was the case for young boys and their more advanced cognitive skills protected them from feelings of self-blame. Unlike boys, girls were more vulnerable to the indirect effects of economic loss if it occurred later, rather than earlier in their lives, in part, because, unlike adolescent boys, few adolescent girls in the older cohort found employment outside the home, in part because mothers provided their young daughters with exceptionally high levels of support in the face of fathers' harsh, arbitrary discipline (Elder, 1974; Elder et al., 1985).

An important addition to research in this area is examination of adolescents' coping responses as mediators and moderators of the link between economic stress and mental health, a line of work that complements studies of the association between coping responses and psychosocial adjustment in low-income adolescents (e.g., Tolan, Gorman-Smith, Henry, Chung, & Hunt, 2002). Conceptualizing coping as a mediator assumes that coping is affected by stressful conditions, such that stress determines which strategies are enacted. Use of those strategies, in turn, presumably accounts for the link between stress and mental health (Wadsworth & Compas, 2002; Wadsworth, 2005). Wadsworth et al. (2005) found that secondary control coping (e.g., acceptance, cognitive restructuring, distraction, positive thinking) and involuntary engagement (e.g., emotional and physiological arousal, rumination, intrusive thought, impulsive action) mediated the association between adolescent-reported economic strain and both internalizing and externalizing behavior in adolescents.

None of the six coping responses they investigated moderated the relation between economic strain and psychosocial adjustment in adolescents (Wadsworth & Compas, 2002; Wadsworth et al., 2005). However, among parents of these adolescents, coping responses

influenced the strength of the association between parent-reported economic strain and depressive symptoms, with high levels of primary control coping (e.g., problem solving, emotional expression, emotional regulation) weakening the association, and disengagement coping (e.g., avoidance, denial, wishful thinking) accentuating it. In explaining the absence of buffering effects of coping responses in adolescents, in contrast to the presence of buffering effects in parents, Wadsworth et al. (2005) argue that cognitive processes such as those involved in stress appraisal and coping are malleable during adolescence, shaped in part through interactions with stressful and nonstressful environmental events and conditions. They further contend that as coping strategies become more traitlike over time, they culminate as moderators of stressors in adulthood. These plausible and intriguing ideas warrant study.

Another developmentally sensitive issue concerns children's responses to socioeconomic disadvantage in relation to their network orientations (i.e., beliefs, attitudes, and expectations concerning the potential usefulness of network members in helping one cope with a problem), social networks, and friendship patterns. Given the increased significance of peers and the expansion of social networks during the adolescent years, it is surprising how little is known about the role that friends and network members play in helping adolescents cope with poverty and socioeconomic disadvantage. There is some suggestion that gender moderates the effectiveness of peer support in the context of economic loss (Simons, Whitbeck, & Wu, 1994) and that low family income militates against children adopting an optimistic view of social network members as potential support providers (Belle, Dill, & Burr, 1991). The focus on peers as contributors to adolescent deviance in studies of disadvantaged adolescents needs to be balanced by efforts to understand the conditions under which peers play positive roles that contribute to resilience in adolescents who are poor, low income, or living in families experiencing economic loss. We also need to better understand what factors influence how poor and low-income adolescents view their social networks and identify ways to encourage support-seeking and to enhance the support functions of these adolescents' social networks.

Stress-Vulnerability Response Models

As our understanding of the neurobiological underpinnings of cognitive development has grown, researchers have proposed new connections between exposure to stressors and adolescent mental health. A stress-vulnerability model proposed by Singha (2001) links stress exposure to substance abuse problems through negative impacts on the stress response system. This model proposes that optimal development of executive cognitive functions, the ability to perceive emotional cues, and social skills are impaired under conditions of chronic, high stress, such as chronic poverty. The stress response system that develops under high stress becomes maladapted. As a result of these deficits, adolescents in poverty are at a higher risk of problems related to poor decision making, such as substance abuse (Bar-On Tranel, Denburg, & Bechara 2003). There is also evidence that the link between poverty and drug abuse may result in part because stress and drugs activate the same neural pathways, sensitizing individuals who grow up under chronic stress to the effects of drugs (Kreek & Kobb, 1998).

Fishbein Herman-Stahl, & Eldreth, (2006) tested a stress-vulnerability model using a sample of male adolescents who were from low-income, high crime neighborhoods and considered high risk for exposure to stress and drug use. Participants completed a battery of tests measuring impulsivity, risky decision making, delay of gratification, and social competence. Experiences with stressful life events during early adolescence were associated with increased risky decision making and lower levels of social competence at age 16 yet, only social competence mediated the relationship

between stress experiences and later substance use (alcohol, marijuana, and polydrug use). Within this group of high-risk male adolescents, Fishbein and colleagues found support for the assertion that exposure to stress can lead to substance use by negatively impacting prosocial decision making and behavior. These findings further suggest that a similar pathway may operate to increase risk for conduct problems and antisocial behaviors.

One unique aspect of this model is that it potentially explains why the period of adolescence may be a time of heightened vulnerability to stress. The prefrontal cortex, thought to be responsible for executive cognitive functions of problem solving, high-level judgments, and decision making, is under development during the adolescent years. The developing prefrontal cortex is particularly sensitive to stress, leading to dysfunction in areas of decision making (Arnsten & Shansky, 2004). The stress-vulnerability model also posits a mechanism that would explain why stressors experienced during adolescence can have enduring effects on mental health (Fishbein, 2000).

Allostatic Load as an Emergent Model

Evans and colleagues have recently undertaken a provocative program of research that draws attention to the impact that cumulative exposure to suboptimal physical and psychosocial conditions associated with poverty can have on child and adolescent biological systems (Evans, 2004; Evans & English, 2002; Evans, Kim, Ting, Tesher, & Shannas, 2007). In their study of rural White 8- to 10-year-olds, Evans and English (2002) found that those who were poor were more likely than their middle-class counterparts to experience psychosocial stressors (family turmoil, early childhood separation, and community violence) and physical stressors (substandard housing, high levels of noise, crowding). Cumulative exposure to these stressors partially mediated the link between poverty and children's psychosocial adjustment (anxiety, depression, behavioral conduct problems, feelings of low self-worth). Moreover, cumulative stressor exposure was a much more powerful mediator of the link between poverty and children's adjustment than were the individual physical and psychosocial stressors.

More path breaking is these researchers' work indicating that young adolescents exposed to greater accumulated physical and psychosocial stressors manifest higher levels of allostatic load, a physiologic marker (e.g., chronic resting blood pressure, overnight cortisol levels) of cumulative wear and tear on the body caused by repeated mobilization of multiple physiological response systems. This relationship held controlling for allostatic load 3–4 years earlier, when the youth were in elementary school, but only among adolescents with mothers were low in sensitivity and responsiveness. The constant turning on and turning off of stress-related physiological responses creates allostatic load, including more long-term changes (e.g., persistent elevation of blood pressure) (Evans et al., 2007). In sum, exposure to accumulated physical and psychosocial stressors associated with poverty appears to have implications for adolescents' physical health status through allostatic load. It also appears to be a pathway through which poverty can create psychosocial difficulties in children and adolescents, presumably by creating adaptation demands that are beyond the adolescent's coping capacities. This is a promising area of research that may prove highly influential in modifying how we conceptualize poverty-related stress and advancing our understanding of connections between physical and mental health and the particular vulnerabilities of adolescence.

Bioecological Model

Bronfenbrenner and Ceci's (1994) bioecological model may provide the most complete framework for examining the relationship between poverty and mental health. It aptly reflects the widely held view that psychological adjustment is multiply determined and is directly and indirectly affected by many levels of influence (Eamon, 2002; Compas, Hinden,

& Gephardt, 1995; Petersen et al, 1993). "Proximal processes," a cornerstone of the bioecological model, posit mechanisms that explain how influences from various levels interact and ultimately impact individual functioning. The bioecological model has encouraged research that expands our understanding of the connections between family-, school-, and neighborhood-level influences, and how genetics, gender, age, and ethnicity moderate these connections.

Eamon (2002) used the bioecological model to guide an analysis of multiple levels of influence linking poverty to depressive symptoms in adolescents. Consistent with a family stress model, the findings concerning family level factors indicated that maternal depressive symptoms, spousal conflict, and physical punishment mediated the link between poverty and adolescent depressive symptoms two years later. Neighborhood-level disadvantage so exerted influence on depressive symptoms through two mechanisms. First, a positive relationship between neighborhood disadvantage and noninvolvement in outside activities in turn predicted depressive symptoms in subsequent years. Second, neighborhood disadvantage predicted an increase in maternal depressive symptoms, which, consistent with a family stress model, operated indirectly to increase adolescent depressive symptoms.

Eamon's (2002) study is also significant for its focus on the link between physical health status and adolescent depressive symptoms and documentation of factors that mediated this link (i.e., maternal depression, parental conflict, and school satisfaction). This finding is particularly salient in light of recent research showing that poor youth are almost 20% less likely than nonpoor youth to be rated in very good or excellent health during their teen years (Currie & Lin, 2007). The association between physical health and mental health is now widely accepted, but the mechanisms underlying the connection are not well understood. It will require a more holistic approach, such as the bioecological model, to illuminate interactions between domains previously viewed as unrelated.

Social Evaluation Theory

Social evaluation is another process that may underlie links between family socioeconomic disadvantage and adolescent mental health. Our stratified society inevitably places a group at the bottom, and social evaluation theories assert that the psychological well-being of members of low status groups is shaped by the messages members receive about their place in society, through reflected appraisals and social comparison (Cartwright, 1950; Rosenberg, 1979). Persons in lower status groups are expected to have more negative appraisals of self-worth, culminating in anger, psychological stress, loss of control, and resentment. It is further hypothesized that these negative cognitive states may manifest in either internalizing or externalizing symptoms (Lindheim & Syme, 1983). Social evaluation theory was developed and has been tested primarily with adult populations. Nonetheless, it lends itself to a developmental perspective, given that, relative to earlier developmental periods, adolescence is distinguished by increased salience of peers, greater exposure to the media, and heightened understanding of what it means to be poor or from a low SES background in a stratified society (Larson & Verma, 1999; Steinberg & Silk, 2002; Wiltfang & Scarbecz, 1990). All of these trends likely increase the prevalence and psychological consequences of social evaluation processes as children transition to and move through adolescence.

Adolescent Awareness and Responses to Stigma Associated with Socioeconomic Disadvantage

Poverty, low-income status, and low SES may adversely affect adolescent psychosocial adjustment by increasing exposure to demeaning, humiliating, and otherwise negative treatment precipitated by the stigmas of socioeconomic disadvantage. These themes are sounded in qualitative studies (e.g., Glasgow, 1981; Gouldner, 1978; MacLeod, 1987), but are largely missing in quantitative research focusing on mediators of the effects of poverty and economic stress. Economically impoverished individuals contend with stigmatizing living conditions and circumstances that publicly "mark" or symbolize their membership in the category of poor or economically deprived individuals (e.g., food stamps, separate line in school cafeterias for children who receive government-subsidized lunches, public housing, living in a "bad" neighborhood) (Goodban, 1985; MacLeod, 1987; Marshall, 1982). These stigmas serve as cues for maltreatment at the interpersonal level largely because of widespread negative attitudes toward the poor and a strong bias in American society toward explanations of poverty that blame the person for his or her economic circumstances (Feather, 1974; Leahy, 1990; Pelton, 1989).

By the time children enter early adolescence, if not earlier, they have more than an inchoate understanding of the negative social meaning of economic disadvantage. This understanding derives from their interpersonal experiences and often prompts efforts to mask their membership in a stigmatized group. Consider the observations of a father whose family was receiving food stamps. According to the father:

> When my kids go with me to the grocery store shopping, and we go through the checkout line, my kids usually take off. They told me they are embarrassed when I use our food stamps. They don't want to be seen with me. (Wiltfang & Scarbecz, 1990, p.176)

Children are not oblivious to their living environment and, like adults, make judgments of their neighborhoods that are consistent with their neighborhoods' objective characteristics (e.g., high rates of unemployment and crime, low public safety, minimum and low quality health and education services) (Homel & Burns, 1987). When asked to evaluate their local neighborhood as "a place to grow up in," children living in poor inner-city areas are most negative, while those living in rural areas and in affluent suburbs are most positive (Zill, 1984). MacLeod (1987) found that adolescent males living in a predominantly white, low-income housing development in a working-class neighborhood were acutely aware of the stigmas and disadvantages of living in public housing. One of them said:

> Out here, there's not the opportunity to make money. That's how you get into stealing and all that . . . To get a job, first of all, this is a handicap, out here. If you say you're from the projects or anywhere in this area, that can hurt you. Right off the bat: reputation. (p. 5)

Class- and culture-based stigmatization in the classroom are also salient in the recollections of a group of poor, inner-city, African American male dropouts studied by Glasgow (1981). These youth believed that "mainstream" education actually is intended to demoralize African Americans and to ensure that they have bleak economic futures. They pointed to myriad ways in which instructors "put down" or stigmatized African American culture (e.g., African American dance, music, dress, speech patterns), core aspects of their definition of self, poor people more generally, and their community at large. Understandably, they reacted to explicit and implicit messages of cultural inferiority with resentment, defensiveness, and feelings of alienation. Reflecting on these demeaning experiences, one young man said, "I don't need the man [the White teacher] to tell me directly that my way of life is uncivilized, but I know what he's putting down; I ain't nobody's fool" (Glasgow, 1981, p. 58).

Brantlinger's (1991) investigation of high and low SES adolescents' reports of problems and punishment in school revealed processes reminiscent of those recounted by Glasgow. Epithets from high SES students referring to low SES students (e.g., "scum") evoked intensely negative reactions from the latter (all of whom lived in government subsidized housing projects) and were often the precipitant of fights between schoolmates differing in SES. Poor students, compared to their affluent schoolmates, reported a greater number of penalties; more severe, stigmatizing punishment; and more stringent consequences for similar infractions. The self-reported penalties experienced by low SES students more often involved *public* humiliation (e.g., being yelled at in front of the class), ostracism (e.g., being made to stand in the hall for long periods of time), and rejection. Low SES students were less likely than high SES students to believe that discipline meted out by school personnel was fair and more likely to believe that teachers did not like them because of prejudice against either their social class or the groups with which they affiliated.

In addition to engendering negative self-appraisal, the stigmatizing process described in these investigations may encourage students to drop out of school and foment anxiety, depressive symptoms, aggression, and disruptive behavior. Given the large amount of time children spend in school, it is likely that cumulative exposure to demeaning experiences in the school setting is a major factor underlying the increase with age in SES differences in behavior problems (Stevenson, Richman, & Graham, 1985). Indeed, in view of evidence that SES differences in behavior problems emerge and become more pronounced as children enter and progress through school, it is difficult to envision that such exposure plays no causal role in the overrepresentation of internalizing and, especially, externalizing problems among children who are poor or from low SES backgrounds. This issue deserves more systematic study.

Self-Esteem and Stigma Associated with Socioeconomic Disadvantage

Self-esteem might be the category of psychological functioning most commonly affected by the stigma of poverty and low SES. Whereas numerous empirical studies have investigated the relation between SES and self-esteem, remarkably few have examined stigma per se as a factor linking socioeconomic hardship to self-esteem in adolescents. This is surprising because derogatory self-relevant information in the form of social stigma, marginalization, and disparate treatment is thought to be a critical element in the processes through which poverty and low SES influence adolescent identity formation (Phillips & Pittman, 2003). Haney's (2006) recent study, although focused on adults, is noteworthy in this regard. Utilizing interview data from a probability sample of about 9,000 adults from four major metropolitan areas, Haney found that perceived neighborhood disorder partly mediated the relationship between neighborhood poverty and self-esteem. The findings support the view that "blighted and decaying urban neighborhoods are read as disinvestments both by residents and by city governments, and therefore, these images are internalized and incorporated into residents' psychological makeup" (Haney, 2006, p. 968).

Rosenberg and Pearlin's (1978) well-known review of studies examining the relation between SES and self-esteem suggested that the relation is strong for adults, relatively weak for adolescents, and virtually nonexistent for children. Their interpretation of this pattern of findings is that the psychological meaning of social class and the social experiences attendant to social class depend on the individual's developmental status. In particular, they argue that adults are more exposed to social inequality than children, pointing out that the world of work calls attention to a social stratification system and the worker's place in it, whereas the major extrafamilial context for children's socialization and development—school—tends to be socioeconomically homogeneous, because children typically attend schools whose average SES level is similar to their own. They also note that social class is generally viewed as achieved for adults and ascribed for children and adolescents; consequently,

adults, more so than children and adolescents, are evaluated and tend to evaluate themselves along class lines.

Wiltfang and Scarbecz (1990) argued that Rosenberg and Pearlin's conclusions were premature, claiming that studies underestimated the effects of social class on adolescents' self-esteem as a result of relying on traditional measures of parental social class (e.g., father's education and occupation) that do not tap the dimensions of social class most likely to affect adolescents' self-esteem. Their assessment of social class in a study of 12- to 19-year-olds included traditional as well as nontraditional indicators. The latter included whether the family was receiving public welfare, whether the father was employed or unemployed, the adolescent's description of the neighborhood (whether it was described as luxurious, comfortable, average, run down, or a slum), and whether the adolescent perceived that lots of men in the neighborhood did not have work. These nontraditional indicators of social class were thought to better reflect the "hidden injuries" of social class (Sennett & Cobb, 1972), to have greater psychological relevance, and to carry more stigma for adolescents than low parental education or occupational status, especially in American society "where people measure one another by what they have or do, or by where they live" (Wiltfang & Scarbecz, 1990, p. 175). Consistent with their predictions, nontraditional measures of social class were much stronger predictors of adolescent self-esteem than were traditional measures.

It is conceivable that stigma linked to socioeconomic disadvantage is more detrimental to adolescents' self-esteem than stigma associated with other characteristics (e.g., being African American, being physically disabled). In their now classic paper, Crocker and Major (1989) made the compelling argument that, paradoxically, members of stigmatized groups generally do not have lower global self-esteem than members of nonstigmatized groups because they have at their disposal several self-protective strategies such as attributing negative feedback to prejudice against their group, selectively devaluing those dimensions on which their group fares poorly, and selectively valuing those dimensions on which their group excels. However, adolescents who are poor or from low SES backgrounds may lack the self-protective strategies that membership in other stigmatized groups can provide because class consciousness is low among American youth—the myth of America as a classless society persists—(Leahy, 1990) and because adolescents, like adults, generally view poverty and socioeconomic disadvantage as emanating from individual differences in merit and are more likely than children to endorse this view (Leahy, 1983, 1990). Indeed, research suggests that low-income adolescents are even more likely than middle-income adolescents to endorse individualistic explanations of poverty (Flanagan & Tucker, 1999).

All of these considerations suggest that the psychological costs of stigma associated with socioeconomic disadvantage may be greater than those for other types of stigma where the targets of stigma consciously identify with other members of their stigmatized group. Crocker and Major (1989) highlight the distinction between responsibility for causing a stigmatizing condition and responsibility for maintaining it. They point out that "whereas the person who is born into poverty may not be blamed for his or her condition, both observers and poor people themselves may attribute blame for not rising above it" (p. 620). Perceived responsibility for poverty and socioeconomic disadvantage may not begin to shape individuals' reactions to stigma until they reach adulthood, given that adolescents generally bear no responsibility for their family's socioeconomic status.

It remains unclear how an individual's different roles or social characteristics interact in the process of social evaluation, but it is likely that social status affects well-being through a series of complex contingencies that may be particularly fragile throughout the adolescent years (McLeod & Owens, 2004). Because

direct tests of mediating processes are lacking, it also is unclear whether social evaluation is a primary mechanism by which mental health is impacted, or whether relations among self-esteem, stress, and mental health are driven by a different, less direct, process.

EDUCATIONAL ACHIEVEMENT

Adolescents from poor and low-income families have lower levels of educational attainment than their nonpoor counterparts. In 2005, 18% of youth whose families' income was in the lowest quartile were high school dropouts, as compared to only 2.7% of youth whose families' income was in the highest quartile (NCES, 2006). Among adolescents who graduated high school in 2005, 53% of those from low-income families immediately enrolled in college in the fall, as compared to 65% of adolescents from middle-income families and 81% of adolescents from high-income families (NCES, 2007). Educational achievement is also linked to duration of economic deprivation. Schoon et al.'s (2002) longitudinal analyses indicated that youth who experienced risks in both childhood and adolescence due to adverse socioeconomic conditions fared worst in terms of academic outcomes.

Adolescents who are poor or from low SES backgrounds find it more difficult to engage and succeed in the educational system than adolescents from advantaged backgrounds for a host of reasons, including limited material resources, attendance at schools of lower quality, and salient examples of peers, family members, and persons in their community who failed to reap economic benefits from education (MacLeod, 1987). Mickelson (1990) describes two types of attitudes adolescents possess regarding education—abstract and concrete. Abstract attitudes, which are held by most youth, reflect the dominant ideology that education is a critical component to success in American society. Concrete attitudes, in contrast, reflect the reality that adolescents observe around them regarding opportunity structures and the payoff of education. Mickelson found that minority adolescents and adolescents from lower social classes had less positive concrete attitudes about education. Moreover, concrete attitudes were linked to academic achievement, whereas abstract attitudes were not.

The attitudes and perceptions of disadvantaged children shift during adolescence in ways that have important implications for educational achievement. Youth from low socioeconomic backgrounds experience declines in educational aspirations across adolescence, whereas youth from higher socioeconomic backgrounds do not (Kao & Tienda, 1998). In addition, research points to adolescence as a time when achievement values become tied to perceived barriers. In particular, in their study of low-income ethnic-minority adolescents, Taylor and Graham (2007) found that perceived barriers to educational and occupational success were associated with diminished achievement values among middle school students, but not among elementary school students.

Recognition of barriers and how they may interact with one's own future may grow in salience during the adolescent period, in part, because youth are now actively forming their own identities and being granted increasing autonomy at home and school. This autonomy provides students in middle school and high school more flexibility in terms of their engagement in schooling, a development that may be problematic for youth who are poor or from low SES backgrounds if it coincides with increasing perceptions of barriers to educational and occupational success (Eccles et al., 1993). With these considerations as a backdrop, in the sections below, we present a brief overview of family, school, and neighborhood characteristics that facilitate and hinder academic success among youth who are poor or from low SES backgrounds.

Family Influences

Findings from both correlational research and welfare experiments suggest that family processes are important sources of variation in academic achievement among economically disadvantaged adolescents. These findings are briefly reviewed below.

Correlational Research

A voluminous research literature points to a complex web of parental attitudes and behaviors as antecedents of academic outcomes among low-income adolescents and as mediators of the link between family income and academic outcomes among adolescents (e.g., Benner & Mistry, 2007; Conger, Conger, & Elder, 1997; Crosnoe, Mistry, & Elder, 2002; Furstenberg et al., 1999; Hango, 2007; Hill et al., 2004; Schoon, Parsons, & Sacker, 2004; Smokowski, Reynolds, & Bezruckzo, 1999). Levels of academic achievement are higher among low-income adolescents whose parents have higher educational expectations for them (Schoon et al., 2004; Wood, Kaplan, & McLoyd, 2007). Higher educational expectations among low-income parents are also associated with better adjustment to secondary school, which in turn fosters higher educational attainment (Schoon et al., 2004).

Furstenberg and colleagues' (1999) in-depth investigation of economically disadvantaged adolescents in urban Philadelphia revealed a number of ways in which parents promoted academic success among their adolescent children. Youth who had an open, supportive relationship that encouraged autonomy and problem solving with their parents experienced greater academic success. In addition, parental management of adolescents' social ties and community involvement predicted better academic outcomes. Youth whose parents enrolled them in private schools and encouraged ties to churches and other community institutions showed higher levels of academic success.

In a mixed methods investigation of factors that promoted academic resilience, Smokowski and colleagues (1999) examined autobiographical essays prepared by youth who faced high levels of economic risk, such as parental unemployment and low family income, but were still performing above average in terms of reading and math achievement. These adolescents consistently identified family support as an important factor in their achievement motivation and their ability to overcome adversity. Another salient theme in their essays concerned the psychological consequences of watching family members make less optimal decisions, such as dropping out of high school or using drugs. Adolescents viewed these experiences as motivational, in that they saw the negative repercussions that others faced and were motivated to avoid the same circumstances.

Although studies indicate that parental factors can contribute to academic achievement in low-income adolescents, there also is evidence that socioeconomic disadvantage weakens the link between positive parental behaviors and adolescent achievement. For example, Hill and colleagues (2004) found that greater parental academic involvement in 7th grade was predictive of higher academic achievement in 9th grade among youth whose parents had high levels of education, but not among youth whose parents had low levels of education. Similarly, in McNeal's (1999) analysis of national data, parental involvement was linked to higher achievement scores and lower chances of dropping out of high school, but this relationship was stronger among youth from higher SES households than youth from lower SES households. Among youth whose socioeconomic status was more than one standard deviation below the mean, the positive influences of parental involvement were nonexistent. Parent–child discussions about schooling and parental involvement in parent–teacher organizations were linked to positive academic outcomes for high SES youth, but were unrelated to academic outcomes for low SES youth. Perhaps the wide spectrum of multilevel barriers to achievement that exists within the context of socioeconomic disadvantage overrides the impact of parental involvement seen in more benign contexts.

Welfare Experiments

Findings from welfare experiments suggest that in terms of school achievement, adolescents fare less well than preschool and elementary school-age children when their parents move from welfare to work or increase their hours of employment. By the early 1990s, welfare policy in the United States was under intense scrutiny and strong efforts were being made to reform current policy into a policy that pushed welfare recipients toward higher levels of employment-based support (Morris et al., 2001). Although the Personal Responsibility and Work Opportunity Reconciliation Act (PRWORA), the new federal welfare act, was not passed until 1996, a large number of states had been granted waivers of Aid to Families with Dependent Children (AFDC) rules to experiment with changes in welfare provisions (Morris et al., 2001). States' receipt of waivers from the federal government to experiment with changes in welfare provisions was conditional on use of a random assignment design and evaluation of the program (Gennetian & Morris, 2003). States mixed and matched several kinds of welfare and employment policies, and the resulting diversity of programs provided an opportunity to assess the comparative effects of different program features on child and adolescent well-being.

To compensate for some of the shortcomings of the labor market (e.g., low wages) and to make work more financially rewarding, some experimental programs offered earnings supplements, contingent on employment, either by providing working families cash benefits or by increasing the amount of earnings that were not counted as income in calculating the amount of a family's welfare benefit. Other programs provided only mandatory employment services (e.g., education, training, or immediate job search), and others put time limits on families' eligibility for welfare benefits.

Morris et al.'s (2001) synthesis of findings for preschool and elementary school-age children assessed 2–4 years after random assignment, and who ranged in age from approximately 5 to 12 years at the time of assessment, indicated that programs that provided earnings supplements, unlike programs with mandatory employment services and time limits, had consistent and positive effects on children's school achievement. However, similar positive effects were not evident in Gennetian and colleagues' synthesis (Gennetian et al., 2002) focusing on children who were adolescens age or approaching adolescence at the time their parents entered the experimental programs. Using meta-analytic techniques, Gennetian et al. integrated survey data collected from parents about their adolescent children in 8 studies of 16 different welfare and employment programs, all of which used a random assignment design. Of the 16 programs tested in the 8 experimental studies, 12 required parents to work or to participate in work-related activities in order to receive welfare, 8 offered earnings supplements to parents who worked (6 allowed parents to continue receiving welfare benefits along with the earning supplements), and 2 put time limits on the length of time that families could receive welfare. Children were roughly 10–16 years old at random assignment and 12–18 years old when the follow-up survey data on which the synthesis is based were collected. The length of the follow-up period varied, ranging from 24 months to 60 months after random assignment.

The pattern of findings that emerged from Gennetian et al.'s synthesis sharply contrasts with that found in Morris et al.'s (2001) synthesis. Specifically, parents in the programs generally reported worse school performance, a higher rate of grade retention, and more use of special education services among their adolescent children than did control-group parents. Effects were especially pronounced among adolescents with younger siblings. Of the 9 programs examined in the 7 studies that measured adolescents' school performance, six lowered performance; for grade repetition, 9 of the 15 impacts were unfavorable; and for receipt of special services for an emotional, physical, or mental condition, the impacts were unfavorable in 8 of 12 comparisons. The largest negative impact was on maternal reports of

school performance (one-tenth of a standard deviation). Overall, the sizes of the average effects were small and many of the programs did not produce statistically significant effects. No consistent effects were found for the three policies. That is, negative effects could not be traced to any one welfare or employment policy. For example, negative effects were found both for programs that required parents to work or to participate in work activities and programs in which parents' work participation was voluntary. On average, the programs had no effect on school dropout rates, suspension rates, or the proportion of adolescents who completed school or had children.

Gennetian et al. (2002) undertook a series of analyses to examine what might account for the negative effects on school outcomes across the different employment-based welfare and antipoverty poverty programs. Their findings are only suggestive, because several studies lacked data needed to assess mediating processes. Gennetian et al. found some evidence that negative impacts were the result of changes in adolescents' home and out-of-home environments, such as increased pressure to work long hours outside the home, greater domestic responsibilities (e.g., sibling care), and less supervision by adults. For example, the Self-Sufficiency Project (SSP), the only project that provided information about adolescent employment, increased the likelihood that adolescents were employed more than 20 hours per week. This increase in adolescent employment may have been responsible for the elevated rates of delinquent behavior and lower school achievement found in the SSP program group, in keeping with prior research linking adolescent employment to delinquent behavior (Steinberg & Dornbusch, 1991).

Gennetian et al. also found that programs that increased maternal employment and that had negative effects on adolescents' school functioning were the same programs that increased adolescents' home responsibilities. When single mothers move into employment, adolescent children may assume greater domestic responsibilities and this may, in some circumstances, hinder academic achievement and school progress among adolescents already struggling with schoolwork. Gennetian et al. reasoned that if additional home responsibilities are a pathway by which the programs adversely affected adolescents' academic achievement and school progress, negative effects should be especially pronounced among adolescents with younger siblings, on the assumption that expanded domestic responsibilities probably included sibling care. Indeed, they found this to be the case. Whereas control-group adolescents who had younger siblings at study entry functioned similarly to control-group adolescents who did not, the detrimental effects of the programs were larger and more consistently negative across outcomes for adolescents who had younger siblings at study entry than those who did not.

In sum, these experimental welfare programs tended to change adolescents' ecologies in ways that were largely incompatible with their developmental needs, whereas the reverse seemed true for preschoolers and elementary school-age children. Among adolescents, the programs tended to increase intensive adolescent employment, decrease adult supervision, and increase domestic responsibilities—all factors that have the potential to impose time pressures that interfere with adolescents' engagement in school and homework and increase the likelihood of involvement in delinquent activity. In contrast, for preschool and school-age children, many of these programs led to increases in the amount of time they spent in formal child care and organized after-school activities, both of which have been linked to enhance cognitive, academic, and social functioning (Lamb, 1997; Pierce; Hamm, & Vandell, 1999; Posner & Vandell, 1999).

Findings from the evaluation of the New Hope program are illustrative of the positive effects of programs that offered earnings supplements. The New Hope program, a 3-year demonstration experiment in Milwaukee, Wisconsin, designed to test the effectiveness of an employment-based antipoverty program, provided adults wage supplements sufficient to raise family income above the poverty threshold and subsidies for child care and health insurance, conditioned on proof of 30 or more hours of weekly work. This program is noteworthy because, of all the earnings supplement programs in which children were preschool and elementary school-age at random assignment, it has the longest follow-up (8 years after random assignment) and the follow-ups extend into adolescence. When the program started, children were between 1 and 10 years old.

At earlier follow-ups, both during the program and two years after it ended, New Hope had significant positive effects on children's school achievement and educational expectations (Huston et al., 2003, 2005). At the 2-year follow-up (during the program), teachers rated program group children higher on academic skills than control-group children. This effect persisted at the five-year follow-up, but only among boys and older children. At the 5-year follow-up, children in the program group performed better than their control-group counterparts on a standardized test of reading achievement, and among the youth who were ages 13–16, those in the program group were more likely to be "making school progress." In particular, they were less likely than control-group adolescents to be retained in grade, less likely to be using remedial services, and less likely to receive poor grades (Huston et al., 2005). At the 8-year follow-up, most impacts on academic achievement observed in earlier waves were no longer evident, but New Hope boys continued to perform better on a standardized test of reading achievement than did control-group boys.

These positive effects on achievement appear to stem largely from improvements in family income, increased use of organized child care, and children's greater involvement in structured activities away from home. Almost half of the parents in the experimental group used the child care subsidy, and at 2 years post random assignment, children ages 3–12 in the experimental group had spent almost twice as many months in state-licensed or county-certified center-based care (for preschool and school-age children) and more than twice as many months in school-based extended day care as children in the control group. Moreover, among the 9- to 12-year-olds, children in the program group spent more time in adult-supervised, organized after-school activities (e.g., lessons, sports, clubs, youth groups) than did children in the control group (Huston et al., 2001). In is also likely that earlier gains in academic achievement placed children in the experimental group on a more positive academic trajectory throughout the schooling years.

New Hope's impact on achievement can be framed more broadly in terms of Laureau's (2003) concept of "concerted cultivation." This concept refers to a child-rearing approach in which parents actively foster and assess children's talents, opinions, and skills and provide children with multiple leisure activities that adults orchestrate and supervise. Lareau's research suggests that elements of "concerted cultivation" are highly salient in middle-class families, whereas working-class and low-income parents are likely to rely on "the accomplishment of natural growth" as a primary child-rearing strategy. This class differential likely reflects differences in financial resources with which to provide children growth-enhancing opportunities, disparities in available time to engage in activities with children, and differing perspectives on how parents should be involved in their child's schooling and activities. By increasing income, promoting more stable employment, and providing options for structured child care, New Hope may have increased low-income children's opportunities for "concerted cultivation."

Although there are costs and benefits to both child-rearing strategies, one of the most significant benefits of concerted cultivation may be the promotion of skills and sensibilities that foster positive experiences outside of the family, especially in school settings. For example, Lareau's (2003) in-depth ethnographies indicate that children who participate in extracurricular activities learn new skills and experience new things (e.g., the feelings associated with losing a sporting event) that are useful in other contexts. They learn appropriate ways to present themselves and to interact with non-family members. Within the context of structured activities, children develop relationships with other adults who may serve as role models and mentors, and they may begin to develop a trust of institutions beyond their family. These experiences help youth to understand what is expected of them in school, handle authority in appropriate ways, and maintain positive social relations with classmates. In addition, they tend to nurture initiative, which fosters success in academic pursuits.

Lareau's work focuses on children, but the concepts and processes described in her work are applicable to adolescents as well. Because of the increased need for adult guidance in relation to major decisions pondered during adolescence, such as going to college and choosing a career, connections to responsible, caring adults and institutions increase the likelihood of positive adolescent development (Jarrett, 1995). Thus, increased experiences of "concerted cultivation" may be a possible path to higher academic attainment for low-income youth. The section that follows gives more detailed attention to the role of extracurricular activities in facilitating achievement in economically disadvantaged adolescents.

Extracurricular Activities

Extracurricular activities are gaining recognition as a potential vehicle for fostering positive development. Evidence is amassing that participation in extracurricular activities is related to positive outcomes in multiple domains. Both longitudinal investigations and experiments have substantiated these linkages (for reviews see Eccles & Templeton, 2002; Feldman & Matjasko, 2005; and vol. 2, chapter 7).

Participation in extracurricular activities has been found to be related to higher academic achievement and greater likelihood of college attendance and graduation (Barber, Eccles, & Stone, 2001; Fredricks & Eccles, 2006; Mahoney, Cairns, & Farmer, 2003), as well as reduced likelihood of engagement in problem behaviors and school dropout (Mahoney, 2000; Mahoney & Cairns, 1997; Marsh & Kleitman 2002). Studies have also shown that adolescents who participate in more activities and who participate consistently over time experience greater benefits than adolescents who do not (Fredricks & Eccles, 2006; Pedersen et al., 2005; Troutman & Dufur, 2007).

Although the overall nature of these and similar findings is promising, concerns remain about selection bias or the extent to which preexisting differences account for the purported educational and psychological benefits of activity involvement (Feldman & Matjasko, 2005; Marsh & Kleitman, 2002). However, studies that have attempted to account for self-selection by following children longitudinally or by controlling for potentially confounding variables have still found links to positive outcomes (Epps, 2006; Fredricks & Eccles, 2006; Larson, 2000).

Another limitation of this area of study is that little of the prior work on extracurricular activities has focused on poor or low SES adolescents or on how income may affect the relationship between participation in extracurricular activities and developmental outcomes. Although we know very little about predictors of extracurricular participation for poor youth, we do know that poor youth participate in activities at lower rates than other youth (Pedersen & Seidman, 2005). For poor adolescents the costs of some extracurricular activities may be prohibitive (Lareau, 2002), or they may face limited options in their schools and neighborhoods for quality activities (Furstenberg, 1993; Gutman & McLoyd, 2000; Lareau, 1987).

A very small number of studies have sampled low-income adolescents, and for the most part the results of these investigations seem to parallel what has been found in studies of higher income samples (Pedersen et al. 2005; Pedersen & Seidman, 2005). For example, Pedersen and Seidman (2005) observed that participation in school-based activities, religious youth groups, and team sports were positively related to school grades for low-income adolescents. Other studies have examined whether income moderates the relation between extracurricular activities and various academic outcomes, providing some evidence that low-income adolescents may experience more benefits from extracurricular activities in terms of grades and academic attainment than other adolescents (Marsh, 1992; Marsh & Kleitman, 2002).

In neighborhoods where resources are scarce, parents of successful children have been found to be particularly adept at facilitating their children's involvement in school-based, church, and community programs within and outside of their neighborhoods, specifically for the purposes of fostering positive development (Furstenberg, 1993; Gutman & McLoyd, 2000; Jarrett, 1995). And, interestingly, parents who are involved in organized activities tend to have children who are involved in organized activities (Furstenberg et al., 1999). Most studies do not account for parents' influence on adolescents' participation in extracurricular activities beyond some limited socioeconomic factors, again raising the issue of selection bias.

More work is needed not only to understand parents' roles but also to understand the processes through which adolescents benefit from participation in extracurricular activities (Larson, 2000). Thus far, it appears that engagement in extracurricular activities may promote interpersonal competence and raise educational expectations (Mahoney, Cairns, & Farmer, 2003). There is also evidence that adolescents who participate in extracurricular activities develop a sense of initiative, associate with more academically oriented peers, and build valuable social and cultural capital (Charles, Roscigno, & Torres, 2007; Feldman

& Matjasko, 2005; Jarrett, Sullivan, & Watkins, 2005; Larson, 2000; Roscigno & Ainsworth-Darnell, 1999).

Further research is also needed to determine the types and characteristics of activities that best promote positive development (Eccles & Templeton, 2002). Whether and the extent to which adolescents benefit from extracurricular activities may vary depending on the type of extracurricular activity (Barber, Eccles, & Stone, 2001; Eccles & Barber, 1999; Marsh, 1992), the particular combination of activities (Pedersen et al., 2005; Seidman & Pedersen, 2003), and whether the activity is structured or unstructured (Mahoney & Stattin, 2000).

Neighborhood Influences

The effects of residing in economically poor and depressed neighborhoods may be particularly strong during adolescence, as this is a period when time away from home increases, and peers, nonfamilial adults, and employment opportunities in the community grow in salience and importance. Research investigating the size of neighborhood effects in both middle childhood and adolescence has found that links between neighborhood risk (high concentration of families in poverty, low concentration of high SES neighbors, and high levels of male joblessness) and educational outcomes are stronger in early adolescence than in middle childhood (Halpern-Felsher et al., 1997; and see chapter 12, this volume).

Poor neighborhoods may impact adolescents' educational outcomes through a number of pathways, above and beyond the effects of family-level income (Connell & Halpern-Felsher, 1997). These neighborhoods may have fewer adults who have completed high school or college, which lowers the number of models that adolescents can look to when making decisions about their own schooling. Additionally, neighborhoods with high poverty concentrations, particularly urban neighborhoods, have fewer occupational opportunities, which may affect adolescents' value of education, engagement in school, and ultimately,

their educational attainment. Researchers have argued that adolescents who perceive more opportunities to work and have more exposure to the regularities of work are more likely to stay in school because they see the payoff of educational attainment (Wilson, 1987). In keeping with this claim, longitudinal research conducted in Chicago found that residing in a neighborhood with a higher percentage of residents who work in white-collar jobs increased the odds of high school graduation among low-income male youth (Ensminger, Lamkin, & Jacobson, 1996).

Another pathway of neighborhood influence is the quality and availability of institutions that support the schooling of adolescents, such as churches and organizations targeted to help youth. Not only are youth-supporting institutions like Boys and Girls Clubs and Little Leagues less common in poor neighborhoods, but they possess fewer resources than their counterparts in middle-class neighborhoods and therefore do not have the capacity to serve as many children and adolescents as needed (Connell & Halpern-Felsher, 1997).

Similar to the moderation effects of family-level SES on the relation between parental involvement and adolescent educational achievement, discussed in the previous section, research suggests that both parents' institutional connections and effective discipline strategy are more strongly related to educational achievement in more economically advantaged neighborhoods (Furstenberg et al., 1999). Using data drawn from five neighborhoods in Philadelphia, Fisher and Kmec (2004) found that neighborhood characteristics moderated the relationship between parental financial resources and adolescent dropout. Among families residing in high SES neighborhoods, mother's educational attainment, family financial stability, and parental marital status all increased the likelihood of high school completion. These links did not exist among families residing in low SES neighborhoods.

At the same time, there is evidence that poor youth are more vulnerable to the negative effects of neighborhood characteristics. Using national panel data, Crowder and South (2003) found that neighborhood socioeconomic characteristics predicted school dropout independent of individual and family level characteristics, but the magnitude of this relationship varied across individuals. African American youth from single-parent homes and White youth from poor families were most sensitive to the neighborhood context. One possible explanation is that youth from these backgrounds are the most involved in the neighborhood and may be more affected by the collective socialization practices of peers around them, which could interfere with school achievement in low SES neighborhoods. Future research needs to continue to focus on the interplay of neighborhood characteristics with family and individual characteristics, as well as family practices, to gain a more detailed understanding of the processes by which neighborhoods influence youth.

Other work has focused on more specific community characteristics, such as neighborhood stress, in relation to family processes and adolescent outcomes. Gutman and colleagues (Gutman, McLoyd, & Tokoyawa, 2005) found that among inner-city African American families, neighborhood stress, conceptualized as a latent construct reflecting variables such as neighborhood crime, social control, and barriers to services, is associated with parental psychological stress, which influences the quality of relationships between parents and adolescents. The quality of parent–adolescent relationships in turn, was linked to adolescent adjustment, including self-efficacy beliefs and academic achievement.

One problem that plagues the literature on neighborhood effects is potential selection effects. Because families living in the same neighborhood likely have more in common than just the neighborhood characteristics and families living in different neighborhood have differences beyond the differences in neighborhoods, unbiased estimates of neighborhood effects depend on how well the researcher is able to disentangle neighborhood characteristics

from endogenous factors. Most observational work attempts to do this by controlling for family background characteristics, but controlling for all relevant characteristics is nearly impossible. Other analytic techniques provide more stringent tests of neighborhood impacts and provide estimates that are more causal in nature. Foster and McLanahan (1996) used an instrumental variable approach to estimate the impact of neighborhood conditions on adolescents' chances of completing school. By using city-level characteristics as an instrument, they removed the bias in the estimation of local neighborhood characteristics on adolescent school completion. Their results indicated that a higher local neighborhood dropout rate predicted female adolescents' likelihood of completing school. Harding (2003) employed a different approach to overcome the problem of selection effects. Using propensity score analysis and sensitivity analyses, he found strong evidence that living in a high-poverty neighborhood increased the chances of high school dropout.

Another source of information on the effects of neighborhoods on school achievement is housing experiments. To address neighborhood effects experimentally, the U.S. Department of Housing and Urban Development created the Moving to Opportunity demonstration. In this randomized housing mobility experiment, conducted in five cities across the country (i.e., Baltimore, Boston, Chicago, Los Angeles, and New York), families living in high-poverty public housing projects were given vouchers to help them move to private housing units in low-poverty neighborhoods. An "experimental" group was offered vouchers valid only in low-poverty neighborhoods; a "Section 8" group was offered traditional housing vouchers without geographic restriction; a control group was not offered vouchers. Families were followed so that researchers could assess the impact on child and adolescent functioning of moving to a low-poverty neighborhood versus staying in a high-poverty area (Leventhal, Fauth, & Brooks-Gunn, 2005).

To date, impacts on youth academic achievement are mixed. The first assessments were completed at individual sites two and a half years after the program started. Some sites showed consistent negative effects of moving to a low-poverty neighborhood on adolescents. For example, in Baltimore, adolescents in the experimental group were more likely to repeat a grade and were more likely to drop out of school than adolescents in the control group (Ludwig, Ladd, & Duncan, 2001). In contrast, in New York, adolescent boys in the experimental group seemed to fare well, achieving higher reading and math achievement scores than boys in the control group (Leventhal & Brooks-Gunn, 2004).

At five years post random assignment, a cross-site evaluation was conducted to identify and understand the pattern of lasting effects. At this time point, there was a consistent pattern of gender differences. Whereas adolescent boys in the experimental group showed less academic progress than boys in the control group, adolescent girls in the experimental group were more likely to stay in school and graduate than their control-group counterparts (Kling & Liebman, 2004; Leventhal et al., 2005). The positive effects found at the 2½-year follow-up among adolescent boys in the New York sample were no longer evident at the 5-year follow-up. At the latter follow-up, boys in the experimental group showed lower levels of academic progress than boys in the control group, a pattern similar to results found at the other sites of the experiment (Leventhal et al., 2005).

Understanding the processes underlying the negative impacts of moving to a low-poverty neighborhood is particularly important for the formulation of future social policy in this area. Moving and having to form new social networks may be particularly stressful for adolescents, which plausibly could disrupt academic efforts. Furthermore, it is noteworthy that moving to a low-poverty neighborhood did not lift individual families out of poverty. The stress of being poor in a nonpoor area may have had additional detrimental effects on youth psychological well-being beyond the stress engendered by poverty per se, moving, and adapting to a new environment (Leventhal et al., 2005).

School Influences

In America, the primary source of funding for schools is local property taxes. This causes disparities in the amount of financial resources available to school districts serving poor communities as compared to districts serving wealthier communities. Although recent legislation has sought to decrease these disparities, current funding mechanisms still place most of the burden of school financing on local revenues. This forces poor districts to tax themselves at much higher rates to raise the same amount of revenue as wealthier districts (Slavin, 1999). Recent work has shown that even within districts, schools with high concentrations of poor students have lower per-pupil expenditures as compared to other schools in the same district (Condron & Roscigno, 2003). Because of decreased funding, there are many structural differences in schools that low-income adolescents attend as compared to the schools that middle- or upper-class adolescents attend.

A wealth of research exists about inequalities in education (e.g., Betts, Ruben, Danenberg, 2000; Kozol, 1991), but we only cite a few examples most relevant for adolescents. High-poverty school districts experience higher rates of teacher turnover and are less capable of attracting and retaining high quality teachers, factors that can lead to lower levels of student achievement (Clotfelter, Ladd, & Vigdor, 2006; Ingersoll, 2004; Clotfelter, Ladd, Vigdor, & Wheeler, 2006). Evidence from California indicates that not only do low-income students have less access to teachers with advanced degrees, but they also are more likely to have a teacher who is teaching out of subject (e.g., teaching a chemistry class without a science degree) (Socias, Chambers, Esra, & Shambaugh, 2007).

Another challenge facing low-income students is the lack of advanced placement classes (Solorzano & Ornelas 2002). These classes provide opportunities for higher learning and enable students to begin earning college credits. Research has shown that low-income and ethnic minority students are less likely to attend schools that offer a wide variety of advanced placement classes and that within the schools that do offer them, low-income and ethnic-minority students are disproportionately underrepresented in them. In short, schools that low-income students often attend provide fewer of the resources needed to promote successful academic careers that typically are prerequisites to high school and postsecondary degrees.

Besides understanding school characteristics that contribute to the achievement gap between economically disadvantaged adolescents and more affluent adolescents, it also is important to know what school characteristics promote academic success among poor adolescents. Evidence from a group of pilot schools in Boston suggests that having smaller class sizes, longer classes, making more advisory opportunities available, and providing teachers with more time to discuss teaching methods promotes higher levels of high school achievement among economically disadvantaged adolescents than more traditional schooling options (Center for Collaborative Education, 2007).

In summary, low-income students face a number of barriers that can impede their academic progress. These barriers stem from multiple contexts—the home, the neighborhood, the school—and factors within these contexts can have both individual and interactive effects. It is also important to recognize the factors that foster academic achievement in poor adolescents, such as parent involvement, teacher support, and certain school characteristics. As research continues to unravel the complicated web of mediators and moderators of the link between income and adolescent achievement, a clearer and more comprehensive analysis

will emerge of what poor adolescents need to succeed in school.

FUTURE ORIENTATION

Future orientation is a cognitive–motivational–affective construct that refers to an individual's thoughts, feelings, plans, and attitudes about his or her future. As individuals anticipate the future, they may identify goals and aspirations and plan activities to help achieve those goals, while also assessing the possibilities of goal fulfillment. These processes in turn, may shape decision making and behavior (Nurmi, 1991; Trommsdorff, 1986). Adolescence is a critical time in the development and expansion of future orientation. As youth move through adolescence, their orientation to the future grows stronger, future plans become increasingly detailed and they become more realistic about the prospects of achieving their goals (Nurmi, 1991; Steinberg et al., in press). Appraisal of one's future prospects may influence a host of choices about peers, romantic partners, school, out-of-school activities, and their own behavior that, in turn, may significantly alter one's life course (McCabe & Barnett, 2000; Quinton, Pickles, Maugham, & Rutter, 1993).

Adolescents' future orientation is highly relevant to competencies many youth development leaders regard as necessary for positive development. Among the key developmental goals that youth development leaders have identified and that are especially relevant to future orientation is preparation for a lifetime of meaningful work and specific competencies that signify this preparation (e.g., understanding and awareness of life options; knowledge of steps needed to make educational and occupational choices; preparation for work and family life; understanding the value and purpose of work and family) (Roth et al., 1999).

Correlates of Future Orientation

More positive future orientation is associated with a host of positive social and psychological indicators among economically diverse adolescents, including selection of nondeviant mates, more positive socioemotional adjustment at school, fewer conduct problems, less substance use, more positive self-esteem, and greater feelings of efficacy and responsibility for one's life and decisions (Dorham, 2006; Kerpelman & Mosher, 2004; Nurmi, 1991; Quinton et al., 1993; Robbins & Bryan, 2004; Seginer, 2003; Wyman et al., 1993). Among lower SES adolescents, planning for the future predicts upward social mobility in adulthood (Clausen, 1991). In a similar vein, research suggests that maintaining "vocational hope" is pivotal in advancing career development among urban, at-risk youth (Diemer & Blustein, 2007). A strong and positive future orientation appears to lower the risk of some negative outcomes associated with poverty and low-income such as substance abuse, delinquency, teen pregnancy, and truncated educational attainment, a consideration that undergirds efforts within prevention and intervention programs to help urban youth identify career goals and plans for reaching those goals (Murray, 1996; Wyman et al., 1992).

Socioeconomic Differences in Future Orientation

By mid-adolescence, children who are poor or from low SES backgrounds have begun to appreciate the truncated life chances that confront the poor. When asked to describe rich and poor individuals, low-income children, but especially low-income adolescents, are more likely than their economically advantaged peers to mention the life chances and thoughts of individuals, suggesting that they are more keenly aware of the consequences of poverty (Leahy, 1981, 1990). Among low-income ethnic-minority children, levels of perceived barriers to educational and occupational achievement increase between 2nd and 7th grade (Taylor & Graham, 2007). In addition, many low SES youth express high levels of cynicism about work, the opportunity structure, and the extent to which the social mobility system rewards effort and talent (MacLeod, 1987).

On average, children and youth from low SES backgrounds report lower occupational aspirations and expectations, have a larger gap between occupational aspirations and expectations, and perceive more barriers to occupational success compared to those from more economically advantaged backgrounds. Moreover, the gap between occupational aspirations and expectations increases at a faster rate among low-income children than among economically advantaged children (Bigler et al., 2003; Cook et al., 1996). Perceptions of limited educational and economic opportunities and skepticism about one's ability to attain educational goals and labor market success are troubling, in part, because among some groups, they are associated with increased valuing of low-achieving classmates, lower career aspirations, and disengagement from school and work (Hill, Ramirez, & Dumka, 2003; Holzer, in press; Taylor & Graham, 2007; Wilson, 1996). Cook et al. (1996) found evidence that low-income status lowers occupational expectations though its influence on educational expectations (Cook et al., 1996).

Parental Influences

Considerable evidence links adolescents' future orientation to parental behavior, role modeling, and family economic circumstances. African American adolescents living in households in which parents are employed and not receiving welfare, compared to their counterparts residing in mother-only households dependent on welfare, have higher expectations of being successful in obtaining well-paying jobs when they become adults (Quane & Rankin, 1998). Among adolescents whose parents work primarily in nonmanagerial and nonprofessional occupations, more favorable parental work experiences are linked to greater optimism about future careers (Neblett & Cortina, 2006).

Regardless of teenage childbearing status, African American female youth (ages 15–23) from families with some history of welfare receipt have higher expectancies of future economic self-sufficiency and are more likely to have definite and reasonably well-informed plans for educational and occupational attainment if they received more frequent messages from parents about the value of work, experienced greater tangible support of their work efforts from family members, and had multiple examples of extended family members with strong work attachments. Relational parental support, maternal involvement, and kinship support predict a more positive future orientation among poor and low-income adolescents generally, as well as higher expectancies of being successful in their future line of work. Research also indicates that poor and low-income adolescents whose parents provide more instrumental support for career development (e.g., attending programs about employment opportunities for adolescents, discussing job opportunities with adolescent) subsequently attach greater importance to finding steady work—an effect that holds after taking account of the quality of parent–adolescent relations (e.g., joint adolescent–parent activities, discussion of problems with parent) (Diemer & Blustein, 2007; McCabe & Barnett, 2000).

In light of social class differences in youth's occupational aspirations and expectations, it is not surprising that family economic circumstances can influence children's future orientation. Adolescents who perceive their families as experiencing more financial strain are less optimistic about their economic future (Flanagan, 1990; Larson, 1984; McLoyd & Jozefowicz, 1996). Similarly, less economically advantaged parents and parents who report more perceived financial strain, compared to parents who are more economically advantaged and report less financial strain, are less optimistic about their children's economic future. Changes in parental outlook and behavior when parents experience job and income loss appear to be partly responsible for declines in children's aspirations and expectations (Galambos & Silbereisen, 1987).

Conversely, improvements in family economic circumstances can enhance low-income adolescents' future orientation, as demonstrated by the New Hope program, an employment-based antipoverty program described previously. Eight years after parents were randomly assigned to program or control groups, and 5 years after the program ended, adolescents in program-group families were more involved in employment and career preparation activities (e.g., talked with adults outside of school about careers, work, and what they will do after high school; got instruction or counseling on how to find a job; studied about different kinds of jobs and requirements for the jobs in class) and held less cynical attitudes about work than adolescents in control-group families. For example, they were less likely than adolescents in control-group families to agree with statements such as "If I had the chance, I would go through life without ever working" or "Workers are entitled to call in sick when they don't feel like working." In addition, boys in program-group families were more optimistic about their economic futures (e.g., lower expectations of losing a job as an adult or encountering difficulty finding a good job or supporting a family financially) and more certain that they would have high educational attainment than boys in control-group families (Huston, Walker, Dowsett, Imes, & Ware, 2008; McLoyd, Kaplan, & Purtell, 2008).

This parent-focused program may have positively affected adolescents' future orientation through its beneficial effects on parents' employment and earnings. At the 5-year follow-up, New Hope parents had more stable jobs paying higher wages and lower rates of poverty than control-group parents (Huston et al., 2005). Perhaps these positive impacts enhanced parents' status or salience as positive role models of employment and encouraged them to focus more attention on, and rendered them more optimistic about, their children's employment and financial future (e.g., discussing job opportunities and career plans with adolescents), factors found in other research to be linked to more positive future orientation in adolescents. Youth development programs offering a wide range of services and opportunities (e.g., social, academic, recreational, cultural, and competence building supports), and evaluated using random assignment, have also been shown to positively impact future orientation among poor, urban adolescents (e.g., increases in optimism about the future, higher educational expectations) (Roth et al., 1999).

DELINQUENCY

Socioeconomic disadvantage can increase the risk of adolescent delinquency through individual-, family-, and community-level processes. Certain factors, such as level of socioeconomic disadvantage, persistence of poverty, timing of poverty in children's development, and type of delinquency are important considerations when examining the link between socioeconomic disadvantage and delinquency. Whereas individual, family, and community variables may have direct effects on delinquent behavior, they can also mitigate the effects of socioeconomic disadvantage on delinquency. Understanding poverty at both the individual/family level and community level can help explain certain findings in the literature, such as race differences in serious delinquency, as well as aid in developing and evaluating social policy intended to prevent at-risk youth from committing delinquent acts.

Family-Level Socioeconomic Disadvantage

Studies of the association between family socioeconomic disadvantage and delinquent behavior have produced discordant findings, with some reporting a positive link and others finding that the variables are unrelated. This discordant pattern appears to reflect complexities in the nature of the relationship between socioeconomic disadvantage and delinquent behavior and the influence of moderating factors not incorporated into research designs. Bjerk's (2007) recent analyses suggest that the association between income and delinquency can be obscured because of its nonlinearity and because of error in the measurement of household economic resources. Dividing household income into quintiles, he found that a positive relationship existed between income and participation in serious crime only when comparing adolescents at the lowest end of the income distribution with those at the highest end of the income distribution. In addition, the relationship between economic disadvantage and delinquency was much stronger if the measure of family economic well-being included other relevant economic indicators in addition to income (e.g., savings, debts owed, inheritances).

Poverty is linked to adolescent delinquency independent of other familial factors such as maternal education, family configuration status, and earlier childhood behavior patterns (Pagani, Boulerice, Vitaro, & Tremblaya, 1999). In general, the relationship between socioeconomic disadvantage and adolescent delinquency is stronger when the dependent variable is serious delinquency (Bjerk, 2007; Farnworth, Thornberry, Kohn, & Lizotte, 1994; Jarjoura, Triplett, & Brinker, 2002), if youth live in persistent poverty (Duncan et al., 1994; Farnworth, et al., 1994; Jarjoura et al., 2002; Thornberry, Huizinga, & Loeber, 1995), and if adolescents experienced poverty during early childhood or during adolescence (Brooks-Gunn, Duncan, & Maritato, 1997; Duncan et al, 1998; Jarjoura et al., 2002). Family poverty in middle childhood appears to be less important as an antecedent to serious delinquency than poverty during early childhood or adolescence (Jarjoura et al., 2002).

Mediating Processes

Variants of the family stress model have been used to explain the association between family-level socioeconomic disadvantage and delinquency. Findings consistently show that much of the increased risk of delinquency associated with poverty is mediated through negative parental and family functioning (e.g., parental hostility, parental depression, marital conflict) (Conger et al., 1992, 1994, 1995; Rutter, Giller,

& Hagell, 1998). Numerous studies have found that socioeconomic disadvantage is associated with an increase in coercive, punitive parenting and a decrease in effective parenting (e.g., reasoning and negotiation)—associations mediated partly by psychological distress and fewer material and social resources (Larzelere & Patterson, 1990; McLoyd, 1990; Rutter & Giller, 1983).

Coercive, punitive parenting is a strong and consistent correlate of delinquency (Patterson, 1982; Patterson & Dishion, 1985). In their reanalyses of data from the Glueck's classic study of delinquents and nondelinquents reared in low-income neighborhoods, Sampson and Laub (1994) found that family-level poverty had an indirect effect on delinquency by increasing erratic harsh discipline, reducing effective monitoring and weakening parent–child attachment. The family process variables mediated about 75% of the effect of poverty and other structural background factors on delinquency. Parenting practices (e.g., ineffective discipline, low involvement, and low monitoring) have also been found to mediate the negative relation between "neighborliness" (e.g., sense of belonging, feeling of support, involvement in neighborhood) and gang involvement (Tolan, Gorman-Smith, & Henry, 2003).

Protective Factors

From a social control perspective (Hirschi, 1969), adolescents from poorer families may have a greater propensity toward delinquent behavior because their families have less social support and fewer resources (e.g., money for recreational sports, summer camp) needed to maintain social control over their adolescent children (Heimer, 1997). Subsequently, the provision of certain resources may discourage disadvantaged adolescents from participating in delinquent activities. Participation in sports, for example, is associated with a decrease in the likelihood of cigarette smoking and drug use. Likewise, increases in family time are associated with less cigarette smoking, drinking, drug use, and delinquent activity (e.g., theft,

violence) (Barnes et al., 2006). Greater amounts of social capital also appear to divert youth from delinquent involvement (Rosenfeld, Messner, & Baumer, 2001; Wright, Cullen, & Miller, 2001). Youth are less likely to be involved in fights if they interact on a regular basis with nonparental adults and if their parents have established links to their friends' parents and know at least some of the children's friends (McNulty & Bellair, 2003).

Evidence also exists that participation in religious activities operates as a protective factor. Sinha, Cnaan, and Gelles, (2007) found that attendance at religious services was negatively associated with the likelihood of adolescent smoking, alcohol use and marijuana use and that attaching strong importance to religion predicted decreases in the likelihood of smoking and marijuana use. Compared to nonreligious adolescents, religious adolescents are more likely to endorse conventional values and less likely to affiliate with delinquent peers, which in turn predicts lower levels of involvement in delinquent activity (Simons, Simons, & Conger, 2004).

Community Disadvantage as an Amplifier

Significant variation exists among poor families in the United States in the level of poverty in the communities in which they reside. In the United States, about 20% of the poor live in communities with high concentrations of poverty, leaving 80% living in communities without high concentrations of poverty. Fifty percent of the latter are communities in which the majority of households have incomes above the poverty line (Jargowsky, 1997). There is growing evidence that variation in the context where poor families live influences the degree of association between family-level poverty and delinquency. Specifically, research indicates that community disadvantage amplifies already existing relationships between parenting behavior and delinquent activity (Brody et al., 2001; Hay et al., 2007; Rankin & Quane, 2002). Lower family income puts families at risk of low levels of supervision of youth, weak parent–child bonds, and inconsistent and physical discipline. These relationships are more pronounced in disadvantaged neighborhoods where there are fewer controls to prevent delinquent behavior and more opportunities to commit delinquent acts (Bursik & Grasmick, 1993; Sampson, Raudenbush, & Earls, 1997).

Hay et al., (2007) tested the independent effects of family-level and community-level poverty, as well as their interaction effects on delinquency (e.g. theft, vandalism, assaults, drug use). Family-level unemployment had a particularly strong main effect on delinquency. Whereas there was no main effect of community poverty, Hay et al. found a significant interaction effect of family-level unemployment and family-level income on delinquency, with stronger effects of family disadvantage as community disadvantage increased. For those in especially poor communities with a level of poverty two standard deviations above the mean, having unemployed parents increased adolescents' level of delinquency by 2.71 standard deviation units.

In further evidence of an amplification effect of community disadvantage, Rankin and Quane (2002) found that weak monitoring predicted delinquency only for juveniles living in neighborhoods that had lower collective efficacy. In a similar vein, research indicates that the positive effects of good family functioning are diminished, and the effects of family problems are amplified in neighborhoods with higher levels of crime and poverty (Gorman-Smith, Tolan, & Henry, 2000; Hay et al., 2007). Research even indicates that level of neighborhood poverty moderates the relationship between individual personality traits and delinquency. In two studies examining this issue, Lynam et al. (2000) found that the relationship between impulsivity and delinquency was nonsignificant in the highest SES neighborhoods but very strong in impoverished neighborhoods. This finding is particularly interesting because even if impulsive individuals are more likely to select into impoverished communities,

the disadvantaged context appears to further amplify the positive relation between impulsivity and delinquent activity.

Community-Level Socioeconomic Disadvantage

Community-level socioeconomic disadvantage has been linked to an increase in individual level delinquent activity (Elliot et al., 1996; Simons et al., 1996, McNulty & Bellair, 2003). Leventhal et al. (this volume) summarized the literature linking low neighborhood SES to delinquent activity, citing a series of studies utilizing multiple data sets such as the Family and Community Health Study (FACHS) (Brody et al., 2001; Ge, Brody, Conger, Simons, & Murry, 2002; Gibbons et al., 2004), the National Longitudinal Study of Adolescent Health (Add Health) (Haynie, Silver, & Teasdale, 2006; Knoester & Haynie, 2005), and the Project on Human Development in Chicago Neighborhoods (PHDCN) (Obeidallah, Brennan, Brooks-Gunn, & Earls, 2004). They also cite a specific neighborhood study in Chicago (Sampson, Morenoff, & Raudenbush, 2005), as well as two studies utilizing a national British survey that have found links between low neighborhood SES and delinquency. Studies have also demonstrated that specific aspects of community disadvantage are linked to delinquent behavior. For example, youth exposed to high levels of community violence are at greater risk of perpetrating violence themselves (Gorman-Smith, Henry, & Tolen, 2004).

The preceding discussion concerning amplification effects of community disadvantage anticipates some of the processes by which concentrated disadvantage affects delinquent behavior. Although most poor families do not reside in areas of concentrated disadvantage, those that do face unique risks that increase the likelihood of adolescent delinquency. Impoverished communities are the result of the concentration of impoverished residents in inner cities, who become socially and economically isolated from the rest of society (Wilson,

1987, 1996). These disadvantaged communities are characterized by extreme poverty, welfare dependency, isolation from conventional role models, disproportionately high rates of female-headed households (Massey & Denton, 1993; Wilson, 1987), and high rates of crime and violence (Liska & Bellair, 1995; Morenoff & Sampson, 1997; South & Messner, 2000).

The constrained residential choices perspective suggests that minority and poor individuals are more likely to engage in violence largely because of residential constraints that concentrate them in these disadvantaged communities (De Coster, Heimer, & Wittrock, 2006). Family poverty restricts residential opportunities for certain families and steers them into communities that foster violence and crime among youth (Krivo &Peterson, 2000; Velez, Krivo, & Peterson, 2003). Because disadvantaged neighborhoods typically afford legitimate opportunities for obtaining desired goals, and because poor individuals residing in these neighborhoods are often presented illegitimate opportunities, they are at risk of turning to delinquent activity to achieve their goals (Cloward & Ohlin, 1960; Merton, 1957).

Mediating Processes

One way in which concentrated community disadvantage increases the risk of adolescent delinquency is through a breakdown in formal and informal community control (Sampson & Groves, 1989; Sampson et al., 1997). Hirschi's social control theory (1969) emphasizes that weak social bonds do not compel people to commit crime; rather, they remove constraints from participating in opportunities to commit crime. Therefore, if community social bonds are weak, there are fewer constraints on delinquent activity. Community social capital, defined as the interrelations or ties between families or individuals within a community, is more likely to be compromised in disadvantaged communities (Kingston, 2006). Some of the key dimensions of community social capital that are diminished in these neighborhoods are closure of social networks, community

supervision, and connectedness of individuals in the community (Kubrin & Weitzer, 2003; Sampson et al., 1997). Sampson et al. (1997) found that collective efficacy, measured as informal social control and social cohesion, accounted for a large portion of the effect of socioeconomic disadvantage on violent crime victimization in Chicago neighborhoods. Utilizing a social disorganization framework, Kingston (2006) found a significant negative relationship between individual-level bonding to conventional society and delinquency, but this link was mostly mediated by association with delinquent peers.

Disadvantaged neighborhoods have greater difficulty attracting and maintaining conventional institutions that help control crime, while at the same time, institutions that are more conducive to violence, such as bars, are more prevalent (Peterson, Krivo, & Harris 2000). Peterson et al. found that communities may reduce violent crime somewhat by developing a larger base of certain types of local institutions, such as recreation centers, and preventing other types of institutions, such as bars.

Concentrated community disadvantage can also increase the risk of adolescent delinquency through the establishment of a "street context" or environment conducive to violent behavior. "Street context" is a concept that is being incorporated into the community and crime literature as relevant for understanding the link between community disadvantage and violence. Anderson (1999) posited that the most disadvantaged areas of the inner city ghettos have the greatest amount of violent crime. Thus although parents can compensate to some extent by giving their children a clear message of care and concern, youth in these communities, even those with vigilant, highly engaged parents, will still eventually have to confront the reality of the streets, where violence becomes a central component of life. Youth in highly disadvantaged communities are more likely to see violence as a way of life because they are more likely to be exposed to role models who do not control their own violence (Sampson et al., 1997), and because they are more likely to witness violent acts in their community, have access to weapons, and associate with delinquent peers who promote violence (Hagan & McCarthy, 1997). DeCoster et al. (2005) found that measures of street context mediated the effect of community disadvantage on adolescent violence. In particular, community-level violence increased adolescents' tendency to engage in violent acts by increasing adolescents' embeddedness in deviant peer networks.

Deviant peer associations are a key mediator of the link between community-level socioeconomic disadvantage and delinquency. For example, in Chung and Steinberg's (2006) study of economically disadvantaged minority youth, youth-reported neighborhood disorder (e.g., gang activity, abandoned buildings) increased individual level delinquency by decreasing effective parenting practices (e.g., monitoring) and increasing association with deviant peers. Case and Katz (1991) found evidence for peer contagion effects at the community level, whereby youth who lived in neighborhoods where high numbers of teens were engaged in crime, using drugs, or were out of work or school had an increased probability of the same outcome, controlling for family- and individual-level characteristics. Community disadvantage has been linked to increased probability of associating with deviant peers (Brody et al., 2001).

At the individual level, association with deviant peers is consistently found to predict delinquent activity among both urban and rural youth (Kingston, 2006; Wilson & Donnermeyer, 2006). Deviant peer associations appear to be even more important than family bonds for understanding the relationships between community characteristics and individual crime (Caterello, 2000; Elliott et al., 1996; McNulty & Bellair, 2003a). Youth embedded in deviant peer groups are more likely to engage in violent acts than those not embedded in deviant peer groups (DeCoster et al., 2005) and an adolescent's

delinquency is strongly correlated with the delinquency of the adolescent's "best friend" (Duncan, Boisjoly, & Harris, 2001). In a natural experiment, Levy, Duncan, Boisjoly, & Kremer, (2005) found that being randomly paired with a roommate who is a binge drinker increased the likelihood that a male college freshman who engaged in binge drinking in high school would continue to do so in college.

Race discrepancies exist in the commission of serious delinquent behavior, with African Americans disproportionately more likely to offend than other groups. Sampson and Wilson (1995) posited that the causes of violence are invariant across racial–ethnic groups, and that African American youth and other ethnic-minority youth exhibit higher levels of violence than Whites because they are more likely to reside in community contexts with higher levels of poverty, unemployment, family disruption, and residential instability, and therefore more likely to be exposed to weakened conventional institutions and a "street context" where violence is more normative. McNulty and Bellair (2003) tested whether concentrated disadvantage (percentage income below poverty, single-women households, percentage unemployed, percentage African American) and family well-being (family structure, parental education) mediated the link between race and violent behavior. Concentrated disadvantage completely accounted for the Black–White disparity in fighting, and the effect of concentrated disadvantage on fighting was completely mediated by family well-being.

The deleterious effects of disadvantaged communities on delinquent outcomes can be buffered by family processes. As noted previously, youth exposed to high levels of community violence are more likely to perpetrate violence. However, research also indicates that youth who are exposed to community violence but live in families that function well across multiple dimensions of parenting and family relationships perpetrate less violence than similarly exposed youth from less well-functioning families (Gorman-Smith et al., 2004).

*Altering Adolescents' Context
for Development: The Moving
to Opportunity Experiment*

Programs have attempted to reduce the likelihood of delinquent behavior among disadvantaged youth by altering neighborhood context. The Moving to Opportunity (MTO) demonstration, described previously, provides important information about the effects of altering neighborhood context on delinquent behavior. Although this randomized housing mobility experiment program was successful in moving families into lower poverty, safer neighborhoods, it has not led to overall improvements in children's problem behavior 4–7 years after random assignment (Sanbonmatsu, Kling, Duncen, & Brooks-Gunn 2007).

The findings showed divergent effects on delinquency for program boys and girls. Whereas experimental girls reported a lesser likelihood of marijuana smoking than control girls, experimental boys reported a *greater* likelihood of cigarette smoking and alcohol drinking (Clampet-Lundquist, Edin, Kling, & Duncan, 2006), *more* self-reported behavior problems, and *more* arrests (Kling, Ludwig, & Katz, 2005), relative to control boys. Clampet-Lundquist et al. (2006) examined the qualitative interviews with MTO adolescents to discern why this gender difference existed. Experimental boys were more likely than experimental girls to forge neighborhood-based friendships with delinquent peers, whereas experimental girls were more likely than experimental boys to form school-based friendships with nondelinquent peers (possibly leading to greater school engagement, which may have served as a protective factor). Boys' close friendships more often originated in elementary or middle school (from their previous neighborhoods), rather than the current school they were attending.

Forging friendships in the neighborhood can be riskier than forging friendships at school, especially for boys. In poor neighborhoods, certain delinquent activity, such as the drug trade, is heavily male dominated. Therefore, even for boys and girls living in similar neighborhoods, forging same-sex, neighborhood-based friendships is a greater risk to boys in terms of committing certain types of delinquent activities. Whereas experimental girls were more likely than experimental boys to portray their new neighborhoods in positive terms (e.g., quiet, peaceful), experimental boys often expressed negative views of their new neighborhoods (e.g., boring) (Clampet-Lundquist et al., 2006).

Cultural conflict was also evident for experimental boys, whose main forms of leisure—hanging out on street corners or playing sports in unsupervised settings—drew negative attention from neighbors and police in the forms of police harassment and surveillance far more than leisure activities of any other group. In addition, assuming that a strong attachment to positive male role models is important for motivating boys to stay out of trouble, it is important to note that experimental boys were far less likely than control boys to have strong connections to nonbiological father figures. There were no differences in the proportion of adolescents who had contact with their biological fathers, but four to seven years after random assignment, control boys were almost twice as likely as those in the experimental group to have a close relationship with a male other than a biological father (63% vs. 33%). Apparently, a high proportion of experimental boys lost contact with father figures when they moved to low-poverty neighborhoods. Four to 7 years after random assignment, with only one exception, experimental families with boys who had father figures had moved out of the low-poverty neighborhoods and back to high-poverty neighborhoods, perhaps motivated in part by a desire to reestablish ties with boys' father figures (Clampet-Lundquist et al., 2006). An interesting question that deserves study is why experimental boys, after moving to low-poverty neighborhoods, are able to maintain friendships from their previous neighborhoods, but are not able to form or maintain relationships with potential father figures.

ADOLESCENT EMPLOYMENT

Throughout adolescence, many youth participate in some form of employment. Participation in the labor market is one of the many transitions adolescents negotiate as they prepare for the transition to adulthood. Youth often begin gaining work experience as early as 12 or 13, although child labor laws prohibit participation in formal employment contexts until later in adolescence. In the National Longitudinal Survey of Youth 1997, half of the 13-year-olds interviewed reported engaging in informal employment activities while they were aged 12 (BLS, 2000). Nationally representative surveys also indicate that youth from low SES backgrounds are less likely to work than those from higher SES backgrounds (BLS, 2000; D'Amico, 1984). Entwisle and colleagues' (1999) study of low-income youth indicates that a majority of them do engage in paid work during early adolescence, although the nature of their work may be informal and sporadic. They did various kinds of work, ranging from helping out at local shops to selling door-to-door to construction (Entwisle, Alexander, Olson, & Ross, 1999). The prevalence and variety of employment experiences during early adolescence are important to consider when examining later employment experiences as developmental correlates.

As youth from low-income families enter late adolescence, they are more likely to be employed than they were at younger ages, although they still are less likely to work than their middle-class peers (BLS, 2000). Because of less stringent labor regulations, they can work under more formal arrangements and for more hours. Despite the lower prevalence of employment among low-income youth, those who do work often work longer hours than more affluent youth (Entwisle, Alexander, & Olsen, 2000), presumably to meet material needs and provide financial help to their families.

Employment Opportunities

Numerous factors contribute to the lower employment rates of low-income adolescents. Youth living in poor urban areas face a difficult job market. In recent years, many employers have left the inner cities in favor of the suburbs or overseas markets. This upheaval has left residents of urban areas, especially minorities, with high levels of unemployment and few opportunities (Wilson, 1996). Because no other jobs are available, adults often apply for service jobs that are typically reserved for the youth workforce in more affluent residential areas. This high level of competition makes it difficult for low-income adolescents to obtain employment, a factor exacerbated by youth unfavorable position vis-à-vis adults in terms of experience (Newman, 1999). Using detailed geocode data, Weinberg and colleagues (Weinberg, Regan, & Yankow, 2002) found that male teenagers who resided in economically and socially disadvantaged neighborhoods worked less than those in more affluent areas. Spatial isolation from non-poor households decreases the likelihood that urban minority youth will work during the late adolescent years (Regan & Quigley, 1996). Although the specific mechanisms through which spatial isolation influences adolescent employment need to be further explored, it is likely that reduced contact with employed adults who could provide information and connections needed to obtain work is one pathway (O'Regan & Quigley, 1996).

Other research has shown that residing in high poverty neighborhoods, regardless of urbanicity, decreases youth employment. Youth living in areas where average travel times are greater are less likely to work as well, probably because of transportation difficulties (Gardecki, 2001). In addition to transportation difficulties, adolescents living in rural areas face unique challenges to employment. Many economically disadvantaged rural youth participate in farm work, but this is often seasonal and more prevalent among boys than girls (Elder et al., 1994). National data indicates that most youth engaged in farm work are from families facing economic hardship (BLS, 2000).

Because of the difficult labor markets, the importance of personal and family characteristics in securing and maintaining employment may be magnified for low-income youth. Economically disadvantaged adolescents who have failed a grade in school and who exhibit problem behaviors are less likely to be employed than their peers (Leventhal et al., 2003), whereas having a parent who is employed increases the likelihood of adolescent work (Johnson & Lino, 2000; Leventhal et al., 2003). Ethnographic work with low-income youth also highlights the importance of preexisting connections to people in the labor market for acquiring employment (Newman, 1999).

Ethnic-minority youth appear to experience more difficulties securing and maintaining employment than White youth, regardless of socioeconomic background. Across social classes and family income groups, African American and Latino adolescents are less likely to be employed than White adolescents (Gardecki, 2001; Lerman, 2002). In a longitudinal exploration of work among low-income youth in Baltimore, researchers found that African Americans put more effort into job seeking, but were less likely to secure employment and were more likely to experience spells of unemployment than their White peers (Entwisle, et al., 2000). This suggests that discrimination practices in hiring that hinder minority adults may also operate in the youth sector of the labor market (Bertrand & Mullainathan, 2004). More work is needed to identify factors that contribute to ethnic differences in adolescent employment.

Employment Experiences

Most jobs that low-income adolescents hold are in the service sector and are considered unskilled labor (Entwisle et al., 2000). In her ethnographic study of low-income adolescents and young adults working in fast-food restaurants, Newman found that the time spent working provided a variety of experiences, both positive and negative (Newman, 1999).

Employees may face strict and demanding managers, rude and demeaning customers, as well as ridicule from their nonemployed peers. Despite the possibility of harmful psychological experiences, Newman also highlighted the support that many managers provided their young employees and the social support gained through friendships formed with coworkers.

Youth employment poses risks of physical injury. The actual rate of injuries is hard to assess because most go unreported. Data on injuries that are reported suggest that employment-related injury rates among adolescents range from 6 to 10 injuries per 100 workers (Brooks, Davis, & Gallagher 1993; Parker, Carl, French, & Martin, 1994; Schober et al., 1988). In the United States, approximately 100,000 youth visit the emergency room because of work-related injuries per year and an average of 70 work-related deaths of children and adolescents are reported each year. The rate of work-related injuries is approximately twice as high for adolescents as compared to adults, in part due to lack of experience and training as well as the fact that adolescents are still developing cognitively (Committee on the Health and Safety Implications of Child Labor, 1998). One potential source of harm is burns, which often occur among food preparers, a common job among adolescents employed in the service industry (Parker et al., 1994). Rural adolescents face other risks at their workspace. Children whose parents work in agriculture have higher levels of exposure to pesticides. It is likely that adolescents with similar types of work experience high levels as well (Dilworth-Bart & Moore, 2006).

Spending Patterns

The ways in which earnings are spent reflects another important difference between economically impoverished youth and youth from more affluent circumstances. In affluent contexts, adolescents are usually working to purchase luxury goods, such as cars and entertainment gear (Greenberger & Steinberg, 1986; Johnson & Lino, 2000). In families where financial resources are scarce, adolescents are more likely to be working to contribute to the household. Among adolescents who are employed, those from low-income families and families who have left Temporary Aid to Needy Families (TANF) tend to work more intensely than those from more affluent circumstances, with the former often making significant contributions to overall household income (Entwisle, Alexander, & Olson, 2000; Johnson & Lino, 2000; Lerman, 2000). Questions have been raised about the desirability of this pattern, on the grounds that high-intensity employment may undermine the educational progress of low-income and poor youth due to decreased time to attend to school responsibilities (Lerman, 2000).

Correlates of Employment

Investigations have reported both positive and negative consequences of adolescent employment (Greenberger & Steinberg, 1986; Marsh, 1991; Mortimer, 2003; Steinberg & Cauffman, 1995; Stone & Mortimer, 1998; also see chapter by Staff, Messersmith, & Schulenberg in this volume). Few of these investigations have focused on poor youth, raising questions about whether employment influences poor and nonpoor youth differently. The job market is more challenging for poor and low-income youth, and the motivation for working and employment experiences may be different for poor versus nonpoor youth—all factors that could bear on how employment influences adolescent functioning.

Numerous studies have focused on the relationship between employment and educational outcomes (e.g., Greenberger & Steinberg, 1986; Marsh, 1991; Schoenhals, Tienda, & Schneider, 1998). Despite this rich literature, very few studies have focused on impoverished youth, but the most prominent of these indicate a complex relationship. In their study of low-income African American youth, Leventhal et al. (2003) found that stable employment in adolescence predicted an increase in the likelihood of graduating high

school for both males and females, and of college attendance for males. Entwisle and colleagues (Entwisle, Alexander, & Olson, 2005) found a more complex relationship between employment and school dropout, one that is dependent on type of job and timing. At age 15, low-income adolescents in adult-like jobs were more likely to drop out of school than their peers in teen jobs (e.g., lawn mowing, babysitting), but once adolescents reached age 16, the pattern reversed so that adult-like jobs were related to staying in school. This change is likely related to investment in school and perceptions of one's future employment prospects. Fifteen-year-olds working in adult-like jobs may perceive graduation to be far off in the future and are still going through the challenging transition to high school. Within this context, adult-like employment may be seen as a more appealing option with more immediate opportunities than schooling. By the time youth are 16, they are likely better adjusted to high school and closer to finishing their degree. When employed in an adult-like job at this point, the perceived and actual payoff from education may be strong enough to counteract the perceived benefits of dropping out of school (Entwisle et al., 2005).

Understanding the psychological underpinnings of the relationship between work and schooling is critical to accurately estimating the influences of employment. Although most research has tested a zero-sum hypothesis (Marsh, 1991), which posits that investment in employment will take away from investment in school, it is likely that adolescents who work more intensely and have lower educational attainment choose to engage in work because they do not enjoy school or do not want to continue their education (Warren, 2002). Future research needs to consider psychological constructs such as educational and occupational expectations and school engagement when studying adolescent employment. These notions are especially important to investigate in low-income youth, as they may deinvest in school because they see limited payoff from education and are aware of financial barriers that may prevent them from continuing in the educational system beyond high school. They may view employment as a path that offers more opportunities and provides them with a better chance to obtain their long-term goals.

An important positive outcome of adolescent employment may be the accumulation of human capital. In her ethnographic study of low-income youth working in fast-food restaurants, Newman (1996) observed the time-management, teamwork, and interpersonal skills that were fostered on the job. These skills are likely important for later success in the labor market. Additionally, although many of the youth had to balance work with school, many believed their bosses were supportive of their school commitments and helped maintain that balance. Furthermore, participation in the low-wage service sector served to motivate some adolescents to continue with their education to secure a better career trajectory.

Other ethnographic work has stressed the importance of structured adolescent employment as a way to prevent delinquent behaviors among urban youth (Sullivan, 1989). Although employment does reduce the amount of time available to participate in illegal activities, Roche and colleagues (Roche, Ensminger, Chilcoat, & Storr, 2003) found links between employment and aggressive behaviors among low-income youth who worked early in adolescence. However the relationships were conditional on other roles and experiences in the adolescents' lives. Employed adolescents who were more involved in dating and partying with peers showed increased levels of aggressive behaviors, whereas employed adolescents who assumed more domestic responsibilities (e.g., chores, caring for siblings) showed less aggressive behavior than youth who were not employed. This finding highlights the need for further empirical work that assesses the psychosocial correlates of adolescent employment in tandem with other roles in the lives of low-income youth.

Future research also needs to consider alternative analytic strategies that can better disentangle preexisting differences between adolescents who work and those who do not and hence provide less biased estimates of the impacts of adolescent employment. One example of such a strategy is a sibling design used by Foster (1995) to assess the impact of employment at age 16 on earnings in early adulthood. Using a subsample of brothers from the Panel Study of Income Dynamics, Foster made within-family comparisons. Comparing brothers from the same family when one brother worked and one did not removed from the estimated effect of employment on later outcomes many of the background characteristics that influence whether or not one works, such as family SES.

Foster's analysis indicated a link between employment during adolescence and higher earnings in young adulthood, but this relationship did not hold for all youth. In particular, the results indicated that adolescent employment did not improve later earnings for poor, African American youth. There are many plausible explanations for this finding. African American youth work less than other adolescents and, thus, may not work long enough to gain the skills and experience needed to advance in the labor market. Alternatively, it may be due to the types of jobs they secure. Understanding *why* the relationship between adolescent employment and future earnings operates differently for poor, African American youth is an important question for future research to address. Using inventive methods, such as sibling analyses or other quasi-experimental techniques, will enable researchers to reach more definitive answers about the relationship between adolescent employment and outcomes in later life.

Considering the implications of being unemployed during adolescence is equally important. Need for financial resources and a difficult labor market may cause psychological distress among poor and low-income teenagers who want to contribute to their family's economic situation but are unable to maintain a job. Struggles in the job market can lead to a loss of hope, low self-esteem, and overall life dissatisfaction (Bowman, 1999). These links might be especially strong among older adolescents who are beginning to form their adult identity, given the salience of occupational and economic attainment as markers of successful adulthood. Furthermore, disengagement from the labor market during adolescence may promote youth "idleness," which is linked to lowered economic success and less stable employment later in life (Edelman, Holzer, & Offner, 2006). Thus, the consequences of not working during adolescence when one wishes to or when one feels it is vital for the family's economic well-being are both psychological and structural in nature, and have implications for the short- and long-term well-being of youth from economically disadvantaged backgrounds.

DIRECTIONS FOR FUTURE RESEARCH

Numerous changes that occur as children move from childhood into and through adolescence (e.g., growth in abstract thought, increased understanding of social stratification and its link to life chances, increased awareness of the social meaning of being poor or from a low SES background) modify the meaning and influence of socioeconomic disadvantage. However, it is less clear whether adolescence is a period of heightened vulnerability to the negative impact of poverty and socioeconomic disadvantage on certain outcomes. Despite a voluminous research literature linking socioeconomic disadvantage with adolescent functioning, rigorous examination of this issue is exceedingly rare. The few studies of this issue suggest that living in poor families and residing in economically depressed neighborhoods during early adolescence are more detrimental to school achievement and educational outcomes than similar circumstances during childhood. These timing of poverty effects perhaps are due, in part, to adolescents' increased awareness of barriers and the challenges their social and economic environments pose, which

can undermine achievement values and lessen academic effort (Guo, 1998; Halpern-Felsher et al., 1997; Taylor & Graham, 2007).

Poor and low-income children benefit academically from educationally oriented interventions implemented early in their childhood (McLoyd et al., 2006), but Guo and Halpern-Felsher et al.'s findings suggest that they might also benefit from programs implemented when they are adolescents. The focus of interventions probably needs to be different at different life stages of development to achieve maximum benefits. Early childhood interventions are more effective in promoting school readiness and achievement if there is a strong emphasis on *cognitive stimulation*, whereas Guo and Halpern-Felsher et al.'s work suggests that programs to promote academic achievement among poor and low-income adolescents need to give strong emphasis to cultivating and bolstering *achievement motivation*, predicated on the assumption that psychological and social processes play major roles in undermining school achievement during adolescence. Although Guo and Halpern-Felsher et al.'s findings appear to challenge the view that adolescence is too late in the life course for effective remediation of the effects of persistent poverty and to make a strong case for interventions that specifically target poor or low-income children during their adolescent years, evidence of the replicability and robustness of their findings is needed. Also needed are investigations of the processes that account for timing of family-level and neighborhood-level poverty effects.

The stressors attendant to poverty and socioeconomic disadvantage and the subjective experience of these stressors have long been viewed as key mechanisms through which economic stress adversely affects parental mental health, parenting, family relations, and in turn, child and adolescent mental health. The research literature on economic stress and child-adolescent development is saturated with studies that document these mediating processes, guided largely by psychological perspectives. The family stress model has found strong empirical support, such that it is now well established, at least on the basis of correlational studies, that the model holds for contemporary families from diverse ethnic and socioeconomic backgrounds living in varied geographic contexts.

A notable shortcoming in this area of study is the failure to develop and test variants and extensions of the model that more fully incorporate developmental considerations. Changes in children's psychological characteristics, social contexts, and time use as they move from childhood into and through adolescence are likely to moderate the strength of particular relationships represented in the basic model. Adolescents' coping responses as mediators and moderators of the link between economic stress and mental health have received surprisingly little scholarly attention. In addition to addressing this area of neglect, we need to better understand the antecedents, consequences, and developmental course of children's coping responses in the face of chronic poverty and its attendant stressors. Testing Wadsworth et al.'s (2005) claim that adolescents' coping strategies become less malleable and more traitlike over time and culminate as moderators of stressors in adulthood could be an important step toward expanding the family stress model to accommodate different developmental periods.

Psychologists have been criticized for their persistent attention to parental behavior as a mediator of the relation between poverty and children's socioemotional and cognitive functioning, while ignoring the developmental and psychological significance of the overwhelming array of aversive physical conditions that surround poor children (Evans, 2004). Researchers are beginning to redress the lack of attention to the latter issue, but in general, psychologists have given short shrift to forces outside the immediate household or family (with the exception of deviant peers) as potential mediators of links between poverty and children's development. A fuller

understanding of the pathways through which poverty and socioeconomic disadvantage affects adolescents requires attention to the multiple ecological contexts within which adolescents are embedded. In this regard, we need research that clarifies the extent to which chronic poverty and socioeconomic disadvantage adversely affect adolescents' mental health, school achievement, and other areas of functioning by increasing their exposure to demeaning, humiliating, and otherwise negative treatment precipitated by the stigmas of poverty and socioeconomic disadvantage. Adolescents who are poor or from socioeconomically disadvantaged backgrounds may be hampered in the use of self-protective strategies found among members of other stigmatized groups because of low class consciousness and the widespread endorsement of individualistic explanations of poverty and socioeconomic disadvantage. The rich empirical literature on stigma provides fertile ground to investigate these issues.

Neurobiological models and studies promise to expand our understanding of the pathways through which exposure to chronic stressors linked to poverty impacts adolescent mental health. Scholars working in this area hypothesize, for example, that chronic stressors dysregulate physiological stress response systems, putting adolescents at higher risk of poor decision making and its consequences (e.g., substance abuse), psychosocial maladjustment, and physical health problems. Early work lends preliminary support for some of these hypotheses, although much more work will be required to adequately test them and determine the generalizability of various processes. Research about brain development during adolescence, links between this development and behavior, and the neurobiological effects of poverty-related stress on the developing brain is also likely to significantly advance our understanding of the pathways through which poverty affects adolescent mental health. It may also illuminate the extent to which timing of poverty effects are biologically based and, in turn, aid in the design of more efficient and potent prevention programs. Given the complexities and multifaceted nature of these issues, and the different methods that will be required to adequately address them, interdisciplinary research collaborations and research training that crosses disciplinary boundaries seem particularly appropriate and advantageous.

There is increasing evidence that participation in extracurricular activities promotes academic achievement and educational attainment among poor and low-income adolescents. Moreover, economically disadvantaged adolescents appear to experience greater academic benefits from extracurricular activities than adolescents from more economically advantaged backgrounds. In light of these findings, it is important to identify factors that influence poor children's participation in extracurricular activities and find ways to encourage and expand participation. More work is needed to understand the processes through which poor adolescents benefit from extracurricular activities and to determine the types and characteristics of activities that best promote poor adolescents' academic and socioemotional competence. Testing the effects of extracurricular participation in a random assignment experimental design is an attractive and highly feasible strategy to address the problems of selection bias.

Socioeconomic disadvantage can have deleterious effects on family processes, which in turn, put adolescents at greater risk of committing delinquent behavior. However, research indicates that level of socioeconomic disadvantage, duration and timing of poverty, and the type of delinquency influence the strength of the relationship between family socioeconomic disadvantage and adolescent delinquency. Participation in sports, increased family time, greater social capital, and involvement in religious activities help mitigate the risks associated with family-level socioeconomic disadvantage, and certain factors such as residing in a high-poverty community can exacerbate the risks. Studies further suggest

that the environmental context in which a family resides can have unique effects on delinquent behavior, but also moderate the effects of family level disadvantage. Correlational research has provided a comprehensive and compelling analysis of why and how family- and community-level socioeconomic disadvantage increases the risk of delinquency. What is now needed is experimental field research that draws on the findings from the Moving to Opportunity experiment to design and test the effectiveness of alternative strategies for modifying poor adolescents' socioeconomic environment at the community and school levels. The research design of these studies should allow a determination of whether the effectiveness of various strategies depends on the child's developmental stage at the point when strategies were implemented.

Many healthy and productive adults grew up in poverty. Nonetheless, research on positive adaptation in the context of socioeconomic disadvantage and protective processes that mitigate negative outcomes among economically disadvantaged adolescents is extremely limited. More work has focused on resilience in the face of specific stressors (e.g., parental alcoholism, child maltreatment, and maternal depression) than resilience in the context of socioeconomic disadvantage. Poverty and low-income status are risk factors that are strongly associated with a highly diverse combination of other risk factors. This reality does not preclude examination of protective processes that mitigate the effects of poverty and the cumulative risks associated with poverty. Indeed, scholars have argued that focusing on a single risk factor does not address the reality of most children's lives and that "to truly appreciate the determinants of competence requires attention to the broad constellation of ecological factors in which these individuals and families are embedded" (Sameroff, Gutman, & Peck, 2003, p. 338).

What factors might account for the paucity of research on positive adaptation in the context of socioeconomic disadvantage? Yoshikawa and Seidman (2000) cite the disproportionate attention paid to problem behaviors and the idea that competence among poor or low-income adolescents is not consistent with certain developmental theories as reasons for the paucity of research in this area. Research on adolescents has traditionally focused heavily on antisocial and problem behaviors (Furstenberg, 2000), especially when the adolescents in question are poor or from low SES backgrounds (Yoshikawa & Seidman, 2000). Domains in which adolescents may be highly functional despite difficult circumstances have largely been overlooked (Burton, Obeidallah, & Allison, 1996). Even studies of resilience have tended not to center on positive development, but rather on whether or not problem behaviors exist (Mahoney & Bergman, 2002; Yoshikawa & Seidman, 2000).

Others have raised the possibility that the capacity of positive individual, family, or community factors to either mitigate risks or foster positive outcomes may be compromised under circumstances of extremely high risk (Li, Nussbaum, & Richards, 2007; Luthar, Cicchetti, & Becker, 2000). Still others have argued that some poor and low SES adolescents are growing up in circumstances so dire that positive outcomes are highly unlikely (Cauce, Stewart, Rodriguez, Cochran, & Ginzler, 2003). Because the research literature on adolescents living under conditions of socioeconomic hardship has given so little attention to positive adaptation or competence, in general, it is unclear which protective factors are overwhelmed under certain circumstances and which positive outcomes are more common than others. Both policy and theoretical considerations warrant vigorous and systematic efforts to identify and understand protective processes that mitigate negative outcomes among economically disadvantaged adolescents.

REFERENCES

Alexander, K. L., Entwisle, D. R., & Horsey, C. (1997). From first grade forward: Early foundations of high school dropout. *Sociology of Education, 70,* 87–107.

Anderson, E. (1999). *Code of the street: Decency, violence, and the moral life of the inner city.* New York: W.W. Norton.

Arnsten, A.F., & Shansky, R. M. (2004). Adolescence: Vulnerable period for stress-induced prefrontal cortical function? Introduction to part IV. In R. E. Dahl. & L. P. Spear (Eds.), *Adolescent brain development: Vulnerabilities and opportunities* (pp. 143–147). New York: New York Academy of Sciences.

Barber, B. L., Eccles, J. S., & Stone, M. R. (2001). Whatever happened to the jock, the brain, and the princess? Young adult pathways linked to adolescent activity involvement and social identity. *Journal of Adolescent Research, 16,* 429–455.

Barnes, G. M., Hoffman, J. H., Welte, J. W., Farrell, M. P., & Dintcheff, B. A. (2006). Adolescents' time use: Effects on substance use, delinquency, and sexual activity. *Journal of Youth and Adolescence, 36,* 697–710.

Bar-On, R., Tranel, D. Denburg, N. L., & Bechara, A. (2003). Exploring the neurological substrate of emotional and social intelligence. *Brain, 126,* 1790–1800.

Belle, D., Dill, D., & Burr, R. (1991). Children's network orientations. *Journal of Community Psychology, 19,* 362–372.

Benner, A. D., & Mistry, R. S. (2007). Congruence of mother and teacher educational expectations and low-income youth's academic competence. *Journal of Educational Psychology, 99,* 140–153.

Benson, P. L., Mannes, M., Pittman, K., & Ferber, T. (2004). Youth development, developmental assets, and public policy. In R. M. Lerner & L. Steinberg (Eds.), *Handbook of adolescent psychology* (pp. 781–814). Hoboken, NJ: John Wiley & Sons.

Bertrand, M., & Mullainathan, S. (2004). Are Emily and Greg more employable than Lakisha and Jamal? A field experiment of labor market discrimination. *American Economic Review, 94,* 991–1013.

Betts, J. R., Rueben, K. S., & Danenberg, A. (2000). *Equal resources, equal outcomes? The distribution of school resources and student achievement in California.* San Francisco: Public Policy Institute of California.

Bigler, R. S., Averhart, C. A., & Liben, L. S. (2003). Race and the work force: Occupational status, aspirations, and stereotyping among African American children. *Developmental Psychology, 39,* 572–580.

Bjerk, D. (2007). Measuring the relationship between youth criminal participation and household economic resources. *Journal of Quantitative Criminology, 23,* 23–39.

Bloom, B. S. (1964). *Stability and change in human characteristics.* New York: John Wiley & Sons.

Bolger, K. E., Patterson, C. J. & Thompson, W. W. (1995). Psychosocial adjustment among children experiencing persistent and intermittent family economic hardship. *Child Development, 66,* 1107–1129.

Bolger, K. E., Patterson, C.J., Thompson, W. W., & Kupersmidt, J. B. (1995). Psychological adjustment among children experiencing persistent and intermittent family economic hardship. *Child Development, 66,* 1107–1129.

Bowman, P. J. (1990). The adolescent-to-adult transition: Discouragement among jobless Black youth. *New Directions for Child Development, 46,* 87–105.

Bradley, R., & Corwyn, R. (2002). Socioeconomic status and child development. *Annual Review of Psychology, 53,* 371–399.

Brantlinger, E. (1991). Social class distinctions in adolescents' reports of problems and punishment in school. *Behavioral Disorders, 17,* 36–46.

Brody, G. H., Ge, X., Conger, R., Gibbons, F.X., McBride Murry, V., Gerrard, M., Simons, R. L. (2001). The influence of neighborhood disadvantage, collective socialization, and parenting on African American children's affiliation with deviant peers. *Child Development, 72,* 1231–1246.

Brody, G., Stoneman, Z., Flor, D., McCrary, C., Hastings, L., & Conyers, O. (1994). Financial resources, parent psychological functioning, parent co-caregiving, and early adolescent competence in rural two-parent African-American families. *Child Development, 65,* 590–605.

Bronfenbrenner, U., & Ceci, S. J. (1994). Nature-nurture reconceptualized in developmental perspective: A bioecological model. *Psychology Review, 101,* 568–586.

Brooks, D. R., Davis, L. K., & Gallagher, S. S. (1993). Work-related injuries among Massachusetts children: A study based on emergency department data. *American Journal of Industrial Medicine, 24,* 313–324.

Brooks-Gunn, J., Duncan, G. J., & Maritato, N. (1997). Poor families, poor outcomes: The well-being of children and youth. In G. J. Duncan & J. Brooks-Gunn (Eds.), *Consequences of growing up poor* (pp. 1–17). New York: Russell Sage Foundation.

Brooks-Gunn, J., & Furstenberg, F. F. (1989). Adolescent sexual behavior. *American Psychologist, 44,* 249–257.

Brooks-Gunn, J., Guo, G., & Furstenberg, F. (1993). Who drops out and who continues beyond high school? A 20-year follow-up of Black urban youth. *Journal of Research on Adolescence, 3,* 271–294.

Bureau of Labor Statistics (BLS) (2000). *Report on the youth labor force.* Washington, DC: U.S. Department of Labor.

Bursik, R. J., & Grasmick, H. G. (1993). *Neighborhoods and crime: The dimensions of effective community control.* New York: Macmillan.

Burton, L. M., Obeidallah, D. A., & Allison, K. (1996). Ethnographic insights on social context and adolescent development among inner-city African American teens. In R. Jessor, A. Colby, & R. A. Shweder (Eds.), *Ethnography and human development: Context and meaning in social inquiry* (pp. 395–418). Chicago: University of Chicago Press.

Cartwright, D. (1950). Emotional dimensions of group life. In M. L. Reymert (Ed.), *Feelings and emotions* (pp. 437–337). New York: McGraw-Hill.

Case, A.C., & Katz, L.F. (1991). *The company you keep: The effects of family and neighborhood on disadvantaged youth.* Working paper.

Cauce, A. M., Stewart, A., Rodriguez, M. D., Cochran, M., & Ginzler, J. (2003). Overcoming the odds? Adolescent development in the context of urban poverty. In S. S. Luthar (Ed.), *Resilience and vulnerability: Adaptation in the context of childhood adversities* (pp. 343–363). New York: Cambridge University Press.

Charles, C. Z., Roscigno, V. J., & Torres, K. C. (2007). Racial inequality and college attendance: The mediating role of parental investments. *Social Science Research, 36,* 329–352.

Chung, H. L., & Steinberg, L. (2006). Relations between neighborhood factors, parenting behaviors, peer deviance, and delinquency among serious juvenile offenders. *Developmental Psychology, 42,* 319–331.

Clampet-Lundquist, S. C., Edin, K., Kling, J. R., & Duncan, G. J. (2006). *Moving at-risk teenagers out of high-risk neighborhoods: Why girls fare better than boys.* Working paper #509, Industrial Relations Section, Princeton University.

Clausen, J. S. (1991). Adolescent competence and the shaping of the life course. *American Journal of Sociology, 96,* 805–842.

Clotfelter, C. T., Ladd, H. F., & Vigdor, J. L. (2006, June). *How and why do teacher credentials matter for student achievement?* Paper presented at World Bank Conference, Dijon, France

Clotfelter, C., Ladd, H. F., Vigdor, J., & Wheeler, J. (2006). *High poverty schools and the distribution of teachers and principals.* Calder Institute Working Paper.

.Cloward, R. A., & Ohlin, L. E. (1960). *Delinquency and opportunity: A theory of delinquent gangs.* New York: Free Press.

Committee on the Health and Safety Implications of Child Labor. (1998). *Protecting youth at work: Health, safety, and development of working children and adolescents in the United States.* Washington, DC: National Academy Press.

Compas, B. E., Hinden, B. R., & Gerhardt, C. A. (1995). Adolescent development: Pathways and processes of risk and resilience. *Annual Reviews of Psychology, 46,* 265–293.

Condron, D. T., & Roscigno, V. J. (2003). Disparities within: Unequal spending and achievement in an urban school district. *Sociology of Education, 76,* 18–36.

Conger, R. D., Conger, K. J., & Elder, G. H. (1997). Family economic hardship and adolescent adjustment: Mediating and moderating processes. In G. J. Duncan & J. Brooks-Gunn (Eds.), *Consequences of growing up poor* (pp. 288–310). New York: Russell Sage.

Conger, R. D., Conger, K. J., Elder, G. H., Lorenz, F. O., Simons, R. L., & Whitbeck, L. B. (1992). A family process model of economic hardship and adjustment of early adolescent boys. *Child Development, 63,* 526–541.

Conger, R. D., Ge, X., Elder, G. H., Lorenz, F. O., & Simons, R. L. (1994). Economic stress, coercive family processes, and developmental problems of adolescents. *Child Development, 65,* 541–561.

Conger, R. D., Patterson, G. R., & Ge, X. (1995). It takes two to replicate: A mediational model for the impact of parents' stress on adolescent adjustment. *Child Development, 66,* 80–97.

Conger, R. D., Wallace, L. E., Sun, Y., Simons, R. L., McLoyd, V. C., & Brody, G. H. (2002). Economic pressure in African American families: A replication and extension of the family stress model. *Developmental Psychology, 38,* 179–193.

Connell, J. P., & Halpern-Felsher, B. L. (1997). How neighborhoods affect educational outcomes in middle childhood and adolescence: Conceptual issues and an empirical example. In J. Brooks-Gunn, G. J. Duncan, & J. L. Aber (Eds.), *Neighborhood poverty,* vol.1: *Context and consequences for children* (pp. 174–199). New York: Russell Sage.

Cook, T. D., Church, M. B., Ajanaku, S., Shadish, W. R., Kim, J., & Cohen, R. (1996). The development of occupational aspirations and expectations among inner-city boys. *Child Development, 67,* 3368–3385.

Crocker, J., & Major, B. (1989). Social stigma and self-esteem: The self-protective properties of stigma. *Psychological Review, 96,* 608–630.

Crosnoe, R., Mistry, R. S., & Elder, G. H. (2002). Economic disadvantage, family dynamics, and adolescent enrollment in higher education. *Journal of Marriage and Family, 64,* 690–702.

Crowder, K., & South, S.J. (2003). Neighborhood distress and school dropout: The variable significance of community context. *Social Science Research, 32,* 659–698.

Currie, J, & Lin, W. (2007). Chipping away at health: More on the relationship between income and child health. *Health Affairs, 26,* 331–344.

D'Amico, R. J. (1984). Does employment during high school impair academic progress? *Sociology of Education, 57,* 152–164.

Dearing, E. (2004). The developmental implications of restrictive and supportive parenting across neighborhoods and ethnicities: Exceptions are the rule. *Journal of Applied Developmental Psychology, 25,* 555–575.

DeCoster S. Heimer, K. & Wittrock, S.M. (2006). Neighborhood disadvantage, social capital, street context, and youth violence. *Sociological Quarterly, 47,* 723–753.

Diemer, M. A., & Blustein, D. L. (2007). Vocational hope and vocational identity: Adolescents career development. *Journal of Career Assessment, 15,* 98–118.

Dilworth-Bart, J. E. & Moore, C. F. (2006). Mercy mercy me: Social injustices and the prevention of environmental pollutant exposures among ethnic minority and poor children. *Child Development, 77,* 247–265.

Dorham, C. L. (2006). Future orientation as a protective factor in the relationship between deviant peer association and adolescent adjustment. *Dissertation Abstracts International: Section B: The Sciences and Engineering, 66*(9-B), 5121.

Douglas-Hall, A., & Chau, M. (2007). *Basic facts about low-income children: Birth to age 18.* National Center for Children in Poverty, Columbia University Mailman School of Public Health, New York.

Duncan, G. (1991). The economic environment of childhood. In A. Huston (Ed.), *Children in poverty: Child development and public policy* (pp. 23–50). New York: Cambridge University Press.

Duncan, G. J., Boisjoly, J., & Harris, K. M. (2001). Sibling, peer, neighbor, and schoolmate correlations as indicators of the importance of context for adolescent development. *Demography, 38,* 437–447.

Duncan, G., & Brooks-Gunn, J. (Eds.). (1997). *Consequences of growing up poor.* New York: Russell Sage Foundation.

Duncan, G. J., Brooks-Gunn, J. & Klebanov, P. K. (1994). Economic deprivation and early childhood development. *Child Development, 65,* 296–318.

Duncan, G., & Rodgers, W. (1988). Longitudinal aspects of childhood poverty. *Journal of Marriage and the Family, 50,* 1007–1021.

Duncan, G., Yeung, W., Brooks-Gunn, J., & Smith, J. (1998). How much does childhood poverty affect the life chances of children? *American Sociological Review, 63,* 406–423.

Eamon, M. K. (2002). Influences and mediators of the effect of poverty on young adolescent depressive symptoms. *Journal of Youth and Adolescence, 31,* 231–242.

Eccles, J. S., & Barber, B. L. (1999). Student council, volunteering, basketball, or marching band: What kind of extracurricular involvement matters? *Journal of Adolescent Research, 14,* 10–43.

Eccles, J. S., Midgley, C., Wigfield, A., Buchanan, C. M., Reuman, D., Flanagan, C., & Iver, D. M. (1993). The impact of stage-environment fit on young adolescents' experiences in schools and in families. *American Psychologist, 48,* 90–101.

Eccles, J. S. & Templeton, J. (2007). Extracurricular and other after-school activities for youth. *Review of Research in Education, 26,* 113–180.

Edelman, P., Holzer, H. J., & Offner, P. (2006). *Reconnecting disadvantaged young men.* Washington DC: Urban Institute Press.

Elder, G. (1974). *Children of the Great Depression.* Chicago: University of Chicago Press.

Elder, G. (1997). The life course and human development. In W. Damon (Series Ed.) & R. Lerner (Vol. Ed.), *Handbook of child psychology,* vol. *1: Theoretical models of human development* (5th ed., pp. 939–991). New York: John Wiley & Sons.

Elder, G., Foster, E. M., & Ardelt, M. (1994). Children in the household economy. In R. D. Conger & G. Elder (Eds.), *Families in troubled times* (pp. 127–148). New York: Aldine de Gruyter.

Elder, G., Nguyen, T., & Caspi, A. (1985). Linking family hardship to children's lives. *Child Development, 56,* 361–375.

Elliot, D. S., Wilson, W. J., Huizinga, D, Sampson, R. J., Elliott, A., & Rankin, B. (1996). The effects of neighborhood disadvantage on adolescent development. *Journal of Research in Crime and Delinquency, 33,* 389–426.

Ensminger, M. E., Lamkin, R. P., & Jacobson, N. (1996). Schooling leaving: A longitudinal perspective including neighborhood effects. *Child Development, 67,* 2400–2416.

Entwisle, D. R., Alexander, K. L., & Olson, L. S. (1999). Paid work in early adolescence: Developmental and ethnic patterns. *Journal of Early Adolescence, 19,* 363–388.

Entwisle, D. R., Alexander, K. L., & Olson, L. S. (2000). Early work histories of urban youth. *American Sociological Review, 65,* 279–297.

Entwisle, D. R., Alexander, K. L., & Olson, L. S. (2005). Urban teenagers: Work and dropout. *Youth & Society, 37,* 3–32.

Epps, S. R. (2006). *Low-income children's participation in out-of-school activities: Predictors, developmental differences, and consistency over time.* Unpublished dissertation, University of Texas, Austin.

Evans, G. W. (2004). The environment of childhood poverty. *American Psychologist, 59,* 77–92.

Evans, G. W., & English, K. (2002). The environment of poverty: Multiple stressor exposure, psychophysiological stress, and socioemotional adjustment. *Child Development, 73,* 1238–1248.

Evans, G. W., & Kim, P. (2007). Childhood poverty and health: Cumulative risk exposure and stress dysregulation. *Psychological Science, 18,* 953–957.

Evans, G. W., Kim, P., Ting, A. H., Tesher, H. B., & Shannas, D. (2007). Cumulative risk, maternal responsiveness, and allostatic load in young adolescents. *Developmental Psychology, 43,* 341–351.

Farmer, T. W., Price, L. N., O'Neal, K. K., Leung, M., Goforth, J. B., Cairns, B. D., & Reese, L. E. (2004). Exploring risk in early adolescent African American youth. *American Journal of Community Psychology, 33,* 51–59.

Farnworth, M., Thornberry, T., Krohn, M., & Lizotte, A. (1994). Measurement in the study of class and delinquency: Integrating theory and research. *Journal of Research in Crime and Delinquency, 31,* 32–61.

Fass, S., & Cauthen, N. K. (2007). *Who are America's poor children: The official story.* National Center for Children in Poverty, Columbia University Mailman School of Public Health, New York.

Feather, N. (1974). Explanations of poverty in Australian and American samples. *Australian Journal of Psychology, 26,* 199–216.

Feldman, A. F., & Matjasko, J. L. (2005). The role of school-based extracurricular activities in adolescent development: A comprehensive review and future directions. *Review of Educational Research, 75,* 159–210.

Fishbein, D. (2000). The importance of neurobiological research to the prevention of psychopathology. *Prevention Science, 1,* 89–106.

Fishbein, D., Herman-Stahl, M., & Eldreth, D. (2006). Mediators of the stress-substance-use relationship in urban male adolescents. *Prevention Science, 7,* 113–126.

Fisher, M. J., & Kmec, J. A. (2004). Neighborhood socioeconomic conditions as moderators of family resource transmission: High school completion among at-risk youth. *Sociological Perspectives, 47,* 507–527.

Flanagan, C. A. (1990). Families and schools in hard times. In McLoyd, V. C. & Flanagan, C. A. (Eds.), *New directions for child development,* vol. 46: *Economic stress: Effects on family life and child development* (pp. 7–26). San Francisco: Jossey-Bass.

Flanagan, C., & Tucker, C. (1999). Adolescents' explanations for political issues: Concordance with their views of self and society. *Developmental Psychology, 35,* 1198–1209.

Foster, E. M. (1995). Why teens do not benefit from work experience programs: Evidence from brother comparisons. *Journal of Policy Analysis and Management, 14,* 393–414.

Foster, E. M., & McLanahan, S. (1996). An illustration of the use of instrumental variables: Do neighborhood conditions affect a young person's chance of finishing high school? *Psychological Methods, 1,* 249–260.

Fredricks, J. A., & Eccles, J. S. (2006). Is extracurricular participation associated with beneficial outcomes? Concurrent and longitudinal relations. *Developmental Psychology, 42,* 698–713.

Furstenberg, F. F. (1993). How families manage risk and opportunity in dangerous neighborhoods. In W. J. Wilson (Ed.), *Sociology and the public agenda* (pp. 231–258). Newbury Park, CA: Sage.

Furstenberg, F. F. (2000). The sociology of adolescence and youth in the 1990s: A critical commentary. *Journal of Marriage and Family, 62,* 896–910.

Furstenberg, F. F., Cook, T. D., Eccles, J., Elder, G. H., Jr., & Sameroff, A. (1999). *Managing to make it: Urban families and adolescent success.* Chicago: University of Chicago Press.

Galambos, N. L., & Silbereisen, R. K. (1987). Income change, parental life outlook, and adolescent expectations for job success. *Journal of Marriage and the Family, 49,* 141–149.

Gardecki, R. (2001, August). Racial differences in youth employment. *Monthly Labor Review,* 51–67.

Gennetian, L. A., & Morris, P. A. (2003). The effects of time limits and make work pay strategies on the well being of children: Experimental evidence from two welfare reform programs. *Children and Youth Services Review, 25,* 17–54.

Gennetian, L. A., Duncan, G. J., Knox, V. W., Vargas, W. G., Clark-Kauffman, E., & London, A. S. (2002). *How welfare and work policies for parents affect adolescents: A synthesis of research.* New York: MDRC.

Glasgow, D. (1981). *The Black underclass: Poverty, unemployment and entrapment of ghetto youth.* San Francisco: Jossey-Bass.

Goodban, N. (1985). The psychological impact of being on welfare. *Social Service Review, 59,* 403–422.

Goodman, E. (1999). The role of socioeconomic status gradients in explaining differences in U.S. adolescents' health. *American Journal of Public Health, 89,* 1522–1528.

Goosby, B. J. (2007). Poverty duration, maternal psychological resources, and adolescent socioeconomic outcomes. *Journal of Family Issues, 28,* 1113–1134.

Gorman-Smith, D., Henry, D. B., & Tolan, P. H. (2004). Exposure to community violence and violence perpetration: The protective effects of family functioning. *Journal of Clinical Child and Adolescent Psychology, 33,* 439–449.

Gouldner, H. (1978). *Teachers' pets, troublemakers, and nobodies: Black children in elementary school.* Westport, CT: Greenwood.

Greenberger, E., & Steinberg, L. (1986). *When teenagers work: The psychological and social costs of adolescent employment.* New York: Basic Books.

Guo, G. (1998). The timing of the influences of cumulative poverty on children's cognitive ability and achievement. *Social Forces, 77,* 257–288.

Gutman, L. M., Friedel, J. N., & Hitt, R. (2003). Keeping adolescents safe from harm: Management strategies of African American families in a high-risk community. *Journal of School Psychology, 41,* 167–184.

Gutman, L. M., & McLoyd, V. C. (2000). Parents' management of their children's education within the home, at school, and in the community: An examination of African-American families living in poverty. *Urban Review, 32,* 1–24.

Gutman, L., McLoyd, V. C., & Toyokawa, T. (2005). Financial strain, neighborhood stress, parenting behaviors, and adolescent functioning of urban African American boys and girls. *Journal of Research on Adolescence, 15,* 425–449.

Hagan, J., & McCarthy, B. (1997). *Mean streets: Youth crime and homelessness.* Toronto: Cambridge University Press.

Halpern-Felsher, B. L., Connell, J. P., Spencer, M. B., Aber, J. L., Duncan, G. J., Clifford, E., et al. (1997). Neighborhood and family factors predicting educational risk and attainment in African American and White children and adolescents. In J. Brooks-Gunn, G. J. Duncan, & J. L. Aber (Eds.), *Neighborhood poverty,* vol.1: *Context and consequences for children.* New York: Russell Sage.

Haney, T. (2006). "Broken windows" and self-esteem: Subjective understandings of neighborhood poverty and disorder. *Social Science Research, 36,* 968–994.

Hango, D. (2007). Parental investment in childhood and educational qualifications: Can greater parental involvement mediate the effects of socioeconomic disadvantage? *Social Science Research, 36,* 1371–1390.

Harding, D. J. (2003). Counterfactual models of neighborhood effects: The effect of neighborhood poverty on dropping out and teenage pregnancy. *American Journal of Sociology, 109,* 676–719.

Hay, C., Fortson, E. N., Hollist, D. R., Altheimer, I., & Schaible, L. M. (2007). Compounded risk: The implications for delinquency of coming from a poor family that lives in a poor community. *Journal of Youth and Adolescence, 36,* 593–605.

Heimer, K. (1997). Socioeconomic status, subcultural definitions, and violent delinquency. *Social Forces, 75,* 799–833.

Hill, N., Castellino, D. R., Lansford, J. E., Nowlin, P., Dodge, K. A., Bates, J. E., et al. (2004). Parent academic involvement as related to school behavior, achievement, and aspirations: Demographic variations across adolescence. *Child Development, 75,* 1491–1509.

Hill, N., Ramirez, C., & Dumka, L. (2003). Early adolescents' career aspirations: A qualitative study of perceived barriers and family support among low-income, ethnically diverse adolescents. *Journal of Family Issues, 24,* 934–959.

Hirschi, T. (1969). *Causes of delinquency.* Berkeley: University of California Press.

Holzer, H. J. (in press). The labor market and young black men: Updating Moynihan's perspective. *Annals of the American Academy of Political and Social Science.*

Homel, R., & Burns, A. (1987). Is this a good place to grow up in? Neighborhood quality and children's evaluations. *Landscape and Urban Planning, 14,* 101–116.

Huston, A. C., Duncan, G. J., Granger, R., Bos, J., McLoyd, V. C., Mistry, R., et al. (2001). Work-based antipoverty programs for parents can enhance the school performance and social behavior of children. *Child Development, 72,* 318–336.

Huston, A. C., Duncan, G. J., McLoyd, V. C., Crosby, D. A., Ripke, M. N., Weisner, T. S., et al. (2005). Impacts on children of a policy to promote employment and reduce poverty for low-income parents: New Hope after 5 years. *Developmental Psychology, 41,* 902–918.

Huston, A. C., Miller, C., Richburg-Hayes, L., Duncan, G. J., Eldred, C. A., Weisner, T. S., et al. (2003). *New Hope for families and children: Five-year results of a program to reduce poverty and reform welfare.* New York: MDRC.

Huston, A. C., Walker, J. T., Dowsett, C. J., Imes, A. E., & Ware, A. (2008). *Long-term effects of New Hope on children's academic achievement and achievement motivation.* New York: MDRC.

Ingersoll, R. M. (2004). *Why do high poverty schools have difficulty staffing their classrooms with qualified teachers?* Washington DC: Center for American Progress.

Jargowsky, P. A. (1997). *Poverty and place: Ghettos, barrios, and the American city.* New York: Sage Foundation.

Jarjoura, G. R., Triplett, R. A., & Brinker, G. P. (2002). Growing up poor: Examining the link between persistent childhood poverty and delinquency. *Journal of Quantitative Criminology, 18,* 159–187.

Jarrett, R. L. (1995). Growing up poor: The family experiences of socially mobile youth in low-income African American neighborhoods. *Journal of Adolescent Research, 10,* 111–135.

Jarrett, R. L., Sullivan, P. J., & Watkins, N. D. (2005). Developing social capital through participation in organized youth programs: Qualitative insights from three programs. *Journal of Community Psychology, 33,* 41–55.

Johnson, D. S., & Lino, M. (2000, September). Teenagers: Employment and contributions to family spending. *Monthly Labor Review,* 5–25.

Kao, G., & Tienda, M. (1998). Educational aspirations of minority youth. *American Journal of Education, 106,* 349–384.

Kerpelman, J. L., & Mosher, L. S. (2004). Rural African American adolescents' future orientation: The importance of self-efficacy, control, responsibility, and identity development. *Identity: An International Journal of Theory and Research, 4,* 187–208.

Kingston, B. (2006). The effect of the neighborhood context on adolescent delinquency and drug use. *Dissertation Abstracts International, A: The Humanities and Social Sciences, 66*(9), 3482-A.

Kling, J. R., & Liebman, J. B. (2004). *Experimental analysis of neighborhood effects on youth.* Princeton, NJ: Princeton University.

Kling, J. R., Ludwig, J., & Katz, L. F. (2005). Neighborhood effects on crime for female and male youth: Evidence from a randomized housing voucher experiment. *Quarterly Journal of Economics, 120,* 87–130.

Kozol, J. (1991). *Savage inequalities: Children in America's schools.* New York: Crown.

Kreek, M. J., & Kobb, G. F. (1998). Drug dependence: Stress and dysregulation of brain reward pathways. *Drug and Alcohol Dependence, 51,* 23–47.

Krivo, L. J., & Peterson, R. D. (2000). The structural context of homicide: Accounting for racial differences in process. *American Sociological Review, 65,* 547–559.

Kubrin, C. E., & Weitzer, R. (2003). New directions in social disorganization theory. *Journal of Research in Crime and Delinquency, 40,* 374–402.

Lamb, M. E. (1997). Non-parental child care: Context, quality, correlates, and consequences. In W. Damon (Series Ed.), I. Sigel, & K. A. Renninger (Vol. Eds.), *Handbook of child psychology,* vol. 4: *Child psychology in practice* (5th ed.). New York: John Wiley & Sons.

Lareau, A. (1987). Social class differences in family-school relationships: The importance of cultural capital. *Sociology of Education, 60,* 73–85.

Lareau, A. (2002). Invisible inequality: Social class and child rearing in black families and white families. *American Sociological Review, 67,* 747–776.

Lareau, A. (2003). *Unequal childhoods: Class, race, and family life.* Berkeley: University of California Press.

Larson, J. (1984). The effect of husband's unemployment on marital and family relations in blue-collar families. *Family Relations, 33,* 503–511.

Larson, R. W. (2000). Toward a psychology of positive youth development. *American Psychologist, 55,* 170–183.

Larson, R. W., & Verma, S. (1999). How children and adolescents spend time across the world: Work, play, and developmental opportunities. *Psychological Bulletin, 125,* 701–736.

Larzelere, R.E., & Patterson, G.R. (1990). Parental management: Mediator of the effect of socioeconomic status on early delinquency. *Criminology, 28,* 301–324.

Leahy, R. (1981). The development of the conception of economic inequality: I. Descriptions and comparisons of rich and poor people. *Child Development, 52,* 523–532.

Leahy, R. (1983). Development of the conception of economic inequality: II. Explanations, justifications, and concepts of social mobility and change. *Developmental Psychology, 19,* 111–125.

Lerman, R. I. (2000). *Are teens in low-income and welfare families working too much?* (Series B, No. B-25). Washington DC: Urban Institute Press.

Lerner, R. M., Almerigi, J. B., Theokas, C., & Lerner, J. V. (2005). Positive youth development: A view of the issues. *Journal of Early Adolescence, 25,* 10–16.

Leventhal, T., & Brooks-Gunn, J. (2004). A randomized study of neighborhood effects on low-income children's educational outcomes. *Developmental Psychology, 40,* 488–507.

Leventhal, T., Fauth, R. C., & Brooks-Gunn, J. (2005). Neighborhood poverty and public policy: a 5-year follow-up of children's educational outcomes in the New York City Moving to Opportunity Demonstration. *Developmental Psychology, 41,* 933–952.

Leventhal, T., Graber, J. A., & Brooks-Gunn, J. (2001). Adolescent transitions to young adulthood: Antecedents, correlates, and consequences of adolescent employment. *Journal of Research on Adolescence, 11,* 297–323.

Levy, D. M., Duncan, G. J., Boisjoly, J., & Kremer, M. (2005). *Peer effects in drug use and sex among college students.* Paper presented at the fall conference of the Applied Public Policy and Management Association, November, Washington, DC.

Li, S. T., Nussbaum, K. M., & Richards, M. H. (2007). Risk and protective factors for urban African-American youth. *American Journal of Community Psychology, 39,* 21–35

Lindheim, R., & Syme, S.L. (1983). Environments, people and health. *Annual Reviews of Public Health, 4,* 335–359.

Liska, A. E., & Bellair, P. E. (1995). Violent-crime rates and racial composition: Convergence over time. *American Journal of Sociology, 101,* 578–610.

Ludwig, J., Ladd, H., & Duncan, G.J. (2001). Urban poverty and educational outcomes. In W. G. Gale & J. R. Pack (eds.), *Brookings-Wharton papers on urban affairs* (pp. 147–201). Washington, DC: Brookings Press.

Luthar, S. S., Cicchetti, D., & Becker, B. (2000). The construct of resilience: A critical evaluation and guidelines for future work. *Child Development, 71,* 543–562.

Lynam, D. R., Wikstrsöm, P. H. Caspi, A., Moffitt, T. E., Loeber, R., & Novak, S. (2000). The interaction between impulsivity and neighborhood context on offending: The effects of impulsivity are stronger in poorer neighborhoods. *Journal of Abnormal Psychology, 109,* 563–574.

MacLeod, J. (1987). *Ain't no makin' it: Aspirations and attainment in a low-income neighborhood.* Boulder, CO: Westview Press.

Mahoney, J. L. (2000). Participation in school extracurricular activities as a moderator in the development of antisocial patterns. *Child Development, 71,* 502–516.

Mahoney, J. L., & Bergman, L. B. (2002). Conceptual and methodological considerations in a developmental approach to the study of positive adaptation. *Applied Developmental Psychology, 23,* 195–217.

Mahoney, J. L., & Cairns, R. (1997). Do extracurricular activities protect against early school dropout? *Developmental Psychology, 33,* 241–253.

Mahoney, J. L., Cairns, B. D., & Farmer, T. W. (2003). Promoting interpersonal competence and educational success through extracurricular activity participation. *Journal of Educational Psychology, 95,* 409–418.

Mahoney, J. L., & Stattin, H. (2000). Leisure activities and adolescent antisocial behavior: The role of structure and social context. *Journal of Adolescence, 23,* 113–127.

Makosky, V. P. (1982). Sources of stress: Events or conditions? In D. Belle (Ed.), *Lives in stress: Women and depression* (pp. 35–53). Beverly Hills, CA: Sage.

Marsh, H. W. (1991). Employment during high school: Character building or subversion of academic goals? *Sociology of Education, 64,* 172–189.

Marsh, H. W. (1992). Extracurricular activities: Beneficial extension of the traditional curriculum or subversion of academic goals? *Journal of Educational Psychology, 84,* 553–562.

Marsh, H. W., & Kleitman, S. (2002). Extracurricular school activities: The good, the bad, and the nonlinear. *Harvard Educational Review, 72,* 464–514.

Marshall, N. (1982). The public welfare system: Regulation and dehumanization. In D. Belle (Ed.), *Lives in stress: Women and depression* (pp. 96–108). Beverly Hills: Sage.

Massey, D. S., & Denton, N. A. (1993). *American apartheid: Segregation and the making of the underclass.* Cambridge, MA: Harvard University Press.

McCabe, K., & Barnett, D. (2000). First comes work, then comes marriage: Future orientation among African American young adolescents. *Family Relations, 49,* 63–70.

McKown, C. (2004). Age and ethnic variation in children's thinking about the nature of racism. *Journal of Applied Developmental Psychology, 25,* 597–617.

McLeod, J. D., & Owens, T. J. (2004). Psychological well-being in the early life course: Variations by socioeconomic status, gender, and race/ethnicity. *Social Psychology Quarterly, 67,* 257–278.

McLeod, J. D., & Shanahan, M. (1993). Poverty, parenting, and children's mental health. *American Sociological Review, 58,* 351–366.

McLoyd, V. C. (1990). The impact of economic hardship on black families and children: Psychological distress, parenting, and socioemotional development. *Child Development, 61,* 311–346.

McLoyd, V. C. (1998). Socioeconomic disadvantage and child development. *American Psychologist, 53,* 185–204.

McLoyd, V. C., Aikens, N. L., & Burton, L. M. (2006). Childhood poverty, policy, and practice. In W. Damon (Series Ed.), I. Sigel, & K. A. Renninger (Eds.), *Handbook of child psychology,* vol. 4: *Child psychology in practice* (5th ed.) Hoboken, NJ: John Wiley & Sons.

McLoyd, V. C., Jayaratne, T., Ceballo, R., & Borquez, J. (1994). Unemployment and work interruption among African American single mothers: Effects on parenting and adolescent socioemotional functioning. *Child Development, 65,* 562–589.

McLoyd, V. C., & Jozefowicz, D. M. (1996). Sizing up the future: Predictors of African American adolescent females' expectancies about their economic fortunes and family life course. In B. Leadbeater & N. Way (Eds.), *Creating identities, resisting stereotypes: Urban adolescent girls.* New York: University Press.

McLoyd, V. C., Kaplan, R., & Purtell, K. M. (2008). *New Hope's effects on children's future orientation and employment experiences.* New York: MDRC.

McNeal, R. B. (1999). Parental involvement as social capital: Differential effectiveness on science achievement, truancy, and dropping out. *Social Forces, 78,* 117–144.

McNulty, T. L., & Bellair, P. E. (2003a). Explaining racial and ethnic differences in serious adolescent violent behavior. *Criminology, 41,* 709–746.

McNulty, T. L. & Bellair, P. E. (2003b). Explaining racial and ethnic differences in adolescent violence: Structural disadvantage, family well-being, and social capital. *Justice Quarterly, 20,* 1–31.

Merton, R. K. (1957). *Social theory and social structure.* Glencoe, IL: Free Press.

Mickelson. R. A. (1990). The attitude-achievement paradox among Black adolescents. *Sociology of Education, 63,* 44–61.

Mistry, R. S., Vandewater, E. A., Huston, A. C., & McLoyd, V. C. (2002). Economic well-being and children's social adjustment: The role of family process in an ethnically diverse low-income sample. *Child Development, 73,* 935–951.

Morenoff, J. E., & Sampson, R. J. (1997). Violent crime and the spatial dynamics of neighborhood transition: Chicago, 1970–1990. *Social Forces, 76,* 31–64.

Morris, P. A., Huston, A. C., Duncan, G. J., Crosby, D. A., & Bos, J. M. (2001). *How welfare and work policies affect children: A synthesis of research.* New York: MDRC.

Mortimer, J. T. (2003). *Work and growing up in America.* Cambridge, MA: Harvard University Press.

Murray, B. (1996). Program helps kids map realistic goals. *American Psychological Association Monitor, 27,* 40.

National Center for Educational Statistics. (2006). *Digest of educational statistics.* Washington, DC: Institute of Educational Sciences.

National Center for Education Statistics. (2007). *The condition of education.* Washington, DC: Institute of Educational Sciences.

Neblett, N. G., & Cortina, K.S. (2006). Adolescents' thoughts about parents' jobs and their importance for adolescents' future orientation. *Journal of Adolescence, 29,* 795–811.

Newman, K. S. (1996). Working poor: Low-wage employment in the lives of Harlem youth. In J. A. Graber, J. Brooks-Gunn, & A. C. Peterson (Eds.), *Transitions through adolescence* (pp. 323–343). Mahwah, NJ: Lawrence Eribaum.

Newman, K. S. (1999). *No shame in my game: The working poor in the inner city.* New York: Knopf/Russell Sage Foundation.

Nurmi, J. E. (1991). How do adolescents see their future? A review of the development of future orientation and planning. *Developmental Review, 11,* 1–59.

O'Regan, K., & Quigley, J. (1996). Teenage employment and the spatial isolation of minority and poverty households. *Journal of Human Resources, 31,* 692–702.

Pagani, L., Boulerice, B., Vitaro, F., & Tremblay, R. E. (1999). Effects of poverty on academic failure and delinquency in boys: A change and process model approach. *Journal of Child Psychology and Psychiatry, 40,* 1209–1219.

Parker, D. L., Carl, W. R., French, L. R., & Martin, F. B. (1994). Nature and incidence of self-reported adolescent work injury in Minnesota. *American Journal of Industrial Medicine, 26,* 529–541.

Patterson, G. R. (1982). *Coercive family process.* Eugene, OR: Castalia.

Patterson, G. R., & Dishion, T. (1985). Contributions of families and peers to delinquency. *Criminology, 23,* 63–79.

Pedersen, S., & Seidman, E. (2005). Contexts and correlates of out-of-school activity participation among low-income urban adolescents. In R. Larson (Ed.), *Organized activities as contexts of development: Extracurricular activities, after school, and community programs* (pp. 85–109). Mahwah, NJ: Lawrence Erlbaum.

Pedersen, S., Seidman, E., Yoshikawa, H., Rivera, A. C., Allen, L., & Aber, J. L. (2005). Contextual competence: Multiple manifestations among urban adolescents. *American Journal of Community Psychology, 35,* 65–82.

Pelton, L. H. (1989). *For reasons of poverty: A critical analysis of the public child welfare system in the United States.* New York: Praeger.

Petersen, A. C., Compas, B. E., Brooks-Gunn, J. Stemmpler, M., Ey, S., & Grant, K. E. (1993). Depression in adolescence. *American Psychologist, 48,* 155–168.

Peterson, R. D., Krivo, L .J. & Harris, M. A. (2000). Disadvantage and neighborhood violent crime: Do local institutions matter? *Journal of Research in Crime and Delinquency, 37,* 31–63.

Phillips, T. M., & Pittman, J. (2003). Identity processes in poor adolescents: Exploring the linkages between economic disadvantage and the primary task of adolescence. *Identity: An International Journal of Theory and Research, 3,* 115–129.

Pierce, K. M., Hamm, J. V., & Vandell, D. L. (1999). Experiences in after-school programs and children's adjustment in first-grade classrooms. *Child Development, 70,* 756–767.

Pittman, K., Irby, M. & Ferber, T. (2001). Unfinished business: Further reflections on a decade of promoting youth development. In P. L. Benson & K. J. Pittman (Eds.), *Trends in youth development: Visions, realities and challenges.* Norwell, MA: Kluwer Academic.

Pogash, C. (2008, March 1). Poor students in high school suffer stigma from lunch aid. *New York Times,* p.1.

Posner, J. K., & Vandell, D. L. (1999). After-school activities and the development of low-income urban children: A longitudinal study. *Developmental Psychology, 35,* 868–879.

Quane, J., & Rankin, B. (1998). Neighborhood poverty, family characteristics, and commitment to mainstream goals. *Journal of Family Issues, 19,* 769–794.

Quintana, S. M. (1998). Development of children's understanding of ethnicity and race. *Applied & Preventive Psychology: Current Scientific Perspectives, 7,* 27–45.

Quinton, D., Pickles, A., Maughan, B., & Rutter, M. (1993). Partners, peers, and pathways: Assortative pairing and continuities and discontinuities in conduct disorder. *Developmental Psychology, 5,* 763–783.

Rankin, B. H., & Quane, J. M. (2002). Social contexts and urban adolescent outcomes: The interrelated effects of neighborhoods, families, and peers on African-American youth. *Social Problems, 49,* 79–100.

Rist, R. (1970). Student social class and teacher expectations: The self-fulfilling prophecy in ghetto education. *Harvard Educational Review, 40,* 411–451.

Robbins, R. N., & Bryan, A. (2004). Relationships between future orientation, impulsive sensation seeking, and risk behaviors among adjudicated adolescents. *Journal of Adolescent Research, 19,* 428–445.

Roche, K. M., Ensminger, M. E., Chilcoat, H., & Storr, C. (2003). Establishing independence in low-income urban areas: The relationship to adolescent aggressive behavior. *Journal of Marriage and Family, 65,* 668–680.

Roscigno, V. J., & Ainsworth-Darnell, J. W. (1999). Race, cultural capital, and educational resources: Persistent inequalities. *Sociology of Education, 72,* 158–178.

Rosenberg, M. (1979). *Conceiving the self.* New York: Basic Books.

Rosenberg, M., & Pearlin, L. (1978). Social class and self-esteem among children and adults. *American Journal of Sociology, 84,* 53–77.

Rosenfeld, R., Messner, S. F., & Baumer, E. P. (2001). Social capital and homicide. *Social Forces, 80,* 283–309.

Roth, J., Murray, L. F., Brooks-Gunn, J., & Foster, W. H. (1999). Youth development programs. In D. J. Besharov (Ed.), *America's disconnected youth: Toward a preventive strategy.* Washington, DC: CWLA Press.

Rutter, M., & Giller, H. (1983). *Juvenile delinquency: Trends and perspectives.* New York: Guilford.

Rutter, M., Giller, H., & Hagell, A. (1998). *Antisocial behavior by young people.* Cambridge: Cambridge University Press.

Sameroff, A., Gutman, L. M., & Peck, S. C. (2003). Adaptation among youth facing multiple risks: Prospective research findings. In S. S. Luthar (Ed.), *Resilience and vulnerability: Adaptation in the context of childhood adversities* (pp. 364–391). New York: Cambridge University Press.

Sampson, R. J., & Groves, W. B. (1989). Community structure and crime: Testing social-disorganization theory. *American Journal of Sociology, 94,* 774.

Sampson, R. J., & Laub, J. H. (1994). Urban poverty and the family context of delinquency: A new look at structure and process in a classic study. *Child Development, 65,* 523–540.

Sampson, R. J., Raudenbush, S. W. & Earls, R. F. (1997). Neighborhoods and violent crime: A multilevel study of collective efficacy. *Science, 277,* 918–924.

Sampson, R.J., & Wilson, W.J. (1995). Toward a theory of race, crime, and urban inequality. In J. Hagan & R.D. Peterson (Eds.), *Crime and inequality* (pp. 37–54). Stanford, CA: Stanford University Press.

Sanbonmatsu, L., Kling, J. R., Duncan, G. J., & Brooks-Gunn, J. (2007). Neighborhood and academic achievement: Results from the moving to opportunity experiment. *Journal of Human Resources, XLI,* 649–691.

Schober, S. E., Handke, J. L., Halperin, W. E., Moll, M. B., & Thun, M. J. (1988). Work-related injuries in minors. *American Journal of Industrial Medicine, 14,* 585–595.

Schoenhals, M., Tienda, M., & Schneider, B. (1998). The educational and personal consequences of adolescent employment. *Social Forces, 77,* 723–762.

Schoon, I., Bynner, J., Joshi, H., Parsons, S., Wiggins, R.D., & Sacker, A. (2002). The influence of context, timing, and duration of risk experiences for the passage from childhood to mid-adulthood. *Child Development, 73,* 1486–1504.

Schoon, I., Parsons, S., & Sacker, A. (2004). Socioeconomic adversity, educational resilience, and subsequent level of adult adaptation. *Journal of Adolescent Research, 19,* 383–404.

Seginer, R. (2003). Adolescent future orientation in culture and family settings. In W. Friedlmeier, P. Chakarath, & B. Schwartz (Eds.), *Culture and human development: The importance of cross-cultural research to the social sciences.* Lisse, Netherlands: Swets & Zetlinger.

Seidman, E., & Pedersen, S. (2003). Holistic contextual perspectives on risk, protection, and competence among low-income urban adolescents. S. S. Luthar (Ed.), *Resilience and vulnerability: Adaptation in the context of childhood adversities* (pp. 318–342). New York: Cambridge University Press.

Sennett, R., & Cobb, J. (1972). *The hidden injuries of class.* New York: Vintage Books.

Shaw, C., & McKay, H. (1942). *Juvenile delinquency in urban areas.* Chicago: University of Chicago Press.

Simons, L. G., Simons, R. L., & Conger, R. D. (2004). Identifying the mechanisms whereby family religiosity influences the probability of adolescent antisocial behavior. *Journal of Comparative Family Studies, 35,* 547–563.

Simons, R. L., Johnson, C., Beaman, J., Conger, R. D., & Whitbeck, L. B. (1996). Parents and peer group as mediators of the effect of community structure on adolescent problem behavior. *American Journal of Community Psychology, 24,* 145–165.

Simons, R. L., Murry, V., McLoyd, V. C., Lin, K., Cutrona, C., & Conger, R. D. (2002). Discrimination, crime, ethnic identity, and parenting as correlates of depressive symptoms among African American children: A multilevel analysis. *Development and Psychopathology, 14,* 371–393.

Simons, R. L., Whitbeck, L. B., & Wu, C. (1994). Resilient and vulnerable adolescents. In R. Conger & G. Elder, (Eds.), *Families in troubled times: Adapting to change in rural America* (pp. 223–234). New York: Aldine de Gruyter.

Singha, R. (2001). How does stress increase risk of drug abuse and relapse? *Psychopharmacology, 158,* 343–359.

Sinha, J. W., Cnaan, R.A., & Gelles, R.J. (2007). Adolescent risk behaviors and religion: Findings from a national study. *Journal of Adolescence, 30,* 231–249.

Slavin, R. E. (1999). How can funding equity ensure enhanced achievement? *Journal of Education Finance, 24,* 519–528.

Smith, J., Brooks-Gunn, J., & Klebanov, P. (1997). Consequences of living in poverty for young children's cognitive and verbal ability and early school achievement. In G. Duncan & J. Brooks-Gunn (Eds.), *Consequences of growing up poor* (pp. 132–189). New York: Russell Sage Foundation.

Smokowski, P. R., Reynolds, A. J., & Bezruckzo, N. (1999). Resilience and protective factors in adolescence: An autobiographical perspective from disadvantaged youth. *Journal of School Psychology, 37,* 425–448.

Socias, M., Chambers, J., Esra, P., & Shambaugh, L. (2007). *The distribution of teaching and learning resources in California's middle and high schools* (Issues & Answers Report, REL 2007–No. 023). Washington, DC: U.S. Department of Education, Institute of Education Sciences, National Center for Education Evaluation and Regional Assistance, Regional Educational Laboratory West. Retrieved from http://ies.ed.gov/ncee/edlabs

Solorzano, D.G., & Ornelas, A. (2002). A critical race analysis of advanced placement classes: A case of educational inequality. *Journal of Latinos and Education, 1,* 215–229.

South, S. J., & Messner, S. F. (2000). Crime and demography: Multiple linkages, reciprocal relations. *Annual Review of Sociology, 26,* 83–106.

Steinberg, L., & Cauffman, E. (1995). The impact of employment on adolescent development. In R. Vasta (Ed.), *Annals of child development,* vol. *11* (pp. 132–166). London: Jessica Kingsley.

Steinberg, L., Graham, S., O'Brien, L., Woolard, J., Cauffman, E. & Banich, M. (in press). Age differences in future orientation and delay discounting. *Child Development.*

Steinberg, L., & Silk, J. (2002). Parenting adolescents. In M. Bornstein (Ed.), *Handbook of parenting,* vol. 1: *Children and parenting.* Mahwah, NJ: Lawrence Erlbaum.

Stevenson, J., Richman, N., & Graham, P. (1985). Behaviour problems and language abilities at three years and behavioural deviance at eight years. *Journal of Child Psychology and Psychiatry, 26,* 215–230.

Stone, J. R., & Mortimer, J. T. (1998). The effect of adolescent employment on vocational development: Public and educational policy implications. *Journal of Vocational Behavior, 53,* 184–214.

Strohschein, L. A. (2005), Household income histories and child mental health trajectories. *Journal of Health and Social Behavior, 46,* 359–375.

Sullivan, M. L. (1989). *"Getting paid": Youth crime and work in the inner city.* Ithaca: Cornell University Press.

Taylor, A. Z., & Graham, S. (2007). An examination of the relationship between achievement values and perceptions of barriers among low-SES African American and Latino students. *Journal of Educational Psychology, 99,* 52–64.

Taylor, R. D., Rodriguez, A. U., Seaton, E., & Dominguez, A. (2004). Association of financial resources with parenting and adolescent adjustment in African-American families. *Journal of Adolescent Research, 19,* 267–283.

Thornberry, T. P., Huizinga, D., & Loeber, R. (1995). The prevention of serious delinquency and violence: Implications from the Program of Research on the Causes and Correlates of Delinquency. In J. C. Howell, B. Krisberg, J. D. Hawkins, & J. J. Wilson, (Eds.). *Sourcebook on serious, violent, and chronic juvenile offender* (pp. 213–237). Thousand Oaks, CA: Sage.

Tolan, P. H., Gorman-Smith, D., & Henry, D. B. (2003). The developmental ecology of urban males' youth violence. *Developmental Psychology, 39,* 274–291.

Tolan, P., Gorman-Smith, D., Henry, D., Chung, K., & Hunt, M. (2002). The relation of patterns of coping of inner-city youth to psychopathology symptoms. *Journal of Research on Adolescence, 12,* 423–449.

Trommsdorff, G. (1986). Future orientation and its relevance for development as action. In R. K. Silbereisen, K. Eyferth, & G. Rudinger (Eds.), *Development as action in context: Problem behavior and normal youth development* (pp. 121–136). Berlin: Springer-Verlag.

Troutman, K. P., & Dufur, M. J. (2007). From high school jocks to college grads: Assessing the long-term effects of high school sport participation on females' educational attainment. *Youth and Society, 38,* 443–462.

Tung, R., & Ouimette, M. (2007). *Strong results, high demand: A four-year study of Boston's pilot high schools.* Boston: Center for Collaborative Education.

Velez, M. B., Krivo, L. J., & Peterson, R. D. (2003). Structural inequality and homicide: An assessment of the black-white gap in killings. *Criminology, 41,* 645–672.

Wadsworth, M. E., & Compas, B. E. (2002). Coping with economic strain and family conflict: The adolescent perspective. *Journal of Research on Adolescence, 12,* 243–274.

Wadsworth, M. E., Raviv, T., Compas, B. E., & Connor-Smith, J. K. (2005). Parent and adolescent responses to poverty-related stress: Tests of mediated and moderated coping models. *Journal of Child and Family Studies, 14,* 283–298.

Warren, J. R. (2002). Reconsidering the relationship between student employment and academic outcomes: A new theory and better data. *Youth and Society, 33,* 366–393.

Weinberg, B. A., Regan, P. B., & Yankow, J. J. (2004). Do neighborhoods affect hours worked? Evidence from longitudinal data. *Journal of Labor Economics, 22,* 891–924.

Wilson, J. M., & Donnermeyer, J. F. (2006). Urbanity, rurality, and adolescent substance use. *Criminal Justice Review, 31,* 337–356.

Wilson, W. J. (1987). *The truly disadvantaged: The inner city, the underclass and public policy.* Chicago: University of Chicago Press.

Wilson, W. J. (1996). *When work disappears: The world of the new urban poor.* New York: Knopf.

Wiltfang, G., & Scarbecz, M. (1990). Social class and adolescents' self-esteem: Another look. *Social Psychology Quarterly, 53,* 174–183.

Wood, D., Kaplan, R., & McLoyd, V.C. (2007). Gender differences in the educational expectations of urban, low-income African American youth: The role of parents and the school. *Journal of Youth and Adolescence, 36,* 417–427.

Wright, J. P., Cullen, F. T., & Miller, J. T. (2001). Family social capital and delinquent involvement. *Journal of Criminal Justice, 29,* 1–9.

Wyman, P. A., Cowen, E. L., Work, W. C., & Kerley, J. H. (1993). The role of children's future expectations in self-system functioning and adjustment to life stress: A prospective study of urban at-risk children. *Development and Psychopathology, 5,* 649–661.

Wyman, P. A., Cowen, E. L., Work, W. C., Raoof, B. A., Gribble, P. A., Parker, G. R., & Wannon, M. (1992). Interviews with children who experienced major life stress: Family and child attributes that predict resilient outcomes. *Journal of the American Academy of Child and Adolescent Psychiatry, 31,* 904–910.

Yoshikawa, H., & Seidman, E. (2000). Competence among urban adolescents in poverty: Multiple forms, contexts, and developmental processes. In R. Montemayor, G.R. Adams, & T.P. Gullotta (Eds.), *Advances in adolescent development: Vol. 10. Adolescent diversity in ethnic, economic, and cultural contexts* (pp. 9–42). Thousand Oaks, CA: Sage.

Zigler, E., & Berman, W. (1983). Discerning the future of early childhood intervention. *American Psychologist, 33,* 894–906.

Zill, N. (1984). *American children: Happy, healthy and insecure.* New York: Doubleday Anchor.

CHAPTER 14

The Transition to Adulthood

Challenges of Poverty and Structural Lag

STEPHEN F. HAMILTON AND MARY AGNES HAMILTON

This chapter discusses the transition of adolescents to adulthood. It is more speculative than empirical because the issues we raise regarding the transition to adulthood have not been extensively studied. It is grounded in two observations: The transition to adulthood is central to both the reproduction of the social class hierarchy and the alleviation of poverty, and the transition is fundamentally institutional. These two observations generate our framing question: How can the institutions supporting the transition to adulthood more effectively contribute to overcoming poverty? The United States is our primary point of reference, but we include data and institutions from other countries as well. We rely on, but do not attempt to summarize or reproduce, the rich material in the excellent volumes on the transition to adulthood in the United States, edited by Furstenberg, Rumbaut, and Settersten (2005), and globally, edited by Lloyd (2005). Chapter 17 in this *Handbook* complements this one, especially by calling attention to contrary trends in the transition to adulthood viewed globally, variation both within and across nations and cultures, and variation by gender.

The transition to adulthood is pivotal in the reproduction of socioeconomic status (SES) and in social and economic mobility. If young people who have grown up in poverty are to rise above the SES of their parents, their best chance to do so, or at least to move on the path in that direction, is at the transition to adulthood. Children's SES is secondhand; it is determined directly by that of their parents. In societies that allow social mobility, adults' SES depends on their own education and employment. Of course, young adults carry with them an array of assets related to SES bequeathed to them by their parents, but their SES is attributed to them based on their own characteristics, not automatically extended to them based on their parents' SES, as in an aristocracy. Therefore, social mobility (in either direction) depends critically on what happens at the transition to adulthood. Overcoming poverty clearly requires attention to the needs of young children, but the transition to adulthood is when most people either begin to rise above their status at birth or fail to do so, because the capacity to be economically productive is largely set by the time young people become adults.

THE LONG AND VARIED TRANSITION TO ADULTHOOD

The transition to adulthood is defined by changes in institutional roles and relationships. Adults, in the standard scenario, have left their parents' household and established their own. They have married and become parents. They have completed full-time education and are employed full time. Listing these changes immediately calls attention to variations. First, by the age of 30 or 35, nearly everyone is considered adult even without having taken any of these steps. Second, rather than being required, every step is increasingly optional.

Divorce, cohabitation, and same-sex couples increase the variety of household options. Third, what was once considered an ideal sequence of steps no longer matches reality. Children are born before marriage. Education and employment alternate in all combinations of full and part time. Fourth, each of these steps is in some senses reversible. The parents' home serves as a refuge for young adults who had previously moved away and completed their educations, perhaps following a divorce or loss of a job. Parenthood is not completely reversible, but even parental responsibilities can be formally relinquished through adoption or informally turned over to a grandparent. In addition to varying in sequence and universality, the timing of these markers of adulthood varies among individuals, groups, and historical periods (Modell, 1989).

Adolescence is defined by a biological process, puberty, just as the differences between infancy and early childhood and the other stages of childhood are marked by visible physiological changes. In contrast, the transition to adulthood is defined by changes in social roles, notably within the institutions of family, education, employment, and civil society. The markers of adulthood listed above constitute a shift from being dependent upon parents or parent substitutes for basic needs to being capable of caring for self and others. This shift from dependency to being depended upon is structured by the institutions of education, employment, civil society, and the family—families of origin and the new families formed by new adults. No other life-course transition is so fully defined by social institutions as the transition from adolescence to adulthood.

Consider an 18-year-old and a 28-year-old. Physiologically, both are fully mature, capable of reproduction. Yet in the United States, few 18-year-olds are considered fully adult, despite legal rights and obligations associated with the age, and most 28-year-olds are, even if they have not achieved all the markers of adulthood. The centrality of institutional roles is illustrated by extreme cases, as when an 18-year-old is already a parent living in her own apartment and employed full time while her unmarried 28-year-old sister is living at home and attending college classes. The institutional nature of the transition to adulthood explains why it is reasonable to claim that the transition has grown longer around the world (Arnett, 2004; Lloyd, 2005) with no concomitant change in the timing of physical maturation.

The lengthening period of time when young people are physically mature and capable of reproduction but not yet acting like and treated as adults reflects changes in employment that increasingly reward extended education. Marriage and parenthood are delayed to allow more years of education. The change is all the more dramatic for involving young women as well as men. If young women were not able to take advantage of both advanced education and the employment opportunities it affords, then older ages at marriage might be observed only among men, or, conceivably, women might marry students who were supported economically by their families. Simultaneous increases in marriage age for both women and men indicate increasing gender equality. The growing participation of women in higher education and in paid employment serves as a reminder too that the lengthening transition to adulthood results not only from impersonal economic forces but also from choices young people make. Control over fertility and the separation of sexual relations from marriage, which entail individual choices, also contribute to lengthening the transition.

Delayed marriage is widely cited as the principal indicator that the transition to adulthood is being prolonged in the United States and around the world. With few exceptions, notably in South America, where age at first marriage was already high in comparison to other countries, both women and men are marrying later as the twenty-first century dawns than in previous decades (Lloyd, 2005, p.). A compelling and mostly upbeat story explains this phenomenon. Jobs paying enough to support a family increasingly require more formal education. Young people accordingly remain in school longer to acquire the credentials they will need to support a family.

But the story is more complicated than that. Marrying later has a different impact and a different meaning for Japanese women, who are able to enjoy unprecedented personal freedom and employment opportunities, than for Egyptian men, who are unable to marry because they cannot earn the money needed to pay for a wedding, much less to support a family (Lloyd, 2005, pp. 442–443). Marriage can be postponed to provide for the accumulation of additional human capital, but it can also be postponed simply because young people lack the resources to establish a new household. These two sources of the same phenomenon can reflect quite different personal situations. Young people from very poor backgrounds may be unable to take advantage of the educational opportunities that would improve their long-term life prospects. Lack of money to pay for education and living expenses interferes with continued schooling. Yet the same lack of money makes marriage impossible or at best unwise. Young people in this situation may be in a prolonged transition to adulthood, but they will have to complete the transition without the support of educational institutions and without the added human capital that education provides. In contrast to the development-enhancing nature of an extended transition as often described (Arnett, 2004), this situation seems like a delayed or blocked transition. Some young people may acquire added human capital in the form of work experience and job skills, but others simply mark time. The same objective condition—delayed marriage—can yield significant benefits to one group of young people, those who are not married because they are enrolled in school, and none for another group, who are unemployed or working to survive in low-skilled jobs without receiving any benefits from the freedom they enjoy from adult responsibilities.

Another delayed marriage scenario is in some ways even more poignant. In some African and Middle Eastern countries that have invested heavily in higher education without building strong economies, young people postpone marriage to complete higher education but after graduation take jobs as shopkeepers and taxi drivers because of a mismatch between the education system and the labor market. In these cases, the postponement of marriage in favor of higher education leads to further postponement of marriage because of poverty.

Delayed marriage is an excellent example of historical change in the patterns of lives. According to Elder (1999, p. 302), "The life course refers to a pattern of socially defined, age-graded events and roles which is subject to historical change in culture and social structure." Elder (1999, p. 306) goes on to identify timing as one of the key principles in the life course perspective: "The developmental impact of a succession of life transitions or events is contingent on when they occur in a person's life." Transitions can be normatively "on-time" or "off-time." Young people who marry today at an age that was appropriate or "on-time" for their parents and grandparents are now "off-time." Off-time transitions pose special challenges and "early" marriage is an excellent illustration. Young people who go against the norms and marry (or produce children without marriage) have a more difficult time economically because they must cope with the same dearth of well-paid jobs that leads most of their age-mates to postpone marriage and because marriage makes school enrollment more difficult.

Choosing early marriage is one way to shorten the transition to adulthood. And we must remember that some continue to do so even as the trends shift (Carr & Kefalas, 2006). There is another set of young people who are forced by poverty to assume adult responsibilities prematurely, interfering with their opportunities to improve their life chances. Very poor families are not only unable to finance higher education, they may expect older teenagers to become independent or even to earn money to contribute to the family. Foster children are a special case; they are required by law to become financially independent at age 18, when middle-class youth are relying on their parents to finance their higher education (Schoeni & Ross, 2005; see also Osgood, Foster, Flanagan, & Ruth, 2006). Young women from poor families may be expected to care for young children or disabled adults, delaying or foregoing education, employment, civic engagement, and marriage.

In view of all these possibilities, it is incorrect to interpret the trend toward delayed marriage as having the same consequences for all who experience it. And it is important to consider the negative consequences that normative changes in marriage age can have on those who marry early or assume other adult responsibilities prematurely. Part of a prolonged transition to adulthood is continued reliance on parents after reaching physical maturity. When parents are too poor to aid their grown children, the benefits of a prolonged transition are unattainable and the norms favoring it further disadvantage the poor. Education is the institution most implicated in both the opportunities and the barriers.

STRUCTURAL LAG AND INEQUALITY

Riley, Kahn, and Foner (1994) introduced the useful construct of "structural lag" to designate challenges facing people at the age of retirement and beyond whose wishes and actions no longer conform to expectations for their age group or to the affordances of the institutions they inhabit. Rather than terminating work entirely and devoting themselves to leisure, many people of "retirement age" continue to work, often part time, and to engage in significant voluntary service. Defined most succinctly by Hareven (1994, p. 130), structural lag is "the mismatch between changing lives and changing social structures." Like Settersten (2005) we believe structural lag applies to the beginning of adulthood as well as it does to aging. Changes in the transition

to adulthood have not been matched by appropriate changes in the institutions that support that transition. Serious mismatch results when those institutions no longer provide the support that is needed for a large proportion of the young people who are becoming adults.

We believe the institutions that shape and support entry into adulthood have failed to keep pace with changes in the transition to adulthood, making it more perilous for many than in the past. Those who make full use of the well-functioning institutions, notably selective residential colleges, generally do quite well. Those who for whatever reason do not rely on such institutions have a much more difficult time. The problem is that the kinds of jobs that once enabled young men and women who did not graduate from higher education to earn a decent living have disappeared. The gap has been inadequately filled with low-wage, low-skill, part-time, short-term jobs (Osterman, 1980). In the worst case, just as with retired people, rolelessness results, the state of having no significant responsibilities in social institutions. This situation is a sad waste of energy, talent, and wisdom, whether it befalls our elders or our young people. Rolelessness or disconnectedness in youth tends to lead to problem behavior, especially for young men (Chinman & Linney, 1998; Nightingale & Wolverton, 1993).

Institutional adaptation and invention are needed to strengthen support for the transition to adulthood among the most disadvantaged. The term *institution* applies to formal organizations and to customs and practices. Hence, schools and families are both institutions. As noted above, the institutions most germane to the transition to adulthood include family, education, civil society, and employment. Government at all levels is also implicated as a source of laws and policies and as a sponsor of educational and other institutions. Not-for-profit organizations and profit-making businesses contribute as employers and as sources of opportunity. Inclusion of these institutions serves as a reminder that adulthood entails new roles not only as workers and family members but also as citizens. Although it is not true as often stated that youth are "citizens of the future"—citizenship is conferred by birth or naturalization, not by reaching voting age—the rights and responsibilities of citizenship increase at adulthood, not only by the addition of voting but by qualification to serve in public office and by the acquisition of civic competence that both enables and compels civic engagement (Verba, Schlozman, & Brady, 1995).

Examples of institutions supporting the transition to adulthood include families of origin, higher education and apprenticeship, the military, and some forms of service (e.g., the Peace Corps, AmeriCorps, CityYear, YouthBuild, Service and Conservation Corps, and certain religious missions). Structural lag occurs when such institutions are not available to all who can benefit from them and when those in them no longer gain the benefits they need from them. Families of origin can be stressed by the financial needs of young people whose education continues longer than expected or who complete their education but are unable to find employment paying enough to support themselves. The rise of cohabitation in Europe and the United States suggests that traditional marriage no longer matches the needs and expectations of many young people who would previously have been expected to marry. Non-enrollment and high dropout rates in secondary school and higher education indicate mismatch between prospective students and education. But, most important of all, persistent poverty demonstrates the failure of institutions to provide pathways of upward mobility at the time of life when they are most needed.

We are especially interested in educational and employment institutions and in the governmental and nongovernmental institutions of civil society. Families are clearly important, but they are less amenable to intentional change. Before examining some of these institutions, we propose a set of developmental assets that we believe are particularly needed by young people as they assume adult roles and responsibilities as workers and active citizens.

Considering the employment and civic roles of adults, and the contributions of education to enabling their performance, two generalizations are valid, allowing for the variety already acknowledged. One, echoing the work of Riley, Kahn, and Foner (1994) and others on aging, is that the previous (ideal) sequence of learning–work–leisure, or education–employment–retirement no longer holds for many people. Education is increasingly a recurring activity rather than something one grows out of. Young people and elderly people work, perhaps part time, in combination with schooling and other activities. Hence, although we think of education as preparing young people for adulthood, it is also true that adults participate in education and that students who are not yet adults work and participate in civil society.

The second generalization is that the assets or competencies demanded by contemporary workplaces increasingly overlap with those needed in civil society. Although the hopes for a steady march toward worldwide democracy that were spawned by the fall of the Soviet Union have proved premature at best, with Russia reverting to autocracy and China managing to embrace capitalism in economics while retaining tight control over its people, the world today offers far more opportunities for ordinary people to act as responsible citizens than it did a few decades ago. As a result, a larger proportion of the world's population can make use of civic competencies such as the ability to analyze and discuss public issues, the ability to work in groups, and the ability to plan and carry out civic actions, in addition to general social and communicative competencies. These same competencies, with different content, are increasingly valued in workplaces where information and communication take precedence over making things (Reich, 2001).

DEVELOPMENTAL ASSETS FOR YOUNG ADULTS

The metaphor of "developmental assets" has been employed by the Search Institute as a conceptual tool for organizing communities to promote positive youth development (Benson, Scales, Hamilton, & Sesma, 2006; Scales & Leffert, 2004). It was subsequently adopted and refined by the Committee on Community-Level Programs for Youth of the National Research Council and Institutes of Medicine (Eccles & Gootman, 2002). We adopt the same metaphor here, but apply it to development during the transition to adulthood, emphasizing selected assets that are especially critical during this stage of life and for successful performance of adult roles as workers and citizens. We do not attempt to be comprehensive, as Search Institute and Eccles and Gootman were.

We believe the assets most distinctive to this time of life, and to this time in history, can be grouped in three clusters:

1. Sense of purpose and agency
2. Human capital
3. Social capital

These assets are not unique to adults; indeed, sense of purpose and personal power are two of the assets constituting "positive identity" among the Search Institute's 40 assets, and both human capital and social capital are implied by other assets in the Search Institute list. However, these assets take on additional importance and somewhat different form during the transition to adulthood, when either building or failing to build these assets is exceptionally significant for the remainder of the life course. It is important to keep in mind that developmental assets, like financial ones, are continuous, not dichotomous. The question is not whether one has an asset but to what extent, and in what forms, and how the asset can be deployed. The analogy to financial assets eventually breaks down because there is no easy way to count how much of a developmental asset a person has. But imprecise quantitative comparisons are possible; it is reasonable to claim that some people have a stronger sense of purpose than others, to describe the ways in which that stronger sense

of purpose is demonstrated, and to assess the consequences of the difference.

Sense of Purpose and Agency

Having a sense of purpose entails finding meaning in life and having a set of principles to live by. Religious beliefs and moral principles are essential to many in answering such questions. Having a life plan, a direction, is a major part of a sense of purpose.

Rawls (1971, p. 408) attributed to Josiah Royce the idea that "a person may be regarded as a human life lived according to a plan." For Rawls, a life plan is essential to humanity and a touchstone for determining what is rational and what is good (pp. 407–416). A life plan should not be construed as detailed and rigid. It is unrealistic for anyone to project too much too far into the future. Rather, it is a set of goals based on values and aspirations with at least some of the intermediate steps filled in; it helps to guide a person's choices but is subject to change in response to unanticipated obstacles and opportunities. The value and meaning of having a life plan depend on being in a society that affords enough personal freedom so that choices are possible and enough stability so that the future is partly predictable.

In his classic long-term longitudinal study, *American Lives*, Clausen (1993) found that "planful competence" characterized those people, even in adolescence, who as adults became most successful, not only in educational and occupational attainment and earnings, but also in marital stability and life satisfaction. Planfulness is an approach to life based on conscious assessment of opportunities and resources, not a simple *a priori* mapping of one's life. Planful people do not always know what is coming but they use the best information they can find to prepare for the future. In the Sloan study of the transition from adolescence to the adulthood, Schneider and Stevenson (1999) found that young people with "aligned ambitions" were most likely to achieve their educational and vocational goals, meaning that their plans and expectations for education were congruent with their vocational interests and plans. Those who either underestimated or overestimated the amount of education they would need to achieve their career goals were less likely to achieve them.

In societies where vocations and marital partners as well as the timing of transitions are mostly established by tradition and by families rather than by individual choice, a sense of purpose is based on meeting those expectations and often by traditional religious beliefs. A life plan under such circumstances is highly constrained by gender, by social class, and by the few possibilities that exist. As the number of options grows, the need for an individual plan increases as does the complexity and contingency of plans. Institutions can constrain possibilities during the transition to adulthood, but institutions that function well in today's world support young people in making use of proliferating options and their growing freedom to choose.

Ideally, purpose extends beyond oneself and one's family to incorporate the well-being of others and broader social goals. Youniss and Yates (1999, p. 365), who have studied youth involvement in service, suggest that their research "may provide some insight into the process by which long-term social orientations are initially shaped." This process includes giving youth the opportunity to act in accordance with religious, political, or other ideological traditions of caring and commitment. "This form of morality is expressed when adults join voluntary associations that are focused on explicit causes which promote community well-being. . . ." (Youniss & Yates, 1999, p. 365).

Agency is related to planfulness but is distinguishable. In life-course theory, agency is the capacity of a person to shape her or his own life course (Elder, 1999). A young man in a neighborhood plagued by gang violence, for example, might decide to enlist in the military as a way of getting away from the temptations and the dangers of that environment, gaining vocational skills and obtaining financial aid for higher education. This illustrates initiative,

self-efficacy, or internal locus of control, but in addition to being a near-term decision to get away from a bad environment, it is also a long-term decision to enter a different kind of life path that opens previously unavailable opportunities. More broadly, agency is defined as the belief that one can act effectively; in this sense it is similar to self-efficacy and internal locus of control. Without a sense of agency, planning seems pointless. If one is at the mercy of immutable forces, then survival is enough; planning is superfluous. Increasing prosperity in many parts of the world combined with declining returns to traditional agriculture and crafts make agency far more important to more people than in the past. As opportunities grow for living and working in new places, doing new things, those with a stronger sense of agency are better able to avoid the poverty they would face if they did not change, and to exploit the new opportunities available to them. Agency is critical in market economies. To thrive or even just survive in labor markets in which employers and jobs disappear rapidly, workers must be able to reinvent themselves quickly (Reich, 2001).

In the field of youth development, the goal of fostering agency is often discussed in terms of youth voice or youth participation in activities or programs, not for survival. Whatever the context, agency grows when youth have choices about what they do and opportunities to take leadership and make decisions about how programs will operate. Youth-initiated programs are the ultimate expression of agency, but youth–adult partnerships are desirable in all aspects of a program (Zeldin, McDaniel, Topitzes, & Calvert, 2000). Youth who have voice, power, and adult support also have a stronger sense of community (Evans, 2007).

A sense of agency is central to civic engagement. Only people who feel that their actions can make a difference are motivated to participate in civil society. Some of the same kinds of experiences that foster a sense of social purpose also encourage youth to see themselves as capable of taking effective action in their community, their nation, and the larger world. The kinds of experiences studied by Youniss and Yates (1999) not only promote a sense of purpose extending to others but also a belief in one's capacity to act on behalf of others, and to participate in the political process (see also Larson & Hanson, 2005; Reinders & Youniss, 2005, 2006; and Watts & Flanagan, 2007).

Human Capital

In contemporary societies, education is the most important producer of human capital (Becker, 1993), the knowledge and skills that enable a person to make a living. As large-scale industrial production methods have displaced traditional agriculture and crafts, so formal education in schools has replaced the informal transfer, often from parent to child, that characterizes human capital formation in simpler societies. Human capital is acquired throughout a lifetime and from multiple sources. Both the quantity and type of human capital vary among children of the same age.

During the transition to adulthood, peers begin to diverge widely in what and how much they know and are able to do. Some set themselves apart with advanced education and training, enabling them to participate in the professions and other rewarding economic roles. Higher education is not the only institution involved in this sorting process, but it is the most important one in prosperous countries, and its importance is growing in developing countries. Access to education and training is related to family income and education. Youth in poverty face daunting barriers to accumulating human capital because their schools, families, and communities often cannot provide the support they need to make use of education and training opportunities (Hamilton & Hamilton, 2008; Schoeni & Ross, 2005).

Social Capital

Like human capital, the term *social capital* makes an analogy between economic capital—such as money, buildings, and machinery—that enables the owner to engage in productive

moneymaking activities and human acquaintances and connections that are beneficial to their owner. Social capital inheres in direct and indirect social relations that enable those who possess them to achieve their goals.

Coleman (1990) spelled out the differences among physical, human, and social capital:

> Physical capital is wholly tangible, being embodied in observable material form; human capital is less tangible, being embodied in the skills and knowledge acquired by an individual; social capital is even less tangible, for it is embodied in the *relations* among persons. Physical capital and human capital facilitate productive activity, and social capital does so as well. (p. 304)

One of the best illustrations of social capital is the personal connections that enable a person to find a job. A job seeker whose relatives and acquaintances are unemployed or employed only in low-level positions or one without extensive social connections at all is at a severe disadvantage in the labor market compared to a job seeker with many acquaintances and family members who are employed, especially if they hold decision-making positions. The prospects of finding a job are much higher if people tell a job seeker about openings and if acquaintances are in a position to recommend the person to those who are hiring. A well-established phenomenon in social networking is "the strength of weak ties" (Granovetter, 1973), meaning the importance to finding employment and other purposes of knowing people, even slightly, who are aware of and can make accessible opportunities outside one's own circles. The link between social capital and employment is stronger than job finding. A young person who would like to become an engineer but whose family knows no engineers may not learn until too late how central mathematics is to engineering. He may lack advice about which colleges have the best engineering programs, what kinds of employers hire engineers, and how to get a summer internship that will help build a resume.

Putnam (2000, pp. 22–24) distinguished bridging social capital from bonding social capital. Bonding social capital unites a group and excludes outsiders, as in a lodge or sorority, a tribe or small community. Bridging social capital makes connections among people identified with different groups. Young people who seek to improve their station in life by gaining enough education to earn a better living than their parents and when they move away from home to live and work in large cities need bridging social capital. Bonding social capital continues to be important, both with their family and their community of origin. It is also critical that they develop new groups with which they share bonding social capital. But social mobility by definition entails making social connections with people in groups to which one does not yet belong. That process is multiplicative. One acquaintance from a new social circle can introduce a person to many more. Each of those new acquaintances, in turn, may be able to open the door to another social circle. Of course, social capital alone is not sufficient; poor populations in South Africa that are rich in social capital still find themselves in poverty traps because they lack access to financial capital (Adato, Carter, & May, 2006).

Mentoring is a special case of social capital; it can serve both bonding and bridging functions (Hamilton & Hamilton, 2008; see also Rhodes & Lowe, this *Handbook*). A mentor who is a neighbor or a family friend can strengthen solidarity within a young person's social circle of friends and neighbors. A mentor provides bridging social capital when she or he is better educated than most friends and family and can introduce a young person to new people and organizations, ideas and opportunities. For example, such a mentor might join parents in encouraging aspirations for higher education but go beyond them by offering specific information about financial aid, taking a young person to visit campuses, and writing a letter of recommendation that carries added weight because of the mentor's

status. A mentor might provide bridging social capital by arranging for a job interview with an employer that is inaccessible to the young person's friends and family members.

HIGHER EDUCATION AND THE TRANSITION TO ADULTHOOD

The royal road to adulthood leads through higher education. The American residential college epitomizes institutional support for the transition to adulthood. (We use the term *college,* in its uniquely American meaning, applying to any institution of higher education from a small 2-year or 4-year school to the undergraduate component of a large university.) Young people privileged to enroll in such institutions are engaged in purposeful effort that will enhance their ability to earn a living and to take positions of influence and responsibility in their communities. They are surrounded by their peers, as is appropriate to their developmental needs. Many of those relationships are likely to continue over their lifetime, repeatedly providing useful information and opportunities. Residential college students live away from the immediate supervision of their parents, which is also appropriate to their age and maturity level, but they are far from independent; Mom and Dad pay the bills and welcome them home whenever they choose to return. In Kett's (1977, p. 29) term, they are *semidependent.* The adults around them are trained and accountable to enhance their welfare, education, and planning for the future. Not only faculty, but residence staff, tutors, counselors, career advisors, registrars, even cafeteria workers and security guards share in these responsibilities. In addition to courses, students have access to a vast array of informal educational and recreational opportunities, some adult-led (museums, varsity sports) and some student-led (campus newspapers, Greek letter societies, clubs). In addition, and not to be slighted, they enjoy identification with a respected social role: student.

Even in the United States, which pioneered mass higher education, the college experience described above applies only to a minority. Nearly one-third of youth of college age cannot think about enrolling because they have failed to graduate from high school (Barton, 2005). About 7% of dropouts earn a GED by the age of 24 (Laird, DeBell, Kienzl, & Chapman, 2007). During the fall after high school graduation, between 64% and 69% of youth enroll in 2-year and 4-year colleges. Fluctuation has been in this range for more than a decade (*The Condition of Education, 2000–2008*, Indicator 24, Table 24-1). About 57% of all undergraduates in the fall of 2006 were in 4-year institutions and 43% in 2-year. About 20% of 4-year students were enrolled part time; 59% of 2-year students were part time (calculations from data in Table 1, Knapp, Kelly-Reid, Ginder, & Miller, 2008, p. 4). About 58% of students enrolled in 4-year institutions earned a bachelor's degree within 6 years (Table 5, Knapp et al., 2008, p. 10). Less than one-third of the population has earned a bachelor's degree by the age of 29; for Blacks it is 19.5%, and for Hispanics, 11.6% (*Digest of Education Statistics, 2007*, p. 22, Table 8). Despite compensatory and remedial education programs and financial aid, income remains highly correlated with higher education. Of 1990 high school sophomores, only 7.4% of those whose parents were in the lowest SES quartile had obtained a bachelor's or master's degree 10 years later (*Digest of Education Statistics 2007*, p. 458, Table 313).

Higher education is doubtless the surest route out of poverty. The existence of a wide range of institutions, including highly selective ones whose high cost is balanced by generous financial aid and less selective or unselective ones, most having low costs, makes it possible for almost anyone to aspire to graduate from college. However, aspirations are too often frustrated. Modest graduation rates, which are lower for those entering the least selective institutions, mean that going to college is not at all the same thing as earning a degree. After dramatic increases in the enrollment of women and minority students in higher education

and especially in the elite institutions, progress has stalled (Karen, 2002). Social class is highly associated with enrollment in the most prestigious institutions (Bowen, Kurzweil, & Tobin, 2005).

Several western European countries have quietly surpassed the United States in the proportions of the student-age population enrolled in higher education. In 2001, the rate of entry of U.S. youth into higher education institutions preparing students for postgraduate education and the professions was 42%, compared to the Organization for Economic Cooperation and Development (OECD) average of 47%. The U.S. rate for primarily vocational institutions was 13% compared to the OECD average of 15% (*The Condition of Education, 2000–2008*, Indicator 17).

European universities are generally less like total institutions than American residential colleges (Cook & Furstenberg, 2002). Faculty are less accessible, and professional staff support for students is much sparser. Nonacademic activities and housing are much less institutionalized, left more in the hands of students. Commuting to university varies among countries depending upon how dispersed universities are and how restrictive majors are. Countries with *numerus clausus* provisions limiting enrollment in the most popular majors (e.g., medicine) require students to relocate.

Postsecondary enrollment rates are growing rapidly in many developing nations, especially for women, but falling in others. South Asia, the Middle East, and the Caribbean regions have seen the most impressive growth. Sub-Saharan Africa, formerly Soviet Asia, and South America have seen declines (Lloyd, 2005, pp. 88–89). None will soon achieve the levels in the United States, western Europe, and other prosperous countries. Moreover, poor countries cannot afford ideal institutions. They struggle both to provide places for those wishing to enroll and to provide an acceptable quality of education for those who do. Housing, advising, and extracurricular activities are often simply beyond their capacity.

Basic needs such as seats in lecture halls, libraries, and Internet access may go unmet (Polgreen, 2007).

As daunting as these kinds of conditions are, and as far as they are from providing the support young people need to become productive adults, there is a second kind of limitation to their effectiveness at this function. In some countries, after students manage to overcome all of these barriers and earn their degrees, they enter labor markets that simply cannot absorb so many graduates. Colonial economies and educational systems established universities as pathways to civil service. Neoliberal economic policies have severely constrained the size of government in many countries, eliminating the positions formerly awaiting graduates. In the absence of vibrant economies, those graduates either remain unemployed or are underemployed, working at jobs that do not require or reward their educational attainments. Large numbers of university graduates drive taxis, run shops, or remain unemployed. Having delayed adulthood to obtain a university degree, they are unable to earn enough money to support a family and therefore remain not-yet-adults (Assaad, 1997; Siphambe, 2000; Sjöholm, 2005).

No doubt the continuous improvement of institutions of higher education and the continuous increase in the proportion of the population with postsecondary education are goals to be pursued everywhere. But the proportions graduating in the United States, including those whose college experience fails to approximate the ideal represented by residential colleges make clear that even Herculean efforts will not succeed in enrolling the majority of youth in most countries. And the reality of imbalances between educational attainment and labor market demand prove that a purely "supply side" approach does not work. Only if growing demand for employees with higher education matches the growing supply of graduates can higher education improve life prospects. Education certainly has noneconomic benefits, but those benefits seldom satisfy either the graduates who are unemployed or the taxpayers who underwrote the expenses of their education.

The same shift in employment that heightens the value of higher education reduces the employment prospects and earnings of those without higher education. For too many young people, the conclusion of their full-time schooling leads to extended unemployment and underemployment because they do not have the knowledge and skills that are needed in the labor market. This phenomenon can be seen clearly in the United States, where the real earnings of young men without education beyond high school have declined drastically over the past 3 decades. The automation and offshoring of manufacturing have reshaped the labor market to favor information and communication over manual tasks, thereby privileging more educated workers and women, increasing the difference in earnings between those with college degrees and those without.

College students and graduates may enjoy a prolonged transition to adulthood as an extension of the psychosocial moratorium that Erikson (1963) described in adolescence. Young people in this situation may try out relationships, lifestyles, and occupations while consolidating their identities independent of their families (Arnett, 2004), an opportunity for further development. But when young people are unable to assume adult roles and responsibilities because of poverty and lack of education, their transition might better be seen as blocked than prolonged. The time between the attainment of physical adulthood and ability to act as adults does not necessarily increase their human capital and other assets and may become a trap from which they never emerge.

PROMISING INSTITUTIONS

If higher education is inadequate to the task or enabling poor young people to acquire these essential assets, then new or adapted institutions are needed to support the transition of low-income youth to adulthood. We describe four, focusing on the opportunities they afford young people to build a sense of purpose and agency, human capital, and social capital. Then we inductively identify some of the key "features" of these institutions, using the term in the same way as the Eccles and Gootman (2002) panel did as the sources of asset building for youth in communities.

The first institution, German apprenticeship, is the most highly developed. Indeed, we consider it also an excellent example of a system, compared to the other three, which are programs. Next, we describe YouthBuild, which has some parallels to apprenticeship, but is aimed at dropouts in American cities and uses local housing construction and rehabilitation as a focus for asset building. Our search for institutions supporting the transition to adulthood in developing countries was disappointing, but we found two in Nairobi, Kenya. One, Tap and Reposition Youth (TRY), adapts microfinance to young women who have migrated from rural villages and are highly vulnerable to sexual exploitation and HIV infection. The Community Cleaning Service was created by young men in partnership with a community-based organization and a multinational corporation that meets a community need while creating jobs and fostering entrepreneurship.

The purpose of this exploration is to begin to create a strategy to remedy the structural lag that has left current institutions inadequate to aid the transition to adulthood of poor youth, in the United States and around the world. Although the empirical evidence of their success is far from comprehensive, the four institutions described below appear to offer opportunities for asset building. By identifying the features they have in common we can see more clearly how new and adapted institutions for this purpose might be designed.

German Apprenticeship[1]

Just as the residential college exemplifies an institution designed to support the transition to adulthood, German apprenticeship is an exemplary institution for young people who do not benefit from higher education. Part of what makes it exemplary is that it is an alternative that leads to desirable careers, but does not rule out the more prestigious option; 5.4% of young people who complete an apprenticeship go on to higher education (Bundesinstitut für Berufsbildung, 2008).

As the rise of factories greatly diminished the importance of apprenticeship in most other industrializing countries, Germany adapted the traditional practice by creating new apprenticeable occupations and combining them with schooling as the "dual system." Similar systems evolved in Switzerland and Denmark. Currently, after 10 years or more of full-time school, young men and young women enter apprenticeship contracts with employers to learn one of some 350 recognized occupations, including not only crafts but technical and white-collar occupations as well. Occupations regarded as feminine, such as sales clerk and beautician are apprenticeable. Agreements among employers, unions, and government specify the knowledge and skills to be learned in the workplace and in a specialized vocational high school, usually attended one day per week. After a term of 3 years (with some variation), apprentices must pass written and performance tests to be certified as skilled workers in their occupation. Certification is required for employment in apprenticeable occupations. The examinations also test the employers' ability to deliver high-quality training. If too many of its apprentices fail the examinations, the firm will lose its right to train, which is considered a generalized validation of its commitment to quality, a very important issue in Germany.

The quality of apprentices' experiences varies widely. In general, large firms invest heavily in training their apprentices because they expect to hire them as lifelong employees and they rely upon highly skilled workers to maintain quality standards. In such firms, apprentices are selected from among vast numbers of applicants and would most likely enroll in selective second-tier colleges if they were in the United States. At the opposite end of the spectrum, local bakeries and barber shops use apprentices to do routine work at low wages and seldom have sufficient demand for new workers to hire them after their training is complete. Young people who serve apprenticeships but are unable to find employment in their trade are disadvantaged compared to those who are hired as skilled workers by their training employer, but they are far better off than their peers who have no training. Employers in fields without apprenticeships prefer applicants who have been trained in other fields.

Apprenticeship has social as well as technical functions. It embeds young people in a world of adults and adult roles and responsibilities at a time when they are beginning the transition to adulthood, enabling them to observe adults other than parents and teachers and to try out adult roles. It provides appropriate support by requiring responsibility and performance but recognizing apprentices' need to learn. Apprentices are paid for the work they perform, but their wage levels are low, reflecting their primary commitment to learning and their employers' investment in their training. Adults in the workplace have an explicit responsibility to help them learn. In a small firm, this responsibility rests with the owner or shop supervisor, who must, by law, have been trained as an apprentice and have had the additional training and passed the higher level examination to qualify as a master, an achievement that carries high status in German society and that is critical to the economy. In practice, the master usually delegates responsibility for training apprentices to one or more skilled workers. Large firms may have full-time trainers who supervise apprentices. The apprentices rotate among various departments with different immediate supervisors in each. Because all skilled workers have themselves been apprentices and because the training of apprentices is widely recognized as an important function, most adults readily help out as supervisors or "just-in-time" instructors.

The role of apprentice is respected and valued in Germany. The concept of vocation (*Beruf*) is extremely important in Germany as a part of a person's identity and apprentices share in the identity of the vocation for which they are preparing. A newspaper article that names a young person, perhaps as a member of a victorious soccer team, will state the occupation in which she or he is an apprentice as an essential piece of information. In some of the traditional crafts, successful apprentices are welcomed into the guild with a ceremony and a mark of belonging, such as an earring or the right to perform a folk dance.

Being surrounded most days by adults in the workplace rather than peers in school, apprentices have ample opportunity to observe and get to know adults outside their families at the time when they are beginning to think of themselves as adults. Earning their own money gives them a measure of autonomy from their parents, but most still live at home. Apprentices attend their part-time vocational school with other apprentices in the same occupation, not with their previous schoolmates, so their peer networks grow along with their connections to adults.

Current Challenges to the System

Over the past two decades the German economy has been challenged by international competition, which, in addition to its other effects, has raised questions about whether the investment that apprenticeship requires is repaid. Lexus and Acura have cut into the market for Mercedes-Benz and BMW automobiles, and Japanese workers are not trained as apprentices.

Although the proportion of youth who serve apprenticeships has declined over the past 2 decades, some of them have enrolled in higher education instead. It helps to put the current "crisis" in perspective by noting that in the face of these and other challenges, in 2006 the proportion of young people of the appropriate age who were apprentices was just under 60% (Bundesinstitut für Berufsbildung, 2008). It would appear that reports of the death of German apprenticeship have been highly exaggerated.

Exacerbating the challenges of global competition, the reunification of East and West Germany beginning in 1990 caused economic and institutional upheaval that continues today. (For an excellent treatment of this transformation as a natural experiment testing the influence of social structural changes on life courses, see Diewald, Goedicke, & Mayer, 2006.) Under the smothering protection of communism, East German industry was a powerhouse of the Eastern bloc, but the fall of the wall revealed how hopelessly outdated it was. The Trabant epitomized the shoddy but also scarce products of the East German system, which was as careless of its workers as it was of its customers. Apprenticeships in the construction trades and agriculture were judged to be adequate; in fact, skilled construction workers readily found employment in the west. But in manufacturing, white-collar, and technical occupations, both the workers who had completed training and the training system were often found to be unsuited to a market economy. As West German firms bought up East German enterprises, they often declined to train apprentices, arguing that it was too expensive under the circumstances and that, besides, they had to give higher priority to retraining adult workers.

Integrating Youth With Immigration Backgrounds

Youth with immigration backgrounds are another challenge to the system. This terminology is used to include not only young people who were born outside Germany, but the children and grandchildren of immigrants. Poorer school performance, limited language skills, conflicting cultural traditions, and discrimination impede such young people's participation in apprenticeship. As a result, youth with immigration backgrounds experience greater difficulty in finding an apprenticeship after they finish school than their classmates with German ancestry. Among applicants for apprenticeships in the spring of 2006, only 42% with immigration backgrounds were

successful by the fall compared to 54.1% of applicants without immigration backgrounds who succeeded (Granato et al., n.d., p. 2).

Applicants for apprenticeships whose school records are inferior are understandably less desirable to employers, but in a system that relies upon the willingness of small business owners and their employees to take young people into a close personal relationship, as well as a formal employer–employee relationship, cultural difference (gender difference as well) can be a potent barrier. Both higher level school certificates and better grades help native German applicants for apprenticeship more than they help applicants with immigration backgrounds (Granato et al, n.d., pp. 3–4). The consequences of these differences carry over into early adulthood, when only 15% of young men between the ages of 25 and 35 with German ancestry lack a formal occupational certificate compared to 41% of immigrants and fully 57% of Turks (Granato et al., p. 5). These discrepancies are disturbing enough but they have actually worsened over the past decade, demonstrating clearly that more effective measures are desperately needed.

At this point, the main alternative to apprenticeship is vocational schooling, and youth with immigration backgrounds are more likely than those without to enroll in full-time postcompulsory vocational schools (Granato et al., p. 2). Unfortunately, the schools they are most likely to enroll in do not provide occupational certification and are, therefore, far less desirable and less useful in the labor market. Transitional programs (e.g., the vocational preparation year) designed to help school leavers move into apprenticeship are widely decried as mere parking lots that occupy young people but leave them no better off. They, too, are disproportionately used by youth with immigration backgrounds. New initiatives are envisioned to address some of these issues (Kremer, 2007). An intriguing aspect of these efforts is the attempt to convince employers that "intercultural competence" is a desirable quality of apprentices, one that gives an advantage to applicants who speak another language and are not of German ancestry.

The institutional framework for apprenticeship is a deep and multifaceted partnership among employers, employees, and the education system, each taking responsibility for part of the education and training of apprentices in collaboration with the others. These three partners jointly determine specifications of learning objectives, school-based curricula, work-based training experiences, and examinations to certify apprentices as skilled workers in their occupation. Schools are represented by the education ministries of the various states (*Länder*). Employers are represented by chambers (*Kammern*), organizations that can sound like the Chamber of Commerce in the United States, but are not voluntary; employers in each field are required to belong to their respective chamber. Employees are represented in the system by their unions. The combination of strong employers' organizations and strong unions working with each other and with government agencies has been a hallmark of the German economy since reconstruction following World War II, when they manifested a strong collective ethos of working together to rebuild the country.

Apprenticeship in the East[2]

Some of the most interesting current innovations are occurring in the former Eastern states, where apprenticeship, like everything else, was dominated by the government and the "social partnership" among employers, unions, and schools was underdeveloped. Faced with lower levels of economic activity and a scarcity of large firms, which in the West provide many of the best apprenticeships, people in the East have tried new approaches. One of the boldest innovations is the sponsorship of apprenticeships by *Bildungsträger* (Berger & Grünert, 2007) rather than firms. The term translates literally as training carrier or provider but might be better understood in U.S. terms as intermediary organization. A *Bildungsträger* might be a community-based organization, a

church, even a city government that formally assumes responsibility for the training of a set of apprentices in a specific occupation. This represents a dramatic break with traditional practice. The presumption that employers are best able to train is very strong, and the system relies in large part on the expectation that training firms will hire most of the apprentices they train. But the involvement of *Bildungsträger* has several advantages.

They sometimes create training workshops, comparable to vocational school shops, in which training begins and advanced techniques are taught to apprentices who are protected from the stresses of production. Many large firms have such workshops, but they are not feasible for small firms. *Bildungsträger* may also perform a brokering function, enlisting multiple small firms in the training of the same apprentices. Instead of remaining in one firm for the duration of training, as is traditional, apprentices in this arrangement rotate among different firms, learning in each skills not found in the others. In this way, small firms that are unqualified to train apprentices may participate in and contribute to apprenticeship in collaboration with other firms, facilitated by a *Bildungsträger*. (This arrangement has precedents in the West but has been expanded and elaborated in the East.)

The greatest drawback to relying on third parties to train apprentices is identical to the reason they are needed: Too few jobs are available. Trained apprentices, as a result, cannot expect their training firm to offer them a job; they must take their hard-earned certificate into an unfriendly labor market.

Purpose and Agency

The need to select and qualify for an apprenticeship demands from German youth an early serious commitment to an occupation. Although this is not an unalloyed good, it does constitute a purpose that may be lacking in young people in the United States at the same age who have also concluded that they are not college material. The distance and vagueness of adult occupations for most American youth in that situation deprive them of that sense of direction.

Being treated as almost adult at work and, when successful, beginning an adult career with a well-paid job around the age of 20 can add to young people's sense of agency. They no longer need to rely on their parents economically. They belong in the respected social category of skilled worker in a recognized occupation.

The impact of apprenticeship on civic attitudes and behaviors is a controversial topic in German sociology (Hamilton & Lempert, 1997). The controversy illuminates some large differences between Germany and the United States. On the one hand, observers from the political right have expressed concern that labor union involvement in apprenticeship builds in a socialist bias that recruits impressionable youth to the Social Democratic Party and encourages an adversarial attitude toward employers. The contrary perspective is that giving employers so much influence over the education of so many youth leads to indoctrination in pro-capitalist, pro-business ideology. However, the consensus of multiple studies is that apprenticeship does not have a strong impact on political orientation or action in one direction or the other. This is reassuring if the concern is with indoctrination but cause for concern if one presumes that youth should be a time of political learning and socialization and that apprenticeship and associated institutions (e.g., apprentice representation on the union-based works councils that participate in the management of many German firms) should have a salutary effect on apprentice citizens.

It may be that the new opportunities for collective consciousness and action are counterbalanced by the clear power imbalances between employers and employees, even in Germany where unions are strong and codetermination remains a widely shared ideal. The old slogan, *"Lehrzeit ist keine Herrzeit"* (apprentice time is no time for being in charge), still holds. Making greater use of apprenticeship as an arena for developing civic competence would require the creation of new opportunities and a heightened awareness of the importance of this aspect of youth development in Germany (Hofer, 1999; Oswald, 1999).

Human Capital

Apprenticeship is primarily an institution designed to build human capital. It is supported by firms because it helps them meet their need for highly skilled employees. Young people choose to participate for the opportunity it affords to gain human capital that provides direct returns in the form of earnings, job security, and prospects for continued learning and higher level employment in the future.

Social Capital

Being colocated in workplaces as well as schools, German apprenticeship can create social capital for young people in the form of new relationships with fellow apprentices and with adult workmates, notably with the skilled workers who are assigned to teach them. Workplaces are adult centered, in contrast with schools, giving apprentices opportunities to observe and develop relationships with adults outside their family. In addition to working alongside adults, apprentices share break periods and lunchtime with them.

YouthBuild

YouthBuild is an American program for low-income urban youth that engages them in building and rehabilitating housing in their communities. Currently about 8,000 youth, ages 16–24, are enrolled in 226 local YouthBuild programs. Each year, YouthBuild turns away 14,000 applicants because funding is inadequate to meet the demand (Dorothy Stoneman, interview, August 31, 2007). Between 2002 and 2006: 90% of the youth enrolled had not graduated from high school or earned a GED; 36% had been adjudicated, and 14% convicted of a felony; 26% were on public assistance; 25% were parents; and the average age was 19.1, with a grade 7.2 average reading level upon entrance; the average length of stay was

8 months (*YouthBuild USA Demographics and Outcomes, 2002–2006*, n.d.). In a survey of graduates, respondents indicated that they had faced on average four of seven categories of challenges prior to entering YouthBuild: job challenges, substance abuse, criminal justice, home problems, care responsibilities, education, and mental health (Hahn, Leavitt, Horvat, & Davis, 2004, pp. 19–20). The extraordinary impact of the program becomes clear when considering Cohen and Piquero's (in press) estimate of the "present value of saving a high-risk youth . . . to be $2.6 to $5.3 million at age 18."

YouthBuild began as a single program in Harlem in 1978. "Since 1994, more than 76,000 YouthBuild students have helped rebuild their communities, transformed their lives, and created more than 17,000 units of affordable housing in 226 of America's poorest communities" (National Alumni Council, & Young Leaders Council of the YouthBuild USA Affiliated Network, 2008, p. i). Most local programs are supported through competitive federal grants from the U.S. Department of Labor YouthBuild Program (p. i).

Components of the program include, in addition to job training and a preapprenticeship in construction skills, an alternative school to help youth earn their GED or high school diploma; engagement in community service; leadership development; building a mutually supportive mini-community of adults and peers; and construction and rehabilitation of housing in their neighborhood (YouthBuild USA, 1996, pp. 1–2). After some time in the program, many participants describe experiencing a kind of epiphany, a turning point that gives them a sense of purpose and agency. Handbooks and manuals provide curricula on multiple topics revealing the ambitious goals of the program: blueprint for democracy, money skills, career development, expanding opportunities in trade unions, construction training, counseling, education, planning housing and community projects, tools and technology, teamwork and leadership, construction-related math and

measurement, health and safety, and leadership development.

An underlying premise of YouthBuild is that staff foster the personal transformation of participants. John Bell, the vice president for leadership development and the Academy for Transformation, wrote:

> In our heart of hearts, what we most want for the young people we work with is to provide the environment for them to reach their highest aspirations. When we look back at our own transformations, for most of us there was at least one caring, skillful adult who hung in there with us over a period of time, on whom we relied for some combination of encouragement, challenge, information, guidance, teaching, validation, and love; who believed in us until we believed in ourselves (Bell, 2003, p. 1).

Leadership development is explicitly linked to personal transformation.

> A large part of what makes the Youthbuild program effective is the attitude, communicated immediately by the staff to the young people as they enter the program, that they are potential leaders and role models whose contribution to the program and the community can and will make a difference. This attitude is often so different from the way disadvantaged young people believe adults view them, that it provides the opportunity and motivation for the young people to rise to the challenge of transforming their own lives, rebuilding their communities, and taking responsibility for the future of their communities. (YouthBuild USA, n.d., pp ix–x).

Membership on committees provides opportunities for youth to set policy and to participate in community advocacy and action (pp. 4–5). Leadership competency workshops develop skills. Opportunities also include accompanying staff to visit local government offices and foundations (p. 6).

Testimonials by graduates from YouthBuild provide heartrending detail about families living in crowded apartments, parents' drug addiction, pressure to join gangs involved in violent behaviors, caring for younger siblings, rotating foster care, dropping out of high school or being expelled, gunshot deaths of family members and friends, and being jailed.

> I eventually became tired of the life I was leading. After twenty one years I wanted a change. Making this change was hard because it meant shifting learned behaviors I had practiced since I was a child. Then one day, I saw an advertisement in the *Employment News* about the YouthBuild program. Since then, my perspective on life has changed dramatically. I took advantage of all that YouthBuild had to offer. I attained my GED and received intense training in construction. I became employable, and secured work with the Carpenters Union for 3 years. I made the change. From 1997 to now, I've accomplished many goals I never thought I'd reach. I am now the Program Manager of my local YouthBuild. I am happily married and the father of four beautiful children. I am a minister at . . . [my church] and was elected to serve as the Vice President of YouthBuild USA's National Alumni Council. In 2000, I started a city-wide outreach/mentoring program for young men in my community. Recently in 2005, I successfully launched my own construction business that employs local YouthBuild graduates and students. I have made all of these changes and I am still striving both locally and nationally. (Graduate's letter to Dorothy Stoneman, personal communication)

One youth described the YouthBuild boot camp he attended during his first week. Passing this Mental Toughness wilderness experience dramatically served to separate him from the temptations of the street and immersed him in an environment of positive people who believed he could gain a focus to succeed in life.

> That was my first time like being away from where I normally live. . . . When I got out there I was happy just to be out of my environment. . . . I can get used to this because nobody knows me and I don't know nobody. I can make friends. Positive people lead to positive things. . . .

> People who want to see you do good. People that will help you if you need help and such things like that, counsel you and all that. Everything is in here for me to do. I am in the right place. . . . So now I can do what I need to do. (Hamilton & Hamilton, 2008, p. 20)

Interviews of 57 graduates from eight sites from the Hahn et al. study (2004), chosen because they were "established, respected programs with sound leadership that represented the norm of a solid YouthBuild program as well as the geographical and cultural diversity of YouthBuild's national network" (p. 5) corroborate the generality of these expressions of purpose and agency. The youth both "envision another life" for themselves in the future and assert "a right to claim that better life" (p. 12).

Multiple youth describe the caring and support they experienced in the YouthBuild program, as filling a void and contributing to life changes.

> If I had the motivation and I had the support like, "You can do this," I would have been out of high school and gone to college. . . . But I have slipped up, so now I am here; now they are focusing, they getting me back on the right track. . . . I shot up [in test scores] 'cause I started studying and I got focused with my work. . . . [A staff member] sat me down and talked to me on a one-on-one basis and told me, "You have a real good potential and I don't want to see anything happen to you in society, like when you become a part of statistics by like getting locked up and going through the whole system." (Hamilton & Hamilton, 2008, p. 20)

A graduate program (YouthBuild USA, 1996, p. 117) creates additional opportunities for graduates through continuing education, job and career counseling, support services, leadership development and social life. As Hahn et al. (2004, p. 26) report, "Close to half of graduates cited lack of education, lack of training, and lack of computer skills as affecting them 'a lot' or 'some'; a clear indication that many graduates have realized after being in the post-YouthBuild world for a while that YouthBuild is the beginning but that the real world often requires more."

Youth in the program keep journals to reflect on their past lives and help them think about future directions. Peers in the program and staff suggest questions.

Like past experiences, like what has gone on in our life that we want to change. Or things that we look back on and I wish that they had never happened because I would have been doing this right now. And that's what I do. Like I just reflect on the past. Like well I did this but I knew that I could have been doing this when I was doing that. And that's probably what got me sidetracked. But now that I am back into the program, now I can really have time to focus on my work. And to get prepared for the future because life is short. You never [know] who's gonna pass. You never know what's gonna happen. So I got to work hard now and rest when I am dead. (Interview conducted by M. A. Hamilton)

This youth attributed his positive direction and focus in part to his relationship with a staff person in YouthBuild.

I mean if I am having a problem, I need to talk to him. . . . If you need a push, he is the one to push you, "Go ahead and do it." If you fall he's picking you back up to try again. Like that, so when I go to him there's nothing but positive information that he gives me. . . . He was just a good mentor. He shows me the ins and outs, like this is what you not supposed to do and this is what you can do. (Interview conducted by M. A. Hamilton)

The words of another youth suggest how a haven of stability and positive relationships can change a youth's life path, creating an intent to give back to the community.

My objective is to develop and deliver educational presentations for at-risk youth and adults working with at-risk youth. Conduct activities that develop critical and strategic thinking for youth empowerment. Expose youth to learning experiences that increase their expectation for a viable, stable future. Create an environment that encourages, nurtures and contributes to positive relationships of at-risk youth and adults. Expose youth and young adults to the possibilities of education, post secondary education as well as career alternatives. Promote activities that develop new learning skills and advance traditional ones while engaging youth in activities that provide team building, networking, communication, and other soft people skills. (Participant's response to survey, provided by Dorothy Stoneman)

Sense of Purpose and Agency

The purpose of the program, illustrated above, is to provide both opportunity and inspiration for upward mobility among a highly disadvantaged population, namely, very poor youth who have dropped out of high school. Many have also been involved in crime and drug use. Mental health problems are common. A survey of graduates found that 75% were enrolled in higher education, receiving additional job training, or employed in jobs paying an average wage of $10/hour; and 48% reported being involved in their community. Reported criminal activity and drug use was dramatically lower than on entry to the program (Hahn et al., 2004, pp. 22–23).

Dorothy Stoneman, the founder, emphasizes that a "crucial YouthBuild 'product' is a network of ethical and inspired young leaders who have been raised poor and understand their communities' needs and can step forward to take responsibility for the well-being of these communities" (Hahn et al., 2004, p. 3). Stoneman refers to current alumni efforts locally and nationally that provide training opportunities and networking, while admitting that many youth still are pressed to finish their GED or work through other personal problems that did not disappear during their year or less in the program (p. 3). The graduate's letter above indicates such an achievement, another participant's survey response quoted above states similar intentions.

Human Capital

The manifest purpose of YouthBuild is to increase the human capital of youth who have very little, in the form of construction skills and a GED or high school diploma. However, the program's goals and its structure reach farther, raising aspirations and teaching leadership skills, which are applicable to a wider range of subsequent activities. The postgraduation accomplishments of participants are very impressive in contrast to their prospects upon enrollment.

Social Capital

Participants' testimony conveys the significance of a caring staff, people who, without being formally designated mentors, establish the climate for participants' personal transformation, as expressed in the stories. The program also builds a positive peer culture in which young people who have experienced some of the same disadvantages and missteps work together toward common goals and develop a sense of solidarity that gives them self-confidence and a sense of self-worth not experienced before by many when in the company of non-related adults, especially teachers, or of peers. The experience of these relationships provides a foundation for future achievement.

Community Cleaning Service

In Mathare, a slum of Nairobi, Kenya, a group of young men in their late teens and early twenties founded the Community Cleaning Service (CCS) to clean bathrooms on contract with apartment house residents, who share toilets among multiple households. The young men's enterprise makes it possible for them to earn enough for daily subsistence while they also learn how to create a sustainable business that benefits the residents.

The Base of the Pyramid (BoP) refers to the 4 billion people in the world who live in poverty, on less than the equivalent of $2 a day. Business strategists (Hart, 2005; Prahalad & Hart, 2002) have pointed out that a business can make a profit by selling very expensive products and services to the very wealthy but very small number of people at the top of the population pyramid or by selling very inexpensive products and services to the very poor but huge number of people at the base of the pyramid. Examples include selling shampoo sachets to people in India wishing to improve their cleanliness and appearance but whose week's earnings would not pay for a whole bottle, and selling insecticide packets to help poor Kenyans control insect-borne diseases.

But people at the BoP can be more than customers whose purchases increase profits for corporations. Muhammad Yunus (1999) received the Nobel Prize for figuring out how to use microfinance to draft members of the BoP population in Bangladesh as entrepreneurs in the capitalist system. Women stool makers, his first borrowers, were able to purchase bamboo and pay back their $27 loans after building their businesses' profitability and freeing themselves from the crushing burden of debt they previously owed to vendors of their raw materials. In 1983, Yunus founded the Grameen bank to provide loans to the poorest of the poor and to build support networks that would help them make the best use of their small capital funds (www.grameenfoundation.org/who_we_are/gf_and_grameen_bank/).

Lessons learned about how corporations can work with BoP populations have been incorporated into a newly revised protocol by the Center for Sustainable Global Enterprise at Cornell University (Simanis & Hart, 2008). The principles and cases explain how to use a combination of business development and community development strategies to identify market niches and then co-create businesses with the community that meet both the needs of the community and the company. Using the Community Cleaning Service as one example, Simanis and Hart set out a "co-creation logic" that so far has been partially tested in Kenya and India.

In 2005, a team from Cornell's Johnson School of Management, the University of

Michigan and others, sponsored by the SC Johnson Company, went to Kenya to identify partners to try to implement the first version of this BoP protocol (Simanis, Hart, Enk, Duke, Gordon, & Lippert, 2005). In Kibera, Nairobi, East Africa's largest slum, they came into contact with youth groups collecting "Trash for Cash," known locally as "Taki ni Pato." These youth groups were operating with the support of several nonprofit nongovernmental organizations (NGOs), notably Carolina for Kibera, which was founded by a student from the University of North Carolina (http://cfk.unc.edu/) and Pamoja Trust, a local NGO. Justin DeKoszmovszky, who participated in the three month "immersion" as a Cornell MBA student and is now employed by the SC Johnson Company, explained in an interview (May 19, 2008) that the business idea during the first year was for the youth to run a "bug killing" company using SC Johnson insecticide products in and around the homes of people who could not afford to buy the products themselves. But this business was not successful. SC Johnson and the young entrepreneurs with whom they were working needed to evolve the initial "service concept."

> And what we saw was one of the groups in another slum actually, not in Kibera, but in Mathare, had started cleaning shared toilets. Mathare is what we have come to call a "vertical slum," whereas Kibera is a "horizontal slum." So if you can imagine, Kibera is almost 100% single-storey, mostly mud walled, some cement block, corrugated steel roofs. And it is about the size of Central Park, with some estimates of about 1 million people, maybe a little less, living there. Mathare, by contrast is mostly 4-6-storey buildings, cement blocks, with about 5–6 apartments per floor. There is usually one toilet point and one shower point on each floor, so it is shared across five or six households, which could each have about five people within them. So it is a serious amount of sharing going on. And like any shared resource, unfortunately, the toilets are not maintained or cared for in the way that anyone would like them to be. So these

toilets in Mathare, in these vertical buildings, had become really, really unhealthy, unsanitary, unpleasant, to say the least. To the point where some people, some parents were not letting their children use toilets by themselves, for fear that they would touch a wall, slip and fall, or anything like that and that could be a serious health hazard.

The entrepreneurs we had been working with in Mathare evolved a new business by responding to the situation in their neighborhood, which was very different from the one in which we had focused originally, and started doing this shared toilet cleaning service, using our products, mainly Toilet Duck, and then actually a locally-sourced general-purpose cleaner. It was the same theory, the same idea, creating a service in a community based on an SC Johnson product, that also really delivered a significant amount of benefit for the community at a price point everyone could afford, because it was shared across multiple people. But it was an idea that we had not had. Now we are really focused on shared toilet cleaning, and developing that as a business and growing that as a business. . . . CCS offers the service, telling residents of each floor: "Everyone puts in about 30 cents and we clean the toilet." There was no regular cleaning before and in most buildings there is no running water. So it is an added value to the residents. (Justin DeKoszmovszky, interview, May 19, 2008)

Describing the changes that occurred in both the location of the project and the business plan, DeKoszmovszky explained how he and other outsiders had learned one of the key principles in community organizing from the local entrepreneurs they worked with.

> One of the learnings we had in year one, as we were going from. . . . having a business concept to creating a business that is an on-going, operating entity, we were talking a lot about "sweat equity"—put in the time to develop the business, and the income will come later on. What we realized very quickly was at the Base of the Pyramid, when you are working with very poor partners, poor from an income standpoint, they cannot make the investment of sweat equity. That is too expensive. Most of these folks are day

laborers or have very diverse income streams; even within one day they might do 2 or 3 jobs or 2 or 3 income-generating activities. Dedicating half of a day to working with us to go door-to-door and sell a service, if they did not make 3 or 4 sales a day, it affected what they ate that night, very, very literally. And so sweat equity, not a capital investment, even a time investment is not something that at this level is necessarily even possible. I think one of the myths about the Base of the Pyramid or poor people in general and working with them is that they have a lot of time. That's not necessarily true. In one of the families there is someone abroad who is sending money home or someone else who's making money in the family and therefore everyone is relying on the one income. But at least in my experience in Nairobi with youth that has not been the case. They use the term, "hustling." If you ask them, "How do you make your money?" most of them will say, "I hustle." That means that in the morning they might be down at the local potato market. So they haul 3 sacks of potatoes before 11am up to the store of someone who's hired them to do that.

And then in the afternoon they're going to sell newspapers to rush hour traffic. Or in the middle of the day they might try to pick up some work. Or now a lot of them are working with CCS, cleaning toilets or selling services and making some money that way. There is something of a fallacy that there is this sweat equity component that people can put in and that companies and development agencies, all they have to do is put in money and invest in the capital and the (workers') time is available. I think that's one of the things that I learned is not necessarily the case. (Justin DeKoszmovszky, interview, May 19, 2008).

Creating a business requires identifying and developing leadership. DeKoszmovszky commented on this process, emphasizing that business leadership calls for different qualities than some informal youth leaders possess.

One of the things we had to do early on was to get away from the existing hierarchy in the pre-established youth groups, and having leadership of the business not be based on where someone was within the pecking order in the youth group, but rather how effective they were at selling the

business, doing the business, managing the business. And that has been a key shift. Now we find that some of people who are leaders of the business today are not those who are leaders of youth groups. They are often somewhat quieter, less outgoing than the typical group leader, and they are often somewhat on the outskirts of the youth group. (Justin DeKoszmovszky, interview, May 19, 2008).

The challenge of finding and building human capital is enormous because of low levels of education in the population. According to DeKoszmovszky, most youth participants have no more than a primary school education and even then it might be a minority who are able to write (Interview, 2008).

What began as a partnership between a company and a community organization has evolved into an independent business. Recently, the community-based nature of the CCS business and its members' involvement with and support from the community created a new opportunity.

A newly-elected member of parliament contacted one CCS group, one of the most successful and longest running ones in Mathare, and is offering them [a contract to operate] a public toilet, which is closer to the center of town, It could be a very lucrative business. Because she [member of parliament] knows the work they do in the community, and because she is confident that the income that is generated by giving them the right to operate this toilet will go back to community rather than an outside business owner, she is willing to help them get this business. . . . They clearly did some, not formal lobbying, but they were very, very savvy [about local politics]. Incredibly savvy. Clearly they were in touch with her and or her office, and let her know, "By the way, we are still out here. . . ." And it paid off for them. Now they have an opportunity to do this potentially rather lucrative other business. They are locally involved. (Justin DeKoszmovszky, interview, May 19, 2008).

Purpose and Agency

Survival is the primary purpose motivating the young men in CCS. Their sense of agency is evident in the diligence and creativity they demonstrate by finding a variety of different ways to "hustle" a living. CCS adds some new dimensions. First, it is another source of earnings for people who are so poor that they need multiple sources in case one disappears or a sudden need overwhelms their earning capacity. Second, after it is established, CCS provides a more regular source of income. The work is steady and the payment is contracted in advance. Third, and most significant from the perspective of promoting agency, at CCS the youth are not supplicants asking store owners for work or salesmen hawking newspapers to drivers stuck in traffic. They are the owners and executives of the company that they conceived and founded and that they can modify if they choose. One indicator that this new experience can change participants' behavior is that several entrepreneurs independently started new businesses, such as juice stands and barber shops. In contrast to the CCS entrepreneurs, Herbert (2008) described the plight of urban underclass dropout youth in the United States who "hustle" by turning to illicit activity when they see no other options.

One of the most remarkable aspects of the partnership that created CCS is the respect paid by the representatives of an American corporation and universities to the needs, preferences, and wisdom of young men in an African slum. At least as described, this behavior seems the opposite of the historical colonizing approach that deprives people of agency. It is admirable, but seems to emerge not only from commitments to dealing fairly with people but also from the pragmatic realization that this is the only way to create a viable and enduring business. Whatever its origins, this experience of being respected and wielding influence can be an important source of agency.

Human Capital

The BoP protocol (Simanis & Hart, 2008) is not only a template for developing new businesses but also a process through which people who never imagined starting a business both contribute their knowledge and skills and develop them by co-creating a business with their partners. Initially, the protocol calls for pre-field processes of selecting the site, forming and preparing a team and selecting local partners. Phase I—"Opening Up" involves embedding the company in the community to co-create the business concept. Phase II—"Building the Ecosystem"—involves building the business prototype and shared commitment. Phase III—"Enterprise Creation"—emphasizes the further development of the business model, including testing, and expansion (Simanis & Hart, 2008). Throughout the process entrepreneurship on the part of local participants is nurtured, leading to the creation of additional new businesses.

Social Capital

One advantage to the link between community-based organizations and a large multinational corporation is that the resulting social capital—personal connections—can help people build their human capital. One of the leaders of a project that preceded CCS stood out for his academic promise, though he had not graduated from high school. With sponsorship from team members and Carolina for Kibera, he was admitted to Manchester University, where he earned a master's degree in development.

It is not clear to what extent CCS gives participants access to mentors. It seems that the entrepreneurs who will lead a group are tied to managers, and get a fair amount of direction from them, particularly in terms of their own personal short-range goals for the business. When participants have learned to be entrepreneurs, they are also able to become mentors for other youth in the program.

Tap and Reposition Youth (TRY)[3]

Microfinance, described above in association with the Grameen Bank of Bangladesh created by Muhammad Yunus, typically works with groups of poor women who are married and have children (Erulkar et al., 2006, p. 11). Their maturity, family commitments, and roots in the community stabilize the groups and account for high rates of repayment.

TRY was created in the slums of Nairobi, Kenya, by two organizations, K-Rep Development Agency and the Population Council. K-Rep had extensive experience with microfinance with adults as the largest and longest-running microfinance organization in Kenya. Being concerned about reproductive health, the Population Council identified young women (ages 16–22) in the area as especially vulnerable to HIV/AIDS infection and more generally to sexual exploitation. As in many other developing countries, Nairobi's slums are the destination for young people emigrating from rural villages. In patriarchal societies, young women have few rights at best. When they leave their families and their communities to settle among strangers, they lose whatever support they once had. Adding to their vulnerability, the "informal settlements" where they live are so designated in part to justify their exclusion from law enforcement and other government services. In the midst of population churning, even informal social institutions and social networks have not yet formed.

A few statistics convey the situation well. Kenya has a well-developed primary education system. Ninety percent of 12- to 13-year-olds are enrolled in school (Mensch, Bruce, & Greene, 1998, cited by Erulkar et al., 2006, p. 7). But only 22% of 15- to 17-year-old girls in the slums of Nairobi are in school. Fifty-eight percent of those girls do not live with either parent (Erulkar et al., p. 7). The HIV infection rate among 15- to 19-year-old girls living in Nairobi, measured in 2003, was 5.1% (p. 8).

TRY was designed as a means of helping poor young women who were not in school to enhance their economic situations so that they could better protect themselves from sexual exploitation and the risk of HIV infection that results. Erulkar et al. (2006) and coauthors reported three phases of the program's development. In the first phase, the model originally designed for adults was used. Enthusiasm for microfinance in Asia and Africa has led to large-scale expansion of this model and to a growing emphasis on self-sustaining institutions; that is, on building institutions with rates of repayment and capital formation adequate to support their continuation and growth without infusions of aid funds. As a consequence of this understandable emphasis, microfinance organizations have increasingly concentrated solely on saving and lending, to the exclusion of other functions.

Following this model, participants began by attending a 6-day training program to learn about business planning and management, bookkeeping, and how to fill out and evaluate a loan application. Trainers emphasized that the program is about self-help, not aid. Personal issues including sexual health and relationships were also discussed. After the 25 or so members got to know one another and the staff, they began to build up a loan pool with weekly contributions that were collected and placed in a group savings account at a local bank. Originally, each member put in the equivalent of about 26 U.S. cents weekly. But members decided to raise that number to 65 cents. After about 2 months of contributions, when sufficient funds had accumulated, subgroups of five participants met to select the two with the strongest applications to receive the first loans, averaging 147 U.S. dollars. Repayment began the next week so that the fund could be replenished for the next round of loans. After all members received a loan the first recipients became eligible for a second. Loans were used mainly to start small businesses, including a hairdressing salon, a used clothing store, and a fruit juice business.

Participants voluntarily added a parallel savings plan for nonbusiness purposes. Recognizing their inability to cope with financial emergencies or make nonessential purchases, they created a "merry-go-round" in which each member contributed a small amount weekly that was given to one of the members in turn. In this manner, each member eventually accumulated a reserve amounting to nearly 4 U.S. dollars. The weekly recipient of the fund often made the event into a party, which helped build group solidarity. In addition to putting the accumulated money away, some members used it to purchase clothing or improve their homes.

The creation of the merry-go-rounds reflected not only the need for social support to help members save, but the difficulty many of them had in protecting savings from husbands or boyfriends. The group and its savings account offered a safe place to keep extra money that a man might otherwise take and use for his own purposes.

Repayment rates and participation were high at first, but then began to fall off. The microfinance design depends completely on the continuous cycle of contributions and repayments building up to be loaned out. When some loan recipients default and when members withdraw, the cycle is broken and it may not be repairable. Some members who had repaid their loans were denied second applications because other members failed to repay theirs. As members dropped out, they withdrew their contributions, threatening to leave remaining members with the responsibility for outstanding loans that were not repaid by others.

Analysis of the emerging problems revealed that the youngest and most vulnerable members were experiencing the greatest difficulties, leading to the conclusion that "the program's social-performance objectives of increasing girls' security and financial assets conflicted with its financial-performance objectives focused on credit and loan repayment" (Erulkar et al., 2006, p. 26). This conflict was manifest in the role of the credit officers who were expected simultaneously to encourage and support the members in all aspects of their lives and to enforce repayment schedules. It interfered with the formation of personal relationships among members: One might make a new friend over tea and cookies in the home of the week's merry-go-round winner only to have to pressure the new friend to keep up loan repayments so that the account would have enough money to make a loan when her turn came.

Responding to this analysis, K-Rep and the Population Council created a new role for mentors who would focus on members' personal and social issues and leave financial management to the credit officers. They recruited mentors to address the issues that members had struggled with: health, relationships, conflict management, learning opportunities, and business management. Meetings addressing these topics were added to the weekly meetings on saving and loans. This adaptation recognized that young women recently arrived from the countryside who are mostly unmarried and not yet mothers have small social networks and are mobile. It is very common for them to marry and then move away.

However, it did not recognize another need that members had expressed. Living so close to the edge of survival, they were always only a few hundred shillings away from disaster. They welcomed the encouragement and support they received to save and invest in their long-term economic benefit and to put aside some extra money for purchases. But they also needed savings for emergencies, and the only way to gain access to the money they put into the loan account was to quit the program. A member faced with a medical bill or the need to rent a new place to live had no way of getting the money she needed except to withdraw all of her contributions from the common account. Concerns about these issues were magnified when repayment and participation began to drop and remaining members worried that their contributions would be used to cover other members' debts.

Recognition of this problem set the stage for TRY phase 3 in which Young Savers Clubs were created with many of the same young women and many of the same procedures as the original model, such as weekly meetings to deposit savings in a joint account. The difference was that deposits were not for loan but personal savings, available at any time to the depositors. Despite staff concerns that girls would put all their money into savings and stop contributing to the revolving loan fund, the most common response was for young women to participate in both.

Two of the key themes that emerged from the TRY experience are the importance of the social interaction it promotes and the different needs and capacities of the participants. Under the anomic conditions facing the young women targeted by TRY, simply having a group of peers to meet with weekly and one or more older women to talk to was a significant improvement in their lives and would have been regardless of the reasons for meeting. Many of the additions to the program acknowledged and responded to the need for human contact, for friendship and caring.

But repeatedly the differences among participants, especially by age, came to the surface. Dropouts from the original program were younger, had less education, were likely to live with a parent, and were poorer compared to those who persisted. Their most pressing financial need was not for a business loan but for a safe place to keep savings that could be readily accessed in an emergency. Mixed groups encountered problems when some women, mostly older, were hoping to create a business while others simply wanted to save money and were anxious about whether they could regain access to it or whether other members would pay back their loans. Older participants were readier to save and to repay loans. Like classic beneficiaries of microfinance they wanted to maintain their access to capital, taking out and repaying a series of loans. Younger participants gained the most simply from the discipline of saving and of having to repay their loans. One loan might be sufficient. They needed more mentoring and social support. Their default rate was higher, but their needs were too.

TRY was accompanied by a well-designed evaluation (Erulkar & Chong, 2005). Participants were matched with nonparticipants and both groups were interviewed before the program began. Small sample size and extreme difficulty in locating nonparticipants for the postintervention interview make evaluation findings less robust than desired; because of

high residential mobility only 17% could be located. But the amount of data collected on participants, including records on what they did, and comparisons by age within the participant group yielded valuable insights.

Reflecting the ambitious and diverse goals of the program, financial outcomes were assessed along with gender attitudes and knowledge about reproductive health issues. After the program, TRY participants compared to matched nonparticipants reported higher income, more household assets, and more savings, which were also more secure. They were more likely to endorse the principle that women should be able to refuse sex with her husband. And they were somewhat more likely to say they could negotiate sexual relations, including condom use. However, they did not demonstrate greater knowledge of sexual health issues.

One number captures both the limitations and the potential of the program. After 5 years of operation, the repayment rate for loans had fallen to 50%, far too low to sustain a revolving loan fund. Yet if the nonfinancial benefits are compared to those from many other social and health programs, the fact that participants put up part of the costs themselves makes it a more reasonable investment. Most poignantly, the young women who proved least able to meet the requirements of microfinance were also the most vulnerable.

With both the benefits and limitations in mind, and recognizing the age differences in participants' experience, Erulkar et al. (2006), concluded by recommending a differentiated and staged approach. TRY demonstrates that the standard approach to microfinance that has demonstrated its value and efficacy with older women in established communities is simply not suitable to the target group in the Nairobi slums, especially those still in their teens. They require far more social support and mentoring and they are far less able to generate value with their loans. For this group, savers clubs and opportunities for social interaction and learning, links to youth-serving organizations, training programs, and other supports could magnify the effectiveness of these program elements. Strictly organized microfinance, in this scenario, would be reserved for more mature and confident young women, some of whom would make the transition from the previous stage. Additional means of learning about employment and business would also be made available to the more mature group, including vocational training, work experience, apprenticeships, and other forms of on-the-job training.

Purpose and Agency

Just like the young men creating the Community Cleaning Service, the young women who are their peers and neighbors are motivated by what Maslow (1954) identified as the fundamental human need, survival. Most of them relocated to the vicinity of Nairobi in search of a better life than they could make for themselves in their home villages. Arriving in a strange place without family and friends, they need guidance and support to find the most rewarding possibilities for earning a living. Grasping these possibilities requires and builds a sense of agency.

It is difficult to imagine a more shattering absence of agency than the experience reported by several TRY participants of having exchanged sex for subsistence. Among the 85% of participants who reported being sexually experienced when they began the program, only 37% said they had willingly consented to their sexual initiation (Erulkar et al., 2006, pp. 26–27). Confronted with the power imbalances that underlie such exploitation, the threats to physical health posed by HIV infection cannot be resisted solely with education. Young women need to know that they have the support they need to provide for themselves and that they can resist unwanted sexual advances.

Although the evaluation did not assess agency or purpose, the reports of participants succeeding in building small businesses suggest that some of them gained the ability to plan and to carry out their plans.

Human Capital

TRY focuses on accumulating financial capital but simultaneously on building the attitudes and habits of saving and investing wisely. Training in business practices, the modeling by peers of successful entrepreneurship, and the experience of making business plans and decisions individually and as part of a group also add to participants' human capital.

Social Capital

As significant and relevant as purpose and agency and human capital are in TRY, it epitomizes the power of social capital. Microfinance relies upon the power of personal relationships and the trust that develops within them. TRY recruits young women who have left most of their social capital back in their home villages and helps them build a new fund of social capital. This is where TRY departs from classical microfinance, which builds on existing social capital of long standing. The obvious explanation for the much lower repayment rates in TRY and for the need to build in additional supports is that TRY participants are defined by the very absence of the social capital that made microfinance work so well among mature women in Bangladeshi villages.

Participating in a saving and lending group adds to young women's social capital, but the experience of TRY demonstrates that the group itself and its activities are insufficient. Especially for teenagers, the chance to make friends with peers and to share purely social time are essential. Adults who can serve as mentors are another important form of social capital, greatly augmented by the addition of older women to the program staff who were formally designated as mentors and selected to meet needs expressed by the participants.

FEATURES OF ASSET-BUILDING INSTITUTIONS

The four institutions described above seem to promote asset building. They differ in many ways, but they also share some common features, meaning the ways they are structured and the kinds of experiences that participants have. We find six common features: public/private partnerships; learning and earning; responsible social roles; youth leadership and civic engagement; proliferating pathways; and mentoring. The four institutions also illustrate the difference between systems and programs.

The term *institution* has multiple, broad meanings. We introduce here another such term, *system,* and contrast it with *program.* In this context, we mean by system an entity that is large enough to accommodate nearly all of those who can benefit from it. For example, school systems are expected to find a place for every child of the appropriate age. A system endures; its existence is not dependent on annual fund raising or a variable legislative appropriation. A system also has clear and robust connections to other systems (Hamilton & Hamilton, 1999).

German apprenticeship exemplifies systems. Despite current struggles to find adequate placements, it continues to serve more than half of the eligible age cohort. Its financial support is solid enough to carry it through some employers' decisions to opt out. And it very clearly and strongly links the country's education system with the labor market. It also provides paths to other parts of the educational system, including a range of postsecondary vocational institutions and even universities.

Our other three institutions are programs, not systems. We present them as potential seeds for new systems, but acknowledge that they remain small and vulnerable. YouthBuild is both the oldest and the largest. The success of YouthBuild's leaders in gaining federal funds and private donations bodes well for continued growth. Ideally, that growth will be in the direction of becoming a widely valued and recognized institution to meet the needs of young people who have failed in and been failed by schools. It is encouraging in this context that the educational component is being enhanced and formalized. The participants who wrote and signed their *Declaration of*

Inter-Dependence demonstrated an awareness of the need for stronger systems by pointing out that YouthBuild alone cannot achieve all of its goals. Better schools and better jobs are also needed.

Progress toward system status is harder to envision for CCS and TRY. Both are small scale. We have not been able to determine how they fared during and after the political and ethnic violence that recently swept parts of Kenya. However, they illustrate some of the possibilities and demonstrate that even under the most challenging conditions creative and committed people can find solutions.

Expanding on the theme of system building, we also urge attention to the ecology of institutions in which these programs—possibly nascent systems—function. Bronfenbrenner's (1979) ecological conception of the world in which people develop included four nested levels of systems, including the mesosystem, which he defined as a system of systems. Institutions supporting the transition to adulthood are part of a mesosystem that includes other institutions. Bronfenbrenner propounded a series of hypotheses regarding the optimal nature of mesosystems for development, emphasizing links among microsystems and reinforcement of positive influences in multiple settings (pp. 214–218). In Bronfenbrenner's terms, the YouthBuild staff member mentoring a participant would be a microsystem. To the extent that the staff member links the YouthBuild participant quoted above to new educational opportunities (additional microsystems), he is helping him build links within the mesosystem he inhabits.

Public/Private Partnerships

When we searched for programs that might foreshadow what new institutions supporting the transition to adulthood could do and what they would look like, we did not have in mind as a criterion the melding that we found of public with private. Although it is most highly developed in German apprenticeship, the only system we examined as an alternative and complement to higher education, the same melding also characterizes the other three institutions. Private organizations and entrepreneurship are increasingly seen as more effective and more cost-efficient than government programs.

The term *social entrepreneurship* (Bornstein, 2007) illustrates this convergence of sectors. Whereas philanthropy and social service were once seen as quite distinct, despite the examples of people like John D. Rockefeller and Andrew Carnegie, taking action to improve the lives of others is now seen as requiring some of the same competencies and same approaches as creating a business. As Bill Gates, Warren Buffett, and less celebrated business moguls have turned their attention to and invested their wealth in social causes, they have brought to these kinds of activities the same creativity, analytical powers, and careful attention to costs and benefits that made them wealthy and applied them in the nonprofit arena. Muhammad Yunus and others with a social mission have freely adapted business methods.

Learning and Earning: Combining Education with Employment

In the United States, working one's way through school is a time-honored tradition. As enrollment in higher education has exploded and commuter institutions have proliferated, working while going to college has become normative, even in elite institutions. This practice reflects not only the adaptation of institutions of higher education to students who are employed, part time or even full time, but also a labor market that makes numerous part-time and "swing-shift" jobs available. It is harder for students in Germany and many other countries to work part time because higher education is organized for full-time students and the labor market is organized for full-time workers.

The cost of attending school is not limited to tuition charges. Enrolling in school also incurs "opportunity costs," namely, lost earnings from not working. Young people from families living on the edge cannot rely on family support. They may be fortunate to have it during the primary grades, but if they go as far as postsecondary education they are on their own. Therefore, they need low- or no-cost education, but they also need a way to earn money while they are enrolled. Young people who are expected to contribute to the family's well-being need money for that purpose, over and above tuition and their own sustenance.

German apprenticeship is designed as a work/learning experience, with wages held low enough to ensure that learning prevails. Youth-Build was created specifically for poor youth who are no longer enrolled in school. Earning wages is a critical incentive for participation. Assistance in obtaining the GED or a high school diploma is a central goal of the program, enabling and encouraging graduates to enter post-secondary education. Both TRY and CCS are designed primarily to help young adults earn a decent living. Yet they educate and train young people as certainly as if they were formal educational institutions. They have only informal links to formal education. Strengthening those links seems a desirable direction for future development both as a means of increasing the emphasis on learning but also as a basis for conferring formal educational credentials on participants. One of the strengths of German apprenticeship is that it yields a formal credential that is negotiable in the labor market. It formalizes what was originally an informal mode of teaching and learning both by certifying the knowledge and skills apprentices gain and by linking work-based learning to schooling.

German apprenticeship is also exemplary in exploiting quite systematically the pedagogical power of workplaces. Rather than treating the need to earn money as a distraction from learning, new institutions can be designed to teach through work. YouthBuild espouses this philosophy and both CCS and TRY have made progress in this direction.

Responsible Social Roles

As has been noted, rolelessness is a threat during the transition to adulthood. With "regular" jobs hard to find and the role of student inaccessible, apprenticeship, Youthbuild, CCS, and TRY provide respected social roles. Young people who would otherwise be unemployed or picking up odd jobs have stable employment as well as earnings. They are part of an organization that values them and in which their peers as well as adults encourage and support them. Filling new institutional roles builds a young person's sense of identity; it is part of the answer to the key question: "Who are you?"

Youth Leadership and Civic Engagement

Karen Pittman (Pittman, Irby, Tolman, Yohalem, & Ferber, 2002), who is one of the best thinkers about youth issues and unmatched as a communicator about those issues, has distinguished things done *to* youth—services—from things done *for* youth—supports—and both from things done *with* youth—opportunities. Services, supports, and opportunities are all needed and often provided by the same institutions. However, Pittman reminds us that when youth are viewed as problems to be solved rather than resources to be developed, services tend to predominate. We have written of institutions supporting the transition to adulthood, but the cases discussed are excellent examples of creating opportunities for youth to take responsibility for themselves and others. That is how they promote agency.

YouthBuild pays the most explicit attention of the institutions described to enhancing young people's ability and willingness to participate in democratic decision making. The leadership program not only prepares participants to take leadership roles in YouthBuild, it aims to make them more engaged and more effective citizens of their communities. German apprentices in larger firms may be elected by their peers to sit on a youth committee of the works council, a fixture in German workplaces that gives workers, through their unions, a voice in corporate governance. The *Jugendbeirat* speaks on behalf of apprentices but also provides a kind of apprenticeship in joint decision making.

TRY and CCS appear to be remarkably youth directed. Young workers developed the CCS business model while the partners were trying to get a different model started. TRY has been redesigned at least twice in response to participants' needs. Although youth empowerment such as this may not lead directly to civic engagement, the agency it fosters and the experience it gives young people in defining their interests and expressing them publicly seem likely to carry over into other arenas, especially civil society.

Proliferating Pathways

Some young people follow career paths that are very clear and very direct. Consider a young woman who has wanted to be a doctor since she was five years old. Given good advice, intelligence, hard work, support, a high school internship in a hospital, and some luck, she is likely to graduate from high school with a strong record, enroll in a selective college and excel at her premed courses, do well on the MCATs, enroll in the best medical school that admits her, accept the internship that best suits her needs, pass her state exams, and begin a residency that will lead to a satisfying and productive practice. The professions are distinct precisely in the specificity of preparation that qualifies people to practice them. Entry is allowed only through certain gateways. Some who succeed may do other things first, but everyone must pass through the same gateways, without exception.

Most occupations do not have such clear, and rigid, entry requirements, and most people's career paths are far less direct. German apprenticeship and associated laws and practices create specific gateways for skilled and semi-skilled occupations. The presence of significant gateways has two competing effects on young people's career paths. On the one hand, they clearly mark career paths. They make them transparent. The would-be doctor knows precisely what she must do. On the other hand, they make those paths difficult to traverse. Gates not only swing open to allow people through, they remain closed to those without the key. The presence in Germany of precise requirements for certification as an auto mechanic tells a young man just what he must do to be able to work on cars. But if he changes his mind and decides he would rather work on auto bodies, he has to start over and follow a different path through a different set of gates. Career paths are, under these circumstances, relatively impermeable; it is hard to move along them (Hamilton, 1994).

An ideal institution supporting the transition to adulthood gives young people both a map to make career paths more transparent—advice and assistance on career paths—and the kind of experience and training that helps them through the gates that mark the path. Institutions that create multiple pathways to the same career goals are especially desirable. Recent adaptations of German apprenticeship have enabled apprentices to move back into full-time schooling. Pathways are being created in some occupations so that, for example, cabinet makers can become interior designers.

Mentoring

Among the four institutions, only TRY formally designated a set of adults as mentors. The role was created after high default and dropout rates forced the rethinking of the microfinance scheme, resulting in more explicit attention to nonfinancial issues. Selecting mentors to match the issues participants had identified as important to them was an enlightened design feature. Tellingly, the women who qualified as mentors were also strong candidates for other positions, leading to high turnover despite attractive rates of pay.

But mentoring does not depend upon people who are formally designated as mentors (Hamilton & Hamilton, 2004). By our definition, mentors are adults outside the family who offer the kind of advice and assistance that a parent or other family might be expected to provide. As mentoring programs have proliferated, a positive development, mentoring has come to be identified with programs. But the programs exist to synthesize a natural relationship that has been impeded by age and social class segregation and by hyper-busyness. Most mentors are naturally part of a young person's social network, not introduced by a mentoring program. In all four of the institutions we have described, adults are available who are responsible for working with young people to help them achieve their goals. Some of them become mentors.

Mentoring connotes a relationship that goes beyond the limits of a position description and endures through changes in the organizational relationships of the people involved. A teacher who instructs a student in class and works with the student after class is doing her job. When the teacher also advises the student on her educational pathway and on other topics, such as relations with parents and personal values, she has moved beyond the teaching role to become a mentor as well. Becoming a mentor often means that the relationship extends beyond the walls of the school and the duration of the school year as well.

When mentoring is defined in this way, rather than in terms of a formally defined organizational role as in TRY, it becomes difficult, if not impossible, to determine whether and to what extent mentoring is happening within a program or system without conducting empirical research. However, the structure and functions of all four institutions appear to provide opportunities for mentoring relationships to develop between participants and adult staff but also other adults who are involved by bringing them together around common goals. German apprenticeship illustrates the possibilities well. Taking on an apprentice obligates an employer to provide learning opportunities. A designated person has day-to-day responsibility for teaching an apprentice. In a small shop, that might be the owner. In a large firm, a coordinator of apprentices arranges placements in rotation so that each apprentice learns about the functions of multiple departments, with a series of different supervisors. But apprentices may form their closest relationships with other adults they get to know at work.

CONCLUSIONS

For large numbers of young people, the transition to adulthood is a journey of discovery, a time to learn more about themselves, others, the worlds of work and citizenship, and their places in those worlds. Higher education, employment, family, and institutions of civil society provide them with support, notably in the form of opportunities to gain a sense of purpose and agency, to build their human capital, and to acquire social capital. As norms change regarding the duration of the transition and the sequence of steps that constitute it, advantages accumulate with those who are able to use higher education as an institution in which to make or at least start the transition. The labor market, which once offered jobs that would support a family to young men whose education stopped at high school, has become a more forbidding place in the United States and other countries. Many employers will hire older teenagers or people in their early twenties, but they are concentrated in low-wage, low-skill positions with few opportunities for moving up a career ladder. Young women of the same age are unlikely to devote themselves to raising children; economic necessity forces most to work and to build the human capital they will need to contribute steadily to the family's sustenance.

A prolonged transition to adulthood without benefit of higher education can be valuable but it can also be a fruitless delay. To enable more young people and especially those from poor families to take full advantage of a longer period between the time when they are physically mature and the time when they assume adult roles, young people experiencing it need to inhabit institutions that more closely match the new realities of this period of life. New

and adapted institutions can provide the sense of purpose and agency, the human and social capital that young people need to be productive workers, engaged citizens, and nurturing family members.

Enrolling more young people in higher education is certainly desirable, but it is no substitute for the declining capacity of employment institutions and families to support the transition to adulthood. Large increases in enrollment would require larger investments in higher education than taxpayers are prepared to make. Some young people do not like and do not do well in school. And if everyone went to college, some graduates would still have to do work that does not require a college degree.

New institutions must be attuned to the needs of young people from poor families as they enter adulthood. Like residential colleges, these new institutions must offer the supports and opportunities required during the transition. Ideally, they will contribute to reducing the reproduction of social class, making it possible for young people to exceed the SES into which they were born. We have examined one well-developed system, German apprenticeship, for clues to what such institutions might look like. Three programs for low-income youth, YouthBuild in the United States and the Community Cleaning Service and Tap and Reposition Youth in Kenya, point in some new directions.

Perhaps the most important lesson to be learned from examining these institutions is that more than one institution is needed. Rather than trying to create a single institution that does everything for all young people, we should think about the ecology of institutions in which young people become adults. German apprenticeship gains strength from bestriding the educational system on one side and workplaces on the other. It provides a gateway into respected and well-paid occupations. But it does so with a certain rigidity. Young people who neither graduate from universities or from postsecondary vocational institutions nor complete an apprenticeship have few options. The path to a skilled worker's certificate is well marked; deviations are discouraged. Young people with immigrant family backgrounds have not been well served by this institution and adaptations to improve their prospects are just being created to adapt to the structural limitations of the former East.

In the United States, young people who do not earn college degrees make their way into adulthood via multiple paths, but many lose valuable time and fail to acquire in a timely way the assets they need. Paths with more clearly visible gates and clear information about how to pass through those gates would help. YouthBuild is an example of an organization that helps mostly minority high school dropouts in poor urban communities gain the purpose and agency they need to move into productive paths and gain a powerful combination of construction-related skills but also academics and civic competence, enabling graduates to go on to many different fields, especially human services. But, as participants pointed out, YouthBuild cannot do it all alone. Other supportive institutions must be visible and accessible to participants.

The exemplars described here suggest that such institutions will have some common features. Although many will be no more than programs, they will have the potential to become systems. Rather than maintaining the separation between work and learning that typifies institutions for children, they will enable young people to earn a living while they continue to learn. Being a participant in these institutions will give young people responsible and respected roles, avoiding the fate of rolelessness. Becoming an adult means assuming additional civic responsibilities, and these institutions give at least some young people experience and instruction in civic competencies, including leadership. New institutions, like those we have described, will be hybrids, linking public with private in ways that challenge that dichotomy. Rather than constituting a single channel through which all young people must pass to adulthood, they will create a plethora of pathways from which young people may choose. That variety heightens the need for mentoring from caring

adults beyond the family, including both formally designated and informal or natural mentors. Like the creators of YouthBuild, CCS and TRY, we need to turn our collective capacity for social entrepreneurship to the task of overcoming the structural lag that now leaves too many poor young people with inadequate support during the transition to adulthood.

ENDNOTES

1. Additional detail and extensive documentation may be found in Hamilton (1990).

2. We are greatly indebted to Professors Drs. Burkhart Lutz and Holle Grünert for convening an informal seminar with their colleagues on institutional support for the transition to adulthood and recent developments in apprenticeship in eastern Germany, at th University of Halle, Germany, September 24, 2007.

3. We rely for this description on the report by Erulkar, et. al. (2006) and the evaluation conducted by Erulkar and Chon (2005). Page numbers are provided only for specific information in those documents.

REFERENCES

Adato, M., Carter, M. R., & May, J. (2006). Exploring poverty traps and social exclusion in South Africa using qualitative and quantitative data. *Journal of Development Studies, 42*(2), 226–247.

Arnett, J.J. (2004). *Emerging adulthood: The winding road from the late teens through the twenties.* Oxford: Oxford University Press.

Assaad, R. (1997). The effects of public sector hiring and compensation policies on the Egyptian labor market. *The World Bank Economic Review, 11*(1), 85–118.

Barton, P.E. (2005). *One-third of a nation: Rising dropout rates and declining opportunities.* Princeton, NJ: Educational Testing Service.

Becker, G.S. (1993). *Human capital: A theoretical and empirical analysis, with special reference to education* (3rd ed.). Chicago: The University of Chicago Press.

Bell, J. (2003). *Youth transformation & us.* Retrieved June 13, 2008, from www.youthbuild.org/atf/cf/%7B22B5F680-2AF9-4ED2-B948-40C4B32E6198%7D/Youth%20Transformation%20&%20Us,%202003.pdf.

Benson, P. L., Scales, P. C., Hamilton, S. F., & Semsa, A., Jr. (2006). Positive youth development: Theory, research, and applications. In R. M. Lerner (Ed.), *Handbook of child psychology* (6th ed.), vol. 1: *Theoretical models of human development* (pp. 894–941). (Editors-in-chief: W. Damon & R. M. Lerner). Hoboken, NJ: John Wiley & Sons.

Berger, K., & Grünert, H. (Eds.) (2007). *Zwischen Markt und Förderung—Wirksamkeit und Zukunft von Ausbildungsplatzstrukturen in Ostdeutschland. Ergebnisse eines gemeinsamen Workshops des Bundesinstituts für Berufsbildung und des Zentrums für Sozialforschung Halle.* Bielefeld: Bertelsmann.

Bornstein, D. (2007). *How to change the world* (rev. ed.). New York: Oxford University Press.

Bowen, W. G., Kurzweil, M. A., & Tobin, E. M. (2005). *Equity and excellence in American higher education.* Charlottesville: University of Virginia Press.

Bundesinstitut für Berufsbildung. (2008). *Ausbildungsbeteiligungs quoten nach Geschlecht, Deutschland 1993 – 2006.* Retrieved May 5, 2008, from www.bibb.de/dokumente/pdf/a21_ausweitstat_schaubilder_ab0901.pdf.

Bronfenbrenner, U. (1979). *The ecology of human development: Experiments by nature and design.* Cambridge, MA: Harvard University Press.

Carr, P., & Kefalas, M. (2006). *Straight from the heartland: Coming of age in Ellis, Iowa*. Working Paper for the MacArthur Foundation Network on Transitions to Adulthood. Retrieved June 25, 2008, from www.transad.pop.upenn.edu/downloads/Iowa%20Final%209-21-06%20br.pdf.

Chinman, M. J., & Linney, J. A. (1998). Toward a model of adolescent empowerment: Theoretical and empirical evidence. *The Journal of Primary Prevention, 18*(4), 393–413.

Clausen, J. S. (1993). *American lives: Looking back at the children of the Great Depression*. New York: Free Press.

Cohen, M.A., & Piquero, A. R. (in press). New evidence on the monetary value of saving a high risk youth. *Journal of Quantitative Criminology*.

Coleman, J. S. (1990). *Foundations of social theory*. Cambridge, MA: Belknap Press of Harvard University.

The Condition of Education 2000–2008. National Center for Education Statistics, Institute of Education Sciences, U.S. Department of Education. Retrieved June 17, 2008, from www.nces.ed.gov/programs/coe/.

Cook, T. D., & Furstenberg, F. F., Jr. (2002). Explaining aspects of the transition to adulthood in Italy, Sweden, Germany, and the United States: A cross-disciplinary, case synthesis approach. *Annals of the American Academy of Political and Social Science 580*(1), 257–287.

Diewald, M., Goedicke, A., & Mayer, K. U. (Eds.). (2006). *After the fall of the Wall: Life courses in the transformation of East Germany*. Stanford, CA: Stanford University Press.

Digest of Education Statistics 2007. (2008). National Center for Education Statistics, Institute of Education Sciences, U.S. Department of Education. Retrieved June 17, 2008, from www.nces.ed.gov/programs/digest/d07/tables/dt07_008.asp?referrer=report.

Eccles, J., & Gootman, J. A. (Eds.). (2002). *Community programs to promote youth development*. Washington, DC: National Academy Press.

Elder, G. H., Jr. (1999). *Children of the Great Depression: Social change in life experience* (25th Anniversary Edition). Boulder, CO: Westview Press.

Erikson, E. H. (1963). *Childhood and society*. New York: W. W. Norton.

Erulkar, A., Bruce, J., Dondo, A. Sebstad, J., Matheka, J., Khan, M.B., & Gathuku, A. (2006). *Tap and Reposition Youth (TRY): Providing social support, savings, and microcredit opportunities for young women in areas with high HIV prevalence*. New York: The Population Council. Retrieved June 19, 2008, from www.popcouncil.org/pdfs/seeds/seeds23.pdf.

Erulkar, A.S., & Chong, E. (2005). *Evaluation of a savings and micro-credit program for vulnerable young women in Nairobi*. New York: The Population Council. Retrieved June 19, 2008, from www.popcouncil.org/pdfs/TRY_Evaluation.pdf.

Evans, S. D. (2007). Youth sense of community: Voice and power in community contexts. *Journal of Community Psychology, 35*(6), 693–709.

Furstenberg, F. F., Jr., Rumbaut, R. G., & Settersten, R. A. (Eds.). (2005). *On the frontier of adulthood: Theory, research and public policy*. Chicago: University of Chicago Press.

Granato, M., Bethscheider, M., Friedrich, M., Gutschow, K., Paulsen, B., Schwerin, C., Settelmeyer, A., Uhly, A., & Ulrich, J.G. (no date). *Integration und berufliche Ausbildung*. Bundesinstitut für Berufsbildung. Retrieved June 19, 2008, from www.bibb.de/dokumente/pdf/a24_integration-und-berufliche-ausbildung.pdf.

Granovetter, M. (1973). The strength of weak ties. *American Journal of Sociology, 78,* 1360–1380.

Hahn, A., Leavitt, T. D., Horvat, E. M., & Davis, J. E. (June, 2004). Life after YouthBuild: 900 YouthBuild graduates reflect on their lives, dreams, and experiences. Retrieved June 26, 2008, from www.youthbuild.org/atf/cf/{22B5F680-2AF9-4ED2-B948-40C4B32E6198}/GraduateResearchReport_full.pdf.

Hamilton, M. A., & Hamilton, S. F. (2008). A precarious passage: Aging out of the child-only case load. *Applied Development Science, 12*(1), 10–25.

Hamilton, S.F. (1994). Employment prospects as motivation for school achievement: Links and gaps between school and work in seven countries. In R.K. Silbereisen & E. Todt (Eds.), *Adolescence in context: The interplay of family, school, peers, and work in adjustment* (pp. 267–283). New York: Springer.

Hamilton, S. F. (1990). *Apprenticeship for adulthood: Preparing youth for the future*. New York: Free Press.

Hamilton, S. F., & Hamilton, M. A. (1999). *Building strong school-to-work systems: Illustrations of key components*. Washington, DC: National School-to-Work Office.

Hamilton, S. F., & Hamilton, M. A. (2004). Contexts for mentoring: Adolescent-adult relationships in workplaces and communities. In R. M. Lerner & L. Steinberg (Eds.), *Handbook of adolescent psychology* (2nd ed., pp. 395–428). Hoboken, NJ: John Wiley & Sons.

Hamilton, S. F., & Lempert, W. (1997). The impact of apprenticeship on youth: A prospective analysis. *Journal of Research on Adolescence, 6,* 427–455.

Hareven, T. K. (1994). Family change and historical change: An uneasy relationship. In M. W. Riley, R. L. Kahn, & A. Foner (Eds.), *Age and structural lag: Societies' failure to provide meaningful opportunities in work, family, and leisure* (pp. 130–150). New York: John Wiley & Sons.

Hart, S. L. (2005). *Capitalism at the crossroads: The unlimited business opportunities in solving the world's most difficult problems*. Upper Saddle River, N.J.: Wharton School.

Herbert, B. (2008, June 10). Out of sight. *New York Times,* Op. Ed.

Hofer, M. (1999). Community service and social cognitive development in German adolescents. In M. Yates & J. Youniss (Eds.), *Roots of civic identity: International perspectives on community service and activism in youth* (pp. 114–134). Cambridge UK: Cambridge University Press.

Karen, D. (2002). Changes in access to higher education in the United States: 1980–1992. *Sociology of Education, 75*(3): 191–210.

Kett, J.F. (1977). *Rites of passage: Adolescence in America, 1790 to the present*. New York: Basic Books.

Knapp, L.G., Kelly-Reid, J.E., Ginder, S.A., & Miller, E. (2008). *Enrollment in Postsecondary Institutions, Fall 2006; Graduation Rates, 2000 & 2003 Cohorts; and Financial Statistics, Fiscal Year 2006* (NCES 2008-173). Washington, DC: National Center for Education Statistics, Institute of Education Sciences, U.S. Department of Education. Retrieved June 17, 2008, from www.nces.ed.gov/pubs2008/2008173.pdf.

Kremer, M. (2007). Reducing the educational hurdles facing young migrants. Speech by the President of the Federal Institute for Vocational Education and Training Manfred Kremer on the occasion of "Diversity in training and work" conference staged by the Coordination Agency for Continuing Training and Employment in Hamburg. Retrieved June 19, 2008, from www.bibb.de/en/29714.htm.

Larson, R.W., & Hanson, D. (2005). The development of strategic thinking: Learning to impact human systems in a youth activism program. *Human Development, 48*(6), 327–349.

Laird, J., DeBell, M., Kienzl, G., and Chapman, C. (2007). *Dropout Rates in the United States: 2005* (NCES 2007-059). U.S. Department of Education. Washington, DC: National Center for Education Statistics. Retrieved June 17, 2008, from www.nces.ed.gov/pubsearch.

Lloyd, C.B. (Ed.) (2005). *Growing up global: The changing transitions to adulthood in developing countries*. Washington, DC: National Academies Press.

Maslow, A. H. (1954). *Motivation and personality*. New York: Harper.

Mensch, B., Bruce, J., & Greene, M. E. (1998). *The uncharted passage: Girls' adolescence in the developing world*. New York: Population Council.

Modell, J. (1989). *Into one's own: From youth to adulthood in the United States, 1920–1975*. Berkeley, CA: University of California Press.

National Alumni Council, & Young Leaders Council of the YouthBuild USA Affiliated Network. (2008). The Declaration of Inter-Dependence: Policy statement. March. Retrieved on June 26, 2008, from www.youthbuild.org/atf/cf/{22b5f680-2af9-4ed2-b948-40c4b32e6198}/DECLARATION08.PDF.

Nightingale, E.O., & Wolverton, L. (1993). Adolescent rolelessness in modern society. *Teachers College Record, 94*(3), 472– 486.

Osgood, D. W., Foster, E. M. Flanagan, C., & Ruth, G. R. (Eds.). (2006). *On your own without a net: The transition to adulthood for vulnerable populations*. Chicago: University of Chicago Press.

Osterman, P. (1980). *Getting started: The youth labor market*. Cambridge, MA: MIT Press.

Oswald, H. (1999). The political socialization in the new states of Germany. In M. Yates, & J. Youniss (Eds.), *Roots of civic identity: International perspectives on community service and activism in youth* (pp. 97-113). Cambridge UK: Cambridge University Press.

Pittman, K., Irby, M., Tolman, J., Yohalem, N., & Ferber, T. (2002). *Preventing problems, promoting development, encouraging engagement: Competing priorities or inseparable goals?* Washington, DC: Forum for Youth Investment.

Polgreen, L. (2007, May 20). Africa's storied colleges, jammed and crumbling. *The New York Times.* p. 1. Retrieved June 19, 2008, from www.nytimes.com/2007/05/20/world/africa/20senegal.html?_r=1&oref=slogin.

Prahalad, C. K., & Hart, S. L. (2002). The fortune at the bottom of the pyramid. *Strategy + Business, 26,* 54–67.

Putnam, R. D. (2000). *Bowling alone: The collapse and revival of American community*. New York: Simon & Schuster.

Rawls, J. (1971). *A theory of justice*. Cambridge, MA: Belknap Press of Harvard University Press.

Reich, R. B. (2001). *The future of success*. New York: Alfred A. Knopf.

Reinders, H., & Youniss, J. (2005). Community service and political participation of American and German adolescents. *Psychologie in Erziehung und Unterricht, 52*(1), 1–19.

Reinders, H., & Youniss, J. (2006). School-based required community service and civic development in adolescents. *Applied Developmental Science, 10*(1), 2–12.

Riley, M. W., Kahn, R. L., & Foner, A. (Eds.). (1994). *Age and structural lag: Society's failure to provide meaningful opportunities in work, family, and leisure*. New York: John Wiley & Sons.

Scales, P.C. & Leffert, N. (2004). *Developmental assets: A synthesis of the scientific research on adolescent development* (2nd ed.). Minneapolis: Search Institute.

Schneider, B., & Stevenson, D. (1999). *The ambitious generation: America's teenagers, motivated but directionless*. New Haven, CT: Yale University Press.

Schoeni, R., & Ross, K. (2005). Material assistance received from families during the transition to adulthood. In F. F. Furstenberg, Jr., R. G. Rumbaut, & R. A. Settersten (Eds.), *On the frontier of adulthood: Theory, research and public policy* (pp. 396–416). Chicago: University of Chicago Press.

Settersten, R. (2005). Social policy and the transition to adulthood: Toward stronger institutions and individual capacities. In F. F. Furstenberg, Jr., R. G. Rumbaut, & R. A. Settersten (Eds.), *On the frontier of adulthood: Theory, research, and public policy* (pp. 534–560). Chicago: University of Chicago Press.

Simanis, E., & Hart, S., with DeKoszmovszky, J., Donohue, P., Duke, D., Enk, G., Gordon, M., and Thieme, T. (2008). The base of the pyramid protocol: Toward next generation BoP strategy (2nd ed.). Retrieved June 27, 2008, from www.bopnetwork.org/files/publications/BoPProtocol2ndEdition2008.pdf.

Simanis, E., Hart, S., Enk, G., Duke, G., Gordon, M., & Lippert, A. (2005, February 17). *Strategic initiatives at the base of the pyramid: A protocol for mutual value creation* (Version 1.0). Retrieved June 27, 2008, from www.bop-protocol.org/docs/BoP_Protocol_1st_ed.pdf.

Siphambe, H.K. (2000). Rates of return to education in Botswana. *Economics of Education Review 19*(3), 291–300.

Sjöholm, F. (2005). Educational reforms and challenges in Southeast Asia. In F. Sjöholm & J. L. Tongzon (Eds.), *Institutional change in Southeast Asia* (pp. 28–48). London: Routledge.

Verba, S., Schlozman, K.L., & Brady, H.E. (1995). *Voice and equality: Civic voluntarism in American politics*. Cambridge, MA: Harvard University Press.

Watts, R. J., & Flanagan, C. (2007). Pushing the envelope on youth civic engagement: A developmental and liberation psychology perspective. *Journal of Community Psychology, 35*(6), 779–792.

Youniss, J. & Yates, M. (1999). Youth service and moral–civic identity: A case for everyday morality. *Educational Psychology Review, 11*(4), 361–376.

YouthBuild USA. (n.d.). *Leadership Development at a Youthbuild Program*. U.S. Department of Housing and Urban Development: Washington, D.C. Retrieved June 27, 2008, from www.youthbuild.org/atf/cf/{22B5F680-2AF9-4ED2-B948-40C4B32E6198}/LeadershipDev.pdf.

YouthBuild USA. (1996). *Youthbuild Program Manual*. U.S. Department of Housing and Urban Development: Washington, D.C. Retrieved June 26, 2008, from www.youthbuild.org/atf/cf/{22B5F680-2AF9-4ED2-B948-40C4B32E6198}/ProgramManual.pdf.

YouthBuild USA Demographics and Outcomes, 2002–2006. (n.d.). Retrieved June 26, 2008, from www.youthbuild.org/site/c.htIRI3PIKoG/b.1310741/apps/s/content.asp?ct=1716263.

Yunus, M., with Jolis, A. (1999). *Banker to the poor: Micro-lending and the battle against world poverty*. New York: PublicAffairs.

Zeldin, S., McDaniel, A. K., Topitzes, D., & Calvert, M. (2000). *Youth in decision-making: A study on the impacts of youth on adults and organizations*. Chevy Chase, MD: National 4-H Council.

CHAPTER 15

Ethnicity and Immigration

ANDREW J. FULIGNI, DIANE L. HUGHES, AND NIOBE WAY

The proportion of ethnic-minority adolescents in the general population of the United States and many other countries has continued to rise in recent years. Some estimates suggest that the number of individuals from ethnic-minority backgrounds will equal the number of individuals from European backgrounds in the United States by the year 2050 (U.S. Bureau of the Census, 2004). A key source of the growing ethnic-minority population has been immigration. Over the past 40 years, the number of immigrants entering the United States has risen dramatically such that a record of 35.7 million foreign-born individuals lived in the country in 2005 (Batalova & Terrazas, 2007). As a result, approximately one-fifth of American children are currently from an immigrant family (Hernandez, 2004). Today, the vast majority of immigrants to the United States come from nations in Asia and Latin America, with the top five countries of origin being Mexico, the Philippines, China and Hong Kong, India, and Vietnam (Batalova & Terrazas, 2007).

Researchers initially were slow to respond to the growing population of adolescents from ethnic-minority and immigrant families, but the past decade has witnessed a notable increase in such studies. The goal of this chapter is to summarize research in a select number of key domains in the lives of adolescents from ethnic-minority and immigrant families. We selected four topics based on their significance for adolescent development as well as the availability of sufficient previous work that allows for the drawing of

at least tentative conclusions: (1) family relationships and parenting, including parental control and autonomy, family obligation and assistance, and ethnic and racial socialization; (2) friendships, including their characteristics, qualities, and the contexts that influence these relationships; (3) educational achievement and attainment, including motivation, values, and actual performance and attainment; and (4) identity, focusing on the predictors and outcomes of racial-ethnic identity. Attention is paid to ethnic and racial variations and similarities as well as the role of immigrant generation in these aspects of development. Although we do not have separate sections devoted to psychological and behavioral adjustment, each section addresses the extent to which the relevant developmental factors play a role in these outcomes.

Finally, each section explores the role of two broad contexts that are known to vary across ethnic and generational lines and that often influence the specific aspects of development being addressed. Variations in cultural norms, values, and beliefs likely play a role in the motivations, behaviors, and activities of adolescents. Yet these norms, values, and beliefs do not exist in a vacuum, and any consideration of the development of ethnic-minority children and adolescents must also take into account two key contexts of their lives (García Coll, Ackerman, & Cicchetti, et al., 1996). The first of these is the collection of socioeconomic resources possessed by the family. As discussed in the following sections, ethnic and generational groups in the United States often differ in terms parental education, occupation, family income, and family wealth. These resources, in turn, may both influence values and beliefs and directly affect aspects of adolescents' development. The second context is the set of structural and social factors that can constrain the opportunities available to adolescents and their families, ranging from school and neighborhood quality to larger societal stereotypes about the ability and potential of teenagers from different ethnic and immigrant backgrounds. The amount of attention paid to these socioeconomic, structural, and social factors in each section depends on the availability of existing evidence for their influence.

FAMILY RELATIONSHIPS AND PARENTING

As perhaps the primary socializing agent of adolescents that mediates the effects of many structural and social factors in the larger society, the family is a likely source of ethnic variability in development during the teenage years. Relationships and socialization techniques within the family have been described as being highly dependent on both cultural traditions and the immediate adaptation challenges facing family members (Kagitcibasi, 1990; Levine, 1974). Interestingly, however, the few studies that have focused on dyadic relationships between individual family members (e.g., mother–adolescent, father–adolescent) have found relatively few variations across ethnic groups, either in relationship quality or in the links between variations in relationship quality and adolescent adjustment. For example, Fuligni (1998) observed similar levels and developmental patterns of parent–adolescent conflict and cohesion across families from Latin American and Asian backgrounds. Also, Smetana (2002) has noted similarity in the reasoning and justification behind parent–adolescent conflicts within African American and European American families. Some studies have suggested that ethnic variations may be evident at specific periods of adolescence

(e.g., late adolescence; Greenberger & Chen, 1996), or that there may be important differences in how conflict may be resolved (Lee, Su, & Yoshida, 2005). But these findings remain to be further studied, and they do not change the overall picture of dyadic interactions between parents and adolescence during the teenage years as being fairly similar across ethnic and immigrant generational groups.

Rather than dyadic relationships, other aspects of family relationships appear to show more significant variability according to ethnic background. Specifically, research has suggested important variability in three aspects of family relationships during adolescence: parent control and discipline, family obligation and assistance, and ethnic or racial socialization. As described below, each of these aspects of family relationships have sources in the cultural backgrounds and socioeconomic resources of families, as well as the immediate social context and structural challenges faced by the families by virtue of their ethnic-minority and immigrant status.

Parental Control and Discipline

Families from all ethnic and cultural backgrounds must deal with the fact that during the teenage years, their children become increasingly mature and capable of independent decision making and action. In addition, all families endeavor to socialize their adolescents to eventually take on adult-life roles and responsibilities and to be capable of taking care of themselves and others who depend upon them. Yet it is clear that complete independence is neither desirable nor healthy for adolescent development, so families face the challenge of striking the right balance between autonomy and relatedness during the teenage years. The ideal balance will be specific to individual adolescents' competence and maturity and to the families' cultural values and life circumstances. Numerous ethnic and immigrant generational differences have been noted in regards to the allowance of individual autonomy and the exertion of parental control.

An important aspect of adolescent autonomy is the age at which parents allow children to engage in various personal and social behaviors. A number of studies have shown that adolescents with Asian backgrounds generally expect to receive autonomy at later ages as compared to their U.S. peers from other ethnic backgrounds. For example, adolescents from Chinese backgrounds are expected to be able to do things like go on overnight trips with friends, date, go to parties, and choose to do things with friends rather than family at significantly later ages than their peers from European backgrounds (Feldman & Quatman, 1988; Fuligni, 1998). These findings are consistent with international comparisons that have shown that adolescents in Asian societies (e.g., China, Hong Kong) expect to receive autonomy in these areas at significantly later ages than adolescents in Western societies such as Australia and the United States (Feldman & Rosenthal, 1990; Zhang & Fuligni, 2006). Yet generational differences in these expectations exist such that immigrant adolescents in the United States have later expectations for autonomy as compared to U.S.-born adolescents of the same ethnic background, suggesting that at least in the area of behavioral autonomy, Asian families may acculturate to the norms of U.S. society across generations. Indeed, controlling for generational differences reduced ethnic differences to nonsignificance in the Fuligni (1998) study, suggesting that the original ethnic difference was due to the later expectations for autonomy among the immigrants.

Differences in autonomy expectations exist largely in the domain of socializing with peers, suggesting that ethnic and generational variations in autonomy and parental control may be specific to certain domains. This argument has been made by Smetana (2002), who has argued that among adolescents from all ethnic and cultural groups, there exists a "personal" domain over which they believe parents should have limited authority. Indeed, numerous studies have shown few ethnic differences in adolescents' endorsement of parental authority over issues such as control over one's body, privacy, and the choice of one's friends and activities. Smetana argues that the prevalence of the belief in personal jurisdiction over certain aspects of one's like is a critical aspect of the development of agency and personhood, which are generally agreed to be fairly widespread developmental imperatives. Fuligni and Flook (2005) suggested that this is consistent with viewing ethnic differences in family relations from a social identity perspective. That is, even within ethnic and cultural groups that emphasize interdependence and reciprocity, it is important for family members to be allowed a degree of individual agency and respect that serves to enhance their identification with and obligation to the larger family.

A great deal of research has focused on variation in parenting styles across different ethnic and generational groups within the United States. A general finding has been that adolescents from Asian, Latin American, or African American families report higher levels of authoritarian parenting, which is a global characterization of a parenting style that focuses on control, obedience, and conformity among children. Adolescents from European American families, in contrast, report a comparatively higher frequency of authoritative parenting, a style that emphasizes the development of autonomy and self-direction (e.g., Dornbusch, Ritter, Leiderman, Roberts, & Fraleigh, 1987; Steinberg, Mounts, Lamborn, & Dornbusch, 1991). Many reasons for the ethnic variation in parenting styles have been offered. Chao (1994; Chao & Tseng, 2002) suggested cultural explanations for the higher level of parental control in many Asian American families, focusing on a traditional belief that parents should engage in what is called "child training" that focuses upon inculcating hard work and discipline in children. Other sources of ethnic variations may lie in the lower socioeconomic resources of many ethnic-minority parents, and parents who have lower levels of education and lower status occupations are more likely to report authoritarian-type parenting (Dornbusch et al., 1985; Steinberg et al., 1991), a finding consistent with earlier work by Kohn and Schooler (1978) that suggested parents who work in lower status occupations are more likely to value conformity in their children. Finally, the higher level of control and emphasis upon obedience among some ethnic-minority families may be due to the fact that they are more likely to live in threatening neighborhoods. Strict parental control may be an adaptive strategy in these families in order to protect teenagers from the dangers of the neighborhoods in which they live (Furstenberg, Cook, Eccles, Elder, & Sameroff, 1999).

Despite the general agreement about ethnic differences in the distribution of different parenting styles, there has been more controversy about whether the impact of different styles of parenting on adolescent adjustment varies across ethnic and cultural background. The basic question has been whether the cultural or social context in which the parenting occurs modifies the effect of the parenting on adolescent adjustment. Two reviews (Sorkhabi, 2005; Steinberg, 2001) have suggested that the power assertion and excessive control that is typical of authoritarian parenting have generally negative implications for adolescent adjustment across a variety of domains, including psychological well being, externalizing behavior, and psychosocial maturity.

The one exception to the rule, acknowledged by Steinberg (2001) and Sorkhabi (2005), is in the area of academic achievement. A number of studies have noted that whereas authoritarian parenting is associated with lower grade point averages (GPAs) among several groups, it is unassociated with GPA among Asian Americans (Dornbusch, et al., 1985; Steinberg, 1991). Sorkhabi (2005) has argued that these findings may be an artifact of the use of adolescents' self-reported grade point average (GPA) in these studies, and that other studies using official measures of achievement in Asian societies have found that authoritarian parenting is associated with poorer achievement in these countries. Yet

another explanation is that the lack of association between authoritarian parenting and GPA may be limited to Asian families in the United States, who are largely immigrant families, in contrast to Asian adolescents in Asia and non-Asian adolescents in the United States. Indeed, Chao (2001) reported that the association between authoritarian parenting and GPA actually became stronger in later generations of Chinese families in the United States. It is possible that for immigrant Chinese families, who emphasize the importance of educational success perhaps more than any other ethnic or generational group in the United States, their focus on academic achievement outweighs any negative impact of authoritarian parenting. This focus can be seen in the high aspirations of the parents, their belief in the dire consequences of *not* doing well in school, and the high level of academic support among Asian peer groups in the United States (Fuligni, 1997; Fuligni & Yoshikawa, 2004; Kao & Tienda, 1995; Steinberg, Dornbusch, & Brown, 1992). It is also possible that the "model minority myth" of the high academic competence of Asian American students fosters high expectations among teachers and this in turn enhances academic achievement among Asian American students (Qin, Way, & Muhkerjee, 2008; Rosenbloom & Way, 2004). Together, these factors may serve to buffer the students from the negative implications of authoritarian parenting for their achievement at school.

Finally, there has been a recent surge of interest in variability in the frequency and implications of different disciplinary practices for adolescent development. In particular, studies have examined the role of physical discipline, such as spanking or hand slapping, that does not cross the line into abuse or maltreatment. Studies of earlier ages observed how although African American families, particularly low-income families, may more frequently employ such disciplinary techniques when compared to European Americans, such techniques did not seem to have the same negative implications for children's adjustment as they did in European American families (Deater-Deckard, Dodge, Bates, and Pettit, 1996; Gunnoe & Mariner,1997). Lansford, Deater-Deckard, Dodge, Bates, and Pettit (2004) extended this work to the adolescent years, observing that African American parents of early adolescents reported infrequent, but nevertheless greater use of physical discipline as compared to European American parents. Yet whereas physical discipline was associated with greater externalizing behavior among European American adolescents, it was linked to lower levels of externalizing among African American adolescents. Lansford and colleagues suggest that the social and cultural context of physical discipline is different in African American families, where it can be seen as a more legitimate expression of parental authority and is done out of concern for the behavior of the child as opposed to being done out of anger. It should also be noted that Lansford and colleagues distinguished between physical discipline such as spanking from more extreme practices that are abusive, which have negative implications for adjustment among adolescents from both African American and European American groups (Lansford, Dodge, Pettit, Bates, Crozier, & Kaplow, 2002). Additional work is needed to replicate these intriguing results, as well as explore the possible explanations for them. In addition, understanding the variation of the use of physical discipline by socioeconomic status and how the impact of physical discipline may be moderated by socioeconomic status is lacking. Research is also needed to explore the frequency of physical discipline and implications for adjustment for adolescents from immigrant families within the United States and for adolescents outside of the United States. Preliminary findings suggest that physical discipline is common among many poor Chinese American families as well Chinese families with parents who were raised in China before the economic and social transformations of the 1980s (Way & Yoshikawa, in progress). Yet little is known if

and how these parenting techniques are associated with adolescent adjustment.

Family Obligation and Assistance

Many ethnic-minority families in American society have cultural traditions that emphasize the role of children to support and assist the family. Within families with Latin American roots, there is a traditional emphasis upon family solidarity and togetherness that is sometimes referred to as "familism" (Sabogal, Marín-Otero-Sabogal, & Marín, et al., 1987). Families with Asian backgrounds, such as those from China and Korea, may have Confucian traditions of filial piety and respect that focus on the importance of children providing instrumental and financial support their parents and siblings throughout their lives (Chao & Tseng, 2002; Ho, 1996). Immigrant parents from Latin American and Asia, having been raised in their native societies, are thought to place particular emphasis upon these traditions when raising their children (Fuligni & Yoshikawa, 2004). Similar values of family togetherness and mutual support have also been cited as existing within the cultural backgrounds of African American and Native American families (Harrison, Wilson, Pine, Chan, & Buriel, 1990; Joe & Malach, 1998).

Ethnic-minority and immigrant families also face numerous social and economic challenges that may enhance and maintain the tradition of adolescents supporting and assisting the family. The challenging economic circumstances of many families with Latin American, African American, and Native American backgrounds create the very real need to help the family. Parents who work in low status jobs with irregular work hours may need their adolescents to assist with the maintenance of the household by engaging in tasks such as sibling care, cleaning, and meal preparation. The irregular income of some poorer families may mean that adolescents, once they become of employable age, may work in order to contribute financially to the family. Immigrant parents often know very little about the workings of American society, have limited English skills, and often need to rely upon their adolescents to negotiate interactions with government agencies, services, and utility companies. Finally, simply knowing that one is a member of an ethnic or racial group that is derogated and under threat by elements of the larger society leads family members to believe they must band together and support one another in order to faces the challenges of being an ethnic minority in American society.

Numerous studies have reported that indeed, adolescents from many ethnic-minority groups have a stronger sense of obligation to support, assist, and respect the authority of the family when compared to their European American peers. Ethnographies of several immigrant groups have noted the emphasis adolescents place on providing help to their parents and siblings both currently and in the future when they become adults (Caplan, Choy, & Whitmore, 1991; Suárez-Orozco & Suárez-Orozco, 1995; Zhou & Bankston, 1998). For many of these adolescents, part of their sense of obligation stems from a desire to repay their parents for the many sacrifices they made in order immigrate and provide better lives for their children. This sense of obligation is strong regardless of the adolescents' country of origin, with one study noting that those from Asian and Latin American backgrounds together reported substantially stronger values regarding family assistance and support than their peers from European American backgrounds (Fuligni, Tseng, & Lam, 1999).

Although many observers suggested that the cultural tradition of family obligation and assistance would wane across immigrant generations, there is very little evidence to suggest that this is the case. Instead, a sense of obligation to support and assist the family appears to remain strong across several generations such that even U.S.-born adolescents from U.S.-born parents with Latin American and Asian backgrounds reported a stronger value of family assistance than their peers from European backgrounds (Fuligni et al., 1999; Sabogal et al., 1987). Fuligni and Flook (2005) have

suggested that the retention of traditions of family obligation and assistance across generations may be due to the fact that family membership serves as a social identity for adolescents from ethnic-minority backgrounds. That is, even though U.S.-born parents and adolescents grow up in a more individualistically oriented American society, they are still members of ethnic and racial minority groups who face numerous challenges and experience social threat. Hundreds of studies that have focused on other social identities, whether real or experimentally manipulated, have shown that experiencing threat results in a greater identification with the group and a greater willingness to support the group (Hogg, 2003). Fuligni and Flook suggest that the same may be true for adolescents from U.S.-born families with ethnic-minority backgrounds who understand that their families still face challenges succeeding in American society simply by virtue of their ethnic group membership.

Nevertheless, there is some evidence for relatively lower sense of family obligation among some adolescents in the United States from East Asian backgrounds who are able to pursue postsecondary schooling at 4-year colleges and are able to take advantage of the social and economic opportunities this affords them. Fuligni and Pedersen (2002) observed that even though the sense of obligation of these youth increased from high school into young adulthood, as it did for all youth regardless of ethnic background, the sense of obligation of those from East Asian backgrounds did not increase the same rate as their peers from Latin American backgrounds, resulting in a value of family obligation that was quite similar to that of their peers from European backgrounds. As a college graduate from a Chinese immigrant family reported to Fuligni, Rivera, and Leininger (2007):

> You know, like a lot of Asian people start to feel torn . . . I mean I do feel compelled to help them out, but yet, I also feel compelled to do what I wanna do . . . because it's like you're supposed

to do that, you're supposed to go out and make a name for yourself and be the person you're supposed to be, but then at the same time, it's kind of like you, there's this obligation there. (p. 256)

The implication for other aspects of adolescent adjustment of an emphasis on family obligation and assistance is an important consideration. On the one hand, family obligation and assistance may be seen as inherently negative for several aspects of development during a developmental period that emphasizes the development of autonomy in an individualistically oriented American society. On the other hand, a sense of obligation may provide adolescents from immigrant and ethnic-minority backgrounds a sense of purpose and meaning that provides them with a meaningful role to fulfill in an American society that is often criticized as offering teenagers few opportunities to be productive. Numerous studies have suggested that a sense of family obligation has a number of positive correlates among adolescents from both ethnic-minority and -majority backgrounds, but high levels of actual assistance to the family may be problematic for some youth in more difficult life circumstances.

Most work has focused on adolescents' values regarding family obligation. A sense of duty to support and assist the family has consistently been related to a higher level of academic motivation in both qualitative and quantitative studies. In a study of adolescents from immigrant Vietnamese families, in which teenagers were asked to rank the relative importance they placed upon several values, the top five values were "respect for family members," "education and achievement," "freedom," "family loyalty," and "hard work" (Caplan et al., 1991). A factor analysis of these values, in turn, yielded a "family-based" achievement factor that included "education and achievement," "loyalty," and "cohesion and respect." Similar patterns of a link between obligation and educational motivation have been observed in studies of immigrants from

Latin America and South Asia (Gibson & Bhachu, 1991; Suárez-Orozco & Suárez-Orozco, 1995). Finally, Fuligni (2001) has noted a significant correlation between adolescents' sense of obligation to the family and their belief in the utility of education, such that a stronger sense of obligation significantly accounts for the higher level of academic motivation among adolescents from Asian and Latin American backgrounds as compared to their equally achieving peers from European backgrounds.

A sense of obligation to help the family also has been linked to better psychological and behavioral health. Fuligni and Pedersen (2002) noted that those with a greater sense of obligation report better positive psychological well being, and other studies have linked a sense of family duty to higher self-esteem (Bush, Supple, & Lash, 2004). Similarly, a number of studies have linked higher levels of familialism among Latino adolescents to lower levels of problem behavior and substance use. For example, Gil, Wagner, and Vega (2000) found that familism was associated with less alcohol use and a lower deviance, and Ramirez et al. (2004) reported that higher familism led to less use of marijuana and inhalants among families. Sommers, Fagan, and Baskin (1993) observed that familism was associated with less violence, theft, and drug use. More recently, Germán, Gonzales, and Dumka (in press) showed that familism mitigated the negative effects of deviant peers on adolescents' externalizing behaviors.

Much less work has been done on the actual provision of assistance to the family, but this research has suggested that, whereas modest levels of assistance may have no negative impact on youth, high levels of actual assistance in the context of difficult family circumstances may be more problematic. For example, young adults from poorer families who provided financial support to their families have a more difficult time completing their postsecondary degrees (Fuligni & Witkow, 2004). Adolescents from economically distressed families who shoulder the burden of too much household maintenance may have difficulties (Burton & Skinner, 2005). Other research has suggested negative outcomes when family assistance is provided because of parental mental or physical distress (Jurkovic, 1997). Therefore, it appears that the implications of assistance behaviors should depend upon the family context. The implications may be negative when assistance takes place in families characterized by severe economic strain, parental distress, and problematic family relationships. Future research should concentrate more closely on the implications of actual family assistance for adjustment, and how it may depend on the family context in which that assistance occurs.

Ethnic and Racial Socialization

Ethnic-minority and immigrant families face unique challenges in the socialization of their adolescents that are not shared by European American families. As members of racial and ethnic groups that often experience derogation and discrimination, parents must prepare their adolescents for the kind of negative treatment that the adolescents may receive from peers, adults, and societal institutions. In addition, some of the values and traditions of ethnic-minority and immigrant families differ from the norms of the larger society. Therefore, rather than being able to rely on larger institutions such as schools and the media to teach their adolescents about their cultural background, parents in ethnic-minority families need to make special efforts to teach their adolescents about their ethnic heritage.

These particular socialization challenges of ethnic-minority parents were largely ignored until only recently, and there has been a rise in research into what has been called racial or ethnic socialization. Several theories and models of racial/ethnic socialization have been offered, but they all share an emphasis on the key dimensions of preparation for discrimination and teaching about one's ethnic and cultural background. One popular conceptualization has been offered by Hughes and Chen (1997), who outlined three dimensions of racial and ethnic socialization. The first dimension, called *cultural socialization*, includes teaching that focuses on the cultural traditions of the group to instill feelings of ethnic and racial pride. The second dimension, *preparation for bias*, includes efforts to teach children about ethnic and racial stratification in the larger society, and how to deal with negative treatment. Finally, *promotion of mistrust* messages are more negative in tone and teach children to be suspicious of other groups. Other models have included additional dimensions such as egalitarianism, religiosity, caring for extended family, and achievement (for a review, see Hughes et al., 2006).

Ethnic and racial socialization should be particularly relevant during the teenage years. Teaching about discrimination and the fact that one's child may be a target of negative treatment simply because of his or her ethnic background is a difficult and sensitive topic for parents to broach. Many ethnic-minority parents are reluctant to discuss such topics until their children are cognitively and socially mature enough to understand their complexity. Even though children can understand discrimination during elementary school (Brown & Bigler, 2005), parents understandably want their children to maintain a positive and optimistic view of their place in the world. But experiences with actual mistreatment and discrimination increase during the teenage years as adolescents increasingly interact with the larger society outside of the protection and purview of their parents (Greene, Way, & Pahl, 2006; Way, Santos, Niwa, & Kim-Gervey, in press). In addition, adolescents become aware of the disparities and stereotypes that are attached to ethnic and racial background as they witness the unequal distribution of students across achievement levels and academic tracks (Rosenbloom & Way, 2004). Finally, the unequal response to adolescents' risky behavior by the criminal justice system makes some adolescents (e.g., African American males) aware that society expects them to get in trouble by virtue of their race or ethnicity.

As noted by Hughes et al. (2006) in their comprehensive review, research on ethnic and racial socialization has been conducted primarily with African American families. In addition, studies have rarely included multiple groups to allow for the comparison of rates of ethnic and socialization across different ethnic groups. Nevertheless, two studies have suggested that ethnic and racial socialization is more common in African American families than families with Latin American backgrounds (Hughes, 2003; Phinney & Chavira, 1995). In particular, messages about preparation for bias appear to be more common in African American families than other ethnic-minority families (Hughes et al., 2006).

It is assumed that ethnic and racial socialization is more common among ethnic-minority families than European American families. That assumption has rarely been tested, but Huynh and Fuligni (in press) found that U.S. adolescents with Chinese and Mexican backgrounds reported more frequent cultural socialization and preparation for bias messages from their parents than did their U.S. peers from European backgrounds. Among the different types of ethnic and racial socialization, cultural socialization appears to be the most common, being reported by the majority of families in many different studies (Hughes et al., 2006). Preparation for bias occurs somewhat less frequently, and promotion of mistrust tends to be reported by only a small percentage of ethnic-minority parents and adolescents.

Because of the predominant emphasis upon African American families, there has been little work on the nature of ethnic or racial socialization among immigrant families living in the United States. It is reasonable to expect that the dimension of cultural socialization may be higher among immigrant families, given that the parents were raised in the native society and often maintain ties to their countries of origin. Indeed, several studies have suggested that immigrant parents are more likely to try to teach their adolescents about their families' cultural norms, values, and traditions (Knight, Bernal, Garza, Cota, & Ocampo, 1993; Umaña-Taylor & Fine, 2004). It is unclear, however, how immigration might influence other dimensions of ethnic and racial socialization. On the one hand, given the status as both newcomers and ethnic minorities in American society, immigrant parents may be expected to engage in relatively higher levels of preparation for bias as compared to their counterparts born in the United States. On the other hand, some studies have suggested that immigrant parents' relative lack of historical experience with American discrimination and their optimism about succeeding in their new countries may lead them to deemphasize discrimination against their racial or ethnic group. Along these lines, Hughes (2003) found that immigrant Latin American parents were less likely to deliver preparation for bias messages than African American parents. Future work that compares adolescents and families from different generations with the same ethnic background should be done in order to examine the impact of immigration more closely.

The implications of ethnic and racial socialization for other aspects of adolescent development are not well understood. Studies have often obtained mixed results because of inconsistency in the operationalization of ethnic and cultural socialization, and because researchers have not clearly distinguished between specific dimensions of socialization that may have different outcomes (Hughes et al., 2006). Yet when studies have clearly measured cultural socialization, this dimension has been fairly consistently related to positive developmental outcomes such as higher ethnic identity, self-esteem, and lower rates of externalizing behavior. The links between cultural socialization and academic outcomes are inconsistent, as are the associations between preparation for bias and a host of developmental outcomes, largely because of the difficulty of distinguishing between a proactive, positive preparation for bias and a more negative promotion of mistrust. This would seem to be a key direction for future research, in that preparation for bias theoretically should enable adolescents from ethnic-minority and immigrant backgrounds to more effectively deal with episodes of discrimination.

FRIENDSHIPS

Theory and research have repeatedly under-scored the importance of friendships in satisfying adolescents' desire for intimacy; enhancing their interpersonal skills, sensitiv-ity, and understanding; and contributing to their cognitive and social development and psychological adjustment (Crockett, Losoff, & Petersen, 1984; Csikszentmihalyi & Larson, 1984; Hartup, 1996; Savin-Williams & Berndt, 1990). During adolescence, the significance of friendships becomes even more paramount as adolescents begin to spend increased time with their friends (Crockett et al., 1984). However, despite the fact that friendships are critical for adolescents across multiple cultures (Hinde, 1987; Patterson, Dishion, & Yoerger, 2000; Sherer, 1991), researchers rarely focus on friendship processes among ethnic-minority adolescents. Although there has been some research on peer group processes, such as peer victimization, among ethnic-minority adoles-cents (Graham, Bellmore, & Juvonen, 2007; Graham, Bellmore, & Mize, 2006), there exists only a handful of research on the friendships, in particular, of ethnic-minority adolescents.

The research that does exist on the friend-ships of ethnic-minority youth (Cauce, 1986; Cote, 1996; DuBois & Hirsch, 1990; Hamm, 2000; Mounts, 2004; Way & Chen, 2000; Way & Greene, 2006; Way & Pahl, 2001) tends to be comparative in nature, aiming to detect ethnic/racial differences in *the charac-teristics* (e.g., number of cross-ethnic/racial friendships) and *quality* (e.g., level of support or intimacy) of friendships among ethnically diverse youth. In addition, a small but grow-ing body of research draws from ecological theories of human development to explore the ways in which families and school shape the friendships of adolescents, including those of ethnic-minority adolescents (Mounts, 2004; Updegraff, Madden-Derdich, Estrada, Sales, & Leonard 2002; Way & Greene, 2006).

The Characteristics of Friendships

Research on the characteristics of friend-ships among ethnic-minority adolescents has typically focused on the extent to which eth-nic-minority and -majority youth have cross-ethnic/racial friendships. These studies suggest that, for the most part, adolescents, including those who attend ethnically diverse schools, are less accepting of peers from other ethnic/racial groups than they are of peers from their own ethnic/racial group (Bellmore, Nishina, Witkow, Graham, & Juvonen, 2007; Brown, 1990; Hamm, 1998; Tatum, 1997). Inconsistency, however, is evident regarding the prevalence of cross-ethnic/racial friendships. Some stud-ies show African American and/or European American youth as unlikely to have any cross-ethnic friendships (Bellmore et al., 2007; Shrum, Cheek, & Hanter, 1987; Way & Chen, 2000), whereas others depict adolescents who attend ethnically diverse schools as commonly experiencing ethnically diverse friendship net-works (Hamm, 1998).

In addition, the likelihood of cross-ethnic/racial friendships appears to differ depending on the race/ethnicity of the adolescent (Clark & Ayers, 1991; DuBois & Hirsch, 1990; Hamm, 1998). Hamm (1998) showed, for example, that 75% of the Asian American and Latino adolescents in her study reported having at least one cross-ethnic friend, whereas only 50% of the African American and European American adolescents did so. Other schol-ars, however, have shown African American adolescents to be almost twice as likely to report having other-race friends than White adolescents (Clark & Ayers, 1991; DuBois & Hirsch, 1990). Way and colleagues found that the vast majority (73%) of Black, Latino, and Asian American students report having same-race/ethnic friendship networks (Way & Chen, 2000). However, in contrast to Hamm's (1998) findings, in Way's study Asian American students were most likely *not* to have cross racial/ethnic friendships (85% of Asian American students in comparison to 73% and 64% of Latino and African American students, respectively).

The discrepancy in findings regarding prevalence of cross-ethnic friendships as well as the ethnic/racial group least or most likely to report having such friendships draws attention to the importance of examining the context in which these friendships are embedded. Cross-ethnic friendships may be more likely in school contexts in which there are academic and extracurricular activities that implicitly or explicitly encourage such relationships. Furthermore, the ethnic/racial diversity of the school, as well as the dominance of particular ethnic/racial groups within the school, is likely to influence the prevalence of cross-ethnic/racial friendships. The discrepancy in findings may also be due to the type of friendship being examined. Closest friendships may be less likely to cross the racial/ethnic divide than less intimate ones (Way & Chen, 2000).

The prevalence of cross-ethnic/racial friendships within particular ethnic/racial groups is also likely influenced by social status, language preference, and gender. Research finds that Asian American students who may be a numerical majority in the school but have very low social status often report high levels of peer discrimination by their non-Asian peers and thus few cross-ethnic friendships (Rosenbloom & Way, 2004). Furthermore, language barriers are likely to further enhance ethnic segregation, with Asian American immigrant students often reporting that they prefer to speak Chinese with their peers (Rosenbloom & Way, 2004; Qin & Way, in press). Although most studies have not explored gender differences, Way and colleagues find that girls are slightly more likely to report having same-race/ethnicity friendships than boys, with approximately 78% of the girls and 67% of the boys reporting same-race/ethnic friendship networks (Way & Chen, 2000). Qualitative interview data reveal boys as being

more flexible or open regarding friendship selection than girls, which may be the product of boys being more likely than girls to be involved in informal or formal sporting activities that forced them to have more contact with adolescents from different ethnic/racial groups (Way, 2004).

Research on the characteristics of ethnic-minority adolescent friendships has also shown context-specific differences in the source of friendships. DuBois and Hirsch (1990), for example, found Black adolescents to be more likely than their White peers to report having a large network of neighborhood friends, whereas White adolescents reported having more school-based friendships. Supporting this finding, Clark and Ayers (1991) showed that African American adolescents had more contact with their best friends outside of school, whereas European American adolescents' best friendships were more likely to take place within the school context. Way and colleagues find that while most of the ethnic-minority adolescents in their studies report having school-based friendships, less than half, particularly in the first 2 years of high school, indicate having *best* friends who attend the same school (Way & Greene, 2006; Way & Pahl, 2001). In the 9th grade, only 25% of the Black students, 40% of the Latino students, and 38% of the Asian American students reported having best friends who attended the same school (Way & Chen, 2000). These findings are consistent with previous research showing ethnic-minority adolescents as less likely than European American adolescents to have school-based close friendships (particularly in the early years of high school) and underscore not only the importance of examining the diversity of characteristics of friendships among youth, but also of distinguishing between types of friendships (e.g., school vs. neighborhood, closest vs. general friendships).

The Quality of Friendships—Quantitative Research

Research on the quality of adolescent friendships has typically been grounded in Weiss's

(1974) contention that children and adolescent seek social provisions in their close friendships (Furman, 1996). Such provisions include intimacy (e.g., sharing secrets together), affection (e.g., showing warmth toward one another), companionship (e.g., having fun together), and satisfaction (e.g., deriving pleasure from the relationship) (Shulman, 1993). A large body of research over the past decade has focused on understanding the prevalence and correlates of these dimensions of friendship quality (see Buhrmester, 1990; Bukowski, Newcomb, & Hartup, 1996; Collins & Laursen, 1992; Furman & Buhrmester, 1985), and the extent to which they vary by gender and, more recently, by ethnicity.

Studies have found that the quality of friendships do vary by gender and ethnicity. Jones & Costin, (1994), for example, explored friendship quality among Mexican American, African American, and European American sixth and ninth graders and found that African American males were more likely to reveal their personal thoughts and feelings with their male friends than were Mexican American or European American boys. Furthermore, significant gender differences in levels of self disclosure in their same-sex friendships were apparent only among European American adolescents; European American girls were more likely to reveal their personal thoughts and feelings to their friends than European American boys. Similarly, in their study of Black and White, socioeconomically diverse, middle school children, DuBois and Hirsch (1990) showed White girls as having significantly more supportive friendships than White boys. No gender differences were detected among Black youth. Black boys were also shown to be more likely to have intimate conversations with their best friends than were White boys; no differences were found between Black and White girls.

Way and colleagues find ethnic differences in perceptions of friendship support with Black and Latino adolescents reporting higher levels of friendship support than their Asian American peers (Way & Chen, 2000;

Way & Greene, 2006; Way & Pahl, 2001). Their qualitative research also suggests that Asian American immigrant adolescents often report being unhappy with their friendships and yearning for friendships that are more supportive (Qin et al., 2008; Qin & Way, in press; Way & Pahl, 1999). They find, however, few gender differences in friendship support, with only the Latino youth in the first years of high school indicating such differences (Way & Chen, 2000). Research is needed to explore why gender differences in friendship support are consistently found among White youth but not among among ethnic-minority or immigrant youth.

Longitudinal research on friendship quality across adolescents from different ethnic groups is extremely limited, with most longitudinal studies conducted with young children (e.g., Ladd, 1990), over brief periods of time, or with middle class, European American adolescents (e.g., Buhrmester & Furman, 1987; Rice & Mulkeen, 1995). Research conducted primarily with European American, middle-class adolescents has shown that from early to late adolescence, (1) friendships are perceived as increasingly more intimate and/or supportive and (2) gender differences in friendship quality become less apparent as boys and girls begin to rely more on friends to help solve their problems (Azmitia, Kamprath, & Linnet, 1998; Berndt, 1989; Furman & Burhmester, 1992; Rice & Mulkeen, 1995; Sharabany, Gershoni, & Hofman, 1981; Youniss & Smollar, 1985). Longitudinal studies of friendships among ethnic-minority adolescents have also indicated that the perceived level of support in both close friendships and friendships in general increases over time from age 13 to age 18 (Way & Greene, 2006). These findings support theory and research indicating that as young people become increasingly self-aware, cognitively skilled, and confident in their identities (McCarthy & Hoge, 1982), they become better able to have mutually supportive and satisfying friendships. In Way's studies of the development of friendships of ethnic-minority adolescents, the rate of improvements over time in friendship quality was similar across African American, Latino, and Asian American adolescents. Boys, however, showed steeper improvements over time than girls in the quality of closest same-sex friendships even though the mean level of friendship quality at age 16 did not differ by gender (Way & Greene, 2006). This latter finding is consistent with previous longitudinal research with European American adolescents that suggests that intimacy in best friendship increases at a sharper rate for boys than for girls from 8th grade to 12th grade (Rice & Mulkeen, 1995).

The Experience of Friendships— Qualitative Research

Although research has examined the extent to which adolescents feel supported in their friendships, very little research has focused on how adolescents make meaning of or experience their friendships. In-depth interviews over 4–5 years with over 200 ethnic-minority youth living in an urban context revealed themes of *closeness, desire,* and *distrust* in their friendships (Way, 2006; Way, in progress; Way, Greene, & Pahl, 2004; Way & Pahl, 2001). Each of these themes suggested subthemes that underscored the complexity of each theme. For example, closeness was experienced in friendships not only as a result of intimate disclosures within the friendship but also as a result of borrowing and loaning money. Furthermore, the three themes were interwoven such that, for example, the theme of distrust formed a type of "context" for the experience of closeness for adolescents.

Closeness

Closeness was defined by the youth in Way's studies as believing that one could trust his or her best friends with secrets and money (Way, 2004; Way, Becker, & Greene, 2004; Way et al., 2005; Way & Pahl, 1999). For example, when Amanda, a Puerto Rican young woman, was asked what she liked about her best friend,

she replied, "she keeps everything a secret, whatever I tell her." Maria, a Puerto Rican young woman, responded similarly saying that: "I can talk to her about anything, like if I call her, I'm hysterically crying or something just happened or whatever, . . . and maybe she'll be doing something, she'll stop doing that to come and talk to me and to help me." Brian, an African American male, stated about his best friends: "I tell them anything about me and I know they won't tell anybody else unless I tell them to." (Way et al., 2004). Similarly, adolescents, particularly the boys, consistently indicated that borrowing and loaning money was a key component of closeness between themselves and their peers.

In addition, adolescents, particularly the boys, voiced feelings that they could trust that closest friends to protect them from harm and that they would "be there" when needed. When Raphael, a Puerto Rican young man, was asked by an interviewer, "What kinds of things could you trust with your [closest] friends?" he replied: "Let's just say I had a big fight, I got beat up, I had like five guys against me, they'll come and they'll help me out." Similarly, Akil, an African American male, responded to the same question: "You get into a fight with somebody else; [my best friend] will tell me to calm down, chill . . . like when someone jumps me, he will help me." Although trust was consistently the foundation of closeness in friendships, the ways in which the adolescents trusted their friends, or *how they felt close to them*, varied across gender (Way et al., 2004).

Finally, adolescents conveyed feelings of closeness to their best friends due to the fact that their family knew their friends and their friends' families (and vice versa) (Way et al., 2004). Michael, an African American young man, said about his best friend: "Since we were real small I have known his whole family, he knows everybody in my house, we just walk over to his crib, open his fridge without asking or something, that's how long we've know each other." Similarly, Armando, a Dominican young man, responded when asked what makes him close to his best friend: "Um, basically 'cause he knows my family. If you know somebody's parents, then you know how far the trust can be stretched." Bringing their friends into the fold of their families and becoming part of their friends' family allowed the adolescents to trust and feel close to their friends.

Desire

Way and her colleagues also find that the boys in their qualitative studies consistently expressed a strong yearning for intimate, same-sex friendships. For example, Albert, a Puerto Rican young man, told the interviewer: "I would like a friend that if I got anything to say to him or like any problems or anything I'll tell him and he'll tell me his problems." (Way et al., 2004). In contrast to what the research literature suggests about boys' friendships (Belle, 1989; Buhrmester & Furman, 1987), Albert's wish for a close friend was not based on a desire for friends with whom to "do things," but instead, to discuss personal problems. After describing the betrayals of friends who will "talk behind your back," Victor, a Puerto Rican male, similarly stated: "Basically I hate it, I hate it, cause you know I wouldn't mind talking to somebody my age that I can relate to 'em on a different basis." Boys, like Albert and Victor, expressed yearning for friends who "would really be there" and with whom they could share their "true feelings."

Significantly, these stories of desire for friendships that involve high levels of self-disclosure were not stories revealed exclusively by acutely sensitive boys who were socially isolated in the school context. They were stories heard from popular boys who were members of athletic teams as well as those involved in theater arts. These stories were heard from straight "A" students and students who were struggling academically. The language of yearning for intimacy with other males was used by laid back, macho, "hip hop" boys wearing low-riding pants, baseball caps drawn low over their brows, and sneakers untied. Boys,

who have been portrayed in popular culture as more interested in shooting each other than in sharing their thoughts and feelings spoke to us about wanting male friendships with whom they could "share their secrets," "tell everything," and "get inside" (Way et al., 2004).

Distrust

Finally, a key theme in the teens' discussions of friendships was distrust (Way et al., 2004). For example, adolescents spoke of a world in which peers will "try to take over you and take you for everything you've got and step on you." For example, in response to a question about his male peers in general, Anthony responded: "I don't trust [them], I trust me, myself, and I. That's the way I am. I trust nobody." Although he reported having a best friend during all four years of the study, a friend in whom he voiced being able to confide and to whom he felt close to, his overall perception of his peers in general involved much mistrust. Richard, too, spoke about distrusting his male peers, saying: "Can't trust anybody nowadays. They are trying to scam you, or scheme, or talk about you." Richard admitted that although he had never directly experienced these types of betrayals from his male peers, he "know[s] what most of [them] are like." These youth, however, often also spoke of having close friendships despite their perceptions of distrust. Thus, distrust of peers appeared to be a type of context in which close friendships develop (Way, 2004; Way et al., 2004). In other words, the distrust of their peers in general is the larger context in which they develop close and trusting same-sex friendships.

The Context of Friendships

Drawing from ecological theories of human development, a small but growing body of research examines the links among family, school, and neighborhood contexts and the development of friendship among ethnic-minority youth. Findings suggest that many of the associations between contextual factors and variations in friendships are similar across ethnic groups. However, studies with ethnic-minority youth, particularly those from urban contexts, shed light on the ways in which families, schools, and neighborhoods shape the development of friendships.

The Family Context

Research on the links between the quality of relationships with family members and with peers has been based primarily on attachment and/or social support theories (Updegraff: McHale, Crouter, & Kupanoff, 2001) and has typically found the quality of family relationships to be positively associated with the quality of friendships (Greenberg, Siegel, & Leitch, 1983; Kerns, 1994; Kerns & Stevens, 1996; Procidano & Smith, 1997; Youngblade, Park, & Belsky, 1993). According to attachment theorists, children internalize their parents' responsiveness toward them in the form of internal working models of the self (Ainsworth & Bowlby, 1991). These internal working models, in turn, influence non-familial relationships, as children provided with security, warmth, and trust are more likely than others to experience similar qualities in their relationships with their peers (Armsden & Greenberg, 1987; Greenberg et al., 1983; Kerns & Stevens, 1996; Sroufe & Waters, 1977). Moreover, attachment theorists also emphasize the enduring and stable nature of attachment styles, showing significant associations between current parent attachment and peer relationships (Armsden & Greenberg, 1987; Cauce, Mason, Gonzales, Hiraga, & Liu, 1996). In a similar vein, social support theorists also maintain that a positive association exists between adolescents' perceived support from families and the extent to which they feel supported by friends (Procidano, 1992; Procidano & Smith, 1997). In the social support literature, perceived family support is generally understood as the extent to which adolescents feel they can depend on family members for advice, guidance, and emotional support. When a child's need for support is met at home, that child will likely experience others outside of the home as supportive as well (Bartholomew, Cobb, & Poole, 1997; Sarason, Pierce, & Sarason, 1990).

The few studies of ethnic-minority friendships have found significant links between parent–child closeness and adolescent friendships among ethnic-minority youth (see Cote, 1996; Updegraff et al., 2001). This research has suggested that the association between parent and peer relationships varies as a function of race/ethnicity, and gender. For example, using a sample of early adolescents from Latino and European American families, Updegraff and her colleagues (2002), examined adolescents' experiences with their mothers, fathers, and best friends and found both mother and father acceptance to be significantly linked to friendship intimacy among European American adolescents. For the Latino adolescents, however, only mother acceptance was related to friendship intimacy.

Similar to Updegraff and colleagues (2002), Way and colleagues find that father support is unrelated to friendship support among Latino, Black, and Asian American adolescents. However, support from mothers is significantly associated with change over time in adolescent reports of friendship support (Way & Pahl, 2001). These findings extend the relevance of mother support for friendships to other ethnic-minority groups (e.g., African American and Asian American). Strikingly, however, adolescents who reported the least amount of support from their mothers in 9th grade (at time 1) show the sharpest increases over time in reported levels of support from friends, suggesting a compensatory pattern of relationship (Way & Greene 2006; Way & Pahl, 2001). However, increases in perceived family support are associated with improvements in friendship quality over time (Way & Greene, 2006). Although these findings seem contradictory, they are consistent with much of what we know about the development of relationships. Improvements in one type of relationship (i.e., family members) may be associated with improvements in another type of relationship (i.e., friends). However, the sharpest improvements may be seen in those relationships (i.e., friends) that are compensating for the lack of support in other relationships (see also Cicchetti, Lynch, Shonk, & Manly, 1992).

In addition to studies examining the association between the quality of family support and peer relationships, a growing body of research based on social learning theory has examined the links between parental attitudes about peers and friendships and adolescent friendships. According to social learning theorists, children acquire the requisite skills for friendships through modeling and observational learning (Mischel, 1966). Such research has primarily focused on issues of parental monitoring, examining how parental monitoring at home influence the quality and characteristics of peer relationships (Brown, Mounts, Lamborn, & Steinberg, 1993; Fuligni & Eccles, 1993; Snyder & Hoffman, 1990). Findings from these studies have suggested that there is a clear association between the extent of parental monitoring and a range of adolescent outcomes, including involvement with deviant peers (Ary, Duncan, Duncan, & Hops, 1999; Snyder, Dishion, & Patterson, 1986) and positive peer contact (Brown et al., 1993; Mounts, 2001). The degree of parental monitoring has also been related to friendship development, with the two extremes of monitoring—excessively high and excessively low—interfering with children's abilities to establish friendships (Patterson & Stouthamer-Loeber, 1984). Research with ethnic-minority youth has also found parental monitoring to be significantly related to the perceived quality of closest and general friendships (Rosenbaum, 2000). Adolescents who reported that their parents knew their whereabouts, what they are doing after school, how they spend their money, and where they are during the day and evening hours reported having more supportive closest and general friendships (Rosenbaum, 2000).

Parental guidance, or the degree to which parents directly assist adolescents with friendships, has also been linked with the quality

of adolescents' friendships. Vernberg, Beery, Ewell, and Absender (1993), for example, documented various strategies used by parents to help their seventh and eighth grade children develop friendships after moving to a new school district, such as meeting with other parents, facilitating proximity to peers, talking with their adolescent children about peer relationships, and encouraging their children to participate in activities with other adolescents. More recently, in a study of Latino and European American adolescents and their parents, Updegraff and colleagues (2001) reported that parents— mothers in particular—often got to know and spent time with their children's friends as a way to influence these friendships. Mounts (2001, 2002, 2004) has also described various strategies parents use to influence their adolescents' friendships, such as guiding (i.e., talking about the consequence of being friends with particular people), neutrality (i.e., not interfering with their children's peer relationships), prohibiting (i.e., forbidding adolescents' associations with particular peers), and supporting (i.e., providing an environment at home where adolescents can have their friends over).

Studies have also indicated that parental rules and attitudes regarding their adolescents' friends are critical correlates of the quality of adolescent friendships for both ethnic-minority and -majority adolescents (Mounts, 2004; Way et al., 2007). In one study of ethnic-minority adolescents, adolescents' perceptions of parental rules and attitudes predicted the quality of closest friendships over and above the effect of mother and family support (Way, Greene, & Muhkerjee, 2007). Those adolescents who perceived themselves as having parents with a more encouraging attitudes (e.g., "my parents think it is important to have friends") and rules (e.g., "my parents allow me to spend time with my friends during the weekends or after school") regarding friendships reported having more supportive close friendships. Furthermore, research with both ethnic-minority and -majority middle school students indicates that parents' practices related to their children's friendships (e.g., being involved in their children's friendships), as reported by the parents, was significantly associated with change over time in adolescent perceptions of the quality of their friendships (Muhkerjee, Way, & Hughes, under review). No ethnic differences were found in this analysis. Parents' perceptions of their practices related to friendships had, in fact, a stronger association with the adolescents' perceptions of the quality of their friendships than did the adolescents' perceptions of their parents' practices. Thus, in addition to adolescent perceptions of family support, parental monitoring, and guidance, parents' attitudes, rules, and practices related to their children's friendships shape ethnic-minority and -majority adolescents' perceptions of the quality of their friendships.

Qualitative data also underscores the significance of parental rules and attitudes about friendships for ethnic-minority adolescents. In Way and colleagues' research, Black, Latino, and Asian American adolescents reported their parents as wanting them to have friendships. However, they also perceived their parents as being extremely wary of nonfamilial friendships (Gingold, 2003; Way, 1998; Way & Pahl, 1999) and of the tendency for nonfamilial friends to be deceptive and to pressure them to engage in deviant behaviors. Previous research has suggested that many families from low-income and/or ethnic-minority backgrounds maintain the belief—due to a history of discrimination and oppression—that those who are not part of one's immediate or extended family should not be trusted (Salguero & McCusker, 1996; Stack, 1974; Way, 1998). Thus, the particular parental messages and attitudes regarding friendships may be unique to a low-income, urban sample.

The School Context

It is typically assumed that family relationships—both the quality of these relationships and the level of parental guidance and monitoring—are the most important factors shaping adolescents' experiences of friendships.

However, such beliefs ignore the significant role of the school context (Rosenbloom & Way, 2004; Way et al., 2004; Way & Pahl, 2001). Perceptions of the school climate, or the quality of interactions and feelings of trust, respect, and support that exist within the school community, have been found to influence (both concurrently and prospectively) students' self-esteem, psychological adjustment, level of anxiety, problem behavior, academic self-concept (Grobel & Scharzer, 1982; Kuperminc, Leadbeater, Emmons, & Blatt, 1997; Roeser & Eccles, 1998), and school behavior (Hoge, Smit, & Hanson, 1990; Sommer, 1985). Theorists also argue that students who perceive the school environment as respectful, supportive, equitable, safe, and dependable find it easier and are more willing to make and maintain supportive friendships with their peers than those who perceive the school as hostile (Epstein & Karweit, 1983; Minuchin & Shapiro, 1983; Hamm, 2000). Indeed, Epstein and Karweit (1983) note: "Negative features in a school environment—ridicule, discrimination, low expectations, stereotypes, repressions, punishment, isolation—may increase the disassociative quality of the setting and affect the thought processes and social behavior of the students" (p. 60). Although the objective reality of the school (e.g., number of students in school, ethnic diversity) is likely related to the characteristics and quality of friendships, adolescents' perceptions of the relational (e.g., teacher/student and student/student relationships) and the organizational (e.g., sense of safety in the school) climate may also have a powerful influence (Andersen, 1982; Roeser & Eccles, 1998).

Whereas much research has investigated the ways in which perceptions of school climate influence adolescents' psychological adjustment and academic development (Hoge et al., 1990; Kuperminc et al., 1997; Roeser, Eccles, & Strobel, 1998; Way & Robinson, 2003), substantially less attention has been directed at exploring the ways in which adolescents' perceptions of school climate shape their social development (Crosnoe et al., 2003; Eccles & Roeser, 2003). The existing research with ethnic-minority and -majority adolescents indicates that the effects of adolescents' perceptions of school climate on friendship quality is significant over and above the influence of family relationships and psychological adjustment (Way & Pahl, 2001). Moreover, changes in teacher/student relations and student/ student relations in particular is significantly associated with changes over time in adolescent perceptions of friendship quality for African American, Latino, and Asian American adolescents (Way & Greene, 2006). Strikingly, when examined together with perceptions of family relationships, only teacher/student relationships remained a significant predictor of the quality of friendships for adolescents across ethnic groups. When students perceived their teachers as supportive, they also perceived their friendships as being supportive as well, even after controlling for the effects of family relationships (Way & Greene, 2006).

Ethnographic work also has revealed that the racial/ethnic dynamics of the school are strongly associated with the quality and characteristics of ethnic-minority adolescent friendships (Rosenbloom & Way, 2004). In the urban, low-income, exclusively ethnic-minority high school studied by Way and colleagues, Black and Latino students are typically in either mainstream or special education classes while Asian American students are generally over-represented in honors classrooms. According to teachers, these divisions are often made irrespective of the actual abilities of students, with Asian American students with very low literacy skills being placed in honors classes so that they can "be with their peers" (Way et al., 2004). Such actions openly and actively reinforce the model minority myth of Asian American students and the idea that Black and Latino students were not in honors classes because they lacked motivation (Tatum, 1998). As a consequence, Black and Latino students have often been found to harass Asian American students due, at least in part, to their frustration

and anger regarding the obvious preference for the Asian American students by the teachers (Rosenbloom & Way, 2004).

Such a negative and hostile relational climate in the school even makes it difficult for students to form friendships *within* their own ethnic/racial group (Way et al., 2004). Research finds that those students who report school as being a particularly hostile (usually based on incidents of racism and discrimination) place often indicate having contentious friendships—irrespective of whether they are same-ethnicity/race friendships (Rosenbloom, 2004). However, students who recount more positive school experiences tend to describe more stable and secure friendships (Rosenbloom, 2004).

The Neighborhood Context

Studies have also indicated that friendship experiences vary depending on the quality and characteristics of the neighborhood (Berg & Medrich, 1980; DuBois & Hirsch, 1990; Epstein, 1989; Homel & Burns, 1989). For example, children living in neighborhoods with easily accessible "play spaces" have more contact with friends outside of school and more friends in general than those who live in neighborhoods without such places (Berg & Medrich, 1980; Homel & Burns, 1989). Similarly, youth residing in dangerous neighborhoods with a high prevalence of violence tend to have fewer neighborhood friends and less contact with their friends outside of school than their peers who live in less violent neighborhoods (Rosenbaum, 2000; Way, 1998).

Neighborhood climate has also been found to influence friendship satisfaction. In their study of urban low-income early adolescents, Homel and Burns (1989) found neighborhood social problems (e.g., crime, delinquency) to predict lower levels of perceived satisfaction with friends and a lower probability of liking one's classmates. Other studies have found family's residence to be strongly linked to the quality of social opportunities (Berg & Medrich, 1980; DuBois & Hirsch, 1990; Hirsch & DuBois, 1990).

Ethnographic work indicates that urban Black and Latino boys often choose not to spend time with their neighborhood friends because doing so often means being stopped and harassed by policemen or by groups of boys "looking for trouble" (Way, 1998). As a consequence, some of these boys choose instead to spend time alone or with family members. For example, one male Puerto Rican sophomore stated in his interview in Way's studies that he did not have friends from the neighborhood because he did not like "hangin' with people getting killed" (Way, 1998, p. 119) and thus he often stayed home during nonschool hours. Similarly, when a Black 11th-grade male was asked why he thought he had not found a close friend he could trust, he replied that the betrayal or "backstabbing" that was typical in his neighborhood led people to further "diss" one another in order to "feel important" (Way, 1998, p. 118). After learning that his closest friend was talking about him "all throughout my neighborhood," this young man decided not to "really bother with it, you know, trying to make best friends" (Way, 1998, p. 116). Survey research has also found that Black, Latino, and Asian American youth's perceptions of neighborhood cohesion, defined as levels of trust, familiarity, and reliability among neighbors and level of safety in the neighborhood, were significantly associated with reported levels of friendship support (Rosenbaum, 2000).

In summary, research with ethnic-minority and -majority adolescents has found that the context of families, schools, and neighborhoods play a significant role in predicting the quality and characteristics of adolescent friendships. Strikingly, few ethnic differences have been found in this body of research suggesting that the impact of the context on friendships is similar across adolescents. However, the ways in which these contexts shape adolescent friendships may not be similar. Whereas families, schools, and neighborhoods may influence the friendships of adolescents regardless of the cultural context, the ways in which these contexts influence friendships may look dramatically different across contexts. The role of teachers, for example, in the social wellbeing of adolescents may be more important for those being raised in cultures in which teachers are highly valued (e.g., China) than for those being raised in cultures that place less value on the role of teachers. Future research should explore the processes by which the contexts of development shape adolescent friendships.

EDUCATIONAL ACHIEVEMENT AND ATTAINMENT

Because it is predictive of numerous indicators of a successful transition to adulthood, academic achievement is one of the most significant developmental tasks facing adolescents in contemporary American society. Individuals who receive high school and college degrees are more likely as adults to be employed, work in higher status occupations, have higher incomes, and even to be married and have better physical health (Halperin, 1998). Unfortunately, substantial differences in academic achievement exist according to adolescents' ethnic background, with the members of some ethnic groups facing particularly acute educational challenges. Variations in different aspects of academic achievement are described below, followed by a discussion of the potential role of motivation and values, the socioeconomic resources of adolescents' families, and social and institutional barriers in creating these often substantial differences according to ethnic and generational background.

Variation in Achievement and Attainment

Ethnic differences in educational achievement and attainment exist at all levels of schooling during adolescence, from middle school through the college years. American students from African American and Latino backgrounds generally receive lower grades and have lower scores than European American and Asian American students on standardized achievement tests during the middle and high school years. Although the difference in drop-out rates between European American and African American students narrowed during the 1970s and 1980s, a gap in high school completion between these two groups has remained stable for the past 15 years (see Figure 15.1). The dropout rate for Latino students has fluctuated over the past 30 years, but it remains essentially unchanged since 1970 and is higher than any other ethnic group in the United States. In contrast, the grades and test scores of Asian American students are higher than any other ethnic group, and they complete high school at rates equal to their European American peers. The higher high school dropout rates among African American and Latino students are one reason why their levels of college enrollment and completion are lower than those of their peers from other ethnic backgrounds. Asian students, in contrast, attend college and received postsecondary degrees at higher rates than their European American peers.

Despite the many challenges that adolescents from immigrant families face in their adaptation to American society, numerous studies have suggested that they often do just as well, if not better, in school than their peers from American-born families. Both national and local studies have suggested that first- and

second-generation adolescents receive either similar or even higher grades and test scores than their third-generation peers from similar ethnic backgrounds (Fuligni, 1997; Kao & Tienda, 1995). College attendance and completion rates show similar patterns, with those from the first and second generations enrolling in college and receiving degrees at rates similar to their third-generation coethnic peers (Fuligni & Witkow, 2004; Glick & White, 2004).

There is some suggestion, however, that the immigrant advantage may be stronger and more consistent among Asian students than among those with Latino backgrounds. Fuligni (1997) noted that despite the fact that they did as well in English classes as their third-generation peers, first-generation Latino students received significantly lower grades in mathematics, and Kao and Tienda (1995) reported that the immigrant advantage in grades was most consistent among Asian students in a national sample. Census Bureau statistics suggest that the high school completion rate of foreign-born Latinos is dramatically lower (49% of those 25–44 years of age) than their second- and third-generation counterparts (82% and 82%, respectively; U.S. Bureau of the Census, 2007). Yet census statistics often include immigrants who

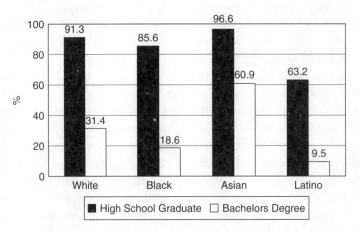

Source: U.S. Census Bureau (2007). Current Population Survey, 2006. Annual Social and Economic Supplement.

FIGURE 15.1   Percentages of the population, aged 25–29 years, with high school and bachelors degrees, according to ethnic background.

entered the United States as adults and never enrolled in school. A recent national study of adolescents who attended U.S. schools, in contrast, observed little generational variation in dropout rates among Latinos (Perreira, Harris, & Lee, 2006). The inconsistency in research findings regarding the achievement of the foreign born from Latin America may be due to the rapid fluctuation of population flows due to immigration, regional variation in the nature of the Latino population, and significant differences within the larger population of Latin American immigrants according to country of origin (e.g., Mexico vs. Cuba). Future research needs to isolate the role of these factors in order to most accurately determine which aspects of the immigrant Latino population have more difficulty in school than others.

Ethnic differences in educational achievement among the immigrant population itself generally mirror those observed in the larger population, with immigrants from Asia demonstrating higher levels of educational attainment compared to those from Latin America (Larsen, 2004). Yet these overall comparisons can mask often dramatic variations within each panethnic group. For example, students from South America and Cuba typically receive better grades and enroll in college at higher rates than those from Mexico or Central America (Portes & Rumbaut, 2001). In addition, students in immigrant families that hail from Southeast Asian countries, such as the Hmong and the Lao, have more difficulty in school than those from China or Korea. Although it is often difficult to break samples down into specific ethnic groups because of their relatively limited sizes in the larger population, it is important to remember that achievement estimates for panethnic groups such as "Asian" or "Latino" youth may not readily apply to all of the specific immigrant groups included in these broad categories.

Motivation and Values

Explanations for ethnic differences in adolescent achievement have often focused on the role of students' value of education and their motivation to succeed. For example, a noted theory offered by Ogbu (1987) suggested that the academic difficulties of African American adolescents were partially attributable to the students' devaluing of education and academic effort. Despite the popularity of this theory, however, subsequent research provided very little evidence to suggest that African American students have lower values of education (Ainsworth-Darnell & Downey, 1998). Similar results have been obtained in studies of adolescents from other ethnic-minority backgrounds. For example, Latino and Asian adolescents often report higher educational aspirations and a stronger belief in the utility of education for their future lives (Fuligni, 2001).

Once source of the academic motivation of many ethnic-minority students is their identification with their ethnic and cultural background. Rather than developing an "oppositional identity," in which a strong cultural identity among ethnic-minority students includes an opposition to engaging with educational institutions, most students attempt to create an ethnic identity that includes a value placed on trying hard and doing well in school. Most studies have been conducted with African American adolescents. For example, Chavous et al. (2003) found that adolescents with a stronger ethnic identity possessed greater academic motivation and were more likely to enroll in college. Oyserman, Harrison, and Bybee (2001) reported a positive link between ethnic identification and feelings of academic efficacy, and Wong, Eccles, and Sameroff (2003) observed that African American adolescents with higher levels of ethnic identity actually received better grades in school. Recent work has observed similar links among those from Asian and Latin American backgrounds. For example, Fuligni, Witkow, and Garcia (2005) found that a stronger attachment to one's ethnic background was associated with greater interest in school, a stronger belief in the utility of education, and a greater identification with the actual high school among adolescents with Mexican and Chinese backgrounds. In fact, the greater level of ethnic identification among those from Mexican and Chinese backgrounds was a significant source of the higher levels of motivation of these students as compared to their equally achieving European American peers.

Family is another significant source of motivation for many ethnic-minority adolescents. As described in the previous section on family relationships, adolescents from a variety of backgrounds have a strong sense of obligation to support, assist, and contribute to their families. Trying hard and doing well in school is seen as a key obligation of these students, both to fulfill the hopes and dreams of their parents and to obtain better jobs in the future so that they can provide financial support to their parents, siblings, and extended family (Suárez-Orozco & Suárez-Orozco, 1995; Zhou & Bankston, 1998). The link between family obligation and academic motivation has been particularly studied among adolescents from immigrant families, and it appears to exist regardless of the families' country of origin. Similar to ethnic identity, a greater sense of family obligation among adolescents from Asian and Latin American backgrounds is a significant source of the extra motivation it takes these students to achieve at the same level as their European American peers (Fuligni, 2001).

Although academic motivation does not explain the profound ethnic differences in adolescents' actual achievement at school, it appears to be one source of the surprising success of many students from immigrant families when compared to their peers from similar ethnic and economic backgrounds. Immigrant parents have high aspirations for their adolescents' educational attainment, wanting their teenagers to received college degrees at higher rates than American-born parents (Fuligni, 1997; Kao & Tienda, 1995; Suárez-Orozco & Suárez-Orozco, 1995). Educational opportunity is a primary reason why many foreign-born parents immigrate to the United States in the first place, and their belief in the opportunities available in American society leads them to expect there will be greater returns from their educational investments as compared to American-born parents (Fuligni & Yoshikawa, 2004). The value placed on education by immigrant parents is readily shared by their adolescents, who also have higher educational aspirations and greater academic motivation than their peers from American-born families. The greater motivation of students from immigrant families has been shown to account for their higher level of achievement in secondary school (Fuligni, 1997).

Interestingly, it may be that the belief in the importance of education among immigrant parents is largely instrumental as opposed to being an abstract value placed on exploration and self-improvement. Consistent with this idea, Caplan et al. (1991) reported that a Vietnamese refugee mother stated:

> According to our culture, a well-educated person always gets respect, even when not rich. But this country is different; education goes along with the wealth. I would like my children to be well education, both to be respected in our community and also to get a high position in this society. (p. 116)

The emphasis on the utility of education can be seen in the tendency for many college students from immigrant families to pursue technical and business degrees that have a clear link to stable, well-paying occupations (Tseng, 2006).

It is important to note that substantial variability exists among different immigrant groups in their academic motivation and educational aspirations, however, with adolescents from Asian immigrant families tending to report a stronger belief in the utility of education, higher educational aspirations, and more time each week studying and doing homework as compared to those from other immigrant groups (Fuligni, 1997; Kao & Tienda, 1995). Differences exist even within these panethnic larger groups. For example, adolescents from Chinese immigrant families place more emphasis upon education than their peers from immigrant Filipino backgrounds (Fuligni, 1997).

In contrast to the generational differences in motivation, these ethnic differences among those from immigrant families have a lot to do with the often significant differences in socioeconomic background and resources among various immigrant groups, as discussed below.

Socioeconomic Resources of the Family

In contrast to motivational differences, variations in socioeconomic resources play an important role in ethnic differences in adolescent achievement. Parents of adolescents in the two panethnic groups that have the most difficulty in school, African Americans and Latinos, tend to have lower levels of education as compared to European American and Asian American adults (U.S. Bureau of the Census, 2007). African American and Latino adults also are more likely to work in lower status occupations and have lower incomes as compared to other adults (Webster & Bishaw, 2007). These differences in the educational and financial resources of families, which are important predictors of school success, partially account for some of the differences in educational success among adolescents from different ethnic groups. Yet families' socioeconomic resources do not explain all ethnic differences, which often remain after controlling for indices such as parental education and occupation. For example, the achievement gap between African American and European American students exists at virtually every level of the economic distribution (Ferguson, 2007). Many observers note that this may be due to the underestimation of economic variability. For example, even when parents of different ethnic groups have similar levels of education and income, they can have substantial differences in wealth (e.g., home ownership and value, inheritance), financial stability and income regularity, and generational continuity of social class (McLoyd & Ceballo, 1998). These additional, potentially significant aspects of the socioeconomic resources of adolescents' families have rarely been considered in studies of ethnic differences in academic achievement.

Interestingly, variations in the socioeconomic resources of adolescents' families do little to explain the differences in achievement between those from immigrant and American-born families. On average, immigrant parents tend to have lower levels of education, work in lower status occupations, and are more disadvantaged than American-born parents on most other socioeconomic indicators, such as income, poverty, home ownership, and neighborhood quality (Hernandez, 2004). Yet, as discussed above, students from immigrant families tend to do just as well, if not better, in school than their counterparts from American-born families. In fact, the generational differences in academic achievement become even greater after accounting for families' socioeconomic background, suggesting that students from immigrant families do better than would be predicted on the basis on their parents' educational, occupational, and financial standing (Fuligni, 1997; Kao & Tienda, 1995). The greater educational aspirations and academic motivation of immigrant parents and their adolescents is an important reason for this surprising result, as discussed above.

Yet another reason for the inability of traditional socioeconomic indicators to account for generational differences in achievement may be in the complexity of measuring human and financial capital among immigrant families (Fuligni & Yoshikawa, 2003). For example, parental education may be an underestimate of the human capital of immigrant families. Human capital, as assessed by parental education, is thought to be the extent to which parents can provide the skills, abilities, and values that children need to achieve in school settings and later in their own employment (Entwisle & Astone, 1994). The problem is that educational opportunity differs dramatically around the world, and many immigrant parents attended school in countries in which only a minority of the population receives education beyond the primary school years, much less the secondary school years (e.g., Mexico, China, Vietnam). This means that an immigrant parent who has attended school for the same number of years as an American-born parent actually has gone much further in their educational system. As such, absolute educational level may be an underestimate of the educational values, motivation, and cognitive skills of immigrant parents as compared to American-born parents. Similarly, the occupational status of an immigrant parent may be an underestimate of the skills and abilities of immigrant parents because of the reluctance of American employers to recognize foreign credentials and training (e.g., medical degrees). The socioeconomic resources of immigrant families, therefore, are difficult to assess and require a close attention to issues of parental education, occupation, and family income both before and after immigration (Fuligni & Yoshikawa, 2003).

Even with the caveats expressed above, socioeconomic differences do explain some of the ethnic differences in academic achievement within the immigrant population itself. Immigrants from Asia tend to have higher levels of education and work in better paying jobs than those from Latin America, and these variations account for some of the differences in school grades and standardized test performance (Fuligni, 1997; Kao & Tienda, 1995).

Structural Disparities and Stereotyping

An important reason that ethnic differences families' socioeconomic resources cannot completely account for variations in academic achievement is that students do not compete on a level educational playing field. Substantial differences exist in the quality of schools attended by students from different ethnic backgrounds. Even when they attend similar schools, adolescents may encounter different expectations and opportunities, due to the implicit stereotypes held by the larger society regarding educational abilities and potential of students from different ethnic and immigrant groups. Although some of the variations in the social context of education faced by adolescents from different ethnic backgrounds are linked

to differences in family economic resources (e.g., low-income families living in poor neighborhoods with low-quality schools), they are not completely confounded as evidenced by the different expectations encountered by students who attend the same school. That is, even within the same school, students from ethnic-minority backgrounds may by channeled toward and away from challenging coursework by virtue of the stereotypical assumptions made about the academic motivation and potential of their ethnic group. Galletta and Cross (2007) have noted how African American students can be steered away from advanced classes, whereas Way and colleagues found in their ethnographic studies of high schools that the "model minority myth" often led teachers to assign Chinese American students to the "advanced" classes when many of them were not academically prepared for such classes. Teachers justified such tracking claiming that the Chinese students felt more comfortable being among other Chinese students (Rosenbloom & Way, 2004).

The inability of family-level economic factors to fully account for ethnic differences in academic achievement has led to an increased interest in how extrafamilial factors such as structural disparities and societal stereotypes play a role in the lower educational success of students from certain ethnic backgrounds. Students from African American and Latino backgrounds are significantly less likely to attend secondary schools that provide qualified teachers, a positive school climate, and the availability of advanced and college preparation courses. Analyses of school-level differences have shown that experienced teachers are much less likely to be located within schools that have high proportions of ethnic-minority students and those with limited English proficiency (LEP) (National Center for Education Statistics, 2003). The social environment and climate of schools attended by these students are also less conducive to learning. Ethnic-minority and LEP students are more likely to attend schools that are large (i.e., more than 900 enrolled students) and severely overcrowded (National Center for Education Statistics, 2003a). Studies have also shown that African American and Latino students are more likely to report the presence of gangs in their schools and to be afraid of being beaten up or attacked at their schools (Kaufman et al., 1998).

The opportunities for taking advanced coursework in secondary school also are more limited for African American and Latino students. Even among those who graduate from high school, students from these two groups are the least likely to take the advanced courses in science and math that are necessary for college admission and attendance, even after controlling for prior levels of achievement (National Center for Education Statistics, 2003b). In contrast, Asian American students are significantly more likely to enroll these types of course in high school than those from any other ethnic group, including Whites. Some of these differences can be attributable to ethnic differences in achievement prior to the high school years that create variations in eligibility for advanced coursework, but there is still differential access to these courses across schools. Upper tracks (e.g., advanced and college track) tend to be smaller, and lower tracks tend to be larger in schools with large numbers of ethnic-minority students (Dornbusch, Glasgow, & Lin, 1996; Oakes, Selvin, Karoly, & Guiton, 1991).

Yet even within the same school, ethnic differences exist in students' enrollment in upper track and advanced placement courses. Misplacement of students across tracks may occur, whether due to official decisions by school personnel or by voluntary course selection patterns on the part of the students. Studies have suggested the African American and Latino students are less likely to enroll in advanced placement courses than students from other ethnic backgrounds with equivalent levels of ability and prior achievement, whereas Asian American students are more likely to be found in such course as compared to similar peers (Dornbusch et al., 1996; Oakes et al., 1991).

The differential patterns of enrollment in advanced coursework among students even in the same schools highlight the role that societal stereotypes regarding academic potential, motivation, and engagement play in the persistent ethnic differences in academic achievement in American society. It has been argued that long-standing stereotypes and myths about the intellectual abilities and academic motivation of certain marginalized ethnic groups, such as African Americans and Latinos, act to essentialize the groups. That is, societal myths and stereotypes about marginalized groups serve to identity the "true" or "essential" character of the group in the social imagination (Mahalingham, 2007). The "essential" character of a groups is impermeable to change or improvement, thereby justifying long-standing differences in educational resources and opportunity.

The influences of such stereotypes can be seen as influencing the differential patterns of enrollment in advanced coursework during the secondary school years. Galletta and Cross (2007), in an ethnographic analysis of the integration efforts of an ethnically mixed school district, show how that even within efforts to promote equality in education, social stereotypes can shape the opportunities available to African American students within the same school and even within the same classroom. One African American student recounted to them an experience in the beginning of the school year in an advanced class:

> [The teacher] called all of the black students' names and told us – in front of the whole class – that we were in the wrong class, that were supposed to be in the other teacher's and [the teacher] said [the other teacher's] name, and the other kids in the class knew that wasn't the enriched class, and I'm, I'm thinking to myself, this is wrong, this is not – how could that be? (p. 33).

These social barriers for full participation of many ethnic-minority students can, at times, take on very real physical significance. In an ethnography of a large, middle-class, predominantly

White high school, O'Connor, Deluca, Fernández, and Girard (2007) examined how the physical spaces in large high schools can become "racialized." The organization of the school into instructional wings meant that classrooms serving different academic tracks were located in different locations of the school. The differential enrollment in tracks based on ethnicity created distinct social spaces within the school in which the African American and White students congregated in the different areas. As a result, African American students who wished to enroll in upper-track classes literally had to travel greater distances and cross distinct social barriers that served to reify existing stereotypes about their academic potential and motivation.

In addition to structural and social barriers, ethnic-minority adolescents must contend with direct experiences of mistreatment due to their ethnic or racial background. Several studies have shown that ethnic-minority students, particularly those from African American backgrounds, report more frequent discrimination from adults, including teachers and school personnel (Fisher, Wallace, & Fenton, 2001; Rosenbloom & Way, 2004). Perceived discrimination, in turn, is often associated with lower levels of educational adjustment across a variety of indicators, including disengagement, GPA, and dropping out before graduation (Katz, 1999; Wayman, 2002; Wong, Eccles, & Sameroff, 2003).

The effects of stereotyping on the achievement of many ethnic-minority students, particularly those from African American and Latino backgrounds, do not have to be explicit. In their work on the impact of stereotype threat on minority achievement, Steele and Aronson (1995) have argued that there is always a threat "in the air" to minority-student achievement. In a seminar study, they demonstrated how simply asking college students to report their ethnicity before taking a standardized test resulted in lower levels of performance on the exam. Steele and Aronson argued that making ethnicity salient resulted in pressure for the

students to feel that they needed to disprove the stereotype, thereby creating excessive anxiety and perhaps even disengagement that depressed their performance on the exam. This phenomenon has since been replicated among many different groups in different situations, including those as young as middle school (McKown & Weinstein, 2003). Stereotypes, therefore, can impede the achievement of derogated ethnic-minority students even when they are not currently experiencing even implicit prejudicial treatment.

Interestingly, recent studies have suggested that an effective way to counter the effects of such stereotype threat is to emphasize the malleability of intelligence to students. Experimental studies have shown that the effect is minimized when students are told before a test that the test does not assess innate ability. In addition, recent intervention studies have indicated that an intervention that teaches students about the malleability of intelligence through the life span also minimize the effects of stereotype threat (Good, Dweck, & Aronson, 2007). In a sense, these studies have shown the effectiveness of providing students with the tools to fight back efforts of the larger society to "essentialize" their ethnic groups in terms of innate intelligence.

IDENTITY PROCESSES

Among the most widely recognized tasks adolescents face is that of coming to terms with who they want to be and how they fit into existing social groups and settings. This identity-seeking process involves trying on and discarding multiple identities and weighing the values, goals, and behaviors that they could potentially adopt vis-à-vis the various roles and contexts of their lives (e.g., son/daughter, student, citizen, or friend). Researchers have sought to understand identity processes both in terms of resolution of personal identities—self-representations that allow individuals to distinguish themselves from others—and social identities—self-representations that are derived from membership in social groups.

Both personal and social identities affect individuals' appraisals of their world and their social and psychological experiences across time and settings.

An important component of social identity development during adolescence involves coming to an understanding of one's position vis-à-vis one's racial and ethnic group. Although young children are certainly aware of ethnicity and race, can categorize themselves as group members, and often participate in their groups' practices and traditions, the process of actively exploring one's ethnicity and race and of determining their significance in one's life becomes far more complex during adolescence (McKown & Weinstein, 2003; Ruble et al., 2004). Due to the emergence of abstract reasoning and dialectical thinking, adolescents are able to take a more active role in reflecting on their own and others' views about their group, in deciding how important group membership is to their sense of self and in making choices about participating in group-relevant activities and settings. Each of these tasks is integral to the process of developing a ethnic and racial identity, which is generally conceived as the development of positive (or negative) views of one's group, knowledge about its history and traditions, feelings of group attachment and belongingness, and participation in practices or settings that reflect group membership (Phinney, 1990).

Although the work of racial and ethnic identity development occurs among all adolescents, it is especially salient and complex for ethnic-minority adolescents, native born or immigrant. Ethnic-minority and non-White immigrant adolescents must reconcile their group membership with knowledge that their group is stigmatized and devalued and with experiences of racism, discrimination, and stereotypes. Immigrant youth face additional challenges in negotiating potentially conflicting expectations across the worlds of their more traditional parents and those of mainstream peer and adult agents of socialization (Fuligni, 1998; Lee, 2001; 2002; Suarez

Oroszco & Suarez Oroszco, 2001). Thus, studies find that ethnic-minority and immigrant adolescents score significantly higher on measures of ethnic identity than do their White counterparts (Phinney & Alipuria, 1990; Phinney et al., 1994), view race and ethnicity as more central to their self-concept (Fuligni et al., 2005), and are more likely to view their experiences through a racial or ethnic lens (London, Downy, Bolger, & Velella, 2005). Studies also find that components of ethnic identity are more strongly associated with psychological, social, and academic outcomes among ethnic-minority as compared to White adolescents (Yasui, Dorham, & Dishion, 2004). Indeed, scholars have suggested that resolving issues relevant to racial and ethnic identity is necessary for healthy psychological functioning among ethnic-minority and immigrant youth (Phinney, 1989; Umaña-Taylor, 2004).

Due to differences in groups' social status, experiences in the United States, and sending and receiving communities, ethnic and racial identity processes quite likely vary across different ethnic-minority and immigrant groups. However, the empirical literature to date is limited in the information it provides in this regard. Although studies have documented ethnic group differences in identity components and in the experience of ethnicity (e.g., Fuligni, Whitkow, & Garcia, 2005; Pahl & Way, 2006; Way et al., in press), a priori hypotheses that link predicted between-group differences to differences in groups' histories and experiences are generally lacking. Moreover, to date, the general patterns for ethnic and racial identity processes are more similar than different across groups. Thus, in this section, rather than focusing on between-group differences, we focus instead on processes that adolescents share, highlighting differences ethnic–racial group where documented.

Before proceeding, it is useful to clarify our use of the terms racial and ethnic identity, which are used interchangeably in the literature but are theoretically distinct. The term *race* denotes groups derived from similarity in phenotypic characteristics but only minimally identifies biologically or genetically distinct groups. Although race is largely socially constructed, it nonetheless has powerful meaning in the United States (Allen, Bat-Chava, Aber & Seidman, 2005), rendering the process of negotiating social identities based on *racial* group membership especially relevant to many adolescents. We would expect this to especially be the case for adolescents from groups with distinctive phenotypic characteristics (e.g., Blacks, Asians), in part because they are most often subject to others' ascriptive ethnic/racial designations (Espiritu, 1992, Lee, 1999, Nagel, 1994). The term *ethnicity* implies a set of characteristics that include cultural values, language, traditions, and behaviors shared by a geographically contiguous group that is transmitted intergenerationally. Ethnic identities are often represented as chosen, malleable, and fluid, with ethnic choices changing as the audience changes (Nagel, 1994; Waters, 1993, 2003). Notably, the term *racial identity* is primarily used in studies of U.S.-born Blacks (e.g., Sellers, Smith, Shelton, Rowley, & Chavous, 1998; Vandiver, Cross, Worrell, & Fhagen-Smith, 2002), and Whites (e.g., Helms, 1999; Stoddart, 2002), and the term *ethnic identity* is used more broadly across multiple ethnic groups. However, there is little consensus regarding when one term should be used in lieu of the other (Cross, 2007; Quintana, 2007), and we do not seek to engage or resolve issues of nomenclature here. Instead, we use the hyphenated term *ethnic–racial identity*, reflecting our belief that both are important in providing adolescents with psychological resources and in imposing obstacles to their successful development.

Theoretical Underpinnings

Empirical knowledge about ethnic–racial identity processes during adolescence is embedded in multiple theoretical frameworks, each characterized by slightly different approaches to understanding the phenomena and slightly different research questions. These frameworks recognize that ethnic–racial identities are multifaceted, dynamic, and shift across time and context. Within psychology, the predominant frameworks are social identity theory (Tajfel, 1978), ego identity frameworks (Erikson, 1968; Marcia, 1966, Phinney, 1989), and acculturation frameworks (Berry, 1990).

At its core, social identity theory (Tajfel, 1978) proposes that individuals derive their self-concept from knowledge that they are members of particular social groups and categories that share characteristics that are meaningful in particular social contexts. Given the salience of race and ethnicity in the United States, these are central social categories that individuals evaluate. Membership in stigmatized social categories is thought to be problematic for a positive sense of self, whereas membership in categories that are held in high esteem is thought to enhance self-esteem. Correspondingly, studies have sought to differentiate varying components ethnic identity (Ashmore, Deaux, & McLaughlin-Volpe, 2004; Sellers et al., 1998), the mechanisms through which individuals from stigmatized groups maintain a positive sense of themselves and their group (e.g., Crocker, Luhtanen, Blaine & Broadnax, 1994; Crocker & Major, 1989); and variations across contexts and situations in the salience of identity (Way et al., in press; Yip, 2005; Yip & Fuligni, 2002). This work has yielded important concepts for distinguishing multiple ethnic identity components that may profoundly shape adolescents' experiences and worldviews. An example is Sellers, Chavous, and Cooke's (1998) distinction between centrality (the importance of ethnicity and race to one's self-definition), salience (the importance of identity at a particular moment), regard (one's own and views of others evaluations of one's group), and ideology (the content of one's beliefs about how one should behave as a group member). For instance, several studies have found that Chinese adolescents have lower private regard compared to their Mexican counterparts (Fuligni et al., 2005) and to their African American, Dominican, or Puerto

Rican counterparts (Rivas Drake, Hughes, and Way, 2008; in press; Way et al., in press). French, Seidman, Allen and Aber (2006) found higher private regard among Latino middle adolescents as compared to their African American counterparts. Altshul, Oyserman, and Bybee (2006) found higher connectedness and awareness of racism among African American as compared to Latino students.

Research embedded in ego-identity frameworks (French et al., 2006; Phinney, 1990; Umaña-Taylor, 2004) focuses primarily on elaborating the processes through which individuals consolidate their ethnic–racial identities. Central to this framework is the idea that individuals attain an achieved ethnic/ratial identity only after having explored and actively accepted its meaning. In Cross's (1971, 1991) "nigresence" model, grounded in the experiences of U.S.-born Blacks, individuals are thought to move from a state of relative ignorance of race (pre-encounter) to one characterized by an achieved sense of their race and its meaning. Movement is precipitated by a discrete encounter event that sets in motion processes of self-reflection and search for greater racial understanding (Cross & Fhagen-Smith, 2001). In a similar stage model, Phinney (1989, 1990) differentiates three identity statuses: *unexamined*, in which the meaning of group membership is unexplored; *exploration*, characterized by an active search for information about the meaning of group membership; and *achievement*, the resolution of the identity search, usually resulting in commitment to and affirmation of one's ethnic group. Recent iterations of both theories emphasize that ethnic–racial identities are reformulated throughout the life cycle (Cross & Fhagen-Smith, 2001; Parham, 1989; Phinney, 2006; Umaña-Taylor, Diversi, & Fine, 2002). Empirically based knowledge about shifts in ethnic–racial identity during adolescence is largely embedded within this framework.

Finally, recognizing that immigrant adolescents navigate two cultures, the dominant host culture and the culture of origin, researchers studying ethnic–racial identity within an acculturation framework emphasize the psychological and social consequences of adolescents' efforts to negotiate identification with and preference for the values, beliefs, language, and cultural practices of each culture. Berry's (2003) distinction between integration, assimilation, separation, and marginalization; Suaŕez-Orozco and Suaŕez Orozco's (2001) distinction between ethnic flight, adversarial identities, and transcultural identities; and Rumbaut's (1994) attention to the specific identity labels immigrant youth choose exemplify this research tradition. Research questions focus on the extent to which adolescents' identity labels and acculturation profiles shift with length of time in the United States and are differentially associated with outcomes such as school success or deviance (Fuligni et al., 2005; Rumbaut, 1994; Sullivan, Schwartz, Prado, Huang, Pantin & Szapocznik, 2007). Most often, identities characterized by integration of the host culture and the culture of origin are promoted as more healthy than other identities.

The Course and Timing of Ethnic–Racial Identity Development During Adolescence

Ethnic-racial identity processes are intimately intertwined with other aspects of identity seeking that are ongoing during adolescence. In general, however, early and middle adolescents are thought to have less clear and committed sense of ethnic identity compared to their older adolescent counterparts, with mid- to late adolescence characterized by search and exploration. Both cross-sectional studies that compare ethnic–racial identity across age groups and longitudinal studies that examine intraindividual change suggest that during adolescence there is a progression from an unexplored and uncommitted ethnic–racial identity to a more secure view of the role of race and ethnicity and affirmation of one's group membership.

Cross-sectional studies that have compared older adolescents to their adult or younger adolescent counterparts provide the bulk of information about developmental shifts in ethnic–racial identity development, the advantage being that they cover a larger swath of the developmental spectrum than existing longitudinal studies have covered. For instance, in Lysne and Levy's (1997) comparison of 9th- and 12th-grade Native American students, 12th-grade Native American adolescents reported significantly greater identity commitment than did 9th-grade students. Moreover, difference in identity exploration as a function of school ethnic composition was evident only among 12th graders, suggesting that the process of exploration precipitated by being a minority in the school had not yet been set in motion among the 9th graders. Yip, Seaton, and Sellers (2006) compared the identity statuses of African American adolescents, college students, and adults, using cluster profiles derived from Phinney's (1989) proposed stages of identity development. Findings indicated that 42% of adolescents were in the moratorium stage, characterized by active exploration of their ethnicity and race, compared to about 25% of college students or adults. Fewer than 1 in 3 adolescents were characterized as being in the achieved status, characterized by an active commitment to the meaning of ethnicity based on intensive exploration, compared with about one-half of college students or adults.

Longitudinal studies confirm cross-sectional findings that ethnic–racial identities shift during mid- to late adolescence. Studies based on latent growth curve models across multiple ethnic groups find increases in ethnic affirmation during junior high and early high school (Altshul et al., 2006; French et al., 2006; Whitesell, Mitchell, Kaufman, & Spicer, 2006), whereas Pahl and Way (2006) documented stability in ethnic affirmation between 10th grade and 1 year post high school. In French et al., increases in affirmation were most pronounced following the transition to junior high or high school and among Black and Latino, as compared to European American, adolescents. In Altshul et al. (2006) group connectedness

and awareness of racism were higher among African American as compared to Latino 8th- and 9th-grade adolescents, but their rates of were similar over time. In contrast to ethnic affirmation, several studies have documented that exploration occurs only among older adolescents. In French et al. (2006), increases in exploration were documented among adolescents transitioning to high school but not among those transitioning to junior high school. Pahl and Way (2006) documented decreases in ethnic exploration between 10th grade and 1 year post high school, although this decrease was more pronounced among Latino than Black youth. Together, cross-sectional and longitudinal studies locate the processes of exploration that Phinney (1989) emphasizes in the later high school years, and indicate that Black and Latino students may differ from each other in the patterns of change over time.

Length of Time in the United States

For immigrant adolescents, the form and shape of ethnic identity also shifts as a function of the length of time their family has been in the United States (Fuligni, Tseng, & Lam, 1999; Tseng & Fuligni, 2000). Over time, immigrant adolescents interact within an increasing number and broader range of mainstream institutions, including schools, organized activities, and workplaces, where peers and adult socialization agents expose them to U.S. norms and values that they must integrate with those of their own culture (Fuligni, et al., 1999; Lee, 2001, 2002; Phinney, Horenczyk, Liebkind, & Vedder, 2001; Rumbaut, 1994). Negotiations that occur within and between these cultures have important implications for immigrant adolescents' views of their ethnic group and perceptions of their group's status (Berry, Phinney, Sam, & Vedder, 2006; Phinney, 2001), in addition to having important implications for adolescents' family relationships (Tseng & Fuligni 2000; Fuligni et al., 1999). Studies find differences in the identity labels adolescents choose and in the nature of their ethnic identity as a function of generational status and the length of time in the United States. Youth with more years in the United States are more likely to prefer combined (e.g., Dominican American) or pan-ethnic (e.g., Latino) labels over labels that refer only to national origin (e.g., Mexican) compared to their counterparts who have been in the United States for fewer years (Rumbaut, 1994), although there is some evidence that identity content better predicts adolescent outcomes (Fuligni et al., 2005; Marsiglia, Kulis, & Hecht, 2001). In a recent study of 5,000 immigrant adolescents, those with high levels of comfort in the host culture and the culture of origin reported better sociocultural and psychological adaptation than adolescents who were primarily oriented either toward the host culture or toward the culture of origin, or those who were unclear about their identity (Berry et al., 2006).

Parental Influences on Ethnic–Racial Identity

As we have mentioned, many ethnic-minority and immigrant parents transmit information and knowledge to their children about their racial and ethnic group and do so in ways that are both intentional and inadvertent (Hughes, et al., 2006). Parents from multiple ethnic-minority and immigrant groups emphasize the importance of ethnic pride and knowledge about group history, values, traditions, and practices in their childrearing. They also make deliberate efforts to expose children to museums, language classes, books, and trips to the home country in order to connect them do their culture. These deliberate and intentional strategies are reinforced by cultural practices that are deeply embedded in families' daily routines, including celebrations, cooking of ethnic food and listening to ethnic music, and artifacts in the home (Hughes, Rivas, Foust, Hagelskamp, Gersick, & Way, 2008).

Studies clearly suggest that adolescents whose parents place a strong emphasis on socializing them about ethnicity and race report that their ethnicity is more important to them,

and they have more positive feelings about their ethnic group (e.g., Hughes et al., 2006; 2007; Phinney & Chavira, 1995). Stevenson's program of research on African American youth has consistently documented significant relationships between parents' reinforcement of cultural pride and measures of African American adolescents' ethnic identity (e.g., Stevenson, 1995, 1998, 2002). Umaña-Taylor and colleagues have documented similar relationships between covert and overt forms of ethnic socialization and Mexican American adolescents' ethnic identity (Gonzalez, Umaña-Taylor, & Bámaca, 2006; Umaña-Taylor & Yazedijan, 2006). Rivas-Drake, Hughes, and Way (in press) examined relationships between specific types of ethnic–racial socialization and specific dimensions of ethnic identity in a sample of African American, Chinese, Dominican, Puerto Rican, and White 6th-grade adolescents. Adolescents who reported greater parental socialization about culture and pride reported that ethnicity and race were more central to their self-concepts and more positive views of their ethnic group. Parents discussions about discrimination were unrelated to centrality or ethnic affirmation, but were associated with adolescents' perceptions of others views about their groups.

Situational and Contextual Influences on Adolescents' Ethnic–Racial Identities

Although studies have primarily focused on individual-level variation in components of adolescents' ethnic–racial identities, scholars increasingly recognize that characteristics of the settings adolescents inhabit have important influences of the course, timing, and content of adolescents' developing ethnic/racial identities. Aspects of settings can both support and challenge adolescents' emerging ethnic identities—rendering them more or less salient and variously challenging and supporting them. For instance, aggregate characteristics of others in the settings as well as ambient setting features (e.g., posters or curriculum in schools that celebrate the contributions of multiple groups) can shape adolescents' emerging ethnic–racial identities in important ways.

The most commonly examined setting characteristic to date is the ethnic and racial composition of other setting participants. Adolescents in settings in which few other group members are present and adolescents in settings in which their group is a clear majority have both been found to differ from adolescents in more ethnically diverse settings in levels of exploration (Lysne & Levy, 1997) and in their positive feelings about their ethnic group (Umaña-Taylor, 2004). Ethnic composition has also been found to moderate relationships between components of ethnic identity and self-esteem. Allen et al. (2005) reported that Black adolescents' less favorable views about their ethnic–racial group were associated with depression when they lived in mixed neighborhoods or neighborhoods in which they were in the minority, but such views were unrelated to depression among Black adolescents who lived in majority Black neighborhoods. Latino students who lived in mixed or predominantly non-Latino neighborhoods reported more depression if they held their group in high esteem, but group esteem was associated with lower depression among those who lived in majority Latino neighborhoods. White adolescents' school ethnic composition was more relevant to their depression than was neighborhood ethnic composition. Way et al. (in press), however, find that ethnic and racial composition is less relevant for the development of identities than the social and political status of the ethnic groups within the setting. They find that the Chinese American students, who formed the vast majority of students in the urban, low-income school they studied but who also had the lowest social standing among their Puerto Rican, African American, and Dominican peers, reported the least positive feelings about themselves and their ethnic group. Way et al. (in press) underscore the importance of examining the "qualitative" components of a setting (i.e., social status)

as well as the more quantitative components (i.e., number of students from each ethnic group in a school) in studies of ethnic identity development.

In addition to comparing ethnic–racial identities across adolescents in different types of settings, studies have begun to pay attention to the ways in which an individual adolescent's ethnic/racial identities vary across different types of settings and situations. These studies recognize that adolescents, like adults, are likely to carry a portfolio of ethnic–racial identities that are more or less likely to emerge at a given moment, depending on the situation they are in and the audience they are facing (Ashmore et al., 2004; Nagle, 1994). For instance, Huang (1998) documented situational variation in ethnic/racial identity among Asian immigrant youth, who felt more ethnic at home, more American at school, and equally ethnic and American with peers. Similarly, Kiang, Harter, and Whitesell (2007) documented that Chinese American college students reported that they were significantly more likely to express their feelings about their ethnic identities in the context of other Chinese American peers as compared to parents or non-Asian peers, and in the context of parents as compared to non-Asian peers. They reported feeling significantly more support for their ethnic identities in contexts that involved other Chinese American peers or parents, as compared to non-Asian peers. Yip and colleagues, in a series of daily diary studies, although ethnic identity is generally more salient among Chinese American high school and college students with higher affirmation and achievement, they report greater identity salience in situations in which they are engaging in ethnic behaviors (e.g., speaking Chinese, eating Chinese food, reading Chinese newspapers) and in situations in which other Chinese people were present (Yip & Fuligni, 2002; Yip, 2005).

A final setting feature that has been examined in relationship to adolescents' emerging ethnic identities concerns the extent to which adolescents perceive that they are exposed to ethnically or racially based discrimination across the various settings in which they participate. Although perceived discrimination can be construed as a feature of settings or a feature of individuals, in that some adolescents may simply be inclined to perceive more discrimination, studies show that perceiving discrimination plays an important role in shaping adolescents' ethnic identities. For instance, based on ethnographic work with Chinese and Korean high school students, Lee (1999) describes the ways in which students' perceptions that non-Asian peers would always view and treat them differently came to view connections with other Asians, and the development of panethnic identities, as politically and psychologically beneficial. In longitudinal studies with African American high school and college students, Sellers and colleagues have documented that those for whom race is more central, and those who believe that others hold more negative views of African Americans, are more likely to report experiencing discrimination. This may be because they are more likely to interpret ambiguous events as being discriminatory or, in line with theories of race rejection sensitivity (Mendoza-Denton, Downey, Purdie, Davis, & Pietrzak, 2002) because their a priori expectations predispose them to actually being treated unfairly. Using latent growth curve models, Pahl and Way (2006) showed significant relationships between growth in exploration and growth in perceived discrimination over time among students between 10th grade and 1 year post high school. Specifically, increases in discrimination by peers was associated with increases in identity exploration, especially among Black students. In addition, students who perceived more discrimination by peers showed less deceleration in their identity exploration over time compared to their counterparts. Conversely, initial levels of exploration or affirmation did not predict changes in trajectories of perceived discrimination over time.

Functional Consequences of Ethnic Identity

The importance of ethnic/racial identities during adolescence lies in the potential role that they play in shaping adolescents current psychological outcomes and behaviors, and their views of their future roles and opportunities. We have already discussed the documented importance of ethnic–racial identities in influencing adolescents' orientations toward their academics and their actual academic outcomes, given the powerful stereotypes that exist among educators, practicioners, and community members regarding the academic goals, work habits, and abilities of students from different ethnic backgrounds. Thus, our discussion here focuses on the consequences of adolescents' racial–ethnic identities for their overall feelings about themselves and their general psychological well-being.

In line with social identity theory, a secure sense of one's ethnic identity serves to promote self-esteem and psychological well-being during adolescence and throughout adulthood. Scores of studies have documented correlations between concurrent measures of ethnic identity and self-esteem or well-being (e.g., Ethier & Deaux, 1990, 1994; Goodstein & Ponterotto, 1997; Phinney, 1991; Phinney & Chavira, 1992; Umaña-Taylor, Diversi, & Fine, 2002). More specifically, greater ethnic exploration (Umaña-Taylor, 2004), the importance placed on one's identity as an ethnic–racial group member (Ethier & Deaux, 1990, 1994), having positive views of one's ethnic group (Lee & Yoo, 2004), and having reached an achieved ethnic identity status (Lee & Yoo, 2004; Seaton, Scottham & Sellers, 2006) have each been associated with higher self-esteem and greater psychological well-being.

Longitudinal studies, however, indicate that components of ethnic identity may not be as critical over the long run as cross-sectional studies might suggest. For instance, although Umaña-Taylor and colleagues found contemporaneous relationships between ethnic identity exploration, affirmation, and resolution vis-à-vis self-esteem among Latino students, none of these dimensions of ethnic identity predicted self-esteem over time, either directly or through psychological resources provided for coping with discrimination (Umaña-Taylor, Vargas-Chanes, Garcia, & Gonzales-Backen, 2008). Whitesell et al. (2006) also found weak relationships between trajectories of self-esteem and trajectories of group esteem among Native American high school students. However, Pahl and Way (2006) find that different elements of ethnic identity are significantly associated with change over time in self-esteem for African American, Latino, and Asian American adolescents. Discrepancy between findings in the longitudinal studies of ethnic identity may be due to the length of time examined with those studies that examined shorter periods of time (i.e., and thus less variability to predict change) less likely to find an association while those studies examining extended periods of time more likely to find significant associations between components of ethnic identity and self-esteem.

Additional research in this area has begun to unpack the conditions under which adolescents' orientation toward their ethnic group matters most in predicting their well-being. For example, the content of ethnic identity appears to matter most for adolescents who view ethnicity as central to their self-definition (Sellers, Chavous, & Cooke, 1998; Yip & Cross, 2004). Yip (2005) and Yip and Fuligni (2002) found that Chinese American high school and college students reported greater well-being on days when their Chinese identities were salient to them, but this was especially true for those who held their group in high regard. In addition, although holding ethnicity as central to one's self-concept and feeling connected to one's ethnic group may not be a prerequisite for positive self-views, a strong ethnic identity permits adolescents to resist and better interpret instances of marginalization, exclusion, and discrimination they encounter in their daily lives (Downy, Chatman, London, et al., 2005; Strauss & Cross, 2005). Numerous studies using cross-sectional, longitudinal, and daily diary approaches have found that having an achieved sense of identity and holding positive views of one's ethnic group attenuates the

otherwise negative consequences of daily stressors and of specific experiences with discrimination (Kiang, Yip, Gonzales-Bracken, Witkow, & Fuligni, 2006; Sellers, Copeland-Linder, Martin & Lewis, 2006; Sellers & Shelton, 2003; Wong, Eccles, & Sameroff, 2003). For instance, Greene et al. (2006) report that an increase in perceived discrimination by peers over time is associated with declines in self-esteem among adolescents with lower initial scores on measures of ethnic affirmation. Sellers et al. (2006) found that more positive feelings toward African Americans were associated with more favorable psychological functioning in the face of racial discrimination. In addition, there was a significantly weaker association between racial discrimination and psychological functioning among those adolescents who had a greater awareness that other groups held less favorable attitudes toward African Americans than among those who believe others held more positive attitudes. Identity components have been found to buffer relationships between exposure to discrimination and academic outcomes (Wong, et al., 2003) and between discrimination and engagement in violent behaviors (Caldwell, Kohn-Wood, Schmeelk-Cone, Chavous, & Zimmerman, 2004).

CONCLUSION

As the amount of material covered in the previous sections demonstrates, the surge in research on adolescents from ethnic-minority and immigrant backgrounds has matured to the point where rich descriptions can be made about the lives and patterns of development of these teenagers. It is clear that variations in cultural background, socioeconomic resources, and social and structural contexts can sometimes produce significant differences in family relationships, friendships, academic achievement, and identity development. These differences include the frequency and implications of parental control, the importance placed upon family obligation and ethnic socialization, educational attainment, and the relevance of racial–ethnic identity for the development of the self. At the same time, substantial similarities exist across ethnic and immigrant groups in other aspects of development and adjustment, such as the quality of their dyadic relationships with their parents and several characteristics of their friendships. As these findings suggest, the question is no longer whether adolescents from different ethnic and immigrant groups differ from one another. Rather, the questions are in what respects do they differ, in what respects are they similar, and what does the answer to these questions tell us about the larger role played by ethnicity and immigration in the fundamental developmental processes of adolescence. As the population of the United States continues to diversify in the coming decades, there will continue to be opportunities for researchers to address these overarching questions.

REFERENCES

Aboud, F. E. (1987). The development of ethnic self-identification and attitudes. In J. S. Phinney & M. J. Rotherman (Eds.), *Children's ethnic socialization: Pluralism and development* (pp. 32–55). Newbury Park, CA: Sage.

Ainsworth, M. D., & Bowlby, J. (1991). An ethological approach to personality development. *American Psychologist, 46,* 333–341.

Ainsworth-Darnell, W. J., & Downey, D. B. (1998). Assessing the oppositional culture explanation for racial/ethnic differences in school performance. *American Sociological Review, 63,* 536–553.

Allen, L., Bat-Chava, Y., Aber, L., & Seidman, E. (2005). Adolescent racial and ethnic identity in context. In G. Downey, J. Eccles, & C. Chatman (Eds.), *Navigating the future: Social identity, coping, and life tasks.* New York: Russell Sage Foundation.

Altschul, I., Oyserman, D., & Bybee, D. (2006). Racial–ethnic identity in mid-adolescence: Content and change as predictors of academic achievement. *Child Development, 77,* 1155–1169.

Andersen, C. S. (1982). The search for school climate: A review of the research. *Review of Educational Research,* 368–420.

Armsden, G. C., & Greenberg, M. T. (1987). The Inventory of Parent and Peer Attachment: Individual differences and their relationship to psychological well-being in adolescence. *Journal of Youth & Adolescence, 16,* 427–454.

Ary, D. V., Duncan, T. E., Duncan, S. C., & Hops, H. (1999). Adolescent problem behavior: The influence of parents and peers. *Behaviour Research & Therapy, 37,* 217–230.

Ashmore, R. D., Deaux, K., & McLaughlin-Volpe, T. (2004). An organizing framework for collective identity: Articulation and significance of multidimensionality. *Psychological Bulletin, 130,* 80–114.

Azmitia, M., Kamprath, N., & Linnet, J. (1998). Intimacy and conflict: The dynamics of boys' and girls' friendships during middle childhood and early adolescence. In L. Meyer, H. Park, M. Grnot-Scheyer, I. Schwartz & B. Harry (Eds.), *Making friends: The influences of culture and development* (pp. 171–189). Baltimore: Paul H. Brookes.

Banks, K. H., Kohn-Wood, L. P. (2007). The influence of racial identity profiles on the relationship between racial discrimination and depressive symptoms. *Journal of Black Psychology, 33*(3), 331–354.

Barenboim, C. (1981). The development of person perception in childhood and adolescence: From behavioral comparisons to psychological constructs to psychological comparisons. *Child Development, 52,* 129–144.

Bartholomew, K., Cobb, R. J., & Poole, J. A. (1997). Adult attachment patterns and social support processes. In G. R. Pierce, B. Lakey, I. Sarason, & B. R. Sarason (Eds.), *The sourcebook of social support and personality* (pp. 359–378). New York: Plenum Press.

Batalova, J., & Terrazas, A. M. (2007). *The recently arrived foreign born in the United States.* Washington, DC: Migration Policy Institute. Available online: www.migrationinformation.org.

Belle, D. (1989). *Children's social networks and social supports.* New York: John Wiley & Sons.

Berg, M., & Medrich, E. A. (1980). Children in four neighborhoods: The physical environment and its effect on play and play patterns. *Environment and Behavior, 12,* 320–348.

Berndt, T. (1989). The nature and significance of children's friendships. In R. Vasta (Ed.), *Annals of Child Development,* vol. 5 (pp. 155–186). Greenwich, CT: JAI Press.

Berry, J. W. (2003). Conceptual approaches to acculturation. In K. M. Chun, B. O. Pamela, & G. Marín (Eds.), *Acculturation: Advances in theory measurement and applied research* (pp. 17–37). Washington, DC: American Psychological Association.

Berry, J. W., Phinney, J. S., Sam, D. L., & Vedder, P. (2006). Immigrant youth: Acculturation, identity, and adaptation. *Applied Psychology: An International Review, 55,* 303–332.

Blyth, D. A., Hill, J. P., & Thiel, K. S. (1982). Early adolescents' significant others: Grade and gender differences in perceived relationships with familial and non-familial adults and young people. *Journal of Youth & Adolescence, 11,* 425–450.

Bronfenbrenner, U. (1977). Toward an experimental ecology of human development. *American Psychologist, 32,* 513–530.

Bronfenbrenner, U. (1979). *The ecology of human development: Experiments by nature and design.* Cambridge, MA: Harvard University Press.

Bronfenbrenner, U. (1989). Ecological systems theory. *Annals of Child Development, 6,* 187–249.

Brooks-Gunn, J., Duncan, G. J., Klebanov, P., & Sealand, N. (1993). Do neighborhoods influence child and adolescent development? *American Journal of Sociology, 99,* 353–395.

Brown, B. B. (1990). Peer groups and peer cultures. In S. S. Feldman & G. R. Elliot (Eds.), *At the threshold: The developing adolescent* (pp. 171–195). Cambridge, MA: Harvard University Press.

Brown, B., Eicher, S. A., & Petrie, S. (1986). The importance of peer group ("crowd") affiliation in adolescence. *Journal of Adolescence, 9,* 73–96.

Brown, B., Mounts, N., Lamborn, S., & Steinberg, L. (1993). Parenting practices and peer group affiliation in adolescence. *Child Development, 69,* 771–791.

Brown, C.S., & Bigler, R.S. (2005). Children's perceptions of discrimination: A developmental model. *Child Development, 76,* 533–553.

Brown, L., Tappan, M., Gilligan, C., Miller, B., & Argyris, D. (1989). Reading for self and moral voice: A method for interpreting narratives of real-life moral conflict and choice. In M. Packer & R. Addison (Eds.), *Entering the circle: Hermeneutic investigation in psychology* (pp. 141–164). Albany: SUNY Press.

Buhrmester, D. (1990). Intimacy of friendship, interpersonal competence, and adjustment during preadolescence and adolescence. *Child Development, 61,* 1101–1111.

Buhrmester, D., & Furman, W. (1987). The development of companionship and intimacy. *Child Development, 58,* 1101–1113.

Bukowski, W. M., Newcomb, A. F., & Hartup, W. W. (1996). The company they keep: Friendship in childhood and adolescence. In New York: Cambridge University Press.

Burton, L. M., Allison, K. W., & Obeidallah, D. (1995). Social context and adolescence: Perspectives on development among inner-city African-American teens. In L. J. Crockett & A. C. Crouter (Eds.), *Pathways through adolescence: Individual development in relation to social contexts* (pp. 119–138). Mahwah, NJ: Lawrence Erlbaum.

Burton, L. M., & Skinner, D. (2005). *Children's kinwork in low income urban and rural families: Ethnographic perspectives on positive development.* Paper presented at the Biennial Meeting of the Society for Research in Child Development, Atlanta, GA.

Bush, K. R., Supple, A. J., & Lash, S. B. (2004). Mexican adolescents' perceptions of parental behaviors and authority as predictors of their self-esteem and sense of familism. *Marriage & Family Review, 36,* 35–65.

Cairns, R. B., Xie, H., & Leung, M. (1998). The popularity of friendship and the neglect of social networks: Toward a new balance. In W. M. Bukowski & A. H. Cillessen (Eds.), *Sociometry then and now: Building on six decades of measuring children's experiences with the peer group: No 80. New directions for child development* (pp. 5–24). San Francisco: Jossey-Bass.

Caldwell, C. H., Kohn-Wood, L. P., Schmeelk-Cone, K. H., Chavous, T. M., Zimmerman, M. A. (2004). Racial discrimination and racial identity as risk or protective factors for violent behaviors in African American young adults. *American Journal of Community Psychology, 33*(1/2), 92–105.

Caplan, N., Choy, M. H., & Whitmore, J. K. (1991). *Children of the boat people: A study of educational success.* Ann Arbor, MI: The University of Michigan Press.

Cauce, A. M. (1986). Social networks and social competence: Exploring the effects of early adolescent friendships. *American Journal of Community Psychology, 14,* 607–628.

Cauce, A. M. (1987). School and peer competence in early adolescence: A test of domain-specific self-perceived competence. *Developmental Psychology, 23,* 287–291.

Cauce, A. M., Mason, C. A., Gonzales, N., Hiraga, Y., & Liu, G. (1996). Social support during adolescence: Methodological and theoretical considerations. In K. Hurrelmann & S. F. Hamilton (Eds.), *Social problems and social contexts in adolescence* (pp. 131–153). Hawthorne, NY: Aldine.

Chao, R. K. (1994). Beyond parental control and authoritarian parenting style: Understanding Chinese parenting through the cultural notion of training. *Child Development, 65,* 1111–1119.

Chao, R. K. (2001). Extending research on consequences of parenting style for Chinese American and European Americans. *Child Development, 72,* 1832–1843.

Chao, R., & Tseng, V. (2002). Parenting of Asians. In M. H. Bornstein (Ed.), *Handbook of parenting, vol. 4: Social conditions and applied parenting* (pp. 59–93). Mahwah, NJ: Lawrence Erlbaum.

Chavous, T. M., Bernat, D. H., Schmeelk-Cone, K., Caldwell, C. H., Kohn-Wood, L., & Zimmerman, M. A. (2003). Racial identity and academic attainment among African American adolescents. *Child Development, 74,* 1076–1090.

Chu, J. (2004). A relational perspective on adolescent boys' identity development. In N. Way & J. Chu (Eds), Adolescent boys: Exploring diverse cultures of boyhood. New York: New York University Press.

Cicchetti, D., Lynch, M., Shonk, S., & Manly, J. T. (1992). An organizational perspective on peer relations in maltreated children. In R. D. Parke & G. W. Ladd (Eds.), *Family–peer relationship: Modes of linkage* (pp. 345–383). Hillsdale, NJ: Lawrence Erlbaum.

Clark, M. L., & Ayers, M. (1991). Friendship similarity during early adolescence: Gender and racial patterns. *Journal of Psychology, 126,* 393–405.

Collins, A. W., & Laursen, B. (1992). Conflicts and relationships in adolescence. In C. Shantz & W. W. Hartup (Eds.), *Conflict in child and adolescent development* (pp. 216–241). New York: Cambridge University Press.

Cooper, C. (1999). Multiple selves, multiple worlds: Cultural perspectives on individuality and connectedness in adolescent development. In A. Masten (Ed.), *Cultural processes in child development: The Minnesota symposia on child psychology,* vol. 29 (pp. 25–57).

Cote, J. E. (1996). Sociological perspectives on identity formation: The culture-identity link and identity capital. *Journal of Adolescence, 19,* 417–432.

Crocker, J., & Major, B. (1989). Social stigma and self-esteem: The self protective properties of stigma. *Psychological Review, 96,* 608–630.

Crockett, L. J., Losoff, M., & Petersen, L. (1984). Perceptions of the peer group and friendship in early adolescence. *Journal of Early Adolescence, 4,* 155–181.

Crocker, J., Luhtanen, R., Blaine, B., & Broadnax, S. (1994). Collective self esteem and psyhchological well-being among White, Black, and Asian college students. *Personality and Social Psychology Bulletin, 20,* 503–513.

Crosnoe, R., Cavanagh, S., & Elder, G. H. (2003). Adolescent friendships as academic resources: The intersection of social relationships, social structure, and institutional context. *Sociological Perspectives, 46,* 331–352.

Cross, W. E., Jr.. (1971). The Negro-to-Black conversion experience. *Black World, 20,* 13–27.

Cross, W. E., Jr. (1991). *Shades of black: Diversity in African-American Identity.* Phildelphia: Temple University Press.

Cross, W. E., Jr., & Fhagen-Smith, P. E. (2001). Patterns of African American identity development: A life span perspective. In C. L. Wijeyesinghe & B. W. Jackson (Eds.), *New perspectives on racial identity development: A theoretical and practical anthology* (pp. 243–270). New York: New York University Press.

Csikszentmihalyi, M., & Larson, R. (1984). *Being adolescent: Conflict and growth in the teenage years.* New York: Basic Books.

Deater-Deckard, K., Dodge, K. A., Bates, J. E., & Pettit, G. S. (1996). Physical discipline among African American and European American mothers: Links to children's externalizing behaviors. *Developmental Psychology, 32,* 1065–1072.

Dornbusch, S. M., Glasgow, K. L., & Lin, I. C. (1996). The social structure of schooling. *Annual Review of Psychology, 47,* 401–429.

Dornbusch, S. M., Ritter, P. L., Leiderman, P. H., Roberts, D. F., & Fraleigh, M. J. (1987). The relation of parenting style to adolescent school performance. *Child Development, 58,* 1244–1257.

Downey, G., Chatman, C., London, B., Cross, W., Hughes, D., Moje, E., et al. (2005). Navigating self and context in a diverse nation: How social identities matter. In G. Downey, J. Eccles & C. Chatman (Eds.), *Navigating the future: Social identity, coping, and life tasks.* New York: Russell Sage Foundation.

DuBois, D. L., & Hirsch, B. J. (1990). School and neighborhood friendship patterns of blacks and whites in early adolescence. *Child Development, 61,* 524–536.

Eder, D. (1985). The cycle of popularity: Interpersonal relations among female adolescents. *Sociology of Education, 58,* 154–165.

Eder, D., Evans, C. C., & Parker, S. (1995). *School talk: Gender and adolescent culture.* New Brunswick, NJ: Rutgers University Press.

Elias, M. J., & Dilworth, J. E. (2003). Ecological/developmental theory, context-based best practice, and school-based action research: cornerstones of school psychology training and policy. *Journal of School Psychology, 41,* 293–297.

Entwisle, D. R., & Astone, N. M. (1994). Some practical guidelines for measuring youth's race/ethnicity and socioeconomic status. *Child Development, 65,* 1521–1540.

Epstein, J. L. (1989). The selection of friends: Changes across the grades in different school environments. In T. J. Berndt & G. W. Ladd (Eds.), *Peer relationships in child development* (pp. 158–187). New York: John Wiley & Sons.

Epstein, J. L., & Karweit, N. (1983). *Friends in school: Patterns of selection and influence in secondary schools.* New York: Academic Press.

Erikson, E. H. (1968). *Identity: Youth and crisis*. Oxford, UK: Norton & Co.

Espiritu, Y. L. (1992). *Asian American panethnicity: bridging institutions and identities*. Philadelphia: Temple University Press.

Ethier, K., & Deaux, K. (1990). Hispanics in the ivy: Assessing identity and perceived threat. *Sex Roles, 22,* 427–440.

Ethier, K. A., & Deaux, K. (1994). Negotiating social identity when contexts change: Maintaining identification and responding to threat. *Journal of Personality and Social Psychology, 67,* 243–251.

Farmer, E. M., & Rodkin, P. C. (1996). Antisocial and prosocial correlates of classroom positions: The social network centrality perspective. *Social Development, 5,* 174–188.

Feldman, S. S., & Quatman, T. (1988). Factors influencing age expectations for adolescent autonomy: A study of early adolescents and parents. *Journal of Early Adolescence, 8,* 325–343.

Feldman, S. S., & Rosenthal, D.A. (1990). The acculturation of autonomy expectations in Chinese high schools residing in two Western nations. *International Journal of Psychology, 25,* 259–281.

Ferguson, R. (2007). *Toward excellence with equity: An emerging vision for closing the achievement gap*. Cambridge, MA: Harvard Education Press.

Fisher, C. B., Wallace, S. A., & Fenton, R. E. (2001). Discrimination distress during adolescence. *Journal of Youth and Adolescence, 29*(6), 679–695.

Fitzgerald, H. E., Lester, B. M., & Zuckerman, B. S. (1995). *Children of poverty: Research, health, and policy issues*. New York: Garland.

French, S. E., Seidman, E., Allen, L., & Aber, L. (2000). Racial/ethnic identity, congruence with the social context and the transition to high school. *Journal of Adolescent Research, 15*(5), 587–602.

French, S. E., Seidman, E., Allen, L., & Aber, L. (2006). The development of ethnic identity during adolescence. *Developmental Psychology, 42,* 1–10.

Fuligni, A. J. (1997). The academic achievement of adolescents from immigrant families: The roles of family background, attitudes, and behavior. *Child Development, 68,* 261–273.

Fuligni, A. J. (1998). Parental authority, adolescent autonomy, and parent-adolescent relationships: A study of adolescents from Mexican, Chinese, Filipino, and European backgrounds. *Developmental Psychology, 34,* 782–792.

Fuligni, A. J. (1998). The adjustment of children from immigrant families. *Current Directions in Psychological Science, 7,* 99–103.

Fuligni, A. J. (2001). Family obligation and the academic motivation of adolescents from Asian and Latin American, and European backgrounds. In A. Fuligni (Ed.), *Family obligation and assistance during adolescence: Contextual variations and developmental implications* (New Directions in Child and Adolescent Development Monograph) (pp. 61–76). San Francisco: Jossey-Bass.

Fuligni, A. J., & Eccles, J. S. (1993). Perceived parent–child relationships and early adolescents' orientation toward peers. *Developmental Psychology, 29,* 622–632.

Fuligni, A.J., & Flook, L. (2005) A social identity approach to ethnic differences in family relationships during adolescence. In R. Kail (Ed.), *Advances in child development and behavior* (pp. 125–152). New York: Academic Press.

Fuligni, A.J., & Pedersen, S. (2002). Family obligation and the transition to young adulthood. *Developmental Psychology, 38,* 856–868.

Fuligni, A. J., Rivera, W., & Leininger, A. (2007). Family identity and the educational progress of adolescents from Asian and Latin American backgrounds. In A. J. Fuligni (Ed.), *Contesting stereotypes and creating identities: Social categories, social identities, and educational participation* (pp. 239–264). New York: Russell Sage Foundation Press.

Fuligni, A. J., Tseng, V., & Lam, M. (1999). Attitudes toward family obligations among American adolescents from Asian, Latin American, and European backgrounds. *Child Development, 70,* 1030–1044.

Fuligni, A. J., & Witkow, M. (2004). The postsecondary educational progress of youth from immigrant families. *Journal of Research on Adolescence, 14,* 159–183.

Fuligni, A., Witkow, M., & Garcia, C. (2005). Ethnic identity and the academic adjustment of adolescents from Mexican, Chinese, and European backgrounds. *Developmental Psychology, 41,* 799–811.

Fuligni, A. J., & Yoshikawa, H. (2003). Socioeconomic resources, parenting, and child development among immigrant families. In M. Bornstein & R. Bradley (Ed.), *Socioeconomic status, parenting, and child development* (pp. 107–124). Mahwah, NJ: Lawrence Erlbaum.

Fuligni, A. J., & Yoshikawa, H. (2004). Investments in children among immigrant families. In A. Kalil & T. DeLiere (Eds.), *Family investments in children's potential*. Mahwah, NJ: Lawrence Erlbaum.

Furman, W. (1996). The measurement of friendship perceptions: Conceptual and methodological issues. In W. M. Bukowski & F. Newcomb (Eds.), *The company they keep: Friendships in Childhood and adolescence* (pp. 41–65). New York: Cambridge University Press.

Furman, W., & Buhrmester, D. (1985). Children's perceptions of the personal relationships in their social networks. *Developmental Psychology, 21,* 1016–1024.

Furman, W., & Burhmester, D. (1992). Age and sex differences in perceptions of networks of personal relationships. *Child Development, 65,* 103–115.

Furstenberg, F., Cook, T., Eccles, J., Elder, G.H., Sameroff, A.J. (1999). *Managing to make it: Urban families and adolescent success*. Chicago, IL: University of Chicago Press.

Galletta, A., & Cross, Jr., W.E. (2007). Past as present, present as past: Historicizing black education and interrogating "integration." In A. Fuligni (Ed.), *Contesting stereotypes and creating identities: Social categories, social identities, and educational participation*. New York: Russell Sage Foundation Press.

García Coll, C., Akerman, A., & Cicchetti, D. (2000). Cultural differences on developmental processes and outcomes: Implications for the study of development and psychopathology. *Development and Psychopathology, 12,* 333–356.

García Coll, C., Lamberty, G., Jenkins, R., McAdoo, H. P., Crnic, K., Wasik, B. H., et al. (1996). An integrative model for the study of developmental competencies in minority children. *Child Development, 67,* 1891–1914.

Gavin, L. A., & Furman, W. (1989). Age difference in adolescents' perceptions of their peer groups. *Developmental Psychology, 25,* 827–834.

Germán, M, Gonzales, N.A. & Dumka, L.E. (in press). Familism values as a protective factor for Mexican-origin adolescents exposed to deviant peers. *Journal of Community Psychology*.

Gest, S. D., Graham-Bermann, S. A., & Hartup, W. (2001). Peer experience: Common and unique features of number of friendships, social network centrality, and sociometric status. *Social Development, 10,* 23–40.

Gibson, M. A., & Bhachu, P. K. (1991). The dynamics of educational decision making: A comparative study of Sikhs in Britain and the United States. In M. A. Gibson & J. U. Ogbu (Eds.), *Minority status and schooling: A comparative study of immigrant and involuntary minorities*. (pp. 63–96). New York: Garland.

Gifford-Smith, M. E., & Brownell, C. A. (2003). Childhood peer relationships: social acceptance, friendships, and peer networks. *Journal of School Psychology, 41,* 235–284.

Gil, A. G., Wagner, E. F., & Vega, W. A. (2000). Acculturation, familism and alcohol use among Latino adolescent males: Longitudinal relations. *Journal of Community Psychology, 28,* 443–458.

Gingold, R. (2003). *The influence of parenting beliefs and messages about friendships on adolescent friendships*. Unpublished dissertation completed at Yeshiva University.

Glick, J. E., & White, M. J. (2004). Post-secondary school participation of immigrant and native youth: The role of familial resources and educational expectations. *Social Science Research, 33,* 272–299.

González, A. G., Umaña-Taylor, A. J., & Bámaca, M. Y. (2006). Familial ethnic socialization among adolescents of Latino and European descent: Do Latina mothers exert the most influence? *Journal of Family Issues, 27,* 184–207.

Good, C., Dweck, C.S., & Aronson, J. (2007). Social identity, stereotype threat, and self-theories. In A. Fuligni (Ed.), *Contesting stereotypes and creating identities: Social categories, social identities, and educational participation.* New York: Russell Sage Foundation Press.

Goodstein, R., & Ponterotto, J. G. (1997). Racial and ethnic identity: Their relationship and their contribution to self-esteem. *The Journal of Black Psychology, 23,* 275–292.

Graham, S. (1992). "Most of the subjects were White and middle class": Trends in published research on African Americans in selected APA journals. *American Psychologist, 47,* 629–639.

Graham, S. (1994). Motivation in African Americans. *Review of Educational Research, 64,* 55–117.

Greenberg, M. T., Siegel, J. M., & Leitch, C. J. (1983). The nature and importance of attachment relationships to parents and peers during adolescence. *Journal of Youth and Adolescence, 12,* 373–385.

Greenberger, E., & Chen, C. (1996). Perceived family relationships and depressed mood in early and late adolescence: A comparison of European and Asian Americans. *Developmental Psychology, 32,* 707–716.

Greene, M. L., Way, N., & Pahl, K. (2006). Trajectories of perceived adult and peer discrimination among Black, Latino, and Asian American adolescents: Patterns and psychological correlates. *Developmental Psychology, 42,* 218–238.

Grobel, J., & Scharzer, R. (1982). Social comparison, expectations, and emotional reactions in the classroom. *School Psychology International, 3,* 49–56.

Gunnoe, M. L., & Mariner, C. L. (1997). Toward a developmental-contextual model of the effects of parental spanking on children's aggression. *Archives of Pediatrics and Adolescent Medicine, 151,* 768–775.

Hagan, J. W., & Conley, A. C. (1994). Ethnicity and race of children studied in Child Development, 1980–1993. *Society for Research in Child Development Newsletter,* 6–7.

Halperin, S. (Ed.) (1998). *The forgotten half revisited: American youth and young families, 1988–2008.* Washington, DC: American Youth Policy Forum, Inc.

Hamm, J. V. (1994). *Similarity in the face of diversity? African American, Asian American, European-American, and Hispanic-American adolescents' best friendships in ethnically diverse high school.* Paper presented at the biennial meeting of the Society for Research on Adolescence, San Diego, CA.

Hamm, J. V. (1998). Negotiating the maze: Adolescents' cross-ethnic peer relations in ethnically diverse schools. In L. H. Meyer, H. S. Park, M. Grenot-Scheyer, I. S. Schwartz, & B. Harry (Eds.), *Making friends: The influences of culture and development* (pp. 243–261). Baltimore: Paul H. Brookes.

Hamm, J. V. (2000). Do birds of a feather flock together? The variable bases for African American, Asian American, and European American adolescents' selection of similar friends. *Developmental Psychology, 36,* 209–219.

Harrison, A. O., Wilson, M. N., Pine, C. J., Chan, S. Q., & Buriel, R. (1990). Family ecologies of ethnic minority children. *Child Development, 61,* 347–362.

Harter, S. (1990). Causes, correlates, and the functional role of global self-worth: A life-span perspective. In R. J. Sternberg & J. Kolligan (Eds.), *Competence considered* (pp. 67–97). New Haven, CT: Yale University Press.

Hartup, W. W. (1996). The company they keep: Friendships and their developmental significance. *Child Development, 67,* 1–13.

Hawley, P. H. (2002). Social dominance and prosocial and coercive strategies of resource control in preschoolers. *International Journal of Behavioral Development, 26,* 167–176.

Haynes, N., Emmons, C., & Comer, J. P. (1993). *Elementary and middle-school climate survey.* Unpublished manuscript. Yale University Child Study Center.

Helms, J. E. (1999). Another meta-analysis of the White Racial Identity Attitude Scale's cronbach alphas: Implications for validity. *Measurement and Evaluation in Counseling and Development, 32,* 122–137.

Hernandez, D. (2004). Demographic change and the life circumstances of immigrant families. *The Future of Children: Children from Immigrant Families, 14*(2), 17–47.

Hinde, R. A. (1987). *Individuals, relationships, and culture.* Cambridge: Cambridge University Press.

Hirsch, B. J., & DuBois, D. L. (1990). The school-nonschool ecology of early adolescent friendships. In D. Belle (Ed.), *Children's social networks and social supports* (pp. 260–274). New York: John Wiley & Sons.

Hirsch, B., & Rapkin, B. (1987). The transition to junior high school: A longitudinal study of self-esteem, psychological symptomatology, school life, and social support. *Child Development, 58,* 1235–1243.

Ho, D. (1996). Filial piety and its psychological consequences. In M. H. Bond (Ed.), *The handbook of Chinese psychology* (pp. 155–165). Hong Kong: Oxford University Press.

Hoge, D. R., Smit, E. K., & Hanson, S. L. (1990). School experiences predicting changes in self-esteem of sixth- and seventh-grade students. *Journal of Educational Psychology, 82,* 117–127.

Hogg, M. A. (2003). Social identity. In M. R. Leary & J. P. Tangney (Eds.), *Handbook of self and identity* (pp. 462–479). New York: Guilford Press.

Homel, R., & Burns, A. (1989). Environmental quality and the well-being of children. *Social Indicators Research, 21,* 133–158.

Hughes, D. (2003). Correlates of African American and Latino parents' messages to children about ethnicity and race: A comparative study of racial socialization. *American Journal of Community Psychology, 31,* 15–33.

Hughes, D., & Chen, L. (1997). When and what parents tell children about race: An examination of race-related socialization among African American families. *Applied Developmental Science, 1,* 200–214.

Hughes, D., Rivas, D., Foust, M., Hagelskamp, C., Gersick, S., & Way, N. (2008). How to catch a moonbeam: A mixed-methods approach to understanding ethnic socialization in ethnically diverse families. In S. Quintana & C. McKnown (Eds.), *Handbook of race, racism, and child development* (pp. 226–277). Hoboken, NJ: John Wiley & Sons.

Hughes, D., Rodriguez, J., Smith, E. P., Johnson, D., Stevenson, H. C., & Spicer, P. (2006). Parents' ethnic–racial socialization: A review of research and directions for future study. *Developmental Psychology, 42,* 747–770.

Huynh, V., & Fuligni, A. J. (in press). Ethnic socialization and the academic adjustment of adolescents from Mexican, Chinese, and European backgrounds. *Developmental Psychology.*

Jencks, C., & Mayer, S. E. (1990). The social consequences of growing up in a poor neighborhood. In L. E. Lynn & M. McGeary (Eds.), *Inner city poverty in the United States.* Washington, DC: National Academy Press.

Joe, J. R., & Malach, R. S. (1998). Families with native American roots. In E. W. Lynch & M. J. Hanson (Eds.), *Developing cross-cultural competence* (2nd ed., pp. 127–158). Baltimore, MD: Brookes.

Jones, D. C., Costin, S. E., & Ricard, R. J. (1994, February). *Ethnic and sex differences in best friendship characteristics among African American, Mexican American, and European American adolescents.* Paper presented at the Society for Research on Adolescence, San Diego, CA.

Jurkovic, G. J. (1997). *Lost childhoods: The plight of the parentified child.* New York: Bruner/Mazel.

Kagitcibasi, C. (1990). Family and socialization in cross-cultural perspective: a model of change. In J. Berman (Ed.), *Cross-cultural perspectives: The Nebraska symposium on motivation, 1989* (pp. 135–200) Lincoln: University of Nebraska Press.

Kao, G., & Tienda, M. (1995). Optimism and achievement: The educational performance of immigrant youth. *Social Science Quarterly, 76,* 1–19.

Katz, S. R. (1999). Teaching in tensions: Latino immigrant youth, their teachers, and the structure of schooling. *Teachers College Record, 100,* 809–840.

Kaufman, P., Chen, X., Choy, S.P., et al. (1998). *Indicators of school crime and safety: 1998.* NCES 98-251/NCJ-172215. Washington, DC: U.S. Departments of Education and Justice.

Kerns, K. A. (1994). A longitudinal examination of links between mother-child attachments and children's friendships in early childhood. *Journal of Social and Personal Relationships, 11,* 379–381.

Kerns, K. A., & Stevens, A. C. (1996). Parent-child attachment in late adolescence: Links to social relations and personality. *Journal of Youth & Adolescence, 25,* 323–342.

Kiang, L., Harter, S., & Whitesell, N. R. (2007). Relational expression of ethnic identity in Chinese Americans. *Journal of Social and Personal Relationships, 24*(2), 277–296.

Kiang, L., Yip, T., Gonzales-Backen, M., Witkow, M., & Fuligni, A. J. (2006). Ethnic identity and the daily psychological well-being of adolescents from Mexican and Chinese backgrounds. *Child Development, 77,* 1338–1350.

Kim-Ju, G. M., & Liem, R. (2003). Ethnic self-awareness as a function of ethnic group status, group composition, and ethnic identity orientation. *Cultural Diversity and Ethnic Minority Psychology, 9,* 289–302.

Knight, G. P., Bernal, M. E., Garza, C. A., Cota, M. K., & Ocampo, K. A. (1993). Family socialization and the ethnic identity of Mexican-American children. *Journal of Cross-Cultural Psychology, 24,* 99–114.

Kohn, M. L., & Schooler, C. (1978). The reciprocal effects of the substantive complexity of work and intellectual flexibility: A longitudinal assessment. *American Journal of Sociology, 84,* 24–52.

Kuperminc, G., Leadbeater, B. J., Emmons, C., & Blatt, S. J. (1997). Perceived school climate and problem behaviors in middle-school students: The protective function of a positive educational environment. *Journal of Applied Developmental Science, 1,* 76–88.

Ladd, G. W. (1990). Having friends, Keeping friends, making friends, and being liked by peers in the classroom: Predictors of children's early school adjustment? *Child Development, 61,* 1081–1100.

Lansford, J. E., Deater-Deckard, K., Dodge, K. A., Bates, J. E., & Pettit, G.S. (2004). Ethnic differences in the link between physical discipline and later adolescent externalizing behaviors. *Journal of Child Psychology and Psychiatry, 45,* 801–812.

Lansford, J. E., Dodge, K. A., Pettit, G. S., Bates, J. E., Crozier, J., & Kaplow, J. (2002). A 12-year prospective study of the long-term effects of early child physical maltreatment on psychological, behavioral, and academic problems in adolescence. *Archives of Pediatrics and Adolescent Medicine, 156,* 824–830.

Larsen, L. J. (2004). *The foreign-born population in the United States: 2003.* Current Population Reports, P20-551, U.S. Census Bureau, Washington, D.C.

Lee, R. (2003). Do ethnic identity and other-group orientation protect against discrimination for Asian Americans? *Journal of Counseling Psychology, 50*(2), 133–141.

Lee, R. M. R., & Liu, H.-T. T. (2001). Coping with intergenerational family conflict: Comparison of Asian American, Hispanic, and European American college students. *Journal of Counseling Psychology, 48,* 410–419.

Lee, R. M., Su, J., & Yoshida, E. (2005). Coping with intergenerational family conflict among Asian American collage students. *Journal of Counseling Psychology, 52,* 389–399.

Lee, R. M., & Yoo, H. C. (2004). Structure and measurement of ethnic identity for Asian American college students. *Journal of Counseling Psychology, 51,* 263–269.

Lee, S. J. (1999). Are you Chinese or what? Ethnic identity among Asian Americans. In R. H. Sheets & E. R. Hollins (Eds.), *Racial and ethnic identity in school practices: Aspects of human development* (pp. 107–121). Mahwah, NJ: Lawrence Erlbaum.

Levine, R. (1974). Parental goals: A cross-cultural view. *Teachers College Record, 76,* 226–239.

Lewin, K. (1951). *Field theory in social science. Selected theoretical papers.* Westport, CT.: Greenwood Press.

London, B., Downey, G., Bolger, N., & Velilla, E. (2005). A framework for studying social identity and coping with daily stress during the transition to college. In G. Downey, J. Eccles, & C. Chatman (Eds.), *Navigating the future: Social identity, coping, and life tasks.* New York: Russell Sage Foundation.

Luthar, S. S., & McMahon, T. (1996). Peer reputation among inner city adolescents: Structure and correlates. *Journal of Research on Adolescence, 6,* 581–603.

Lysne, M., Levy, G. D. (1997). Differences in ethnic identity in Native American adolescents as a function of school context. *Journal of Adolescent Research, 12*(3), 372–388.

Mahalingham, R. (2007). Essentialism and cultural narratives: A social marginality perspective. In A. Fuligni (Ed.), *Contesting stereotypes and creating identities: Social categories, social identities, and educational participation.* New York: Russell Sage Foundation Press.

Marcia, J. E. (1966). Development and validation of ego-identity status. *Journal of Personality and Social Psychology, 3,* 551–558.

Marsiglia, F. F., Kulis, S., & Hecht, M. (2001). Ethnic labels and ethnic identity as predictors of drug use among middle school students in the southwest. *Journal of Research on Adolescence, 11,* 21–48.

Masuoka, N. (2006). Together they become one: Examining the predictors of panethnic group consciousness among Asian Americans and Latinos. *Social Science Quarterly, 87*(5), 993–1011.

McCarthy, J. D., & Hoge, D. R. (1982). Analysis of age effects in longitudinal studies of adolescent self-esteem. *Developmental Psychology, 18,* 372–379.

McKown, C., & Weinstein, R. S. (2003). The development and consequences of stereotype consciousness in middle childhood. *Child Development, 74,* 498–515.

McLoyd, V. C. (1998). Changing demographics in this American population: Implications for research on minority children and adolescents. In V. C. McLoyd & L. Steinberg (Eds.), *Studying minority adolescents: Conceptual, methodological, and theoretical issues* (pp. 3–28). Mahwah, NJ: Lawrence Erlbaum.

McLoyd, V. C., & Ceballo, R. (1998). Conceptualizing and assessing economic context: Issues in the study of race and child development. In V. C. McLoyd & L. Steinberg (Eds.), *Studying minority adolescents: Conceptual, methodological, and theoretical issues* (pp. 251–278). Mahwah, NJ: Lawrence Erlbaum.

Mendoza-Denton, R., Downey, G., Purdie, V. J., Davis, A., & Pietrzak, J. (2002). Sensitivity to status-based rejection: Implications for African American students' college experience. *Journal of Personality & Social Psychology, 83,* 896–918.

Miles, M. B., & Huberman, A. M. (1995). *Qualitative data analysis: An expanded sourcebook of new methods* (2nd ed.). Thousand Oaks, CA: Sage.

Minuchin, P. P., & Shapiro, E. K. (1983). The school as a context for social development. In P. H. Mussen (Ed.), *Handbook of child psychology,* vol. 4: *Socialization, personality, and social development* (pp. 197–275). New York: John Wiley & Sons.

Mischel, W. A. (1966). A social learning view of sex differences in behavior. In E. E. Maccoby (Ed.), *The development of sex differences.* Stanford, CA: Stanford.

Montemayor, R., & Van Komen, R. (1980). Age segregation of adolescents in and out of school. *Journal of Youth and Adolescence, 9,* 371–381.

Mossakowski, K. N. (2003). Coping with perceived discrimination: does ethnic identity protect mental health? *Journal of Health and Social Behavior, 44*(3), 318–331.

Mott, F. L. (1994). Sons, daughters, and fathers' absence: Differentials in father-leaving probabilities and in home environments. *Journal of Family Issues, 15,* 97–128.

Mounts, N. S. (2001). Young adolescents' perceptions of parental management of peer relationships. *Journal of Early Adolescence, 21,* 92–122.

Mounts, N. S. (2002). Parental management of adolescent peer relationships in context: The role of parenting style. *Journal of Family Psychology, 16,* 58–69.

Mounts, N. S. (2004). Adolescents' perceptions of parental management of peer relationships in an ethnically diverse sample. *Journal of Adolescent Research, 19,* 428–445.

Nagel, J. (1994). Constructing ethnicity: Creating and recreating ethnic identity and culture. *Social Problems, 41,* 152–176.

National Center for Education Statistics. (2003a). *Condition of education: 2003* (Indicator 29). Washington, DC: U.S. Department of Education.

National Center for Education Statistics. (2003b). *Digest of education statistics: 2002.* NCES Number 2003-060. Washington, DC: U.S. Department of Education.

Newcomb, A., & Bagwell, C. L. (1996). The developmental significance of children's friendship relations. In W. Bukowski, A. Newcomb & W. Hartup (Eds.), *The company they keep: Friendship in childhood and adolescence* (pp. 289–321). New York: Cambridge University Press.

Oakes, J., Selvin, M. J., Karoly, L., & Guiton, G. (1991). *Educational matchmaking: Toward a better understanding of curriculum and tracking decisions.* Santa Monica, CA: RAND Corporation.

O'Brian, S. F., & Bierman, K. L. (1988). Conceptions and perceived influence of peer groups: Interviews with preadolescents and adolescents. *Child Development, 59,* 1360–1365.

O'Connor, C., DeLuca Fernandez, S., & Girard, B. (2007). The meaning of "Blackness": How Black students differentially align race and achievement across time and space. In A. Fuligni (Ed.), *Contesting stereotypes and creating identities: Social categories, social identities, and educational participation.* New York: Russell Sage Foundation Press.

Ogbu, J. U. (1987). Variability in minority school performance: A problem in search of an explanation. *Anthropology and Education Quarterly, 18,* 312–334.

Ontai-Grzebik, L. L., Raffaelli, M. (2004). Individual and social influences on ethnic identity among Latino young adults. *Journal of Adolescent Research, 19*(5), 559–575.

Oyserman, D., Harrison, K., & Bybee, D. (2001). Can racial identity be promotive of academic efficacy? *International Journal of Behavioral Development, 25,* 379–385.

Pahl, K., & Way, N. (2006). Longitudinal trajectories of ethnic identity among urban Black and Latino adolescents. *Child Development, 77,* 1403–1415.

Parham, T. A. (1989). Cycles of psychological Nigrescence. *The Counseling Psychologist, 17,* 187–226.

Parke, R. D., McDowell, D. J., Kim, M., Killian, C., Dennis, J., Flyr, M. L., et al. (2002). Fathers' contributions to children's peer relationships. In C. S. Tamis-LeMonda & N. Cabrera (Eds.), *Handbook of father involvement: Multidisciplinary perspectives* (pp. 141–168). Mahwah, NJ: Lawrence Erlbaum.

Patterson, G. R., Dishion, T. J., & Yoerger, K. L. (2000). Adolescent growth in new forms of problem behavior: Macro- and micro-peer dynamics. *Prevention Science, 1,* 3–13.

Patterson, G. R., & Stouthamer-Loeber, M. (1984). The correlation of family management practices and delinquency. *Child Development, 55,* 1299–1307.

Perreira, K., Harris, K. M., & Lee, D. (2006). Making it in America: High school completion among immigrant youth. *Demography, 43,* 511–536.

Phelan, P., Davidson, A. L., & Cao, H. T. (1991). Students' multiple worlds: Negotiating the boundaries of family, peer, and school cultures. *Anthropology and Education Quarterly, 22,* 224–250.

Phelan, P., Yu, H. C., & Davidson, A. L. (1994). Navigating the psychosocial pressure of adolescence: The voices and experiences of high school youth. *American Educational Research Journal, 31,* 415–447.

Phinney, J. S. (1989). Stages of ethnic identity development in minority group adolescents. *Journal of Early Adolescence, 9*(1–2), 34–49.

Phinney, J. S. (1990). Ethnic identity in adolescents and adults: Review of research. *Psychological Bulletin, 108,* 499–514.

Phinney, J. S. (1991). Ethnic identity and self-esteem: A review and integration. *Hispanic Journal of Behavioral Sciences, 13,* 193–208.

Phinney, J. S. (2006). Ethnic identity exploration in emerging adulthood. In J. J. Arnett & J. L. Tanner (Eds.), *Emerging adults in America: Coming of age in the 21st century* (pp. 117–134). Washington, DC: American Psychological Association.

Phinney, J. S., & Alipuria, L. (1990). Ethnic identity in college students from four ethnic groups. *Journal of Adolescence, 13,* 171–183.

Phinney, J. S., Cantu, C. L., Kurtz, D. A. (1997). Ethnic and American identity as predictors of self-esteem among African American, Latino, and White adolescents. *Journal of Youth and Adolescence, 26*(2), 165–185.

Phinney, J. S., & Chavira, V. (1992). Ethnic identity and self-esteem: An exploratory longitudinal study. *Journal of Adolescence, 15,* 271–281.

Phinney, J. S., & Chavira, V. (1995). Parental ethnic socialization and adolescent coping with problems related to ethnicity. *Journal of Research on Adolescence, 5,* 31–54.

Phinney, J. S., Chavira, V., & Williamson, L. (1992). Acculturation attitudes and self-esteem among high school and college students. *Youth & Society, 23,* 299–312.

Phinney, J. S., DuPont, S., Espinosa, C., Revill, J., & Sanders, K. (1994). Ethnic identity and American identification among ethnic minority youth. In A. Bouvy, R. van de Vijver, J.R., Fons P. Boski & P. G. Schmitz (Eds.), *International congress of the international association for cross-cultural psychology* (pp. 167–183). Lisse, Netherlands: Swets & Zeitlinger Publishers.

Phinney, J. S., Ferguson, D. L., Tate, J. D. (1997). Intergroup Attitudes among ethnic minority adolescents: A causal model. *Child Development, 68*(5), 955–969.

Phinney, J. S., Horenczyk, G., Liebkind, K., & Vedder, P. (2001). Ethnic identity, immigration, and well-being: An interactional perspective. *The Journal of Social Issues, 57,* 493–510.

Phinney, J. S., & Ong, A. D. (2007). Conceptualization and measurement of ethnic identity: Current status and future directions. *Journal of Counseling Psychology, 54*(3), 271–281.

Phinney, J. S., Romero, I., Nava, M., & Huang, D. (2001). The role of language, parents, and peers in ethnic identity among adolescents in immigrant families. *Journal of Youth and Adolescence, 30,* 135–153.

Portes, A., & Rumbaut, R. G. (2001). *Legacies: The story of the second generation.* Berkeley: University of California Press.

Procidano, M. (1992). The nature of perceived social support: Findings of meta-analytic studies. In C. D. Spielberger & J. N. Butler (Eds.), *Advances in personality assessment* vol. 9 (pp. 1–26). Hillsdale, NJ: Lawrence Erlbaum.

Procidano, M., & Heller, K. (1983). Measure of perceived social support from friends and family. *American Journal of Psychology, 11,* 1–24.

Procidano, M., & Smith, W. W. (1997). Assessing perceived social support: The importance of context. In G. R. Pierce, B. Lakey, I. Sarason & B. R. Sarason (Eds.), *The sourcebook of social support and personality* (pp. 93–106). New York: Plenum Press.

Qin, D., & Way, N. (in press). The peer context for Chinese American immigrant youth. In H. Yoshikawa & N. Way (Eds), *Contexts of development for immigrant families.* New Directions for Child and Adolescent Development Series. San Francisco: Jossey-Bass.

Qin, D. B., Way, N., & Mukherjee, P. (2008). The other side of the model minority story: The familial and peer challenges faced by Chinese American adolescents. *Youth and Society, 39,* 480–506.

Quintana, S. M. (2007). Racial and ethnic identity: Developmental perspectives and research. *Journal of Counseling Psychology, 54*, 259–270.

Ramirez, J. R., Crano, W. D., Quist, R., Burgoon, M., Alvaro, E. M., & Grandpre, J. (2004). Acculturation, familism, parental monitoring, and knowledge as predictors of marijuana and inhalant use in adolescents. *Psychology of Addictive Behaviors, 18,* 3–11.

Raymond, D. (1994). Homophobia, identity, and the meanings of desire: Reflections on the culture construction of gay and lesbian adolescent sexuality. In J. Irvine (Ed.), *Sexual cultures and the construction of adolescent identities* (pp. 115–150). Philadelphia: Temple University Press.

Reyes, G. M., Goyette, M. K., & Bishop, J. A. (1996, March). *Friendship, peer acceptance, and social behaviors: Contributors to self-esteem.* Paper presented at the Society for Research on Adolescence, Boston, MA.

Rice, K., & Mulkeen, P. (1995). Relationships with parents and peers: A longitudinal study of adolescent intimacy. *Journal of Adolescent Research, 10,* 338–357.

Rivas-Drake, D., Hughes, D., & Way, N. (2008). A closer look at peer discrimination, ethnic identity, and psychological well-being among urban Chinese American sixth graders. *Journal of Youth and Adolescence, 37,* 12–21.

Robinson, N. S. (1995). Evaluating the nature of received support and its relation to perceived self-worth in adolescents. *Journal of Research on Adolescence, 5,* 253–280.

Rodkin, P. C., Farmer, T. W., Pearl, R., & Van Acker, R. (2000). Heterogeneity of popular boys: Antisocial and prosocial configurations. *Developmental Psychology, 36,* 14–24.

Roeser, R. W., & Eccles, J. S. (1998). Adolescents' perceptions of middle school: Relation to longitudinal changes in academic and psychological adjustment. *Journal of Research on Adolescence, 8,* 123–158.

Roeser, R. W., Eccles, J. S., & Strobel, K. R. (1998). Linking the study of schooling and mental health: Selected issues and empirical illustrations at the level of the individual. *Educational Psychologist, 33,* 153–176.

Rogosa, D. R., & Willett, J. B. (1985). Understanding correlates of change by modeling individual differences in growth. *Psychometrika, 50,* 203–228.

Rosenbaum, G. (2000). *An investigation of the ecological factors associated with friendship quality in urban, low-income, racial and ethnic minority adolescents.* Unpublished doctoral dissertation completed at New York University.

Rosenbloom, S. R. (2004). *The influence of the school context on urban adolescent friendships.* Unpublished dissertation completed at New York University.

Rosenbloom, S. R., & Way, N. (2004). Experiences of discrimination among African American, Asian American, and Latino adolescents in an urban high school. *Youth & Society, 35,* 420–451.

Rotheram-Borus, M. J., Lightfoot, M., Moraes, A., Dopkins, S., LaCour, J. (1998). Developmental, ethnic, and gender differences in ethnic identity among adolescents. *Journal of Adolescent Research, 13*(4), 487–507.

Ruble, D. N., Alvarez, J., Bachman, M., Cameron, J., Fuligni, A. J., García Coll, C., & Rhee, E. (2004). The development of a sense of "We": The emergence and implications of children's collective identity. In M. Bennett & F. Sani (Eds.), *The development of the social self.* East Sussex, UK: Psychology Press.

Rumbaut, R. (1994). The crucible within: Ethnic identity, self-esteem, and segmented assimilation among children of immigrants. *International Migration Review, 28,* 748–794.

Sabogal, F., Marín, G., Otero-Sabogal, R., Marín, B. V., et al. (1987). Hispanic familism and acculturation: What changes and what doesn't? *Hispanic Journal of Behavioral Sciences, 9,* 397–412.

Salguero, C., & McCusker, W. (1996). Symptom expression in inner-city Latinas: Psychopathology or help-seeking? In B. J. Leadbeater & N. Way (Eds.), *Urban girls: Resisting stereotypes, creating identities.* New York: New York University Press.

Sarason, B. R., Pierce, G. R., & Sarason, I. G. (1990). Social support: The sense of acceptance and the role of relationships. In B. R. Sarason, I. G. Sarason & G. R. Pierce (Eds.), *Social support: An interactional view.* New York: John Wiley & Sons.

Savin-Williams, R. C., & Berndt, T. (1990). Friendship and peer relations. In S. S. Feldman & D. S. Elliot (Eds.), *At the threshold: The developing adolescent.* Cambridge, MA: Harvard University Press.

Schwartz, S. J., Zamboanga, B. L., & Jarvis, L. H. (2007). Ethnic identity and acculturation in Hispanic early adolescents: Mediated relationships to academic grades, prosocial behaviors, and externalizing symptoms. *Cultural Diversity and Ethnic Minority Psychology, 13*(4), 364–373.

Schwartz, S. J., Zamboanga, B. L., Rodriguez, L., & Wang, S. C. (2007). The structure of cultural identity in an ethnically diverse sample of emerging adults. *Basic and Applied Social Psychology, 29*(2), 159–173.

Sears, D. O., Fu, M., Henry, P. J., & Bui, K. (2003). The origins and persistence of ethnic identity among the "new immigrant" groups. *Social Psychology Quarterly, 66*(4), 419–437.

Seaton, E. K., Scottham, K. M., & Sellers, R. M. (2006). The status model of racial identity development in African American adolescents: Evidence of structure, trajectories, and well-being. *Child Development, 77,* 1416–1426.

Seidman, E. (1991). Growing up the hard way: Pathways of urban adolescents. *American Journal of Community Psychology, 19,* 169–205.

Sellers, R. M., Chavous, T. M., & Cooke, D. Y. (1998). Racial ideology and racial centrality as predictors of African American college students' academic performance. *The Journal of Black Psychology, 24,* 8–27.

Sellers, R. M., Copeland-Linder, N., Martin, P. P., Lewis, R. L. (2006). Racial identity matters: The relationship between racial discrimination and psychological functioning in African American adolescents. *Journal of Research on Adolescence, 16*(2), 187–216.

Sellers, R. M., & Shelton, J. N. (2003). The role of racial identity in perceived racial discrimination. *Journal of Personality and Social Psychology, 84,* 1079–1092.

Sellers, R. M., Smith, M. A., Shelton, J. N., Rowley, S. A. J., Chavous, T. M. (1998). Multidimensional model of racial identity: A reconceptualization of African American racial identity. *Personality and Social Psychology Review, 2*(1), 18–39.

Sharabany, R., Gershoni, R., & Hofman, J. (1981). Girlfriend, boyfriend: Age and sex differences in intimate friendship. *Developmental Psychology, 17,* 800–808.

Sherer, M. (1991). Peer group norms among Jewish and Arab juveniles in Israel. *Criminal Justice and Behavior, 18,* 267–286.

Shrum, W., Cheek, N. H., & Hunter, S. M. (1987). Friendship in school: General and racial homophily. *Sociology of Education, 61,* 227–239.

Shulman, S. (1993). Close friendships in early and mid adolescence: Typology and friendship reasoning. In B. Laursen (Ed.), *Close friendships in adolescence* (pp. 55–71). San Francisco: Jossey-Bass.

Smalls, C., White, R., Chavous, T., & Sellers, R. (2007). Racial ideological beliefs and racial discrimination experiences as predictors of academic engagement among African American adolescents. *Journal of Black Psychology, 33*(3), 299–330.

Smetana, J. (2002). Culture, autonomy, and personal jurisdiction in adolescent-parent relationships. In R. Kail (Ed.), *Advances in Child Development and Behavior, 29,* 51–87. San Diego, CA: Academic Press.

Snyder, J., Dishion, T. J., & Patterson, G. R. (1986). Determinants and consequences of associating with deviant peers during preadolescence and adolescence. *Journal of Early Adolescence, 6,* 29–43.

Snyder, T. D., & Hoffman, C. M. (1990). *Digest of educational statistics, 1990.* Washington, DC: National Center for Educational Statistics, U.S. Department of Education.

Sommer, B. (1985). What's different about truants? A comparison study of eighth graders. *Journal of Youth & Adolescence, 14*(411–422).

Sommers, I., Fagan, J., & Baskin, D. (1993). Sociocultural influences on the explanation of delinquency for Puerto Rican youth. *Hispanic Journal of Behavioral Sciences, 15,* 36–62.

Sorkhabi, N. (2005). Applicability of Baumrind's parent typology to collective cultures: Analysis of cultural explanations of parent socialization effects. *International Journal of Behavioral Development, 29,* 552–563.

Sroufe, L. A., & Waters, C. (1977). Attachment as an organizational construct. *Child Development, 48,* 1184–1199.

Stack, C. (1974). *All our kin: Strategies for survival in a black community.* New York: Basic Books.

Steele, C., & Aronson, J. (1995). Stereotype threat and the intellectual test performance of African-Americans. *Journal of Personality and Social Psychology, 69,* 797–811.

Steinberg, L. (2001). We know some things: Parent–adolescent relationships in retrospect and prospect. *Journal of Research on Adolescence, 11,* 1–19.

Steinberg, L., Dornbusch, S. M., & Brown, B. B. (1992). Ethnic differences in adolescent achievement: An ecological perspective. *American Psychologist, 47,* 723–729.

Steinberg, L., Mounts, N., Lamborn, S., & Dornbusch, S. (1991). Authoritative parenting and adolescent adjustment across various ecological niches. *Journal of Research on Adolescence, 1,* 19–36.

Stevenson, H. C. (1995). Relationship of adolescent perceptions of racial socialization to racial identity. *Journal of Black Psychology, 21,* 49–70.

Stevenson, H. C. (1998). Raising safe villages: Cultural-ecological factors that influence the emotional adjustment of adolescents. *Journal of Black Psychology, 24,* 44–59.

Stevenson, H. C. (2004). Boys not men: Racial socialization and neighborhood safety as buffers for rejection sensitivity in African American males. In N. Way & J. Chu (Eds.), *Adolescent boys in context.* New York: New York University Press.

Stevenson, H. C., Cameron, R., Herrero-Taylor, T., & Davis, G. Y. (2002). Development of the teenage experience of racial socialization scale: Correlates of race-related socialization frequency from the perspective of Black youth. *Journal of Black Psychology, 28,* 84–106.

Stoddart, K. K., & Stoddart. (2002). Researching White racial identity. *The American Behavioral Scientist, 45,* 1254–1264.

Strauss, L. C., & Cross, W. E., Jr. (2005). Transacting black identity: A two-week daily-diary study. In G. Downey, J. S. Eccles, & C. M. Chatman (Eds.), *Navigating the future: social identity, coping, and life tasks.* New York: Russell Sage Foundation.

Suárez-Orozco, C. (2004). Formulating identity in a globalized world. In M. Suárez-Orozco & D. B. Qin-Hillard (Eds.), *Globalization: Culture & Education in the New Millennium.* Berkeley: University of California Press.

Suárez-Orozco, C., & Suárez-Orozco, M.M. (1995). *Transformations: Immigration, family life, and achievement motivation among Latino adolescents.* Stanford, CA: Stanford University Press.

Suárez-Orozco, C., & Suárez-Orozco, M. M. (2001). *Children of immigration.* Cambridge, MA: Harvard University Press.

Sullivan, S., Schwartz, S. J., Prado, G., Huang, S., Pantin, H., & Szapocznik, J. (2007). A bidimensional model of acculturation for examining differences in family functioning and behavior problems in Hispanic immigrant adolescents. *Journal of Early Adolescence, 27*(4), 405–430.

Syed, M., Azmitia, M., Phinney, J. S. (2007). Stability and change in ethnic identity among Latino emerging adults in two contexts. *Identity: An International Journal of Theory and Research, 7*(2), 155–178.

Tajfel, H. (1978). *Differentiation between social groups: Studies in the social psychology of intergroup relations.* London: Academic Press.

Tatum, B. D. (1997). *Why are all the Black kids sitting together in the cafeteria?* New York: Basic.

Triandis, H. (1976). *Variations in Black and White perceptions of the social environment.* Urbana: University of Illinois Press.

Triandis, H. C., Vassiliou, V., Vassiliou, G., Tanaka, Y., & Shanmungan, A. (1972). *The analysis of subjective culture.* New York: John Wiley & Sons.

Tseng, V. (2006). Unpacking immigration in youth' academic and occupational pathways. *Child Development, 77,* 1434–1445.

Tseng, V., & Fuligni, A. J. (2000). Parent-adolescent language use and relationships among immigrant families with East Asian, Filipino and Latin American backgrounds. *Journal of Marriage and Family, 62,* 465–476.

U.S. Bureau of the Census. (1999). *CenStats Databases*, from http://tier2.census.gov/dbappweb.htm.

U.S. Bureau of the Census. (2004). *CenStats Databases*, from http://tier2.census.gov/dbappweb.htm.

U.S. Bureau of the Census. (2004). *U.S. interim projections by age, sex, race, and Hispanic origin.* Available online at www.census.gov/ipc/www/usinterimproj/.

U.S. Bureau of the Census. (2007). *Current Population Survey, March 2006.* Available online at http://www.census.gov/population/www/socdemo/education/cps2006.html. Accessed on February 21, 2007.

Umaña-Taylor, A., & Bamaca, M. Y. (2004). Conducting focus groups with Latino populations: Lessons from the field. *Family Relations: Interdisciplinary Journal of Applied Family Studies, 53*(3), 261–272.

Umaña-Taylor, A., Diversi, M., & Fine, M. A. (2002). Ethnic identity and self-esteem of Latino adolescents: Distinctions among the Latino populations. *Journal of Adolescent Research, 17,* 303–327.

Umaña-Taylor, A., & Fine, M. A. (2004). Examining ethnic identity among Mexican-origin adolescents living in the United States. *Hispanic Journal of Behavioral Sciences, 26,* 36–59.

Umaña-Taylor, A., & Shin, N. (2007). An examination of ethnic identity and self-esteem with diverse populations: Exploring variation by ethnicity and geography. *Cultural Diversity and Ethnic Minority Psychology, 13*(2), 178–186.

Umaña-Taylor, A., & Updegraff, K. A. (2007). Latino adolescents' mental health: Exploring the interrelations among discrimination, ethnic identity, cultural orientation, self-esteem, and depressive symptoms. *Journal of Adolescence, 30,* 549–567.

Umaña-Taylor, A., Vargas-Chanes, D., Garcia, C. D., & Gonzales-Backen, M. (2008). A longitudinal examination of Latino adolescents' ethnic identity, coping with discrimination, and self-esteem. *The Journal of Early Adolescence, 28,* 16–50.

Umaña-Taylor, A., & Yazedjian, A. (2006). Generational differences and similarities among Puerto Rican and Mexican mothers' experiences with familial ethnic socialization. *Journal of Social and Personal Relationships, 23,* 445–464.

Updegraff, K. A., Madden-Derdich, D. A., Estrada, A. U., Sales, L. J., & Leonard, S. A. (2002). Young adolescents' experiences with parents and friends: Exploring the connections. *Family Relations: Journal of Applied Family & Child Studies, 51,* 72–80.

Updegraff, K. A., McHale, S. M., Crouter, A. C., & Kupanoff, K. (2001). Parents' involvement in adolescents' peer relationships: A comparison of mothers' and fathers' roles. *Journal of Marriage & the Family, 63,* 655–668.

Vandiver, B. J., Cross, W. E., Jr., Worrell, F. C., & Fhagen-Smith, P. E. (2002). Validating the Cross Racial Identity Scale. *Journal of Counseling Psychology, 49,* 71–85.

Vernberg, E. M., Beery, S. H., Ewell, K. K., & Absender, D. A. (1993). Parents' use of friendship facilitation strategies and the formation of friendships in early adolescence: A prospective study. *Journal of Family Psychology, 7,* 356–369.

Waters, M. C. (1990). *Ethnic options: Choosing identities in American.* Berkeley: University of California Press.

Waters, M. C. (2003). Black identities: West Indian immigrant dreams and American realities. *American Journal of Sociology, 108,* 1373–1375.

Way, N. (1996). Between experiences of betrayal and desire: Close friendships among urban adolescents. In B. J. Leadbeater & N. Way (Eds.), *Urban girls: Resisting stereotypes, creating identities* (pp. 173–193). New York: New York University Press.

Way, N. (1998). *Everyday courage: The lives and stories of urban teenagers.* New York: New York University Press.

Way, N. (2004). Intimacy, desire, and distrust in the friendships of adolescent boys. In N. Way & J. Y. Chu (Eds.), *Adolescent boys: Exploring diverse cultures of boyhood* (pp. 167–196). New York: New York University Press.

Way, N. (2006). The cultural practice of friendships among urban youth. In D. French, B. Schneider, & X. Chen (Eds.), *Friendships in cultural context.* New York: Cambridge University Press.

Way, N. (in progress). *Real boys: Resisting stereotypes, Creating identities.* To be published by Harvard University Press.

Way, N., & Chen, L. (2000). Close and general friendships among African American, Latino, and Asian American adolescents from low-income families. *Journal of Adolescent Research, 15,* 274–301.

Way, N., Cowal, K., Gingold, R., Pahl, K., & Bissessar, N. (2001). Friendship patterns among African American, Asian American, and Latino adolescents from low-income families. *Journal of Social and Personal Relationships, 18,* 29–53.

Way, N., & Greene, M. (2006) Changes in perceived friendship quality during adolescence: The patterns and contextual predictors. *Journal of Research on Adolescence, 16,* 293–320.

Way, N., Greene, M. L., & Pahl, K. (2004, March). *School as a context for the development of social identities.* Paper presented at the Baltimore, MD, Society for Research on Adolescence.

Way, N., & Pahl, K. (1999). Friendship patterns among urban adolescent boys: A qualitative account. In M. Kopala & L. Suzuki (Eds.), *Using qualitative methods in psychology* (pp. 145–161). Thousand Oaks, CA: Sage.

Way, N., & Pahl, K. (2001). Individual and contextual-level predictors of perceived friendship quality among ethnic minority, low-income adolescents. *Journal of Research on Adolescence, 11,* 325–349.

Way, N., & Robinson, M. (2003). The influence of family and friends on the psychological adjustment of ethnic minority, low-income adolescents. *Journal of Adolescent Research, 18,* 324–347.

Way, N. Santos, C., Niwa, E., & Kim, C. (in press). A contextualized understanding of ethnic identity among Chinese American, African American, Puerto Rican, and Dominican youth. In M. Azmitia (Ed.). *The intersection of social and personal identities.* New Directions for Child and Adolescent Development.

Wayman, J. C. (2002). Student perceptions of teacher ethnic bias: A comparison of Mexican American and Non-Latino White dropouts and students. *The High School Journal,* 27–37.

Webster, B. H., Jr., & Bishaw, A. (2007). *Income, Earnings, and Poverty Data from the 2005 American Community Survey.* U.S. Bureau of the Census, American Community Survey Reports, ACS-02. Washington, DC: U.S. Government Printing Office.

Weiss, R. S. (1974). The provisions of social relationships. In Z. Rubin (Ed.), *Doing unto others* (pp. 17–26). Englewood Cliffs, NJ: Prentice Hall.

Wheelock, M. A., & Erickson, C. (1996). *Self-esteem: Examining gender, ethnic, socioeconomic status, and developmental differences.* Paper presented at the Association for Women in Psychology, Indianapolis, IN.

Whitesell, N. R., Mitchell, C. M., Kaufman, C. E., & Spicer, P. (2006). Developmental trajectories of personal and collective self-concept among American Indian adolescents. *Child Development, 77,* 1487–1503.

Willett, J. B., Singer, J. D., & Martin, N. C. (1998). The design and analysis of longitudinal studies of development and psychopathology in context: Statistical models and methodological recommendations. *Development and Psychopathology, 10,* 395–426.

Wong, C. A., Eccles, J. S., & Sameroff, A. (2003). Adolescents' school and socioemotional adjustment. *Journal of Personality 71,* 1198–1232.

Yasui, M., Dorham, C. L., & Dishion, T. J. (2004). Ethnic identity and psychological adjustment: A validity analysis for European American and African American adolescents. *Journal of Adolescent Research, 19,* 807–825.

Yip, T. (2005). Sources of situational variation in ethnic identity and psychological well-being: A palm pilot study of Chinese American students. *Personality and Social Psychology Bulletin, 31*(12), 1603–1616.

Yip, T., & Cross, W. E., Jr. (2004). A daily diary study of mental health and community involvement outcomes for three Chinese American Social Identities. *Cultural Diversity & Ethnic Minority Psychology, 10,* 394–408.

Yip, T., & Fuligni, A. J. (2002). Daily variation in ethnic identity, ethnic behaviors, and psychological well-being among American adolescents of Chinese descent. *Child Development, 73*(5), 1557–1572.

Yip, T., Seaton, E. K., & Sellers, R. M. (2006). African American racial identity across the lifespan: Identity status, identity content, and depressive symptoms. *Child Development, 77,* 1504–1517.

Yoo, H. C., & Lee, R. M. (2005). Ethnic identity and approach-type coping as moderators of the racial discrimination/well-being relation in Asian Americans. *Journal of Counseling Psychology, 52*(4), 497–506.

Yoo, H. C., & Lee, R. M. (2008). Does ethnic identity buffer or exacerbate the effects of frequent racial discrimination on situational well-being of Asian Americans? *Journal of Counseling Psychology, 55*(1), 63–74.

Youngblade, L. M., Park, K. A., & Belsky, J. (1993). Measurement of young children's close friendship: A comparison of two independent assessment systems and their associations with attachment security. *International Journal of Behavioral Development, 16,* 563–587.

Youniss, J., & Smollar, J. (1985). *Adolescent relations with mothers, fathers, and friends.* Chicago: University of Chicago Press.

Zhang, W., & Fuligni, A. J. (2006). Authority, autonomy, family relationships among adolescents in urban and rural China. *Journal of Research on Adolescence, 16,* 527–537.

Zhou, M., & Bankston, C. L. (1998). *Growing up American: How Vietnamese children adapt to life in the United States.* New York: Russell Sage Foundation.

Zisman, P. M., & Wilson, V. (1994). Table hopping in the cafeteria: An exploration of "racial" integration in early adolescent social groups. *Multicultural Education Annual Editions,* 104–115.

CHAPTER 16

Cross-Cultural Issues in the Study of Adolescent Development

ALICE SCHLEGEL

Anthropologists have long considered cross-cultural studies to be among their disciplinary specialties. However, since any foreign culture is seen through the lens of the observer's home culture, one could argue that all observations of foreign cultures are by their very nature cross-cultural, not only those by anthropologists. Cross-cultural studies, therefore, could include the ethnographies, or descriptive reports, by observers throughout history, such as the writings of Herodotus, the letters the Jesuits and Franciscans sent home from the New World, and the reports of traders, travelers, and colonial administrators since at least the sixteenth century. Nevertheless, the *systematic* study of other cultures is a special feature of anthropology.

Explicit comparison has been a feature of anthropology from its beginning. Attempts to classify similarities and differences across cultures include even the long-discredited attempts in the nineteenth century to understand cultural evolution, which divided cultures into those at the stages of Savagery, Barbarism, and Civilization (Morgan, 1877). The earliest scholarly paper using statistical techniques to analyze culture traits in a sample of cultures also dates from the late nineteenth century (Tylor, 1889).

One impact of anthropology on the other social sciences has been to influence other disciplines to test assumptions and findings, based on research in modern Western societies, with data from non-Western cultures. Psychologists responded by looking at psychological issues with subjects from other cultures. In the early 1960s, John Berry was testing Western models of perception among the Eskimo (Berry, 1966), and not many years later Pierre Dasen was addressing Piaget's research from a cross-cultural perspective (Dasen, 1972). The *Journal of Cross-Cultural Psychology*, the earliest of such journals, appeared in 1966 (Berry, Poortinga, Segall, & Dasen, 1992; Segall, Dasen, Berry, & Poortinga, 1990).

Anthropologists also benefited from the research theories and methods of psychology. Psychological anthropology depended heavily on personality theory developed by psychologists. Some anthropologists refined their observational techniques by making systematic observations of target individuals who represented specific categories (e.g., by sex and age) within the population they studied, thus moving from the cultural to the individual level. Others used Thematic Apperception Test cards to elicit stories that reflected cultural themes of personality traits or interpersonal relations (Schlegel, 1977).

The deliberate bridging of disciplines was expressed in the mid-twentieth century by the introduction of interdisciplinary programs in some respected universities, such as the

I thank Herbert Barry III for reading and providing valuable comments on this chapter. He was co-author with me of most of the cross-cultural studies from which information presented here was drawn, and I gratefully acknowledge his indispensable contribution to those studies.

Department of Social Relations at Harvard. Anthropologists, psychologists, and sociologists collaborated on research and teaching, and graduate students in the department received cross-disciplinary training.

It was in this intellectual climate that the Society for Cross-Cultural Research (SCCR) was founded in 1972 by George Peter Murdock and others. Although for most of his career Murdock was in the Department of Anthropology at Yale, his graduate training was in sociology, and he had a keen interest in psychology. The founding members of SCCR were mainly anthropologists and psychologists, with some other social scientists. The membership has retained that proportion of disciplinary representation and is deliberately interdisciplinary in its meeting programs and its journal, *Cross-Cultural Research.*

CROSS-CULTURAL STUDIES OF ADOLESCENCE

Psychologists and sociologists, using Western subjects, have conducted most of the research on adolescence. As these disciplines gained wider distribution throughout the world, non-Western psychologists, in particular, studied the adolescents of their own cultures. This type of cross-cultural research blends theories and methods, derived mainly from European and American sources, with a deep understanding of the local culture and conditions. Research on Indian adolescent girls by Saraswathi and Dutta (1988) and Sharma (1996) provide good examples of the insights such an approach can reach.

In spite of the success of Margaret Mead's *Coming of Age in Samoa* (1928), which was a study of Samoan adolescent girls, cultural anthropologists have until recently showed little interest in adolescence or adolescent development. They continued to refer to the rituals performed at around puberty in many societies as initiation into adulthood. This was so even after the work of Mead and, later, a few other anthropologists (e.g., Elwin, 1947; Wilson, 1951) clearly showed that a socially marked stage of life between childhood and adulthood existed in the preindustrial and preliterate societies they examined. Exceptions to this general absence of anthropological studies of adolescence are cross-cultural studies of initiation ceremonies by Cohen (1964) and Young (1965), the latter a social psychologist. In both, the authors refer to a subsequent adolescent stage, but they do not discuss it.

The lack of interest by anthropologists in adolescence may have been due in part to assumptions about adolescence. It was assumed by many that an adolescent stage is the social construct of modern societies, with schools that separate postpubertal individuals from adults for much of the time. According to this assumption, before widespread schooling appeared, teenage girls and boys were thought of as young adults, with adult-like responsibilities and interests. Anthropologists, who for the most part studied preliterate and preindustrial cultures, gave little attention to the developmental stage of individuals past puberty.

Another reason for the neglect of adolescence may have come from psychology. Psychological anthropologists of the mid-twentieth century, whose primary interest lay in the development of personality, were strongly influenced by Freudian and other branches of psychology that regard early influences as the determinants of adult personality and behavior. According to Freud, for example, significant socialization declines once young people have passed through the period of latency and reach the genital stage (Hall, 1954). Anthropologists, particularly psychological anthropologists, reported on the behavior of children, but they neglected adolescents. Thus, while there was plenty of evidence of adolescence in the ethnographic and historical literature—indeed, a later cross-cultural study of adolescence (Schlegel & Barry, 1991) would have been impossible without such evidence—it was usually buried in discussions of other topics or mentioned in passing.

Coming of Age in Samoa (Mead, 1928) presented a challenge that most other anthropologists did not take up. Mead's doctoral dissertation, the basis for her book, was a test of the assumption that adolescence was a time of *Sturm und Drang*, and that this itself was biologically determined by hormonal changes and their consequences. Mead's work, which purported to discredit that assumption, was heralded by many anthropologists as a triumph of cultural over biological determinism.

By the 1970s, interest in adolescence had experienced something of a revival among anthropologists. Two major cross-cultural research projects on adolescence were established at this time, one by Beatrice and John Whiting (two anthropologists) at Harvard, and one by Herbert Barry III (a psychologist) and Alice Schlegel (an anthropologist) at the University of Pittsburgh. All of these researchers had done comparative studies of earlier stages in human development. The Whitings had organized the Six Cultures Project in the 1950s, which resulted in monographs by anthropologists and psychologists on child socialization in six cultures. Schlegel and Barry had conducted cross-cultural research on adolescent initiation ceremonies (Schlegel & Barry, 1980) and adolescent games (Schlegel & Barry, 1989), and Barry had participated in a large body of cross-cultural research on childhood, some of it reproduced or cited in Barry and Schlegel (1980). Schlegel (1973) had also written "The Adolescent Socialization of the Hopi Girl," based on her field observations of Hopi daily life and the recollections of middle-aged and old women. In both the Pittsburgh and the Harvard projects, interest in adolescence seemed to grow naturally out of research on earlier stages and the questions that arose out of this research, just as many longitudinal studies of psychological development that began in infancy grew into studies of adolescence as their samples aged.

The Harvard and Pittsburgh cross-cultural projects differed in their method. The Harvard Adolescence Project sent anthropologists to seven widely dispersed sites of very different cultures to conduct detailed studies of adolescent life. Of these seven studies, four have

been published as books by Rutgers University Press in the series "Adolescents in a Changing World." The Pittsburgh project, referred to as the Adolescent Socialization Project, used the Standard Ethnographic Sample (Murdock & White, 1969). Coders collected data drawn from ethnographic material on these cultures, and the principal investigators analyzed and interpreted these data. The data were reported in Barry and Schlegel (1990) and the analytic findings in Schlegel and Barry (1991). (Specific works resulting from the Harvard and Pittsburgh projects will be discussed further in a later section of this chapter.)

At about the same time that these projects were designed, there was a renewed burst of interest among some anthropologists in biological explanations. This was the result of research by animal behaviorists and biological anthropologists on reproductive behavior in animal populations, including our closest relatives among the primates. This research program, neo-Darwinian in its premises, put into motion the development of a new field, sociobiology, which has now matured into the more nuanced disciplines of evolutionary psychology and evolutionary ecology. Any study of reproductive behavior in humans, and indeed in our primate kin, the monkeys and apes, cannot ignore adolescence, when hormonal changes underlie the motivation to find a sexual partner and begin a reproductive career, even though the individual has not yet reached full physical and social development (cf. Weisfeld, 1999).

Anthropologists during these years were faced with a new form of an old dilemma, the question of human universals versus the uniqueness of cultures. Those who stressed the universalities of human behavior were often at odds with those who argued for the importance of local cultural determination in molding not only beliefs and values but also behavior generally. Somewhere in the middle were those who, like the present author, hold that there are evolved psychological constants that are expressed behaviorally in various ways depending on features of the natural and social environments. These include anything from the prevalence of war to the availability of game for hunting or the practices carried along in converting to a new religion. Some of these features may be cultural, but behavior may also be influenced by demographic conditions or other features to which culture itself responds. A pictorial model is not so much one of linear cause and effect as of multidirectional influences and responses with feedback loops, without a strict division between nature and nurture.

WHAT IS CROSS-CULTURAL RESEARCH?

The term *cross-cultural* is used rather loosely to describe several modes of research and analysis. At its simplest, cross-cultural studies analyze behavior in another culture as an implied comparison with the culture of the investigator. Berry's (1966) study of perception among the Eskimo serves as an example in psychology, as do many of the case studies done by anthropologists. The book-length case studies of adolescence that resulted from the Harvard Adolescence Projects are among the best investigations of non-Western adolescent life in the anthropological literature. They describe and analyze adolescence among Arctic Inuit (Condon, 1987), an Australian Aboriginal community (Burbank, 1988), the Ijo of Nigeria (Hollos & Leis, 1989), and in a town in Morocco (Davis & Davis, 1989). A brief description of the Harvard Adolescence Project appears as a foreword in each of these volumes.

Other cross-cultural studies examine a particular variable, a behavior or culture trait, in two or several cultures or nations (the latter is technically *cross-national*), and usually offer an explanation for the similarities or differences. One study of this type developed by anthropologists is the controlled comparison. Its most common form is a comparison of (usually) two cultures that are similar in most important respects but differ in the behavior or culture trait of interest (i.e., the similarities are

controlled for). An alternative is a comparison of (usually) two cultures that are different in most respects but are similar in the variable of interest, controlling for the differences. In both instances, the point is to explain the difference or similarity, respectively, in the dependent variable. The study by Hollos and Leis (1989) of adolescence in two Ibo villages, one more modern and one more traditional, is an example of the first form.

Cross-cultural research has a more specific meaning than the general one, which applies to all research that compares cultures. In its specific sense, it refers to tests of hypotheses using ethnographic materials from a large representative sample of cultures. Data are coded from these materials according to a codebook, which consists of the variables to be coded (e.g., present/absent or along a scale) and their operational definitions. The data are then analyzed using appropriate statistical techniques, and the findings are interpreted. For example, appendices I, II, and III of Schlegel and Barry (1991) contain information on the sample, the codebook, and the statistical techniques used in their cross-cultural study of adolescent socialization.

CENTRAL ISSUES IN THE CROSS-CULTURAL STUDY OF ADOLESCENCE

Biological adolescence is universal. Recent research into the structure and processes of the developing brain make it clear that there are neurobiological changes as well (Steinberg et al., 2006), and we can safely assume that these too are universal. The consensus is not so clear regarding adolescence as a stage of social development, however.

Scholars conducting cross-cultural research on adolescence have asked several fundamental questions in this respect. Is social adolescence universal, or is it only found in a limited number of societies, modern ones with schooling and perhaps a few others? When does social adolescence begin and when does it end? What are the characteristics of social adolescence, and how is it similar or different across cultures? Which features of adolescence differ between girls and boys, and which are similar? And finally, if social adolescence is universal, why does our species, *Homo sapiens*, have this period between puberty and the socially recognized stage of adulthood?

The primary source of data for addressing these questions here is the research of the Adolescent Socialization Project. Unless otherwise noted the data in this section are drawn from the resulting publication of the findings (Schlegel & Barry, 1991). This book reported on only a portion of the 341 variables in the project, coded separately for girls and boys. Data came from ethnographic materials on cultures in the Standard Ethnographic Sample (Murdock & White, 1969), a worldwide representative sample of known reported preindustrial cultures. Of the 186 cultures in the sample, 181 had information on adolescence that could be coded. (Details are found in the text and appendices in Schlegel and Barry [1991].) These are all traditional cultures, and the ethnographic material on each refers to a specific community at a particular time.

Is Adolescence as a Social Stage Universal?

Here we have the "black swan" problem: One contrary case can negate the generalization, unless it can be accounted for by special circumstances. All of the cultures in the sample, with one possible exception with respect to girls, recognized a social stage between childhood and adulthood for both sexes, during which time the behavior and treatment of young people differed from that of both younger children and adults. In several cases there was an additional stage between adolescence and full adulthood, which we termed *youth*, for one or both sexes. Such a stage, somewhat similar to what Arnett (2001) has called "emerging adulthood," is a feature of most regions and social classes of modern societies. It also existed in some traditional ones such as ancient Athens and Sparta, Europe since at least the Middle

Ages, and militaristic states of Africa like Zulu. Arnett (2001) has conceptualized the youth stage of modern societies as "emerging adulthood," with characteristic features that differentiate it quite markedly from the institutionalized youth stages of preindustrial societies.

Given the great variety of cultures in the sample by geographical placement, by subsistence techniques from hunting to advanced agriculture, and by level of technological development, we can be fairly confident that social adolescence is a constant across cultures for both sexes. Its absence rather than its presence requires an explanation.

There may be at least two exceptions, one in the Standard Ethnographic Sample and one other, to the generalization that adolescence is a social universal. Girls of the Gros Ventre Indians of Montana and girls of some Australian aboriginal tribes (Burbank, 1988) married and had sexual relations with their husbands before menarche, Aboriginal girls as young as 9 or 10 in some cases. We do not have information on the lives of these girls, except that Gros Ventre co-wives, older than the new bride, treated her as a little sister. It is impossible to say whether an adolescent stage was acknowledged for these very young wives or whether they were treated as adults and expected to behave like them. Nor do we know if the transition from childhood was marked by very early signs of puberty, which would mean that girls entered an adolescent stage before menarche, whether or not it ended at marriage. We do know that in at least one Aboriginal tribe, the Aranda, social adolescence began with the appearance of the breast buds, an early sign of puberty.

Many cultures have a special term for adolescence as a period between childhood and adulthood, but most do not. We should not confuse the presence or absence of linguistic markers with social reality, however. The Navajo Indians of New Mexico and Arizona, whose language does have terms for *adolescent girl* and *adolescent boy*, did not have many distinctive markers in appearance or age-specific behaviors to set off this stage. On the other hand, their neighbors the Hopi, whose language does not have terms for adolescents, held public events where adolescent girls and boys could display themselves. Hopi girls after menarche wore their hair in a style that signaled that they were ready for courtship. In another case, the Trobriand Islanders of Melanesia spoke of adolescents as "the flower of the village," without giving this stage a label.

The Parameters of Adolescence

When Adolescence Begins

The difficulty in determining age at the beginning and end of adolescence lies in the absence of good data on chronological age for most of the cultures in the Standard Ethnographic Sample. Age can only be estimated. A better measure, more in line with the way most peoples regard social age, is level of physical development. Although such features of physical development as tooth eruption (Bogin, 1999) and brain development (Steinberg et al., 2006) seem to be universally consistent, reproductive maturation for both sexes is variable according to diet and possibly other conditions (Vizmanos & Marti-Hennenberg, 2001). For this reason, we defined social adolescence as beginning at around first menstruation and first ejaculation, unless otherwise indicated. We estimated menarche to be around age 14 in these relatively well-nourished populations, with spermarche 1 or 2 years later, unless there was information to the contrary, basing our estimates on Eveleth and Tanner (1976). There are several cases of girls' social adolescence beginning before menarche with earlier signs of pubertal change, such as breast development. The Aranda, mentioned earlier, is one such case.

Length of Adolescence and Youth

In most cultures social adulthood began at marriage, particularly for girls. In a few, full social adulthood was reached after one or more

children were born to a couple. In other cases, a ceremony other than marriage marked the transition from boy to man. For the Hopi Indians of Arizona, a girl became a woman at marriage, but a boy became a man when he was initiated into one of the four male ceremonial societies. He did not marry until after this event.

Length of social adolescence can vary between the sexes within a culture. In fact, boys' adolescence is frequently longer than girls' adolescence. Boys, whose growth spurt follows spermarche, do not reach their full physical development until some time after puberty, rarely before their late teens in the populations of the sample. Girls, whose growth spurt precedes menarche, develop adult-like bodies much earlier (although they go through a period of adolescent sub-fecundity before they are capable of maintaining a pregnancy) (Bogin, 1999). Thus, they are likely to be considered ready for adult life earlier than are their male peers, who have not yet attained an adult-like body. This, then, is a reason, grounded in biological development, for a longer adolescence for boys than for girls.

A cultural reason for a longer male adolescence is that boys generally have to prove themselves capable of meeting the obligations of husband and father before the parents of a prospective bride will accept him as a son-in-law. For both biological and social developmental reasons, the end result is that boys may still be considered adolescents or youth while the girls of their cohort are already married adults and bearing children.

A youth stage, when present, typically begins and adolescence ends when the young person has attained full or almost full physical growth. This is rarely before the late teens. Individuals at that age are more developed, not only physically but also cognitively (Hooper, 2004), than boys and girls in their early teens. When full social adulthood is not reached until after the late teen-age years, usually sometime in the early to middle 20s or even later, cultures generally recognize a social stage that intervenes between adolescence and adulthood.

During this stage, young people have more responsibilities, and usually more freedom, than adolescents, without the privileges and social recognition of adulthood. This stage of "youth" or "emerging adulthood" (Arnett, 2001) was common for males in cultures in which they spent a period of time before marriage as warriors or in other specialized roles, while girls did not have such an intervening stage but married within a few years of menarche. When marriage for most girls was delayed as well, as it has been for most social classes in Europe since at least the sixteenth century, girls as well as boys passed through a youth stage (Levi & Schmitt, 1997; Mitterauer, 1992).

Marriage and the Beginning of Adulthood

If marriage marks the beginning of adulthood, the length of adolescence or youth depends on the factors that determine the timing of marriage. One of these factors is the economic opportunities provided to boys and youth that allow them to meet the obligations of marriage. Another factor is whether youth are given special social roles, such as warrior, that preclude marriage. A factor determining the age of marriage for girls is the benefit of keeping a daughter at home for the labor or income she provides. This has to be weighed against the present or future benefits a son-in-law provides through his labor, economic or social connections, or goods, the last in the form of bride wealth (Schlegel & Eloul, 1988).

Marriage strategies and negotiations were important elements in the social lives of most traditional peoples, who sought to use the marriages of their children for economic and political benefit and to maintain or improve the social position of their families (Schlegel & Eloul, 1988). This is generally true for societies of all types, from simple foragers (hunters and gatherers) to complex traditional states.

In European and European-derived societies, and more recently in modernizing ones, industrialization weakened the economic hold that most families had on their adolescent and older unmarried children. This new economic formation provided boys, and later girls as well, with opportunities for economic independence that had been undreamed of for most. Family resources that helped get a spouse, whether economic or social (e.g., kinship connections), receded in importance. Personal effort plus ability became a path to success for many more than just a few exceptional individuals. Family control over daughters as well as sons declined as educational and occupational opportunities opened up to them. As girls became more independent, boys and young men could direct their appeal as suitors to the girls themselves, without as much regard for their parents as in earlier times. Adults lost considerable authority over the young of both sexes as marital prospects depended more on personal resources other than familial ones, such as those the potential marriage partners could obtain by themselves.

Before we generalize too broadly about the dependence of the young on their families, we must recognize that there have always been sectors in many societies, not just the less privileged in class-based ones, in which the marital prospects of young males were poor and only ability and luck could help them succeed. Even the Hopi have tales of orphan boys without kinship support, on whom Spider Grandmother, like a fairy godmother, takes pity and helps them find a wife and a place in the community. These legends tell of success through individual ability and luck. They are not unlike tales of upward social mobility that have become popular legends in technologically more advanced societies, like those of Cinderella or Dick Whittington (the legendary London scullery boy who rose to become lord-mayor of London).

CONSTANTS AND VARIANTS OF ADOLESCENCE ACROSS CULTURES

This section examines the constants and variants across cultures and between the sexes. The data are cultural rather than individual in nature; that is, each "subject" is a culture in the sample, and the code for each variable of each culture—present/absent or point on an ordinal scale—represents the best judgment of the coders. For the purpose of rendering the data manageable, ordinal scales were converted into two categories, and these variables were analyzed statistically as above or below the mean.

The following discussion highlights those findings from the Adolescent Socialization Project that, in this author's judgment, have the greatest relevance to issues in the study of contemporary adolescents. They are not necessarily presented in the form they were in the original cross-cultural report (Schlegel & Barry, 1991).

Adolescents and Their Families

The Household—the Primary Locus of Socialization

In Western cultures, that is, European and European-derived cultures, a common family form for many centuries has been the nuclear-family household, which consists of a married couple and their children, plus perhaps other unmarried or widowed adult kin, boarders, and household workers. Household authority rests with the central couple. The other common form has been the stem-family household. That contains an older couple and one of their children (more often a son, but a daughter if there is no male heir) plus that child's spouse and children. Household workers and unmarried kin may also belong to the household. This household form occurred in many world regions of peasant agriculture, including many parts of Asia, where the household required more than two working adults but limits on land or other household resources kept the household fairly small.

In underpopulated African pastoral and farming regions, and in other places where vast tracts of arable land or grasslands constituted the landscape, the constraints were on shortage of labor rather than shortage of land.

Extended-family households provided for household expansion by keeping some married children, most often sons, and their spouses and children in the parental home. These societies often promoted polygynous marriage, which expanded the domestic female labor force and provided more children for help in farming or herding. Wealthy families in traditional advanced societies like India and China also formed extended-family households to bring together the male kin, fathers, sons, and brothers that formed the family corporation and ran its enterprises.

These are broad generalizations, for there are variations of these forms suited to local needs and the rules or customs of inheritance of property. Household structure and activities provided the social milieu within which children and adolescents were socialized and girls and boys learned their varying social roles. In the nuclear-family and extended-family households, before a demographic shift away from high fertility, the ratio of children to adults in the household was equal or high. For example, given four dependent children per woman, the nuclear-family household had a ratio of two children per one adult with whom they were likely to have reciprocal obligations and emotional ties. In the extended-family household, the ratio of children to adults might even be higher, particularly where there were polygynous marriages. The stem-family household, where polygyny was usually absent or uncommon, contained two parents and two grandparents, so the ratio was one-to-one. Since it often also contained unmarried adult children of the founding couple, uncles and aunts of the children, the ratio could be even lower.

Thus, the social and emotional settings in which children were socialized were structured in different ways that depended on the household form. It is not surprising that where there were extended-family households, much rearing of young children was done by older siblings (Weisner, 1982) and cousins, and older children had authority over and responsibility for younger ones. Children as young as four could be left to mind the baby and could expect to be punished for serious mishaps. Sibling care was also common in highly fecund nuclear-family households. In stem-family households, grandparents as well as older siblings could do much of the child care.

The effects on adolescents of household demography show up in the association between household form and the traits of competition and aggression. Competitiveness in boys is associated with the nuclear-family household (0.052) and weakly associated negatively with the stem-family household (-0.087, a trend). Competitiveness in girls is weakly associated with the nuclear-family household (0.072, a trend). Aggressiveness in boys is negatively associated with the stem-family household (-0.031). In girls, aggressiveness is positively associated with the nuclear-family household (0.020). For both sexes, the strongest positive associations of both competitiveness and aggressiveness are with competition with peers. However, family social structure, as setting the stage for the family emotional structure, does appear to be a factor. The ratio of adults to children affects the quantity and quality of adult-child interactions, and this in turn affects sibling interactions. Children learn in the family what they will carry over into adolescence.

Relations with Family Members

Regardless of household form, in most cultures adolescents of both sexes spent most of their waking hours with adults of the same sex, boys in somewhat fewer societies than girls because, in foraging or pastoral cultures in the sample, the boys were often out with other boys hunting or herding. Most production in sedentary societies, whether farming or craft production, took place in the home, and adolescents worked alongside adults there.

Almost all production was sex typed, and girls and boys worked primarily with family members of the same sex. Overall, boys had the most contact with fathers and older brothers, the greatest subordination to and the least intimacy with fathers, and the most conflict with fathers and older brothers, although the level of conflict overall was low. Girls had the most contact with mothers and older sisters and, like boys, the greatest subordination to and the least intimacy with fathers. Level of conflict with all kin was very low. Although there were important exceptions, in general, family life was quite harmonious and showed little rebellion by adolescent sons or daughters. This is in marked contrast to the stereotypic (if overstated) portrayal of adolescence in modern societies.

It should be remembered that adolescents in most of these cultures depended heavily on parents and other kin for help in moving into the adult stage of life. Open defiance, without other resources to fall back on, would have been self-destructive. Nevertheless, parental interests could conflict with those of adolescents and youth, particularly when the children felt that they were being exploited or denied their legitimate dues, and open conflict or passive resistance could ensue.

Having said that, it should be emphasized that in most cases, as far as we can tell from the ethnographic literature, the older generation helped the younger one. We often hear that children provided social security in old age when other institutional means were lacking, and it is likely that that possibility factored into family decisions about fertility. However, over the course of a lifetime the resource flow was probably at least as much down the generational ladder as up, especially as most people did not live much past their productive years. The economic and social benefits of children came through their labor and marital connections as much as through later help to aged parents.

A striking feature of adolescent life in these traditional societies is the degree to which adolescents were embedded in adult-based structures and activities. We see this with the family and kin circle, and we shall see it again when we examine other social forms.

Peers and Peer Groups

Peer groups were an important feature of adolescent life in the cultures of the sample; but aside from those places where boys hunted or herded away from the home base or spent time in schools (like the Aztecs), peers often did not have many hours of the day when they were together. Unless adolescents were called out by adults for group instruction or community service, most peer contact occurred during leisure time.

Peer relations were more important in adolescence than in childhood in these traditional cultures, as they are in modern ones. Before adolescence, children rely heavily on their families for their needs, and they turn to family members for evaluation and validation. Adolescents in all cultures are more self-sufficient. In foraging societies, children were generally able to provide enough food to feed themselves by the time they reached adolescence, while European history and folklore tell of adolescent boys sent out to make their own way in the world.

In traditional cultures, as it is in modern ones, adolescence was a time when evaluation and validation by peers as well as adults became a critical issue. This may be because one's peers, the allies or competitors in adolescence, become one's adult allies or competitors in the near future, when economic and marital opportunities and decisions come into play.

Contact with Peers

Locations where adolescents joined with other adolescents differed somewhat between the sexes. Girls and boys both had groups of friends unless the local community was too small to have more than one or two adolescents at a time, like a small foraging band. In these cases, adolescents waited until bands congregated to meet up with their age-mates. In most communities, girls' groups or pairs of friends were just as likely to meet in the company of adult women, their mothers and neighbors, as apart from them. Boys' groups, however, tended to congregate away from adults or at the periphery of an adult male group. This spatial placement is described, or can be inferred from other descriptions, in

the ethnographic literature. The author has also observed it in a tribal Philippine village, an upper-class community in Malaysia, Hopi villages (all described in Schlegel & Barry, 1991), a town in Egypt, and one village each in modern Germany and Italy.

The Italian case is instructive, because this is a village in an advanced industrial culture. Its inhabitants were formerly peasants, but in the last half-century or more they have worked in a nearby city or held paid jobs in the local economy. The following scene describes the village piazza as the present author observed it on a summer evening in 2003. It depicts a pattern of spatial placement by sex and age-stage found over the world.

> On one side of the piazza stood the bar-restaurant, a gathering place for the local inhabitants. As evening fell, villagers began to drift in. After getting drinks at the bar, often coffee or soda, they took chairs outside. The men sat on one side of the main door and the women and adolescent girls sat on the other, although occasionally a man moved his chair over to the women's side to talk to his wife or mother. The male adolescents and youths sat or stood by the wall of the buildings opposite. In earlier times someone often would bring out an accordion or guitar for impromptu singing and dancing, but if there is music today it is likely to come from a transistor radio, as it did on this occasion. As the evening wore on, some girls and boys broke away from where they were standing or sitting and met off to one side of the piazza. A few left in pairs or small groups. The adults began to head homeward, and by ten o'clock the piazza was deserted.

The Structure and Character of Peer Groups

Both girls and boys in the cultures of the sample formed friendship dyads and peer groups, but girls were more likely than boys to meet in pairs. Peer groups of boys tended to be larger than peer groups of girls of the same culture, and they were more structured; that is, they more often had an established hierarchy and a name, more so in permanent than in nomadic or semipermanent settlements. Boys' peer groups were in general more important in socializing their members for adult community life than were girls' groups. Girls participated more in community life by accompanying mothers and other close kin, while boys were more likely to participate as groups of peers. When boys were under adult male supervision, the men in authority over them were not necessarily kin.

Peer-group activities also differed between the sexes. Girls joined together primarily for leisure-time activities, and these were usually unstructured like simple games or chatting and storytelling. Boys more than girls were engaged in structured activities like competitive games with rules (cf. Schlegel & Barry, 1989). As will be discussed later in this section on peer groups, boys' groups provided community service in more cultures than girls' groups did, although sometimes both girls' and boys' groups, together or separately, acted to benefit the community.

The dynamics of peer-group relations differed between girls and boys. Girls in most cultures exhibited little competitiveness in peer relations, although they were certainly capable of it; on an 11-point scale for this trait, two cultures received a rating of 9, the highest any culture received (20 received this rating for boys). Girls were frequently the minor members of groups dominated numerically and socially by adult women, which offered little opportunity for them to compete for social position. Boys, however, were often with other boys away from adult supervision during leisure time, and here jockeying for position in the status hierarchy could receive full play. Even when boys were under adult supervision, they might compete for excellence in whatever tasks the adults had assigned them, in order to win the approval of the men and the respect of their age-mates.

However, the same boys' groups that were internally competitive could also be cooperative—the two modes of operating were not mutually exclusive. This is illustrated by observations the author and her researchers

made in 1994–1996 of a class of 15 adolescent boy apprentices in Frankfurt am Main, Germany. They were members of an in-house vocational training program of a major electronics firm. The following description is drawn from the author's notes:

> It did not take many weeks from the beginning of the training program for this class to sort themselves into a hierarchy, which lasted through the two-and-a-half years they were being observed. The boy who seemed the most assertive at first ended up in the middle group, while the undisputed leader who emerged was the boy who clearly excelled over the others. The boys at neither the top nor the bottom displayed a good deal of good natured competition in their humorous but pointed banter and controlled horseplay. Toward the bottom were the one or two less competent, and the least competent was frequently the butt of jokes and pranks. Nevertheless, the better apprentices helped the others, including the boy at the bottom, and everyone was usually invited when they got together outside of their work-training hours. Social rank in this group depended on competence on the job, particularly the hands-on projects.

Participation in Community Life

Peer-Group Participation in the Community

Adolescent peer groups often engage in activities that benefit the entire community. One universal or almost universal way is to provide entertainment for adults through displays of beauty and prowess in dancing and sports. These displays serve several purposes. Beyond providing entertainment, they allow adults to look the adolescents over and judge them as worthy or unworthy of attention. In small communities where future social success and even marital prospects depend on how they are viewed by adults, young people are eager to be looked on favorably. And they all want to be admired by their fellow adolescents, particularly those of the opposite sex.

In some cultures in the sample and elsewhere, adolescent groups assumed responsibility for certain rituals, community festivals, or other community projects. Groups of adolescent boys in some Japanese villages, and groups of adolescents of both sexes in some tribal regions of India, were responsible for keeping village paths clean. Ritual involvement by teenage girls and boys was common throughout Latin America, where the adolescent groups took on such duties as helping to clean the church or organize religious processions. Some tasks of community life, like taking charge of certain aspects of public festivals, were done by groups of adolescent girls and boys, separately or together. This practice continues in Siena, Italy, today in the public dinners held as fundraisers by the city's district associations (*contrade*), where adolescents take part by helping set up, clean up, and serve food.

Adolescent groups may also be given some responsibility for enforcing community rules of behavior. Reports of adolescent boys being allowed to engage in what otherwise would be considered antisocial acts—destroying property of rule violators, beating those who have aggressed against the community in some way, or publicly mocking those persons whose behavior threatens community moral standards—come from such disparate places as Pygmy villages in the Congo, American Chinatowns, and European peasant villages, respectively. In all these cases, groups of boys were permitted to aggress against disruptive adults with community approval.

Participation as Individuals

In traditional communities, adolescents were everywhere, working with adults or sharing responsibility. Adolescent girls and boys sold in the marketplace, participated with their family members in public rituals, and made themselves available to adults for tasks beyond the capabilities of younger children.

Adolescents also participated as individuals in religious sodalities and civil organizations. Hopi girls and boys began to take part in sodality activities as children, taking on increasing responsibility as adolescents. In contemporary Germany, many adolescents from about age 15 or 16 join one or more of the clubs (*Vereine*), from hunting or singing to chess or stamp collecting, that are a prominent feature of German town and village life.

The ethnographies used in the Adolescent Socialization Project, as well as others of cultures not in the sample, reveal that adolescents interacted freely and often with adults in the community. These adults were not just family members or adults who had authority over them in specific domains, like employers, religious leaders, or instructors, but also adults engaged in the same activities as the adolescents. Adolescents may have in many respects behaved differently, and were treated differently, than either children or adults, but they were not segregated.

Sexual Attitudes and Practices
Managing Adolescents' Sexual Behavior
Families and communities everywhere must deal with adolescent children who are not considered ready for marriage, but who are highly motivated to engage in sexual relations. Adolescent girls are also capable of producing offspring, once they lose the protection of adolescent subfecundity.

A matter of concern to a girl's family was the possibility of her pregnancy outside of marriage. Bastardy by itself was not a social problem where children of unwed mothers either stayed with the maternal grandparents when the mother married, or accompanied the mother into her new household. However, even where such children were not stigmatized in any way, they were still at a disadvantage. This is because there was usually no obligation for the biological father or his kin to provide whatever material or social benefits they normally provided to a man's children; if they did provide any, what they gave often depended on how they valued any particular child. This was true for matrilineal societies, where children belong to their mothers' kin group, as well as those with other forms of kinship.

Managing the strong sexual urges of boys and youth, unsupervised by adults during much of their leisure time, concerned the larger community. If boys and youth had no class of females sexually available to them, such as their female age-mates, it was tempting to try to flout the rules and seduce unmarried girls or the young wives of adult men. The sexuality of young males in these cultures was a matter of concern to the fathers of daughters and the older husbands of young wives (Schlegel, 1991). The families of boys were also interested parties, as angry fathers and husbands could cause trouble for them as well as for their adolescents.

The Value on Virginity

Whether or not sexual intercourse, or heterosexual activity of any kind, was permitted depended on the way people valued virginity, particularly virginity of girls. A cross-cultural study with the same sample by the present author (Schlegel, 1991) found that virginity was valued to a statistically significant degree when family property accompanied daughters into marriage, as in dowry or indirect dowry. It tended to be valued in far fewer cultures in which goods or labor (i.e., bride wealth and bride service) were provided to the family of the bride by the groom or his family. Fewer than half of the cultures in which bride wealth was given valued virginity. In other words, families were more likely to pay to give a virgin daughter than to acquire a virgin daughter-in-law. Virginity was also not likely to be valued when no goods, beyond perhaps voluntary wedding gifts to the couple, were given at marriage.

What this means is that cultures, and social classes in class-stratified societies, in which the bride's family gave property generally demanded virginity and attached a moral value to it. This value was found in most of the traditional civilizations of Europe, Asia, and the pre-Columbian civilizations of the New World, at least in their propertied classes where marriage transactions that involved the transfer

of property from the bride's family were the norm. Some areas of Southeast Asia were an exception; Red (1988), writing of the fifteenth and sixteenth centuries, attributes this to the economic independence of women there, and it is likely that the availability of safe and socially approved abortions was also a factor.

Sexually Permissive Cultures

Where virginity had little or no value, adolescent girls were allowed to engage in sexual activity, which may or may not have included full sexual intercourse. The most permissive cultures were those that had adolescent dormitories where girls and boys congregated in the evening, after the day's work and the evening meal with the family were over. After singing and games it was usual for couples to pair off to sleep together, with or without intercourse. Such dormitories were found in parts of tribal Southeast Asia and India. The East African Kikuyu also had adolescent dormitories where couples could fondle and engage in interfemoral intercourse, but here the girls wore leather aprons that prevented penetration.

The best descriptions of an adolescent dormitory, somewhat romanticized, come from Elwin's (1947) ethnography of the Muria tribe of Madhya Pradesh, India, and a later study of the same people by Gell (1992). The sexual freedom of adolescence was fondly remembered by older Muria. Once married, however, a couple was expected to be faithful. Adultery was strongly disapproved, and according to reports it was rare.

We should not think that these were adolescent paradises, however. There is plenty of evidence that girls and boys often felt rejected when their favored partner preferred someone else. A Muria girl in love with her preferred partner, and the boy who loved her, were despondent when her parents married her to someone else.

Even where adolescents had sexual freedom, boys did not necessarily have access to girls. Girls could require gifts and tests of devotion before they were willing to accept a suitor. Alternatives to heterosexual intercourse in these and other societies were masturbation and homoerotic activity.

Homoerotic Activity

There is little ethnographic reporting on masturbation among adolescents, as this is a private practice that is rarely observed by ethnographers or discussed with them. There is, however, information on adolescent homoerotic activity in a number of cultures in the sample. From the evidence we have, it appears that where adolescent homoerotic behavior was tolerated or expected for one or both sexes, it was considered to be either youthful experimentation or an acceptable outlet for sexual urges, without social consequences like an out-of-wedlock pregnancy (Schlegel, 1995). There was no evidence that homoerotic activity in adolescence led to adult homosexuality as a preferred or frequent form of sexual behavior.

Ritualized homoerotic behavior, involving adolescent boys, has been reported for several parts of Melanesia (Herdt, 1984). The fullest ethnography that discusses this is Herdt's (1981) book on the Sambia (a fictitious name). Young males until marriage slept in the men's house, which during the day was used as a meeting place for adult men. Preadolescent Sambia boys fellated adolescent boys, a behavior the Sambia explained by their belief that boys need to ingest semen in order to grow. When the boys married, their wives had not yet reached menarche. They, too, needed semen, so both these immature wives and the younger boys fellated the youngest husbands. After the wife's menarche, or at least after a child was born, fellatio was discontinued and heterosexual intercourse was the normal sexual practice for adults.

Sexual Abuse of Adolescents

The somewhat developed bodies of adolescents plus their lack of social power make them potential victims of sexual predators. Most of the ethnographic information for the sample came from observations made in small communities, villages or long-established neighborhoods in traditional towns and cities. Predatory acts here would be difficult to accomplish and would be seriously punished by family, kin, and community members. However, there is information on sexual abuse for one of the societies, ancient Rome during the early Empire.

The third century was close to the time span pinpointed for the sample (A.D. 110), when the morals and customs of the Romans were adapted by Christian society and colored the writings of the first Church Fathers. Clement of Alexandria, not of Rome but socialized to upper-class Roman culture, warned Christians against frequenting brothels, for the girls or boys they engaged might be sons or daughters they had abandoned as unwanted infants (Boswell, 1988). Other evidence of the sexual use of adolescent slaves or prostitutes is plentiful for Ancient Greece and Rome. It is likely that similar information could be found for any of the large cities of pre-industrial Europe or Asia, where abandonment of unwanted children, slavery, or destitution of the underclass provided a pool of exploitable adolescents.

One domain in which sexual abuse is known from much anecdotal evidence to occur, but for which systematically collected data are very scanty, is abuse within the family, or more often the circle of kin. Relatives such as uncles and older cousins have opportunities to abuse young adolescents sexually in cultures that promote family cohesiveness, where relatives come into frequent contact and children are expected to respect older kin and obey them without question. Many of these cultures like those of India and the Middle East, value virginity, the loss of which brings shame on the family (Schlegel, 1991). Family members blame the abused girls themselves, and their mothers for not adequately supervising them, rather than risk tearing the social fabric of the larger kin group. While such abuse is no doubt rare, there is enough anecdotal information to indicate that it can happen where there are opportunities for such abuse. It is the deviant side of close kin connections and the involvement of adolescents with adult kin.

Adolescent Misbehavior

Misbehavior has to be judged according to the cultural standards of the community: what is delinquent for one society or sector may not be for another. We have already seen that adolescents may be called upon to do the social "dirty work" that is below the dignity of adults to do, or that would result in major ruptures of social harmony if performed by adults. In such cases, boys' peer groups may be encouraged to punish those who pose some sort of threat to the community, as in the American Chinatowns or Pygmy villages already mentioned. For purposes of the cross-cultural study, antisocial behavior was defined as expected misbehavior, not the actions of deviants who probably exist in every society. It included such diverse activities as hostile speech, fighting or crimes against persons, theft, disapproved sexual behavior, and disapproved drunkenness or misuse of other drugs.

Information on this subject was rather sparse, from only 54 cultures for boys and 28 for girls. It was impossible to generalize about the girls, for expected antisocial behavior was present in only six cultures. For boys, it was coded as present in 24 and absent in 30. We cannot assume that absence of reporting means absence of the feature, but it is probable that in detailed ethnographies, expected antisocial behavior would have been mentioned if it were a prominent feature of the culture. In our best judgment, boys' adolescent misbehavior was limited and occasional in most societies. Girls were even less likely to cause problems for the community. The most common forms of boys' misbehavior were theft (nine) and physical violence (seven).

Theft is significantly associated with the opportunity to own property, such as domesticated animals, but work is not emphasized as an area of skill. In other words, it seems that theft resulted from the desire for goods without a means by which the individual could gain them by effort other than theft. Theft of animals is endemic in pastoral societies, for example, and one way of starting a herd is to steal from your neighbor (disapproved) or a neighboring community (often approved). Violence was most likely to occur where peer competition was high and cooperation was low. Boys also followed the example of adults, for adolescent violence is significantly associated with frequent deviance by men.

Theft and violence do not show any relation to hostile or strained relations within the family or with adults in general. They appear to have resulted from present situations that stimulated impulsive behavior, the failure of socialization in teaching how to control impulses, and, where adult deviance was high, the example of grown men.

Boys' antisocial behavior in general is positively related to a low degree of contact that boys had with adult men generally and adult men outside the home, that is, men who were not members of their household. It is also positively related to a lack of emphasis on productive skills. This means that in cultures that involved boys with adult men and taught them productive skills, teaching that was usually done by grown men, boys were not likely to be expected to misbehave. Most girls in the sample societies had close and frequent, often almost continuous, contact with adult women, and they were usually kept busy learning and doing productive work.

Some Implications for Contemporary Adolescence

Our examination of a number of features of adolescence that differ across cultures or between the sexes suggests several implications for adolescence in modern and modernizing cultures.

Involvement with Adults

Adolescents in modern cultures generally spend less time with adults, and adults of the same sex, than adolescents in traditional cultures, since they are in school for much of the day, and adult family members and neighbors often work away from home. The contrast of adolescents in the sample cultures with American adolescents is particularly striking. In the United States, extreme age segregation limits contacts across generations in civic or leisure-time activities. In many sectors of American society, adolescents are remarkably uninvolved with adults other than immediate family members and authority figures like teachers, coaches, youth leaders, and the like.

Yet, it would be wrong to assume that adults other than parents play no meaningful roles in the lives of American adolescents. It would be easy to stereotype American teenagers as A Tribe Apart, the title of a recent book (Hersch, 1998). As the work of Greenberger, Chen, and Beam, (1998) on VIPs (very important persons) shows, adolescents often have one or two adults other than parents to whom they turn for counsel. Hamilton and Darling (1998), among others, have also written about the importance of adult mentors in the lives of adolescents. Nevertheless, for many adolescents, the workplace and civil society provide few opportunities for adolescents to develop long-term close relationships with unrelated adults; and while young people may love grandparents and other kin, these are often not readily available.

In the European nations where the author has done research, Italy and Germany, adolescents are much more involved with adults than American teenagers are, even though European adolescents attend school and spend considerable leisure time with peers. Kin and neighborhood networks in these countries provide more scope for adolescent–adult interaction, and institutions exist that promote such interaction. This is pronounced in Germany and other German-speaking countries and regions, which have extensive apprenticeship programs for adolescents. German adolescents are also involved with adults in social clubs and civic organizations, the *Vereine*.

Socialization for adulthood begins early when adolescents interact often and freely with adults. It eases the transition to adulthood, as adolescents have many opportunities to observe adult behavior and select realistic role models from those they admire. Such interaction also sets the stage for possible friendships between the generations. These may be especially valuable as escape valves when pressures within the family and with peers mount, and adolescents can turn to adults, rather than other adolescents, for solace and advice. Institutions that involve adolescents with adults also provide settings for socialization that could be particularly important for the children of dysfunctional families.

Work

Most adolescents in traditional societies, where production generally took place in the home or the small job shop, were at work for much of their time. Schooling, where it existed, took up only part of the day. Among traditional elites, whose children did not do productive labor, the boys learned the skills they would need to be successful managers of family enterprises, soldiers, diplomats, or whatever elite men did, and girls learned the practical and social skills they would need as wives of these men.

Such practical learning is found in apprenticeship programs in modern societies. While informal apprenticeships are widespread throughout the world, Germany, Austria, and Switzerland have established apprenticeship systems that employ the majority of their adolescent boys and girls aged 16 and older. These adolescents, who are either in blue-collar or white-collar apprenticeships, typically attend vocational school (with some academic subjects) for part of the time and work the rest of the time at their place of employment, where they receive apprentice wages. These systems bring together employers, unions, and state educational bureaucracies in a relationship that is not always harmonious, but it does produce an institution that succeeds in preparing young people for future vocations.

Apprenticeship programs modeled after the German system have been adapted to American high-school settings in a few places (Schlegel,

1996). They offer adolescents the opportunity to enter jobs that are not dead-end but rather are the first rung on a vocational career ladder. A broader application of similar programs would be particularly helpful for adolescents who lack the ability or the motivation to continue on to higher education, and it would give them an incentive to finish high school and get their vocational certificate.

Sexual Behavior

Sexual activity among adolescents to the point of sexual intercourse now is more common, and in many quarters more tolerated, than it was fifty years ago. The decline in the value on virginity corresponds in time with increased opportunities of young people to be independent of family resources, and the corresponding decline of adult authority over them. There has been a trickle-down effect from the sexual freedom of youth to the sexual freedom of adolescents, particularly as means of escaping adult supervision have increased through access to cars and now the Internet, and adults themselves are more permissive toward sexual behavior outside of marriage.

Sexual permissiveness is not without consequences. The most obvious are the risks of pregnancy and contracting a sexually transmitted disease; another is the danger of sexual coercion by other adolescents. There are emotional risks as well. As we saw in the case of the Muria, sexual intimacy can intensify emotional attachment for one or both participants, and the almost inevitable break-up can be very disturbing to adolescents unprepared to cope with such an emotional jolt.

Judging from the limited amount of available information, homoerotic behavior among adolescents is not uncommon in traditional cultures, nor is it usually stigmatized. There is no evidence that such acts in adolescence lead to a preference for homosexuality or even to an interest in it, unless the individual already has that preference. For many adolescents with heterosexual preference, homoerotic acts may be a kind of waystation between the sexual play of children and full adult heterosexuality. Experimentation with a same-sex friend can be a way of socializing young people for sexual behavior with a partner of the opposite sex, without the same emotional load that a heterosexual relationship may carry for one or both participants. This would only be true of the kind of homoerotic activities reported for cultures of the sample; that is, they occur among adolescent friends, where the dangers of sexual predation and the risk of sexually transmitted disease are minimal, not between adolescents and adults.

Antisocial Behavior

The two most common forms of misbehavior in the sample cultures are theft and fighting. Theft is associated with the difficulty or impossibility of obtaining desired objects. Juvenile theft in modern societies is generally dealt with through attempts at prevention, and punishment. It is probably impossible to curtail desire, as television and advertising keep desirable material objects constantly in view, and one mark of high status in the group is ownership of these objects. But a better way to prevent theft, by reducing the motive, would be to increase the means by which adolescents who otherwise would not have access to these objects could attain them in a legitimate manner, through earnings of some kind. Unlike adolescents in some nations, American teenagers who are not bound for college have little access to programs that vocationally train and gainfully employ them and prepare them for adult vocations.

Violence was found where peer competition was high and cooperation was low. Some competition for status, and for attractiveness to the opposite sex, is probably inherent in adolescent social relationships. However, young people are less likely to become angry and fight when they are working together on a project and depending on one another for success in completing it. Activities that place less emphasis on competition and more on cooperation, particularly cooperation with tangible results that bring recognition and reward to the whole cooperating group, would be a place to start.

It would be very difficult to reduce adolescent misbehavior when adults frequently commit antisocial acts, for these variables are significantly correlated. Attempts to reduce youth delinquency alone are less likely to be effective than attempts that also address adult delinquency. Adolescent delinquency may be more than simply an epiphenomenon of adult delinquency; it may have causes of its own, but it exists within an environment of adult delinquency, as the cross-cultural study finds.

DISCUSSION

The cross-cultural method is correlational, not experimental, and it has the strengths and weaknesses of all correlational methods. Cross-cultural studies are most valuable when they are one of a set of studies that use different methods to address a topic (i.e., triangulation), but this can be said of any kind of study in the social sciences. The findings of cross-cultural studies of adolescence, instructive by themselves, also point to directions that other studies can take using more restricted samples, such as a sample from a single culture.

Some of the findings presented here have been illustrated with single-case studies, based on the field research of the author and others. Those that are relevant to research on modern adolescents received particular attention.

Overall, cross-cultural data indicate that social adolescence is a panhuman phenomenon. The few ambiguous cases seem to be anomalies that could be explained by specific local conditions. Projecting into the past, it seems likely that our late-Pleistocene ancestors, and even earlier ones, recognized a social adolescence. This possibility is reinforced by studies of a developmental stage in the behavior of higher primates that is analogous to human social adolescence (Walters, 1987).

We have also seen that social adolescence is generally coterminus with biological adolescence, but its beginning and ending can vary according to social conditions. Since biological adolescence is broadly defined as the period during which the human reproductive system becomes active and matures, it is not surprising that social adolescence in most cases begins with some physical signs of puberty and ends with marriage, when the reproductive careers of most people become established. In cultures or social sectors where marriage is delayed for one or both sexes, a second pre-adult period intervenes between adolescence and full social adulthood. This we have termed *youth*.

The presence of adolescence as a social stage has often been explained as a needed time for young people to learn adult skills and roles. This explanation is called into question when we learn that in many traditional societies, by puberty both sexes had acquired the survival skills they needed. Furthermore, it was common worldwide for adult married couples to live with the groom's or the bride's parents, permanently (until these parents died) or up to the time they were able to set up their own household. Presumably, a very young couple just past puberty would be as capable of survival as an older couple, for both would be embedded in the social networks that promote survival. So there is more to adolescence than just a time for extended learning of survival skills.

As we have seen, this social stage has a biological basis. For girls, menarche, or other physical signs of puberty, signal the readiness to move out of childhood; for boys, secondary sex characteristics also indicate that the boy has reached sexual maturity and is no longer a child. For humans as for higher primates, eggs and sperm do not by themselves lead to full adult reproductive behavior (which in humans is generally preceded by the formation of some kind of pair bond). At the very minimum, female bodies have to develop sufficiently to carry a pregnancy, and male bodies must be sufficiently large and developed to indicate that they can fulfill the requirements of manhood. Biological adolescence is the time when both sexes make this transition. Social adolescence generally tracks biological adolescence, with some variations across cultures as to the beginning and ending of this social stage.

The biology of reproductive development was probably no different for Pleistocene *Homo sapiens* than it is for us today, although the timing may have been. The reproductive maturity of children of both sexes comes early in modern well-nourished societies, with diets that promote the higher levels of body fat that are associated with early puberty. By comparison, reproductive maturity occurs late in many foraging societies of recent times. This can be accounted for by their low-fat and low-sugar diet—wild vegetal foods and the lean meat that comes from wild game. It is likely that puberty came much later to our Pleistocene ancestors, and social adolescence may have been rather short, especially for girls. A longer period of social adolescence may be a cultural artifact, brought on by the domestication of calorie-rich plant and animal foods that promoted earlier puberty without a corresponding early entrance into adulthood.

A stage of social adolescence for girls is a cultural feature, but it may be based in part on the recognition that early pregnancies can be difficult and dangerous. The dangers of pregnancies may be greater where biological adolescence comes early, before the female body has fully developed. If menarche is late, and full fecundity is not achieved before the late teens, pregnancy at age 18 or 19 is probably safe if the pregnant mother receives adequate nutrition. In such cases, social adolescence could be short without endangering the woman's health or that of her child.

Adolescent boys, whose growth spurt follows spermarche, do not look like men and are not ready to participate fully in adult male activities. As we have seen, men usually exclude adolescent boys from their leisure-time groups or allow their presence only at the margins of the men's group. By the very late teens, though, most boys are ready to join the society of adult men, unless cultural factors create an intervening youth stage.

Human evolution and behavior are dependent on neither nature nor nurture alone, but rather on the complex interplay and mutual influence of biological and cultural factors. An understanding of adolescent behavior, and how social adolescence comes to be a stage in the human life cycle, requires a biocultural approach.

CONCLUDING REMARKS

The data for this chapter come from a sample of preindustrial cultures. Many of these cultures still exist, but they do so in a form that would be unrecognizable to the residents of the communities in which the ethnographic observations were made. The people of these cultures are all moving into the industrial world, for better or for worse, if they have not already done so. Pygmy foragers of the Congo have become sedentary farmers. The Yanomami of tropical South America are connected to the Internet and fight for indigenous rights. Grandchildren of Uttar Pradesh villagers go to New Delhi for jobs or education, and some emigrate to England or the United States. Kazaks, former pastoralists, are very much in the news as the nation of Kazakhstan enters the world market with its oil and gas reserves. In large stretches of the Sudan, some adolescents who in earlier times would have, at worst, tried to steal a cow are now killing innocent victims: "Child" soldiers are often teenagers capable of wielding a loaded AK-47 rifle that weighs 9.5 pounds.

Today's teenagers are no longer isolated from modern political and economic forces; they are participants in the global reach of contemporary adolescent culture (Schlegel, 1999; see also Amit-Talai & Wulff, 1995). Their lives have changed irrevocably, and the future of their cultures depends on how they are prepared to meet these changes.

REFERENCES

Amit-Talai, V., & Wulff, H. (Eds.). (1995). *Youth cultures: A cross-cultural perspective.* London: Routledge.

Arnett, J. J. (2001). *Adolescence and emerging adulthood: A cultural approach.* Upper Saddle River, NJ: Prentice Hall.

Barry, H., III, & Schlegel, A. (Eds.). (1980). *Cross-cultural samples and codes.* Pittsburgh: University of Pittsburgh Press.

Barry, H., III, & Schlegel, A. (1990). *Adolescence.* HRAF Research Series in Quantative Cross-Cultural Data, vol. *IV.* New Haven, CT: Human Relations Area Files Press.

Berry, J. W. (1966). Temne and Eskimo perceptual skills. *International Journal of Psychology, 1,* 207–229.

Berry, J. W., Poortinga, Y. H., Segall, M. H., & Dasen, P. R. (1992). *Cross-cultural psychology: Research and applications.* Cambridge: Cambridge University Press.

Bogin, B. (1999). *Patterns of human growth.* Cambridge: Cambridge University Press.

Boswell, J. (1988). *The kindness of strangers: The abandonment of children in western Europe from late antiquity to the Renaissance.* New York: Pantheon.

Burbank, V. K. (1988). *Aboriginal adolescence: Maidenhood in an Australian community.* New Brunswick: Rutgers University Press.

Cohen, Y. A. (1964). *The transition from childhood to adolescence: Cross-cultural studies of initiation ceremonies, legal systems, and incest taboos.* Chicago: Aldine.

Condon, R. G. (1987). *Inuit youth: Growth and change in the Canadian Arctic.* New Brunswick: Rutgers University Press.

Dasen, P. R. (1972). Cross-cultural Piagetian research: A summary. *Journal of Cross-Cultural Psychology, 7,* 75–85.

Davis, S. S., & Davis, D. A. (1989). *Adolescence in a Moroccan town: Making social sense.* New Brunswick: Rutgers University Press.

Elwin, V. (1947). *The Muria and their ghotul.* London: Oxford University Press.

Eveleth, P. B., & Tanner, J. M. (1976). *Worldwide variation in human growth.* Cambridge, UK: Cambridge University Press.

Gell, S. M. S. (1992). *The ghotul in Muria society.* Chur, Switzerland: Harwood Academic Publishers.

Greenberger, E., Chen, C., & Beam, M. R. (1998). The role of "very important" non-parental adults in adolescent development. *Journal of Youth and Adolescence, 4,* 321–343.

Hall, C. S. (1954). *A primer of Freudian psychology.* New York: World Publishing.

Hamilton, S., & Darling, N. (1998). Mentors in adolescents' lives. In K. Hurrelmann & U. Engels (Eds.), *The social world of adolescents; International perspectives* (pp. 121–139). Berlin: Walter de Gruyter.

Herdt, G. (1981). *Guardians of the flutes: Idioms of masculinity.* New York: McGraw-Hill.

Herdt, G. (1984). *Ritualized homosexuality in Melanesia.* Berkeley: University of California Press.

Hersch, P. (1998). *A tribe apart: A journey into the heart of American adolescence.* New York: Fawcett Columbine.

Hollos, M., & Leis, P. E. (1989). *Becoming Nigerian in Ijo society.* New Brunswick, NJ: Rutgers University Press.

Hooper, C. (2004). *Cognition-emotion interactions: Late maturation of decision-making.* Paper presented at the 10th annual meeting of the Society for Research on Adolescence, Baltimore, MD, March 11–14.

Levi, G., & Schmitt, J.-C. (Eds.) (1997). *A history of young people,* vols. 1 and 2. Cambridge, MA: Belknap Press.

Mead, M. (1928). *Coming of age in Samoa.* Ann Arbor, MI: Morrow.

Mitterauer, M. (1992). *A history of youth.* Oxford: Blackwell.

Morgan, L. H. (1877). *Ancient society.* New York: World Publishing.

Murdock, G. P., & White, D. R. (1969). The standard cross-cultural sample. *Ethnology, 8,* 329–369.

Reid, A. (1988). *Southeast Asia in the age of commerce 1450–1680, vol. 1: The lands below the winds.* New Haven, CT: Yale University Press.

Saraswathi, T. S., & Dutta, R. (1988). *Invisible boundaries; grooming for adult roles. A descriptive study of socialization in a poor rural and urban slum setting in Gujarat.* New Delhi: Northern Book Centre.

Sharma, N. (1996). *Identity of the adolescent girl.* New Delhi: Discovery Publishing House.

Schlegel, A. (1973). The adolescent socialization of the Hopi girl. *Ethnology, 12,* 449–462.

Schlegel, A. (1991). Status, property, and the value on virginity. *American Ethnologist, 18,* 719–734.

Schlegel, A. (1995). The cultural management of adolescent sexuality. In P. Abramson and S. Pinkerton (Eds.), *Sexual nature/ sexual culture* (pp. 177–194). Chicago: University of Chicago Press.

Schlegel, A. (1996). *The Fox Valley apprenticeship program.* Unpublished report to the Menasha Corporation Foundation and the Fox Cities Chamber of Commerce and Industry.

Schlegel, A. (1999). The global spread of adolescent culture. In R. Silbereisen & L. Crockett (Eds.), *Negotiating adolescence in times of social change: Cross-national perspectives on developmental process and social intervention* (pp. 71–88). New York: Cambridge University Press.

Schlegel, A., & Barry, H., III. (1980). The evolutionary significance of adolescent initiation ceremonies. *American Ethnologist, 7,* 696–715.

Schlegel, A., & Barry, H., III. (1989). Adolescents at play: A cross-cultural study of adolescent games. In R. Bolton (Ed.), *The content of culture: Constants and variants* (pp. 33–48). New Haven: Human Relations Area Files Press.

Schlegel, A., & Barry H., III. (1991). *Adolescence: An anthropological inquiry.* New York: Free Press.

Segall, M. H, Dasen, P. R., Berry, J. W., & Poortinga, Y. H. (1990). *Human behavior in global perspective: An introduction to cross-cultural psychology.* Boston: Allyn and Bacon.

Steinberg, L., Dahl, R., Keating, D., Kupfer, D. J., Masten, A. S., & Pine, D. (2006). Psychopathology in adolescence: Integrating affective neuroscience with the study of context. In D. Cicchetti & D. Cohen (Eds.), *Developmental psychopathology,* vol. 2: *Developmental neuroscience* (pp. 710–741). Hoboken, NJ: John Wiley & Sons.

Tylor, E. B. (1889). On a method of investigating the development of insitutions; applied to laws of marriage and descent. *Journal of the Royal Anthropological Institute, 18,* 245–269.

Vizmanos, B., & Marti-Hennenberg, C. (2001). Puberty begins with body fat mass in each sex. *European Journal of Clinical Nutrition, 54,* 203–208.

Walters, J. R. (1987). Transition to adulthood. In B. B. Smuts, D. L. Cheney, R. M. Seyfarth, R. W. Wrangham, & T. T. Struhsaker (Eds.), *Primate societies* (pp. 358–369). Chicago: University of Chicago Press.

Weisner, T. S. (1982). Sibling independence and child caretaking: A cross-cultural view. In M. E. Lamb & B. Sutton-Smith (Eds.), *Sibling relationships: Their nature and significance across the lifespan* (pp. 305–328). Hillsdale: Lawrence Earlbaum.

Weisfeld, G. (1999). *Evolutionary principles of human adolescence.* New York: Basic Books.

Wilson, M. (1951). *Good company: A study of Nyakyusa age villages.* London: Oxford University Press.

Young, F. W. (1965). *Initiation ceremonies: A cross-cultural study of status dramatization.* Indianapolis: Bobbs-Merrill.

CHAPTER 17

Globalization, Societal Change, and Adolescence Across the World

REED W. LARSON, SUZANNE WILSON, AND AIMEE RICKMAN

As we move into the twenty-first century, it is clear that the life period of adolescence can no longer be seen as just a Western phenomenon. A transitional life stage between childhood and adulthood is now evident in nearly all societies of the world. Schlegel and Barry (1991) argued that some form of adolescence, often brief, existed across nonindustrial societies. The new adolescences now taking hold across societies, however, are distinguished by a common set of historically recent elements associated with modernization and globalization that create a longer period of liminality and transition. These include earlier puberty, longer schooling, and later marriage (Larson, 2002; Lloyd, 2005). For many youth these changes also include delayed participation in the labor force, greater separation from the world of adults, and prolonged experience of uncertainty about one's future.

We use the plural *adolescences* deliberately to emphasize the diversity in the experience of this life period across societies and subpopulations. Adolescence takes different forms in different contexts as a function of the distinct combination of cultural, social, and economic processes at work. In many societies, for example, this period does not carry the connotations of emotional turmoil associated with adolescence in the West, nor does it involve the task of psychic separation from parents (Dasen, 2000). Relationships with peers are a central element of adolescence in some societies (Nsamenang, 2002) but not in others (Booth, 2002; Verma & Saraswathi, 2002).

A common feature across settings is societal change. Rapid economic change is occurring in all parts of the world. Governance is unstable in many nations. New technologies, ideas, and instant cross-global communication contribute to upheaval and careening social change. As a product of this change, adolescence everywhere has been in flux. Outside influences have sparked sexual revolutions in Japan and parts of Latin America (Stevenson & Zusho, 2002; Welti, 2002). In Islamic nations, significant numbers of youth are attracted to a Muslim fundamentalism that embraces distinct gender roles, veiling of young women, and resistance to Western world views (Booth, 2002; Hoffman, 1995). Changes in the economic well-being of nations influences their ability to provide an infrastructure of schools, health care, and other resources for youth. Frequent movement of jobs from one country to another creates instability in the types of employment youth can expect to obtain as adults. The adolescences evolving across the world are postmodern hybrids of local and global, traditional and modern, combined in different and changing ways.

The work on this paper was partly supported by the William T. Grant Foundation. Thanks to Marcela Raffaelli and Philip Hoffman for input and assistance with the preparation of this chapter.

This change and flux, in some cases, creates opportunities for young people to shape lives for themselves that were unimaginable by their parents. Young women in many nations, for example, are gaining more opportunities to exercise choice and enter the labor force than was true a generation ago (International Labour Office [ILO], 2007; United Nations [UN], 2007). But change also creates uncertainty and peril. Many youth are taking uncharted pathways that put them at risk for exploitation, for sexual victimization, or, simply, for reaching adulthood ill-prepared for the demands of life in the twenty-first century.

For developmental scientists, the emergence of new and diverse adolescences represents a major challenge. There are currently over one billion youth in the second decade of life—the largest number ever—and we know very little about the great majority of them. A new generation of scholars in the developing world is learning more about the lives of adolescents in their nations (cf. Arnett, 2007), often reporting their studies in regional languages. Yet, most scholars of adolescence are in Western nations, and their knowledge of this age period is based almost entirely on youth in their corners of the world. Given increased global interaction, migration, and interdependency, it is essential that the field of adolescence awake from its parochialism and pay attention to the multiplicity of adolescences in Asia, Africa, the Middle East, Latin America, and the former Soviet states. None of us can be experts on the myriad of adolescences of the world, but we can learn about the general processes that are shaping them and the range of influences they have on youth.

This chapter is aimed at that challenge. We examine the processes of globalization occurring across nations, and how these are shaping the experience of the adolescent transition. Our primary focus is on the second decade of life, but given that our concern is with the transition between childhood and adulthood, we periodically include youth of later chronological ages. (Following similar reasoning, the United Nations reports that we cite often aggregate youth ages 15–24 as a single age group.) In Part I we examine the larger macro system processes driving changes. To understand adolescence in any part of the world, developmental scientists need to be aware of the demographic, economic, political, technological, cultural, and other processes that are shaping this age period in that locale. Our goal in Part I is to provide an overview of these macro processes and to examine how they may influence the adolescent transition across different international contexts. Given its wide scope, this first half of the chapter is inevitably general. In Part II, we examine the impact of these processes within four specific domains of adolescent research. We first look at how diverse societies represent adolescence and how these representations are changing. Then we examine the impacts of macro changes in the domains of adolescent family relationships, adolescent work, and gender differences. Although globalization is influencing these four domains in all parts of the world, we chose to focus on non-Western nations in Part II because of the need for the field to catch up on its knowledge of adolescence in these contexts.

A primary concern across the chapter is how different societal changes are improving or harming conditions for youth to prepare for meaningful adulthood. Following both the international literature on "human development" (Sen, 1999; UN, 2005) and the psychological literature on positive development (Benson, Scales & Sesma, 2005; Guerra & Bradshaw, in press; Silbereisen & Lerner, 2007), we ask how these changes are creating increasing supports (versus obstacles) for youth. The underlying postulate is that, under the right conditions, youth have enormous capacities for agency: for hard work, growth, adaptation, and contributing to society. How are these societal changes restricting or expanding young people's potentials for self-determination, positive relationships, development of psychological well-being, and preparation for meaningful employment and civic engagement?

It should be noted that the chapter is limited by the incomplete state of research on adolescents in developing countries. On the one hand there are good cross-national data on youth's educational achievement (United Nations Educational, Scientific and Cultural Organization [UNESCO], 2007), employment (ILO, 2006a, 2006b), health (World Health Organization [WHO], 2003), marriage, and other demographic indicators (UN, 2005, 2007). But there are comparatively few longitudinal studies, particularly ones that focus on developmental issues or allow testing of how macro societal variables influence adolescents' experiences. A recent panel of the National Research Council and Institute of Medicine describes large gaps between expansive conceptual frameworks and research evidence (Lloyd, 2005). It should also be acknowledged that our attempt to survey this enormous topic is inevitably constrained by our experiences and blind spots. This is a topic that begs for input from scholars with diverse perspectives, especially those from outside the West (Nsamenang, 2002, 2004; Saraswathi, 2005).

PART I: MACRO PROCESSES

Elder (1998) wrote that students of human development "generally fail to apprehend social structure as a *constitutive force* in development" (p. 944, emphasis added). To understand the ongoing changes in adolescents' experiences across the world, we need to apprehend the societal processes at work in creating these changes. This task requires attention to the processes described by multiple scholarly fields, as well as at multiple levels and units of analyses (e.g., world regions, nations, local communities, peer groups, families, individual youth) across which these processes occur (Bronfenbrenner, 1999; Lerner, 2002). The constructs of modernization and globalization provide broad theoretical umbrellas for examining these macro processes. We address the first briefly and then discuss globalization in greater depth.

Modernization: Theory About the "Development" of Societies

Modernization is an older, more ambitious, and more controversial construct used to describe a set of macrostructural "developmental" changes theorized to occur across societies. Like early epigenetic theorists of human development (such as Freud and Piaget), early economists and sociologists (e.g., Karl Marx, Max Weber, Herbert Spencer) postulated that societies go through predictable stages of development leading toward a common endpoint (the modern). More recent theories of modernization posit that societies go through interrelated transformations in their economic systems, social organization, religious beliefs, and even the personalities of their members (Inglehart & Welzel, 2007). Applying concepts about modernization to children and youth, Gielen and Chumachenko (2004) present a chart contrasting the environments that young people are likely to experience on 16 dimensions in "poor, traditional" societies versus "wealthy, postindustrial" ones. Thus, for example, the influence of the peer group is identified as "moderate" in traditional societies and "pervasive" in postindustrial societies; exposure to war is identified as "common" in traditional societies and "rare" in postindustrial ones. The concept of modernization posits that societal development involves a set of interrelated predictable changes.

But just as our stage theories of human development have been criticized and scaled back, so have theories of societal development and modernization. Some of the criticisms are the same. Theories of societal development were often based on an ethnocentric assumption that Western society represented the highest (most modern) level of societal development. A deficit model was then applied to societies that did not match the Western model. They were considered to be "underdeveloped"; indeed we *still* refer to them as "developing nations" and consider them to be in need of "developmental aid." A particular concern is that disputed theories of economic development have been used by the World Bank and other international aid organizations to force poor nations to reduce funding for schools, health care, and other social services for children, youth, and families (Stiglitz, 2003).

A second problem is evidence that different types of societal changes labeled modernization are not always correlated with each other. The modernization of a society in one domain is not necessarily related with modernization in others domains. Thus, for example, China and the state of Kerala in India achieved long life expectancies and high rates of education—cardinal features of modernization—without market capitalism, another feature typically linked to modernization (Sen, 1999). Research also shows that some of the values theorized to be modern are not consistently related to other dimensions of modernization. For example, Japan has become as technologically "modern" (and postmodern) as any nation, while maintaining distinct Eastern cultural values, business practices, and ways of life (Kâğitçibaşi, 1997; Nederveen Pieterse, 2004). Extensive psychological research indicates that some collectivist cultural values endure even as societies become modern in other ways (Inglehart & Baker, 2000; Kâğitçibaşi, 2007; Smith & Schwartz, 1997). This last point is important, as we will discuss later, because it suggests that adolescents in collectivist societies may not face the developmental task of establishing psychological autonomy from family that is described in the West.

Keeping these limits in mind, however, evidence does support the idea that there is a shared "family" of demographic, economic, technological, and other "developmental" changes that are loosely related and have occurred or are occurring across all or most societies (Inglehart, 1997; Inglehart & Welzel, 2007). These include:

- A demographic transition in which non-industrialized populations undergo, first, reduced rates of child mortality, lengthened life spans, and rapid population growth, followed by declining birth rates, smaller families, and decreased population growth

- The development of national economies, including capital accumulation and progression from an agrarian to a manufacturing to a service economy

- A shift of populations from rural to urban areas (accompanied by erosion of primary communities and traditional systems of education, social control, and intergenerational transmission)

- Development and spread of technology, improved health care, and new, faster means of communication

- Development of an "information society" in which knowledge is a fundamental commodity

This family of changes influences many of the shared elements of the new "modern" adolescences occurring across societies. The demographic transition, for example, affects the number of youth in the population relative to other age groups, and this affects youth's access to resources. Many nations in the middle of this transition (e.g., Africa, South Asia, and the Middle East) continue to have high birth rates, making it difficult for them to build enough schools and create enough jobs for their growing numbers of youth (Brown, Garder, & Halweil, 1999; Lloyd, 2005). Yet for nations that are further along in the transition, lower birth rates (coupled with development of their economies) have allowed governments to provide extended schooling, a cardinal element of modern adolescence. Longer schooling, then, means that the markers of adulthood, like marriage and full-time employment, are pushed later—creating a longer transitional period. Urbanization (along with more time in school) typically increases the time teens spend with peers. The development of national economies increases youth's access to communication technology and other material goods, and these allow young people to make life style choices and participate in youth culture. Extended schooling, delayed adulthood, more time with peers, and participation in youth culture are all elements of modern adolescences.

Globalization

If the construct of modernization is analogous to epigenetic theories of human development that posit unidirectional growth, then ideas under the umbrella of "globalization" are closer to poststructuralist theories of human development. They posit processes of societal change that occur in complex ecological contexts, involve multilevel interactions and social construction, and are not inherently predetermined. Discussions of globalization often incorporate the processes of modernization just discussed. But they also recognize that "the modern" is a tremendously powerful image that individuals and nations strive to identify with (or, in some cases, deliberately reject).

Globalization is a trendy word that can mean everything and nothing. The core observation is that the world is getting smaller: that relationships of exchange and interdependency across distances are increasing. The term *globalization* is used by scholars from different fields to refer to increasing interconnections in economies, cultures, government, and use of technology, among other things. Different parts of the planet are connected by greater flows of goods, people, capital, information, images, fads, and problems (Tomlinson, 1999). There is a time-space compression in which information passes, often instantly, from one part of the world to another. What this means is that individuals—including adolescents—are less embedded in the local than in the past (Friedman, 1990, 2005; Tomlinson, 2007; Watson, 2004).

Interconnection does not mean only relationships of cooperation and trust. Globalization, as of yet, has not made people from different parts of the world into one happy family. Individuals in different locales may purchase some of the same products and watch some of the same programs and news footage on television, but they experience these from different perspectives. One group's "freedom fighters" are viewed as "terrorists" by other groups. Tomlinson (1999) suggests that the experience of globalization is analogous to living in a crowded "global neighborhood," where we do not choose and may not like our neighbors, but are obliged to live alongside them. For adolescents, the processes of globalization means that their lives are more influenced by actions—whether cooperative, competitive, or hostile—outside their local community.

We will discuss some of the primary processes, trends, and concepts discussed in the globalization literature, and examine how they relate to adolescence.

Top-Down and Bottom-Up Societal Change

The mechanisms creating global interconnections include both top-down and bottom-up processes. By top-down we mean societal changes driven by large businesses, powerful elites, and international organizations that influence local communities, families, and youth. In contrast, bottom-up processes are those driven by the actions of ordinary individuals or grassroots movements that cumulate to create macro societal changes.

Top-Down Change   The most contentious top-down processes of globalization involve large corporations from powerful nations—often with backing from their governments—doing business in developing countries. This business has involved extracting natural resources, setting up factories and outsourced service industries, and marketing goods to the local populace. In numerous current and past instances, Western and other powerful governments have used coercive military force to support and protect these business enterprises (McGrew, 2007). (The United States currently maintains over 700 foreign military bases; U.S. Department of Defense, 2007). These businesses also use mass media as powerful tools to market products in developing nations, often by linking them to attractive images of modern ways of life.

Modernist economic theorists argue that this cross-national business and trade supports a process of economic development in the targeted nations: It stimulates capital growth and "lifts all boats" (e.g., Bhagwati, 2004). Yet the record, stretching from the era of European colonialism, indicates that this growth does not always materialize and the benefits are unequally distributed, often leaving an exploited local populace as poor or poorer than before (Coatsworth, 2004; Ghosh, 2006; Stiglitz, 2003). (The process, after all, is not driven by altruism, but the economic interests of wealthy entrepreneurs, large corporations, and corporate stockholders, including those of us with holdings in mutual funds.)

The impact of this top-down economic globalization on adolescents in developing nations can be extreme. As multinational business operations permeate new regions, the effects often disrupt traditional subsistence economies and the accompanying ways of life (Côté, 1994). In many cases, new mass market goods underprice goods produced by local farmers, potters, and weavers. As a result, families lose their livelihoods and are forced to migrate to urban centers (sometimes in other nations). Adolescents in some cases become laborers in factories, mines, street trades, brothels, or criminal networks (Castells, 1998). These economic changes, coupled with exposure to modern materialistic life styles, have the ancillary effect of disrupting local, historically evolved cultural systems for socializing young people. They undermine traditional mechanisms for teaching youth, providing supports, and directing them into paths to adulthood (Blum, 2007; Côté, 1994).

Of course, the nature of this disruption varies greatly by nation and circumstances. In some cases the opening of markets has increased economic opportunities for a portion of families and youth, allowing them more choice. In India, China, and other nations, global trade is feeding the growth of a middle class, who are able to exercise agency in negotiating choices between traditional and modern values and lifestyles (Bhagwati, 2004; Ghosh, 2006; Lloyd, 2005).

A second important form of top-down globalization is the efforts by international organizations, working in consort with developing nations to directly improve conditions for young people and people in general. UNICEF, UNIFEM, numerous international nongovernmental organizations (NGOs), and other consortia have worked to provide protections and resources to facilitate young people's development. These efforts have created social pressure among nations, which has persuaded many to establish legal rights for youth; build schools; improve health care; grant youth more participation in decision making; and pass laws that prohibit child labor, female circumcision, child marriage, and discriminatory practices against girls and women (Lloyd, 2005; Venkatesh & Kassimir, 2007; UN, 2005).

Perhaps the most successful example of this positive top-down international influence has been the gradual, dramatic increase in the number of youth enrolled in school across most developing nations (UNESCO, 2007). The most recent demonstration of this influence followed the World Education Forum, held in Dakar in 2000, when 164 governments and partner organizations endorsed a comprehensive vision of education. Since then there has been a clear "Dakar effect." Over a 6-year period, enrollment of youth in secondary school increased by more than 17% worldwide, with the largest increases occurring in sub-Saharan Africa (55%), South and West Asia and the Arab States (25% each), and East Asia (21%) (UNESCO, 2007). This large increase in education is important because it potentially gives adolescents skills and capacity for agency to improve their lives, as well as giving them greater abilities to contribute to bottom-up change.

Bottom-Up Change Simultaneous with top-down processes, globalization includes bottom-up processes of economic, social, and political change. Individuals are actors in the global world, and they can be influential when actions by thousands or millions of people have cumulative impact. These include decisions to ignore traditional norms, buy (or not buy) specific products, migrate, or join grassroots political movements (including antiglobalization movements that resist top-down changes). Bottom-up influence has been enhanced by education and new information and communication technology (ICT). ICT allows individuals to carry out activities and have influences with wider reach and scope (UN, 2005). This occurs, for example, when women weavers in Morocco use the Internet to sell their rugs in the United States and thus improve their socioeconomic status (Schaefer Davis, 2005), and when youth activists in China, South Africa, and Chile have used fax and e-mail to organize protest movements (Vogler, 2008; Youniss et al., 2002).

Adolescents, then, are not solely subjects of macro change: They sometimes are active participants and producers of it (Elder & O'Rand, 1995; Lerner & Walls, 1999). Youth have effects on society through their collective decisions to obtain education, use contraception, or identify with modern versus traditional values and lifestyles. These decisions have a cumulative effect in changing norms, influencing society, and altering the pathways to adulthood for future adolescents. In the United States, for example, the decision by millions of older youth in the 1960s and 1970s to defy societal prescriptions that one should marry at age 18–22 led to the waning of those norms for future generations (Modell, 1989). And a new generation of young bloggers in Egypt is challenging and changing the positions of the powerful Society of Muslim Brothers, the largest opposition party in that nation (Lynch, 2007). As Mannheim (1952) argued, each new generation of youth represents an instrument of social change.

This agency, of course, is constrained by societal circumstances: It is "bounded agency" (Shanahan, 2000). Economic conditions, political events, the machinations of powerful businesses, and other top-down factors influence the array of choices available to youth. Large-scale research demonstrates that many poor youth have restricted options due to lack of resources

and social capital (Elder, 1998; Furstenberg, 2006). This is particularly evident in employment options. An uneducated teenage girl seeking employment in Bangkok has limited choices: domestic service, factory work, laboring, or prostitution (Cook, 1998). Across developing nations many older youth, even those with education, find themselves unemployed (UN, 2005, 2007), reflecting the inability of the economy to generate jobs fast enough for the bulging youth populations in these nations (Brown et al., 1999). Youth aged 15–24 make up 25% of the global working-age population but account for 44% of the unemployment (UN, 2007). So youth may have opportunities for agency, but their options are bounded by the local community and societal ecology in which they live.

This interplay of top-down and bottom-up processes (as well as middle-out processes that emanate from local communities, businesses, and governments) play out differently across localities and regions. In the later half of the twentieth century, Japan, then Korea, Taiwan, Singapore, and other nations known as "the Asian Tigers," made top-down decision to invest heavily in education. This expanded the human resources possessed by a generation of youth, unlocked their potentials, and allowed them to lift themselves into the middle class (and their nations with them) (Cummings, 1997). In contrast, when the International Monetary Fund (IMF) imposed budgetary policies on South American countries in the 1980s and 1990s, it drastically reduced the abilities of those nations to provide education, thus limiting the skills that a generation of young people brought into adulthood, and limiting the opportunities for them to develop their potentials and contribute to societal change (Kohl & Farthing, 2006; Stiglitz, 2003).

Directions of Societal and Global Change: Integration Versus Differentiation

At a basic level, what many of us (including adolescent scholars) ask is whether the myriad of top-down and bottom-up changes are ultimately bringing the world together or splintering it apart. Is globalization creating greater integration in the economic, political, and cultural organization of the world? And is it doing so in ways that are improving the developmental opportunities and supports for youth? Or is it creating greater differentiation, individualization, inequality, or polarization? Modernization theorists are generally optimistic about the overall direction of change. Globalization theorists are typically less so. The globalization literature documents diverse trends toward both integration and differentiation, trends that are occurring simultaneously (Hoffman, 1998).

Integration, Systematization, and Homogenization There is no question that the world is becoming more integrated in numerous ways, with indirect and direct benefits for youth. We have mentioned the increasing flows of information, goods, and ideas. Integration can also be seen in the proliferation of new international organizations, systems, and networks. For example, the number of international governmental bodies (for regulating trade, postal delivery, communication, containment of infectious diseases, etc.) has grown from near zero in 1865 to approximately 50 in 1940 to 350 in 2000 (Diehl, 2005). Similar growth has occurred for other types of cross-national economic, business, professional, avocational, religious, and other organizations and systems.

For adolescents, this growth of organized systems means that their diets, clothing, health, education, and life options are embedded in large, geographically distributed networks of cooperation. Basic human activities, from eating to health care to entertainment, depend on diverse people's trusting each other and coordinating their actions (Giddens, 1990). This integration benefits youth in numerous ways. Some of these systems help protect them from epidemics, give youth access to new information, increase their opportunities for employment and travel, make

their knowledge and education more transferable from one locale to another, and generally expand their opportunities for agency and development. Venkatesh and Kassimir (2007, p.8) describe an "explosion" across the world of organizations that have provided new legal instruments to support youth's rights. The United Nations Convention on the Rights of the Child (UNCRC), though unsigned by the United States, has had substantial effects in creating rights for young people.

Two major questions, however, have been raised about this growing integration, and how it affects youth. A first question is whether these systems are growing fast enough in reach and power to keep up—or catch up—with the growing world problems. Political scientists express strong concern that the current systems of global governance (which depend largely on nations' voluntary compliance) have proven unable to prevent global warming, genocide, nuclear proliferation, the emergence of failed states (like Somalia and Haiti), continuing international terrorism, and massive economic inequalities (Held, 2007; Kuper, 2007).

Given these failures, can we expect the world's governmental systems to be successful in better meeting young people's needs? Indeed, while we noted progress by collective international efforts to provide education, resources, and protections to youth, reports on these positive trends are usually accompanied by significant qualifiers. Thus, although many more youth are obtaining secondary education, the quality of these schools is often poor due to lack of resources and qualified teachers. Although some health indicators for young people show strong improvement (e.g., declining mortality), globalization has increased youth's participation in risky health behaviors, including poor eating habits, greater substance use, and unprotected sex that have long-term negative consequences for youth's health (Call, Riedel, Hein, McLoyd, Petersen, & Kipke, 2002; Lloyd, 2005; UN, 2005). The inefficacy of international governmental structures is a weak link in improving conditions for youth.

A second, different question raised by adolescent scholars, is whether growing global integration might be leading to the homogenization or convergence of adolescence around a shared shallow materialist lifestyle. Suárez-Orozco (2004) observes that middle-class youth from Argentina to China see some of the same films, visit the same Internet sites, and often come to desire the same "cool" brand-name products. This shared experience, it is argued, has created a shared transnational youth culture, heavily influenced by Western consumerism (Suárez-Orozco & Qin-Hilliard, 2004; UN, 2005).

This concern may overstate the degree to which young people's material culture affects their underlying beliefs and values. Pilkington, Omel'chenko, Flynn, Bliudina, and Starkova (2002) found that, although Russian youth often purchased and imitated things Western, they saw this as fun, not serious. They described themselves as being strongly identified with Russian culture and values, which they held to be more spiritually rich. Verma and Saraswathi (2002) made similar observations about adolescents in India.

At the same time, we should not too quickly dismiss the ways in which integration is creating deeper convergences in youth's knowledge and values. Caldwell, Caldwell, Caldwell, and Pieris (1998) argue that the portrayals of love in Western cinema contributed to the undermining of arranged marriages in Africa, and Watson (2004) shows that Western influence has led to a change from extended to conjugal families in Asia. Some of this convergence may be viewed as positive. For example, substantial uniformity has developed across nations in the basic elements of the school curriculum (i.e., science, math, language), which creates an internationally shared knowledge base among youth (Gardner, 2004; Lloyd, 2005). And some scholars have expressed optimism that values of tolerance, mutual respect, activism, and respect for human rights and the environment can be taught and adopted by youth across the world (Hershock, Mason, & Hawkins, 2007; Spring, 2004).

Differentiation and Polarization

Simultaneous with these trends toward integration, globalization also generates differences among people. The term *differentiation* subsumes a diverse range of processes. We will discuss three. First, the same technology that facilitates integration also facilitates customization and bottom-up individualization. ICT allows youth to find or create a niche for themselves, to be different. They can have their own Web page or blog; join groups who share their unique affinities; and explore, discover, and create individual identities.

A second kind of differentiation, which we began discussing above, is economic. Marshall McLeon predicted that the global world would create greater economic equality (cited by Watson, 2004). But nations and individuals have not become equal. Capitalism is not a leveler; it produces winners and losers. Economic globalization has led to increased economic stratification *both between and within nations* (UN, 2005). At the cross-national level, the competition between developing nations for manufacturing and other outsourced jobs from wealthy nations leads to downward pressure on wages, what has been called "a race to the bottom" (Ghosh, 2006, p. 8; Mosely, 2007). As a result of these processes, the difference in per-capita income between the wealthiest and poorest countries grew by a *factor of five* between 1870 and 1990; at the same time, stratification within many nations also grew (Fussell & Greene, 2002; Guillèn, 2001). Within nations, wages paid to knowledge workers have increased, while those to unskilled workers have remained stable or decreased. So the world's economies may be more integrated, but in ways that involve profound asymmetries in power and wealth (Nederveen Pieterse, 2004). Economic processes have accentuated a "global divide" between rich and poor (UN, 2005).

The limited opportunities and resources experienced by youth in poor families create a separate adolescence, with limited options for economic mobility. Forty-four percent of the world's youth aged 15–24 live on less than $2.00 US per day (UN, 2005). Limited access to schooling, heath care, employment, and computers severely restricts their life pathways. The range of obstacles to economic mobility affecting poor youth include (UN, 2005, 2007):

- Being born in a poor nation that provides few job opportunities.
- Living in rural, isolated areas.
- Being unable to migrate due to gender, family responsibilities, or other types of impairment.
- Being a member of a marginalized group that is subject to discrimination based on religion, caste, or ethnicity.
- Urban gang activity.
- Experiencing events or "shocks" that create a significant lasting setback. These include experience of local violence, breakdown of law and order, an injury, loss of a parent, loss of financial assets, child bearing, and being unable to complete a program in school and thus forfeiting costly investment of time and money.

Adolescence and early adulthood are a critical life period for economic mobility, yet disruptive events during this period can result in youth's not having the material, social, or psychological resources they need, and thus missing the opportunities this life stage provides to better their conditions. In some cases, families can provide resources that facilitate mobility: they provide youth with money, aspirations, literacy, other knowledge, and social capital. But poor families may also handicap their children with bonded labor obligations, dowry demands, or a history of poor nutrition (UN, 2005). Claims that globalization has made the world "flat" (Friedman, 2005) belie these many factors that perpetuate the global divide and restrict poor youth's opportunities for choice, development, and upward mobility.

A third process of differentiation described by globalization scholars involves people's cultural identifications. Globalization is definitely not a one-way process in which the cultures of the world converge toward a shared form of modernity. Cultural groups periodically experience *cultural renewal and revival movements* (Botz-Bornstein & Hengelbrock, 2006). Many Chinese intellectuals, for example, are currently rediscovering their classic philosophy (Chin, 2007).

In some cases cultural revival and differentiation is a reactive process. Similar to Erikson's (1968) "negative identity," ethnic and religious groups may express values *in counterreaction to* those of other groups. The "crowded-neighborhood" of the global world can feed processes of group differentiation, leading to the proliferation of identities (Tomlinson, 2003, p. 272) or what Hoffman (1998) termed the *clash of civilizations* (his example was the mounting tension between the worlds of Islam and Christianity). Indeed, there has been a dramatic resurgence of diverse religious movements over the past 30–40 years, partly as a backlash against modernity (Lloyd, 2005, p. 50). In quite a number of cases, these reactive group identities are fueling civil wars (Sen, 2006).

Because youth are at a stage of identity exploration, they are often overrepresented in reactionary cultural and religious groups (Lloyd, 2005). Indeed, extremist religious groups are often skilled at drawing on youth's identity needs to attract and socialize young people into their cause. In many cases, their leaders are, in effect, experts in youth development (Patel, 2007). Likewise, adolescents are often recruited (or drafted) as combatants in civil conflicts (Barber, in press). In sum, at the same time globalization is creating integration, it also promotes counterreactions that feed differentiation.

Hybridization   Globalization, as we have seen, is often conceptualized in dialectic terms: as countervailing tugs-of-war between top-down and bottom-up, global and local, integration and differentiation. *Hybridization* is a concept used by globalization theorists to describe processes that synthesize. It occurs when elements from different cultures or ways of thinking are adapted, reappropriated, and combined (Kraidy, 2005; Pilkington et al., 2002). Rather than wholly rejecting or adopting a global influence, people often selectively adapt what is useful. Hybridization is a component of globalization discussed across disciplinary domains. Political scientist talk about hybrid governments (Held, 2007); criminologists about hybrid juvenile justice systems (Muncie, 2007); economists about hybrid economies (capitalist/socialist); historians about the melding of cultures, languages, and beliefs that occurs when different peoples have come into contact.

We are going to focus on youth's hybridization of cultural forms—styles, symbols, ways of thinking, and the identities these represent—because this is a process in which youth are often active agents of globalization. Their production and use of cultural hybrids are a mechanism through which they adapt and negotiate their way in the global world.

The transnational adaptation of hip hop is a useful illustration of hybridization. Youth from different parts of the world have developed their own forms of rap music, addressed to the moral, cultural, or identity issues they face. These adaptations employ a shared musical lexicon from the roots of hip hop in African American urban culture, including an attitude of "telling it like it is," protest, and resistance. But its form has been reappropriated in different settings to incorporate local instruments, rhythms, sensibilities, and concerns (Lam, 2006; Pennycook, 2003). Maori rap groups in New Zealand combine African American rap inflections with the style of traditional Maori songs. Their lyrics articulate resistance to Euro–New Zealand dominance, pride in Maori culture, and desire for self-government (Mitchell, 2001). The lyrics of Muslim hip hop groups in England protest the racism and hostility that Middle Eastern youth experience in that context (Swedenburg, 2001), while rap

music in Korea protests the "slavery" imposed by the Korean college entrance exam (Morelli, 2001).

Listening to a specific hybrid form of music, it should be recognized, does not necessarily express adherence to its views. Rather music and other hybrids often provide a "cultural space" that allows youth to explore and experiment with different values, emotions, taboos, and combinations of the local and global (Schade-Poulsen, 1995; Swedenburg, 2007). This experimentation can be a fluid process, influenced by personal experiences, world events, and the shifting power of different images to evoke or express personal issues (Jensen, 2003; Lam, 2006). Nederveen Pieterse (2004) writes that hybridity "is a history of ambivalence, attraction and repulsions, double-takes, and zigzag moves" (p. 93).

Much research on hybridization, like on hip hop, has focused on non-Western youth's selective and creative reappropriation of "modern" and Western cultural forms (e.g., Levy, 2001; Lukose, 2005). But increasingly, hybridization occurs in many directions (Tomlinson, 2003). Evidence suggests that the influence of things Western may be diminishing, and that cultural borrowing and hybridization is involving more multidirectional exchanges (Jenkins, 2004; Leeds, 2007). British Chinese youth have created their own versions of Hong Kong–based "Canto-pop" as a means to articulate their bicultural identities (Pilkington et al., 2002). Youth in the Middle East have turned to Indian Bollywood culture and Bhangra music to provide alternative versions of modernity (Lam, 2006; Lukose, 2005). European American young women have adapted indo-chic (e.g., henna body painting, bindis, and body jewelry) as a way of experimenting with exotic femininity (Maira, 2002).

An important point is that most, if not all, societies of the world have engaged in long, complex debates and struggles between the traditional and modern. These have been waged in diverse arenas, including foods, holidays, entertainment, language, morality, religious practices, legal rights, and the social construction of gender (Lukose, 2005). Each new generation of youth are actors in these community debates. As they experiment with clothing, music, values, and postings on Web pages, they are negotiating these cultural tensions (Lam, 2006). Whether they are adopting a cultural form from another tradition, rejecting it, or adapting it into a creative hybrid, they are exploring and choosing where they fit into the enormous cultural variety offered by the global interconnected world. In the process, they also reshape the debate for the next generation.

Globalization and Globaloney

The discerning reader will notice that these general concepts—integration, differentiation, hybridization, and globalization itself—are facile and imprecise. They do not provide a theory of how the world works; they are often descriptions of trends, applied post hoc; they frequently blur conceptual boundaries (Ghosh, 2006; Kraidy, 2005). Some authors have even questioned whether the proliferating literature on globalization might be a bunch of "globaloney" (Nederveen Pieterse, 2004). In contrast to modernization theory, these concepts provide a less orderly account of how the world is changing and how adolescents in a given locale will be affected.

But that is part of the point. The processes described in the globalization literature are complex and unruly. They are driven by such a diverse range of multilevel and multidirectional processes that predication can be a fool's game. Although the topic of globalization often lends itself to evocative sound bites and headlines, scholarly analysis of globalization requires that we attend to the wide array of eclectic components involved. Every thesis about globalization, as we have seen, calls up contradictory evidence and arguments. Understanding the changes in the adolescences of the world requires attending to the wide constellations of interacting factors that shape young people's experiences across diverse contexts.

Conclusion: Taking a Disciplinary and Interdisciplinary Approach

Many developmental scientists, of course, may have less ambitious objectives and be primarily concerned with understanding adolescence within only one or a couple specific contexts. By way of concluding Part I, let us address ourselves to this more manageable goal. How would an adolescent scholar whose primary orientation is psychological go about understanding the array of macro societal changes at work in influencing adolescence in a particular context?

A good starting point, we suggest, is to build on the expertise of the different social science disciplines that focus on macro processes. Each discipline helps us see a different segment of Bronfenbrenner's macro system. Each provides a body of theory and research on a particular set of societal change processes, and helps us think about how they might influence adolescents' experiences and development in a specific context. To provide a beginning framework for doing this, we surveyed the literature from pertinent disciplines and have identified the macro societal change processes occurring in some or most locales of the world that we felt were most relevant to adolescence (Table 17.1). Many of these we have already discussed.

Each discipline directs us to ask about a distinct set of macro processes that might be affecting youth in a context of interest. Demography directs our attention to the important impact of shifting numbers of adolescents in a population. One should ask, where is the population in the demographic transition and how are the changing proportions of youth affecting the resources and opportunities available to them? Economics directs us to ask about the structure of wealth in a society and how it shapes opportunities for youth and their families. Changes in the local economy and labor market can open or close career pathways for youth, require families to migrate, or alter the revenue that allows the government to invest in education and health care. Anthropology poses

Table 17.1   Macro Change Processes That Are Influencing Adolescence in Most or Some Parts of the World

Discipline	Major Processes & Changes	Influences on Adolescents and their Families
Demography	Demographic transition (longer life span, reduced birth rates)	Bulge in numbers of youth in the population that reduces opportunities (currently occurring in developing nations) followed by reduction in number of youth relative to the number of elderly (now occurring in developed nations).
Economics	Globalization of markets, including labor markets	New job opportunities for families & adolescents. Traditional forms of subsistence are undermined, creating unemployment. Demands that youth learn new skills.
	Widening economic disparities between nations	Wider differences in capability of nations to provide education, health care, and other services to adolescents and their families.
	Widening economic disparities within nations	Wider differences between families in provision of resources and opportunities to young people.
Geography	Rural families migrate to urban areas	Adolescents have access to better education and jobs, but may live in dense urban areas, with less connection to community and more exposure to crime, crowding, and other urban ills.
	Migration of family members for employment	Families are split up.
	Confluence of diverse peoples due to internal and cross-national migration	Adolescents challenged to get along with people from diverse cultures; need to develop skills for cross-group communication and cooperation.
Anthropology	Erosion of traditional cultures	Disruption of traditional pathways to adulthood and systems of socialization
	Continued intergenerational transmission of values and beliefs	Persistence in some cultural values and world views, including indigenous psychologies of socialization and development
	Cross-cultural flow of information, images, and cultures	Adolescents adopt, resist, or incorporate elements of new cultures into hybrid activities and identities.
Political Science	Democratization	Greater opportunities for civic participation by adolescents and their parents.
	Increased pressure across nations to adhere to international norms	Increased resources, rights, and protections for adolescents.
	Growth of NGOs	New sources of resources and opportunities for youth and their families.
	Fundamentalist & reactionary movements	Adolescents adopt or form values that are particularistic or deliberately in opposition to those of others.
	Armed conflicts between groups	Adolescents recruited as insurgents and soldiers.
Sociology	Information society	Longer schooling; youth who do well in school have access to higher paying jobs.
	Changes in social institutions that permit greater choice	Families take more varied and voluntary forms; adolescents need skills to function in more heterogeneous and fluid contexts.

(Continued)

Table 17.1   *(Continued)*

Discipline	Major Processes & Changes	Influences on Adolescents and Their Families
	Changing roles of women in some societies	More opportunities for girls and young women; greater requirements for independence.
Technology, Science, & Society	Spread of mass media (radio, TV, & print media)	Youth are exposed to diverse life styles, youth cultures; consumption patterns influenced by commercialization.
	Spread of information and communication technology (ICT)	Youth with resources gain access to information; are able to communicate & exercise agency across boundaries of age, distance, gender, etc.
	Ecological degradation	Adolescents and families face new economic, health and other challenges.
	Advances in biotechnology and medicine	New options to address adolescents' physical and psychological limits when resources are available.

Based on Larson, 2002, Lloyd, 2005, Suárez-Orozco & Qin-Hillard, 2004; UN, 2005; and other sources cited in the text.

vital questions about what culture (or changing cultural hybrids) are operative for a population. How do these practices and values influence the way families raise their children and how adolescents think about themselves and their priorities? The perspective of political science is essential to understanding changing policies and provisions for youth, as well as the brewing of conflict and disorder which can disrupt adolescents' development.

A discipline-by-discipline approach, however, is only a starting point. The framework presented by Table 17.1 is inevitably incomplete. It focuses primarily on top-down processes. It does not do justice to biopsychosocial processes in individual adolescents and youth's role as bottom-up agents of societal change. So one needs to ask, not only about the large forces of societal changes shaping adolescence in a given context, but how youth and their families and peer groups are responding to and reshaping societal change?

The table also does not do justice to the numerous diagonal pathways that link macro processes and adolescents' experience across disciplines. Separation of disciplines contradicts a central message that we have tried to make earlier—that globalization is an interdisciplinary phenomena. One needs to ask how the current demographic, economic, cultural,

and political forces at work in a society interact with each other. What is the total ecology of processes and counterprocesses at work that facilitate or obstruct youth's opportunities for agency and development?

PART II: HOW GLOBALIZATION IS INFLUENCING ADOLESCENCE IN FOUR DOMAINS

We shift now from focusing on processes to outcomes: from focusing on the dynamics of macro societal change to how specific domains of adolescents' experience are being affected by these processes. How is globalization influencing domains of young people's lives that adolescent researchers care about? The domains we chose include basic, textbook-chapter topics of adolescent scholarship: family relationships, employment, and gender. We start, however, by examining the more fundamental issue of how globalization is changing societies' general conceptions of this age period.

Shifting Cultural Representations of Adolescents and the Adolescent Age Period

Young people's experiences in a society are shaped in part by how that society thinks about them, and these ways of thinking are changing as a product of globalization. Cultural representations of the period between childhood and adulthood—how it is named, conceptualized, and rendered in public images—influence the resources and pathways made available to adolescents. Until recently for example, girls among the Gusii of Kenya, were inducted into adulthood by the ordeal of circumcision into the stage of *omoiseke,* a term that means "marriageable girl"—someone whose parents await an offer of bride price (Levine, 1980). Male youth among the Sambia of New Guinea were defined as "initiates" and taught that ingestion of semen following fellatio performed on older men helps prepare them for manhood (Herdt, 1982). Across societies, adolescents are now increasingly identified as "students," a label that links them to the age-segregated institution of schooling and prioritizes their role as learners of academic knowledge, while also disconnecting them from active participation in society (Brown & Larson, 2002; Chen & Chang, 2007; Missani, 2007). Across cultures, adolescence is often represented as a time of preparation (Schlegel, 1995; although see Cole, 2005). But, beyond this, wide variability exists.

Variability in how youth are perceived occurs not only between but within cultures. Traditional and modern representations, such as "initiate" and student, may coexist and contend with each other. Aubrun and Grady (2000) found that American adults often "toggle" between contrasting positive and negative images of youth. At one moment the adults in their research would adopt an "empathetic frame" that draws on their own experiences during adolescence and that views youth sympathetically, as struggling, learning, and growing toward a positive adulthood. Yet, at other moments they would switch to a negative frame that views youth as self-centered, disrespectful, and having lower morals than did their generation. A troubling finding is that American adults toggle to this negative view even when presented with evidence that it is an inaccurate portrayal of the majority of youth (Gilliam & Bales, 2001). These and other findings suggest that adults' views of adolescents are often shaped more by adults' needs than young people's behavior (Males, 1996). Enright, Levy, Harris, and Lapsley (1987) found that, historically, American adults' representations of adolescents have been more positive when the country needs young people's labor or military participation and more negative when it does not.

Similar competing positive and negative images occur in other cultures. In Arabic, the terms *fata* for males and *fatat* for females signify youth in the midst of growth and development. Yet the closest term to adolescence is *murahaqa*, which refers to puberty, and invokes an image of this age period as fraught with sexual temptations and disobedience (Booth, 2002). In Istanbul, young men from lower socioeconomic status (SES) neighborhoods are sometimes identified as *delikanli* (a sprightly brave, trustworthy youth) and sometimes as *serseri*, a perjorative term meaning vagabond and vagrant (Boratav, 2005). Schlegel and Barry (1991) concluded from an analysis of 175 cultures that virtually all contained positive views of youth, and some but not all also had ambivalent or negative views. Thus, the presence of competing representations of adolescents—and the potential for toggling between different frames—appears to be common across many societies.

What is particularly relevant for scholars of adolescence is that, in a number of societies, new negative images of youth have been entering the public mind via the mass media and other channels. Indian society has traditionally held very favorable attitudes toward the young (Shukla, 1994), but the image of the delinquent male "superpredator" has recently been introduced by the media (Thapa, Raval, & Chakravarty, 1999). In the Middle East, the theme of youth as a "dangerous" group has entered the public discourse (Swedenburg, 2007). And in Nigeria, a traditional honorific term for male adolescents, *Oma ara* or "son of the soil," which conferred respect and admiration, now denotes a miscreant and hoodlum in urban Lagos (Ibeagha, 2007).

In many societies the rituals used to publicly mark transitional stages in a boy's or girl's passage to adult status are weakening. In parts of Africa and Indonesia, the age of initiation has been deliberately lowered with the goal of cementing bonds between youth and the local community before youth are lured away by the city (Levine, 1980; Mikarsa, 2007). In rural Eritrea, the puberty rights that functioned to give 16-year-old boys the rights of a man are disappearing (Araia, 2007). In some cases, however, these rites have been adapted and hybridized to adapt to modern contexts. The Navajo rite of passage for girls, *Kinaalda*, is still practiced and serves to reinforce a community expectation that adult relatives help guide the young woman in learning skills for womanhood in the bicultural context they face (Markstrom & Irbooa, 2003).

Across societies, the legal system has taken an increasing role in defining adolescence. New laws have formalized the age period, limiting youth's behavior as well as giving them new protections and rights. In Malaysia, for example, young people are now given an identity card at 12 and the right to vote at 21 (Mikarsa, 2007). In Iran, a law passed in 2002 now prohibits parents from marrying a daughter before age 13 without court permission (Sondaite, 2007). Top-down encouragement by the United Nations and other agencies has led to a more convergent international legal conception of children and adolescents as active individuals with rights (Boyle, Smith, & Guenther, 2007; Lloyd, 2005). Muncie (2007), however, points out these changes have also been negotiated, reinterpreted, and hybridized within different localities and nations, as a product of ongoing internal debates. In general, a shift has occurred across the twentieth century from a legal framework focused on the obligations of children to their parents to one focused on the obligations of parents to their children (Boyle et al., 2007; Muncie, 2007).

Underneath these shifting representations of adolescence is the negotiation of modern ways of thinking with traditional cultural foundations. On the one hand, the globalization of media presents the public in different parts of the world with a larger palette of new images to draw upon: adolescents drinking Coke and enjoying themselves, young people in love, and youth as criminals or suicide bombers. On the other hand, Islamic, Christian, Hindu, Buddhist, and other traditions have systems of values that shape how the young are viewed within specific cultural milieu. Among Hindus, for example, the ancient Dharmashastras, which prescribe a code of conduct for each stage of development, continue to have a strong influence on young people's family behavior (Verma & Saraswathi, 2002). The interplay of modern and traditional images of youth results in distinct evolving conceptions of adolescents in different cultural contexts. For instance, the media image of the American "teenager"—blue jean clad, independent, and willful—is viewed across much of the world, and it is both imitated and, in some contexts, invoked as a depiction of what a society does *not* want its youth to become (Hoffman, 1995; Salamon, 1995).

Adolescents, of course, are anything but passive in this arbitration of representations of their age period. Side-by-side with following the Hindu prescriptions for young people's behavior, many upper-strata Indian youth in Bangalore are experimenting with a Westernized lifestyle of parties and joyriding (Saldanha, 2002). Youth in Beruit are exploring new ways of combining Islamic piety with middle-class forms of recreation and leisure (Deeb & Harb, 2007).

The central point is that public conceptions of youth in many societies are undergoing revision. They are, in a sense, "up for grabs." The lengthening of adolescence and the new roles associated with it create an opening in which new images can catch the attention of a national public and compete with the old. These new images are important because they influence the resources and options adults make available to young people. The increased prevalence of negative images of delinquents within both American and Brazilian society, for example, has contributed to adoption of harsher, more punitive, approaches to juvenile justice (Cullen & Wright, 2002; Diversi, Moraes, & Morelli, 1999). In quite a number of nations, there has been a punitive turn in juvenile justice, in which youth are viewed through a lens of "crime and disorder" (Muncie, 2007, p. 35).

Scholars of adolescence need to be aware of this interplay of old and new images within whatever society they are examining and attuned to how this interplay shapes youth–adult relationships. What are the societal debates shaping these representations, and how are these representations shaping the resources and opportunities available to youth? How might the media or other intervention tools be used to influence the public's images so that they are more accurate and understanding of adolescents' needs (Gilliam & Bales, 2001)?

We turn now to the cultural construction of adolescence within the domain of the family.

Adolescents' Family Relationships: Developmental Tasks in a Changing World

To understand adolescents' family experience across societies, it is essential that we look beyond Western models of what is supposed to happen in these relationships. In Western developmental psychology (which is often a frame of reference even for non-Western developmentalists; Saraswathi, 1999a), it is understood that emotional "individuation" from family is a central developmental task of adolescence (Freud, 1946; Havighurst, 1953). More recent writings have stressed that achieving emotional self-sufficiency does not mean severing connections to family (Hauser, 1991; Raeff, 2006). Nonetheless extreme caution is needed to not let culturally loaded Western concepts like autonomy and independence define the terms for understanding other cultures (Sharma, 2003a). Bellah, Madsen,

Sullivan, Swidler, and Tipton (1985) warn that Westerners are constrained by a "language of radical individual autonomy," which limits their ability to think about the self as anything other than a center of volition (p. 81). We need to heed the call of Elder (1998), Bronfenbrenner (1979), Lerner (2002), and others to consider the macro system, including culture, as a constitutive element of individual's family experience.

Let us use our findings from a study of middle-class families in northern India to illustrate the importance of being attuned to the interplay of cultures and societal change in adolescents' family relationships.

The Developmental Tasks for Adolescents' in Indian Families

Middle-class adolescents in India are a group whose material lives are not too dissimilar from middle-class Western adolescents. Television and the Internet are a part of their lives; they have opportunities for international travel and a sense of being connected to the global (Sharma, 2003a). Yet in our research in the large regional city of Chandigarh, we found that the basic characteristics of daily adolescent–parent interactions were markedly different from the Western scenario in which adolescents are on a course toward independence. In an experience sampling study, we found, first, that these Indian 8th graders spent 39% of their waking hours with family members, much more than the 23% found for a comparable study of American 8th graders. The Indian adolescents also spent twice as much time talking with their families (Larson, Verma, & Dworkin, 2003). What was most striking was that these Indian adolescents rated themselves as significantly happier than the American 8th graders during time with their families (and less happy during time with friends). Furthermore, half of these Indian adolescents reported *preferring* to spend time with their families, and only 29% preferred to spend time with their peers (Larson et al., 2003). Consistent with other studies of Indian youth (Roland, 1989; Sharma, 2003b), achieving behavioral or emotional separation from family did not appear to be a priority for these Indian 8th graders.

Anthropological research provides an explanation for this developmental pattern. It shows that Indian culture places connections to family, including extended family, at the center of people's lives across the life span (Seymour, 1999; Sinha, 1994). Respect, deference, and dependence on older family members is taught to children from an early age (Bharat, 1997). Independence is not valued in Indian families and is equated with disobedience (Ramanujam, 1978). In the Indian value system, it is considered a virtue to subordinate one's own individual needs to the needs of the kinship group (Saraswathi, 1999b). This primacy of family ties is not unique to India, but has also been reported among contemporary adolescents in China (Fuligni & Zhang, 2004), Indonesia (French, Rianasari, Pidada, Nelwan, & Buhrmester, 2001), Bangladesh (Stewart, Bond, Abdullah, & Ma, 2000), Morocco (Davis & Davis, 1989), and Argentina (Facio & Batistuta, 1998). In many collectivist societies, children *are* given major responsibilities, starting at an early age (Gauvain, 1999), but this is a distinct dimension from emotional independence.

Rather than striving for autonomy, Indian adolescents appear to face different family developmental tasks. Based on three decades of anthropological research, Seymour (1999) concluded that the self in Indian society is defined, not through differentiation from others, but through interdependence with them. One's worth as a person, she concluded, is defined through the development of a "we-self." Roopnarine and Suppal (2003) argue that, instead of an Oedipus complex, in Indian culture there is an Oedipal alliance. The psychic task of Indian adolescents is not to become separate but to reduce separation—to work on strengthening emotional bonds and overcoming impulses that create differentiation. Hindu culture places less emphasis on individual volition, and more on staying true to one's dharma or duties (Derné, 2003).

Culture, Societal Change, and Hybridization

Some of our Western colleagues have responded to this different Indian family script by seeing it as interesting, but quaint and of limited importance, because "everyone knows" that in 50 years, perhaps sooner, adolescence in other countries will be just like it is in the West. This possibility of convergence toward a Western "modern" script is also voiced by some Indian scholars who worry that urbanization, mobility, and mothers' employment are weakening family cohesion (Bharat, 1997; Biswas, 1992). Research does suggest several ways in which Indian and Western family relationships have been converging. Smaller families and affluence have permitted Indian middle-class parents to become less authoritarian and more responsive to children (Kashyap, 1993; Saraswathi & Ganapathy, 2002). Urban middle-class parents, as compared to rural and lower SES parents, do not see children as an economic asset, but rather value children as a source of love and personal fulfillment (Kapadia & Shah, 1998; Srivastava, 1997).

This shift to more responsive parenting, however, has not altered the centrality that middle-class Indians give to the family, nor the lifelong interdependency in families. Parents still often choose careers and spouses for their children, in the majority of cases (Ramu, 1988; Uplaonkar, 1995). In fact, two-thirds of youth in an Indian middle-class sample reported that they preferred having their parents arrange their marriages (Verma & Saraswathi, 2002). Rather than succumbing to a Western mold of modernization, Indian society has *selectively integrated* facets of modernization into its value system. Families increasingly use the media, including the Internet, to identify potential spouses for arranged marriages (Saraswathi, 1999b). In addition, although the number of "joint" extended family households has fallen with urbanization, many have found that it provides a useful adaptation to urban life—live-in grandparents and adult siblings provide child care and additional sources of emotional support to hurried urban parents and their adolescents (Sharma & Srivastava, 1991). Sharma (2003a) reports a recent resurgence in India of investment in national and cultural identities, including a new wave of popular culture that extols unique India values. She writes, "The middle class aspires to be authentically Indian yet thoroughly modern" (p. 4). The cultural scripts guiding Indian adolescents' relationships with their families are a complex hybrid of global and local (including the distinct mores of the many religious, caste, and cultural groups across India).

Research documents a similar pattern of hybridization in urban Chinese adolescents' relationships with their families. Chinese parents emphasize cooperation, harmony, and shared social and moral goals (Smetana, 2002). Fuligni and Zhang (2004), however, posed the interesting question as to whether the sudden shift to competitive market capitalism in Chinese urban areas might lead families to accept and encourage greater independence in their youth. They found some support for this prediction. In a comparison of urban and rural adolescents, urban youth (whose families were more exposed to economic change) reported being more willing to openly disagree with their parents and urban males reported that their parents imposed fewer rules. But these authors also found that both urban and rural adolescents reported a strong sense of obligation to support, assist, and respect the authority of their parents (Fuligni & Zhang, 2004; Zhang & Fuligni, 2006). These researchers also found these traditional values to be strong in Taiwan, which shifted to a market economy sooner (Fuligni & Zhang, 2004), and among Asian American high school students as compared to European American students (Fuligni, 2007). Across collectivist societies, middle-class families experiencing urbanization appear to make functional shifts to adapt to urban life, for example accepting more material independence in adult children. However, emotional interdependence and mutual responsibility typically remain (Kâğıtçıbaşı, 1997; Mistry & Saraswathi, 2002).

Therefore, in China, as in India, the developmental task of adolescents is more likely to involve cultivating connection than achieving autonomy. Indeed, Nelson and Chen (2007) found that Chinese college students described their primary developmental goals as learning to become less self-oriented, developing greater emotional control, and having greater consideration for others, including becoming capable of financially supporting their parents. Greenfield (1994) argues these developmental tasks, which involve breaking down egotistical impulses and harmonizing oneself with family and community, are by no means easy. They go against fundamental human dispositions that prioritize personal needs. Clearly, more research is needed, but it is possible we will find that the family developmental task of adolescents in cultures that value interdependence is harder and more challenging than the task of youth in the West.

Adolescents' Family Relationships in a Changing World

Clearly, modernization and globalization do not mean that adolescent–family relationships are being Westernized. Depending on culture and circumstances, different peoples may demonstrate differing patterns of cultural convergence, persistence, or hybridization. In many parts of Asia, Africa, and the Middle East, adolescents' families continue to be quite patriarchal and authoritarian (Lloyd, 2005). Across societies, parents grant adolescents jurisdiction over some domains of decision making, and young people's jurisdiction expands with age. However, the specific domains and timetables differ as a function of culture and family situation (Darling, Cumsille, Pena-Alampay, & Coatsworth, 2005; Nucci, Hasebe, & Lins Dyer, 2005; Smetana, 2002). Adolescents and parents draw on the strengths and moral authority of their culture, but they also adapt to the circumstances of their lives. A paradox, occurring in some contexts, is that youth's desire for behavioral independence is coming at an earlier age, but they often continue to live in their parents' home and be financially dependent for longer (Tomanovic & Ignjatovic, 2006).

As with other sections in this chapter, this one provides only a sketch and unavoidably overlooks many important issues and valuable studies (regrettably including those published in languages other than English). Existent research on adolescent family relationships teaches us that, as we look closer, adolescent–parent relationships become more complex and multifaceted than was originally thought (Silverberg & Gondoli, 1996; Steinberg, 2001). Even in English, terms like autonomy, dependence, and obligation carry diverse meanings, nuanced by context. Surely, the same will be true as our knowledge of adolescents' family relationships across diverse global contexts expands.

Young Adolescents in the Labor Force

Broadening the lens of research on adolescent work to include the developing world brings into focus the issue of child labor (see also chapter 8, this volume). Over the past 2 decades, the increased visibility of this issue with its accompanying action by governments and NGOs has begun to bring about significant change. According to the ILO (2006a), the incidence of work among children declined in both absolute and relative terms between 2000 and 2004—a trend that is consistent across all major age groups. Fewer children and adolescents were working, and the percentage of working children among the total child population (ages 5–17) also declined across this time period. However, the situation across regions was highly uneven. While some regions made significant progress (e.g., Latin America and the Caribbean), others, such as sub-Saharan Africa, showed little improvement. The best news is the general trend toward less dangerous forms of work. The biggest decline was observed among children in hazardous work, a subcategory of the worst forms of child labor (WFCL). The global number plummeted by about one-third in the 5–14 age group, from 111 million to 74 million children (ILO, 2006a).

However, the notion of youth employment continues to be deeply entrenched in many parts of the globe. In parts of Africa and Asia, youth's early introduction to an occupation and to making economic contributions to the family is seen as crucial to their socialization (Nieuwenhuys, 1996). For many children, initiation into work begins as early as age 5, often as an extension of simple domestic tasks, and remains a core feature into adolescence. "Work is viewed as a necessary part of childhood, a part of everyday life, a way of learning skills and responsibility, as well as being essential to family survival" (Woodhead, 2004, p. 5). Research illustrates the diversity of functions that work plays in youth's lives. It can be both an asset and a hazard to well-being, making unqualified generalizations about harm of limited value.

Modernization, globalization, and especially urbanization continue to alter the types of employment available to youth, and often they move work further from the family hearth. There are important questions, then, to be asked. Some are familiar to research on adolescent employment in the West, such as the influence of employment on school work and the effects of different numbers of work hours. But there are also less familiar issues, including adverse effects on physical health, the conditions of employment in the informal sector, and the differing family dynamics that may result when young adolescents are major breadwinners in the family. We will first describe who works and why, then turn to these important questions.

Who Works and Why

We focus on employment among young adolescents, because, although employment sometimes starts earlier in childhood, there is a large increase in employment rates for this age period. For the world as a whole, the UN's International Labour Office (ILO, 2006a) estimates that 20.8% of all 10- to 14-year-olds are economically active—a total of 126.1 million youth. In 2004, sub-Saharan Africa had the highest incidence of working children aged 5–14 at 26.4%, followed by Asia and the Pacific with 18.8%, and Latin America and the Caribbean with 5.1%. (Due to data gaps, there are no new estimates for the Middle East and North Africa.) Statistics from the 1990s suggested that about three-quarters of employed young adolescents worked over 14 hours a week. More recent trend data are not available on hours of work; therefore, it is hard to assess whether the demands of this work may have changed to make it more compatible with being in school (Lloyd, 2005).

The types of employment these young adolescents hold are extremely diverse. They range from apprenticeships and working in a family craft, farm, or business to factory labor, live-in domestic service, street activities, and prostitution. Much of this work occurs in the informal sector (ILO, 1996) and is not counted in national unemployment statistics or accounts of gross national product/gross domestic product. Indeed, employment of young adolescents is illegal in most nations, which, by definition, makes it part of the informal market. Some youth are entrepreneurial, working as venders or scavengers. Others work in unofficial relationships with family members, a local merchant, a factory foreman, or someone they may be indentured to in another village or city. In some cases these informal arrangements are quite complex, involving linkages between employers, community power brokers, and parents. In other cases youth simply assist parents at their jobs. Though informal, the conditions of employment can be binding. The ILO (2002) estimates that 5.7 million children and young adolescents are in bonded and forced labor.

There are both push and pull factors that promote young adolescents' work. The most cited push factor is family need (Lloyd, 2005). Conditions of extreme poverty often leave no alternative but for young adolescents to work. In Bangladesh, approximately 30% of both urban and rural heads of household with working children reported that the household would

suffer a decline in living standard or would not be able to survive at all if the children stopped working (Bangladesh Bureau of Statistics, 2003). It is important to realize that in collectivist societies it is often parents, not adolescents, who make the decisions in young people's lives. Mensch, Bruce, and Greene (1998) stress that in Southeast Asia it is typically the parents who decide to sell their daughters into prostitution as a means of addressing acute family financial needs.

In addition to poverty, poor school quality and other obstacles to school attendance are push factors that lead to young adolescents' employment. For example, in rural Morocco, distance to school tends to increase the likelihood of child work. Reducing the travel time from school by about 20 minutes decreases the probability of working by about three percentage points (Understanding Children's Work [UCW], 2003). In Cambodia, an increase of school quality seems to induce children already attending school not to also take on an economic activity. In addition, schools with health- and learning-related facilities have consistently lower dropout rates (UCW, 2006). Meyers and Boyden (1998, p. 18) argue these factors are often "as or more significant than family poverty" in preventing youth from choosing work over school.

But there are also factors that pull youth into employment. In many settings, work is one of the most critical domains in which adolescents, especially poor youth, integrate themselves into their families and communities. They gain status and respect by becoming family breadwinners (Meyers & Boyden, 1998; Nieuwenhuys, 1996). We discussed in the last section how adolescents in collectivist societies often face the developmental task of strengthening their bonds to their families. By providing economic assistance to the household, young adolescents fulfill filial duties and prove they belong. Another pull factor is the jobs themselves. Some of the new jobs being created by neoliberal international trade policies are attractive. Compared to jobs in agriculture, those in the export industry and in the growing service sector are seen as pathways to modernity (French, 2002; Rosas & Rossignotti, 2005). These jobs can provide opportunities to learn a skill, ensure steady and higher income, offer better working conditions, and may provide better opportunities than family employers.

Developmental Costs and Benefits

This diversity of types and conditions of employment continues to present a difficult challenge to researchers attempting to evaluate their effects on young people. Research to date shows that employment of young adolescents in developing nations can have both positive and negative effects, not all of which can be isolated from each other. Most of the existing empirical evidence regarding the impact of work on children and adolescents in the developing world has focused on its physical effects. Yet, available data do not indicate a consistent negative relationship between children's work and health. For example, an 18-country study of health hazards failed to find a uniform relationship between work and ill-health (O'Donnell, Van Doorslaer, & Rosati, 2002). In five countries working children were more at risk of health problems than nonworking children, but in another five countries working children were more healthy than nonworking children. In three other countries children who were in school (and not working) were the least healthy. Such inconclusive evidence does not mean health hazards associated with work have been exaggerated. Horrific conditions have been documented in the recent past, conditions that had permanent toxic effects on children (Sundaram, 1995). Nor does it mean that schooling promotes ill health. Rather, this study draws attention to the limitations of "broad brush" approaches to monitoring and evaluating the effects of work on youth. They suggest that local contexts need to be considered and research is needed on the causal pathways between work and health in children's lives (Woodhead, 2004).

When we shift to examining the psychosocial effects of young adolescent employment, the picture is no less complex. Much more research and conceptual work needs to be done. Consider, for example, the case of a 13-year-old boy in Brazil who has been working in his father's repair shops:

> I like to work with my father because he has patience. I say to Dad, "What is this? What does this thing do?" And he explains just like a teacher. Everything that he knows, he passes on to me. When I grow up, I hope to have my own shop and have workers and pass on to them everything that I know. (French, 2002, p. 319)

In another case, a 15-year-old girl training as a dental assistant explains:

> I'm learning a lot. When helping with the patients, I learn how to take care of them — I already know how to do some things. Maybe some day I'll be a dentist. I'm learning so much. The dentist is more of a friend than a boss. He helps me, he explains everything and when I have a question I just ask him. (French, 2002, p. 319)

These youth are developing skills and strengthening bonds to their family. The girl appears to have a healthy mentoring relationship with her employer. When employed young adolescents are interviewed, some describe their work as a means to develop responsibility, gain self-esteem, and develop economic autonomy (Woodhead, 1999). In the case of adolescent girls, it has been noted that employment can play a vital role in giving young women pride, a sense of agency, and the chance to develop an identity apart from that of daughter and wife (French, 2002; Mensch, et al., 1998). But many youth in the developing world are employed in jobs that are highly repetitive, involve little skill development, and have employers who see them only as a source of cheap docile labor. Youth's working environment, their conditions of work, and especially their treatment by employers are a major influence on their well-being, but these can be highly variable in potential harm/benefit, even when and where the work is broadly similar in nature. Consequently, the extent to which children and adolescents are at psychosocial risk may vary significantly within sectors, as well as between sectors (Woodhead, 2004).

Research is needed that differentiates the effects of the various types and conditions of employment. A central research issue concerns the pathways that different types of youth employment provide to adult work. Worldwide, studies show that heavy work schedules lower adolescents' school performance and may contribute to school dropout (UCW, 2003). But work in certain economic activities (e.g., in an engineering or carpenter shop) is considered by adolescents and their families to be a valuable opportunity for learning employable skills (Rahman, Khanam, & Absar, 1999); to them it can be a preferred alternative to secondary education. Reasonably well-off children in Surat, India, quit school to work in the diamond industry, because the entire family believes the diamond polishing industry offers long-term prospects for employment at an acceptable wage (Bachman, 2000). Only when investments in education promise greater future returns may families be willing to keep their adolescents in school. However, youth who drop out of school to work as a weavers, wagon makers, potters, or in numerous other traditional crafts may face a future in which their expertise becomes antiquated, leaving them qualified only to work as pedicab drivers or factory laborers.

Under current conditions, the question of whether employment is categorically good or bad for young adolescents is not the right question. Woodhead (2004, p. 6) suggests the right question is, "Which children—in which kinds of work—and in which situations—are most at risk of being harmed by their work?" The key issue, then, is not whether youth work, but the nature of their work, its physical and developmental impact, and how it relates

to other aspects of their lives, especially their family relationships and long-term economic prospects. The extent to which work constitutes a risk to a youth's well-being is conditional on a whole range of circumstances. Research on adolescent employment needs to make comparisons, not only between young adolescents who work and those who do not, but among those who work in different sectors of the economy and under different conditions. We can expect the costs and benefits of adolescent employment to be moderated by the factors leading adolescents to work, the social and physical conditions of their employment, the skill set they are acquiring, and how likely this skill set is to match the jobs available as economies continue to change.

Adroit policy research is also critical. Adolescent work is embedded in a complex web of family needs, cultural assumptions, and community relationships. Culturally sensitive interventions need to be tested that address these multiple layers and involve coordination among governments, nongovernmental organizations, social workers, community leaders, and unions (Rosas & Rossignotti, 2005; Saraswathi & Larson, 2002). Clearly, efforts should be made to eliminate forms of adolescent employment that are physically harmful and expose youth to unacceptable risks. But how to achieve this is a difficult empirical question. The goal generally needs to be to bring child and adolescent labor under both formal and informal controls. Creative efforts are also needed to find ways for adolescents to work while allowing them to stay in school. It is also vital to determine how schools can provide education that broadens adolescents' opportunities to secure a job in the future.

Gender Differences: Girls' Adolescence in Contrast to Boys'

To this point we have given little attention to gender, but across societies gender is a central coordinate of adolescence that cannot be ignored. For adolescent girls in many cultural settings the pathways to adulthood continue to be quite distinct from that of boys, as the following examples poignantly illustrate:

- An 11-year-old Ethiopian girl ran away from her rural home to Addis Ababa in order to avoid being married off by her parents (Erulkar, Mekbib, Simie, & Gulema, 2006).
- Girls in rural Guatemala say that their parents will not pay for their education because they believe boys are more intelligent and therefore only boys should study (Colom et al., 2005).
- A 16-year-old Turkish girl wants someday to own the family business, but it has already been named after her 7-year-old brother (White, 1995).

In Western and other industrial societies, gender differences have been decreasing over the last 100 years, at least within many life domains. As a result, Western scholars often see gender differences in terms of "overlapping bell curves" (Bernstein, 1998). Yet in many regions of the globe, globalization has not reduced traditional gender differences. Girls' and boys' experiences remain so dissimilar as to constitute separate adolescences. We focus on gender differences in the two domains of family experience and education.

The Role of Girls and Young Women in Families

In many cultures, differential treatment of girls intensifies at puberty. Budding sexuality induces deeply rooted cultural concerns and invokes diverging scripts of socialization for girls and boys. In the Middle East and parts of Latin America, Africa, and Asia, families' honor, status, and long-term financial interests (through marriage contracts) are tied to girls' virginity, thus requiring that girls' sexuality be tightly monitored and controlled. In most of the same societies, males' sexual exploits tend to be tolerated by adults and admired by peers as affirmations of manhood (WHO, 2000), whereas in Turkey, for example, forced virginity

examinations may be conducted on girls as a condition for marriage (Bunting, 2005).

Puberty also intensifies preparation for separate adult family roles, requiring girls and boys to spend their time in different daily contexts of socialization. In much of the world, women's primary adult role is seen to be domestic, and men carry little responsibility for childcare and household labor (UNICEF, 1995). To prepare for their role, girls' time is enlisted in an intensive regime of household work. In Laos, for example, an adolescent girl may spend up to 2½ hours every day husking, washing, soaking, and steaming rice (Ireson-Doolittle & Moreno-Black, 2004). In Istanbul, a girl must learn how to cook and clean the house, care for younger children, and serve tea or water with the proper gestures and ceremony, because she will be required to display these skills when the family of a prospective husband comes to call (White, 1995). By early adolescence, girls' principal developmental agenda is learning how to manage the variety of household and nurturing tasks that will define them as adults.

Timing of marriage is of considerable relevance to understanding the experience of girls and young women in the developing world. In most regions the age of marriage for both girls and boys has increased as a function of increased family wealth, urbanization, rising educational attainment and international social pressure. As a result, during the last 30 years, all regions except the former Soviet Asia and South America have experienced substantial declines in the proportion of adolescent girls who are married (Mensch, Singh, & Casterline, 2005). However, the number of adolescent girls affected by early marriage remains large in Africa, South Asia, and Southeast Asia. In some areas, a large proportion of girls are married before their 15th birthday – 50% of girls in Amhara, Ethiopia; 40% in Bihar, India; and 25% in Jinotega, Nicaragua (Bunting, 2005; Erulkar et al., 2004; Haberland, Chong, & Bracken, 2004). Half of all adolescent girls between 15 and 19 years are married in Niger,

Mali, Bangladesh, and Afghanistan. In these same countries, less than 10% of boys of the same age group are married. In fact, marriage for males in adolescent years has been and continues to be rare (Mensch et al., 2005).

Early marriage has profound implications for girls' physical, psychological, and social development. Married adolescents girls, compared to unmarried girls and married women from the same locale (Bunting, 2005; Haberland et al., 2004):

- Consistently have less education and fewer schooling opportunities. For adolescent girls in Nigeria, marriage is more prohibitive to school enrollment than motherhood. Only 3% of married girls without children are in school compared to 34% of unmarried girls with children (Population Council, 2006).
- Have less mobility than their unwed counterparts.
- Have less exposure to modern media.
- Have limited social networks.
- Face greater risk of gender-based violence.
- Face greater reproductive health risks.

Marriage, in effect, terminates adolescence: It is a right of passage from childhood into adulthood. It changes virtually all the known and safe parameters of girls' lives. In India, Nepal, Ethiopia, and Burkina Faso, young wives move from their natal homes to the village or compound of their husband. They lose contact with friends, are initiated into sexual activity, and many become mothers within 18 months. But, while becoming a wife and mother gives them the markings of adult status, because of their young age, these girls may find themselves particularly isolated with little power to negotiate for their own well-being within their husband's household (Haberland et al, 2004; Levine, Lloyd, Green, & Grown, 2008).

As a result of these restrictions, girls' early marriage translates into marked differences in their developmental experiences. It means they have fewer chances to develop independent thinking; they may even find it difficult to conceptualize any clear notion of their own

individual welfare (Mensch et al., 1998; Sen, 1990). In these contexts, girls may face what Erikson called "identity foreclosure"; their restricted social interactions and culturally imposed identities of wife and mother prohibit them from the exploration and experimentation necessary for the development of agency—a capacity increasingly needed for adulthood in a changing society.

Girls' Schooling and Pathways to Employment

Traditional conceptions of gender also remain an obstacle to both girls' education and employment, restricting their pathways to adulthood and creating additional divergence between girls' and boys' lived experiences. Formal education systems continue to maintain and reproduce a subordinate status for girls and, even where societies have encouraged higher educational aspirations for girls, the structures and patterns of the economy have not yet yielded proportionate socioeconomic attainment.

But there is limited good news. As we said earlier, rates of school enrollment have been increasing dramatically across most nations, and girls have caught up with and achieved parity with boys in many nations, particularly in Latin America and East Asia. In other nations, girls' rates of enrollment have been increasing, but remain behind those of boys. Girls' rates of enrollment in secondary education is 79% that of boys in sub-Saharan Africa and is 83% that of boys in South and West Asia. Sub-Saharan Africa actually moved away from gender parity in secondary education between 1999 and 2005 (UNESCO, 2007).

Greater education for young women is a crucial step toward gender equality, women's empowerment, and societal development as a whole. The multiple benefits of girls' education include (United Nations Population Fund [UNFPA], 2004):

- Reducing poverty—educated girls are less likely to live in poverty as adults.
- Improving health of women and their children—worldwide, the risk of a child dying

prematurely is reduced by around 8% for each year that her or his mother spent in primary school.

• Delaying marriage—increasing education has played a vital role in reducing child marriage.

• Reducing female genital cutting—educated women are less than half as likely to be subjected to female circumcision and four times more likely to oppose it for their daughters.

• Increasing self-confidence and decision-making power—evidence from across the world shows that, though women everywhere continue to be constrained by unequal power relations, increased education helps women to gain in status and secure greater decision-making power in the family and the wider community.

For many previously confined young women, the opportunity to attend school has helped break down and undermine some of the taboos and restrictions on girls' behavior and gives them exposure to more diverse contexts and role models outside the family (Adely, 2004). Increased education is leading girls (more so than boys) to have more egalitarian gender role attitudes and expectations (Booth, 2002; Mensch, Ibrahim, Lee, & El-Gibaly, 2000). Most importantly, education increases young women's life choices by making them better prepared for jobs in the emerging information society.

Yet the good news is qualified by differences in the quality of the educational experiences girls receive. First, families are often not as supportive of girls' education. Girls' domestic responsibilities often limit the amount of time girls have to study and do homework, and sometimes prevent them from graduation (Lloyd, Grant, & Ritche, 2008; Mensch et al, 2000; Rothchild, 2006). Furthermore, research in Nepal, Bangladesh, and Egypt shows that families perceive girls' education as utilitarian rather than emancipatory. Parents speak of girls' education in terms of their presumed and future roles as daughters, wives, mothers,

and daughters-in-law. In many contexts, girls' education is seen as an investment that allows families to yield higher returns for the family by attracting better-educated and financially successful husbands for their daughters (Lloyd, El Tawila, Clark, & Mensch, 2003, Mahmud & Amin, 2006; Rothchild, 2006).

Second, girls' experiences in the classroom often differ from those of boys. Research shows that boys experience more challenging interactions with teachers, dominate classroom activities, and receive more attention than girls (Rothchild, 2006; UNESCO, 2007). In some settings, education may simply continue to perpetuate existing cultural gender roles. Studies have found that school books and teaching materials underrepresented women and too frequently characterized them only in their roles as wives and mothers, a phenomenon not restricted to developing countries (UNESCO, 2007). In Saudi Arabia, boys and girls attend separate schools with different curricula, and the girls' curriculum includes fewer academic subjects and has a heavy domestic science component. In some Turkish middle and high schools, boys are assigned extra time for science labs or field trips and are instructed in crafts such as bookbinding, woodworking, and paper marbling, while girls are instructed in modern techniques of housekeeping, including cooking, baking, sewing, and child care (Arat, 1998).

Finally, schools are not safe havens—they are often places of physical and psychological violence, perpetuated by teachers, other staff, and by adolescents themselves. Boys are more likely to experience frequent and severe violence, particularly corporal punishment. Girls are more likely to be affected by sexual violence and harassment, often resulting in early dropout. A study in Ecuador reported that 22% of adolescent girls had been victims of sexual abuse in an educational setting (UNESCO, 2004). The physical environment of schools is also important, especially for girls. Researchers in sub-Saharan Africa have documented that lack of girl-only toilets, sanitary pads, and water for washing hands has driven a number of girls from school (LaFraniere, 2005; Sangraula & Subedi, 2007; UNESCO, 2007).

In sum, gender equality in education remains elusive. While more girls than ever before are gaining access to education, this access does not always translate into high achievement or preparedness for adulthood. A further issue is that even with the same education, when young women reach the job market, gender discrimination often means they find themselves in less remunerative jobs than those obtained by young men (Hannum & Buchmann, 2005; Santa Maria, 2002; UNESCO, 2007). Gender differences are deeply embedded in language, family concepts, and cultural scripts and myths. Lack of access to education and employment create developmental challenges and threats. Even with access to education, young women still find themselves bearing a disproportionate burden of family care, which serves to limit education's benefit. Trying to escape the prospect of early marriage or even attending school itself create risks of exploitation and victimization, against which women need to be prepared to protect themselves.

Challenges for Research and Policy

New challenges and risks are emerging for adolescent girls that urgently need to be understood. Our cursory summary did not provide space to consider the role of media images in affecting the experience of gender, nor ways in which gender has served as a focus for cultural counterreactions (e.g., as a rallying point for the reassertion of traditional norms by fundamentalist groups). We have also given little attention to the many important issues facing boys, yet research in diverse regions shows that the societal transition from traditional to modern typically brings significant changes in gender socialization and adult gender roles for males as well (Condon & Stern, 1993; Hansen, 2005; WHO, 2000). Researchers need to track how larger social forces, like urbanization and economic development, are changing, disrupting, or realigning the pathways to adulthood for both boys and girls.

The implications are important for youth policy, too. Mensch et al. (1998) argue that youth policy has been weakened by the assumptions, first, that male and female adolescents form a homogeneous group and, second, that girls have control over their lives. Bridging the gap requires long-term dialogue among all institutions involved in imparting codes of conduct and setting standards. Policy for adolescent girls needs to be organized around the distinctive features of their lives within a cultural setting, which may include their confinement to domestic roles, their restricted mobility, and the barriers they experience to education and meaningful employment.

CONCLUSION

Anthropologists such as Margaret Mead (1928) and Ruth Benedict (1939) characterized adolescence in Western nations as a difficult period due to discontinuity in roles between childhood and adulthood. In other societies they had studied, children and youth gradually learned the work and family roles of their parents; in some there were rites of passage that shaped and supported this transition to adulthood. Mead and Benedict observed that in Western societies, however, adolescents experienced a long period of uncertainty when they were required to learn new roles and make choices between numerous alternate pathways.

Saraswathi (1999b) argues that similar discontinuity between childhood and adulthood is coming about in India, and the same might be said of many other nations. Globalization, modernization, and related macro societal changes are disrupting and reconfiguring the pathways from childhood to adulthood. They are creating a longer, more uncertain adolescent period during which more knowledge needs to be acquired and decisions made to fit oneself into a viable pathway to adulthood. Children are less able to simply follow in parents' footsteps. The fast pace of cultural change also means that knowledge learned as a child—and the advice parents are able to give in adolescence—may be less helpful in preparing youth for the world they will live in as adults. This is particularly true for youth in a generation that makes the transition from rural to urban residence.

This chapter has illustrated some of the ways in which the pathways through adolescence are becoming more discontinuous, complex, and challenging across different parts of the world. For large numbers of the world's youth, poverty is creating a widening "global divide" that limits their access to the education, information technology, and jobs that would provide a route out of poverty. Tumultuous labor markets (shaped by changing technologies and global competition) are creating greater uncertainty in the types of jobs youth can expect as adults (Ghosh, 2006). Greater contact and competition between diverse people is fueling new regional conflicts, disrupting resources for youth and in some cases enlisting youth as combatants. In these, and other ways, societal changes are making the pathways to adulthood more unpredictable, longer, and labyrinth-like. Adolescence requires young people to achieve longer and bigger "leaps" between what they are as children and what they need to become as adults.

Mead and Benedict saw discontinuity as a contributor to the high levels of stress they believed that Western adolescents experienced. This theme has been repeated by some current authors, with a focus particularly on the cultural dislocation that globalization can create for the world's youth. Arnett (2002) argues that youth may experience themselves as alienated or excluded from both the local and global culture, and he points to increased rates of suicide and substance use in some groups of youth. In carefully controlled research, McDade and Worthman (2004) provide impressive demonstration of how Samoan adolescents who experience cultural dissonance between their lives at home and away from home showed elevated indicators of physiological stress.

It would be a mistake, however, to underestimate the ways in which adolescents, families, and cultural groups can be resourceful

in adapting to change. At the same time that societies are being transformed by top-down change, ordinary people respond with bottom-up actions through which cultural values, ways of thinking, and practices (like the *Kinaalda* of the Navajo; Markstrom & Irbooa, 2003) are passed on and/or adapted to provide supports and continuity to youth. In the United States, adolescents tend to distance themselves from their families during a period when they may most need family support (Larson, Richards, Moneta, Holmbeck, & Duckett, 1996). However, in India, most adolescents do not break away but rather nurture and work on maintaining strong ties to immediate and extended kin, ties that are a source of stability and resources as they make the transition into adulthood. Chandler and coauthors (2003) show that among Native Canadian youth the high rates of suicide attributed to the cultural disruption of globalization were not evident for youth in tribal communities that maintained an active sense of cultural cohesion and self-determination.

It is important to understand the wide range of new challenges that youth face in our rapidly changing global world and the enormous costs and disadvantages they impose. But it is also vital that research identify ways that families, communities, and institutions sustain continuities, while adapting and supporting youth. There is much to be learned about how young people, given the right supports, mobilize their creative and adaptive capabilities and become positive agents, not only of their own development, but of local and global change.

REFERENCES

Adely, F. (2004). The mixed effects of schooling for high school girls in Jordan: The case of Tel Yahya. *Comparative Education Review, 48,* 353–373.

Araia, B. B. (2007). Eritrea. In J. J. Arnett (Ed.), *International encyclopedia of adolescence* (pp. 269–276). New York: Routledge.

Arat, Z. F. (1998). Educating daughters of the republic. In Z. F. Arat (Ed.), *Reconstructing images of a Turkish woman* (pp. 157–180). New York: St. Martin's Press.

Arnett, J. J. (2002). The psychology of globalization. *American Psychologist, 57,* 774–783.

Arnett, J. J. (Ed.) (2007). *International encyclopedia of adolescence.* New York: Routledge.

Aubrun, A., & Grady, J. (2000). *How Americans understand teens: Findings from cognitive interviews*. Washington, DC: Frameworks Institute.

Bachman, S. L. (2000). A new economics of child labor: Searching for answers behind the headlines. *Journal of International Affairs, 53*, 545–572.

Bangladesh Bureau of Statistics (2003). *Report on national child labour survey 2002–2003*. Dhaka: Author.

Barber, B. K. (in press). *Adolescents and war: How youth deal with political violence*. New York: Oxford University Press.

Bellah, R. N., Madsen, R., Sullivan, W. M., Swidler, A., & Tipton, S. M. (1985). *Habits of the heart: Individualism and commitment in American life*. New York: Harper & Row.

Benedict, R. (1939). Continuities and discontinuities in cultural conditioning. *Psychiatry, 1*, 161–167.

Benson, P. L., Scales, P. C., Hamilton, S. F., & Sesma, A., Jr. (2006). Positive youth development: Theory, research and applications. In W. Damon & R.M. Lerner (Eds.), *Handbook of child psychology* (6th ed.), vol. 1: *Theoretical models of human development* (pp. 894–941). (Editors-in-chief: W. Damon & R. M. Lerner). Hoboken, NJ: John Wiley & Sons.

Bernstein, D. (1998). *Gender and motivation*, vol. 5: *Nebraska symposium on motivation*. Lincoln: University of Nebraska Press.

Bhagwati, J. (2004). *In defense of globalization*. New York: Oxford.

Bharat, S. (1997). Family socialization of the Indian child. *Trends in Social Science Research, 4*, 201–216.

Biswas, P. C. (1992). Perception of parental behaviour and adolescents' frustration. *Indian Journal of Social Work, L111*, 669–678.

Blum, R. W. (2007). Youth in sub-Saharan Africa. *Journal of Adolescent Health, 41*, 230–238.

Booth, M. (2002). Arab adolescents facing the future: Enduring ideals and pressures to change. In B. B. Brown, R. W. Larson, & T. S. Saraswathi (Eds.), *The world's youth: Adolescence in eight regions of the globe* (pp. 207–242). New York: Cambridge University Press.

Boratav, H. B. (2005). Negotiating youth: Growing up in inner-city Istanbul. *Journal of Youth Studies, 8*, 203–220.

Botz-Bornstein, T., & Hengelbrock, J. (Eds.). (2006). *Re-ethnicizing the minds? Cultural revival in contemporary thought*. New York: Rodopi.

Boyle, E. H., Smith, T., & Guenther, K. M. (2007). The rise of the child as an individual in global society. In S. A. Venkatesh & R. Kassimir (Eds.), *Youth, globalization, and the law* (pp. 255–283). Stanford, CN: Stanford University Press.

Bronfenbrenner, U. (1979). *The ecology of human development*. Cambridge, MA: Harvard University Press.

Bronfenbrenner, U. (1999). Environments in developmental perspective: Theoretical and operational models. In S. Friedman & T. Wachs (Eds.), *Measuring environment across the life span* (pp. 3–28). Washington, DC: American Psychological Association.

Brown, B. B., & Larson, R. (2002). The kaleidoscope of adolescence: Experiences of the world's youth at the beginning of the 21st century. In B. B. Brown, R. W. Larson, & T. S. Saraswathi (Eds.), *The world's youth: Adolescence in eight regions of the globe* (pp. 1–20). New York: Cambridge University Press.

Brown, L., Garder, G., & Halweil, B. (1999). 16 impacts of population growth. *The Futurist, 33*, 36–41.

Bunting, A. (2005). Stages of development: Marriage of girls and teens as an international human rights issue. *Social Legal Studies, 14*, 17–38.

Caldwell, J. C., Caldwell, P., Caldwell, B. K., & Pieris, I. (1998). The construction of adolescence in a changing world: Implications for sexuality, reproduction, and marriage. *Studies in Family Planning, 29*, 137–153.

Call, K., Riedel, A., Hein, K., McLoyd, V., Petersen, A. C., & Kipke, M. (2002). Adolescent health and well-being in the 21st century: A global perspective. *Journal of Research on Adolescence, 12*, 69–98.

Castells, M. (1998). *End of millennium*. Oxford: Blackwell.

Chandler, M. J., Lalonde, C. E., Sokol, B. W., & Hallett, D. (2003). Personal persistence, identity development, and suicide: A study of native and non-native North American adolescents. *Monographs of the Society for Research in Child Development, 68*.

Chen, X., & Chang, L. (2007). China. In J. J. Arnett (Ed.), *International encyclopedia of adolescence* (pp. 179–194). New York: Routledge.

Chin, A. (2007). The newest Mandarins. *New York Times*, December 16, 2007.

Coatsworth, J. H. (2004). Globalization, growth, and welfare in history. In M. Suárez-Orozco & D. B. Qin-Hilliard (Eds.), *Globalization: Culture and education in the new millennium* (pp. 38–55). Berkeley: University of California Press.

Cole, J. (2005). The jaombilo of Tamtave (Madagascar), 1992–2004: Reflections on youth and globalization. *Journal of Social History, 38*, 891–914.

Condon, R. G., & Stern, P. R. (1993). Gender-role preference, gender identity, and gender socialization among contemporary Inuit youth. *Ethos, 21*, 384–416.

Cook, N. (1998). "Dutiful daughters," estranged sisters: Women in Thailand. In K. Sen & M. Stivens (Eds.), *Gender and power in affluent Asia* (pp. 250–290). New York: Routledge.

Côté, J. E. (1994). *Adolescent storm and stress: An evaluation of the Mead/Freeman controversy*. Hillsdale, NJ: Lawrence Erlbaum.

Cullen, F. T., & Wright, J. P. (2002). Criminal justice in the lives of American adolescents. In J. Mortimer & R. Larson (Eds.), *The changing adolescent experience: Societal trends and the transition to adulthood* (pp. 88–128). New York: Cambridge University Press.

Cummings, W. K. (1997). Human resource development: The J-Model. In W. K. Cummings & P. G. Altbach (Eds.), *The challenge of Eastern Asian education: Implications for America* (pp. 275–291). Albany: State University of New York Press.

Darling, N., Cumsille, P., Pena-Alampay, L., & Coatsworth, D. (2005). Individual and issue-specific differences in parental knowledge and adolescent disclosure in Chile, the Philippines, and the United States. *New Directions in Child and Adolescent Development, 108*, 47–60.

Dasen, P. R. (2000). Rapid social change and the turmoil of adolescence: A cross-cultural perspective. *International Journal of Group Tensions, 29*, 17–49.

Davis, S. S., & Davis, D. A. (1989). *Adolescence in a Moroccan town: Making social sense*. New Brunswick, NJ: Rutgers University Press.

Deeb, L., & Harb, M. (2007). Sanctioned pleasures: Youth, piety and leisure in Beirut. *Middle East Reports, 245*, 12–19.

Derné, S. (2003). Culture, family structure, and psyche in Hindu India: The "fit" and the "inconsistencies." In D. Sharma (Ed.), *Childhood, family, and sociocultural change in India* (pp. 88–114). New Delhi: Oxford University Press.

Diehl, P. F. (Ed.). (2005). *The politics of global governance: International organizations in an interdependent world*. Boulder, CO: Lynne Rienner.

Diversi, M., Moraes, N., & Morelli, M. (1999). Daily reality on the streets of Campinas, Brazil. *New Directions for Child and Adolescent Development, 85*, 19–34.

Elder, G. H., Jr. (1998). The life course and human development. In R. M. Lerner (Ed.), *Handbook of child psychology*, vol. 1: *Theoretical models of human development* (5th ed., pp. 939–991). New York: John Wiley & Sons.

Elder, G. H., Jr., & O'Rand, A. M. (1995). Adult lives in a changing society. In K. S. Cook, G. A. Fine, & J. S. House (Eds.), *Sociological perspectives on social psychology* (pp. 452–475). Boston: Allyn and Bacon.

Enright, R. D., Levy, V. M., Harris, D. & Lapsley, D. K. (1987). Do economic conditions influence how theorists view adolescents? *Journal of Youth and Adolescence, 16*, 541–559.

Erikson, E. H. (1968). *Identity: Youth and crisis.* New York: W. W. Norton.

Erulkar, A., Mekbib, T., Simie, N., & Gulema, T. (2004). *The experience of adolescence in rural Amhara region Ethiopia.* New York: Population Council.

Facio, A., & Batistuta, M. (1998). Latins, Catholics and from the far south: Argentinian adolescents and their parents. *Journal of Adolescence, 21,* 49–67.

French, D. C., Rianasari, M., Pidada, S., Nelwan, P., & Buhrmester, D. (2001). Social support of Indonesian and U.S. children and adolescents by family members and friends. *Merrill-Palmer Quarterly, 47,* 377–394.

French, J. L. (2002). Adolescent workers in third world export industries: Attitudes of young Brazilian shoemakers. *Industrial and Labor Relations Review, 55,* 308–323.

Freud, A. (1946). *The ego and the mechanisms of defense.* New York: International Universities Press.

Friedman, T. (2005). *The world is flat: A brief history of the twenty-first century.* New York: Farrar, Straus & Giroux.

Fuligni, A. J. (2007). Family obligation, enrollment, and emerging adulthood in Asian and Latin American families. *Child Development Perspectives, 1,* 96–100.

Fuligni, A. J., & Zhang, W. (2004). Attitudes towards family obligation among adolescents in contemporary urban and rural China. *Child Development, 74,* 180–192.

Furstenberg, F. F. (2006). *Diverging development: The not so invisible hand of social class in the United States.* Paper presented at the biennial meetings of the Society for Research on Adolescence, San Francisco. Available at www.transad.pop.upenn.edu.

Fussell, E., & Greene, M. E. (2002). Demographic trends affecting youth around the world. In B. B. Brown, R. W. Larson, & T. S. Saraswathi (Eds.), *The world's youth: Adolescence in eight regions of the globe* (pp. 21–60). New York: Cambridge University Press.

Gardner, H. (2004). How education changes: Considerations of history, science, and values. In M. Suárez-Orozco & D. B. Qin-Hilliard (Eds.), *Globalization: Culture and education in the new millennium* (pp. 235–258). Berkeley: University of California Press.

Gauvain, M. (1999). Everyday opportunities for the development of planning skills: Sociocultural and family influences. In A. Göncü (Ed.), *Children's engagement in the world: Sociocultural perspectives* (pp. 173–201). New York: Cambridge University Press.

Ghosh, B. N. (2006). Introduction: The end of geography and the beginning of conflicts. In B. N. Ghosh & H. M. Guven (Eds.), *Globalization and the third world: A study of negative consequences* (pp. 1–14). New York: Palgrave Macmillan.

Giddens, A. (1990). *The consequences of modernity.* Stanford, CA: Stanford University Press.

Gielen, U. P., & Chumachenko, O. (2004). All the world's children: The impact of global demographic trends and economic disparities. In U. P. Gielen & J. Roopnarine (Eds.), *Childhood and adolescence: Cross-cultural perspectives and applications* (pp. 81–109). Westport, CT: Praeger.

Gilliam, F. D., & Bales, S. (2001). Strategic frame analysis: Reframing America's youth. *Social Policy Report, XV*(3), Ann Arbor, MI: Society for Research in Child Development.

Greenfield, P. M. (1994). Independence and interdependence as developmental scripts: Implications for theory, research, and practice. In P. M. Greenfield & R. R. Cocking (Eds.), *Cross-cultural roots of minority child development* (pp. 1–37). Hillsdale, NJ: Lawrence Erlbaum.

Guerra, N., & Bradshaw, C. (Eds.). (in press). Youth at risk: Core competencies to prevent problem behaviors and promote positive youth development. *New Directions for Child and Adolescent Development.*

Guillèn, M. F. (2001). Is globalization civilizing, destructive, or feeble? A critique of five key debates in the social science literature. *Annual Review of Sociology, 27,* 235–260.

Haberland, N., Chong, E., & Bracken, H. (2004). *A world apart: The disadvantage and social isolation of married adolescent girls.* Brief based on background paper prepared for the WHO/UNFPA/Population Council Technical Consultation on Married Adolescents. New York: Population Council.

Hannum, E., & Buchmann, C. (2005). Global educational expansion and socio-economic development: An assessment of findings from the social sciences. *World Development, 33,* 333–354.

Hansen, K. (2005). Getting stuck in the compound: Some odds against social adulthood in Lusaka, Zambia. *Africa Today, 51,* 3–16.

Hauser, S. T., Powers, S. I., & Noam, G. G. (1991). *Adolescents and their families: Paths of ego development.* New York: Free Press.

Havighurst, R. J. (1953). *Human development and education.* New York: McKay.

Held, D. (2007). Reframing global governance: Apocalypse soon or reform! In D. Held & A. McGrew (Eds.), *Globalization theory: Approaches and controversies* (pp. 240–260). Cambridge: Polity Press.

Herdt, G. H. (1982). Fetish and fantasy in Sambia initiation. In G. H. Herdt (Ed.), *Rituals of manhood: Male initiation in Papua New Guinea* (pp. 44–98). Berkeley: University of California Press.

Hershock, P., Mason, M., & Hawkins, J. (Eds.). (2007). *Changing education: Leadership, innovation and development in a globalizing Asia Pacific.* Hong Kong: Comparative Education Research Centre.

Hoffman, S. (1998). *World disorders: Troubled peace in the post-Cold War era.* Lanham, MD: Rowman & Littlefield.

Hoffman, V. (1995). Muslim fundamentalists: Psychosocial profiles. In M.E. Marty & R.S. Appleby (Eds.), *Fundamentalisms comprehended* (pp. 199–230). Chicago: University of Chicago Press.

Ibeagha, P. N. (2007). Nigeria. In J. J. Arnett (Ed.), *International encyclopedia of adolescence* (pp. 681–698). New York: Routledge.

Inglehart, R. (1997). *Modernization and postmodernization: Cultural, ecomomic and political change in 43 societies.* Princeton, NJ: Princeton University Press.

Inglehart, R., & Baker, W. (2000). Modernization, cultural change, and the persistence of traditional values. *American Sociological Review, 65,* 19–51.

Inglehart, R. F., & Welzel, C. (2007). Modernization. In G. Ritzer (Ed.), *Blackwell encyclopedia of sociology* (pp. 3071–3078). New York: Blackwell.

International Labour Office (ILO) (1996). *Child labor: Targeting the intolerable.* Geneva, Switzerland: Author.

ILO. (2002). *Every child counts: New global estimates on child labour.* Geneva, Switzerland: Author.

ILO. (2006a). *Global child labour trends 2000 to 2004.* Geneva, Switzerland: Author.

ILO. (2006b). *Global employment trends for youth.* Geneva, Switzerland: Author.

ILO. (2007). *Global employment trends for women brief 2007.* Geneva, Switzerland: Author.

Jenkins, H. (2004). Pop cosmopolitanism: Mapping cultural flows in an age of media convergence. In M. Suárez-Orozco & D. B. Qin-Hilliard (Eds.), *Globalization: Culture and education in the new millennium* (pp. 114–140). Berkeley: University of California Press.

Jensen, L. A. (2003). Coming of age in a multicultural world: Globalization and adolescent cultural identity formulation. *Applied Developmental Science, 7,* 189–196.

Kâğıtçıbaşı, Ç. (1997). Individualism and collectivism. In J. W. Berry, M. H. Segall, & C. Kâğıtçıbaşı (Eds.), *Handbook of cross-cultural psychology: Social behavior and applications,* vol. 3 (2nd ed.; pp. 1–49). Boston: Allyn and Bacon.

Kâğıtçıbaşı, Ç. (2007). *Family, self, and human development across cultures: Theory and applications* (2nd ed) Mahwah, NJ: Lawrence Erlbaum.

Kapadia, S., & Shah, R. (1998). Strengths and weaknesses of the Indian family: An insider's perspective. *Perspectives in Education, 14,* 173–182.

Kashyap, L. D. (1993). Adolescent/youth and family dynamics and development programmes. *Indian Journal of Social Work, LIV,* 94–107.

Kohl, B., & Farthing, L. (2006). *Impasse in Bolivia: Neoliberal hegemony and popular resistance.* London: Zed Books.

Kraidy, M. (2005). *Hybridity, or the cultural logic of globalization.* Philadelphia: Temple University Press.

Kuper, A. (2007). Reconstructing global governance: Eight innovations. In D. Held & A. McGrew (Eds.), *Globalization theory: Approaches and controversies* (pp. 225–239). Cambridge: Polity Press.

LaFraniere, S. (2005, December 23). Another school barrier for African girls: No toilet. *New York Times.* Retrieved February 8, 2008, from www.nytimes.com/2005/12/23/international/africa/23ethiopia.html?_r=1&scp=1&sq=LaFraniere%2C+S.+Another+school+barrier+for+African+girls%3A+No+toilet.+&st=nyt&oref=slogin.

Lam, W. S. E. (2006). Culture and learning in the context of globalization: Research directions. *Review of Research in Education, 30,* 213–237.

Larson, R. (2002). Globalization, societal change, and new technologies: What they mean for the future of adolescence. *Journal of Research on Adolescence, 12,* 1–30.

Larson, R. W., Richards, M. H., Moneta, G., Holmbeck, G., & Duckett, E. (1996). Changes in adolescents' daily interactions with their families from ages 10 to 18: Disengagement and transformation. *Developmental Psychology, 32,* 744–754.

Larson, R., Verma, S., & Dworkin, J. (2003). Adolescence without disengagement: The daily family lives of Indian middle-class teenagers. In T.S. Saraswathi (Ed.), *Cross-cultural perspectives in human development: Theory, research and applications* (pp. 258–286). New Delhi: Sage.

Leeds, J. (2007, December 5). As U.S. pop wanes abroad, talent scout looks wide. *New York Times,* pp. B1, B9.

Lerner, R. (2002). *Concepts and theories of human development* (3rd ed.). Mahwah, NJ: Lawrence Erlbaum.

Lerner, R. M., & Walls, T. (1999). Revisiting individuals as producers of their development: From dynamic interactionism to developmental systems. In J. Brandstädter & R. M. Lerner (Eds.), *Action and self-development: Theory and research through the life span* (pp. 3–36). Thousand Oaks, CA: Sage.

Levine, R. A. (1980). Adulthood among the Gusii of Kenya. In N. Smelser & E. Erikson (Eds), *Themes of work and love in adulthood* (pp. 77–104). Cambridge: Harvard University Press.

Levine, R., Lloyd, C., Greene, M., & Grown, C. (2008). *Girls count: A global investment and action agenda.* Washington, DC: Center for Global Development.

Levy, C. (2001). Rap in Bulgaria: Between fashion and reality. In T. Mitchell (Ed.), *Global noise: Rap and hip-hop outside the USA* (pp. 134–148). Middletown, CT: Wesleyan University Press.

Lloyd, C. B. (Ed.) (2005). *Growing up global: The changing transitions to adulthood in developing countries.* Panel on Transitions to Adulthood in Developing Countries. National Research Council and Institute of Medicine. Committee on Population and Board on Children, Youth, and Families. Division of Behavioral and Social Sciences and Education. Washington, DC: National Academies Press.

Lloyd, C., El Tawila, S., Clark, W., & Mensch, B. (2003). The impact of educational quality on school exit in Egypt. *Comparative Education Review, 47,* 444–467.

Lloyd, C., Grant, M. & Ritche, A. (2008). Gender differences in time use among adolescents in developing countries: Implications of rising school enrollment rates. *Journal of Research on Adolescence, 18,* 99–120.

Lukose, R. (2005). Consuming globalization: Youth and gender in Kerala, India. *Journal of Social History, 38,* 915–935.

Lynch, M. (2007). Young brothers in cyberspace. *Middle East Reports, 245,* 26–33.

Mahmud, S., & Amin, S. (2006). Girls' schooling and marriage in rural Bangladesh. In E. Hannum & B. Fuller (Eds.), *Children's lives and schooling across societies* (pp. 71–100). San Diego: Elsevier.

Maira, S. (2002). Temporary tattoos: Indo-Chic fantasies and late capitalist Orientalism. *Meridians: Feminism, Race, Transnationalism, 3,* 134–160.

Males, M. (1996). *The scapegoat generation: America's war on adolescents.* Monroe, ME: Common Courage Press.

Mannheim, K. (1952). The problem of generations. In P. Keckskemeti (Ed.), *Essays on the sociology of knowledge* (pp. 276–320). New York: Oxford University Press.

Markstrom, C. A., & Irbooa, A. (2003). Adolescent identity formation and rites of passage: The Navajo Kinaalda ceremony for girls. *Journal of Research on Adolescence, 13,* 399–425.

McDade, T. M., & Worthman, C. M. (2004). Socialization ambiguity in Samoan adolescents: A model for human development and stress in the context of cultural change. *Journal of Research on Adolescence, 14,* 49–72.

McGrew, A. (2007). Organized violence in the making (and remaking) of globalization. In D. Held & A. McGrew (Eds.), *Globalization theory: Approaches and controversies.* (pp. 15–40). Cambridge: Polity Press.

Mead, M. (1928). *Coming of age in Samoa.* New York: William Morrow.

Mensch, B. S., Bruce, J., & Greene, M. E. (1998). *The uncharted passage: Girls' adolescence in the developing world.* New York: Population Council.

Mensch, B. S., Ibrahim, B. L., Lee, S. M., & El-Gibaly, O. (2000, March). *Socialization to gender roles and marriage among Egyptian adolescents.* Paper presented at the Annual Meeting of the Population Association of America, Los Angeles.

Mensch, B., Singh, S., & Casterline, J. (2005). *Trends in the timing of first marriage among men and women in the developing world.* New York: Population Council.

Meyers, W., & Boyden, J. (1998). *Child labour: Promoting the best interests of working children* (2nd ed.). London: International Save the Children Alliance.

Mikarsa, H. L. (2007). Indonesia. In J. J. Arnett (Ed.), *International encyclopedia of adolescence* (pp. 460–469). New York: Routledge.

Missani, B. (2007). Tanzania. In J. J. Arnett (Ed.), *International encyclopedia of adolescence* (pp. 989–995). New York: Routledge.

Mistry, J., & Saraswathi, T. S. (2002). Culture and child development. In R. M. Lerner, M. A. Easterbrooks., & J. Mistry (Eds), *Comprehensive handbook of psychology,* vol. 6. *Developmental psychology.* New York: John Wiley & Sons.

Mitchell, T. (2001). Another root—hip-hop outside the USA. In T. Mitchell (Ed.), *Global noise: Rap and hip-hop outside the USA* (pp. 1–38). Middletown, CT: Wesleyan University Press.

Modell, J. (1989). *Into one's own.* Berkeley: University of California Press.

Morelli, S. (2001). "Who is a dancing hero?" Rap, hip-hop, and dance in Korean popular culture. In T. Mitchell (Ed.), *Global noise: Rap and hip-hop outside the USA* (pp. 248–258). Middletown, CT: Wesleyan University Press.

Moseley, L. (2007). The political economy of globalization. In D. Held & A.G. McGrew (Eds.), *The global transformations reader* (pp. 106–125). Cambridge: Polity.

Muncie, J. (2007). Youth justice and the governance of young people: Global, international, national, and local contexts. In S. A. Venkatesh & R. Kassimir (Eds.), *Youth, globalization, and the law* (pp. 17–56). Stanford, CN: Stanford University Press.

Nederveen Pieterse, J. (2004). *Globalization and culture: Global mélange.* Lanham, MD: Rowman & Littlefield.

Nelson, L. J. & Chen, X. (2007). Emerging adulthood in China: The role of social and cultural factors. *Child Development, 74,* 86–91.

Nieuwenhuys, O. (1996). The paradox of child labor and anthropology. *Annual Review of Anthropology, 25,* 237–251.

Nsamenang, A.B. (2004). *Cultures of human development and education: Challenge to growing up African.* New York: Nova Science Publishers.

Nsamenang, B. (2002). Adolescence in sub-Saharan Africa: An image constructed from Africa's triple inheritance. In B.B. Brown, R. W. Larson, & T. S. Saraswathi (Eds.), *The world's youth: Adolescence in eight regions of the globe* (pp. 61–104). New York: Cambridge University Press.

Nucci, L., Hasebe, Y., & Lins Dyer, M. T. (2005). Adolescent psychological well-being and parental control of the personal. *New Directions for Child and Adolescent Development, 108,* 17–30.

O'Donnell, O., Van Doorslaer, E., & Rosati, F. (2002). *Child labour and health: Evidence and research issues.* Geneva: ILO/UCW.

Patel, E. (2007). *Acts of faith: The story of an American Muslim, the struggle for the soul of a generation.* Boston, MA: Beacon Press.

Pennycook, A. (2003). Global Englishes, Rip slyme and performativity. *Journal of Sociolinguistics, 7,* 513–533.

Pilkington, H., Omel'chenko, E., Flynn, M., Bliudina, U., & Starkova, E. (2002). *Looking west? Cultural globalization and Russian youth.* University Park, PA: Penn State University Press.

Population Council. (2006). *Facts about adolescents from the Demographic and Health Survey—Statistical tables for program planning: Nigeria 2003.* New York: Author.

Raeff, C. (2006). *Always separate, always connected: Independence and interdependence in cultural contexts of development.* Mahwah, NJ: Lawrence Erlbaum.

Rahman, M. M., Khanam, R., & Absar, N. (1999). Child labor in Bangladesh: A critical appraisal of Harkin's Bill and the MOU-type schooling program. *Journal of Economic Issues, 33,* 985–1105.

Ramanujam, B. K. (1978). The Ahmedabad discussions on change: An Indian viewpoint. In E. J. Anthony & C. Chiland (Eds.), *The child in his family* (pp. 415–419). New York: John Wiley & Sons.

Ramu, G. N. (1988). *Family structure and fertility.* New Delhi: Sage.

Roland, A. (1989). *In search of self in India and Japan.* Princeton, NJ: Princeton University Press.

Roopnarine, J. L., & Suppal, P. (2003). Kakar's psychoanalytic interpretation of Indian childhood: The need to emphasize the father and mother caregivers in the socialization equation. In D. Sharma (Ed.), *Childhood, family, and sociocultural change in India* (pp.115–137). New Delhi: Oxford University Press.

Rosas, G., & Rossignotti, G. (2005). Starting the new millennium right: Decent employment for young people. *International Labour Review, 144,* 139–160.

Rothchild, J. (2006). Gendered homes and classrooms: Schooling in rural Nepal. In E. Hannum & B. Fuller (Eds.), *Children's lives and schooling across societies* (pp. 101–132). San Diego: Elsevier.

Salamon, L. M. (1995). *Partners in public service: Government-nonprofit relations in the modern welfare state.* Baltimore: Johns Hopkins University Press.

Saldanha, A. (2002). Music, space, identity: Geographies of youth culture in Bangalore. *Cultural Studies, 16,* 337–550.

Sangraula, B., & Subedi, A. (2007, August 3). Lack of toilets means fewer girls in school. *Kathmandu Post.*

Santa Maria, M. (2002). Youth in Southeast Asia: Living within the continuity of tradition and the turbulence of change. In B. B. Brown, R. W. Larson, & T. S. Saraswathi (Eds.), *The world's youth: Adolescence in eight regions of the globe* (pp. 171–206). New York: Cambridge University Press.

Saraswathi, T. S. (1999a). Introduction. In T. S. Saraswathi (Ed.), *Culture, socialization and human development* (pp.1–42). New Delhi: Sage.

Saraswathi, T. S. (1999b). Adult–child continuity in India: Is adolescence a myth or an emerging reality? In T. S. Saraswathi (Ed.), *Culture, socialization and human development* (pp. 213–232). New Delhi: Sage.

Saraswathi, T. S. (2005). Hindu worldview in the development of selfways: The "atman" as the real self. In L. Arnett Jensen & R. W. Larson (Eds.), *New horizons in developmental theory and research: new directions in child and adolescent development, 109,* 43–50.

Saraswathi, T. S., & Ganapathy, H. (2002). The Hindu world view of child and human development: Reflections in contemporary parental ethnotheories. In H. Keller, Y. Poortinga, & A. Scholmerich (Eds.), *Between biology and culture: Perspectives on ontogenetic development* (pp. 80–88). London: Cambridge University Press.

Saraswathi, T. S., & Larson, R. (2002). Adolescence in global perspective: An agenda of social policy. In B.B. Brown, R. W. Larson, & T. S. Saraswathi (Eds.), *The world's youth: Adolescence in eight regions of the globe* (pp. 344–362). New York: Cambridge University Press.

Schade-Poulsen, M. (1995). The power of love: Raï music and youth in Algeria. In V. Amit-Talai & H. Wulff (Eds.), *Youth cultures: A cross-cultural perspective* (pp. 81–113). New York: Routledge.

Schaefer Davis, S. (2005). Women weavers online: Rural Moroccan women on the Internet. In C. Ng & S. Mitter (Eds.), *Gender and the digital economy: Perspectives from the developing world* (pp. 159–185). New Delhi: Sage.

Schlegel, A. (1995). A cross-cultural approach to adolescence. *Ethos, 23,* 15–32.

Schlegel, A., & Barry, H. (1991). *Adolescence: An anthropological inquiry.* New York: Free Press.

Sen, A. (1990). Gender and cooperative conflict. In I. Tinker (Ed.), *Persistent inequalities: Rethinking assumptions about development and women* (pp. 123–149). New York: Oxford University Press.

Sen, A. (1999). *Development as freedom.* New York: Random House.

Sen, A. (2006). *Identity and violence: The illusion of destiny.* New York: W. W. Norton.

Seymour, S. C. (1999). *Women, family, and child care in India.* Cambridge: Cambridge University Press.

Shanahan, M. J. (2000). Adolescence. In E. Borgatta & R. Montgomery (Eds.), *Encyclopedia of sociology* (pp. 1–18). New York: Macmillan.

Sharma, D. (2003a). Infancy and childhood in India: A review. In D. Sharma (Ed.), *Childhood, family, and sociocultural change in India* (pp. 13–47). New Delhi: Oxford University Press.

Sharma, D. (2003b). Introduction. In D. Sharma (Ed.), *Childhood, family, and sociocultural change in India* (pp.1–12). New Delhi: Oxford University Press.

Sharma, M., & Srivastava, A. (1991). The family, social network and mental health. In S. Bharat (Ed.), *Research on families with problems in India. Issues and implications,* vol. 1 (pp. 68–78). Bombay: Tata Institute of Social Sciences.

Shukla, M. (1994). India. In K. Hurrelmann (Ed.), *International handbook of adolescence* (pp. 191–206). Westport, CT: Greenwood Press.

Silbereisen, R., & Lerner, R. (Eds.). (2007). *Approaches to positive youth development.* Thousand Oaks, CA: Sage.

Silverberg, S. B., & Gondoli, D. M. (1996). Autonomy in adolescence: A contextualized perspective. In G. R. Adams, R. Montemayor, & T.P. Gullota (Eds.), *Psychosocial development during adolescence: Progress in developmental contextualism* (pp. 12–61). Thousand Oaks, CA: Sage.

Sinha, D. (1994). The joint family in tradition. *Seminar, 424,* 20–23.

Smetana, J. G. (2002). Culture, autonomy, and personal jurisdiction in adolescent–parent relationships. In H. W. Reese & R. Kail (Eds.), *Advances in child development and behavior,* vol. 29 (pp. 51–87). New York: Academic Press.

Smith, P. B., & Schwartz, S. H. (1997). Values. In J. W. Berry, M. H. Segall, & C. Kâğitçibaşi (Eds.), *Handbook of cross-cultural psychology: Social behavior and applications,* vol. 3 (2nd ed.; (pp. 77–118). Boston: Allyn and Bacon.

Sondaite, J. (2007). Iran. In J. J. Arnett (Ed.), *International encyclopedia of adolescence* (pp. 681–698). New York: Routledge.

Spring, J. (2004). *How educational ideologies are shaping global society.* Mahwah, NJ: Lawrence Erlbaum.

Srivastava, A. K. (1997). The changing place of child in Indian families: A cross-generational study. *Trends in Social Science Research, 4,* 191–200.

Steinberg, L. (2001). We know some things: Parent-adolescent relationships in retrospect and prospect. *Journal of Research on Adolescence, 11,* 1–9.

Stevenson, H., & Zusho, A. (2002). Adolescence in China and Japan: Adapting to a changing environment. In B. B. Brown, R. W. Larson, & T. S. Saraswathi (Eds.), *The world's youth: Adolescence in eight regions of the globe* (pp. 141–170). New York: Cambridge University Press.

Stewart, S. M., Bond, M. H., Abdullah, A., & Ma, S. (2000). Gender, parenting, and adolescent functioning in Bangladesh. *Merrill-Palmer Quarterly, 46,* 540–563.

Stiglitz, J. E. (2003). *Globalization and its discontents.* New York: W. W. Norton.

Suárez-Orozco, C. (2004). Formulating identity in a globalized world. In M. Suárez-Orozco & D. B. Qin-Hilliard (Eds.), *Globalization: Culture and education in the new millennium* (pp. 173–202). Berkeley, CA: University of California Press.

Suárez-Orozco, M., & Qin-Hilliard, D. B. (Eds.), (2004). *Globalization: Culture and education in the new millennium* (pp. 1–37). Berkeley: University of California Press.

Sundaram, I. S. (1995). Child labour: Facing the harsh reality. In R. C. Heredia & E. Mathias (Eds.), *The family in a changing world: Women, children and strategies of intervention* (pp. 120–128). New Delhi: Indian Social Institute.

Swedenburg, T. (2001). Islamic hip-hop vs. Islamophobia: Aki Nawaz, Natacha Atlas, Akhenaton. In T. Mitchell (Ed.), *Global noise: Rap and hip-hop outside the USA* (pp. 57–85). Middletown, CT: Wesleyan University Press.

Swedenburg, T. (2007). Imagined youth. *Middle East Reports, 245,* 4–11.

Thapa, V. J., Raval, S., & Chakravarty, S. (1999, January 18). Young men. *India Today,* 52–58.

Tomlinson, J. (1999). *Globalization and culture.* Chicago: University of Chicago Press.

Tomlinson, J. (2003). Globalization and cultural identity. In D. Held & A.G. McGrew (Eds.), *The global transformations reader* (pp. 269–277). Cambridge: Polity.

Tomlinson, J. (2007). Globalization and cultural identity. In D. Held & A.G. McGrew (Eds.), *Globalization theory* (pp. 148–168). Cambridge: Polity.

Tomanovic, S. & Ignjatovic, S. (2006). The transition of young people in a transitional society: The case of Serbia. *Journal of Youth Studies, 9,* 269–285.

Understanding Children's Work (2003). *Understanding children's work in Guatemala.* Geneva: ILO/UCW.

Understanding Children's Work (2006). *Children's work in Cambodia: A challenge for growth and poverty reduction.* Geneva: ILO/UCW.

UNICEF (1995). *A picture of health: A review and annotated bibliography of the health of young people in developing countries.* Geneva, Switzerland: Author.

United Nations (2005). *World youth report 2005.* New York: Author.

United Nations (2007). *World youth report 2007.* New York: Author.

United Nations Educational, Scientific and Cultural Organization (UNESCO) (2004). *Education for all: Global monitoring report, 2003–2004.* Retrieved January 16, 2008, from www.efareport.unesco.org.

UNESCO (2007). *Education for all: Global monitoring report, 2008,* Retrieved January 22, 2008, from www.efareport.unesco.org.

United Nations Population Fund (2004). *Women and HIV/AIDS: Confronting the crisis.* Retrieved January 16, 2008, from www.unfpa.org.

United States Department of Defense (2007). *Base structure report: Fiscal year 2007 baseline.* Retrieved January 20, 2008, from www.defenselink.mil/pubs/BSR_2007_Baseline.pdf.

Uplaonkar, A. T. (1995). The emerging rural youth: A study of their changing values towards marriage. *Indian Journal of Social Work, 56,* 415–423.

Venkatesh, S. A. & Kassimer, R. (2007). Youth and legal institutions: Thinking globally and comparatively. In S. A. Venkatesh & R. Kassimir (Eds.), *Youth, globalization, and the law* (pp. 3–16). Stanford, CN: Stanford University Press.

Verma, S., & Saraswathi, T. S. (2002). Adolescence in India: Street urchins or Silicon Valley millionaires? In B. B. Brown, R. W. Larson, & T. S. Saraswathi (Eds.), *The world's youth: Adolescence in eight regions of the globe* (pp. 105–140). New York: Cambridge University Press.

Vogler, J. (2008). Chile: The rise of the penguin revolution. *Upside down world.* Retrieved April 3, 2008 from http://upsidedownworld.org/main/content/viewe/330/34/.

Watson, J. L. (2004). Globalization in Asia: Anthropological perspectives. In M. Suárez-Orozco & D. B. Qin-Hilliard (Eds.), *Globalization: Culture and education in the new millennium* (pp. 141–172). Berkeley: University of California Press.

Welti, C. (2002). Adolescents in Latin America: Facing the future with skepticism. In B.B. Brown, R. W. Larson, & T. S. Saraswathi (Eds.), *The world's youth: Adolescence in eight regions of the globe* (pp. 276–306). New York: Cambridge University Press.

White, J. B. (1995). An unmarried girl and a grinding stone: A Turkish girl's childhood in the city. In E. W. Fernea (Ed.), *Children in the Muslim Middle East* (pp. 257–267). Austin: University of Texas Press.

WHO (2000). *What about boys? A literature review on the health and development of adolescent boys.* Geneva: Author.

WHO (2003). *Strategic directions for improving the health and development of children and adolescents.* Geneva: Author.

Woodhead, M. (1999). Combating child labour: Listen to what the children say. *Childhood, 6,* 27–49.

Woodhead, M. (2004). *Psychosocial impacts of child work: A framework for research, monitoring and intervention.* Geneva: ILO/UCW.

Youniss, J., Bales, S., Christmas-Best, V., Diversi, M., McLaughlin, M., & Silbereisen, R. (2002). Youth civic engagement in the twenty-first century. *Journal of Research on Adolescence, 12,* 121–148.

Zhang, W. & Fuligni, A. J. (2006). Authority, autonomy, and family relationships among adolescents in urban and rural China. *Journal of Research on Adolescence, 16,* 527–537.

CHAPTER 18

A Shared Commitment to Youth

The Integration of Theory, Research, Practice, and Policy

AIDA B. BALSANO, CHRISTINA THEOKAS, AND DEBORAH L. BOBEK

As demonstrated by the preceding chapters in this *Handbook*, there is a wide range of theories and research on adolescence—ones starting from an individual perspective, from a contextual perspective, and most taking a perspective that integrates individuals and contexts across the adolescent years. But how are these theories and research integrated with programs and policies that affect the lives of today's adolescents? That is, how is the scientific knowledge of adolescent development used to impact policies and programs aimed at promoting the positive and healthy development of youth and how does the experiential knowledge generated in the field influence new research and policy development?

If we seek to maximize the positive development of adolescents, it is imperative that all contexts in which they are embedded—from the micro to the macro—are integrated. Consistent with the framework of applied developmental science, which recognizes the expertise of those living in real-world contexts and seeks to embed research about adolescent development in the ecologies in which they live (Lerner, Fisher, & Weinberg, 2000; Lerner, Jacobs, & Wertlieb, 2003), we discuss in this chapter the ways in which research, policy, and practice have been successfully integrated for the benefit of youth. We also discuss barriers to such integration, address some of the sources of those barriers, and offer suggestions for how researchers, policy makers, and program leaders can work together to further the integration of efforts among their three groups.

As the chapter shows, the actual, real-life positive development of today's adolescents hinges heavily on intentional, long-term, and collaborative commitments by individuals and agencies advocating for and/or supporting the integration of adolescent research, practice, and policies.

APPLIED DEVELOPMENTAL SCIENCE AND POSITIVE YOUTH DEVELOPMENT

To begin a discussion of the importance of integrating research, policy, and practice, it is important to understand the developmental theories that ground this work. Applied developmental systems theories, which focus on the developmental relationships between individuals and contexts, are a starting point for integrating research, policy, and practice. In addition, since we are interested in enhancing through this integration the development of a specific population—adolescents—it is important to understand the theory of positive youth development (PYD) and its links with applied developmental science (see chapter 15, vol. 1 of this *Handbook*).

To truly understand any aspect of adolescent development, it is necessary to look at the interaction between adolescents as individuals and their contexts. Those interactions provide explanations of change and ideas on how to alter the direction of change in a positive way. This is the essence of a developmental systems approach (Lerner, 2002). In a developmental systems approach individuals are influenced by contexts while, at the same time, they influence the contexts of which they are a part. As a consequence of this mutually influential relationship between individual and context, attempts to understand adolescent development, and/or efforts to enhance such development, require assessment of the individual, the context and, most importantly, of the relations between these two levels of the fused developmental system.

Within contemporary developmental science, mutually influential relations between individuals and their ecological or contextual settings are represented as individual ← → context relations. When these individual ← → context relations are also of mutual benefit to all parties involved (that is, when they are beneficial to both the individuals and their context), they provide the supports needed for young people to advance ideally toward positive adulthood (Lerner, Alberts, & Bobek, 2007). This line of thinking is consistent with a positive youth development approach.

Historically, there has been a tradition in the United States of regarding the second decade of life as a period during which adolescents are destined for a variety of developmental risks. This tradition led to a range of programs and policies aimed at problem prevention or remediation in regard to risks viewed as "inevitable" among young people (e.g., drug and alcohol use and abuse or unsafe sexual practices). The problem with this approach is that if we see young people as destined to succumb to these developmental risks and if program developers and policy makers focus their resources only on preventing and/or remediating these risks once they begin, young people will not develop the skills, resources, and knowledge they need to become positive, healthy adults.

As noted by McKnight (1995), in treating young people as problems to be managed, we are not only treating them as "clients" of a professional helping system, but we are also robbing families, communities, and societies of having young people be a useful part of their communities. By defining young people as problems, we take away their ability not only

to be valued contributors to their own healthy development but also to be part of solutions to community challenges that programs and policy makers are often tackling.

Within the past 10–15 years, a new view of young people has emerged, one that sees young people as capable of making positive contributions to themselves, their families, and society (e.g., Benson, 2003; Lerner, 2004). This view, supported by scholarship from multiple fields, suggests that the positive development of adolescents can be promoted when policies or programs are enacted that do not treat young people as problems to be managed but rather as resources to be developed (Roth & Brooks-Gunn, 2003). As Roth and Brooks-Gunn (2003) emphasize, this positive approach to youth and youth development reflects "our hopes and aspirations for a nation of healthy, happy, and competent adolescents on their way to productive and satisfying adulthoods."

This new strength-based vision for young people is predicated on the idea that because of the plasticity of human development and, thus, the potential for systematic change in behavior (Lerner, 2004), all adolescents have the potential for positive development. By supporting this potential for change through programs and policies that account for the individual and contextual needs of young people, we are contributing to the healthy development of young people and to the healthy development of the various contextual levels of society.

One area in which the experience of youth development practitioners and researchers has come together is in the conceptualization of this potential for positive healthy development by the Five Cs of PYD. Lerner, Fisher, and Weinberg (2000) noted that positive developmental outcomes could be characterized by "five Cs": competence, connection, character, confidence, and caring (or compassion):

> These five attributes represent five clusters of individual attributes—for example, intellectual ability and social and behavioral skills; positive bonds with people and institutions; integrity

and moral centeredness; positive self-regard, a sense of self-efficacy, and courage; and humane values, empathy, and a sense of social justice, respectively. (pp. 16–17)

Consistent with a developmental systems perspective, scholars and practitioners have recently added a sixth C of PYD: contribution to self, family, and society (see Lerner, 2002). This addition to the theory of PYD was made because raising healthy young people and enacting policies and programs that increase the chances that young people will reach positive adulthood requires that adolescents go beyond development focused just on their own health and become active, committed individuals, that is, members of a civil society. That is, the expectation is that if young people are manifesting the five Cs of PYD across time, then a sixth C should emerge—contributions to self, family, and society (Lerner, 2002, 2004). When an adolescent is able to successfully regulate the individual ⟵→ context relations necessary for healthy individual development, he or she is likely to flourish in the 5Cs of positive development and, thereby, be on a path toward making positive contributions to his or her context (Lerner, 2004).

Thus, while promoting the positive development of youth through a focus on their individual characteristics (e.g., cognitive development, gender role development, and moral development) is important, by itself, it is not enough. Interventions into the development of humans must also promote the likelihood of enhancing positive individual ⟵→ context relations. We need to go beyond positive adolescent development for its own sake and promote development for the betterment of young people and for the betterment of the institutions of society. Recent scholarship has supported the connection between PYD and contributions to self, family, and society (Bobek, 2007; Jelicic, et al., 2007; Phelps et al., 2007;). The institutions of society, and the policies that support them, need to be integrated with our understanding of adolescent development in order to maximize

positive results for both individuals and contexts. This is the essence of applied developmental science (Lerner, 2002; Lerner, Jacobs, & Wertlieb, 2003).

By recognizing the strengths of young people, researchers, program leaders, and policy makers can begin to do the following:

1. Think of young people as a resource for tackling some of the issues that face communities and society more broadly today.

2. Integrate their respective knowledge to ensure that research, programs, and policies address the real day-to-day lives of the adolescent population they seek to understand or support.

3. Ensure that individuals and contexts are aligned in a way that will provide appropriate opportunities for young people to develop the Six Cs of PYD.

4. Integrate research about individual development, community contexts, organizational development, economic benefit, and political viability in a way that enhances the likelihood that changes in youth and their communities will be synthesized in the service of promoting positive outcomes.

For several decades now, applied developmental science has been serving as an important advocate in the process of promotion of positive outcomes in youth, most notably by recognizing the expertise of individuals, program leaders, and policy makers and by seeking to integrate their knowledge in order to help us both understand individual development and enhance contextualized knowledge that can be used in practical ways to enhance human development.

INTEGRATING THEORY, RESEARCH, PRACTICE, AND POLICY

Integration of research and theory on adolescence with practice and policy is happening, albeit piecemeal and somewhat fragmented. While this process has been encumbered at times by complexities associated with translating innovative theories into often non-complementary practices and policies, given a sufficient commitment to change and time, the integration can and usually occurs. In the United States, examples of what could be considered successful integrations of practice, policy, and research from the field of developmental science, youth development, and civic engagement abound.

In recent years, the PYD approach has gained much public recognition and support. Translating this theory into practice and policy and utilizing the wisdom of practitioners to advance the theory, however, has taken many forms. To focus our inquiry, we examined ways in which different agencies use concepts and strategies laid out in theories of PYD to better serve and support the healthy development of adolescents. In the part of the chapter that follows, we describe how several different groups operationalize PYD through their youth- and community-focused activities, projects, and initiatives. For example, the Milton S. Eisenhower Foundation uses PYD theory and research to frame and promote an after-school program model designed specifically to address the needs of high school students in disadvantaged communities; the National Research Council provides expert advice, based on evidence from research, practice, and policy, on the role of after-school programs in promotion of PYD; the Forum for Youth Investment advocates for PYD-driven youth-focused initiatives at state and local levels; Public/Private Ventures provides communities interested in implementing PYD with knowledge pertinent to PYD and effective implementation strategies; and the Family and Youth Service Bureau funds multiparty collaborations across the country aimed at promoting PYD at a community level. These examples are by no means meant to be exhaustive. Rather, they serve as evidence of efforts by federal, state, and local agencies to inform and shape practices, policies, and future research of significance to the healthy development of adolescents and their communities.

Milton S. Eisenhower Foundation

The Milton S. Eisenhower Foundation, a Washington, DC-based continuation of two presidential commissions—the 1967–1968 National Advisory Commission on Civil Disorders (established after the big city riots of the 1960s) and the 1968–1969 National Commission on the Causes and Prevention of Violence (formed after the assassinations of the Reverend Martin Luther King, Jr., and Senator Robert Kennedy)—was established as a nonprofit operating institution and intermediary organization in 1981. The Foundation invests in identifying, replicating, evaluating, and communicating community-based program models proven to represent successful solutions to problems experienced by poor youth and families, racial and ethnic minorities, the jobless, the undereducated, formerly incarcerated individuals, and other disenfranchised and marginalized groups.

The structure of the Eisenhower Foundation's community-based program replications serving adolescents are grounded in PYD theory and research. Since 2001, its cornerstone program model designed specifically to address the needs of adolescents growing up in disadvantaged communities has been the Quantum Opportunities Program (Quantum). Originally developed by the Opportunities Industrialization Centers of America in late 1980s, the Quantum program model reflects the understanding of researchers and practitioners, which recognizes that to change the future for youth in disadvantaged communities, we must change the opportunities available to them. Similarly, to take full advantages of such opportunities, it was understood that youth must possess certain basic life and academic skills.

Quantum is a comprehensive, 4-year after-school youth development program model for adolescents. High school students who perform academically at the bottom of their freshman class are recruited into the program. The program's mission is to support youth in poor neighborhoods in completing their high school education and, in the process, motivating these teens to continue on to post-secondary education or some other type of post-secondary training. Hence, the model provides youth with a comprehensive and intensive design that devotes an equal number of hours to educational achievement, youth development, and community service, delivered through the following activities:

- 250 hours per year of adult mentor–assisted, self-paced, competency-based computer learning in basic academics (including reading and math). The education goal is attained through a computer-assisted remedial education program that assesses the academic needs of each student and provides assistance through the eXtraLearning Curriculum.
- 250 hours per year of personal development and life skills activities. The development activities focus on providing Quantum students with the personal development and social skills necessary for success in the home, school, workplace, and community.
- 250 hours per year of community service (recently expanded in its scope and termed Youth Leadership and Democracy Building) that enables youth to develop leadership skills and civic responsibility and to become change agents within their communities.
- Year-round programming, especially throughout summers and vacations when youth tend to be idle and most at risk.
- Financial incentives (in the form of stipends) for all Quantum youth to stay in the program. Upon completion of certain academic milestones, additional amounts equal to the youth's total accumulated earnings are added. For each participant, the money that he or she has earned is deposited in a bank account and accrues toward college or other type of post-secondary training.

The Milton S. Eisenhower Foundation began funding, technically assisting, and evaluating replications of Quantum after identifying the Quantum model as being exceptionally successful in working with teens. Evaluations of the first cohort of Quantum programs, launched

in 1989 and funded by the Ford Foundation, were carried out by Brandeis University in the early 1990s. Results of these evaluations reported that Quantum youth, when compared to youth in the control groups, were more likely to graduate from high school (63% vs. 42%), less likely to drop out of school (23% vs. 50%), more likely to go on for postsecondary education (42% vs. 16%), more likely to attend 4-year college (18% vs. 5%), more likely to attend 2-year postsecondary program (19% vs. 9%), less likely to become teen parents (24% vs. 38%), more likely to be civically engaged 6 months post Quantum (21% vs. 12%), and more likely to volunteer their time as mentors and tutors (28% vs. 8%) (Hahn, Leavitt, & Aaron, 1994). The evaluation study also provided a cost–benefit analysis of the Quantum program model, showing that for every dollar spent on youth in Quantum there was at least a $3.04 benefit.

Following the first cohort of the Ford Foundation's funded Quantum sites, the Eisenhower Foundation has supported these Quantum sites—in New Hampshire, Maryland, the District of Columbia, Virginia, South Carolina, Alabama, Mississippi, and Oregon. Preliminary data from across five of these Eisenhower Foundation Quantum sites show that 96% of the youth who attended Quantum have completed the program, of which 92% have graduated from high school and 74% have enrolled in college or some other type of advanced training. The PYD-infused design of the Quantum program model has demonstrated (and continues to demonstrate) that structured opportunities for high levels of commitment from individuals and their context can, and do, increase the likelihood that youth from poor, marginalized communities will develop into healthy, thriving, contributing members of civil society.

National Research Council

The National Research Council (NRC), established in 1916, has a mission to "improve government decision-making and public policy, increase public education and understanding, and promote the acquisition and dissemination of knowledge . . . providing elected leaders, policymakers, and the public with expert advice based on sound scientific evidence" (National Research Council, n.d).

In 2002, NRC and the Institute of Medicine (IOM) issued a report about community programs to promote youth development. The report coalesced results of a 2-year evaluation and integration of extensive research and theory on the health and development of young people ages 10–18. Research findings addressed design, implementation, and evaluation of community-based programs that serve this age group. The work was led by 15 members of the Committee on Community-Level Programs for Youth, a project of NRC and IOM. The 15 committee members represented top experts in the field of youth-centered research, practice, and public policy.

In addition to discussing the features of positive developmental settings, the report described individual and environmental characteristics necessary to support healthy, positive development and thriving of all youth. The report also described ways in which individual and environmental characteristics ought to come together if they are to be of the most benefit to youth development.

Settings supportive of positive and healthy development in youth, the report notes, must provide the following:

- Physical and psychological safety
- Age-appropriate structure
- Supportive relationships
- Opportunities for being connected to others and building relationships
- Positive social norms
- Support for efficacy and mattering
- Opportunities for skill building (including physical, intellectual, psychological, emotional, and social skills)
- The integration of family, school, and community efforts

While the authors of the NRC and IOM's report agreed that it is hard for any one single community program to incorporate all of the eight features of positive developmental settings and, especially, to serve all youth within a particular community, the authors also emphasized that "diverse opportunities are more likely to support broad adolescent development and [positive] outcomes for a greater number of youth" (National Research Council & Institute of Medicine, 2002, p. 145). The report concludes by calling for a community-wide approach to securing diverse, rich opportunities/ solutions for youth.

Comprehensive and systematic evaluations of community-based programs for youth are somewhat of a rarity, primarily due to lack of funds necessary to develop and conduct evaluations. Few integrated programs, as the NRC and IOM's report noted, have undergone such evaluations. Given these realities, the Committee on Community-Level Programs for Youth extended its endorsement for national replication to a handful of PYD program models, encouraging others to seek to understand the benefits of program evaluations for securing the success of after-school programs serving adolescents.

The Forum for Youth Investment

Founded in 1998, the Forum for Youth Investment is a national nonprofit organization with a mission of supporting communities in helping their youth be problem free, fully prepared and civically engaged, and, thereby, ready for college, work, and life by the time they are 21 (an initiative also known as Ready by 21™). "The Forum provides information, technical assistance, training, network support and develops the partnership opportunities needed to increase the quality and quantity of youth investment and youth involvement" (Pittman, 2005a, p. 3).

Endorsing the theory of PYD, the Forum advocates for youth-focused initiatives that challenge the risk behavior prevention approach, eschew the traditional thinking about youth risks and responsibilities, and emphasize a whole, nonfragmented approach to youth development services that go beyond focusing on academic success as the primary youth outcome. Rather, the Forum encourages practitioners and policy makers to infuse their work with a holistic picture of youth, to take into account a coherent picture of state and local resources and mandates, and to share accountability when making decisions that affect youth, families, and communities.

Exploration of the agency's website (see www.forumfyi.org) reveals that the Forum's staff come from diverse professional and academic backgrounds (such as sociology, education, policy analysis, media, business, and communications), which has helped the agency establish itself in a relatively short time as one of the leaders on topics of youth development research and policy, out-of-school time programs and policies, youth civic engagement, high school education reform, and community assets development, to name just a few.

Perhaps the most innovative contribution of the Forum to the interaction between research, practice, and policy and its impact on the quality and quantity of youth investment and youth development comes in the form of multi-party conference calls. Set up by the Forum, the primary role of these calls is to bring together diverse groups of stakeholders around a research, program, or policy issue of common interest. These sessions provide opportunities for decision makers to connect, share, and coordinate their goals, strategies, and activities in youth development. The sessions also often represent a catalyst for collaborations and new community efforts among parties which otherwise might not have come together. As Karen Pittman (2005b), the Forum's Executive Director and a pioneer thinker in the youth development field, describes, "Getting people to think from a youth-centered rather than system-centered perspective requires ongoing education and reinforcement, . . . [and] helping those engaged in one sphere recognize the value of connecting to the others" (p. 4).

In 2006, in cooperation with the National Conference of State Legislatures and representatives from Chapin Hall Center for Children

(University of Chicago), Missouri Division of Youth Services, and District of Columbia Department of Youth Rehabilitation Services, the Forum hosted a discussion on how juvenile justice agencies can improve their services for juvenile offenders by incorporating positive youth development standards into their work. That same year, in collaboration with Voices for America's Children, Kids Count, and the National Conference of State Legislatures, the Forum brought together state child and youth advocates to discuss the effects of the changing political landscape on the current state of and future directions for child and youth advocacy. In 2007, in collaboration with Ann Lochner, director of the Applied Research Collaborative on Youth Development at the University of Minnesota, Kristen Grimm, the president of Spitfire Strategies (an agency that helps community organizations build the internal capacity necessary to communicate effectively), Voices for America's Children, and Kids Count, the Forum hosted a conference call for youth advocates on successful communications strategies for increasing communities' understanding of and support for PYD programs.

Conference calls (recordings of which the public can listen to online via the Forum's website) represent just one of the ways in which the Forum extends itself to the greater community. The Forum also partners with and provides technical assistance to state change makers who are seeking to increase community capacity and the effectiveness of their state-specific youth and community development initiatives. One example is the Forum's partnership with the New Mexico Community Foundation, formed to strengthen the New Mexico Forum for Youth and Community, create a statewide Youth Alliance, and develop organizations that provide space for community members to come together and strategize about local capacity building (known as Regional Point Organizations).

Recently, the Forum's success in connecting communities to youth development research and relevant practices and policies has been garnered for a project at the national level. In the fall of 2007, the Robert Wood Johnson Foundation and the Atlantic Philanthropies provided $2.5 million in grants to support implementation of the Ready by 21™ Quality Counts initiative in seven cities (Austin, Texas; Columbus, Indiana; Georgetown Divide, California; Grand Rapids, Michigan; Indianapolis, Indiana; Nashville, Tennessee; and St. Louis, Missouri) and five states (Iowa, Kentucky, New York, Oklahoma, and Rhode Island) across the country. The improvement of local or state youth programs will be brought about as participating sites "create a database of available youth programs offered by different organizations and systems, assess the quality of individual youth programs, document the characteristics of the staff who work with youth, and identify public and private resources available to support youth programs and the staff who work in them" (Forum for Youth Investment, 2007). Management of the initiative has been awarded to the Forum for Youth Investment, while two other agencies will provide training in youth program quality assessment and youth development curriculum to the sites.

Public/Private Ventures

Public/Private Ventures (P/PV) is a national, nonprofit organization that partners with nonprofit organizations, and the public, business, and philanthropic sectors to "improve the effectiveness of social policies, programs and community initiatives, especially as they affect youth and young adults" (P/PV, n.d.). In the early 1990s, Public/Private Ventures initiated the Community Change for Youth Development Initiative (CCYD). The initiative's mandate was to supply communities in its network with knowledge pertinent to "core concepts" of PYD (such as community involvement and leadership, opportunities for skill development, exposure to structured after-school activities, and access to supportive relationships with adults), as well

as to offer proven strategies for implementing PYD. The initiative targeted youth aged 12–20 and was built on the premise that by increasing supports and opportunities for youth's healthy and positive development within communities, the number of thriving youth in those communities would increase as well.

Between 1996 and 2001, the CCYD initiative was piloted in six communities (Austin, Texas; Kansas City, Missouri; the Lower East Side in New York City; Savannah, Georgia; St. Petersburg, Florida; and Staten Island, New York). All these sites were chosen because they had neighborhoods with high poverty rates and some existing youth program infrastructure already in place. Within each of the neighborhoods, lead agency partners were identified. While Public/Private Ventures provided some funding for the initiative, those funds were limited and focused on supporting initiative planning (for which each site received $10,000). Sites were also awarded up to $175,000 annually for their operating costs but with an expectation that those funds would be used to leverage money from local institutions and agencies necessary to fund the rest of the cost.

The main questions that the CCYD initiative set out to answer were: (1) What does it take for a community to mobilize its resources to create vital quality supports and opportunities for youth? (2) What opportunities and activities are developed? and (3) Do community youth take advantage of those opportunities and activities? Lessons learned from the implementation of the pilot CCYD went beyond the answers to these three main questions. As reported by Watson (2002), 10 core lessons emerged as the result of the Public/Private Ventures initiative:

1. It is possible to implement and sustain a neighborhood-wide youth development initiative, based on a common substantive framework, in resource-poor neighborhoods.

2. A set of research-based core concepts is extremely useful in helping communities generate consensus around what to do, move quickly to action and stay on track.
3. It takes local leadership with credibility, resources, and with a commitment to partner with residents to get results within a reasonable period of time and to sustain a youth development effort.
4. Variation and flexibility in the roles residents play, and a commitment to clarifying and supporting those roles, are essential to integrating residents into neighborhood-based youth development initiatives.
5. Local infrastructure and previous programming experience play a critical role in a community's ability to address serious youth development issues and should be considered when developing technical assistance approaches.
6. Older youth and higher risk youth are more difficult to attract to PYD initiatives and require targeted outreach.
7. It is critical to distinguish between youth involvement and youth leadership strategies and to provide adults with the training they need to help youth become good decision makers.
8. Large-scale initiatives need a structured approach to assessing program quality on an ongoing basis.
9. Place-based initiatives cannot draw a fence around a neighborhood.
10. Researching community initiatives may require new strategies, including closer engagement and timely, ongoing connection between researchers (e.g., evaluators) and sites.

The Family and Youth Services Bureau

The Family and Youth Services Bureau (FYSB), an agency of the U.S. Department of Health & Human Services, uses PYD theory and research to provide leadership on youth and family issues at the federal level. In the past several decades, FYSB has adopted the PYD approach as the cornerstone of all of

its programmatic efforts to support healthy and positive outcomes in children, youth and families experiencing difficult life circumstances (e.g., homelessness, domestic violence, and parental imprisonment). The focus of the Bureau's utilization of PYD is on supporting services that create opportunities for life skill building, youth leadership, and community involvement and that use those opportunities as tools in assisting youth in building self-confidence, trust and, in the long run, attaining self-sufficiency. FYSB instills PYD into a variety of state and national youth services that are designed to help youth thrive (FYSB, n.d.a).

One way in which FYSB delivers its support for youth and families is by funding collaborations and comprehensive youth services at the local, tribal, state and national levels. Its emphasis on collaborations reflects the agency's firm belief that neighborhoods, policy makers, youth-serving organizations, media, schools, faith-based institutions, business leaders, and parents all have a role to play in assisting a community in the promotion of PYD.

As the Bureau's outreach and support have grown over the past three decades, the need for creating more effective ways for communities to provide youth and their families with best practices has grown as well. In response, the agency has offered grants for research, evaluation, and demonstration projects that enhance our knowledge about positive youth and community development and identify best programmatic practices for communities interested in helping their youth thrive. One exemplar of such an initiative is FYSB's Positive Youth Development State and Local Collaboration Demonstration Projects.

As described by FYSB (n.d.b, n.d.c), the mission of the PYD demonstration projects is "to develop and support innovative youth development strategies through collaborations" between state and local government and non-government agencies, community organizations, schools, and youth. To date, FYSB has distributed a total of $10.8 million in support of demonstration projects that seek to develop new strategies or to enhance existing innovative PYD strategies for groups of youth in diverse life circumstances.

Between 1998 and 2003, the Bureau awarded $7.8 million to support innovative PYD strategies in 13 states. Strategies included activities such as "assessing existing statewide policies and procedures to determine how best to integrate youth development principles into current approaches; providing training on the [PYD] approach; involving young people in program and policy development; organizing regional, state, or community-wide conferences and forums; creating new outlets for sharing information on youth development; developing and supporting statewide coalitions of agencies serving runaway and homeless youth; and identifying data to measure positive outcomes" (FYSB, n.d.c). In 2004 and 2005, to assist in local implementation of some of the strategies developed during the first funding period, an additional $3 million was awarded to 9 of the initial 13 states (Arizona, Iowa, Kentucky, Illinois, Louisiana, Massachusetts, Nebraska, New York, and Oregon) for projects such as improving police presence in a neighborhood in Arizona, working with community organizations to advocate around issues of youth employment and quality education in Illinois, providing community-wide training in youth development in Iowa, evaluating existing youth programs across the state of Kentucky, and creating additional educational and after-school opportunities for local youth in Massachusetts.

As different activities, projects, and initiatives of the Family and Youth Service Bureau, the Milton S. Eisenhower Foundation, the National Research Council, the Forum for Youth Investment, and Public/Private Ventures show us, PYD can be operationalized, supported, and promoted in a myriad of creative ways. However, the true short- and long-term success of these diverse efforts by federal, state, and local agencies in informing and shaping practices, policies, and future research of significance to the healthy development of adolescents and their communities heavily hinges on the level of understanding, recognition, and respect that researchers, practitioners, and policy makers hold for each others' role in maximizing positive youth development outcomes.

ROLES OF RESEARCH, POLICY, AND PRACTICE IN YOUTH DEVELOPMENT

Developmental theory, which specifies how ontogenetic change occurs, and the tenets of positive youth development both resonate across the boundaries and divisions in research, policy, and practice, but there are no prescriptions or clear mechanisms that specify how integration among the fields should happen. Indeed, as demonstrated above, organizations and agencies often spend a significant amount of time developing these integrations, and replication is a challenge. There are many barriers to integration that arise from the particularities of each of the three settings, barriers that are unique to the work done for and with youth in each particular context.

To facilitate the integration process, it is important to understand where the limitations lie, so that as this burgeoning perspective and collaborative partnerships continue to develop, individuals in each of the three settings can make choices that will lead to further integration and help the ideals of ADS and PYD to be achieved. The benefits of these collaborations will reach many stakeholders: youth, families, schools, program developers and staff, policy makers, and researchers. As research is moved out of the academic silo and is integrated with the knowledge of practitioners and reflected in policies that impact human behavior, different questions will be posed that are inspired by real issues and circumstances faced by youth. Knowledge generated in response to these questions will feed back into the system, ultimately making research, policies, and practices with youth more on point with societal needs.

Contexts of the "Triumvirate"

The three contexts of policy making, research generation, and practice with youth share many things in common, in particular the goal to positively influence opportunities for development and improve young people's quality of life. However, each has a unique vantage point on the issues as they work at different levels of the ecology, and each with their unique cultures and different demands, communication styles and measures of success (Zervigon-Hakes, 1995). As such, they are faced with different choices and compromises that must be made to advance their work. The nature of the work and varied approaches also suggest different fundamental assumptions about how to effect change. These differences often lead to lack of respect, miscommunication, and misperceptions about common ground among the three contexts. We will discuss the different settings and roles of policy makers, researchers, and practitioners to explicate both the commonalities and differences. This will be followed by a discussion of the barriers that arise from each of the settings that inhibit collaboration and steps that can be taken by each of the actors to advance the mission of Applied Developmental Science and improve outcomes for youth.

Policy Makers

Policy makers work at local, state, and federal levels and are elected or appointed. For example, in the field of education, city school board members set policy for localities, state representatives approve and institute state academic standards and accountability measures, and congressmen, senators, and the president establish federal education legislation. Conventionally, federal policy focuses on the level of investment and state and local policy considers how to adapt a policy to its constituents. Currently, reauthorization of the No Child Left Behind Act, the most significant presence of the federal government in education, is being debated. Of particular concern is implementation of the existing guidelines. States' interpretations of the federal guidelines in terms of achievement proficiency levels, Adequate Yearly Progress targets, and the definition of highly qualified teachers have varied significantly (Porter & Polikoff, 2007). Policy makers must now consider what is working, what is not working, and the factors associated with each to determine if reauthorization should occur and, if so, what changes should be made. This example points out just how mutually beneficial partnership with researchers and the field would be, as these persons could significantly inform the discussion with objective data, experiential knowledge, and real-world examples.

The work of policy makers is political, pragmatic, and action oriented, designed to affect fundamental social problems, particularly those of their constituents. The key question asked by policy makers is: What are the conditions that can be affected by policy that will improve circumstances for young people's development (Huston, 2005)? As can be seen from the question, policy makers are not concerned with individuals, but rather with broader environmental conditions that can be manipulated, which in turn may bring about a change in behavior. They decide which aspects of behavior and which environments to target. Powerful advocacy groups can significantly impact their decisions and priorities. Scientific data is only one source of knowledge; compelling stories and arguments can also significantly influence policy (Shonkoff, 2000). Data is gathered together from multiple sources to support an agenda.

In their role, policy makers have the authority to make decisions about what problems will be addressed within a particular sector and how those problems will be handled. They are faced with advocating for distribution of funds in equitable and meaningful ways to address an existing problem. As such, they often focus on cost–benefit analyses and strive to understand thresholds and minimum requirements (how much is good enough?) that will bring about the *maximum amount* of change. A high return on their investment is sought for all policies. They must also consider when increased effort or spending does not yield socially significant improvements. Terminating spending when a certain percentage of the target population is reached, even though continued work and investment may allow more people to benefit, is a controversial but common problem.

Often, policy makers are focused on the big picture (e.g., reducing teen pregnancy or improving school performance) and take an economist's point of view by trying to understand how the long-term economic productivity of individuals can be improved by changing existing societal conditions (Currie, 1997). What are the short-term and long-term costs? Do the dollars invested save later spending? For example, do early investments in child care improve school readiness, achievement, and job attainment and reduce crime and the need for special education and social service? When these questions are linked with dollar cost savings, as in the case of the High/Scope Preschool studies, they are particularly powerful (Schweinhart, 1999).

The arena of policy making is also unique. Changing leaders, changing budgets, and changing time frames contribute to what decisions are made and how. Policy making is a time-consuming process from selection of goals, to determining the means to achieve them, to implementation, and, ideally, to evaluation of the efforts. However, this process can be disrupted or derailed by circumstances and differing political ideologies. Programs initially developed during one administration can change in priority and focus, and funding streams for programs may dry up or require different outcomes, thus challenging efforts directed at sustainability and impact on the target population.

Researchers

Researchers typically work in colleges and universities or for private or nonprofit research organizations think tanks and as consultants for hire. Research is intellectual investigation aimed at discovering, interpreting, and revising human knowledge. Researchers are guided by what is not known (Shonkoff, 2000). Historically, the work done by researchers has been classified as either basic or applied

research. Basic research is typically theory testing or trying to understand a phenomenon of interest (e.g., personality development). The main motivation is to expand human knowledge. The method of data collection is often in highly controlled laboratory settings. Applied research, often less well regarded by the scientific community, attempts to understand current conditions that affect children (e.g., the impact of different types of child care) and to solve practical problems. The main goal is to improve the human condition. Research in this vein strives to be ecologically valid, reflecting the population, values, and conditions of the community, and externally valid, being relevant to communities not included in the original studies (Smith, 1990). Achieving these goals and addressing questions of causality can be difficult as data collection is often conducted in the messy, natural environments of peoples' lives, and it is inappropriate and unethical to sort people into conditions for random assignment experiments (McCall & Green, 2004).

Applied developmental science eschews these false distinctions and emphasizes collaborative effort among multiple disciplines and community institutions to address quality of life issues (Miller & Lerner, 1994). It is assumed that science in the service of children, and families can be both theoretically derived and generate knowledge about basic developmental processes, as well as improve circumstances for children. Commitment to the pursuit of knowledge and the promotion of human welfare are simultaneous, integrated processes for applied developmental researchers (Fisher & Brennan, 1992). Five interrelated "what" questions drive scholarship to inform our understanding of developmental processes and to address issues of diversity and context present in the human condition, so that relevance to application can be meaningful (Theokas & Lerner, 2004). The questions are:

1. What attributes?; of
2. What individuals?; in relation to
3. What set of contextual conditions?; at

4. What points in time?; may be integrated to promote

5. What instances of positive human development?

More and more calls have been made for universities to move beyond discipline based scholarship for the academic community to an agenda that is focused on helping to ameliorate problems in the communities within which they reside (Boyer, 1990; Lynton & Elman, 1987). Indeed, one such example is the William T. Grant Foundation, which does not fund atheoretical work and operates on the premise that the best social science research is inspired by societal needs, is useful, and is theoretically derived (Granger, 2005).

While policy makers attempt to directly influence conditions that will change human behavior, researchers' work is more indirect. Through the generation of knowledge, researchers contribute to our understanding of developmental processes and antecedents and outcomes of behavior. Through the dissemination of research, those ideas are integrated into practice with youth that will ideally promote positive development and decrease risk.

Researchers ask questions that are small and build on existing research. They apply different methodologies to collect data that will be reliable and valid and bring information to bear on the constructs of interest. Instead of a uniform macro-level goal of improved economic productivity often found in the policy world, researchers' outcomes of interest are quite varied, encompassing physical health and well-being, life skills, relationships (peer, family, intergenerational), spirituality/morality, and achievement to name a few. As discussed earlier, PYD is becoming increasingly defined by the 6Cs: competence, confidence, connection, caring, character, and contribution (Lerner et al., 2005).

Further, developmental research is beginning to move beyond the individual level and beginning to ask what characteristics of settings are optimal for PYD. As noted earlier, the National Research Council and Institute of Medicine (2002) has specified eight characteristics of positive youth development settings. They hypothesize that young people will develop personal and social assets if they experience: physical and psychological safety; clear and consistent structure and appropriate supervision; supportive relationships; opportunities to belong; positive social norms; support for efficacy and mattering; opportunities for skill building; and integration of family, school, and community efforts. When adolescents' developmental needs are matched with resources in the environment and when there is synergy between settings, thriving is more likely to occur (Theokas & Lerner, 2004, 2006). Advancements in developmental research that include models and measurements of social settings should support integration with policy because policies are often attempts to influence human behavior through changes in the context (Little, Bovaird, & Card, 2007).

As policy making is guided by political, economic, and social forces, the research process is guided by ethical guidelines and standards that must be adhered to for credibility. The scientific process, like policy making, is also not perfect. The academic establishment is slow to change and values traditional research methodology that emphasizes random assignment of participants, quantitative assessment, and statistical tests of significance (McCall & Groark, 2000; McCartney & Rosenthal, 2000). Yet, a single research study or finding has the ability to push the field in one direction or another. In addition, the findings from research must be interpreted cautiously due to issues of generalizability from the sample, research design utilized, effect size observed, and factors not accounted for in the research (Bertenthal, 2002). This ambiguity appeals to researchers who like to stop and reflect, whereas policy makers and practitioners are searching for answers and are expected to act. And while researchers who work within an applied developmental science methodology need to develop relationships and trust with both community practitioners and policy makers, this effort is not rewarded by the traditional tenure system.

Practitioners

Practitioners are probably the most widely varied group, with different backgrounds, training, settings, and interactions with youth. Coaches, youth program workers, educators, youth ministry, and mentors are a few of the different types of roles played by practitioners. As the roles suggest, they employ different methods to achieve their goals of promoting the personal, educational, social, and citizenship competencies of youth. Methods may include recreational activities, informal guidance, counseling, mentoring, or teaching and may take place in clubs, youth centers, schools, churches, and outreach locations.

Practitioners have the most direct connection to youth and youth outcomes of the three. Through their work and actions, they have the potential to impact change on a daily basis and to shape the lives of youth. Like researchers, the outcomes they desire for youth are varied and context dependent. They respond to the immediate needs and interests of the young people they are working with in their program. They may implement programs about substance use or bullying; they may teach academic subjects or provide guidance about choices and challenges faced by an individual youth. Practitioners are concerned with the individual. They may choose to go above and beyond their job responsibilities to reach one youth, and their actions are likely to differ by youth, as they determine what each individual needs from them. The demands on them are dynamic and the consequences of their actions immediate. For example, mentors often have to provide constructive feedback, which may be interpreted negatively by youth, which may cause them to pull away and avoid meetings. Practitioners need to be able to build relationships and trust and have good listening skills; enthusiasm and creativity are also useful. These skill sets are very different from the researcher who is engaged in an intellectual activity.

Whereas the qualifications for both researchers and policy makers tend to be consistent among each group, the experience of youth workers is varied. However, professionalization of the youth work field is occurring, and core competencies and standards are being developed (Quinn, 2004). This is partially dependent on the type of work done (e.g., educators vs. out-of-school activity leaders), but also reflects the culture change occurring in the field regarding how youth are perceived and what their needs are (Lerner, 2007; Roth, et al., 1998). A huge after-school movement and corresponding programs for youth have been created in the past 10 years in response to concerns about youth safety (Pittman, 2004).

However, youth workers have always been around; for example, parents or volunteers in national organizations such as Boy and Girl Scouts, 4-H, Boys and Girls Club of America, and religious organizations are all examples of people whose work has an immediate impact on youth. Nonetheless, historically, the professional component of youth work was focused on treatment and prevention. Trained psychologists provided the "professional" intervention and other work done with youth was left to "well intentioned individuals." While often quite successful on an individual level, these youth workers typically based their interventions on common sense approaches to youth development work, with little connection to research about best practices or other resources that could help them maximize their results as well as bring their interventions to scale and sustain them across time. With the new conceptualization of positive youth development and a focus on the promotion of normal, healthy development, more research-based approaches have been advocated for. In addition, there is a call for more professional strategies to prepare and support the frontline youth worker as well as techniques that can be shared with others (such as parents, neighbors, or employers) who have a stake in the positive development of youth.

One example of a professional development program for youth workers is the Advancing

Youth Development training curriculum produced by the National Training Institute for Community Youth Work at the Academy for Educational Development (Center for Youth Development and Policy Research, 1996; Johnson, Rothstein, & Gajdosic, 2004). In addition to this curriculum that identifies core competencies and best practices, other resources have emerged for the field including the National Youth Development Information Center (www.nydic.org) developed by the National Collaboration for Youth. Further, the Department of Labor has funded a pilot project of the National 4-H Leadership Trust to implement a Youth Development Practitioner Apprenticeship program (www.nae4ha.org/ydpa).

Youth workers and practitioners must be realistic. As policy makers must deal with changing circumstances and researchers must adhere to the scientific process, practitioners are confronted with the day-to-day realities of youth. Motivation, interests, and program attendance varies. Youth struggle with issues of poverty, instability, and racism. Through these issues, practitioners must remain consistent, focused, and caring while at the same time worrying about garnering resources to sustain their programs.

As complex as they are, the day-to-day realities of youth and communities, changing political and economic circumstances and multilayered scientific processes must be addressed and tended to if we expect integrations of practice, policy, and research to yield us a success in our efforts to promote PYD. The above discussion about differing but essential roles of policy makers, researchers, and practitioners hints at some of the barriers that can arise in each of the three contexts and, ultimately, limit integration. The next section specifically articulates those concerns.

Barriers to Successful Integration of Research, Policy, and Practice in Youth Development

By being explicit about barriers that stand in a way of a successful integration of research, policy, and practice in youth development, we

hope to generate discussion that will begin to break down those barriers, so that more fruitful integration can occur. As can be seen from the preceding discussion, there are obvious, even necessary, links between the three contexts. Without one another, the work done in each setting is limited. With one another, their work will be more informed and, ultimately, beneficial to youth.

Lack of Respect and Suspicion

Of utmost concern is the lack of respect and even suspicion of one another that arises most likely as a result of the unfamiliarity with the work, language utilized, communication style, and demands of each other's fields. There are perceptions of each group held by one another and the public at large that contribute to the lack of respect as well. For example, policy makers are often thought to be more concerned with reelection and special interest groups than with developing good policy that will meet the needs of youth and families. Researchers, although typically considered knowledgeable, often suffer from the perception of being impractical and out of touch. Recommendations offered by researchers often fall into the category of "more is better." This is not new news and is not helpful in making difficult funding decisions or choosing among program alternatives. Practitioners are considered the recipients of the knowledge of researchers or actors in policy recommendations. Their intuitive, experiential knowledge typically has not been valued, so they have often not been asked to the table. In addition, ideological differences among the three groups can also lead to mistrust and thinking of each other as adversaries. Thus, rather than setting aside ideological differences and attempting to find common-ground solutions to a common goal—improving the lives of youth—conversations are often not even begun.

Limited Communication Channels

Historically, communication has only gone one way between researchers and practitioners or researchers and policy makers (McCall & Groark, 2000). That is, the academics considered themselves the knowledge holders and "gave away" knowledge to practitioners so they could do their jobs better. They did not make it imperative to ask questions of practitioners or try to understand their world view, viewing it as less relevant and informed than theory. The lack of understanding by researchers of the issues and challenges facing practitioners as well as their lack of real hands-on experience made it easy for practitioners to dismiss researchers' expertise. Often, research confirms things that practitioners already knew (e.g., relationships are important), or, in the worst case, they are told things that are not practical, relevant, or feasible given the constraints of their setting and work with youth (e.g., youth must attend 5 days a week for 1–2 years to achieve desired outcomes).

More recently, some researchers have engaged in program evaluations of youth programs. Inviting researchers into programs is essential to improving their knowledge of the ins and outs of program operations and implementation. However, in doing so, practitioners are fearful that their weaknesses will be exposed. Programs are frequently confronted with staff and youth turnover, which has implications for implementation, continuity, and stability. This exposure could have ramifications for funding and even the viability of the program (Denner, Cooper, Lopez, & Dunbar, 1999).

Similarly, with policy makers, the knowledge generated from research may not answer the policy questions asked. Understanding the amount of variance accounted for between two variables does not translate well to requirements and standards. Moreover, research does not generally yield the black-and-white information that policy makers need. Academic writing includes a lot of technical terms, and conclusions tend to be qualified based on the population sampled and limitations of the research. Data often yield inconsistencies or rival hypotheses that can water down the message to lay audiences (Zervigon-Hakes,

1995). Whereas researchers are intrigued by conflicting findings, for those who want to act on the knowledg, they do not provide clear guidance. In addition, even when research does elucidate potential strategies for promoting positive development, it often does not take into consideration cost–benefit ratios of different strategies, leaving policy makers to try to figure this out on their own.

The third leg of the triangle between policy and practice has also been limited, primarily focused on funding investments, rather than discussions of best practices and development of programs. Policy makers do not get into the "nitty-gritty" of programs or program operations. Their focus on the big picture is very different from academic research that tries to understand nuances and how individual and contextual differences might bring about different outcomes for different groups of individuals. Practitioners fault policy makers for not following through and searching for the "big bang" rather than understanding that change sometimes happens one individual at a time. To practitioners, no individual is expendable, but for policy makers who need to make pragmatic decisions, youth are sometimes conceived as numbers. Practitioners also desire flexibility to deal with the diversity they experience, while policy is uniform and standardized.

Communication Lost in Translation

Researchers have historically published in journals inaccessible to the public, both due to restricted access and the language/terminology utilized in the writing. Scientific rigor is essential in research, and this must be conveyed to the academic community, but it is equally important to capture the message and reasonable hypotheses that can be made and communicate those to general audiences who seek information to improve their work (Shonkoff, 2000). Researchers are not trained to write concise briefs or executive summaries that are needed by policy makers (Huston, 2005; Susman-Stillman et al., 1996). Intermediary organizations often provide the links among the three groups. For example, the media often report or publish findings from research, tells stories about successful programs, or inform the public about policy issues. The format utilized is more simple and digestable to reach the largest audience possible, and they tend to focus on the message, not the process. However, messages can become changed or distorted as they move through this process and it is important for consumers to be cautious. In addition, as demonstrated by the No Child Left Behind legislation for example, new government policies are often complicated and vague, leaving practitioners to figure out how to comply. Failure to comply adequately can have severe consequences.

Different Time Continuums

Another key issue that divides the groups is the time frame in which decisions need to be made. Research is a slow, methodical process. The time needed for planning and conceptualizing a study, developing data collection methods, and obtaining informed consent and participation of subjects is extensive and subject to oversight by internal review boards or human subjects committees at universities or research organizations. Then, after data is collected, results are not immediately available. Researchers must clean the data to ensure its reliability and validity. There are few ways to speed this process, and if attempts are made, the credibility of the data can be compromised. Researchers often target deadlines that coincide with presentations at society conferences, deadlines for publications, or required funding reports. While this process is happening, practitioners and policy makers need to make decisions in real time. Although they are asked to make data-driven decisions or use evidenced-based programs, the tools and data to do so are simply often not available.

Practitioners, however, often receive a sum of money and must have a program up and running, at full capacity, in a short period of time to justify the funding. Although there are significant numbers of underserved youth or

youth who would benefit from the focus of a particular program, recruiting those specific youth may be quite difficult. For example, the goal of after-school tutoring programs is to provide intervention to underperforming students. However, these youth are typically the most disengaged and disinterested in attending a program that is going to require them to do things they do not like and are not good at. Thus, the most engaged students and families sign up for the program. Programs might enroll these students to reach their participation numbers; however, it takes away from the investment of time necessary to find and retain those youth who would benefit most.

In addition, programs compete for students' time and attention. There is a limited pool of hours when youth are available after school to participate in programs. Thus, sports programs, tutoring programs, arts programs, jobs, and volunteering all occur at the same time. Also competing for this time is homework and family responsibilities. Students may choose a tutoring program for the fall, but when basketball begins in the winter they switch programs. This decision is based on interest, rather than need. In fact, recent data supports the idea that the rule when it comes to youth activity participation is variety and change (Theokas, et al., 2006).

Similarly, the cycle for policy development is integral to the political process, which may or may not match the research cycle. Opportunities to make program changes or get legislation passed can be unpredictable. Public events (e.g., a school shooting) or electoral changes may bring about an opportunity that was not foreseeable. Policy makers may also place practitioners and researchers on unrealistic timetables based on funding cycles or reporting rules.

Constraints of Research Methodology/ Conflict with Program Operations

As mentioned, the research process is slow and methodical and may not match the program development/improvement cycle or policy development cycle. In addition to this issue, the appropriate research methodology to address the question of interest may conflict with program operations in applied, intervention, or evaluation research. There are different research designs (experimental, quasi-experimental, ethnographic, pretest/posttest comparisons, and longitudinal) and types of data collected (quantitative vs. qualitative), which contribute different types of knowledge. In reality, multiple methods are needed to fully understand a program, policy, or developmental process (Cook, 2002, 2004). However, experimental research has come to be known as the "gold standard" for evaluation and policy research (McCall & Green, 2004; Rossi, 1997). Indeed, its strengths are significant, specifically the ability to make causal inferences and to apply any statistically significant outcome to the program or policy studied.

However, the application of random assignment is quite demanding and potentially incompatible with program goals and the service delivery model. Human services are not randomly assigned in society, and often the voluntary commitment of an individual to a program is an essential ingredient of the ultimate success of the program. Aside from ethical issues with random assignment and practical issues associated with the sample size necessary for such research, it is expected that random assignment, experimental studies be standardized from recruitment to implementation and uniform across sites. However, programs require flexibility to adapt to the local needs and preferences of participants. Interventions tend not be singular and stable, as the population of participants is not homogeneous. Successful programs are often the result of the unique relationships and culture created within the program. In experimental designs, application of the intervention must not vary between conditions except on variables of interest (e.g., length, dosage), this necessary rigidity can take away from the enthusiasm and commitment of staff and buy-in by participants. Experimental purity, which increases internal validity and the ability to determine causality, can also decrease external validity and understanding of the context in which a program is embedded. So, not only do random assignment studies require significant planning and stability, but the data collected may not provide the most important details that lead to understanding successes or failures.

In addition, when research is being conducted within a program, program staff may not fully understand the research process and the need for a standardized protocol and might put the interests of participants before data collection or modify a process to make it easier to fit in with existing practices. For example, study participants are required to provide informed consent prior to becoming involved in the program and data collection. Informed consent for minors must be provided by both the youth and a parent/guardian. Programs often do not have access to parents/guardians, and many parents may be suspicious of research. This may be particularly true of marginalized populations or individuals who are receiving social services, who may believe that as a result of their participation they may lose some of their benefits or be subject to certain consequences.

Finally, there could be a mismatch between the type of research valued by a researcher and the academic community and the type of research a program wishes to participate in. For example, longitudinal research is particularly powerful and desirable to the academic community. However, multiple data collection points and the need to track and follow individuals over time can be particularly burdensome to programs.

Lack of Sustainable Funding for Joint Projects

Funding for meetings, conferences, studies, projects, and initiatives that bring together researchers, policy makers, and practitioners around the issues of PYD theory and application is often unreliable and rather fragmented. Availability of funds necessary to support multiparty engagement in promotion of activities and policies that promote healthy development of youth closely fluctuates in response to fluctuations of the economy and ever-changing funding priorities. The unreliability, fragmentation, and fluctuation of funds and funding sources pose a serious challenge to long-term sustainability and success of any collaborative endeavor.

Partnerships between researchers, practitioners, and policy makers are usually supported by a diverse number of agencies at the federal, state, and local levels. Many state- or local-level community collaborations around youth development theory, practices, and policies patch together funds from several sources in order to support their work. Part of the funds may come through different departments of the U.S. government, such as the Department of Agriculture, the Department of Justice, the Department of Housing and Urban Development, the Department of Education, the Department of Labor, and the Department of Health and Human Services. Initiatives may also receive supplemental support from state and local funds, as is the case with the U.S. Department of Health and Human Services' Youth Development Collaboration Projects, featured earlier in this chapter. Foundations, such as the William T. Grant Foundation, Charles Stewart Mott Foundation, Open Society Institute, Annie E. Casey Foundation, Wallace Foundation, and Atlantic Philanthropies represent important funding sources as well. They often serve as both funders and catalysts for particular multiparty PYD collaborations. Similarly, many private-sector companies have been investing in PYD initiatives by making contributions to community-level partnerships located in cities/towns where they do substantial business or have major activities. For instance, Timberland has invested over $10 million to help with City Year's national expansion, while Best Buy's Children's Foundation gives away over $2 million annually in grants to support local and national organizations that serve youth aged 5–18 (National Research Council & Institute of Medicine, 2002).

Although funding has increased for projects that bring together researchers, practitioners and/or policy makers interested in PYD implementation, neither the new funding nor the presence of other institutional supports are occurring on a scale equivalent to the size of the commitment that is required (both in expertise and money). All funding agencies have their own missions, objectives, eligibility requirements, application processes, types of outcomes they look for and, most important, ideas about sustainability of the projects they fund. Most agencies offer short-term funding, usually between 1 and 5 years (a 3-year time frame seems to be the most common grant period). Grants provided are usually intended to be used as seed money for new projects, and/or are focused on project development and quality improvement. Needless to say, for initiatives focused on start-up or expansion, the time frame of 1–3 years does not allow sufficient time to plan for new approaches, launch new efforts, set up services, and possibly hire staff, not to even mention the time that would be needed for conducting an evaluation of the initiative or assessing outcomes on PYD indicators.

Even though funding agencies rarely provide grantees with funds for ongoing operating support or training in fund raising, grantees are expected to sustain their initiatives and services beyond initial funding. However, what usually happens is that as the first round of administered grants expire, many state and local partnerships find themselves ill prepared to achieve sustainability for their programs or projects while simultaneously scrambling for additional funding (Langford, 2007; Sherman, Deich, & Langford, 2007).

Funding practices of many agencies can reflect funders' lack of knowledge about the cost of individual local, state, and federal initiatives. Similarly, they can reflect a true lack of knowledge in the short- and long-term benefits of initiatives being funded. This seems somewhat paradoxical given that every funding agency investing in implementation of

PYD-supportive initiatives at a state or community level uses their grantees' ability to sustain the initiative long term as a measure of their own success and as a tool to determine if they have, regardless of the specific outcomes, achieved a positive return on their investment (Langford, 2007). Funding agencies seem to misjudge the extent to which the lack of reliable, stable funding streams to support multiparty PYD initiatives can affect the design and stability of partnerships (National Research Council & Institute of Medicine, 2002) and how poor stability of partnerships affects the extent to which researchers, policy makers, and practitioners, individually and jointly, are truly able to promote healthy developmental outcomes in youth and secure positive return on the funders' investment.

As exemplified earlier in the chapter by some of the examples of partnerships between researchers, policy makers and practitioners, the field does not lack ideas for PYD implementation initiatives nor the knowledge about how to establish partnerships, or whether there are financial sources available to support such partnerships. What is lacking is sustainable funding, or, actually, a stable institutional framework that would offer financing and operational strategies required to successfully scale up and sustain the growing number of integrated research-, practice- and policy-related youth-serving initiatives (Deich & Hayes, 2007; National Research Council & Institute of Medicine, 2002). In the section that follows, we provide some initial recommendations for strategies that can bring us a step closer to developing an institutional framework that has positive youth development as its national priority.

Recommendations for Continued Integration

The differences and inherent barriers among researchers, practitioners, and policy makers at times can seem insurmountable. For example, how can research be relevant to a constantly changing social environment and provide timely research for current social problems given the demands of the scientific method (Prewitt, 1995; Zigler & Hall, 2000)? Similarly, how do youth policy makers garner support for issues that don't directly generate revenue or demonstrate an immediate impact? And finally, how do practitioners give their child development knowledge away, but still devote 100% to the children and youth who need them? Indeed, building bridges and devising creative solutions to the barriers that separate researchers, practitioners, and policy makers requires an even greater level of investment than if each were to do it on their own, but it is an investment well worth the effort.

Recommendations for Researchers

There are some clear directions that researchers can pursue to support integration and to move beyond one-way communication channels with practitioners and policy makers, which has been the normative practice in the academic community. First and foremost, researchers need to communicate their findings in clear, nontechnical, jargon-free language. In addition to peer-reviewed publications, researchers need to find other venues for their work and to produce reports and briefs that are accessible to general audiences. One existing organization that produces research syntheses is the National Research Council, Board on Children, Youth and Families. They assemble panels of experts to review research and draw conclusions that have meaningful applications. One recent example was the publication of the book *Neurons to Neighborhoods* (Shonkoff & Phillips, 2000).

Developing relationships with the media and other intermediary organizations (e.g., the American Youth Policy Forum) that work with the public and policy makers and disseminate information is another important communication channel to develop. The media tends to shape public opinion and drive society's agenda. To be included in the public decision making process, researchers must share their findings and further engage in conversation, and sometimes heated debate with other interested parties (McCall & Groak, 2000). Both positive and null findings must be shared, as it is equally important to know what to do and what not to do.

It also takes more than just brief summaries of research findings and communication with various media outlets to "give child development knowledge away." Researchers need to find ways to communicate what is important from the research. Given the complexities of the research process and limitations inherent with any research design or sample collected, it is essential that researchers convey what was learned in the context of the already existing literature base, to offer ways that the information can be utilized, and to caution against exaggerated claims and overadvocacy (Campbell, 1969; Sechrest & Bootzin, 1996). Framing the message is necessary, because the same data can and has been interpreted to support divergent positions (e.g., the Head Start evaluations; Zigler & Muenchow, 1992, or the Twenty First Century Community Learning Program; Moore, Dynarski, Mullen, James-Burdamy, & Rosenberg, 2000). When dollars are on the line, the stakes are raised, and researchers need to represent the body of existing knowledge, interpret its practical significance, and provide explanatory conclusions.

Shonkoff (2000) offers a taxonomy that differentiates three categories of child development knowledge that can support the translation of research to application and guard against exaggerated claims. The underlying assumption is that our knowledge is constantly evolving and becoming more refined, but this incomplete state of affairs cannot be a deterrent from participating in the conversation. The three levels of knowledge are established knowledge, reasonable hypotheses, and unwarranted assumptions. This perspective recognizes that application and practice often need information and feedback prior to the conclusion of complex and time-consuming research. Reasonable hypotheses fill this gap area. Although information may be incomplete,

reasonable action can be suggested. Given the demand and myriad pressures for new knowledge, scientists must be extremely cautious to not make promises and overstatements from research findings that lead to ill-advised or premature interventions and policies (Fabes, Martin, Hanis & Updegraff, 2000). Well-intentioned advocates may knowingly or unknowingly distort findings for their purposes, so the message must be clear to guard against unwarranted assumptions. Researchers have expertise in the scientific process and must maintain scientific rigor and credibility.

In regard to scientific rigor, one point often not addressed is the fact that psychological measures and education metrics, although seemingly precise, are still inevitably one or more steps removed from the actual construct of interest (Hess, 2008). In psychology, we often rely on surveys, which are only one method of data collection, but it is one of the more feasible and less costly approaches. Moreover, research is always faced with the role of unmeasured variables. In any given study, it is impossible to measure all desired variables. Thus, as the push for "scientifically based research" continues, researchers can work to develop better measures for desired outcomes.

Hard science and data can also seem far away from the real lives of children and families. Discussing the amount of variance accounted for does not generate excitement or commitment to children. Including anecdotal stories or case examples can help bring research alive to other audiences (Zervigon-Hakes, 1995). Mixed method studies that produce effect sizes necessary to evaluate the practical importance of the findings (McCartney & Rosenthal, 2000), as well as offer qualitative information that provides texture to the statistical analyses, are one method. However, there are numerous methodologies available that all must be capitalized on to answer the diverse questions of practitioners and policy makers (Huston, 2005; McCall & Groak, 2000). Reliance on the "gold standard" or experimental studies, which have recently been emphasized in request for proposals, limits the knowledge that can be gained and the ecological validity of the findings (McCall & Green, 2004). Meta-analysis is one useful, underutilized methodology because it summarizes average effect sizes from a set of studies and can help eliminate often confusing and contradictory findings from different studies (Hunter & Schmidt, 1996; for an example of a meta-analysis of PYD programs, see Durlak & Weissberg, 2007).

In addition to managing the dissemination of information, as Huston (2005) and many others recommend, researchers must work to answer policy-relevant and practical implementation questions that can guide the development of effective programs (Zervigon-Hakes, 1995). This requires a mind-set change to refocus research questions on specific actions that policy makers can take to affect child development outcomes rather than just providing information about the general conditions that affect development. It means being more intentional and focused on what processes bring about the desired outcomes and addressing issues of cost. For example, in the PYD field, the reigning philosophy is that "more is better" (Benson, 2006). Youth with more assets have fewer risk behaviors and more thriving behaviors (Benson, Leffert, Scales, & Blyth, 1998; Scales, Benson, Leffert, & Blyth 2000). However, a more compelling question or the next question to be addressed is: What are the conditions that need to be created to develop assets and what is the associated cost/benefit ratio for developing 1, 5, or 10 assets for all youth in a community?

Finally, one productive avenue that applied developmental science has suggested and has had some time to work on and build is university–community partnerships (Boyer, 1990; Denner et al., 1999; Lerner et al., 2000; Zeldin, 1995). Successful partnerships focus on the goals of community members, while researchers bring theoretical and methodological tools so that community-specific questions can be answered and theoretical information can

be generated that can be generalized to other populations. It is important that universities reward this applied/evaluation work and public service and outreach. McCall (1996) suggests that research needs to be evaluated both by its scholarly significance, as well as by standards related to the research's social relevancy. In addition, students would benefit from cross-training (Sussman-Stillman et al., 1996). In training students to be future researchers, policy makers, or practitioners (whether they take the role formally or informally), universities are in a unique position to provide multidisciplinary training allowing students a richer view of what it takes to support PYD. Knowledge in a student's chosen discipline could be supported with courses and/or practical experiences in for example, human development theory, how policy is developed, how to attract diverse sources of funding, or how to manage media relations.

Senior scholars, junior scholars, and graduate students alike should be exposed to cross-disciplinary knowledge that will inform their exploration and expansion of existing theories and research in applied developmental sciences and youth development. If we want them to be part of the conversation about PYD implementation at a local, state, and federal levels, researchers need the knowledge base necessary to tackle questions such as: What is the cost–benefit ratio of implementing the PYD perspective within a community, a county, or a state? What are the short- and long-term costs in prospective economic and social capital of under-funded PYD initiatives? and What type of financing strategies will yield the best outcomes for youth and the most positive return on investments for the funding agencies?

To answer these questions, researchers within the field of youth development cannot work in isolation. Rather, they must open themselves up to working with experts from other fields (especially econometricians, and including policy makers and practitioners). Above all, researchers should seek to provide leadership in developing standard methodologies for estimating the full costs and benefits of promoting healthy and positive development among youth.

Similar steps have already been taken in regard to after-school programs for children and youth. For example, agencies such as Private/ Public Ventures inform us that in order to make sound investment decisions, it is important that researchers, policy makers, and practitioners have a good understanding of the costs of a variety of out-of-school-time options, because "up-to-date, reliable cost information is essential for estimating the full costs of quality out-of-school-time programs, as well as the incremental costs of improving or expanding programs" (Lind et al., 2006, p.1). Just as the lack of information regarding the full cost of after-school programs poses a challenge in implementing options to finance expansion and improvements of such programs (Lind et al.), lack of information regarding costs and benefits of supporting short- versus long-term sustainability of cross-disciplinary initiatives challenges our ability to successfully argue for more funding for PYD-driven research and collaborative projects.

Recommendations for Policy Makers

As researchers are being asked to take steps away from their comfort zone and communicate in new and different ways to share their knowledge, policy makers must do the same. Policy makers are often guided by two competing forces. First, common sense or culturally transmitted beliefs about behavior guide policy development. Scientific inquiry and facts are one small piece of the vast array of information that informs policy makers' decisions and indeed research may be ignored if it conflicts with personal beliefs (Shonkoff, 2000; Zervigon-Hakes, 1995). Alternatively and currently in vogue is the new mantra or cry for accountability and evidence-based research and programs (McCall, Groark, & Nelkin, 2004). Moreover, evidence-based programs are defined as those that have been evaluated with a random assignment experiment.

Accountability, demonstrating that publicly funded programs achieve their goals, has permeated all aspects of education and programs for youth. Essentially, for programs to receive funding, they must be replications of programs that research has already demonstrated to be effective. These two extreme positions are fatally flawed. Research can provide nuances that are not readily apparent from experience and intuition, and evidence for programs requires the prior dedication of money, time, and resources to effectively evaluate the program. In addition, programs are often not packaged or easily exportable to communities with different conditions and individuals (Hess, 2008; McCall, Groark & Nelkin, 2004).

We ask that policy makers respect the expertise of researchers. If one can demand evidence-based research, one must also be receptive to the idea that other methodologies can contribute equally relevant pieces of information. As scientists learn to equivocate less about research findings, policy makers must invest time in broadly understanding the different types of research available and the questions that can be answered by each approach. We encourage policy makers to ask questions, have open debate about the appropriate inferences made from multidisciplinary developmental research, and blend objective data and political ideology. Further, it is incumbent on policy makers to realize that research can only inform decisions, it cannot relieve individuals of making them. It is natural for individuals to look for answers or quick solutions to complex problems, but both research and policy making are processes the require time and trial-and-error learning.

Also, policy makers must recognize that it is inappropriate to require new programs to be evaluated for outcomes. Programs go through developmental stages, and until a program is established, conducting an impact evaluation is unwarranted (Jacobs, 1988). Programs must learn how to implement a program with fidelity and collect formative data along that the way that provides information about what is working, for whom, and why before being required to collect outcome evaluation data.

In addition to open debate about research findings, policy makers can involve researchers in think tank sessions to help frame policy-relevant research questions (Zervigon-Hakes, 1995). Policy makers can share what they want to learn, and researchers can contribute different ideas on how that information can best be gathered.

Policy makers must also be open to funding high-quality research that will take time before yielding meaningful information. To secure such funds, however, policy makers need to create a stronger platform from which all three parties (policy makers, researchers, and practitioners) can advocate for increased support for initiatives aimed at supporting healthy development and thriving of youth, families, and communities. Despite federal- and state-level funding for PYD initiatives, the United States still has not adopted an overall PYD policy at the national level. This means that there is no dedicated funding stream for community programs and initiatives that promote youth development. Yet, we know that our ability to promote thriving and well-being among adolescents hinges to a great extent on dependable, steady and broad-based support at federal, state, and community levels (National Research Council & Institute of Medicine, 2002).

Similarly, policies ought to be put in place that require funders (be they federal, state, local, or corporate) to clarify how they plan to assess and strengthen their grantees' capacity for sustainability of their work after funding has ended (Langford, 2007). In addition, for initiatives that fail to yield success, funders should be encouraged to work with researchers and practitioners on providing an assessment of the failure and determining whether corrections can be made or the program/activities in question should cease. As Langford (2007, p. 5) remarks, putting such protocols in place would "encourage both investors and program leaders to be thoughtful and intentional in making decisions about what programs and services *should* be sustained."

Recommendations for Practitioners

Practitioners are in a unique and difficult situation. Their voice has not typically been heard, as they are not typically asked to the table. Practitioners have been both the recipients of research and the ones expected to carry out policy. In moving forward toward greater integration, it is a priority that practitioners must become full partners in the process. The greatest gift practitioners have to share is their institutional knowledge. They know what has worked, what has not worked, and what programs and ideas have come around again and again. They also understand youth. Their knowledge is not theoretical, but rather practical. It is important that they document their work and knowledge to help inform the interpretation of data. Practitioners also understand all of the intervening variables and how to differentiate instruction and programs to match the needs of youth. Learning how the political process works and how to engage with decision makers will also increase the chances that practitioners, voices and concerns are heard and that they can advocate for the resources they need.

In addition to the documentation of their work and communicating their perspective, practitioners are also encouraged to welcome research and evaluation. Evaluation research can help practitioners elucidate theories of change (why they expect to have results based on the programs they are offering), understand how their programs are being carried out, document what is working, and provide data on areas that need improvement (Weiss, 1997). In addition, engaging with researchers and policy makers can help practitioners make the difficult decisions regarding terminating a program or shifting priorities to ones that are more likely to be effective.

In addition to being open to initiatives from researchers, practitioners need to seek out resources in their local community universities and colleges. Practitioners can pose the questions they need or want answered. For example, practitioners can call on researchers and policy makers to work with them on identifying specific components that all quality youth-serving programs for adolescents should have. Lately especially, youth-serving programs have been bombarded with requests for implementing academic enrichment activities that would yield better short- and long-term academic outcomes. However, to make academic achievement a realistic goal for youth programs, practitioners should call on researchers, policy makers, and funders to help them determine what it would take to get there. As practitioners already know well, many after-school programs do not have the structure, activities, and staffing necessary to provide quality academic activities. Also, very few receive funding sufficient to implement best practices for targeting academic achievement.

Instead of leaving it to researchers, policy makers, and funders to define academic component priorities for them, practitioners should feel empowered by their knowledge of challenges facing youth programs and advocate more aggressively for allocation of funds to cover costs associated with hiring staff skilled in academic fields of focus and experienced in working as educators and trainers, and funds to cover costs associated with ongoing staff training (Sheldon & Hopkins, 2008), such as training in PYD theory and application. Practitioners are also being encouraged to implement programming strategies that will help them address financing issues for their youth programs, such as:

- Make better use of existing resources that they already control.
- Maximize public revenue that is in the system but has not been tapped.
- Build partnerships between public- and private-sector organizations.
- Create more flexibility in existing funding streams to better meet their programs' needs.
- Develop new dedicated revenue sources (Deich & Hayes, 2007).

CONCLUSIONS

The field of youth development has come a long way from the time when adolescence was regarded as a period of storm and stress. More and more researchers, practitioners, and policy makers are supportive of, and intentional about, supporting the positive development of young people, promoting healthy behaviors, and giving young people the opportunities, skills, and resources needed to thrive in a variety of contexts and to be valued, contributing members of society. However, as demonstrated in this chapter, there is still work to be done. Groups such as the Eisenhower Foundation, the National Research Council, the Forum for Youth Investment, Public/Private Ventures, the Family and Youth Services Bureau, and others like them demonstrate that meaningful and fruitful partnerships among researchers, practitioners, and policy makers desirable and feasible. Each brings different perspectives, resources, and knowledge to the partnership, which allows for a more holistic understanding of ways to improve the lives of young people and the contexts in which they exist.

Researchers, policy makers, and practitioners all have a vested interest to see youth be safe and have access to caring adults and enriching activities, to ensure the job readiness of the future workforce, to improve outcomes for at-risk youth, and to provide youth with various supports, experiences, and opportunities they need in order to develop to their full potential. Given this vested interest, it is important to acknowledge that the combination of wisdom about adolescent development and methods for effecting change in different ways and at different levels of the ecology are most effective when combined toward a singular goal. In order to be successful, each group needs to shift from an organization-centered approach to a youth-centered approach and to be flexible and open to the different expertise that each group brings. Each also needs to be understanding of the different ways in which each group works in terms of level of investment, timelines, and communication styles while at the same time working toward removing those barriers that limit integration.

No one set of knowledge supersedes another (e.g., empirical knowledge versus experiential knowledge). Similarly, no method is more powerful than another (e.g., macrolevel systems change focused on by policy makers or the micro- and meso-systems worked in by practitioners). If each group is committed to making changes that will lead to increased integration, trust and communication among the three groups will likely increase, hopefully leading to a virtuous cycle of increased collaboration, trust, shared resources, and mutual respect in the service of providing sustained and to scale initiatives promoting the positive development of all young people.

REFERENCES

Benson, P. L. (2003). Toward asset-building communities: How does change occur? In R. M. Lerner, & P. L. Benson (Eds.), *Developmental assets and asset-building communities: Implications for research, policy, and practice* (pp. 213–221). New York: Kluwer Academic/Plenum.

Benson, P. L., Leffert, N., Scales, P. C., & Blyth, D. A. (1998). Beyond the "village" rhetoric: Creating healthy communities for children and adolescents. *Applied Developmental Science, 2,* 138–160.

Benson, P. L., Scales, P. C., Hamilton, S. F., & Semsa, A., Jr. (2006). Positive youth development: Theory, research, and applications. In R. M. Lerner (Ed.), *Handbook of child psychology* (6th ed.), vol. 1: *Theoretical models of human development* (pp. 894–941). (Editors-in-chief: W. Damon & R. M. Lerner). Hoboken, NJ: John Wiley & Sons.

Bertenthal, B. I. (2002). Challenges and opportunities in the psychological sciences. *American Psychologist, 57*(3), 215–218.

Bobek, D. L. (2007). *Maintaining civil society and democracy: Examining the role of youth development organizations in promoting civic identity development.* Doctoral dissertation, Tufts University, Medford, MA.

Boyer, E. L. (1990). *Scholarship reconsidered: Priorities of the professoriate.* Princeton, NJ: Princeton University Press.

Campbell, D. T. (1969). Reforms as experiments. *American Psychologist, 24,* 409–429.

Center for Youth Development and Policy Research (1996). *Advancing Youth Development: A Curriculum for Training Youth Workers.* Academy for Educational Development: Center for Youth Development and Policy Research, Washington, D.C.

Cook, T. D. (2002). Generalization in the social sciences. In N. Smelser & P. Baltes (Eds.), *Encyclopedia of the social and behavioral sciences.* Oxford: Elsevier.

Cook, T. D. (2004). Causal generalization: How Campbell and Cronbach influenced my theoretical thinking on this topic. In M. C. Alkin (Ed.), *Evaluation roots: Tracing theorists' views and influences.* Thousand Oaks, CA: Sage.

Currie, J. (1997). Choosing among alternative programs for poor children. *Future of Children, 7,* 113–132.

Deich, S. G., & Hayes, C. D. (2007). *Thinking broadly: Financing strategies for youth programs.* Downloaded January 15, 2008 from

http://76.12.61.196/publications/Thinkingbroadly_PM.pdf. Washington, DC: The Finance Project.

Denner, J., Cooper, C. R., Lopez, E. M., & Dunbar, N. (1999). Beyond "giving science away:" How university-community partnerships inform youth programs, research, and policy. *Social Policy Report, 13*(1), 1–17.

Durlak, J., & Weissberg, R. P. (2007). The impact of after-school programs that promote personal and social skills. Chicago: Collaborative for Academic, Social and Emotional Learning.

Fabes, R. A., Martin, C. L. Hanis, L. D., & Updegraff, K. A. (2000). Criteria for evaluating the significance of developmental research in the twenty-first century: Force and counterforce. *Child Development, 71*(1), 212–221.

Family and Youth Services Bureau. (n.d.a). About FYSB. Downloaded December 15, 2007, from www.acf.hhs.gov/programs/fysb/, Washington, DC.

Family and Youth Services Bureau. (n.d.b). History of FYSB. Downloaded December 15, 2007, from www.acf.hhs.gov/programs/fysb/content/aboutfysb/history.htm, Washington, DC.

Family and Youth Services Bureau. (n.d.c). Fact sheet: Positive youth development state and local collaboration demonstration projects. Downloaded December 15, 2007, from www.acf.hhs.gov/programs/fysb/content/youthdivision/initiatives/statecollabfactsheet.htm, Washington, DC.

Fisher, C. B., & Brennan, M. (1992). Application and ethics in developmental psychology. In D. L. Featherman, R.M. Lerner, & M. Perlmutter. (Eds.), *Life-span development and behavior,* vol. 2 (pp. 189–219), Hillsdale, NJ: Lawrence Erlbaum.

Forum for Youth Investment. (2007). Ready by 21™ Quality Counts Initiative sites announced. Downloaded January 15, 2008, from www.forumfyi.org/node/188.

Foster, E. M. (2003). How economists think about family resources and child development. *Child Development, 73,* 1904–1916.

Granger, R. C. (2005). Commentary. *Social Policy Report, 19,* 8–9.

Hahn, A., Leavitt, T., & Aaron, P. (1994). *Evaluation of the Quantum Opportunities Program (QOP). Did the program work? A report on the post secondary outcome and cost-effectiveness of the QOP program (1989–1993).* Waltham, MA: Brandeis University.

Hess, F. H. (Ed.) (2008). *When research matters: How scholarship influences education policy.* Cambridge, MA: Harvard Education Press.

Hunter, J. E., & Schmidt, F. L. (1996). Cumulative research knowledge and social policy formation: The critical role of meta-analysis. *Psychology, Public Policy and Law, 2,* 324–347.

Huston, A. C. (2005). Connecting the science of child development to public policy. *Social Policy Report, 19*(4), 3–18.

Jacobs, F. (1988). The five-tiered approach to evaluation: Context and implementation. In H. B. Weiss & F. H. Jacobs (Eds.), *Evaluating family programs* (pp. 37–68). Hawthorne, NY: Aldine de Gruyter.

Jelicic, H., Bobek, D., Phelps, E. D., Lerner, J. V., Lerner, R. M. (2007). Using positive youth development to predict contribution and risk behaviors in early adolescence: Findings from the first two waves of the 4-H Study of Positive Youth Development. *International Journal of Behavioral Development, 31*(3), 263–273.

Johnson, E., Rothstein, F., & Gajdosik, J. (2004). The intermediary role in youth worker professional development: Successes and challenges. *New Directions for Youth Development, 104,* 51–64.

Langford, B. H. (2007). *Investing in the sustainability of youth programs: An assessment tool for funders.* Downloaded January 15, 2008, from http://financeproject.org/. Publications/FundersTool.pdf. Washington, DC: The Finance Project.

Leffert, N., Benson, P. L., Scales, P. C., Sharma, A. R., Drake, D. R., & Blyth, D. A. (1998). Developmental assets: Measurement and prediction of risk behaviors among adolescents. *Applied Developmental Science, 2*(4), 209–230.

Lerner, R. M. (2002). *Concepts and theories of human development* (3rd ed.). Mahwah, NJ:Lawrence Erlbaum.

Lerner, R.M. (2004). *Liberty: Thriving and civic engagement among America's youth*. London: Sage Publications.

Lerner, R.M. (2007). *The good teen: Rescuing adolescence from the myths of the storm and stress years*. New York: Stonesong Press.

Lerner, R. M., Alberts, A. E., & Bobek, D. (2007). *Thriving youth, flourishing civil society: How positively developing young people may contribute to democracy and social justice: A Bertelsmann Foundation White Paper*. Gutersloh, Germany: Bertelsmann Foundation.

Lerner, R. M., Fisher, C. B., & Weinberg, R. A. (2000). Toward a science for and of the people: Promoting civil society through the application of developmental science. *Child Development, 71*, 11–20.

Lerner, R. M., Jacobs, F., & Wertlieb, D. (2003). *Handbook of applied developmental science: Promoting positive child, adolescent, and family development through research, policies, and programs*. Thousand Oaks, CA: Sage.

Lerner, R. M., Lerner, J. V., Almerigi, J., Theokas, C., Phelps, E., Gestsdottir, S., et al. (2005). Positive youth development, participation in community youth development programs and community contributions of fifth grade adolescents: Findings from the first wave of the 4-H Study of positive youth development. *Journal of Early Adolescence, 25*(1), 17–71.

Lind, C., Relave, N., Deich, S., Grossman, J., & Gersick, A. (2006). *The cost of out-of-school-time programs: A review of the available evidence*. Commissioned by the Wallace Foundation. The Finance Project and Public/Private Ventures. www.ppv.org/ppv/publications/assets/199_publication.pdf.

Little, T. D., Bovaird, J. A., & Card, N. A. (Eds.). (2007). *Modeling contextual effects in longitudinal studies*. Mahwah, NJ: Lawrence Erlbaum.

Lynton, E. A., & Elman, S. E. (1987). *New priorities for the university*. San Francisco: Jossey-Bass.

McCall, R. B. (1996). The concept and practive of education, research, and public service in university psychology departments. *American Psychologist, 51*(4), 379–388.

McCall, R. B., & Green, B. L. (2004). Beyond the methodological gold standards of behavioral research: Considerations for practice and policy. *Social Policy Report, 18*(2), 3–19.

McCall, R. B., & Groark, C. J. (2000). The future of applied child development research and public policy. *Child Development, 71*(1), 197–204.

McCall, R. B., Groark, C. J., & Nelkin, R. P. (2004). Integrating developmental scholarship and society: From dissemination and accountability to evidence-based programming and policies. *Merril-Palmer Quarterly, 50*(3), 326–340.

McCartney, K., & Rosenthal, R. (2000). Effect size, practical importance, and social policy for children. *Child Development, 71*, 173–180.

McKnight, J. (1995). *The careless society: Community and its counterfeits*. New York: Basic Books.

Miller, J. R., & Lerner, R. M. (1994). Integrating research and outreach: Developmental contextualism and the human ecological perspective. *Home Economics Forum, 7*(1) 21–28.

Moore, M., Dynarski, M., Mullen, J., James-Burdamy, S., & Rosenberg, L. (2000). *Enhancing the 21st Century Community Learning Centers evaluation: A concept paper*. Princeton, NJ: Mathematica Policy Research.

National Research Council. (n.d.). *Welcome to the National Research Council*. Retrieved January 15, 2008, from http://sites.nationalacademies.org/nrc/index.htm.

National Research Council and Institute of Medicine. (2002). *Community programs to promote youth development*. Washington, DC: National Academy Press.

Phelps, E., Balsano, A., Fay, K., Peltz, J., Zimmerman, S., Lerner, R. M., et al. (2007). Nuances in early adolescent development trajectories of positive and of problematic/risk behaviors: Findings from the 4-H Study of Positive Youth Development. *Child and Adolescent Clinics of North America, 16*(2), 473–496.

Pittman, K. (2004). Reflections on the road not yet taken: How a centralized public policy and make youth work focus on youth *New Directions for Youth Development, 104*, 87–99.

Pittman, K. (2005a, March 3). *Moving youth development principles into adolescent health*. Talk given at the State Adolescent Health Coordinators Annual Meeting.

Pitman, K. (2005b, June 13). *Moving ideas to impact to change the odds for youth: Charting the Forum's course to 2010*. Talk given at the Annual Board Dinner of the Forum for Youth Investment.

Porter, A. C., & Polikoff, M. S. (2007). NCLB: State interpretations, early effects, and suggestions for reauthorization. *Social Policy Report, 21*(4), 3–14.

Prewitt, K. (1995). *Social sciences and private philanthropy: The quest for social* (Essays on Philanthropy, No. 15, Series on foundations and their role in American life). Indiana University Center on Philanthropy.

Public/Private Ventures. (n.d.). *Mission statement*. Downloaded February 1, 2008, from www.ppv.org/ppv/about/about.asp.

Quinn, J. (2004). Professional development in the youth development field: Issues, trends, opportunities, and challenges. *New Directions for Youth Development, 104*, 13–24.

Rossi, P. H. (1997). Program outcomes: Conceptual and measurement issues. In E. J. Mullen & J. L. Magnabosco (Eds.), *Outcomes measurement in the human services*. Washington, DC: NASW Press.

Roth, J. L., & Brooks-Gunn, J. (2003). What is a youth development program? Identification and defining principles. In R. M. Lerner, F. Jacobs, & D. Wertlieb (Series Eds.) & F. Jacobs, D. Wertlieb, & R. M. Lerner (Vol. Eds.), *Handbook of applied developmental science: Promoting positive child, adolescent, and family development through research, policies, and programs, vol. 2: Enhancing the life chances of youth and families: Public service systems and public policy perspectives* (pp. 197–223). Thousand Oaks, CA: Sage.

Roth, J., Brooks-Gunn, J., Murray, L., & Foster, W. (1998). Promoting healthy adolescents: Synthesis of youth development program evaluations. *Journal of Research on Adolescence, 8*(4), 423–459.

Scales, P. C., Benson, P. L., Leffert, N., & Blyth, D. A. (2000). The contribution of developmental assets to the prediction of thriving among adolescents. *Applied Developmental Science, 4*, 27–46.

Schweinhart, L.J. (1999). *Evaluating early childhood programs: Key step on the professional path*. Ypsilanti, MI: High/Scope ReSource.

Sechrest, L.B., & Bootzin, R.R. (1996). Psychology and inferences about public policy. *Psychology, Public Policy, and Law, 2*(2), 377–392.

Sheldon, J., & Hopkins, L. (2008). *Supporting success: Why and how to improve quality in after-school programs*. Downloaded February 1, 2008 from http://www.ppv.org/ppv/publications/assets/227_publication.pdf. Philadelphia, PA: Public/Private Ventures.

Sherman, R. H., Deich, S. G., & Langford, B. H. (2007). *Creating dedicated local and state revenue sources for youth programs*. Downloaded January 15, 2008, from http://76.12.61.196/publications/DLR_PM.pdf.Washington, DC: The Finance Project.

Shonkoff, J. P. (2000). Science, policy, and practice: Three cultures in search of a shared mission. *Child Development, 71*(1), 181–187.

Shonkoff, J. P., & Phillips, D. A. (2000). *From neurons to neighborhoods: The science of early childhood development*. Washington, D.C: National Academy Press.

Smith, B.M. (1990). Psychology in the public interest: What have we done? What can we do? *American Psychologist, 45*(4), 530–536.

Sussman-Stillman, A. R., Brown, J. L., Adam, E. K., Blair, C., Gaines, R., Gordon, R. A., et al. (1996). Building research and policy connections: Training and career options for developmental scientists. *Social Policy Reports, 10*(4), 1–18.

Theokas, C., & Lerner, R. M. (2004). Promoting positive development across variations in socioeconomic status and poverty: Framing the Corwyn and Bradley structural equation modeling approach with a developmental systems perspective. In A. Acock, K. Allen, V. L. Bengtson, D. Klein, & P. Dilworth-Anderson (Eds), *Sourcebook of family theory and research* (pp. 488–492). Thousand Oaks, CA: Sage.

Theokas, C., & Lerner, R. M. (2006). Observed ecological assets in families, schools and neighborhoods: Conceptualization, measurement and relations with positive and negative developmental outcomes. Special Issue, *Applied Developmental Science, 10*(2), 61–74.

Theokas, C., Lerner, J. V., Lerner, R. M., & Phelps, E. (2006). Cacophony and change in youth after school activities: Implications for development and practice from the 4-H Study of Positive Youth Development. *Journal of Youth Development: Bridging Research and Practice, 1.*

Watson, B. H. (2002). *Community change for youth development: Ten Lessons from the CCYD Initiative.* Downloaded January 31, 2008, from www.ppv.org/ppv/publications/assets/115_publication.pdf, Philadelphia: Public/Private Ventures.

Weiss, C. (1997). *Evaluation* (2nd Ed.). Upper Saddle River, NJ: Prentice Hall.

Zeldin, S. (1995). Community-university collaborations for youth development: From theory to practice. *Journal of Adolescent Research, 10,* 449–469.

Zervigon-Hakes, A.M. (1995). Translating research findings into large-scale public programs and policy. *The Future of Children, 5*(3), 175–191.

Zigler, E. (1998). A place of value for applied and policy studies. *Child Development, 69*(2), 532–542.

Zigler, E., & Hall, N. (2000). *Child development and social policy.* New York: McGraw-Hill.

Zingler, E., & Muenchow, E. (1992). *Head Start: The inside story of America's most successful educational experiment.* Albany: State University of New York Press.

Author Index

Subject Index

Sodality activities, 581
"Soft skills," 276
South Africa, 393–394
South America, 493, 547, 596
South Asia, 595, 614
Southeast Asia, 547, 610
Southern Regional Economic
    Board, 389
Special needs, 179–180
Special remedial programs, 198
Spending patterns, 478–479
Spermarche, 575
Spillover model, 6, 22
Spirituality, 395
Spitfire Strategies, 629
Sports, 255–256
Sports participation:
    and coaches' behavior, 247
    and problem behaviors, 251
    risky behavior and intense, 256
    and socioeconomic status, 242
SRA (Society for Research on
    Adolescence), 141
SSP (Self-Sufficiency Project),
    461
Stable relationships, 114
Stage–environment fit theory,
    230
Standard curriculum, 216
Standard Ethnographic Sample,
    572, 574
State accountability tests, 212
Status:
    and aggression, 81
    and peer relationships, 76–77,
        92–93, 95
    and romantic relationships,
        115, 123, 140–141
    in schools, 194–195, 198, 199,
        205–206, 210
Status phase, of romantic self-
    image, 115
Steinberg, L., 94
Steinberg, L. D., 280
STEM careers, 295
Stem-family household, 577, 578
Stepfathers, 33
Stereotyping, 550–552
Stigma, of socioeconomic disad-
    vantage, 455–458
Stoneman, Dorothy, 390, 510
Store clerks, 300, 301
Street-blocks, 412
"Street context," 474–475
Stress:

neighborhood, 466
and sports participation, 256
Stress models, 450–455
    allostatic load, 453–454
    bioecological, 454–455
    family stress, 451–453
    stress-vulnerability response,
        453
Stress-vulnerability response
    models, 453
Structural lag, 495–496
The Structure of Social Action
    (Parsons), 376
Structuring opportunities, 95
Student Voices, 391–392
Stylized questions, 241
Sub-baccalaureate labor market,
    302
Subject-matter tests, 220
Sub-Saharan Africa, 595, 609–
    610, 614–616
Subsidized meal programs, 448
Substance Abuse and
    Mental Health Services
    Administration (SAMHSA),
    162
Substance use:
    and arts activities, 256
    media effects on, 333–335
    and neighborhoods, 419, 426
    and out-of-school activities,
        254
    and self-care, 238
    and sibling relationships, 59–60
    and socioeconomic
        disadvantage, 453
    and sports participation, 256
Sudan, 588
Suicide, 616
Sullivan, H. S., 112
Supports, youth, 521
Support groups, 380
Supportive relationships with
    adults, 259–260
Support networks, 428
Support processes, 127–129
Survey of Adolescent Health, 394
Survey of Parents and Youth, 394
Suspicion, 637
Sweat equity, 512–513
Switzerland, 585
Systems, programs vs., 519
Systematic social observations,
    413
Systematization, of change, 597

T
Talent Development Program,
    200–201
TANF (Temporary Aid to Needy
    Families), 479
Tap and Reposition Youth (TRY),
    503, 515–524
Teacher attitudes, 199–200
Teacher behavior, 387
Teacher quality, 467
Teaching practices, 217–218
Teasing, 123
Technology, 603
Teen jobs, 300–301
Teen language, 106
Teen Outreach Program (TOP),
    257
Teen pregnancy. *See also*
    Abortion, access to;
    Childbearing
    cultural differences with, 581
    dangers of, 588
    and sibling relationships, 61–62
Telephones, 322
Television, 315, 317–320, 327,
    329–332, 335
Temperament, sibling relation-
    ships and, 51–52
Temporary Aid to Needy Families
    (TANF), 479
Test preparation courses, 220–221
Text messaging, 321, 323
Theft, 584, 586
Thinness ideal, 331
Third International Mathematics
    and Science Study (TIMSS),
    204
360-degree evaluations, 223
Three C's of PYD, 379
Timberland, 641
Time diaries, 241
Time issues, of youth programs,
    639
Time management, 289
Time span:
    of mentoring relationships, 171
    of out-of-school activities, 240
    of self-care, 237–238
Timing:
    of neighborhood influences, 433
    of out-of-school activities, 233
    of self-care, 237–238
TIMSS (Third International
    Mathematics and Science
    Study), 204